PRACTICAL PROFESSIONAL COOKERY

LexingtonCollege

310 S. Peoria St. Ste. 512
Chicago, Il 60607 3534

Phone 312-226-6294
Fax 312-226-6405

Practical Professional Cookery

H. L. Cracknell
R. J. Kaufmann

REVISED THIRD EDITION

THOMSON

Australia • Canada • Mexico • Singapore • Spain • United Kingdom • United States

Practical Professional Cookery revised 3rd edition

Copyright © 1999 H.L. Cracknell and R.J. Kaufmann

The Thomson logo is a registered trademark used herein under licence.

For more information, contact Thomson Learning, High Holborn House, 50-51 Bedford Row, London WC1R 4LR or visit us on the World Wide Web at:
http://www.thomsonlearning.co.uk

British Library Cataloguing-in-Publication Data
A catalogue record for this book is available from the British Library

---

ISBN 1-86152-873-6

First edition published by Macmillan Press Ltd 1972
Reprinted 5 time
Second edition in 1981
Reprinted 9 times
Third edition in 1992
Reprinted 6 times
Revised third edition 1999
This edition published by Thomson Learning
Reprinted 2002 by Thomson Learning

Printed in Great Britain by Creative Print and Design Wales, Ebbw Vale

Contents

Preface to the Third Edition   ix
Preface to the Revised Third Edition   xi
Abbreviations and Conversion Tables   xii

1 **Introduction**   1

2 **The Methods and General Principles of Cookery**   7
  Boiling; Poaching; Steaming; Stewing; Braising; Poêling or Pot-Roasting;
  Roasting; Baking; Grilling; Shallow Frying; Deep Frying; Stir-frying;
  Microwave Cooking.

3 **Initial Procedures and Preparations**   19

4 **Stocks, Glazes, Thickening and Binding Agents**   43

5 **Sauces**   50
  Classification; Storage; Quantity Guide; Basic Sauces, Sauces based on
  Demi-glace and Jus lié; Sauces based on Béchamel and Velouté; Egg and
  Butter Sauces; Fish Sauces; Coulis; Cold Sauces; Cocktail Sauces;
  Hors-d'oeuvre Dips; Miscellaneous Sauces.

6 **Hors-d'oeuvre**   87
  Hors-d'oeuvre variés; Single Hors-d'oeuvre.

7 **Soups**   109
  Classification; Garnishes; Quantity Guide; Consommés and Bouillons –
  Clear Soups; Potages, Soupes and Broths; Purée-based Soups; Veloutés;
  Cream Soups; Bisques; Brown Soups; Special Unclassified Soups; Cold
  Soups.

8 **Eggs**   148
  Classification; Oeufs brouillés – Scrambled Eggs; Oeufs en Cocotte –
  Eggs in Cocotte; Oeufs à la Coque – Boiled Eggs served in the Shell;
  Oeufs durs or farcis – Hard-boiled or Stuffed Eggs; Oeufs frits – Fried
  Eggs; Oeufs mollets – Soft-boiled Eggs; Omelettes; Oeufs sur le Plat –
  Eggs cooked in the Dish; Oeufs pochés – Poached Eggs.

9 **Farinaceous and Rice Dishes**   163
  Gnocchi; Pastas; Sauces for Pasta; Pasta Dishes; Nouilles – Noodles
  Tagliatelli; Stuffed Pastas; Riz – Rice.

10 **Fish**   181
   Classification; Quality Points; Storage; Cleaning and Preparation; Cuts
   and Special Preparations; Preparation Losses; Courts-bouillons; Cooking

Methods; Portion Guide; Aiglefin – Fresh Haddock; Anguille – Eel; Bar
– Sea Bass; Barbue – Brill; Blanchailles – Whitebait; Brochet – Pike;
Cabillaud – Cod; Colin – Hake; Flétan – Halibut; Haddock, Smoked and
Finnan; Hareng – Herring; Limande – Lemon Sole; Lotte – Monkfish;
Maquereau – Mackerel; Merlan – Whiting; Plie – Plaice; Raie – Skate;
Rouget – Red Mullet; Saint-Pierre –John Dory; Saumon – Salmon; Sole;
Fillets of Sole; Thon – Tunny; Truite – Trout and Rainbow Trout; Truite
Saumonée – Salmon Trout; Turbot et Turbotin – Turbot and Chicken
Turbot; Miscellaneous Fish Dishes; Grenouilles – Frogs' Legs.

11 **Shellfish**   244
Classification; Quality Points; Storage; Cleaning and Preparation; Cooking
Methods; Weight Loss and Portion Guide; Calmar – Squid; Sea Urchin –
Oursin; Coquilles St Jacques – Scallops; Crabe – Crab; Crevettes –
Prawns; Ecrevisses – Freshwater Crayfish or Yabbies; Homard – Lobster;
Huîtres – Oysters; Moules – Mussels; Scampi; Mixed Shellfish Dishes.

12 **Meats**   264
Quality Points; Hanging and Conditioning; Storage; Cooking Methods;
Portion Guide; Agneau et Mouton – Lamb and Mutton; Boeuf – Beef;
Porc – Pork; Bacon; Ham; Veau – Veal.

13 **Poultry**   402
Quality Points; Storage; Plucking, Drawing, Singeing and Cleaning;
Preparation and Cuts for Cooking; Cooking methods; To Carve and
Portion Cooked Poultry; Poulet – Chicken; Canard et Caneton – Duck
and Duckling; Oie – Goose; Pintade – Guinea-fowl; Pigeon; Dindonneau
– Turkey.

14 **Game**   471
Classification and Quality Points; Hanging and Maturation; Plucking,
Drawing and Cleaning of Feathered Game; Drawing and Skinning of
Furred Game; Storage; Cuts and Preparation for Cooking; Cooking
Methods; Coq de Bruyère – Blackgame and Capercaillie; Grouse;
Perdreau – Partridge; Faisan – Pheasant; Caille – Quail; Canard Sauvage
– Wild Duck; Bécasse et Bécassine – Woodcock and Snipe; Venaison –
Venison; Lièvre – Hare; Lapin – Rabbit.

15 **Cold Dishes and Buffet Work**   534
Selection of Commodities; Preparation, Cooking and Presentation;
Carving; Hygiene and Health Considerations; Preparation Times; Initial
Preparations for Buffet Work; Gelées d'Aspic – Aspic or Savoury Jellies;
Chaud-froid Sauces; Decoration for Cold Buffet Work; Garnishes for
Cold Buffet Work; Socles; Cold Mousses and Mousselines; Oeufs froids
– Cold Eggs; Poissons et Crustacés froids – Cold Fish and Shellfish;
Viandes froides – Cold Meats; Volailles et Gibiers à Plume froids – Cold
Poultry and Game Birds; Pies, Pâtés, Terrines and Galantines.

16 **Salads and Salad Dressings**   582
Cleaning and Preparation; Salad Dressings; Simple Salads; Composed
Salads; Salades tièdes – Warm Salads.

17 **Vegetables** 596
Classification and Quality Points; Storage; Preparation; Portion Guide;
Cooking Methods; Artichauts – Globe Artichokes; Asperges – Asparagus;
Aubergine – Eggplant; Bean Sprouts; Betteraves – Beetroot; Broccoli;
Carottes – Carrots; Céleri – Celery; Céleri-rave – Celeriac; Champignons
– Mushrooms; Chou – Cabbage; Chou-fleur – Cauliflower; Chou de Mer
– Seakale; Chou-rave – Kohlrabi or Cabbage Turnip; Choux de Bruxelles
– Brussels Sprouts; Concombre – Cucumber; Courgette – Young
Marrow; Endive Belge – Belgian Endive (Chicory); Epinards – Spinach;
Fenouil – Fennel; Fèves – Broad Beans; Haricots Blancs – Haricot
Beans; Haricots d'Espagne – Runner Beans; Haricots Flageolets –
Flageolet or Green Kidney Beans; Haricots de Lima – Lima Beans;
Haricots Rouges – Red Kidney Beans; Haricots Verts – French Beans;
Laitue – Lettuce; Lentilles – Lentils; Maïs – Sweetcorn; Marrons –
Chestnuts; Navets – Turnips; Oignons – Onions; Okra – Okra or Lady's
Fingers; Panais – Parsnips; Petits Pois – Peas; Piment Doux – Pimento;
Pois Mange-Tout – Mange-Tout Peas; Poireau – Leek; Salsifis – Salsify;
Tomates – Tomatoes; Topinambours – Jerusalem Artichokes; Mixed
Vegetable Dishes.

18 **Potatoes** 659
Varieties; Quality and Selection; Storage; Preparation; Cooking Methods;
Preparation Losses and Portion Guide; Pommes de Terre – Potatoes.

19 **Canapes, Sandwiches and Savouries** 689

20 **Pastry and Sweet Dishes** 715
Commodities; Storage; Hygiene Considerations; Basic and Miscellaneous
Preparations; Sweet and Butter Sauces; Basic Pastes; Yeast Goods; Flans,
Bandes, Tarts, Tartlets and Barquettes; Gâteaux and Pastries; Entremets
chauds – Hot Sweets; Entremets froids – Cold Sweets; Glaces et
Entremets à Glace – Ices and Ice-Cream Sweets; Petits Fours.

Glossary 875
Appendix 1 Australian and New Zealand Fish 881
Appendix 2 Salad leaves 883
Select Bibliography 884
Index 886

Preface to the Third Edition

Since the First Edition of this book appeared in 1972, there have been many changes in the world of catering, changes which are felt to be of sufficient importance to merit recognition in the content of this new edition.

In the restaurant sector those who were pioneers of the style of artistic presentation have had to accede in some measure to the demand for the well-tried and trustworthy dishes selected from the international repertoire rather than completely restrict their offerings to the fashions of the time. But to do this successfully they have also had to keep abreast of developments and experiment with the new commodities which are constantly coming onto the market and then to decide how best to incorporate them in their menus. In this age of the global kitchen, customers expect to be offered a wide choice of dishes and many of them like to know that those they choose are felt to be beneficial to their health and well-being.

In the realm of catering education there has been continual change both in the titles of courses and their contents. There is a wide choice of degree courses in various aspects of the catering and hospitality industry, there are the national certificates and diplomas in catering and institutional management, and last but not least, the various craft courses ranging from the elementary to very advanced level which lead to the examinations of the City and Guilds or to those of the college. In addition there are now various vocational and training schemes run by training centres and employers on government grants and the growing number of private colleges and institutes which offer a variety of courses in the culinary arts leading to various internationally recognised diplomas.

This edition then has been extensively revised and greatly enlarged so as to take account of these changes and emphases. It provides a wider range of recipes, many of them supported by detailed information on how to obtain optimum results. New and original recipes are included together with a number of the more popular national and ethnic dishes and a greater selection of vegetable dishes. The inclusion of a Select Bibliography is for the benefit of those who wish to widen their knowledge of any of the aspects covered in this present edition.

The section on kitchen organisation in the Second Edition has not been included in this edition but it can still be found in this book's companion volume *Practical Professional Catering*. However, the number of chapters in the present book has been increased, mainly by splitting some of the existing chapters into their logical divisions. The original layout and presentation of recipes has proved its value as being a logical sequence of operations and has been retained in its entirety. Recipe titles are given as they should be written on the menu together with accents where applicable so as to help with spelling and pronunciation; it is hoped that this will assist in good menu compilation. French titling has been translated into English where felt sensible and appropriate but fanciful translations have been eschewed.

The majority of recipes are for ten covers as this is thought to be helpful for Table d'Hôte production but where there is good reason for it the number of portions is given to suit the commodity, e.g. a medium-sized chicken yields four portions whereas a sucking-pig will serve 20–30.

Regarding the contents as a whole it is emphasised that this book, within its limits, has endeavoured to cover as wide a spectrum of culinary knowledge as possible, from the elementary to the advanced. No cross-reference is made to processes or methodology nor are recipes forced into awkward groupings. The logical sequence in this book is the time-honoured one of placing recipes in their natural categories. Thus it is not intended to be a work schedule, nor is it planned as a work-progress manual, but it is hoped that its broad coverage will be useful for the drawing-up of teaching programmes in colleges, in the compilation of menus for all kinds of restaurants and in providing a study of commodities and the differing techniques and methods by which they may be correctly processed and cooked.

An original feature of this book was the use of metric units only, without any side-by-side conversions. Another important feature was the use of the decilitre and its fractions as being a more professional measure for liquids than the millilitre; this has been retained in this edition. Nevertheless the use of spoon measures for smaller quantities has been included where it was felt to be more useful.

This new edition recognises and applauds the demand for healthy eating and accepts that any excess can be harmful, so whilst no details of how to minimise the use of certain ingredients which are deemed to be deleterious to the healthy diet are given, we suggest that it is perfectly in order for the user of this book to reduce the quantity say of salt or sugar in a recipe without unbalancing it or spoiling the eating quality. In the case of the use of fats, margarine is not considered to be just an equal-value alternative to butter, although margarine or vegetable oil can be substituted for butter where this is felt to have a beneficial effect on some aspect of health; it should be borne in mind nevertheless that this can alter the flavour. Again, the substitution of wholemeal flour for white flour will give a darker colour and more distinctive flavour to dishes and is not therefore an ideal alternative in most cases. The same applies to the use of yoghurt, fromage frais, quark and so on as a means of reducing the calorie count of such things as sauces, soups and stews, as again the flavour is bound to be affected. In effect then it becomes a matter of fine judgement for the caterer or chef whether to use these alternative ingredients as being more appropriate for their own particular clientele.

We hope then that this, the Third Edition of *Practical Professional Cookery*, will be well-received and will meet the requirements of another generation of chefs, commis, trainees, lecturers and students of catering and home economics, housewives and practising gourmets, and all who are interested in good food. Having spent the whole of our working lives in the world of professional cookery, latterly as teachers in the sphere of catering education, we wish to acknowledge our debt to the great chefs of the past, to our own teachers and to the many colleagues we have worked alongside. But in addition, we also wish to place on record our respect for the great unsung army of those cooks of many nationalities, who translated the ideas and menus of their masters into worthwhile dishes, who endured the heat of the kitchen, made the best of the stressful conditions under which they worked and yet always stayed loyal to their chosen profession.

H.L.C.
R.J.K.

Preface to the Revised Third Edition

As the world enters a new millennium this book celebrates its twenty-eighth year of continuous publication. In the Preface to the First Edition it was stated that the aim of the book was to meet the needs of students and chefs responsible for the preparation and service of food in all kinds of catering establishments. The aim of this revised edition is exactly the same as it was all those years ago, and despite all the changes that have come about in food fashions this book should flourish for many more years.

This new version sees the incorporation of details about Australian foods which will widen the appeal of the book. Food importers are always on the lookout for new ingredients which impart new flavours, textures and colour to the diet, and chefs are always willing to use them to titillate customers' tastebuds.

Since this book was first written many changes have come about in the way that even the most traditional chef works. For instance, suppliers will do the chores of vegetable preparation, butchery of carcasses and visceration of poultry, and items of *mise en place* can be purchased as cheaply as doing them in the old-fashioned way on the job. This is not de-skilling the craftsmanship of chefs and no chef would consciously serve fully prepared, factory-produced dishes as homemade ones, but it is acceptable for them to use value-added ingredients that have been taken a stage from raw to make their life easier.

So practices change but the essential nature of the chef's job remains the same. Chefs still have to demonstrate their expertise and widen their repertoire constantly to keep pace with customers' demands and *Practical Professional Cookery* helps them meet these and other targets. As evidence of its standing this book received an accolade from the former editor of *La Cuisine*, journal of the Association Culinaire Française de Grande Bretagne, who wrote that if Escoffier's *Guide Culinaire* is accepted as the chef's Bible then *Practical Professional Cookery* is the chef's Shakespeare.

Ronald Kaufmann died during the preparation of this revised edition. The wide knowledge and extensive experience of the industry which gave him his living are evident on every page of this established book, and this was his way of giving thanks to those he learned from and of showing the way forward to succeeding generations.

A meticulous attention to detail and an unbending aim to achieve perfection in everything he undertook ruled his life. His fastidious insistence on excellence made working with him a stimulating experience, whether on the stove or at the writing table. A joint of beef roasted by Mr Kaufmann, or any other dish he made, was unique because his inborn flair always stamped the result with his personality. So it is with this book. He will be greatly missed by his colleagues and friends.

Harry Cracknell

Abbreviations and Conversion Tables

Abbreviations

g	=	gram
kg	=	kilogram
dl	=	decilitre
mm	=	millimetre
cm	=	centimetre
°C	=	°Celsius (Centigrade)
°F	=	°Fahrenheit
tbsp	=	tablespoon
tsp	=	teaspoon

Conversion Tables

Volume (Liquids)

1 litre = 10 decilitres = 1000 millilitres (or 1000cc) = 1.76 pints

METRIC CAPACITY	IMPERIAL EQUIVALENT MEASURES		AUSTRALIAN	
	Actual	*Approx.*		
¼ dl	0.88fl oz	1fl oz	1 teaspoon	5 ml
½dl	1.76fl oz	1¾fl oz	1 tablespoon	20 ml
¾dl	2.66fl oz	2½fl oz	1 cup	250 ml
1 dl	3.52fl oz	3½fl oz	4 cups	1 litre
¼ litre	8.81fl oz	9fl oz		
½ litre	17.63fl oz	18fl oz		
¾ litre	26.44fl oz	1⅓ pt		
1 litre	35.27fl oz	1¾ pt		
5 litres	176.35fl oz	8¾ pt		

Weight

1 kilogram = 1000 grams = 2 lb 3.27 oz (2 ¼ lb approx)

METRIC WEIGHT	IMPERIAL EQUIVALENT	
	Actual	*Approx.*
1g	0.035oz	⅟₂₅ oz
5g	0.17oz	⅕ oz
10g	0.35oz	⅓oz
20g	0.70oz	¾oz
50g	1.76oz	1¾oz
100g	3.52oz	3½oz
250g (¼kg)	8.81oz	9oz
500g (½kg)	17.63oz	1lb 2oz
750g (¾kg)	26.44oz	1lb 10oz
1000g (1kg)	35.27oz	2lb 4oz

Length

1 metre = 100 centimetres = 1000 millimetres = 39.37 inches

METRIC LENGTH	IMPERIAL EQUIVALENT	
	Actual	*Approx.*
1mm	0.039inch	⅟₂₅inch
2mm	0.078inch	⅟₁₂inch
5mm	0.197inch	⅕inch
1cm	0.39inch	⅖inch
5cm	1.97inches	2inches
10cm	3.93inches	4inches
20cm	7.86inches	8inches
50cm	19.68inches	20inches
1 metre	39.37inches	3¼ft

Temperature

°C	°F	°C	°F	°C	°F	°C	°F
−20	−4	60	140	130	266	200	392
−18	0.4	65	149	135	275	205	401
0	32	70	158	140	284	210	410
5	41	75	167	145	293	215	419
10	50	80	176	150	302	220	428
15	59	85	185	155	311	225	437
20	68	90	194	160	320	230	446
25	77	95	203	165	329	235	455
30	86	100	212	170	338	240	464
35	95	105	221	175	347	245	473
40	104	110	230	180	356	250	482
45	113	115	239	185	365	255	491
50	122	120	248	190	374	260	500
55	131	125	257	195	383	275	527

Oven Temperatures (Standard Conversions)

Gas Mark or Regulo No.	Celsius (Centigrade)	Fahrenheit	Definition
½	130	250	very cool
1	140	275	cool
2	150	300	warm
3	170	325	moderate
4	180	350	moderate
5	190	375	moderately hot
6	200	400	hot
7	220	425	hot
8	230	450	very hot
9	240	475	very hot

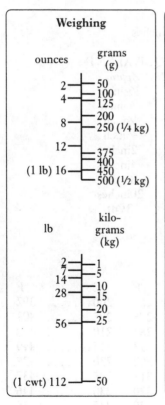

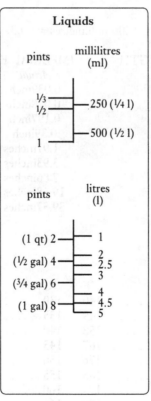

1
Introduction

The social and economic changes which alter the standard of living of a nation have a bearing at all levels of society on people's attitudes towards their food and the way they eat. Outside influences can also alter a nation's attitude to food as evidenced by the United Kingdom's progress towards being a multiracial society, largely the result of the new wave of post-war immigrants from the Caribbean and the Indian subcontinent, and to a lesser extent from other former colonies of Great Britain. The indigenous population has thus been made more aware of the values and qualities of the foods and dishes of other races.

In the shape of tourism there has been a tremendous upsurge in the number of people travelling abroad for holidays and in reverse the number of people visiting this country. The ease of travel has helped to broaden people's outlook especially in understanding the customs and eating habits of other nations; in return, visiting tourists to Britain are introduced to our customs and foods.

The improved standard of living and the high amount of disposable income enjoyed by most Western countries have led not only to more frequent holidays at home and abroad but also to a higher incidence of eating out as a normal feature of daily life. This has created a greater interest in food and drink, and in turn this has created demands on the catering industry for new and exotic foods and novelty in their preparations and presentation. This demand for novelty is not a new fashion but is one that has occurred many times throughout the ages, according to the prevailing state and wealth of society. It has always had an effect upon the way cookery has developed and on people's attitudes to food and eating as a subject worthy of attention, in contradiction to those periods when society was mainly concerned with the problems of providing sufficient to feed its population. Thus these changes now mean that it is acceptable to be knowledgeable on the subject of gastronomy, to be adventurous in eating habits and to show a liking for foreign foods.

Environmental topics should be borne in mind when discussing the subject of food; the need to protect the land and its species and prevent indiscriminate over-use by, for example intensive farming methods for livestock must be seen as being incompatible with self-indulgence. Modern methods of farming can cause aversion to meat-eating and the indiscriminate use of fertilisers and pesticides has led to the demand for organically grown foodstuffs among which are many vegetarian products and the speciality restaurants for those who seek to combine what is perceived as healthy living with pleasurable eating. Of course, some of the features pertaining to the environment have been made necessary by the increase in world population and by the demand for better-quality food which the higher standard of living creates.

The wider availability of commodities, brought about by more rapid methods of transportation, usually under controlled conditions, has also had a great influence on the advancement of cookery. Improved strains and methods of cultivating vegetables and fruits have virtually ousted the need for a knowledge of seasonal availabilities as it is now possible to obtain most goods at all times of the year, albeit at a price. Processed foods including raw meat and fish products, exotic fruits and uncommon vegetables can now be grown within the EC, which has become practically self-supporting for food. In addition to the many ready-prepared products there are now newer and better machines that can do all the hard work of many cooking processes, so releasing the worker from the drudgery that was once inherent in the preparation of food.

Doctors, dietitians and food scientists exert an influence on people's lifestyle, usually by publicising their views as to what they consider to be good or bad eating practices. Much of their advice unfortunately tends to be contradictory and very often seems to be discounted by further research or the findings of a new authority. What can be accepted however is that healthy eating is now a commonplace phrase which embraces a wide range of subjects, including those already mentioned such as methods of rearing livestock, the controlled use of fertilisers, pesticides and insecticides, and others including the moral aspects of vegetarianism, organic foods and drinks, personal standards of hygiene, fitness activities, health farms and clinics together with the pros and cons of eating butter, sugar, salt, and many other foods. More emphasis is being given to the standards of hygiene in the professional kitchen and in cooking practices and techniques regarding the safety of very underdone meat, fish and raw egg dishes; all this is further compounded by a general fear regarding the use of additives such as preserving agents which are mainly used in processed foods.

Among these many facets of the changes in society related to food and cookery, a number have shown through in contemporary cookery practices.

THE NEW COOKERY

History shows that every age gives birth to new ideas on the way we live; these new ideas often ebb and flow like the tide and usually all that remains is what succeeding generations consider to be of value. In the realms of cookery, one generation may emphasise complication and heaviness while a succeeding one will require a new and lighter style. The most recent of these styles is the advent of a cookery that was identified by Henri Gault of Gault and Millau, the restaurant critics, aided by several well-known French chefs-patron including Messieurs Bocuse, Guérard, Vergé and the brothers Troisgros and, in direct line, based on the practices and principles expounded by Fernand Point of La Pyramide Restaurant at Vienne.

These chefs who laid down these practices had all been disciples of the great masters of modern cookery who codified and established the methodology and standards governing food production in the kitchens of the grand hotels and restaurants of the late nineteenth century and in the first half of this. All the fundamentals as laid down by these master-chefs have been well-publicised in recent years as the basic tenets of Nouvelle Cuisine. They include: Lightness; the Use of Fresh Ingredients; the Need to be Imaginative; a Rejection of Complicated Techniques; Ease of Service; a Good Balance of Colour, Taste and Texture; the Need to Adapt to the Changes in Society; Faithfulness to Established Principles of Quality; a Recognition of Customer's Requirements; Willingness to Use Machines to Lighten the Workload; a Scientific Approach to Cooking Practices; Less Menu Choice; and to feature dishes which reflect New Thinking on Health Considerations, such as a diminution in the use of fat, flour, salt, sugar and so on.

But regrettably, this opportunity to be innovative under the banner of Nouvelle Cuisine has been misinterpreted by some practitioners where attitudes to these basic culinary principles have prevented them from realising their fullest possible value. The result is that it is sometimes considered essential to over-emphasise the garnishing and decoration of each plateful of food to the detriment of the main item of food itself. In many cases the size of main portions becomes less than the customer would wish or expect. However, at its best, the new style of cookery has much to commend it because it is possible to be entirely in accordance with the best traditions of classic cookery but it needs to be based on sound fundamental principles and techniques and a knowledge of how to obtain the best results from the available raw materials. Expertise is essential in the way it is taught and carried out, for at its worst, it can easily become the target of perceptive food writers and critics.

Provided the basic principles are well-understood and the harmonious use of ingredients is mastered, Nouvelle Cuisine is a valuable addition to the present-day eating experience. A study of Japanese and Chinese methods can be of use in formulating ideas of presentation as these civilisations have always given a high degree of importance to the artistic presentation of food. History will record how well Nouvelle Cuisine has met the demands of this day and age.

GARNISHING, PRESENTATION AND SERVICE

This very important subject is the final phase in the chain of food production and, as has been noted, is under the influence of new attitudes to cookery which unfortunately have been very often to its detriment, mainly again because of a lack of attention to fundamental principles.

First of all, ease of service must be considered, especially when a number of persons are to be served from a single dish of food; the garnish should not be dispersed around the dish but laid in lines or grouped in bouquets so that the server can ensure that each person is given an equal amount without having to scrape all around the dish to find the garnishes; a very elaborate garnish could well be arranged separately from the main food with each item grouped separately.

The difference between a garnish and an accompaniment is that the latter is invariably handed round or served quite separately, usually being offered as part of a choice related to the customer's requirements, and therefore not obligatory. But a garnish itself, if it is from the classical repertoire, must be strictly adhered to so as to register its identity. Outside the use of the repertoire, when creating a new dish or garnish, great care should be taken regarding its particular suitability to the main item so as to create harmony even though there may be a contrast of taste and texture between them. All garnishes should be thought of as being created with a particular commodity in mind and never taken to the extreme where it becomes difficult to determine any theme or emphasis; the main focus of a dish must never be overwhelmed by the garnish.

Long verbose descriptions of dishes and their garnishes is really to be deplored – after all, a menu description is meant to give a quick impression of the dish to be served, over-long literary pretension can only obscure the essential information needed by the customer. If a dish has been well-created, is really something original and begins to create a reputation for itself, then the well-tried traditional method of naming a dish has much to commend it. Only in this way, when a dish is accepted into the culinary repertoire under its title and described in sufficient detail, can a dish become truly popular and have a widely disseminated appeal. Its presentation and garnishing can then be standardised and accepted – it will still depend on each individual chef for its final interpretation and allow an establishment to create or maintain its own reputation.

The presentation and garnishing of a dish is determined by the demands of the service which could be either on a silver or an earthenware dish, or as is often the case now, even in the best of restaurants, on a china plate. Here the whole plate is totally arranged in the kitchen and allows of no after-additions because otherwise the eye-appeal as determined by the chef would be destroyed; it is he or she who should always ensure that the main focus of attention, which is the main item, is not overwhelmed by its garnish.

All in all, the garnishing and presentation of every dish depend on good artistic taste allied to common sense, so that it fulfils the guest's expectations, satisfies his or her appetite, and gives a feeling of occasion that is in keeping with the type of establishment.

ETHNIC CUISINES

The arrival of ethnic groups in the United Kingdom, especially those from the former British Colonies who brought their own style of cookery, has resulted in the opening of their own restaurants but ones which have been geared mainly to the eating habits of these people, based on their own particular requirements, though these may become slightly blurred at the edges by certain racial or national interrelationships. But basically their cultural ethos remains authentic together with their styles of cookery. Other than immigrants from the former British Colonies, French, Italian, Greek, Cypriot immigrants and temporary workers also brought their styles of cookery and found it profitable to offer it in their own restaurants. This interchange of eating styles and cookery does of course happen internationally and France is an example, which, whilst exerting its own culinary influence abroad, welcomed ethnic influences from its former colonies such as Indo-China and Algeria and Tunisia in North Africa; as previously stated, a number of Japanese ideas were incorporated into its concept of Nouvelle Cuisine. Thus French cooking absorbed these influences, refined them and spread them.

The cookery of some European countries was absorbed so long ago that it is no longer noticeable but new experiences of other countries' dishes are constantly being evaluated, thus leading to importers satisfying the demand for authentic ingredients. Spices which were once regarded as exotic ingredients are now much more widely available as are rare herbs, condiments, fruits and vegetables and these together with the plethora of ethnic cookery books make it possible now to produce authentic dishes successfully.

Food importers and manufacturers have found it profitable to offer a wide range of foreign foods, many as ready-made dishes which can range from Paella to Moussaka to Sweet and Sour dishes perhaps not entirely authentic but nevertheless now acceptable to the average British taste which has been broadened by overseas holidays, books, magazines and television.

In those parts of the country where immigrant groups have settled, authentic restaurants have been opened; where there is a mixed population, recipes tend often to be modified and the menu enlarged with some less specifically ethnic dishes. In industrial and institutional catering establishments such as works canteens, schools, college refectories and hospitals where there is often a high ratio of an ethnic group or groups to cater for, it may be advisable to feature dishes which are suitable for them. This, in turn, would indicate a need to employ cooks of that group which again might necessitate local education authorities providing courses in ethnic cookery for which they would need to engage professionals in such subjects. At the general level it should be possible to give teachers of cookery short courses in the intricacies of the subject. Obviously, at a higher level, where strict observance of religious considerations is a precept, nationals would have to be engaged.

——NUTRITION, DIET AND HEALTH——

The relationship between nutrition, which is the nourishing of the body and the study of the foods needed to nourish it, and diet, which is the selection of the foods consumed, is central to the creation of good health. Historically, this relationship has at times been impaired by fads and fashions and often by wishful thinking which chose to ignore the connection, yet it has been known from early Greco-Roman times. This relationship came to be well-understood by the early Middle Ages, and found a full and authentic expression in the teachings of the Medical School of Salerno. Already a well-established centre of learning by the twelfth century, it came to represent the focus of both Western and Eastern medical and nutritional thought. It produced a collection of aphorisms related to diet which were subsequently published in most languages and in succeeding editions to the present day. Much of the book is based on good common sense and observation and the following verse in English, translated by Sir John Harington and published in 1607, gives something of its particular quality. The *italicized* words can be seen as being central to diet and nutrition and are no less applicable to our modern understanding of sensible diet and to those who prescribe diets.

> They that in Physick will prescribe you food,
> Six things must note we here in order touch,
> First *what it is* and then *for what 'tis good,*
> And *when* and *where, how often,* and *how much*:
> Who note not this, it cannot be withstood,
> They hurt, not heal, yet are too many such.

In those days considerations of nutrition, diet and health went hand in hand with wealth and prosperity and often led to over-indulgence, thus a physician had to prescribe methods of curing illnesses caused by this over-indulgence. Over the centuries there have been many books on healthy eating, some giving sound basic advice but others suggesting principles which were suspect because they paid heed to the fashions and fads of the time and were largely based on the practical knowledge then available. The Victorians were obsessed both by gluttony and by regimes many of which, unfortunately, were not based on scientific principles. Thus fashions in diet have not always been well-founded and it has taken much in the way of scientific research to bring the study of nutrition to its present high levels of understanding.

The number of people who are vegetarian is increasing rapidly, the reasons being either moral, religious or based on health grounds rather than on expense. Caterers need to be ready to satisfy the demands of non-meat-eaters and ensure that staff are capable of providing a reasonable range of vegetarian meals; they should bear in mind that vegetarians are usually knowledgeable on the subject of diet.

Veganism demands an even deeper knowledge of nutrition than vegetarianism since a vegan diet excludes all animal products so that while a vegetarian may accept milk, eggs, butter or cheese, a vegan will not eat any of these nor meat, fish or poultry and it is much more difficult to cater for such persons; it usually requires specialised restaurants and special training to satisfy these particular needs.

Every caterer needs at least a good basic knowledge of nutrition and the dietary requirements of people since apart from purely medical considerations, a healthy diet is based on a balanced intake of the right food in correct proportions, in other words the exercise of moderation and discrimination, backed up by discipline. Dissent surrounds the dietary value of many foods including salt, sugar, and saturated fat and dietitians recommend that it makes good sense to limit the intake of these and to increase that of dietary fibre; salt can increase the risk of high blood pressure, sugar is correlated with heart disease and saturated fat can contribute to high blood cholesterol in the body. Dietary fibre as found in wholemeal bread, crispbreads, pastas and beans is of benefit to the functioning of the intestines and digestion. Other than a diet imposed for medical reasons, a balanced diet is the responsibility of the individual and each may have differing needs for their different lifestyles. Medical opinion tends to alter its opinions as to what constitutes a balanced diet but a sensible approach usually ensures that people eat the right things in the right amount and if they also have the right outlook on life and lead a sober life, take sufficient rest and have an even temperament allied to good humour, such a way of life should help towards longevity and well-being.

The chef or caterer has a responsibility then to assist customers by offering a good variety of fresh foods that have been prepared so as to retain their nutritional value and without having to resort to expensive health foods or wholefoods; he should be able to produce low-calorie dishes for a slimming diet, or indeed any non-medical diet. This he can do in entire accordance with sound culinary principles and by those well-tried methods which never change and should not be lost sight of. Only in this way can the best of nutrition be matched with the physical enjoyment of food and the psychological pleasures of taste and discrimination.

2
The Methods and General Principles of Cookery

To be acceptable and agreeable to the palate and digestive system many of the foods in our diet need to be cooked, that is, subjected to a certain degree of heat for a predetermined period. The method of cooking selected and qualities of these foods may be modified by the addition of various seasonings, herbs and spices and other ingredients. These modifications have the advantage of making food more easy to eat and to digest, and make its nutrients more easily available; they stimulate the appetite and satisfy our need for variety and change. In addition, cooking can make food safer to eat by destroying harmful organisms which may be in or on the food. Care in preparation and cooking can eliminate or destroy natural poisons, or residual chemicals on vegetables.

But apart from these needs and reasons, cooking is the art of matching an item of food to a method of cooking, assessing its possible range of compatible flavours, textures and appearance, judging the length of time for cooking it to perfection by the selected method, and achieving the optimum of palatability.

Recipes are the blueprints for guiding the practitioner in the details of achieving best results. Most recipes are founded on traditional techniques and processes; but it is not only permissible but even desirable that these recipes be sensibly interpreted. However, before adjusting a recipe it is suggested that a knowledge of the commodity and the cooking process is necessary. And this can only be acquired through study, guidance and experience.

The methods of cookery are sometimes referred to as either moist or dry, the moist methods being those where some form of liquid is used or produced by the food, and the dry methods in which liquid is not necessary to the process; these two wide categories cover the accepted modern methods of cookery. The dividing line between these methods is often quite blurred and in many cases a combination of two or more methods are used.

Cooking by microwaves is not considered to be a truly separate method of cookery in the traditional sense, however an outline of the guidelines covering the use of the microwave oven is included in this chapter.

It is to be hoped then, that a study of the following methods and precepts, together with the more detailed cooking methods in the chapters devoted to specific commodities will be of help in achieving the best results.

BOILING

This is the subjection of food to the action of heat in a liquid at 100°C – the boiling-point of water. The state of boiling is shown by the bubbling movement of the liquid which may range from rapid to gentle. Gentle boiling is referred to as simmering – in some cases this needs to be so gentle that only a barely discernible movement of the liquid is required – at this point the temperature can drop a few degrees below boiling-point and the process is closer to poaching.

Boiling is one of the most widely used methods of cookery, and is used in the preparation of stocks, sauces and soups, for the cooking of eggs, pastas, rice, shellfish, some fish, all types of vegetables and for items of meat and poultry which generally require extended cooking times to make them tender.

In boiling, the commodity must be covered by sufficient liquid throughout the process. If cooking times are prolonged excess evaporation can occur. If this happens the liquid should be replenished to prevent any food surfaces being undercooked or drying out. Items which are inclined to partially float can be covered with a cloth which will trap some of the rising steam and assist the cooking process. Meats and poultry can be partially covered with a lid to prevent excess evaporation but this can increase the rate of boiling and the heat source will need to be adjusted downwards.

After adding the food, the pot can be covered to speed up reboiling but green vegetables must be kept uncovered whilst actually cooking. Pastas and rice need some degree of stirring or movement to prevent them sticking together and should not be covered.

For most items it is essential to skim the cooking liquid when it first comes to the boil and frequently thereafter in relation to the amount of scum or fat being brought to the surface. Failure to skim can spoil the liquid and subsequently the item being cooked. Failing to remove the scum thrown up by vegetables can leave a dirty deposit attached to the vegetables when they are drained. In the preparation of boiled meats or stocks any scum attaching itself to the side of the pot should be removed by wiping with a damp cloth.

Any flavouring ingredients should be added only after the initial skimming; if added before this there is always the likelihood of the rising scum being trapped and adhering to them and subsequently spoiling the cooking liquid.

The rate of boiling is determined by the needs of the item being cooked. In general all meats and poultry are best cooked by gentle simmering especially if the flesh is more tender. Where the flesh is tougher the boiling of the liquid can be a little more rapid but never to the point of being turbulent; this can only result in uneven cooking and a breaking-down and stringiness of the outside surfaces. If taken to the extreme it can result in the actual breaking-up of the flesh.

To preserve the maximum flavour of fresh meat and poultry the items should be placed in a boiling liquid, brought quickly to the boil again, skimmed, boiled for a few minutes rapidly and then simmered gently. Placing in a boiling liquid helps to seal the surfaces of the food more so than if placed in a cold liquid and then brought to the boil. Salt and cured meats are best placed to boil in cold water, which will assist in extracting excess salt.

As a general rule, root vegetables, with the possible exception of new potatoes, are best placed to boil in cold water. Green vegetables must be placed in boiling, salted water immediately it comes to the boil and then brought back to the boil as quickly as possible. This helps to preserve the green colour and minimises the loss of valuable vitamins and mineral salts.

A general assessment of the time require to cook a particular item of food by boiling is essential so that the cooking process can be checked then halted when the item of food is just done. Failure to do this and leaving things to chance can easily result in the food being quickly overcooked and in extreme cases, to its breaking-up and ultimate disintegration.

The term 'boiled' when applied to fish can be misleading. The movement of a boiling liquid will tend to break up the flesh of all but the firmest fish; because of this the method of poaching is better applied.

POACHING

This process, closely related to that of boiling, is the subjection of food to the action of heat in a liquid, held as close to boiling-point as possible but without any perceptible movement of the liquid. For most purposes the temperature of the liquid for poaching is 93–95°C.

This method is most suitably applied to tender items of first quality where extended cooking times are not required. In most cases this means that the item of food becomes tender and easy to eat within a relatively short time after its internal temperature reaches that of the poaching liquid.

Poaching is widely used for the cooking of fish, poultry and game birds, certain offals, eggs and fruit and for made items such as quenelles, mousselines and gnocchi.

Various liquids can be used for this process including water, stock, milk or wine, either singly or in combination and their suitability for any particular item of food is determined by the needs of the recipe and the degree of compatibility required.

There are two related types of poaching:

1. Where the item is totally immersed in the liquid and is identical at all points to boiling but carried out at a lower temperature and with no movement of the liquid. Because of the more tender nature of the items cooked by this method, it is better that stock or some sort of a flavoured liquid is used rather than water. This adds flavour which might be naturally lacking in the commodity or at least can prevent the loss of too much of its flavour to the liquid.

2. Where the process is used for the shallow poaching of small cuts of fish, meat, poultry and game. In this method the item of food is placed in a buttered shallow tray with a little liquid and any flavouring or garnishing ingredients, covered with a buttered paper or close-fitting lid to prevent the surfaces from drying out or colouring, then cooked in a moderate oven at approx. 195°C. The cooking time should be judged and checked so that the food is just cooked only. The cooking liquid should always be utilised in the preparation of any accompanying sauce.

   This shallow poaching process is also applied in the same way to quenelles and mousselines of fish, meat and poultry etc.

The term 'stewed' when applied to fresh fruits is erroneous; in practice poaching is essential to prevent any damage to the fruit even to the extreme point where some soft berried fruits need only to be covered with a flavoured sweet stock at boiling-point, covered and then allowed to cool without any further application of heat. The only exceptions are for dried fruits such as figs and prunes etc. and for them the process of stewing can be correctly applied.

STEAMING

This is the subjection of food to the action of heat in the form of steam under pressure. The pressure varies according to the type of equipment used and it can range from just above atmospheric pressure to 1.05kg/cm^2. In its simplest form food can be steamed by placing it in a perforated container or sieve which fits tightly over a pan of boiling liquid covered in turn by a tightly fitting lid. This method only marginally raises the pressure above atmospheric pressure but it is sufficient to cook many foods satisfactorily. The majority of work however, is carried out in steaming ovens operating with moist steam at pressures varying from 0.17 to 0.35kg/cm^2, and high-pressure steamers operating with dry steam at anything between 0.70kg and 1.05kg/cm^2. As a general principle the higher the pressure the higher the temperature and thus the quicker the cooking time. The steam for low-pressure steaming ovens can be generated centrally and piped to the equipment but is more usually generated from its own self-contained unit.

Steaming is suitable for the cooking of fish, meat, poultry, vegetables and various puddings and can reproduce in some respects the results of cooking food by boiling or poaching. Its advantages can be a useful retention of the nutrients in food and making it easier to digest. High-pressure steaming can shorten cooking times considerably and its speed can conserve the colour of green vegetables adequately. The disadvantages of steaming are mainly related to the difficulty of retaining cooking juices and modifying taste and flavour with added ingredients; in the case of large joints and poultry there can be an overall loss of taste resulting in blandness.

Low-pressure steaming ovens produce condensation and the use of perforated trays is necessary to prevent its accumulation especially where cooking times tend to be long. A cooking liquid of sorts can be obtained by placing the food in a deepish unperforated tray but the results are not always satisfactory; careful boiling with added ingredients can produce better cooking liquids and more flavoursome joints of meat. Puddings in basins need to be covered with paper or foil and then tied with cloth to prevent contact with any condensation.

All steaming equipment needs to be properly maintained and operating, safety and hygiene aspects require careful attention at all times. The following points need to be emphasised.

Operating and Safety Factors

1. If the steam is generated by the unit itself, always check that the water reservoir is full and that its refilling mechanism is functioning properly. Any drying out of the water reservoir during the operation will lead to the burning and damage of the equipment and subsequent spoilage of the food.
2. Check that the operating temperature of the water and its production of steam is obtained before placing the food in the steamer.
3. It is essential that the door of the steamer is tightly shut and that there is no leakage of steam from the seals. Any leakage of steam will result in loss of pressure and subsequent increases of cooking time; if loss of pressure is severe it can even prevent the food from being cooked at all. The seals should be periodically checked for damage and wear.
4. Before opening the door of the steamer, allow sufficient time for the pressure to drop then always stand behind the door when opening it; there is always the danger of unperceived pressure and the likelihood of scalding if this is not done.
5. Although high-pressure steamers have in-built safety operating factors, no attempt should ever be made to force open the door during cooking or before the pressure has dropped to zero at the end of the cooking time.

6. Carefully adhere to cooking times for both types of steamer; the times for high-pressure steaming are naturally more critical.

Hygiene Factors
1. All types of steaming equipment should be thoroughly cleaned out after use and the doors should be left ajar when not in use so as to prevent stale odours developing.
2. The water reservoir for low-pressure steamers should always be checked to ensure that the water is fresh and clean. If the steamer is out of use for any length of time, empty and clean the water reservoir. Here the guiding principle is to prevent any sort of contamination from developing.

————————STEWING————————

This is the subjection of food to the action of heat while it is immersed in a minimum amount of simmering liquid or sauce. Invariably the food and its sauce or liquid are served together. The cooking can take place on top of the stove or in the oven.

Stewing is particularly suitable for the slow cooking of tougher meats or poultry which would always be cut into small pieces or sections on or off the bone. In many cases the liquid is thickened by flour in the form of a roux. In others the ingredients can be sufficient or thickening takes place after the food is cooked.

The amount of liquid in proportion to the main ingredient is critical. This should be just sufficient to allow the cooking process to be carried out efficiently; the size of the pan should not be too large but just enough to comfortably hold the total of ingredients. After an initial skimming the cooking needs to be slow and regular. Covering with a tight-fitting lid will keep evaporation to a minimum and will concentrate flavour and aroma. The longer cooking time will ensure an interchange of flavour between the food and its liquid so essential to the qualities of a stew.

Fish of a cheaper or coarser nature are also well-served by stewing and is exemplified by the many types of popular fish stews. However, the process generally consists of a fairly rapid boiling resulting in a general thickening of the liquid by the partial disaggregation of the more light textured fish. In some respects this type of stew can be similar to certain of the more robust soups which can afford a meal in themselves. Firm fish such as eel, squid, tunny, can be successfully stewed in many of the ways applicable to the meats because longer cooking times are necessary.

Vegetables are best stewed where the cooking is very slow and there is no added liquid. There is usually enough moisture in vegetables to prevent any drying out or burning especially where the pan is covered with a tight-fitting lid and cooked in the oven.

Dried fruits such as prunes and figs after an initial soaking require longer cooking times than they would if fresh. The usual basic techniques of stewing are naturally required, that is a minimum of liquid, slow and even cooking, and covering to prevent excess evaporation.

The cooking of garnishes with the main item of food is a desirable part of the process not only because of its ability to add flavour to the dish but also to alter the emphasis and particular quality of a stew; the technique and style may be similar but the finished results can be widely different. Nevertheless garnishing with vegetables and pastas when serving can do much to add variety to the menu.

A careful check should always be kept on the progress of the cooking with care taken to avoid overcooking. For meat and poultry a little firmness in the commodity is preferred to that where it loses bite and texture or becomes pappy.

—— BRAISING ——

This is the subjection of food, while it is enclosed in a container with liquid or sauce, to the action of heat in an oven. The container should be of a size and shape in keeping with the food being cooked and should be covered with a tight-fitting lid to prevent undue evaporation. The braising liquid or sauce should always be utilised and served with the item of food.

Braising is a suitable method for cooking the tougher joints of meats and poultry and which require longer cooking times. Fish of a firm nature such as salmon, turbot, bass or tunny fish lend themselves to braising either whole or cut in sections or portions and many vegetables such as leeks, celery and cabbage can also be braised.

For meats and poultry the process normally starts with shallow frying to seal and flavour the outer surfaces, then placing on a bed of root vegetables and herbs. The liquid can be either stock, wines, marinades, sauces or a combination of any and should never completely cover the food. Half to two-thirds of the way up is sufficient. The actual cooking must be slow and regular and the item of food should be turned occasionally and basted. This is necessary to build up the required degree of colouring and glazing of the joint.

Vegetables and herbs serve to impart flavour and aroma to both liquid and food; and as with stews, an interchange of flavours between the food and its liquid takes place. In some cases garnishes may be introduced during the cooking process, but the garnish of the joint is more frequently added on completion of the cooking when being served.

For meat, there are two main categories of braising, brown and white. Brown braising is used in the main for beef, lamb, game and offals, and poultry items such as duck, goose and guinea-fowl, and in some cases, chicken. In this process the acquiring of an appetising brown to both the joint and its sauce, produces its own particular qualities of robustness and concentration. White braising is used mainly for veal, pork, poultry and offals such as sweetbreads. Here the emphasis is on preserving the light colour of the flesh and finishing with light-coloured or cream-based sauces. Lightness and delicacy in the finished result are to be aimed for.

The braising of fish does not require prior sealing in hot fat but the main techniques of using the correct size of pan with the right amount of liquid, slow cooking and basting and glazing are all essential. It is not correct to use any prepared sauce as a liquid but the braising liquid should always be used in the preparation of the accompanying sauce. White and red wines are commonly used for the braising of fish.

It is useful to blanch most vegetables for a few minutes before braising them. This helps to remove excessive acidity and in some cases makes them more pliable and easier to manipulate. In the majority of cases only white stock should be used as a braising liquid for vegetables.

POÊLING OR
—— POT-ROASTING ——

This is the subjection of food, which is enclosed in a container with butter, to the action of heat in an oven. The container should be of a size in keeping with the food being cooked and should be covered with a tight-fitting lid to conserve the juices and aroma of the joint and any added flavourings usually in the form of a bed of root vegetables and herbs; these should always be utilised in the preparation of any accompanying sauce. No liquid should be used at the initial stages of poêling as this would result in a process more akin to braising. Nevertheless the addition of a little wine or spirit at the later stages is permissible.

The most suitable items of food for poêling are first-quality tender joints of meat, poultry, game and some offals such as calf's kidney, liver and sweetbreads. Smaller cuts such as veal cutlets and chops may be treated in the same way.

In general the process of poêling needs to be carried out at a slightly higher temperature and for longer times than for the roasting of the same joints. It needs to be accompanied with basting to build up a certain degree of colour and glazing; particularly in the case of larger joints, the lid must be removed towards the end of the process to ensure adequate colouring. The temperature should be reduced downwards as required and to prevent the overcolouring of the flavourings and aromats being used.

For smaller joints and cuts, the cooking can be carried out with advantage in smaller or individual cocottes or casseroles. This is a suitable technique for incorporating a garnish during the process and subsequently the food can be presented and served from its container. In some cases, where a fortified wine or spirit such as brandy or Madeira is incorporated it is useful to seal the lid to the container with a band of dough or pastry. This keeps evaporation to the minimum and retains the maximum of aroma and flavour.

ROASTING

This is the subjection of food to the action of heat in an oven, or while it is rotating on a spit over or at the side of a fire. In both cases fat is used as a basting agent.

The most suitable foods for roasting are the prime-quality tender joints of butcher's meat, poultry and game. A major requisite for any joint of meat used for roasting is that it should have an adequate covering of fat as well as a certain amount dispersed in the flesh. Where this is insufficient, either insert strips of fat into the meat (larding), or cover it with slices of fat (barding) so as to prevent the flesh from unduly losing moisture. The barding of most game birds is essential and is usefully applied in some cases to the roasting of poultry.

Vegetables such as potatoes, sweet potatoes and parsnips may also be roasted and to a lesser extent certain whole fish or sections of fish such as tunny fish, sturgeon, stuffed carp, lobster and so on.

Oven Roasting
Well maintained clean ovens with adequate ventilation are a first consideration for this process to be successful. Without adequate ventilation, trapped steam or the fumes from burning fat or particles of food, can spoil the flavour of the roasting food.

The most important points to be observed for the oven roasting of meats are:
a) The food should be seasoned generally with salt only, just prior to the commencement of cooking,
b) For meat, place the joint on a trivet or bones so as to raise it from direct contact with the roasting tray.
c) Cover with a little clean fat.
d) Place in a very hot oven to initially seal the surfaces of the meat.
e) Baste frequently with the fat and juices and lower the temperature in relation to the size of the joint and the time needed to cook it.
f) Use the roasting juices and sediment for the preparation of any gravy.

Covering or wrapping joints of meat or poultry with foil or paper can make it difficult to attain the authentic qualities of a roast and its gravy and can prevent adequate colouring of surfaces. Taken to its extreme the process could start resembling poêling without the advantages of added flavourings and basting with butter. Forced-air convection ovens can speed up the roasting process but tend to have an increased drying effect on the food being roasted.

Spit-Roasting
This method has many enthusiastic devotees who, with justification, consider it to be the only true way to roast. It can be a more complicated procedure and undoubtedly requires a high degree of competence and experience to obtain the best results, but the same principles of seasoning, basting and cooking with very high temperatures to start must be observed.

Modern rotary spits for poultry which operate in a partly enclosed cabinet do not give the same results as traditional spit-roasting; the process is modified by the steam produced and trapped in the cabinet.

BAKING

This is the subjection of food to the action of dry convected heat in an oven. The dryness of the heat may be modified by the amount of steam produced from the food being baked; in some cases, especially the baking of certain types of bread, steam is introduced to the oven with advantageous results. Likewise the convected heat may be moderated to a greater or lesser extent by radiated heat from the surfaces of the oven and by conducted heat from the equipment which contains the food. Foods such as pâtés and baked egg custard mixtures should be placed first in a water bath (known as a bain-marie) so as to moderate and control the degree of cooking.

Baking is widely used for almost all commodities but its main use is for confectionery, pastry and bakery items. For general-purpose baking the large-capacity kitchen oven is quite satisfactory but it is important to remember that temperatures are not easy to control within fine limits, and there is usually a wide variation in temperature from top to bottom and at the sides of the oven. For specialised pastry work, purpose-built ovens in narrow separate decks which can be stacked on each other offer higher temperatures where needed, controlled oven heat and correct ventilation.

Careful maintenance of all ovens is essential for best results; all equipment such as baking trays and moulds for pastry work need to be kept absolutely clean and free of any particles of adhering foods and where needed kept greased to prevent food sticking to them.

GRILLING, ALSO KNOWN AS BROILING

This is the subjection of food placed on grill bars to the action of radiated heat. The heat may be directed from above or below and the source of heat may be charcoal, wood, gas or electricity. An authentic grill has the heat source located below the grill bars. Where the heat source is located above the grill bars, the equipment is usually referred to as a salamander. True grilling cannot be carried out by placing items on a tray to cook in the oven or on a griddle plate or char broiler or by sandwiching them between the plates of an infra-red contact grill.

The fuel used to fire the grill will have an effect upon the taste of the food grilled; e.g. cuttings of vine wood and other aromatic woods add their own particular flavour.

The flesh of fish is much more fragile than meat. Because of this it is advisable to use folding double wire grids for flat fish or cuts of fish, and hollow wire cradles to contain whole round fish. These make it possible to turn the items without damaging them during cooking. Items for grilling must be small to medium in size; large items cannot be grilled successfully as the outside tends to become too charred before the inside is cooked. Those most suitable for grilling successfully are tender first-quality cuts of butcher's meat, poultry, game, offals, small cuts of fish, whole flat and round fish of small to medium size and some vegetables such as mushrooms and tomatoes. Made items such as Hamburgers, Bitoks, Pojarskis and sausages can also be successfully grilled although in practice they will probably be cooked on griddle plates or shallow-fried. It is not good culinary practice to use mechanical tenderisers which disaggregate the fibres of meat or liquid tenderisers which soften the texture of tough meat.

The process of grilling is a very popular method of cooking; for best results the following points need to be observed.

a) The grilling equipment should be preheated to its best operating temperature.

b) Season all food just prior to grilling except for any made items like sausage.

c) Lightly oil the grill bars and brush or coat all items with clean oil or other fat where called for. Fish should first be passed through flour.

d) Place on the bars; initially the heat must be sufficient to immediately seal the surfaces of the food and to commence colouring; temperatures can then be reduced or the food moved up or down from the heat as determined by the size of the item.

e) The grill marks of the bars should show upon the item which should be turned where possible so as to form a trellis pattern on both sides.

f) Where necessary use tongs to move or turn the food. Never pierce meat or fish with a fork; this will cause the escape of juices.

g) Occasional basting with oil or butter can help to build up the required succulent coating of the food.

After use, all grilling equipment should be carefully cleaned of any burnt particles of food and greased ready for re-use.

SHALLOW FRYING

This is the subjection of food to the action of heat from a shallow layer of fat in a pan. The fat used can be butter, clarified butter, oil or where called for, lard or other clean animal fat.

Shallow frying is an excellent method of cooking for first-quality tender cuts of meat, poultry, game and offals, fillets of fish, small to medium whole fish, made items such as Pojarskis and sausages, vegetables and occasionally fruit. It is also frequently used in the part-preparation of a wide variety of dishes.

A shallow, heavy-bottomed pan with straight sides called a sauté pan is the most suitable for the shallow frying of items which are large enough to be separately turned over, e.g. escalopes of veal or steaks. A heavy frying-pan with curved sides is more suitable for food cut in small pieces and requiring rapid frying with frequent tossing over and over to obtain even cooking and colouring, e.g. small pieces of liver and kidney.

Protective coatings are not a necessity for the shallow frying of foods but in some cases, especially for small cuts of veal, fish or liver, flouring the surfaces will help to colour them. Breadcrumbing is frequently used and gives a particular eating quality of the dish when cooked.

Seasoning should be carried out just prior to cooking except where this is done before breadcrumbing or coating.

Attention needs to be given to the following points:

a) The fat should be sufficiently hot to quickly seal and colour the outer surfaces of the food.

b) Small cuts of food should be placed best side down first in the fat. The side fried first usually obtains a more even and better colour, and after turning it can make the best presentation.

c) The size of the pan should be selected with an eye to the amount of food to be cooked. When shallow frying, the bottom of the pan should be more or less covered with the food. Unused areas of fat can overheat quickly and start to burn.

d) As and if necessary, because of thickness, reduce the heat or pull the pan to one side of the stove to continue cooking more slowly.

e) Small cut pieces of food must be placed in very hot fat, tossed over and over and cooked continuously and quickly at high temperature.

f) If cooking breadcrumbed items, strain the fat after each panful has been cooked. Loose breadcrumbs quickly colour in the fat and will spoil any subsequent frying if not removed; the fat can be strained and used again.

g) Any sediment and juices left in the pan from food which has not been breadcrumbed should be used for the preparation of any sauce as called for.

The term 'sauter' is used to describe the shallow frying of meat or poultry and the subsequent utilisation of its cooking juices and sediment for the accompanying sauce. The term 'sauter' also indicates the necessity of tossing certain small items of food so as to colour them evenly during the process of shallow frying. The term 'meunière' is loosely used to describe the shallow frying of fish; correctly speaking it refers to the finishing of shallow-fried fish with butter, lemon juice and parsley. The actual French term for shallow frying is 'cuisson or friture à la Poêle'.

——————————DEEP FRYING——————————

This is the subjection of food to heat while it is completely submerged in hot fat. The process is very quick because the penetration of heat is from all sides simultaneously. Normal frying temperatures range from approx. 160 to 195°C and the most suitable temperatures are selected in relation to the size and thickness of the item being cooked.

Suitable items for deep frying include meat and poultry which should be of prime, tender quality, fish either as fillets or whole, vegetables, potatoes, fruits especially in the form of fritters, and made items such as rissoles, Cromesquis and Fritots.

Good-quality clean fat must be used and strained regularly and not allowed to overheat. Thermostatically controlled units should be regularly maintained to ensure that temperatures can be held within the defined limits.

There must be sufficient depth of fat in the frying unit but it should be no more than half to two-thirds full.

Most foods except for a few items like potatoes or onion rings need to be seasoned first then coated either with flour, egg, batter, or egg and breadcrumbs before deep frying. The fat must be hot enough to seal the outside surfaces of the food being fried. If not, the food will absorb fat and begin to leach its juices into the fat with subsequent spoilage both of the food and fat. This will also happen if the frying unit is overloaded with food which will drastically reduce the temperature and in addition the food can begin to break up.

All deep-fried food needs careful draining, where possible on absorbent kitchen paper, before being served.

The use of deep-frying kettles (fritures) which are placed over heat on the stove is now largely outdated because of their inefficiency and relative danger in use. They were frequently the cause of fires in the kitchen either through the fat bubbling over on to the hot stove or through being left unattended until the flash-point of the fat was reached. Modern free-standing deep fryers, thermostatically controlled and with safer and easier ways of straining the fat, are in more common use. Nevertheless great care must be taken to prevent accidents; the possibility of fires when using older equipment is always present but the following points are applicable to all frying equipment:

1) The bubbling over of a fat with its attendant dangers of fire and burns can be caused by using old or dirty fat, by having too much fat in the frying unit, by not drying certain wet foods like potatoes properly before frying them, by overloading the unit or using it at too high a temperature.
2) A frying-basket and wire spider should be kept close at hand so that items can be removed quickly should the fat start bubbling excessively and start to rise.
3) Care should be taken to avoid any sudden movement of the frying unit if on the stove which might cause the fat to spill over and catch alight, or splash the hands.
4) Lower the items of food into the fat carefully so as to avoid splashing the arms or hands.
5) A certain amount of steam rises from the fat during the frying process so it is necessary to avoid placing the arms or hands directly over the fat when frying.
6) In the case of fire use a fire blanket or foam extinguisher which should be at hand and accessible. Never use water to try and extinguish a fat fire. This can only make the matter worse and spread the fire.

STIR-FRYING

Stir-Frying is an Asian particularly Chinese method of cookery carried out rapidly at very high temperature while constantly stirring the food.

Ingredients for stir-frying must be cut into small pieces before cooking, placed in the hot wok at staggered intervals according to their firmness and density.

The food should be cooked to order for immediate consumption while still crisp and keeping its nutritional value.

A wok is used in the process, the heat is diffused over the entire area, very little oil is required. First heat the wok without oil then add the oil, as a result the metal is always hotter than the oil and the ingredients do not stick to the surface, the wok also sits deeply into the opening on the stove so that heat is distributed over the entire surface thus making full use of the intense heat of the Chinese stove and ensuring the even cooking of the food.

————————MICROWAVE COOKING————————

This is the subjection of food to the action of microwave energy. This is brought about by the transforming of electricity via a magnetron into radio waves operating at a frequency of 2450 Megahertz (MHz) which cook the food in an oven by electro-magnetic radiation.

In many respects the microwave oven is unable to reproduce the results of conventional cooking methods; because of the capacity of even the largest oven it is also limited in application to large-scale catering. However, it has a useful part to play in modern cooking particularly for defrosting frozen food, reheating pre-prepared dishes and other items, and it can in many cases cook food to a required standard where browning is not necessary.

The time required to cook by microwave energy is dependent upon the latent heat of the food, its moisture content, volume density and the total amount being cooked at any one time; the higher the energy output of the oven the quicker the cooking time.

With a combined dual-purpose oven there are two sources of energy, the microwaves and forced-air convection heating. These can be used separately or together and will cook and colour food quickly and satisfactorily.

Metal deflects microwaves and it cannot be used in ordinary microwave ovens. Glass, china, some plastics and card are good transmitters of microwave energy. However, metal containers can be used in combined microwave and forced-air convection ovens.

It is of the utmost importance that any microwave equipment is kept clean and correctly maintained. Door rims and seals must be kept clean to ensure suitable contact on closing. Any possible leakage from door seals or distortion of the door is a potential danger; these should be checked regularly and whenever anything not quite right is suspected.

Actual times for cooking, defrosting and reheating and related techniques can vary according to the power output and controls of the equipment and the degree of its sophistication. It is suggested that maker's or establishment's instructions and their microwave cookery books are studied carefully.

3

Initial Procedures and Preparations

The importance of initial procedures and preparations cannot be overstressed; both areas are essential to the quality of the finished results.

If correctly stored, many of the preparations can be held successfully for a reasonable length of time and be part of what is referred to in the professional kitchen as the 'Mise en Place', that is, advance preparations which can be used in the actual making of a dish.

1   Barding

This is the covering of items of meat, poultry or game and in some cases fish, with thin slices of fat bacon or salt pork fat. Its main functions are to prevent drying out during cooking, to supply any deficiency of natural fat where perceived, and in the process to add something in the way of flavour and improved eating qualities. It is mainly used in roasting but can also be used in poêling and braising. In the case of poultry the breast and legs should be completely covered with a single shaped slice of fat loosely tied on with two or three strings. For items of meat such as fillets of beef, joints of veal and game, where larding has not been carried out, they should be completely wrapped in the slices of fat, tied on carefully. In almost all cases, these slices should be removed before the end of the cooking time so that the item may obtain its desired colour.

2   BUTTERS

The following group of butters are widely used in the finishing of sauces or the accompanying of dishes and include those for thickening and cooking.

Flavoured or composite butters, such as parsley butter, have a wide range of uses including accompanying grills of meat and fish and the finishing of sauces. Generally, in the professional kitchen these compound butters are moulded into a cylindrical shape approximately 3cm in diameter by wrapping in greaseproof paper, and firming in a refrigerator. It is then cut into fairly thick ½–1cm slices with a hot knife and placed on crushed ice in a sauceboat. However, it should be borne in mind that a better result in eating quality can be obtained, especially when these butters are served with grills, if they are freshly made and then the required amount is placed on the food immediately on being served. If necessary these butters may be held for several days in a refrigerator either as moulded rolls or in a basin covered with greaseproof paper.

3   Beurre d'Ail – Garlic Butter

For 500g of softened butter, mix together thoroughly with 75g of peeled and very finely pounded garlic; pass through a very fine sieve and reserve for use as required.

4   Beurre d'Anchois – Anchovy Butter

For 500g of softened butter, mix together with 150g of anchovy fillets which have been well-drained, finely pounded and passed through a fine sieve. Or mix sufficient anchovy essence into softened butter to give a good colour and flavour. Reserve for use as required.

5   Beurre Bercy

Place 2dl of white wine and 50g of finely chopped shallot in a pan and reduce by three-quarters; allow to cool and mix together with 200g of softened butter; 200g of bone marrow, cut in dice, poached and drained; the juice of half a lemon and 20g of chopped parsley. Season as necessary with salt, pepper and a touch of cayenne. Reserve for use as required.

6   Beurre à la Bourguignonne

For 500g of softened butter, mix together with 50g of finely chopped shallot, 15g of crushed and very finely chopped garlic, 20g of chopped parsley, and salt and pepper to taste. Reserve for use as required.

SPECIAL POINT
This butter is used in the preparation of Escargots à la Bourguignonne as well as being suitable for grills of red meat.

7   Beurre Clarifié – Clarified Butter

Place the required amount of butter in a pan and allow to melt in a bain-marie of hot water. When the butter is clear, skim the surface and decant the butter carefully into a clean container leaving any liquid or sediment behind.

8   Beurre de Crevette – Shrimp Butter

Pound together equal quantities of shelled shrimps and butter. Pass through a fine sieve and season with salt, pepper and a touch of cayenne. Reserve for use as required.

9   Beurre Fondu

Carefully heat the required amount of butter in a pan until just melted and shake in a few drops of lemon juice. The result should have a slightly creamy appearance and in no way should resemble clarified butter.

10   Beurre Maître d'Hôtel – Parsley Butter

For 500g of softened butter add and mix in the juice of half a lemon, 20g of chopped parsley and season with salt, pepper and a touch of cayenne. Reserve for use as required.

11   Beurre Manié

Place two parts of soft butter and one of flour in a basin and mix together to a smooth paste.

12 Beurre Noir

Cook the required amount of butter in a frying-pan until well browned, shaking occasionally to ensure even colouring. Add a few drops of vinegar away from the fire and pour over the food immediately. The capers and chopped parsley which are an integral part of a dish designated 'au Beurre Noir' may be added to the butter before pouring it over the food.

13 Beurre Noisette – Brown Butter

Cook the required amount of butter in a frying-pan until brown, shaking occasionally to ensure even colouring. Pour over the food immediately. A little lemon juice may be added to the butter, according to the requirements of the dish.

14 Beurre Ravigote or Beurre Chivry

Blanch together for a few minutes 200g of mixed leaves of parsley, chervil, tarragon, salad burnet and chives; refresh them and squeeze firmly to remove most of the moisture. Pass through a fine sieve then mix together with 75g of very fine chopped and blanched shallot and 500g of softened butter. Season as necessary with salt, pepper and a touch of cayenne and reserve for use as required.

15 Blanc

5 litres
10 mins.

Stage	Ingredient	Quantity	Method
1	cold water	5 litres	Mix the flour with a little water to a
	flour	100g	smooth paste. Add the remainder of the
	juice of lemon	3	water and the lemon juice and whisk to
	salt	25g	remove any lumps. Season with the salt and bring to the boil while stirring.

16 Blanching

This term has five distinct applications:
1) To whiten meats for white stews such as blanquette or Irish stew. Cover the meat with cold water, bring to the boil, allow to boil for 3–4 mins. and immediately refresh and wash under cold running water. Drain well.
2) To partially remove excess of flavour such as when preparing certain vegetables for braising. Place the vegetables into boiling water, boil for 3–4 mins. and refresh and wash under cold running water. Drain well.
3) To remove the skins from foods, e.g. grapes or tomatoes. Plunge the items into boiling water for a few seconds. Try one to see if the skin is removable; if so, drain and skin.
4) To parcook, as in the case of fried potatoes where they are cooked in deep fat without colour in readiness for finishing for service.
5) To retain or improve the colour of certain items such as mint and tarragon leaves, cucumber or green of leek. Plunge the items into boiling water for a few seconds, refresh in cold water and drain.

17 Blinis

20 blinis
1½ hours

Stage	Ingredient	Quantity	Method
1	flour, strong	50g	Dissolve the yeast in the milk. Add the flour and mix to a loose paste. Place in a basin, cover with a warm damp cloth and allow to prove until double its size.
	yeast	30g	
	milk at 37°C	1dl	
2	flour, strong	250g	Sift the flour and salt into a basin and make a bay in the centre. Add the egg yolks and milk and whisk together to a smooth batter. Add the prepared paste from Stage 1 and whisk until smooth. Allow to prove in a warm place for 30 mins.
	milk at 37°C	3dl	
	egg yolks	4	
	salt	2g	
3	egg whites	4	Whisk until stiff and fold into the mixture.
4	clarified butter	250g	Heat a little in a pancake pan or special Blinis pans. Add ½dl of the mixture and cook gently until brown on both sides. Continue until all the mixture has been used.

18 Bone Marrow – Moelle

The best bone marrow is obtained from the shin of beef, because of its quality and its roughly cylindrical shape. This makes it possible to cut into rondels or dice which are ideal for garnishing. A certain amount of marrow can also be obtained from the shank although because of its shape it is not so useful. That obtained from a shin of veal is much smaller but makes up for its lack of size by its more creamy, buttery texture and flavour.

Extraction of the marrow from a shin of beef needs a certain amount of care so as to keep it as a whole as possible. To do this, first saw off 10–12cm from each end of the shin; it may be possible to extract a little marrow from each of these joint ends. Now hit the shin-bone firmly in three or four places along its length with the back of a cleaver, or similar, to crack it open. Open it up and remove the marrow in one piece if possible and carefully check and remove any splintered bone. Now place it in a basin, cover with well-salted water and leave in a cold room for a few hours, long enough to disgorge itself of all blood. After this, wash the marrow under gently-running cold water for 1–2 hours when the result should be a pale creamy white colour. Ideally it should be used as soon as possible but it can be stored successfully in cold water in a refrigerator for 2–3 days.

19 Bouquet Garni

A bouquet garni is a very convenient and useful means of adding background flavours to a cooking liquid. It can consist of various aromatic vegetables and herbs and other flavourings as determined by the requirements of the dish under preparation and the particular emphasis and subtlety of flavours required. The ingredients are tied together thus preventing them from dispersing in the liquid, and also making them easy to remove. Small items such as some spices and seeds cannot be included in a bouquet garni successfully and are best tied in a muslin bag separately. The firmest item should be on the outside enclosing the more delicate items and the whole should be tied securely along its length and especially at both ends; the size and amount of the ingredients should be in proportion to the amount of food to which it is to be added.

The most commonly used ingredients recognised as being suitable for most purposes are bayleaf, parsley stalks, and a sprig of thyme, in the centre of a few pieces of leek and celery.

20 Breadcrumbs

a) Dry: place light-coloured crusts of bread in a slow oven or hot-cupboard until dry and crisp but do not colour them. Pass through the crumbing attachment of a mincer, or pound in the mortar. Shake through a sieve and store in tins in a dry place.
b) White: Remove the crust from stale bread and rub the remaining white bread through a medium sieve or use a food processor. These breadcrumbs can be stored successfully in the refrigerator for up to one week.

21 Breadcrumbs, Fried

Heat 250g butter or clarified butter in a frying-pan and add 100g white breadcrumbs. Move and toss over continuously and at not too high a temperature until an even golden brown. Drain carefully and use as required.

22 Brunoise

This is the neat even cutting of vegetables into approximately 2mm dice or slightly larger. Where these cut vegetables are served as part of a dish their size not only helps in the rapid extraction of their flavours but also enhances appearance and eating quality.

23 Chiffonade

This refers to finely shredded vegetable leaves such as lettuce, spinach or sorrel. A chiffonade of lettuce, for example, is used raw in seafood cocktails. Chiffonades are stewed in a little butter without colouring and used as garnish in soups.

24 Chou Paste (general purpose)

1½ litres
30 mins.

Stage	Ingredient	Quantity	Method
1	water	½litre	Place in a deep pan and bring to the boil
	butter	100g	slowly in order that the butter is melted
	salt	5g	by the time the water is boiled.
2	flour	320g	Add, away from the fire, beating well with a wooden spatule. Return the pan to the fire and continue mixing until the mixture becomes smooth and does not stick to the sides of the pan. Cool slightly.
3	eggs	8	Add the eggs to the mixture one at a time and mix in thoroughly. Use as required.

25 Crêtes et Rognons de Coq – Cockscombs and Kidneys

1) Prick the cockscombs all over with a trussing needle and place in a basin of salt water with the cock's kidneys. Place in the refrigerator and allow to soak for 12 hours.
2) Wash the combs and kidneys well then blanch the combs for 5 mins., refresh, drain and rub off the skin with the aid of a little salt.
3) Prepare a Blanc (15) with the addition of a bouquet garni and an Oignon Clouté (65). Add the combs and cook until tender. Add the kidneys and simmer gently for a further 5 mins. Allow to cool in the cooking liquid and use as required.

26 Croûtons

a) Heart-shaped croûtons for stews, etc.: Remove the crust from a sandwich loaf and cut the bread into two triangular halves along the complete length. Using a long rigid knife, trim each half along its length into the shape of a heart when viewed from the end. Cut off single heart-shaped croûtons ½cm thick. Shallow fry in clarified butter until golden brown and drain well.
b) Round croûtons for tournedos, etc.: Cut ½cm-thick slices from a sandwich loaf and cut out circles of bread to the required size with a plain round cutter. Fry in clarified butter until golden brown and drain well.
c) Croûtons for roast game: Remove the crusts from a sandwich loaf and cut the bread into fairly thick oblongs; the size and thickness should be in keeping with the size of the bird. These oblong croûtons may be hollowed along the length so as to cradle the roast bird and the sides may be decorated by cutting with a knife. Fry in clarified butter until golden brown. Drain well and spread the hollow side with Farce à Gratin (38).
d) Croûtons for vegetable purées: Remove the crusts from a sandwich loaf then trim and cut the bread into small triangles 3mm thick and with 2½cm sides. Fry in clarified butter until golden brown and drain well.

Croûtons for soups, see (311).

27 Deglazing

This is the utilisation of the juices exuded during the roasting, poêling or shallow frying, in particular of meat, poultry and game, and occasionally of fish. Shallow frying results in the depositing of juices which go through the stages of first forming a glaze and then caramelising. In roasting and poêling, when carried out correctly, the juices are left in a viscous state; in this case it is firstly necessary to reduce and lightly caramelise them; in either case this results in the adding of colour and the modifying of the final taste and flavour. On no account should caramelisation be taken to the stage where it burns the glaze or, in poêling, burns also the vegetables and herbs which are part of the cooking.

The actual process of deglazing consists of adding appropriate liquids which can be stock, wine, spirits or prepared sauces, and the incorporation of the caramelised juices in the bottom of the pan. In the case of shallow frying where no cooking of added ingredients is to take place in the remaining fat, this fat should first be drained off, the liquid added immediately then flamed, reduced or simmered as called for in the recipe.

In roast meats, poultry and game, once the juices and sediment have been lightly caramelised, the fat should be drained off and the appropriate stock added then allowed to simmer. It is not necessary to remove every vestige of the fat, in fact it is a desirable feature that the gravy should be identifiable as being from a roast and no attempt made to obtain a clear consommé.

In the poêling of meats, drain off as much of the fat as possible, add the required liquid and/or sauce and allow to simmer very gently so as to extract the flavour of any vegetables and herbs used. In this case, it is essential to skim off all the fat from the final result.

28 Disgorging

This refers to the cleansing or purging of unwanted matter from an article of food and is a process carried out particularly for the removal of blood from items such as brains, sweetbreads and calf's head, so as to whiten them. It consists of careful soaking in cold running water, for preference up to 12 hours, but this can be speeded up by placing in a receptacle of well-salted water for 3–4 hours in a refrigerator. The salt water speeds up the process of osmosis and the item of food needs only to be washed then under very cold water for a short time for effective whitening to take place.

Disgorging is the term also applied to the purging of snails and shellfish such as mussels before cooking. For snails soak for 2 hours or so in salt water with the addition of a little vinegar and a pinch of flour. For mussels soak in salted water for 2–3 hours; this will help to rid them of sand as well as purging them. Wash in clean water afterwards before cleaning and cooking.

Vegetables such as aubergine and courgettes will release unwanted juices if the cut surfaces are sprinkled with salt and allowed to drain for a suitable time.

29 Duxelles

300g
25 mins.

Stage	Ingredient	Quantity	Method
1	butter	75g	Melt the butter in a small pan and cook
	onion, finely		the onion without colour.
	chopped	100g	
2	mushrooms, finely	750g	Add the mushrooms to the onions,
	chopped		lightly season and cook gently until fairly
	parsley,	1 tbsp	dry. Finish with the chopped parsley.
	chopped		Place in a basin, covered with a buttered
			paper and reserve in the refrigerator.

30 Fat Clarification

Good clean trimmings of fat, especially beef, should be utilised for cooking purposes. It must be rendered and clarified in the following manner – pass the fat through a mincer or chop with a knife, place in a pan with a little water and allow to cook slowly until bubbling ceases and the fat is clear. Do not overheat. Allow to cool and strain.

31 Fines Herbes

This refers to certain fresh herbs usually parsley, chervil, tarragon and chives. They are frequently finely chopped and used in the preparation and finishing of a wide number of dishes. The proportion of herbs used should be approx. three parts of parsley to one part of each of the other herbs, when chopped.

32 Flamber

This French culinary term means to flame or singe and denotes the final singeing with a naked flame to remove the last vestiges of feather and hair from poultry and game birds.

However, the term is more commonly used to denote the flaming of spirits or liqueurs which are set alight during or at the end of the cooking process. It is applied to many fish and shellfish, meat, poultry, game and sweet dishes.

The spirit can be added already alight just before serving or added neat to the finished dish if hot enough which will allow the alcohol to vaporise and then be lit. During the cooking process when using an open-top stove, it is only necessary to tilt and pull the pan to one side after adding the spirit for it to automatically ignite. If there is no direct flame from the stove, a lighted taper rather than a match can do the same job. Care should be taken to keep the hands out of reach of the flames. In all cases the flames should be allowed to die out completely before continuing the cooking or serving.

The effect of flaming is twofold. Firstly it results in the concentration of the essential flavours of the spirit or liqueur used; it allows them to be absorbed by whatever is being prepared although there is a marginal loss of perfume. And secondly a very subtle intermarriage of these flavours with those of the dish under preparation takes place. Thus it does not impart an overlaid flavour and perfume as is the case when a spirit or liqueur is added raw just before serving.

33 Fleurons

These are small puff pastry shapes used mainly for garnishing fish dishes although they can be a useful alternative to croûtons for fricassées of poultry.

Roll out Puff Pastry (1736) to approx. 2mm thick and cut out crescent shapes with a 4–5cm round fluted cutter. Place on a dampened baking tray, eggwash, allow to rest for 30 mins. then bake at 215°C until a light golden brown. Other shapes such as diamonds or rounds can be cut and used as thought fit and proper.

34 FORCEMEATS AND STUFFINGS – FARCES

The term forcemeat is generally used to describe fine mixtures of meat or fish used for such things as pies, pâtés, terrines and galantines, or for quenelles and mousses as well as for stuffing foods. Stuffing, on the other hand, is a term particular to a mixture often based on breadcrumbs and used solely for the stuffing of articles of food. The French term Farce is applicable to both.

35 Farce Américaine

1kg
25 mins.

Stage	Ingredient	Quantity	Method
1	breadcrumbs, white	500g	Place all the ingredients in a basin,
	thyme, rubbed	1 tbsp	season with salt and pepper and mix
	parsley, chopped	2 tbsps	together.
	mustard, dry	5g	
2	butter	100g	Heat the butter in a pan. Add the onions
	onions, finely chopped	350g	and cook gently without colour then add
			to the breadcrumbs.

3   small Lardons, sautéed 150g   Add to the rest of the ingredients and
       (51)   mix well together.

This stuffing is suitable for roast and poêléed poultry.

---

36 Farce Californienne

Prepare Farce Américaine (35) adding 150g of cleaned chicken livers cut in small dice and lightly sautéed in butter.
This stuffing is suitable for roast and poêleed poultry.

---

37 Farce Duxelloise – Mushroom Stuffing

450g
15 mins.

Stage	Ingredient	Quantity	Method
1	Duxelles (29) white wine Demi-glace (112) garlic, finely chopped	300g 1dl 1dl ½ clove	Place in a sauteuse, add the white wine, demi-glace and garlic. Season and reduce slightly.
2	breadcrumbs	100g	Add the breadcrumbs and reduce to a piping consistency. Adjust the seasoning.

This is suitable for stuffing tomatoes, aubergines and courgettes.

---

38 Farce à Gratin

850g
25 mins.

Stage	Ingredient	Quantity	Method
1	butter fat bacon, diced	50g 250g	Melt the butter in a frying-pan. Add the bacon and fry gently with a little colour.
2	onions, finely chopped thyme bayleaf	 75g sprig ½	Add and fry with the bacon until light brown.
3	chicken livers	500g	Remove the gall bladders and any discoloured surfaces. Add the livers to the bacon and onions, season and fry quickly to colour, keeping slightly underdone.
4			Pass all the ingredients through a fine sieve and allow to cool.
5	butter	100g	Add the butter and mix in. Place the mixture in a basin. Cover with a buttered paper and keep for further use.

This is suitable for croûtons and the stuffing of poultry and game birds.

---

39 Farce Mousseline – Fine Mousseline Forcemeat   850g
35 mins.

Stage	Ingredient	Quantity	Method
1	flesh of poultry, veal, fish, or game, etc. (free of skin, bones or sinew)	500g	Either pound finely or pass twice through the fine plate of a mincer and place in a basin. Chill thoroughly.
2	egg whites, cold salt pepper	2	Season with a little salt and pepper. Add the whites little by little, beating together thoroughly with a wooden spatule until stiff and elastic in texture.
3			Pass the mixture through a fine sieve or food processor, replace in the basin and again chill thoroughly in the refrigerator.
4	double cream, cold	3½dl	Gradually add to the mixture, beating thoroughly with a wooden spatule. Check the seasoning and use as required.

Suitable for quenelles, mousselines, mousses and fine stuffings for meat, poultry and fish.

SPECIAL POINTS
a) Whichever type of forcemeat is being prepared it is always advisable to first poach a small piece to check its texture and quality before moulding; if too firm add a little extra cream, if too soft and watery it may be necessary to add a little more egg-white. The quality to be aimed for is the very lightest possible texture without any signs of disaggregation and wateriness.
b) It is essential that the flesh is as fresh as possible; the albumen present develops elasticity and is the main quality for allowing the cream to be incorporated in an homogenous manner. As the flesh ages so the albumen tends to disintegrate.
c) At all stages the ingredients should be as cold as possible without of course freezing. It is good practice to stand the basin at Stage 4 in a receptacle of crushed ice.
d) Mousseline forcemeats of shellfish are best made where 25% of the total weight of flesh consists of whiting or sole. For lobster forcemeat incorporate the coral and eggs of the lobster into the mixture.
e) The use of a food processor for making this forcemeat or similar can save a considerable amount of time and energy.

---

40 Farce de Poisson – Fish Forcemeat   1kg
35 mins.

Stage	Ingredient	Quantity	Method
1	whiting fillets, free of all skin and bones	500g	Pass twice through the fine plate of the mincer and place in a basin.
2	Panada (68) salt pepper nutmeg	250g 5g pinch pinch	Add to the fish and mix in thoroughly. Pass through a fine sieve or food processor. Chill thoroughly.

3	eggs	3	Add the eggs to the mixture one at a
	double cream, cold	2½dl	time mixing well. Finish by working the cream in thoroughly.

This forcemeat can be used for stuffing any white fish.

41 Farce de Volaille – Chicken Forcemeat

This is prepared in the same way as Farce de Poisson (40), using 500g of raw breast of chicken flesh instead of the fish. It is suitable for stuffing poultry.

42 Apple, Raisin and Walnut Stuffing
1kg
30 mins.

Stage	Ingredient	Quantity	Method
1	apples, cooking	500g	Peel, core and cut the apple into 1cm
	butter	50g	dice. Heat the butter in a heavy shallow
	mixed spice	good pinch	pan and when just turning brown add
	Calvados	½dl	the apples. Fry and toss over quickly for 2–3 mins. only, sprinkle with the spice then add the Calvados and turn out into a basin.
2	shallot, very		Cook the shallots with the butter until
	finely chopped	75g	just soft and without colour, then add to
	butter	25g	the apples along with the raisins and the
	raisins, soaked		walnuts cut in approx. ½cm pieces.
	and drained	125g	
	walnuts, skinned	125g	
3	bread, slices	15	Discard the crusts then toast the bread
	fresh basil,		and cut into approx. 1cm dice. Add to
	roughly chopped	2 tbsps	the mixture along with the basil and season with salt and pepper. Mix together and use as required.

This mixture is especially suitable for stuffing goose or duck for roasting. Leaving the mixture in a suitably dry state will allow it to soak up the juices and fat of the bird as it cooks.

43 Chestnut Stuffing
1¼kg
30 mins.

Stage	Ingredient	Quantity	Method
1	pork, lean	350g	Mince the pork and fat very finely and
	pork, back fat	150g	place in a basin with the breadcrumbs.
	white breadcrumbs	200g	
2	onions, finely		Cook the onions in the butter until just
	chopped	150g	soft and translucent, allow to cool then
	butter	75g	add to the meat together with the thyme,
	powdered thyme	pinch	basil, mace and eggs. Season with salt
	powdered basil	pinch	and pepper and mix well together.
	ground mace	pinch	
	eggs	2	

3	chestnuts, half-cooked (1486)	450g	Add to the mixture either whole or broken in largish pieces, and mix carefully together.

This mixture is suitable for stuffing turkey.

---

44 Sage and Onion Stuffing

1kg
20 mins.

Stage	Ingredient	Quantity	Method
1	duck or pork dripping onions, finely chopped	250g 350g	Melt the dripping in a pan. Add the onions and cook gently without colour. Remove from the stove and place in a basin.
2	breadcrumbs, white parsley, chopped sage, rubbed	500g 5g 15g	Add, season with salt and pepper and mix in well.

This stuffing may be used to stuff ducks and geese. If intended to be cooked separately or for stuffing joints of pork, mix two-thirds of the finished quantity with one-third the amount of good pork sausage-meat and 1 egg.

---

45 Thyme and Parsley Stuffing

1kg
20 mins.

Stage	Ingredient	Quantity	Method
1	breadcrumbs, white chopped suet parsley, chopped thyme, rubbed lemon, grated rind nutmeg, grated	500g 250g 5g 5g 1 pinch	Place all these ingredients in a basin, season and mix together.
2	onion, chopped butter eggs milk	200g 50g 3	Cook the onion in the butter until just soft, then add to the breadcrumb mixture with the eggs and mix together with a little milk if too dry. Check the seasoning.

This stuffing may be used for veal, lamb and poultry.

---

46 Garlic, to prepare

The technique of working crushed garlic to a paste with salt is not necessarily the best way of preparing garlic for use; it tends to disperse and waste much of the essential volatile oils. The following methods for preparing garlic are to be preferred:

To separate the head of garlic into cloves: strike the head of garlic firmly with the heel of the hand. This should break open the head into separate cloves.

To peel the cloves whole for inserting into food: use a small knife to peel back the skin from the root end piece by piece to leave the cloves of garlic whole and undamaged. Cut off any root.

To crush the cloves: lay on a chopping board and strike firmly with the flat side of a medium heavy cook's knife. Remove the skin, the root end and any green central shoot if present.

To chop: crush and remove the skin, root ends and any green shoots. Flatten the garlic properly with the flat side of the knife then chop through finely. Use immediately.

47 Green Vegetable Colouring

Pound or finely mince 1kg washed and drained spinach. Place in a cloth and squeeze firmly into a small pan to completely extract the juices. Place in a bain-marie of hot water and allow these juices to coagulate. Carefully pour onto a clean damp muslin stretched over a basin to drain. Remove the resultant green paste to a small basin and use as required. Mixed with double its quantity of soft butter it will keep for some days if covered with greaseproof paper and stored in a refrigerator.

48 Jardinière

This refers to a mixture of vegetables which can be served as a vegetable in its own right or as a garnish for meat dishes such as stews and braised meats. It consists of equal quantities of carrots and turnips cut into batons approx. 2cm long × 4mm × 4mm, French beans cut in diamonds, and peas (see 1531).

49 Julienne

This term refers to items of food cut into thin strips. The actual size depends to some extent upon the type and texture of the food being used, but the strips should not be longer than approx. 4cm.

50 Larding

Larding is a process for inserting strips of pork fat or fat bacon into joints or cuts of meat which are deficient in fat. The strips of fat may be marinated with brandy, various spices and herbs before being inserted which allows the opportunity of varying flavours. The fat should be well-chilled first to facilitate cutting.

Method for larding large joints:
1) Cut the fat into strips ½cm square and a little longer than the joint to be larded.
2) Push a large larding-pin (daubing needle) right through the joint along the grain of the meat and twist it round two or three times so as to make a hole; withdraw the needle.
3) Insert the strip of fat in the hollow of the needle along its length attaching it to the hook at the end.
4) Push the needle through the prepared hole and out the other end so that the lardon protrudes 2–3cm outside the joint. Disengage the fat from the hook and hold firmly while carefully withdrawing the needle.
5) Repeat as necessary, inserting five or six strips through a joint of average size, making a neat pattern.

Method for larding small joints:
1) Cut the fat into strips approx. 8cm long × 3mm square.
2) Insert a strip of fat into a small larding needle, push it into the surface of the joint and out on the same side so as to leave only the two ends showing.

3) Repeat the larding process in an even sequence along the length and around the sides of the joint until it is completely covered with an even pattern.

51 Lardons

These are baton-shaped pieces cut from streaky bacon. The size should be in keeping with the dish with which they are to be served.

Cut the streaky bacon into slices of the appropriate thickness and then into batons. Each lardon should show the layers of fat and lean meat running across its height. Blanch in boiling water, drain and fry until golden brown in a little fat. Drain.

52 Lemons

Lemons are frequently used for garnishing and are cut into various shapes according to requirements.
a) Peeled slices: Remove all peel and pith from the lemon taking care not to damage the inner skin. Cut into slices and remove any pips. These slices are suitable for fish meunière.
b) Grooved slices: Cut grooves in the skin of the lemon from top to bottom at regular intervals all the way round. Cut into slices and remove any pips. These slices are suitable for poached and grilled fish.
c) Quarters: Cut off both ends of the lemon square without cutting into flesh. Cut from top to bottom into quarters. Cut off the strips of pith from the centres and remove any pips which are showing.
d) Halves: Cut off both ends of the lemon square without cutting into the flesh. Cut in half horizontally, remove any pips and cut a thin strip from around the edge without detaching it completely from the lemon. Curl the strip round and pull the end through the centre to make a little knot. Or, cut off both ends of the lemon square without cutting into the flesh, then using a small sharp knife make zig-zag cuts into the lemon around its middle. These should be deep enough into the lemon to allow it to separate into two tooth-edged halves. Remove any pips showing.
e) Segments: These are prepared in the same way as Orange Segments (66).

53 Marinating

Marinating is a process for adding flavour to food, or for tenderising it as with some joints of meat. In many cases it is a combination of both. As an added factor it can extend the storage life of certain meats and fish. However, this last possibility should not be a first consideration.

There are two main types of marinade, a) quick or short marinades which are used particularly for flavouring small cuts of fish, meat, poultry and sometimes vegetables, and b) raw and cooked marinades which are suitable for large joints or poultry. They require covering with the liquid and a much longer period of time for the process to be satisfactory.

54 Marinade, quick (for small cuts of meat, poultry and fish etc.)

Basically this can consist of sprinkling the items with 3 parts olive oil to 1 of lemon juice or wine vinegar together with salt, pepper and chopped parsley. These ingredients can be augmented as seen fit with finely chopped shallots and other herbs such as thyme, bayleaf, basil etc.

For other purposes, especially in the use of strips of fat or meats for pies, terrines and galantines, the marinating can consist of just a little sprinkled brandy and seasoning. This again can be augmented with such things as spices, powdered herbs and dry white wine.

In both cases the item of food should be frequently turned over but the period of time for marinating should not be more than 2 hours – that is to say just sufficient time for the food to be impregnated fully with the flavours of the marinade.

---

55 Marinade, Red Wine (for joints of meat, game and poultry)   1 litre

Stage	Ingredient	Quantity	Method
1	red wine	1 litre	Place half the vegetables and herbs in
	vinegar, red wine	1 dl	the bottom of a stainless steel or glazed
	oil	1 dl	basin. Season the pieces of meat with
	carrots } sliced	150g	salt, place on top then add the wine,
	onions } small	150g	vinegar and oil which have been mixed
	celery }	150g	together. Finish with the remaining
	garlic, crushed	2 cloves	vegetables and herbs and cover with
	peppercorns	15	greaseproof paper.
	bayleaf	1	
	thyme	1 sprig	
	cloves	3	
	parsley stalks	15g	
2			Keep in a refrigerator and turn the meat over now and again.

---

56 Marinade, White Wine (for joints of meat, game and poultry)

Prepare as Red Wine Marinade (55) but substitute dry white wine and white wine vinegar for the red wine and vinegar.

---

57 Marinade, Cooked

Both the red wine and white wine marinades can be cooked before use. This has the effect of making the flavourings more assimilable and thus helps to speed up the process.

Method
Lightly colour the vegetables in the oil then tip into a suitable pan with the rest of the ingredients plus 2½dl of water. Simmer gently for 40–45 minutes to extract the maximum of flavours. Strain carefully and allow to become completely cold before use.

SPECIAL POINTS RELATING TO ALL RAW AND COOKED MARINADES
a) It is essential that the joints being marinated should be just covered with the liquid.
b) The length of time for the process to be satisfactory depends naturally on the size of the joint. As a guide: joints of beef for braising, 1–2 days; joints of venison, 2–3 days; chicken and hare cut in portions, 12–15 hours.
c) Other ingredients may be added as seen fit, e.g. rosemary, basil, juniper berries and mace when marinating venison. A little added brandy can be an excellent addition.
d) The marinating liquid and its flavouring are better used in the cooking of the dish rather than being used again and again for the marination of other joints.

58 Mirepoix

This term refers to a mixture of vegetables and herbs used for flavouring various dishes. The standard proportions for a mirepoix are: 250g carrots, 250g onion, 250g celery. Cut into rough dice with the addition of ½ bayleaf and a small sprig of thyme. The mirepoix for poêléed meat or poultry should include 100g of diced bacon trimmings in addition to the above ingredients.

The ingredients and their proportions can be varied as necessary and according to the dish under preparation. Other herbs such as rosemary or tarragon or flavourings like fennel and parsnip can be used or items like carrot can be omitted if it is thought that its colour would interfere with the result.

59 Monter au Beurre

This is a French culinary term which refers to the thickening of a reduced cooking liquor with butter to make a sauce and does not imply the simple buttering of a sauce.

In practice this technique is reserved for the utilisation and thickening of: a) the cooking liquor from the shallow poaching of fish or poultry; b) the liquid resulting from the deglazing with wine, stock etc. of the pan used for shallow frying; or c) very light meat and fish glazes.

The process consists of first reducing the cooking liquid or deglazed juices to a light viscous syrup then removing it from direct heat, allowing it to cool slightly and finally adding softened butter little by little whilst whisking or shaking the pan. In effect it becomes a process of emulsification similar to the making of Sauce Hollandaise. It results in the thickening of the reduced liquid which can absorb up to four times its own volume of butter.

SPECIAL POINTS
a) It is advisable to use best-quality unsalted butter – the reduction of cooking liquids concentrates any seasonings used and salted butter could possibly mean a too salty finish.
b) Sauces prepared in this way tend to be unstable and break down if not used immediately. Extremes of temperatures should be avoided. A useful working temperature for adding the butter would be 40–50°C and maintaining it.

60 Mushrooms, cooked à Blanc

This is the cooking of white mushrooms either whole, quartered, sliced or in julienne, so that the colour can be retained. The following method and amounts will give the desired result: place 500g of prepared mushrooms, the juice of half a lemon, 50g of butter, ½dl of water and a pinch of salt in a suitable pan. Cover with a buttered paper and bring to the boil rapidly. Cook until soft, remove from the fire and leave in the cooking liquor until required.

61 Mushrooms, sautéed

Mushrooms can be sautéed whole, quartered or sliced. For each 500g of mushrooms allow 50g of butter. Heat the butter in a frying-pan and, just as it turns brown, add the mushrooms, season and fry quickly, tossing them over and over to ensure even cooking.

62 Onions, to peel

Large onions: using a small knife, cut almost through the top of the onion then pull this with the adhering brown skin down to the root end. Continue to pull down the remaining brown skin to the root end then cut off square from the onion without removing the root; the root is necessary to hold the onion together for cutting, chopping or when being cooked etc.

Button onions: for ease of manipulation, first soak the onions in hot water for 10 mins. or so. Using a small sharp knife, cut closely across the root end without cutting deep into it, then separate the brown skin a piece at a time from the onion, peeling it off to the top end. Repeat until completely free of skin. Cut off the very tip only of the top end; this will make sure that the centre of the onion cannot be forced out whilst cooking.

63 Onion, to chop

1) Peel the onion and cut in half vertically, down and through the root end; lay one half on the board with the root end facing away.
2) Slice downwards but stopping short of the root end.
3) Turn the onion sideways, hold it together and cut two or three times horizontally towards the root end but again stopping short of it.
4) Now cut down vertically across the slices to give small particles. Do not cut the root end, it can be used for flavourings. Proceed with the other half.

The fineness of the particles depends on the closeness of the cuts.

64 Onion, to slice

Peel the onion and cut in half vertically, down and through the root end. Lay one half on the board, cut off the root end and reserve for other uses. Now slice finely from top to bottom along the grain of the onion.

If the onions are very large and likely to give slices which are too long, cut across from side to side before slicing.

65 Onion, Studded – Oignon Piqué or Clouté

Attach a bayleaf to a peeled onion by pushing cloves through the bayleaf and into the onion. The onion should not be too large and the number of onions, bayleaf and cloves should be in accordance with the quantity of liquid or sauce to be flavoured.

66 Orange Segments

Cut off both ends of the orange squarely. Stand it on a chopping board and cut downwards following the shape of the orange to remove all the skin and pith and as little of the fruit as possible. Hold the orange in one hand, remove each segment by cutting along each side of it close to the dividing membrane; do not cut through the centre core. Place in a basin and continue to remove all the segments in the same manner. Squeeze the juice from the remainder of the orange.

67 PANADES – PANADAS

Panadas are thickened mixtures used in the binding of fish and meat stuffings and forcemeats. They can add a useful firmness where required and can be helpful in levelling out the over-assertive flavours of some fish. They should only be used as an extender where economy is an absolute and overriding factor.

68 Panade à la Farine – Flour Panada
500g
20 mins.

Place 50g butter and 3dl water into a pan, season with salt and pepper and bring to the boil. Add 150g flour and mix well off the fire with a wooden spatule. Return to the stove and mix well until smooth and cooked (approx. 5 mins.). Spread on a buttered tray, butter the surface and allow to cool before use.

69 Panade à la Frangipane
500g
20 mins.

Place 125g flour in a basin, add 4 egg yolks, 1dl of milk and season with salt, pepper and a little grated nutmeg. Mix together to a smooth paste. Bring 1½dl milk and 75g butter to the boil slowly so that the butter is melted then whisk quickly into the paste. Place this mixture in a pan and cook slowly on the stove, mixing well with a wooden spatule until thick, smooth and cooked, approx 5–8 mins. Spread on a buttered tray, butter the surface and allow to cool before using.

70 Panade au Pain – Bread Panada
500g
20 mins.

Add 300g white breadcrumbs to 3dl boiling milk and season with salt and pepper. Mix well with a wooden spatule over the fire until the mixture is thick and smooth. Spread on a buttered tray, butter the surface and allow to cool before use.

71 Pancakes, Plain
Approx. 25 pancakes
25 mins.

Stage	Ingredient	Quantity	Method
1	flour	250g	Sift the flour and salt into a basin. Make
	salt	2g	a bay and add the eggs. Add the milk
	eggs	2	slowly and whisk continuously to a
	milk	½ litre	smooth batter.
2	lard, melted	150g	Heat the pancake pan, add a little of the lard and reheat until very hot. Tip out the surplus lard, add approx. ⅓dl of batter sufficient to thinly coat the bottom of the pan. Cook quickly until brown on both sides then turn out on a tray. Continue until all the batter has been used.

72 Paner à l'Anglaise – to Breadcrumb

This refers to the process of coating items of food with egg and breadcrumbs.
1) Season the item of food if necessary.
2) Pass through flour and shake off the surplus.
3) Pass through eggwash and remove the surplus. (Eggwash: to 5 eggs, add ¼dl of oil, ¼dl of water and mix well together.)
4) Place in white breadcrumbs, cover with crumbs, and pat in.
5) Shake off surplus crumbs, flatten the item lightly with a palette knife, neaten the edges and mark one side trellis-fashion with the edge of the palette knife.

73 Parsley, chopped

Wash parsley in cold water, discard the stalks and chop as required with a sharp knife. Place in the corner of a clean cloth and squeeze out the surplus moisture. Rub the cloth to separate the particles of parsley then place in a basin. Chopped parsley should always be used fresh.

74 Parsley, fried

Dry picked parsley in a cloth. Place into a frying-basket and plunge into very hot deep fat for a few seconds; remove while still green and crisp. Drain on kitchen paper and use as a garnish with deep-fried foods.

75 Parsley, picked

Wash the parsley in cold water and pick off sprigs. Keep these in a basin of cold water to use as a garnish. Shake off surplus water before using.

76 Pâte à Frire – Frying Batter

1 litre
1¼ hours

Stage	Ingredient	Quantity	Method
1	flour, strong	400g	Sift into a basin and make a bay.
	salt	2g	
	sugar	5g	
2	eggs	4	Break the eggs into the bay. Dissolve the
	yeast	15g	yeast in the water and pour into the bay
	water at 37°C	5dl	with the oil. Gradually mix in the flour,
	oil	½dl	whisking to a smooth batter.
3			Allow to prove for 1 hour in a warm place.

77 Paysanne

This term can be applied to a method of cutting vegetables for certain dishes. Vegetables such as carrots, turnips, swede, potato, leek, cabbage and celery are cut into thin slices or pieces which can be square or round in shape. The approximate size is 1cm square or 1–1½cm in diameter for rounds.

78 Pimento, to skin

Place the pimento into very hot fat and turn over and over until the outer skin blisters. Remove from the fat and rub off the skin. Or impale the pimento on a fork and place over a gas jet until the skin blisters. Rub or scrape off the skin and wash. Fresh, firm ones can be peeled with a potato peeler.

79 Pimento, as a garnish

Skin and remove the seeds from the pimento and cut the flesh into julienne or dice. Place a little butter in a sauteuse, add the pimento, season lightly, cover with a lid and cook gently on the side of the stove until tender.

80 Pluches

This descriptive term is generally applied to very small sprigs of parsley or chervil, blanched and used as a garnish.

81 Printanière

This refers to a mixture of spring vegetables cut as a garnish for items such as stewed and braised meats and soups. It consists of equal quantities of small balls of carrots and turnips cut with a small round vegetable cutter, small diamonds of French beans and peas. Cook in boiling salted water and drain. Toss in butter if required for garnishing meats or poultry. Jardinière de Légumes (1531) or Macédoine de Légumes (1532), cut smaller, can also be used when designating a dish à la Printanière.

82 Quenelles for Garnishing

Quenelles can be prepared and moulded from various forcemeats in shapes and sizes as determined by their ultimate use. They are especially useful for garnishing soups and fish, meat and poultry dishes as well as being prepared as dishes in their own right. As a garnish for prepared dishes they are best moulded using teaspoons.

Mousseline Forcemeat (39) is more suitable for those quenelles used in garnishing consommés and for dishes in their own right. In this last case the menu titling of Mousseline instead of Quenelle can be more descriptive.

The following recipe which gives a firmer texture is more suitable for the preparation of quenelles to be used as part of a garnish which is mixed with a sauce.

Other quenelles can be prepared using the following recipe but substituting the whiting with lean veal, chicken, ham, game or other fish as needed. The proportions of ingredients should be followed and an appropriate stock used for the poaching, e.g. chicken stock for quenelles of chicken.

83   Quenelles de Poisson – Quenelles of Fish   850g
1 hour

Stage	Ingredient	Quantity	Method
1	whiting fillets, skinned	500g	Pass the fish twice through the fine plate of the mincer and place in a basin. Add

	egg whites	2	the egg whites, season and beat thoroughly together with a wooden spatule.
2	Panada (68)	200g	Add to the mixture and mix in thoroughly. Pass through a fine sieve, replace in the basin and thoroughly chill in the refrigerator.
3	double cream, cold	2½dl	Gradually add to the mixture beating in thoroughly with a wooden spatule. Check seasoning.
4			Butter a deep tray. Mould the mixture into small oval shapes using two teaspoons and place on the tray.
5	Fumet de Poisson (101)	2 litres	Barely cover the quenelles with fish stock, cover with a buttered paper and poach in a moderate oven at 175°C until firm.
6			Drain the quenelles if required for immediate use, or place in a basin and cover with the cooking liquor and reserve for further use.

SPECIAL POINT

If for use as a garnish for consommé, the quenelles are best piped, using a plain or fancy tube, into small neat shapes onto a buttered tray. They should then be poached with the appropriate stock. Mousseline Forcemeat (39) is more suitable for these quenelles.

---

84 Sabayon

Place the required number of egg yolks in a clean, well-tinned copper or stainless steel sauteuse. Whisk in just sufficient water to make the yolks fairly liquid using a thin flexible sauce whisk. Place in a bain-marie of hot water and whisk continuously until cooked; this stage is reached when the sabayon clings to the whisk when raised from the pan. Use immediately.

---

85 Salt Curing and Pickling

There are two main methods of salting – dry salting and using a brine solution. In both cases flavour and taste are modified by the addition of other items such as sugars, spices, herbs and wines. Saltpetre provides the pleasing red colour to the meats. In both methods it is essential that the containers and cover should be perfectly clean before use – ideally they should be sterilised. Metal containers should never be used.

---

86 Dry Salt Curing – Salaison à Sec

Especially suitable for smaller joints of beef, pork and poultry.

Stage	Ingredient	Quantity	Method
1	sea salt	2kg	Mix all these ingredients thoroughly
	saltpetre	75g	together. Prick the meats well with a
	sugar	100g	trussing needle then rub all surfaces well
	peppercorns,		with the prepared salt.
	crushed	5g	
	cloves, crushed	8	
	juniper berries,		
	crushed	10g	
	mace, ground	pinch	
	bayleaf, crushed	2	
	thyme, crushed	2 pinches	
2			Cover the bottom of a sterilised poly-thene or glazed earthenware container with some of the prepared salt, place the joints on top then cover with the remaining salt. Place a clean wooden lid on top and weigh down slightly. Keep in the refrigerator and turn the meats occasionally.

SPECIAL POINTS
a) The amount of salt needed depends on the number and volume of the joints to be salted. Generally there should be enough salt to cover the meat – this works out at approximately 500g salt per 1kg of meat.
b) The length of time necessary depends on size and shape. In general, small items like the breast of goose, will need 24–36 hours. Larger and thicker joints will need in the region of 1 day for each 1cm of thickness, say 5–6 days for a belly of pork.

---

87 Brine Pickling – Salaison Liquide   25 litres

Especially suitable for joints of beef, pork, and ox-tongue.

Stage	Ingredient	Quantity	Method
1	water	25 litres	Place all these ingredients into a stain-less steel or well-tinned pan and bring to
	sea salt	5kg	the boil. Skim well, simmer for 15 mins.
	saltpetre	200g	and allow to become completely cold.
	brown sugar	250g	
	black peppercorns	5g	
	bayleaf	3	
	thyme	sprig	
	cloves	6	
2			Strain the brine into a very clean poly-thene or glazed earthenware receptacle or brine tank then immerse the joints for

pickling. Cover with a clean lid and keep cool or place in a refrigerator. It is useful to occasionally move the joints around.

Average pickling times:

Silverside of beef	8–10kg	10–14 days
Brisket or plate of beef	8–10kg	5– 7 days
Leg of pork	4kg	5– 7 days
Belly of pork	3kg	3– 5 days
Ox-tongue	2kg	3– 5 days

SPECIAL POINTS

a) An 80% salt-saturated solution should be aimed for. This can be judged by placing a potato in the cold brine; it should just float near to the surface. If it sinks, more salt is required and if it floats proud of the brine adjust the density with more water.
b) Adequate salting at the centre of large joints can be effected by the occasional use of a brine syringe to inject the brine where needed.
c) Ox-tongues should be well-pricked with a trussing needle before placing in the brine.

88 Suet, chopped

Use beef kidney suet. Remove and discard all skin and membranes then place the suet on a chopping board and chop finely with the addition of a little flour to prevent it sticking together.

89 Suet Pastry, for 25–30 Dumplings and Puddings 1kg
15 mins.

Stage	Ingredient	Quantity	Method
1	flour	500g	Sift the flour, baking powder and salt
	baking powder	15g	into a basin. Add the suet and mix in
	salt	10g	lightly.
	beef kidney suet, chopped	300g	
2	water, cold	2½dl	Make a bay in the centre, add the water and mix lightly to form a firm paste. Use as required.

90 Tomates Concassées – Chopped or Diced Tomatoes

Remove the eyes from the tomatoes then blanch and peel them. Cut in half horizontally, remove the seeds and cut or roughly chop the flesh into ¾–1cm dice. 1kg of fresh tomatoes will yield approx. 750g of diced flesh.

91 Tomates Concassées, Cooked – Fondue de Tomates   500g
45 mins.

This refers to roughly chopped tomatoes which are cooked for use as a garnish or in some cases as part of a dish.

Stage	Ingredient	Quantity	Method
1	butter	75g	Melt the butter in a small pan, add the
	onion, finely		onion and garlic and cook without col-
	chopped	50g	our.
	garlic, finely		
	chopped	½ clove	
2	Tomates Concassées		Add the tomatoes and bouquet garni and
	(90)	750g	season with salt, pepper and a pinch of
	sugar	pinch	sugar. Cook gently on the side of the
	celery ⎫	25g	stove until most of the moisture has
	parsley ⎬ Bouquet		evaporated. Discard the bouquet.
	stalks ⎬ Garni	5g	
	bayleaf ⎭	1	

SPECIAL POINT
Cooked Tomates Concassées may be placed in a basin, covered with greaseproof paper and stored for use as required in the refrigerator.

---

92 Truffles –Truffes

There are a number of varieties of this underground fungus of which only two are considered to be of real value for cookery. These are the so-called white Piedmont truffle much used in Italian cookery, and the black truffle which is the best in terms of colour and perfume, those from Périgord enjoying the best reputation.

Black truffles can be cooked as a dish in their own right but tend to be used mostly as an ingredient of such things as salpicons, forcemeats, stuffings, pâtés and galantines. They are obtainable as a commercially prepared product and these are mainly used in the garnishing and decoration of hot and cold dishes.

For the garnishing and decoration of hot dishes cut the truffle in thin slices and as appropriate, pass through jus lié or melted butter just prior to placing on the prepared item of food.

4
Stocks, Glazes, Thickening and Binding Agents

FONDS – STOCKS

Stock is the most important liquid base used in the preparation of many dishes such as soups, sauces, stews and braisings. When correctly made from good-quality fresh ingredients in the correct proportions, good stock can only enhance the quality of the dish with which it is used; if badly-made or stale stock is used, it may ruin the dish – the constant simmering for days on end with the continuous addition of dubious ingredients resulting in an indefinable, overcooked, cloudy and tasteless stock should have no place in the kitchen.

In the preparation of stocks which require bones, these should be as meaty as possible if some sort of body and flavour is to be imparted; the addition of tougher meats like shin of beef, old boiling fowls and hocks of raw unsmoked ham or bacon can be more than justified these days when the general importance of stocks has never been so high. It should be remembered that these meats can be removed when cooked and used later for other dishes.

It is essential that the ingredients and flavourings used take account of the ultimate use of the stock; the same flavourings and their proportions can never be equally suitable for all stocks. They should be capable of defining and accentuating the particular qualities of a dish where they are used to deglaze a cooking-pan or used as a lightly buttered glaze. Stock cubes and proprietary essences are useful in an emergency when there is a temporary shortage of stock, but in general these are not suitable for large-scale use since they can produce a stock which, being already seasoned, is against the rules regarding the use of stock. Produced in the traditional manner stock is very economical compared with the cost of instant stock.

Care should be taken in the preparation of stock as follows:
1) For preference use a stockpot with a bottom emptying tap, this facilitates the drawing-off of the stock and lessens the possibility of disturbance and waste.
2) Use fresh ingredients of good quality and always in the right proportions to give stocks of reproducible quality and taste.
3) Break meat bones small so that the maximum of flavour can be extracted and imparted to the stock. The marrow of any beef shin-bone should be removed and reserved for other uses.
4) If any meats are used these should be tied so they can be easily removed when cooked.

5) The stock should be brought to the boil slowly so as to leach out the clarifying qualities of the blood contained in any meat$.
6) As it comes to the boil, remove the fat and scum as it rises to the surface, then skim regularly; if not skimmed regularly the stock will become cloudy and dirty in appearance and taste.
7) The stock should be allowed to simmer gently; if boiled too quickly it becomes cloudy and excessive evaporation takes place.
8) Top up with cold water as and when necessary.
9) It is essential that all stocks be cooked for approximately the required amount of time only. Overcooking can result in a deterioration of taste and quality. Undercooking results in lack of flavour and body.
10) As a general rule only a very little salt should be added during the cooking of a stock. Although just a little helps in developing flavour, even the possibility of too much can unbalance the seasoning of the dish in which it is used.

SPECIAL POINTS
a) The addition of eggshells does not enhance the quality or assist in the clarification of stock which has become cloudy through lack of care in preparation.
b) The fat skimmed from stock should be strained, clarified and used for cooking.
c) Although it may be thought better to prepare stock on a daily basis, it can be made twice weekly provided it is cooled quickly, refrigerated and stored correctly.
d) To cool the stock quickly before storing in a refrigerator, stand the container of finished stock on a triangle in a sink. Run the cold water so that it constantly circulates under and around the container until the stock is sufficiently cold to be safely stored.

---

93 Fonds Blanc – White Stock

20 litres
8–9 hours

Stage	Ingredient	Quantity	Method
1	beef bones, meaty	2kg	Chop the bones small, remove any fat or
	veal bones	2kg	marrow and reserve for further use.
	stewing beef, tied	1kg	Place the bones, beef and boiling fowl in
	boiling fowl	1	a stockpot, add the water, bring to the
	water, cold	25 litres	boil slowly and skim well.
2	carrots	750g	Add the peeled and cleaned whole
	onions	500g	vegetables with the bouquet garni and
	leeks	500g	peppercorns. Simmer very gently for 8–9
	celery	350g	hours skimming as necessary. Remove
	Bouquet Garni	1 large	the tied beef and the chicken when
	peppercorns	5g	cooked.
3			Strain, cool rapidly and use as required.

SPECIAL POINTS
a) This is a general-purpose stock for use in recipes where a compatible flavour and colour is not essential. For example, Crème de Tomate is best made from this stock whereas Crème de Volaille should be made from Fonds Blanc de Volaille – White Chicken Stock.
b) The boiling fowl and stewing beef may be omitted if it is felt necessary but in this case the total of bones should be increased to 7kg.

---

94 Fonds Blanc de Mouton – White Mutton Stock

This is made in the same way as Fonds Blanc (93) using 7kg of mutton bones and 22 litres of water instead of the ingredients at Stage 1. Cook for 3–4 hours only.

95 Fonds Blanc de Veau – White Veal Stock

This is made in the same way as Fonds Blanc (93) using 7kg of veal bones and trimmings instead of the bones, meat and chicken at Stage 1.

96 Fonds Blanc de Volaille – White Chicken Stock

This is made in the same way as Fonds Blanc (93) using 5kg of chicken bones, 2kg of veal bones and 22 litres of water instead of the ingredients at Stage 1. The addition of a boiling fowl can make an improvement. Cook for 3–4 hours only.

97 Estouffade or Fonds Brun – Brown Stock

20 litres
8–9 hours

Stage	Ingredient	Quantity	Method
1	beef bones, meaty	4kg	Chop the bones small and remove any fat or marrow and reserve for further use. Place the bones in a roasting tray with the stewing beef cut small and colour to a good brown in a hot oven at approx. 200°C. Drain off any fat, place the bones and meat in the stockpot and deglaze the roasting tray with a little water. Add this also to the stockpot together with the hock of ham and cover with the water. Bring to the boil and skim well.
	veal bones	2kg	
	stewing beef	1kg	
	hock of ham or bacon, unsmoked and blanched	1	
	water, cold	25 litres	
2	carrots ⎫	750g	Fry the vegetables to a golden brown in a little hot fat; drain off the fat then add the vegetables and the rest of the ingredients to the stock. Simmer very gently for approx. 8–9 hours, skimming as necessary.
	onions ⎬ roughly	500g	
	leeks ⎬ chopped	500g	
	celery ⎭	350g	
	tomatoes, ripe	500g	
	mushroom trimmings	250g	
	Bouquet Garni	1 large	
	garlic, crushed	2 cloves	
	cloves	4	
	peppercorns	5g	
3			Strain, cool rapidly and use as required.

98 Fonds Brun de Veau – Brown Veal Stock

This is made in the same way as Estouffade (97) using 7kg bones and trimmings of veal instead of the bones and meats at Stage 1.

99 Fonds de Gibier – Game Stock

5 litres
4–5 hours

Stage	Ingredient	Quantity	Method
1	game bones and trimmings (hare, venison, pheasant etc.)	3kg	Chop or cut the game into small pieces, place in a roasting tray with a little dripping and colour brown in a hot oven. Drain off any fat, place the game in a
	clean dripping		suitable pot and deglaze the roasting tray
	white wine, dry	½ bottle	with the wine. Add this together with the
	water, cold	6 litres	water, bring to the boil and skim well.
2	carrots ⎫ roughly	250g	Colour the vegetables in a little hot fat
	onions ⎬ chopped	250g	together with the garlic, sage, rosemary
	celery ⎭	150g	and juniper berries. Drain off the fat and
	Bouquet Garni	1	add the vegetables to the stock together
	sage	sprig	with the remaining ingredients. Simmer
	rosemary	sprig	very gently for approx. 4–5 hours
	juniper berries, crushed	10	skimming when necessary.
	garlic, crushed	1 clove	
	dried mushrooms, soaked	150g	
	cloves	2	
	peppercorns	10	
3			Strain, cool rapidly and use as required.

100 Fonds de Légumes – Vegetable Stock

10 litres
1 hour

Stage	Ingredient	Quantity	Method
1	onions	300g	Roughly chop the vegetables and lightly
	carrots	300g	colour with the butter or oil in a suitable
	celery	300g	pot.
	parsnip	200g	
	leek	300g	
	butter or oil	75g	
2	water	10½ litres	Add the herbs, other ingredients and the
	bayleaf	1	water. Bring to the boil, skim and
	thyme	sprig	simmer gently for 45 minutes. Pass
	peppercorns	10	through a fine strainer and use as
	clove	2	required.
	dried mushrooms, soaked	50g	
	parsley stalks	10g	
	tomatoes	150g	
	salt	pinch	

SPECIAL POINT
The use of this stock can be a marked improvement over that of water in the preparation of vegetarian dishes.

101 Fonds or Fumet de Poisson – Fish Stock

5 litres
30 mins.

Stage	Ingredient	Quantity	Method
1	butter	75g	Melt the butter in a deep pan. Place the
	onion, finely sliced	250g	onions in the pan with the bayleaf,
	bayleaf	1	peppercorns, parsley stalks and lemon
	peppercorns	8	juice. Add the washed bones, cover with
	parsley stalks	20g	a lid and lightly stew for approx. 5 mins
	juice of lemon	1	without colour.
	fish bones, sole,		
	turbot or whiting	3kg	
2	water, cold	5 litres	Add, bring to the boil, skim and simmer gently for 20 mins.
3			Strain and reserve for use.

SPECIAL POINTS

a) Cooking for more than 20 mins. will extract a bitter flavour from the bones and render the stock unpalatable.

b) The quality of the stock will be considerably improved by substituting ¾ litre of dry white wine for the same amount of water.

102 GLACES – GLAZES

Glazes are used in cookery for enhancing the flavour of sauces and dishes, for enriching sautéed meats and for decorating finished dishes and sauces. Light glazes can be lightly buttered and used with advantage as sauces.

Glazes are prepared by reducing the appropriate stock to a barely flowing consistency. The stock is passed through muslin into a clean, well-tinned pan, allowed to reduce gently, paying attention to regular skimming; as the volume diminishes the stock must be transferred to a smaller and then still smaller pan. Ten litres of good stock will yield approximately 2dl of glaze. When finished, glazes should be kept in a china basin and can be stored in a refrigerator for several days.

The following are the glazes normally used:

103 Glace de Viande – Meat Glaze

Use Estouffade (97).

104 Glace de Volaille – Chicken Glaze

Use Fonds Blanc de Volaille (96).

105 Glace de Poisson – Fish Glaze

Use Fumet de Poisson (101).

106 LIAISONS – THICKENING AND BINDING AGENTS

Thickening agents are used to give body and consistency to flavoured liquids and in some cases can be used to bind mixtures of ingredients into a cohesive mass. Those in common use are the following:

Beurre Manié: This consists of two parts of butter to one of flour mixed to a smooth paste. It must be mixed well into the boiling liquid and brought back to the boil without further cooking. Used mainly for fish sauces.

Blood: The blood of hare, deer and poultry is sometimes used not only to finish a sauce but also to thicken it. It should first be mixed with a little vinegar to prevent congealing and then whisked into the liquid or sauce. Care should be taken to thicken by reheating without actually boiling. If boiled, curdling, i.e. separation into unsightly flecks, will take place.

Butter: This can be whisked into a reduced cooking liquid to thicken and enrich it; this is effected by the process of emulsification.

Cream: Good-quality double cream can be added to deglazings or liquids and becomes thick by careful reducing.

Egg Yolks: These are used in three main preparations as a thickening agent:
a) in Mayonnaise where the yolks are emulsified with oil,
b) in Sauce Hollandaise where they are cooked to a Sabayon then emulsified with butter,
c) in Sauce Anglaise – Custard Sauce, where they are incorporated with hot milk and then reheated without actually boiling.
They are also used as a binding agent in such items as stuffings, pâtés etc. They are added to the mixture which is then cooked, with the result that the ingredients are bound together and have a firm texture.

Egg Yolks and Cream: these are used for thickening and enriching soups, sauces and stews. They are whisked together and added to a liquid which has been removed from the boil, mixed in well, reheated but not allowed to reboil. For thickening thin liquids such as bouillons, 8 egg yolks and 2dl of cream per litre should be used. For thickening sauces, soups and stews, 2 egg yolks and 1dl of cream per litre is sufficient.

Fécules – Starches: The four starches in common use for thickening soups, sauces and gravies are arrowroot, cornflour, potato flour and rice flour (Crème de Riz). The starch must be diluted with cold water, stock or milk, to a thin paste, stirred into the boiling liquid and allowed to simmer for a few minutes.

Roux: A roux is a combination of fat and flour cooked together to one of three stages: (1) white; (2) blond; (3) brown. They are used mainly in the preparation of soups, sauces and stews.

107 Roux Blanc – White Roux

Use equal quantities of butter and flour. Melt the butter in a heavy pan, add the flour and mix in well. Cook gently on the side of the stove or in an oven at approx. 160°C to a sandy texture, without colour. Mix frequently.

108 Roux Blond – Blond Roux

This roux is made in the same way as Roux Blanc (107) cooking it a little more to a light fawn colour.

---

109 Roux Brun – Brown Roux

Using five parts of flour to four parts of clean dripping, make the roux in the same way as Roux Blanc (107), but cook it to a light brown colour.

SPECIAL POINTS FOR ALL ROUX

a) A small quantity of roux can be cooked successfully at the side of the stove but larger quantities should always be cooked in an oven at approx. 160°C.

b) Mix a roux frequently while cooking it so as to prevent burning and flecking.

c) Allow a roux to cool before adding the hot liquid; this will ensure that the sauce takes on the desired smooth-running consistency. It also prevents the possibility of scalding.

d) In order not to impair the absorption quality of the starch cells it is most important that a roux is not cooked too quickly nor at too high a temperature.

5
Sauces

Sauces play a very important part in cooking, a fact which is exemplified by the standing of the Chef Saucier as the senior chef de partie in the kitchen brigade; he has the responsibility for the production of much of the food accompanied by sauces and for many dishes which have a sauce as an integral part.

A good sauce can enhance the quality of the food with which it is served; it can be the means of creating variety and thus becomes a valuable tool in the widening of the culinary repertoire. Sauces also play a part as an aid to digestion – by utilising a careful selection of flavourings and ingredients they can diminish the natural indigestibility of certain foods, for example where the acidity of things like lemon, vinegar or apple can counteract the fatty nature of certain meats.

In years gone by sauces were richer and more highly concentrated than now. Today the trend is towards a more delicate natural flavour which serves to complement the food rather than mask its flavour. Techniques of deglazing with wines, spirits, stocks, creams and so on and then finishing with a little butter have found much favour. Also the natural thickening obtained by making a purée from the ingredients of a sauce seems to satisfy some of the demands of modern diet; the old traditional descriptive term Coulis for this type of sauce is now enjoying a popular revival.

A sauce can be a liquid thickened by one or a combination of the following:
a) A roux – either white, blond or brown.
b) A starch – such as arrowroot or cornflour diluted with liquid.
c) Yolks of eggs – usually in the form of a liaison with cream.
d) Cream – by reducing.
e) Beurre Manié – butter and flour mixed together.
f) Butter – softened butter shaken or whisked into a reduced cooking liquid.
g) Puréeing the ingredients used for the sauce.

Sauces such as Mayonnaise and Hollandaise are prepared and thickened by using the emulsifying qualities of egg yolks and oil or butter.

──────────CLASSIFICATION──────────

a) Basic Sauces: These are sauces from which many other sauces are derived and, as the quality of derived sauces depends to a great extent on the quality of their basic sauce, strict attention should be paid to their preparation.
b) Sauces based on Demi-glace and Jus lié: This section includes all the small brown sauces which have either Demi-glace or Jus lié as a base and are finished with additional flavourings and garnishes.
c) Sauces based on Béchamel and Veloutés: This section includes all the white and blond sauces which have either Béchamel or Veloutés as a base, and are finished with additional flavourings and garnishes.

d) Egg and butter sauces: This section includes all the sauces made by the process of emulsifying yolks of egg and butter. Sauce Hollandaise and its derivatives and Sauce Béarnaise are included in this classification.

e) Fish Sauces: This section comprises those sauces which are specifically served with fish.

f) Coulis: These are sauces whose thickening is effected solely by their ingredients, usually in the form of a fine purée.

g) Cold Sauces: This section is comprised of Sauce Mayonnaise and its derivatives and other cold sauces, many of which are English in origin.

h) Miscellaneous Sauces: This section includes those sauces which cannot be placed under the previous classifications mainly because of the individuality of their colour and flavour.

STORAGE

Basic sauces such as Demi-glace and Béchamel can be an integral part of the 'Mise en Place' of the kitchen and are usually made in large quantities for use over a period of time and kept under refrigeration. Strict attention must be paid to the storage of all sauces. They should be placed in clean containers made from stainless steel or glazed earthenware and cooled quickly before being placed in the refrigerator. All basic sauces should be covered with a film of butter and marked with their names if stored.

QUANTITY GUIDE

As a guide to calculating the quantity of sauce required for a given number of portions, 1 litre is sufficient for 18 average-sized servings or approximately ½ dl per person.

110 BASIC SAUCES

The reputation of these sauces, most of which are roux-based, has presumably suffered in recent years from the perception that good diet and healthy eating means the elimination of flour where possible. Perhaps a better reason is that for so long insufficient attention and expertise was placed on their preparation resulting very often in strongly flavoured and over-assertive sauces. This in turn resulted in many derived sauces being devoid of their own particular quality and they frequently looked and tasted alike.

With correct attention paid to their preparation these sauces are still capable of assuming their rightful role, that is to widen the repertoire of the professional kitchen and in turn satisfy the customer's need for variety.

111 Espagnole – Brown Sauce

5 litres
6–8 hours

Stage	Ingredient	Quantity	Method
1	clean dripping	300g	Prepare a Brown Roux (109) using a
	flour	350g	deep heavy pan. Allow to cool.

2	tomato purée	125g	Add to the roux and mix in well.
3	Estouffade (97)	8 litres	Bring to the boil and gradually mix into the roux using a wooden spatule, avoiding lumps.

4	clean dripping	75g	Fry the vegetables and bacon a light
	carrots ⎫	400g	brown in the fat. Drain and add the
	onions ⎬ cut in rough	400g	ingredients to the sauce.
	bacon, ⎬ dice		
	streaky ⎭	200g	
5	Bouquet Garni (19)	1	Add to the sauce and simmer gently for 6–8 hours, skimming when necessary and stirring frequently with a wooden or metal spatule to prevent sticking. Pass through a fine strainer.

SPECIAL POINTS

a) It is important that the sauce be simmered very gently. This will prevent the impurities which rise to the surface from boiling back into the sauce.
b) Regular skimming of the impurities is essential to produce the desired final appearance and consistency of the sauce. The colour should be a clean, reddish-brown. It should have a light coating consistency and be glossy and free of flecks.
c) On no account should the sauce be allowed to become too thick; this can be prevented by the addition of extra stock when necessary.

112 Sauce Demi-glace

Reduce equal quantities of Espagnole (111) and Estouffade (97) to approximately half its total volume. Skim frequently, adjust seasoning and pass through a fine strainer.

SPECIAL POINT

This sauce is the basis of many of the small brown sauces. As a sauce in its own right it should be of a sufficiently good quality to be served without further refinement or additions.

113 Jus Lié – Thickened Gravy   5 litres
2½ hours

Stage	Ingredient	Quantity	Method
1	dripping, clean	75g	Melt the dripping in a heavy deep pan.
	raw veal or chicken bones,		Add the bones and fry to a brown colour.
	chopped small	2kg	
2	carrots ⎫ cut in	400g	Add and finish colouring together.
	onions ⎬ rough	400g	Drain off the fat.
	celery ⎭ dice	200g	
	bayleaf	2	
	thyme	sprig	
	garlic, crushed	1 clove	
3	Estouffade (97) or		Add to the bones and vegetables in the
	Brown Veal Stock (98)	6 litres	pan and simmer gently for 1½–2

	tomato purée	200g	hours, skimming regularly. Season lightly.
	mushroom		
	trimmings	350g	
4	cornflour or		Dilute with a little cold water and stir into the simmering stock. Simmer for a further 15 mins. Adjust the colour and seasoning and pass through a fine strainer.
	arrowroot	100g	

SPECIAL POINTS

a) The colour of the sauce should be a clear reddish-brown and its consistency should be quite light.

b) This sauce is best when made fresh and does not lend itself to prolonged reduction.

c) Jus lié is often used in preference to Demi-glace for some of the more delicate meat and chicken dishes.

---

114 Sauce Béchamel – White Sauce
5 litres
1 hour

Stage	Ingredient	Quantity	Method
1	butter	450g	Prepare a White Roux (107) using a deep and heavy pan. Allow to cool.
	flour	450g	
2	milk	5 litres	Bring to the boil with the onion, clove and bayleaf, cover and allow to infuse for 10 mins. Strain and gradually mix the milk into the roux using a wooden spatule, avoiding all lumps.
	onion, shredded	175g	
	clove	2	
	bayleaf	1	
3			Simmer gently for 30 mins. stirring frequently with a wooden or metal spatule to prevent sticking. Pass through a fine strainer and cover with butter to prevent the formation of a skin.

SPECIAL POINTS

a) This recipe gives a Béchamel of a fairly stiff consistency. If a thinner sauce is required e.g. for Spaghetti au Gratin, it is necessary only to thin it by the addition of hot milk.

b) When making large quantities of Béchamel, e.g. 20–30 litres, it is good practice to cover the sauce with a lid and cook gently in a moderate oven at approximately 175°C for 1 hour.

---

115 Velouté de Volaille – Chicken Velouté
5 litres
1½ hours

Stage	Ingredient	Quantity	Method
1	butter	400g	Prepare a Blond Roux (108) using a deep, heavy pan. Allow to cool.
	flour	400g	
2	Fonds de Volaille (96)	5 litres	Bring to the boil and gradually mix into the roux using a wooden spatule, avoiding all lumps.

3	mushroom trimmings (white)	125g	Add to the sauce and simmer gently for 1 hour stirring frequently with a wooden or metal spatule to prevent sticking. Pass through a fine strainer and cover with butter to prevent the formation of a skin.

SPECIAL POINTS

a) This recipe gives a velouté of a fairly stiff consistency. If a thinner sauce is required it is necessary only to thin it by the addition of chicken stock.

b) When making large quantities of velouté it is good practice to cover it with a lid and cook in a moderate oven at approximately 175°C for 1½ hours.

116 Velouté de Veau – Veal Velouté

Prepare in the same way as Velouté de Volaille (115) using Fonds Blanc de Veau (95) instead of Fonds Blanc de Volaille. The same special points regarding Velouté de Volaille are applicable to this sauce.

117 Velouté de Poisson – Fish Velouté

Prepare in the same way as Velouté de Volaille (115) using Fumet de Poisson (101) instead of Fonds Blanc de Volaille and cooking for 30 mins only.

SPECIAL POINTS

When making Velouté de Poisson, overcooking will result in the loss of the clean, fresh taste which is essential for its use in a fish sauce. Reduction of fish velouté together with wine and stock at a later stage does, however, improve the finished sauce.

118 Sauce Tomate – Tomato Sauce

5 litres
1½ hours

Stage	Ingredient	Quantity	Method
1	butter	350g	Melt the butter in a deep, heavy pan.
	bacon trimmings (cut in rough dice)	250g	Add the bacon and fry until lightly coloured.
2	onions	400g	Add and continue to fry until all the ingredients are lightly coloured.
	carrots } cut in	400g	
	celery } rough dice	200g	
	bayleaf	1	
	thyme	sprig	
	garlic, crushed	1 clove	
3	flour	400g	Add and cook to a Blond Roux (108) Allow to cool.
4	tomato purée	600g	Mix in well.
5	Fonds Blanc (93)	5 litres	Bring to the boil and gradually mix in, using a wooden spatule and avoiding all lumps.

| 6 | sugar | 50g | Add to the sauce, season and simmer gently for 1 hour, stirring frequently with a wooden or metal spatule to prevent sticking. Skim frequently. Pass through a fine strainer and cover with butter to prevent formation of a skin. |

SPECIAL POINTS
a) The degree and concentration of colour and flavour of canned tomato purée varies considerably and experience will determine the exact quantity to use.
b) When served in a sauceboat the consistency should be fairly thick.
c) See Coulis de Tomates (179) for a non-roux-based sauce made with fresh tomatoes.

SAUCES BASED ON DEMI-GLACE AND ————————JUS LIÉ————————

119 Sauce Bercy

1 litre
30 mins.

Stage	Ingredient	Quantity	Method
1	shallots, finely chopped white wine, dry	75g 2dl	Place in a small pan and reduce by two-thirds.
2	Jus lié (113)	1 litre	Add and simmer gently to the correct consistency. Skim and remove from fire.
3	Glace de Viande (103) butter	20g 50g	Add and mix in thoroughly.
4	bone marrow, diced	100g	Poach in a little stock, drain and add to the sauce. Adjust the finish with milled pepper.

Suitable for serving with grilled meats. See Recipe 163 for Sauce Bercy suitable for serving with fish.

120 Sauce Bordelaise or Sauce Moelle

1 litre
30 mins.

Stage	Ingredient	Quantity	Method
1	shallots, finely chopped peppercorns, crushed bayleaf thyme red wine	50g 6 ½ sprig 2dl	Place in a small pan and reduce by two-thirds.
2	Demi-glace (112)	1 litre	Add and simmer gently to correct the consistency. Skim and pass through a fine strainer.

3	Glace de Viande (103)	20g	Add and mix in thoroughly.
4	bone marrow, diced	100g	Poach in a little stock, drain and add to the sauce.
5	juice of lemon	squeeze	Adjust the seasoning of the sauce and finish with lemon juice.

Suitable for serving with grilled and sautéed cuts of beef.

121 Sauce Champignons – Mushroom Sauce

1 litre
30 mins.

Stage	Ingredient	Quantity	Method
1	butter button mushrooms, sliced	75g 400g	Melt the butter in a small pan, add the mushrooms and cook without colour.
2	white wine, dry	2dl	Add and reduce by two-thirds.
3	Demi-glace (112)	1 litre	Add and simmer gently to a coating consistency. Skim and remove from the heat.
4	butter	50g	Mix in thoroughly, adjust the seasoning and finish with milled pepper.

This sauce is suitable for serving with grilled fish and meat.

122 Sauce Charcutière

1 litre

Add 75g of gherkin, cut in julienne, to 1 litre of Sauce Robert (136). This sauce is suitable for serving with grilled pork chops.

123 Sauce Chasseur

1 litre
30 mins

Stage	Ingredient	Quantity	Method
1	butter button mushrooms, sliced	50g 250g	Melt the butter in a small pan, add the mushrooms, lightly season and cook without colour.
2	shallots, finely chopped	 50g	Add and cook together gently for 2–3 mins.
3	Tomates Concassées (90) tarragon, chopped white wine, dry	 250g 1 teaspoon 2dl	Add and reduce by half.
4	Jus lié (113)	1 litre	Add and simmer gently to a coating consistency. Skim and adjust the seasoning.

This sauce is suitable for serving with grills and sautés of meat and poultry.

124 Sauce Chateaubriand

1 litre
30 mins.

Stage	Ingredient	Quantity	Method
1	shallots, finely chopped	50g	Place in a small pan and reduce by two-thirds.
	mushroom trimmings	50g	
	bayleaf	½	
	thyme	sprig	
	white wine, dry	2dl	
2	Jus lié (113)	1 litre	Add and simmer gently to a coating consistency. Skim and pass through a fine strainer.
3	Beurre Maître d'Hôtel (10)	100g	Mix in thoroughly, a little at a time and away from the heat. Adjust the seasoning.
4	tarragon, chopped	1 teaspoon	Add to the sauce.

This sauce is suitable for serving with grilled steaks.

125 Sauce Diable – Devilled Sauce

1 litre
30 mins.

Stage	Ingredient	Quantity	Method
1	shallots, chopped	50g	Place in a small pan and reduce until almost dry.
	peppercorns, crushed	25	
	bayleaf	½	
	thyme	sprig	
	white wine, dry	1dl	
	vinegar	2dl	
2	Demi-glace (112)	1 litre	Add, simmer gently for 10 mins. and skim. Correct the consistency by adding a little stock if necessary and pass through a fine strainer.
3	butter	75g	Mix the butter in thoroughly adding a little at a time, adjust the seasoning and finish with a touch of cayenne pepper.
	cayenne pepper	pinch	

This sauce is suitable for serving with grilled fish, meat and poultry.

SPECIAL POINT
This sauce should have a pronounced flavour of pepper but no pronounced taste of vinegar.

126 Sauce Grand Veneur

1 litre
30 mins.

Stage	Ingredient	Quantity	Method
1	Sauce Poivrade (133)	1 litre	Reduce to the original consistency of the sauce.
	Fonds de Gibier (99)	½ litre	

2	redcurrant jelly	50g	Add, reboil, skim and pass through a fine strainer.
3	butter	50g	Mix in thoroughly away from the heat.
4	cream	1dl	Add and adjust the seasoning.

This sauce is suitable for game dishes.

---

127 Sauce Italienne

1 litre
30 mins.

Stage	Ingredient	Quantity	Method
1	butter	75g	Melt the butter in a small pan. Add the shallots and cook without colour.
	shallots, finely chopped	50g	
2	mushrooms, finely chopped	400g	Add and cook until almost dry.
3	lean ham, finely chopped	100g	Add and simmer gently for 5 mins. Skim and adjust the consistency with stock if too thick.
	Demi-glace (112)	4dl	
	Sauce Tomate (118)	4dl	
4	Fines Herbes, chopped (31)	1 tbsp	Add and adjust the seasoning.

This sauce is suitable for serving with various small entrées, e.g. brains, lamb cutlets, liver.

---

128 Sauce Lyonnaise – Brown Onion Sauce

1 litre
30 mins.

Stage	Ingredient	Quantity	Method
1	butter	75g	Melt the butter in a small pan. Add the onions and cook until lightly coloured.
	onions, finely sliced	400g	
2	white wine, dry	1½dl	Add and reduce by two-thirds.
	vinegar	½dl	
3	Demi-glace (112) or Jus lié (113)	8dl	Add and simmer gently to a coating consistency. Skim and adjust the seasoning.

Suitable for serving with sautéed liver and Hamburg Steaks.

---

129 Sauce Madère – Madeira Sauce

1 litre
15 mins.

Reduce 1 litre of demi-glace until slightly thickened and add ½dl of Madeira to correct its consistency. The sauce should not be boiled after the wine has been added as this will destroy the flavour and bouquet of the Madeira. Adjust the seasoning and pass through a fine strainer. It may be finished with a little butter.

Suitable for entrées made of small items of beef, veal, poultry, game, ham and also for large joints such as Filet de Boeuf poêlé and Jambon braisé.

130 Sauce au Marsala – Marsala Sauce

As for Sauce Madère (129), substituting Marsala for Madeira. Used for small cuts of veal and lamb which have been sautéed, braised ham.

131 Sauce Périgueux

1 litre
45 mins.

Stage	Ingredient	Quantity	Method
1	truffles, fresh	75g	Wash the truffles thoroughly and scrub if necessary then peel carefully.

2	butter
	raw ham, lightly
	   smoked
	onions, finely
	   chopped
		50g
		
		100g
		
		75g
			Heat the butter in a small pan, add the ham, chopped, and fry gently for a few minutes then add the onion and a little milled pepper and allow to cook to a light golden colour. Add the truffles and peelings, cover with a tight-fitting lid and allow to sweat slowly for a few minutes.

3	Madeira, Bual	3dl	Add the Madeira, cover tightly again and allow to simmer very gently for 25–30 minutes. Remove the pan from the heat, allow to cool, then remove the whole truffles only and reserve.
4	Demi-glace (112) butter	1 litre 50g	Add the demi-glace to the wine and other ingredients and simmer together to a light coating consistency. Pass firmly through a fine strainer, mix in the butter and adjust the seasoning as necessary. Finally add the reserved truffle cut in very small dice.

Suitable for serving with sautés of meat, poultry and game.

SPECIAL POINTS
a) This sauce is also known as Sauce Périgourdine and traditionally was garnished with truffle cut in the shape of small balls or trimmed in small olive shapes.
b) If fresh truffles are unavailable this sauce can be prepared in the following manner. Reduce the liquid from a 100g tin of truffles with 1 litre of demi-glace to the original consistency of the sauce. Season, pass through a fine strainer and add 75g finely diced truffle. Finish by mixing in 50g of butter.

132 Sauce Piquante

1 litre
30 mins.

Stage	Ingredient	Quantity	Method
1	shallots, chopped	50g	Place in a small pan and reduce by two-
	vinegar	1dl	thirds.
	white wine, dry	1dl	
2	Demi-glace (112)	1 litre	Add and reduce to a coating consistency.
	or Jus lié (113)		Skim.
3	gherkins, finely		Add to the sauce and adjust the season-
	chopped	50g	ing.
	capers, finely		
	chopped	25g	
	Fines Herbes,		
	chopped (31)	1 tbsp	

Suitable for serving with grilled pork chops.

133 Sauce Poivrade

1 litre
45 mins.

Stage	Ingredient	Quantity	Method
1	butter	50g	Melt the butter in a small pan. Add the
	carrots ⎱ finely	75g	rest of the ingredients and fry until
	onions ⎰ chopped	75g	coloured brown.
	celery	50g	
	bayleaf	½	
	thyme	sprig	
2	red wine	1dl	Add and reduce until nearly dry.
	vinegar, red wine	1dl	
3	Demi-glace (112)	1 litre	Add and simmer gently for approx. 10 mins. Skim.
4	peppercorns, crushed	15	Add and simmer for 10 mins. Skim and pass through a fine strainer.
5	butter	50g	Mix in thoroughly away from the heat and adjust the seasoning.

Suitable for serving with game, e.g. sautés of venison, Râble de Lièvre, Gigue de Chevreuil rôtie.

SPECIAL POINTS
a) If the meat has been previously marinaded, e.g. for Gigue de Chevreuil rôtie, it is good practice to use the marinade in place of the red wine.
b) If the sauce is to be used specifically for game dishes, 200g of chopped small raw game bones and trimmings should be added when frying the vegetables.

134 Sauce au Porto – Port Wine Sauce

As for Sauce Madère (129), substituting port for Madeira. Suitable for small game birds, e.g. canard sauvage; veal escalopes.

---

135 Sauce Réforme – Reform Sauce

1 litre
1 hour

Stage	Ingredient		Quantity	Method
1	butter		50g	Melt the butter in a small pan. Add the
	carrots	} finely	75g	rest of the ingredients and fry until
	onions		75g	coloured brown.
	celery	} chopped	50g	
	bayleaf		½	
	thyme		sprig	
2	vinegar		1dl	Add and reduce by two-thirds.
	peppercorns, crushed		10	
3	Demi-glace (112)		8dl	Add and skimmer gently for 20–25 mins.
	Estouffade (97)		2dl	Skim.
4	redcurrant jelly		50g	Add, reboil, skim and adjust the season-ing. Pass through a fine strainer.
5	ham		25g	Cut into julienne, warm in a little butter
	tongue		25g	and add to the sauce. The mushroom
	beetroot, cooked		25g	should be cut into julienne while raw
	white of egg, cooked		25g	and cooked à Blanc. (60)
	gherkin		25g	
	mushroom, cooked		25g	
	truffle		10g	

Used specifically for Côtelettes d'Agneau Réforme. (p. 228)

---

136 Sauce Robert

1 litre
30 mins.

Stage	Ingredient	Quantity	Method
1	butter	50g	Melt the butter in a small pan. Add the
	onions, finely chopped	75g	onions and cook without colour.
2	white wine, dry	2dl	Add and reduce by two-thirds.
3	Demi-glace (112)	1 litre	Add, simmer to a light coating consistency and skim.
4	mustard, dry	5g	Dilute the mustard with a little cold
	sugar	10g	water and add, with the sugar, to the sauce. Do not reboil. Adjust the season-ing and pass through a fine strainer.

Suitable for grilled and sautéed pork chops, grilled fish.

137 Sauce Xérès – Sherry Sauce

As for Sauce Madère (129), substituting dry sherry for Madeira. Suitable for small cuts of lamb, beef and veal, small game birds and braised ham.

---

138 Sauce Tortue

1 litre
45 mins.

Stage	Ingredient	Quantity	Method
1	Estouffade (97)	2dl	Place the turtle herbs in the boiling
	turtle herbs	1 sachet	stock, remove from the heat immediately, cover and allow to infuse for 10 mins. Strain and keep on one side.
2	white wine, dry	2dl	Place in a small pan and reduce by half.
	mushroom trimmings	100g	
3	Demi-glace (112)	6dl	Add to the reduction, simmer until
	Sauce Tomate (118)	3dl	reduced by one-third and skim. Add the prepared infusion (Stage 1), re-boil and pass through a fine strainer.
5	butter	50g	Mix in thoroughly away from the heat and adjust the seasoning.
6	Madeira	1dl	Finish with the Madeira and a little
	cayenne		cayenne pepper.

Suitable for use with Ris de Veau Financière.

SAUCES BASED ON BÉCHAMEL
————————AND VELOUTÉS————————

139 Sauce Allemande

1 litre
30 mins.

Stage	Ingredient	Quantity	Method
1	Velouté de Volaille (115)	8dl	Place in a small pan, mix well, bring to the boil and reduce gently by one-third,
	Fonds Blanc de Volaille (96)	4dl	stirring frequently with a wooden or metal spatule to prevent sticking. Pass
	egg yolks	4	through a fine strainer.
	mushroom trimmings, white	50g	
2	butter	50g	Mix the butter in thoroughly away from
	cream, double	2dl	the heat. Add the cream and adjust the seasoning.
3	juice of lemon	squeeze	Finish the sauce with the lemon juice.

Suitable for serving with poached chicken.

140 Sauce Aurore

1 litre
30 mins.

Stage	Ingredient	Quantity	Method
1	butter	50g	Melt the butter in a small pan, add the
	Tomates Concassées		tomatoes and cook to a smooth and fairly
	(90)	400g	dry paste. Pass through a fine sieve and
			return to a clean pan.
2	Velouté de Volaille		Add, simmer gently for a few mins. and
	(115)	8dl	pass through a fine strainer.
3	butter	75g	Mix in thoroughly away from the heat.
4	cream, double	2dl	Add and adjust the seasoning.

Suitable for serving with poached chicken.

141 Sauce aux Câpres – Caper Sauce

1 litre

Prepare 1 litre of Velouté de Mouton in the same way as Velouté de Volaille (115), using white mutton stock instead of chicken stock. Squeeze the surplus vinegar from 100g of capers, add the capers to the sauce and adjust the seasoning. Suitable for serving with boiled mutton.

142 Sauce Champignons – Mushroom Sauce

1 litre
20 mins.

Stage	Ingredient	Quantity	Method
1	butter	75g	Melt the butter in a small pan, add the
	button mushrooms,		mushrooms and lemon juice. Lightly
	sliced	400g	season and cook gently without colour.
	juice of lemon	¼	
2	Velouté de Volaille		Add and simmer gently to a light coating
	(115)	7dl	consistency. Adjust the seasoning as
	cream, double	2dl	necessary and finish with a touch of
	cayenne		cayenne.

Suitable for serving with Bitoks, Escalopes of veal, Suprêmes of chicken, poached chicken.

143 Sauce Crème – Cream Sauce

1 litre

Add 50g of butter and 2dl of double cream to 8dl of hot Sauce Béchamel (114). Adjust the seasoning and pass through a fine strainer. Suitable for serving with poached fish, boiled vegetables.

144 Sauce Hongroise

1 litre
45 mins.

Stage	Ingredient	Quantity	Method
1	butter	75g	Melt the butter in a small pan, add the
	onions, finely		onions and cook without colour.
	chopped	100g	

2	paprika	50g	Add, mix in thoroughly and cook gently for 2–3 mins.
3	white wine, dry	2dl	Add and reduce by two-thirds.
4	Velouté de Volaille (115)	8dl	Add and simmer gently for 10 mins. Pass through a fine strainer.
5	butter cream, double	50g 1dl	Mix the butter in thoroughly away from the heat, add the cream and adjust the seasoning.

Suitable for serving with poached chicken, Escalopes of veal.

145 Sauce Ivoire   1 litre

Finish 1 litre of Sauce Suprême (151) with 50g of meat glaze (103). Suitable for serving with poached chicken.

146 Sauce Mornay – Cheese Sauce   1 litre
                                                                          30 mins.

Stage	Ingredient	Quantity	Method
1	Béchamel (114) Parmesan, grated Gruyère grated	9dl 40g 40g	Add the cheeses to the hot Béchamel and mix in well.
2	butter cream, double	50g 1dl	Mix the butter in thoroughly away from the heat and add the cream.
3	egg yolks cayenne	3	Prepare a sabayon with the egg yolks (84) and add to the sauce. Adjust the seasoning and finish with a little cayenne.

Suitable for serving with poached eggs, vegetables. See also Sauce Mornay for Fish (171).

147 Sauce aux Oignons – Onion Sauce   1 litre
                                                                          30 mins.

Stage	Ingredient	Quantity	Method
1	butter onions, finely sliced water	50g 600g 2dl	Place in a deep pan, cover and cook gently until the onions are tender and the water is almost evaporated.
2	Béchamel (114)	8dl	Add, mix in gently and bring to the boil.
3	cream, double	1dl	Add away from the heat and season well.

SPECIAL POINT
This sauce should be of a very thick consistency. Suitable for serving with roast mutton, Oeufs à la Tripe.

148 Sauce Persil – Parsley Sauce

1 litre

Add 50g of butter and 1dl of double cream to 9dl of hot Sauce Béchamel (114) and finish with 3 tablespoons of blanched and pressed chopped parsley. Adjust the seasoning and add a little cayenne. Suitable for serving with vegetables and calf's head. Also served with boiled fish.

149 Sauce Poulette

1 litre

Finish 1 litre of Sauce Allemande (139) with 2 tablespoons chopped parsley. Suitable for serving with calf's head.

150 Sauce Soubise

1 litre
1½ hours

Stage	Ingredient	Quantity	Method
1	onions, chopped	750g	Blanch in boiling water for 2–3 mins. Drain well.
2	butter	100g	Melt in a deep saucepan, add the onions and cook gently without colour.
3	Béchamel (114)	8dl	Add, mix in well, season, cover and cook in a slow oven 140°C for 1 hour. Pass through a fine sieve and place in a clean pan. Reheat.
4	cream	2dl	Add and adjust the seasoning.

Suitable for serving with eggs, roast lamb and mutton.

151 Sauce Suprême

1 litre
30 mins.

Stage	Ingredient	Quantity	Method
1	Fonds Blanc de Volaille (96) mushroom trimmings, white	5dl 100g	Place in a small pan and reduce by half.
2	Velouté de Volaille (115) cream	8dl 1dl	Add and reduce to a coating consistency. Pass through a fine strainer.
3	butter cream	75g 1dl	Mix the butter in thoroughly away from the heat. Finish with the cream and adjust the seasoning.

Suitable for serving with poached chicken.

————152   EGG AND BUTTER SAUCES————

The sauces in this section present certain difficulties in their preparation and in their keeping for use during the service. The following points must be observed in order that their quality may be ensured:

1) Use a clean, well-tinned copper or stainless steel sauteuse; this will ensure that the sauce keeps a good colour. If a copper pan is not properly tinned there is a risk of discolouration and contamination from the copper.

2) It is essential to use a thin and flexible sauce whisk so as to ensure that the sauce reaches the maximum degree of lightness.

3) Use sufficient water only to make the yolks fairly liquid so that they become light and fluffy when whisking. The sabayon must be whisked vigorously and continuously, keeping the bottom and sides of the pan clean so as to prevent the yolks from becoming scrambled. The sabayon is sufficiently cooked when it clings to the whisk when this is raised from the pan.

4) Before adding the butter care must be taken that all scum is removed from its surface. The sediment and liquid at the bottom should not be used as the texture, flavour and appearance of the sauce may be spoilt.

5) These sauces are susceptible to extremes of temperature at all stages of their preparation. During the cooking of the sabayon, its temperature must not be allowed to go higher than 85°C and this means that the pan should be removed from the bain-marie from time to time to keep the temperature below boiling point. It is essential to allow the sabayon to cool to lukewarm while still whisking before adding the butter, which should be at a temperature of 30–37°C.

6) When finished, the sauce should be passed through a muslin or fine strainer into a slightly warmed container. The finished sauce should be held at a constant temperature of 30–37°C. If it becomes too cold, the butterfat will set and, on reheating, the sauce will separate. If it becomes too hot, the sauce will also separate.

7) If the sauce separates it may be reconstituted by making a one yolk sabayon and gradually adding the separated sauce whilst whisking vigorously and continuously.

---

153   Sauce Béarnaise

½ litre
45 mins.

Stage	Ingredient	Quantity	Method
1	butter	500g	Place in a pan and melt in a bain-marie. Skim and keep lukewarm
2	shallots, finely chopped	25g	Place these ingredients in a well-tinned copper or stainless steel sauteuse and reduce until almost dry. Allow to cool and add approx. ¼dl water.
	tarragon and chervil stalks, finely chopped	1 tbsp	
	peppercorns, crushed	8	
	vinegar, white wine	½dl	
3	egg yolks	6	Add the egg yolks and whisk continuously in a bain-marie until cooked (sabayon). Remove from the heat and allow to cool until lukewarm while whisking.

4			Add the melted butter gradually, whisking continuously. Pass through a muslin or fine strainer into a warm container. Adjust the seasoning with salt only.
5	tarragon and chervil leaves, chopped	1 tbsp	Mix in gently. Keep at an even temperature of 30–37°C.

Suitable for serving with grilled fish, grilled and sautéed meats.

SPECIAL POINTS
a) This should be much thicker than Sauce Hollandaise and should not require thinning.
b) Because of its thickness this sauce is inclined to separate if kept for a long period of time and needs to be whisked occasionally during the service.

---

154 Sauce Chantilly

See Sauce Mousseline (159).

---

155 Sauce Choron

½ litre
45 mins.

Cook 250g of Tomates Concassées (90) in butter to a smooth and almost dry paste; pass through a fine sieve and add to ½ litre of Sauce Béarnaise (153) from which the final addition of chopped tarragon and chervil leaves has been omitted. Suitable for grilled and sautéed meats.

---

156 Sauce Foyot or Sauce Valois

¼ litre
45 mins.

Add 1 tablespoon of warm meat glaze (103) to ½ litre of finished Sauce Béarnaise (153). Suitable for serving with grilled and sautéed meats.

---

157 Sauce Hollandaise

½ litre
45 mins.

Stage	Ingredient	Quantity	Method
1	butter	500g	Place in a pan and melt in a bain-marie. Skim and keep lukewarm.
2	peppercorns, white crushed vinegar	8 ½dl	Place in a well-tinned copper or stainless steel sauteuse and reduce until almost dry. Allow to cool and add approx. ¼dl water.
3	egg yolks	5	Add the egg yolks and whisk continuously in a bain-marie until cooked (sabayon). Remove from the bain-marie and allow to cool until lukewarm while whisking.
4			Add the melted butter gradually, whisking continuously. Pass through a muslin or fine strainer into a warm container. Adjust the seasoning with salt only.

5	juice of lemon	squeeze	Finish with the lemon juice and keep at an even temperature of 30–37°C.

Suitable for serving with boiled vegetables and poached fish.

SPECIAL POINT
The addition of a little warm water may be necessary to lighten the texture and make the consistency suitable for coating.

---

158 Sauce Maltaise

½ litre
45 mins.

Stage	Ingredient	Quantity	Method
1	butter	500g	Place in a pan and melt in a bain-marie. Skim and keep lukewarm
2	blood oranges	2	Finely peel the zest of one orange and cut into the finest julienne possible, simmer in a little water for 2–3 mins. then refresh, drain and reserve. Grate the zest of the other orange and squeeze the juice from both.
3	lemon juice peppercorns, crushed	½ tbsp 6	Place the grated zest and orange juice into a well-tinned copper or stainless steel sauteuse together with the lemon juice and peppercorns and reduce to approx. two tablespoons. Allow to cool.
4	egg yolks	6	Add the egg yolks and whisk continuously in a bain-marie until cooked (sabayon). Remove from the bain-marie and allow to cool until lukewarm while whisking.
5			Add the melted butter gradually, whisking continuously. Pass through a muslin or fine strainer into a warm container. Adjust seasoning with salt only.
6			Finish with the reserved julienne of zest and keep at an even temperature of 30–37°C

Suitable for serving with hot asparagus and seakale.

---

159 Sauce Mousseline or Sauce Chantilly

Lightly whip 1dl of cream and fold gently into ½ litre of Sauce Hollandaise. Suitable for serving with boiled vegetables and poached fish.

---

160 Sauce Paloise

Proceed as for Sauce Béarnaise (153) at all stages, with the following alterations:
1) For the reduction at Stage 2 replace the chopped tarragon and chervil with 2 tablespoons of finely chopped mint stalks and add 1 teaspoon of sugar.

2) Finish the sauce at Stage 5 with 1 tablespoon of chopped mint leaves instead of tarragon and chervil.

Suitable for serving with roast and grilled meats, especially lamb.

161 Sauce Valois

See Sauce Foyot (156).

FISH SAUCES

162 Sauce aux Anchois – Anchovy Sauce

1 litre
10 mins.

Add 3–4 tablespoons of anchovy essence to 9dl of hot Sauce Béchamel (114). Finish with 50g butter and 1dl cream, adjust the seasoning and add a little cayenne. Pass through a fine strainer. Suitable for serving with grilled fish.

---

163 Sauce Bercy

1 litre
30 mins.

Stage	Ingredient	Quantity	Method
1	butter	50g	Melt the butter in a small pan, add the shallots and cook without colour.
	shallots, finely chopped	75g	
2	white wine, dry	2dl	Add and reduce by two-thirds.
	Fumet de Poisson (101)	4dl	
3	Velouté de Poisson (117)	9dl	Add and simmer to a coating consistency. Skim carefully.
4	butter	50g	Mix the butter in thoroughly away from the heat. Add the cream and adjust the seasoning.
	cream	1dl	
5	chopped parsley		Finish with chopped parsley when serving.

Suitable for use with poached fish. See 119 for Sauce Bercy suitable for serving with meats.

---

164 Sauce au Beurre Blanc – Butter Sauce

¼ litre (2½dl)
20 mins.

Stage	Ingredient	Quantity	Method
1	shallots, finely chopped	75g	Place in a small sauteuse and reduce by approx. three-quarters until the liquid becomes somewhat viscous. Cool slightly.
	vinegar, white wine	1dl	
	white wine, dry	1dl	

2	butter, unsalted and softened	250g	Whisk in the butter vigorously little by little away from direct heat and do not allow it to become too hot. When all the butter has been absorbed, the mixture should be creamy and well-emulsified. Season with salt and pepper as necessary and serve immediately.
	salt		
	pepper		

Suitable for serving with all poached fish and some vegetables such as asparagus and seakale.

SPECIAL POINTS
a) This emulsified sauce can be somewhat unstable and does not lend itself too much to being prepared in advance. It is best if made as required and to order.
b) If felt necessary it may be passed to remove the shallots.
c) Further reduction at Stage 1 with the addition of cream may help stabilise the sauce but this alters its particular quality and character. It is not to be recommended where the sauce is served under its correct name.

---

165 Sauce Cardinal

1 litre
5 mins.

Finish 8dl of hot basic Sauce Homard (169) with 50g of butter, 1dl of cream and ¼dl of brandy; adjust the seasoning as necessary plus a touch of cayenne. Suitable for serving with poached fish, lobster.

---

166 Sauce aux Crevettes – Shrimp Sauce

1 litre
30 mins.

Stage	Ingredient	Quantity	Method
1	Béchamel (114)	8dl	Place all the ingredients in a small pan and simmer gently to a coating consistency, stirring frequently with a wooden or metal spatule to prevent sticking. Skim.
	Fumet de Poisson (101)	3dl	
	cream	2dl	
2	Beurre de Crevette (8)	75g	Mix in thoroughly away from the heat and pass through a fine strainer.
3	butter	25g	Melt the butter, add the shrimps and heat. Add to the sauce, adjust the seasoning and finish with a little cayenne pepper.
	shrimps, shelled	75g	
	cayenne		

Suitable for serving with boiled fish.

---

167 Sauce Génevoise

1 litre
1½ hours

Stage	Ingredient	Quantity	Method
1	butter	75g	Melt the butter in a small pan, add the rest of the ingredients and cook without colour.
	onions ⎫ finely	150g	
	carrots ⎬ chopped	150g	
	celery ⎭	75g	

	bayleaf	½	
	thyme	sprig	
	peppercorns, crushed	10	
2	salmon, head and bones	500g	Add, cover with a lid and cook gently on the side of the stove for 10 mins.
3	red wine	½ litre	Add and simmer gently for 30 mins.
	Demi-glace (112)	½ litre	Strain into a clean pan.
4	Fumet de Poisson (101)	1 litre	Add to the sauce and reduce to a coating consistency.
5	anchovy essence	2 tbsps	Add to the sauce and pass through a fine strainer.
6	butter	50g	Mix in thoroughly away from the heat and adjust the seasoning.

Suitable for serving with poached salmon, salmon trout and trout.

---

168 Sauce Gratin

1 litre
30 mins.

Stage	Ingredient	Quantity	Method
1	butter	75g	Melt the butter in a small pan. Add the shallots and cook without colour. Add the mushrooms, season and cook until almost dry.
	shallots, finely chopped	75g	
	mushrooms, finely chopped	500g	
2	Demi-glace (112)	8dl	Add the demi-glace, bring to the boil, skim and simmer for 10 mins. until slightly thickened. Adjust the seasoning and finish with chopped parsley.
	parsley, chopped		

---

169 Sauce Homard de Base – Basic Lobster Sauce

5 litres
1½ hours

Stage	Ingredient	Quantity	Method
1	lobsters, live	8 × 650g (approx)	Remove any spawn from the lobsters and place on one side. Heat the oil and butter in a large shallow pan until very hot but not burning. Place the lobsters in the pan and cook quickly until red on all sides.
	oil	2dl	
	butter	75g	
2	onions } finely	400g	Add and cook with the lobsters without too much colour. Drain the fat from the pan.
	carrots } chopped	400g	
	celery	200g	
	peppercorns	20	
	bayleaf	1	
	parsley stalks	20g	
	garlic, crushed	1 clove	
3	brandy	2dl	Add and flamber (32).

4	white wine, dry	½ litre	Add to the lobsters, season lightly with
	Fumet de Poisson		salt, bring to the boil, skim, cover and
	(101)	4 litres	simmer gently for 20–25 mins. until the
	Tomates Concassées		lobsters are cooked. Remove the
	(90)	1kg	lobsters, wash and keep for other uses.
	tomato purée	250g	Reduce the cooking liquor by half.
5	Velouté de Poisson		Add to the cooking liquor and reduce
	(117)	4 litres	gently by one-third, stirring frequently
			with a wooden or metal spatule. Crush
			the lobster spawn, add to the sauce and
			reboil. Pass firmly through a strainer and
			cover with butter to prevent the forma-
			tion of a skin.

SPECIAL POINTS

a) This sauce can be part of the mise en place of the fish section and can be successfully stored for several days in a refrigerator.

b) In classical recipes whole lobsters were used, the shells and flesh being pounded and used solely for making this sauce. Because of the high cost of lobsters, it is good practice to use this recipe which produces an excellent sauce suitable for the modern palate and, at the same time, the lobsters are cooked and available for serving for Homard Thermidor, Cardinal, etc.

c) The shells from the cooked lobster can be removed, crushed well and returned to the sauce at the end of Stage 4 with advantage to the finished sauce. The flesh from the lobsters can then be utilised for such dishes as Homard Newburg or for lobster cocktails, salpicons or mayonnaises etc.

---

170 Sauce Homard – Lobster Sauce

1 litre
15 mins.

Finish 8dl of hot basic Lobster Sauce (169) with 50g of butter and 1dl of cream, adjust the seasoning and add a little cayenne pepper. Warm 75g of diced cooked lobster in a little butter and add to the sauce with ¼dl of brandy at the last moment. Suitable for serving with poached fillets of fish.

---

171 Sauce Mornay, for fish

Finish Sauce Mornay (146) with the well-reduced cooking liquor from the fish with which it is to be used.

---

172 Sauce Moutarde – Mustard Sauce

1 litre
5 mins.

Add 50g of butter and 1dl of cream to 9dl of hot Sauce Béchamel (114). Finish with 20g of English mustard diluted with a little water, adjust the seasoning and add a little cayenne. Suitable for serving with grilled herrings.

---

173 Sauce aux Oeufs – Egg Sauce

1 litre
15 mins.

Add 50g of butter and 1dl of cream to 8dl of hot Sauce Béchamel (114). Finish with four warm hard-boiled eggs cut into ½cm dice. Adjust the seasoning and add a little cayenne. Suitable for serving with boiled white fish.

---

174 Sauce au Vin Blanc – White Wine Sauce

1 litre
30 mins.

Stage	Ingredient	Quantity	Method
1	white wine, dry	3dl	Place in a small pan and reduce by two-thirds.
	Fumet de Poisson (101)	3dl	
2	Velouté de Poisson (117)	1 litre	Add and simmer gently to a coating consistency using a wooden or metal spatule to prevent sticking. Pass through a fine strainer.
	cream	2dl	
3	butter	75g	Mix in thoroughly away from the heat, adjust the seasoning and add a little cayenne pepper.
	cayenne		

Suitable for use with poached fish.

SPECIAL POINTS
a) If the sauce is required for glazing, add a sabayon (84) of three egg yolks per 1 litre of sauce.
b) If required in a large quantity for glazing as for a banquet, approx. 20% of the volume of sauce required may consist of Sauce Hollandaise (157).

---

175 Sauce au Vin Rouge – Red Wine Sauce

1 litre
30 mins.

Stage	Ingredient	Quantity	Method
1	shallots, finely chopped	50g	Place in a small pan and reduce by two-thirds.
	red wine	5dl	
2	Demi-glace (112)	1 litre	Add and simmer gently to a coating consistency.
3	anchovy essence	3 tbsps	Add the anchovy essence and pass through a fine strainer. Mix the butter in thoroughly away from the heat, adjust the seasoning and add a little cayenne.
	butter	50g	
	cayenne		

Suitable for serving with poached fish.

COULIS

176 Coulis Moravienne

1 litre
1 hour

Stage	Ingredient	Quantity	Method
1	almonds, ground water	75g 2dl	Place the almonds in a basin. Boil the water, pour over the almonds and allow to steep until needed.

2	butter
	pears, firm and
	  not too ripe
	sugar
	juniper berries
	  crushed
		50g
		
		1kg
		50g
		
		5g
			Peel and core the pears and cut into rough cubes. Heat the butter in a deepish pan then add the pears together with the sugar, juniper berries and a pinch of salt. Cook together quickly for a few minutes turning over and over.

3	gin bilberries	1dl 300g	Add the gin and flamber (32) then add the bilberries and the almonds and their liquid. Cook gently until soft and reduced, approx. 25 mins.
4	lemon juice butter	2 tbsps 50g	Pass the sauce carefully through a fine sieve. Reheat and finish with the lemon juice and the butter. Adjust the seasoning.

Suitable especially for grills and roast joints of venison.

* SPECIAL POINTS
  a) Cranberries may be used if bilberries are unobtainable.
  b) The use of aluminium or iron pans for making this sauce will result in discolouration and metallic contamination. It is essential to use a well-tinned copper or stainless steel pan.·

177 Coulis Palermitaine – Fennel Sauce

1 litre
45 mins.

Stage	Ingredient	Quantity	Method
1	fennel	850g	Remove the very centre and the feathery leaves of the fennel to about 50g and reserve.
2	butter shallot, chopped	75g 50g	Chop the rest of the fennel and cook gently with the butter for 5 or 6 minutes and without colour then add the shallot and cook slowly together until all is soft.
3	Pernod Fonds Blanc (93)	1dl 3dl	Add the Pernod and flamber (32), then add the stock. Season lightly and cook together until the liquid is well-reduced.
4	cream, double butter cayenne	3dl 25g	Pass the sauce firmly through a fine sieve and then a fine strainer. Reheat, add the cream and reduce to a thick

coating consistency. Adjust the seasoning as necessary, add a touch of cayenne and mix in the butter. Finally, chop the reserved centres and leaves of the fennel and mix into the sauce.

Suitable for serving with grills and sautés of poultry and veal. Served cold it is suitable for serving with Crudités and fried fish.

SPECIAL POINT
By substituting the white stock with fish stock (101), the sauce makes a useful accompaniment for poached white fish.

---

178 Coulis de Poivrons

1 litre
45 mins.

Stage	Ingredient	Quantity	Method
1	butter	50g	Melt the butter in a deep pan, add the
	onions, chopped	75g	onions and garlic and cook without
	garlic, crushed	1 clove	colour.
2	red pimentos, skinned (78) and deseeded	750g	Roughly chop the pimentos and add to the pan. Cook gently until soft then add the peppercorns and vinegar and reduce almost completely.
	green peppercorns, bruised	10g	
	vinegar, white wine	1dl	
3	honey	1 tbsp	Add the honey and tomatoes to the
	Tomates Concassées (90)	500g	pimentos, season lightly and cook together until soft and fairly well-
	cayenne		reduced. Pass through a fine sieve then a fine strainer. Reheat and simmer to a thick coating consistency, adjust the sea- soning and finish with a little cayenne.

Suitable for serving with grilled and ungarnished cuts of fish and meat. Cold it is a suitable accompaniment for Crudités.

---

179 Coulis de Tomates

1 litre
30 mins.

Stage	Ingredient	Quantity	Method
1	butter	30g	Heat the butter in a pan, add the bacon
	streaky bacon, unsmoked	50g	cut in small dice and cook until golden in colour.
2	onions, chopped	75g	Add the onion, carrot and garlic and
	carrot, finely chopped	50g	cook gently together without any
	garlic, crushed	1 clove	pronounced colour.

3	Tomates Concassées		Add the tomatoes, bouquet garni, glace
	(90)	1¼kg	de viande and sugar to the pan. Season
	parsley stalks	25g	lightly with salt and pepper and cook
	marjoram	sprig	slowly for 25–30 minutes until slightly
	basil	Bouquet sprig	reduced.
	thyme	Garni sprig	
	celery	1 stick	
	bayleaf	1	
	light Glace de		
	Viande (103)	1 tbsp	
	sugar	20g	
4	butter	50g	Remove the bouquet garni then pass the sauce firmly through a fine sieve then a fine strainer. Reheat and reduce again if necessary to a fairly thick coating consistency. Adjust the seasoning as necessary and finish with the butter.

Suitable for serving with grills, fried fish and for flavouring cocktail sauces and white and brown sauces.

SPECIAL POINT
The sauce may be finished with a little chopped fresh majoram or basil.

---------------------------COLD SAUCES---------------------------

180 Aïoli

½ litre
15 mins.

Stage	Ingredient	Quantity	Method
1	garlic, peeled	30g	Cut the garlic cloves open and discard any central green shoots. Place the garlic in a mortar with a pinch of salt and pound as finely as possible.
2	egg yolks	3	Mix in the egg yolks and then the oil, drop by drop to begin with and then
	olive oil, best quality	5dl	increase to a trickle as the sauce begins to emulsify. Take care that the pestle is
	lemon, juice	2 tbsps	turned vigorously and continuously, add-
	warm water	½ tbsp	ing the lemon juice little by little along with the oil until all is completely incorporated. Finish with the warm water and adjust the seasoning with a little salt and a touch of ground white pepper as necessary.

Suitable for serving with cold meats, poached fish, eggs, for incorporation into broth-type soups, fish soups and as a sauce for Crudités.

SPECIAL POINTS
a) The oil should be used at room temperature.
b) If the sauce should separate, start again with a yolk of egg and a few drops of lemon juice, adding the separated mixture slowly and a little more oil to keep the proportions correct.
c) The sauce should be of the consistency of a thick mayonnaise and of a golden-yellow colour to justify its other name, Beurre de Provence.

---

181 Sauce Andalouse

1 litre
30 mins.

Prepare 600g Tomates Concassées (90) and cook to a fairly dry paste. Pass through a fine sieve, cool and add to 8dl of mayonnaise. Finish with 75g small dice of red pimento. Suitable for serving with cold meat.

---

182 Cambridge Sauce

1 litre
20 mins.

Stage	Ingredient	Quantity	Method
1	hard-boiled egg yolks	6	Pound together and pass through a fine sieve.
	anchovy fillets	20g	
	capers	20g	
	Fines Herbes (31)	50g	
2	Mayonnaise (185)	9dl	Add the purée to the mayonnaise and
	parsley, chopped	1 tbsp	finish with the chopped parsley.

---

183 Cumberland Sauce

1 litre
45 mins.

Stage	Ingredient	Quantity	Method
1	redcurrant jelly	1kg	Place in a pan and warm so as to
	port	3dl	dissolve the jelly. Allow to cool.
2	shallots, finely chopped	25g	Blanch, refresh, squeeze dry and add to the mixture.
3	lemon	1	Peel thinly, cut the zests into julienne,
	oranges	2	blanch and refresh. Squeeze the juices from the lemon and oranges and add with the julienne to the mixture.
4	mustard, dry	1 tsp	Dilute the mustard and ginger with a
	ginger, ground	1 tsp	little water, add and mix in thoroughly.

Suitable for serving with cold game.

---

184 Sauce Gribiche

1 litre
10 mins.

Stage	Ingredient	Quantity	Method
1	mustard, French	1 tsp	Mix thoroughly in a basin.
	vinegar, wine	2dl	
	oil	7dl	

2	gherkins ⎱ chopped	50g	Add, mix in well and season with salt
	capers ⎰	50g	and pepper.
	Fines Herbes,		
	chopped (31)	25g	
	eggs, hard-boiled	3	
	and sieved		

Suitable for serving with calf's head and cold fish.

---

185 Sauce Mayonnaise

1 litre
30 mins.

Stage	Ingredient	Quantity	Method
1	egg yolks	7	Place in a basin and mix thoroughly with
	vinegar	¼dl	a whisk.
	mustard, dry	1 tsp	
	salt	5g	
	pepper	pinch	
2	olive oil	1 litre	Add slowly a little at a time whisking continuously until all the oil is incorporated.
3	water, hot	½dl	Add and adjust the seasoning if necessary.

SPECIAL POINTS
a) Any good quality oil may be used in place of olive oil.
b) The oil should be used at a lukewarm temperature of approx. 20°C and, in the initial stages, it is important to add it drop by drop.
c) The proportion of oil to yolks should not be exceeded.
d) The hot water is added to act as a stabiliser.
e) This sauce should be stored in a cool place away from extremes of temperature and covered with a lid.
f) If the sauce separates, e.g. as happens if the oil is added too quickly, place a fresh yolk in a basin with 2–3 drops of vinegar and whisk in sufficient oil to thicken; then whisk in the separated mayonnaise little by little.

Suitable for serving with cold fish, meat, hors-d'oeuvre.

---

186 Sauce Menthe – Mint Sauce

1 litre
15 mins.

Stage	Ingredient	Quantity	Method
1	mint leaves	250g	Chop together and place in a basin.
	sugar, caster	150g	
2	water	2dl	Bring to the boil, pour over the mint and allow to cool.
3	vinegar	7dl	Add to the mint and mix together.

Suitable for serving with hot and cold lamb and mutton.

---

187 Pesto

½ litre
25 mins.

Stage	Ingredient	Quantity	Method
1	fresh young		Pound or blend the basil, garlic, pine
	basil leaves	120g	kernels and a pinch of salt, to a fine
	garlic, peeled	30g	paste.
	pine kernels	75g	
	salt		
2	olive oil	4dl	Gradually add the oil little by little, working vigorously to a smooth texture. Adjust the seasoning with salt and pepper as necessary.

Suitable for serving with cold meats, as a dip with Crudités, for adding to Minestrone or similar soups or mixing into cooked pasta.

SPECIAL POINT
50g each of grated Parmesan and Pecorino cheese may be blended in at Stage 1 if desired and more especially if to be used with any pasta dish.

188 Sauce Provençale

As for hot Sauce Provençale (211). Allow to become cold. Suitable for serving with cold meats and hors-d'oeuvre.

189 Sauce Raifort – Horseradish Sauce

1 litre
30 mins.

Stage	Ingredient	Quantity	Method
1	cream	7dl	Lightly whip the cream. Grate the
	horseradish	150g	horseradish and add to the cream.
2	breadcrumbs, white	150g	Soak the breadcrumbs in the milk,
	milk	2dl	squeeze out and add to the mixture.
3	vinegar	½dl	Add and season with salt, pepper and a
	cayenne		little cayenne.

Suitable for serving with smoked eel and trout, hot and cold roast beef.

190 Sauce Ravigote or Sauce Vinaigrette

1 litre
10 mins.

Stage	Ingredient	Quantity	Method
1	vinegar	2dl	Mix thoroughly in a basin.
	oil	7dl	
2	onions ⎫ finely	75g	Add, mix in well and season with salt
	capers ⎭ chopped	50g	and pepper
	Fines Herbes,		
	chopped (31)	2 tbsps	

Suitable for serving with calf's head and calf's feet.

191 Sauce Remoulade   1 litre

To 9dl of Mayonnaise (185) add 25g of chopped capers, 50g of chopped gherkin, 1 tablespoon of chopped fines herbes, 2 tablespoons of anchovy essence and mix in thoroughly. Suitable for serving with fried fish.

192 Sauce Tartare

As for Sauce Remoulade (191) omitting the anchovy essence.

193 Sauce Tyrolienne   1 litre
                                                       45 mins.

Stage	Ingredient	Quantity	Method
1	oil	½dl	Heat the oil in a small pan and cook the
	shallots, finely		shallots without colour.
	chopped	50g	
2	Tomates Concassées		Add, stew gently to a fairly dry paste,
	(90)	400g	pass through a fine sieve and allow to
	bayleaf	½	cool.
	thyme	sprig	
3	Mayonnaise (185)	9dl	Add the paste to the mayonnaise and
	Fines Herbes,		finish with the fines herbes.
	(31) chopped	1 tbsp	

Suitable for serving with fried fish, cold meats.

194 Sauce Verte – Green Sauce   1 litre
                                                       30 mins.

Stage	Ingredient	Quantity	Method
1	watercress	50g	Place in boiling water to blanch for 1
	spinach	100g	min. Refresh, drain, squeeze out and
	parsley	20g	pound well. Pass through a very fine
	tarragon	20g	sieve.
	chervil	20g	
	chives	20g	
2	Mayonnaise (185)	9dl	Add the purée to the mayonnaise and
			mix in thoroughly.

Suitable for serving with cold trout, salmon trout, salmon and shellfish.

195 Sauce Vinaigrette

See Sauce Ravigote (190).

196 Sauce Vincent   1 litre

Pass the yolks of six hard-boiled eggs through a sieve and add to 9dl of Mayonnaise (185). Finish with 1 tablespoon of Worcestershire sauce. Suitable for serving with cold fish and shellfish.

197 COCKTAIL SAUCES

Cocktail sauces are mostly used in the preparation of Hors-d'oeuvre, shellfish and fish cocktails and occasionally for some types of poultry cocktail; they are frequently used as dips for Crudités and Fondues. As cocktail sauces they should have a compatibility of flavours with the items of food used but at the same time should offer some contrast and a well-seasoned sharpness to fulfil the function of an appetite-provoking Hors-d'oeuvre. In general they should not be too thick nor used in over-generous quantities; the main item of food should be identifiable both in flavour and quantity.

198 Cocktail Sauce for Fish and Shellfish (1)   1 litre

Add 2dl of tomato ketchup and 1dl of cream to 7dl of Mayonnaise (185). Flavour with Worcestershire sauce and lemon juice to taste.

199 Cocktail Sauce for Fish and Shellfish (2)   1 litre

Add 2 tablespoons of anchovy essence and 2dl of half-whipped cream to 7dl of Mayonnaise (185). Season with a little cayenne, salt and pepper and finish with 1 tablespoon of brandy, 1 tablespoon of chopped parsley and ½ tablespoon of chopped fresh tarragon.

200 HORS-D'OEUVRE DIPS

Hors-d'oeuvre dips are an increasingly popular and wide-ranging type of thick sauce useful for giving zest to food which either lacks this in itself or needs additional or contrasting flavours to justify its use at the beginning of a meal. They are mainly based on mayonnaise but increasingly on yoghurt, crème fraîche, cream, blue and other cheeses as well as purées or pastes of vegetables, fruits and seeds. They should be capable of stimulating the appetite and this means contrast in flavours and textures, heightened seasoning and an emollient quality to assist mastication. They are particularly suitable for serving with Crudités, Fondues, Goujonettes of fish or poultry, Attereaux and various small Croquettes etc. In general dips should be thick enough to adhere in a fairly generous amount to the items of food when dipped in. An inventive and sympathetic attitude to foods and their flavours will allow the practitioner to create his own mixes. Many traditional and classic sauces are suitable, such as Andalouse, Gribiche, Ravigote, Remoulade, Tartare, Tyrolienne, Verte, Vinaigrette and Vincent, as well as Mayonnaise flavoured with such things as curry paste, sesame seed paste, fennel, finely chopped nuts, horseradish, garlic and various herbs. The following three recipes are more specific and give an idea of further possibilities.

201 Anchoïade   1 litre
25 mins.

Stage	Ingredient	Quantity	Method
1	garlic	30g	Remove any green centres from the
	basil, leaves	15g	garlic. Pound or blend the garlic, shallots
	shallot, chopped	100g	and basil together with the drained
	anchovy fillets	150g	anchovies and work to a smooth paste.

2	vinegar, white		Mix in half the vinegar then add the oil
	wine	½dl	little by little, vigorously working the
	oil, olive	6dl	whole to an homogenous mixture.
	cayenne		Season well with pepper and cayenne
			and finish with the remaining vinegar.

SPECIAL POINT
This sauce is best prepared with a blender or processor; failing this a mortar and pestle should be used.

---

202 Blue Cheese, Celery and Chive Sauce

1 litre
25 mins.

Pass 450g blue cheese through a fine sieve and mix together with 4dl soured cream. Add 100g chopped heart of celery and 2 tablespoons chopped chives. Mix together and season with salt, pepper and cayenne.

---

203 Guacamole

1 litre
25 mins.

Stage	Ingredient	Quantity	Method
1	avocado pears, ripe	6	Remove the flesh from the avocado
	tomatoes, skinned		pears then pass together with the tomato
	and deseeded	250g	flesh and garlic through a fine sieve.
	garlic, crushed	2 cloves	
2	Mayonnaise (185)	3dl	Add the Mayonnaise and onion to the
	onion, very finely		avocado mixture together with a pinch
	chopped	50g	each of the coriander and chilli powder.
	ground coriander		Heighten the seasoning with salt, pepper
	chilli powder		and a few drops of Tabasco.
	Tabasco		

——————MISCELLANEOUS SAUCES——————

204 Sauce aux Airelles – Cranberry Sauce

1 litre
1 hour

Place 750g of cranberries, 200g of sugar and 5dl water in a pan, bring to the boil and simmer gently for approx. 1 hour until soft and well-cooked. Suitable for serving with roast turkey.

SPECIAL POINTS
a) This sauce may be used either hot or cold and may be served passed or unpassed.
b) The use of aluminium or iron pans for making this sauce will result in discolouration and metallic contamination. It is essential to use a well-tinned copper or stainless steel pan.

205 Bread Sauce (1)

1 litre
30 mins.

Stage	Ingredient	Quantity	Method
1	milk	8dl	Boil the milk with the studded onion in
	Oignon Clouté		a deep pan. Draw to the side of the
	(65)	1	stove, cover and allow to infuse for 15 mins. Discard the onion.
2	breadcrumbs, white	250g	Add and mix in well.
3	butter	50g	Add, mix in and season.

Suitable for serving with roast chicken, turkey and game.

SPECIAL POINT
This sauce should be fairly thick but not stodgy and may require thinning with hot milk or thickening with the addition of more breadcrumbs.

---

206 Bread Sauce (2)

1 litre
30 mins.

Stage	Ingredient	Quantity	Method
1	milk	8dl	Place the milk and cloves in a deep pan,
	cloves, crushed	2	bring to the boil, cover and allow to infuse away from the heat for 15 mins.
2	onion, finely		Heat the butter in a pan and cook the
	chopped	75g	onion gently without colour. Strain the
	butter	25g	milk and add to the onions.
3	breadcrumbs, white	250g	Add to the milk, season with a little salt
	mace, ground	pinch	and the mace and simmer gently for approx. 15 mins.
4	cream	1dl	Finish with the cream and butter and
	butter	50g	adjust the seasoning with salt, pepper and a touch of cayenne as necessary.

Suitable for serving with roast chicken, turkey and game.

SPECIAL POINTS
a) This recipe can be a marked improvement on the previous one; if well-seasoned it will add much in the way of relish to the fairly bland taste of roast poultry.
b) The sauce should be of a fairly thick texture but not stodgy; it may require thinning with a little hot milk or thickening with more breadcrumbs.

---

207 Sauce Bretonne

1 litre
30 mins.

Stage	Ingredient	Quantity	Method
1	butter	75g	Melt the butter in a small pan, add the
	onions, finely		onions and cook without colour.
	chopped	100g	

2	white wine, dry	2dl	Add and reduce by two-thirds.
	Tomates Concassées		
	(90)	250g	
3	Demi-glace (112)	4dl	Add and simmer gently for 10 mins.
	Sauce Tomate (118)	3dl	Season well.

Suitable for use in the preparation of Haricots Bretonne (1469).

---

208 Sauce Currie – Curry Sauce

1 litre
1½ hours

Stage	Ingredient	Quantity	Method
1	butter	75g	Melt the butter in a small pan, add the
	onions, finely		onions and garlic and cook until lightly
	chopped	100g	coloured.
	garlic	½ clove	
2	curry powder	30g	Add and cook as for a Roux (107), allow
	flour	50g	to cool.
3	tomato purée	2 tbsps	Add and mix in well.
4	Estouffade (97)	1 litre	Add slowly, mixing well. Bring to the boil and skim.
5	apples, cooking ⎱ finely	50g	Add and simmer gently for 45 mins.
	chutney ⎰ chopped	30g	Skim and adjust the seasoning.
	coconut,		
	desiccated	10g	

Suitable for serving with eggs, shellfish.

SPECIAL POINTS
a) The amount of curry powder will vary according to the brand; some are hotter than others.
b) This sauce may be passed before use.
c) This sauce may be finished with a little cream to obtain a smoother texture.

---

209 Sauce aux Pommes – Apple Sauce

1 litre
1 hour

Stage	Ingredient	Quantity	Method
1	apples, cooking	2kg	Peel, core, slice, wash and place in a deep pan.
2	water	2dl	Add, cover with a lid and cook rapidly
	juice of lemon	1	until the apples are soft. Pass through a
	sugar	75g	fine sieve. Return to a clean pan and reheat.
3	butter	50g	Add and mix in.

Suitable for serving with roast pork, duckling and goose.

---

210 Sauce Portugaise

1 litre
30 mins.

Stage	Ingredient	Quantity	Method
1	oil	1dl	Heat the oil in a small pan, add the
	onion ⎱ finely	100g	onions and garlic and cook to a light
	garlic ⎰ chopped	1 clove	golden colour.
2	Tomates Concassées (90)	400g	Add, lightly season, cover and cook gently for 5 mins.
3	Sauce Tomate (118)	8dl	Add, simmer gently for 5 mins. and adjust the seasoning.

Suitable for serving with eggs, poached fish, hors-d'oeuvre.

SPECIAL POINT
This sauce may have a little chopped parsley added to it when serving.

---

211 Sauce Provençale

1 litre
30 mins.

Stage	Ingredient	Quantity	Method
1	oil, olive	1dl	Heat the oil in a small pan, add the
	garlic, finely chopped	2 cloves	garlic and cook gently without colour.
2	Tomates Concassées (90)	1kg	Add, lightly season, simmer gently and reduce by approx. half.
	white wine, dry	2dl	
3	Sauce Tomate (118)	3dl	Add, reboil and simmer gently for 10
	parsley, chopped	1 tbsp	mins. Correct seasoning and finish with the chopped parsley.

Suitable for serving with eggs, fish, shellfish.

---

212 Sauce Smitaine

1 litre
30 mins.

Stage	Ingredient	Quantity	Method
1	butter	50g	Melt the butter in a small pan, add the
	onion, finely chopped	75g	onion and cook without colour.
2	white wine, dry	2dl	Add and reduce by two-thirds.
3	sour cream	1½ litres	Add, season lightly and reduce by approx. one-third. Pass through a fine strainer.
4	lemon juice cayenne	1 tbsp	Add the juice and adjust the seasoning plus a touch of cayenne.

Suitable for serving with Bitoks, Pojarskis, Râble de Lièvre, sautés of game.

SPECIAL POINT
If sour cream is unobtainable, use fresh cream and add more lemon juice.

---

213 Sweet and Sour Sauce

1 litre
25 mins.

Stage	Ingredient	Quantity	Method
1	oil	½dl	Heat the oil in a pan and add the onion,
	onion, finely		ginger, chilli and garlic. Stir-fry gently
	chopped	125g	until soft but without colour.
	root ginger, finely		
	chopped	1 tsp	
	chilli, deseeded		
	and finely chopped	½ pod	
	garlic, finely		
	chopped	1 clove	
2	sherry, dry	½dl	Add the sherry and almost completely
	vinegar	1dl	reduce then add the vinegar and sugar
	sugar	100g	and reduce by half.
3	Jus lié (113)	1 litre	Add to the sauce, bring to the boil and
	tomato purée	½ tbsp	carefully skim.
4	juice of lemon	½	Add the lemon juice, grated orange and
	orange zest,		soy sauce. Simmer gently for a few mins.
	grated	1 tsp	and season.
	soy sauce	1 tbsp	

6
Hors-d'oeuvre

Although it plays only a relatively minor part in a full meal, the hors-d'oeuvre course merits much care and thought since being the first part of a meal, its quality gives an impression of what is to follow. An hors-d'oeuvre should be light, colourful and stimulating to the appetite, not so abundant as to spoil the appetite for any dishes which may follow.

Hors-d'oeuvre are often listed under the heading of Starters or Appetisers but it should be remembered that while all hors-d'oeuvre are the first course or prelude to a meal, not all starters can be classified as hors-d'oeuvre; many of them, especially hot ones, are actually small entrées and do not always fulfil the true function of a start to the meal.

There are two main kinds of cold hors-d'oeuvre – the mixed selection known traditionally as Hors-d'oeuvre Variés and the Single Hors-d'oeuvre which is usually a single item but which can also consist of two or more compatible items. Nowadays the mixed selection is not as extensive as it used to be but the more limited variety of items is offset usually by higher quality. In addition to the single hors-d'oeuvre in this chapter the cold eggs and the mousses and mousselines of ham, chicken and lobster given in Chapter 15 are suitable.

The inclusion of hot hors-d'oeuvre on menus is becoming more popular. These embrace not only items such as hot single vegetables but various Bouchées, Vols-au-vent and Quiches as well as many of the savouries dealt with in Chapter 19. Smaller items such as deep-fried Goujonettes of fish, shellfish and poultry served with hot sauces or cold dips also enjoy an increased demand.

Fruit juices such as orange, grapefruit and tomato are frequently offered as single hors-d'oeuvre as well as a wide variety of melons, cold or hot vegetables such as artichokes and asparagus; fruit, fish, eggs, meat, prepared pork butchers' meats and the more expensive items such as foie gras, smoked salmon and oysters.

The skill of the person who prepares the hors-d'oeuvre lies in making a wide range of commodities into attractive, well-flavoured dishes; a versatile practitioner with an artistic touch is afforded great opportunity to show originality of combination and presentation over the whole range. By tradition, hors-d'ocuvre were considered to be more suitable for lunch but this is no longer the case and it is quite in order to serve any type for dinner; the de luxe single ones such as asparagus, caviar, foie gras, oysters and smoked fish and meats are perhaps the most suitable for the formal dinner or special occasion.

HORS-D'OEUVRE VARIÉS

Hors-d'oeuvre variés is a traditional and standard title for defining the Hors-d'oeuvre selection and the items in this section are suitable for inclusion whether presented on a trolley, tray or table. It is usual to offer a minimum of 10–12 varieties with a possible choice from salads, meat, fish, eggs and vegetables, although a smaller well-chosen selection can be plated. Many of these items can be served equally well as a single hors-d'oeuvre.

Portion yield is not given here, as the amount served can vary widely according to the number of varieties offered and customers' preferences.

214 HORS-D'OEUVRE À LA GRECQUE

This type of hors-d'oeuvre requires the initial preparation of a highly seasoned and flavoured cooking liquor in which the vegetables are cooked, and is characterised by the abundant use of olive oil and lemon juice. In most cases the vegetables need to be blanched first and should then be cooked only for the length of time necessary to maintain a certain amount of firmness. Artichokes, artichoke bottoms, cauliflower, button onions, mushrooms, leeks, celery and fennel are suitable and may be served as a single hors-d'oeuvre.

Stage 1 of the following recipe for Artichokes à la Grecque gives the standard ingredients and proportions for the cooking liquor.

215 Artichauts à la Grecque   1½ hours

Stage	Ingredient	Quantity	Method
1	water	1 litre	Place in a pan, bring to the boil, skim
	oil	1½dl	and simmer for 10 mins.
	juice of lemon	3	
	bayleaf	2	
	thyme	sprig	
	fennel ⎫ cut into	50g	
	celery ⎭ batons	50g	
	coriander seeds	10	
	peppercorns	10	
	salt	15g	
2	globe artichokes, very small	30	Remove any dark green leaves from the outside and trim the top ends of the remaining leaves. Place in boiling, salted water and blanch for 5 mins. Drain.
3			Add the artichokes to the cooking liquor and simmer gently until just tender. Allow to cool in the cooking liquor. Dress neatly in a ravier with a little of the cooking liquor.

SPECIAL POINT
The cooking liquor is best left unstrained and some of its garnish dressed with the artichokes.

216 Fonds d'Artichauts à la Grecque

Use 12–14 globe artichokes trimmed and prepared for cooking, see 1379. Blanch for 5 minutes in lemon-acidulated water and cook in the same way as the artichokes (215).

217 Céleris à la Grecque

Use 600g of celery cut into batons approx. 4cm × 1cm or 8 hearts of celery trimmed to approx. 10cm in length. Blanch for 5 minutes and cook in the same way as the artichokes (215).

218 Champignons à la Grecque

Use 850g small white button mushrooms trimmed of excess stalk. Do not blanch. Cook in the same way as the artichokes (215).

219 Choux-fleurs à la Grecque

Use 600g small florets of cauliflower. Blanch for 5 minutes and cook in the same way as the artichokes (215).

220 Fenouils à la Grecque

Use 8 small fennel trimmed carefully and blanched for 10 minutes. Cook in the same way as the artichokes (215). Cut in neat portions when arranging in the hors-d'oeuvre dish.

221 Oignons à la Grecque

Use 600g peeled button onions, blanch for 5 minutes and cook in the same way as the artichokes (215).

222 Poireaux à la Grecque

Use 10–12 small trimmed leeks cut to approx. 10cm in length. Tie carefully into 2 small bundles, blanch for 5 minutes and cook in the same way as the artichokes (215).

223 HORS-D'OEUVRE À LA PORTUGAISE

This type of preparation is similar in some respects to Hors-d'oeuvre à la Grecque inasmuch as it also requires the initial preparation of a well-seasoned and flavoured cooking liquor although this time characterised by olive oil, tomatoes and white wine. It is especially suitable for the preparation of fish which need to be cut in suitably-sized sections, also for vegetables such as artichoke bottoms, mushrooms, celery, fennel, button onions, cauliflowers and leeks all of which, except for mushrooms, need to be blanched first. They should only be cooked for sufficient time to maintain a certain firmness. Any fish or vegetable prepared in this style can also be served as a single hors-d'oeuvre.

224 Harengs à la Portugaise   1½ hours

Stage	Ingredient	Quantity	Method
1	oil	1dl	Heat the oil in a pan, add the onions
	onions, finely		and garlic and cook without colour.
	chopped	100g	
	garlic, finely chopped	1 clove	

2	white wine, dry	4dl	Add, season, bring to the boil, skim and
	Tomates Concassées		simmer gently for 10 mins.
	(90)	500g	
	tomato purée	2 tbsps	
	bayleaf	2	
	thyme	sprig	
	celery,		
	cut into batons	50g	
3	herrings	750g	Clean and cut into sections 2cm wide. Place in a shallow tray. Pour the mixture over the herrings, cover with an oiled paper and cook in a moderate oven at 170°C for 30 mins. Allow to cool in the sauce.
4	parsley, chopped		Dress neatly in a ravier with some of the sauce. Sprinkle with the chopped parsley.

SPECIAL POINTS
a) Other fish such as mackerel, red mullet, grey mullet as well as white fish cut in sections may be cooked in the same way.
b) Those vegetables suitable for preparation à la Grecque are also suitable for preparation à la Portugaise. Follow the same points for blanching but cook in a shallow tray covered with oiled paper as in the above recipe.

---

225 Charcuterie

This is a general term used to describe a range of items made mainly from pork but also including other kinds of meat as well as venison and poultry. They are usually processed into various forms of cooked hams and sausages but sometimes are cured or smoked in the raw state. Pâtés and terrines are often included under this heading.

Items such as Bierwurst, Coppa, Garlic sausage, Mortadella, and all types of Salami as well as cooked or raw ham and pâtés can be used as part of the Hors-d'oeuvre selection.

Any skins should be removed first and then the item should be sliced thinly or cut into small portions as appropriate. Arrange sausage-type meats overlapping in the raviers and garnish with picked parsley. Raw or cooked ham can be cut in small slices and arranged in the ravier either as cornets or rolls. It is best not to mix different items in the same dish.

---

226 Coleslaw

Discard the outside leaves of crisp, white cabbage, cut the cabbage into quarters and remove the centre stalk. Cut the cabbage into julienne (49), wash, drain well and place in a basin. Add a little chopped onion and moisten with equal quantities of French Dressing (1329) and Mayonnaise (185). Dress neatly in a ravier. A julienne of carrots may be added in the proportion of 1 part carrots to 4 of cabbage.

---

227 Filets d'Anchois – Anchovy Fillets

Dress the fillets of anchovy trellis-fashion in a ravier, moisten with oil and garnish with sieved yolk and white of hard-boiled egg, capers, thin slices of lemon and picked parsley.

228 Gherkins

Small pickled gherkins can be placed in raviers as part of the Hors-d'oeuvre selection.

229 Maïs à la Crème – Creamed Sweetcorn

Cook the corn on the cob in boiling, salted water until tender, refresh and remove the grains with a spoon. Place in a basin and mix with a little half-whipped cream, season and dress neatly in a ravier. Tinned sweetcorn may be used in place of fresh corn on the cob.

230 Mayonnaises

Poached fish, shellfish, and poultry may be prepared as Mayonnaises for the Hors-d'oeuvre selection. Any fish used must be completely free of skin and bone and should then be flaked. Poultry should be cut in neat easily manageable pieces for service and in both these cases they should be arranged dome-shaped on a bed of shredded lettuce before coating with mayonnaise and garnishing. Where appropriate the garnish can consist of bordering the ravier with small lettuce leaves and decorating with thin strips of anchovy, red pimento, green, black or stuffed olives, capers and chopped parsley.

231 Mayonnaise d'Oeufs – Egg Mayonnaise

Cut hard-boiled eggs in half lengthways and arrange round side upward in raviers. Coat neatly with Mayonnaise (185) and decorate with thin strips of anchovy fillet arranged trellis-fashion, stoned green olives and capers.

232 Olives

Black, green and stuffed olives may be placed in raviers as part of the Hors-d'oeuvre selection.

233 Radis – Radishes

Wash the radishes well, trim the stalks to 2cm length and clean the top of the radish where it joins the stalk. Remove the end of the root then place the radishes in a basin of ice water to become crisp. Dress in raviers sprinkled with a little crushed ice.

234 Rollmops

Stage	Ingredient	Quantity	Method
1	herrings, medium	10	Remove the heads and scales, gut and wash the herrings. Remove the centre bones, cutting from the top of the fish, without separating the two fillets. Lay them flat on a tray, sprinkle well with coarse salt and allow to stand for approx. 10 hours in a cool place. Wash well under running cold water for one hour. Remove and dry.
2	onions, finely sliced	150g	Place a few slices of onion at the head end of each prepared herring and roll them up securing the tail with a cocktail stick. Pack into an earthenware basin or jar.
3	onions, finely shredded	100g	Place all these ingredients into a pan, bring to the boil and simmer for 5 mins. Allow to cool thoroughly then pour over the herrings. Leave for a minimum of two days to marinate.
	vinegar, white	7dl	
	white wine, dry	3dl	
	bayleaf	2	
	chillies	5	
	peppercorns	10	
	allspice	10	
4			For service: remove the sticks, unroll and remove the onions from the herrings. Reroll and cut into rings approx. 1cm thick. Dress neatly in raviers with a little of the marinade, the onions and a bayleaf.

235 SALADS FOR HORS-D'OEUVRE

Most kinds of salads make very good hors-d'oeuvre either individually or as part of a selection, however some thought must be given as to their suitability and those that contain lettuce, either finely shredded or as leaves, may look attractive to begin with but once dressed and left for a while will quickly lose their fresh appearance. Besides the usual single-vegetable salads there is an almost infinite number of suitable combinations based mainly on vegetables, fish, shellfish, meat and poultry together with compatible or contrasting adjuncts such as nuts and fruits, and dressings based on cream, mayonnaise, vinaigrette or yoghurt. All the elements used in making these kinds of salads must be of good quality with the main ingredient which gives its name to the dish comprising roughly half of the total, though where there are a good number of items, it could well be equal amounts of each. The skill of the practitioner should ensure an appetising and attractive series of hors-d'oeuvre salads and he will be aware, for example, of the versatility of rice as a basic ingredient because it allows of many additions such as apple, chicken, meat, fish, pimentos, pineapple, dried fruit, smoked fish, canned fish and nuts, etc., as well as many flavoured dressings. Many of these mixed salads can also be served as single hors-d'oeuvre.

236 Salade de Betterave – Beetroot Salad

Wash the beetroots and place in a pan of cold water. Bring to boil and allow to simmer gently until tender for approx. 1 hour. Allow to cool and peel by rubbing off the skin with the hands. Cut into batons approx. 2½cm long × ½cm and arrange neatly in a ravier; moisten with French Dressing (1329). Garnish with small onion rings and sprinkle with chopped parsley. This salad may be moistened with mustard dressing (1334) instead of French dressing.

SPECIAL POINTS
Cooked and peeled beetroot may be stored successfully be covering with vinegar in a basin and keeping in the refrigerator.

237 Salade de Boeuf – Beef Salad

Mix together an equal quantity of diced cooked beef, diced cooked potato and Tomates Concassées (90). Add a little chopped onion and moisten with French Dressing (1329), keep in a refrigerator for a few hours before using, then dress neatly in a ravier and sprinkle with chopped parsley.

238 Salade Bretonne

Mix 3 parts of cold cooked Haricots Blancs (1467) with 1 part of Tomates Concassées (90). Add a little chopped onion and moisten with French Dressing (1329). Mix well and store in a refrigerator for a few hours before using, then dress neatly in a ravier and sprinkle with chopped parsley.

239 Salade de Céleri-rave – Celeriac Salad

Wash and peel celeriac and cut into Julienne (49). Place into a basin of water with a little lemon juice to keep it white. Drain well and mix with a little mayonnaise, season with salt and pepper and flavour with a little finely chopped garlic. Dress neatly in a ravier.

240 Salade de Chou-fleur – Cauliflower Salad

Prepare, wash and cook cauliflower in boiling, salted water, refresh under cold running water and drain. Cut into small bouquets. Place into a basin, season with salt and pepper and moisten with French Dressing (1329). Dress neatly in a ravier and a sprinkle with chopped parsley.

241 Salade de Chou-rouge – Pickled Red Cabbage

Discard the outside leaves of red cabbage, cut the cabbage into quarters and remove the centre stalk. Cut the cabbage into Julienne (49) wash well, drain and place in a basin. Add a little salt, a few peppercorns and cloves of garlic. Cover with vinegar and keep in the refrigerator for a minimum of two days before using. Dress neatly in a ravier.

242 Salade de Concombres – Cucumber Salad

Peel and thinly slice cucumber. Arrange neatly overlapping in raviers and moisten with a little French Dressing (1329). Sprinkle with chopped parsley.

243 Salade Fécampoise

Mix together equal quantities of diced cooked potatoes, cooked shrimps, diced pimento and diced hard-boiled egg. Add a little chopped onion and moisten with equal quantities of French Dressing (1329) and Mayonnaise (185). Dress neatly in raviers and decorate with strips of pimento arranged trellis-fashion and shrimps.

244 Salade de Haricots Verts – French Bean Salad

Top and tail small French beans and just cook in boiling, salted water. Drain and place spread out on a cloth or tray to cool. Place in a basin, add a little finely chopped onion, season and moisten with French Dressing (1329). Dress in a ravier and sprinkle with chopped parsley.

245 Salade Italienne

Mix together 4 parts of Salade Russe (249), 1 part small dice of Salami and 1 part small dice of anchovy fillets. Dress neatly in raviers.

246 Salade de Piments – Pimento Salad

Remove the stalks from an equal quantity of red and green pimentos. Cut in half and remove the seeds. Cut in Julienne (49) and place in a basin. Moisten with French Dressing (1329). Mix well and dress neatly in a ravier.

247 Salade de Pommes de Terre – Potato Salad

a) Cut cold boiled potatoes into ½cm dice, add a little chopped onion, season and mix with Mayonnaise (185). Dress neatly in raviers and sprinkle with chopped parsley.

b) Wash some firm waxy potatoes, cook in boiling, salted water until just cooked. Skin carefully then cut into dice while still hot. Place immediately into a basin, add a little finely chopped onion and chopped parsley. Season with salt and milled black pepper, moisten with French Dressing (1329) and mix gently together. Allow to cool and dress neatly in raviers.

248 Salade de Riz – Rice Salad

Mix together 3 parts of cold cooked rice (534), 1 part of Tomates Concassées (90) and 1 part of cooked peas; season and moisten with French Dressing (1329). Mix gently and dress neatly in raviers.

SPECIAL POINT
This type of salad may be varied by the use of other ingredients such as fresh fruits cut in dice, other cooked vegetables, raw salad vegetables, hard-boiled eggs, and cooked meat and fish but provided always that the rice represents half the total quantity. The flavouring may also be varied by the use of other dressings such as Cream Dressing (1326) and Lemon Dressing (1331).

249 Salade Russe – Russian Salad

This consists of equal quantities of carrots, turnips, peas and French beans; the carrots and turnips cut into 8mm dice, and the beans into small diamond shapes. Cook separately in boiling, salted water. Drain, spread out on a tray and allow to cool. season and mix with Mayonnaise (185) and dress neatly in raviers.

SPECIAL POINT
These ingredients can be augmented or varied, if desired, with a selection of the following: salami, cooked sausage, gherkins, cooked mushroom, tongue, ham, all cut in dice; and capers.

250 Salade de Tomates – Tomato Salad

Remove the eyes from firm tomatoes, blanch and peel. Slice neatly and dress in raviers slightly overlapping. Moisten with French Dressing (1329) and sprinkle with chopped parsley.

251 Sardines

Dress the canned sardines fan-shape in a ravier, moisten with a little of the oil and garnish with picked parsley.

252 Thon à l'Huile – Tunny Fish

Dress the tunny fish neatly in a ravier, moisten with a little of the oil and garnish with picked parsley.

————SINGLE HORS-D'OEUVRE————

This kind is usually regarded as a more luxurious and costly hors d'oeuvre than those normally used for a selection though in some cases items are used in both kinds, those for a selection being scaled down in portion size, shape and presentation. Single hors-d'oeuvre are usually listed and priced separately and are very often regarded as being more appropriate for dinner rather than for lunch, but there is nothing really to justify this position; the customer's needs here are paramount.

253 Artichauts – Globe Artichokes

Prepare and cook globe artichokes (1377) and serve hot accompanied with a suitable sauce such as Sauce Hollandaise (157) or Beurre Fondu (9), or serve cold and presented in the same manner but accompanied with French Dressing (1329).

254 Asperges – Asparagus

Prepare and cook asparagus (1382–3) and serve either hot accompanied with a suitable sauce such as Sauce Hollandaise (157) or Beurre Fondu (9), or serve cold and presented in the same manner but accompanied with French Dressing (1329). Allow 6–8 sticks of asparagus per portion.

255 Avocat Vinaigrette – Avocado Pear with French Dressing

Cut avocado pears in half lengthways and remove the stones. Dress on leaves of lettuce or in special avocado dishes and serve with French Dressing (1329) as an accompaniment. Serve half a pear per portion. Sauce Gribiche (184) and Sauce Mayonnaise (185) are suitable alternatives.

256 Avocat aux Crevettes – Avocado Pear with Prawns

Cut avocado pears in half lengthways and remove the stones. Fill the centre with shrimps or prawns bound with Cocktail Sauce (198 or 199). Dress on leaves of lettuce or in special avocado dishes and garnish with slices of peeled tomato and cucumber.

SPECIAL POINT
Other cooked shellfish or a mixture of shellfish such as lobster, scampi and mussels may be used. Designate the dish accordingly, e.g. Avocat au Crabe, aux Fruits de Mer, au Homard.

257 Avocat Côte d'Azur

10 portions
25 mins.

Stage	Ingredient	Quantity	Method
1	Sauce Gribiche (184) anchovy fillets	1½dl 6	Chop the anchovy fillets and add to the Sauce Gribiche. Mix together lightly and check that it is well-seasoned.
2	avocado pears, ripe but firm pine kernels cucumber, peeled and deseeded tomatoes, peeled and deseeded	5 50g 100g 150g	Cut the avocados in half, discard the stones and scoop out the flesh. Reserve the skins. Cut the flesh into cubes and place in a basin. Cut the tomato and cucumber into small dice and add to the avocado together with the pine kernels. Mix lightly together.
3			Add the prepared sauce and mix very carefully together so as not to mash the avocado. Refill the skins dome-shape and dress on leaves of lettuce or in special avocado dishes.

258 Caviar

Caviar is the lightly salted roe of the sturgeon and its allied species. There are a number of caviars named after their particular fish, the best known being Beluga, Ocietrova, and Sevruga with the term Malossol denoting the amount of salt used in the curing process. It is mainly imported from Russia and Iran and is usually packed in tins. Caviar can be served from the tin or from special earthenware jars. In either case, the container should be presented in a deep dish surrounded by crushed ice. Serve accompanied with quarters of lemon, sieved yolk and white of hard-boiled egg, finely chopped onion and Blinis (17) or hot toast. It is usual to serve 25–30g of caviar per portion. A bone or ivory spoon should be used for serving caviar.

259 Charcuterie

As a single hors-d'oeuvre this can be selected from a wide range of processed pork butcher's meats and sausages such as Bierwurst, Bratwurst, Coppa, Mortadella, various salamis, raw hams such as Bayonne, Mayence, Parma and Ardennes and cooked hams. It can also include such things as Pastrami and Engadine dried beef (Bündnerfleisch). In all cases the skins should be removed where present, the meat cut in thin slices then arranged neatly on a plate or dish and garnished with gherkins and a few leaves of salad vegetables.

Charcuterie may be served as just a single item, e.g. salami, Jambon de Bayonne etc., or as a well-chosen selection of similar items.

260 Cocktail de Crevettes – Prawn Cocktail

10 portions
20 mins.

Stage	Ingredient	Quantity	Method
1	lettuce	1	Wash and drain the lettuce and coarsely shred. Place in cocktail glasses approx. half to two-thirds full.
2	prawns, shelled	450g	Place neatly on top of the lettuce.
3	Cocktail Sauce (198 or 199)	4dl	Cover the prawns carefully with the cocktail sauce. Decorate with quarters of tomato, lemon and chopped parsley.
	tomatoes, peeled	3	
	lemons	2	
	parsley, chopped		

261 Cocktail de Crabe – Crab Cocktail

This is prepared in the same way as Cocktail de Crevettes (260) using the white crabmeat instead of prawns; pass 2–3 tablespoons of the dark creamy flesh of the crab through a very fine sieve and add to the sauce before using.

262 Cocktail de Fruits de Mer – Seafood Cocktail

This is prepared in the same way as Cocktail de Crevettes (260), using a mixture of diced lobster, small cooked mussels, prawns and diced scallops instead of the prawns.

263 Cocktail de Homard – Lobster Cocktail

This is prepared in the same way as Cocktail de Crevettes (260), using diced lobster instead of the prawns. An additional garnish of a shelled lobster claw can be placed on top.

264 Confit d'Oie – Preserved Goose

18–20 portions
1 day

Stage	Ingredient	Quantity	Method
1	goose	1 × 5kg	Clean and singe the goose carefully, remove any fat and place on one side. Remove the 2 legs and 2 suprêmes from the breast. Do not remove the skin.

2	sea salt	1kg	Mix these ingredients well together. Rub
	saltpetre	pinch	the pieces of goose with it on both sides
	thyme, ground	pinch	then place in a deep dish and cover with
	bayleaf, ground	pinch	the remaining salt mixture. Leave for
	clove, ground	pinch	approx, 24 hours in the refrigerator.
	milled black		
	pepper	pinch	

3 — Melt the reserved goose fat in a heavy shallow pan. Wash the pieces of goose well, dry them, then place to cook very slowly in the fat which should be fairly abundant. Time 1½–2 hours. Turn and test occasionally; do not overcook.

4 lard, best — 500g (approx.) — When ready, place the pieces into a deep, very clean glazed earthenware marmite or terrine. Strain over the goose fat and when set make sure that the goose is finally covered completely by pouring over some melted lard. Allow to mature in the refrigerator for at least a week.

5 lettuce — 1 — As a single hors-d'oeuvre the breast of the goose is the best. For service remove the pieces of goose, clean off any fat, cut into very thin slices on the slant and arrange overlapping on a suitable dish or plate. Garnish lightly with a few leaves of salad vegetable and accompany with hot toasted white or brown bread. Allow approx. 50–60g per portion.

SPECIAL POINT

If kept covered with fat and a paper and kept in a refrigerator this preparation of goose will keep in a perfect condition for at least three months. It is frequently used as a component or garnish of some types of stew.

---

265 Crevettes Roses – Prawns

Arrange unshelled cooked prawns in a glass bowl full of crushed ice, allowing approx. 10–12 per portion according to size. Garnish with picked parsley and serve with lemon and brown bread and butter.

---

266 Crudités – Raw Vegetables

This is a colourful selection of raw vegetables cut into slices, sections or batons as the case may be and served with different cold sauces and dressings. They are also served as a selection of several dishes of cut raw vegetables that have been seasoned and dressed just before service. The vegetables in this case are shredded, cut into slices or sections, or into julienne, according to the nature of each. Such a selection may also be presented on a plate.

Suitable vegetables include bean sprouts, red and white cabbage, carrot, cauliflower, celeriac, celery, chicory, Chinese leaves, cucumber, fennel, kohlrabi, mushrooms, pimentos and radishes. Dressings and sauces can be based on vinaigrette, sour cream, yoghurt or mayonnaise, with suitable additions and flavourings. See Chapter 5 for suitable sauces.

---

267 Dressed Crab

10 portions
1½ hours

Stage	Ingredient	Quantity	Method
1	crab, cooked vinegar, malt	2 × 2 kg few drops	Remove the large claws and the small legs. Place the legs at one side. Pull the breast away from the shell (underside) and discard the dead man's fingers (gills) and sac. Remove all the white meat from the breast and from the claws after cracking them. Season with salt, milled pepper and just a little vinegar.

2	breadcrumbs, white
	Mayonnaise (185)
	made English
	  mustard
	Worcestershire
	  sauce
		75g
		1dl
		
		½ tbsp
		
		few drops
			Remove the dark creamy flesh from inside the shell and pass it through a fine sieve. Mix together with the bread-crumbs, mayonnaise and mustard. Season with salt, pepper and Worcestershire sauce.

3			Break off the shells to the natural line at each end of the underside. Thoroughly scrub, wash and dry. Fill the centres with the creamy mixture and place the white flesh neatly at each side.
4	eggs, hard-boiled parsley, chopped	3	Decorate the creamy mixture with lines of sieved yolk and white of hard-boiled egg and chopped parsley.
5	tomatoes, peeled lettuce Mayonnaise (185)	5 2 7dl	Arrange some nice leaves of lettuce on a suitable flat dish. Use the reserved small legs to make two ovals by pushing their pointed ends into the open ends. Place these on the lettuce and use as cradles on which to rest the filled crab shells. Garnish with quarters of peeled tomatoes. Serve accompanied with mayonnaise.

---

268 Escargots à la Bourguignonne

12–15 pieces
25 mins.

Snails are invariably purchased ready-cooked in tins accompanied separately by an appropriate number of clean shells. Remove the snails from the tin and drain. Prepare approx. 100g of Beurre à la Bourguignonne (6). Place a little of the butter in each shell followed by a snail and then add sufficient butter to fill the shells. Arrange the snails on a special snail dish with the filled apertures uppermost and place into a hot oven at 200°C for 7–8 mins. until bubbling. Serve immediately.

269 Escargots à la Bordelaise

12–15 pieces
25 mins.

Place in a basin 75g butter, 50g finely diced bone marrow, 50g finely chopped shallot reduced with 1dl dry white wine until nearly dry, 1 tablespoon melted Glace de Viande (103), 1 tablespoon chopped parsley and a good squeeze of lemon juice. Mix together thoroughly and season well with salt, pepper and a touch of cayenne. Using this butter proceed as for Escargots à la Bourguignonne (268).

270 Escargots à la Chablaisienne

12–15 pieces
25 mins.

First place a few drops each of dry white wine and melted Glace de Viande (103) in each snail shell followed by a snail and then add sufficient Beurre Bourguignonne (6) to fill the shells. Arrange on a special snail dish with the filled apertures uppermost and place into a hot oven at 200°C for 7–8 minutes, until bubbling. Remove from the oven, sprinkle the snails with a little of the same white wine and serve immediately.

271 Figues – Figs

Only fresh ripe figs are suitable as an hors-d'oeuvre. They can be presented whole, arranged on vine leaves covering crushed ice, or chilled, cut in halves and arranged on a suitable dish or plate.

272 Foie Gras

Foie gras is made from the livers of specially fattened geese, prepared commercially mainly in Alsace in France. It is available cooked in a pastry crust (Foie gras en Croûte), in earthenware terrines (Terrine de Foie gras) and in various shaped tins.

FOR SERVICE:
a) Foie gras en Croûte should be placed on a folded serviette.
b) Terrine de Foie gras should be placed in a deep dish and surrounded with ice.
c) Tinned foie gras may be served cut into ½cm slices, arranged on a dish and garnished with diced aspic jelly and a little plain salad. The slices of foie gras may be coated with aspic jelly for service.
d) Foie gras may also be served lukewarm as an hors-d'oeuvre. Shallow fry ½cm thick slices of seasoned raw foie gras in hot butter and on both sides until just set. Place on a dish and pour over the butter from the pan, deglazed with a little wine vinegar. Garnish with a few leaves of salad vegetable.
e) Hot toast should always be served with foie gras.

273 FRUIT COCKTAILS

Citrus fruits are the most suitable for fruit cocktails with oranges and grapefruit being the most popular. They can be combined with other fruits including tangerines, pineapple, melon, grapes, nectarines and mangoes, and ripe berries such as bilberries, redcurrants and raspberries can be added. Normally, the natural sharp flavour of these fruits is ideal but if they are too sour it is in order to add sugar. What is not suitable, however, is something which resembles a sweet fruit salad. The use of a few drops of a complementary-flavoured spirit or liqueur such as Kirsch, Maraschino or Grand Marnier is quite in order as well as garnishing with maraschino cherries and sprigs of mint.

274 Grapefruit Cocktail

10 portions
30 mins.

Stage	Ingredient	Quantity	Method
1	grapefruit	8–10	Cut off both ends of the grapefruit squarely. Stand it on a chopping board and cut downward following the shape of the grapefruit to remove all the peel and pith and as little of the flesh as possible.
2			Holding the grapefruit in one hand, remove one segment by cutting along each side of it close to the dividing membrane; do not cut through the centre core. Place in a basin and continue to remove all the segments. Squeeze the juice from the remainder of the grapefruit onto the segments.
3	sugar	50g	Sprinkle the sugar over the grapefruit. Arrange the segments neatly in coupes or goblets with some of the juice and place a cherry in the centre. Serve well-chilled.
	maraschino cherries	10	

275 Coupe Miami

Prepare as Grapefruit Cocktail (274), using 4–5 oranges, 3–4 grapefruit according to size and 250g of fresh pineapple cut into small segments instead of only grapefruit.

276 Florida Cocktail

Prepare as Grapefruit Cocktail (274), using 6–7 oranges and 4–5 grapefruit instead of only grapefruit.

277 Orange Cocktail

Prepare as Grapefruit Cocktail (274), using 10–12 oranges according to size instead of the grapefruit.

278 Melon Cocktail

10 portions
30 mins.

Stage	Ingredient	Quantity	Method
1	melons, ripe	2	Cut in half, remove the seeds and scoop out the flesh with a parisienne cutter into a basin. Squeeze the juice from the remainder over the melon balls.

| 2 | maraschino cherries | 10 | Place into coupes or goblets with a cherry on top and serve well-chilled. |

Serve approx. 100g of melon per portion. This cocktail may be flavoured with Kirsch, Maraschino, Madeira, Marsala or port.

279 Grapefruit

It is usual to serve half a grapefruit per portion. Lightly roll into a good shape, cut in half horizontally and remove the pips. Remove the centre core with a small sharp knife and cut carefully around each segment to free it from the skin. Place in coupes with a cherry in the centre of each half-grapefruit.

280 Grilled Grapefruit

Prepare the grapefruit as indicated in Recipe 279, omitting the cherry; sprinkle well with brown sugar and cook gently under a grill until the topping is caramelised to a golden brown colour. Serve hot in coupes.

281 Gravlax

20–25 portions
2–3 days

Stage	Ingredient	Quantity	Method
1	salmon fillet	2kg	Make sure that the fillet of salmon is
	sea salt	100g	scaled, free of bones, washed and dried.
	sugar	50g	Cut in two equal halves. Place one half,
	white peppercorns,		skin-side down, in a suitably-sized deep
	finely crushed	5g	dish. Sprinkle with some of the mixed
	dill, coarsely		seasonings, dill and Aquavit. Cover with
	chopped	100g	the other piece of salmon, flesh-side
	Aquavit	2 tbsps	down, and sprinkle with the remaining ingredients.
2			Cover with foil or paper and place in the refrigerator to marinate for approx. 2–3 days. Separate the fillets and baste occasionally with the exuded juices.
3			To serve, clean the salmon of any adhering salt, pepper and dill. Cut into thin slices on the slant, allowing 2–3 slices per portion and serve with lemon and brown bread and butter. The following sauce should always be offered.

282 Sauce for Gravlax

Stage	Ingredient	Quantity	Method
1	Dijon mustard	2 tbsps	Place the mustard in a basin. Add the
	vinegar, wine	¼dl	rest of the ingredients and mix together
	salt	pinch	well with a small whisk.
	milled black		
	pepper	good pinch	
	sugar	1 tsp	

| 2 | salad oil | 4dl | Add the oil in a steady stream whisking |
| | dill, chopped | 2 tbsps | continuously. This should result in a |

Add the oil in a steady stream whisking continuously. This should result in a nice creamy emulsion. Adjust the seasoning as necessary and finish with the dill.

283 Huîtres – Oysters

The main species of oysters available are the flat or plate British natives from Colchester, Helford and Whitstable, together with the Portuguese and the Belon variety imported from France. They are purchased in graded sizes, Number 1 being the largest down to Number 4, only about half the size. For use it is of the utmost importance that they should be alive; this is determined by tightly closed shells and heaviness in relation to size.

Oysters should be opened carefully with an oyster knife by inserting the edge of the knife at the hinged end and levering it open. Discard the flat shell. Release the oysters from the shell by cutting through the muscle close to the shell. Turn the oysters over. Place them on a dish of crushed ice. Serve accompanied with brown bread and butter and lemon. It is normal to serve six per portion.

284 Jambon de Parme – Parma Ham

Parma ham is purchased ready prepared either on the bone or boneless. Cut very thinly and serve garnished with a little plain salad. Other smoked and cured raw hams such as Jambon de Bayonne and Jambon de Westphalie are served in the same way.

285 Mayonnaise d'Oeufs – Egg Mayonnaise

Arrange three halves of hard-boiled eggs per portion on lettuce leaves, coat with Mayonnaise (185) and decorate with strips of anchovy fillet arranged trellis-fashion, capers and stoned olives. Garnish with slices of peeled tomato and cucumber.

286 Mayonnaise de Poisson – Mayonnaise of Fish

Arrange 75g of flaked poached fish per portion on lettuce leaves and coat with Mayonnaise (185). Decorate with thin strips of anchovy fillets, arranged trellis-fashion, capers and stoned olives. Garnish with slices of peeled tomato and cucumber.

SPECIAL POINT
The fish used should be designated on the menu, e.g. Mayonnaise de Turbot.

287 Melon

There are many varieties of melons including Bellegard, Cantaloupe, Charentais, Chypre, Galia, Honeydew and Ogen, each having its own particular size, shape, aroma, colour and flavour. To serve, cut the melon in half through the stem ends, discard the seeds, cut each half into three or four wedge-shaped pieces according to size and cut the curved base flat to make each piece stand level. If small, cut in half horizontally. Serve well-chilled or on crushed ice accompanied with caster sugar and ground ginger.

288 Melon Charentais au Porto – Charentais Melon with Port

Choose small Charentais melons, cut off the tops and scoop out the seeds with a spoon. Half fill the melons with port and add a little demerara sugar. Replace the tops and keep in the refrigerator for a minimum of one hour before serving on a bed of crushed ice. Madeira may be used instead of port in which case the name would become Melon Charentais au Madère.

Small Ogen melons are also very suitable for this type of preparation.

289 Melon et Jambon de Parme – Melon with Parma Ham

This is a portion of honeydew or sugar melon served with slices of Parma ham. It is usual to remove the skin from the melon before serving. Parma ham may also be served with fresh figs or thick slices of peeled and cored, firm but ripe pear.

290 Mousses

Cold mousses made from cooked ingredients are suitable for serving as a cold hors-d'oeuvre either as individual moulded portions set in ramekins or served from a large dish. They should be well-flavoured, light in texture, lightly decorated or ungarnished and may be glazed with aspic jelly. In some instances a mousse may be served as a filling in a cornet of ham, salami, smoked salmon etc., or used to fill tomatoes or artichoke bottoms. They can be served garnished with leaves of salad vegetables.

The main items for making cold mousses are:
   Fish: fresh or smoked salmon, tuna, lobster, shrimps.
   Meat: ham, chicken, game, foie gras.
   Vegetables: avocado, tomato, asparagus.

See 1266–1271 for standard recipes.

291 Oeufs de Cailles – Quails' Eggs

Quails' eggs are obtainable fresh, hard-boiled, canned or bottled. To cook fresh quails' eggs, place in cold water, bring to the boil, cook for 30 seconds then allow them to cool in the water. They are served in the same way as Gulls' Eggs (293).

They may also be prepared and presented in accordance with the recipe for Oeuf en Gelée à l'Estragon (1272) using 2–3 hard-boiled quails' eggs per portion instead of the poached eggs.

292 Oeufs Farcis – Stuffed Eggs

Hard-boiled eggs may be cut in half lengthways and stuffed with a purée of the yolks mixed with a little butter, mayonnaise and chopped parsley. This is best done by using a piping bag and star tube. The mixture may be varied by the addition of flavourings such as tomato, curry, Worcestershire sauce, chopped fresh herbs and chopped nuts as well as purées of meat, fish and poultry. Serve three halves per portion dressed with a few salad leaves and garnish with tomato and cucumber.

293 Oeufs de Mouettes – Gulls' Eggs

Gulls' eggs are usually purchased hard-boiled; if purchased raw they should be boiled for 7–8 mins. They are served in the shell on a bed of mustard and cress. Serve with cayenne pepper and brown bread and butter. Allow 2–3 per portion. Gulls' eggs have largely replaced plovers' eggs on the menu as the plover is now a protected bird.

294 Pâtés and Terrines

The number and variety of pâtés and terrines is extensive and almost all are suitable as a single hors-d'oeuvre. They can be served from the terrines as they are or cut in portions. In either case a few salad leaves may be served as an accompaniment and crisp French bread, hot toast and toast Melba should be offered. See Recipes 1315–19 for suitable examples.

295 POTTED MEATS AND FISH

These are pounded or finely chopped purées of cooked or smoked meat, poultry, fish, shellfish or game, well-seasoned, spiced and flavoured, and mixed with up to half their quantity of cool melted butter according to the nature of the item being used. They are then pressed into small individual or larger containers, with porcelain ramequins and cassolettes being the most suitable, and are finally covered with melted butter. Some small items such as shrimps can also be used whole. They keep well if stored in a refrigerator.

Suitable items for potting are:
  Fish: smoked mackerel, trout, tunnyfish and salmon.
  Shellfish: shrimps, prawns, lobster, crab.
  Meat: ox-tongue, ham, beef, pork.
  Game: venison, pheasant, grouse.
  Poultry: chicken, duck, goose.

The most suitable seasonings are milled white pepper, cayenne, ground mace, nutmeg and ginger, and salt as needed. Ground bayleaf and thyme can be useful if sparingly used for pork, ham and game. The butter used should not be too salty.

Potted meats and fish are served best in their small containers accompanied by hot toast and brown bread and butter.

296 Potted Smoked Salmon

10–12 portions
15 mins.

Finely chop or pound 600g smoked salmon or good trimmings of the salmon. Mix well with 150g cool melted butter and season well with a pinch each of ground mace and nutmeg, a touch of cayenne, a little milled white pepper and salt if required. Press neatly into porcelain ramequins, cover with a little melted butter and refrigerate. Serve accompanied with hot toast and brown bread and butter.

297 Potted Shrimps

10–12 portions
15 mins.

Mix well together 700g freshly cooked and shelled shrimps with 200g cool melted butter, season well with ground mace and nutmeg, milled white pepper, cayenne and salt if required. Press flat into porcelain ramequins, cover with a little melted butter and refrigerate. Serve in the ramequins with hot toast and brown bread and butter.

Ready-prepared potted shrimps are usually purchased in waxed card containers. In this case it is better to turn them out and garnish with a few leaves of vegetable salad.

298 Rillettes

12–14 portions
4½ hours

Stage	Ingredient	Quantity	Method
1	belly of pork, no skin or bones	1kg	Cut the pork into approx. 2cm cubes and place in a pan with the water and a
	water	1dl	pinch of salt. Cover and cook very, very slowly, moving the meat occasionally, either on low heat or in a slow oven. Allow 2½–3 hours when the meat should be very soft and almost melting.
2	mace, ground	pinch	Drain off all the fat carefully and reser-
	mixed spice	pinch	ve. Pound the meat vigorously then place
	bayleaf, ground	touch	in a basin. Add a little of the reserved fat
	thyme, ground	touch	to give a soft smooth texture and season
	cayenne	touch	well with the spices and herbs. Add salt
	milled white pepper		as required. Reheat for 10–15 mins., stirring frequently.
3			Press flat into individual porcelain rame-quins and finally cover with a thin layer of the reserved fat. Place in the refri-gerator to set. Serve in the ramequins accompanied with hot toast.

299 SMOKED FISH

There is a wide range of smoked fish available in addition to the more popular smoked eel, salmon and trout. They include smoked sturgeon, salmon trout, mackerel, halibut and tuna as well as sprats and Buckling herrings. Smoked mackerel may be served in thickish slices or by the whole fillet; sprats and Buckling herrings are served whole, other large smoked fish are sliced. In all cases serve with lemon and accompanied with brown bread and butter. Horseradish either grated or as a sauce can be offered.

300 Anguille Fumée – Smoked Eel

Whole smoked eel can be purchased ready for use. Where appropriate they can be arranged on a board for service in the dining room where they are cut into approx. 8cm lengths. The skin is removed and the eel may be filleted or cut into thin slices. Serve with quarters of lemon, brown bread and butter and grated horseradish or horseradish sauce. Allow two pieces of fillet or its equivalent in slices per portion, approx. 50–75g.

301 Saumon Fumé – Smoked Salmon

Smoked salmon is purchased ready-prepared, usually by the side. It requires trimming and the removal of all the bones. Cut into thin slices on the slant across the side giving 2–3 slices per portion. Serve with quarters of lemon and brown bread and butter.

302 Truite Fumée – Smoked Trout

Smoked trout are purchased ready-prepared. They may be dressed on a dish for service in the restaurant, where the trout is skinned and the head removed; it may be filleted. Serve with quarters of lemon, brown bread and butter and grated horseradish or Horseradish Sauce (189).

303 Soused Herrings

10 portions
2½ hours

Stage	Ingredient	Quantity	Method
1	herrings	10 × 200g	Remove the heads. Clean, scale and wash the herrings. Place in a fairly deep tray.
2	carrots, grooved and cut into thin rings	100g	Place all ingredients over the herrings and cover with greaseproof paper. Place in the oven at 150°C and cook for approx 1½–2 hours.
	button onions, cut into thin rings	100g	
	vinegar	5dl	
	water	5dl	
	chillies	6	
	bayleaf	2	
	parsley stalks	10g	
	cloves	2	
	sugar	15g	
	peppercorns	10	
	salt	15g	
3			Remove from the oven and allow to cool in the cooking liquor. Serve with a little of the cooking liquor and decorate with the carrot and onion.

304 Taramasalata – Smoked Cod's Roe Relish

10–12 portions
15 mins.

Stage	Ingredient	Quantity	Method
1	bread, crust removed	150g	Soak the bread in water then squeeze firmly to remove most of the moisture.
2	smoked cod's roe	450g	Carefully remove any skin from the roe. Place the roe, onion, garlic and the prepared bread in a food processor and blend together until smooth.
	onion, finely chopped	50g	
	garlic, crushed	1 clove	
3	olive oil	2½dl	Gradually add the oil to the mixture as for mayonnaise, adding the lemon juice to taste until it reaches a smooth spreadable mixture. Season as necessary plus a touch of cayenne.
	juice of lemon	1	
	cayenne		

| 4 | black olives, stoned
lemon | | Arrange dome-shaped in individual ramequin dishes and garnish with the olives. Serve accompanied with halves of lemon and offer hot pitta bread or toast. |

305 Pitta Bread

10 pieces

Stage	Ingredient	Quantity	Method	1 hour
1	flour, strong salt water at 37°C yeast olive oil	500g 10g 2½dl 25g 1 tbsp	Sift the flour and salt into a warm basin and make a bay. Dissolve the yeast in the water and add the oil. Mix into the flour and knead well.	
2			Cover the dough with a damp cloth and allow to prove in a warm place to double its size, approx. 25 mins. Knead the dough again to knock it back to its original bulk.	
3			Divide into ten pieces and roll out into ovals, approx. 18cm long × ¾cm thick.	
4			Allow to prove for approx. 10 mins. then place onto a hot oiled tray. Brush with water and bake at 240°C for approx. 5 mins.	
5			Keep wrapped in a warm cloth for service.	

306 Tomates Farcies – Stuffed Tomatoes

Select firm medium-sized tomatoes, remove the eyes and blanch and skin them. Cut off the rounded ends and reserve and empty the insides. They can then be filled to choice with salpicons or purées of fish, meat, vegetables or cheese bound with mayonnaise or other suitable sauces. Mousses of the same items are also suitable and contrasts of texture can be added by the use of nuts, celery etc.

Stuffed tomatoes may also be used as part of the Hors-d'oeuvre selection. Good examples are Tomates farcies à la Russe (with Russian Salad), à la Niçoise (with tuna fish), Yorkaise (with ham mousse), Monégasque (with a purée of tuna fish and egg), à la Reine (with chicken mousse), Ecossaise (with salmon purée). Serve 2–3 stuffed tomatoes per portion, garnished with leaves of vegetable salad.

307 Tomato Juice

Wash ripe tomatoes, remove the eyes, cut into quarters and pass through a fine sieve. Season with salt, pepper, a few drops of Worcestershire sauce and a squeeze of lemon juice. Pour into goblets and serve well-chilled.

SPECIAL POINT
Commercially produced tomato juice is generally used instead of fresh tomatoes but often requires additional seasoning.

7
Soups

The number of different soups and their possible further range of new creations is virtually unlimited; in effect they can utilise either singly or in combination almost any of the available food commodities.

Historically soups are derived from preparations which were meals in themselves; although they still perform the same function in some cases, they can more importantly serve as the first course in the menu where their function is to stimulate the appetite but not satisfy it. They should be of delicate flavour and a clean natural colour; thick soups should not be too heavy in texture. In all cases where soups are part of a set meal they should have a clear relationship to the following dishes; repetition of ingredients, colour and flavourings need to be avoided. Where choices of soup are offered it is wise to offer a selection drawn from some of the categories as shown in the following classification.

The more robust soups are best for lunch while the clear soups and light creams, veloutés and bisques are better suited to dinner. Some account also needs to be taken of seasonal pressures – the more substantial hot soups can be popular in the winter months whilst cold soups are a welcome addition to summer menus.

Any ingredient used should be fresh and of good quality; the making of soups should not be the opportunity for using poor-quality trimmings. Due attention also needs to be paid to any stocks used; again these should be of irreproachable quality.

Hot soups need to be served very hot and any accompanying garnish should be added when serving; cold soups should be served chilled rather than at room temperature.

CLASSIFICATION

Soups can be classified into two main categories: a) clear soups and b) thick soups.

Clear Soups – Consommés and Bouillons

These soups are prepared from stock, flavoured with various meats, poultry, game or fish, with vegetables, herbs and seasonings. Consommés are clarified and should be crystal-clear when finished. They may be served plain or with a garnish. Bouillons are carefully cooked and clear without being clarified and can be served plain or with a garnish.

Thick Soups – Potages liés

Unpassed Soups – Potages, Soupes, Broths
These soups are prepared from vegetables cut in varying shapes, cooked in stock, sometimes with the addition of cereals and pieces of meat or poultry, and served unpassed.

Passed Soups
1) Purée-based soups.
   These soups are made from fresh or dried vegetables cooked with stock and sometimes with the addition of meat, poultry or cereals. The ingredients act as the sole thickening agent and, as the name implies, they are passed. Ungarnished soups of this type should be served with croûtons as an accompaniment. Purée-based soups are better designated Potage when included on the menu; when finished with cream it is in order to designate them as a Crème.
2) Veloutés.
   These soups are prepared from a base of roux diluted with the appropriate flavoured stock and cooked with the addition of blanched vegetables, meat, poultry, game or fish. They are passed, finished with a liaison of egg yolks and cream and are invariably garnished.
3) Crèmes – Cream Soups.
   These soups must be of a smooth consistency and it is essential that they are finished with cream. There are three acceptable methods of preparation:
   a) The classical method using approx. 50% Béchamel, 25% purée of the appropriate cooked ingredients and 25% of the appropriate stock and finished with cream.
   b) A purée-based soup finished with cream.
   c) A velouté-based soup finished with cream instead of cream and egg yolks.
4) Bisques.
   These soups are made specifically from raw shellfish, vegetables, fish stock, wines, herbs, and seasonings, thickened with rice, passed and finished with wine and cream.
5) Brown Soups.
   These soups are mainly of British origin and are usually prepared from a base of roux diluted with stock and cooked with the addition of vegetables and meat. They are passed and are usually garnished.

Special Unclassified Soups

These are a number of soups which do not easily fit into the previous classifications.

Cold Soups

This includes specially prepared cold soups as well as those which can be successfully served cold as well as hot.

GARNISHES

Garnishes and accompaniments for soups also cover a wide variety of commodities and possible combinations, ranging from simple vegetable shapes to small patties, raviolis, quenelles and cooked meats and cheese. They should, however, without exception be small, neat and dainty and appropriate to the soups which they garnish or accompany. The following have been selected as those in need of a more detailed explanation. Other items such as cheese straws, can be found under their appropriate reference.

308 Cereals

The most commonly used are long-grain rice, sago, tapioca pearls (Perles du Japon), and seed tapioca.

In all cases, place into plenty of lightly salted boiling water, then allow to cook gently, moving occasionally to prevent sticking together. Rice grains should be separate and kept slightly firm. Tapioca and sago are cooked when the grains are completely transparent. Refresh under cold running water and drain or keep in a little cold water until required.

309 Chiffonades

Finely shredded vegetable leaves of lettuce, spinach or sorrel stewed in a little butter should be kept fairly short when used as a garnish for soup or they tend to be unsightly and awkward when spooning soup from the plate.

310 Croûtes de Flûte

Cut slices ½cm thick from a long thin French loaf, lay them on a tray and toast lightly on both sides. They may be brushed on one side with a little melted butter before toasting.

311 Croûtons

Remove the crust from a sandwich loaf then cut the bread into ½cm cubes. Fry carefully in clarified butter until golden brown and drain well.

312 Diablotins

Cut slices ½cm thick from a long thin French loaf, lay on a tray and toast on both sides until golden brown. Sprinkle with a mixture of grated Parmesan and Cheddar cheese, season well with cayenne pepper and gratinate under the salamander. Used as an accompaniment for consommés.

313 Pancakes, Savoury

Prepare pancakes (71), adding 1 tablespoon chopped Fines Herbes and ½ tablespoon finely chopped truffle to the finished batter. For garnishing soup, allow the required number of pancakes to first dry a little then cut into fine short julienne or into small rounds, whichever is applicable.

314 Pastas

The small fine Italian pastas such as the vermicelli, stelline and alphabet shapes are widely used for garnishing consommé. They are best if cooked separately – cooking in the consommé itself, although technically correct, tends to cloud it, ruining its particular quality of clarity. To cook, place the selected pasta into boiling salted stock for preference, or salted water, and simmer until cooked, stirring to prevent it sticking together. When cooked, drain and wash quickly under running water. These cooked pastas may be kept until required in a little of the consommé being used.

315 Pluches

This refers to small sprigs of parsley or chervil used as a garnish. For soups make sure that any signs of stalk are removed and do not blanch them. Place directly into the boiling soup at the very last moment before serving.

316 Profiteroles, for Consommé

Take unsweetened Pâte à Chou (1735) and season well. Place in a piping bag with a 3mm plain tube and pipe out to the size of a pea on a greased baking tray. Eggwash and bake in the oven at 185°C until crisp and dry. They may be stuffed with fine purées using a very fine piping tube, e.g. purée of foie gras.

317 Quenelles

Although quenelles for soups may be made from most forcemeats, Farce Mousseline (39) is undoubtedly the best, mainly because of its very light texture when cooked. They can be prepared from all meats, poultry and fish and can be varied by the addition of finely puréed items like truffle, pistachios, or foie gras.

To make quenelles, pipe out into small shapes using a 3mm tube and piping bag, or mould with coffee spoons or teaspoons into small egg shapes, in either case onto buttered shallow trays. Cover carefully with an appropriate hot and lightly salted stock, cover with a buttered greaseproof paper and poach carefully in a moderate oven at 190°C until firm. Drain and use as required; they may be held for a short period of time in the cooking liquid.

318 Royale

This refers to an egg custard mixture cooked and cut into various shapes and used for garnishing consommés.

Whisk together one egg and ¾ dl of consommé or milk and season. Pass through a fine strainer into a lightly buttered mould. Place in a tray of warm water and cook in the oven at 150°C until set. Allow to cool thoroughly, turn out of the mould and cut carefully into the required shapes.

For Consommé Royale cut the royale into small cubes or diamond shapes.

319 Royale Crécy

Mix together 60g of very fine purée of plain boiled carrots with 2 tablespoons of Béchamel. Whisk together two eggs and ½dl of cream. Blend the two mixtures together, season and pour into a lightly buttered mould. Place in a tray of warm water and cook in the oven at 150°C until set. Allow to cool thoroughly, turn out of the mould and cut carefully into the required shape.

SPECIAL POINT
Other royales may be prepared using 60g of the required purée, e.g. purée of chicken, and proceeding in the same way as for Royale Crécy.

320 Vegetable Garnishes

There are a number of cut vegetable shapes used either as a light garnish especially for consommés or as a main constituent of thick, mainly peasant-style soups and broths. Whichever their use, careful cutting into neat, even and regular shapes is essential to the finished result. Where added to a finished soup, vegetable garnishes should be cooked either in a little stock or consommé and drained. The following are the most important:

Brunoise: Cut equal quantities of carrot, turnip, leek and celery into approximately 2mm dice for consommé. Cut a little larger for broths, approximately 3mm dice.

Julienne: Cut equal quantities of carrot, turnip, leek and celery into thin strips no longer than 4cm in length.

Paysanne: Vegetables such as carrots, turnips, swede, potato, leek, cabbage and celery cut into thin slices either approximately 1cm squares or 1–1½cm rounds. Used mainly for soups such as Potage Paysanne, Minestrone, etc.

─────────────QUANTITY GUIDE─────────────

When estimating the required amount of soup for a given number of covers it should be calculated on the basis of five portions per litre of soup.

CONSOMMÉS AND BOUILLONS –
─────────────CLEAR SOUPS─────────────

The most important requirements of these clear soups are:

a) That they be as clear as possible. For Consommés this means absolute clarity obtained by careful attention to the methods incorporated in clarifying, and for Bouillons, by very gentle and careful simmering to obtain a liquid which is as clear as possible without actually having to clarify it.

b) That consommés be completely free of fat except where this is derived from an added garnish such as a cooked chiffonade or bone marrow.

c) That in all cases the colour should be appropriate to the main ingredients used and that this should be naturally obtained by careful attention to correct ingredients and preparation and cooking times. Only where absolutely necessary should artificial colouring be used. No consommé or bouillon should ever be dark brown in colour.

d) That if garnished, this should not be overgenerous. In general 100–120g of a single item or a combination of items is sufficient for ten covers, that means for 2 litres of consommé or bouillon.

The repertoire of clear soups and bouillons is very extensive and the following have been chosen as a representative cross-section of the more well-known ones.

321 Consommé Ordinaire – Consommé

2 litres
2½ hours

Stage	Ingredient	Quantity	Method
1	egg whites	2	Place the egg whites in a pan with the
	Fonds Blanc, cold (93)	½ litre	cold stock and whisk briskly. Add the
	shin of beef,		beef and salt, mix thoroughly together
	minced	500g	and leave for a few minutes.
	salt	5g	

2	onions, medium	2	Cut the onions in half and place on the
	carrot ⎫	100g	stove to colour dark brown. Add the
	leek ⎬ chopped	100g	onions and remainder of ingredients to
	celery ⎭ small	100g	the beef and egg whites and mix in well.
	peppercorns	10	Leave for 15 mins.
	bayleaf	½	
	thyme	sprig	
3	Fonds Blanc (93)	2½ litres	Add and mix well together. Bring to the boil quickly, keeping the bottom of the pan clean by carefully using a straight-edged spatule from time to time and taking care that the consommé is disturbed as little as possible. Remove the spatule immediately the consommé comes to the boil.
4			Simmer very gently for approx. 2 hours and strain through a double muslin. Remove any fat and season, if necessary, using salt only. Reboil before using.

SPECIAL POINTS

a) It is important that the egg whites are well broken down with the cold stock so that they can be completely dispersed through the mixture; failure to do this may result in imperfect clarification.
b) The stock used may be added either hot or cold. The use of hot stock serves to speed up the clarification process and there is less risk of the egg whites and blood settling to the bottom of the pot and discolouring; this will spoil the flavour of the consommé.
c) As the consommé comes to the boil, the egg whites and blood coagulate and bring the other ingredients, fat and any impurities with it to the surface. To prevent this being broken up and finding its way into the consommé during straining, it is advisable to use a stockpot with a tap.
d) This consommé should be a golden amber in colour.

---

322 Consommé de Volaille – Chicken Consommé

Prepare in the same way as Consommé Ordinaire (321) with the addition of 500g of chicken carcase lightly coloured in the oven and added at Stage 2. The colour of Consommé de Volaille should be light amber and it should have an identifiable flavour of chicken.

---

323 Consommé de Gibier – Game Consommé

Prepare in the same way as Consommé Ordinaire (321) with the addition of 500g of game carcase, bones and trimmings well-coloured in the oven and added at Stage 2 and using Fonds de Gibier (99) instead of the Fonds Blanc. The colour of Consommé de Gibier should be amber and it should have an identifiable flavour of game.

---

324 Consommé de Poisson – Fish Consommé

2 litres
2½ hours

Stage	Ingredient		Quantity	Method
1	egg whites		3	Place the egg whites in a pan with the stock and whisk briskly together. Add the minced whiting and salt, mix thoroughly together and leave for a few mins.
	Fonds de Poisson (101), cold		½ litre	
	salt		4g	
	whiting flesh, minced		500g	
2	celery	roughly chopped	50g	Add these ingredients and mix well together. Bring to the boil quickly, keeping the bottom of the pan clean by carefully using a straight-edged spatule from time to time and taking care that the consommé is disturbed as little as possible. Remove the spatule immediately the consommé comes to the boil.
	leek, white		75g	
	shallots		75g	
	parsley stalks		50g	
	peppercorns		8	
	Fonds de Poisson (101)		2½ litres	
3				Simmer very gently for approx. 45 mins. and strain through a double muslin. Remove any fat and season, if necessary, using salt only. Reboil before using.

325 Consommés aux Fumets – Flavoured Consommés

These consommés are made in the usual way (321) with additional ingredients added at Stage 2 so as to give a distinctive flavour of the particular addition. These can be well-flavoured vegetables such as celery, tomatoes, pimentos, mushrooms, or pheasant, quail and so on. They can be served as they are or with various garnishes to provide an extension of the repertoire of consommés. Examples are Consommé au Fumet de Céleri (with extra celery), Consommé au Fumet de Caille (with added lightly roasted carcases of quail).

326 Consommé aux Ailerons

Consommé de Volaille (322) garnished with cooked boned chicken winglets allowing 2–3 pieces per person. The winglets are cut into halves.

327 Consommé Brunoise

Consommé Ordinaire (321) garnished with 100g of cooked brunoise of vegetables (22).

328 Consommé Carmen

Prepare Consommé Ordinaire (321) with the addition of 500g of squashed ripe tomatoes and 100g of chopped raw pimento added at Stage 2. Garnish the finished consommé with 50g flesh only of skinned tomatoes cut in small dice, 50g of cooked julienne of green pimento (79), 50g of plain boiled rice (534) and pluches of chervil.

329 Consommé Célestine

Consommé Ordinaire (321) garnished at the time of serving with 100g of Savoury Pancake (313) cut into fine short julienne.

330 Consommé Colbert

Consommé Ordinaire (321) garnished with one small poached egg per person.

331 Consommé Crécy

Consommé de Volaille (322) garnished with 50g of small diamonds of Royale Crécy (319), 50g of small balls of cooked carrot and pluches of chervil.

332 Consommé Croûte-au-Pot

Prepare and serve as Petite Marmite (344) omitting the garnish of beef, chicken and bone marrow. Serve with Croûtes de Flûte (310) only.

333 Consommé Diane

Consommé de Gibier (323) garnished with 50g of short julienne of game and 50g of very small dice of truffle. Finish with 1dl of Madeira when serving.

334 Consommé Julienne

Consommé Ordinaire (321) garnished with 100g of cooked julienne of vegetables (49).

335 Consommé Madrilène

Prepare Consommé Ordinaire (321) with the addition of 500g of squashed ripe tomatoes, 100g of chopped raw pimento and an additional 200g of chopped celery all added at Stage 2. Garnish the finished consommé with 50g of short julienne of skinned tomato flesh, 50g of cooked broken vermicelli (314) and 25g of Chiffonade of sorrel (309).

336 Consommé Niçoise

Consommé Ordinaire (321) garnished with 50g of cooked French beans cut into ½cm diamonds and 75g flesh only of skinned tomatoes cut in small dice.

337 Consommé des Pêcheurs

Consommé de Poisson (324) garnished with small fish quenelles made from a Mousseline forcemeat of whiting (39), flavoured with paprika and moulded with teaspoons. Allow three pieces per cover. Serve accompanied with Diablotins (312).

338 Consommé Royale

Consommé Ordinaire (321) garnished at the time of serving with 100g of Royale (318) cut into small diamond shapes.

339 Consommé au Tapioca

Consommé Ordinaire (321) garnished with 100g of cooked seed tapioca (308).

340 Consommé au Vermicelle

Consommé Ordinaire (321) garnished with 100g of cooked small broken vermicelli (314).

341 Consommé Viennoise

Consommé Ordinaire (321) with the addition of 25g of paprika included at Stage 1 and garnished with 75g julienne of Savoury Pancake (313) flavoured with Parmesan and 75g very small Gnocchi de Pommes de Terre (490) flavoured with Parmesan.

342 Consommé des Viveurs

Consommé Ordinaire (321) with the addition of 500g of giblets and bones of raw duck, an extra 200g of celery and 2dl of beetroot juice at Stage 2. Garnish with 100g of cooked julienne of celery and serve Diablotins (312) as an accompaniment.

343 Consommé Xavier

Take 3 eggs and beat well with a little salt. Pour through a conical strainer into 2 litres of boiling Consommé Ordinaire (321) and allow to cook until the egg is lightly set.

344 Petite Marmite

10 portions
1½ hours

Stage	Ingredient	Quantity	Method
1	chicken winglets fillet of beef, cut in 1cm dice	10 120g	Blanch the beef and winglets. Refresh, remove and discard the bones from the chicken winglets and cut these in half.
2	carrots turnips cabbage leaves celery	200g 200g 75g 100g	Turn the carrots and turnips approx. 2cm long. Cut the cabbage and celery into oblong pieces approx. 2cm × ½cm. Blanch and refresh all the vegetables.
3	Consommé (321)	2½ litres	Divide and place the beef, winglets and vegetables equally into the required number of marmites. Add the consommé to the marmites, bring to the boil, cover and simmer very gently until the garnish is cooked.
4	bone marrow cut in ½cm slices Croûtes de Flûte (310) Parmesan, grated	10 30 75g	Add one slice of bone marrow per cover to the marmites just before serving. Serve the croûtes and Parmesan separately as accompaniments.

SPECIAL POINT

Marmites are usually made of earthenware or porcelain and are available in sizes from one to ten portions. The custom of the establishment will decide whether single or larger sizes are used when catering for large numbers.

345 Tortue Claire – Clear Turtle Soup

2 litres
3 hours

Stage	Ingredient	Quantity	Method
1	turtle meat, dried Fonds Blanc de Volaille (96)	75g 5dl	Soak the turtle meat in cold water for 24 hours. Remove, simmer gently in the stock until tender, then drain and cut into 1cm dice. Replace in the stock.
2	turtle herbs Consommé de Volaille (322)	1 pkt 5dl	Place the turtle herbs in the boiling consommé, cover, remove from the heat and infuse for 15 mins.

3	Consommé de
	  Volaille
	arrowroot
	sherry or Madeira,
	  dry
		1½ litres
		10g
		1dl
			Strain the infusion into the consommé, reboil and lightly thicken with the diluted arrowroot. Add the drained turtle meat from Stage 1, and finish with the wine.

SPECIAL POINTS

a) Cheese straws and quarters of lemon may be served separately as an accompaniment.

b) Turtle herbs are usually bought ready prepared in small muslin sachets and consist of basil, marjoram, sage, rosemary, thyme, bayleaf, peppercorns and coriander seed, in varying proportions according to the formula of the manufacturer. Experience will decide which yields the best result.

346 Bortsch Polonais

2 litres
2 hours

Stage	Ingredient			Quantity	Method
1	duck, prepared			½ × 2kg	Roast quickly in a hot oven for 15 mins. to colour well. Drain off fat.
2	butter			50g	Melt the butter in a deep pan. Add the vegetables and cook without colour.
	beetroot, raw	cut		75g	
	leek	in		75g	
	cabbage	julienne		50g	
	onion, finely sliced			50g	
3	Fonds Blanc (93)			2¼ litres	Add the stock and beetroot juice to the vegetables. Blanch the beef and place in the soup together with the duck. Add the bouquet garni and season lightly. Simmer gently, skimming from time to time, until all ingredients are tender (approx. 1 hour).
	beetroot juice			2dl	
	beef, thick flank			200g	
	Bouquet Garni			1	

4			Remove the beef, bouquet garni and duck. Cut the beef into ½cm dice and the flesh only of the duck into coarse julienne. Replace both in the soup, reboil, skim and correct seasoning.
5	beetroot juice	3dl	Serve the beetroot juice, sour cream and small duck patties separately as accompaniments.
	cream, sour	3dl	
	small duck		
	patties	10	

SPECIAL POINTS

a) To make beetroot juice, peel and finely grate raw beetroots, barely cover with cold water and squeeze firmly through a cloth.

b) To make the small duck patties:
   1) Cook a little finely chopped onion in butter without colour, add finely chopped cooked duck, a little demi-glace to moisten, season well and cook gently until a little stiff.
   2) Roll out puff paste 2mm thick and eggwash one half. Pipe small balls of the duck mixture, the size of a hazelnut, at 3cm intervals on the eggwashed half.
   3) Cover with the other half of the paste, seal well and cut out with a 3cm-diameter round fancy cutter.
   4) Place the patties on a damp baking tray, brush with eggwash and prick a hole in the centres. Allow to rest for 30 mins. in a cool place then bake at 210°C for approx. 10 mins. until nicely coloured.

---

347 Potage Queue de Boeuf Clair – Clear Oxtail Soup 2 litres
5½ hours

Stage	Ingredient	Quantity	Method
1	oxtails, thin ends	800g	Cut the oxtail into sections, place in a tray with the vegetables and colour well in a hot oven. Drain off the fat and place the ingredients in a deep pan.
	carrot ⎫	50g	
	onion ⎪ roughly	50g	
	leek ⎬ chopped	50g	
	celery ⎭	50g	
2	Estouffade (97)	6 litres	Add, bring to the boil, skim and allow to simmer for approx. 2 hours until the ox-tail is tender. Place the oxtail aside for use as the garnish. Strain the stock and remove the fat.
3	egg whites	2	Use this stock, together with the ingredients listed, to make a Consommé (321).
	shin of beef,		
	minced	500g	
	salt	5g	
	onions	2	
	carrot ⎫	100g	
	leek ⎬ chopped	100g	
	celery ⎭ small	100g	
	peppercorns	10	
	bayleaf	½	
	thyme	sprig	

4	carrot } small turnip } balls sherry, dry	150g 150g 1dl	Cook the carrots and turnips separately in boiling salted water, drain and add to the soup with one section of the thinnest end of the cooked oxtail per person. Finish with the sherry just before serving.

SPECIAL POINT

Potage Queue de Kangourou or Kangaroo Tail soup is made in the same way using the thin ends of Kangaroo tails.

———POTAGES, SOUPES AND BROTHS———

These types of soup are almost invariably based on cut vegetables cooked in stock and when finished are served as they are without being passed. Because of this it is essential that care is taken in the cutting of the vegetables; they should be neat and even shapes as required by the particular soup. Also the soup should not be over-garnished. In general the proportion of the vegetables and any other garnish should be no more than one-third the quantity of the finished soup. If over-evaporation should take place it is only necessary to add sufficient stock to balance out these proportions.

Typically, these soups are of a more substantial nature and thus are perhaps more suitable for lunch.

348 Chicken Broth

2 litres
2½ hours

Stage	Ingredient	Quantity	Method
1	boiling chicken Fonds Blanc de Volaille (96)	½ × 2kg 2½ litres	Place the chicken in a deep pan, add the stock, bring to the boil and skim. Lightly season with salt and simmer gently until tender. Remove the chicken and reserve for the garnish.
2	carrot } turnip } cut in 3mm celery } Brunoise leek } (22) onion, chopped	75g 75g 75g 75g 75g	Add these vegetables to the prepared stock and simmer gently for 20 mins.
3	rice, long-grain	50g	Wash and add to the soup and continue cooking until all ingredients are tender. Stir occasionally.
4	parsley, chopped		Skin and bone the chicken. Cut the flesh into ½cm dice and replace in the soup. Reboil, skim, adjust the seasoning and sprinkle with chopped parsley when serving.

349 Mutton Broth

2 litres
2 hours

Stage	Ingredient	Quantity	Method
1	mutton, scrag end water	400g 3 litres	Blanch and refresh the mutton, place it in a deep pan, add the water, bring to

	Bouquet Garni	1	the boil and skim off the fat. Lightly
	pearl barley	50g	season, add the barley and bouquet garni and simmer gently for approx. 1 hour. Skim carefully.
2	carrot ⎫ turnip ⎬ cut in 3mm celery ⎬ Brunoise leek ⎭ (22) onion, chopped	75g 75g 75g 75g 75g	Add and simmer until all the ingredients are tender (approx. 30 mins.).
3	parsley, chopped		Remove the bouquet garni and meat from the soup. Cut the meat from the bone and discard any fat. Cut the meat into ½cm dice and replace in the soup. Reboil, skim and adjust the seasoning. Sprinkle with chopped parsley when serving.

350 Scotch Broth

2 litres
2 hours

Stage	Ingredient	Quantity	Method
1	pearl barley Fonds Blanc (93)	50g 3 litres	Wash the barley and place in a deep pan. Add the stock, bring to the boil, skim, season and simmer gently for 1 hour.
2	carrot ⎫ turnip ⎬ cut in 3mm celery ⎬ Brunoise leek ⎭ (22) onion, chopped	75g 75g 75g 75g 75g	Add and simmer until all the ingredients are tender (approx. 30 mins.).
3	parsley, chopped		Skim and adjust the seasoning. Sprinkle with chopped parsley when serving.

351 Cockie Leekie

2 litres
2½ hours

Stage	Ingredient	Quantity	Method
1	boiling chicken Fonds Blanc de Volaille (96)	½ × 2kg 2½ litres	Place the prepared chicken in a deep pan, add the stock, bring to the boil and skim. Lightly season and simmer gently until cooked. Remove the chicken.

2	butter
	white of leek, cut
	    in Julienne
	    (49)
		50g
		
		400g
			Melt the butter in another pan, add the leek and cook without colour. Cover with the strained stock, bring to the boil, skim and simmer gently until the leek is cooked.

3	prunes, cooked and cut in Julienne (49)	10	Add the prunes to the soup together with the flesh of the chicken cut into julienne. Reboil. Skim and adjust the seasoning.

---

352 Minestrone

2 litres
1½ hours

Stage	Ingredient	Quantity	Method
1	butter	50g	Melt the butter in a deep pan, add the
	onions	50g	vegetables and cook without colour for a
	carrot	50g	few minutes, stirring occasionally with a
	turnip } cut in Paysanne (77)	50g	wooden spatule.
	leek	50g	
	celery	50g	
	cabbage	50g	
2	Fonds Blanc (93)	2 litres	Add, bring to the boil, skim, season and
	tomato purée	½ tbsp	simmer gently for approx. 20 mins.
3	peas	30g	Add and continue to simmer until all the
	spaghetti, 2cm lengths	50g	ingredients are tender. Skim and adjust the seasoning.
	potato, cut in Paysanne (77)	50g	
	Tomates Concassées (90)	50g	
4	fat bacon (free from flesh)	25g	Chop together to a fine paste, add to the boiling soup in small pieces until
	garlic	2 cloves	completely dispersed and remove from
	parsley, picked	15g	boil immediately.
5	Parmesan, grated	50g	Serve separately as accompaniments.
	Croûtes de Flûte (310)	20	

---

353 Potage Bonne-Femme

This soup is made in the same way as Potage Poireaux et Pommes (357) and is finished with the addition of 1dl of cream and 25g of butter.

---

354 Potage Cultivateur

2 litres
1½ hours

Stage	Ingredient	Quantity	Method
1	butter	50g	Melt the butter in a deep pan. Cut the
	belly of pork, salted	100g	salt pork into small lardons, add to the butter and fry until light brown in colour.

2	carrot	} cut in Paysanne (77)	75g	Add and cook without colour for a few minutes, stirring occasionally with a wooden spoon.
	turnip		75g	
	leek		75g	
	celery		75g	
	onion		75g	
3	Fonds Blanc de Volaille (96) potato, cut in Paysanne (77)		2½ litres 75g	Add the stock, bring to the boil, skim, season and simmer gently for approx. 20 mins. Add the potato and continue to simmer until all the ingredients are tender.
4	chopped parsley			Skim off the fat, adjust the seasoning and sprinkle with chopped parsley when serving.

---

355 Potage Fermière

2 litres
1¼ hours

Stage	Ingredient		Quantity	Method
1	butter		50g	Melt the butter in a deep pan, add the vegetables and cook without colour for a few minutes, stirring occasionally with a wooden spatule.
	carrot	} cut in Paysanne (77)	75g	
	turnip		75g	
	leek		75g	
	celery		75g	
	onion		75g	
	cabbage		50g	
2	Fonds Blanc de Volaille (96) potato, cut in Paysanne (77)		2½ litres 75g	Add the stock, bring to the boil, skim, season and simmer gently for approx. 20 mins. Add the potato and continue to simmer until all the ingredients are tender.
3	chopped parsley			Skim off the fat and adjust the seasoning. Sprinkle with chopped parsley when serving.

---

356 Potage Paysanne

2 litres
1½ hours

Stage	Ingredient		Quantity	Method
1	butter		50g	Melt the butter in a deep pan, add the vegetables and cook without colour for a few minutes, stirring occasionally with a wooden spatule.
	carrots	} cut in Paysanne (77)	75g	
	turnips		75g	
	leek		75g	
	celery		75g	
	onion		75g	
2	Fonds Blanc de Volaille (96)		2½ litres	Add, bring to the boil, skim, season and simmer gently for approx. 20 mins.

Stage	Ingredient	Quantity	Method
3	French beans, cut in diamond-shaped pieces	50g	Add and continue to simmer until all the ingredients are tender.
	peas	50g	
4	parsley, chopped		Skim off the fat, adjust the seasoning and sprinkle with chopped parsley when serving.

357 Potage Poireaux et Pommes – Leek and Potato Soup

2 litres
1 hour

Stage	Ingredient	Quantity	Method
1	butter	50g	Melt the butter in a deep pan, add the leek and cook without colour for a few minutes, stirring occasionally with a wooden spoon.
	white of leek, cut in Paysanne (77)	400g	
2	Fonds Blanc de Volaille (96)	2½ litres	Add, bring to the boil, skim, season and simmer gently for approx. 20 mins.
3	potato, cut in Paysanne (77)	400g	Add and continue to simmer until all the ingredients are tender.
4	parsley, chopped		Skim off the fat, adjust the seasoning and sprinkle with chopped parsley when serving.

358 Soupe à l'Oignon Gratinée

10 portions
1½ hours

Stage	Ingredient	Quantity	Method
1	butter	50g	Melt the butter in a deep pan, add the onions and cook to a light golden-brown colour.
	onion, finely sliced	750g	
2	flour	20g	Add and cook gently while mixing to a fawn colour.
3	Estouffade (97)	2 litres	Mix in slowly, bring to the boil, skim off fat, season and simmer gently until cooked (approx. 20 mins). Adjust the seasoning.
4	Croûtes de Flûte (310)	50 pieces	Divide the soup equally between the required number of marmites or soup bowls. Cover the surface of the soup with the croûtes neatly overlapping. Sprinkle with the grated cheeses and gratinate in a hot oven. Do not cover with lids.
	Gruyère, grated	100g	
	Parmesan, grated	50g	

────────── PURÉE-BASED SOUPS ──────────

These soups are prepared from a base of either fresh or dried vegetables which also acts as their thickening agent.

The actual puréeing or passing of the soup is very important and the finished result should always be very smooth and fine – a coarse granular texture tends to make these soups more like their older counterparts which, as dishes in themselves, were just mixed vigorously to break down the cooked ingredients. Purée-based soups should be first passed through a sieve, liquidiser or soup machine, then finally passed firmly through a fine strainer. This final passing also helps to remove any remaining hard bits of fibre.

These soups must not be too thick or stodgy; this can easily be rectified by a little extra stock. Conversely they should not be watery – this is best taken care of by making sure that the original proportions of vegetables to liquid is correct. Thickening with starches such as cornflour to correct wateriness is not really satisfactory as it tends to alter the particular texture of a purée.

Generally speaking these soups are better for inclusion on luncheon menus. The addition of 2dl of fresh cream per 2 litres, however, allows them to be designated as cream soups and in this form they are also very suitable for dinner menus bearing in mind that those prepared from dried leguminous vegetables place a greater strain on the digestive system.

SPECIAL POINT
Good-quality dried pulses such as split peas, haricot beans and lentils, of the current season, do not require soaking. They provide their own natural colour and recourse to artificial colouring should not be necessary.

PURÉE SOUPS USING FRESH VEGETABLES

359 Potage Bruxelloise

2 litres
1¾ hours

Stage	Ingredient		Quantity	Method
1	butter		50g	Melt the butter in a deep pan, add the
	onion		100g	vegetables and cook without colour for a
	white of leek	roughly	100g	few minutes, stirring occasionally.
	celery	sliced	100g	
	Brussels			
	sprouts		600g	
2	Fonds Blanc (93)		2½ litres	Add the stock, bring to the boil and
	potatoes, sliced		600g	skim. Add the potatoes, season and simmer until all the ingredients are tender (approx. 45 mins.).
3	Croûtons (311)		150g	Pass the soup through a fine sieve or liquidiser and then firmly through a fine strainer into a clean pan. Reboil and adjust the consistency and seasoning. Serve the croûtons as an accompaniment.

360 Potage Crécy – Carrot Soup

2 litres
1¾ hours

Stage	Ingredient	Quantity	Method
1	butter	50g	Melt the butter in a deep pan, add the
	carrot, sliced	1kg	vegetables and cook without colour for a
	onion, sliced	100g	few minutes, stirring occasionally.
2	Fonds Blanc (93)	2½ litres	Add the stock, bring to the boil and
	rice, short-grain	150g	skim. Add the washed rice, season and cook until tender (approx. 1 hour). Stir occasionally.
3	Croûtons (311)	150g	Pass the soup through a fine sieve or liquidiser and then through a fine strainer into a clean pan. Reboil, adjust the consistency and seasoning. Serve the croûtons as an accompaniment.

361 Potage Cressonière – Watercress and Potato Soup

Wash 2 bunches of watercress and remove the best leaves. Blanch these and place aside to garnish the soup. Add the remainder of the watercress to the onion and leek at Stage 1 of Potage Parmentier (365). Finish the soup as per this recipe and finish with the blanched leaves of watercress instead of chopped parsley.

362 Potage Freneuse – Turnip Soup

2 litres
1¾ hours

Stage	Ingredient	Quantity	Method
1	butter	50g	Melt the butter in a deep pan, add the
	turnip ⎱ roughly	1kg	vegetables and cook without colour for a
	onion ⎰ chopped	100g	few minutes, stirring occasionally.
	white of leek	50g	
2	Fonds Blanc (93)	2½ litres	Add the stock, bring to the boil and
	potato, sliced	400g	skim. Add the potatoes, season and simmer until all ingredients are cooked (approx. 45 mins.).
3	Croûtons (311)	150g	Pass the soup through a fine sieve or liquidiser and then through a fine strainer into a clean pan. Reboil, adjust the consistency and seasoning. Serve with the croûtons as an accompaniment.

363 Potage Garbure – Vegetable Soup

2 litres
1¾ hours

Stage	Ingredient	Quantity	Method
1	butter	50g	Melt the butter in a deep pan, add the
	onion, sliced	200g	vegetables and cook without colour for a

	carrot ⎤	200g	few minutes stirring occasionally.
	turnip ⎟ roughly	200g	
	leek ⎬ sliced	200g	
	celery ⎦	200g	
2	Fonds Blanc (93)	2½ litres	Add the stock, bring to the boil and
	potato, sliced	400g	skim. Add the potatoes, season and simmer until all the ingredients are cooked (approx. 45 mins.).
3	Croûtons (311)	150g	Pass the soup through a fine sieve or liquidiser and then through a fine strainer into a clean pan. Reboil, adjust the consistency and seasoning. Serve with the croûtons as an accompaniment.

364 Potage Julienne d'Arblay

Potage Parmentier (365) with the addition of 100g of cooked julienne of vegetables (49). Finish with chopped parsley when serving.

365 Potage Parmentier – Leek and Potato Soup

2 litres
1¾ hours

Stage	Ingredient	Quantity	Method
1	butter	50g	Melt the butter in a deep pan, add the
	white of ⎤		vegetables and cook without colour for a
	leek ⎬ roughly sliced	300g	few minutes, stirring occasionally with a
	onion ⎦	200g	wooden spatule.
2	Fonds Blanc (93)	2½ litres	Add the stock, bring to the boil and
	potatoes, roughly		skim. Add the potatoes, season and
	cut	1kg	simmer until all ingredients are tender (approx. 45 mins.).
3	parsley, chopped		Pass the soup through a fine sieve or
	Croûtons (311)	150g	liquidiser and then firmly through a fine strainer into a clean pan. Reboil, and adjust the consistency and seasoning. Serve sprinkled with chopped parsley. Serve the croûtons as an accompaniment.

366 Potage Santé

Potage Parmentier (365) garnished with 75g of Chiffonade of sorrel (309).

367 Potage Solferino

Prepare as Potage Parmentier (365), adding 2 tablespoons of tomato purée with the stock at Stage 2. Garnish with 50g of cooked small balls of potatoes and 50g of cooked small balls of carrot.

PURÉE SOUPS USING DRIED PULSES

368 Potage St Germain – Green Pea Soup

2 litres
2–2½ hours

Stage	Ingredient	Quantity	Method
1	peas, green split Fonds Blanc (93)	 600g 3 litres	Wash the peas, place in a deep pan, cover with the stock, bring to the boil and skim.
2	onion, whole Bouquet Garni carrots, whole bacon or ham bone	200g 1 200g 150g	Add to the soup, season and simmer gently until the peas are tender and break easily (approx. 1½–2 hours).
3	Croûtons (311)	150g	Remove the bone, carrots and bouquet garni. Pass the soup through a fine sieve or liquidiser and then firmly through a fine strainer. Replace the soup in a clean pan, reboil, adjust the consistency and seasoning. Serve the croûtons as an accompaniment.

369 Potage Bretonne

Prepare as Potage St Germain (368), using haricot beans in place of green split peas and adding 2 tablespoons of tomato purée with the stock.

370 Potage Choiseul

Prepare as Potage St Germain (368), using 750g of lentils in place of green split peas. Garnish with 50g of Chiffonade of sorrel (309) and 100g of boiled long-grain rice (534). The carrots can be passed with the soup.

371 Potage Condé

Prepare as Potage St Germain (368), using red beans instead of green split peas and add 3dl of red wine after the beans have been brought to the boil with the stock and skimmed.

372 Potage Conti

Prepare as Potage St Germain (368), using 750g of lentils in place of green split peas. Garnish with 100g of small fried Lardons (51) and Pluches of chervil (315). The carrots can be passed with the soup.

373 Potage Dartois

Prepare as Potage St Germain (368), using haricot beans instead of green split peas. Garnish with 100g of cooked Brunoise of vegetables (22).

374 Potage Egyptienne

Prepare as Potage St Germain (368), using yellow split peas instead of green split peas. Serve with Croûtons (311) as an accompaniment. The carrots can be passed with the soup.

375 Potage Esaü

Prepare as Potage St Germain (368), using 750g of lentils instead of green split peas. Garnish with 100g of boiled long-grain rice (534). The carrots can be passed with the soup.

376 Potage Faubonne

Prepare as Potage St Germain (368), using haricot beans instead of green split peas. Garnish with 100g of cooked Julienne of vegetables (49).

377 Potage Gentilhomme

Prepare as Potage St Germain (368), using 750g of lentils instead of green split peas and Fonds de Gibier (99) instead of Fonds Blanc. Garnish with 100g of small dice of ham and finish with 1dl of Madeira. The carrots can be passed with the soup.

378 Potage Lamballe

Potage St Germain (368) garnished with 100g of cooked seed Tapioca (308).

379 Potage Longchamps

Potage St Germain (368) garnished with 75g of cooked broken Vermicelli (314), 50g of Chiffonade of sorrel (309) and Pluches of chervil (315).

380 Potage Maria

Prepare as Potage St Germain (368), using haricot beans instead of green split peas. Garnish with 100g of Printanière of cooked vegetables (81).

381 Potage Soissonaise – Haricot Bean Soup

Prepare as Potage St Germain (368), using haricot beans instead of green split peas. Serve with Croûtons (311) as an accompaniment.

VELOUTÉS

The essential qualities of these types of soups are an extremely velvety and smooth texture and a light, delicate flavour. The requirements for producing these results are excellent stocks, well-chosen ingredients, careful simmering, and above all careful finishing with a liaison of egg yolks and cream. Once the liaison is added the soup needs to be carefully reheated but on no account must it be allowed to boil; this would result in a granular texture and the whole particular quality of a velouté would be ruined. They should not be too thick and again this only needs the addition of a little stock at the final stage if deemed necessary.

Velouté-style soups are best suited to dinner menus. The egg yolks of the liaison may be omitted and the soup finished only with 2–3dl of fresh cream per 2 litres of soup. They can then be designated as Crèmes.

382 Velouté Agnès Sorel

2 litres
1½ hours

Stage	Ingredient	Quantity	Method
1	butter flour	120g 120g	Prepare a Roux Blond (108). Allow to cool.
2	Fonds Blanc de Volaille (96)	2½ litres	Mix in the boiling stock gradually using a wooden spatule, avoiding lumps. Bring to the boil and simmer.
3	mushrooms, white	500g	Wash, drain, pass through a sieve and add to the soup.
4			Bring the soup to the boil again, skim, season and simmer gently for 45 mins. Pass through a fine strainer into a clean pan and reboil.
5	egg yolks cream	4 2dl	Whisk together in a large basin and add approx. one-third of the soup, whisking in quickly. Return to the remainder of the soup mixing in quickly. Reheat, stirring continuously with a straight-edged wooden spatule until the liaison thickens the soup, taking care that it does not reboil.
6	butter	50g	Mix into the soup.
7	cooked white of chicken ox-tongue, cooked mushrooms, white	50g 50g 50g	Cut in short julienne (the mushrooms need to be cooked à Blanc) (60). Warm and add to the soup; adjust the consistency and seasoning.

383 Velouté Dame Blanche

This soup is prepared in the same way as Velouté Agnès Sorel (382). Garnish with 50g of small dice of cooked white of chicken and 75g of small Quenelles de Volaille (82) instead of the julienne of chicken, ox-tongue and mushroom. Finish with a few drops of pure almond essence, sufficient only to impart a discernible flavour.

384 Velouté Doria

2 litres
1½ hours

Stage	Ingredient	Quantity	Method
1	butter flour	120g 120g	Prepare a Roux Blond (108). Allow to cool.

2	Fonds Blanc de Volaille (96)	2½ litres	Mix in the boiling stock gradually, using a wooden spatule, avoiding lumps. Bring to the boil and simmer.
3	cucumbers butter	2 50g	Peel the cucumbers, discard the seeds and slice and stew in the butter without colour. Add to the soup.
4			Bring the soup to the boil again, skim, season and simmer gently for 45 mins. Pass through a sieve and then through a fine strainer into a clean pan and reboil.
5	egg yolks cream	4 2dl	Whisk together in a large basin and add approx. one-third of the soup, whisking in quickly. Return to the remainder of the soup mixing in quickly. Reheat, stirring continuously with a straight-edged wooden spatule until the liaison thickens the soup. Take care that it does not reboil.
6	butter	50g	Mix into the soup.
7	long-grain rice, poached and drained pea-sized balls of cucumber, stewed in a little butter	50g 75g	Add to the soup. Adjust the consistency and seasoning.

385 Velouté Fédora

2 litres
1½ litres

Stage	Ingredient	Quantity	Method
1	butter flour	120g 120g	Prepare a Roux Blond (108). Allow to cool.
2	Fonds Blanc de Volaille (96)	2½ litres	Mix in the boiling stock gradually using a wooden spatule, avoiding lumps. Bring to the boil and simmer.
3	butter Tomates Concassées (90)	25g 600g	Heat the butter in a small pan, add the tomatoes and cook to a fairly dry paste. Add to the soup.
4			Bring to the boil again, skim, season and simmer gently for 45 mins. Pass through a fine strainer into a clean pan and reboil.

5	egg yolks	4	Whisk together in a large basin and add
	cream	2dl	approx. one-third of the soup, whisking in quickly. Return to the remainder of the soup mixing in quickly. Reheat, stirring continuously with a straight-edged wooden spatule until the liaison thickens the soup, taking care that it does not reboil.
6	butter	50g	Mix into the soup.
7	red tomatoes, skinned, deseeded and cut in very small dice	100g	Gently heat the tomatoes in the stock, drain and add to the soup. Adjust the consistency and seasoning.
	Fonds Blanc de Volaille (96)	½dl	

386 Velouté Marie-Stuart

2 litres
1¼ hours

Stage	Ingredient	Quantity	Method
1	barley flour	175g	Dilute the barley with 2½dl of the stock. Bring the remainder of the stock to the boil then mix in the diluted barley flour quickly. Bring to the boil, skim, season and simmer very gently for 25 mins.
	Fonds Blanc de Volaille (96)	2½ litres	
2	egg yolks	4	Whisk together in a large basin and add approx. one-third of the soup whisking in quickly. Return to the remainder of the soup mixing in quickly. Reheat, stirring continuously with a straight-edged wooden spatule until the liaison thickens the soup, taking care that it does not reboil.
	cream, double	2dl	
3	butter	75g	Mix into the soup.
4	pea-sized balls of carrots cooked in a little chicken stock and drained	75g	Add to the soup and adjust the consistency and seasoning.

CREAM SOUPS

These soups are exemplified by their extremely smooth, creamy texture and a light creamy appearance. Classically, this exceptional quality of creaminess was imparted by using Béchamel as 50% of the total volume of the soup. In modern times however, most cream soups as such are prepared as a velouté and finished with 2–3dl of excellent fresh cream per 2 litres of soup.

Well-prepared, smooth purée-based soups finished with cream, as well as velouté-style soups finished with cream instead of a liaison, can also be designated as cream soups.

Conversely, cream soups 387–393 and 398–399 can be finished with a liaison of egg yolks and cream and be designated as veloutés.

Cream soups are equally suitable for lunch or dinner.

---

387 Crème d'Asperges (Crème Argenteuil) – Cream of Asparagus

2 litres
1½ hours

Stage	Ingredient	Quantity	Method
1	butter	120g	Prepare a Roux Blond (108). Allow to
	flour	120g	cool.
2	Fonds Blanc de		Mix in the boiling stock gradually using
	Volaille (96)	2½ litres	a wooden spatule, and avoiding lumps.
3	asparagus stalks,		Blanch, drain and add to the soup.
	cut in pieces	750g	
4			Bring the soup to the boil, skim, season and simmer gently for 45 mins. Pass through a fine strainer into a clean pan and reboil.
5	cream	2dl	Add to the soup and adjust the consistency and seasoning.
6	Asparagus Sprue		Cut into 5mm pieces, cook in boiling
	(1388), edible part	100g	salted water, drain and add to the soup.

SPECIAL POINT
This soup can be served as Velouté d'Asperges by finishing with a liaison of egg yolks and cream instead of only cream.

---

388 Crème de Céleri – Cream of Celery

Prepare as Crème d'Asperges (387), using 750g of roughly cut celery instead of asparagus stalks. Garnish with 100g short julienne of celery cooked in a little stock, drained and added to the soup. This soup may be served as Velouté de Céleri by finishing with a liaison of egg yolks and cream instead of only cream.

---

389 Crème de Champignons – Cream of Mushroom

2 litres
1½ hours

Stage	Ingredient	Quantity	Method
1	butter	120g	Prepare a Roux Blond (108). Allow to
	flour	120g	cool.
2	Fonds Blanc de		Mix in the boiling stock gradually using
	Volaille (96)	2½ litres	a wooden spatule and avoiding lumps.
3	mushrooms, white	500g	Wash, drain, pass through a sieve and add to the soup.

4			Bring the soup to the boil, skim, season and simmer gently for 45 mins. Pass through a fine strainer into a clean pan and reboil.
5	cream	2dl	Add to the soup and adjust the consistency and seasoning.
6	mushrooms, white	100g	Cut in short julienne and cook à Blanc (60). Add to the soup.

SPECIAL POINT
This soup can be served as Velouté de Champignons by finishing with a liaison of egg yolks and cream instead of only cream.

---

390 Crème Dubarry – Cream of Cauliflower

Prepare as Crème d'Asperges (387), using 750g of roughly cut white cauliflower instead of asparagus stalks. Garnish with 100g of florets of cauliflower cooked in boiling salted water and drained before adding to the soup. This soup can be served as Velouté Dubarry by finishing with a liaison of egg yolks and cream instead of only cream.

---

391 Crème Favorite – Cream of French Beans

Prepare as Crème d'Asperges (387), using 750g of roughly cut French beans instead of asparagus stalks. Garnish with 100g of small diamond-shaped pieces of French beans plain-boiled and drained before adding to the soup. This soup can be served as Velouté Favorite by finishing with a liaison of egg yolks and cream instead of only cream.

---

392 Crème de Laitue – Cream of Lettuce

Prepare as Crème d'Asperges (387), using 750g of lettuce leaves instead of asparagus stalks. Garnish with 100g of Chiffonade of lettuce (309). This soup can be served as Velouté de Laitue by finishing with a liaison of egg yolks and cream instead of only cream.

---

393 Crème Palestine – Cream of Jerusalem Artichokes

Prepare as Crème d'Asperges (387), using 750g of Jerusalem artichokes instead of asparagus stalks. It is not customary to garnish this soup. This soup may be served as Velouté Palestine by finishing with a liaison of egg yolks and cream instead of only cream.

---

394 Crème de Pois frais – Cream of Green Peas   2 litres
1½ hours

Stage	Ingredient	Quantity	Method
1	butter	50g	Melt the butter in a deep pan, add the
	leek, roughly cut	100g	leek and lettuce and cook without colour.
	lettuce, roughly cut	1	
2	Fonds Blanc de Volaille (96)	1 litre	Add the stock and peas. Bring to the boil, skim, season and simmer gently

	peas, fresh	750g	until tender for approx. 30 mins. Pass through a fine sieve into a clean pan.
3	Béchamel (114)	1 litre	Add, bring to the boil and simmer gently for 10 mins. Pass through a sieve and then through a fine strainer, reboil and adjust the consistency.
4	butter	50g	Add the butter and cream to the soup.
	cream	1dl	Adjust the seasoning.
5	peas	100g	Cook the peas in boiling salted water,
	Pluches of chervil		drain and add to soup with the pluches
	(315)		of chervil.

395 Crème Pompadour

Crème de Tomate (397) garnished with 75g of cooked Perles du Japon (308) and 50g of Chiffonade of lettuce (309).

396 Crème Portugaise

Crème de Tomate (397) garnished with 50g of boiled long-grain rice (534) and 50g of Tomates Concassées (90).

397 Crème de Tomate – Cream of Tomato

2 litres
2 hours

Stage	Ingredient	Quantity	Method
1	butter	100g	Melt the butter in a deep pan, add the
	bacon trimmings,		bacon and fry to extract the fat. Add the
	diced	75g	rest of the ingredients and continue fry-
	onion ⎱ roughly	150g	ing to a light brown colour.
	carrot ⎰ diced	150g	
	bayleaf	½	
	thyme	sprig	
2	flour	120g	Add and cook as a Roux Blond (108). Allow to cool.
3	tomato purée	150g	Add the purée and mix in. Add the boil-
	Fonds Blanc (93)	2½ litres	ing stock, mixing well with a wooden spatule and avoiding lumps. Bring to the boil, skim, season and simmer gently for 1 hour.
4			Pass through a fine strainer into a clean pan and reboil.
5	cream	2dl	Add and adjust the consistency and seasoning. Add a little sugar if too sharp.

398 Crème de Volaille – Cream of Chicken

2 litres
1½ hours

Stage	Ingredient	Quantity	Method
1	butter flour	120g 120g	Prepare a Roux Blond (108) and allow to cool.
2	Fonds Blanc de Volaille (96)	2½ litres	Mix in gradually using a wooden spatule and avoiding lumps.
3	chicken bones	1kg	Blanch, drain and add to the soup.
4			Bring to the boil, skim, season and simmer gently for 45 mins. Pass through a fine strainer into a clean pan and reboil.
5	cream	2dl	Add to the soup. Adjust the consistency and seasoning.
6	cooked white of chicken	100g	Cut into short julienne, warm and add to the soup.

This soup can be served as Velouté de Volaille by finishing with a liaison of egg yolks and cream instead of only cream.

399 Crème Washington – Cream of Maize

This soup is made in the same way as Crème d'Asperges (387), using 750g of raw or tinned maize grains instead of asparagus stalks. Garnish with 100g of cooked maize. It is not necessary to blanch tinned maize, and the liquid from the tin should be added to the soup. This soup can be served as Velouté Washington by finishing with a liaison of egg yolks and cream instead of only cream.

BISQUES

The term Bisque is almost always used these days to denote thick soups prepared from crustaceans although these can with some justification be referred to as Coulis. Even though it is possible to prepare these soups from cooked crustaceans the finished result is never so good as when the raw article is used. Allow 750–800g live lobster, crayfish, Dublin Bay prawns, small crabs, prawns or shrimps for 2–2½ litres of finished soup; it is not really possible to prepare larger quantities from these amounts and still maintain the necessary quality.

It should be remembered that a large proportion of the flavour of crustaceans is contained in their shells and it is for this reason that after the flesh is cooked the shells are always well-pounded or crushed before being returned to the soup; this ensures that maximum flavour is extracted. This also explains why Bisques prepared from molluscs such as clams or scallops are never really successful; it is not useful to pound their shells as there is little flavour in them to speak of and the flavour of the actual shellfish itself is fairly bland and inclined to sweetness.

---

400 Bisque de Homard – Lobster Soup

2 litres
2 hours

Stage	Ingredient	Quantity	Method
1	butter	100g	Melt the butter in a deep pan, add the
	carrot ⎱ finely	100g	rest of the ingredients and cook to a
	onion ⎰ chopped	100g	light brown colour.
	bayleaf	½	
	thyme	sprig	
	parsley stalks	10g	
2	lobster, live	1 × 750g	First wash the lobster then kill it (page 246). Cut the tail into sections, split the head in half and discard the sac. Add the pieces of lobster to the pan, season with salt and pepper and fry together until the lobster turns red on all sides.
3	brandy	½dl	Pour over the lobster and Flamber (32).
4	tomato purée	1½ tbsps	Add, bring to the boil, skim, season
	white wine, dry	2dl	lightly and simmer gently for 20 mins.
	Fumet de Poisson (101)	2 litres	
5			Remove the lobster from the soup. Take 100g of the flesh, cut into small dice and reserve for the garnish. Pound the remainder of the flesh and the shells and return to the soup. Simmer gently for 20 mins.
6	rice flour	140g	Dilute with a little water, mix into the boiling soup and simmer gently for a further 10 mins. Pass firmly through a fine strainer into a clean pan.
7	butter	50g	Reboil the soup and add the butter and
	cream	1dl	cream. Finish with the brandy and
	brandy	½dl	warmed garnish. Adjust the consistency
	cayenne		and seasoning and finish with a little cayenne.

SPECIAL POINTS
a) The rice flour may be replaced by 1½ litres of Velouté de Poisson (117) and the fish stock reduced to ½ litre only.
b) Bisques may be prepared from the same weight of other live crustaceans such as crayfish, crab, prawns etc.

---

401 Bisque de Crabe – Crab Soup

Prepare as Bisque de Homard (400) using 750g live small crabs and with the following
points to notice:
1) Leave the crabs whole.
2) On removing the crabs from the cooking liquid at Stage 5 reserve the flaked flesh
   from the claws for the garnish and discard the gills from the breasts before pounding
   the shells and returning to the soup.

——————————— BROWN SOUPS ———————————

In recent years these mainly British soups seem to have suffered an eclipse in popularity,
perhaps because of the bad reputation of the so-called Brown Windsor Soup.
Nevertheless the following selection of brown soups have much to offer in terms of
flavour and robustness and thus are ideal for placing on luncheon menus. Their
excellence depends solely on the use of correctly prepared and well-flavoured stocks,
good ingredients and careful slow cooking. The dark brown colour usually obtained
from the use of gravy browning is not necessary; a naturally light reddish-brown can be
obtained by paying attention to detail and has a more pleasing appearance.

402 Potage Fausse Tortue – Mock Turtle Soup   2 litres
                                                              3 hours

Stage	Ingredient	Quantity	Method
1	dripping, clean	100g	Prepare a Roux Brun (109). Allow to
	flour	120g	cool.
2	tomato purée	1 tbsp	Add the purée and mix in well. Add the
	Estouffade (97)	3 litres	hot stock gradually, mixing well with a wooden spatula to avoid lumps. Bring to the boil, season and skim. Simmer gently.
3	onion ⎞ roughly	200g	Fry in a little fat until coloured brown,
	carrot ⎠ diced	200g	drain and add to the soup.
4	calf's head, boned	½	Blanch, place in the soup and continue to simmer the soup for 1½–2 hours until the head is tender. Skim as necessary. Remove the head, wash and keep on one side for the garnish.
5	turtle herbs	1 pkt	Place the herbs in the boiling stock.
	Estouffade (97), boiling	2dl	Remove from the stove. Cover and allow to infuse for 10 mins. Strain.
6			Pass the soup through a fine strainer into a clean pan. Add the infusion, reboil and adjust the consistency and seasoning.

| 7 | sherry | ½dl | Add to the soup together with the calf's head cut in 1cm dice. |

---

403 Mulligatawny

2 litres
1½ hours

Stage	Ingredient	Quantity	Method
1	butter	100g	Melt the butter in a deep pan, add the
	onion, finely		onion and garlic and cook to a light
	chopped	300g	brown colour.
	garlic, finely		
	chopped	1 clove	
2	curry powder	25g	Add and mix in well. Cook as for a Roux
	flour	120g	Blond (108). Allow to cool.
3	tomato purée	1 tbsp	Add the purée and mix in well. Add the
	Estouffade (97)	2½ litres	hot stock gradually, mixing with a wooden spatule to avoid lumps. Bring to the boil, skim and season.
4	chutney, finely		Add to the soup and simmer for approx.
	chopped	75g	45 mins. Pass through a fine strainer
	apple, finely		into a clean pan and reboil.
	chopped	100g	
5	rice, long-grain	50g	Cook the rice in boiling salted water,
	cream	1dl	drain, add to the soup and finish with the cream. Adjust the consistency and seasoning.

---

404 Soupe aux Rognons – Kidney Soup

2 litres
3 hours

Stage	Ingredient	Quantity	Method
1	dripping, clean	100g	Prepare a Roux Brun (109). Allow to
	flour	120g	cool.
2	tomato purée	1 tbsp	Add the purée and mix in well. Add the
	Estouffade (97)	3 litres	hot stock gradually, mixing well with a wooden spatule to avoid lumps. Bring to the boil, skim and season.
3	onion ⎫ roughly	200g	Fry the vegetables in a little fat until
	carrot ⎬ diced	200g	coloured brown, drain and add to the
	Bouquet Garni (19)	1	soup with the bouquet garni.
4	ox kidney, minced	500g	Fry the kidney quickly in the hot butter,
	butter	50g	and also add to the soup. Simmer for 2 hours skimming as necessary.
5			Remove the bouquet garni and discard, then pass the soup through a fine strainer into a clean pan. Reboil and adjust the consistency and seasoning.

6	ox kidney, cut into small dice	150g	While the soup is cooking, prepare the following garnish: season and sauté the kidney in the butter, drain, place in a
	butter	25g	small pan and cover with the stock.
	Estouffade (97)	½ litre	Simmer gently until cooked, drain and add to the finished soup.

405 Potage Queue de Boeuf Lié – Thick Oxtail Soup   2 litres
4 hours

Stage	Ingredient	Quantity	Method
1	dripping, clean	100g	Prepare a Roux Brun (109). Allow to
	flour	120g	cool.
2	tomato purée	1 tbsp	Add the purée and mix in well. Add the
	Estouffade (97)	3½ litres	hot stock gradually, mixing well with a wooden spatule to avoid lumps. Bring to the boil, skim, season and simmer gently.
3	onion ⎱ roughly	200g	Fry the vegetables in a little fat until
	carrot ⎰ diced	200g	coloured brown, drain and add to the
	Bouquet Garni (19)	1	soup with the bouquet garni.
4	oxtail, thin ends	1kg	Cut into sections, fry in a little fat, drain and add to the soup. Simmer gently for 2½–3 hours until the oxtail is cooked.
5			Remove the oxtail and bouquet garni. Place the oxtail aside for the garnish. Pass the soup through a fine strainer into a clean pan and reboil. Adjust the consistency and seasoning.
6	carrot ⎱ cut in	75g	Cook the carrot and turnip separately in
	turnip ⎰ small balls	75g	salted water. Drain and add to the soup
	sherry	½dl	with one section of the oxtail per person. Finish with the sherry.

SPECIAL POINT
Kangaroo Tail can be used to make Potage Queue de Kangourou Lié.

——————SPECIAL UNCLASSIFIED SOUPS——————

This section contains those soups of a special nature and which do not fall easily into the previous categories.

406 Clam Chowder
2 litres
1½ hours

Stage	Ingredient	Quantity	Method
1	belly of pork, salted	250g	Cut into ½cm dice, blanch and drain. Heat the butter in a pan, add the pork
	butter	25g	and cook gently until a golden brown.
2	onion, chopped	250g	Add to the pan and cook gently without colour.

3	potatoes	500g	Add the potatoes cut into ½cm dice
	milk	1 litre	together with the milk and bouquet gar-
	Bouquet Garni (19)	1	ni. Season lightly and simmer gently for
			approx. 20 mins.

4	clams	1kg	Wash the clams well then place in a
	water	1dl	deep pan with the water. Cover with a
			lid and cook quickly until the shells
			open.

5			Remove the clams from their shells;
			wash the clams to remove any sand then
			cut into small dice and add to the soup.

6			Allow the cooking liquid to stand for a
			few minutes to settle out any sand, then
			carefully strain through a fine strainer
			and also add to the soup.

7	fresh thyme		Reheat the soup, simmer gently for a
	leaves, roughly		further 10 mins. Remove the bouquet
	chopped	½ tbsp	garni and at the last minute add the
	cream	1dl	chopped thyme leaves. Finish with the
	cayenne		cream and adjust the seasoning as
			necessary with salt, milled black pepper
			and a touch of cayenne.

SPECIAL POINTS

a) Broken cream cracker biscuits may be served separately.
b) 400g Tomates Concassées (90) may be added at Stage 5 as a variation.

---

407 Potage Germiny

2 litres
30 mins.

Stage	Ingredient	Quantity	Method
1	sorrel	250g	Pick, wash and shred finely.
2	butter	50g	Melt in a pan, add the sorrel. Cover and cook until tender.
3	Fonds Blanc de Volaille (96)	1½ litres	Bring to the boil, add to the sorrel, reboil, season and simmer gently for 5 mins.
4	egg yolks	12	Whisk together in a large basin and add
	cream	3dl	approx. one-third of the soup, whisking in quickly. Return to the remainder of the soup mixing in quickly. Reheat, stirring continuously with a wooden or metal spatule until the liaison thickens the soup. Take care that it does not reboil.
5	butter	50g	Add the butter, adjust the seasoning and
	Cheese Straws (1655)	20	serve the cheese straws as an accompaniment, allowing two per portion.

408 Potage Goanese

2 litres
1½ hours

Stage	Ingredient	Quantity	Method
1	almonds, ground	100g	Place the almond and coconut in a basin and cover with the boiling water. Allow to steep.
	coconut, grated	120g	
	water	½ litre	
2	butter	50g	Heat the butter in a pan, add the onions and cook until transparent then add the spices and cook gently for a few minutes to draw out their flavours.
	onions, finely chopped	150g	
	curry powder	½ tbsp	
	ginger, ground	½ tsp	
	turmeric, ground	½ tsp	
3	Fonds de Volaille (96)	1½ litres	Add the steeped nuts and their liquid together with the stock to the pan. Bring to the boil and skim carefully. Season lightly and simmer gently for 30 mins.
4	rice flour	40g	Dilute with a little stock and add to the soup so as to lightly thicken it. Simmer gently for a further 15 mins. then pass very firmly through a fine strainer so as to extract the maximum of liquid and flavour. Return to a clean pan and reheat.
5	egg yolks	8	Whisk together in a large basin and add approx. one-third of the soup, whisking in quickly. Return to the remainder of the soup mixing in quickly. Reheat, stirring continuously with a straight-edged wooden spatule until the soup thickens. Make sure that it does not boil and adjust the seasoning as necessary.
	cream, sour	3dl	
6	almonds, skinned	150g	Serve accompanied with a dish of the almonds which have been browned in the butter, drained and sprinkled with a little salt and a pinch of ground coriander.
	butter	50g	
	coriander, ground		

409 Soupe aux Moules – Mussel Soup

2 litres
1 hour

Stage	Ingredient		Quantity	Method
1	butter		75g	Heat the butter in a heavy pan, add the vegetables and cook gently without colour.
	onion	cut into fine brunoise	150g	
	celery		75g	
	white of leek		50g	
2	flour		25g	Add, mix in and cook slowly for a few minutes without colour.

3	milk, hot	1 litre	Mix in gradually with a wooden spatule avoiding any lumps whatsoever and lightly season with salt and pepper. Bring to the boil, skim and allow to simmer gently for 30 mins.
4	mussels, small	1kg	Scrape well and wash.
5	shallot, chopped bayleaf parsley stalks white wine, dry	50g 1 20g 2dl	Place in a pan, add the mussels, cover with a lid and cook quickly until the shells open.
6			Remove the mussels from their shells and discard their beards.
7			Add the mussels to the soup. Allow the cooking liquid to stand for a few mins. to settle out any sand, then carefully strain through a fine strainer into the soup and reheat.
8	egg yolks cream	6 2dl	Whisk together in a large basin and add approx. one-third of the soup, whisking in quickly. Return to the soup whisking in quickly. Reheat, stirring continuously with a wooden spatule until the liaison thickens the soup; take care that it does not reboil. Adjust the seasoning as necessary.

COLD SOUPS

For the hot summer months especially, cold soups can be a welcome addition to either luncheon or dinner menus. Flavoured consommés, well-chilled and lightly jellied are very suitable and many of the veloutés and cream soups are equally so, if served well-flavoured, with extra cream and not too thick. In addition, there is a wide range of soups especially created for serving cold only. Generally all cold soups are best if ungarnished or at the very most with a simple compatible garnish.

410 Consommé froid en Gelée – Cold Jellied Consommé

Prepare as Consommé Ordinaire (321) with the addition of up to 20g of leaf gelatine soaked in water and added just before straining. Allow to cool and set to a jelly in the refrigerator.

SPECIAL POINT
It is very important that jellied consommés are not in any way firm. They need to be only lightly jellied and should melt in the mouth without any feeling of texture whatsoever. Usually a well-prepared consommé will set sufficiently by itself, thus it is well to try it both before and after adding any gelatine by placing a little of the consommé in the refrigerator for sufficient time to set.

411 Consommés en Gelée aux Vins

These are cold jellied consommés which are flavoured with wine and take the name of the wine in the menu designation, e.g. Consommé en Gelée au Porto. Other suitable wines are sherry and Madeira. They are prepared by adding 1 dl of the appropriate wine per 2 litres of cool Consommé froid en Gelée (410) prior to placing in the refrigerator.

412 Consommé Madrilène en Gelée

Prepare Consommé Madrilène (335), adding 20g of leaf gelatine soaked in cold water. Allow to cool and place in the refrigerator until required. Omit the garnish of tomato, vermicelli and sorrel as for hot Consommé Madrilène.

413 Consommés froids aux Fumets – Flavoured Cold Consommés

These are cold consommés, very lightly jellied which are flavoured and take the name of the flavour in its menu designation, e.g. Consommé froid au Fumet de Caille, au Fumet de Céleri and so on. They should be prepared as Consommé Ordinaire (321) with just sufficient of the chosen flavouring item added at Stage 2 to give a discreet noticeable quality to the finished result.

414 Chilled Avocado and Tomato Soup

2 litres
1 hour

Stage	Ingredient	Quantity	Method
1	avocado pears, ripe	5	Peel the avocados, discard the stones and pass the flesh quickly through a sieve.
2	Fonds de Volaille (96)	1 litre	Bring the stock to the boil, add the avocado purée and tomates concassées.
	Tomates Concassèes (90)	500g	Season and simmer gently for 15 mins. Pass through a fine strainer and allow to cool.
3	crème fraîche	5dl	Add the cream to the soup when quite
	lime juice	2 tbsps	cold, flavour with the lime juice and
	cayenne		adjust the seasoning with salt and a good touch of cayenne.
4	fines herbes, chopped	1 tbsp	Serve immediately, well-chilled and sprinkled with the herbs.

415 Chilled Cucumber and Mint Soup

2 litres
2 hours

Stage	Ingredient	Quantity	Method
1	cucumbers	4	Peel and cut out 150g of pea-sized balls using a spoon cutter. Cook these in a

			little salted water, refresh, drain and reserve. Roughly chop the remaining cucumber.
2	onion, chopped	100g	Place in a pan with the chopped cucumber.
3	Fonds de Volaille (96)	2 litres	Add, bring to the boil, skim and season.
4	mint	1 bunch	Wash, pick off 15g of the small leaves and reserve; tie the remainder and add to the soup.
5			Allow to simmer for 15–20 mins. then remove the mint. Pass the soup through a sieve or liquidiser and then through a fine strainer. Season well and allow to cool thoroughly.
6	cream, double	2½dl	Add to the soup mixing in carefully. Then add the reserved cucumber balls.
7			Serve well-chilled sprinkled with the reserved mint leaves, roughly chopped.

416 Chilled Tomato and Basil Soup

2 litres
2 hours

Stage	Ingredient	Quantity	Method
1	butter onions, chopped garlic, crushed	50g 150g 1 clove	Heat the butter in a deep pan and cook the onions and garlic without colour.
2	tomatoes, quartered tomato purée	1½kg 1 tbsp	Add the tomatoes and purée and cook down for a few mins.
3	Fonds de Volaille (96) basil	1 litre 1 bunch	Add the chicken stock. Strip off a few of the basil leaves and reserve. Tie the remainder together and add to the soup. Season and bring to the boil. Skim carefully and simmer for 10–15 mins.
4			Remove the basil. Pass the soup through a sieve then through a fine strainer. Cool thoroughly. Adjust the seasoning as necessary.
5	sour cream	2dl	Serve well-chilled, sprinkled with the chopped reserved basil leaves and add a little of the cream when serving.

417 Gazpacho Andalouse

2 litres
1 hour

Stage	Ingredient	Quantity	Method
1	garlic	6 cloves	Peel and crush the garlic in a basin. Cut
	bread	200g	the bread into small pieces and place
	oil, olive	2dl	with the garlic, mixing well. Add the oil gradually and mix in well. Season with salt and allow to stand for 10 mins.
2	tomatoes	500g	Cut the tomatoes into quarters, chop the
	cucumber, peeled	250g	cucumber, remove the seeds from the
	pimentos, green	200g	pimento and chop finely. Add all ingred-
	vinegar	1dl	ients to the previous mixture, season and allow to stand for 10 mins.
3	cumin seeds	15g	Crush the cumin seeds, add to the
	ice	500g	mixture and pass the whole through a fine sieve or mix in a blender. Add ice to chill the soup and correct the consistency.
4	Croûtons (311)	100g	Serve the soup very cold accompanied
	onion, finely chopped	100g	with dishes of croûtons, finely chopped
	cucumber, diced	100g	onion, diced cucumber, tomatoes
	Tomates Concassées (90)	100g	concassées and diced green pepper.
	pimento, diced	100g	

418 Vichyssoise

2 litres
2 hours

Stage	Ingredient	Quantity	Method
1	butter	50g	Melt the butter in a deep pan, add the
	white of ⎫ roughly		vegetables and cook without colour,
	leek ⎬ sliced	300g	stirring occasionally with a wooden
	onion ⎭	200g	spatule.
2	Fonds Blanc de Volaille (96)	1 litre	Add the stock and milk, bring to the boil and skim. Add the potatoes, season and
	milk	¾ litre	simmer until all ingredients are tender
	potato, sliced	500g	(approx. 45 mins.).
3	cream	2dl	Pass the soup through a fine sieve and
	chives, chopped		then firmly through a fine strainer. Replace in a clean pan, reboil and allow to cool. Correct the consistency with the cream, adjust the seasoning and serve well-chilled, sprinkled with chopped chives.

419 Soupe aux Cerises – Cherry Soup

2 litres
1 hour

Stage	Ingredient	Quantity	Method
1	Morello or sour cherries	750g	Stone the cherries. Reserve 100g of the cherries and crush half the stones.
2	port wine	3dl	Place in a pan with the crushed stones, bring to the boil, cover, remove from the heat and allow to steep.
3	white wine, medium cinnamon lemon zest orange zest sugar	5dl 1 piece 1 strip 1 strip 50g	Place in a pan, add the rest of the stoned cherries and boil quickly for 10 mins. Remove the zests and cinnamon then pass the soup first through a sieve or liquidiser then through a fine strainer into a clean pan.
4	arrowroot	15g	Strain the port from the stones into the soup. Bring to the boil then thicken lightly with the diluted arrowroot.
5	lemon juice	1 tbsp	Add to the soup together with the reserved cherries and gently cook together for a further 5 mins.
6	sour cream Croûtes de Flûte (310) or slices of brioche, toasted	3dl	Allow the soup to cool thoroughly then stir in the cream. Serve well-chilled accompanied with the croûtes or toasted brioche.

8

Eggs

The hen's egg is one of the most versatile and widely used commodities and its special properties are utilised for thickening, colouring, shortening, emulsifying, coagulating, clarifying and aerating. All sections of the kitchen use eggs, often in combination with other ingredients, to produce dishes where these special properties are fundamental to the dish. For example, the property of aeration found in whisked egg whites is used to produce the light fluffy texture of a soufflé. But in addition to these very special qualities, eggs can be prepared and served either hot or cold, with or without garnishes and as dishes in their own right. This chapter, however, relates only to savoury egg dishes which are served hot.

The hen's egg is used almost exclusively for these hot dishes; it is possible to use the eggs of other birds such as duck, gull and quail where demanded, but in general, flavour and size preclude anything but a very occasional use.

The non-assertive and delicate flavour of the cooked egg lends itself with advantage to being garnished or mixed with almost any savoury item including all kinds of fish and shellfish, meat, poultry, game and offals such as kidney and liver, as well as many vegetables and cheese. In addition, a number of sauces can also be used to enhance the quality of hot egg dishes, either mixed with a garnish or as a surround to the dish.

Variety in presentation is effected not only by special serving dishes but by the use of tartlet cases, fried or toasted croûtons and sometimes half-tomatoes or artichoke bottoms for dressing poached or soft-boiled eggs.

Plainly-cooked eggs without particular garnishes are more appropriate for breakfast and the garnished ones mainly for lunch, early evening meals or late supper. It is not usual to include egg dishes on a dinner menu. In the classical tradition hot egg dishes come after the hors-d'oeuvre and soup and are usually featured alongside the farinaceous dishes.

There are a number of general points to bear in mind concerning the preparation of egg dishes. Firstly, the eggs used should be as fresh as possible, be just cooked but not overcooked, then served immediately. However, it is possible to cook poached and soft- and hard-boiled eggs in advance, keeping them in cold water until required. Secondly, it is inadvisable to use silver or metal dishes for the cooking and serving of eggs as direct contact with silver particularly can lead to discolouration of the dish which will present badly when serving to the customer. Fireproof porcelain or earthenware dishes are available and should be used where possible. Omelettes are best served on plates or oval or round earthenware dishes.

CLASSIFICATION

a) Brouillé – Scrambled,
b) en Cocotte – in cocotte,
c) à la Coque – Boiled and served in the shell,
d) Dur or farci – Hard-boiled or stuffed,

e) Frit – Fried,
f) Mollet – Soft-boiled,
g) Omelette,
h) Sur le Plat – Cooked in the dish,
i) Poché – Poached.

Cold egg dishes will be found in Chapters 6 and 15 and sweet omelettes in Chapter 20.

Unless otherwise stated the following recipes are based on the use of medium-sized eggs.

OEUFS BROUILLÉS – SCRAMBLED EGGS

420 Oeufs brouillés Nature – Scrambled Eggs

1 portion
5 mins.

Stage	Ingredient	Quantity	Method
1	eggs	2	Break into a basin, season with salt and pepper and mix thoroughly with a whisk, without making it frothy.
2	butter	15g	Melt in a small sauteuse and add the eggs. Cook gently, stirring continuously with a wooden spoon until lightly set. Remove from the heat.
3	butter cream	15g 1 tbsp	Finish with the butter and cream and serve in a warm, eared egg dish.

SPECIAL POINTS
a) The texture of the finished eggs should be light and moist, not over-coagulated and hard – they are best cooked to order or at least in small batches.
b) Holding even for short periods in a heated container or bain-marie will result in further cooking and deterioration of quality.
c) The addition of milk to extend the quantity will inevitably mean a watery result, although a little double cream added with the eggs at Stage 1 can improve it.
d) For large quantities it can be useful to cook scrambled eggs in a pan in a bain-marie of hot water. They may take longer to cook but there is less chance of the eggs adhering to the base of the pan and becoming discoloured. It is not necessary to stir continuously, but the coagulated egg must be broken up as soon as it begins to form.
e) Use two eggs per portion for a set menu and three eggs per portion if priced as a separate dish.

421 Oeufs brouillés aux Champignons – Scrambled Eggs with Mushrooms

Prepare Oeufs brouillés Nature (420), place 1 tablespoon of sliced, sautéed button mushrooms (61) in the centre and finish with a pinch of chopped parsley.

422   Oeufs brouillés aux Croûtons – Scrambled Eggs with Croûtons

Prepare Oeufs brouillés Nature (420) and place 1 tablespoon of Croûtons (311) in the centre when serving.

423   Oeufs brouillés aux Foies de Volaille – Scrambled Eggs with Chicken Livers

Cut chicken livers in small dice, season and fry quickly in a little hot butter. Drain and mix with a little Sauce Madère (129). Prepare Oeufs brouillés Nature (420) and place 1 tablespoon of the prepared chicken livers in the centre. Finish with a cordon of Sauce Madère and a pinch of chopped parsley on the livers.

424   Oeufs brouillés aux Pointes d'Asperges – Scrambled Eggs with Asparagus Tips

Prepare Oeufs brouillés Nature (420) and place a bouquet of hot buttered asparagus tips in the centre.

425   Oeufs brouillés aux Tomates or Portugaise – Scrambled Eggs with Tomatoes

Prepare Oeufs brouillés Nature (420) and place 1 tablespoon of cooked Tomates Concassées (91) in the centre. Finish with a pinch of chopped parsley.

426   Scrambled Eggs on Toast

Prepare Oeufs brouillés Nature (420) and place on a slice of hot buttered toast for service. Garnish with picked parsley.

OEUFS EN COCOTTE – EGGS IN COCOTTE

427   Oeufs en Cocotte Nature – Eggs in Cocotte   1 portion
5 mins.

Stage	Ingredient	Quantity	Method
1	butter	10g	Butter well two egg cocottes and season lightly with salt and pepper.
2	eggs	2	Break one egg into each cocotte and then place them in a sauté pan with sufficient boiling water to come half-way up the cocottes. Cover with a lid and simmer gently until the eggs are lightly set (approx. 4 mins.).
3			Remove and drain off any water which has condensed on the surface of the eggs. Wipe the outside of the cocottes before serving.

SPECIAL POINTS

a) Very fresh eggs are essential for making sure that when ready to serve, the yolks will have become covered with a light veiling or coating of just-setting white.

b) Unless asked for differently, be sure to remove the eggs in cocotte when they are no more than lightly set and serve immediately. Being thick the cocottes will hold a certain amount of latent heat – the time from stove to customer will be sufficient to ensure that the eggs are cooked to the right degree.

428 Oeufs en Cocotte Bergère

Cook a little finely chopped mushroom in butter, add an equal quantity of finely diced cooked lamb or mutton, mix with Demi-glace (112), and season. Place a tablespoon of this mixture in each prepared cocotte, break the eggs on top and cook as for Oeufs en Cocotte Nature (427). Finish with a cordon of demi-glace when serving.

429 Oeufs en Cocotte à la Crème

Prepare Oeufs en Cocotte Nature (427) and place 1 dessertspoon of warm cream over each egg when serving.

430 Oeufs en Cocotte au Jus

Prepare Oeufs en Cocotte Nature (427) and place 1 dessertspoon of well-seasoned Jus lié (113) over each egg when serving.

431 Oeufs en Cocotte Portugaise

Place a dessertspoon of cooked Tomates Concassées (91) in each prepared cocotte, break the eggs on top and cook as for Oeufs en Cocotte Nature (427). Finish with a cordon of Sauce Tomate (118) when serving.

432 Oeufs en Cocotte à la Reine

Mix some finely diced cooked white of chicken with a little Sauce Suprême (151), reheat and season. Place a dessertspoon of this mixture in each prepared cocotte. Break the eggs on top and cook as for Oeufs en Cocotte Nature (427). Finish by placing a dessertspoon of warm cream over each egg.

433 Oeufs en Cocotte Soubise

Coat the base and sides of the cocottes with Sauce Soubise (150). Break in the eggs and cook as for Oeufs en Cocotte Nature (427). Finish with a cordon of warm Glace de Viande (103) when serving.

OEUFS À LA COQUE – BOILED EGGS SERVED IN THE SHELL

434 Boiled Eggs

Boiled eggs served in the shell are a popular breakfast dish but the right degree of cooking is still surrounded with some sort of mystique. Many people feel that they themselves alone know how to prepare a soft-boiled egg properly. Nevertheless, the following are the important details which need to be taken into account when catering for the discerning customer:

1) The eggs need to be as fresh as possible.
2) The eggs should be kept at room temperature for at least 2 hours before boiling. Do not use straight from the refrigerator.
3) Place the eggs in a wire basket or other suitable item and plunge into already boiling water, bring to the boil quickly then reduce to a simmer.
4) Cook them according to the customer's requirements – this can vary, for a medium-sized egg, from 3 minutes for lightly-boiled to 10 minutes for hard-boiled; adjust the times for larger or smaller eggs.
5) Serve immediately, remembering that the eggs will be hot enough to carry on cooking for some little time.

SPECIAL POINT
Special egg-boiling equipment is used in most establishments but all the above points, excepting of course the equipment at 3. above, still apply.

OEUFS DURS OR FARCIS – HARD-BOILED OR STUFFED EGGS

435 Oeufs durs – Hard-boiled Eggs

For medium-sized eggs, place the eggs into a frying-basket and then into a pan of sufficient boiling water to cover them. Simmer gently for 10–12 minutes then remove the basket of eggs and place under running cold water. Shell them quickly and reserve for use in a china basin, covered with cold water. If required hot, reheat the eggs in boiling salted water for approx. 3 mins.

SPECIAL POINT
It is essential that the eggs are not overcooked as this will result in a greyish-blue covering to the yolks which becomes thicker the longer the correct cooking time is exceeded.

436 Oeuf farci Chimay

10 portions
30 mins.

Stage	Ingredient	Quantity	Method
1	eggs, hard-boiled	10	Cut in half lengthways, remove the yolks and pass them through a sieve.
2	Duxelles (29)	80g	Mix with the egg yolks, season and pipe into the centre of the whites.
3	Sauce Mornay (146) Parmesan, grated	7dl 50g	Place a little sauce in the bottom of the required number of fire-proof dishes, arrange the eggs neatly on top, coat with the Sauce Mornay, sprinkle with cheese and gratinate in a hot oven.

437 Côtelette d'Oeufs Forestière – Egg and Mushroom Cutlet

10 portions
45 mins.

Stage	Ingredient	Quantity	Method
1	butter	50g	Heat the butter in a shallow pan and cook the shallots without colour. Add the washed mushrooms cut into roughly 3mm dice, season lightly and cook together until almost dry.
	shallots, finely chopped	50g	
	mushrooms, white	350g	
2	eggs, hard-boiled	12	Cut the eggs into roughly 3mm dice, and add together with the sauce to the mushrooms. Bring to the boil stirring with a wooden spatule.
	Béchamel (114), hot	3dl	
3	egg yolks	4	Add the egg yolks, mix in well, season and continue cooking until the mixture thickens. Remove from the heat and mix in the parsley.
	parsley, chopped	½ tbsp	
4	butter	50g	Spread the mixture on a buttered tray, butter the surface and allow to become cold. Divide the mixture into 10 equal pieces. Mould cutlet-shape using flour to prevent sticking. Paner à l'Anglaise (72).
	flour	} for crumbing	
	eggwash		
	breadcrumbs		
5	parsley, picked		Deep fry in hot fat until golden brown. Drain well and serve on a dish paper on a dish garnished with fresh or fried parsley. Serve the sauce as an accompaniment.
	Sauce Tomate (118)	6dl	

438 Croquettes d'Oeufs – Egg Croquettes

10 portions
1½ hours

Stage	Ingredient	Quantity	Method
1	eggs, hard-boiled	15	Cut into ½cm dice and place in a sauteuse.
2	Béchamel (114) hot	½ litre	Add and bring to the boil, stirring with a wooden spatule.
3	egg yolks	4	Add, mix in well, season and continue cooking until the mixture thickens.
4	flour	} for crumbing	Spread the mixture on a buttered tray, butter the surface and allow to become cold. Divide the mixture into 20 equal pieces and mould croquette-shape using flour to prevent sticking. Paner à l'Anglaise (72).
	eggwash		
	breadcrumbs		

| 5 | parsley, picked | | Deep fry in hot fat until golden brown. |
| | Sauce Tomate (118) | 6dl | Drain well and serve on a dish paper on a flat dish, garnished with fresh or fried parsley. Serve Sauce Tomate as an accompaniment. |

439 Scotch Egg

10 portions
45 mins.

Stage	Ingredient	Quantity	Method
1	eggs, hard-boiled	10	Lightly flour the eggs and envelop each
	sausage-meat,		one completely in 80g of the sausage-
	pork	800g	meat, moulding egg-shape.
2	flour ⎫		Paner à l'Anglaise (72) and deep fry in
	eggwash ⎬ for		moderately hot fat until golden brown,
	breadcrumbs ⎭ crumbing		taking care that the sausage-meat is completely cooked. Drain well.
3	parsley, picked		Cut the eggs in half lengthways. Serve
	Sauce Tomate (118)	6dl	on a dish paper on a flat dish and garnish with fresh or fried parsley. Serve Sauce Tomate as an accompaniment.

SPECIAL POINT

Scotch eggs may also be served cold accompanied with a mixed salad.

440 Oeufs à la Tripe

Reheat hard-boiled eggs in boiling salted water for 3 mins. Drain, slice and place neatly on a buttered egg dish. Coat with Sauce aux Oignons (147) and sprinkle with chopped parsley when serving.

OEUFS FRITS – FRIED EGGS

441 Oeufs frits à la Poêle – Pan-fried Eggs

Heat sufficient clean bacon fat or butter in a frying-pan to cover the bottom. Break in the eggs and fry gently, basting the surfaces with the fat in the frying-pan until the whites are set but the yolks still soft.

SPECIAL POINTS

a) Good results can only be obtained with fresh eggs where the white surrounds the yolk tightly and stands proud of the pan. Stale watery eggs are completely worthless.

b) This type of fried egg can be cooked easily to customer's requirements, ranging from being just cooked as above to having crispy whites, being fried on both sides, or well-done. It is only a question of adjusting heat, length of time and manipulation.

c) Fried eggs are mainly used for serving as a breakfast dish with grilled rashers of bacon, sausages, tomatoes, etc. They are also used for garnishing certain dishes, e.g. Escalope de Veau Holstein.

442 Oeufs frits à la Française – French Fried Eggs

Fill an omelette pan two-thirds full of oil, place the round part of a wooden spoon in the pan and heat the oil gradually so as to ensure that the surface of the wooden spoon will not stick when being used to fry the eggs. Remove the spoon and heat the oil to a temperature of approx. 175°C. Break one egg into a small basin, tip the pan slightly and place the egg in the deepest part of the oil. With the spoon in the other hand envelop the yolk with the white, turning it in the oil until the outside of the egg becomes light brown in colour and the yolk remains soft inside. Drain well and lightly season with salt. Repeat as required.

There are a small number of dishes in the repertoire in which this kind of fried egg is served with a garnish as an egg dish. It is also used for garnishing certain dishes, e.g. Poulet sauté Marengo.

443 Oeufs frits Andalouse – Fried Eggs Andalouse

Arrange the French Fried Eggs (442) on a bed of Aubergines frites (1391) and serve accompanied with Sauce Tomate (118).

OEUFS MOLLETS–SOFT-BOILED EGGS

444 Oeufs mollets – Soft-boiled Eggs

Place the eggs into a frying-basket and then into a pan of sufficient boiling water to cover them. Simmer gently for 5 mins., remove, place under cold running water, shell and reserve in a china basin covered with cold water. Allow one egg per portion when garnished. Reheat when required by placing in very hot salted water for approx. 1 min. Drain on a clean cloth before serving.

Oeufs mollets may be prepared and served in accordance with any of the recipes for Oeufs pochés (473–482).

445 OMELETTES

Omelettes are a very quick and relatively simple dish to prepare. They can be served plain or garnished with a wide variety of commodities and sauces. They can be featured on breakfast and lunch menus and on à la Carte menus as a light dish or main meal for any time of the day. However, omelettes are not suitable for set dinner menus.

There are three types of omelettes which can be classified as follows:
1) Oval or rolled omelettes – these can be prepared:
   a) with a garnish mixed in with the eggs;
   b) stuffed with a garnish;
   c) with a garnish placed in a pocket along the top of the finished omelette, or
   d) as a stuffed omelette, coated or surrounded with a sauce.
2) Flat omelettes – these are invariably made with a garnish mixed in with the egg. They are made flat and turned and cooked on both sides.
3) Omelettes mousseline – these are also prepared as a flat omelette but the yolks are first separated then mixed with the stiffly whipped whites.

SPECIAL POINTS
a) The finished omelette should be light and fluffy and unless requested, not overcooked or overcoloured on the outside. A familiar request however, is for an omelette to be undercooked, i.e. softer than normal – the technical term for this is 'baveuse'.
b) Water or milk added to extend the quantity of egg will only spoil the texture – however, ½ tablespoon of good double cream per 2 eggs can lighten and improve the texture.
c) It is essential that omelettes are prepared to order and served immediately. They should not be prepared in advance, held in a hot-cupboard or reheated.
d) It is both useful and practical to make larger omelettes than for one portion. It only needs a larger pan but it is not advantageous to make them larger than with 10–12 eggs. To prepare a large omelette to the right degree of perfection requires considerable practice and expertise.
e) If single omelettes are required in large numbers for a busy service it is a useful technique to prepare a large quantity of beaten egg in advance but they should not be seasoned at this stage – salt breaks down the albumen in the whites and the beaten eggs quickly become thin and watery which adversely affects the texture of the omelette. It is better to season each measured amount of egg just before making the omelette. For measurement of the egg mixture use a ladle with a capacity equal to the number of eggs used for a single omelette, i.e. the equivalent of two or three eggs as the case may be.

The Omelette Pan
The best types of omelette pan have curved sides and are made from heavy-gauge, black wrought iron or steel. They should be kept especially for making omelettes and not used as general purpose frying-pans. A pan 20cm in diameter is suitable for making one-portion omelettes. New pans need cleaning in the following manner to prevent sticking: place sufficient lard in the pan to almost fill it and allow to become hot without burning. Leave it for 1 hour and then pour out the fat. Place a handful of salt in the pan and rub vigorously with a piece of kitchen paper. Throw away the salt and wipe the pan clean with a piece of soft cloth.

It is usual to serve two-egg omelettes as an egg dish and three-egg omelettes as a main dish.

OVAL OMELETTES

446 Omelette Nature – Plain Omelette

1) Break two eggs into a china or stainless steel basin, season with salt and pepper and beat with a fork so as to blend the whites and yolks thoroughly. This will prevent streaks of white showing in the finished omelette. Do not overbeat.
2) Heat the omelette pan, add 15g of butter and move the pan round and round so as to allow it to coat the base and sides completely. When the butter is very hot but just before it commences to turn brown, pour in the eggs.
3) Shake the pan briskly and stir with a fork, at the same time removing the egg from the sides of the pan to the centre as it begins to set. When the egg is slightly firm underneath but still soft in the centre leave it for a few seconds on full heat.
4) Pull away from the heat, take hold of the handle of the pan and, using the fork to release the omelette from the sides, fold one-third of it over away from the handle.

Fold the other end of the omelette towards the centre and shape the ends to form an oval shape. Tap the pan on the stove to make the omelette slide to the edge of the pan, leave for a few seconds on full heat.
5) Turn the omelette over onto a warm, buttered oval china or stainless steel dish. Brush the surface lightly with melted butter.

447 Omelette Arnold Bennett

Mix some flaked cooked smoked haddock free from skin and bones with cream. Season and reheat. Prepare the omelette as for Omelette Nature (446), placing 1 tablespoon of the prepared mixture in the centre of the omelette before folding. Coat the omelette with Sauce Mornay (146). Sprinkle with a little grated Parmesan and gratinate very quickly under the salamander.

448 Omelette aux Champignons – Mushroom Omelette

Add 1 tablespoon of sautéed sliced button mushrooms (61) to the beaten eggs and proceed as for Omelette Nature (446). Place a whole sautéed button mushroom in the centre of the finished omelette.

449 Omelette Chasseur

Sauté an equal quantity of diced chicken liver and sliced button mushrooms in hot butter, season, drain and mix with a little Sauce Madère (129). Prepare the omelette as for Omelette Nature (446), slit the top of the omelette along half its length, open it slightly and place 1 tablespoon of the prepared garnish in the opening. Finish with a pinch of chopped parsley and surround with a cordon of Sauce Madère.

450 Omelette Fines Herbes

Add 1 teaspoon of chopped Fines Herbes (31) to the beaten eggs and proceed as for Omelette Nature (446).

451 Omelette au Fromage – Cheese Omelette

Add 1 tablespoon of grated cheese (an equal quantity of Cheddar and Parmesan) to the beaten eggs and proceed as for Omelette Nature (446)

452 Omelette au Jambon or Yorkaise – Ham Omelette

Add 1 tablespoon of small dice of ham to the beaten eggs and proceed as for Omelette Nature (446). Place diamonds of warmed ham on top of the finished omelette.

453 Omelette Lyonnaise – Onion Omelette

Add 1 tablespoon of Oignons sautés (1491) to the beaten eggs and proceed as for Omelette Nature (446).

454 Omelette au Parmesan

Add 1 dessertspoon of grated Parmesan to the beaten eggs and proceed as for Omelette Nature (446). Sprinkle a little grated Parmesan over the surface of the finished omelette.

455 Omelette aux Pointes d'Asperges – Asparagus Omelette

Add 1 tablespoon of cooked asparagus tips cut into ½cm-long pieces to the beaten eggs. Proceed as for Omelette Nature (446). Place a bouquet of warm buttered asparagus tips diagonally on top of the finished omelette.

456 Omelette à la Reine

Mix some finely diced cooked white of chicken with a little Sauce Suprême (151), season and reheat. Prepare the omelette as for Omelette Nature (446), placing 1 tablespoon of the prepared mixture in the centre of the omelette before folding. Finish with a cordon of Sauce Suprême.

457 Omelette aux Rognons – Kidney Omelette

Sauté some small dice of lamb's kidneys in butter, season, drain and mix with a little Sauce Madère (129). Prepare the omelette as for Omelette Nature (446). Cut the top of the omelette along half its length, open it slightly and place 1 tablespoon of the prepared garnish in the opening. Finish with a pinch of chopped parsley on the kidney and surround with a cordon of Sauce Madère.

458 Omelette aux Tomates or Portugaise – Tomato Omelette

Prepare the omelette as for Omelette Nature (446). Slit the top of the omelette along half its length, open out slightly and place 1 tablespoon of hot cooked Tomates Concassées (91) in the opening. Finish with a pinch of chopped parsley and surround with a cordon of Sauce Tomate (118).

FLAT OMELETTES

459 Omelette Espagnole – Spanish Omelette

1) Break two eggs into a china or stainless steel basin, season with salt and pepper and beat with a fork so as to blend the whites and yolks thoroughly. This will prevent streaks of white showing in the finished omelette. Do not overbeat.
2) Add 1 dessertspoon of cooked Tomates Concassées (91), 1 dessertspoon of cooked julienne of green pimento (79) and 1 dessertspoon of Oignons sautés (1491) to the beaten eggs.
3) Heat the omelette pan, add 15g of butter and move the pan round and round so as to allow it to coat the base and sides completely. When it is very hot but just before it commences to turn brown, add the egg mixture.
4) Shake the pan briskly and stir with a fork, at the same time removing the egg from the sides of the pan to the centre as it sets. When slightly firm underneath but still soft on top, leave it for a few seconds on full heat.
5) Pull away from the heat, release the omelette from all round the pan with the fork and tap the pan on the stove to ensure that it is free.

6) a) Toss over and leave on full heat for a few seconds more then slide onto a warm buttered plate or round dish, or
   b) place under the salamander for a few seconds to lightly set the top, then turn over onto a warm buttered plate or round dish.
   In both cases brush the surface with melted butter.

460 Omelette Fermière

Add 1 tablespoon of small dice of ham and a little chopped parsley to the beaten eggs and proceed as for Omelette Espagnole (459).

461 Omelette Paysanne

Add 1 dessertspoon of ½cm Pommes Parmentier (1588), 1 dessertspoon of small lardons (51), a little Chiffonade of sorrel (309) and some chopped Fines Herbes (31) to the beaten eggs and proceed as for Omelette Espagnole (459).

462 Omelette Parmentier

Add 2 tablespoons of ½cm Pommes Parmentier (1588) and a little chopped parsley to the beaten eggs and proceed as for Omelette Espagnole (459).

463 Omelette Suissesse

Add 1 tablespoon of small dice of Gruyère cheese to the beaten eggs and proceed as for Omelette Espagnole (459). Sprinkle the top of the finished omelette with a little grated Gruyère and lightly gratinate as quickly as possible under the salamander.

OMELETTES MOUSSELINES

464 Omelette Mousseline

1) Take two eggs and separate the yolks from the whites. Beat the yolks with salt and pepper in a basin. Whisk the whites until stiff in a separate basin then carefully fold the whites into the yolks.
2) Heat the omelette pan, add 15g of butter and move the pan so as to coat the base and sides completely. When it is hot and before it turns brown, add the egg mixture.
3) Shake the pan briskly and stir lightly with a fork, at the same time removing the egg from the side of the pan to the centre. Do not overmix.
4) Add another 10g of butter to melt round the sides of the pan, shake the pan to allow the butter to run underneath the omelette and cook it gently for a few more seconds. Either toss the omelette over, or slide onto a plate and turn over back into the pan.
5) Carry on cooking gently until lightly coloured then slide onto a warm buttered plate or round dish. Brush the surface with a little melted butter.

SPECIAL POINTS
a) Very fresh eggs and best-quality butter are both essential for this type of omelette.
b) When cooked the omelette should be very light, well souffléed and slightly soft in the very centre, a light golden colour on both sides, and the extra amount of butter should have been absorbed into the eggs.

c) Omelettes Mousselines can also be garnished. Most items are suitable, such as vegetables, shellfish, offal, meat, poultry and so on but the garnish is best when cut small and mixed with a little appropriate sauce or cream which is fairly thick; for example, sautéed sliced mushrooms with cream, shrimps or prawns with lobster sauce, buttered and creamed asparagus tips, sautéed chicken livers and Madeira sauce, chopped tomato cooked with diced pimentos and onion. Just place 2 or 3 tablespoons of the selected garnish in the middle of the omelette when cooked.

OEUFS SUR LE PLAT – EGGS COOKED IN THE DISH

465 Oeuf sur le Plat

1) Well butter an egg dish and lightly season with salt and pepper.
2) Break in an egg.
3) Place on the side of the stove until the white is lightly set. Finish cooking under the salamander or in a hot oven until the surface is lightly set.

Allow one or two eggs per portion.

SPECIAL POINTS
a) Very fresh eggs are an essential requirement. The whites need to surround the yolk tightly and leave a coating on the yolk.
b) Unless required otherwise eggs cooked in this manner need to have the white lightly set but the yolk still soft and covered with a light milky veil of just-set white.
c) Egg dishes for sur le Plat are usually made of fireproof porcelain or earthenware. As with egg cocottes they hold heat for some time – it is thus imperative that they be served as soon as ready. Any delay can result in overcooking of the white.

466 Oeuf sur le Plat Bercy

Prepare Oeuf sur le Plat (465) and garnish with two small grilled chipolatas and a cordon of Sauce Tomate (118).

467 Oeuf sur le Plat au Beurre Noir

Prepare Oeuf sur le Plat (465) and finish with 15g of Beurre Noir (12) when serving.

468 Oeuf sur le Plat aux Foies de Volaille

Sauté some small dice of chicken livers in butter, season, drain and mix with a little Sauce Madère (129). Garnish the Oeuf sur le Plat (465) with a tablespoon of this mixture and finish with a pinch of chopped parsley on the liver, and a cordon of Sauce Madère.

469 Oeuf sur le Plat au Jambon

Place a thin slice of ham in the buttered egg dish sufficient to cover the base, add the egg and proceed as for Oeuf sur le Plat (465).

470 Oeuf sur le Plat au Lard

Place two slices of grilled back bacon in the buttered egg dish, add the egg and proceed as for Oeuf sur le Plat (465).

471 Oeuf sur le Plat Lorraine

Place two slices of grilled back bacon in the buttered egg dish and cover with a thin slice of Gruyère cheese. Break in the egg, coat with cream and cook gently in the oven until the egg is lightly set.

472 Oeuf sur le Plat Opéra

Sauté some small dice of chicken livers in butter, season, drain and mix with a little Sauce Madère (129). Garnish the Oeuf sur le Plat with a tablespoon of this mixture and a bouquet of warm buttered asparagus tips. Finish with a pinch of chopped parsley on the liver, and a cordon of Sauce Madère.

OEUFS POCHÉS – POACHED EGGS

473 Oeufs pochés Nature – Poached Eggs

1) Break the eggs into gently boiling acidulated water (approx. 1 part white vinegar to 10 parts water) using a suitably-sized sauteuse three-quarters full.
2) Simmer very gently for approx. 4 mins. until the whites are just firm and the yolks are still soft.
3) Remove the eggs carefully with a perforated spoon and place into a basin of cold water. Trim off the loose edges.
4) Reheat when required by placing the eggs in very hot salted water for approx. 1 min. Drain on a clean cloth before serving.

Allow one or two eggs per portion for an egg dish.

SPECIAL POINTS
a) All the recipes given here for poached eggs are suitable for soft-boiled eggs (444).
b) The finished poached egg should have a nice oval egg shape. This requires firstly the use of very fresh eggs and secondly, acidulating the water for poaching with a little vinegar – this assists in making the whites contract tightly around the yolk thus preventing it from spreading. Stale watery eggs will spread, break up and loosen from the yolks – no amount of vinegar will make them look anything other than stale.
c) It is very important, however, that poached eggs are not served straight from the acidulated water. They should still be placed into clean hot salted water to remove the taste of the vinegar.

474 Oeuf poché Argenteuil

Prepare tartlet cases (1763) and fill with hot diced cooked asparagus tips tossed in butter. Place each in an egg dish, put a reheated egg on top and coat with Sauce Suprême (151). Garnish with a small bouquet of warm buttered asparagus tips.

475 Oeuf poché Bénédictine

Place a round piece of buttered toast in an egg dish and cover with a slice of warmed cooked ox-tongue. Place a reheated egg on top and coat with Sauce Hollandaise (157). Garnish with a slice of truffle on the egg.

476 Oeuf poché Bombay

Place a bed of hot plain boiled rice (534) in an egg dish with a reheated egg on top, and coat with creamed Curry Sauce (208).

477 Oeuf poché Florentine

Place a bed of Epinards en Branches (1454) in an egg dish with a reheated egg on top. Coat with Sauce Mornay (146). Sprinkle with Parmesan and gratinate under the salamander.

478 Oeuf poché Mornay

Place a little Sauce Mornay (146) in the bottom of an egg dish with a reheated egg on top. Coat with Sauce Mornay, sprinkle with grated Parmesan and gratinate under the salamander.

479 Oeuf poché à la Reine

Prepare tartlet cases (1763) and fill with hot diced cooked white of chicken mixed with a little Sauce Suprême (151). Place each in an egg dish with a reheated egg on top and coat with Sauce Suprême.

480 Oeuf poché Viroflay

Prepare tartlet cases (1763) and fill with hot Epinards en Branches (1454). Place each in an egg dish with a reheated egg on top and coat with Sauce Suprême (151).

481 Oeuf poché Washington

Mix some cooked grains of maize with a little Sauce Crème (143). Season and reheat. Place a bed of this in an egg dish with a reheated egg on top. Coat with Sauce Crème.

482 Poached Egg on Toast

Place a reheated egg on a round of trimmed hot buttered toast. Garnish with picked parsley.

9

Farinaceous and Rice Dishes

The word 'farinaceous' is derived from the Latin 'farina' meaning flour and the French words *farineux* and *farinages* and the English term 'farinaceous' indicate a wide range of dishes made with differing flours, usually as a main ingredient. These include the vast range of Italian pastas in their many different forms, shapes and sizes and a range of small dumplings known in Italian as Gnocchi. Rice dishes are included because of their similar uses and value for the menu.

In the traditional menu these three types of dish are normally served as a subsidiary item for lunch coming after the soup, or frequently acting as an hors-d'oeuvre. Nevertheless, especially when garnished and with a suitable sauce, they can serve as substantial main dishes for any time of the day. When plainly prepared and not over-garnished themselves they make suitable garnishes for a number of fish, meat and poultry dishes. It is usual to serve grated Parmesan cheese or similar as an accompaniment for most farinaceous and rice dishes.

483 GNOCCHI

There are three main types of small dumplings or Gnocchi;
a) Gnocchi Parisienne made from flour, egg and butter, which in effect is a basic chou paste,
b) Gnocchi Romaine made from milk, semolina and egg,
c) Gnocchi Italienne made from potato, flour and egg.

Basically these are all gratinated with butter and cheese but they can all be lightly garnished or mixed with such things as mushrooms, cooked sausage, poultry or meat. Tomato sauce, Jus lié, Béchamel and cream are used as variations. Besides these three main types of Gnocchi there are a number of plain pastes made from flour, egg and water or milk, with or without various additions, which belong to the cuisines of Central and Eastern Europe; generally they were used and derived as garnishes and more frequently than not functioning as a means of extending the small amounts of meat and sauce which they accompanied.

484 Gnocchi Parisienne

10 portions
1 hour

Stage	Ingredient	Quantity	Method
1	water	½ litre	Place in a deep pan and bring to the boil
	butter	100g	slowly in order that the butter is melted
	salt	10g	by the time the water is boiled.

2	flour	320g	Add, away from the heat, mixing well with a wooden spatule. Return the pan to the heat and continue mixing until the mixture becomes smooth and does not stick to the sides of the pan. Cool slightly.
3	eggs Parmesan, grated	8 50g	Add the eggs to the mixture one at a time mixing in thoroughly. Add the cheese.
4			Place the mixture into a piping bag with a 1cm plain tube. Pipe into gently simmering salted water, cutting into 2cm lengths as it leaves the tube.
5			Allow to poach very gently until firm. Drain well.
6	Sauce Crème (143)	6dl	Place the gnocchi into a pan, add the sauce and mix very carefully.
7	Parmesan, grated butter, melted	60g 75g	Place the gnocchi into earthenware dishes, sprinkle with Parmesan and melted butter and gratinate under the salamander.

485 Gnocchi Florentine

Prepare Gnocchi Parisienne (484), adding 75g finely chopped, cooked and well-squeezed leaf spinach to the finished mixture at Stage 3.

486 Gnocchi Carravese al Sugo

Prepare Gnocchi Parisienne (484), adding 3 tablespoons of finely chopped fresh sage leaves to the mixture at the end of Stage 3. When cooked and drained, toss in melted butter, place in suitable dishes and lightly coat with jus lié. Sprinkle with grated Gruyère cheese and melted butter and heat sufficiently under the salamander to just melt the cheese.

487 Gnocchi Romaine

10 portions
1 hour

Stage	Ingredient	Quantity	Method
1	milk semolina nutmeg, grated	1 litre 200g	Bring the milk to the boil. Rain in the semolina, mixing in well with a whisk to avoid lumps. Season with salt, pepper and nutmeg and cook gently for 6–8 mins. stirring continuously. Remove from the heat.
2	egg yolks Parmesan, grated butter	2 50g 50g	Add and mix in well. Spread the mixture on a buttered tray and flatten to an even thickness of 1cm. Butter the surface and allow to cool.

3			Cut out with a 5cm round cutter. Place the remnants in buttered earthenware dishes to form a base and arrange the gnocchi neatly on top.
4	Parmesan, grated	60g	Sprinkle with the Parmesan and melted
	butter, melted	75g	butter and gratinate in a hot oven.

SPECIAL POINT

A cordon of Sauce Tomate (118) is often placed around this dish before serving.

---

488 Gnocchi Ticinese

Prepare Gnocchi Romaine (487) but shallow fry the rounds of semolina gnocchi in butter to a golden brown on both sides. Arrange overlapping in round dishes, each round interspersed with a 5cm-diameter round slice of cooked ham. Coat with a little jus lié, sprinkle with a little grated Parmesan and melted butter and lightly gratinate.

---

489 Gnocchi Palermitaine

Prepare Gnocchi Romaine (487) but shallow fry the rounds of semolina gnocchi in butter to a golden brown on both sides. Arrange neatly overlapping in suitable dishes, coat with a little Sauce Italienne (127) and sprinkle with chopped parsley.

---

490 Gnocchi Italienne or Gnocchi de Pommes de Terre

10 portions
1 hour

Stage	Ingredient	Quantity	Method
1	potatoes, floury, unpeeled	800g	Boil the potatoes in salted water until just done, drain and remove the skins. Pass quickly through a sieve into a basin.
2	butter	30g	Add the butter, flour and beaten eggs,
	flour, strong	150g	season with salt, pepper and a little
	eggs	2	grated nutmeg and quickly and lightly
	egg yolks	2	mix together.
	nutmeg		
3	flour, strong		Using the flour, mould the mixture into small balls, mark and slightly flatten them on one side with a fork.
4			Place into boiling salted water and simmer for 5–6 mins. Drain well.
5	Parmesan, grated	50g	Place the gnocchi in well-buttered
	butter, melted	100g	earthenware dishes and sprinkle with melted butter and cheese. Gratinate lightly under the salamander.

SPECIAL POINTS

a) It is very important that the mixture is prepared and cooked as quickly as possible. The mixture tends to become very sticky if left for any length of time and its light texture becomes impaired.

b) They are always best if served freshly made but they can, with a reasonable amount of care, be held in cold water for a short period then reheated in hot salted water.

491 Gnocchi Piémontaise

Prepare Gnocchi Italienne (490). Serve accompanied with Sauce Tomate (118).

492 Gnocchi Vénitienne

Prepare Gnocchi Italienne (490), adding 75g of finely chopped ham, 75g of finely chopped leaf spinach and 1 tablespoon of finely chopped fresh sage leaves to the mixture at Stage 2. When cooked, drain and place in buttered dishes. Coat with a little jus lié, sprinkle with grated Parmesan and melted butter and very lightly gratinate.

493 Spätzle

10 portions
30 mins.

Stage	Ingredient	Quantity	Method
1	flour	450g	Sift the flour and salt together, make a
	eggs	4	bay, add the eggs, milk and a little
	milk	4dl	grated nutmeg and mix to a loose paste.
	salt	15g	Do not overmix.
2			Place the mixture in a large-holed vegetable strainer over a pan of boiling salted water so as to let the paste run through in small pieces. Allow to poach gently for 6–8 mins. Drain.
3	butter	100g	Melt in a sauteuse, add the spätzle and toss lightly to coat. Place in earthenware dishes and finish with a little Beurre Noisette (13) when serving.

SPECIAL POINTS
a) This type of small dumpling can be held for a short period of time if refreshed and covered with cold water. It can then be reheated in hot salted water. It does tend to become harder however; freshly made spätzle are always better in texture.
b) Spätzle can be served with any of the sauces suitable for pasta.

494 PASTAS

The very popular and ubiquitous spaghetti is only one of more than 200 different shapes, sizes and styles of pasta. The list of names seems to increase constantly yet the basic paste from which they are all made is often the same, even though the resultant textures and eating qualities may be perceived as being different. Most commercially produced pastas are made from pastes using durum wheat which has a very high gluten content. Generally most of these products are not produced in the home or in catering establishments. The exceptions are the pastes for the varying forms of tagliatelli or noodles and raviolis. These are made fresh and more satisfactorily from a general purpose plain flour with a medium gluten content, mainly because of the ease of manipulation.

The number of sauces used for pastas is fairly limited but there is a wide range of garnishes and in general most sauces and garnishes are interchangeable with the varying shapes. This is in addition to the vast range of speciality and regional pasta dishes of Italy, of which the preparation, garnishing and sauce relate to a single particular pasta.

The four broad categories of pasta are:
1) small sizes and shapes for soups such as vermicelli, stelline, alfabete,
2) long thin sizes and shapes such as spaghetti, macaroni, linguine, tagliatelle,
3) lasagne which are thin oblongs mainly used in layering with sauce and garnish, and
4) stuffed pastas which include ravioli, tortellini, cappelletti and cannelloni.

The basic pastes from which thse broad varieties can be prepared are plain, egg, green (spinach), tomato or wholemeal.

Portion weights
Allow 30g uncooked weight per person as a garnish, 60–80g per person as a farinaceous course or main dish and 90–100g of fresh pasta such as ravioli or noodles.

495 THE COOKING OF PASTA

All pastas should be placed to cook in boiling salted water allowing as a rough guide at least 1 litre of water and 10g of salt per 100g of raw pasta. They should be gently moved with a wooden spoon to prevent sticking together and allowed to simmer gently; stuffed pastas such as ravioli require very gentle simmering only, to prevent breaking. The actual cooking time is determined by the size or thickness of the pasta but in all cases they should not be overcooked. What should be aimed for is to be just cooked only, having a certain amount of firmness and bite in the pasta. This is referred to in Italian as 'al dente'. When cooked, drain well and use immediately.

If not served immediately the cooked pasta can be refreshed under running cold water and kept in a basin of cold water in the refrigerator. It can then be reheated in hot salted water as required but it tends to swell if this is done and the texture and eating quality is badly impaired. Where possible, pastas should always be freshly cooked and used immediately.

496 SAUCES FOR PASTAS

In addition to the standard finishings of butter, cream and grated Parmesan there are a number of sauces which are extensively used such as Béchamel, Sauce Crème, Jus lié, Demi-glace, Sauce Italienne, Sauce Champignons, Sauce Tomate, Pesto, and Provençale. Besides these there are a few sauces which are special to pasta dishes, as well as some which become an integral part of the dish. The following are some of the special sauces for pasta.

497 Sauce Bolognaise (1)

1 litre
1¼ hours

Stage	Ingredient	Quantity	Method
1	butter	75g	Melt the butter in a pan, add the onions
	onions, finely		and garlic and cook until very lightly
	chopped	200g	coloured.
	garlic, chopped	1 clove	

2	beef, thick flank, minced	500g	Add, season and continue cooking until the beef is lightly coloured.
3	tomato purée	1½ tbsp	Add, mix together, bring to the boil and
	Demi-glace (112)	½ litre	simmer gently for approx. 45 mins. until
	Estouffade (97)	3dl	the meat is tender. Adjust the seasoning
	cayenne		as necessary with salt, milled black pepper and a touch of cayenne.

498 Sauce Bolognaise (2)

1 litre
1½ hours

Stage	Ingredient	Quantity	Method
1	oil, olive	½dl	Heat the oil and butter in a pan, add the
	butter	25g	onions, celery and garlic and cook
	garlic, finely chopped	2 cloves	without colour.
	onion, finely chopped	150g	
	celery, finely chopped	75g	
2	beef, thick flank, minced	350g	Add to the pan, season with salt and pepper and cook until lightly coloured,
	streaky bacon, unsmoked, minced	150g	mixing frequently.
3	mushrooms, coarsely chopped	150g	Add to the pan and cook for a few mins. Drain off any excess fat.
4	tomato purée	1 tbsp	Add to the pan, mix together, bring to
	red wine	3dl	the boil and simmer gently for approx.
	Demi-glace (112)	5dl	45 mins. or until the meat is tender.
	cayenne		Adjust the seasoning as necessary with salt, milled black pepper and a touch of cayenne.

499 Sauce Niçoise or Tomato and Basil Sauce

½ litre
30 mins.

Stage	Ingredient	Quantity	Method
1	oil, olive	½dl	Lightly heat the oil in a pan. Add the
	garlic, finely chopped	2 cloves	garlic and cook very gently for a few seconds and without any colour whatsoever.
2	Tomates Concassées (90)	600g	Add the tomato concassée, purée and white wine, season with salt and pepper
	tomato purée	1 tbsp	and cook quickly to reduce out half of
	white wine, dry	2dl	the liquid.
3	fresh basil leaves, chopped	1 tbsp	Add, mix in and cook for another ½ min. only. Adjust the seasoning as necessary.

SPECIAL POINT
This sauce should not be so reduced as to become a dryish purée, rather it should resemble a semi-liquid coulis with the chopped tomatoes well-discernible.

500 Sauce Monégasque

½ litre
25 mins.

Stage	Ingredient	Quantity	Method
1	olive oil	1dl	Heat the oil in a pan, add the garlic and cook gently without colour.
	garlic, finely chopped	2 cloves	
2	anchovy fillets, chopped	12	Add the chopped anchovy fillets and cook for a few seconds then add the tomatoes, wine and the olives, cut in four and blanched. Reduce by half.
	black olives, stoned	24	
	Tomates Concassées (90)	400g	
	white wine, dry	3dl	
3	fresh oregano, chopped	½ tbsp	Adjust the seasoning with salt and milled black pepper, add the oregano and basil and simmer for a further 1 min.
	fresh basil leaves, chopped	½ tbsp	

PASTA DISHES

The following recipes and variations are interchangeable between most of the pastas such as spaghetti, macaroni, noodles, and various shapes such as bows, spirals, shells and so on. The recipes are presented using spaghetti as the standard type.

501 Spaghetti Italienne

10 portions
20 mins.

Stage	Ingredient	Quantity	Method
1	spaghetti	600g	Place into a pan of boiling salted water and allow to simmer gently for 12–15 mins. stirring occasionally with a wooden spoon. Drain.
2	butter	100g	Melt in a sauteuse. Add the spaghetti, season with salt and milled pepper and toss over to mix. Place the spaghetti in earthenware dishes.
3	Parmesan, grated	75g	Serve the grated Parmesan as an accompaniment.

SPECIAL POINT
When serving Spaghetti Italienne as a garnish, half the quantity is sufficient. The grated Parmesan can be mixed in or sprinkled over the spaghetti.

502 Spaghetti Bolognaise

Prepare as Spaghetti Italienne (501) and serve Sauce Bolognaise (497 or 498) and grated Parmesan as accompaniments. Allow approx. ½ litre of the sauce for ten. Alternatively the sauce may be placed in the centre of the spaghetti when dishing up.

503 Spaghetti Carbonara

10 portions
45 mins.

Stage	Ingredient	Quantity	Method
1	streaky bacon, unsmoked	200g	Cut the streaky bacon into very small Lardons (51) and cook in the butter until light brown. Add the garlic away from the heat and allow to cook for a few seconds then add the wine and reduce by three-quarters.
	garlic, finely chopped	1 clove	
	butter	25g	
	white wine, dry	1dl	
2	eggs	2	Mix together thoroughly in a basin.
	egg yolks	4	
	Parmesan cheese, grated	50g	
	Pecorino cheese, grated	50g	
	cream, double	2dl	
3	spaghetti	600g	Place into a pan of boiling salted water and simmer gently for 12–15 mins. stirring occasionally.
4	butter	50g	Heat in a shallow pan, add the spaghetti immediately it is cooked and drained, mix quickly then add the lardons and the cream mixture. Fork in carefully to mix and heat slightly to thicken but do not allow to boil.
5	Parmesan, grated	75g	Place the spaghetti in earthenware dishes accompanied with the cheese.

SPECIAL POINT

Usually there is enough heat in the spaghetti to thicken the sauce if used immediately it is cooked, although a little extra heat may be necessary to effect this. Any boiling however, would lead to separation of the liaison.

504 Spaghetti Milanaise

Prepare as Spaghetti Italienne (501) and mix with 4dl Sauce Tomate (118) and 350g of cooked Tomates Concassées (91). Finally mix in very gently 50g julienne of ham, 50g julienne of cooked ox-tongue and 50g julienne of mushrooms cooked à Blanc (60). Serve accompanied with grated Parmesan.

505 Spaghetti Monégasque

Prepare as Spaghetti Italienne (501) and mix with ½ litre of Sauce Monégasque (500). Serve accompanied with grated Parmesan.

506 Spaghetti Napolitaine

Prepare as Spaghetti Italienne (501) and mix with 4dl Sauce Tomate (118) and 350g cooked Tomates Concassées (91). Serve accompanied with grated Parmesan.

507 Spaghetti Niçoise

Prepare as Spaghetti Italienne (501) and either mix with 5dl of Sauce Niçoise (499) or dish up the spaghetti and place the sauce in the centre of the spaghetti. Serve accompanied with grated Parmesan.

508 Spaghetti Sicilienne

10 portions
30 mins.

Stage	Ingredient	Quantity	Method
1	butter chicken liver, cleaned	50g 350g	Cut the chicken livers carefully into very small dice. Season well with salt and milled pepper and shallow fry quickly in the butter. Drain.
2	spaghetti	600g	Place into a pan of boiling salted water and allow to simmer gently for 12–15 mins. stirring occasionally.
3	butter Parmesan, grated cream, double	100g 75g 3dl	Heat the butter in a shallow pan, drain the spaghetti as soon as cooked and add to the pan with the Parmesan and cream. Season as necessary, mix carefully together and finish by forking in the prepared livers. Serve accompanied with extra grated Parmesan.

509 NOUILLES – NOODLES – TAGLIATELLI

Commercially produced varieties and qualities of this type of pasta are readily available but there is something to be said for producing them on the premises. If well-made with care they can usually be of better quality and here the easy control of the ingredients used can be of major importance.

Noodle paste is best made from a good-quality general purpose flour having a good average gluten content. Important points to bear in mind when preparing the paste are:
a) The initial kneading should be thorough and for sufficient time to develop a soft silky texture.
b) It should be left covered in a cool place for at least 45 mins. before using.
c) The paste should be rolled very thinly – for ravioli as thin as possible.
d) Use very fine milled semolina, hard flour or rice flour for rolling out.
e) Except for ravioli allow the rolled paste to dry for 30 mins. before cutting.

f) Allow the prepared pasta of whichever sort, to dry for a further 30 mins. or so before cooking.

g) Noodles can be completely dried and stored very successfully for some time if kept in a covered container in a dry cool place.

The rolled paste can be cut into strips of varying widths and can be used also for ravioli and other stuffed pasta. The paste can also be coloured and flavoured by the addition of tomato or spinach or extra egg yolks, and can also be made with wholemeal flour.

---

510 Pâte à Nouilles – Noodle Paste

850g
1 hour

Stage	Ingredient	Quantity	Method
1	flour, plain	500g	Sift the flour and salt and make a bay. Whisk the eggs, egg yolks and oil and water together and pour into the centre of the flour. Using the fingers, mix the flour with the egg mixture to form a dough. Knead well with both hands until firm and very smooth and silky to the touch. Cover with a damp cloth and rest it for 45 mins. in a cool place before using.
	salt	10g	
	eggs	5	
	egg yolks	3	
	olive oil	1 tbsp	
	water	2 tbsps	

---

511 Nouilles au Beurre – Noodles with Butter

10 portions
1½ hours

Stage	Ingredient	Quantity	Method
1	Pâte à Nouilles (510)	850g	Dusting with strong flour, roll out the paste thinly to a rectangle, approx. 80cm × 40cm and not more than 2mm thick. Allow to dry for 30 mins. Fold over into six thicknesses from the long side and cut into strips ½cm wide. Spread out well on a tray dusted with fine semolina or ground rice and leave to dry for at least 30 mins.
2			Place the noodles into a pan of boiling salted water and allow to simmer for 10–12 mins. stirring the noodles occasionally with a wooden spoon. Drain.
3	butter	100g	Melt in a sauteuse, add the noodles, season with salt and milled pepper and toss over to mix.
4	Parmesan, grated	100g	Place the noodles in earthenware dishes. Serve the grated Parmesan as an accompaniment.

SPECIAL POINT
Noodles may be prepared and served as in any of the recipes for spaghetti.

---

512 Green Noodle Paste

Add 250g very fine and dry purée of very green boiled spinach to the flour and eggs at Stage 1 of Noodle Paste (510). Use 1 egg less.

---

513 Tomato Noodle Paste

Add 150g double concentrated tomato purée to the flour and eggs at at Stage 1 of Noodle Paste (510). Use 1 egg less.

---

514 Yellow Noodle Paste

Use 2 whole eggs and 10 egg yolks instead of the eggs at Stage 1 of Noodle Paste (510).

---

515 Wholemeal Noodle Paste

Use 350g wholemeal flour and 150g strong white flour instead of the flour at Stage 1 of Noodle Paste (510).

---

516 Lasagnes

Lasagnes are made from noodle paste (510). Roll out the paste into a rectangle not more than 2mm thick and cut into pieces approx. 8cm × 3cm. Cook and serve in accordance with any of the recipes for spaghetti.

When serving lasagnes with a sauce such as Bolognaise, Monégasque or Niçoise, cook the lasagnes in boiling salted water, drain and toss in butter. Lay them flat in earthenware dishes with interposed layers of sauce finishing with sauce on top. Sprinkle with grated Parmesan and melted butter and gratinate in the top of a hot oven.

---

517 STUFFED PASTAS

These are made from noodle paste in various shapes and sizes, commonly as 2½–3cm squares or smaller; they consist of a top and bottom of paste enclosing a prepared mixture and are known as Ravioli. They can also be made as small round shapes, half-circles or moons, and small oblongs twisted at each end as bows. Tortellini or Cappelletti are other varieties where small half-circles of stuffed paste are twisted round the finger, the ends joined and the edge folded over to give the shape of a cap. Cannelloni are made from thin squares of noodle paste, cooked, refreshed, drained then rolled round a stuffing mixture.

---

518 Ravioli au Jus

10 portions
2½ hours

Stage	Ingredient	Quantity	Method
1	butter	75g	Melt the butter in a sauteuse, add the
	onions, chopped	100g	onion and garlic and cook without
	garlic	2 cloves	colour.

2	beef, stewing	200g	Cut into 1cm cubes and add to the onions and garlic. Season and cook until lightly coloured.
3	Demi-glace (112) leaf spinach, cooked bayleaf thyme	½ litre 100g 1 sprig	Add, cover with a lid and cook gently until the meat is tender and the sauce well-reduced and thick. (approx. 1 hour). Discard the herbs.
4			Pass the mixture through the fine plate of a mincer. Adjust the seasoning and allow to cool.
5	Pâte à Nouilles (510)	850g	Dusting with a strong flour, roll out thinly to a rectangle approx. 80cm × 40cm and not more than 2mm thick. Cut into even-sized halves and egg-wash one. Place the filling into a piping bag with a 1cm plain piping tube. Pipe small amounts the size of a hazelnut onto the eggwashed half at 3cm intervals. Carefully cover with the other half of the paste. Press the two pieces of paste together between the filling, starting at the centre and avoiding any pockets of air. Cut in between each line of filling, down and across using a serrated pastry wheel. Spread out well on a tray dusted with fine semolina or ground rice and leave to dry for 30 mins.
6			Place the ravioli into a pan of boiling salted water and poach gently for 12–15 mins. stirring them occasionally to prevent sticking together. Drain.
7	butter	100g	Melt in a sauteuse, add the ravioli, season with salt and milled pepper and toss over gently to mix.
8	Jus lié (113)	½ litre	Cover the bottom of earthenware dishes with a little jus lié and add the ravioli. Barely cover with the remainder of the sauce.
9	butter, melted Parmesan, grated	75g 60g	Sprinkle with the Parmesan cheese and melted butter and lightly gratinate under the salamander.

SPECIAL POINT
Braised beef or veal may be used in preparing the filling.

519 Various Stuffings for Ravioli, Cannelloni, etc.

1) Mix 350g of flaked cooked fish, 80g of grated Parmesan cheese and 3 raw eggs to a paste, seasoning well with salt, pepper and nutmeg.
2) Mix together 250g of Ricotta cheese, 25g of softened butter and 1 egg yolk then add and mix in 50g of grated Parmesan and 1 tablespoon finely chopped parsley.
3) Mix together 300g of finely chopped cooked spinach, 50g of butter and 50g of grated Parmesan. Season with salt, pepper and nutmeg and bind with 1–2 yolks of egg.
4) Cook 350g of finely chopped spinach in 50g of hot butter, then mix in 250g of grated Cheddar cheese and 2 eggs. Season well and finish with 30g of grated Parmesan.

---

520 Cannelloni au Jus

10 portions
1½ hours

Stage	Ingredient	Quantity	Method
1	Pâte à Nouilles (510)	850g	Dusting with strong flour, roll out into a square 2mm thick, then cut into squares approx. 8cm × 8cm. Allow to dry on a tray dusted with fine semolina or ground rice for approx. 30 mins.
2			Place into a pan of boiling salted water and allow to simmer for approx. 10–12 mins., moving them occasionally to prevent sticking. Refresh under cold running water, drain and lay out singly on a slightly damp cloth.
3	ravioli filling (518), stages 1–4	500g	Place into a piping bag with a 1cm plain tube and pipe out along one side of the squares of paste, roll up.
4	Jus lié (113)	½ litre	Cover the bottom of earthenware dishes with a little jus lié and arrange the cannelloni neatly on top. Barely cover with the remainder of the jus lié.
5	Parmesan, grated butter, melted	60g 75g	Sprinkle with the Parmesan and melted butter and gratinate in a moderate oven for 10–15 mins.

521 RIZ – RICE

Rice is a versatile commodity which can be used in every course of the menu from the hors-d'œuvre to the sweet. As a savoury dish though, its main uses are equally divided between garnishing and as a subsidiary dish in the same place on the menu as the pastas. However, if garnished well and with imagination it can serve as a main dish. A good example of this is the Spanish Paella.

The main varieties of rice used in catering are:

1) The short-grain, frequently called Carolina, which swells and softens considerably in cooking. It is often called pudding rice.

2) Long-grain rices. The most famous for quality is the Basmati rice, which has a distinctive smell and flavour and is naturally ideal for Indian dishes. This long-grain rice and other varieties are excellent for Riz Pilaff and can be successful also for Risotto.

3) The Italian rices such as Arborio, Piedmont, Vallone and Avorio which are good-quality medium- to large-grain round rices are ideal for the making of Risotto. They have the very desirable quality for this dish of not easily breaking up with prolonged cooking.

4) Pre-fluffed rice which is a long-grain rice parsteamed to remove some of the starch. It is easy to use as a boiled rice as the grains separate very easily. It lacks however the taste of untreated rice.

Portion weights
As a guide allow 30g raw weight of rice as a garnish, 45g as a subsidiary dish or 60g as a main dish.

522 Riz Pilaff (as a garnish)

10 portions
30 mins.

Stage	Ingredient	Quantity	Method
1	butter onions, finely chopped rice, long-grain	75g 75g 300g	Melt the butter in a sauteuse. Add the onion and cook without colouring. Add the picked rice and fry gently, stirring occasionally until the rice takes on a golden colour.
2	Fonds Blanc de Volaille (96) bayleaf garlic	 7dl ½ 1 clove	Add the boiling stock. Season and add the bayleaf and crushed garlic. Bring to the boil, cover with a buttered grease-proof paper and lid and cook in the oven at 190°C for 18-20 mins.
3	butter	50g	Remove the bayleaf and garlic and turn out the rice onto a tray so as to prevent further cooking. Lightly fork in the butter, correct the seasoning, return to the pan and serve as required.

SPECIAL POINT
It is good practice to measure the rice by volume and to use a scant 2 parts of stock to 1 part of rice.

523 Riz Créole

Riz Pilaff (522) with the addition of 150g of sliced mushrooms sautéed in butter, 50g of dice of cooked red pimento, and 100g of Tomates Concassées (90).

524 Riz à la Grecque

Riz Pilaff (522) with the addition of 100g of grilled pork chipolatas cut into 1cm sections, 75g of cooked peas and 50g of cooked red pimento cut in small dice.

525 Riz Egyptienne

Riz Pilaff (522) with the addition of 100g of small dice of chicken's liver seasoned, sautéed quickly in butter and drained; 150g of small dice of mushrooms seasoned and sautéed in butter, and 50g of small dice of lean ham.

526 Riz à la Turque

Riz Pilaff Safrané (527) with the addition of 125g of Tomates Concassées (90).

527 Riz Pilaff Safrané

Riz Pilaff (522) with sufficient saffron added at Stage 2 to give a golden yellow colour.

528 Riz Valenciennes

Riz Pilaff (522) with the addition of 50g dice of lean ham, 75g dice of cooked red pimento (79), 50g Tomates Concassées (90) and 50g cooked peas.

529 Risotto

10 portions
40 mins.

Stage	Ingredient	Quantity	Method
1	butter onion, finely chopped rice, Italian	100g 100g 600g	Melt the butter in a small pan, add the onion and cook without colouring. Add the picked rice and fry gently stirring occasionally until the rice takes on a golden colour.
2	Fonds Blanc de Volaille (96)	2 litres	Add the boiling stock. Season with salt and pepper and bring to the boil. Cover and cook gently at the side of the stove stirring occasionally with a wooden spoon until the rice is soft and all the stock has been absorbed.
3	Parmesan, grated	100g	Add half to the rice, fork in and adjust the seasoning. Serve the remainder of the cheese as an accompaniment.

SPECIAL POINT
It is good practice to measure the rice by volume and to use 3 parts of stock to 1 part of rice.

530 Risotto Milanaise

Prepare a Risotto (529) with sufficient saffron added at Stage 2 to give a golden yellow colour. Add 50g julienne of ham, 50g julienne of cooked ox-tongue and 50g julienne of mushrooms cooked à Blanc (60). Serve a sauceboat of Sauce Tomate (118) and grated Parmesan as accompaniments.

SPECIAL POINT
This is a popular version well-suited to being served as a main dish. It should not be used to garnish any dish of ham or tongue.

531 Risotto alla Milanese

10 portions
40 mins.

Stage	Ingredient	Quantity	Method
1	butter	50g	Heat the butter and bone marrow in a
	bone marrow, cut in		small deep pan, add the onion and cook
	small dice	50g	without colour. Add the picked rice and
	onion, finely chopped	100g	fry gently, stirring frequently until the
	rice, Italian	600g	rice takes on a golden colour.
2	saffron powder or		Steep the saffron for a few minutes with
	threads	pinch	a little of the hot stock. If using threads,
	Fonds Blanc de		carefully cut finely before steeping. Add
	Volaille (96)	2 litres	one-third of the boiling stock and the
			saffron and its liquid. Season, cover and
			cook gently over a very low heat. Add
			the rest of the stock in two more lots as
			each amount is absorbed and stirring
			gently when being added. Cover each
			time but do not stir while cooking. The
			stock should finally be almost completely
			absorbed but still leave the rice moist
			and creamy.
3	butter	50g	Carefully fork in the butter and half the
	Parmesan, grated	100g	Parmesan and adjust the seasoning at the
			same time. Send the remainder of the
			Parmesan in a sauceboat.

SPECIAL POINT
The above recipe is the more authentic version and should always be the one to
accompany Ossi Buchi alla Milanese.

532 Risotto Piémontaise

Prepare Risotto (529) with sufficient saffron added at Stage 2 to give a golden yellow
colour. When dished up sprinkle with very fine shavings of white truffle. Serve
accompanied with grated Parmesan.

533 Paella

4 portions
1 hour

Stage	Ingredient	Quantity	Method
1	olive oil	½dl	Cut the pork into 1cm cubes. Heat the
	salt belly of		oil in a 'Paellera' if available or a heavy
	pork	200g	wide shallow pan and fry the pork until
	chicken, cut for		brown. Remove from the pan. Season
	sauté (1014)	4 portions	the chicken and fry in the same fat until
			coloured on all sides; remove and place
			on one side with the pork.

2	red pimento, skinned and cut in short julienne	1	Add to the remaining fat and cook for a few minutes until soft.
	garlic, finely chopped	1 clove	
3	rice, Valencia or Piedmont	250g	Add to the pan and stir in for a few minutes to coat with the fat and become transparent.
4	Fonds Blanc de Volaille (96)	7½dl	Have the saffron previously soaked in a little of the hot stock then add together with the remaining stock and other ingredients. Season with salt and pepper and bring to the boil. Allow to simmer for approx. 10 mins.
	saffron	pinch	
	Tomates Concassées (90)	150g	
	bayleaf	1	
5	prawns, raw	100g	Add to the pan together with the reserved pork and chicken and cook for another 10–15 mins. or so until all is cooked and most of the moisture has evaporated. Remove one shell from each mussel then serve the Paella as it is and from the pan it was cooked in.
	mussels, raw	20	
	peas	60g	

SPECIAL POINTS
a) A Paellera is a shallow heavy pan made of wrought or enamelled iron or stainless steel, with a handle on each side.
b) There are many regional variations of Paella which include the use of slices of Chorizo sausage, lobster, chipolatas, rabbit, squid, artichokes and so on.

---

534 Riz Poché – Boiled Rice (as a garnish)

10 portions
30 mins.

Pick and wash 300g of long-grain rice. Place into a deep pan containing at least 5 litres of boiling salted water and poach gently for approx. 15 mins. stirring occasionally to prevent sticking together. The rice should be tender but still firm. Refresh under running cold water and reheat again under hot water. Drain well, place on a clean cloth on a sieve or colander and dry out in a hot-cupboard or in a cool oven. When finished, each grain of rice should be separate and fluffy. When served with curry this is known as Riz à l'Indienne.

---

535 Poach-steamed Rice (as a garnish)

10 portions
45 mins.

Stage	Ingredient	Quantity	Method
1	rice, long-grain	300g	Wash the rice in 3–4 changes of cold water. Drain, place in a deep heavy pan, add the water and salt and leave to soak for 20 mins.
	water	4dl	
	salt	10g	

2   Bring to the boil, cover with a tight-fitting lid and allow to cook on a very low heat for 15 mins.

3   Remove from the heat completely, leave for another 10 mins. then fork through carefully to separate the grains.

10
Fish

Fish is a commodity of major importance to the food and catering industries as well as being an important contributor to the well-balanced diet. A well-organised sea fishing industry lands its catch in prime condition, either fresh, frozen or in chilled form, and distribution in these days of modern transport is easy and rapid; air transport has even made it possible for quality fish from many parts of the globe to be made available in fresh form; fish like dorado, snapper, grouper and swordfish have attained some sort of exotic popularity and other species once thought unsuitable are now accepted. The proportion of freshwater fish landed and consumed is not so large but the extensive farming of salmon and trout is making a marked impact on the total availability of fish.

In general, fish, especially white fish, can be considered as a delicate commodity requiring expertise and great care in its preparation. The wide range and variety of fish and their garnishes and sauces form a considerable part of the culinary repertoire and possible further combinations and preparations seem to be limitless. But what is essential in fish cookery is the marrying of subtlety and elegance to lightness and delicacy at all stages of preparation. Garnishing must always be neat and compatible and, above all, sauces need to enhance and not overwhelm the natural flavour and quality of the fish. Oily fish like herrings, salmon and trout can withstand in some cases a more robust treatment but even then delicacy and subtlety are still prime requirements.

The modern antipathy to the use of flour-based sauces has a bearing on the preparation of fish dishes inasmuch as fish velouté has traditionally always played an important part in the making of fish sauces. It is possible, by making reductions of cooking liquids and then thickening with butter, cream or liaisons, to dispense altogether with fish velouté. But when correctly made with due care and attention, a fish velouté can still make a useful contribution to the finishing of fish sauces, especially where large numbers or banquets are concerned and where a stable consistency which can be maintained for a period of time is required.

The rightful place of fish on the menu is as a subordinate course directly before and in contrast to the meat course which is usually more robust. However, fish is used in other sections of the menu, most noticeably as an hors-d'oeuvre, for the garnishing of egg and farinaceous dishes, and for salads and savouries. It is also frequently served as a main dish and in almost all cases it is equally suitable for lunch or dinner.

CLASSIFICATION

Fish have certain characteristics which lend themselves to particular methods of cooking and they are usually classified for culinary purposes as round or flat fish. These two broad classifications are further subdivided into white and oily fish.

The following are the fish in general use:

Round: a) White: bass, bream, cod, haddock, hake, huss, whiting, croaker, emperor, snapper.

b) Oily: eel, grayling, herring, mackerel, red mullet, salmon, salmon trout, sardine, trout, whitebait.

Flat: a) White: brill, Dover sole, halibut, John Dory, lemon sole, plaice, turbot.

b) Oily: skate.

Alligator and Crocodile

Appendix 1 lists the popular fish found in Australia and New Zealand.

Alligator

White meat similar to veal with a flavour of shellfish, usually marinated before cooking by braising, grilling and stewing.

Crocodile

Light coloured flesh of delicate flavour similar to monkfish, the best part is the tail. A freshwater creature, it can be cooked as for alligator.

─────────QUALITY POINTS─────────

Absolute freshness is the first and overriding quality to be sought after in fresh fish. This freshness can be determined by careful attention to the following points:

1) All fish should have a clean pleasant smell – no hint of ammonia or any offensive odour.
2) The fish should be plump with no signs of emaciation.
3) The fish should be firm and just moist – no signs of stickiness if in fillet form.
4) Whole fish should have a slight slimy coating to the skin with the scales moist and shiny.
5) Whole fish – the eyes should be bright and full, not sunken and dull.
6) The gills should have a bright pink to red colour, be moist and full and with no signs of being shrunken or dry.

In general, fresh fish give better results both in terms of quality and eating. However, frozen fish, when properly processed, frozen immediately after catching, defrosted properly and prepared correctly, can be a useful substitute when the fresh item is not available.

Frozen fish deteriorates after prolonged storage and should be checked for signs of this. There should be no evidence of dehydration or freezer-burn. If in blocks of fillets, patchy yellowing or discolouration is a sign of overlong or improper storage. All frozen fish whether whole, in fillets, steaks or blocks, should be evenly coated with a thin layer of clean-looking, frosted ice.

─────────STORAGE─────────

Fresh fish should be used on the day of delivery where possible but if this is not always practical then it should be washed well and stored in a refrigerator designed for the storage of fish only. The temperature should be maintained at just above freezing-point, 1–2°C, and the fish should ideally be covered with crushed ice to prevent any surfaces from drying. The fish should subsequently be used as soon as possible.

Frozen fish need to be stored at a temperature of not higher than −18°C, and used in rotation.

Any tanks for live freshwater or salt-water fish should be cleaned regularly and suitably sterilised to prevent the build-up of harmful conditions. Freshwater tanks should have an efficient running water system and salt-water tanks, if any, should have an efficient air supply for oxygenisation.

Any live fish delivered should be transferred to a tank immediately on arrival to prevent distress and subsequent spoilage.

536 CLEANING AND PREPARATION

There are several steps to the correct cleaning and preparation of fish for cooking which should follow a logical sequence as suggested in the following notes:

1) Washing

Before trimming or cutting it is advisable to wash all fish under cold running water to remove any coating of the slime which is found on fresh fish. This makes it easier to handle. Fish should subsequently be washed at all stages of preparation and cutting and particularly at the last when ready prepared for cooking.

2) Scaling

Place the fish flat on the work surface, hold the fish by its tail and scrape towards the head using a knife held at an angle of about 15°. Be careful not to make the scales fly. Finally, wash the fish and equipment thoroughly to remove any loose scales – if allowed to dry they become difficult to remove.

3) Trimming

This means dealing with the gills, fins, eyes and head of fish as necessary.

Gills: Lift up the gill flaps and cut out the gills completely from both sides using fish scissors or a small sharp knife as necessary. The gills of some small fish like herrings can be detached more easily with the fingers.

Fins: Remove all fins with fish scissors. Trim the tail straight across but not too near the actual body of the fish. Alternatively, for flat fish lay the fish flat with the tail outwards, draw the point of a knife backwards from tail to head to make the fins stand out from the body then cut carefully along the lines where the fins join the body. The pectoral fins will still have to be trimmed with scissors.

Eyes: Where felt necessary these are best removed with the point of a small knife.

Head: If the head needs to be removed for round fish, cut in at an angle from each side of the fish just behind the pectoral fins and as near as possible to where the bony skeleton of the head begins. For flat fish such as sole, cut at an angle from as near to the head as possible and from behind the pectoral fin and abdominal flap. If desired, the snout of the head can be trimmed off flat from just behind the eyes.

4) Gutting

Many fish such as cod, haddock, sole, plaice and whiting etc. are landed already opened and gutted but not necessarily as cleanly as desired. Where this has been done remove any roes as necessary, scrape out any congealed blood from under the spinal vertebrae and wash carefully to remove any traces of dark membrane from the inner surface of the abdominal cavity. Round fish, however, such as herrings, mackerel, salmon and trout, are often delivered as they are and require gutting. To do this make sure that the gills and fins are first removed, then make a small cut from the anal vent along the belly of the fish. The gut can then be pulled out with the fingers or if needed with the handle of a spoon for small fish or the hooked handle of a small ladle for large fish. After the guts have been removed make sure that the blood tract lying directly under the vertebrae is scraped away with the spoon or ladle handle.

5) Filleting

This is the careful and neat removal of the flesh of the fish from its bony skeleton. Correctly removed fillets are judged by being smoothly cut without ridges and with no flesh to speak of remaining on the bones. With Dover sole it is usual to first remove the skin from both sides. Round fish yield two fillets and flat fish four fillets. *Round fish:* Remove the head, scales and fins, gut if needed and wash. Place the fish on its side with the head end pointing away and its back to the right. Using the knife flat cut along the fish just on top of the backbone and continue cutting through and following the bones to detach the fillet. Turn the fish over and remove the other fillet. *Flat fish:* Note: for large flat fish such as brill, halibut and turbot it is better to remove the head first, cutting as near to the head bones as possible.

Lay the fish flat, then cut down along the length of the fish from head to tail following the natural central line. Turn the blade of the knife almost flat then cut from the centre to the left just on top of the bone as a guide – cut with smooth sweeping strokes rather than jerky short strokes and lift the fillet back as the cutting proceeds. When the fillet is detached, face the fish the other way and detach the second fillet, then turn the fish over and repeat the operation for the other two fillets.

6) Skinning

It is usual to remove the skin from most fillets of fish where this is practical and can be done without harming the flesh. The skin is also removed from whole flat fish but in most cases it is only the black skin which is removed. But there are exceptions which are noted in the recipes of this chapter.

Fillets: Place the fillet skin-side down on the work surface, hold at the tail and then cut down through the flesh at the tail and to the skin. Turn the knife down to an angle of about 45° then cut and push forwards with the knife, at the same time keeping the skin fairly taut. Be careful not to cut through the skin. Trim carefully as required.

Dover Sole: Place the sole, black skin up on the work surface, cut across the centre of the tail to the bone; then scrape back towards the head so as to raise some of the skin. Grip this with one hand and pull upwards and towards the head using a cloth if necessary to give a better grip. At the same time it may be useful to ease the skin away from the side edges with the thumbs to prevent tearing the skin and leaving it behind. Usually the white skin is only removed if the sole is to be filleted.

Lemon Sole, Flounder, Dab, etc.: Medium to small fish of these types can be cooked whole on the bone but need to have the dark skin and the head removed first. These can be removed in one operation as follows:

Place the fish dark skin down on the work surface; cut straight through and diagonally behind the head and pectoral fin, down to the dark skin but not through it. Turn the fish over, bend the head back then insert a knife between the dark skin and flesh and detach the skin along the length of the cut. Insert the thumb and loosen the skin sufficiently, then hold the head firmly in a cloth and peel back the skin. Use the thumb or the knife to ease the skin back if it begins to tear the flesh. Remove the scales if any from the white skin and wash.

Whiting: Remove the gills, fins and eyes and trim the tail. Carefully clean the inside of the abdominal cavity. Cut just through the skin only on each side of the head and behind the gill flap then along the back from head to tail. Loosen the skin at the head carefully then pull the skin back from head to tail and from both sides.

Eel: These are usually bought live or kept live in a tank and used as required. To kill, insert a sharp pointed knife or skewer into and between the vertebrae just behind the head. Hold the head with a cloth and cut just through the skin right round the head. Cut open along the length of the belly then turn back the skin for an inch or so from the head. Hold the skin firmly – a little salt or a cloth will help to stop slipping – and pull steadily to strip off the entire skin from head to tail. Clean out the gut and wash quickly.

7) Scoring – Ciseler.
This is the cutting of shallow incisions in the thicker part of whole fish, particularly round fish, to facilitate evenness of cooking. It is especially useful in the case of grilling and shallow frying. The cuts should be slightly slanting towards the head and slightly diagonal in direction towards the tail and at the broadest and thickest part of the fish.

The number of cuts and the depth of each cut should be in accordance with the size of the fish and should diminish in depth and length towards the tail. In any case they should never be so deep as to open too wide and deform the shape and look of the fish when cooking. As a guide 4–5 cuts on each side of a 200g herring or trout is sufficient.

537 CUTS AND SPECIAL PREPARATIONS
The following are particular named preparations of fish or fillets of fish which are used in the designation of fish dishes:

1) Filet
This refers to the flesh of the fish removed completely from the skeletal structure in long flat pieces. Flat fish yield four fillets and round fish two fillets. Fillets from smaller flat fish such as Dover sole can be left a) whole in the length for frying, shallow frying, grilling and poaching, b) folded in half with the wider head end uppermost, for poaching, and c) folded in three with the two ends folded under.

NOTES
a) Fillets of lemon sole, plaice or whiting are best if folded for poaching. If poached in the whole length they tend to break very easily when being dished up and served.
b) For large services or banquets, folded fillets of any poached fish are much easier to serve at the table than long fillets; they can be accommodated in smaller dishes, and they tend to present better.

2) Délice
This is really just a fanciful name, synonymous with Filet, although the term is frequently used to denote a fillet folded in three.

3) Paupiette
This is a small fillet of flat fish such as sole, usually spread with fish farce (40) on the skinned side and rolled up from tail end to head and poached. The compact shape of paupiettes can be retained during cooking by packing them close together or tying round carefully with a strip of buttered greaseproof.

4) Suprême
This is a section of fish cut across and on the slant from the fillet of a large round or flat fish such as salmon, cod, turbot or brill. Suitable for poaching, shallow and deep frying and grilling.

5) **Médaillon**
   This is cut in the same way as a suprême, but a little more on the slant and then trimmed carefully to a neat oval or round shape. The trimmings can be used in the preparation of fish farce.

6) **Goujons and Goujonettes**
   Goujons are fillets of fish, usually sole, cut into strips diagonally across the fillet, approx. 8cm × 1cm. Goujonettes are a smaller version cut approx. 6cm × ½cm. Suitable for deep or shallow frying.

7) **Darne**
   This is a section of fish cut across and through the bone of a large whole round fish such as cod or salmon, approx. 2–3cm thick. It can also denote a large middle-cut of a proportionate size for a given number of persons. Suitable for grilling and poaching.

8) **Tronçon**
   This is a section of fish cut on the bone from a large flat fish such as turbot, brill or halibut. The fins and head are first removed from the fish, it is then split down the centre bone from the tail end and each side is then cut across into sections approx. 4–5cm wide. The term is sometimes applied to small fish when cut into sections for fish stews or hors-d'oeuvre. Suitable for grilling and poaching.

9) **Colbert preparation**
   This method of preparation can be applied to small round fish or flat fish, usually Dover sole.

   Round fish:
   a) Scale the fish, remove the fins, gills and eyes and trim the tail. Wash carefully and dry.
   b) Cut down along both sides of the backbone from just before the head to within 3 cm of the tail and remove the backbone without splitting the fish in half then open it out flat.
   c) This preparation is usually egg-and-breadcrumbed for deep frying but may be dipped in melted butter, breadcrumbed and grilled under the salamander.

   Dover sole:
   a) Remove the black skin, trim the fins and tail and scale the white skin. Remove any roes, clean the abdominal cavity and scrape out the blood tract under the spine. Wash well and dry.
   b) Cut down along the backbone of the skinned side from 1–2cm below the head to 1–2cm before the tail.
   c) Partially detach the fillets and fold each back to the edge of the fish so as to form an open pocket.
   d) Nick through the backbone in three places, near the head, near the tail and in the centre, without cutting into the flesh underneath. This allows the bone to be removed when cooked.
   e) This preparation is invariably egg-and-breadcrumbed then deep-fried.

10) **'en Colère' preparation**
This is invariably a preparation of whiting. Remove the fins, gills and eyes and clean out the abdominal cavity. Skin carefully then wash and dry. Curl the tail round and place between the teeth, fixing in place if necessary with a cocktail stick. The fish is then seasoned, egg-and-breadcrumbed and deep-fried.

PREPARATION LOSSES

The following percentages of weight loss in the preparation of whole fish for cooking are only approximate and will tend to vary a little according to the species of fish being handled.

Round fish: For serving whole there is a 5% weight loss entailed in gutting and trimming, with a further 10% if the head is removed. If filleted the total weight loss can be 40–45%.

Flat fish: For serving whole there can be a weight loss of 3–5% entailed in trimming, with a further 10% if the head is removed. If filleted the total weight loss can be as high as 45–50%, represented by fins, skin, the complete head and skeleton and the final trimming of the fillets.

COURTS-BOUILLONS

There are a number of prepared cooking liquors which have their own special qualities suitable for particular types of fish. The following are those in more general use.

538 Vinegar Court-bouillon
5 litres

Suitable for salmon, salmon trout, trout and shellfish.

Stage	Ingredient	Quantity	Method
1	water	5 litres	Place the ingredients in a pan, bring to the boil and simmer gently for 25 mins.
	vinegar	3dl	
	carrots } sliced	350g	
	onions }	250g	
	thyme	sprig	
	bayleaf	2	
	parsley stalks	15g	
	salt	50g	
	peppercorns	12	
2			Pass through a fine strainer and use as needed.

539 White Wine Court-bouillon
5 litres

Suitable for freshwater fish and oily fish.

Stage	Ingredient	Quantity	Method
1	white wine, dry	1½ litres	Place all the ingredients in a pan, bring
	water	3½ litres	to the boil and simmer gently for 25
	juice of lemon	3	mins.
	onions, sliced	350g	
	thyme	sprig	
	bayleaf	2	
	parsley stalks	15g	
	salt	50g	
	peppercorns	12	
2			Pass through a fine strainer and use as required.

540 Court-bouillon for White Fish

The following proportions are suitable for the poaching of whole and cuts of white fish. For 5 litres of water add the juice of 3 lemons and 50g salt.

─────────── COOKING METHODS ───────────

In general all the standard methods of cookery may be applied to all fish although with a few exceptions oily fish are not really suitable for deep frying.

Boiling/Poaching
Whole fish should be cooked by placing in cold liquid, bringing to the boil and barely simmering till cooked. Cuts of fish should be placed in simmering liquid; this prevents the juices from escaping and coagulating into a white coating on the cut surfaces. After reboiling and skimming, the liquid should barely move; a temperature of 90–95°C is sufficient. It is inadvisable to boil fish rapidly as this damages the texture and shape of the flesh. Thus the principle involved more closely approximates true poaching. In fact, the French term for boiling, 'bouillir', is seldom used in conjunction with fish; 'pocher' is the most widely used term, e.g. Darne de Saumon pochée. Fish may be poached in deep or shallow liquid. After deep poaching it is usual to serve the fish with lemon, plain boiled potatoes, picked parsley and a suitable sauce. Fish is shallow poached when it is to be covered with a sauce. It should be barely covered with a liquid and cooked in a moderate oven. The cooking liquid is invariably utilised for finishing the coating sauce.

Steaming
Small whole fish and fillets as well as small cuts, on or off the bone, can be cooked successfully by steaming. It can be carried out in a low-pressure steaming oven in bulk, at high pressure which makes it possible to cook with garnishes, or individually in a covered container set over a simmering liquid such as water or fish stock which can be flavoured and perfumed with herbs as seen fit.

For steaming large numbers of small cuts of white fish, place in a buttered tray, season lightly, sprinkle with a little lemon juice and cover with a buttered paper. Steam until just cooked through. There will be a small amount of cooking liquid available for the preparation of any accompanying sauce.

Braising
Whole turbot and brill as well as round oily fish such as salmon, sturgeon and tunny can be braised very successfully. The usual method is to place the fish in a covered buttered braising pan either directly onto a bed of herbs and aromats, or on a perforated tray over them, and to use various wines and fumets as the braising liquid. Very slow oven cooking with frequent basting is an essential part of the process.

Baking
Round white fish may be stuffed with forcemeat or stuffing and baked in the oven, using butter. Whole flat fish such as sole may be baked by the 'au Gratin' method. See Sole au Gratin (592).

Grilling
Whole small fish and most cuts and types of fish are suitable for grilling. They need to be seasoned, floured, brushed with oil and cooked over heat on the grill or placed on an oiled tray to be grilled under the salamander. Grilled fish should be garnished with lemon and parsley and accompanied with a suitable sauce or butter.

Stewing
There are a number of national and regional fish stews using a mixture of different fish, of which the best known is Bouillabaisse à la Marseillaise. The usual method is to cook an assortment of fish and shellfish with vegetables, herbs and seasoning in water, fish stock or wine and any thickening takes place naturally from the ingredients.

Shallow Frying
Whole small round and flat fish, tronçons, fillets and suprêmes of larger fish are suitable for shallow frying. The term 'meunière' is used to denote fish cooked by this method. The fish is passed through flour and then shallow-fried in oil or clarified butter. Fish meunière is finished with slices of lemon, lemon juice, brown butter and chopped parsley.

Deep Frying
Whole small round and flat fish, suprêmes, fillets and goujons of fish are suitable for deep frying. Fish must be coated before frying, using one of the following combinations:
a) flour, eggwash and breadcrumbs,
b) milk and flour,
c) flour and batter,
d) flour and beaten egg.
Deep-fried fish should be served garnished with lemon and parsley, and accompanied with a suitable sauce, e.g. Sauce Tartare, Sauce Remoulade.

——————————— PORTION GUIDE ———————————

The following average-portion weights of fish are suitable:
For set menus:
a) small whole fish, e.g. herring, mackerel, trout, slip sole: 200–250g
b) fillets, suprêmes and paupiettes: 90–100g
c) darnes and tronçons: 150–200g
For separately priced items, i.e. for à la Carte menus:
a) whole fish, e.g. trout, sole: 300–350g
b) fillets: 2 × 80g

c) paupiettes: 2 × 80g
d) suprêmes: 2 × 90g or 1 × 175g
e) darnes and tronçons: 250–275g

AIGLEFIN – FRESH HADDOCK

Suprêmes of fresh haddock may be served in the same way as suprêmes of cod and fillets of whiting. The recipes for fillets of sole are also suitable.

ANGUILLE – EEL

541 Matelote d'Anguille à la Bourguignonne

10 portions
1 hour

Stage	Ingredient	Quantity	Method
1	eels, skinned	1kg	Cut the eels into sections 3cm thick.
	butter	100g	Melt the butter in a sauté pan, add the
	shallots, finely		shallots and cook without colour. Add
	chopped	75g	the eels, season, cover and cook gently for 5 mins.
2	red wine	8dl	Add and season lightly with salt and
	Bouquet Garni (19)	1	pepper. Cover, bring to the boil and allow to simmer gently for 15–20 mins. or until tender.
3	butter ⎫ into Beurre	100g	Remove the eel, place in a clean pan,
	flour ⎬ Manié (11)	50g	cover and keep warm. Reduce the cooking liquor by one-third. Whisk in the beurre manié, bring to the boil, adjust the seasoning and pass through a fine strainer over the eels.
4	button onions, glacé à Brun (1493)	30	Add to the eels and simmer together very gently for 2–3 mins.
	button mushrooms, sautéed (61)	250g	
5	Heart-shaped Croûtons (26)	10	Dress the eels in earthenware dishes. Rub the fried croûtons with the cut side
	garlic	1 clove	of a clove of garlic and arrange around
	parsley, chopped		the dishes. Serve sprinkled with chopped parsley.

542 Anguille à la Normande

10 portions
1 hour

Stage	Ingredient	Quantity	Method
1	butter	100g	Heat the butter in a sauté pan, add the
	button onions, peeled	40	onions and mushrooms and cook together for a few mins.
	button mushrooms	40	

2	eel, skinned	1kg	Add the eel cut in 3cm sections. Season with salt and pepper and cover with a lid. Allow to sweat together for 5 mins.
3	cider, dry Bouquet Garni (19)	7½dl 1	Add, season again lightly, bring to the boil, cover with the lid and simmer very gently until the eel is tender approx. 15–20 mins.
4			Discard the bouquet garni, remove the eel, onions and mushrooms to a clean pan, cover and keep warm.
5	cream, double	6dl	Reduce the cooking liquor by two-thirds then add the cream and reduce again until lightly thickened. Adjust the seasoning as necessary together with a touch of cayenne. Pass through a fine strainer over the eels and garnish and heat gently for 2–3 mins.
6	butter Heart-shaped Croûtons (26) parsley, chopped	75g 10	Shake in the butter away from the heat then arrange in suitable dishes. Surround with the croûtons and sprinkle with the parsley.

BAR – SEA BASS

543 Bar au Beurre Blanc

4 portions
1 hour

Stage	Ingredient	Quantity	Method
1	sea bass	1 × 1½kg	Scale, trim the fins and tail and gut the bass – leave the head on. Wash well.
2	White Wine Court- bouillon, cold (539)	4–5 litres	Place the cleaned bass on a perforated rack in a fish kettle and cover with the court-bouillon. Bring to the boil slowly, skim and simmer very gently to poach (90–95°C) for approx. 10–12 mins.
3	shallot, finely chopped white wine, dry white wine, vinegar	 75g 1dl 1dl	Place in a small pan together with 2dl of the strained cooking liquor from the bass and reduce rapidly (by about three-quarters approx.) until slightly viscous. Remove from direct heat.
4	butter, unsalted, softened	200g	Whisk in the butter vigorously little by little but do not allow it to become too hot. Season with salt and pepper as necessary.
5	picked parsley boiled potatoes, small turned	 12–16	Drain the bass and place on a suitable dish or tray and garnish with the parsley. Serve accompanied with the sauce and a dish of the potatoes.

SPECIAL POINT
The bass may be cut diagonally into sections after removing the head but they will need to be placed in simmering court-bouillon, then brought to the boil and poached gently for about 10 mins.

---

544 Bar grillé au Fenouil – Grilled Bass, Fennel Sauce

4 portions
1½ hours

Stage	Ingredient	Quantity	Method
1	sea bass	1 × 1½kg	Scale, trim the fins and tail and carefully gut the bass. Leave the head on. Wash, dry well and cut 5–6 diagonal incisions on each side of the fish at the thickest parts.
2	ground fennel seed		Hold the fish across one hand so that the incisions open and season these with a little of the ground fennel. Repeat on the other side then place the fish in a shallow tray. Sprinkle with the chopped fennel, a little salt and milled black pepper, the oil and the Pernod. Allow to marinate for approx. 1 hour in a cool place, turning over occasionally and basting with the liquid.
	fennel, chopped	50g	
	olive oil	½dl	
	Pernod	3 tbsps	
3			Place the bass between a double fish grill then on the bars of the grill proper. Grill well for 8–10 mins. on both sides, brushing frequently with the marinating liquor.
4	feathery leaves of fennel or picked parsley		When cooked arrange the fish on a suitable dish and garnish with the fennel leaves or parsley. Serve accompanied with the sauce.
	Fennel Sauce (177)	2dl	

BARBUE – BRILL

For whole brill, all the recipes for whole turbot are suitable. For brill which are to be served as fillets and suprêmes, the recipes for fillets of sole are applicable. Tronçons of brill may be poached or grilled in the same way as tronçons of turbot.

BLANCHAILLES – WHITEBAIT

545 Blanchailles Diablées – Devilled Whitebait

10 portions
20 mins.

Stage	Ingredient	Quantity	Method
1	whitebait	1kg	Wash the whitebait well, drain, place in a basin and add the milk.
	milk	2½dl	

2	flour		Take one-third of the whitebait from the milk, drain and pass through the flour. Shake well in a sieve to remove the surplus flour. Place in a frying-basket and plunge into very hot fat. Fry quickly until crisp and golden brown, taking care to shake the basket to prevent the white-bait sticking together.
3			Remove and drain. Fry the rest of the whitebait in the same manner.
4	cayenne lemons parsley picked	2½	Season with salt and cayenne. Dress on a serviette and garnish with fried or picked parsley and quarters of lemon.

SPECIAL POINTS
a) The preparation must be carried out as quickly as possible and once they are floured, the whitebait must be cooked immediately. If left floured even for a little while before cooking, the flour with become sticky and they will be difficult to separate when frying.
b) It is advisable not to cook too many whitebait at a time so as to allow for separation of the fish when frying.

---

546 Blanchailles frites – Fried Whitebait

This is prepared in the same way as Blanchailles Diablées (545), but season with salt only and garnish with quarters of lemon and picked parsley.

BROCHET – PIKE

Small pike can be baked or poached whole or prepared 'en Matelote' in the same manner as for eels (541). Because of its coarse flesh and numerous small bones however, it lends itself more to the preparation of quenelles.

---

547 Quenelles de Brochet au Vin Blanc
10 portions
1½ hours

Stage	Ingredient	Quantity	Method
1	pike flesh (free from skin and bone) beef suet, free of membrane egg whites salt pepper nutmeg, ground	400g 400g 4 15g pinch	Pass the fish and suet through the fine plate of the mincer twice. Place in a basin, add the egg whites, season with the salt, pepper and nutmeg and beat thoroughly with a wooden spatula until stiff and elastic. Pass through a fine sieve, replace the mixture into a basin and chill thoroughly.
2	Frangipane Panada (69)	400g	Add the panada, and beat thoroughly together with a wooden spatule.

3		Butter a deep tray. Mould the mixture into egg-shapes using two tablespoons, and place on the tray. Continue until twenty quenelles are moulded.
4	Fumet de Poisson (101) 1 litre	Season lightly, bring to the boil and pour gently around the quenelles. Cover with buttered paper and poach in a moderate oven 175°C for approx. 10 mins. until cooked and lightly souffléed.
5	Sauce Vin Blanc (174) 6dl Fleurons (33) 10	Drain well and arrange neatly in earthenware dishes. Coat with the sauce and garnish with fleurons.

SPECIAL POINTS

a) Quenelles de Brochet may be served with various fish sauces, e.g. Sauce Vin Rouge, Sauce Homard, Sauce Bercy, or Sauce Cardinal.

b) The use of a food processor can be an advantage in preparing this type of mixture.

CABILLAUD – COD

In addition to the following recipes those for fillets of sole are also suitable for suprêmes of cod.

---

548 Cabillaud Crème au Gratin

10 portions
1 hour

Stage	Ingredient	Quantity	Method
1	cod fillet, skinned Fumet de Poisson (101)	750g 3dl	Wash the fillets and place in a buttered shallow tray. Season, add the fish stock and cover with buttered greaseproof paper. Cook in a moderate oven at 195°C for approx. 12–15 mins.
2	Pommes Duchesse (1560)	1kg	Place in a piping bag with a star tube and decorate the inner sides of earthenware dishes up to the rim.
3	Sauce Mornay (171) Parmesan, grated	7dl 75g	Place a little Sauce Mornay in the bottom of the dishes. Drain and lightly flake the cod and place dome-shaped on the sauce. Coat the cod with sauce and sprinkle with the grated Parmesan. Place under the salamander and gratinate to a golden brown.

SPECIAL POINT

It is a good practice to place the decorated dishes at Stage 2 under the salamander to dry the Pommes Duchesse but not to colour. When the finished dish is placed under the salamander this will help to give an even colour to the potatoes and the sauce.

---

549 Darne de Cabillaud grillée – Grilled Cod Steak 10 portions
30 mins.

Stage	Ingredient	Quantity	Method
1	cod darnes flour oil	10 × 150g 1dl	Wash the darnes well, dry, season and lightly flour. Brush well with the oil.
2			Place on a fish grill and grill on both sides to a good colour. (approx. 10 mins.)
3	butter, melted parsley, picked lemons	50g 2	Dress the darnes neatly on dishes, remove the centre bones and brush the fish with melted butter. Garnish with slices of fluted lemon and picked parsley.

Serve with Beurre Maître d'Hôtel (10), Beurre d'Anchois (4) or Sauce Diable (125).

---

550 Darne de Cabillaud pochée – Poached Cod 10 portions
1 hour

Stage	Ingredient	Quantity	Method
1	water juice of lemon	approx. 6 litres 2	Place the water and lemon juice in a suitably-sized shallow pan. Season with salt and bring to the boil.
2	cod darnes	10 × 150g	Wash well, place into the boiling liquid and reboil. Skim, draw to the side of the stove and allow to poach gently until cooked (approx. 10 mins.).
3	small turned potatoes	20	Place in boiling, salted water and cook until tender.
4	lemons parsley sprigs Sauce Hollandaise (157) or other suitable sauce	2 6dl	Dress the cooked cod neatly in earthenware dishes, remove the centre bones and add a little cooking liquor to cover the bottom of the dish. Garnish with slices of fluted lemon, the potatoes and picked parsley. Serve with an appropriate sauce, e.g. Hollandaise, Homard, Persil, Crème, aux Oeufs.

---

551 Darne de Cabillaud Portugaise 10 portions
1 hour

Stage	Ingredient	Quantity	Method
1	cod darnes	10 × 150g	Wash well and place in a buttered tray.
2	butter onion, finely chopped garlic, very finely chopped	75g 150g 1 clove	Melt the butter in a small pan, add the onion and garlic and cook without colour. Sprinkle over the fish.

3	Tomates Concassées (90)	750g	Sprinkle the tomatoes and parsley over the fish. Add the wine and fish stock and season. Cover with buttered greaseproof paper and cook in a moderate oven 195°C for 15–18 mins.
	parsley, chopped		
	white wine, dry	2dl	
	Fumet de Poisson (101)	2dl	
4	butter	100g	Remove the darnes only, take out the centre bone and place the fish in earthenware dishes. Cover and keep warm. Place the cooking liquor and tomatoes in a pan and slightly reduce. Draw the pan to the side of the stove and add the butter while shaking the pan to form a lightly thickened sauce. Adjust the seasoning.
5	parsley, chopped		Remove the cover from the fish and ladle the sauce over. Sprinkle with chopped parsley.

552 Suprême de Cabillaud au Beurre d'Anchois   10 portions
35 mins.

Stage	Ingredient	Quantity	Method
1	oil	2dl	Heat the oil in a frying-pan. Wash, dry, season and lightly flour the suprêmes, and when the oil is very hot place them in the oil best side downwards, fry to a golden brown on both sides. (approx. 7–8 mins.).
	cod suprêmes	10 × 100g	
	flour		
2			Remove and dress neatly in earthenware dishes, keeping the dishes on the side of the stove.
3	butter, soft	150g	Place the butter in a suitable frying-pan and cook, shaking the pan to ensure even colouring. Just as the butter turns nut-brown in colour add the anchovy essence, shake to mix well and pour quickly over the fish. Sprinkle with chopped parsley.
	anchovy essence	2 tbsps	
	parsley, chopped		

SPECIAL POINT
An essential quality of this dish is that it should reach the customer while the butter is still bubbling. The butter should be poured over the fish in a very hot dish at the moment of service.

553 Suprême de Cabillaud frit – Fried Cod

10 portions
30 mins.

Stage	Ingredient	Quantity	Method
1	cod suprêmes	10 × 100g	Wash, dry, season and paner à l'Anglaise (72).
	flour ⎫		
	eggwash ⎬ for		
	breadcrumbs ⎭ crumbing		
2			Place the suprêmes on frying grills and deep fry at 175°C until crisp and golden brown, approx. 4 mins.
3	lemons	2½	Drain the suprêmes well and place on dish papers on flat dishes. Garnish with quarters of lemon and fried or picked parsley.
	parsley, picked		

Fried cod may be served with Sauce Tartare (192) or Sauce Remoulade (191).

COLIN – HAKE (ALSO CALLED GEMFISH)

Hake is a fish of the cod family and all preparations for cod are suitable. Because of the firmness of the flesh, fillets of hake cut into suprêmes may be cooked in accordance with the recipes for poached fillets of sole.

FLÉTAN – HALIBUT

Halibut is usually filleted and cut into suprêmes or cut on the bone into tronçons. For suprêmes of halibut any of the recipes for poached fillets of sole are suitable. Tronçons of halibut can be poached or grilled as for tronçons of turbot.

HADDOCK, SMOKED AND FINNAN

554 Poached Finnan Haddock

Cut off the fins and flaps and trim the tail straight. Place in a shallow pan, cover with milk, bring to the boil and poach gently until cooked (10–12 mins. according to size). Place in an earthenware dish, remove the centre bone and serve the haddock with a little of the cooking liquor. Poached haddock is usually served as a breakfast dish.

555 Haddock Monte Carlo

1 portion
30 mins.

Stage	Ingredient	Quantity	Method
1	smoked haddock	1 × 250g	Trim the fins, flaps and tail and place in a buttered pan.
2	Tomates Concassées (90)	100g	Add to the fish and cover with a buttered greaseproof paper. Cook in a
	cream	2dl	moderate oven at 195°C for 12–15 mins.

| 3 | parsley, chopped | | Remove the fish to an earthenware dish and lift off the centre bone. Reduce the sauce slightly and ladle over the fish. Sprinkle with chopped parsley and place a hot poached egg on top when serving. |
| | eggs, poached | 1 | |

SPECIAL POINT

This recipe is usually used for à la Carte service and does not lend itself to preparation in large numbers.

556 Kedgeree

10 portions
40 mins.

Stage	Ingredient	Quantity	Method
1	smoked haddock	750g	Poach in water and when cooked remove all skin and bone. Lightly flake the flesh.
2	rice, long-grain	300g	Cook the rice as for Riz Poché (534).
	eggs, hard-boiled	10	Cut the eggs into small dice.
3	butter	150g	Melt the butter in a sauteuse. Add the flaked fish, rice and eggs. Season and toss over to reheat.
4	parsley, chopped		Dress the mixture in earthenware dishes,
	Curry Sauce (208)	½ litre	sprinkle with chopped parsley and serve the curry sauce separately as an accompaniment.

HARENG – HERRING

557 Hareng grillé – Grilled Herring

10 portions
30 mins.

Stage	Ingredient	Quantity	Method
1	herrings	10 × 200g	Scale, cut off the fins, trim the tail and remove the gut, leaving any roes inside. Wash, dry and cut four to five shallow incisions on each side of the thicker part of the fish.
2	flour		Season the herrings, lightly flour and
	oil	1dl	brush with oil. Place on a fish grill and grill on both sides to a good colour (approx. 5–6 mins. each side).
3	melted butter	50g	Dress the herrings neatly on dishes and
	lemons	2	brush with melted butter. Garnish with
	parsley, picked		slices of grooved lemon and picked parsley.

Grilled herrings may be served with Mustard Sauce (172).

558 Bloaters

Bloaters are cured whole herrings and are usually served as a breakfast dish. To cook, first clean and trim them, remove the heads then place on a fish grill and grill on both sides brushing with a little butter. They are frequently filleted before grilling.

559 Kippers

Kippers are herrings which have been split open, then cured and smoked. They are usually grilled with a little butter, after cutting off the head and trimming the tail, and are served mainly as a breakfast dish.

LIMANDE – LEMON SOLE

Fillets of lemon sole may be served in any of the ways applicable to Fillets of Sole (595–632).

LOTTE – MONKFISH

The head of the monkfish is discarded when caught and the tail end is obtainable ready skinned. Its flesh is very firm and can be successfully cut into slices or médaillons; the recipes for fillets of sole are thus applicable. It can be cut on the bone into steaks and grilled.

560 Lotte à la Bordelaise

10 portions
50 mins.

Stage	Ingredient		Quantity	Method
1	monkfish, fillet		1kg	Cut the monkfish into 20 small but thickish médaillons.
2	butter		50g	Heat the butter and oil in a shallow pan; season and lightly flour the fish and colour quickly on both sides. Remove.
	oil		½dl	
	flour			
3	onions	cut in	100g	Place the vegetables and garlic in the pan and cook quickly to a light golden colour. Replace the médaillons of fish on top. Add the brandy and Flamber (32).
	carrots	Brunoise	100g	
	celery	(22)	75g	
	garlic, finely chopped		1 clove	
	brandy		1dl	
4	Fumet de Poisson (101)		2dl	Add, season with salt and pepper, cover with a lid and simmer very gently for 12–15 mins.
	white wine, dry		3dl	
	Tomates Concassées (90)		500g	
	tomato purée		2 tbsps	
	bayleaf		1	

5	butter cayenne lemon juice	75g few drops	Remove the monkfish to earthenware dishes and keep warm. Discard the bayleaf then reduce the cooking liquor by approx. a quarter. Shake in the butter, add a few drops of lemon juice and adjust the seasoning plus a touch of cayenne.
6	tarragon, chopped	1 tbsp	Ladle the sauce and its garnish over the fish and sprinkle with the chopped tarragon.

561 Médaillon de Lotte aux Concombres

10 portions
45 mins.

Stage	Ingredient	Quantity	Method
1	monkfish, fillet	1kg	Cut into 10 round slices and flatten slightly.
2	cucumber	1½	Peel, cut in quarters lengthways, remove the pips then cut the remaining flesh into 2cm diamond shapes.
3	butter flour	75g	Heat the butter in a sauté pan. Season the fish, flour lightly and fry quickly to colour on both sides. Add the cucumbers to the pan, season lightly then cover with a lid. Place in a moderate oven and cook gently for approx. 7–8 mins.
4	shallots, finely chopped sherry, dry cream cayenne	50g 1dl 3dl	Remove the fish and cucumber and keep warm. Add the shallots to the pan and cook without colour, then add the sherry and reduce by three-quarters. Finally add the cream, reduce to a coating consistency and season well plus a touch of cayenne. Pass through a fine strainer into a pan. Add the cucumber, mix in lightly and keep warm.
5	fresh basil, chopped butter, melted	1 tbsp 25g	To serve: dress the médaillons of monkfish in dishes with the creamed cucumber to one side. Sprinkle the cucumber with the chopped basil and brush the fish with the melted butter.

562 Lotte à la Provençale

10 portions
20 mins.

Prepare as Scampi Provençale (678), using 1kg monkfish cut into 30 small collops.

MAQUEREAU – MACKEREL

563 Maquereau grillé – Grilled Mackerel

Prepare and cook as for Hareng grillé (557). Serve with Beurre Maître d'Hôtel (10) or Beurre d'Anchois (4).

---

564 Filet de Maquereau Meunière

Prepare as Filet de Sole Meunière (613) using 10 × 100g fillets of mackerel. They can also be served with the different garnishes for Filets de Sole Meunière (614–616).

MERLAN – WHITING

565 Merlan à l'Anglaise – Fried Whiting, English-Style

10 portions
1 hour

Stage	Ingredient	Quantity	Method
1	whiting, small	10 × 300g	Remove the fins, eyes and gills and trim the tails of the whiting. Wash and dry. Cut an incision along the back of the fish and remove the back bone from just before the head to within an inch of the tail and open out flat. Season and paner à l'Anglaise (72). Lightly flatten and stand the head upright. Mark the fish trellis-fashion with the back of a knife.
	flour		
	eggwash } for		
	breadcrumbs } crumbing		
2	clarified butter	400g	Heat in a frying-pan and when hot, place in the whiting best side downwards. Fry to a golden brown on both sides (approx. 5–6 mins.).
3	parsley, picked		Drain the fish on kitchen paper. Arrange neatly on flat dishes. Garnish with picked parsley and serve slices of Beurre Maître d'Hôtel separately.
	Beurre Maître d'Hôtel (10)	150g	

---

566 Merlan Colbert

10 portions
1 hour

Stage	Ingredient	Quantity	Method
1	whiting, small	10 × 300g	Remove the fins, gills and eyes and trim the tail of the whiting. Wash and dry. Cut an incision along the back of the fish and remove the back bone from just before the head to within an inch of the tail and open out flat. Season and paner à l'Anglaise (72). Lightly flatten and stand the head upright. Mark the fish trellis-fashion with the back of a knife.
	flour		
	eggwash } for		
	breadcrumbs } crumbing		

2			Place between two frying grills, skin side uppermost and deep fry at 175°C until golden brown.
3	lemon parsley, picked Beurre Maître d'Hôtel (10)	2½ 150g	Drain the fish well and arrange on dish papers on suitable dishes. Garnish with quarters of lemon and fried or picked parsley. Serve slices of Beurre Maître d'Hôtel separately.

567 Merlan en Colère – Curled Whiting

10 portions
1 hour

Stage	Ingredient	Quantity	Method
1	whiting, small	10 × 300g	Remove the fins, gills and eyes and trim the tail. Remove the skin and clean the inside of the abdominal cavity. Wash and dry the whiting and place the tail between the teeth fixing in place with a cocktail stick if necessary.
2	flour eggwash ⎬ for breadcrumbs ⎬ crumbing		Season and paner à l'Anglaise (72). Place in frying-baskets and deep fry at 175°C until crisp and golden brown.
3	lemons parsley, picked	2½	Drain well and place on dish papers on suitable dishes. Garnish with quarters of lemon and fried or picked parsley.

Merlan en Colère may be served with Sauce Tartare (192) or Sauce Remoulade (191).

568 Filet de Merlan frit – Fried Fillet of Whiting

Prepare as Filet de Sole frit (608), using 10 × 100g fillets of whiting.

569 Filet de Merlan frit à la Française – Fried Fillet of Whiting, French-Style

10 portions
20 mins.

Stage	Ingredient	Quantity	Method
1	whiting fillets milk flour	10 × 100g 2dl	Wash and dry the fillets, dip in milk and pass through the flour.
2	lemons parsley, picked Sauce Tomate (118)	2½ 6dl	Shake off surplus flour and deep fry at 175°C until golden brown. Drain, season lightly with salt and place on dish papers on suitable dishes. Garnish with quarters of lemon and fried or picked parsley. Serve accompanied with Sauce Tomate.

570 Filet de Merlan Meunière

Prepare as Filet de Sole Meunière (613), using 10 × 100g fillets of whiting. They can also be served with the different garnishes for Filet de Sole Meunière (614–616).

PLIE – PLAICE

In addition to the following, recipes for fillets of sole with sauces are also suitable for fillets of plaice.

---

571 Filet de Plie frit – Fried Fillet of Plaice

Prepare as Filet de Sole frit (608), using 10 × 100g fillets of plaice.

---

572 Filet de Plie grillé – Grilled Fillet of Plaice

Prepare as Filet de Sole grillé (611), using 10 × 100g fillets of plaice.

---

573 Filet de Plie Meunière

Prepare as Filet de Sole Meunière (613), using 10 × 100g fillets of plaice. They can also be served with the different garnishes for Filet de Sole Meunière (614–616).

---

574 Filet de Plie Niçoise

10 portions
30 mins.

Stage	Ingredient	Quantity	Method
1	plaice fillets oil flour	10 × 100g 2dl	Heat the oil in a frying-pan. Wash, dry, season and lightly flour the fillets, and when the oil is very hot place them in best side downwards.
2			Fry to a golden brown on both sides (approx. 5 mins.). Remove the fillets, dress neatly in earthenware dishes and keep on the side of the stove.

3	Tomates Concassées,
	  cooked (91)
	anchovy fillets
	olives, black
	lemons, peeled
	  slices
		250g
		10
		10
		
		10
			Place a spoonful of the hot tomates concassées in the centre of each fillet, then a slice of lemon, a circle of anchovy fillet on the lemon and a stoned black olive in the centre of the anchovy.

4	Beurre d'Anchois (4)	150g	Serve accompanied with the anchovy butter.

---

575 Filet de Plie à l'Orly

Prepare as Filet de Sole à l'Orly (619) using 10 × 100g fillets of place.

---

576 Goujons de Plie frits

Prepare as Goujons de Sole frits (630) using fillets of plaice.

---

577 Goujonettes de Plie frites

Prepare as Goujonettes de Sole frites (631) using fillets of plaice.

RAIE – SKATE (ALSO CALLED ROKER)

578　Raie au Beurre Noir – Skate with Black Butter　10 portions
30 mins.

Stage	Ingredient	Quantity	Method
1	skate wings	1½kg	Skin the skate on both sides and cut into ten even-sized pieces. Wash well.
2	water	6 litres	Place all the ingredients into a shallow pan of a suitable size and add the pieces of skate. Bring to the boil and skim. Draw to the side of the stove and poach gently until cooked (approx. 10 mins.).
	onion, sliced	200g	
	peppercorns	18	
	parsley stalks	10g	
	vinegar	6dl	
	salt	25g	
3			Remove the skate, drain and place in earthenware dishes. Leave on the side of the stove.
4	capers	150g	Sprinkle the capers over the fish. Place the butter in a suitable frying pan and cook until brown, shaking the pan to ensure even colouring. Remove from the heat, add the vinegar and pour over the fish immediately. Sprinkle with chopped parsley.
	butter	150g	
	vinegar	2 tbsps	
	parsley, chopped		

ROUGET – RED MULLET (ALSO CALLED GOATFISH)

579　Rouget Grenobloise
10 portions
30 mins.

Stage	Ingredient	Quantity	Method
1	red mullet	10 × 200g	Scale, cut off the fins, remove the eyes and gut. Wash and dry and cut four to five shallow incisions on each side at the thick part.
2	oil	2dl	Heat the oil in a frying-pan. Season and lightly flour the mullets. When the oil is very hot, place them in the pan all facing the same way. Fry to a golden brown on both sides (approx. 10–12 mins.).
	flour		
3			Remove and arrange neatly in earthen-ware dishes and keep on the side of the stove.
4	lemons in peeled segments (52)	3	Place two or three segments of lemon on each fish and sprinkle the capers over.
	capers	150g	

5	butter parsley, chopped	150g	Place the butter in a suitable frying-pan and cook until nut-brown shaking the pan to ensure even colouring. Pour quickly over the fish and sprinkle with chopped parsley.

580 Rouget grillé – Grilled Red Mullet

10 portions
30 mins.

Stage	Ingredient	Quantity	Method
1	red mullet	10 × 200g	Scale, cut off the fins, remove the eyes and gut. Wash, dry and cut four to five shallow incisions on each side at the thickest part.
2	flour oil		Season the fish, lightly flour and brush with oil. Place on a fish grill and grill on both sides to a good colour (approx. 6–8 mins. each side).
3	lemons parsley, picked melted butter	2 50g	Dress neatly on dishes and brush with melted butter. Garnish with slices of grooved lemon and picked parsley.

Serve Beurre Maître d'Hôtel (10) or Sauce Diable (125) separately.

SPECIAL POINT
Connoisseurs like the red mullet to be grilled with the entrails left inside as this imparts a distinctive flavour which is much appreciated.

581 Rouget Niçoise

10 portions
30 mins.

Grill the red mullet as for Rouget grillé (580) and garnish with cooked Tomates Concassées (91), slices of peeled lemon, anchovy fillets and stoned black olives.

582 Rouget en Papillote

1 portion
30 mins.

Stage	Ingredient	Quantity	Method
1	red mullet	1 × 200g	Scale, cut off the fins, remove the eyes and gut. Wash and dry and cut four to five shallow incisions on each side at the thick part.
2	flour oil	 ½dl	Season the fish, lightly flour, brush with oil and place on a fish grill. Grill on both sides to a good colour (approx. 6–8 mins. each side).

3	butter	10g	Melt the butter in a small pan, add the
	onion, finely		onion and cook without colour. Add the
	chopped	25g	mushrooms, season and cook until
	mushrooms, finely		almost dry. Add the wine and demi-glace
	chopped	150g	and reduce gently to a fairly thick
	white wine	½dl	consistency. Adjust the seasoning and
	Demi-glace (112)	1dl	finish with a little chopped parsley.
	parsley, chopped		
4	greaseproof paper	1 sheet	Cut the paper into the shape of a large
	oil		heart big enough to hold the fish. Lay it
			flat on the table and oil well. Spread half
			of the prepared mushroom mixture on
			one side of the centre of the paper,
			roughly the same shape as the mullet.
			Place the mullet on top and cover with
			the remainder of the mixture. Fold the
			paper over to cover and seal by folding
			and pleating the edges tightly.
5			Place the Rouget en Papillote on an
			oiled flat dish and place in a moderate
			oven at 175°C for approx. 5–7 mins. in
			order to colour the outside and to allow
			the steam, which is trapped inside, to
			swell the papillote. Serve immediately.

SPECIAL POINTS
a) The papillote should be presented and opened in front of the customer.
b) Aluminium foil may be used instead of greaseproof.

SAINT-PIERRE – JOHN DORY

This fish gives excellent white fillets of good texture and delicate flavour which can rival those of the Dover sole. All the recipes for fillets of sole are thus suitable.

583 Saint-Pierre en Papillote Arnaudy

1 portion
40 mins.

Stage	Ingredient	Quantity	Method
1	aluminium foil		Cut a large heart-shape from the foil
	butter, melted	10g	large enough to fold over and contain
			the fillet. Lay it flat and brush with the
			butter.
2	mushrooms, white		Slice the mushrooms fairly thick and lay
	button	4	flat as a bed to one side of the centre of
	John Dory fillet	1 × 100g	the foil. Lightly season, then place the
	soft herring		fillet of John Dory on top. Place one roe
	roes	2	at each side of the fillet.
3	Glace de Poisson		Brush the fish glaze over the surface of
	(105)	½ tbsp	the fish and roes. Sprinkle with the
	sherry, dry	1 tbsp	sherry and butter and lightly season.

butter, melted	10g		Finally, sprinkle with the tarragon.
fresh tarragon, chopped	pinch		

4		Fold the foil over to cover and seal, folding and pleating the edges tightly. Place on an oiled dish or tray, then in a moderate oven at 175°C for approx. 15–18 mins. to cook the fish. Serve immediately.

SPECIAL POINTS

a) The papillote should be presented and opened in front of the customer.
b) Greaseproof paper is not best for this dish, as unfortunately it can become overcoloured and very brittle and then when opened often breaks into small pieces over the food contained inside.

SAUMON – SALMON

584 Coulibiac de Saumon

10–12 portions
2¼ hours

Stage	Ingredient	Quantity	Method
1	vésiga	75g	Soak overnight in plenty of cold water. Drain and roughly chop. Cover well with water, season with salt, bring to the boil and simmer for 3–4 hours. Allow to cool and drain.
2	rice, long-grain	200g	Place the rice into the boiling stock, season with salt and simmer gently until cooked (approx. 18 mins.) Drain in a colander and allow to dry slightly in a very slow oven. Remove from the oven and allow to cool.
	Fonds Blanc (93)	2 litres	
3	butter	50g	Melt the butter in a pan. Add the onion and cook without colour. Add the mushrooms, season and cook until almost dry.
	onions, finely chopped	75g	
	mushrooms, chopped	350g	
4	cream, double	1½dl	Add the chopped vésiga and cream to the mushrooms. Mix in well, adjust the seasoning and cook together until lightly thickened. Allow to cool.
5	salmon fillet	750g	Cut the salmon into small slices, approx. 5cm × ¾cm thick. Melt the butter, add the slices, season and cook gently just to stiffen them. Sprinkle with parsley and allow to cool.
	butter	100g	
	parsley, chopped		
6	egg, hard-boiled	5	Chop roughly.

7	Pâte Feuilletée (1736)	650g	Roll out to a rectangle approx. 45cm in length by 25cm wide. Spread a layer of rice along the centre of the length of the paste, approx. 30cm long and 10cm wide.
8			Cover with some of the mushroom mixture, sprinkle with one-third of the chopped egg then a layer of salmon. Repeat this sequence of layers again, then finish with the mushrooms, remainder of the egg and finally, the rest of the rice.
9			Eggwash the edges of the paste. Pull up the paste from both sides and ends to cover the mixture completely and seal the joins well. Turn the Coulibiac over onto a baking tray so that the joins are underneath. Allow to rest for 30 mins. Make 2–3 holes along the top, eggwash and decorate with the point of a small knife.
10	butter, melted	50g	Bake the Coulibiac in a hot oven at 200°C until lightly coloured and set. Reduce the temperature and continue cooking (total time 45–50 mins.). Allow to rest for a few mins. then pour the butter through the holes into the Coulibiac. Arrange the Coulibiac on an oval flat dish.
11	Beurre Fondu (9) or Sauce au Beurre Blanc (164)	6dl	Serve accompanied with a sauceboat of Beurre Fondu or Sauce au Beurre Blanc.

---

585 Darne de Saumon Chambord

10 portions
1½ hours

Stage	Ingredient	Quantity	Method
1	carrots ⎫ thinly onion ⎬ sliced parsley stalks thyme bayleaf	150g 150g 20g sprig ½	Spread the ingredients over the bottom of a buttered shallow pan.
2	salmon darnes (537)	10 × 150g	Wash well, place in the pan, season and cover. Place the pan on the stove and cook gently to lightly colour the vegetables.

3	red wine	5dl	Remove the lid and add the wine and stock. Re-cover, bring to the boil and braise gently in a moderate oven at approx. 175°C for 25–30 mins.
	Fumet de Poisson (101)	2½dl	
4			Remove the darnes from the cooking liquor and drain. Take out the centre bone and skin. Place the darnes in earthenware dishes, cover and keep warm.
5	Demi-glace (112)	5dl	Strain the cooking liquor into a clean pan and reduce by two-thirds. Add the demi-glace and reduce to a light coating consistency.
6	butter	75g	Mix thoroughly into the sauce away from the heat and adjust the seasoning. Coat the fish with the sauce.
7	button onions, glacé à Brun (1493)	20	Garnish the dish with neat bouquets of the glazed button onions, quenelles and soft roes and place a slice of truffle in the centre of each darne.
	Quenelles de Poisson, small (83)	20	
	soft herring roes, shallow-fried	10	
	truffle slices	10	

586 Darne de Saumon grillée – Grilled Salmon

10 portions
25 mins.

Stage	Ingredient	Quantity	Method
1	salmon darnes (537)	10 × 150g	Wash the darnes well, dry, season and lightly flour. Brush well with the oil.
	flour		
	oil	1dl	
2			Place on a fish grill and grill on both sides to a good colour (approx. 10 mins.).
3	lemons	2	Dress the darnes neatly on dishes, remove the centre bones and brush with melted butter. Garnish with slices of grooved lemon and picked parsley. Serve accompanied with a dish of sliced cucumber and an appropriate sauce, e.g. Sauce Béarnaise, Sauce Diable or Beurre Maître d'Hôtel.
	butter	50g	
	parsley, picked		
	cucumber, peeled	½	
	Sauce Béarnaise (153) or other suitable sauce	6dl	

587 Darne de Saumon pochée

10 portions
30 mins.

Stage	Ingredient	Quantity	Method
1	Court-bouillon (538)	6 litres	Place in a shallow pan, bring to the boil and skim.
2	salmon darnes (537)	10 × 150g	Wash well, place in the boiling liquid, reboil and skim. Draw to the side of the stove and allow the darnes to poach gently until cooked (approx. 10 mins.).
3	lemons	2	Remove the fish from the cooking liquor, drain, take out the centre bones and remove the skin. Arrange the darnes in earthenware dishes, garnish with slices of grooved lemon, plain boiled potatoes and picked parsley. Surround with a little of the strained hot cooking liquid.
	potatoes, small turned	20	
	parsley sprigs		
4	cucumber, peeled	½	Serve accompanied with a dish of sliced cucumber and a suitable sauce, e.g. Beurre Fondu, Sauce Hollandaise or Sauce Génevoise.
	Sauce Hollandaise (157) or other suitable sauce	6dl	

588 Saumon poché – Poached Salmon

10 portions
1 hour

Stage	Ingredient	Quantity	Method
1	salmon, middle-cut piece	1½kg	Wash the salmon well and place in a salmon kettle on a perforated rack. Cover well with hot court-bouillon.
	Court-bouillon (538)	6 litres	
2			Bring to the boil, skim, draw the fish kettle to the side of the stove and allow the salmon to poach gently for 15–20 mins.
3	lemons	2	Lift up the fish on the rack, drain and remove the skin. Place the salmon on a suitable fish dish, garnish with slices of grooved lemon, plain boiled potatoes and picked parsley. Surround with a little of the strained hot cooking liquid.
	boiled potatoes, small turned	20	
	parsley		
4	cucumber, peeled	½	Serve accompanied with a dish of sliced cucumber and an appropriate sauce, e.g. melted butter, Sauce Hollandaise or Sauce Génevoise.
	Sauce Hollandaise (157) or other suitable sauce	6dl	

SPECIAL POINTS

a) Salmon are available whole in varying weights ranging from 3kg to 8kg and are frequently cooked whole, especially for cold buffets.

b) When cooking salmon for cold buffets a 3kg salmon will require approx. 15–20 mins. of actual poaching time after being brought to the boil and a 5kg one approx. 30 mins.

Use cold court-bouillon (538) and after cooking the salmon must be allowed to cool in its cooking liquid.

---

589 Suprême de Saumon Condorcet

10 portions
45 mins.

Stage	Ingredient	Quantity	Method
1	salmon suprêmes tomatoes, peeled cucumber, peeled	10 × 100g 5 ½	Wash and place the suprêmes in a buttered shallow tray. Arrange two ½ cm-thick slices of cucumber and tomato alternately on each suprême and season.
2	white wine, dry Fumet de Poisson (101)	2dl 1dl	Add the wine and stock and cover with buttered greaseproof paper. Poach in a moderate oven at 195°C until cooked, approx. 12–15 mins.
3			Remove the fish, drain and place in earthenware dishes with the garnish on top. Cover and keep warm.
4	Sauce Vin Blanc (174)	7dl	Strain the cooking liquor, reduce well and add to the Sauce Vin Blanc.
5	parsley, chopped		Coat the fish with the sauce and sprinkle with chopped parsley.

---

590 Suprême de Saumon à l'Oseille

10 portions
45 mins.

Stage	Ingredient	Quantity	Method
1	sorrel	300g	Pick off any stalks, wash the leaves and shred these coarsely.
2	butter shallots, finely chopped cream Glace de Poisson (105)	75g 75g 4dl 1 tbsp	Heat the butter in a pan, add the shallots and cook without colour. Add the sorrel, season, cover and cook until tender, then add the cream and cook gently to a light coating consistency. Finally add the glace de poisson and adjust the seasoning. Cover and keep warm.
3	salmon suprêmes butter	10 × 100g 75g	Heat the butter in a sauté pan. Season the suprêmes of salmon and cook on both sides but without colour. Drain.
4			To serve: Cover the bottom of hot dishes or plates with some of the sauce and place the salmon on top.

SOLE (INCLUDING LEMON SOLE, FLOUNDER AND MEGRIM)

There are a number of soles available such as the lemon, Torbay and sand sole all of which enjoy a good reputation or local popularity. They do not however compare with the true Dover sole which possesses a firmness of texture and delicacy of flavour unmatched by any other flat fish.

SPECIAL POINT
In addition to the following recipes for whole sole, the recipes for poached and sauced fillets of sole are also suitable for whole sole. It is necessary however first to remove the head before cooking and when cooked, the fish should then be filleted before covering with the sauce. To do this proceed in the following manner:

1) When cooked, place the sole on a flat tray. Using a knife push down along the line between the outer edge of the fish and next to the flesh proper, and push outwards at the same time. This will remove the outer row of bones.
2) Slide back the two top fillets, remove the central skeleton then replace the top fillets. The fish will then be completely filleted and still in its original shape.

591 Sole Colbert

10 portions
1½ hours

Stage	Ingredient	Quantity	Method
1	Sole	10 × 250g	Remove the black skin, trim the fins and tail and scale the white skin. Wash well and dry. Cut along the backbone of the skinned side from just below the head to the tail. Partially detach the fillets and fold back to the edge of the fish. Cut through the exposed bone in three places (near the head, in the centre and near the tail) without cutting into the flesh.
2	flour eggwash breadcrumbs } for crumbing		Season the fish, paner à l'Anglaise (72), lightly flatten and mark trellis-fashion across the fillets.
3			Place between two frying grills, skin side uppermost and deep fry at 170°C until golden brown.
4	lemons Beurre Maître d'Hôtel (10) parsley, picked	2½ 150g	Drain the soles well, remove the centre bones and place the soles on dish papers on suitable dishes. Place three slices of Beurre Maître d'Hôtel in the centre of each fish. Garnish with quarters of lemon and picked or fried parsley.

592 Sole au Gratin

10 portions
1½ hours

Stage	Ingredient	Quantity	Method
1	Sole butter	10 × 250g 200g	Remove the black skin. Trim the fins and tail and scale the white skin. Wash well and dry. Cut along the backbone of the skinned side from just below the head to the tail. Partially detach the fillets and place 20g of butter under the fillets of each sole.

2	shallots, finely chopped	75g	Butter earthenware dishes, sprinkle with the shallots and just cover with a little
	Sauce Gratin (168)	1 litre	sauce. Place the soles on top, skin side uppermost, and season. Wash the mush-
	button mushrooms	40	rooms, remove the stalks and place four
	white wine, dry	2dl	mushrooms along the centre of each
	white breadcrumbs	75g	sole. Pour the wine over the soles and
	butter, melted	100g	cover them with the remaining sauce. Sprinkle with the breadcrumbs and melted butter.
3	juice of lemon	1	Bake in a moderate oven at 175°C for
	parsley, chopped		15–20 mins. Remove and sprinkle with lemon juice and chopped parsley.

593 Sole grillée – Grilled Sole

10 portions
1 hour

Stage	Ingredient	Quantity	Method
1	Sole	10 × 250g	Remove the black skin. Trim the fins
	oil	1dl	and tail and scale the white skin. Wash
	flour		well, dry, season and lightly flour. Brush well on both sides with oil.
2			Place the soles on fish grills and grill on both sides to a good brown colour (approx 10–12 mins.).
3	butter	50g	Dress the soles neatly on suitable dishes
	lemons	2	with the skin sides uppermost, and brush
	parsley, picked		with melted butter. Garnish with slices of grooved lemon and picked parsley. Serve accompanied with Beurre Maître d'Hôtel, Beurre d'Anchois or Sauce Diable.

SPECIAL POINT
It is advisable to protect the tail ends during the cooking process by keeping them away from the direct heat of the grill.

594 Sole Meunière

10 portions
50 mins.

Stage	Ingredient	Quantity	Method
1	Sole	10 × 250g	Remove the black skin, trim the fins and tail and scale the white skin. Wash well and dry.
2	oil	2dl	Heat the oil in a frying-pan. Season and
	flour		lightly flour the soles, and when the oil is very hot place the soles in skin side downwards. Fry to a golden brown on both sides (8–10 mins.).

3			Remove the soles and dress them neatly in earthenware dishes. Keep on the side of the stove.
4	lemons, peeled		Place two slices of lemon on each sole and sprinkle with lemon juice.
	slices	20	
	juice of lemon	1	
5	butter, soft	180g	Place the butter in a frying-pan and cook
	parsley, chopped		until nut-brown, shaking the pan to ensure even colouring. Pour quickly over the soles and sprinkle with chopped parsley.

Sole Meunière can be served with the different garnishes as listed under Filet de Sole Meunière (614–616).

FILLETS OF SOLE

Fillets of small flat fish such as Dover sole, lemon sole and plaice may be poached flat as they are or folded. If to be folded the fillet should be lightly flattened then folded over, skinned side inwards and the head end of the fillet over the tail end.

With large Dover sole the removal of the skins tends to leave vestiges of fairly tough membrane on the fillets. It is better to remove this with a sharp knife as failure to do so can result in the deformation of the fillets when cooked.

The following recipes for fillets of sole may be successfully applied to fillets and suprêmes of other suitable white fish such as brill, cod, fresh haddock, hake, lemon sole, plaice, turbot, grouper, croaker, jack, murray cod and pomfret.

---

595 Filet de Sole d'Antin

This is prepared in the same way as Filet de Sole Dugléré (605) with the addition of 180g of diced croûtons (311) sprinkled over the cooked sole when serving.

---

596 Filet de Sole Bercy

10 portions
1 hour

Stage	Ingredient	Quantity	Method
1	shallots, finely chopped	100g	Butter a tray. Sprinkle in half of the shallots. Place the washed fillets on top,
	sole fillets	10 × 90g	add the remainder of the shallots,
	white wine, dry	1dl	sprinkle with chopped parsley and
	Fumet de Poisson (101)	2dl	season. Add the wine and fumet de poisson. Cover with a buttered grease-
	parsley, chopped		proof paper and poach in a moderate oven at 195°C until cooked, approx. 12–15 mins.
2			Remove the fillets. Drain them well and dress neatly in earthenware dishes. Cover and keep warm.

3	Velouté de Poisson (117) cream	6dl 1dl	Place the cooking liquor into a small pan. Add the fish velouté and cream and reduce to a coating consistency.
4	egg yolks	2	Make a sabayon (84) and add to the sauce away from the heat.
5	butter juice of lemon parsley, chopped cayenne	75g ¼	Mix in the butter, adjust the seasoning and add a little cayenne. Finish the sauce with lemon juice and chopped parsley.
6			Coat the fish with the sauce and glaze under the salamander.

597 Filet de Sole Bonne-Femme

10 portions
1 hour

Stage	Ingredient	Quantity	Method
1	shallots, finely chopped sole fillets button mushrooms, sliced parsley, chopped white wine, dry Fumet de Poisson (101)	50g 10 × 90g 250g 1 dl 2 dl	Butter a tray, sprinkle in the shallots and place the washed fillets on top. Add the mushrooms, sprinkle with parsley and season. Add the wine and fish stock, cover with a buttered paper and poach in a moderate oven at 195°C until cooked, approx. 12–15 mins.
2			Remove the fillets, drain them well and dress neatly in earthenware dishes with the garnish. Strain the cooking liquor into a small pan and sprinkle any remaining garnish over the fillets. Cover and keep warm.
3	Velouté de Poisson (117) cream	6dl 1dl	Add the fish velouté and cream to the cooking liquor and reduce to a coating consistency.
4	egg yolks	2	Make a sabayon (84) and add to the sauce away from the heat. Pass through a fine strainer.
5	butter cayenne	75g	Mix in thoroughly, adjust the seasoning and finish with a little cayenne.
6			Coat the fish with the sauce and glaze under the salamander.

598 Filet de Sole Bretonne

This is Filet de Sole Meunière (613) with the addition of prawns and sliced mushrooms. These are cooked in butter and sprinkled over the fillets before finishing with the brown butter and chopped parsley.

599 Filet de Sole Bréval

10 portions
1 hour

Stage	Ingredient	Quantity	Method
1	shallots, finely chopped	50g	Butter a tray, sprinkle in the shallots and place the washed fillets on top. Add the mushrooms and tomates concassées. Sprinkle with parsley and season. Add the wine and fish stock, cover with a buttered paper and poach in a moderate oven at 195°C until cooked, approx. 12–15 mins.
	sole fillets	10 × 90g	
	button mushrooms, sliced	200g	
	Tomates Concassées (90)	200g	
	parsley, chopped		
	white wine, dry	1dl	
	Fumet de Poisson (101)	2dl	
2			Remove the fillets, drain well and dress neatly in earthenware dishes with the garnish. Strain the cooking liquor into a small pan and sprinkle any remaining garnish over the fillets. Cover and keep warm.
3	Velouté de Poisson (117)	6dl	Add the fish velouté and cream to the cooking liquor and reduce to a coating consistency.
	cream	1dl	
4	egg yolks	2	Make a sabayon (84) and add to the sauce away from the heat. Pass through a fine strainer.
5	butter	75g	Mix thoroughly into the sauce, adjust the seasoning and finish with a little cayenne.
	cayenne		
6			Coat the fish with the sauce and glaze under the salamander.

600 Filet de Sole Caprice

10 portions
45 mins.

Stage	Ingredient	Quantity	Method
1	sole fillets	10 × 90g	Wash and dry the fillets and season. Pass through flour, melted butter and breadcrumbs and place the skinned side downwards. Flatten slightly and mark trellis-fashion with the back of a knife. Place the fillets on a well-buttered tray and sprinkle with melted butter.
	flour		
	butter, melted	200g	
	breadcrumbs, white		
2			Grill the fillets gently under the salamander to a golden brown. Dress in earthenware dishes and keep warm.

3	bananas	5	Remove the skins and cut the bananas in half lengthways. Pass through flour, place on a well-buttered tray and sprinkle with melted butter. Grill gently under the salamander until soft and brown.
	butter, melted	50g	
4	parsley, picked		Place half a banana on each fillet, garnish with picked parsley and serve with the Sauce Robert as an accompaniment.
	Sauce Robert (136)	7dl	

601 Filet de Sole Cléopâtre

This is Filet de Sole Meunière (613) with the addition of prawns and one soft herring roe per fillet. These are cooked in butter and arranged on the fillets with a few capers, before finishing with brown butter and chopped parsley.

602 Filet de Sole Cubat

This is prepared in the same way as Filet de Sole Mornay (617), placing the poached fillets of sole at Stage 2 on a bed of Duxelles (29) before coating with the sauce and gratinating. The duxelles may be finished with a little cream.

603 Filet de Sole Dieppoise

10 portions
1 hour

Stage	Ingredient	Quantity	Method
1	sole fillets	10 × 90g	Butter a tray, place in the washed fillets and season. Add the wine and fish stock, cover with a buttered paper and poach in a moderate oven at 195°C until cooked, approx. 12–15 mins.
	white wine, dry	1dl	
	Fumet de Poisson		
	(101)	2dl	
2	button mushrooms, cooked à Blanc		Drain the mushrooms and warm the prawns and mussels separately in the butter.
	(60)	20	
	prawns, cooked	150g	
	mussels, cooked to		
	Stage 2 (674)	20	
	butter	50g	
3			Remove the fillets, drain well and dress neatly in earthenware dishes. Decorate the fillets with the mushrooms and arrange the prawns and mussels around the dish. Cover and keep warm.
4	Velouté de Poisson		Strain the cooking liquor into a small pan, add the velouté and cream and reduce to a coating consistency. Pass through a fine strainer.
	(117)	6dl	
	cream	1dl	
5	butter	75g	Mix in the butter thoroughly away from the heat. Adjust the seasoning and finish with a little cayenne.
	cayenne		

6   Coat the fish and the garnish with the sauce. Do not glaze.

604 Filet de Sole Doria

This is Filet de Sole Meunière (613) with the addition of cucumber cut into 2cm diamond shapes. These are cooked in butter and sprinkled over the fillets before finishing with the brown butter and chopped parsley.

605 Filet de Sole Dugléré

10 portions
1 hour

Stage	Ingredient	Quantity	Method
1	sole fillets	10 × 90g	Butter a tray and place in the washed
	shallots, finely		fillets. Sprinkle with the shallots, add the
	chopped	50g	tomatoes, sprinkle with parsley and
	Tomates Concassées		season. Add the wine and fish stock,
	(90)	500g	cover with a buttered greaseproof paper
	parsley, chopped	1 tbsp	and poach in a moderate oven at 195°C
	white wine, dry	1dl	until cooked. Approx. 12–15 mins.
	Fumet de Poisson		
	(101)	2dl	
2			Remove the fillets, drain well and arrange neatly in earthenware dishes with the garnish. Strain the cooking liquor into a small pan and sprinkle any of the remaining garnish over the fillets. Cover and keep warm. Adjust the seasoning.
3	cream	5dl	Reduce the cooking liquor by two-thirds, add the cream and reduce to a light coating consistency.
4	butter	75g	Shake in the butter away from the heat making sure that the butter is blended in well.
5	parsley, chopped		Pour the sauce over the fish and sprinkle with chopped parsley.

606 Filet de Sole Florentine

This is prepared in the same way as Filet de Sole Mornay (617), placing the poached fillets of sole at Stage 2 on a bed of Epinards en Branches (1454) before coating with the sauce and gratinating.

607 Filet de Sole François 1er

10 portions
1 hour

Stage	Ingredient	Quantity	Method
1	sole fillets	10 × 90g	Butter a tray and place in the washed
	shallots, finely chopped	50g	fillets. Sprinkle with shallots and add the
	mushrooms, sliced	250g	mushrooms and tomatoes. Sprinkle with
	Tomates Concassées		chopped parsley and season. Add the
	(90)	200g	wine and fish stock, cover with a but-
	parsley, chopped	1 tbsp	tered greaseproof paper and poach in a
	white wine, dry	1dl	moderate oven at 195°C until cooked,
	Fumet de Poisson		approx. 12–15 mins.
	(101)	2dl	
2			Remove the fillets, drain well and dress neatly in earthenware dishes with the garnish.
3			Strain the cooking liquor into a small pan and sprinkle any of the remaining garnish over the fillets. Cover and keep warm.
4	cream	5dl	Reduce the cooking liquor by two-thirds, add the cream and reduce to a light coating consistency. Adjust the seasoning.
5	butter	75g	Shake in the butter away from the heat
	parsley, chopped		making sure that the butter is blended in well. Pour the sauce over the fish and sprinkle with chopped parsley.

608 Filet de Sole frit – Fried Fillet of Sole

10 portions
25 mins.

Stage	Ingredient	Quantity	Method
1	sole fillets	10 × 90g	Wash and dry the fillets, season them
	flour	} for	and paner à l'Anglaise (72).
	eggwash	} crumbing	
	breadcrumbs		
2			Place in frying-baskets and deep fry at 180°C until crisp and golden brown.
3	lemons	2½	Drain well and place on dish papers on
	parsley, picked		flat dishes. Garnish with quarters of lemon and fried or picked parsley. Fried Dover sole fillets may be served with Sauce Tartare or Sauce Remoulade.

609 Filet de Sole Galliéra

10 portions
45 mins.

Stage	Ingredient	Quantity	Method
1	sole fillets	10 × 90g	Butter a tray and place in the washed
	lettuce, fine		fillets. Add the lettuce, mushrooms and
	julienne	100g	truffle, and season. Add the wine, fish
	mushrooms, fine		stock and lemon juice. Cover with a
	julienne	250g	buttered paper and poach in a moderate
	truffle, fine		oven at 195°C until cooked, approx.
	julienne	50g	12–15 mins.
	white wine, dry	1dl	
	Fumet de Poisson		
	(101)	2dl	
	juice of lemon	½	
2			Remove the fillets, drain well and dress neatly in earthenware dishes, with the garnish.
3			Strain the cooking liquor into a small pan and sprinkle any of the remaining garnish over the fillets. Cover and keep warm.
4	cream	5dl	Reduce the cooking liquor by two-thirds, add the cream and reduce to a light coating consistency. Adjust the seasoning.
5	butter	75g	Shake in the butter away from the heat
	parsley, chopped		making sure that the butter is blended in well. Pour the sauce over the fish and sprinkle with chopped parsley.

610 Filet de Sole Grenobloise

This is Filet de Sole Meunière (613) with 3–4 segments of peeled lemons per portion instead of sliced lemon. Sprinkle with a few capers before finishing with the brown butter and chopped parsley.

611 Filet de Sole grillé – Grilled Fillet of Sole

10 portions
25 mins.

Stage	Ingredient	Quantity	Method
1	sole fillets	10 × 90g	Wash, dry, season and lightly flour the
	flour		fillets. Brush with oil.
	oil	1dl	
2			Place on a fish grill and grill on both sides to a good colour (approx. 4–5 mins. each side).
3	melted butter	50g	Dress the fillets neatly on dishes, brush
	lemons	2	with melted butter and garnish with

parsley, picked

slices of grooved lemon and picked parsley. Serve accompanied with Beurre Maître d'Hôtel, Beurre d'Anchois or Sauce Diable.

612 Filet de Sole Marguery

10 portions
1 hour

Stage	Ingredient	Quantity	Method
1	sole fillets	10 × 90g	Butter a tray, place in the washed fillets and season. Add the wine and fish stock. Cover with a buttered paper and poach in a moderate oven at 195°C until cooked, approx 12–15 mins.
	white wine, dry	1dl	
	Fumet de Poisson (101)	2dl	
2	prawns, cooked	150g	Warm the prawns and mussels in the butter.
	mussels, cooked to Stage 2 (674)	30	
	butter	30g	
3			Remove the fillets, drain well and dress neatly in earthenware dishes. Garnish the fillets with the prawns and mussels, cover and keep warm.
4	Velouté de Poisson (117)	6dl	Strain the cooking liquor into a small pan, add the velouté and cream and reduce to a coating consistency.
	cream	1dl	
5	egg yolks	2	Make a sabayon (84) and add to the sauce away from the heat. Pass through a fine strainer.
6	butter	75g	Mix thoroughly into the sauce. Adjust the seasoning and finish with a little cayenne.
	cayenne		
7	Fleurons (33)	10	Coat the fillets and the garnish with the sauce. Glaze under the salamander and surround with the fleurons.

613 Filet de Sole Meunière

10 portions
25 mins.

Stage	Ingredient	Quantity	Method
1	oil	2dl	Heat the oil in a frying-pan. Wash, dry, season and lightly flour the fillets. When the oil is very hot place them in best side downwards.
	sole fillets	10 × 90g	
	flour		
2			Cook to a golden brown on both sides (approx. 5 mins.). Remove the fillets, dress neatly in earthenware dishes and keep on the side of the stove.

3	lemons, peeled		Place one slice of lemon on each fillet
	slices	10	and sprinkle with lemon juice.
	juice of lemon	½	
4	butter, soft	150g	Place the butter in a suitable frying-pan
	parsley, chopped		and cook until nut-brown, shaking the
			pan to ensure even colouring. Pour
			quickly over the fish and sprinkle with
			chopped parsley.

614 Filet de Sole Belle-Meunière

This is Filet de Sole Meunière (613) with the addition of half a small blanched tomato, a soft herring roe and one button mushroom per portion. These are cooked in butter and arranged on the fillets before finishing with the brown butter and chopped parsley.

615 Filet de Sole Meunière aux Aubergines

This is Filet de Sole Meunière (613) with ½cm-thick rounds of Fried Aubergines (1391) arranged on the fillets before finishing with the brown butter and chopped parsley.

616 Filet de Sole Meunière aux Câpres

This is Filet de Sole Meunière (613) with a few capers sprinkled over the fillets before finishing with the brown butter and chopped parsley.

617 Filet de Sole Mornay

10 portions
1 hour

Stage	Ingredient	Quantity	Method
1	sole fillets	10 × 90g	Butter a tray and place in the washed
	Fumet de Poisson		fillets. Season and add the fish stock.
	(101)	3dl	Cover with a buttered greaseproof paper and poach in a moderate oven at 195°C until cooked, approx 12–15 mins.
2			Remove the fillets, drain well and dress neatly in earthenware dishes. Cover and keep warm.
3	Béchamel (114)	6dl	Strain the cooking liquor into a small
	cream	1dl	pan, add the Béchamel and cream and reduce to a coating consistency.
4	egg yolks	2	Make a sabayon (84) and add to the sauce away from the heat. Pass through a fine strainer.
5	butter	75g	Mix in the butter thoroughly and then
	Parmesan, grated	50g	add the cheese. Adjust the seasoning and
	cayenne		finish with a little cayenne pepper.

| 6 | Parmesan, grated | 25g | Coat the fish with the sauce, sprinkle with the Parmesan and gratinate under the salamander. |

618 Filet de Sole Nelson

10 portions
1 hour

Stage	Ingredient	Quantity	Method
1	sole fillets white wine dry Fumet de Poisson (101)	10 × 90g 1dl 2dl	Butter a tray, wash the fillets, fold and place in the tray. Season, add the wine and fish stock and cover with a buttered greaseproof paper. Poach in the oven at 195°C until cooked, approx. 12–15 mins.
2			Remove the fillets, drain well and dress neatly in earthenware dishes. Cover and keep warm.
3	Velouté de Poisson (117) cream	 6dl 1dl	Strain the cooking liquor into a small pan, add the velouté and cream and reduce to a coating consistency.
4	egg yolks	2	Make a sabayon (84) and add to the sauce away from the heat. Pass the sauce through a fine strainer.
5	butter cayenne	75g	Mix in the butter thoroughly. Adjust the seasoning and finish with a little cayenne.
6			Coat the fillets of sole with the sauce and glaze under the salamander.
7	soft herring roes, poached Pommes Noisette (1580)	 10 200g	Place the poached herring roes between the fillets of sole and arrange the Pommes Noisette in neat bouquets at the side of the dishes.

619 Filet de Sole à l'Orly

10 portions
1 hour

Stage	Ingredient	Quantity	Method
1	sole fillets juice of lemon parsley, chopped oil	10 × 90g 1 1 tbsp ½dl	Wash and dry the fillets and place on a tray. Sprinkle with the lemon juice, parsley and oil and season with salt and pepper. Leave to marinate for approx. 30 mins.
2	flour Pâte à Frire (76)	 ½ litre	Pass the fillets through flour and place in the batter. Remove them one at a time and place gently into hot fat at 180°C. Fry until crisp and golden brown (5–6 mins.). The fillets must be turned over during the frying process to ensure even colouring.

Stage	Ingredient	Quantity	Method
3	parsley, picked		Drain the fillets well and place on dish papers on suitable dishes. Garnish with fried or picked parsley. Serve accompanied with Sauce Tomate.
	Sauce Tomate (118)	6dl	

620 Filet de Sole Otéro

10 portions
2 hours

Stage	Ingredient	Quantity	Method
1	potatoes, large oval	10 × 250g	Wash and dry. Make a shallow incision around the potatoes a little less than one-third of the way down. Place on a tray and bake in a hot oven 220°C until soft (approx. 1 hour).
2	egg yolk	1	Remove the tops from the potatoes and discard. Empty the potatoes with a spoon and pass the pulp quickly through a sieve. Place this in a pan on the stove and add the egg yolk and butter. Season and mix well.
	butter	25g	
3	sole fillets	10 × 90g	Fold the fillets in half, place in a buttered tray, season, add the fish stock, cover with a buttered paper and poach in a moderate oven at 195°C until cooked, approx. 12–15 mins.
	Fumet de Poisson (101)	2dl	
4	Sauce Mornay (171)	6dl	Strain the cooking liquor from the fillets into a small pan and reduce by approx. two-thirds. Add to the Sauce Mornay.
5	Parmesan, grated	25g	Place a little Sauce Mornay in the bottom of each potato case and place a fillet of sole on top. Pipe the potato mixture around the edges of the potatoes in a neat scroll. Cover the fillets of sole with Sauce Mornay, sprinkle with grated Parmesan and gratinate in a hot oven.
6	parsley, picked		Arrange on dish papers on oval dishes and garnish with picked parsley.

621 Filet de Sole Palace

10 portions
1 hour

Stage	Ingredient	Quantity	Method
1	shallots, finely chopped	50g	Butter a tray, sprinkle in the shallots and place the washed fillets on top. Add the mushrooms and tomatoes, season and sprinkle with the tarragon. Add the wine and fish stock. Cover with a buttered greaseproof paper and poach in a
	sole fillets	10 × 90g	
	button mushrooms, sliced	200g	
	tarragon, chopped	1 tbsp	

	Tomates Concassées (90)	200g	moderate oven at 195°C until cooked, approx. 12–15 mins.
	white wine, dry	1dl	
	Fumet de Poisson (101)	2dl	
2			Remove the fillets, drain well and dress neatly in earthenware dishes with the garnish. Strain the cooking liquor into a small pan and sprinkle any remaining garnish over the fillets. Cover and keep warm.
3	Velouté de Poisson (117)	6dl	Add the velouté and cream to the cooking liquor and reduce to a coating consistency.
	cream	1dl	
4	egg yolks	2	Make a sabayon (84) and add to the sauce away from the heat. Pass through a fine strainer.
5	butter	75g	Mix in the butter thoroughly. Adjust the seasoning and finish with a little cayenne and the brandy.
	brandy	¼dl	
	cayenne		
6			Coat the fish with the sauce and glaze under the salamander.

622 Filet de Sole Polignac

10 portions
45 mins.

Stage	Ingredient	Quantity	Method
1	sole fillets	10 × 90g	Butter a tray and place in the washed fillets of sole. Sprinkle the mushrooms and truffle over the fillets, season and add the wine and fish stock. Cover with a buttered greaseproof paper and poach in a moderate oven at 195°C until cooked, approx. 12–15 mins.
	mushrooms, ⎫ fine	200g	
	truffle ⎬ julienne	30g	
	white wine, dry	1dl	
	Fumet de Poisson (101)	2dl	
2			Remove the fillets, drain well and dress neatly in earthenware dishes with the garnish. Strain the cooking liquor into a small pan and sprinkle any remaining garnish over the fillets. Cover and keep warm.
3	Velouté de Poisson (117)	6dl	Add the velouté and cream to the cooking liquor and reduce to a coating consistency. Pass through a fine strainer.
	cream	1dl	
4	butter	75g	Mix in the butter away from the heat, adjust the seasoning and finish with a little cayenne.
	cayenne		

| 5 | Fleurons (33) | 10 | Coat the fish with the sauce and garnish with the fleurons. |

623 Filet de Sole à la Russe

10 portions
1 hour

Stage	Ingredient	Quantity	Method
1	sole fillets white wine, dry Fumet de Poisson (101)	10 × 90g 1dl 2dl	Butter a tray, place in the washed fillets, season and add the wine and fish stock. Cover with a buttered greaseproof paper and poach in a moderate oven at 195°C until cooked, approx. 12–15 mins.
2	carrots, small onions, button butter Fumet de Poisson (101)	150g 150g 25g 1dl	Groove the carrots (canneler) and cut into 2mm-thick slices. Cut the onions into rings 2mm thick. Place in a small pan with the butter and fish stock. Season, cover and cook gently until tender.
3			Remove the fillets, drain well and dress neatly in earthenware dishes. Cover and keep warm.
4	Velouté de Poisson (117)	4dl	Strain the fish cooking liquor into a small pan, add the velouté and reduce by one-third. Pass through a fine strainer.
5	butter cream cayenne	75g 2dl	Mix in the butter thoroughly away from the heat. Warm the cream and add to the sauce. Adjust the seasoning and finish with a little cayenne.
6	parsley, chopped	1 tbsp	Add the garnish of carrots and onions to the sauce together with the parsley. Coat the fish with the sauce. Do not glaze.

SPECIAL POINT
This sauce should be more creamy and thinner than in most other poached fish dishes.

624 Filet de Sole Saint-Germain

This is prepared in the same way as Filet de Sole Caprice (600) to the end of Stage 2. Arrange on a hot dish and garnish with Pommes Noisette (1580). Serve accompanied with a sauceboat of Sauce Béarnaise (153).

625 Filet de Sole Suchet

10 portions
1 hour

Stage	Ingredient	Quantity	Method
1	sole fillets carrot ⎫ leek ⎬ cut in celery ⎭ julienne	10 × 90g 75g 75g 75g	Butter a tray and place in the washed fillets. Blanch the julienne of vegetables in boiling water for 5 mins. Drain and sprinkle over the fish with the truffles.

	truffle, julienne	30g	Season, add the wine and fish stock and
	white wine, dry	1dl	cover with a buttered greaseproof paper.
	Fumet de Poisson		Poach in a moderate oven at 195°C until
	(101)	2dl	cooked, approx. 12–15 mins.
2			Remove the fillets, drain well and dress neatly in earthenware dishes with the garnish. Strain the cooking liquor into a small pan and sprinkle any remaining garnish over the fish.
3	Velouté de Poisson		Add the velouté and cream to the cook-
	(117)	6dl	ing liquor and reduce to a light coating
	cream	1dl	consistency. Pass through a fine strainer.
4	butter	75g	Mix in thoroughly away from the heat,
	cayenne		correct the seasoning and finish with a little cayenne. Coat the fish with the sauce. Do not glaze.

626 Filet de Sole Véronique

10 portions
1¼ hours

Stage	Ingredient	Quantity	Method
1	sole fillets	10 × 90g	Butter a tray. Wash the fillets, fold in
	white wine, dry	1dl	half, place in the tray and season. Add the
	Fumet de Poisson		wine and fish stock. Cover with a buttered
	(101)	2dl	greaseproof paper and poach in a moderate oven at 195°C until cooked, approx. 12–15 mins.
2			Remove the fillets, drain well and dress neatly in earthenware dishes. Cover and keep warm.
3	grapes, white	250g	Blanch, skin and remove the pips from the grapes. Arrange the grapes neatly between the fillets. Cover and keep warm.
4	Velouté de Poisson		Strain the cooking liquor into a small
	(117)	6dl	pan, add the velouté and cream and
	cream	1dl	reduce to a coating consistency.
5	egg yolks	2	Make a sabayon (84) and add to the sauce away from the heat. Pass through a fine strainer.
6	butter	75g	Mix in thoroughly, adjust the seasoning
	cayenne		and finish with a little cayenne.
7			Coat the fish and the garnish with the sauce and glaze under the salamander.

SPECIAL POINT

The classical method of serving Filet de Sole Véronique requires that the prepared grapes are well-chilled and place in a bouquet on the finished fish dish at the moment of service.

---

627 Filet de Sole au Vin Blanc

10 portions
1 hour

Stage	Ingredient	Quantity	Method
1	shallots, finely chopped	50g	Butter a tray, sprinkle in the shallots and place the washed fillets on top. Season,
	sole fillets	10 × 90g	add the wine and fish stock and cover
	white wine, dry	2dl	with a buttered greaseproof paper. Poach
	Fumet de Poisson (101)	1dl	in a moderate oven at 195°C until cooked, approx. 12–15 mins.
2			Remove the fillets leaving the shallots in the tray. Drain the fillets well and dress neatly in earthenware dishes. Cover and keep warm.
3	Velouté de Poisson (117)	6dl	Strain the cooking liquor into a small pan, add the velouté and cream and
	cream	1dl	reduce to a coating consistency. Pass through a fine strainer.
4	butter	75g	Mix in thoroughly away from the heat,
	cayenne		adjust the seasoning and finish with a little cayenne.
5	Fleurons (33)	10	Coat the fish with the sauce and garnish with the fleurons.

SPECIAL POINTS

a) Filet de Sole au Vin Blanc may be finished by glazing under the salamander before adding the fleurons. In this case a sabayon (84) of two egg yolks should be added to the sauce at Stage 3 prior to passing the sauce.

b) Filet de Sole au Chablis, Filet de Sole au Champagne and other similarly named dishes using a particular white wine are made in the same way as Filet de Sole au Vin Blanc by using the named wine.

---

628 Filet de Sole au Vin Rouge

10 portions
1 hour

Stage	Ingredient	Quantity	Method
1	shallots, finely chopped	50g	Butter a tray, sprinkle in the shallots and place the washed fillets on top. Season
	sole fillets	10 × 90g	and add the wine. Cover with a buttered
	red wine	3dl	greaseproof paper and poach in a moderate oven at 195°C until cooked, approx. 12–15 mins.
2			Remove the fillets leaving the shallots in the tray. Drain the fillets well and dress

			neatly in earthenware dishes. Cover and keep warm.
3	Demi-glace (112) anchovy essence	6dl 2 tbsps	Strain the cooking liquor into a small pan and reduce by two-thirds. Add the demi-glace and simmer gently to a coating consistency. Add the anchovy essence and pass through a fine strainer.
4	butter cayenne	50g	Mix the butter in thoroughly away from the heat. Adjust the seasoning and add a little cayenne.
5	Fleurons (33)	10	Coat the fish with the sauce and garnish with the fleurons.

629 Filet de Sole Walewska

Prepare in the same way as Filet de Sole Mornay (617), placing a slice of cooked lobster on each fillet before coating with the sauce and gratinating. Decorate with a slice of truffle on each fillet.

630 Goujons de Sole frits

10 portions
30 mins.

Stage	Ingredient	Quantity	Method
1	sole fillets	10 × 90g	Cut into strips approx. 8cm long and 1cm wide.
2	flour eggwash breadcrumbs } for crumbing		Wash, dry, season and paner à l'Anglaise (72). Roll cigar-shape.
3			Place in frying-baskets and deep fry at 190°C until crisp and golden brown.
4	lemons parsley, picked	2½	Drain the goujons well, season lightly with salt and place on dish papers on suitable dishes with quarters of lemon and fried or picked parsley. Fried Goujons of sole may be served with a suitable sauce, e.g. Sauce Tartare, Sauce Remoulade.

631 Goujonettes de Sole frites

These are prepared in the same way as Goujons de Sole frits (630) except that the fillets are cut into smaller strips, approx 6cm long by ½cm wide. These goujonettes are frequently served as a garnish for large whole fish dishes, e.g. Turbot à la Normande.

632 Goujons de Sole Murat

10 portions
1 hour

Stage	Ingredient	Quantity	Method
1	potatoes oil butter	500g 1dl 75g	Cut the potatoes into batons approx. 3cm long × 8mm × 8mm. Wash, dry, and fry until golden brown in the hot oil and butter. Drain and season and keep on one side.
2	Fonds d'Artichauts (1379)	10	Drain the artichokes and cut them into batons 8mm wide and fry quickly until golden brown in the fat remaining from Stage 1. Drain and lightly season.
3	sole fillets	750g	Cut into strips approx. 8cm long × 1cm wide. Wash and dry.
4	oil flour	2dl	Place the oil in a frying-pan and heat. Season half of the goujons, pass through flour and shake off the surplus in a sieve. When the oil is very hot add the goujons, fry quickly to a golden brown and drain. Repeat with the remainder of the fish.
5	butter juice of lemon parsley, chopped	150g ½	Mix the goujons, artichokes and potatoes together gently. Heat half of the butter in a large frying-pan and just as it turns nut-brown add half the mixture. Toss over quickly to heat thoroughly. Add lemon juice, sprinkle with chopped parsley and toss over again. Place in a hot earthenware dish and sprinkle with chopped parsley. Repeat with the remainder.

633 Mousselines de Sole au Vin Blanc

10 portions
1½ hours

Stage	Ingredient	Quantity	Method
1	sole fillets	750g	Either pound finely or pass twice through the fine plate of a mincer and place in a basin. Chill thoroughly.
2	egg whites, cold	3	Season with a little salt and pepper. Add the whites little by little, beating thoroughly with a wooden spatule until stiff and elastic in texture.
3			Pass the mixture through a fine sieve or food processor, replace in a basin and chill thoroughly in the refrigerator.

4	double cream, cold	5dl	Gradually add to the mixture beating thoroughly with a wooden spatule. Adjust the seasoning.
5			Butter a deep tray and, with a table-spoon, take a twentieth of the mixture. Mould egg-shape with a second table-spoon and remove from the first spoon. Place the mousseline in the tray. Continue until the mixture is finished, 20 pieces in all.
6	Fumet de Poisson (101)	1 litre	Season lightly, bring to the boil and pour gently around the mousselines. Cover with a buttered paper and poach in a moderate oven at 180°C until slightly firm and resilient to the touch, approx. 15 mins.
7	Sauce Vin Blanc (174) Fleurons (33)	6dl 20	Drain the mousselines well and arrange neatly in earthenware dishes. Coat with the sauce and garnish with fleurons.

SPECIAL POINTS

a) It is advisable to check the consistency of the mixture at Stage 4 when only three-quarters of the cream has been added. Poach a small piece in stock – if the result is too firm, carefully add the remainder; if too soft, add a little more egg white. At all stages of the making of the mixture, vigorous and firm beating is necessary.

b) Mousselines can be made with most fish having a reasonably firm texture such as whiting and salmon.

c) Mousselines of fish may be served with any suitable sauce and garnish applicable to poached fillets of sole.

---

634 Paupiette de Sole Sylvia

10 portions
1 hour

Stage	Ingredient	Quantity	Method
1	Fonds d'Artichaut (1379) Farce de Poisson (40)	6 250g	Drain the artichokes well. Pass through a fine sieve and place in a small sauteuse. Cook to a fairly dry consistency. Allow to become cold then mix into the fish farce.
2	sole fillets	10 × 90g	Wash the fillets well, dry and lightly flatten. Place skinned side uppermost and season. Spread the mixture on the fillets and roll them up from the thin end. Place upright in a buttered, shallow pan of a size to allow the paupiettes to be packed fairly tightly together.
3	white wine, dry Fumet de Poisson (101)	1dl 2dl	Add the wine and fish stock and season. Cover with a buttered paper and a lid and poach in a moderate oven at 180°C until cooked, approx. 15–18 mins.

4	Fonds d'Artichauts (1379)	10	Reheat the artichokes in the butter and place in earthenware dishes. Drain the paupiettes well and stand one on each artichoke bottom. Cover and keep warm.
	butter	25g	
5	Velouté de Poisson (117)	6dl	Strain the cooking liquor into a small pan. Add the velouté and cream and reduce to a coating consistency. Pass through a fine strainer.
	cream	1dl	
6	butter	75g	Mix in thoroughly away from the heat. Adjust the seasoning and finish with a little cayenne.
	cayenne		
7	truffle, slices	10	Coat the fish with the sauce and place one slice of truffle on each paupiette.

SPECIAL POINT

Any of the recipes for poached fillets of sole which entail coating with a sauce are suitable; it is only necessary that the fillets are spread with a plain fish farce before rolling them up.

THON – TUNNY

The flesh of this fish is very firm and solid and is similar to meat, thus it can be successfully grilled as steaks on or off the bone and large sections can be suitably braised, e.g. Pièce de Thon braisée au Vin Blanc.

---

635 Rouelle de Thon Mentonnaise

10 portions
2 hours

Stage	Ingredient	Quantity	Method
1	tunny steaks	10 × 120g	Place the steaks in a tray, season with salt and milled pepper and sprinkle with the herbs and lemon juice. Allow to marinate for 45 mins.
	thyme ⎫ very		
	basil ⎬ finely	1 tbsp	
	rosemary ⎭ chopped		
	lemon juice	2 tbsps	
2	butter	100g	Dry the steaks and lightly flour them. Heat the butter in a braising pan and quickly fry the steaks to a light brown on both sides. Remove the steaks to one side.
	flour		
3	mushrooms ⎫	150g	Add all these ingredients to the butter in the pan. Place the steaks on top, cover and place in a moderate oven 180°C for 15 mins.
	onions ⎪ cut in	250g	
	carrots ⎬ Brunoise	150g	
	celery ⎪ (22)	100g	
	fennel ⎭	100g	
	garlic, crushed	1 clove	
4	white wine, dry	3dl	Add to the pan, season lightly, cover and replace in the oven. Braise gently for
	Fumet de Poisson (101)	4dl	

| | Tomates Concassées (90) | 750g | approx. 1 hour basting occasionally. |
| | Bouquet Garni (19) | 1 | |

| 5 | | | Remove the steaks and clean off any vegetables adhering to them. Place in suitable earthenware dishes, cover and keep warm. |

6	small capers, squeezed dry	50g	Discard the bouquet garni, skim off any fat and reduce the cooking liquid and garnish by approx. half then add the capers, olives and anchovies and reboil. Adjust the seasoning as necessary plus a touch of cayenne.
	black olives, stoned, blanched and chopped	10	
	anchovy fillets, chopped	10	
	cayenne		

| 7 | basil leaves, coarsely chopped | 2 tbsps | Make sure that the tunny steaks are hot then ladle the sauce over. Finally sprinkle with the chopped basil. |

TRUITE – TROUT AND RAINBOW TROUT

636 Truite au Bleu

2 portions
45 mins.

Stage	Ingredient	Quantity	Method
1	carrots, small	50g	Groove the carrots (canneler). Cut the carrots and onions into rings 2mm thick and place in a small fish kettle with the water and vinegar. Add the remainder of the ingredients, season with salt and bring to the boil. Simmer very gently for 10 mins.
	onions, button	50g	
	water	1 litre	
	vinegar	2dl	
	peppercorns	10	
	bayleaf	½	
	parsley	few small sprigs	
2	live trout	2	Take the trout from the tank. Stun by holding in the left hand and hitting the head sharply with the back of a knife. Remove the gut and place the trout on a dish with the vinegar. Leave for 2 mins. and then turn them over. The action of the vinegar will set the slimy coating of the trout to a smoky blue film.
	vinegar	1dl	
3			Plunge the trout into the simmering court-bouillon and poach very gently for approx. 8–10 mins.

4	potatoes, plain boiled	4	Send the kettle to the table accompanied by small plain boiled potatoes and a sauceboat each of Beurre Fondu and Sauce Hollandaise.
	Beurre Fondu (9)	75g	
	Sauce Hollandaise (157)	1dl	

---

637 Truite grillée – Grilled Trout

10 portions
1 hour

Stage	Ingredient	Quantity	Method
1	trout	10 × 200g	Scale, cut off the fins, trim the tails and gut. Wash, dry and cut four to five shallow incisions on each side of the thicker part of the fish.
2	flour oil		Season the trout, lightly flour and brush with oil. Place on a fish grill and grill on both sides to a good colour (approx. 5–6 mins. each side).
3	melted butter lemons parsley, picked	50g 2	Dress the trout neatly on dishes and brush with the melted butter. Garnish with slices of grooved lemon and picked parsley.
4	Beurre Maître d'Hôtel (10)	150g	Serve accompanied with the Beurre Maître d'Hôtel.

---

638 Truite Meunière

10 portions
1 hour

Stage	Ingredient	Quantity	Method
1	trout	10 × 200g	Scale, cut off the fins, trim the tails and gut. Wash, dry and cut four to five shallow incisions on each side at the thicker part of the fish.
2	oil flour	2dl	Place the oil in a frying-pan and heat. Season the trout, lightly flour and, when the oil is very hot, place the trout in the pan all facing the same way. Fry quickly until brown. Turn over and colour the other side. Draw the pan to the side of the stove and allow to cook more slowly.
3	lemon, peeled slices juice of lemon	10 ½	Remove the trout and dress neatly in earthenware dishes and keep on the side of the stove; place one slice of lemon on each trout and sprinkle with lemon juice.
4	butter, soft parsley, chopped	150g	Place the butter in a frying-pan and cook until nut-brown in colour shaking the pan to ensure even colouring. Pour

quickly over the fish and sprinkle with
chopped parsley.

Trout Meunière can be served with any of the different garnishes listed under Filet de
Sole Meunière (614–616).

---

639 Truite Meunière aux Amandes

10 portions
1 hour

Stage	Ingredient	Quantity	Method
1	trout	10 × 200g	Scale, cut off the fins, trim the tails and gut. Wash, dry and cut four to five shallow incisions on each side at the thicker part of the fish.
2	oil	2dl	Place the oil in a frying-pan and heat. Season the trout, lightly flour and, when the oil is very hot, place the trout in the pan all facing the same way. Fry quickly until brown. Turn over and colour the other side. Draw the pan to the side of the stove and allow to cook more slowly.
	flour		
3	lemon, peeled		Remove the trout and dress neatly in earthenware dishes and keep on the side of the stove. Place one slice of lemon on each trout and sprinkle with lemon juice.
	slices	10	
	juice of lemon	½	
4	butter, soft	150g	Place the butter into a frying-pan and cook, shaking the pan to ensure even colouring. Just before it begins to turn nut-brown add the almonds and continue cooking until the almonds become lightly coloured. Pour quickly over the fish and sprinkle with chopped parsley.
	almonds, cut in		
	short julienne	100g	
	parsley, chopped		

---

640 Truite au Vin Blanc

10 portions
1½ hours

Stage	Ingredient	Quantity	Method
1	trout	10 × 200g	Scale, cut off the fins, trim the tails and gut. Wash well.
2	shallots, finely		Butter a deep tray. Sprinkle in the shallots and place the trout on top. Season and add the wine and fish stock. Cover with a buttered greaseproof paper and poach in a moderate oven at 195°C until cooked, approx. 12–15 mins.
	chopped	50g	
	white wine, dry	2dl	
	Fumet de Poisson		
	(101)	1dl	
3			Remove the trout leaving the shallots in the tray. Drain the trout and skin both sides. Dress neatly in earthenware dishes. Cover and keep warm.

4	Velouté de Poisson (117)	6dl	Strain the cooking liquor into a small pan. Add the velouté and cream and reduce to a coating consistency. Pass through a fine strainer.
	cream	1dl	
5	butter	75g	Mix in thoroughly away from the heat, correct the seasoning and finish with a little cayenne.
	cayenne		
6	Fleurons (33)	10	Coat the fish with the sauce and garnish with the fleurons.

SPECIAL POINTS

a) Truite au Vin Blanc may be finished by glazing under the salamander before adding the fleurons. In this case a sabayon (84) of two egg yolks should be added to the sauce at Stage 4 prior to passing the sauce.
b) Truite au Chablis, Truite au Champagne and other similarly named dishes using a particular white wine are made in the same way as Truite au Vin Blanc but using the named wine.

TRUITE SAUMONÉE – SALMON TROUT

Large salmon trout 1½–5kg in weight can be served in accordance with the recipes listed under salmon. Small salmon trout up to 1½kg can be served in accordance with the recipes listed under trout.

If for Meunière, salmon trout of ¾–1½kg are more satisfactorily cooked if split open from the back, the central bones removed and then cooked flat.

TURBOT ET TURBOTIN – TURBOT AND CHICKEN TURBOT

Turbotin (chicken turbot) is a young turbot weighing not more than $2\frac{1}{2}$–3kg. Over this weight it is known as turbot. For turbot or turbotin which is to be served as suprêmes or médaillons the recipes for fillets of sole are applicable.

641 Turbot à la Normande

10 portions
1¾ hours

Stage	Ingredient	Quantity	Method
1	turbot	1 × 3kg	Cut off the fins and trim the tail. On the black skin side cut down to the central bone from the head and almost to the tail. Partially detach the fillets by about 2cm on each side and cut through the exposed bone in two or three places. Wash well.
2	Fumet de Poisson (101)	1 litre	Place the turbot on the buttered grill of a turbot kettle, black side down. Add the fish stock and wine, season, cover with the lid and bring to the boil. Poach gently in a moderate oven at approx.
	white wine, dry	5dl	

Stage	Ingredient	Quantity	Method
			175°C for 40–45 mins. basting now and again with the cooking liquid.
3			Remove the turbot, drain well and place on a suitable buttered dish. Cover and keep warm.
4	Velouté de Poisson (117)	5dl	Strain the cooking liquor into a sauteuse and reduce by three-quarters. Add the velouté and mushroom trimmings and reduce to a coating consistency.
	white mushroom trimmings	250g	
5	egg yolks	3	Mix the egg yolks and cream together in a large basin. Add a little of the sauce to the yolks and cream mixing in quickly and return this mixture to the rest of the sauce, mixing in quickly. Reduce the sauce to a good coating consistency, stirring with a spatule, then pass through a fine strainer.
	cream	3dl	
6	butter	75g	Mix in thoroughly away from the heat; adjust the seasoning and finish with a little cayenne.
	cayenne		
7	mussels, cooked to Stage 1 (674)	20	Place the mushrooms along the centre of the turbot and arrange the oysters and mussels in bouquets around the dish. Coat the fish and the garnish with the sauce and finish garnishing with slices of truffle, bouquets of goujonettes and the croûtons tipped with chopped parsley.
	oysters, poached (672)	20	
	button mushrooms, cooked à Blanc (60)	20	
	Goujonettes de Sole frites (631)	30	
	small Heart-shaped Croûtons (26)	10	
	parsley, chopped		
	truffle, slices	10	

SPECIAL POINT

Whole turbot can be poached or braised and served with other appropriate fish sauces and garnishes as seen fit.

642 Tronçon de Turbot grillé – Grilled Turbot 10 portions 45 mins

Stage	Ingredient	Quantity	Method
1	turbot tronçons	10 × 180g	Wash the tronçons well, dry, season and lightly flour. Brush well with the oil.
	flour		
	oil	1dl	

2			Place on a fish grill and grill on both sides to a good colour (approx. 8 mins. each side).
3	butter, melted	50g	Dress the tronçons neatly on dishes, and
	lemons	2	brush with melted butter. Garnish with
	parsley, picked		slices of grooved lemon and picked parsley. Serve accompanied with Beurre Maître d'Hôtel, Beurre d'Anchois or Sauce Diable.

643 Tronçon de Turbot poché – Poached Turbot   10 portions
40 mins.

Stage	Ingredient	Quantity	Method
1	water	6 litres	Place the water and lemon juice in a
	juice of lemons	3	shallow pan. Season with salt and bring to the boil.
2	turbot tronçons	10 × 180g	Wash well, place into the boiling liquid and reboil. Skim, draw to the side of the stove and allow to poach gently until cooked (approx. 20 mins.).
3	potatoes, small turned	20	Place in boiling water and cook until tender.
4	lemons	2	Dress the cooked turbot neatly in
	parsley sprigs		earthenware dishes. Add a little cooking
	Sauce Hollandaise		liquor to cover the bottom of the dish.
	(157) or other		Garnish with slices of grooved lemon,
	suitable sauce	6dl	the potatoes and picked parsley. Serve with an appropriate sauce, e.g. Sauce Hollandaise, Homard, Persil, Crème, aux Oeufs.

644 Médaillon de Turbot Trouvillaise   10 portions
50 mins.

Stage	Ingredient	Quantity	Method
1	turbot, médaillons (537)	10 × 120g	Cut out a deep V-shape from along the top and to one side of the médaillons. Do not cut completely through.
2	whiting flesh, free of skin and bone	250g	Make a Mousseline Forcemeat (39) with these ingredients, plus the flesh removed from the médaillons.
	egg white	1	
	cream, double	1½dl	
3	truffle, chopped	15g	Mix the truffle and nuts into the force-
	pistachio nuts, skinned and chopped	15g	meat. Lightly season the openings of the fish and fill each with an equal amount of the forcemeat. Smooth neatly then

	prawn tails, shelled	30	press three prawns half-way into the surface of each.
4	white wine, dry	1dl	Place the médaillons into a well-buttered shallow pan, add the wine and fishstock, season and cover with a buttered paper. Place in a moderate oven at 195°C and poach gently until just cooked, approx. 15 mins. Drain off the cooking liquid into a small pan. Keep the médaillons covered and warm.
	Fumet de Poisson (101)	2dl	
	butter	50g	
5	Lobster Sauce (169)	4dl	Reduce the cooking liquid well, add the lobster sauce and cream and reduce to a light coating consistency. Season as necessary plus a touch of cayenne and finish with the brandy. Pass through a fine strainer and keep hot.
	cream, double	1dl	
	brandy	¼dl	
	cayenne		
6	oysters, bearded, breadcrumbed and deep-fried	30	Place a little of the sauce on suitable plates or dishes. Arrange the médaillons neatly on top; brush the surface with a little melted butter and place two tarragon leaves neatly on each. Arrange the fried oysters and fleurons to one side.
	Fleurons (33)	10	
	butter, melted	25g	
	tarragon leaves, blanched	20	

MISCELLANEOUS
———————— FISH DISHES ————————

This section includes those fish dishes which do not fall easily into the previous sections.

---

645 Bouillabaisse

10 portions
1¾ hours

Bouillabaisse is a type of fish stew and is a regional speciality from the South of France. The most famous version is Bouillabaisse à la Marseillaise in which an assortment of Mediterranean fish, usually of second quality, is used. The following recipe is an acceptable version much in line with modern practice.

Stage	Ingredient	Quantity	Method
1	mackerel ⎫ John Dory ⎪ red mullet ⎬ whiting ⎭	2½kg	Clean the fish and cut into 5cm thick sections on the bone. Scrape and wash the mussels.
	mussels	500g	

2	oil	1dl	Place the oil in a deep pan and add the
	white of leek,		rest of the ingredients. Place all the fish
	cut in julienne	200g	except the whiting on top. Season, cover
	onions, finely		and cook gently for 5 mins.
	sliced	250g	
	garlic, finely		
	chopped	2 cloves	
	fennel seed	pinch	
	saffron	pinch	
	bayleaf	1	
	thyme	sprig	
	parsley, chopped	1 tbsp	
	Tomates Concassées	500g	
	(90)		
3	white wine, dry	½ litre	Add the wine and sufficient water to
	water		cover the fish. Bring to the boil. Skim
			and simmer gently for 7–8 mins. Add
			the whiting, adjust the seasoning and
			continue cooking for a further 7–8 mins.
4	French bread	2	Serve the Bouillabaisse in a large tureen
			accompanied with slices of French
			bread.

SPECIAL POINT

In France it is usual to place a few slices of bread in a soup plate and to ladle some of the cooking liquor over the bread. This is then eaten as soup. The fish and the rest of the cooking liquor is then served afterwards with more bread.

---

646 Brochette de Poisson à l'Orientale

10 portions
2 hours

Stage	Ingredient	Quantity	Method
1	monkfish, fillet	250g	Cut the monkfish and chicken each into
	scallops	10	20 thickish pieces about 3cm square.
	eel, skinned	350g	Cut the scallops and their roes each in
	chicken breast,		half horizontally. Fillet the eel and cut
	skinned	2	into 20 approx. 3cm squares.
2	sherry	½dl	Place the sherry, soy, and lemon juice in
	soy sauce	2 tbsps	a shallow tray, add the fish and chicken,
	lemon juice	½	sprinkle with the coriander and season
	coriander, ground	good pinch	with the salt, pepper and cayenne. Turn
	pepper, milled		over carefully to mix and leave to
	salt		marinate for 45 mins.
	cayenne		
3	pimento, red,		Thread the fish, scallops, eel, chicken
	cut in 2½cm		and pimento equally onto 10 skewers
	squares	2	interspersing with sage leaves.
	fresh sage leaves		

4	vegetable oil		Sprinkle with oil and grill gently on both sides, brushing frequently with the remaining marinade, approx. 10 mins.
5	Riz Pilaff Safrané (527) Coulis de Tomates (179) or Coulis de Poivrons (178)	10 portions 6dl	Arrange the rice as beds on suitable dishes and dress the brochettes neatly on top. Serve accompanied with either of the sauces.

---

647 Coquille de Poisson Mornay

10 portions
45 mins.

Stage	*Ingredient*	*Quantity*	*Method*
1	Pommes Duchesse (1560)	750g	Pipe the Pommes Duchesse around the edge of ten scallop shells and dry for a few seconds under the salamander.
2	butter fish, cooked and flaked	75g 750g	Melt the butter in a small pan. Add the fish and toss over to reheat.
3	Sauce Mornay (171) Parmesan, grated	7dl 50g	Place a little sauce in the bottom of each shell. Add the flaked fish then coat with the sauce. Sprinkle with the Parmesan and gratinate under the salamander.
4	parsley, picked		Dress the Coquilles on dish papers on suitable dishes garnished with picked parsley.

SPECIAL POINTS
a) Any type of poached fish may be used for preparing Coquille de Poisson Mornay but it is desirable to designate the fish being used in the title of the dish, e.g. Coquille de Turbot or Coquille de Saumon Mornay.
b) Coquille de Poisson may be made with other fish sauces, e.g. Coquille de Cabillaud Bercy.

---

648 Caissette de Turbot et Saumon Granvillaise

4 portions
1½ hours

Stage	*Ingredient*	*Quantity*	*Method*
1	puff pastry (1736)	300g	Prepare and cook four puff pastry cases in the same manner as Vols-au-vent (1714), but cutting the pastry with a knife into oblongs 9cm × 6cm. Remove the lids when cooked and empty the insides of any soft dough. Keep warm.
2	turbot, fillet salmon, fillet	200g 200g	Cut each fillet into eight slices approx. ½cm thick and trim into small médaillons approx. 5cm in diameter. Keep the trimmings.

3	butter	25g	Heat the butter in a pan, add the shallots and cook without colour. Add the mushrooms, season lightly and cook for a few mins. Now add the trimmings of fish cut in small dice and the prawns; toss over until just cooked.
	shallots	25g	
	mushrooms, cut in small dice	50g	
	prawns, cut in small dice	50g	
4	egg yolk	1	Whisk the yolk and cream together and mix quickly into the ingredients. Cook quickly until the mixture thickens, adjust the seasoning, cover and keep warm.
	cream	2 tbsps	
5	butter	75g	Heat the butter in a shallow pan, season the médaillons of fish and gently cook on both sides. Just before ready sprinkle with the basil, cover with a lid, remove pan from the stove but keep warm.
	basil leaves, chopped	½ tbsp	
6	butter	25g	Heat the butter in a small pan, add the shallots and cook without colour. Add the wine, reduce by two-thirds, then the fish stock and reduce by three-quarters. Add the cream and reduce to a medium coating consistency. Season well plus a touch of cayenne. Pass through a fine strainer and keep warm.
	shallots, chopped	25g	
	Noilly Prat	½dl	
	Fumet de Poisson (101)	2dl	
	cream	2dl	
	cayenne		
7	truffle slices	4	To dress: first make sure everything is nicely hot. Cover the bottoms of the pastry cases with the prawns and mushroom mixture. Arrange the turbot and salmon médaillons on top – overlapping and alternately (use two médaillons of each fish and four in total for each case). Spoon over a little of the sauce to cover, place a slice of truffle on top and cover with the pastry lid to one side. Place on suitable dishes or plates as necessary.

649 Fish Cakes

10 portions
45 mins.

Stage	Ingredient	Quantity	Method
1	fish, cooked	600g	Pass the fish through the medium plate of the mincer and add the rest of the ingredients. Season and mix well together.
	potato, dry mashed	600g	
	egg yolks	3	
	parsley, chopped	2 tbsps	
2	flour, eggwash, breadcrumbs } for crumbing		Divide the mixture into ten equal pieces, mould into balls and paner à l'Anglaise (72). Flatten into round cakes and mark trellis-fashion.

3		Place the fish cakes into frying-baskets and deep fry in hot fat at approx. 180°C until golden brown.
4	parsley, picked Sauce Tomate (118) 6dl	Drain the fish cakes, serve on dish papers on suitable dishes and garnish with picked parsley. Serve accompanied with the sauce.

650 Friture des Pêcheurs

Prepare equal quantities of:
1) Goujonettes de Plie frites (577).
2) Blanchailles frites (546),
3) small Médaillons of monkfish, egg-and-breadcrumbed and deep-fried,
4) mussels cooked to Stage 1 (674), marinated with chopped shallot, chopped parsley, lemon juice, salt and pepper, then drained, passed through frying batter and deep-fried,
5) Scampi frits (676).
6) Coquilles St Jacques frites (654),
7) rings of squid, lightly seasoned, floured, passed through frying batter and deep-fried, and
8) small fresh sardines, passed through milk then flour and deep-fried.

These are best presented for a minimum of four persons, arranged neatly in separate bouquets on a folded serviette or dish paper on a large dish. The dish may be garnished with rings of fried onion (1490), rondelles of fried courgettes (1447), and fried parsley.
  A selection of the following sauces should be offered – Sauce Tartare (192), Sauce Remoulade (191), Coulis Palermitaine (177), Coulis de Tomate (179).

SPECIAL POINT
Allow approx. 200–250g raw weight of fish in total per person or put another way, approx. 30–35g of each different fish per person.

651 Grenouilles (Cuisses de) – Frogs' Legs

Correctly speaking the frog is an amphibian and not a fish but it is usually included in the fish section of cookery books. Frogs' legs are generally imported from France and can be cooked in a number of ways, e.g. à la Meunière, fried, poached in white wine, and served with Sauce Poulette, à la Provençale etc.

11
Shellfish

Shellfish have always enjoyed a wide popularity, ranging from the more commonplace cockle to the luxury of the oyster and lobster. In most cases popularity has been attended with relative scarcity, high prices and subsequent controls on overfishing. Regular supplies of fresh fish cannot always be guaranteed as bad weather can often disrupt availability but supplies of frozen items such as prawns, scampi and rock lobster tails can usually be relied on. There is also a certain amount of air freighting of live lobsters and oysters and an increasing trade from Eastern Europe of freshwater crayfish.

For the most part shellfish are suitable for lunch and dinner as subsidiary and main dishes. They also play an important part in the garnishing of hors-d'oeuvre, salads, fish dishes and savouries and increasingly as part of meat and poultry dishes.

CLASSIFICATION

Shellfish are broadly classified into two main groups, crustaceans and molluscs. Crustaceans have an external skeleton or shell and a number of jointed limbs. They are all taken from salt water with the exception of the crayfish which, although like a miniature lobster, is a denizen of the river. The shells of this group contain much of the quality and essential flavour of the particular shellfish in a quite concentrated form and because of this the shells can be pulverised and used in the making of excellent sauces. Molluscs in the main are soft-bodied shellfish contained in single or double shells.

Those shellfish in general use are:
Crustaceans: crab, crawfish or spiny lobster, crayfish, lobster, prawns, scampi or Dublin Bay prawns, and shrimps.
Molluscs: clams, cockles, mussels, oysters and scallops; the squid, although technically in a separate class, is included here.

QUALITY POINTS

Although items such as prawns and shrimps are usually available only in frozen or cook-chilled form it must be stated as a general principle that all shellfish are best if bought in the live state and processed on the premises. This not only ensures the maximum of freshness and eating qualities but it is also the best safeguard against the possibility of contamination and toxicity.

When delivered, lobsters, crabs, crawfish and crayfish should be evidently alive – they should feel heavy in relation to size.

The best weights for lobster are between 650g and 900g; over this weight the flesh tends to become tougher and more stringy. The hen lobster (female) can be distinguished by having a broad tail, the first pair of feelers under the tail and near the head being soft and feathery, and it may carry eggs. In the cock lobster the tail is narrower and the first pair of feelers are smaller and hard. The flesh of the hen lobster is presumed to have the better eating qualities but this is arguable.

By law, the common edible crab must not be landed under 12½cm measured across the back. At this size they tend to be less useful for service as dressed crab – the best size for this is anything between 1 and 2kg live weight. Again, if too large the flesh tends to become too coarse.

Crawfish or spiny lobster are best when no larger than 3kg live weight. Over this the flesh also becomes less palatable and coarse.

Freshwater crayfish are useful at any size, the smallest for soups and sauces and larger ones, 40–120g, for specialised dishes.

Bivalve molluscs should be tightly closed, fairly free of barnacles and mud and should feel heavy in relation to size. Discard any which are open. Fresh ones should always have a fresh seawater smell. Any signs of putrid or foul smell means danger and they should be rejected.

STORAGE

The ideal storage for live crustaceans is obviously the seawater or freshwater tank but this is only possible where the supplier is concerned or where the catering establishment specialises in shellfish. Otherwise lobster, crab and crayfish etc. can be kept alive for 12 hours or so if covered with a wet cloth and kept in a cool place. Mussels and oysters can be kept for up to 24 hours or so if also covered with a damp sack and kept in a very cool place. The rule though should be to use them as soon as possible and to keep a regular cycle of ordering and use.

Cooked shellfish are prone to rapid deterioration with all its attendant dangers – they must be stored in a refrigerator reserved for fish only and the storage period should not exceed 24 hours.

CLEANING AND PREPARATION

In general, shellfish need little preparation other than washing and cleaning before being cooked but this must be carried out carefully. There are also a number of preparations for the crustaceans which involve some degree of special manipulation or cutting.

Lobster
Preparation of cooked lobster for cold:
1) Detach the claws and legs from close to the body.
2) Cut the lobster in half lengthways; a) first pull out the tail and spread the lobster flat on a board, b) insert the point of a knife in the centre of the natural line and just where the head joins the tail, and cut through the head to the board, c) turn the lobster round and cut clean through the remaining tail giving two equal halves.
3) Remove the sacs of grit in the head and also the black trail from the tail. Do not remove the creamy parts from the head.
4) Break back the small pincer of each claw and pull out.
5) Crack the claws carefully with a heavy knife and remove the flesh in one piece. Cut through the remaining segments of the claws and remove any flesh – this can be placed in the cavity in the head together with a few capers, if being served as half a cold lobster.

6) If needed for a lobster salad or mayonnaise, remove the flesh from the tail and cut into sections on the slant. If for half a cold lobster do not remove from the shell; dress as for Recipe 1276.

Cutting raw for à l'Américaine etc.:
1) Wash the lobster.
2) Place the lobster flat on a board and to kill it, insert the point of a knife in the centre of the natural line of the head just behind the eyes and cut through to the board,
3) Remove the claws and crack them,
4) Starting near the head cut the tail into its natural segments and remove the black trail from each segment.
5) Split the head part into two halves and discard the sacs of grit.
6) Remove the creamy parts (tomalley) and coral if any and place in a basin.

Crawfish (Spiny Lobster)
The crawfish, although similar in many respects to the lobster, does not have claws. Small specimens of between 850g and 1¼kg can be prepared for cold or for à l'Américaine in the same way as lobster. If a large specimen is needed to be cooked for cold buffet work such as à la Parisienne, it should first be laid flat on a board then tied down before placing in boiling court-bouillon.

Freshwater Crayfish (also known as Yabbies)
Gutting (châtrer): this must be carried out immediately before cooking. Hold the middle tail flap, twist to dislocate from the shell, then pull carefully so as to remove the gut (trail) in one piece without breaking.
Trussing (trousser): this must be carried out just before cooking. Turn the tail of the crayfish over its head and embed the small pincers into each side of the exposed underside of the tail.

Dublin Bay Prawn – Scampi
Extracting the flesh of the tail:
1) Gut the shellfish in the same way as for crayfish.
2) Remove the head and claws in one piece and reserve for sauce or soups.
3) Place the tail sideways on a board, strike smartly with the hand to break the bony connecting tissues on the underside.
4) Pull open and extract the flesh in one piece.

Crab
The edible crab is liable to shed its claws if not killed before cooking. To kill, use a thin ice pick and 1) stab underneath just above the mouth and 2) lift up the tail flap and also stab in a number of directions in the centre of the exposed parts.
    To dress a boiled crab see Recipe 267.

Mussels and Clams
Before cooking, discard any fish with open shells then wash them well to remove any sand or mud. Scrape the shells clear of any barnacles and any attached hairy fibres. Soak for 2–3 hours in cold salted water to assist in disgorging any sand. Give a final wash before cooking.

Scallops

To remove the scallop from its shell:

1) Place it, round shell downwards, on the side of a hot stove. This will force the fish to detach itself from this shell and the top flat shell will spring open with the fish attached.
2) Slide a sharp knife between the flat shell and the fish. Discard the flat shell.
3) Discard the dark frill leaving the white round centre with the orange tongue (roe) attached.
4) Wash these and use as required.
5) Scrub and boil the deep shell carefully. Allow to dry and use for the presentation of fish dishes where called for.

Squid

Preparation for cooking:

1) Hold the tentacles firmly near the head and pull gently away from the body to extract the inner organs and beak.
2) Cut the tentacles away from the head just behind the eyes leaving them attached to a ring of flesh. Remove and discard the beak.
3) Discard the intestines but reserve the ink sac if required.
4) Remove and discard the transparent bony quill and loose membrane from inside the body.
5) Clean and remove the fine skin from the outside of the body and fins.
6) Wash the body and tentacles which are now ready for use.

Sea Urchin – Oursin

1) Scrape out the flesh without cracking the spiky covering.
2) Serve raw with strips of brown bread and butter.

COOKING METHODS

Generally speaking the most appropriate methods for the cooking of shellfish are boiling, poaching and steaming, and as parts of fish stews. They also lend themselves to gentle shallow frying and deep frying, especially for the smaller items, but braising and roasting are not really suitable because of the long cooking times involved, although it is possible with care to roast a lobster.

WEIGHT LOSS AND PORTION GUIDE

Crustaceans: Lobsters, crawfish, crayfish, scampi and crab will lose on average from 10 to 15% approx. of their original weight after being boiled. The shell and unused parts of the same cooked fish can represent as much as 70–75% of the total weight leaving some 25% approx. of edible flesh. Cooked prawns and shrimps will yield up to 40% edible flesh.

Molluscs: More often than not the yield from mussels and clams is determined by calculating a given weight per number of portions. On average this works out at between 2½ and 3kg live shellfish per 10 portions as a fish dish.

Scallops are usually reckoned as 1–2 fish per portion as a fish course and 2–3 as a main dish. Oysters are always calculated by number whether raw or cooked and can vary from 6 to 12 per portion.

CALMAR – SQUID

652 Calmars Royannaise

10 portions
1½ hours

Stage	Ingredient	Quantity	Method
1	squid, small	1½kg	Clean and prepare the squid (page 247). Reserve the ink from the sacs. Cut the squid into ½cm rings or strips and cut the tentacles into small pieces.
2	butter oil salt pepper	50g 1dl	Heat the butter and oil in a shallow pan. Take one-half of the squid, season and shallow fry quickly to a light brown colour. Remove from the pan and keep on one side. Repeat for the remainder.

3	onions, chopped
	pimento, red,
	  skinned,
	  deseeded and
	  cut into short
	  julienne
	garlic, crushed
		75g
		
		125g
		1 clove
			Add to the fat in the pan and cook gently with just a little colour. Drain off surplus fat and replace the squid in with these ingredients.

4	Tomates Concassées
	  (90)
	white wine, dry
	chilli peppers
	fresh marjoram
	  leaves, chopped
		
		500g
		5dl
		2
		
		good pinch
			Add to the pan together with the reserved ink. Cover with a lid and cook gently for 30–35 mins. in a moderate oven at 170°C.

5	butter	75g	Skim off any fat, discard the chillis and reduce the sauce by half. Shake in the butter and adjust the seasoning as necessary.
6	Riz Pilaff Safrané (527) parsley, chopped marjoram, chopped	10 portions 1 tbsp 1 tbsp	Arrange the squid and sauce in suitable dishes and sprinkle with the chopped herbs. Serve the Riz Pilaff separately.

SPECIAL POINT
The sauce should not be too liquid but fairly thick and well-reduced.

COQUILLES ST JACQUES – SCALLOPS

653 Coquilles St Jacques Bercy

10 portions
1 hour

Stage	Ingredient	Quantity	Method
1	scallops	20	Place deep shells down on the side of a hot stove until they open. Remove the

Stage	Ingredient	Quantity	Method
			fish and cut off the frills leaving the round white pieces and red tongues clean. Scrub the deep shells and dry; discard the flat shells.
2	milk	½ litre	Wash the prepared scallops. Place in a pan, cover with the milk and add the rest of the ingredients. Season with salt, bring to the boil and poach on the side of the stove for approx. 5 mins.
	bayleaf	½	
	thyme	sprig	
	onion, finely sliced	50g	
	parsley stalks	20g	
3	Pommes Duchesse (1560)	750g	Place in a piping bag with a star tube and pipe around the edge of 10 of the shells. Dry for a few seconds under the salamander.
4	egg yolks	2	Make a sabayon (84) with the egg yolks and add to the hot sauce away from the heat.
	Sauce Bercy (163)	6dl	
5			Place a little sauce in the bottom of each shell. Drain the scallops, remove the tongues and cut the white parts into slices; arrange on the sauce in the shells with the tongues on top. Coat with the sauce and glaze under the salamander.
6	parsley, picked		Dress the scallops on dish papers on suitable dishes and garnish with picked parsley.

654 Coquilles St Jacques frites au Lard – Fried Scallops and Bacon

10 portions
40 mins.

Stage	Ingredient	Quantity	Method
1	scallops	20	Place deep shells down on the side of a hot stove until they open. Remove the fish and cut off the frills leaving the round white pieces and the red tongues clean. Do not separate the white part from the tongue.
2	flour ⎫ egg wash ⎬ for crumbing breadcrumbs ⎭		Wash dry and season the scallops. Paner à l'Anglaise (72) and reshape.
3			Place in a frying-basket and deep fry at approx. 185°C until golden brown; drain, lightly season with salt and dress in earthenware dishes.
4	bacon, back rashers	20	Grill the bacon, arrange neatly with the fried scallops and garnish with picked parsley.
	parsley, picked		

655 Coquilles St Jacques Mornay

10 portions
1 hour

Stage	Ingredient	Quantity	Method
1	scallops	20	Place deep shells down on the side of a hot stove until they open. Remove the fish and cut off the frills leaving the round white pieces and red tongues clean. Scrub the deep shells and dry. Discard the flat shells.
2	milk bayleaf thyme onion, shredded parsley stalks	½ litre ½ sprig 50g 20g	Wash the prepared scallops. Place in a pan, cover with the milk and add the rest of the ingredients. Season with salt, bring to the boil and poach on the side of the stove for approx. 5 mins.
3	Pommes Duchesse (1560)	750g	Place in a piping bag with a star tube and pipe around the edge of 10 of the shells. Dry for a few seconds under the salamander.
4	Sauce Mornay (171) Parmesan, grated	5dl 50g	Place a little sauce in the bottom of each shell. Drain the scallops. Remove the tongues and cut the white parts into slices. Arrange on the sauce in the shells with a tongue on top. Coat with the sauce, sprinkle with grated Parmesan and gratinate under the salamander.
5	parsley, picked		Dress the scallops on dish papers on suitable dishes and garnish with picked parsley.

656 Coquilles St Jacques Parisienne

10 portions
1 hour

Stage	Ingredient	Quantity	Method
1	scallops	20	Place deep shells down on the side of a hot stove until they open. Remove the fish and cut off the frills leaving the round white pieces and red tongues clean. Scrub the deep shells and dry. Discard the flat shells.
2	milk bayleaf thyme onion, finely sliced parsley stalks	½ litre ½ sprig 50g 20g	Wash the prepared scallops. Place in a pan, cover with the milk and add the rest of the ingredients. Season with salt. Bring to the boil and poach on the side of the stove for approx. 5 mins.

3	Pommes Duchesse (1560)	750g	Place in a piping bag with a star tube and pipe around the edge of 10 of the shells. Dry for a few seconds, under the salamander.
4	egg yolks Sauce Vin Blanc (174)	2 5dl	Make a sabayon (84) with the egg yolks and add to the hot sauce away from the heat. Pass through a fine strainer.
5			Place a little sauce in the bottom of each shell. Drain the scallops, remove the tongues and cut the white parts into slices. Arrange on the sauce in the shells with a tongue on top. Coat with the sauce and glaze under the salamander.
6	parsley, picked		Dress the scallops on dish papers on suitable dishes and garnish with picked parsley.

CRABE – CRAB

657 Boiled Crab

Wash and kill the crab (page 246) and plunge into sufficient boiling salted water to cover. Simmer for approx. 35–40 mins. for crabs weighing approx. 2 kg. Allow to cool in the cooking liquor if to be used for cold, e.g. Dressed Crab.

658 Quenelles de Crabe Calaisienne

10 portions
2 hours

Stage	Ingredient	Quantity	Method
1	crab, cooked	1 × 1kg	Remove the white meat from the breast and claws and reserve. Discard the gills. Remove the dark creamy flesh from inside the shell and reserve. Pound the shells and breast finely and reserve.
2	whiting fillet, free of skin and bones egg whites salt pepper nutmeg, grated	650g 2 10g pinch pinch	Pass the whiting through the fine plate of the mincer twice. Place in a basin, season with salt, pepper and a little nutmeg and beat together thoroughly with a wooden spatule, adding the whites of egg little by little and until the mixture is stiff and elastic. Pass through a fine sieve, replace the mixture into a basin and chill thoroughly.
3	Frangipane Panada (69), cold	200g	Add the panada and beat thoroughly together.

| 4 | tomato purée | 1 tsp | Pass the reserved dark crabmeat through a fine sieve and add to the mixture together with the tomato and paprika. Beat together thoroughly. |
| | paprika | ½ tsp | |

| 5 | double cream, cold | 2½–3dl | Gradually add to the mixture beating in thoroughly. Cover and place in the refrigerator. |

| 6 | butter | | Butter a deep tray. With a tablespoon, take a twentieth of the mixture, mould egg-shape with a wet second spoon and place in the tray. Continue until the mixture is finished, giving 20 quenelles in all. Keep in the cool until needed. |

7	butter	50g	Heat the butter in a shallow pan. Add the rest of the ingredients and cook quickly just to lightly colour, then add the crushed crab shells. Season lightly, cover with a lid and sweat the ingredients for 5 mins.
	shallots ⎞	75g	
	carrots ⎟ cut	75g	
	celery ⎬ in	50g	
	parsley, ⎟ Brunoise		
	stalks ⎠ (22)	10g	
	tarragon, chopped	5g	
	thyme	sprig	
	garlic, crushed	½ clove	

8	brandy	½dl	Add the brandy and flamber (32), then add the remainder of the ingredients. Cook gently for 20 mins. then pass with firm pressure through a strainer or sieve into a pan. Skim off any fat. Reduce by three-quarters.
	white wine, dry	3dl	
	Fumet de Poisson (101)	3dl	
	Tomates Concassées (90)	75g	

9	double cream	6dl	Add the cream and reduce to a light coating consistency. Mix in the butter carefully, adjust the seasoning as necessary plus a touch of cayenne. Cover and keep hot.
	butter, soft	50g	
	cayenne		

| 10 | Fumet de Poisson (101) | 1 litre | Season lightly, bring to the boil and pour gently around the quenelles. Cover with a buttered paper and poach gently in a moderate oven 175°C for 15–18 mins. until cooked and lightly souffléed. |

11	Bouchées (1674)	10	Heat the butter in a small pan, add the reserved and carefully flaked white crabmeat, season lightly and heat. Fill the bouchées with this mixture, place on the lids and keep warm. Cover the bottom of suitable dishes with a little of the sauce. Drain the quenelles carefully and arrange on top. Decorate each with two tarragon leaves and place the bouchées to one side. Serve any remaining sauce separately.
	butter	25g	
	tarragon leaves, blanched		

SPECIAL POINTS
a) It is advisable to poach a small piece of the mixture after 2½dl of cream have been added. If a little too stiff add the rest or if too loose a little more egg white.
b) The use of a food processor for making the quenelles, Stages 2–5, can save a considerable amount of time and energy.

CREVETTES – PRAWNS

There are a number of differing prawns available varying from the common prawn of European waters to the giant prawn of the Pacific. The common prawn is a useful item for garnishing and as part of a mixture of shellfish for the preparation of mixed fish dishes. The larger varieties lend themselves to grilling and sautéeing and are useful as components of kebabs and brochettes.

---

659 Currie de Crevettes – Curried Prawns
10 portions
30 mins.

Stage	Ingredient	Quantity	Method
1	butter	75g	Melt the butter in a sauteuse, add the
	prawns, shelled	600g	prawns, toss over and reheat.
2	Curry Sauce (208)	7dl	Add and mix in gently.
3	long-grain rice	300g	Cook as for Riz Poché (534).
4			Dress and serve the curried prawns and the rice in separate dishes.

ECREVISSES – FRESHWATER CRAYFISH OR YABBIES

660 Ecrevisses à la Bordelaise
4 portions
1 hour

Stage	Ingredient		Quantity	Method
1	butter		75g	Heat the butter in a shallow pan, add the
	carrots		75g	rest of the ingredients and mix in. Cover
	onion	cut in Brunoise (22)	75g	with a lid and gently stew together until
	parsley stalks		5g	just cooked.
	fresh thyme leaves		good pinch	
	bayleaf, powdered		small pinch	
2	crayfish, medium		16–20	Wash and gut the crayfish and add to the pan. Season with a little salt and a touch of cayenne. Mix together quickly over a good heat until the crayfish turn red.
	cayenne			
	salt			
3	brandy		½dl	Add the brandy and flamber (32), then
	white wine, dry		5dl	add the wine and tomatoes. Bring to the
	Tomates Concassées (90)		250g	boil quickly, cover and cook gently for approx. 10 mins.

4			Remove the crayfish to a deep timbale or earthenware casserole; cover and keep warm.
5	butter	50g	Reduce the sauce by approx. one-third, then shake in the butter. Add the meat glaze and parsley. Season the sauce well, add the crayfish to reheat then pour the whole back into the dish. Serve immediately.
	Glace de Viande		
	(103)	½ tbsp	
	parsley, coarsely chopped	1 tbsp	

661 Ecrevisses à la Nage

4 portions
50 mins.

Stage	Ingredient	Quantity	Method
1	carrots, small	100g	Groove the carrots (canneler) then cut the carrots and onions into thin rings. Place in a suitably-sized fish kettle together with the rest of the ingredients. Bring to the boil and simmer very gently for 20 mins.
	onions, button	100g	
	white wine, dry	7dl	
	Fumet de Poisson		
	(101)	5dl	
	peppercorns	10	
	fresh thyme leaves	good pinch	
	celery ⎫	1 stalk	
	parsley ⎪	5g	
	bayleaf ⎬ Bouquet Garni	1	
	garlic ⎪	1 clove	
	chilli ⎭	1	
	salt	5g	
2	crayfish	16–20	Wash and gut the crayfish (page 246) then place immediately into the boiling court-bouillon. Bring to the boil, cover and simmer very gently for 10–15 mins. moving them around occasionally.
3			Discard the bouquet garni and send the fish kettle to the table as it is.

SPECIAL POINT
If a suitable fish kettle is unavailable, cook the court-bouillon and the crayfish in a well-tinned copper or stainless steel pan and when cooked, transfer the whole to a deep silver or porcelain timbale or casserole.

HOMARD – LOBSTER

662 Boiled Lobster

To cook lobsters for cold or for further preparation such as for Homard Thermidor and Homard Newburg, wash and plunge the live lobsters into sufficient boiling court-bouillon (538) to cover. Simmer for 20–25 mins. for lobsters weighing 600–700g. Allow to cool in the cooking liquor. Lobsters are also called Flapjacks in Australia.

663 Homard à l'Américaine

2 portions
45 mins.

Stage	Ingredient	Quantity	Method
1	lobster, live	1 × 650g	Wash the lobster. Insert the point of a knife in the middle of the head and cut through to the board. Remove the claws and crack them. Cut the tail end into the natural sections. Split the head part into two halves and discard the sac (stomach). Remove any coral and creamy parts and place in a basin.
2	oil	½dl	Place in a shallow pan and heat well.
	butter	30g	Season the pieces of lobster, place in the pan and fry quickly to a red colour on all sides. Drain off surplus fat.
3	shallots ⎤ finely	30g	Add the shallots and garlic to the lobster
	garlic ⎬ chopped	½ clove	and shake in. Add the brandy and
	brandy ⎦	¼dl	flamber (32).
4	white wine, dry	1dl	Add and lightly season. Cover with a lid
	Fumet de Poisson (101)	2dl	and simmer gently for 20 mins.
	Tomates Concassées (90)	150g	
	tomato purée	½ tbsp	
	tarragon, chopped	pinch	
5			Remove the lobster. Pick the meat from the shells and place in a deep dish or timbale. Cover and keep warm.
6	butter	30g	Reduce the cooking liquor by half. Add the butter to the coral and creamy parts and mix thoroughly together. Shake this mixture into the sauce, allow to thicken and remove from the heat. Adjust the seasoning and add a little cayenne.
7	parsley, chopped		Pass the sauce through a coarse strainer to cover the lobster. Decorate with the tops of the head and tail-fan, and sprinkle with chopped parsley.

SPECIAL POINT
It is usual to serve Riz Pilaff (522) as an accompaniment to Homard à l'Américaine.

664 Homard Cardinal

10 portions
1¼ hours

Stage	Ingredient	Quantity	Method
1	lobsters, cooked (662)	5 × 650g	Remove the claws and legs and split the lobster in half lengthways. Crack and remove the flesh from the claws and leave whole. Remove the flesh from the half-shells and cut into fairly thick slices. Wash the half-shells thoroughly and dry.
2	egg yolks	2	Make a sabayon (84) with the egg yolks and add to the hot sauce away from the heat. Pass through a fine strainer.
	Sauce Homard (169)	7dl	
3	cream	½dl	Mix the cream and butter thoroughly into the sauce, adjust the seasoning and finish with a little cayenne.
	butter	50g	
4	mushrooms, small dice	300g	Heat the butter in a small pan, add the mushrooms, season and cook until soft and fairly dry. Mix with a little of the prepared sauce. Divide equally into the bottoms of the ten half-shells.
	butter	50g	
5	butter	75g	Melt in a sauteuse. Add the slices and claws of lobster, lightly season and reheat without colouring. Arrange the lobster neatly on the mushrooms, the slices in the tail part and the claws at the head end.
6	Parmesan, grated	50g	Coat the lobster carefully with the sauce, sprinkle with the grated Parmesan and gratinate under the salamander. Garnish the head of each half-lobster with a slice of truffle and dress on dish papers on suitable dishes. Garnish with picked parsley.
	parsley, picked		
	truffle slices	10	

665 Homard grillé – Grilled Lobster

2 portions
25 mins.

Stage	Ingredient	Quantity	Method
1	lobster, live	1 × 650g	Split the lobster in half lengthways; remove the sac of grit from the head and the black trail from the tail.
2	butter, melted	50g	Place the lobster in a shallow dish, cut sides up. Sprinkle with the butter, season with salt, pepper and a touch of cayenne. Place under the moderate heat of a grill for approx. 15 mins., basting frequently with the butter and juices.
	salt		
	pepper		
	cayenne		

3	picked parsley		When cooked crack the claws to facil-
	lemon quarters	2	itate the removal of the flesh. Arrange
	Sauce Diable (125)		the two halves on a dish paper or folded
	or Sauce		serviette on a suitable dish. Garnish with
	Champignons (121)	1½dl	picked parsley and quarters of lemon
			and serve accompanied with a suitable
			sauce.

SPECIAL POINT
It is better to grill split lobster under overhead heat – if done on an underfired grill it is
liable to lose its juices and becomes overdried.

666 Homard grillé au Pernod

Prepare as Homard grillé (665) but half-way through the cooking time sprinkle with a
little Pernod. Baste frequently and serve accompanied with a sauceboat of Fennel Sauce
(177).

667 Homard Mornay

10 portions
1 hour

Stage	Ingredient	Quantity	Method
1	lobsters, cooked (662)	5 × 650g	Remove the claws and legs and split the lobsters in half lengthways. Crack and remove the flesh from the claws and leave whole. Remove the flesh from the half-shells and cut into fairly thick slices. Wash the half-shells thoroughly and dry.
2	butter	75g	Melt in a small pan. Add the slices and claws of lobster, lightly season and reheat quickly without colouring.
3	Sauce Mornay (171)	7dl	Place a little of the sauce in the bottom of each half-shell. Arrange the slices of lobster neatly in the tail part and a claw in the head end. Coat the lobster care- fully with the sauce, sprinkle with grated Parmesan and gratinate under the salamander.
	Parmesan, grated	50g	
4	parsley, picked		Dress on dish papers on suitable dishes and garnish with picked parsley.

668 Homard Newburg

10 portions
45 mins.

Stage	Ingredient	Quantity	Method
1	lobsters, cooked (662)	5 × 650g	Remove the flesh from the tail and claws, cut the tail end into fairly thick slices and leave the flesh of the claws whole.

2	butter Madeira	75g 1½dl	Melt the butter in a small pan, add the lobster, season lightly and reheat quickly. Add the Madeira and reduce almost completely.
3	cream ⎫ egg yolks ⎬ liaison	½ litre 8	Mix the cream and yolks together well and add to the lobster. Shake the pan gently at the side of the stove and allow to thicken without bringing it to the boil. Adjust the seasoning.
4	Riz Pilaff (522)	10 portions	Place the lobster and the sauce in deep dishes or timbales and serve accompanied with the Riz Pilaff.

SPECIAL POINT
The above recipe is best prepared to order because of the instability of the sauce which will break down if kept too long at the required serving temperature.

669 Homard Thermidor

10 portions
1 hour.

Stage	Ingredient	Quantity	Method
1	lobsters, cooked (662)	5 × 650g	Remove the claws and legs and split the lobsters in half lengthways. Crack and remove the flesh from the claws and leave whole. Remove the flesh from the half-shells and cut into fairly thick slices. Wash the half-shells thoroughly and dry.
2	egg yolks Sauce Bercy (163)	2 7dl	Make a sabayon (84) with the yolks and add to the hot sauce away from the heat.
3	mustard, English	15g	Dilute the mustard with a little water and add to the sauce. Adjust the seasoning.
4	butter	75g	Melt in a small pan and add the slices and claws of lobster. Lightly season and reheat quickly without colouring.
5	parsley, picked		Place a little of the sauce in the bottom of each half-shell. Arrange the slices of lobster neatly in the tail end and a claw in the head end. Coat the lobster carefully with the sauce and glaze under the salamander. Dress on dish papers on suitable dishes and garnish with picked parsley.

HUITRES – OYSTERS
This title includes Coral Rock, Sydney Rock and Pacific Bluff varieties.

670 Huîtres Florentine

Prepare as Huîtres Mornay (671) placing a little Epinards en Branches (1454) under each oyster before coating with the sauce.

671 Huîtres Mornay

12 oysters
20 mins.

Stage	Ingredient	Quantity	Method
1	oysters	12	Remove the oysters from the shells and poach them in their own juices. Wash and dry the deep shells and place level on salt in a tray.
2	Sauce Mornay (171) Parmesan, grated	2dl 20g	Place a little sauce in the bottom of each shell with an oyster on top. Coat with the sauce, sprinkle with grated Parmesan and gratinate under the salamander.
3	parsley, picked		Dress the oysters on a dish paper on a suitable dish and garnish with picked parsley.

672 Huîtres pochées – Poached Oysters

Remove the oysters from their shells and place them in a small pan with their own juice if any. Cover, bring to the boil quickly, leave for a few seconds, remove from the heat and allow to finish cooking in the liquor. Poached oysters are frequently used for garnishing fish dishes.

MOULES – MUSSELS
This title includes the New Zealand greenlip and blacklip varieties.

673 Moules frites en Buisson

10 portions
50 mins.

Stage	Ingredient	Quantity	Method
1	mussels, large onion, chopped parsley stalks white wine, dry pepper	2½kg 75g 20g 2dl pinch	Scrape and wash the mussels well; discard any open ones. Place in a pan with the rest of the ingredients and season with a little pepper. Cover with a lid, bring to the boil and cook for approx. 5 mins. until the shells are open.
2			Drain the mussels well and reserve the cooking liquor for other uses. Remove the mussels from their shells and discard their beards.

3	shallots, finely		Place the mussels in a shallow tray,
	chopped	75g	sprinkle with the shallots, parsley, oil and
	olive oil	½dl	lemon juice, and season with a little salt
	lemon juice	1	and milled pepper. Allow to marinate for
	parsley, chopped	2 tbsps	25 mins. in a cool place.
	salt		
	milled pepper		
4	frying batter,		Drain the mussels, pass through the fry-
	not too thick		ing batter and deep fry quickly in hot fat.
	(76)	½ litre	Drain well and arrange in a neat pile on
	lemon quarters	10	a folded serviette placed on a suitable
	picked parsley		dish, or dress separately on individual
			dishes or plates. Garnish with picked
			parsley and lemon quarters.

SPECIAL POINT
Tomato Coulis (179) may be offered.

674 Moules Marinière

10 portions
1 hour

Stage	Ingredient	Quantity	Method
1	mussels	2½kg	Scrape and wash the mussels well. Place
	shallots, finely		in a pan with the rest of the ingredients
	chopped	75g	and season with a little pepper. Cover
	white wine, dry	½ litre	with a lid, bring to the boil and cook
	parsley stalks	20g	quickly for approx. 5 mins until the
			shells are wide open.
2			Strain the cooking liquor into a small
			pan. Remove the mussels from their
			shells and take off the beards. Replace
			the mussels in half-shells and arrange
			them in deep dishes. Cover and keep
			warm.
3	butter ⎫ into Beurre	50g	Bring the cooking liquor to the boil and
	flour ⎭ Manié (11)	25g	whisk in the beurre manié. Bring to the
			boil and pass through a fine strainer.
4	cream	1dl	Add to the sauce and correct the season-
	parsley, chopped		ing. Pour the sauce over the mussels and
			sprinkle with chopped parsley.

675 Moules Poulette

10 portions
1 hour

Stage	Ingredient	Quantity	Method
1	mussels	2½kg	Scrape and wash the mussels. Place in a
	shallots, chopped	75g	pan with the rest of the ingredients.
	white wine, dry	3dl	Season with a little pepper. Cover with a
	parsley stalks	20g	lid, bring to the boil and cook quickly for

			approx. 5 mins. until the shells are wide open.
2			Strain the cooking liquor into a small pan. Remove the mussels from the shells and take off the beards; place the mussels in a dish, cover and keep warm.
3	Sauce Allemande (139) parsley, chopped	½ litre 1 tbsp	Reduce the cooking liquor by two-thirds and add to the Sauce Allemande. Add the chopped parsley and correct the seasoning.
4	parsley, chopped		Place the mussels in the sauce and reheat gently. Serve in earthenware dishes sprinkled with chopped parsley.

SCAMPI

676 Scampi frits – Fried Scampi

10 portions
30 mins.

Stage	Ingredient	Quantity	Method
1	scampi, shelled flour eggwash breadcrumbs } for crumbing	800g	Season the scampi, paner à l'Anglaise (72) and reshape by rolling.
2			Place the scampi in a frying-basket and deep fry at approx. 185°C until golden brown. Drain and lightly season with salt.
3	lemons parsley, picked	2½	Arrange on dish papers on suitable dishes and garnish with quarters of lemons and fried or picked parsley.

Sauce Tartare or Sauce Remoulade may be served as an accompaniment.

---

677 Scampi Meunière

10 portions
30 mins.

Stage	Ingredient	Quantity	Method
1	oil scampi, shelled flour	2dl 800g	Heat the oil in a frying-pan. Season the scampi and lightly flour. When the oil is very hot put in the scampi and fry quickly to a golden brown on all sides.
2	lemon, peeled slices juice of lemon	10 ½	Remove the scampi, dress neatly in earthenware dishes and keep warm on the side of the stove. Place the slices of lemon neatly on top and sprinkle with lemon juice.

3	butter	150g	Place the butter in a suitable frying-pan
	parsley, chopped		and cook until nut-brown, shaking the
			pan to ensure even colouring. Pour
			quickly over the scampi and sprinkle
			with chopped parsley.

---

678 Scampi Provençale

10 portions
20 mins.

Stage	Ingredient	Quantity	Method
1	oil	2dl	Heat the oil in a frying-pan. Season the
	scampi, shelled	800g	scampi and lightly flour. When the oil is
			very hot place in the scampi and fry
			quickly to a golden brown on all sides.
2	Sauce Provençale		Remove the scampi, dress neatly in
	(211)	6dl	earthenware dishes and coat with the
	parsley, chopped		sauce. Sprinkle with chopped parsley.

MIXED SHELLFISH DISHES

679 Crêpes aux Fruits de Mer Princesse

10 portions
1½ hours

Stage	Ingredient	Quantity	Method
1	Sauce Vin Blanc		Make a sabayon (84) with the egg yolks
	(174)	6dl	and add to the sauce before passing
	egg yolks	2	through a fine strainer. Cover and keep
			warm.
2	white mushrooms	350g	Cut the mushrooms in dice. Melt the
	butter	50g	butter in a small pan, add the mush-
	lemon juice	squeeze	rooms and lemon juice, season and cook.
3	prawns, cooked	175g	Add to the mushrooms. Season lightly
	lobster, cooked		and reheat gently.
	and diced	175g	
	scallops, cooked		
	and diced	175g	
	mussels, cooked		
	and cut in half	175g	
4	Sauce Homard		Add to the shellfish mixture and reheat
	(169)	2½dl	thoroughly. Check the seasoning and
	parsley, chopped	1 tbsp	keep warm.
5	Pancakes (71)	20	Lay out the pancakes on the working
			surface. Divide the mixture equally
			between the pancakes and roll up.
6	butter	50g	Lightly butter two large or ten individual
	Asparagus Sprue		hot earthenware dishes. Place in the
	(1388)	50 pieces	pancakes, two per portion, with five

truffle slices	10	pieces of asparagus lying between each two pancakes and a slice of truffle in the middle of the asparagus.
7		Place the dishes in a hot oven for a few moments then coat with the white wine sauce and glaze quickly under the salamander. Serve immediately.

---

680 Vol-au-vent de Fruits de Mer

10 portions
30 mins.

Stage	Ingredient	Quantity	Method
1	white mushrooms	350g	Cut the mushrooms in dice. Melt the
	butter	50g	butter in a sauteuse, add the mushrooms
	lemon juice	squeeze	and lemon juice, season and cook.
2	prawns, cooked	175g	Add to the mushrooms. Season lightly
	lobster, cooked		and reheat gently.
	and diced	175g	
	scallops, cooked		
	and diced	175g	
	mussels, cooked	175g	
3	Sauce Vin Blanc		Add to the mixture and mix in carefully.
	(174)	5dl	Reheat thoroughly and check the season-
	parsley, chopped	1 tbsp	ing.
4	Vol-au-vent cases		Warm, fill with the mixture and place
	(1714)	10	the lids on top.
5	parsley, picked		Arrange on dish papers on suitable dishes and garnish with picked parsley.

12
Meats

Meat is one of the most significant commodities used in catering and, except for vegetarians, it plays an important role in the diet of most people. Its importance in the diet as far as its nutritional value is concerned is as a source of first-class protein – the substance that provides growth and repair of body tissues.

The four main types of meat in general use are lamb and mutton, beef, pork and veal, and they are generally grouped together and referred to as butcher's meats. Lamb and beef are commonly described as the red meats and pork and veal as the white. Bacon and hams are also included in this section.

All these meats are available throughout the year, seasonal variations in quality not being so pronounced as before, although early season spring lamb is still an item eagerly awaited. Meat is obtainable in various forms, namely fresh, chilled, frozen and vacuum-packed and is sold either as whole carcase, side, quarter, joints or small cuts. The price of meat as with all commodities tends to fluctuate according to supply and demand but it is always a very high-cost item. It should therefore be purchased prudently and be subject to strict storage and usage control.

All of the cooking methods can be applied to meat and the variety and scope of possible dishes is limitless. It ranges from being just another ingredient in an hors-d'oeuvre salad to the many excellent lightly garnished Entrées, through to the prestigious Relevés and richly presented centre-pieces of classical cookery.

Offals

This term refers to certain internal organs and other parts of the animal and should not be confused with the flesh proper of the animal. They make useful and interesting dishes in their own right which add variety to menus and some are also widely used as ingredients and garnishes for other dishes. Offals possess good nutritional value and should not be looked upon as a poor substitute for meat itself.

A number of recipes for the main items of offal can be found interspersed with the other recipes in this chapter.

The following lists the most important and frequently used offals:
Ox – tongue, kidney, liver, tail and tripe.
Calf's – liver, sweetbread, kidney, brain, tongue, head and tail.
Lamb's – kidney, liver, heart, tongue and sweetbread.
Pig's – liver, kidney, tongue and head.

QUALITY POINTS

The quality of meat is influenced by factors such as the breed of animal, the method of rearing, its sex, age at slaughter, the conditions at the abattoir, and the way it is then processed as either fresh or frozen. Quality descriptions such as Prime, Choice and

Standard are used to grade various meats but in general, quality can be judged by the compact shape and the amount of lean meat of a particular cut. However, as first considerations, all fresh meat should have a clean fresh smell devoid of any unpleasant odour, it should have a bright fresh colour, it should be firm and resilient to the touch and there should be no evidence of stickiness.

The characteristics of good-quality fresh meat are as follows:

Lamb
The flesh should be light red in colour and finely grained. The fat in the young animal is white or creamy white and the bones are soft and porous. The carcase as a whole should be evenly fleshed with an even coating of fat.

Mutton
Mutton from an animal of 1 to 3 years in age can be tender and of good flavour and can produce excellent joints for roasting and grilling. The flesh is a little darker than for lamb. The fat is white and brittle and the bones much harder than in lamb. Too large a carcase with an over-abundance of fat and flinty bones indicates an older animal, giving tough and stringy meat.

Beef
The flesh should be firm, cherry-red in colour and finely grained. The thicker parts should show flecks of fat, i.e. marbling. The fat should be firm, smooth and creamy white to creamy in colour. Deep yellow fat is usually a sign of an older animal. The bones in young animals are pink and slightly porous.

Pork
The flesh should be light pink in colour and finely grained. The skin should be thin, smooth and dry and the fat should not be excessive in proportion to the flesh.

Veal
The flesh should be very pale pink in colour, finely grained and smooth. The outer covering of fat should be thin but the kidney should be well-covered with fat. The bones are large in proportion to the size and should be soft, bluish-white and porous.

Bacon
This is best when purchased by the side. It should have a clean, sweet smell and there should be no signs of clamminess.

Hams
These can be obtained cured and smoked, or cured and unsmoked (green). They should be perfectly dry to the touch with a clean sweet smell. Any curing mould should be dry.

Offals
In general fresh offals should be bought as fresh as possible and in all cases they should be devoid of any unpleasant odour, discolouration or stickiness.
Livers: these should have a good even colour with no discoloured patches on the surface.
Kidneys: there should be no smell of ammonia present and they should have a good clean colour, be firm to the touch and with no stickiness evident.
Hearts: these should have a good bright colour, not too much fat and be just moist to the touch.

Sweetbreads: there should be little if any fat showing and any signs of blood should be bright red. They should also be resilient to touch and just moist.
Tongues: these should be firm to the touch and with no sign of stickiness.
Tails: the meaty parts should be a bright red colour with the fat not over-abundant and not too yellow.
Tripe: this is bought ready-dressed meaning that it has been cleaned and blanched. It should have a clean light creamy colour with no greenish or dark discolouration and should be moist with no signs of stickiness or bad smell.
Calf's heads: these should be well-fleshed, have a nice even cream to fawn colour with no dark patches and should be moist to the touch but not sticky.

——————HANGING AND CONDITIONING——————

The flavour and tenderness of meat develops from the hanging of the carcase or its large joints over a period of time during which certain changes take place in the structure of the connective tissue which improve tenderness and eating qualities.

This hanging or conditioning of meat is mainly confined to beef. It is best carried out at a low temperature of approx. 2–3°C in a refrigerator reserved solely for the storage of meat and where a fan-assisted circulation of the air can be maintained. Meat in the correct condition for immediate use can generally be supplied by any high-class wholesaler. However, where an establishment wishes to control the condition of its own meat and has the facilities for so doing the following approximate times for the hanging of meat can be used as a guide. It must however be noted that experience in the handling of meat is the best guide for determining when it is in the best condition for use.

Beef:
Hind and forequarters 12–14 days, foreribs, sirloin and rump 2–3 weeks. All cut edges should be frequently checked. These should always be dry, any sign of stickiness or unpleasant smell should not be allowed to develop.
Lamb and mutton:
The carcase needs to be hung for 4–7 days. Joints should not require further hanging.
Veal:
The carcase requires hanging for a period of 4–7 days and should then be used as soon as possible. When finally cut into joints the flesh of veal does not keep very well and should be used as soon as possible.
Pork:
A total of 7–10 days from slaughtering to utilisation is sufficient for the conditioning of pork. It tends to deteriorate more quickly than other meats and should be used as soon as possible.

——————————————STORAGE——————————————

Fresh meat either as carcases or large joints should be hung where possible in a refrigerator especially reserved for fresh meat only and held at a temperature of 2–3°C. Small cuts should be laid on clean trays and then covered with oiled paper or plastic film to prevent drying but should be used as soon as possible. Small cuts of any meat will deteriorate very quickly and it is for this reason that marked attention should be paid to turnover and ordering so as to prevent overlong storage. Where possible chilled meat should be held at as near freezing temperature without actually freezing the meat hard. Vacuum-packed meats are best stored in trays, fat side uppermost, at the normal refrigerator temperature, and although these meats can be successfully held for a longer period than cuts of fresh meat, the turnover and use should still be as quick as possible. All frozen meats should be stored at a temperature of not higher than −18°C. It should always be defrosted at normal refrigerator temperatures.

Offals deteriorate very quickly and should be ordered frequently and used as soon as possible. Store at 2–3°C on clean trays covered with oiled paper. Handle as little as possible and change to clean trays as and when any seepage of blood or fluid becomes evident.

COOKING METHODS

In general all the standard methods of cooking may be applied to butcher's meats. Their application to offals is limited in many respects but the usual cooking methods for offals are given in the tables relating to each of their respective carcases.

Boiling/Poaching
This process is best applied to those meats of a firmer or tougher nature rather than to the more tender joints. Silverside, brisket and plate of beef as well as legs of pork or mutton are suitable but veal is better suited to other methods. They are all best if placed to cook in sufficient boiling stock to cover the meat and of the same type as the meat; the pot used should be of a size just large enough to hold the joint comfortably. Cooking should be carried out by very slow simmering, in effect by poaching, and on no account should rapid boiling take place – this will only result in stringy, unevenly cooked meat. Seasonings, flavourings and herbs may be added as required but only after the liquid is brought back to the boil and skimmed, then skimming should be frequent and carefully carried out. Ensure that the joint is covered at all times with the cooking liquid and replenish as necessary.

Salted meats such as hams, salt leg of pork, tongues or silverside of beef should always be soaked in running cold water for some hours to extract the excess salt. They are then placed into cold water and brought slowly to the boil – this will assist in leaching out further saltiness. After an initial skimming the process is the same as for fresh meats.

The length of time needed for the actual cooking of joints depends on the size and shape of the joint and its relative structure but varies between 20 and 25 mins. per 500g plus an extra 30 mins. Ox-tongues require approx. 3–3½ hours. To test whether cooked, pierce at the thickest part with a trussing needle – it should be possible to penetrate and withdraw it without any marked resistance.

The foregoing observations for fresh meat also hold good for the parcooking of cuts of veal or lamb for Blanquette, except that an initial blanching can help in whitening the meat.

Steaming
The steaming of meats and their offals, as well as meat puddings, can be successfully carried out at low and high pressure and is commonly used in large-scale catering operations. The same joints as used for boiling are suitable but it should be remembered that the process of steaming can lead to some discolouration and generally a lack of stock unless placed in a deep unperforated tray to conserve escaping juices. For the most part steamed hams and salted meats are the most successful. High steaming pressures have the advantage of shortening cooking times but with large joints can result sometimes in uneven cooking.

Small cuts or thickish slices taken from tender meats such as loin of lamb, fillet of beef, pork or lamb, cushion of veal and the like can be also steamed by placing in a perforated container, covered, then placed over a highly flavoured boiling stock. This method can produce very light, delicate and easily digested dishes, although they tend to lose some of their own particular flavours.

Stewing

This method of cooking is best used for those butcher's meats or offals of a tougher nature and which require longer cooking times to render them tender. The meat is usually cut in small pieces and cooked very slowly, gently and evenly in a minimum of liquid or sauce which is invariably served together with the meat. The final sauce should not be too abundant nor too thick and the aim should be to have the meat just cooked and tender. Fast cooking at too high a temperature will result in rapid evaporation of the liquid and degradation of the texture of the meat. Any garnish as part of the stew should not be over-abundant to the stage where it becomes difficult to decide which is the main ingredient. There are two main types of meat stew, brown and white.

Brown stews: these are exemplified by an initial seasoning and browning of the meat, the use usually of brown stock together with varying seasonings and flavourings, being very slowly cooked in a roux-thickened liquid or liquid which is finally thickened.

White stews: these are best prepared using the white meats, pork and veal, although young lamb can be utilised as well as tripe. There are two useful methods for producing white stews, both of which are finished with either cream or a liaison of egg yolks and cream:

1) As a Fricassée where the meat is just stiffened in butter with very little or no colour, cooked with a little flour and moistened with white stock together with seasonings and flavourings. The Fricassée is then cooked very slowly.

2) As a Blanquette where the meat is usually blanched to whiten it and prevent flecks of coagulated blood from spoiling the final sauce. It is then three-parts cooked in a white stock with flavourings and seasonings and the stock is then utilised together with a blond roux in the preparation of a velouté in which the meat gently completes its cooking.

Suitable meats for brown stews are:
Lamb and mutton – scrag end, middle neck, shoulder and breast.
Beef – topside, silverside, chuck, plate, leg of mutton cut, clod, sticking piece.
Veal – shoulder, neck end, breast and knuckle.
Pork – shoulder, belly
Offals – ox kidney.

Suitable meats for white stews are:
Lamb – shoulder and breast.
Pork – shoulder, belly and spare rib.
Veal – shoulder, neck end and breast.
Offals – tripe.

As a general rule stews are more suitable for inclusion on the luncheon menu.

Braising

This process, like stewing, is best used in general for those cuts or joints of meat or offals which require longer cooking to make them tender. Braising can, however, be successfully applied to more tender items such as fillet, rump and sirloin of beef but this requires very careful attention to length of cooking time and technique. There are two main methods of braising, brown or white. In a few other cases the process becomes a combination of braising and other methods.

Brown braising: for this process, joints, and sometimes cuts, require larding with strips of salt pork fat and the recipes frequently call for prior marination of the meat. In all cases through, the meats are seasoned and shallow-fried until well-coloured on all surfaces. The meat should then be placed in a braising pan of a size just sufficient to hold it comfortably together with the requisite flavourings, seasonings and liquid or sauce then covered and cooked gently in the oven. The liquid used should never completely cover the meat. For joints it should reach no more than two-thirds the way up the joint and for cuts be just below the top surfaces. The cooking should be slow, gentle and regular with occasional turning of the meat in the liquid and fairly frequent basting. These two things are to ensure the building-up of a succulent glossy coating to the meat which is one of the particular qualities of well-braised meat.

Offals such as hearts, oxtail, liver and sweetbreads are also well-suited for brown braising. Hams and tongues need first to be two-thirds to three-quarters cooked by poaching then skinned and braised with sauce or wine, as called for. The braising liquid is always used as an accompanying sauce and is thus an integral part of the dish.

White braising: this process of braising is, as its name suggests, to keep the item of such a colour that it can be served with a white sauce which utilises its cooking liquor. It is mainly applied to sweetbreads and usually the cushion of veal although calf's tongues and feet can be braised white and served with white sauces.

White braising consists of first covering the bottom of a buttered braising pan with a layer of aromatic vegetables and herbs then placing the item of meat or offal on top. Sweetbreads need to be blanched first, veal should be larded and tongues parboiled and skinned. The item should then be seasoned, covered and placed in a moderate oven to sweat for 10–15 mins. A little white stock is added, reduced to a glaze and then further stock is added to come a third to half-way up the item. It should then be covered and cooked very slowly and gently in the oven with occasional turning and sufficient basting to produce a nice golden coating. The cooking liquid can then be reduced to serve with the meat or utilised with the addition of cream, velouté or Béchamel to produce a white sauce.

Suitable meats and offals for brown braising are:
    Lamb and mutton – leg and shoulder, chops.
    Beef – topside, silverside, thick flank, chuck and middle ribs, steaks.
    Pork – shoulder, leg, gammon, ham.
    Veal – neck end, shoulder, saddle, leg and leg joints, chops.
    Offals – lamb's sweetbreads, tongues and hearts. Ox tongue, oxtail
        and ox liver. Calf's sweetbreads, tongues and hearts.
Suitable meats and offal for white braising:
    Veal – cushion, sweetbreads and tongue.

Braised joints, cuts and offals of beef, and small cuts of lamb or mutton are more suitable for lunch. All other braised items can feature equally well for lunch or dinner.

Poêling or Pot-Roasting

This is an excellent process for cuts and joints of first quality and tenderness. It has something in common with roasting inasmuch as it is cooking in the oven without liquid but the process is carried out in a tight-lidded container using butter as a basting agent. This allows it to retain the maximum of its own particular flavours which are augmented or emphasised by the addition of aromatic herbs and vegetables as a base on which the meat is placed and cooked.

Some joints of meat such as the fillet need to be larded and sealed first in hot butter before placing on the mirepoix base. Veal joints also need to be larded. In all cases basting should be frequent and the lid needs to be removed before the meat is completely cooked so as to enable it to colour sufficiently.

The herbs, vegetables and juices from the cooking are utilised together with wines or stocks, as the case may be, in the preparation of a little lightly thickened sauce.

In its more simple form, usually for small joints or cuts of meats, poêling consists of seasoning the item, colouring it quickly in butter on both sides in a small casserole then covering with a lid and completing the cooking in the oven. A little gravy is added just before serving. This process is referred to as 'en Casserole'. The same thing can be carried out but with the addition of a suitable garnish; this is referred to as 'en Cocotte' and should always take the name of its particular garnish, e.g. Côte de Veau en Cocotte Fermière.

Suitable joints, cuts and offals for poêling are:
    Lamb and mutton – saddle, loin, leg, best end.
    Beef – sirloin, fillet, wing rib, rib steak.
    Veal – saddle, loin, best end, cushion, chops, cutlets.
    Offals – kidney, liver.

All poêléed joints and cuts of meat can figure satisfactorily on lunch or dinner menus.

Roasting
This process is well-suited to prime tender joints of butcher's meat; there are two accepted methods of roasting, spit roasting and oven roasting.

Spit roasting: this is the traditional method where the joint is impaled on a metal skewer and rotated over or at the side of a fire, ideally wood but which can be coal or charcoal. The drippings are caught in a trough and are used to baste the joint. Systems for rotating or raising and lowering the joint as well as shields for reflecting or directing the heat are necessary. The whole process requires a high degree of experience and expertise to produce first-class results. Unfortunately this method is rarely used these days although there are a few establishments which make a speciality of it. Modern electrically controlled Rôtisseries regretfully do not produce the best of results because the process usually takes place in a closed cabinet which tends to trap steam from the cooking.

Oven roasting: this has largely superseded the traditional method and although the heat in this case is convected rather than radiated, the result can still be excellent provided of course that correct care and attention is paid to the process, and that the oven being used is properly ventilated. The following aspects need to be considered:
a) Joints should never be placed to roast immediately upon removing from the refrigerator. They should be allowed to reach something like room temperature, i.e. approx. 16–17°C. If the joint is too cold the heat of the oven is conducted more slowly and can result in excessive drying of the outer surfaces before the centre reaches the required cooking temperature.
b) Joints of veal and fillet of beef which are naturally deficient in fat should be larded or barded before roasting; this helps to keep them moist. If barded this should be removed in sufficient time before the completion of cooking so as to allow colouring to take place.

c) The seasoning of the joint should be carried out just before the commencement of roasting and should ideally be rubbed in. It can be simply salt or salt and pepper but these may be augmented with ground herbs and spices as seen fit. Seasoning with salt and then leaving it for any length of time before roasting will result in the salt drawing out the juices from the meat and is not advisable.

d) Place the joint in the roasting tray on a metal trivet or some bones from the same animal except where the joint has bones which allow it to stand free, e.g. ribs of beef, best end of lamb, veal or pork. The use of the trivet or bones is to prevent the joint frying in the fat in the bottom of the tray.

e) Coat the joint with some melted clean dripping and place in a preheated oven at approx. 220–225°C.

f) The temperature should then be reduced progressively after an initial sealing and browning has taken place. This allows roasting to take place without any burning of the joint or fat but it must never be so low as to stop the actual roasting process. This is approx. 170°C. Joints such as fillet of beef or boned sirloin are better if previously quickly coloured in hot fat on the stove prior to placing in the oven.

g) Baste frequently with the fat and juices which collect in the tray. This will help in building up the succulent coating on the surface of the meat and fat. Most joints other than ribs of beef or best ends of lamb etc. need to be turned occasionally to even the colouring and degree of cooking.

h) When cooked, all joints need to rest in a warm place for 20–30 mins. to facilitate carving and to allow the joint to retain its juices.

i) The roasting pan and its juices should always be deglazed as follows. Heat gently on the stove to lightly colour the sediment and juices. Tip off the fat and add brown stock, brown veal stock for preference, and simmer for a few minutes. Strain and season with a little salt. If correctly carried out colouring should not be necessary. It is a mistake to aim for a clear, completely fat-free gravy. A roast gravy should look as if it is produced from roast meat.

j) The flesh of veal tends to be slightly bland in flavour and also lacks much in the way of natural fat. Besides barding and larding, the roasting of veal is best carried out in a much deeper roasting tray than usual and placed on a mirepoix of vegetables and herbs. These three things help to preserve moistness and add flavour which would be otherwise lacking. It is normal to very lightly thicken the gravy of roast veal joints with a little diluted arrowroot.

k) The use of meat thermometers is becoming more common, especially in large-scale operations. It can be a useful guide where uniformity is essential and perhaps the level of professional experience is limited. The thermometer probe should be inserted into the centre of the thickest part of the joint, either at the commencement of the roasting to give a continuous reading or some little time before the calculated completion of cooking.

Approximate thermometer temperatures for degree of cooking:

Lamb and mutton	80°C	just done
Beef	65°C	underdone
Pork	82–85°C	well done
Veal	80°C	just done

Suitable joints of butcher's meats for roasting are:
  Lamb and mutton – leg, shoulder, loin, saddle, best end.
  Beef – first quality: sirloin, fillet, fore-rib, wing rib.
        second quality: middle rib, topside.

Pork – first.quality: leg, loin.
  second quality: shoulder, spare rib.
Veal – leg, cushion, shoulder, loin, saddle, best end.

Approximate roasting times and degree of cooking:

Lamb and mutton	20 mins. per 500g plus 20 mins. extra	just done
Beef	15 mins. per 500g plus 15 mins. extra	underdone
Pork	25 mins. per 500g plus 25 mins. extra	well done
Veal	25 mins. per 500g plus 25 mins. extra	just done

For lunch menus all roast joints are suitable. For dinner, leg, cushion, saddle, best end of veal; leg, loin, saddle and best end of lamb; and fillet and sirloin of beef.

Baking
This method has a limited application to the cooking of meats and certain offals such as liver and always takes the form of the meat or mixture of meat being enclosed or covered with pastry and then being baked. There are two main types of preparation – as pies, pâtés or pasties etc., and as joints and cuts of meat cooked 'en Croûte', i.e. baked in pastry.

For covered pies the meat can either be raw or cooked but must always have enough liquid or sauce to ensure proper cooking without becoming dry. Raised pies are either made from a raw forcemeat or tender meats which do not require lengthy cooking to be correct for eating. A short period when the internal temperature of about 90°C is reached is usually sufficient.

Joints of meat like fillet of beef, ham, gammon, or small cuts of meat always need to be partly or almost completely cooked before covering with pastry and baking. In general fillet of beef and small cuts need to be covered with a moist savoury mixture before enclosing with the pastry so as to prevent the meat from becoming too dry.

Grilling
Together with roasting, grilling is one of the great basic methods of cooking and still enjoys an undiminished popularity. The process is particularly suitable for prime tender cuts of butcher's meats and offals. There are two main methods of grilling, over a radiant heat source, either charcoal, gas or electricity, and under a radiant heat source, either gas or electricity, commonly termed a salamander grill. Cooking between electrically heated plates is not, correctly speaking, true grilling but is more akin to plate griddling albeit from two directions at the same time.

The actual process of grilling either over or under heat is much the same although detail and flexibility in obtaining the final result may differ. For example, the traditional charcoal grill is believed to impart a better flavour to the food and the flavour can be modified by the burning of other different materials such as vine prunings and hickory wood. The grill bars for each type of grill need to have some means for moving them closer or away from the heat source. Meat should never be placed on a flat tray for grilling under a salamander grill. Neither should the meat be marked trellis-fashion with a red-hot poker or bar to simulate traditional grilling – this is unfair to the customer. If a salamander grill is used properly, sufficient marking of the meat will take place.

The following details need some consideration if correct results are to be obtained:
a) The grill should be preheated to an operating temperature and the bars rubbed with oil just prior to the start of cooking; this will ensure the rapid sealing of the meat and will prevent sticking to the bars.

b) The meat should be seasoned just prior to grilling and brushed with oil or butter. Liver should be seasoned and floured first before brushing with oil. Other than this, meats can be flavoured with herbs and may be marinated for a short time for flavour but never in the hope of tenderising tough meat.

c) After an initial sealing the meat can be moved to a cooler part of the grill, or the bars can be lowered or raised as necessary and the meat turned to ensure the right degree of cooking. With gas or electricity the heat source can be controlled. Further brushing with oil or butter is useful to maintain the moistness of thicker items.

d) It is a useful technique to arrange and turn the meats on the bars so as to effect a trellis-shaped pattern on the surfaces.

e) Grilling tongs should preferably be used or failing that a palette knife. Grilling meats should never be pierced with a fork – this will result in the loss of juices from the meat.

f) Grilled meats should be served immediately they are cooked, with the appropriate garnish and accompaniment as called for.

Suitable cuts of butcher's meats and offal for grilling:
Lamb and mutton – chops, cutlets, noisettes, médaillons, filets mignons, liver, kidneys.
Beef – sirloin, fillet, rump, minute, point, porterhouse and T-bone steaks, Chateaubriand.
Pork – chops, cutlets, gammon steak, liver and kidneys.
Veal – steaks (Paillards), grenadins, cutlets, liver, kidney, sweetbreads.

Grilled meats can figure equally well on all types of menu and for lunch or dinner.

Shallow Frying – Sauter

This method is suitable for small cuts of prime-quality meats and offals of a tender nature and the process consists of cooking food quickly on all sides in the minimum of fat or oil. The French term 'Sauter' not only relates to the need to toss small items or pieces of food over and over whilst frying so as to ensure even colouring and cooking but also to the shallow frying process and the subsequent use of the cooking juices for an accompanying sauce.

Although shallow frying is similar for all meats and offals there are many variables relating to the actual techniques of the process and the finishing of the dishes. These are summed up in the following details:

Suitable cuts of meats and offals:
Lamb and mutton – cutlets, noisettes, rosettes, médaillons, filets mignons, liver, sweetbreads, kidneys.
Beef – sirloin steaks, rump steaks, tournedos.
Pork – chops, escalopes, fillet, kidneys, liver.
Veal – cutlets, escalopes, fillet, liver, sweetbreads, kidney, brains.

In addition there are a number of chopped or minced items such as Hamburg steaks, Pojarskis and Bitoks.

Choice of pan: In general, all meats which are cut small such as strips of fillet of beef, and kidney and liver which require very quick cooking, should be shallow-fried in a heavy metal frying-pan. A heavy shallow sauté pan is more suitable for all other items.

The frying medium: The best is undoubtedly butter from the point of view of flavour. It can be used either as it is which needs much in the way of care, or clarified. Good oil is more useful in the shallow frying of breadcrumbed items such as escalopes or cutlets where it is essential to obtain a good clean colour. The oil should be changed as soon as any burnt food particles appear.

Prior preparation of items: Escalopes of veal and pork as well as cutlets of lamb and sweetbreads are frequently egg-and-breadcrumbed, and it is essential that this is properly carried out. The coating of breadcrumbs should not be wet or loose and all edges should be neat and tidy. Untidy finishing will present untidily and too many loose breadcrumbs will quickly spoil the frying medium.

All other items should only be seasoned just before cooking – small cuts of veal and liver should be additionally floured just before cooking.

General method for breadcrumbed items: heat the minimum amount of oil in a sauté pan to a high temperature but without burning. Place in the item and cook quickly to seal and colour, lower the temperature as necessary and turn and colour the other side when needed. Drain well and finish as required with brown butter, jus lié and any garnish called for. The first side down always tends to colour evenly and this side should always be presented face upwards for service.

General method for non-breadcrumbed items: heat sufficient butter in a sauté pan until hot but not burning. Season or season and flour, then place in the butter and cook quickly to seal and colour. As necessary reduce the heat and turn over when ready. Use the pan juices and sediment to prepare the accompanying sauce, if called for.

Degrees of cooking:
Cuts of beef – entrecôtes, tournedos etc.; these should generally be cooked medium and pink but also, when requested, to the customer's requirements.
Cuts of lamb – cutlets, noisettes etc.; pink to just done.
Pork and veal – all items a little more than just done but not dried out.
Liver and kidneys – medium to underdone.
Sweetbreads – just done.

Deglazing the sauté pan: the remaining fat and sediment should always be used to cook any added ingredients like shallots, onions, mushrooms, peppers etc. The excess fat should then be drained off before adding any wines, stocks, creams or sauces. If no ingredients are to be added for cooking, first tip off any fat then deglaze with the required liquid, wine or sauce etc.

Sautés à la Minute: very small strips or slices of beef, veal and pork fillet can make very quick dishes. They just need to be seasoned and sautéed quickly in hot butter, together or separately with other ingredients like mushrooms and pimentos, then drained and the pan juices utilised with wine, stock, cream or sauce as the case may be. The advantage is quickness and scope for inventiveness on the part of the practitioner.

Sautés of veal and young lamb: tender cuts of veal and lamb can be utilised as a sauté. The pieces of meat should be seasoned and completely cooked in clarified butter and the remaining juices and sediment utilised in the preparation of the accompanying sauce. The meat should not be boiled in the sauce.

Raw minced and moulded mixtures: items like Hamburg steaks and Pojarskis should always be moulded with flour, never breadcrumbed. For best results they should be shallow-fried in butter and the sediment from the cooking used for the deglazing and finishing of any accompanying sauce.

Most shallow-fried cuts of meat are useful for luncheon and dinner menus. Sweetbreads, tournedos, noisettes of lamb and veal cutlets are especially suitable for dinner and liver and kidney dishes for lunch.

Deep Frying
This method is very suitable for mixtures or salpicons of cooked meat and offals such as brains and liver, bound with a thick sauce. They can be prepared for example as Beignets, Cromesquis, Croquettes, Fritots or Rissoles where the mixture is moulded and coated with egg and breadcrumbs or frying batter and deep-fried. Or the mixture can be enclosed in various shapes of short or puff pastry and deep-fried.

As a general rule raw meats are unsuitable for deep frying because of the amount of juices which can be expressed from meat at high temperatures even though initially it may be sealed on contact with a hot fat. However, small thin strips of tender fillet of beef or veal can be quickly cooked in hot oil and removed before losing their juices. An example of this is the popular Fondue Bourguignonne where the customer does his own frying of the meat at the table and uses a variety of prepared sauces to go with it. Also thin flat strips of lightly marinated beef, pork or veal can be coated with frying batter and deep-fried. In all cases, whether cooked or raw, deep-fried meats must be cooked at fairly high temperatures and especially when coated, need to be well-drained before serving.

All the above items are best suited to luncheon menus either as hot hors-d'oeuvre or as small garnished entrées. Fondues are really only acceptable as a speciality evening meal.

————————PORTION GUIDE————————

When buying meat for a given number of portions it is useful to allow approx. 130–150g per person, off the bone, which allows for a small trimming loss, or 200–250g if with bone; for example to produce 1 ¼kg of beef cut in cubes for 10 portions of beef stew it requires approx. 1kg 300–1kg 500 of boneless stewing meat.

The more usual weights of small cuts as well as the offals from the same animals are given in the following preliminary details for each type of meat.

AGNEAU ET MOUTON – LAMB AND MUTTON

The main joints obtainable from a carcase of lamb approx. 16kg or mutton approx. 22kg, their average weights and preparation for cooking.

Joint	Average Weight		Preparation for Cooking
	Lamb	Mutton	
681 Leg (Gigot)	2kg	2½kg	Roasting and Boiling: remove the pelvic bone, saw off approx. 3cm of the end of the leg bone. Bare approx. 4cm of the remaining bone. Trim off any surplus fat and tie with a single string at the thick end.
682 Loin (Longe)	2kg	2½kg	Roasting or Poêling: split the saddle through the centre bone to give two loins. Skin and bone completely. Cut the flank straight and leave the fillet in place. Roll and tie, or stuff, roll and tie.
683 Saddle (Selle)	4kg	5kg	Roasting or Poêling: skin, remove the kidneys and surplus fat from inside and remove the pelvic bones. Cut off the flanks straight, re-form the saddle and tie. Or first cut across the saddle to remove the chump ends then proceed as before to give a square-shaped saddle suitable for banquet work.
684 Best End (Carré)	1¼kg	1½kg	Roasting or Poêling: remove the skin, saw off the breast part leaving the thin part of the best end twice the length of the eye of the meat. Remove the sinew from under the fat at the back and remove the tip of the blade bone. Bare the cutlet bones to a depth of 2cm and clean the skin from between the cutlet bones. Score the fat trellis-fashion.
685 Middle Neck (Côte Découverte)	1¼kg	1¾kg	Stewing: split through the middle, cut between the cutlet bones and trim off excess bone and fat.

686	Scrag End (Cou)	750g	1kg	Stewing: split through the centre bone. Chop into 50g pieces and remove excess bone. Trim off the fat.
687	Shoulder (Epaule)	1½kg	2kg	Roasting whole: remove the end of the knuckle bone and trim off excess fat. Roasting, boned and rolled: remove the scapula and humerus bones, trim off excess fat, roll and tie, or stuff, roll and tie. Stewing: bone completely, trim off the fat and cut into 2½cm cubes.
688	Breast (Poitrine)	750g	1¼kg	Roasting: remove the skin, bone completely and trim off excess fat. Roll and tie, or stuff, roll and tie. Stewing: skin, trim excess fat and cut into 5cm squares.
689	Baron	8kg	10kg	This consists of the two legs and the saddle in one piece, and is always roasted whole. Trim the end of the leg bones and the saddle then tie the saddle in two or three places to keep its shape.

The small cuts obtainable from the main joints of lamb and mutton

Name of cut	From which Joint	Average Portion Weight	Preparation for Cooking
690 Lamb or Mutton Chop (Chop d'Agneau ou de Mouton)	loin	200g	Skin the loin, trim off excess fat and cut the flank straight. Do not bone out. Cut the prepared loin into chops approx. 4cm thick, trim. For grilling, half a lamb's kidney may be skewered inside the chop.
691 Chump Chop	loin	200g	Cut the leg end of the loin into chops of the required weight and size. A loin will normally yield two chump chops.
692 Lamb or Mutton Cutlet (Côtelette d'Agneau ou de Mouton)	best end	2 × 80g	Cut between the bones of the prepared and unscored prepared best end. Trim off excess fat and bare the end of the cutlet bones.
693 Double Lamb Cutlet (Côtelette d'Agneau Double)	best end	160g	Cut between every other bone of the unscored prepared best end. Trim excess fat and bare the end of the cutlet bones.
694 Crown Chop or English chop also called Barnsley chop	saddle	300g	Cut straight across the prepared saddle approx. 4cm in width to give two chops joined together. Skewer half a lamb's kidney inside each of the two chops.
695 Fillet of Lamb (Filet Mignon d'Agneau)	saddle	120g	Remove the fillets from the saddle. Trim off any fat and sinew, leave whole or split open lengthways and lightly flatten.
696 Rosettes of Lamb (Médaillons or Rosettes d'Agneau)	loin	2 × 75g	Remove the chump end and bone out the loin completely without detaching the fillet. Trim excess fat and remove surplus flank. Roll and tie carefully with the string equidistant so that the rosettes can be cut between each string to the required weight.
697 Noisettes of Lamb (Noisettes d'Agneau)	loin	2 × 75g	Remove the chump end and the fillet. Bone out the remaining loin. Lay the boned loin flat, meat side uppermost and cut across on the slant into approx. 1½–2cm thick slices. Lightly flatten and trim cutlet shape by removing surplus fat.

The main offals of lamb and mutton, their average portion weights and preparation for cooking

Name	Average Portion Weights	Preparation for Cooking
698 Heart	1 × 125g	Stewing and braising: trim off any fat and cut out any tubes or gristly parts from the insides.
699 Kidney	2 × 60g	Grilling: cut open from along the outside edge to the central core but do not cut in half. Remove the skin and carefully cut out the central core of gristle and fat. Lay out flat and push a skewer over, through and out to keep it flat. Sauté: remove the skin, cut in half and remove the central core of fat and gristle. Cut each trimmed half into two or three pieces on the slant.
700 Liver	125g	Grilling or sauté: cut out any tubes or gristle showing and remove the skin. Cut on the slant into slices approx. ½cm thick.
701 Sweetbread	125g	Braising: disgorge in salted water for 5–6 hours then wash and blanch them. Trim off any fat and excess membrane.
702 Tongue	100g	Boiling or braising: cut away any bone or gristle from the root end and wash well before cooking.

703 Roast Lamb or Mutton

The following joints are suitable for roasting and their titles are given as they can appear on the menu. See Recipe 45 for an appropriate stuffing.

Gigot d'Agneau rôti – Roast Leg of Lamb
Epaule d'Agneau rôtie – Roast Shoulder of Lamb
Epaule d'Agneau rôtie farcie – Roast Stuffed Shoulder of Lamb
Selle d'Agneau rôtie – Roast Saddle of Lamb
Longe d'Agneau rôtie – Roast Loin of Lamb
Longe d'Agneau rôtie farcie – Roast Stuffed Loin of Lamb
Carré d'Agneau rôti – Roast Best End of Lamb

Good quality mutton can be used for roasting and should be so designated on the menu, e.g. Gigot de Mouton rôti.

Small milk fed lamb known as Pauillac in France is often available; it is so small that a shoulder is equal to one portion.

Portion weights
To calculate the quantity of lamb or mutton required to serve a given number of covers, the approximate weight of lamb or mutton prepared for roasting is:

on the bone	e.g. Gigot d'Agneau rôti	200–250g per person
boned and rolled	e.g. Longe d'Agneau rôtie	150–180g per person
boned, stuffed and rolled	e.g. Epaule d'Agneau rôtie farcie	125g plus 50g of stuffing per person

Method for roasting
1) Season the joint, place it fat side up in a roasting tray on a trivet or on top of a few lamb or mutton bones and cover with a little melted dripping.
2) Place into a hot oven at 220–225°C for approx. 20 mins. to set and colour the meat. For thicker and larger joints, for example a leg of lamb, reduce the temperature gradually so as to allow the joint to continue roasting without burning.
3) Baste the joint from time to time and allow it to roast without becoming overcoloured or dried out by the time it is cooked. Allow approx. 20 mins. per 500g plus an extra 20 mins. cooking time. For example a 1½kg unboned shoulder of lamb will take approx. 80 mins.
4) To test when cooked, press the joint firmly so as to squeeze out a little of the juices. If clear the joint is cooked; if there is any blood present in the juice the joint is not sufficiently cooked and should be returned to the oven for further cooking. The reading on a meat thermometer inserted at the thickest part of the joint would show approx. 78–80°C.
5) Allow the cooked joint to rest for 20–30 mins. before carving. This will prevent the meat from shrinking and curling when being carved and also from losing its juices.

Degrees of cooking
In general roast lamb or mutton should never be served underdone to an English clientele unless specifically requested. If on the bone, it should be cooked just to the bone with a little pinkness evident. In all other cases it should be just cooked but on no account to the stage where the meat becomes dry and lacks moistness.

Roast Gravy – Jus de Rôti
1) When the roast joint is cooked and removed, place the roasting tray on the stove and heat gently, allowing the juices and sediment to settle and colour lightly without burning.
2) Drain off the fat without disturbing the sediment.
3) Add brown stock (97) as required and allow to simmer gently for a few mins.
4) Correct the seasoning with salt. There should be no need to colour the gravy.
5) Pass through a fine strainer and skim but it is best not to remove all vestiges of fat. Allow approx. 5dl of gravy per 10 covers.

Carving
Leg: Hold the leg bone and carve slices from the thickest side towards the bone, starting at the knuckle end and at an angle of 45°. Carve about 3–4mm thick. When the slices get too large, carve from alternate sides and when the top part is finished, turn the leg over and continue carving.

Shoulder (on the bone): Carve slices 3–4mm thick starting from the thickest side. Turn over and carve the underside to uncover the blade bone. Finish carving by following the contours of the bones.

Shoulder (boned or boned and stuffed): Cut in slices across the joint approx. ½cm thick.

Saddle: There are two ways of carving a saddle.
1) Carve lengthways either side of the backbone giving long flat strips of meat.
2) Cut down either side of the backbone. Then cut across into slices ½–¾cm thick. The two filets mignons under the saddle should not be forgotten and should be sliced and served as well.

Loin (boned and rolled or boned, stuffed and rolled): Carve across the jont into slices about ½cm thick.

Best end: Carve into cutlets by cutting between each rib-bone.

Service of roast lamb or mutton
Carved in the kitchen: Arrange as required on a suitable dish or plate with a little roast gravy, garnish with watercress and send a separate sauceboat of gravy.

Carved in the restaurant: Send the whole joint on an appropriate dish, garnish with watercress and send also a separate container of gravy.

Accompaniments
Lamb: Mint Sauce (186), Mint Jelly. Redcurrant Jelly can also be served. Mutton: Redcurrant Jelly, Onion Sauce (147). Mint Sauce can also be served.

---

704 Grills of Lamb or Mutton

The following small cuts of lamb or mutton are suitable for grilling and their titles are given as they can appear on the menu:
Chop d'Agneau or de Mouton grillé – Grilled Lamb or Mutton Chop
Côte de Gigot d'Agneau or de Mouton grillée – Grilled Chump Chop of Lamb or Mutton
Grilled Crown Chop of Lamb or Mutton
Noisettes d'Agneau or de Mouton grillées – Grilled Noisettes of Lamb or Mutton
Filet Mignon d'Agneau or de Mouton grillé – Grilled Fillet of Lamb or Mutton
Côtelettes d'Agneau or de Mouton grillées – Grilled Lamb or Mutton Cutlets
Côtelette d'Agneau double grillée – Grilled Double Lamb Cutlet

Method of grilling, using underfired grills (gas, electricity or charcoal)
1) Light the grill so that it will reach its operating temperature by the time grilling is to commence.
2) Wipe the bars of the grill with oil to prevent the meat sticking to them.
3) Season the items and brush with oil or butter.
4) Place on the bars in the centre of the grill and cook quickly turning them at right angles to give a trellis pattern from the bars. Turn the items over and cook more slowly, according to size, either by moving the items to the side of the grill where the heat is not so intense or by raising the height of the grill bars so that they are further away from the heat.

Method of grilling, using a salamander or top-heat grill (gas or electric)
1) Light the salamander in sufficient time for it to reach maximum heat by the time grilling is to commence.
2) Brush the bars or grilling plate with oil. Season the items, brush with oil or butter and place on the bars or plate.
3) Grill the items quickly until well-coloured on top, turn them over and cook the other side until also coloured. If necessary lower the rack and allow to continue cooking until the meat is done.

Service
Serve the grilled items on suitable dishes or plates garnished with watercress. Cutlet frills should be placed on the bones of grilled cutlets.

Suitable butters and sauces as an accompaniment
Beurre à la Bourguignonne, Beurre Maître d'Hôtel, Beurre Ravigote, Sauce Choron, Sauce Paloise.

Suitable garnishes
Continentale – Pommes Soufflées, Tomates grillées, Champignons grillés, watercress.
Henri IV – Pommes Pont-Neuf, watercress.
Tyrolienne – Oignons frits à la Française, Tomates grillées, watercress.
Vert-Pré – Pommes Pailles, Beurre Maître d'Hôtel, watercress.
  The correct menu terms would thus be, for example, Chop d'Agneau grillé Vert-Pré, Côtelettes d'Agneau grillées Continentale.

Cooking times
Grills of lamb or mutton should not be under- or overcooked unless the customer indicates otherwise. The following times can only give an indication and thus are approximate. They will vary according to the customer's requirement and the thickness of the meat.

Lamb cutlets	5–6 mins.
Lamb cutlets, double	10–12 mins.
Lamb chops	15–18 mins.
Chump chops	15–18 mins.
Crown chops	10–12 mins.
Filets Mignons	8–10 mins.
Noisettes	5–6 mins.

These times may need to be slightly increased for grills of mutton.

705 Grills of Lamb's Offals

Lamb's kidneys (699) and liver (700) are suitable for grilling. In either case they should be kept slightly underdone. The liver should be floured first.

Garnish with Pommes Pailles (1586) and watercress and serve accompanied with Parsley butter (10).

706 Blanquette d'Agneau

10 portions
2½ hours

Stage	Ingredient	Quantity	Method
1	shoulder of lamb, boned, trimmed and cut into 2½cm cubes	1¼kg	Place into a pan, cover with cold water, bring to the boil and blanch for 3 mins. Refresh under cold water and drain.
2	Fonds Blanc (93)	1½ litres, approx.	Place the lamb in a clean pan, just cover with stock, bring to the boil and skim.
3	Oignons Cloutés (65)	2	Add to the lamb, season lightly and simmer gently until nearly cooked (1–1½ hours).
4	butter flour	60g 60g	Prepare a Blond Roux (108) and allow to cool.
5			When the lamb is cooked remove from the liquid and place in a clean pan. Strain the cooking liquor and make into a velouté with the blond roux. Allow to simmer for 30 mins.
6	cream juice of lemon parsley, chopped	2dl squeeze	Adjust the seasoning of the velouté and add the cream and lemon juice. Pass through a fine strainer over the lamb. Simmer gently to complete the cooking and serve in entrée dishes sprinkled with chopped parsley.

SPECIAL POINTS
a) A liaison of 3 egg yolks and 2dl of cream can be added instead of just cream but in this case it should be added when the lamb is completely cooked and only reheated sufficiently for the egg yolks to cook. Do not reboil.
b) Lightly coloured Heart-shaped Croûtons (26) or Fleurons (33) can be used to garnish the finished dish.

707 Blanquette d'Agneau à l'Ancienne

Prepare a Blanquette d'Agneau (706) with the addition of 30 button mushrooms cooked à Blanc (60) and 30 button onions cooked à Blanc (1492) added at Stage 6.

708 Blanquette d'Agneau à la Ménagère

Prepare a Blanquette d'Agneau (706) with the addition of 20 small Pommes Nouvelles au Beurre (1581), 30 small glazed carrots (1400) and 20 button onions cooked à Blanc (1492).

---

709 Carré d'Agneau Persillé

10 portions
1½ hours

Stage	Ingredient	Quantity	Method
1	best ends of lamb (684)	3	Roast, leaving slightly underdone.
2	butter shallots, finely chopped breadcrumbs parsley, chopped	150g 75g 200g 2 tbsps	Melt the butter in a sauteuse, add the shallots and cook without colour. Add the breadcrumbs and parsley and season. Mix well together.
3			Lay the underdone best ends on a tray, fat side uppermost, and cover the surfaces with the prepared mixture. Press gently to the shape of the best ends.
4			Place in a moderate oven, approx. 180°C. to finish cooking the lamb and to brown the surface of the mixture.
5	roast gravy watercress	6dl 1 bunch	Dress the best ends on a dish and place frills on the cutlet bones. Garnish with watercress and serve accompanied with a sauceboat of roast gravy made from the juices and sediment in the roasting tray.

SPECIAL POINT

Instead of presenting the best ends whole they may be cut into cutlets and arranged neatly on the dish surrounded with a little of the gravy.

---

710 Carré d'Agneau Boulangère

10 portions
2 hours

Stage	Ingredient	Quantity	Method
1	best ends of lamb (684)	3	Roast, leaving slightly underdone.
2	Pommes Boulangère (1546) (made in 3 dishes)	10 portions	Place one best end on top of each dish of potatoes and place in the oven to continue cooking at approx. 180°C for a further 10–15 mins.
3	parsley, chopped		Remove from the oven, clean the outside of the dishes and place frills on the cutlet bones. Sprinkle the potatoes which

show with a little chopped parsley and serve the dish as it is, accompanied with a sauceboat of roast gravy made from the juices and sediment in the roasting tray.

SPECIAL POINT
Instead of presenting the best ends whole they may be cut into cutlets when cooked and arranged neatly back on top of the potatoes for service.

---

711 Chop d'Agneau braisé – Braised Lamb Chop
10 portions
2½ hours

Stage	Ingredient	Quantity	Method
1	dripping lamb chops (690)	60g 10 × 200g	Heat the dripping in a frying-pan, season the chops and fry brown on both sides. Remove the chops and place in a braising pan.
2	onion, ⎤ roughly carrot, ⎦ diced	250g 250g	Fry in the same fat to a light brown, drain and add the vegetables to the chops.
3	flour	60g	Sprinkle onto the chops and shake the pan to mix in. Place in a hot oven for approx. 10 mins. and remove.
4	tomato purée Fonds Brun (97) Bouquet Garni garlic, crushed	1 tbsp 1½ litres 1 ½ clove	Add the tomato purée and carefully mix in sufficient stock to barely cover the chops. Add the bouquet garni and garlic and season. Bring to the boil, skim, cover with a lid and place in a moderate oven at 180°C. Cook until tender, approx. 1–1½ hours. Baste and turn occasionally.
5			Remove the chops and place in a clean pan. Remove the fat from the sauce and adjust the consistency, colour and seasoning. The sauce should not be too thick and it should be of a reddish-brown colour. Pass through a fine strainer over the meat and reboil.
6	parsley, chopped		Serve the chops in earthenware dishes sprinkled with chopped parsley.

SPECIAL POINT
Braised chops may be served with cooked and lightly buttered vegetable garnishes, e.g. Jardinière, Paysanne, Printanière, and should be designated accordingly on the menu, for example, Chop d'Agneau braisé Printanière.

712 Chump Chop Champvallon

10 portions
2½ hours

Stage	Ingredient	Quantity	Method
1	dripping chump chops (691)	60g 10 × 200g	Place the dripping in a frying-pan and heat. Season the chops and fry brown on both sides in the hot fat. Remove the chops and place on one side.
2	butter onions, finely sliced potatoes, peeled	75g 500g 1½kg	Melt the butter in a pan and sauté the onions quickly without colour. Slice the potatoes 2mm thick on a mandolin.
3			Place a few of the onions and a single layer of potatoes on the bottom of the required number of earthenware dishes. Lightly season, place the chops on top, sprinkle the rest of the onions over the chops, cover with potatoes, season and finish with a neatly arranged layer.
4	Fonds Blanc (93) butter, melted	2 litres, approx. 75g	Add sufficient stock to reach just under the top layer of potatoes and sprinkle with the butter.
5			Place in a moderate oven at 190°C and cook until tender (1½–2 hours), occasionally pressing the top layer of potatoes flat. Reduce the oven temperature as necessary, to prevent burning.
6	parsley, chopped		Brush the surface of the potatoes with butter and sprinkle with chopped parsley.

---

713 Coeur d'Agneau braisé – Braised Lamb's Heart

10 portions
2½ hours

Stage	Ingredient	Quantity	Method
1	lamb's hearts dripping	10 100g	Remove the tubes and excess fat from the hearts. Heat the dripping in a frying-pan, season the hearts and fry until brown on all sides. Remove and place in a braising pan.
2	onion ⎱ roughly carrot ⎰ diced	250g 250g	Fry in the same fat to a light colour, drain the vegetables and add to the hearts.
3	flour	60g	Sprinkle over the hearts and shake the pan to mix in. Place in a hot oven for approx. 10 mins. Remove from the oven.
4	tomato purée Fonds Brun (97)	1 tbsp 1½ litres	Add the tomato purée and carefully mix in sufficient stock to barely cover. Add

	Bouquet Garni	1	the bouquet garni, garlic and season.
	garlic, crushed	½ clove	Bring to the boil, skim, cover with a lid and place in a moderate oven at 180°C and cook until tender (approx. 1–1½ hours).
5			Remove the hearts and place in a clean pan. Remove the fat from the sauce and adjust the consistency, colour and seasoning. The sauce should not be too thick and it should be of a reddish-brown colour. Pass through a fine strainer over the hearts and reboil.
6	parsley, chopped		Serve the hearts in earthenware dishes sprinkled with chopped parsley.

SPECIAL POINT

Braised lamb's hearts may be served with cooked and lightly buttered vegetable garnishes, e.g. Jardinière, Paysanne, Printanière, and should be designated accordingly on the menu, for example, Coeur d'Agneau braisé Paysanne.

---

714 Côtelettes d'Agneau Maintenon

10 portions
2 hours

Stage	Ingredient	Quantity	Method
1	butter	100g	Heat the butter in a sauté pan. When
	lamb cutlets		hot, season the cutlets and fry them
	(692)	20 × 80g	quickly to a good colour on one side only. Drain and place on a buttered tray, cooked side upwards.
2	Sauce Soubise		Spread neatly on the cooked sides of the
	(150)	3dl	cutlets smoothing dome-shape with a wet palette knife.
3	breadcrumbs	100g	Sprinkle the breadcrumbs over the
	butter, melted	100g	Soubise and then sprinkle well with the melted butter.
4			Place the tray of cutlets in the oven at 190°C for 7–8 mins. to complete cooking and to gratinate the surface of the Soubise.
5	butter	120g	Arrange the cutlets on suitable dishes.
	Sauce Périgueux		Place the butter in a suitable frying-pan
	(131)	5dl	and cook until nut-brown, shaking the pan to ensure even colouring. Pour over the cutlets and place a frill on each cutlet bone. Serve accompanied with sauce-boats of Sauce Périgueux.

715 Côtelettes d'Agneau Milanaise

These are cooked and served in the same way as Côtelettes d'Agneau panées (717) with the addition of Spaghetti Milanaise (504) as a garnish.

716 Côtelettes d'Agneau Napolitaine

These are cooked and served in the same way as Côtelettes d'Agneau panées (717) with the addition of Spaghetti Napolitaine (506) as a garnish.

717 Côtelettes d'Agneau panées

10 portions
1 hour

Stage	Ingredient	Quantity	Method
1	lamb cutlets (692)	20 × 80g	Lightly flatten with a cutlet bat and trim excess fat.
2	flour eggwash breadcrumbs } for crumbing		Season the cutlets and paner à l'Anglaise (72). Flatten, reshape and mark trellis-fashion with the back of a knife.
3	oil	3dl	Heat in a sauté pan and when hot place in the cutlets and fry to a golden brown on both sides until cooked (7–8 mins.).
4	Jus lié (113) butter	3dl 120g	Arrange the cutlets on suitable dishes and surround with a cordon of jus lié. Place the butter in a suitable frying-pan and cook until nut-brown, shaking the pan to ensure even colouring. Pour over the cutlets and place a frill on each cutlet bone.

718 Côtelettes d'Agneau Réforme

10 portions
1½ hours

Stage	Ingredient	Quantity	Method
1	lamb cutlets (692)	20 × 80g	Lightly flatten with a cutlet bat and trim excess fat.
2	flour eggwash breadcrumbs ham, finely chopped parsley, chopped } for crumbing	400g 80g 2 tbsps	Mix the breadcrumbs, ham and parsley together. Season the cutlets, pass through flour, eggwash and the breadcrumb mixture. Flatten, reshape and mark the cutlets trellis-fashion with the back of a knife.
3	oil	3dl	Heat in a sauté pan and when hot place in the cutlets. Fry to a golden brown on both sides until cooked (7–8 mins.).
4	butter Sauce Réforme (135)	120g 6dl	Arrange the cutlets on suitable dishes with the decorated sides uppermost. Place the butter in a suitable frying-pan

until nut-brown, shaking the pan to
ensure even colouring. Pour over the
cutlets and place a frill on each cutlet
bone. Serve accompanied with a sauceboat of Sauce Réforme.

719 CURRY

Curried dishes have been popular in this country since their introduction in the days of
Britain's imperial involvement in the Indian subcontinent. People living in India,
Bangladesh and Pakistan and close or adjoining areas, and countries such as Malaya,
Indo-China and Indonesia like to blend a range of local spices, herbs and seeds for use
in the making of hot, spicy and peppery vegetable, egg, fish and meat dishes known and
described under the general name of curry. The word comes from *Kari*, the Tamil word
for a sauce.

Curry powder is made by pounding or grinding together those various herbs, spices
and seeds. Curry pastes use the same ingredients but they are first cooked together
gently with a proportionate amount of ghee or clarified butter. The proportion and
choice of ingredients vary according to tastes and range from pungently hot to mild. The
following list of ingredients is not complete but it gives those which are usually used –
turmeric, cayenne, chilli, cumin, coriander, ginger, pepper, mace, cardamom, fenugreek,
mustard seed, clove, garlic, poppy seed.

In European countries proprietary brands of curry powders and pastes are available
ranging from mild to very hot and which give excellent results. The first of the following
two recipes for curried lamb is a typical one adapted in some respects to European tastes
but which has gained general acceptance and favour. The second is a more authentic
recipe from India.

720 Currie d'Agneau – Curried Lamb

10 portions
2½ hours

Stage	Ingredient	Quantity	Method
1	butter	100g	Heat the butter in a braising pan. Season
	shoulder of lamb,		the lamb and fry quickly in the butter
	boned, trimmed		until brown.
	and cut into		
	2½cm cubes	1¼kg	
2	onions, chopped	500g	Add to the meat, mix in and cook for a
	garlic, finely		few minutes until coloured with the
	chopped	1 clove	meat.
3	curry powder	50g	Add, mix in then place the pan in a hot
	flour	50g	oven for approx. 10 mins. Remove.
4	tomato purée	1 tbsp	Add the tomato purée to the lamb and
	Fonds Brun (97)	2 litres	mix in sufficient stock to barely cover.
	chutney, chopped	75g	Season, bring to the boil and skim. Add
	apple, chopped	150g	the remainder of the ingredients, cover
	sultanas	50g	with the lid and cook in a moderate oven
	desiccated coconut	10g	at 180°C for 1–1½ hours until tender.

5		Skim the fat from the sauce and adjust the seasoning.
6	long-grain rice, for Riz Poché (534) 300g	Serve the curry in entrée dishes accompanied by a dish of poached rice.

SPECIAL POINTS

a) The amount of curry powder given in this recipe is only approximate. Curry powders vary in strength and experience in using a particular brand will determine the required amount.

b) A little warmed yoghurt or cream may be added to the curry when serving.

---

721 Indian Curried Lamb

10 portions
2½ hours

Stage	Ingredient	Quantity	Method
1	chillies, fresh water	4	Remove the stem and seeds. Soak the flesh in a little water for a few mins.
2	ginger root garlic	30g 6 cloves	Pound and blend well together, add the drained chillies and pound again adding a little water to make a smooth paste.
3	almonds cardamom seeds cayenne cloves cumin nutmeg, grated mace, ground peppercorns poppy seeds turmeric	25g 1 tbsp ½ tsp 6 1 tsp pinch pinch 12 1 tsp 1 tbsp	Mix all these ingredients together. Heat a heavy shallow pan then add these ingredients and toss over to heat well and develop their flavours but without colouring. Pound finely and pass through a sieve.
4	ghee (or clarified butter) shoulder of lamb, boned, trimmed and cut into 2½cm cubes	120g 1¼kg	Heat the ghee in a braising pan, season the lamb and fry quickly in the ghee until brown.
5	onions, chopped	250g	Add to the meat, mix in and cook for a few mins. Add the prepared spices, cook for 2–3 mins., then add the paste from Stage 2.
6	chopped tomato, flesh only yoghurt, plain water coconut milk	200g 2dl 2dl 3dl	Add to the lamb, season with salt, bring to the boil and skim. Cover tightly and cook in a moderate oven at 180°C for 1–1½ hours

7	coriander leaves	2 tbsps	Serve the curry in entrée dishes, sprinkle
	Garam Masala (722)	pinch	with some of the Garam Masala and the
	long-grain rice,		chopped coriander leaves. Accompany
	for Riz poché		with a dish of plain boiled rice.
	(534)	300g	

SPECIAL POINTS

a) To prepare coconut milk, pour approx. 3dl of boiling water over 75g desiccated coconut. Allow to infuse for 20 mins. then squeeze firmly through a cloth.

b) Accompaniments for curries. A number of differing items are traditionally offered with curry. The following list is not exhaustive but gives some idea of its range:

poppadums	lime pickle	chopped apple
chapatis	grated coconut	sliced lychees
grilled Bombay duck	sliced lemon	sliced stem ginger
mango chutney	chillies	almonds
sliced pawpaw	shredded pimento	sliced lime
yoghurt		

---

722 Garam Masala

Ingredients: 25g cardamom seeds   25g cinnamon
              25g black peppercorns   15g cumin
              10g cloves   5g nutmeg

Method: Grind the ingredients together fairly finely and store in an airtight jar.

SPECIAL POINT

In India the ingredients of Garam Masala and their proportions tend to vary according to district. It can be used to sprinkle over finished food, used in the cooking of various foods and can be cooked to a paste with a little ghee or clarified butter and used in the preparation of curry dishes.

---

723 Chapatis   25 pieces

Stage	Ingredient	Quantity	Method
1	flour, wholemeal	500g	Sift the flour and salt together. Add the
	salt	10g	water and mix to a smooth soft and
	warm water	2½dl	pliable dough. Knead well then cover
		approx.	with a damp cloth and leave to rest for at least 30 mins.
2			Knead the dough again for a few mins. then divide it into 25 equal-sized pieces. Roll into circles approx. 15–16cm in diameter.
3			Place the chapatis on a hot griddle and cook until brown spots appear then turn over and cook the other sides. As they are cooked keep covered in a warm cloth.

SPECIAL POINT
Chapatis are the unleavened bread of the Indian subcontinent and are commonly offered with most dishes. They should be made freshly for each meal.

724　Epaule d'Agneau Boulangère

Prepare as Carré d'Agneau Boulangère (710), using shoulder of lamb instead of best end.

725　Epigrammes d'Agneau

10 portions
2 hours

Stage	Ingredient	Quantity	Method
1	breasts of lamb Fonds Blanc (93)	2kg 4 litres	Trim off the surplus fat from the breasts of lamb. Place the breasts in a suitable pan, cover with the stock, bring to the boil and skim.
2	carrot, whole 　peeled Oignons Cloutés (65) Bouquet Garni	250g 2 1	Add, season and simmer gently until the breasts are tender, approx. 1 hour. Remove the breasts and drain.
3			Remove and discard all bones and tendons then lay the breasts on a suitably-sized tray to give an evenly thick layer. Cover with another tray and weigh down firmly. The thickness of the lamb should be 1–1½cm. Place in the refrigerator and allow to cool and set completely.
4			Remove the lamb from the trays and cut into 20 equal-sized triangles. Trim off the corners.
5	flour eggwash　} for breadcrumbs } crumbing		Paner à l'Anglaise (72).
6	oil	3dl	Heat in a sauté pan and when hot place in the Epigrammes and fry to a golden brown on both sides (5–6 mins.).
7	Jus lié (113) butter	3dl 100g	Arrange the Epigrammes on suitable dishes and surround with a cordon of jus lié. Place the butter in a suitable frying-pan and cook until nut-brown, shaking the pan to ensure even colouring. Pour over the Epigrammes.

SPECIAL POINT
Epigrammes may be served with suitable garnishes, e.g. Spaghetti Milanaise, Jardinière, and should be designated on the menu accordingly, for example, Epigrammes d'Agneau Milanaise.

726 Filets Mignons d'Agneau

The fillets of lamb (695) can be seasoned, sautéed in butter and served with a suitable sauce, e.g. Chasseur, Madère. Marsala or with any of the garnishes listed under Noisettes d'Agneau (750–754).

727 Filets Mignons d'Agneau Persane

10 portions
1 hour

Stage	Ingredient	Quantity	Method
1	oil	1dl	Heat the oil in a shallow pan. Season and flour the slices of courgettes and shallow fry quickly to colour both sides. Remove and drain. Cook the aubergines in the same way.
	courgettes ⎫ cut in	4 medium	
	aubergines ⎭ 3mm slices	2 medium	
	flour		
2	Tomates Concassées (90)	200g	Fill ten small dariole moulds with alternate slices of the courgettes and aubergines interspersed with a little of the tomato. Press down, place on a tray and cook in a hot oven for approx. 10 mins. Remove and keep warm.
3	butter	75g	Heat the butter in a shallow pan, season the fillets and cook to a golden brown on all sides but kept pink in the centre, approx. 8 mins. Remove and keep warm.
	fillets of lamb, whole, (695)	20	
4	white wine, dry	2dl	Tip out the fat from the pan, add the wine and mint and reduce by half. Pass through a fine strainer into a clean pan.
	chopped mint, stalks and leaves	2 tbsps	
5	sour cream	3dl	Add the cream and jus lié. Simmer gently to a light coating consistency and remove from the heat. Shake in the butter and adjust the seasoning plus a touch of cayenne. Finish with the chopped mint.
	Jus lié	2dl	
	butter	75g	
	cayenne		
	mint, chopped young leaves	2 tbsps	
6	Riz Pilaff (522)	10 portions	Place into suitable dishes and shape as neat flat oval beds. Arrange the fillets on top with the demoulded vegetables to one side of the rice. Make sure that everything is hot, brush the fillets with butter and send the sauce separately in a sauceboat.

728 Foie d'Agneau – Lamb's Liver

The recipes listed under Foie de Veau (965–967) are all suitable for lamb's liver.

729 Fricassée d'Agneau

10 portions
2½ hours

Stage	Ingredient	Quantity	Method

1	butter
	shoulder of lamb,
	  boned, trimmed
	  and cut in
	  2½cm cubes
		100g
		
		1¼kg
			Heat the butter in a sauté pan, season the lamb, place into the pan and stiffen it without colouring.

2	flour	50g	Sprinkle over the meat and shake the pan to mix in. Cover with a lid and place in the oven at 175°C for 10 mins. Remove and allow to cool.
3	Fonds Blanc de Mouton (94) Bouquet Garni	1½ litres 1	Carefully mix in sufficient stock to just cover the lamb, season, bring to the boil and skim. Add the bouquet garni, cover with the lid and place in a moderate oven, approx. 180°C, to cook for 1½–2 hours.
4			Discard the bouquet garni and remove the meat to a clean pan.
5	egg yolks } liaison cream	3 1dl	Whisk together in a large basin and add approx. one-third of the sauce, whisking in quickly. Return to the remainder of the sauce, mixing in quickly. Reheat, moving it continuously with a spatula until the liaison thickens. Take care that it does not reboil.
6			Adjust the seasoning of the sauce and pass through a fine strainer over the meat. Carefully reheat without boiling.
7	parsley, chopped Heart-shaped Croûtons (26)	 10	Serve in earthenware dishes, sprinkle with chopped parsley and garnish with the croûtons.

730 Fricassée d'Agneau à l'Ancienne

Prepare as Fricassée d'Agneau (729) with the addition of 30 button onions cooked à Blanc (1492) and 30 button mushrooms cooked à Blanc (60) added at Stage 6.

731 Gigot d'Agneau Boulangère

Prepare as Carré d'Agneau Boulangère (710), using leg of lamb instead of best end.

732 Gigot d'Agneau Bretonne

Prepare and serve roast leg of lamb and garnish with Haricots Bretonne (1469).

733 Gigot de Mouton Bouilli – Boiled Leg of Mutton

10–12portions
3 hours

Stage	Ingredient	Quantity	Method
1	leg of mutton (681)	1 × 2¼kg	Wash the leg of mutton and place into sufficient boiling stock to cover well.
	Fonds Blanc de Mouton (94)	5 litres	Bring to the boil and skim.
2	carrots, whole peeled	300g	Add, season with salt and simmer gently until the meat is tender, allowing approx.
	Oignons Piqués (65)	2	25 mins. per 500g. Approx. 2 hours.
	Bouquet Garni	1	
3	Caper Sauce (141)	6dl	Serve the leg whole or carved on a suitable dish with a little of the cooking liquor, accompanied with a sauceboat of caper sauce.

SPECIAL POINTS

a) The quality of the mutton and the finished stock for the sauce are vastly improved when using a mutton stock. However, if water is to be used place the leg into cold water, bring to the boil and carry on as in the recipe.

b) The caper sauce should be made with the cooking liquor from the leg of mutton.

c) In traditional English cookery turned carrots and turned turnips are cooked with the leg and served as a garnish.

d) A purée of boiled turnips as well as Parsley Sauce are also suitable for serving with boiled leg of mutton.

---

734 Haricot de Mouton

10 portions
3 hours

Stage	Ingredient	Quantity	Method
1	haricot beans	500g	Place in a pan, cover well with cold water, bring to the boil and skim.
2	carrot, whole peeled	250g	Add to the beans. Season with salt and simmer until half-cooked, approx. 1 hour. Remove the pan from the stove.
	Oignons Piqués (65)	2	
	bacon bones	250g	
3	lard	60g	Heat the lard in a frying-pan. Add the lardons and button onions and fry until light brown. Remove from the pan, drain and keep on one side.
	streaky bacon, cut into lardons (51)	350g	
	button onions	30	
4	middle neck (685) and breast (688) of mutton prepared for stewing	1¾kg	Season and fry until brown in the same pan and fat. Place the meat in a braising pan.
5	carrot } roughly onion } diced	250g 250g	Fry until brown in the same pan and fat. Drain and add the vegetables to the meat.

6	flour	75g	Sprinkle over the meat and shake the pan to mix in. Place in a hot oven for approx. 10 mins. Remove from the oven.
7	tomato purée Fonds Brun (97) Bouquet Garni garlic, crushed	1 tbsp 2 litres 1 1 clove	Add the tomato purée and carefully mix in sufficient stock to just cover the meat. Add the bouquet garni and garlic. Season. Bring to the boil, skim, cover with the lid and place in a moderate oven at 175°C until half-cooked (approx. 1 hour).
8			Remove the meat to a clean pan then add the lardons, button onions and the drained haricot beans.
9			Remove the fat from the sauce, adjust the consistency, colour and seasoning, and pass through a fine strainer over the meat and garnish.
10			Bring to the boil, cover with the lid and replace in the oven at approx. 150°C to finish cooking gently for a further 1–1½ hours.
11	parsley, chopped		Serve in terrines or cocottes sprinkled with chopped parsley.

735 Irish Stew

10 portions
2½ hours

Stage	Ingredient	Quantity	Method
1	middle neck (685) and breast of lamb (688) prepared for stewing	1¾kg	Place in a pan, cover with cold water and bring to the boil.
2			Refresh under running cold water and drain. Place in a clean pan, cover with cold water, bring to the boil and skim.
3	potatoes celery } finely leeks } sliced onions Bouquet Garni	1kg 250g 250g 250g 1	Add, season and simmer gently until the meat and vegetables are tender (approx. 1½ hours). Discard the bouquet garni.
4	button onions small turned potatoes	20 20	Cook the onions and potatoes separately in salted water until tender. Place on one side.
5			Remove the lamb to a clean pan and add the drained button onions and turned potatoes. Skim off any fat from the

vegetables and cooking liquor and pass these through a sieve. Adjust the consistency which should not be too liquid. Adjust the seasoning and pour over the meat and vegetables.

6   parsley, chopped   Reboil and serve in earthenware dishes sprinkled with chopped parsley.

736 KEBABS

Originally of Turkish origin, kebabs in one form or another are not only popular national dishes in the Near and Far East but are enjoying ever-increasing favour in the West. They can consist of various small cubes or pieces of meat, poultry, fish and vegetables either as single items or mixed, seasoned, flavoured with spices and herbs and more often than not marinated with such things as lemon, lime or orange juice, vinegars or yoghurt. These pieces are threaded on wooden or metal skewers and are then gently grilled either over charcoal or under a grill. Frequent basting with oil or clarified butter is an essential part of the process for building up a well-flavoured exterior coating. They are usually accompanied with a Riz Pilaff and a suitable sauce such as Curry Sauce, Devilled Sauce or yoghurts flavoured with spices and chopped aromatic vegetables and herbs.

Other names used to describe this kind of dish are Shashlik, Shishkebab, Brochette, Attereau and Souvlakia.

737 Kebab d'Agneau

10 portions
2½ hours

Stage	Ingredient	Quantity	Method
1	fillets of lamb (695)	1½kg	Trim off the fat and sinew and cut into 1cm-thick slices on the slant. Place on a tray.
2	juice of lemon	1	Sprinkle over the lamb. Season with salt and pepper and allow to marinate for 2 hours.
	oil	1dl	
	powdered thyme	pinch	
	bayleaves	30	
	onions, cut into 2½cm squares	300g	
3			Arrange the lamb, bayleaves and onions equally on 10 skewers then place them on an oiled tray. Grill gently on both sides, brushing with oil occasionally (12–15 mins.).
4	Riz Pilaff (522)	10 portions	Dress the kebabs on a bed of riz pilaff without removing the skewers. Serve accompanied with a sauceboat of demi-glace or Sauce Diable.
	Demi-glace (112) or Sauce Diable (125)	6dl	

738 Lancashire Hot-pot

10 portions
3 hours

Stage	Ingredient	Quantity	Method
1	dripping middle neck of lamb (685) cut for stewing	80g 1¼kg	Heat the dripping in a frying-pan, season the meat and lightly fry without too much colour.
2	potatoes, peeled onions, finely sliced	1½kg 500g	Slice the potatoes 3mm thick on a mandolin. Place alternate layers of potatoes, onions and meat in hot-pot casseroles or deep earthenware dishes, season and finish with a layer of potatoes neatly overlapping.
3	Fonds Blanc (93) butter, melted	2 litres 75g	Add sufficient stock to reach just under the top layer of the potatoes and sprinkle with the butter. Place in a moderate oven at 180°C and cook until tender, 1½–2 hours. Reduce the oven temperature as necessary.
4	parsley, chopped		Brush the surface of the potatoes with butter and serve sprinkled with chopped parsley.

---

739 Langue d'Agneau braisée aux Cornichons – Braised Lamb's Tongue with Gherkins

10 portions
2¼ hours

Stage	Ingredient	Quantity	Method
1	lamb's tongues (702)	10	Place in a pan of cold water, bring to the boil, simmer for 5 mins. refresh and drain.
2	butter bacon trimmings carrots ⎱ sliced onions ⎰	20g 75g 200g 200g	Butter a suitable braising pan, add the rest of the ingredients and place the tongues on top. Cover and place on the stove to allow the vegetables to just colour.
3	Fonds Brun (98) tomato purée Bouquet Garni garlic, crushed	8dl ½ tbsp 1 1 clove	Add to the tongues, bring to the boil, skim and season. Cover with the lid and place in a moderate oven at 180°C for approx. 1½ hours until tender.
4			Remove the tongues and wash and skin them. Trim the root ends neatly, cover and keep warm.
5	white wine vinegar shallots, chopped arrowroot	½dl 50g 10g	Place the shallots and vinegar in a small pan and reduce until almost dry. Add the braising stock, strained and skimmed

of fat. Reduce to give approx. 5dl and lightly thicken with the diluted arrowroot.

Stage	Ingredient	Quantity	Method
6	butter	75g	Shake in the butter and adjust the
	gherkins, small	120g	seasoning plus a good touch of cayenne.
	cayenne		Add the gherkins which have been
			trimmed and cut in half lengthways.
7	parsley, chopped		Cut the tongues in three lengthways and
			place in suitable dishes. Coat with the
			sauce and sprinkle with parsley.

---

740 Langue d'Agneau Poulette

10 portions
2 hours

Stage	Ingredient	Quantity	Method
1	lamb's tongues (702)	10	Place in a pan of cold water, bring to the boil, simmer for 5 mins., refresh and drain.
2	Blanc (15)	2 litres	Place the tongues in the boiling blanc
	carrot, whole	100g	together with the vegetables and bouquet
	Oignons Piqués (65)	2	garni. Cover with a clean cloth or muslin
	Bouquet Garni	1	and simmer gently until tender, approx. 1½ hours.
3			Remove the tongues and wash and skin them. Trim the root ends and keep warm with a little of the cooking liquor.
4	Sauce Poulette (149)	6dl	Cut the tongues in three lengthways and place in suitable dishes. Coat with the
	parsley, chopped		sauce and sprinkle with a little parsley.

---

741 Longe d'Agneau poêléc

10 portions
2 hours

Stage	Ingredient	Quantity	Method
1	loins of lamb, boned and rolled (682)	2 × 800g	Butter a deep pan, add the vegetables, bacon and herbs, season the loins and
	butter	150g	place on top. Melt the remaining butter
	onion	120g	and pour over the loins.
	carrot	120g	
	celery roughly diced	100g	
	bacon	80g	
	bayleaf	1	
	thyme	sprig	

2			Cover with the lid and place in the oven at approx. 200°C. Baste occasionally and remove the lid after 1 hour. Continue cooking and basting until the loins are nicely brown and cooked (total time 1½–1¾ hours). To test if cooked remove the loins to a tray and press firmly to express a little of the juices – this should be slightly pink to clear. Place the loins on one side to keep warm.
3	Fonds Brun (97)	2dl	Place the pan on the stove and allow the juices and vegetables to heat gently and colour without burning. Drain off the fat without disturbing the vegetables and sediment. Add the stock and jus lié and simmer gently for a few minutes to correct consistency. Skim and adjust the seasoning. Pass through a fine strainer and keep hot.
	Jus lié (113)	5dl	
4			Remove the string from the loins, carve the loins into slices and arrange on dishes with the slices overlapping. Surround with a little of the sauce and send the rest separately in a sauceboat.

SPECIAL POINTS
a) The loins may be presented whole for carving in the restaurant.
b) Instead of using jus lié at Stage 3, the total of excellent brown stock can be increased to 7dl, then after a few minutes of simmering it can be lightly thickened with 10–15g diluted arrowroot.

742 Longe d'Agneau Clamart

Prepare Longe d'Agneau poêlée (741) but deglaze the vegetables and juices at Stage 3 with ½dl Madeira before adding the stock and jus lié. Garnish with artichoke bottoms filled with lightly buttered green peas and small Pommes Château (1550).

743 Longe d'Agneau Dubarry

Prepare Longe d'Agneau poêlée (741) and garnish with small Pommes Château (1550) and bouquets of Chou-fleur Mornay (1426).

744 Longe d'Agneau Niçoise

Prepare Longe d'Agneau poêlée (741) and garnish with small Pommes Château (1550), bouquets of Haricots Verts au Beurre (1475) and small peeled tomatoes cooked in the oven with a little butter.

745 Longe d'Agneau Saint-Mandé

Prepare Longe d'Agneau poêlée (741) and garnish with portions of Pommes Macaire (1572) moulded 3½cm in diameter, bouquets of Haricots Verts au Beurre (1475) and Petits Pois au Beurre (1500).

746 Mixed Grill

10 portions
1 hour

Stage	Ingredient	Quantity	Method
1	lamb cutlets (692) oil	10 × 100g 2dl	Season and brush with oil.
2	lamb's kidneys	10	Remove the skins, cut open and place on skewers. Season and brush with oil.
3	chipolatas, pork	10	Place on a grilling tray and brush with oil.
4	grilling mushrooms	10	Remove stalks, wash, place on the grilling tray, brush with oil and season.
5	tomatoes	10	Remove the eyes, cut a shallow incision in the form of a cross on the top. Place on the grilling tray, brush with oil and season.
6	bacon rashers	10	Place on the grilling tray.
7			Grill all the ingredients either on the grill or under the salamander; the kidneys should be cooked slightly underdone.
8	Beurre Maître d'Hôtel (10) Pommes Pailles (1586) watercress	150g 150g 1 bunch	Arrange the grilled items neatly on suitable dishes, place a frill on each cutlet bone and a slice of Beurre Maître d'Hôtel in the centre of each kidney. Garnish the dishes with pommes pailles and watercress.

SPECIAL POINTS

a) The above are the more general components of a mixed grill. Some establishments specialising in grills could exclude some items and include other items like grilled liver and small steaks and even small grilled cuts of veal or veal kidney.

b) The parsley butter may be sent separately in a sauceboat.

747 Moussaka

10 portions
1½ hours

Stage	Ingredient	Quantity	Method
1	butter	60g	Melt the butter in a pan. Add the onions
	onions, finely		and garlic and cook without colour. Add
	chopped	100g	the mushrooms and cook for 2 mins.
	garlic, finely		
	chopped	1 clove	
	mushrooms,		
	chopped	250g	
2	tomato purée	½ tbsp	Add, season well and allow to stew
	cooked mutton,		gently. Reduce until the mixture is
	finely diced	1¼kg	slightly thicker.
	Demi-glace (112)	3dl	
3	aubergines	5	Peel the aubergines and cut into ½cm
	oil	3dl	round slices. Heat the oil in a frying-
	flour		pan; season and pass the aubergines
			through flour and fry in the oil to a
			golden brown on both sides.
4	tomatoes	8	Blanch, skin and cut into 3–4mm-thick
			slices.
5	breadcrumbs	75g	Place the mutton mixture in earthenware
	butter	75g	dishes and cover neatly with alternate
			slices of aubergine and tomato; season
			the surface. Sprinkle with breadcrumbs
			and melted butter and gratinate in a hot
			oven.
6	parsley, chopped		Serve sprinkled with chopped parsley.

748 Navarin d'Agneau

10 portions
2½ hours

Stage	Ingredient	Quantity	Method
1	dripping	60g	Heat the dripping in a frying-pan, season
	middle neck (685)		the meat and fry brown on both sides in
	and breast of lamb (688)		the hot fat. Remove the meat and place
	prepared for stewing	1¾kg	in a braising pan.
2	carrot ⎫ roughly	250g	Fry in the same fat to a light brown,
	onion ⎭ diced	250g	drain and add the vegetables to the
			meat.
3	flour	75g	Sprinkle onto the meat and shake the
			pan to mix in. Place in a hot oven for
			approx. 10 mins.
4	tomato purée	1 tbsp	Add the tomato purée and mix in suffi-
	Fonds Brun (97)	2 litres	cient stock to just cover the meat. Add
	Bouquet Garni	1	the bouquet garni and garlic. Season.

	garlic, crushed	1 clove	Bring to the boil, skim, cover with a lid and place in a moderate oven at 175°C until three-quarters cooked (approx. 1 hour).
5	small turned potatoes	20	Remove the meat to a clean pan. Brown the button onions quickly in a little fat and add with the potatoes to the meat.
	button onions	20	
6			Remove the fat from the sauce. Adjust the consistency and seasoning and pass through a fine strainer over the meat and garnish. Bring to the boil, cover with the lid and replace in the oven at approx. 150°C to finish cooking gently (approx. 1 hour).
7	parsley, chopped		Serve the Navarin in earthenware dishes sprinkled with chopped parsley.

SPECIAL POINT

Vegetable garnishes such as Printanière and Jardinière may be added to the finished Navarin and should be designated accordingly on the menu, for example, Navarin d'Agneau Printanière.

---

749 NOISETTES AND ROSETTES OF LAMB

These small cuts of lamb are well-suited to being sautéed and prepared quickly and to order. They should be just cooked with a slight pinkness showing and should be served as quickly as possible. Butter is the best medium for cooking these because of its flavour but care should be taken not to burn it; a little added oil can help to control this. However, it is essential that the pan is not too large; it should just comfortably hold the number of noisettes. Clarified butter or oil can be used as seen fit.

In most cases it is best to arrange sautéed noisettes or rosettes on croûtons of bread, cut to the approximate shape of the item and fried in clarified butter. These croûtons should not be completely crisped but soft enough inside to soak up any juices escaping from the meat when cooked and thus become an essential part of the dish.

The juices and sediment from the cooking should always be utilised and deglazed as part of the accompanying sauce. Vinegars, wines, stocks, sauces and creams together with herbs, spices and seasonings, singly or in a variety of combinations, are admirably suited to this type of dish. Garnishes should always be neat, of a compatible size and not too complicated.

The following recipes for Noisettes of lamb are given as the standard type and are suitable for either noisettes or rosettes.

---

750 Noisettes d'Agneau Choisy

10 portions
1 hours

Stage	Ingredient	Quantity	Method
1	butter	100g	Heat the butter in a sauté pan, season the noisettes and fry to a golden brown on both sides. Do not overcook.
	Noisettes of lamb (697)	20	

2	Heart-shaped Croûtons (26)	20	Dress the noisettes on the croûtons on suitable dishes and garnish neatly with the braised lettuce and small Pommes Château.
	Braised lettuce (1478)	10 portions	
	small Pommes Château (1550)	30	
3	white wine, dry	1dl	Tip out the fat from the sauté pan, add the white wine. Reduce slightly and add the demi-glace. Reboil, adjust the seasoning and pass the sauce through a fine strainer over the noisettes.
	Demi-glace (112)	5dl	

751 Noisettes d'Agneau Clamart

10 portions
1 hour

Stage	Ingredient	Quantity	Method
1	butter	100g	Heat the butter in a sauté pan. Season the noisettes and fry to a golden brown on both sides. Do not overcook.
	Noisettes of lamb (697)	20	
2	Heart-shaped Croûtons (26)	20	Dress the noisettes on the croûtons on suitable dishes and garnish neatly with the artichoke bottoms filled with peas.
	Fonds d'Artichauts (1379)	10	
	Petits Pois au Beurre (1500)	150g	
3	Madeira	1dl	Tip out the fat from the sauté pan. Add the Madeira, reduce slightly and add the demi-glace. Reboil, adjust the seasoning and pass the sauce through a fine strainer over the noisettes.
	Demi-glace (112)	5dl	

752 Noisettes d'Agneau Dubarry

10 portions
1 hour

Stage	Ingredient	Quantity	Method
1	butter	100g	Heat the butter in a sauté pan. Season the noisettes and fry to a golden brown on both sides. Do not overcook.
	Noisettes of lamb (697)	20	
2	Heart-shaped Croûtons (26)	20	Dress the noisettes on the croûtons on suitable dishes and garnish neatly with the small Pommes Château and the florets of cauliflower Mornay.
	small Pommes Château (1550)	30	
	florets of cauliflower Mornay (1426)	10	
3	Madeira	1dl	Tip out the fat from the sauté pan, add the Madeira, reduce slightly and add the demi-glace. Reboil, adjust the seasoning and pass the sauce through a fine strainer over the noisettes.
	Demi-glace (112)	5dl	

753 Noisettes d'Agneau Mascotte

10 portions
1 hour

Stage	Ingredient	Quantity	Method
1	butter	100g	Heat the butter in a sauté pan. Season the noisettes and fry to a golden brown on both sides. Do not overcook.
	Noisettes of lamb (697)	20	
2	Heart-shaped Croûtons (26)	20	Dress the noisettes on the croûtons on suitable dishes and garnish with the Pommes Cocotte and the artichokes, cut into quarters and sautéed in a little butter.
	Fonds d'Artichauts (1379)	10	
	Pommes Cocotte (1552)	50	
3	white wine, dry	1dl	Tip out the fat from the sauté pan, add the white wine, reduce slightly and add the jus lié. Reboil, adjust the seasoning and pass through a fine strainer over the noisettes. Place a slice of truffle on each noisette.
	Jus lié (113)	5dl	
	truffle slices	20	

754 Noisettes d'Agneau Niçoise

10 portions
1 hour

Stage	Ingredient	Quantity	Method
1	butter	100g	Heat the butter in a sauté pan. Season the noisettes and fry to a golden brown on both sides. Do not overcook.
	Noisettes of lamb (697)	20	
2	Heart-shaped Croûtons (26)	20	Dress the noisettes on the croûtons on suitable dishes and garnish with the small Pommes Château, tomatoes and French beans.
	small Pommes Château (1550)	30	
	small tomatoes, skinned and cooked in the oven with a little butter	10	
	Haricots Verts au Beurre (1475)	200g	
3	white wine, dry	1dl	Tip out the fat from the sauté pan, add the white wine, reduce slightly and add the jus lié. Reboil, adjust the seasoning and pass the sauce through a fine strainer over the noisettes.
	Jus lié (113)	5dl	

Ris d'Agneau – Lamb's Sweetbreads

Recipes for Ris de Veau are suitable for lamb's sweetbreads.

755 Rognons d'Agneau sautés

10 portions
45 mins.

Stage	Ingredient	Quantity	Method
1	lamb's kidneys	20	Remove the skins, cut the kidneys in half and cut each half into three pieces on the slant.
2	butter	100g	Heat the butter in a frying pan, season the kidneys and fry quickly a few at a time keeping them a little underdone. Place in a colander to drain.
3	Demi-glace (112)	6dl	Bring to the boil in a sauteuse and remove from the fire; add the drained kidneys, reheat but do not reboil. Serve in earthenware dishes.

756 Rognons d'Agneau sautés au Madère

This is prepared in the same way as Rognons d'Agneau sautés (755), using Sauce Madère (129) instead of demi-glace.

757 Rognons d'Agneau sautés Turbigo

10 portions
1 hour

Stage	Ingredient	Quantity	Method
1	chipolatas, small	20	Grill the chipolatas. Wash, season and sauté the mushrooms in the butter. Keep warm on one side.
	butter	30g	
	button mushrooms	20	
2	lamb's kidneys	20	Remove the skins and cut the kidneys in half. Heat the butter in a sauté pan, season the kidneys and fry quickly, a few at a time, keeping them a little underdone. Place in a colander and drain.
	butter	100g	
3	white wine, dry	1dl	Tip out the fat from the sauté pan, add the wine and reduce slightly. Add the demi-glace and simmer to a light coating consistency. Season.
	Demi-glace (112)	5dl	
4	oblong Croûtons 8cm × 4cm (26)	10	Arrange the croûtons in earthenware dishes, and place four halves of kidney on each. Garnish neatly with the chipolatas and mushrooms and make hot. Pass the sauce through a fine strainer over all the ingredients.
5	parsley, chopped		Serve sprinkled with chopped parsley.

Rosettes d'Agneau

Rosettes d'Agneau (696) can be cooked and garnished in any of the ways applicable to Noisettes d'Agneau. Place on round croûtons.

758 Shepherd's Pie

10 portions
1 hour

Stage	Ingredient	Quantity	Method
1	butter	75g	Heat the butter in a small pan, add the onions and cook gently without colour. Add the lamb or mutton and the demi-glace. Bring to the boil, season and simmer gently for approx. 10 mins.
	onion, finely chopped	250g	
	cooked lamb or mutton, finely chopped	1¼kg	
	Demi-glace (112)	4dl	
2	Pommes Duchesse (1560)	1½kg	Half fill pie dishes with the meat mixture. Place the Pommes Duchesse in a piping bag with a star tube and pipe neatly over the meat to completely cover.
3	butter, melted	50g	Brush the potatoes with melted butter and place the pies in a hot oven to brown.

---

759 SELLE D'AGNEAU – SADDLE OF LAMB

The saddle of lamb is an excellent joint for roasting or poêling and is effective either as a hot or cold presentation.

As a square cut saddle (683) it is a practical size and shape for carving and re-forming and is thus useful for banqueting work. As a full saddle it is ideally suited for presentation as a whole joint in the restaurant or for small private parties. It lends itself to a wide range of garnishes but is perhaps at its best when surrounded by bouquets of well-selected and contrasting vegetables. The saddle of lamb may also be carved and re-formed with various prepared stuffings, then coated with differing sauces and garnishes.

Where the joint is presented whole it is well to consider the question of being able to carve and serve each portion hot. This requires highly skilled and rapid service techniques, and it may be more useful to present the joint first then to carve and portion it in the kitchen where the temperature of the food can be more easily controlled, or to carve the saddle first and re-form it for presentation.

It is excellent as a cold presentation and also lends itself to being carved and re-formed with various garnishes together with decoration and glazing.

---

760 Selle d'Agneau poêlée Cadmos

10 portions
3 hours

Stage	Ingredient		Quantity	Method
1	saddle of lamb (683)		1 × 4kg	Butter a braising pan, add the mirepoix, season the saddle and place on top. Melt the remaining butter and pour over the saddle.
	butter		200g	
	onion	⎫	250g	
	carrot		250g	
	celery	⎬ mirepoix	250g	
	bacon		100g	
	bayleaf		1	
	thyme	⎭	sprig	

2			Place the pan on top of the stove until the vegetables start colouring. Cover with the lid and place in a hot oven at 210°C. Baste frequently. Remove the lid after approx. 1½ hours and continue to cook and colour the saddle, approx. 1 hour extra. Reduce the temperature of the oven as necessary. Remove the saddle and keep warm.
3	Madeira	1dl	Place the braising pan on the stove and allow the juices and vegetables to heat gently and colour without burning. Drain off the fat without disturbing the vegetables and sediment. Add the Madeira and reduce slightly. Add the stock and tomato purée, bring to the boil, skim and simmer very gently for 10 mins. Thicken with the diluted arrowroot, adjust the seasoning and pass through a fine strainer into a pan. Cover and keep hot.
	Fonds Brun (97)	7dl	
	tomato purée	½ tbsp	
	arrowroot	10g	
4	Sauce Soubise (150)	4dl	Mix together, season well and reheat.
	Duxelles (29)	250g	
	truffles, chopped	50g	
	lean ham, finely chopped	50g	
	parsley, chopped	1 tbsp	
5			Remove the strings from the saddle. Make an incision on the slant away from the tail and across both sides of the saddle, approx. 2–3cm from the tail end. Cut down either side of the backbone and remove each side whole.
6			Cut each side of the removed lamb into ten even slices on the slant. Coat the bared bones of the saddle with a little of the Soubise mixture. Take each slice of the lamb, coat well with the mixture and replace in the correct order and on the correct side of the saddle so as to re-form it.
7	Sauce Mornay (146) thin	5dl	Place the re-formed saddle on a tray. Coat the surface of the saddle carefully with the sauce, sprinkle with Parmesan and place in a hot oven to reheat and gratinate.
	Parmesan, grated		
8	Fenouils braisés (1460)	10 portions	Dress the saddle on a large oval dish and garnish with the braised fennel and bouquets of braised chestnuts. Cover the bottom of the dish with a little of the prepared sauce from Stage 3 and serve the remainder in a sauceboat.
	Marrons braisés (1486)	10 portions	

BOEUF – BEEF

The main joints obtainable from a side of beef, their average weights and preparation for cooking. The side is divided into two – hindquarter and forequarter.

Joint	Average Weight	Preparation for Cooking
		Hindquarter
761 Shin (Jambe)	7kg	Stewing: bone out completely. Trim off the skin and sinew and cut the meat into 2½cm cubes. Clarification for consommé: pass the trimmed meat through a mincer. The shin-bone can be cracked open and the bone marrow extracted; this is soaked in cold water to extract the blood and the marrow is used in garnishes. Chop the bone into small pieces and use for making stock.
762 Topside also called Pocket (Tranche Tendre)	8kg	Roasting: trim the fat, cut into joints of the required size and tie. Braising: trim the fat, cut into joints of the required size and tie. The quality of this joint for braising may be improved by larding. They are marinated for certain recipes. The topside may be cut into steaks for braising. Stewing: trim off the fat, remove any sinew and cut the meat into 2½cm cubes.
763 Silverside (Gîte à la Noix)	10kg	Boiling: trim and pickle in brine. Stewing: trim and cut the meat into 2½cm cubes.
764 Thick Flank (Tranche Grasse)	10kg	Braising: trim off the fat, cut into joints of the required size and tie. The quality of these joints for braising may be improved by larding. They are marinated for certain recipes. The thick flank may be cut into steaks for braising. Stewing: trim the fat, remove any sinew and cut the meat into 2½cm cubes.
765 Rump (Culotte)	9kg	Remove and reserve the piece of fillet, bone out the rump and trim off excess fat. This joint is almost always used for cutting steaks for grilling.
766 Sirloin (Aloyau)	10kg	Roasting: remove the fillet for separate use; saw through the chine bone of the sirloin. Lay back the fat next to the chine bone and remove the exposed thick sinew, fold back the fat and tie up the joint.

cont. p.310

No.	Cut	Weight	Method
767	Baron	18–20kg	A baron of beef consists of a pair of sirloins in one piece. Because of its large size this joint is usually spit roasted for special occasions.
768	Boned Sirloin (Contrefilet)	7½kg	Roasting and poêling: remove the fillet for separate use. Bone out the sirloin completely and trim off excess fat and sinew. It may be rolled and tied if required.
769	Fillet of Beef (Filet de Boeuf)	3kg	Roasting and poêling: remove the fat, skin the fillet and cut off the chain at the side. Lard or bard with salt pork fat and tie.
770	Wing Rib (Côte d'Aloyau)	4kg	Roasting: saw through the chine bone, lay back the fat next to the chine bone and remove the exposed thick sinew. Fold back the fat and tie up the joint.
771	Thin Flank (Bavette d'Aloyau)	8kg	Boiling: trim and remove surplus fat; it can be rolled and tied. Stewing: remove all fat and cut the meat into 2½cm cubes.

Forequarter

No.	Cut	Weight	Method
772	Fore-rib (Côte Première)	6kg	Roasting: saw through the chine bone, lay back the fat next to the chine bone and remove the exposed thick sinew. Fold back the fat and tie up the joint.
773	Middle Rib (Côte découverte)	8kg	Roasting: bone out, trim, remove sinew and cut into joints. Roll and tie. Braising: bone out, cut into joints of the required size and tie. The quality of these joints may be improved by larding and marinating for certain recipes. The middle rib may be cut into steaks for braising.
774	Chuck Rib (Côte du Collier)	13kg	Braising: bone out, cut into joints of the required size and tie. The quality of these joints may be improved by larding and marinating for certain recipes. The chuck rib may be cut into steaks for braising. Stewing: bone out, trim and cut into 2½cm cubes.
775	Clod and Sticking Piece (Collier)	10kg	Stewing: bone out completely, trim carefully, remove fat and cut the meat into 2½cm cubes.
776	Shank (Jambe de Devant)	5kg	Clarification for consommé: bone out completely, trim off the skin and sinew and pass the trimmed meat through the mincer.

| 777 | Leg of Mutton Cut (Macreuse) | 8kg | Braising: bone out completely, trim off the sinew and cut into joints of the required size and tie. The quality of these joints may be improved by larding and marinating for certain recipes. The leg of mutton cut may be cut into steaks for braising. |

| 778 | Brisket (Poitrine) | 12kg | Boiling: bone out and remove surplus fat; if required roll and tie. It may be pickled in brine before boiling. |
| | | | Stewing: bone out, remove fat and cut the meat into 2½cm cubes. |

| 779 | Plate (Plat de Côte) | 8kg | Boiling: trim and remove surplus fat. |
| | | | Stewing: bone out, trim, remove fat and cut the meat into 2½cm cubes. |

The small cuts of beef obtainable from certain of the main joints:

Name of cut	From which Joint	Average Portion Weight	Preparation for Cooking
780 Chateaubriand	fillet	250g	Cut a very thick piece from the thick end of the prepared fillet, allowing 250g per person, then lightly flatten with a cutlet bat. It is usual to cut a chateaubriand for 2–4 persons.
781 Fillet Steak (Filet)	fillet	200g	Cut a piece approx. 3cm thick from the upper middle part of the prepared fillet.
782 Tournedos	fillet	150g	Cut approx. 3cm thick from the lower middle part of the prepared fillet. Trim and tie round.
783 Filets Mignons de Boeuf	fillet	2 × 75g or 3 × 50g	Cut the tail end of the fillet on the slant allowing 2–3 per portion. Lightly flatten.
784 Sirloin Steak (Entrecôte)	sirloin	200g	Cut a piece approx. 1½cm thick from the prepared and boned sirloin (contrefilet) and trim the fat.
785 Double Sirloin Steak (Entrecôte Double)	sirloin	350g	Cut double-sized steaks from the sirloin. Trim the fat.

cont. p.312

			Preparation for Cooking
786 Minute Steak (Entrecôte Minute)	sirloin	200g	Cut a sirloin steak and flatten with a cutlet bat to approx. 3mm thickness. Trim neatly.
787 Porterhouse or T-Bone Steak	sirloin	650g	Cut from the whole sirloin on the bone including the fillet, approx. 4cm thick.
788 Rump Steak	rump	200g	Cut a slice approx. 2cm thick across the whole prepared rump and then divide into pieces of the required size and weight. A whole slice of rump may be grilled and then cut into portions when served in the restaurant.
789 Point Steak	rump	200g	Cut from the triangular part of the rump approx. 2cm thick.

The main offals of beef, their average portion weights and preparation for cooking.

Name	Average Portion Weight	Preparation for Cooking
790 Kidney	125g	Braising and for pies and puddings: remove any skin then cut in half along its length. Cut away any fat and tubes or gristle then cut into small thickish slices, approx. 2½cm square.
791 Liver	150g	Braising: remove the skin then cut away any veins, tubes or gristle. Cut into slices approx. ½cm thick.
792 Oxtail	400g	Braising: cut off any fat from the thick end then cut into segments through the natural joints. Keep the tail end for soup and its garnish, cut into small pieces.
793 Ox-tongue	125g	Boiling and braising: remove any bones and gristle from the root end. Wash well. Ox-tongue may be salted first in a pickling brine.
794 Tripe	150g	Boiling, stewing, braising or for sauté: tripe is normally purchased in dressed form, i.e. trimmed and well-blanched. Cut into 5cm squares or thick julienne as required.

795 Roast Beef

The following are the joints most suitable for roasting and are listed under the titles as they can appear on the menu.

First quality joints:
Aloyau de Boeuf rôti – Roast Sirloin of Beef (on the bone)
Contrefilet de Boeuf rôti – Roast Sirloin of Beef (boned)
Côte de Boeuf rôtie – Roast Ribs of Beef
Filet de Boeuf rôti – Roast Fillet of Beef

Second quality joints:
Côte de Boeuf rôtie – Roast Middle Ribs of Beef
Pièce de Boeuf rôtie – Roast Topside of Beef

Portion weights
To calculate the quantity of beef required to serve a given number of covers, the approx. allowance of beef prepared for roasting is:
   on the bone e.g. Côte de Boeuf rôtie 200–250g per person
   off the bone e.g. Filet de Boeuf rôti 150–180g per person

Method for roasting
1) Season the joint and for
   a) fore and wing ribs or sirloin on the bone: place directly in the roasting tray, standing on its own bones with the outer fat uppermost,
   b) joints of topside, boned middle ribs, boned sirloin (rolled): place fat side uppermost either on a trivet or a flat bed of beef bones in the bottom of the roasting tray,
   c) boned sirloin (unrolled) or fillet of beef (larded): heat a little dripping in the roasting tray on the stove and colour the joint quickly on all sides. Remove then cover the bottom of the tray with a bed of flat beef bones or sliced mirepoix and place the joint on top – for sirloin, with the fat side uppermost,
   d) fillet of beef (barded): place on a flat bed of beef bones or sliced mirepoix.
2) Cover the joint with a little melted dripping then place in a hot oven at 220–225°C for approx. 20 mins. to set and colour the meat, then reduce the temperature gradually and as necessary. This must be done in relation to the size and shape of the joint but never below the temperature where actual roasting ceases – this is determined by the absence of the spitting and crackling sound of roasting and the quick loss of the meat's juices into the tray. This is at approx. 175°C.
3) Baste the joint from time to time and if the joint is rolled and tied, turn occasionally to ensure evenness of cooking and colouring. Allow approx. 15 mins. per 500g plus an extra 15 mins. cooking time, e.g. a 5kg joint of ribs of beef will require approx. 3 hours. If the joint is barded remove this in sufficient time for the joint to colour.
4) Beef should be cooked slightly underdone. To test this, press the joint firmly to squeeze out a little of the juice. This should be tinged with blood. The reading on a meat thermometer inserted at the thickest part of the joint would show approx. 63–65°C.
5) Remove the joint to a tray and allow to rest in a warm place for 20–30 mins. before carving. This will prevent the meat from shrinking and curling when being carved and also from losing its juices.

Jus de Rôti – Roast Gravy
1) When the roast joint is cooked and removed, place the roasting tray on the stove and heat gently, allowing the juices and sediment (and any bones or mirepoix if used), to settle and colour without burning.
2) Drain off the fat without disturbing the sediment.
3) Add brown stock (97) as required and allow to simmer gently for a few mins.
4) Correct the seasoning with salt; it should not be necessary to add extra colouring.
5) Pass through a fine strainer and skim but do not remove every vestige of fat. Allow approx. 5dl of gravy per 10 covers.

Carving
Use a sharp carving knife and cut slices across the grain of the meat. It is usual to carve roast ribs, sirloin or topside of beef into thinnish slices; roast fillet of beef should be cut into slices approx. ½cm thick.

Service of roast beef
   Carved in the kitchen: Serve the slices of beef on a suitable dish with Yorkshire Pudding (796), a little roast gravy and a bouquet of watercress. Serve accompanied by a sauceboat of the gravy and one of Horseradish Sauce (189).
   Carved in the restaurant: Place the whole joint on a suitable dish or on the carving trolley with containers of gravy and portions of Yorkshire Pudding (796). Serve sauceboats of Horseradish Sauce (189) separately.

---

796 Yorkshire Pudding

10 portions
1¾ hours

In Great Britain, Yorkshire Pudding is more often than not served with any joint of roast beef. Traditionally the texture of Yorkshire Pudding was expected to be quite heavy; with advantage and much good sense it was cooked in the same tray under the roasting beef for the last 20 or 30 mins. of its cooking time. Today, however, the expectation is for a light, well risen and crisp pudding, and in the majority of establishments it is served as individually cooked portions.

Stage	Ingredient	Quantity	Method
1	flour	225g	Sift the flour and salt into a basin and
	salt	5g	make a bay. Add the eggs and half the
	eggs	2	milk; whisk until smooth. Gradually add
	milk	2½dl	the remainder of the milk and the water.
	water	1dl	The texture should resemble that of double cream. Allow it to rest for 1 hour.
2	beef dripping, preferably from the joint being roasted	100g	Place in a small roasting tray or 2 × 18cm sauté pans and heat in the oven. When the fat is very hot pour the mixture into the tray (equally divided if using two pans) and place in a hot oven at 210°C. Cook until risen, crisp and brown (15–20 mins.). For the last 5 mins. or so turn the pudding over in the pans. This will allow it to drain off fat

and improve the crispness. Cut into portions for service.

Alternatively, the cooking may be done in individual Yorkshire pudding moulds placed on a tray and using the same method as above. The cooking time may be slightly less.

797 Grills of Beef

The following small cuts of beef are suitable for grilling and their titles are given as they can appear on the menu. See (704) for method of preparation for cooking.

Chateaubriand grillé – Grilled Chateaubriand
Entrecôte grillée – Grilled Sirloin Steak
Entrecôte Double grillée – Grilled Double Sirloin Steak
Entrecôte Minute grillée – Grilled Minute Steak
Filet grillé – Grilled Fillet Steak
Tournedos grillé – Grilled Tournedos
Grilled Point Steak
Grilled Porterhouse Steak
Grilled T-Bone Steak
Grilled Rump Steak

Methods for grilling and garnishes
Cuts of beef are grilled in the same way as cuts of lamb (704) and can be garnished with any of the garnishes applicable to lamb.

Service
Serve the grilled items on suitable dishes or plates with its garnish or just with watercress if accompanied with a butter or sauce.

Suitable butters and sauces as an accompaniment
Beurre d'Ail, Beurre à la Bourguignonne, Beurre Maître d'Hôtel, Beurre Ravigote.
Sauce Béarnaise, Sauce Choron, Sauce Foyot, Sauce Diable, Sauce Champignons, Sauce Paloise.

Cooking times
Grilled steaks are normally cooked slightly underdone – the following times for this degree of cooking are for guidance and these are only approximate.

Chateaubriand 2–3 persons	25–35 mins.
Entrecôte	8–10 mins.
Entrecôte double	15–18 mins.
Entrecôte minute	1½ – 2 mins.
Filet	12–15 mins.
Point steak	10–12 mins.
Porterhouse steak	25–30 mins.
T-bone steak	25–30 mins.
Rump steak	10–12 mins.
Tournedos	10–12 mins.

It is usual, however, for the customer to be asked to what degree he wishes his steak to be cooked. It will be thus seen that the grilling times can be shorter or longer than the above. Experience in the practice of grilling is the best guide and this is usually the acquirement of an ability to recognise the degree of resilience of the meat in relation to the degree of cooking. This is done by pressing the meat and checking its resilience, which ranges from being very soft and spongy or rubbery for very underdone to being firm and with no resilience for well-cooked.

The most common terms used to describe the degree of grilling are:

au Bleu – very underdone or rare: this requires fast grilling to ensure coloured and cooked surfaces only and leaving the centre almost raw.

Black and blue: this requires very rapid grilling to give very well-charred surfaces and a raw centre.

Saignant – underdone: this requires fast grilling to ensure coloured surfaces graded to a nice bloody red at the centre.

à Point – medium-done: this requires grilling at a moderate temperature to ensure coloured surfaces grading to pink at the centre.

Bien Cuit – well-done: this requires longer grilling to ensure well-coloured surfaces and the absence of blood right through to the centre but it should not result in the complete absence of the meat's juices.

Très Bien Cuit – very well-done: this requires extra time to give well-charred surfaces to the meat and an almost dry centre.

---

798 Bitok de Boeuf

10 portions
45 mins.

Stage	Ingredient	Quantity	Method
1	topside of beef, finely minced	1kg	Place the beef in a basin. Add the butter and the breadcrumbs which have been soaked in the milk and squeezed out. Season with salt, pepper and a little grated nutmeg. Mix together thoroughly.
	butter	150g	
	breadcrumbs	150g	
	milk	3dl	
	nutmeg		
2	flour		Divide the mixture into ten even pieces, pass through flour and mould into the form of flat cakes with a palette knife.
3	butter	120g	Heat in a sauté pan and place in the bitoks just as the butter turns brown. Fry gently until golden brown on both sides (10–12 mins.).
4	Sauce Smitaine (212) or other suitable sauce	6dl	Place the bitoks in earthenware dishes and coat with a suitable sauce, e.g. Sauce Piquante, Sauce Smitaine, Sauce Lyonnaise.

---

799 Boeuf Bouilli à la Française – Boiled Beef, French-Style

10 portions
3 hour

Stage	Ingredient	Quantity	Method
1	thin flank or brisket of beef	1½kg	Place the meat into a large pan of boiling water, season with salt and add the bag

	peppercorns	10	of aromates. Bring back to the boil, skim and boil rapidly for 10 mins.
	bayleaf	1	
	thyme	sprig	
	cloves	2	

(peppercorns, bayleaf, thyme, cloves: tied in a muslin bag)

2			Reduce the heat and allow to simmer gently for approx. 2 hours.

3	carrots, turned	350g	Add all the vegetables except the turnips and allow to simmer for 30 mins. Add the turnips and continue cooking until the meat and vegetables are tender.
	turnips, turned	350g	
	small onions	500g	
	leeks, cleaned and tied in a bundle	5	
	celery, cleaned and tied in a bundle	3	
	cabbage, cut into quarters and loosely tied	1	

4	coarse salt		Remove the meat and carve in medium slices approx. 3mm across the grain. Dress the slices overlapping on a large dish and garnish with the vegetables. Moisten with a little of the cooking liquor. Serve accompanied with coarse salt, gherkins and French mustard.
	gherkins		
	French mustard		

SPECIAL POINTS

a) Sauce Ravigote (190) is a suitable accompaniment with Boeuf Bouilli.

b) To test when cooked, pierce the beef with a trussing needle at the thickest part; this should penetrate without marked resistance.

---

800 Boiled Silverside and Dumplings

10 portions
3 hours

Stage	Ingredient	Quantity	Method
1	silverside, salted (87)	1½kg	Soak in cold running water for 2–3 hours to remove excess brine. Place in a large pan of cold water, bring to the boil and skim.
2	Oignons Cloutés (65)	2	Add and allow to simmer gently for 2 hours.
	Bouquet Garni	1	
3	carrots, turned	1kg	Add to the beef and continue cooking gently.
4			Remove the meat and carrots when tender and place in a pan with a little of the cooking liquor. Cover and keep warm.
5	Suet Pastry (89)	500g	Mould into 20 round pieces and place in the remaining cooking liquor. Simmer very gently until cooked (approx. 15 mins.).

6

Carve the beef into medium-thick slices across the grain. Dress the slices overlapping on a suitable dish and garnish with carrots and dumplings. Moisten with a little of the cooking liquor.

SPECIAL POINTS

a) In large establishments, a whole joint of silverside would be used. In this case it would be necessary to soak the silverside overnight. Allow 25 mins. per 500g when cooking.
b) Whole small onions and turned turnips may be added and served with boiled silverside.
c) To test when cooked, pierce the beef with a trussing needle at the thickest part; this should penetrate without marked resistance.

801 Braised Steak

10 portions
2½ hours

Stage	Ingredient	Quantity	Method
1	dripping	100g	Heat the dripping in a frying-pan.
	topside or		Season the steaks and fry until brown on
	thick flank of		both sides. Remove the steaks and place
	beef, cut into		in a braising pan.
	1cm thick slices	10 × 150g	
2	onions, roughly		Fry in the same pan to a light brown,
	diced	200g	drain and add to the steaks.
	carrots, roughly		
	diced	200g	
3	flour	60g	Sprinkle onto the steaks and shake the pan to mix in. Place in a hot oven for approx. 10 mins. and remove.
4	tomato purée	1 tbsp	Add the tomato purée and carefully mix
	Fonds Brun (97)	2 litres	in sufficient stock to barely cover the
	Bouquet Garni	1	steaks. Add the bouquet garni, garlic and
	garlic, crushed	½ clove	season. Bring to the boil, skim, cover with a lid and place in a moderate oven at 180°C. Cook until tender (approx. 1–1½ hours).
5			Remove the steaks and place in a clean pan. Remove the fat from the sauce and adjust the consistency, colour and seasoning. The sauce should not be too thick and it should be a reddish-brown colour. Pass through a fine strainer over the meat and reboil.
6	parsley, chopped		Serve the steaks in earthenware dishes sprinkled with chopped parsley.

SPECIAL POINT

Braised steaks may be served with vegetable garnishes, such as Jardinière and Printanière, and should be designated accordingly on the menu, e.g. Braised Steak Printanière.

802 Carbonnade de Boeuf Flamande

10 portions
2½ hours

Stage	Ingredient	Quantity	Method
1	topside or thick flank of beef	1¼kg	Cut into 20 small steaks.
2	butter flour	100g	Heat the butter in a frying-pan, season the steaks, pass through the flour and fry until brown on both sides. Place in a braising pan.
3	butter onions, finely sliced	75g 1kg	Melt the butter in the same frying-pan, add the onions and sauté to a light brown colour. Add to the beef.
4	beer sugar, demerara Fonds Brun (97)	7dl 25g 1 litre	Add the beer, sugar and sufficient stock to just cover the beef and onions. Bring to the boil, skim, season, cover with the lid and place in the oven at 160°C. Cook until tender (approx. 2 hours).
5	parsley, chopped		Skim off any fat, adjust the seasoning if necessary and serve in earthenware dishes. Sprinkle with chopped parsley.

803 Chilli con Carne

10 portions
2¾ hours

Stage	Ingredient	Quantity	Method
1	red kidney beans, soaked overnight Fonds Brun	350g 2 litres	Cover the drained beans with the stock, bring to the boil, skim and simmer gently for 25 mins.
2	oil topside or thick flank of beef, coarsely minced onions, chopped garlic, finely chopped	¾dl 1kg 300g 1 clove	Heat the oil in a pan, add the beef and cook quickly to colour, stirring to keep it separated. Add the onion and garlic and continue cooking until soft.
3	red pimento, deseeded and chopped chilli powder ground cumin sugar, brown	200g 20g good pinch 15g	Add to the meat and onion and mix in well.

4	Tomates Concassées (90)	400g	Add to the meat, season well, cover and cook for approx. 15 mins.
	tomato purée	1 tbsp	
5			Drain the beans and add to the beef with sufficient of the cooking liquid to just cover. Adjust the seasoning as necessary.
6			Cover with a lid and cook slowly in the oven at 175°C until the ingredients. are tender, approx. 2 hours.
7	parsley, chopped		Serve in earthenware dishes sprinkled with chopped parsley.

SPECIAL POINT

If using canned red beans, use brown stock for moistening the beef and add the drained beans for the last 25 mins. of cooking.

804 Contrefilet de Boeuf – Sirloin of Beef

The sirloin of beef is perhaps best when roasted on the bone, either whole or in smaller joints. However, it is well-suited to being poêléed after being boned or boned, rolled and tied. Thus all the recipes for Fillet of Beef are suitable.

805 Corned Beef Hash

2 portions
30 mins.

Stage	Ingredient	Quantity	Method
1	corned beef, finely diced	200g	Place in a basin, season and mix well together.
	cooked potato, diced	120g	
2	butter	80g	Place in a frying-pan and heat. Add the mixture, smooth flat and fry until turning brown. Fold over to form an omelette shape on one side of the pan. Continue frying and turn over two or three times until crisp and brown all over.
3			Serve on a suitable dish.

806 Cromesquis de Boeuf

10 portions
1½ hours

Stage	Ingredient	Quantity	Method
1	Demi-glace (112)	5dl	Bring the demi-glace to the boil, add the beef and cook to a fairly stiff texture.
	cooked beef, finely chopped	850g	
2	egg yolks	3	Add to the mixture and stir in quickly. Reboil and correct the seasoning.

3			Place the mixture on a buttered tray and cover with a buttered greaseproof paper. Allow to cool thoroughly.
4	flour		Divide the mixture into 20 even-sized pieces and mould rectangle-shape approx. 1½cm thick, using flour.
5	Pâte à Frire (76)	½ litre	Place the cromesquis in the frying batter, remove them one at a time and place gently into hot fat at approx. 180°C. Fry until golden brown. Drain well.
6	parsley, picked Sauce Tomate (118) or other suitable sauce	7dl	Serve on dish papers on flat dishes. Garnish with fried or picked parsley and serve accompanied with a suitable sauce, e.g. Sauce Tomate, Sauce Piquante.

807 Cromesquis de Boeuf à la Polonaise

These are made in the same way as Cromesquis de Boeuf (806), wrapping each rectangle of the mixture in a pancake (71) before passing through the flour and frying batter.

808 Croquettes de Boeuf

Beef croquettes are made in the same way as Cromesquis de Boeuf (806) but mould cork-shape and paner à l'Anglaise (72) instead of passing through frying batter.

809 Currie de Boeuf – Curried Beef

Prepare in the same way as either recipe for Curried Lamb, (720 or 721), using topside or thick flank of beef cut into 2½cm cubes.

810 Daube de Boeuf à la Provençale

10 portions
8½ hours

Stage	Ingredient	Quantity	Method
1	topside or thick flank of beef salt pork fat parsley, finely chopped garlic, finely chopped	1½kg 100g 1 tbsp 1 clove	Cut the beef into 20 equal-sized large cubes then lard (50) each with a strip of the salt pork fat previously rolled in the mixed parsley and garlic.
2	white wine, dry brandy cloves, crushed juniper berries, crushed	5dl ½dl 2 4	Season the larded beef with salt and pepper, place in a basin. Add the wine, brandy and spices and marinate for approx. 3 hours.
3	salt belly of pork pork rind	250g 100g	Cut the belly and rind of pork into 1½cm cubes, blanch and refresh.

4	carrots, cut in thick rings	150g	Remove the beef from the marinade and place in a suitably-sized earthenware casserole with the belly and rind of pork and the rest of the ingredients.
	onions, chopped	250g	
	Tomates Concassées, (90)	450g	
	garlic, crushed	2 cloves	
	black olives, stoned and cut in half	30	
	Bouquet Garni, containing a strip of dried orange zest	1	
5	Fonds Brun de Veau (98)	¾ litre approx.	Strain the marinade and add to the casserole with sufficient stock to barely cover the ingredients. Season.
6	flour	100g	Cover the casserole with its lid and seal with a strip of fairly stiff but moist paste made from the flour and sufficient water. Place in a moderate oven at 165°C and cook very gently for approx. 4½ hours.
	water		
7	parsley, chopped	1 tbsp	Remove the lid, discard the bouquet garni and skim off any excess fat. Check the seasoning, sprinkle with chopped parsley and present and serve from the casserole.

SPECIAL POINTS
a) Traditionally the Daube is cooked in a deep, bellied, glazed earthenware pot which has a fairly narrow top opening. This keeps evaporation to a minimum.
b) It is good practice to cool the cooked Daube and place it in the refrigerator overnight, then remove any fat which has set on the top, and reheat it as required. The flavour and quality is much improved by this technique.
c) A cooked Daube can be poured into a mould, allowed to cool and set, then turned out and served cold cut into slices.

811 ENTRECÔTES – SIRLOIN STEAKS

Other than being grilled, these steaks are very well-suited to being shallow-fried and served with a wide variety of garnishes and sauces. Good-quality butter, as it is or clarified, is the best cooking medium for this, although oil is more suited to particular finishes and garnishes. The steaks should always be seasoned just prior to cooking and unless requested otherwise, shallow-fried slightly underdone. The sediment and cooking juices should be utilised in the finishing of its accompanying sauce and the finished dish should be served immediately.

812 Entrecôte Bordelaise

4 portions
30 mins.

Stage	Ingredient	Quantity	Method
1	butter sirloin steaks (784)	50g 4 × 200g	Heat the butter in a sauté pan. Season the steaks with salt and milled pepper and just as the butter begins to brown shallow fry them keeping slightly under-done. Arrange in an earthenware dish and keep warm.
2	red wine (Bordeaux) Sauce Bordelaise (120)	½dl 2dl	Discard the fat from the pan. Add the wine, reduce slightly and add the sauce.
3	bone marrow, ½cm-thick slices parsley, chopped	 8	Poach the marrow in a little stock and place two pieces on each entrecôte. Coat with the sauce and sprinkle with chopped parsley.

813 Entrecôte aux Champignons – Sirloin Steak with Mushrooms

4 portions
30 mins.

Stage	Ingredient	Quantity	Method
1	butter sirloin steaks (784)	50g 4 × 200g	Heat the butter in a sauté pan. Season the steaks with salt and milled pepper and just as the butter begins to brown, shallow fry them keeping slightly under-done. Arrange in an earthenware dish and keep warm.
2	mushrooms, small button sherry, dry Jus lié (113) butter, softened	 250g ½dl 1dl 50g	Discard half the fat from the pan then add the mushrooms. Season lightly and cook through. Add the sherry, reduce by half then add the jus lié and reduce to a very light coating consistency. Finally shake in the butter and adjust the seasoning as necessary.
3	parsley, chopped		Coat the steaks with the sauce and sprinkle with chopped parsley.

814 Entrecôte Chasseur

4 portions
25 mins.

Stage	Ingredient	Quantity	Method
1	butter sirloin steaks (784)	50g 4 × 200g	Heat the butter in a sauté pan. Season the steaks with salt and milled pepper and just as the butter begins to brown, shallow fry them keeping slightly under-done. Arrange in an earthenware dish and keep warm.

2	white wine, dry	½dl	Discard the fat from the pan, add the
	Sauce Chasseur		wine, reduce slightly then add the sauce.
	(123)	2dl	Reheat and adjust the seasoning.
3	parsley, chopped		Coat the steaks with the sauce and sprinkle with chopped parsley.

815 Entrecôte Marchand de Vins

4 portions
30 mins.

Stage	Ingredient	Quantity	Method
1	butter	50g	Heat the butter in a sauté pan. Season
	sirloin steaks		the steaks with salt and milled pepper
	(784)	4 × 200g	and just as the butter begins to brown, shallow fry them keeping slightly under-done. Arrange in an earthenware dish and keep warm.
2	shallots, finely		Add the shallots to the pan and cook
	chopped	50g	without colour. Add the wine and reduce
	red wine	1½dl	by two-thirds. Add the demi-glace and
	Demi-glace (112)	2dl	allow to simmer gently for 2–3 mins.
	bone marrow, diced	50g	Add the bone marrow and adjust the seasoning.
3	parsley, chopped		Coat the steaks with the sauce and sprinkle with chopped parsley.

816 Entrecôte Mirabeau

4 portions
25 mins.

Stage	Ingredient	Quantity	Method
1	sirloin steaks		Season the steaks, grill as required and
	(784)	4 × 200g	arrange on a suitable dish.
2	anchovy fillets	10	Cut the anchovy fillets into thin strips
	olives, stoned and		lengthways and use them to decorate the
	blanched	24	steaks trellis-fashion. Place bouquets of
	watercress	1 bunch	the olives at each side of the dish and a bouquet of watercress at each end.
3	Beurre d'Anchois		Serve accompanied with a sauceboat of
	(4)	150g	freshly made anchovy butter.

817 Entrecôte au Poivre

4 portions
1½ hours

Stage	Ingredient	Quantity	Method
1	peppercorns	10g	Crush the peppercorns. Season the
	sirloin steaks		steaks with salt and sprinkle with the
	(784)	4 × 200g	peppercorns, lightly pressing them in.
	oil	½dl	Sprinkle with the oil and allow to marinate for 1 hour.
2	butter	50g	Heat in a sauté pan and just as it begins to brown, shallow fry the steaks quickly,

			keeping slightly underdone. Arrange in earthenware dishes and keep warm.
3	brandy Fonds Brun (97) butter, softened	½dl 1dl 50g	Discard the fat from the pan, add the brandy and flamber (32), then add the stock, strain and reduce by half. Shake in the butter and adjust the seasoning.
4	parsley, chopped		Coat the steaks with the sauce and sprinkle with chopped parsley.

818 Entrecôte Tyrolienne

4 portions
30 mins.

Stage	*Ingredient*	*Quantity*	*Method*
1	sirloin steaks (784)	4 × 200g	Season the steaks, grill as required and arrange on a suitable dish.
2	French fried Onions (1490) Grilled Tomatoes (1520) watercress	200g 4 1 bunch	Garnish the dish with bouquets of the fried onions, grilled tomatoes and water-cress.

819 Entrecôte Vert-Pré

4 portions
30 mins.

Stage	*Ingredient*	*Quantity*	*Method*
1	sirloin steaks (784)	4 × 200g	Season the steaks, grill as required and arrange on a suitable dish.
2	Pommes Pailles (1586) watercress	150g 1 bunch	Garnish the dish with the straw potatoes and watercress.
3	Beurre Maître d'Hôtel (10)	150g	Serve accompanied with a sauceboat of freshly-made parsley butter.

820 Estouffade de Boeuf Bourguignonne

10 portions
2½–3 hours

Stage	*Ingredient*	*Quantity*	*Method*
1	butter Lardons (51), blanched button onions	75g 250g 30	Heat the butter in a shallow braising pan. Place in the lardons and quickly fry brown. Remove and reserve. Add the onions to the fat, colour brown and remove to one side with the lardons.
2	topside or thick flank of beef cut in 2½cm cubes onions, roughly diced garlic, crushed	 1¼kg 350g 2 cloves	Season, add to the fat, fry quickly to colour then add the onions and garlic and fry together with the meat.

3	flour	50g	Drain off any excess fat, sprinkle with the flour, shake in and place in a hot oven for approx. 10 mins. Remove from the oven.
4	tomato purée red wine, Burgundy Fonds Brun (97) Bouquet Garni	1 tbsp ¾litre 1 litre 1	Mix in the tomato purée then add the wine and sufficient stock to just cover. Bring to the boil, skim, season and add the bouquet garni. Cover with the lid and place in a moderate oven at 175°C for 1¼–1½ hours until almost cooked.
5	button mushrooms, small butter	 40 25g	Remove the meat to a clean pan, add the reserved lardons and onions and the mushrooms sautéed in the butter.
6			Skim off the fat from the sauce and adjust the seasoning and consistency. Pass through a fine strainer over the meat and garnish. Simmer gently for a further 20–25 mins. to complete the cooking.
7	Heart-shaped Croûtons (26) parsley, chopped	 10	Serve the Estouffade in suitable earthenware dishes and garnish with the croûtons, the points of which have been dipped in chopped parsley.

821 FILET DE BOEUF – FILLET OF BEEF

The fillet is perhaps the finest and the most tender of the joints obtainable from the carcase of beef. Although it has an excellent flavour this is inclined to be somewhat bland and as a joint it has almost no fat. But these minor deficiencies are easily rectified and with advantage, by larding the fillet and cooking it on a bed of a roughly diced Mirepoix of aromatic vegetables and herbs. Poêling is undoubtedly the best method of cooking; this adds flavour to the joint and the flavouring and juices from this process always provide an excellent basis for the accompanying sauce. Roasting is also suitable as a method but this should still be carried out by placing on a Mirepoix. In both cases it is a marked improvement if the larded fillet is seasoned and first quickly coloured on all sides in hot fat – this allows a decent glazed colour to develop even though the cooking time for a fillet of beef can be comparatively short.

The fillet of beef can be presented and garnished whole with just a few slices carved. This however, can lead to the problem of carving in the restaurant with its attendant difficulties of keeping everything hot. In this case it can be better if the joint is returned to the kitchen for final carving and then serving it with its garnish separately from another dish. Alternatively, it may be carved and served in portions directly from the kitchen.

822 Filet de Boeuf au Madère et Champignons

10 portions
2 hours

Stage	Ingredient	Quantity	Method
1	Fillet of Beef, larded (769) butter	1½kg 100g	Heat the butter in a deep pan, season the fillet and brown quickly on all sides. Remove to one side.
2	onions ⎫ roughly carrots ⎬ diced celery ⎭ bayleaf, crushed thyme fat bacon, diced	120g 120g 120g 1 sprig 80g	Add these ingredients to the pan, place the fillet on top. Spoon some of the fat over the fillet then cover with the lid and place in a hot oven at 220°C for approx. 40 mins. basting occasionally. Remove the lid for the last 10 mins. and keep underdone.
3	Madeira	1½dl	Remove the fillet, cover and keep warm. Place the pan on the stove and allow the vegetables and juices to heat gently and colour without burning. Drain off the fat without disturbing the vegetables and sediment. Add the Madeira and reduce by half.
4	Fonds Brun (97) tomato purée arrowroot	6dl ½ tbsp 15g approx.	Add the stock and tomato purée, bring to the boil, skim carefully and simmer very gently for 7–8 mins. Lightly thicken with the diluted arrowroot, adjust the seasoning as necessary, then pass through a fine strainer into a pan. Cover and keep warm.
5	button mushrooms butter Glace de Viande (103)	750g 50g 1 tbsp	Trim and wash the mushrooms. Heat the butter in a pan, add the mushrooms, season and sauté well. When cooked, add the meat glaze and mix in.
6	parsley, chopped		Carve three or four slices from the fillet and arrange the rest on a suitable dish with the carved slices overlapping at one end. Arrange the mushrooms in bouquets at the sides and sprinkle with a little parsley. Serve accompanied with the Madeira sauce.

823 Filet de Boeuf Bouquetière

Prepare as Filet de Boeuf au Madère et Champignons (822) but instead of the mushrooms, garnish with bouquets of glazed carrots (1400), glazed turnips (1488), peas, beans, florets of cauliflower and Pommes Château (1550). Finish the accompanying sauce without the Madeira.

824 Filet de Boeuf Dubarry

Prepare as Filet de Boeuf au Madère et Champignons (822) but instead of the mushrooms, garnish with small Pommes Château (1550) and bouquets of Chou-fleur Mornay (1426). Finish the accompanying sauce without the Madeira.

825 Filet de Boeuf Nivernaise

Prepare as Filet de Boeuf au Madère et Champignons (822) but instead of the mushrooms, garnish with bouquets of glazed carrots (1400) and brown glazed button onions (1493). Finish the accompanying sauce without the Madeira.

826 Filet de Boeuf Richelieu

Prepare as Filet de Boeuf au Madère et Champignons (822) but instead of the mushrooms, garnish with braised lettuce (1478), stuffed mushrooms (1411), small stuffed tomatoes (1518) and small Pommes Château (1550). Finish the accompanying sauce without the Madeira.

827 Filet de Boeuf Wellington

10 portions
2½ hours

Stage	Ingredient	Quantity	Method
1	butter	80g	Melt the butter in a small pan, add the
	onions, finely		onion and cook without colour. Add the
	chopped	100g	mushrooms, season and cook until
	mushrooms, finely		almost dry. Add the wine and reduce.
	chopped	500g	Add the demi-glace and reduce to a stiff
	white wine	1dl	consistency. Add the ham and parsley.
	Demi-glace (112)	2dl	Correct the seasoning and allow the mix-
	lean ham, chopped	100g	ture to cool.
	parsley, chopped	1 tbsp	
2	butter	75g	Heat the butter in a roasting tray.
	fillet of beef,		Season the piece of fillet and brown
	larded (769)	1½kg	quickly on all sides. Place in a hot oven at 220°C until half-cooked (approx. 20 mins.). Remove from the tray and allow to cool completely.
3	Pâte Feuilletée		Roll out to an oblong 3mm thick and
	(1736)	650g	large enough to envelop the fillet of beef. Leave sufficient paste for decoration.
4	eggwash		Spread a layer of the mixture down the centre of the paste the same length as the fillet. Place the fillet on top and spread the remainder of the mixture all over the fillet. Eggwash the edges of the paste, draw the paste over to completely enclose the fillet and seal the edges together neatly. Place on a baking sheet,

			decorate with the remaining pastry and brush with eggwash. Make a neat hole in the top. Leave to rest for 45 mins.
5			Place in a hot oven at 220°C for approx. 15 mins. to set and colour the pastry. Reduce the temperature to approx. 170°C and allow to cook gently for a further 25–30 mins.
6	braised lettuce (1478)	10	Dress the fillet on a suitable dish and garnish with the braised lettuce, Pommes Château and the peeled tomatoes which have been lightly cooked in a little butter. Serve accompanied with the sauce.
	small Pommes Château (1550)	300g	
	small tomatoes, peeled	10	
	Sauce Périgueux (131)	5dl	

SPECIAL POINT

When cooked the fillet should be nicely underdone and pink, and this requires experience and good judgement to relate the particular size and thickness of the fillet to the required period of baking. To provide a fairly accurate confirmation of the degree of cooking, set the probe of a meat thermometer in the centre of the joint to give a reading of 65–67°C.

---

828 Goulash de Boeuf Hongroise

10 portions
2½ hours

Stage	Ingredient	Quantity	Method
1	lard	100g	Heat the lard in a pan. Season the meat and fry until lightly coloured.
	topside or thick flank cut into 2½cm cubes	1¼kg	
2	onions, finely chopped	500g	Add the onions, mix in with the meat and cook together gently for a few minutes. Add the paprika and flour, mix in well and place in a hot oven for 10 mins. Remove from the oven.
	paprika	60g	
	flour	60g	
3	tomato purée	1 tbsp	Add the tomato purée and mix in. Add sufficient stock to just cover the meat and mix together. Bring to the boil, skim, season and add the bouquet garni. Cover with the lid and place in a moderate oven at 180°C for 1½–2 hours until tender. Remove the bouquet garni from the goulash and adjust the seasoning.
	Fonds Blanc (93)	2 litres	
	Bouquet Garni	1	
4	turned potatoes, plain boiled	20	Dress in earthenware dishes, garnish with the potatoes and sprinkle with chopped parsley.
	parsley, chopped		

SPECIAL POINTS
a) A little cream may be added to the finished Goulash.
b) An additional garnish of Gnocchi Parisienne (484), made to Stage 5 only, is frequently served with this dish.

829 Hamburg Steak

10 portions
45 mins.

Stage	Ingredient	Quantity	Method
1	butter	60g	Melt the butter in a sauteuse, add the onion and cook gently without colour.
	onion, finely chopped	100g	Place the meat in a basin, add the onion, eggs and season with salt and pepper
	topside of beef, finely minced	1¼kg	and a pinch of grated nutmeg. Mix well together.
	eggs	2	
2			Divide into ten even pieces, pass through flour and mould in the form of flat cakes, using a palette knife.
3	butter	150g	Heat in a sauté pan and place in the hamburgers just as the butter turns brown. Fry gently until brown on both sides and cooked (10–12 mins).
4	Oignons frits à la Française (1490)	250g	Place the hamburgers in earthenware dishes and garnish with the French fried onions. Serve with a suitable sauce, e.g.
	Sauce Piquante (132) or other suitable sauce	7dl	Sauce Piquante, Sauce Diable, Sauce Tomate, Sauce Lyonnaise.

830 Langue de Boeuf au Madère

10 portions
3½ hours

Stage	Ingredient	Quantity	Method
1	ox-tongue, salted	1	Soak in running cold water for 2–3 hours to remove excess brine. Place in a large pan of cold water, bring to the boil and skim.
2			Allow to simmer gently for 3–3½ hours until tender. Remove the skin and trim the root end.
3	Sauce Madère (129)	5dl	Cut the tongue into 3mm-thick slices and dress in earthenware dishes. Coat with the sauce.

SPECIAL POINT
Ox-tongue may be served with different garnishes, e.g. buttered noodles, spinach and vegetable garnishes such as Jardinière but should always be designated accordingly on the menu, for example, Langue de Boeuf aux Epinards.

831 Paupiette de Boeuf – Beef Olive

10 portions
2½ hours

Stage	Ingredient	Quantity	Method
1	topside, trimmed	1¼kg	Cut across the grain into ten equal slices, flatten with a cutlet bat and trim into rectangles, approx. 12cm × 10cm.
2	pork sausage-meat	300g	Season the slices of beef, divide the sausage-meat into ten equal pieces. Roll and place one piece in the centre of each slice of beef. Roll up and tie carefully with string.
3	butter	30g	Butter a braising pan and cover the bottom with the rest of the ingredients.
	carrot ⎫	150g	
	onion ⎬ sliced	150g	
	celery ⎭	75g	
	bacon trimmings	50g	
	bayleaf	1	
	thyme	sprig	
4	dripping	100g	Heat in a frying-pan, season the paupiettes and fry quickly to colour. Remove and place on top of the vegetables in the braising pan.
5	Espagnole (111)	¾ litre	Add the Espagnole and then sufficient stock to cover a good two-thirds of the way up the paupiettes. Bring to the boil, skim and season. Cover with a lid and place in a moderate oven at approx. 180°C and cook until tender (approx. 1½ hours).
	Fonds Brun (97)	¾ litre	
6			Remove the paupiettes, discard the string, arrange them in earthenware dishes, cover and keep warm. Remove the fat from the sauce. Pass the sauce through a fine strainer into a clean pan, reduce to the correct consistency and adjust the seasoning.
7	parsley, chopped		Pour the sauce over the paupiettes and sprinkle with chopped parsley.

SPECIAL POINT

Beef olives may be served with different garnishes, e.g. buttered noodles, Riz Pilaff, braised celery, and vegetable garnishes such as Jardinière but should always be designated accordingly on the menu, for example, Paupiette de Boeuf aux Nouilles.

832 Pièce de Boeuf braisée – Braised Beef

10 portions
3½ hours

Stage	Ingredient	Quantity	Method
1	dripping	100g	Heat the dripping in a frying-pan, season
	topside or thick		the beef and fry brown on all sides.
	flank, larded (50)	1½kg	Remove and place in a braising pan.
2	carrots ⎱ diced	250g	Fry in the same pan until light brown.
	onions ⎰	250g	Drain and add to the beef.
3	Espagnole (111)	7dl	Add the Espagnole and then sufficient
	Fonds Brun (97)	7dl	stock to cover two-thirds of the beef.
	Bouquet Garni	1	Bring to the boil, skim, season and add the bouquet garni. Cover with the lid and place in a moderate oven at 180°C until tender (approx. 2½ hours). To test when cooked, pierce the beef with a trussing needle at the thickest part; this should penetrate without pronounced resistance.
4			Remove the beef, cover and place on one side to keep warm. Skim off the fat from the sauce. Adjust the seasoning and consistency and pass the sauce through a fine strainer into a suitable pan. Keep warm.
5			Remove the string from the beef then carve across the grain into 3mm-thick slices. Dress neatly overlapping on oval dishes and coat with the sauce. Serve accompanied by the remainder of the sauce in a sauceboat.

SPECIAL POINTS

a) Braised Beef may be served with suitable garnishes, such as noodles, carrots, mixed vegetables, and should be designated accordingly on the menu, for example Pièce de Boeuf braisée aux Nouilles.

b) If the Braised Beef is to be presented whole in the restaurant it is usual to glaze the joint in the following manner. When cooked, remove the string then place the joint on a tray. Coat with a little of the finished sauce and place in a medium oven to set. Repeat the operation several times taking care not to overcolour it. With care, a thin, richly coloured glaze will be obtained.

833 Pièce de Boeuf braisée à la Mode

10 portions
8½–9 hours

Stage	Ingredient	Quantity	Method
1	salt pork fat	300g	Cut the fat into 5–6 long strips ¾cm
	brandy	1dl	square making them slightly longer than

	mixed spice	pinch	the piece of topside. Place in a basin,
	chopped parsley	1 tbsp	add the brandy, sprinkle with the spice
			and chopped parsley and season with salt
			and pepper. Allow to soak for approx.
			20 mins.
2	topside, trimmed	1½kg	Lard the beef (50) along the grain of the
			meat with the marinated strips of fat.
			Tie the joint and place in a basin.
3	red wine	½ litre	Add the brandy from the salt pork fat,
	carrots ⎱	250g	the red wine and remainder of the
	onions ⎰ sliced	250g	ingredients. Leave the beef to marinate
	celery	100g	for 5–6 hours turning it over
	parsley stalks	few	occasionally.
	bayleaf	1	
	thyme	sprig	
	peppercorns	6	
4	dripping	100g	Remove the beef and dry. Heat the
			dripping in a frying-pan. Season the beef
			and fry brown on all sides. Remove and
			place in a braising pan. Strain the
			marinade, fry the vegetables in the same
			pan, drain and add them to the beef.
5	calf's feet	2	Split in half lengthways and blanch in
			boiling water for 5 mins. Refresh, drain
			then add to the beef.
6	Fonds Brun (97)	1½ litres	Add the strained liquid from the
	tomato purée	1 tbsp	marinade and sufficient brown stock to
			come two-thirds of the way up the beef.
			Add the tomato purée. Bring to the boil,
			skim, season and cover with a lid. Place
			in a moderate oven at 180°C and cook
			until tender (approx. 2½ hours). To
			test when cooked pierce the beef with a
			trussing needle at the thickest part; this
			should penetrate without marked
			resistance.
7	arrowroot	20g	Remove the beef and calf's feet, cover
			and place on one side to keep warm.
			Skim off the fat from the cooking liquor
			and reduce to approx. 1 litre. Thicken
			with the diluted arrowroot and adjust the
			seasoning. Pass through a fine strainer.
			Remove the bones from the calf's feet,
			cut the flesh into 1 cm cubes and add to
			the sauce. Simmer gently for 2–3 mins.

8	carrots, glazed (1400)	40	Remove the string from the beef then carve across the grain into 3mm slices. Dress neatly overlapping on oval dishes and garnish with the carrots and onions arrayed in bouquets around the dishes. Coat with the sauce and sprinkle with chopped parsley. Send the remainder of the sauce in a sauceboat.
	button onions Glacé à Brun (1493)	40	
	parsley, chopped		

834 Pièce de Boeuf à la Bourguignonne

10 portions
8–8½ hours

Stage	Ingredient	Quantity	Method
1	topside or thick flank, larded (50)	1½kg	Place in marinade (55) for 5–6 hours.
2	dripping	100g	Remove the beef and dry. Heat the dripping in a frying-pan. Season the beef and fry brown on all sides. Remove and place in a braising pan. Strain the marinade, fry the vegetables in the same pan and add to the beef.
3	Espagnole (111) Fonds Brun (97)	7dl 7dl	Add the strained liquid from the marinade, the Espagnole and sufficient brown stock to cover two-thirds of the beef. Bring to the boil, season, skim and cover with a lid. Place in a moderate oven at 180°C and cook until tender (approx. 2½ hours). To test when cooked pierce the beef with a trussing needle at the thickest part; this should penetrate without marked resistance.
4			Remove the beef, cover and place on one side to keep warm. Skim off the fat from the sauce. Adjust the seasoning and consistency and pass through a fine strainer into a suitable pan. Keep warm.
5	lardons (51) button onions, glacé à Brun (1493) button mushrooms butter	250g 30 30 30g	Blanch the lardons and fry brown in a little fat and drain. Sauté the mushrooms in the butter, season and drain. Add the lardons, mushrooms and onions to the sauce and simmer gently for 5 mins.
6	parsley, chopped		Remove the string from the beef then carve across the grain into 3mm-thick slices. Dress neatly overlapping on oval dishes and coat with the sauce and garnish. Sprinkle with chopped parsley and serve accompanied by the remainder of the sauce and garnish in a sauceboat.

835 Queue de Boeuf braisée – Braised Oxtail

10 portions
4½ hours

Stage	Ingredient	Quantity	Method
1	dripping oxtail	100g 2¼kg	Cut the oxtail into sections through the natural joints. Season. Heat the dripping in a frying-pan and fry the oxtail until brown on all sides. Remove and place in a braising pan.
2	carrots ⎞ roughly onions ⎠ diced	250g 250g	Fry in the same pan to a light brown, drain and add to the oxtail.
3	flour	80g	Sprinkle over the meat and vegetables and shake the pan to mix in. Place in a hot oven for 10 mins. Remove from the oven.
4	tomato purée Fonds Brun (97) Bouquet Garni garlic, crushed	1 tbsp 3 litres 1 1 clove	Mix in the tomato purée and sufficient stock to barely cover the oxtail. Bring to the boil, skim, season and add the bouquet garni and garlic. Cover with the lid and place in a moderate oven at 180°C and cook until tender (3–3½ hours).
5			Remove the oxtail and place in a clean pan. Skim off the fat from the sauce, adjust the seasoning, colour and consistency, and pass through a fine strainer over the oxtail. Reboil and simmer gently for 2–3 mins.
6	parsley, chopped		Serve in deep earthenware dishes sprinkled with chopped parsley.

SPECIAL POINT

Braised oxtail may be served with the usual vegetable garnishes, for example Queue de Boeuf braisée Jardinière, Queue de Boeuf braisée aux Carottes.

---

836 Ragoût de Boeuf – Stewed Beef

10 portions
2½ hours

Stage	Ingredient	Quantity	Method
1	dripping topside or thick flank cut into 2½cm cubes	100g 1¼kg	Heat the dripping in a frying-pan. Season the beef and fry brown on all sides. Remove the beef and place in a braising pan.
2	onions ⎞ roughly carrots ⎠ diced	250g 250g	Fry in the same pan to a light brown, drain and add to the beef.
3	flour	75g	Sprinkle onto the beef and vegetables and shake the pan to mix in. Place in a hot oven for approx. 10 mins. and remove.

4	tomato purée	1 tbsp	Add the tomato purée and carefully mix
	Fonds Brun (97)	2 litres	in sufficient stock to barely cover the
	Bouquet Garni	1	beef. Add the bouquet garni, garlic and
	garlic, crushed	½ clove	season. Bring to the boil, skim, cover
			with a lid and place in a moderate oven
			at 180°C. Cook until tender (approx.
			1–1½ hours).
5			Remove the beef and place in a clean
			pan. Remove the fat from the sauce and
			correct the consistency and seasoning.
			The sauce should not be too thick and
			of a reddish-brown colour. Pass through
			a fine strainer over the meat and reboil.
6	parsley, chopped		Serve the beef in earthenware dishes
			sprinkled with chopped parsley.

SPECIAL POINT

Ragoût de Boeuf may be served with vegetable garnishes, such as Jardinière, Printanière and should be designated accordingly on the menu, for example Ragoût de Boeuf Printanière.

837 Sauté de Boeuf Hongroise

4 portions
25 mins.

Stage	Ingredient	Quantity	Method
1	fillet of beef, tail end	500g	Cut along the grain into strips approx. 5cm long × 1cm square or into small thinnish slices approx. 3mm thick across the grain.
2	butter	50g	Heat the butter in a heavy frying-pan, season the beef and add to the butter just as it begins to turn brown. Fry quickly to colour, tossing over and over and keep slightly underdone. Remove the beef and keep on one side.
3	onion, finely chopped	50g	Add the onions to the remaining fat in the pan and cook until soft then mix in
	paprika	1 tsp	the paprika. Cook gently for a few
	white wine, dry	1dl	seconds then add the wine and reduce
	cream, double	2½dl	by two-thirds. Finally, add the cream and reduce to a light coating consistency.
4	butter	25g	Pass the sauce through a fine strainer into a clean pan, then shake in the butter. Adjust the seasoning as necessary then add the beef and any juices. Mix in carefully, reheat but do not boil.
5	parsley, chopped		Serve in an earthenware dish and sprinkle with chopped parsley.

838 Sauté de Boeuf Stroganoff

4 portions
25 mins.

Stage	Ingredient	Quantity	Method
1	fillet of beef, tail end	500g	Cut into strips approx. 5cm long × 1cm square.
2	butter	50g	Heat in a heavy frying-pan, season the beef and add to the butter just as it begins to turn brown. Fry quickly to colour, tossing over and over and keep slightly underdone. Remove the beef and keep on one side.
3	shallots, finely chopped cream, sour lemon juice	50g 3dl squeeze	Add the shallots to the remaining fat and cook without colour then drain off the fat. Add the cream and reduce to a light coating consistency. Adjust the seasoning as necessary plus a touch of cayenne and finish with a good squeeze of lemon juice.
4	parsley, chopped		Add the beef and any juices to the sauce. Mix in carefully, reheat but do not boil. Serve in an earthenware dish, sprinkled with chopped parsley.

839 Steak Pie (raw filling)

10 portions
3½ hours

Stage	Ingredient	Quantity	Method
1	topside or thick flank cut in 2cm cubes onions, chopped parsley Worcestershire sauce Fonds Brun (97)	1¼kg 150g 1 tbsp few drops ½ litre	Place the beef in a basin, add the onions, parsley, a few drops of Worcestershire sauce and sufficient cold stock to cover. Season and mix together. Place the mixture into two pie dishes.
2	Pâte Feuilletée (1736) eggwash	650g	Roll out the pastry approx. 3mm thick, eggwash the rims of the pie dishes and cover with 1½cm-wide strips of pastry. Eggwash the strips. Cover the pies with the remainder of the pastry, seal firmly and trim off the surplus paste with a knife. Decorate the edge of the pastry around the pie. Eggwash and decorate with designs of pastry. Allow to rest in a cool place for at least 1 hour.
3			Place the pies in a hot oven to lightly brown and set the pastry (approx. 15 mins). Reduce the temperature to approx. 160°C and cook until the meat is tender (approx. 2 hours).

4   Clean the pie dishes, place each on a
                                  dish paper on a suitable dish and
                                  surround with pie collars.

SPECIAL POINTS
a) If the pastry should begin to overcolour, cover the pie with a double sheet of
    greaseproof paper.
b) To test whether cooked, release the pastry from the dish, remove a small piece of the
    meat with a fork and eat it. The meat should not be so soft as to disintegrate but
    tender with a slight degree of firmness.

840 Steak Pie (cooked filling)

10 portions
3½ hours

Stage	Ingredient	Quantity	Method

1	dripping
	onions, chopped
	topside or thick
	  flank cut into 2cm
	  cubes
		75g
		150g
		
		1¼kg
			Heat the dripping in a pan, add the onions and cook without colour. Season the meat and add to the onions. Cook until the meat is lightly coloured.

2	flour	50g	Sprinkle over the meat. Mix in and place in a hot oven for 10 mins. Remove.
3	tomato purée Fonds Brun (97) Worcestershire sauce	1 tbsp 1½ litres few drops	Mix in the tomato purée and sufficient stock to well cover the meat, season and add a few drops of Worcestershire sauce. Bring to the boil, skim and simmer gently until nearly cooked (approx. 1½ hours). Adjust the seasoning.
4	parsley, chopped	1 tbsp	Add and allow the mixture to cool. Place in pie dishes.
5	Pâte Feuilletée (1736) eggwash	650g	Proceed as for Steak Pie (raw filling) and bake for only 30 mins. once the temperature has been reduced.

841 Steak and Kidney Pie

Prepare as Steak Pie (839 or 840), using 850g of beef cut in 2cm cubes and 400g of ox
kidney cut in approx. 1½cm thickish collops.

842 Steak, Kidney and Mushroom Pie

Prepare as Steak Pie (839 or 840), using 850g of beef cut in 2cm cubes, 400g of ox
kidney cut in approx. 1½cm-square collops and 250g of sliced mushrooms.

843 Steak and Kidney Pudding

10 portions
5 hours

Stage	Ingredient	Quantity	Method

1	topside or thick
	  flank cut into 2cm
	  cubes
		800g	Place the beef and kidney in a basin, add the onions, parsley, a few drops of Worcestershire sauce and sufficient cold

	ox kidney		
	cut in neat pieces	400g	stock to cover. Season and mix together.
	onions, chopped	150g	
	parsley, chopped	1 tbsp	
	Worcestershire		
	sauce	few drops	
	Fonds Brun (97)	1 litre	
2	butter	50g	Line two 15cm buttered pudding basins with three-quarters of the paste. Fill with the mixture to within 2cm of the tops. Moisten the edges of the paste, roll out the remainder of the paste and cover the puddings. Seal the edges firmly, cover with buttered greaseproof paper and pudding cloths. Tie securely.
	Suet Paste (89)	750g	
3			Place in a steamer and cook for 3½–4 hours. Remove the cloths and papers, clean the dishes and fasten folded serviettes around the basins.

844 Steak, Kidney and Mushroom Pudding

Prepare as Steak and Kidney Pudding (843), adding 250g of quartered mushrooms at Stage 1.

845 Steak, Kidney and Oyster Pudding

Prepare as Steak and Kidney Pudding (843), adding 30 oysters at Stage 1.

846 Steak Tartare

1 portion
10 mins.

Stage	Ingredient	Quantity	Method
1	fillet of beef, finely chopped	200g	Season and mix well together then mould into a flat cake, approx. 2cm thick. Place in a round dish.
2	egg yolk	1	Make a depression in the centre of the steak and place the egg yolk in it. Garnish around the steak with neat bouquets of the onions, parsley and capers.
	onion, finely chopped	30g	
	parsley, chopped	30g	
	capers	30g	

SPECIAL POINT
This steak is finished in the restaurant by mixing the ingredients together with additional seasonings and flavourings.

847 Toad in the Hole

10 portions
1 hour

Stage	Ingredient	Quantity	Method
1	dripping	100g	Heat the dripping in a shallow roasting
	Yorkshire pudding		tray, arrange the sausages neatly in the
	batter (796)	8dl	tray and fry quickly to colour on all
	beef sausages	20	sides. Pour the Yorkshire pudding batter
			around the sausages taking care to keep
			them separate.
2			Place in a hot oven at 220°C for approx.
			30 mins. until the batter is crisp and
			golden brown and the sausages are
			cooked. Remove from the oven.
3	Jus lié (113)	6dl	Cut the Toad in the Hole into portions
			and arrange on suitable dishes. Serve
			accompanied with jus lié.

SPECIAL POINT
Pork sausages may be used in place of beef sausages. Toad in the Hole may also be prepared using lamb or mutton chops instead of sausages.

---

848 TOURNEDOS OR MÉDAILLONS

These small round steaks cut from the middle end of the fillet are perhaps best when shallow-fried in butter, lightly garnished and served with an accompanying sauce prepared from the deglazed pan juices and sediment.

To keep their shape while cooking it is advisable to tie the tournedos round with fine string. Season with salt and milled pepper just before shallow frying which should be carried out in a sauté pan just large enough to hold the number of steaks. Fresh butter is best for this and should be heated until beginning to turn brown before adding the steaks. They need to be well-coloured on both sides and, if necessary, to be turned on their edges to give an even outer coating, but on no account should the surfaces be overcrisped and dried out. Except for the customer's request to the contrary, tournedos should be kept slightly underdone.

In most cases the tournedos are dressed on round croûtons of bread, shallow-fried in clarified butter. These should be of the same size as the steaks and never larger.

There is a very large repertoire of preparations for tournedos and in general the garnishes and sauces are interchangeable with those for noisettes of lamb.

SPECIAL POINT
It is accepted that the garnishes, sauces and croûtons given as ingredients in the following recipes will be prepared in advance of cooking the steaks.

---

849 Tournedos Chasseur

4 portions
30 mins.

Stage	Ingredient	Quantity	Method
1	butter	50g	Heat the butter in a sauté pan, season
	Tournedos (782)	4 × 120g	the steaks with salt and milled pepper
			and just as the butter begins to brown

<table>
<tr><td></td><td></td><td></td><td>add the steaks and cook to a good colour keeping them slightly underdone. Remove the strings. Place in an earthenware dish. Keep warm.</td></tr>
<tr><td>2</td><td>white wine, dry
Sauce Chasseur
(123)</td><td>½dl

2dl</td><td>Discard the fat from the pan, add the wine, reduce by half then add the sauce. Reboil and adjust the seasoning as necessary.</td></tr>
<tr><td>3</td><td>parsley, chopped</td><td></td><td>Coat the steaks with the sauce and sprinkle with chopped parsley.</td></tr>
</table>

---

850 Tournedos Choisy

4 portions
30 mins.

Stage	Ingredient	Quantity	Method
1	butter Tournedos (782)	50g 4 × 120g	Heat the butter in a sauté pan, season the steaks with salt and milled pepper and just as the butter begins to brown add the steaks and cook to a good colour keeping them slightly underdone. Remove the strings.
2	Croûtons, round (26) Laitues braisées (1478) Pommes Château, small (1550)	4 4 portions 12	Arrange the croûtons on a suitable dish and place the tournedos on the croûtons. Arrange the lettuce and château potatoes neatly around.
3	Madeira Fonds Brun (97) Glace de Viande (103) butter	½dl 1dl ½ tbsp 50g	Discard the fat from pan, add the Madeira, reduce by two-thirds then add the stock. Pass through a fine strainer into a clean pan, add the meat glaze and reduce until slightly viscous. Shake in the butter and adjust the seasoning.
4			Make sure that the steaks and garnish are hot. Coat the steaks with the sauce and serve.

---

851 Tournedos Choron

4 portions
25 mins.

Stage	Ingredient	Quantity	Method
1	butter Tournedos (782)	50g 4 × 120g	Heat the butter in a sauté pan. Season the steaks with salt and milled pepper and just as the butter begins to brown add the steaks and cook to a good colour keeping them slightly underdone. Remove the strings.

2	Croûtons, round (26)	4	Heat the artichoke bottoms in the same pan, drain and fill with the peas. Arrange the croûtons on a suitable dish and place the tournedos on the croûtons. Arrange the filled artichoke bottoms and Pommes Noisette neatly around.
	Fonds d'Artichauts (1379)	4	
	Petits Pois au Beurre (1500)	75g	
	Pommes Noisette (1580)	100g	
3	Fonds Brun de Veau (98)	1dl	Discard the fat from the pan, add stock and reduce to a light glaze. Reserve.
4	Sauce Choron (155)	2dl	Make sure that steaks and garnish are hot. Brush the steaks and potatoes with the reserved glaze and serve accompanied with a sauceboat of Sauce Choron.

852 Tournedos Montpensier

4 portions
25 mins.

Stage	Ingredient	Quantity	Method
1	butter	50g	Heat the butter in a sauté pan. Season the steaks with salt and milled pepper and just as the butter begins to brown add the steaks and cook to a good colour keeping them slightly underdone. Remove the strings.
	Tournedos (782)	4 × 120g	
2	Croûtons, round (26)	4	Arrange the croûtons on a suitable dish with the tournedos on top. Arrange the asparagus tips and Pommes Cocotte in bouquets around.
	Pointes d'Asperges (1386)	20 pieces	
	Pommes Cocotte (1552)	100g	
3	white wine, dry	½dl	Discard the fat from the pan, add the wine and reduce by half then add the stock. Reduce until slightly viscous then shake in the butter. Adjust the seasoning.
	Fonds Brun de Veau (98)	2dl	
	butter	50g	
4	fresh tarragon	good pinch	Make sure that the steaks and garnish are hot, then pass the sauce through a fine strainer over them. Sprinkle with chopped tarragon.

853 Tournedos Rossini

4 portions
25 mins.

Stage	Ingredient	Quantity	Method
1	butter	50g	Heat the butter in a sauté pan. Season the steaks with salt and milled pepper and just as the butter begins to brown add the steaks and cook to a good colour
	Tournedos (782)	4 × 120g	

			keeping them slightly underdone. Remove the strings.
2	Croûtons, round (26) foie gras, round thick slices	4 4 × 20g	Arrange the croûtons on a suitable dish and place the tournedos on the croûtons. Lightly sauté the foie gras in the same pan then place a slice on each steak.
3	Madeira Demi-glace (112) butter	½dl 1½dl 50g	Discard the fat from the pan, add the Madeira, reduce by half then add the demi-glace. Reduce to a light coating consistency, shake in the butter and adjust the seasoning as necessary.
4	truffle slices	4	Make sure that the steaks and dish are hot. Place a slice of truffle on top of each tournedos then pass the sauce through a fine strainer over them and serve immediately.

854 Tripes Provençale

10 portions
5 hours

Stage	Ingredient	Quantity	Method
1	tripe	1½kg	Cut into strips 6cm × 1½cm.
2	oil	1½dl	Heat in a frying-pan and when very hot add half the tripe. Season and fry until light brown. Remove and place in a braising pan. Repeat for the rest.
3	onions, sliced	500g	Place in the remaining oil and cook until lightly coloured. Add to the tripe.
4	garlic, finely chopped Tomates Concassées (90) white wine sugar	2 cloves 500g 3dl 15g	Add to the tripe, season with salt and milled black pepper. Bring to the boil, cover with a tightly fitting lid and cook in the oven at 150°C for approx. 4 hours.
5	parsley, chopped		Serve in earthenware terrines sprinkled with chopped parsley.

855 Tripes à l'Anglaise – Tripe and Onions

10 portions
2 hours

Stage	Ingredient	Quantity	Method
1	tripe	1½kg	Wash well, cut into 5cm squares.
2	onions, finely sliced Bouquet Garni	600g 1	Place into a pan with the tripe and cover with cold water, season and add the bouquet garni. Bring to the boil, skim, cover and simmer gently until tender (approx. 1½ hours). Remove the bouquet garni.

3	Sauċe Crème (143)	1 litre	Drain the tripe and onions, add to the sauce, reheat and simmer gently for a few minutes.
4	parsley, chopped		Serve in earthenware dishes with chopped parsley.

PORC – PORK

The main joints obtainable from a carcase of pork, their average weights and preparations for cooking:

Joint	Average Weight	Preparation for Cooking
856 Leg (Cuissot)	5½kg	Roasting: remove the pelvic bone. Remove the trotter just above the first joint. Saw off the end of the leg bone and bare approx. 3cm of the remaining bone. Score the skin 3mm deep and approx. 1cm apart. Tie the thick end. Boiling: prepare as for roasting but do not score the skin.
857 Long Loin (Longe)	6kg	The long loin comprises the loin proper and the best end or cutlet end of loin, i.e. that part containing the rib bones.
Loin Proper (Longe)	3½kg	Roasting: a) cut the long loin into two pieces. Score the skin 3mm deep and approx. 1cm apart or
Best end or Cutlet end (Carré)	2½kg	b) cut the long loin into two pieces, remove the skin, bone completely, roll and tie. The fillet may be removed first and kept for other uses.
858 Spare-rib or Fore-end (Basse–Côte or Echine)	3½kg	Roasting: a) score the skin 3mm deep and approx. 1cm apart or b) remove the skin, bone completely and tie.
859 Shoulder or Hand (Epaule)	3½kg	Roasting: a) score the skin 3mm deep and approx. 1cm apart or b) remove the skin, bone completely and tie.
860 Belly (Poitrine)	3kg	Boiling: trim and pickle in brine (87).

cont. p. 346

The small cuts obtainable from the main joints of pork:

Name of cut	From which Joint	Average Portion Weight	Preparation for Cooking
861 Pork Chop (Côte de Porc)	loin	200g	Remove the skin and excess fat and cut the loin into 2–2½cm thick chops. Trim fat and bone neatly.
862 Pork Fillet (Filet de Porc)	loin	120g	Remove the fillet from the loin, trim off the fat and sinew and leave whole or split open lengthways, lightly flatten and cut approx. 120g in weight.
863 Pork Escalope (Escalope de Porc)	loin	120g	a) Remove the fillet from the loin, trim off the fat and sinew. Split the fillet open lengthways and cut to approx 120g in weight. One fillet will usually provide four escalopes. Flatten carefully with a moistened cutlet bat approx. 3mm thick and trim.
			b) Cut across the trimmed fillet on the slant, flatten and trim as above.
			c) Bone out the cutlet end of the loin, remove all fat and sinew then cut into approx. 1–1½cm slices on the slant according to size. Flatten carefully with a moistened cutlet bat approx. 3mm thick and trim.
864 Noisette or Médaillon of Pork	best end of loin	120g	Remove the skin and bone out completely. Cut across into approx. 1½–2cm thick slices. Remove all fat and any sinew. Slightly flatten and trim to an oval shape.

The main offals of pork, their average portion weights and preparation for cooking

Name	Average Portion Weight	Preparation for Cooking
865 Brains	100g	Poaching: remove any membrane and soak in cold salted water for 3–4 hours in the refrigerator to disgorge blood. Wash well under cold running water for a further 30 mins.
866 Head	150g	for Brawn: bone out as for calf's head (929) then remove and reserve the tongue and brains. Soak in lightly salted, cold water in the refrigerator for 10–12 hours to disgorge the blood then wash well in cold running water. Blanch carefully, singe to remove any hairs and clean the nostrils and ears carefully of any membrane.
867 Kidneys	2 × 75g	Grilling: cut in half lengthways, remove the skin and cut away the core and any fat from the inner sides. Skewer the four halves of kidney lengthways.
868 Liver	125g	Grilling or sauté: cut out any tubes or gristle showing and remove the skin where possible. Cut on the slant into slices approx. ½cm thick.
869 Tongues	125g	Boiling or braising: cut away any bone or gristle and wash well before cooking.
870 Trotters	125g	Boiling: singe off any hair then blanch in boiling water for 5–6 mins. and refresh under cold water. Scrape carefully with a knife to remove any remaining hair then split in half lengthways between the bones. Trotters are best cooked in a Blanc (15). Grilling: when cooked, wash, remove all bones then dry, season and paner à l'Anglaise (72).

BACON

The main joints obtainable from a side of bacon, their average weights and preparation for cooking.

Joint	Average Weight	Preparation for Cooking
871 Gammon	5½kg	Boiling and braising: a) saw through the knuckle bone 2–3cm from the end. Allow to soak for 12 hours in cold running water. b) boned out: remove the rind and the aitchbone then tunnel out the leg bones with a sharp boning knife. Tie securely with string. Grilling: remove the bones and tendons. Remove the rind. Cut as required.
872 Back	7½kg	Boiling: bone out. Roll out and tie firmly. Soak for 12 hours in cold running water. Grilling: bone out and remove the rind. Cut as required.
873 Collar	3kg	
874 Hock	3½kg	Boiling: bone out. Roll and tie firmly. Soak for 12 hours in cold running water.
875 Streaky	3½kg	Grilling: remove the bones and tendons. Remove the rind. Cut as required.

The small cuts of bacon obtainable from the gammon and middle.

Name of cut	From which Joint	Average Portion Weight	Preparation for Cooking
876 Gammon Steak	Gammon	180g	Remove the skin and bone out carefully. Cut into approx. ½cm-thick slices and make nicks into the fat to prevent it curling when cooking.
877 Bacon Rashers	Back Streaky Collar	2–3 rashers 80–100g	Slice the prepared bacon into rashers of the required thickness.

HAM

878 A ham is the leg of pork cut from behind the aitchbone of a side of pork, usually with a round end as distinct from a gammon which is usually cut square from behind the aitchbone of a side of bacon. Hams are salted, cured and sometimes smoked. There are many different types with many countries having their own special cures.

Preparation for cooking: soak for up to 12 hours in running cold water, clean and scrape the underside to remove any mould and saw through the knuckle bone 2–3cm from the end.

Pork Quality in Australia

Pork is sold by the carcase, side or as ready-to-cook cuts in the following grades:

Sow pork from heavy female over 105kg carcase weight.

Boar pork from heavy males over 105kg carcase weight.

Sucker from young pigs up to 25kg in weight.

Light pork from medium pigs between 25kg and 60kg weight.

Heavy pork from 60kg to 105kg carcase weight pigs.

Grain-fed pigs have a very thin 'covering' of back fat.

879 Roast Pork

The following joints are suitable for roasting and their titles are given as they can appear on the menu. See (44) for suitable stuffing.

First quality joints:
Cuissot de Porc rôti – Roast Leg of Pork
Longe de Porc rôtie – Roast Loin of Pork
Carré de Porc rôti – Roast Best End of Pork

Second quality joints:
Epaule de Porc rôtie – Roast Shoulder of Pork
Epaule de Porc rôtie farcie – Roast Stuffed Shoulder of Pork

Portion weights
To calculate the quantity of pork required to serve a given number of covers the approximate weight of pork prepared for roasting is:
  on the bone   e.g. Cuissot de Porc rôti   200–250g per person
  boned and rolled e.g. Longe de Porc rôtie   150–180g per person

Method for roasting
1) a) Season the joint and place fat side uppermost on a trivet or flat bed of pork bones in the bottom of the roasting tray. If using an unboned cutlet end of the joint stand it on its own bones.
   b) If the skin has been removed but is required for crackling it may be placed loose on top of the joint or tied on loosely.
2) Place the joint in a hot oven at 220°C for 20 mins. Then reduce the heat gradually to allow the joint to continue to roast without becoming overcoloured. If the skin is left on for crackling, a little oil rubbed into the skin is better than dripping for producing the required crispness.
3) Baste the joint from time to time and turn occasionally to ensure evenness of cooking and colouring. Pay attention to the basting of the skin where it is left on – the temperature should be kept high enough to blister it without burning and the basting can be more frequent. If tied on or loose, remove the crackling as soon as it is crisp enough and then the uncovered fat should be coloured. Allow approx. 25 mins. per 500g plus an extra 25 mins. cooking time.
4) Roast pork must be well-done. To test if cooked, press the joint firmly to squeeze out a little of the juices. If clear the joint is cooked; if there is any blood present in the juice the joint is not sufficiently cooked and should be returned to the oven for further cooking. The reading on a meat thermometer inserted at the thickest part of the joint would be approx. 82–85°C.
5) Remove the joint to a tray and allow to rest in a warm place for 20–30 mins. before carving. This will prevent the meat from shrinking and curling when being carved and also from losing its juices.

Jus de Rôti – Roast Gravy
1) When the roast joint is cooked and removed, place the roasting tray on the stove and heat gently, allowing the juices and sediment to settle and colour without burning.
2) Drain off the fat without disturbing the sediment.
3) Add brown stock (97) as required and allow to simmer gently for a few minutes.

4) Correct the seasoning with salt only. It should not be necessary to add any colour.
5) Pass through a fine strainer and skim. Allow approximately 5dl of gravy per 10 covers.

Carving

Leg: Remove the crackling and cut into pieces. Hold the leg bone and carve slices from the thickest side towards the bone starting at the knuckle end at an angle of 45°. Carve about 2–3mm thick. When the slices get too large, carve from alternate sides and when the top part is finished, turn the leg over and continue carving.

Loin (on the bone): Remove the crackling and cut into pieces. Bone out the loin and cut into slices approx. 3mm thick across the grain.

Loin (boned and rolled): Cut into slices across the joint approx. 3mm thick.

Shoulder (on the bone): Remove the crackling and cut into pieces. Carve into slices approx. 3mm thick across the joint and to the bone. Follow the contours of the bone as necessary.

Shoulder (boned and rolled): Carve into slices approx. 3mm thick across the joint.

Service of roast pork

Carved in the kitchen: Serve the slices on a suitable dish with sage and onion stuffing (44), a little roast gravy and watercress. Serve accompanied with a sauceboat of gravy and one of Apple Sauce (209). If the joint is cooked with the skin, a piece of the crackling should be served with the slices.

Carved in the restaurant: Place the whole joint on a suitable dish or on the carving trolley with containers of gravy and sage and onion stuffing. Serve sauceboats of apple sauce separately.

880 Grills of Pork

Generally speaking the most suitable items of pork for grilling are chops cut from the long loin, either the cutlet end or the loin proper, usually with kidney left in. English or French menu-titling very seldom distinguishes between these two parts of the loin and for most purposes the descriptive title when grilled is Côte de Porc grillée – Grilled Pork Chop. The term côtelette or cutlet is seldom used.

The fillet of pork may be split lengthways and slightly flattened for grilling and steaks may be cut from the leg for grilling, but this last tends to spoil a first-class joint more suited to roasting.

All items should be grilled in the same way as grills of lamb (704), ensuring that they are well-done. They may be garnished with any of the garnishes applicable to lamb and may be accompanied with a suitable sauce such as Sauce Diable (125), Sauce Robert (136), Sauce Charcutière (122). Apple Sauce is a useful accompaniment where the garnish is minimal.

881 Grills of Pork Offals

Pig's kidneys (867), and to a lesser extent liver, may be grilled. In either case they should be kept just cooked. The liver should be floured first. Garnish with Pommes Pailles (1586) and watercress and serve accompanied with parsley butter.

Pig's trotters which have been cooked first may be breadcrumbed and grilled. See Pied de Porc (900).

882 Choucroute Garnie

10 portions
3 hours

Stage	Ingredient	Quantity	Method
1	lard	150g	Well grease a braising pan with the lard.
	sauerkraut	1½kg	Place a layer of sauerkraut in the bottom
	streaky bacon	600g	of the pan. Place the piece of bacon on
	carrots, whole		top with the carrots, onions, bouquet
	peeled	250g	garni and the bag of junipers and
	onions, stuck		peppercorns. Cover with the remainder
	with 2 cloves	250g	of the sauerkraut and moisten with the
	Bouquet Garni ⎫ in a	1	wine. Cover with the bacon rinds and
	juniper berries ⎬ muslin	20	then a tightly fitting lid. Place in a
	peppercorns ⎭ bag	10	moderate oven at 180°C and braise
	white wine	½ litre	gently for 1 hour.
	bacon rinds	250g	
2	garlic sauasage	500g	Remove the streaky bacon and replace with the garlic sausage. Continue braising for another hour until the sauerkraut is tender.
3	Frankfurter sausages	20	Place into water and poach gently.
4	Pommes Nature (1538)	20	Remove the sauerkraut from the oven and discard the bacon rinds. Dress the sauerkraut in earthenware dishes and garnish with thick slices of the streaky bacon, slices of garlic sausage, slices of carrot and the Frankfurter sausages. Serve accompanied with plain boiled potatoes.

SPECIAL POINT
It is good practice to taste the sauerkraut before cooking and to wash it under cold water if it is too salty.

883 Côte de Porc Flamande

10 portions
1 hour

Stage	Ingredient	Quantity	Method
1	butter	75g	Heat the butter in a sauté pan, season
	pork chops (861)	10 × 200g	the chops and colour quickly on both sides in the butter and half-cook for approx. 10 mins. Place in earthenware dishes.
2	cooking apples	1kg	Peel, core and cut the apples into
	butter, melted	30g	quarters and arrange neatly around the chops; brush the apples with the butter and place the dishes in a hot oven for 10–15 mins to finish cooking the chops and colour the apple.

| 3 | Jus lié (113) | 6dl | Clean the dishes and place on dish-papers on suitable dishes. Serve accompanied with jus lié. |

884 Côte de Porc Milanaise

10 portions
1¼ hours

Stage	Ingredient	Quantity	Method
1	pork chops (861)	10 ×150g	Lightly flatten the chops and trim.
	flour		Season and paner à l'Anglaise (72).
	eggwash } for crumbing		Reshape and mark trellis-fashion.
	breadcrumbs		
2	oil	2dl	Heat in a sauté pan and shallow fry the chops until brown on both sides and well-cooked.
3	Spaghetti Milanaise (504)	10 portions	Dress the chops on dishes and garnish with the spaghetti Milanaise. Surround
	Jus lié (113)	3dl	with a cordon of jus lié. Place the butter
	butter	150g	in a suitable frying-pan and cook until nut-brown shaking the pan to ensure even colouring. Pour quickly over the chops.

885 Côte de Porc Napolitaine

Prepare as Côtes de Porc Milanaise (884) but garnish with Spaghetti Napolitaine (506) instead of Spaghetti Milanaise.

886 Côte de Porc Provençale

10 portions
1½ hours

Stage	Ingredient	Quantity	Method
1	pork chops (861)	10 × 150g	Make two small incisions in the side of
	young leaves of sage	20	each chop and just large enough to push a sage leaf flat in each. Place in a shallow dish.
2	powdered thyme	good pinch	Season the chops on both sides with salt
	powdered bayleaf	good pinch	and milled pepper and sprinkle with the
	garlic, very finely chopped	2 cloves	herbs, garlic and oil. Allow to marinate for 1 hour, turning occasionally.
	olive oil	1dl	
3	black olives, stoned and blanched	40	Drain the oil from the chops and heat in a sauté pan. Place in the chops and colour light brown on both sides. Cover with a lid and cook gently on a lower heat, approx. 10 mins. Remove the chops and dress neatly in earthenware dishes. Add the olives to the pan and heat gently then remove and place in bouquets at the side of the chops.

4	white wine, dry	2dl	Lightly caramelise the juices in the pan,
	Tomates Concassées		drain off the oil and add the wine.
	(90)	350g	Reduce by half then add the tomatoes,
	Glace de Viande		Glace de Viande, jus lié and anchovies.
	(103)	1 tbsp	Simmer for a few minutes and reduce
	Jus lié (113)	3dl	till slightly thickened. Pass through a fine
	anchovy fillets,		strainer or sieve. Adjust the seasoning
	finely chopped	4	and finish with a little lemon juice.
	lemon juice	squeeze	
5	fresh young sage		Make sure the chops are hot, then
	leaves, chopped	1 tbsp	carefully surround with a little of the
			sauce. Sprinkle with the chopped sage.
			Send the remaining sauce separately.

887 Escalopes of Pork

These can be cut from the fillet or loin of pork and may be prepared in any of the ways applicable to Escalopes of Veal (952–961).

888 Filet de Porc Hongroise

4 portions
50 mins.

Stage	Ingredient	Quantity	Method
1	butter	75g	Heat the butter in a sauté pan, season
	pork fillet, trimmed		the fillet and quickly brown on both
	of fat and sinew	1 × 600g	sides. Cover with a lid and complete the
		or	cooking on a lower heat or in the oven at
		2 × 300g	180°C for approx. 15–18 mins. until just
			nicely cooked. Baste occasionally. When
			cooked remove the fillet to an earthen-
			ware dish and keep warm.
2	onion, finely		Place the onion in the remaining fat and
	chopped	75g	cook without colour. Add the paprika
	paprika	10g	and cook gently for 2–3 mins. then add
	cream, sour	3dl	the cream and simmer to a light coating
	cayenne	touch	consistency. Adjust the seasoning plus a
	lemon juice	squeeze	touch of cayenne and a squeeze of
			lemon juice. Pass through a fine strainer
			into a clean pan and keep warm.
3	Nouilles au Beurre		Cut the fillet into thickish slices on the
	(511)	4 portions	slant and arrange overlapping in the
			dish. Make sure that it is hot and coat
			with the sauce. Garnish with the noodles
			placed to one side of the pork.

889 Filet de Porc Normande

4 portions
50 mins.

Stage	Ingredient	Quantity	Method
1	butter pork fillet, trimmed of fat and sinew	50g 1 × 600g or 2 × 300g	Heat the butter in a sauté pan, season the fillet and quickly brown on both sides. Cover with a lid and complete the cooking on a low heat or in the oven at 180°C for approx. 15–18 mins. until just nicely cooked. Baste occasionally. When cooked remove to an earthenware dish and keep warm.
2	shallots, chopped apples, sharp Calvados Fonds Blanc (93)	50g 200g ½dl 2dl	Add the shallots to the pan and cook without colour. Drain off most of the fat then add the apples, peeled, cored and cut in slices, and cook quickly for a few mins. Add the Calvados and flamber (32), then add the stock. Season and simmer until the apples are soft. Pass the whole through a fine sieve into a clean pan.
3	cream, double lemon juice	2dl squeeze	Add to the apple sauce and reduce to a nice coating consistency. Adjust the seasoning and finish with a squeeze of lemon juice.
4	apples, sharp butter, melted caster sugar	2 medium 25g 15g	Peel and core the apples then cut into quarters. Place on a buttered tray and sprinkle with butter and the sugar. Glaze brown under the salamander.
5			Cut the fillet into thickish slices on the slant and arrange overlapping in the dish. Make sure that it is hot and coat the pork with a little of the sauce. Surround with the glazed apples and send the rest of the sauce separately in a sauceboat.

890 Foie de Porc – Pig's Liver

Pig's liver is generally considered to be inferior to calf's or lamb's liver and is mostly used in the preparation of pâtés. However, its rather strong flavour is appreciated by some people and for these the recipes for calf's liver will be found suitable.

891 Boiled Gammon

1) Soak the gammon (871) for 12 hours in cold running water.
2) Place in a pan and cover with plenty of cold water, bring to the boil, skim and barely simmer until cooked, allowing 20 mins. per 500g, plus an extra 20 mins. For example a 5½kg gammon will take approx. 4 hours. To test if cooked, the small bone at the knuckle end should be easily removable.

3) Allow to cool slightly in the liquor, remove and skin. Carve in thin slices and serve on a dish with a little of the cooking liquor.
4) Serve accompanied with parsley sauce or Sauce Madère (129). Most purées of vegetables are suitable for serving with boiled gammon.

892 Grilled Gammon

10 portions
30 mins.

Stage	Ingredient	Quantity	Method
1	gammon steaks (876)	10 × 180g	Brush with oil and grill quickly on both sides (approx. 8–10 mins.).
2	watercress	2 bunches	Arrange the gammon on suitable dishes
	Pommes Pailles		and garnish with bouquets of watercress
	(1586)	250g	and Pommes Pailles. Serve accompanied
	Sauce Diable		with sauceboats of Sauce Diable.
	(125)	6dl	

893 Grilled Gammon with Pineapple or Peaches

Prepare Grilled Gammon (892) and garnish with slices of pineapple or halves of peach which have been brushed with butter, sprinkled with a little sugar and glazed to a nice brown under the salamander. Serve accompanied with sauceboats of Sauce Madère (129).

894 Jambon braisé aux Epinards – Braised Ham with Spinach

Prepare Jambon braisé au Madère (895) and garnish neatly with either Purée d'Epinards (1456) or Epinards en Branches (1454).

895 Jambon braisé au Madère – Braised Ham, Madeira Sauce

30–35 portions
5 hours

Stage	Ingredient	Quantity	Method
1	ham	1 × 5kg	Soak for 12 hours in cold water.
2			Clean and scrape the underside to remove any mould and saw through the knuckle bone 2–3cm from the end.
3			Place in a pan and cover with plenty of cold water. Bring to the boil, skim and barely simmer until nearly cooked (approx. 3½ hours).
4			Remove from the cooking liquor. Take off the pelvic bone and trim the underside. Remove the skin. Trim the fat smooth. Bare the knuckle bone.
5	Madeira	4dl	Place the ham in a braising pan, add the Madeira, cover with a tightly fitting lid

			and place in a moderate oven at 180°C to braise for 1 hour. Baste occasionally with the wine.
6	icing sugar	75g	Remove the ham from the pan and place on a tray. Dust well with the icing sugar and place in a very hot oven to caramelise the sugar on the surface. Place on one side to keep warm.
7	Demi-glace (112)	2 litres	Add to the wine in the braising pan. Bring to the boil and skim off all fat. Adjust the seasoning and pass through a fine strainer into a pan.
8			Carve the ham into thin slices and dress overlapping on oval china dishes. Coat with the sauce.

SPECIAL POINTS
a) The ham may also be braised with white wine and other fortified wines such as Marsala, Port or Sherry and should be designated accordingly on the menu, e.g. Jambon braisé au Porto.
b) Buttered broad beans, braised lettuce, braised chestnuts, braised Belgian endives and creamed morels are other suitable garnishes and should be designated on the menu, e.g. Jambon braisé aux Marrons. Sauce Madère is the most suitable sauce.

---

896 Jambon en Croûte

1. Cook the ham as for Boiled Ham (1291) but do not allow it to become completely cold.
2. Remove from the cooking liquor, take off the pelvic bone and trim the underneath.
3. Remove the skin and trim the fat smooth. Bare the knuckle bone.
4. Roll out sufficient short pastry (1738) or rough puff pastry (1737) to envelop the ham.
5. Place the ham on the paste upside down and fold the paste over to cover it completely. Seal the edges together.
6. Turn over onto a lightly greased baking tray.
7. Eggwash and decorate by scrolling with the point of a knife or decorate with pastry designs. Make a hole in the top to allow steam to escape.
8. Bake in a hot oven to set and colour the pastry then reduce the temperature to approx. 170°C and continue cooking slowly for ¾ hour.
9. Serve carved in thin slices with a small piece of the pastry and accompanied with a suitable sauce, e.g. Sauce Madère (129), Sauce Champignons (121), Sauce au Porto (134), or Sauce au Xérès (137).

---

897 Jambon Glacé à la Virginienne – Virginian Glazed Ham

1. Cook the ham as for Boiled Ham (1291) and allow to cool slightly for half an hour or so in the cooking liquid.
2. Remove from the liquid, skin completely and trim the fat smooth. Bare the knuckle bone.
3. Place on a deep tray, score the fat grill-fashion and stud with cloves. Sprinkle well with brown sugar.

4. Place in a hot oven at approx. 200°C and glaze to a deep brown colour.
5. Carve into thin slices and serve accompanied with a Sauce Diable (125) containing soaked and plumped sultanas and finished with a little cream and sweet sherry.

SPECIAL POINTS
a) The glazed ham may be served with glazed pineapple or peaches; see Recipe 893.
b) Other sauces such as Sauce Madère, Sauce au Porto or Sauce Xérès are also suitable.

---

898 Longe de Porc aux Pruneaux

10 portions
2 hours

Stage	Ingredient	Quantity	Method
1	prunes, soaked overnight cider, dry cinnamon	30 pieces 5dl small piece	Remove and discard the stones from the soaked prunes. Place the prunes in a pan with the cider and cinnamon. Simmer gently until just cooked and tender. Drain and reserve the cooking liquid. Keep the prunes warm.
2	loin of pork, (857)	2kg	Carefully remove the skin and bone out completely. Trim excess fat then roll and tie firmly.
3	ginger, ground cinnamon, ground milled pepper salt butter	pinch good pinch ½ tsp ½ tbsp 75g	Season the pork on all sides with the mixed seasoning. Heat the butter in a deep oval or oblong casserole, place in the pork and colour on all sides. Cover with a lid and place in a moderate oven at 180°C to cook gently, approx. 1¼–1½ hours. Baste frequently. Remove the pork when cooked and keep warm on one side.
4	crème fraîche lemon juice cayenne	5dl squeeze	Drain off the fat from the casserole, add the reserved liquid from the prunes and reduce by two-thirds. Add the cream, reduce to a light coating consistency, adjust the seasoning and finish with a squeeze of lemon and a touch of cayenne. Pass through a fine strainer.
5			Remove the string from the pork, cut into 20 thick slices and arrange overlapping on suitable dishes. Place the warm prunes to one side and coat the pork with a little of the sauce. Send the rest of the sauce separately in a sauceboat.

899 Mousselines de Jambon Florentine

10 portions
2 hours

Stage	Ingredient	Quantity	Method
1	raw ham, lean and no fat	750g	Either pound finely or pass twice through the fine plate of a mincer and place in a basin. Chill thoroughly.
2	egg whites, cold paprika	3 1 tsp	Season with a little salt and pepper. Add the whites little by little, beating thoroughly with a wooden spatule until stiff and elastic in texture, then beat in the paprika.
3			Pass the mixture through a fine sieve or food processor, replace in a basin and chill thoroughly in the refrigerator.
4	double cream, cold	5dl	Gradually add to the mixture beating thoroughly with a wooden spatule. Adjust the seasoning.
5			Butter a deep tray and, with a table-spoon, take a twentieth of the mixture. Mould egg-shape with a second table-spoon and remove from the first spoon. Place the mousseline in the tray. Continue until the mixture is finished, 20 pieces in all.
6	Fonds Blanc (93)	1 litre	Season lightly, bring to the boil and pour gently around the mousselines. Cover with a buttered paper and poach in a moderate oven at 180°C until slightly firm and resilient to the touch, approx. 15 mins.
7	Epinards en Branches (1454) Sauce Allemande (139) Parmesan, grated	300g 7dl 50g	Place a layer of spinach in earthenware dishes, drain the mousselines well and dress on the spinach. Coat with the sauce and sprinkle with the Parmesan. Gratinate under the salamander.

SPECIAL POINTS

a) Check the consistency of the mixture at Stage 4 when only three-quarters of the cream has been added. Poach a small piece in stock – if too firm, carefully add the remainder; if too soft, add a little more egg white. At all stages, vigorous and firm beating of the mixture is necessary.

b) If the mixture is too pale at Stage 4 it may be useful to add just a touch of tomato purée but this must be done with discretion otherwise the taste and texture can be affected.

900 Pied de Porc Gribiche or Vinaigrette

10 portions
1¼ hours

Stage	Ingredient	Quantity	Method
1	pig's trotters, cleaned and blanched (870)	10	Place the prepared trotters in the boiling blanc with the rest of the ingredients and simmer very gently, covered with a piece of muslin until cooked and tender. Approx. 1 hour.
	Blanc (15)	5 litres	
	carrot, small whole	75g	
	onion, studded	2	
	Bouquet Garni	1	
2			Remove the trotters from the liquid and carefully remove and discard all the bones. Place back in the blanc to reheat.
3	Sauce Gribiche (184) or Sauce Vinaigrette (190)	6dl	Arrange the half trotters in earthenware dishes, skin side upwards, and add just a little of the cooking liquor to keep them moist. Serve accompanied with sauce-boats of Sauce Gribiche or Vinaigrette.

SPECIAL POINT

When cooked and boned the trotters may be served coated with various sauces such as Sauce Poulette, Sauce Persil, Sauce Italienne.

901 Porcelet Pomeranienne – Roast Stuffed Sucking-Pig

20–25 portions
3½–4 hours

Stage	Ingredient	Quantity	Method
1	sucking-pig	1 × 6–7kg	Remove the heart, kidney and liver from the pig and cut into small dice. Heat the butter in a small pan, add the onion and cook without colour. Add the diced offals, season and fry together with the onions until just cooked. Allow to cool.
	butter	150g	
	onion, finely chopped	250g	
2	pork sausage-meat	2kg	Mix all the ingredients with the fried onions and diced offal and stuff the belly of the sucking-pig with the mixture. Sew up with string.
	breadcrumbs, white	500g	
	thyme, powdered	½ tbsp	
	parsley, chopped	2 tbsps	
	mixed spice	1 tsp	
	brandy	½dl	
	eggs	2	
3	oil	1½dl	Season the sucking-pig and place in a long roasting tray with the front legs lying forward and the back legs stretched out. Score the skin lightly on both sides, i.e. 7–8 cuts starting from near the back and diagonally downwards towards the tail end. Brush liberally with oil. Place a small potato in the mouth so as to keep it open. Cover the ears and tail with

			greaseproof paper or foil to prevent burning. Place in the oven at 190°C and roast gently for 2½–3 hours reducing the temperature as necessary and basting frequently. It is essential that the skin becomes crisp and golden brown. Remove the sucking-pig to one side and keep warm. Remove string and foil.
4	Fonds Brun (97)	1½ litres	Place the roasting tray to heat and lightly colour the juices and sediment. Tip off the fat and add the stock. Simmer gently for a few mins. then adjust the seasoning with salt only. Pass through a fine strainer, skim and keep hot.
5	apples, firm pippins butter, melted sugar, caster cinnamon, ground	2½kg 100g 75g pinch	Peel, core and cut the apples into quarters and place on a buttered tray. Sprinkle with the melted butter and the caster sugar mixed with the cinnamon. Place under the salamander until just soft and golden brown.
6	lemon Pommes Château (1550)	1 60	Arrange the sucking-pig on a large dish and replace the potato in the mouth with the lemon. Garnish with bouquets of Pommes Château and grilled apples. Serve accompanied with the roast gravy.

---

902 Pork Chow Mein

10 portions
45 mins.

Stage	Ingredient	Quantity	Method
1	Chinese egg noodles	850g	Plain boil the noodles in salted water for 3–4 mins. keeping them firm. Drain for a few minutes to dry off.
2	vegetable oil	½dl	Heat the oil in a wok or large deep frying-pan, add the noodles. Season and toss over to reheat. Place in suitable dishes and keep warm.
3	oil spring onion ⎫ green beans ⎪ shred- bamboo shoots ⎬ ded Chinese leaves ⎭	2dl 200g 300g 200g 300g	Heat the oil, add the vegetables and stir-fry at high heat in the order as listed, stirring and tossing constantly, time approx. 4 mins. Keep them crisp. Remove from the pan and reserve.
4	garlic, crushed and finely chopped root ginger, grated	1 clove 25g	Add to the same oil and cook gently with little colour then add the reserved vegetables and toss over to mix. Drain and replace the oil in the same pan.

5	pork fillet, trimmed of fat and sinew	1¼kg	Cut into thin strips approx. 5cm long × 3mm square. Season with salt and pepper and stir-fry in the same oil until cooked and lightly coloured. Add the vegetables and toss over to mix. Drain and reserve in a clean pan.
6	chicken stock (96) soy sauce sugar sherry cornflour	3dl ½ tbsp pinch ½dl 15g	Add the stock, soy sauce and sugar to the empty pan. Season with salt and pepper, add the sherry, bring to the boil and thicken with the diluted cornflour. Strain the sauce over the meat and vegetables, mix lightly together.
7			Make sure that everything is hot then neatly ladle the pork and vegetable mixture over the noodles.

903 Rognons de Porc Liègeoise

10 portions
30 mins.

Stage	Ingredient	Quantity	Method
1	pork kidneys	20	Cut in half and remove the skins and central cores. Cut each half into three or four pieces on the slant.
2	butter	75g	Heat the butter in a frying-pan, season the kidneys and fry quickly, a few at a time, keeping slightly underdone. Place in a colander and drain.
3	butter shallots juniper berries, crushed gin Fonds de Veau (95)	25g 75g 10 ½dl 4dl	Heat the butter in the same pan. Add the shallots and cook without colour then add the juniper berries. Heat for a few seconds then add the gin and flamber (32). Add the stock, bring to the boil and reduce by two-thirds.
4	crème fraîche parsley, chopped	4dl	Add the crème fraîche and reduce to a coating consistency. Adjust the seasoning with salt and pepper plus a touch of cayenne then pass through a fine strainer into a clean pan. Add the kidneys, reheat but do not reboil. Serve in earthenware dishes sprinkled with chopped parsley.

904 Sweet and Sour Pork

10 portions
1½ hours

Stage	Ingredient	Quantity	Method
1	fillet of pork trimmed of fat and sinew	1¼kg	Cut the fillet in half lengthways then slice across the grain into approx. ½cm thick slices. Season with salt and the five

	five spice powder	small pinch	spice powder, mix with the soy sauce and leave to marinate for approx. 1 hour.
	soy sauce	2 tbsps	
2	flour	200g	Mix the flour, egg yolk, water, salt and
	egg yolks	1	sugar to a smooth paste then lightly fold
	egg white	1	in the stiffly beaten egg white just before
	water	1½dl	the batter is needed.
	salt	good pinch	
	sugar	pinch	
3	oil	1dl	Heat the oil in a wok or deep frying-pan,
	onion, finely chopped	100g	add the onion and cook until lightly
	red pimento, skinned and cut in short		coloured. Add the pimento and stir-fry until soft. Add the rest of the
	strips	100g	ingredients, bring to the boil and reduce
	vinegar	1dl	by two-thirds.
	lemon juice	2 tbsps	
	orange juice	½dl	
	sugar	25g	
	garlic, finely chopped	1 clove	
4	tomato purée	2 tbsps	Add the tomato purée, sherry and stock,
	sherry	½dl	season, bring to the boil and thicken
	brown stock (97)	2dl	with the diluted cornflour. Allow to
	cornflour	15g	simmer gently for a few mins. then place in a clean pan and keep hot.
5			Dip the pieces of pork into the batter and deep fry in hot oil at 175°C until golden brown. Drain well and lightly mix into the prepared sauce.
6	long-grain rice, for poached rice (534)	300g	Serve the sweet and sour pork in deep dishes accompanied with dishes of poached rice.

VEAU – VEAL (ALSO CALLED BABY BEEF)

The main joints obtainable from a carcase of veal, their average weights and preparations for cooking:

Joint	Average Weight	Preparation for Cooking
905 Leg (Cuisseau)	12kg	Roasting, braising and poêling: a small leg of veal up to 5–8kg can be roasted, poêléed or braised whole. Remove the pelvic bone, saw off the end of the leg bone and bare 5–6cm of the remaining bone. Trim if necessary. Cover with slices of salt pork fat or lard (50) with strips of fat bacon.

The leg is divided into five joints: shin, cushion, under-cushion, thick flank and rump.

Joint	Average Weight	Preparation for Cooking
906 Shin or Knuckle (Jarret)	2¼kg	Stewing: a) bone out completely, trim off skin and sinew and cut into 2½cm cubes. Chop the bones and use for stock. b) cut into sections 3–4cm thick across the bone. Tie round to keep in shape. See Ossi Bucci (979).
907 Cushion (Noix)	2½kg	Roasting, braising and poêling: remove the skin and trim carefully. Lard with strips of fat bacon (50) and tie.
908 Under-Cushion (Sous-Noix)	2½kg	Roasting, braising and poêling: remove the skin and trim carefully. Lard with strips of fat bacon (50) and tie.
909 Thick Flank (Noix Pâtissière)	3kg	Roasting, braising and poêling: remove the skin and trim carefully. Lard with strips of fat bacon (50) and tie. Stewing: the trimmings from the preparation of this joint may be cut into 2½cm cubes and used for stewing.
910 Rump (Quasi or Cul de Veau)	2kg	Roasting, braising and poêling: remove the skin and trim carefully. Lard with strips of fat bacon (50) and tie. Stewing: the trimmings from the preparation of this joint may be cut into 2½cm cubes and used for stewing.

911	Saddle (Selle)	8kg	Roasting, braising and poêling: a small saddle of veal up to 5–6kg can be roasted, poêléed or braised whole. Remove the kidneys from inside and remove the hip bones. Cut off the flank straight, re-form the saddle, cover the back with thin slices of fat bacon (1) and tie.
912	Fillet (Filet)	1–1¼kg	This can be cut from the side of veal before removing the joints. Roasting and poêling: trim carefully of all sinew and lard finely with strips of fat bacon (50).
913	Loin (Longe)	4kg	Roasting, braising and poêling: remove the kidneys. Split the saddle through the centre bone to give two loins. Skin and bone completely. Cut the flank straight and leave the fillet in place. Roll and tie, or stuff, roll and tie.
914	Best End (Carré)	3kg	Roasting and poêling: skin and saw off the breast part of the ribs, leaving the thin part of the best end twice the length of the eye of the meat. Remove the sinew from under the back. Bare the cutlet bones to a depth of 3cm and clean the skin from between the cutlet bones. Stewing: bone completely, remove the sinew and cut into 2½cm cubes.
915	Neck End (Côte Découverte)	2kg	Stewing: bone completely and remove skin and sinew. Cut into 2½cm cubes.
916	Neck (Collet)	3kg	Roasting, poêling and braising: bone completely, remove the skin and either leave whole or cut into joints of the required size. Roll and tie, or stuff, roll and tie. Stewing: bone completely and remove skin and sinew. Cut into 2½cm cubes.
917	Shoulder (Epaule)	7kg	Roasting: bone completely, remove skin and sinew, roll and tie, or stuff, roll and tie. Stewing: bone completely and remove skin, fat and sinew. Cut into even-sized pieces.
918	Breast (Poitrine)	2½ kg	

cont. p. 366

The small cuts obtainable from the main joints of veal:

Name of cut	From which Joint	Average Portion Weight	Preparation for Cooking
919 Veal Cutlet (Côte de Veau)	best end	250g	Cut between the bones of the prepared best end, lightly flatten and trim.
920 Veal Escalope (Escalope de Veau)	cushion, under-cushion, thick flank.	125g	Remove the skin and trim carefully. Cut slices across the grain and flatten carefully with a moistened cutlet bat to a neat oval shape approx. 2–3mm thick and trim.
921 Small Veal Escalopes (Escalopines de Veau or Piccatas)	cushion, under-cushion, thick flank, fillet.	2 × 60g or 3 × 40g	a) Cut from the cushion, under-cushion or thick flank and prepare in the same way as Escalopes de Veau but smaller, allowing 2–3 per person. b) Cut across the grain of the trimmed fillet about 1cm thick and flatten carefully with a moistened cutlet bat approx. 2–3mm thick.
922 Fricandeau	cushion	200–250g	Cut a slice along the grain approx. 4–5cm thick enough for 4 portions (800g–1kg). Lard finely with strips of fat bacon.
923 Grenadin	cushion, under-cushion, thick flank	150g	Cut into slices approx. 1cm thick and then into smaller pieces approx. 150g in weight. Trim neatly into small thick round shapes and lard with fine strips of fat bacon.
924 Médaillons and Noisettes	fillet	2 × 75g	Cut approx. 1½–2cm thick across the fillet and lightly flatten to about ½cm thick.
925 Paillard	cushion	1 × 180g	Cut across the grain to give a steak approx. 1½cm thick.
926 Osso Bucco	knuckle	2 × 250g	Cut and saw into sections 3–4cm thick across the bone. Tie round to keep in shape.

The main offals of veal, their average portion weights and preparation for cooking:

Name	Average Portion Weight	Preparation for Cooking
927 Brains	100g	Poaching: remove any membrane and clotted blood and soak in cold salted water for 3–4 hours in the refrigerator to disgorge blood. Wash well under cold running water for a further 30 mins.
928 Feet	150g	Boiling: singe off any hair then blanch in boiling water for 5–6 mins. and refresh under cold water. Scrape carefully to remove any remaining hair then split in half lengthways between the bones. Calf's feet are best cooked in a Blanc (15). Grilling: when cooked, wash, remove all bones then cool under a lightly weighted tray in the refrigerator. When cold and firm, season and paner à l'Anglaise (72).
929 Head	150g	Singe and clean the head of any hairs. Using a boning knife, cut through the skin down to the bone then along the centre of the head to the nostrils. Carefully detach the flesh from the bone following the contours of the head. Remove the tongue then soak the head and tongue in cold running water for 12 hours. Make an incision around the cranium using a saw or chopper and remove the brains. Place the head and tongue in cold water, bring to the boil, simmer for 5 mins. and refresh under cold water. Cut away any white skin from inside the head and discard. Cut off the ears and cut the head into 5cm squares, taking care that neither the aperture of the eye or nostril remains in the centre of any of the pieces.
930 Heart	150g	Stewing and braising: trim off any fat and cut out any tubes or gristly parts from inside.

cont. p.368

368

Name	Average Portion Weight	Preparation for Cooking
931 Kidney	120g	Whole for braising, roasting or poêling: just trim the kidney of excess fat. For sauté: remove the skin, cut in half lengthways and remove the core and any gristly parts. Cut into small thickish slices on the slant about 2cm square. Grilling: a) remove as much of the core as possible, trim of excess fat then cut in half lengthways towards the core; or cut across into 1–1½cm thick slices. b) remove the fat and skin entirely, remove the core and cut as above.
932 Liver	125g	Grilling or sauté: cut out any tubes or gristle showing and remove the skin. Cut on the slant into slices approx. ½cm thick.
933 Sweetbreads	125g	Soak in cold salted water for 3–4 hours in the refrigerator then under cold running water for an hour so as to remove any blood and whiten them. Blanch and refresh them under cold water. Drain and trim off any tough membrane, fat or gristle. Place on a clean tray between two damp cloths then set a lightly weighted tray on top. Place in the refrigerator for a few hours to become firm and lightly pressed.
934 Tongue	125g	Boiling or braising: cut away any bone or gristle from the root end and wash well.

935 Roast Veal

The following joints are suitable for roasting and their titles are given as they can appear on the menu.

Cuisseau de Veau rôti – Roast Leg of Veal
Epaule de Veau rôtie – Roast Shoulder of Veal
Epaule de Veau rôtie farcie – Roast Stuffed Shoulder of Veal
Selle de Veau rôtie – Roast Saddle of Veal
Longe de Veau rôtie – Roast Loin of Veal
Longe de Veau rôtie farcie – Roast Stuffed Loin of Veal
Poitrine de Veau rôtie farcie – Roast Stuffed Breast of Veal
Carré de Veau rôti – Roast Best End of Veal

See Recipe 45 for an appropriate stuffing.

Portion weights
To calculate the quantity of veal required to serve a given number of covers, the approximate allowance of veal prepared for roasting is:

on the bone	e.g. Selle de Veau rôtie	200–250g per person
off the bone	e.g. Longe de Veau rôtie	150–180g per person
boned and stuffed	e.g. Poitrine de Veau rôtie farcie	100–125g plus 50g stuffing per person

Method for roasting
It is an advantage to lard (50) or bard (1) joints of veal with salt pork fat or fat bacon before roasting. If this is not done veal can become very dry because of the minimal amount of fat naturally covering the joints.

1) Season the joint and place in a deep roasting tray on a Mirepoix (58). Cover well with melted dripping
2) Place in a hot oven at 220–225°C for 20–30 mins. then reduce the heat gradually and as necessary so as to prevent any overcolouring or burning of the mirepoix.
3) Baste the joint frequently and turn occasionally to ensure evenness of cooking.
4) Allow 20 mins. per 500g plus an extra 20 mins. cooking time. For example, a 3kg rolled shoulder joint of veal will require 2–2½ hours cooking time. If barded the slices of fat should be removed when the joint is three-quarters cooked to allow the meat to colour.
5) Veal should be cooked just through and not left underdone. To test when cooked press the joint firmly to squeeze out a little of the juices; these should be clear; any sign of blood means that it is underdone and the joint should be returned to the oven for a little longer. The reading on a meat thermometer inserted at the thickest part of the joint would show approx. 80°C.
6) Remove the joint to a tray and allow to rest for 20–30 mins. before carving. This will prevent the meat from shrinking and curling when being carved and also from losing its juices.

Jus de Rôti – Roast Gravy
1) When the roast joint is cooked and removed, place the roasting tray on the stove and allow the juices and mirepoix to heat gently and colour without burning.
2) Drain off the fat without disturbing the vegetables and sediment.
3) Add brown veal stock (98) as required and allow to simmer gently for a few minutes.

4) Correct the seasoning and very lightly thicken with diluted arrowroot.

5) Pass through a fine strainer and skim. Allow approx. 6dl of gravy per 10 portions.

Carving

Leg: Hold the leg bone and carve slices from the thickest side towards the bone starting at the knuckle end at an angle of 45°. Carve about 2–3mm thick. When the slices get too large, carve from alternate sides and when the top is finished, turn the leg over and continue carving.

Shoulder (boned or boned and stuffed): Cut in slices across the joint approx. ½cm thick.

Saddle: Cut down either side of the backbone. Then cut across into slices about ½cm thick. The two fillets under the saddle should not be forgotten and should be sliced and served as well.

Loin (boned and rolled or boned, stuffed and rolled): Carve across the joint about ½cm thick.

Breast (boned and rolled or boned, stuffed and rolled): Carve across the joint about ½cm thick.

Best end: Carve into cutlets by cutting between each rib-bone or carve in the same way as roast ribs of beef.

Service of roast veal

Carved in the kitchen: Serve on a suitable dish with a little roast gravy, garnish with watercress and send a separate sauceboat of gravy.

Carved in the restaurant: Place the whole joint on a suitable dish or on the carving trolley, garnish with watercress and accompany with containers of roast gravy.

SPECIAL POINT

In the traditional English style roast veal is accompanied with slices of ham and stuffing (45). In this case the stuffing should be cooked separately in a greased tray in the oven.

---

936 Grills of Veal

Because the flesh of veal is somewhat deficient in the amount of natural fat, considerable care must be taken when grilling cuts of veal. Basting frequently with butter or oil is essential and unless otherwise requested, attention must be directed to ensuring that it is grilled only to the point of being just done. This can be gauged by pressing the grilled meat – it should have an overall firmness and the juices expressed should be clear. Past this degree of cooking veal tends to lose its juices rapidly and becomes very dry, chewy and tasteless. For the most part small cuts of veal are best when shallow-fried in butter or better still in the case of cutlets or chops, cooked gently under cover in a cocotte or casserole.

Bearing the foregoing comments in mind, the following small cuts can be suitably grilled and garnished with any of the garnishes appropriate to lamb or beef and may be accompanied with a suitable sauce such as Sauce Champignons, Sauce Robert, Sauce Madère, Sauce Bordelaise:

Côte de Veau grillée – Grilled Veal Cutlet or Chop
Paillard de Veau grillée – Grilled Veal Steak

---

937 Grills of Calf's Offals

Calf's liver (932) cut in thickish slices can be successfully grilled but needs to be seasoned and floured first and is always best when cooked underdone.

Calf's kidney (931) prepared and cut in half lengthways or in slices, may be grilled, keeping underdone. The whole kidney, just trimmed of excess fat, can also be grilled but this requires great care when using an underfired grill to prevent it becoming blackened from the flaring of dripping fat.

Calf's feet which have been cooked first may be breadcrumbed and grilled. See Pied de Veau grillé (981).

Calf's sweetbreads may be grilled after being blanched, trimmed and lightly pressed. They are best if cut in half horizontally, seasoned lightly, floured and coated with melted butter. Grill quickly to a nice brown and serve accompanied with a suitable sauce such as Périgueux, Italienne, Champignons, Coulis de Tomate, Béarnaise or Beurre Maître d'Hôtel. Garnish as seen fit.

---

938 Blanquette de Veau

10 portions
2½ hours

Stage	Ingredient	Quantity	Method
1	shoulder or neck end of veal, boned, trimmed and cut into 2½ cm cubes	1¼kg	Place into a pan, cover with cold water, bring to the boil and blanch for 3 mins. Refresh under cold water and drain.
2	Fonds Blanc de Veau (95)	2 litres	Place the veal in a clean pan, just cover with stock, bring to the boil and skim.
3	Oignons Cloutés (65) carrots,whole Bouquet Garni	2 150g 1	Add to the veal, season lightly and simmer gently until tender (1–1½ hours).
4	butter flour	75g 75g	Prepare a Blond Roux (108) and allow to cool.
5			Remove the pieces of veal and place in a clean pan. Strain the cooking liquor and make a velouté with the blond roux. Allow to simmer for 30 mins.
6	cream juice of lemon parsley, chopped	2dl squeeze	Adjust the seasoning and add the cream and lemon juice. Pass the sauce through a fine strainer over the veal, reheat and serve in entrée dishes sprinkled with chopped parsley.

SPECIAL POINTS

a) A liaison of 3 egg yolks and 2dl of cream can be added to the sauce instead of cream only. In this case the sauce should be reheated sufficiently to cook the egg yolks but should not be allowed to reboil.

b) Blanquette of veal may be served garnished with braised celery, endives, fennel, buttered noodles, salsify and broad beans etc.

---

939 Blanquette de Veau à l'Ancienne

Prepare Blanquette de Veau (938), adding 30 button mushrooms cooked à Blanc (60) and 30 button onions cooked à Blanc (1492) to the veal at Stage 6 before covering with the sauce and reheating.

---

940 Cervelle de Veau au Beurre Noir

2 portions
30 mins.

Stage	Ingredient	Quantity	Method
1	calf's brains, one set	1	Remove the membrane and clots of blood then disgorge in cold salted water for 3 hours and wash under clean water.
2	Court-bouillon (538)	1 litre	Place the brains in a pan and cover with the cold court-bouillon. Bring to the boil, skim and allow to poach gently for 5 mins. Allow the brains to cool in the cooking liquor.
3			Remove the brains, drain well and cut each of the lobes in half lengthways.
4	butter flour	60g	Heat the butter in a sauté pan, season the brains, pass through the flour and fry quickly in the butter until golden brown. Dress neatly in an earthenware dish.
5	butter capers, squeezed vinegar parsley, chopped	50g ½ tbsp ½ tbsp	Sprinkle the capers over the brains. Place the butter in a suitable frying-pan and cook until brown, shaking the pan to ensure even colouring. Remove from the fire, add the vinegar and pour over the brains immediately. Sprinkle with chopped parsley.

---

941 CÔTES DE VEAU – VEAL CUTLETS

These are excellent when shallow-fried and the resulting eating qualities are far superior to those obtained by grilling. Butter is the best cooking medium with clarified butter or oil producing a better colour if the cutlet should be breadcrumbed.

A particularly good result can be obtained by cooking under cover with butter in a casserole especially where the addition of aromatic herbs or fortified wines is called for in the recipe. But this method can only be really successful when no more than one or two at the most are prepared in a single casserole. It is customary for ungarnished cutlets prepared in this manner to be described as 'en Casserole' and when garnished as 'en Cocotte' even though the utensil used may be the same. There is always an attendant danger of earthenware or porcelain casseroles breaking if used for cooking on the stove;

it is for this reason that metal or enamel casseroles or cocottes are recommended. Alternatively, the cutlets may be cooked in a sauté pan, transferred to an earthenware or porcelain casserole and the sauce and garnish, if any, added after deglazing the sauté pan with the required liquid or sauce. It can then be finished off in the oven.

942 Côte de Veau au Basilic – Veal Cutlet with Basil
2 portions
30 mins.

Stage	Ingredient	Quantity	Method
1	butter	50g	Heat the butter in a fireproof cocotte.
	veal cutlets (919)	2 × 250g	Season the cutlets and shallow fry to a golden brown on both sides (12–15 mins.) until almost cooked.
2	white wine, dry	2 tbsps	Tip out most of the fat then add the wine and jus lié and sprinkle the chops with the basil. Cover the cocotte with its lid and place in a hot oven for 4–5 mins. to complete the cooking. Remove and place on a suitable underdish and serve directly from the cocotte.
	Jus lié (113)	½dl	
	fresh basil, chopped	½ tbsp	

943 Côte de Veau Bonne-Femme
4 portions
30 mins.

Stage	Ingredient	Quantity	Method
1	butter	50g	Heat the butter in a sauté pan, season the cutlets and cook to a golden brown on both sides (12–15 mins.). Dress in cocottes.
	veal cutlets (919)	4 × 250g	
2	Lardons (51)	75g	Blanch the lardons, fry until brown in a little fat and drain. Sprinkle over the cutlets with the onions and potatoes.
	Pommes Cocotte (1552)	16	
	button onions, glacés à Brun (1493)	16	
3	Jus lié (113)	2dl	Add the jus lié to the cutlets and the garnish. Sprinkle with chopped parsley and cover with the lids. Place in a hot oven for 4–5 mins.
	parsley, chopped		
4			Remove and place on dish papers on suitable dishes.

944 Côte de Veau Milanaise
Prepare Côte de Veau panée (946) and garnish with Spaghetti Milanaise (504).

945 Côte de Veau Napolitaine
Prepare Côte de Veau panée (946) and garnish with Spaghetti Napolitaine (506).

946 Côte de Veau panée

4 portions
35 mins.

Stage	Ingredient	Quantity	Method
1	veal cutlets (919)	4 × 250g	Trim the cutlets carefully then lightly flatten with a cutlet bat. Season them and paner à l'Anglaise (72). Pat to flatten, reshape and mark trellis-fashion with the back of a knife.
	flour		
	eggwash } for		
	breadcrumbs, } crumbing		
	white		
2	oil	1dl	Heat in a sauté pan and when hot place in the cutlets. Shallow fry to a golden brown on both sides until cooked, 10–12 mins. Arrange in an earthenware dish and keep warm.
3	Jus lié (113)	1dl	Make sure the cutlets are hot and surround with the jus lié. Heat the butter in a suitable frying pan and cook until just brown shaking the pan to ensure even colouring. Pour over the cutlets.
	butter	50g	

947 Côte de Veau en Papillote

1 portion
1 hour

Stage	Ingredient	Quantity	Method
1	butter	30g	Heat the butter in a sauté pan. Season the cutlet and cook to a golden brown on both sides (10–12 mins.).
	veal cutlet (919)	1 × 200g	
2	butter	30g	Melt the butter in a small pan, add the onion and cook without colour. Add the mushrooms, season and cook until almost dry. Add the wine and demi-glace and reduce to a fairly thick consistency. Correct the seasoning and finish with a little chopped parsley.
	onion, finely chopped	30g	
	mushrooms, finely chopped	150g	
	white wine	½dl	
	Demi-glace (112)	1dl	
	parsley, chopped		
3	greaseproof paper	1 sheet	Cut the greaseproof paper into the shape of a large heart big enough to hold the cutlet and oil well. Trim the two slices of ham roughly to the shape of the cutlet. Lay one slice of ham on the paper to one side of the centre. Spread half of the mushroom mixture on top then place the cutlet on top of the mixture. Spread the rest of the mixture on the cutlet and cover with the other slice of ham.
	cooked ham	2 slices	
	oil		
4			Fold the paper over to cover and seal by pleating the edges tightly.

5

Place the Côte de Veau en Papillote on an oiled flat dish and place in a moderate oven at 175°C for approx. 5–7 mins. in order to colour the outside and to allow the steam, which is trapped inside, to swell the papillote. Serve immediately.

948 Côte de Veau au Romarin – Veal Cutlet with Rosemary

4 portions
25 mins.

Stage	Ingredient	Quantity	Method
1	butter	50g	Heat the butter in a sauté pan, season the cutlets and sprinkle on both sides with the rosemary which has been very finely chopped. Pat to make the rosemary adhere well. Shallow fry gently on both sides to a golden brown (12–15 mins.). Place in an earthenware dish.
	veal cutlets (919)	4 × 250g	
	rosemary, fresh	½ tbsp	
2	Fonds Brun de Veau (98)	2dl	Tip out the fat from the pan, add the stock and meat glaze and reduce until slightly viscous then shake in the butter. Adjust the seasoning as necessary.
	Glace de Viande (103)	½ tbsp	
	butter	50g	
3			Make sure the cutlets are hot then pass the sauce through a fine strainer over them.

949 Côte de Veau sautée

4 portions
25 mins.

Stage	Ingredient	Quantity	Method
1	butter	50g	Heat the butter in a sauté pan. Season the cutlets and cook to a golden brown on both sides (10–12 mins.). Place in an earthenware dish.
	veal cutlets (919)	4 × 250g	
2	Jus lié (113)	2dl	Pour a cordon of jus lié around the cutlets. Place the butter in a suitable pan and cook until nut-brown, shaking the pan to ensure even colouring. Pour quickly over the cutlets and sprinkle with chopped parsley.
	butter	50g	
	parsley, chopped		

SPECIAL POINT

Côte de Veau sautée may be served with different garnishes such as Nouilles, Jardinière and Céleris, and should be designated on the menu as such, e.g. Côté de Veau sautée aux Céleris.

950 Côte de Veau Vallée d'Auge

4 portions
45 mins.

Stage	Ingredient	Quantity	Method
1	butter	50g	Heat the butter in a sauté pan, season
	veal cutlets (919)	4 × 250g	the cutlets and shallow fry to a light
			golden colour on both sides until cooked
			(12–15 mins.). Place in an earthenware
			dish and keep warm.
2	shallots	50g	Add the shallots to the pan and cook
	mushrooms, small		gently until soft then add the mushrooms
	white button	125g	and cook together. Add the cider and
	cider, dry	2dl	reduce by two-thirds.
3	Glace de Viande (103)	½ tbsp	Add the meat glaze and cream and
	cream, double	2dl	reduce to a coating consistency. Adjust
	button onions		the seasoning as necessary then add the
	glacés à Blanc (1492)	16	onions and heat for a few moments.
4	parsley, chopped		Make sure the cutlets are hot then spoon
	Fleurons (33)	8	over the sauce and its garnish. Sprinkle
			with chopped parsley and surround with
			the fleurons.

951 ESCALOPES DE VEAU – VEAL ESCALOPES

Escalopes of veal have always been a popular dish, both relatively easy and quick to prepare and cook. There are, however, a number of very important details to bear in mind which are essential for ensuring the best results.

a) The escalopes should always be cut across the grain of the meat. This is necessary to ensure tenderness.

b) Do not flatten the meat too thinly. This is not too disastrous if the escalope is cooked uncoated, but if too thin when breadcrumbed, the proportion of meat to the combined outer coatings can spoil the balance of eating qualities. The thickness should be approx. 2–3mm in this case.

c) Care should be taken that the escalope has a good shape for presentation, either round or oval, and that no ragged edges are discernible.

d) The fat or oil used for shallow frying should always be hot enough to seal the surfaces in contact with the fat. If too cool the juices of the meat are liable to leach out.

e) Escalopes should always be just cooked. They should show moistness when cut but there must be no evidence of blood. Overcooking results in a disagreeable dryness.

f) Escalopes are best cooked to order and served immediately. This is necessary to conserve the moistness of the flesh and also the crispness of any outer coating of breadcrumbs.

952 Escalope de Veau Cordon Bleu

10 portions
1¼ hours

Stage	Ingredient	Quantity	Method
1	veal escalopes (920)	20 × 60g	Lightly season the escalopes and lay ten
	cooked ham, 2mm-		on the table. Place a slice of ham and
	thick slices	10	then a slice of Gruyère cheese on each.

	Gruyère cheese, 2mm-thick slices	10	Cover with the remaining escalopes and press firmly together. Trim to a neat shape.
2	flour eggwash breadcrumbs, white	} for crumbing	Paner à l'Anglaise (72), lightly flatten, reshape and mark the escalopes trellis-fashion with the back of a knife.
3	oil	3dl	Heat the oil in a sauté pan and shallow fry the escalopes on both sides to a golden brown (10–12 mins.). Remove and arrange on suitable dishes with the decorated sides uppermost.
4	Jus lié (113) butter	3dl 150g	Surround the escalopes with a cordon of Jus lié. Place the butter in a suitable frying pan and cook until nut-brown, shaking the pan to ensure even colouring. Pour over the escalopes.

---

953 Escalope de Veau à la Crème

10 portions
30 mins.

Stage	Ingredient	Quantity	Method
1	butter flour veal escalopes (920)	100g 10 × 125g	Heat the butter in a sauté pan, season the escalopes and lightly flour. Just as the butter begins to turn brown, place in the escalopes and shallow fry quickly to a light brown on both sides. Remove and arrange neatly in earthenware dishes.
2	sherry cream, double	½dl 5dl	Tip out the fat from the sauté pan, add the sherry and then the cream and reduce gently to a light coating consistency. Adjust the seasoning and pass through a fine strainer over the escalopes.

---

954 Escalope de Veau à la Crème et Champignons

10 portions
30 mins.

Stage	Ingredient	Quantity	Method
1	butter flour veal escalopes (920)	100g 10 × 125g	Heat the butter in a sauté pan, season the escalopes and lightly flour. Just as the butter begins to turn brown, place in the escalopes and shallow fry quickly to a light brown on both sides. Remove and arrange neatly in earthenware dishes.
2	button mushrooms, sliced	400g	Add to the butter remaining in the sauté pan, lightly season and cook quickly.

3	sherry	½dl	Add the sherry and slightly reduce. Add
	cream, double	5dl	the cream and reduce gently to a light coating consistency. Adjust the seasoning and pour over the escalopes.

955 Escalope de Veau Holstein

10 portions
45 mins.

Stage	Ingredient	Quantity	Method
1	veal escalopes (920) flour eggwash breadcrumbs white } for crumbing	10 × 125g	Season the escalopes and paner à l'Anglaise (72). Lightly flatten, reshape and mark trellis-fashion on one side with the back of a knife.
2	oil	3dl	Heat the oil in a sauté pan and, when very hot, place in the escalopes and shallow fry quickly to a golden brown on both sides. Remove and dress on suitable dishes with the decorated sides uppermost.
3	butter eggs anchovy fillets	100g 10 20	Fry the eggs in the butter and place one on each escalope. Arrange two fillets of anchovy criss-cross on each egg.
4	Jus lié (113) butter	3dl 150g	Surround the escalopes with a cordon of jus lié. Place the butter in a suitable frying-pan and cook until nut-brown, shaking the pan to ensure even colouring. Pour over the escalopes.

956 Escalope de Veau au Madère

10 portions
30 mins.

Stage	Ingredient	Quantity	Method
1	butter flour veal escalopes (920)	100g 10 × 125g	Heat the butter in a sauté pan, season the escalopes and lightly flour. Just as the butter begins to turn brown, place in the escalopes and shallow fry quickly to a light brown on both sides. Remove and arrange neatly in earthenware dishes.
2	Madeira Jus lié (113)	1dl 6dl	Tip out the fat from the sauté pan, add the Madeira and slightly reduce. Add the Jus lié and reduce to a light coating consistency. Adjust the seasoning and pass through a fine strainer over the escalopes.

957 Escalope de Veau au Marsala/Porto/Xérès

Prepare as Escalope de Veau au Madère (956) using Marsala, port or sherry as the case may be, instead of Madeira.

958 Escalope de Veau Milanaise

Prepare Escalope de Veau panée (960) and garnish with Spaghetti Milanaise (504).

959 Escalope de Veau Napolitaine

Prepare Escalope de Veau panée (960) and garnish with Spaghetti Napolitaine (506).

960 Escalope de Veau panée

10 portions
30 mins.

Stage	Ingredient	Quantity	Method
1	veal escalopes (920)	10 × 125g	Season the escalopes and paner à l'Anglaise (72). Lightly flatten, reshape and mark trellis-fashion on one side with the back of a knife.
	flour	} for crumbing	
	eggwash		
	breadcrumbs, white		
2	oil	3dl	Heat the oil in a sauté pan and when very hot place in the escalopes and shallow fry quickly to a golden brown on both sides. Remove and arrange on suitable dishes with the decorated sides uppermost.
3	Jus lié (113)	3dl	Surround the escalopes with a cordon of jus lié. Place the butter in a suitable frying-pan and cook until nut brown, shaking the pan to ensure even colouring. Pour over the escalopes.
	butter	150g	

961 Escalope de Veau Viennoise

10 portions
1 hour

Stage	Ingredient	Quantity	Method
1	veal escalopes (920)	10 × 125g	Season the escalopes and paner à l'Anglaise (72). Lightly flatten, reshape and mark trellis-fashion on one side with the back of a knife.
	flour	} for crumbing	
	eggwash		
	breadcrumbs, white		
2	lemon	10 slices	Decorate each slice of lemon with a ring of anchovy fillet and a stoned olive in its centre. Garnish around the fillet with chopped parsley and sieved white and yolk of the hard-boiled eggs.
	eggs, hard-boiled	2	
	stoned olives	10	
	parsley, chopped	2 tbsps	
	anchovy fillets	10	

| 3 | oil | 3dl | Heat the oil in a sauté pan and, when very hot, place in the escalopes and shallow fry quickly to a golden brown on both sides. Remove and arrange on suitable dishes with the decorated sides uppermost. |
| 4 | Jus lié (113) butter | 3dl 150g | Surround the escalopes with a cordon of jus lié. Place the butter in a suitable frying-pan and cook until nut-brown, shaking the pan to ensure even colouring. Pour over the escalopes. Place one of the prepared lemon garnishes in the centre of each escalope. |

SPECIAL POINT

The following alternative method of garnishing is more suitable for à la Carte service of up to four covers. Dress the parsley and sieved white and yolk of egg in lines at the ends of the dish finishing with a line of anchovy fillets. On each escalope place a slice of peeled lemon with a ring of anchovy fillet and a stoned olive in its centre.

962 Escalopines de Veau

Small Escalopes of Veal (921), using two or three per portion, may be prepared according to certain of the recipes for Escalopes de Veau:

Escalopines de Veau à la Crème (see 953)
Escalopines de Veau à la Crème et Champignons (see 954)
Escalopines de Veau au Madère (see 956)
Escalopines de Veau au Marsala (see 957)
Escalopines de Veau au Porto (see 957)
Escalopines de Veau au Xérès (see 957)

SPECIAL POINT

Escalopines of veal are also known by their descriptive Italian name of Piccatas but in general this term should not be mixed with French titling. It would be better if completely in Italian, e.g. Piccata di Vitello alla Marsala.

963 Filet de Veau Esterhazy

4 portions
1¾ hours

Stage	Ingredient	Quantity	Method
1	butter fillet of veal, larded (912) paprika	100g 850g	Heat the butter in a suitably-sized casserole. Season the fillet with salt and milled pepper. Well sprinkle with paprika and rub in. Shallow fry quickly to a golden brown on all sides. Remove from the casserole.
2	onions, finely sliced	400g	Add to the casserole and cook for a few minutes to a golden colour. Replace the fillet on top. Cover with the lid and place in a moderate oven at 180°C and cook gently for approx. 45 mins. Baste

frequently. Remove the fillet when ready, cover and keep warm.

3	paprika	1 tsp	Stir the paprika into the onions and juices and cook gently for 2–3 mins. then add the wine and tomato and cook for a further five minutes.
	white wine, dry	1dl	
	Tomates Concassées (90)	75g	

4	cream, sour cayenne	1dl	Liquidise the ingredients and liquid from the pan then pass firmly through a fine strainer into a clean pan. Add the cream and reduce to a nice coating consistency. Adjust the seasoning as necessary and finish with a touch of cayenne. Cover and keep hot.

5	pimento, red, skinned and deseeded	50g	Cut into thin strips approx. 2cm long, stew gently in the butter until soft and add to the sauce.
	butter	15g	

6	Gnocchi Parisienne (484)	4 portions	Cut the fillet of veal on the slant into eight fairly thick slices and arrange overlapping in an earthenware dish. Make sure all is hot and coat with the sauce. Serve accompanied with a separate dish of Gnocchi Parisienne.

---

964 Filet de Veau aux Fenouils – Fillet of Veal with Fennel

4 portions
1½ hours

Stage	Ingredient	Quantity	Method
1	butter	75g	Heat the butter in a suitably-sized casserole, season the fillet with salt and milled pepper and shallow fry to a golden brown on all sides. Remove from the casserole.
	fillet of veal, larded (912)	850g	
2	shallots	75g	Add all these ingredients to the casserole and fry for a few minutes to lightly colour. Replace the fillet of veal on top, cover with the lid and cook gently in a moderately hot oven at 180°C for approx. 30 mins. Baste frequently and occasionally turn the fillet.
	mushrooms } roughly	100g	
	fennel } chopped	75g	
	carrot	75g	
	streaky bacon, cut small	50g	
	garlic, crushed	1 clove	
	caraway seeds	pinch	
3	white wine, dry	2dl	Add to the casserole and cook for a further 15–20 mins. then remove the fillet and keep warm.
4	cream, double	1dl	Liquidise the ingredients from the pan together with the cooking juices. Pass through a fine strainer firmly into a clean pan and reduce until fairly thick. Add the cream and simmer to a light coating consistency. Adjust the seasoning as necessary, cover and keep hot.

5   Fenouils braisés (1460) 4 portions   Cut the fillet on the slant into eight fairly
           feathery leaves of   thick slices, arrange overlapping in an
              fennel, chopped   ½ tbsp   earthenware dish. Place the braised
                                                  fennel to one side, make sure that all is
                                                  hot then coat the veal only with the
                                                  sauce. Sprinkle with the chopped fennel
                                                  leaves and send the remainder of the
                                                  sauce in a sauceboat.

---

965 Foie de Veau aux Cassis – Calf's Liver   10 portions
with Blackcurrants   45 mins.

Stage	Ingredient	Quantity	Method
1	calf's liver	1¼kg	Remove the skin and any tubes or gristle and cut into slices approx. ½cm thick allowing two slices per portion.
2	butter flour	100g	Heat the butter in a sauté pan. Season the liver and lightly flour. Just as the butter turns brown place in the liver and shallow fry quickly on both sides leaving slightly underdone (4–5 mins.). Drain and keep warm.
3	wine vinegar, white blackcurrants, cleaned Jus lié (113)	1dl 150g 4dl	Discard the fat from the pan, add the vinegar, reduce by three-quarters then add the blackcurrants and just heat for a few seconds. Add the jus lié. Just bring to the boil and remove from the heat.
4	Crème de Cassis butter	½dl 75g	Add the Crème de Cassis then carefully shake in the butter. Adjust the seasoning as necessary. Do not overheat.
5			Arrange the liver on suitable dishes, make sure that all is hot. Pour the sauce to one side of the liver or round it.

---

966 Foie de Veau au Lard – Calf's Liver and Bacon 10 portions
30 mins.

Stage	Ingredient	Quantity	Method
1	calf's liver	1¼kg	Skin and cut into slices approx. ½cm thick allowing two slices per portion.
2	butter flour	120g	Heat the butter in a frying-pan. Season the liver and pass through the flour. Just as the butter turns brown place in the liver and shallow fry quickly on both sides leaving slightly underdone (4–5 mins.). Dress in earthenware dishes.
3	back bacon rashers	10	Grill and arrange on the calf's liver.

4	Jus lié (113)	3dl	Surround the liver with a cordon of jus lié. Place the butter in a suitable frying-pan and cook until nut-brown, shaking the pan to ensure even colouring. Pour over the liver and bacon.
	butter	120g	

967 Foie de Veau Lyonnaise

10 portions
30 mins.

Stage	Ingredient	Quantity	Method
1	calf's liver	1¼kg	Skin and cut into slices approx. ½cm thick allowing two slices per portion.
2	butter	120g	Heat the butter in a frying-pan. Season the liver and pass through the flour. Just as the butter turns brown, place in the liver and shallow fry quickly on both sides leaving slightly underdone (4–5 mins.). Dress in earthenware dishes.
	flour		
3	Sauce Lyonnaise (128)	7dl	Coat the liver with the Sauce Lyonnaise and sprinkle with chopped parsley.
	parsley, chopped		

968 Fricandeau de Veau

The Fricandeau (922) is a piece cut from the cushion of veal along its grain 4–5cm thick and is usually just sufficient for four portions. It should be well-larded on both sides and should always be braised and well-cooked. Vegetable garnishes such as Printanière, glazed carrots, braised celery and so on are all suitable, as well as buttered noodles, buttered Gnocchi Parisienne and Risotto or Riz Pilaff as accompaniments.

See Noix de Veau braisée, (975 or 976) for the applicable brown and white braising methods.

969 Fricassée de Veau

10 portions
2½ hours

Stage	Ingredient	Quantity	Method
1	butter	100g	Heat the butter in a sauté pan, season the veal, place into the pan and stiffen it without colouring.
	shoulder or neck end of veal, boned, trimmed and cut into 2½cm cubes	1¼kg	
2	flour	75g	Sprinkle over the meat and shake the pan to mix in. Cover with a lid and place in the oven at 175°C for 10 mins. Remove and allow to cool.
3	Fonds Blanc de Veau (95)	2 litres	Carefully mix in sufficient stock to just cover the veal, season, bring to the boil and skim. Add the bouquet garni, cover with the lid and place in a moderate oven approx. 180°C to cook for 1½–2 hours.
	Bouquet Garni	1	

4			Discard the bouquet garni and remove the meat to a clean pan.
5	egg yolks cream	3 1dl	Whisk together in a large basin and add approx. one-third of the sauce, whisking in quickly. Return to the remainder of the sauce, mixing in quickly. Reheat, moving it continuously with a wooden or metal spatule until the liaison thickens, taking care that it does not reboil.
6			Adjust the seasoning of the sauce and pass through a fine strainer over the meat. Carefully reheat without boiling.
7	parsley, chopped Heart-shaped Croûtons (26)	10	Serve the fricassée in earthenware dishes, sprinkle with chopped parsley and garnish with the heart-shaped croûtons.

970 Fricassée de Veau à l'Ancienne

Prepare Fricassée de Veau (969) with the addition of 30 button onions cooked à Blanc (1492) and 30 button mushrooms cooked à Blanc (60) at Stage 6.

971 Grenadin de Veau braisé

10 portions
2 hours

Stage	Ingredient	Quantity	Method
1	butter Grenadins (923)	100g 10 × 150g	Heat the butter in a braising pan, season the Grenadins and fry quickly on both sides to colour. Remove.
2	carrot ⎱ onion ⎰ sliced celery mushroom trimmings bayleaf, crushed thyme garlic, crushed	200g 200g 150g 100g 1 sprig ½ clove	Add the vegetables and herbs to the pan and arrange the Grenadins on top. Cover with the lid and place on the stove for a few minutes to lightly colour the vegetable base and release their flavours.
3	white wine, dry Fonds Brun de Veau (98) tomato purée	3dl 1 litre ½ tbsp	Add the wine and reduce to a glaze, then add the stock and tomato purée to just below the top of the Grenadins. Lightly season, bring to the boil, skim, cover with the lid and place in a moderate oven at 180°C for 50–60 mins. until tender. Remove the Grenadins to a tray and spoon a little of the cooking liquor over them. Place in a hot oven and baste two or three times to glaze. Arrange in earthenware dishes, cover and keep warm.

4	arrowroot	15g	Strain the cooking liquor into a clean pan, reduce well to about 6dl and lightly thicken with the diluted arrowroot. Adjust the seasoning as necessary and pass through a fine strainer.
5			Make sure that the Grenadins are hot and coat with a little of the sauce. Send the rest separately in a sauceboat.

SPECIAL POINTS

a) Grenadins de Veau prepared in the above manner may be garnished with any of the following: Carottes glacées; Céleris braisés; Laitues braisées; Endives braisées; Jardinière de Légumes; and should be designated accordingly on the menu, e.g. Grenadin de Veau braisé aux Céleris.

b) The Grenadins may be braised white in the same manner as the white braised Noix de Veau (976) and finished with the same sauces and types of garnish.

---

972 Médaillons de Veau à l'Estragon

4 portions
35 mins.

Stage	Ingredient	Quantity	Method
1	butter Médaillons of veal (924)	50g 8 × 75g	Heat the butter in a sauté pan. Season the Médaillons and shallow fry on both sides to a golden brown. Arrange neatly in an earthenware dish. Cover and keep warm.
2	white wine, dry tarragon stalks, chopped	1dl ½ tbsp	Tip out the fat from the pan, add the wine and tarragon and reduce gently by half.
3	Jus lié (113) butter	1½dl 50g	Add the jus lié, simmer to a light coating consistency then strain into a clean pan. Shake in the butter and adjust the seasoning as necessary. Cover and keep hot.
4	tarragon leaves, blanched	16	Make sure that the Médaillons are hot then coat with a little of the sauce. Decorate each Médaillon with two blanched tarragon leaves.

---

973 Médaillons de Veau Musette

4 portions
45 mins.

Stage	Ingredient	Quantity	Method
1	butter Médaillons of veal (924)	50g 8 × 75g	Heat the butter in a sauté pan, season the Médaillons and shallow fry on both sides to a golden brown. Arrange neatly in an earthenware dish. Cover and keep warm.
2	Fonds d'Artichauts (1379)	4	Place in the same fat and colour lightly on both sides. Remove and reserve.

3	sherry, dry	½dl	Tip out the fat from the pan, add the
	Jus lié (113)	1½dl	sherry and reduce by half. Add the jus
	butter	50g	lié, simmer to a light coating consistency then pass through a fine strainer into a clean pan. Shake in the butter and adjust the seasoning as necessary. Cover and keep warm.
4	Fondue de Tomates (91)	75g	Fill the artichoke bottoms dome-shape with the tomato mixture and arrange at
	Pommes Noisette (1580)	75g	one side of the Médaillons. Place the Pommes Noisette on the other side.
5	Truffle, slices	4	Make sure that all is hot, then coat the
	parsley, chopped		Médaillons only with a little of the sauce. Place a slice of truffle on top of each tomato and a little of the parsley on the potatoes. Send the remainder of the sauce in a sauceboat.

974 NOIX DE VEAU – CUSHION OF VEAL

In addition to being roasted, the cushion of veal may be braised or poêléed. As a braised joint it suffers somewhat from the disadvantage of being difficult to carve in a presentable manner if cooked sufficiently to absorb the flavours of the braising medium. Undercooking to maintain firmness for carving can render it dry and rather flavourless. The cushion of veal may be braised white making it suitable for serving with white sauces or braised brown for brown sauces, the main differences being the degree of colouring of the meat and its vegetables and the use of white or brown veal stock. There is a marked degree of difference, however, in the finished flavours and taste.

Poêling in general is to be preferred as a more useful process. The joint will more readily absorb the flavours of the aromates and herbs if the cooking is carried out slowly and methodically and it will maintain a suitable texture and tenderness for carving. Whether for braising or poêling the joint should always be larded with strips of salt pork fat or fat bacon on the inner cut surfaces.

975 Noix de Veau braisée (Brown-braised)   10 portions
2½ hours

Stage	Ingredient	Quantity	Method
1	butter	100g	Heat the butter in a braising pan, season
	cushion of veal (907), larded	1½kg	the veal then shallow fry to a light brown on all sides. Remove.
2	carrot ⎫	175g	Spread the vegetables and herbs in the
	onion ⎬ sliced	175g	braising pan and place the veal on top.
	celery ⎭	125g	Cover with the lid and place on the stove
	bayleaf, crushed	1	for a few minutes to lightly colour the
	thyme	sprig	vegetable base.
3	Fonds Brun de Veau (98)	1½ litres	Add sufficient stock to come half-way up the veal. Add the tomato purée, lightly
	tomato pureé	½ tbsp	season and bring to the boil. Cover with

<table>
<tr><td></td><td></td><td></td><td>the lid and place in a moderate oven at 180°C to cook gently. Baste frequently with its cooking liquor and turn it over occasionally to ensure even colouring. To test when cooked, pierce the veal with a trussing needle at the thickest part; this should penetrate without pronounced resistance. Approx. 1¾ hours.</td></tr>
</table>

4	arrowroot	15g	Remove the veal, cover and keep warm. Skim the fat from the cooking liquor, reduce to approx. 6dl and thicken with the diluted arrowroot. Adjust the seasoning and pass the sauce through a fine strainer into a suitable pan. Cover and keep hot.
5			Remove the string from the veal and carve across the grain into 3mm-thick slices. Arrange neatly overlapping on suitable dishes and coat with the sauce. Serve accompanied by the remainder of the sauce in a sauceboat.

SPECIAL POINTS

a) Braised cushion of veal may be served with suitable garnishes, such as Nouilles au Beurre, Carottes glacées, Salsifis sautés, Jardinière de Légumes, Céleris braisés, Endives braisées, and Laitues braisées, and should be designated accordingly on the menu, e.g. Noix de Veau braisée Jardinière.

b) If the braised cushion of veal is to be presented whole, it is useful to glaze the joint in the following manner: when cooked, remove the string and place the joint on a tray. Coat with a little of the finished sauce and place in a medium oven to set. Repeat the operation several times taking care not to overcolour it. With care, a thin richly coloured glaze will be obtained.

---

976 Noix de Veau braisée (White-braised)

10 portions
2½ hours

Stage	Ingredient	Quantity	Method
1	butter cushion of veal (907), larded	100g 1½kg	Heat the butter in a braising pan, season the veal and shallow fry to a light golden brown on all sides. Remove.
2	onion ⎫ carrot ⎬ sliced celery ⎭ bayleaf, crushed thyme	175g 175g 125g 1 sprig	Spread the vegetables and herbs on the bottom of the pan and place the veal on top best side up, cover with the lid and place in a hot oven for 15 mins. Remove the pan from the oven and place on the stove.

3	Fonds Blanc de Veau (95)	1 litre	Add sufficient stock to come one-third the way up the veal. Season lightly and bring to the boil. Cover with the lid and place in a moderate oven at 180°C to cook gently. Baste the veal frequently with its cooking liquor so as to build up a golden glazed coating to the top surface. To test when cooked, pierce the veal at the thickest part with a trussing needle. This should penetrate without marked resistance. Approx. 1¾ hours.
4			Remove the veal, cover and keep warm. Skim the fat from the cooking liquor, pass through a fine strainer and reduce to give approx. 4dl. Adjust the seasoning, cover and keep hot.
5			Remove the string from the veal. Carve across the grain into 3mm slices and arrange neatly overlapping on suitable dishes and coat with the braising juices.

SPECIAL POINTS

a) The cooking liquor can be reduced together with added double cream to a light coating consistency.

b) In either case the veal may be accompanied with suitable garnishes such as Nouilles au Beurre, Riz Pilaff, Salsifis au Beurre, Fèves au Beurre, Céleris braisés, etc.

---

977 Noix de Veau Neuchâtelloise

10 portions
2¾ hours

Stage	Ingredient	Quantity	Method
1	butter	100g	Heat the butter in a braising pan, season the veal and shallow fry on all sides to a light golden brown. Remove the veal.
	cushion of veal, larded (907)	1½kg	
2	shallots ⎱ roughly	175g	Place the vegetables and herbs in the same fat and cook for a few minutes without colour. Place the veal on top.
	carrot ⎬	175g	
	celery ⎰ chopped	125g	
	bayleaf, crushed	1	
	thyme	sprig	
	rosemary, ground	½ tbsp	
	garlic, crushed	1 clove	
3	white wine, dry	3dl	Add the wine, cover with the lid and reduce by half, then add the stock. Bring to the boil, lightly season and cover with the lid. Place in a moderate oven at 180°C to cook gently for approx. 1¾ hours. Baste frequently with the
	Fonds Blanc de Veau (95)	5dl	

cooking liquor. When cooked, remove, cover and keep warm.

4	cream, sour	5dl	Pass the cooking liquor firmly through a fine strainer, reduce by half then add the cream and reduce again to a light coating consistency.
5	button mushrooms, white small	500g	Place in a small pan with a pinch of salt and one tablespoon water, cover and cook quickly until soft and the liquid well-reduced. Add to the sauce. Adjust the seasoning plus a touch of cayenne. Cover and keep hot.
	lemon juice	½ tbsp	
	butter	50g	
	cayenne		
6	Riz Pilaff (522)	5 portions	Remove the string from the veal and carve across the grain into 3mm slices. Arrange neatly on suitable dishes, coat with the sauce and mushrooms and sprinkle with the chives. Place the Riz Pilaff to one side or send in a dish separately, with the remainder of the sauce in a sauceboat.
	chives, cut very small	2 tbsps	

978 Noix de Veau poêlée

10 portions
2½ hours

Stage	Ingredient	Quantity	Method
1	butter	50g	Butter a braising pan and cover the bottom with the aromates and bacon.
	carrots ⎫ roughly	150g	
	onion ⎬ diced	150g	
	celery ⎭	100g	
	bacon trimmings	100g	
	bayleaf, crushed		
	thyme	sprig	
	garlic, crushed	1 clove	
2	cushion of veal, (907) larded	1½kg	Season the veal well and lay on the aromates. Baste with the melted butter. Cover with a lid and place in the oven at approx. 200°C. Baste frequently.
	butter, melted	100g	
3			Remove the lid after 1 hour and allow the veal to colour lightly. Reduce the heat if necessary. Do not allow the vegetables to overcolour. Continue basting until the veal is cooked (approx. 1¾ hours). Turn occasionally to colour evenly.

4	Madeira	1dl	Remove the veal, cover and keep it warm. Place the braising pan on the stove and allow the juices and vegetables to heat gently and colour without burning. Drain off the fat without disturbing the vegetables and sediment. Add the Madeira and reduce slightly. Add the stock and tomato purée, bring to the boil, skim and simmer gently for 10 mins. Thicken with the diluted arrowroot. Adjust the seasoning and pass through a fine strainer into a pan. Cover and keep hot.
	Fonds Brun de Veau		
	(98)	1 litre	
	tomato purée	½ tbsp	
	arrowroot	15g	
5			Remove the string from the veal and carve across the grain into 3mm-thick slices. Arrange neatly on dishes and coat with a little of the sauce. Serve the remainder of the sauce in a sauceboat.

SPECIAL POINT
Noix de Veau poêlée may be served with suitable garnishes as noted for Noix de Veau braisée (975).

979 Ossi Buchi alla Milanese

4 portions
2½ hours

Stage	Ingredient	Quantity	Method
1	butter	75g	Heat the butter in a braising pan, season the veal, pass through flour and fry until brown on both sides. Remove the pieces of veal and keep on one side.
	sections cut from		
	knuckle of veal (906)	8	
	flour		
2	onions, finely chopped	200g	Fry the onion in the same fat without colouring. Replace the veal, add the tomatoes and the wine and reduce the wine by half.
	Tomates Concassées		
	(90)	400g	
	white wine, dry	3dl	
3	Fonds Blanc de Veau		Add sufficient stock to barely cover the veal. Add the bouquet garni, season and bring to the boil. Cover with the lid and cook gently in a moderate oven at 175°C, or on the stove over a gentle heat until tender (approx. 1½ hours).
	(95)	8dl	
	Bouquet Garni	1	
4			Remove the veal, untie the strings and arrange the veal in earthenware dishes. Discard the bouquet garni. Reduce the cooking liquor with the garnish to a consistency which is not too liquid.

5	lemon juice	squeeze	Make sure the veal is hot and pour the sauce over. Sprinkle with a few drops of lemon juice and the chopped mixture of lemon rind, garlic and parsley.
	lemon rind, grated	1 tsp	
	garlic, crushed	1 clove	
	parsley, chopped	1 tbsp	

(lemon rind grated, garlic crushed, parsley chopped — chopped together finely)

6	Risotto alla Milanese (531)	4 portions	Serve accompanied with a dish of the risotto.

SPECIAL POINT

The mixture of grated lemon rind, garlic and parsley is an essential finish for this dish. It is referred to as a 'Gremolata'.

980 Pieds de Veau – Calf's Feet

Calf's feet may be prepared and served in any of the ways applicable to Pied de Porc (900).

981 Pied de Veau Grillé – Grilled Calf's Foot
10 portions
2½ hours

Stage	Ingredient	Quantity	Method
1	calf's feet, cleaned and blanched (928)	5	Split the calf's feet in half lengthways and place in the boiling Blanc. Simmer very gently covering with a piece of muslin until cooked and tender (approx. 1½–1¾ hours).
	Blanc (15)	5 litres	
2			Remove the feet from the liquid and carefully remove and discard all the bones. Wash the feet, dry with kitchen paper and allow to cool.
3	English mustard	50g	Cut each half of the calf's feet into two or three pieces, season and well coat the top surfaces with the mustard diluted not too thinly with water. Turn mustard side down into the breadcrumbs to coat them well, then turn back, pat with the flat of a palette knife and place on a well-buttered tray. Sprinkle well with melted butter then grill to a golden brown under the salamander.
	breadcrumbs, white	125g	
	butter, melted	100g	
4	parsley, picked		Arrange the feet on suitable dishes, garnish with picked parsley and serve accompanied with sauceboats of either sauce as deemed appropriate.
	Sauce Tomate (118) or Sauce Diable (125)	6dl	

982 Paupiette de Veau

Prepare in the same way as Paupiette de Boeuf (831), using cushion or under-cushion of veal. Garnish in any of the ways applicable to Paupiette de Boeuf.

983 Pojarski de Veau Smitaine

10 portions
1 hour

Stage	Ingredient	Quantity	Method
1	veal, trimmed of fat and sinew	1kg	Pass through the fine plate of the mincer twice.
2	breadcrumbs, white milk	150g 2dl	Soak the breadcrumbs in the milk and squeeze out surplus milk. Add the bread to the meat and mix in well.
3	double cream	3dl	Season the mixture with salt, pepper and a little grated nutmeg. Work in the cream a little at a time using a wooden spoon; mix thoroughly and beat well.
4	flour		Divide the mixture into ten equal pieces and mould cutlet-shape using flour. Place on a floured tray.
5	butter	100g	Heat the butter in a sauté pan, place in the Pojarskis and shallow fry to a golden brown on both sides until cooked (12–15 mins.). To test when cooked, press gently and any juices appearing should be clear with no sign of blood. Remove and arrange in earthenware dishes.
6	onion, finely chopped white wine, dry	75g 2dl	Add the onion to the pan and cook without colour. Drain off the fat then add the wine and reduce by two-thirds.
7	cream, sour juice of lemon	7dl	Add and reduce to a light coating consistency. Add a good squeeze of lemon juice and adjust the seasoning. Pass through a fine strainer and keep hot.
8			Make sure the Pojarskis are hot then coat with a little of the sauce. Send the rest of the sauce separately in a sauce-boat.

984 RIS DE VEAU– CALF'S SWEETBREADS

Calf's sweetbreads provide a useful range of light delicate entrées suited to either lunch or dinner menus. They may be braised, shallow-fried or grilled with various garnishes and also serve as ingredients for Salpicons, stuffings and garnishes for other meat dishes.

There are two kinds of sweetbread, the throat sweetbread which is the thymus gland and the heart sweetbread which is the pancreas gland. Where flavour is concerned there is little to choose between them but the larger round shape of the heart sweetbread is more useful for presentation, either whole or as Escalopes or Médaillons, when shallow-fried or grilled. The throat sweetbread is a little smaller, longer and more irregular in shape. They can present well if braised but other than this would be the first choice for use in mixtures for Vols-au-vent and Salpicons.

985 Ris de Veau braisé – Braised Calf's Sweetbread 10 portions
2 hours

Stage	Ingredient	Quantity	Method
1	butter	75g	Butter a braising pan well and line the bottom with the aromates and bacon trimmings. Place the sweetbreads on top. Season, cover with the lid and place in a hot oven for 15 mins. Remove the pan from the oven and place on the stove.
	calf's sweetbreads, prepared for cooking (933)	10 × 125g	
	carrots ⎫	150g	
	onions ⎬ sliced	150g	
	celery ⎭	100g	
	bacon trimmings	75g	
	bayleaf	½	
	thyme	sprig	
2	Fonds Blanc de Veau (95)	2 litres	Add sufficient stock to come one-third of the way up the sweetbreads. Bring to the boil and reduce well to a glaze. Add more stock to come half the way up the sweetbreads, bring to the boil, cover with a buttered greaseproof paper and lid and place in the oven at 175°C for approx. 45 mins.
3			Remove the lid and paper and baste the sweetbreads frequently to glaze to a golden colour for approx. 30–45 mins. until tender. Remove from the oven and dress the sweetbreads in porcelain or earthenware cocottes.
4			Pass the cooking liquor through a fine strainer into a clean pan, skim off the fat and reduce to approx. 3dl. Adjust the seasoning, pour over the sweetbreads and cover with the lids.

986 Ris de Veau braisé au Madère

10 portions
2 hours

Stage	Ingredient	Quantity	Method
1	butter	75g	Butter a braising pan well and line the
	calf's sweetbreads,		bottom with the aromats and bacon
	prepared for cooking		trimmings. Place the sweetbreads on top.
	(933)	10 × 125g	Season, cover with the lid and place on
	carrots⎫	150g	the stove for a few minutes to lightly
	onions⎬ sliced	150g	colour the vegetables.
	celery⎭	100g	
	bacon trimmings	80g	
	bayleaf	½	
	thyme	sprig	
2	Madeira	1½dl	Add the Madeira and reduce by half
	Fonds Brun de Veau		then add sufficient stock to come half-
	(98)	1½ litres	way up the sweetbreads. Bring to the
			boil, cover with a buttered greaseproof
			paper and lid and place in the oven at
			175°C for approx. 45 mins.
3			Remove the lid and paper and baste the
			sweetbreads frequently to glaze to a
			golden brown for approx. 30–45 mins.
			until tender. Remove from the oven and
			dress the sweetbreads in porcelain or
			earthenware cocottes.
4	Demi-glace (112)	4dl	Pass the cooking liquid through a fine
			strainer into a clean pan, skim off the fat
			and reduce by half. Add the demi-glace
			and reduce to a light coating consistency.
			Adjust the seasoning, pour over the
			sweetbreads and cover with the lids.

987 Ris de Veau Bonne-Maman

Prepare Ris de Veau braisé (985). Before adding the reduced cooking liquor, garnish the sweetbreads with 150g each of carrot, leek and celery cut into julienne (4cm long × 2mm square) and stewed together under cover with 25g butter and ½dl of the veal stock. Cover with the lids and place in a medium oven for 10 mins. to reheat well.

988 Ris de Veau à la Crème

Prepare the sweetbreads as for Ris de Veau braisé (985) to the end of Stage 3. Dress the sweetbreads in earthenware dishes and keep warm. Strain the cooking liquor into a clean pan, skim off the fat and reduce by two-thirds. Add 4dl Béchamel (114) and 2dl cream and reduce to a coating consistency. Adjust the seasoning and coat the sweetbreads with the sauce.

989 Ris de Veau Financière

Prepare Ris de Veau braisé au Madère (986) but arrange in earthenware dishes and garnish with bouquets of Quenelles de Veau (82), button mushrooms sautéed in butter, cockscombs and kidneys (25) and stoned and blanched olives. Coat the sweetbreads only with the sauce, then place a nice slice of truffle on each.

990 Ris de Veau panés

10 portions
30 mins

Stage	Ingredient	Quantity	Method
1	calf's sweetbreads, prepared for cooking (933)	10 × 125g	Cut each of the sweetbreads into half horizontally. Paner à l'Anglaise (72), lightly flatten, reshape and mark trellis-fashion on one side with the back of a knife.
	flour	} for	
	eggwash	} crumbing	
	breadcrumbs	}	
2	oil	3dl	Heat in a sauté pan and shallow fry the sweetbreads on both sides to a golden brown, (approx. 5 mins.). Remove and dress in earthenware dishes, decorated side uppermost.
3	Jus lié (113)	3dl	Surround the sweetbreads with a little jus lié. Place the butter in a suitable frying-pan and cook until nut-brown, shaking the pan to ensure even colouring. Pour carefully over the sweetbreads.
	butter	150g	

SPECIAL POINT
It is advisable to use round (pancreas) sweetbreads for Médaillons de Ris de Veau panés. Sweetbreads obtained from the throat (thymus) are longer and more irregular in shape than the pancreas and are difficult to cut into a presentable shape.

991 Ris de Veau Princesse

Prepare Ris de Veau à la Crème (988) and garnish with Asparagus Sprue (1388) and slices of truffle.

992 Médaillons de Ris de Veau Maréchale

Prepare Ris de Veau panés (990) and garnish with bouquets of Asparagus Sprue (1388) and slices of truffle.

993 Médaillons de Ris de Veau Saint-Germain

10 portions
25 mins

Stage	Ingredient	Quantity	Method
1	calf's sweetbreads, prepared for cooking (933)	10 × 125g	Cut each sweetbread in half horizontally. Season, flour very lightly and dip in melted butter. Grill quickly on both sides to a golden brown.
	flour		
	butter, melted	75g	

Stage	Ingredient	Quantity	Method
2	Pommes Parisienne (1587)	350g	Arrange the sweetbreads on suitable dishes and garnish with bouquets of the Pommes Parisienne and glazed carrots. Serve accompanied with the sauce.
	Carottes glacées (1400)	350g	
	Sauce Béarnaise (153)	5dl	

994 Rognon de Veau à la Dijonnaise

4 portions
25 mins.

Stage	Ingredient	Quantity	Method
1	calf's kidney	500g	Remove the skin, cut in half lengthways and cut away any core, gristle or tubes showing. Cut into small thickish slices for sauté (931).
2	butter	75g	Heat the butter in a heavy metal frying-pan. Season the kidney with salt and milled pepper and add to the butter as it begins to turn brown. Sauté quickly by turning over and over. Keep slightly underdone then remove to a colander to drain.
3	shallots, finely chopped	50g	Place the shallots in the same fat and cook gently without colour. Drain off the fat, add the wine and reduce by half.
	white wine, dry	2dl	
4	cream	2dl	Add the cream, reduce to a coating consistency then add the mustard. Reheat but do not boil. Adjust the seasoning plus a touch of nutmeg.
	Dijon mustard	1 tbsp	
	nutmeg, grated		
5	parsley, chopped		Place the kidneys in a cocotte, make sure that it is hot then pass the sauce through a fine strainer over the kidney. Sprinkle with a little parsley.

995 Rognon de Veau à la Fine Champagne

1–2 portions
45 mins.

Stage	Ingredient	Quantity	Method
1	calf's kidney	1 × 250g	Remove any excess fat and any core or gristle with the point of a sharp knife. Leave whole.
2	butter, melted	25g	Place in a small casserole and heat. Season the kidney with salt and milled pepper then place in the butter and colour quickly on all sides. Cover with the lid and place in the oven at approx. 210°C for 20 mins. and baste occasionally.
3	Fine Champagne brandy	½dl	Remove from the oven, add the brandy and flamber (32). Cover with the lid and replace in the oven for another 5 mins.

or so but keep slightly underdone. When
ready, transfer the kidney to a clean
cocotte.

4	Fonds brun de Veau		Do not tip out the fat from the casserole.
	(98)	1dl	Add the stock and rapidly reduce until
	butter	50g	viscous then shake in the butter. Season
	cayenne		well plus a touch of cayenne.
5			Make sure the kidney and dish are hot then pass the sauce through a fine strainer over the kidney. Send immediately.

---

996 Rognonnade de Veau aux Salsifis

10 portions
3½ hours

Stage	Ingredient	Quantity	Method
1	loin of veal, including kidney	2¾kg	Bone out the loin carefully and trim. Remove the skin from the kidney and cut out the core and any gristly parts. Chop the bones small.
2	coriander, ground brandy pork sausage-meat	1 tbsp 750g	Flatten the flank of the veal with a cutlet bat then season and rub the inside of the veal with salt, pepper and a little coriander and sprinkle with the brandy. Season the kidney and enclose in the sausagemeat, then place this in the centre of the veal. Roll neatly, making sure that the kidney does not become exposed at either end but is sealed in with the sausage-meat. Tie securely along the length of the loin.
3	butter coriander, ground carrots celery onion mushroom fennel bacon, chopped garlic, crushed bayleaf, crushed thyme	100g 200g 200g 200g 200g 150g 100g 1 clove 1 sprig	Heat the butter in a suitably-sized braising pan. Season the prepared veal with salt, pepper and a little coriander then colour to a good brown on all sides in the butter. Remove the veal then add the vegetables and herbs to the pan. Replace the veal on top with the chopped bones to one side.
4	white wine, dry	5dl	Add the wine, cover and place in a moderately hot oven at 180°C to cook slowly for approx. 1¾–2 hours. Baste frequently and turn the joint occasionally. Remove the veal, cover and keep warm.

Stage 3: carrots, celery, onion, mushroom, fennel — roughly chopped

5	Fonds Brun de Veau (98)	6dl	Add the stock to the pan and ingredients. Simmer for a few mins. and skim of all fat. Discard the bones then liquidise all the ingredients from the cooking. Pass firmly through a fine strainer into a clean pan, reduce to about 5dl and adjust the seasoning. Cover and keep hot.
6	parsley, chopped Salsifis sautés (1517)	5 portions	Carve the joint neatly into approx. 3mm-thick slices and arrange overlapping in earthenware dishes. Coat with a little of the gravy and place the salsifis to one side. Sprinkle with chopped parsley.

---

997 SAUTÉS OF VEAL

There are a number of veal dishes described as sautés which do not appear to conform to those principles which define an authentic sauté, i.e. the meat is cooked as necessary by shallow frying and the sauce is finished then added without further cooking of the meat.

In many cases the veal is often cooked for a period of time in its sauce until tender and in effect this seems to have something more in common with the preparation of a stew. However, it is not the length of time needed to render the meat tender which distinguishes this type of a sauté from a stew but the fact that a) after the meat is browned, it is not sprinkled with flour for the making of its sauce, and b) the cooking is finished either in a prepared sauce or in a sauce prepared from the pan juices, i.e. deglazed with such things as stock, cream, wine or sauce etc.

For these reasons, it could be unwise to describe a sauté of veal which requires a longer cooking time as a Ragoût, and in any case this rather plebeian term does not sit comfortably on such a valuable commodity.

---

998 Sauté de Veau aux Champignons

10 portions
2¼ hours

Stage	Ingredient	Quantity	Method
1	butter shoulder or neck of veal, cut into 2½cm cubes	75g 1¼kg	Heat the butter in a frying-pan, season the veal and fry quickly until brown on all sides. Drain and place the veal in a braising pan.
2	Estouffade (97) Demi-glace (112) Bouquet Garni	½ litre 1 litre 1	Add to the veal, bring to the boil, skim, cover with the lid and cook in a moderate oven at 175°C for 1–1½ hours until tender.
3	butter button mushrooms	75g 600g	Discard the bouquet garni and remove the veal to a clean pan. Wash the mushrooms and sauté them in the butter. Add to the veal.
4	parsley, chopped		Adjust the seasoning and consistency of the sauce and pass through a fine strainer over the veal and mushrooms.

Simmer gently for 10 mins. Serve in
earthenware dishes sprinkled with
chopped parsley.

999 Sauté de Filet de Veau aux Chanterelles   4 portions
                                                   25 mins.

Stage	Ingredient	Quantity	Method
1	veal fillet	600g	Trim the fillet of any sinew or fat then
	butter	75g	cut into strips approx. 5cm long by ½cm square. Heat the butter in a heavy frying-pan. Season the veal and add to the pan just as the butter begins to turn brown. Sauté quickly tossing over and over until just cooked. Remove from the pan and reserve.
2	shallots, very finely chopped	50g	Add the shallots to the pan and cook without colour then add the chanterelles,
	chanterelles, trimmed and carefully washed	300g	season, cover with a lid and cook for 4–5 mins. Add the sherry and reduce by half.
	sherry, dry	½dl	
3	Crème Fraîche	2dl	Add the cream, reduce to a coating
	butter	50g	consistency, shake in the butter and
	cayenne		season as required plus a touch of cayenne. Replace the veal in with the sauce and chanterelles. Reheat but do not boil.
4	small Heart-shaped Croûtons, lightly coloured (26)	8	Place the sauté in a porcelain cocotte or similar, surround with the croûtons and sprinkle with a little chopped parsley.
	parsley		Cover with the lid and send.

1000 Sauté de Veau à la Portugaise   10 portions
                                          2¼ hours

Stage	Ingredient	Quantity	Method
1	oil	2dl	Heat the oil in a braising pan. When hot,
	shoulder or neck of veal, cut into 2½cm cubes	1¼kg	season the veal and fry until brown on all sides.
2	onions, finely chopped	250g	Add the onions and garlic and colour lightly. Drain off the oil, add the wine
	garlic, finely chopped	1 clove	and reduce by half.
	white wine, dry	3dl	
3	Tomates Concassées (90)	750g	Add to the veal, bring to the boil, skim, cover with the lid and cook in a
	Demi-glace (112)	1 litre	moderate oven at 175°C for
	Bouquet Garni	1	1–1½ hours until tender.

| 4 | parsley, chopped | | Remove from the oven. Discard the bouquet garni and adjust the seasoning. Serve in earthenware dishes sprinkled with parsley. |

1001 Selle de Veau – Saddle of Veal

This can be a very large joint, in some cases as much as 9–10kg in weight, and thus it requires much in the way of professional expertise for its cooking and service. Well-garnished and well-presented it can make an excellent centre-piece for the cold buffet and can be just as impressive when carved hot from the trolley in the restaurant.

It is best when roasted or poêléed and with care can be very successful as a braised joint. All the preparations and garnishes for cushion of veal and saddle of lamb are suitable.

1002 Tête de Veau Poulette

5–6 portions
5 hours

Stage	Ingredient	Quantity	Method
1	Blanc (15)	5 litres	Bring the blanc to the boil with the carrot, onion and bouquet garni then add the ears, tongue and pieces of calf's head. Reboil, cover with a clean cloth or muslin and simmer gently until tender (1½–2 hours). Remove the ears and reserve for other uses.
	carrot ⎫ whole	2	
	onion ⎬	2	
	Bouquet Garni	1	
	calf's head, prepared for cooking (929)	1	
2	calf's brains (927), prepared for cooking	1 set	Place the brains in the court-bouillon, bring to the boil and poach gently for 5 mins. Keep warm.
	Court-bouillon (538)	1 litre	
3	Sauce Poulette (149)	4dl	Arrange the calf's head in earthenware dishes with slices of the skinned tongue and small slices of the cooked brains. Coat with the sauce.

1003 Tête de Veau en Tortue

5–6 portions
5 hours

Stage	Ingredient	Quantity	Method
1	Blanc (15)	5 litres	Bring the blanc to the boil with the carrot, onion and bouquet garni then add the ears, tongue and pieces of calf's head. Reboil, cover with a clean cloth or muslin and simmer gently until tender (1½–2 hours). Remove the ears and reserve for other uses.
	carrot	1	
	onion	1	
	Bouquet Garni	1	
	calf's head, prepared for cooking (929)	1	
2	calf's brains (927), prepared for cooking	1 set	Place the brains in the court-bouillon, bring to the boil and poach gently for 5 mins. Keep warm.
	Court-bouillon (538)	1 litre	
3			Dress the calf's head in earthenware dishes with slices of the skinned tongue and small slices of the cooked brains.

4	Sauce Tortue (138)	4dl	Place the quenelles, mushrooms, olives
	Quenelles de Veau		and gherkins in the sauce and ladle over
	(82)	18	the calf's head. Garnish the dish with
	button mushrooms,		the fried eggs, croûtons and slices of
	sautéed in butter	18	truffle.
	olives, stoned and		
	blanched	12	
	small gherkins,		
	blanched	12	
	Oeufs frits à la		
	Française (442)	6	
	Heart-shaped Croûtons		
	(26)	6	
	slices of truffle	6	

1004 Tête de Veau Vinaigrette – Calf's Head, Sauce Vinaigrette

Prepare as Tête de Veau en Tortue (1003) to Stage 3 only. Moisten with a little of the cooking liquor and garnish with sprigs of parsley. Serve accompanied with a sauceboat of Sauce Vinaigrette (190).

1005 Wiener Schnitzel

10 portions
25 mins.

Stage	Ingredient	Quantity	Method
1	veal escalopes	10 × 125g	The escalopes should be not less than
	flour		3–4mm thick and nicked every 3–4cm
	eggwash	for	about 1cm in around the edge. Season
	breadcrumbs,	crumbing	with salt and paner à l'Anglaise (72).
	white		Lightly flatten and mark trellis-fashion
			on both sides with the back of a knife.
2	lemon, quarters	10	Deep fry in hot fat at 175°C to a golden
	parsley, picked		brown, approx. 6 mins. Drain well on
			kitchen paper and arrange on dish
			papers on under dishes. Garnish with
			wedges of lemon and picked parsley.

SPECIAL POINT

Traditionally the escalope for a Wiener Schnitzel is prepared from a veal cutlet with the bone removed and trimmed of any fat and sinew. It should never be too thin and should be nicked around the edges to prevent undue curling when being fried. Its only garnish is lemon; warm potato salad or pommes sautées, together with a tossed salad, are the more usual accompaniments.

13
Poultry

Poultry is a collective term used to describe domestic birds reared for human consumption. It includes the different varieties and sizes of chickens, turkeys, ducks, geese and guinea-fowl. Although guinea-fowl is classified as poultry, its colour and flavour are somewhat akin to pheasant and it is very often treated as a game bird. Pigeons are also included under the heading of poultry although wood pigeons are shot as game and have dark red flesh. Reared pigeons are not considered to be game birds; the flesh is lighter in colour and the flavour is more delicate and less strong than that of the wild pigeon.

In common with most white meats the flavour of chicken is fairly neutral and this easily assimilates added flavourings and seasonings. In particular chicken provides a readily digestible form of protein and is suitable for use in a wide range of excellent entrées appropriate to lunch and dinner menus.

Presented whole and garnished appropriately, turkey, large chicken, duck and goose also make an important contribution to the repertoire of main dishes and relevés.

Poultry is available in fresh, chilled and frozen form in various weights and sizes and it is usual to purchase fresh items plucked and cleaned ready for final preparation and cooking. When using frozen poultry it is essential to defrost it thoroughly in a refrigerator and to ensure that it is completely cooked.

Offals of Poultry (Giblets)

The giblets or offals of poultry are useful in the preparation of many dishes and at the very least can always be used in the preparation of stocks. It is utterly wasteful to discard them as of no value; it is only necessary that they be fresh, stored correctly and used as soon as possible.

Livers: these can be utilised as garnishes, for small composed entrées such as pilaff, kebabs and sautés, and in the making of pâtés, terrines, stuffings and pies. Large duck and goose livers of the correct quality are used in the preparation of foie gras.

Cockscombs and kidneys: these are used as part of many classical garnishes such as Financière and Tortue.

Hearts: generally used in the making of particular stocks or consommés.

Gizzards: although usually used in the making of stocks, larger ones from turkey, duck or goose can be used as part of giblet stews, braisings or pies.

Necks: these are useful in the making of stocks. Large turkey necks cut in sections may be used in the preparation of turkey giblet stews, e.g. Abatis de Dinde Bourgeoise.

Winglets: chicken winglets are useful as garnishes for consommés and may be used in the preparation of certain pilaffs. Turkey winglets can be used as part of giblet stews or braisings and because of their size may be used separately in their own right, e.g. Ailerons de Dinde à la Chipolata. They may also be boned, stuffed and braised. Other winglets can be useful in the preparation of particular flavoured stocks and consommés.

QUALITY POINTS

Like butcher's meats the quality of poultry is influenced by such factors as the breed of the bird, the methods of rearing, its sex, age at slaughter and the way it is then processed as either fresh, chilled or frozen. As general points to be considered, all fresh poultry should have a fresh smell devoid of any unpleasant odour, the skin should be unbroken with no signs of tearing or damage, and its surface just moist but without any stickiness or, conversely, any dried patches.

Chicken

All chickens should have plump firm breasts with unbroken skin. The end of the breastbone should be flexible and the legs covered with small scales. Any spurs on the legs should be small. Any discolouration of the bird with an attendant stickiness and smell is a sign of deterioration in quality. Boiling fowls usually show marked signs of toughness. For example, the end of the breastbone is firm and hard, the skin usually shows an abundance of long hairs before singeing and the legs are covered with large shiny, hard scales. However, a boiling fowl should still be plump and of a white to creamy appearance – not wasted and scrawny or with discoloured skin. Apart from the usual white breeds there are some speciality-bred chickens which look and taste different, such as corn-fed birds which are pale yellow to light orange in colour, Bresse chickens from France which are fattened on maize and buckwheat, and other named special breeds identified usually by darker skins and leg scales. Free-range chicken are presumed to have a better flavour. Battery-bred chicken may show pecking marks on the lower leg which can detract from their appearance if presented whole with the legs on.

Turkey

Good quality is determined by a large plump well-formed breast with small legs in proportion to the size of the bird. The skin should be unbroken and of a white to bluish colour. A clean fresh smell is essential as a gamey smell will result in a strong flavour when cooked. Hen birds are more tender than cocks though the male has a higher proportion of flesh to bone; the male bird can be recognised by its chest tassel, large wattles and a shorter neck than the hen. The weight can range from 3 to 10kg.

Duck and Goose

Ducklings should have a well-formed breast, unbroken skin with no excessive fat under it and no signs of stickiness. The end of the breastbone should be pliable and the webbed feet clean in colour and easy to tear. The Aylesbury breed is the most popular, with ducklings weighing from 2kg to 2½kg and ducks from 2½kg to 3kg. The Rouennaise duck from France is killed by smothering so as to retain the blood in its flesh. It is larger and more plump than the Aylesbury duck and its flesh is darker in colour.

Geese are available in many different weights from approx. 4kg to 7kg according to breed and age. The quality signs of the young bird are a light skin with the minimum of stubble or feather pins, smooth thin legs and a smooth bill thinning around the nostrils. The upper mandible will break easily under pressure of the finger and thumb.

Guinea-fowl

The breast should be relatively plump with unbroken skin although it is a smaller and thinner bird than the chicken. Its flesh is slightly darker than chicken but should not be too much so. If too dark this usually suggests an older bird with drier flesh.

All other qualities for chicken are applicable. Guinea-fowl is at its best during the months of December to June.

Pigeon

The young farmed pigeon should have a very plump, well-formed breast, light reddish in colour. The flesh at the end of the breast should break easily under the pressure of the thumb and finger and the claws should be clean, pinkish in colour and with no signs of deformation. Wild or wood pigeon are larger in size with much darker flesh and in general are much tougher. These are mostly suitable for braising or for casseroles.

Offals (Giblets)

In the normal course of events giblets would be supplied with the birds from which they derive and as such should reflect their own high quality. If bought separately the following quality points are important. Giblets should have a good, bright colour, with no signs of stickiness, seeping of blood or moisture and above all should be devoid of any bad smell. Livers in particular should have a good colour even if rather pale, be firm to the touch and show no signs of green from damaged gall-bladders. Any frozen giblets should have a good colour and show no signs of drying or freezer-burn; they should always be delivered in a correctly frozen state.

STORAGE

All items of poultry are purchased by numbers of birds of a required average weight each, rather than by total weight. In whichever form poultry is purchased, fresh, chilled or frozen, it must be treated as a highly perishable commodity and be stored correctly. Fresh and chilled birds should be placed in single layers on trays, not stacked on top of each other, and stored at 2–3°C. They should be used within 3 days. If undrawn, fresh birds can be hung in the refrigerator for a short period of time but should be kept well-separated from any other poultry or fresh meat. In this state they should be kept for no longer than 3–4 days and should not be allowed to develop any stickiness, discolouration or unpleasant odour before using. For preference, undrawn poultry are best kept in a completely separate refrigerator used for this purpose only and with all possible care taken to ensure clean and hygienic conditions. Frozen poultry must be stored at −18°C or below in a deep-freeze unit until required for use and used in rotation. It is advisable to allow 24 hours for deep-frozen birds to defrost in the refrigerator at approx. 5–6°C. Frozen poultry often have the giblets enclosed in a packet inside the bird. This must be removed before cooking.

PREPARATIONS AND CUTS FOR COOKING

1006 Plucking, Drawing, Singeing and Cleaning

For the most part all poultry is bought ready-plucked and drawn although chicken and turkey is sometimes delivered to be hung for a short period of time. This does tend to develop flavour but should not be for too long, 3–4 days at the most, and in ideal well-ventilated and refrigerated conditions separate from other food. Too long a period of hanging will develop a pronounced gamey flavour out of keeping with the particular qualities of poultry. Even if delivered in a so-called oven-ready condition, poultry will always require singeing to remove any remaining hairs and any remaining feathers or feather pins will also have to be removed.

Plucking
This is best left to the producers or suppliers of poultry who can do this in satisfactory and hygienic conditions. However, if for some reason or other it is necessary to pluck a bird the procedure is quite simple and consists of four main elements:
1) Use the thumb and side of the forefinger, preferably wet, to hold the feathers.
2) Pull out backwards in the opposite direction to the growth of the feathers.
3) Start from the tail end of the back then the wings and legs followed by the breast and finally the neck.
4) Do not jerk forcibly but always endeavour to remove the feathers in small clumps and without tearing the flesh.

Drawing
1) Turn the bird over, hold the neck firmly so that the skin is tight and make an incision along the back of the neck from the body to the head.
2) Cut off the head, remove the neck from the incision and cut off close to the body.
3) Separate the windpipe and crop from the skin flap and remove.
4) Trim the skin flap to leave sufficient to tuck well under the body.
5) Insert the forefinger or middle finger at the neck end, carefully manoeuvre it round to detach the intestines and lungs from the chest cavity.
6) Cut out the vent taking care not to burst the end of the gut.
7) Insert the forefinger at the vent end and detach the intestines from the abdominal cavity by carefully moving the finger round from one side to the other.
8) Insert the first two fingers over the top of the intestines right to the back of the bird and carefully remove the whole of the insides. Take care not to rupture the intestines or break the gall-bladder on the liver. Check the inside of the bird with the fingers to remove anything left, especially the lungs which are found lying at the back between the rib bones.
9) If carefully done there is no need to clean the inside of the bird but if the intestine or gut at the vent end have soiled any part of the bird, then it should be washed then dried with a clean cloth or kitchen paper.
10) Clean and reserve the giblets:
    a) Neck: this should have nothing attached
    b) Heart: trim off membrane and blood vessels.
    c) Gizzard: completely cut free from any attached gut and remove any fat. Cut through sideways at the thickest part but just to the stomach lining then pull open and discard the lining and its contents. Wash in cold water.
    d) Liver: carefully cut away the gall-bladder and any green discolouration on the surface of the liver. Take care not to burst the gall-bladder; this would make the liver taste bitter. Pigeon liver has no gall-bladder.

NOTE
If any chicken has good-sized combs and/or kidneys they should be reserved and prepared for use. See Recipe 25.

Singeing and Cleaning
Hold the bird at both ends and pass quickly over a suitable flame, usually gas, and turn over and round so that all parts are singed. Be careful not to burn the skin.

Carefully remove any remaining feather pins by trapping them between the back of a small knife and the thumb and pulling out. Finally, wipe clean with a clean cloth.

1007 Trussing

The following two-string methods of trussing always give the best possible shape to poultry whether for roasting, poêling, braising or poaching.

To Truss for Roasting

Chicken, Capon, Poussin, Guinea-fowl
1) Singe the drawn bird to remove any hairs and remove any feather pins with a small knife.
2) Cut off three claws from each leg leaving the centre one with only the tip cut off. Cut the tendon across the top of the legs behind the leg joint.
3) Lift the flap of skin at the neck end and remove the wishbone, turn the flap back under the bird.
4) Cut off the tip and small spur of each winglet and turn the end of the winglets underneath the bird to hold the skin flap in place.
5) Place the bird upright on its back and push the legs back firmly to the carcase.
6) Push the stringed trussing needle through the middle of one leg near the joint and out through the other leg on the opposite side. Leave 7-8cm. of string sticking out for tying.
7) Turn the bird on its side and pass the needle through the centre of the winglet, the tip of the winglet and the flap of the skin, and likewise through the other winglet. Tie the two ends of the string together tightly.
8) Stand the bird on its back again. Push the needle through the carcase under the end of the legs, then pass the needle over the top of the legs without going through the flesh. Pull tight to bring the legs together and tie securely.

Turkey
1) Singe the drawn bird to remove any hairs and remove any feather pins with a small knife.
2 Remove the winglets at the first joint away from the body.
3) Break the bone on the legs between the feet and the first joint by striking firmly with the back of a chopper or heavy knife. Do not cut through the skin or tendons. Twist the ends of the legs round so as to ensure a completely separated break of the bones. Place in the special V-shaped hook or sinew extractor and pull out the sinews from the leg.
4) Lift the flap of skin at the neck end and remove the wishbone, turn the flap back under the bird.
5) Truss securely with very strong string in the same way as for chicken, Stages 5–8.

Duck, Goose and Pigeon
These are prepared and trussed for roasting in the same way as chickens. Before stringing remove the winglets and cut off the ends of the webbed feet of ducks and geese, or claws in the case of pigeon. The livers of pigeon may be left in.

To Truss 'en Entrée' for Poêling, Braising or Poaching

Chicken, Capon, Poussin and Guinea-fowl
1) Singe the drawn bird to remove any hairs. Remove any feather pins with a small knife.

2) Cut off three of the claws from each leg leaving the centre one with just its tip cut off.
3) Lift the flap of skin at the neck end and remove the wishbone, turn the flap back under the bird.
4) Cut the tendon underneath the legs just behind the leg joint. Make an incision in the skin on each side of the bird 3–4cm back from the vent end, fold the legs over and push the end of the folded joint through the incision.
5) Cut off the tip and small spur of each winglet and turn the end of the winglets underneath the bird to hold the skin flap in place.
6) Place the bird upright on its back and push the legs back firmly to the carcase.
7) Push the stringed trussing needle through the middle of one leg near the joint and out through the other leg on the opposite side. Leave 7–8cm of string sticking out for tying.
8) Turn the bird on its side and pass the needle through the centre of the winglet, the tip of the winglet then the flap of skin, and likewise through the other winglet. Tie the two ends of the string together tightly.
9) Stand the bird on its back again. Push the needle through the carcase under the ends of the legs, then pass the needle over the top of the first folded leg then through the incisions at each side and finally over the top of the other folded leg. Pull tight to bring the legs together and tie securely.

Duck
Ducks are trussed for poêling and braising in the same way as roast chicken. Before stringing, remove the winglets, cut off the ends of the webbed feet, fold back the lower legs and twist round and under so as to lie along the bottom sides of the legs.

SPECIAL POINTS
a) The leg sinews of large chicken are sometimes very pronounced and can be removed in the same way as in Stage 3 of trussing for turkey. If the lower legs need to be left on for presentation make a small incision through the skin just behind the joints, push the blunt end of a large trussing needle through and under each sinew then twist the needle round and round until each sinew becomes free enough to be pulled out and detached.
b) It is only necessary to truss poultry with the lower legs on for roasting or turned back for poêling, etc., if the bird is to be presented whole before carving.
c) It can be advantageous to remove the scales from the lower legs of chicken before trussing and where the bird is to be presented whole. This can be done either by placing the lower legs into boiling water for a few seconds or by passing the singeing flame over them for just sufficient time to loosen the scales. They can then be rubbed off with a piece of rough cloth.

1008 Trussing (alternative single string method)

Either of the previous two-string methods of trussing are to be preferred in all cases where the best possible shape is required for presentation and are essential for the trussing of turkey and other large birds. However, the following single-string method can give good results for other birds and in some respects can be a little quicker.
1) Place the prepared bird upright on its back and push the legs back firmly to the carcase.

2) Push the stringed trussing needle through the lower carcase just under the end of the drumstick, then diagonally out through the middle of the joint of the leg on the opposite side, leave 7–8cm of string sticking out.

3) Turn the bird on its side then pass the needle through the centre of the winglet, the tip of the winglet and through the flap of skin and likewise through the other winglet.

4) Stand the bird on its back again. Push the needle through the middle of the joint of the other leg then diagonally to come out of the lower carcase under the end of the other drumstick.

5) Pass the needle over the top of the legs just behind the joints. Pull the strings tightly to pull the bird into shape and tie securely.

1009 To Stuff a Bird for Roasting

Chicken, Turkey and Guinea-fowl: these can be stuffed in one of three ways.

1) Prepare the bird for trussing (1007), fill the inside cavity with the selected stuffing leaving a little room for expansion. Turn the parson's nose in to prevent the stuffing from escaping then truss in the usual manner but catching the end of the parson's nose with the needle at the last stage when going over the legs.

2) Prepare the bird for trussing (1007) and after removing the wishbone loosen the skin from the neck end of the breast and turn it back. Place a suitable amount of stuffing at the neck end, pull the flap of skin over and tuck underneath the bird. Truss carefully and mould the stuffed end to give a good shape.

3) Prepare the bird for trussing (1007). Stuff the bird in both places. This is especially suitable for large chickens, capons and turkeys where the stuffing needs to show as part of a special presentation for carving but where there would be insufficient stuffing in the neck end of the breast.

Duck and Geese: these birds should only be stuffed inside and never at the neck end. Proceed as above for the stuffing of chicken.

1010 Preparation for Grilling

Chicken, Poussin and Pigeon

1) Prepare the bird in the same way as for poêling but do not string.

2) Place the bird on its back, place a knife through the bird from the vent end on one side of the backbone and cut through.

3) Open the bird out flat, cut the backbone away and flatten carefully with a cutlet bat.

1011 Preparation for Grilling 'en Crapaudine'

Chicken, Poussin and Pigeon

1) Prepare the bird in the same way as for poêling but do not string.

2) Stand the bird on its back then cut horizontally from just below the point of the breast over the top of the legs and down to the wing joints without detaching the breast.

3) Lay back the breast and flatten carefully with a cutlet bat. The shape will resemble a toad or frog.

SPECIAL POINT
It is best not to remove the rib bones of any bird before grilling as this encourages the tender white flesh to become dry before the legs are cooked. These bones are better removed after the bird is cooked and just before being carved and served.

1012 Preparation of Suprêmes of Chicken

Young chickens weighing 1¼–1½kg are suitable for cutting into suprêmes; each bird will yield two suprêmes weighing from 100g to 150g each.
1) Cut off both legs; reserve for other uses.
2) Remove the skin from the breast of the bird.
3) Remove the wishbone.
4) Bare the wing bone adjoining the breast and cut off the winglet just before its joint thus leaving 2–3cm of bare bone attached to the breasts.
5) Cut along close to the breastbone and follow the bone down to the wing joint. Place the point of the knife between the carcase and the wing joint and cut through. Turn the chicken on its side, hold the suprême and remove from the carcase by pulling it away, using the knife to cut and assist.
6) Remove the small fillet from under the suprême and detach the tendon from it.
7) Make an incision lengthways along the thick side of the suprême, open and place the fillet inside. Close up, very lightly flatten and trim only as necessary to a neat shape.

1013 Preparation of Fillets of Poultry

Chicken, Duck, Guinea-fowl and Pigeon
These are cut in the same way as the Suprêmes of chicken but without the wing bone (humerus) being attached. The following points may be considered:
1) The term Filet and Suprême can be interchangeable as far as menu titling is concerned.
2) The fillet, i.e. suprême without the wing bone, is best used when it is to be covered with sauce.
3) The suprême with its wing bone attached is best for shallow-fries or sautéed dishes or where the sauce is served separately. It allows for a more interesting presentation.

1014 Preparation of Poultry for Sauté, Fricassée or Pies

1) Singe the bird to remove any hairs and remove any feather pins with a small knife.
2) Cut under the leg to the joint at the body, turn back the leg from the carcase and cut through the joint. Detach the leg completely from the carcase.
3) Bare the thigh bone and break the bone near the joint; lift out the bone from the thigh. Cut through the centre joint of the leg leaving the small piece of bone attached to the thigh. Make an incision in the thickest part of the drumstick and trim both ends.
4) Remove the winglets and reserve for other uses.
5) Cut along the middle of the flesh on each side of the breastbone down to the wing joint. Place the point of the knife between the carcase and the wing joint. Cut through and pull each wing portion away, assisting with the knife.
6) Chop the remaining breast away from the carcase and cut into two lengthways or diagonally. Allow one piece of leg and one piece of wing or breast per portion.

1015 To Bone out a Bird for Stuffing

1) Singe the drawn bird and remove any feather pins with a small knife.
2) Remove the wishbone and parson's nose; cut off the winglets near the joint at the end of the wing bone (humerus). Cut off the lower legs at the joint with the drumstick.
3) Place the bird on its breast and cut along the centre of the back through the skin and to the bone.   ·
4) With a small sharp knife cut flat along the slit from one side to separate the flesh from the carcase.
5) Cut through the leg joint where it is attached to the back and carry on carefully cutting, always close to the bones, to detach the flesh from the rib-cage.
6) When the breastbone has been reached and freed, turn the bird round and proceed on the other side.
7) Cut through the joint where each wing joins the breast.
8) Carefully detach the whole of the carcase from the flesh at the breast without cutting through the skin.
9) With the point of the knife tunnel out and remove the wing bones.
10) Remove the bone from each thigh; pull the leg in from the skin but do not detach, then remove the bone from the drumsticks. Push the legs back into the skin.
11) Use an appropriate forcemeat to fill the opened out bird. Close up, sew together with fine string, shape and truss carefully. The amount of stuffing should be approx. 75% that of the weight of the boned-out bird. If required for poaching it is advantageous after trussing to wrap and tie the bird in a piece of clean cloth. This can help to preserve its shape.

───────── COOKING METHODS ─────────

In most cases all the methods of cookery may be applied to the full range of poultry with chicken being the most versatile and suited to the widest of applications. Because of their texture, flavour and colour, other poultry are more limited in application but nevertheless make a valuable contribution to the range of menu choice. The use of poultry offals in the preparation of dishes is restricted mainly to the use of the livers and winglets; suitable cooking methods are given in the list of details relating to poultry giblets, page 402.

In general the details concerning the cooking methods for meat are applicable to poultry. However, those factors which are specific to the cooking of poultry are noted in the following paragraphs.

Boiling/Poaching
The process of boiling is used almost exclusively for older and tougher chicken such as boiling fowl. They are best if brought to the boil in water or chicken stock, skimmed, then seasoned lightly and simmered gently with added vegetables and herbs. A low poaching temperature is insufficient to tenderise the flesh.

Whole tender chickens or turkeys are best poached by placing in a lightly seasoned, boiling chicken stock. The temperature should be reduced to where only the slightest trembling movement of the stock is discernible and for preference covered with a piece of muslin or cloth to prevent any surfaces from being exposed to the air. They should be just cooked only. This can be determined by piercing at the thickest part of the leg with a trussing needle. Any juices exuded should be clear with no traces of blood. Allow approx. 15 mins. per 500g weight of bird plus an extra 15 mins. actual poaching time.

The stock from the cooking should always be utilised in the making of the sauce where chicken stock is called for. If needed to be presented whole with the skin on, this may be kept very white by rubbing with lemon juice, covering with slices of salt pork fat and then wrapping in a piece of clean cloth before poaching.

Suprêmes and fillets of all tender young poultry can be successfully shallow-poached. They should be placed in a well-buttered shallow pan, cut side down, and the chosen liquid added, which can range from just a little lemon juice, to a little stock, or wine as called for. They should be seasoned at this stage, covered with a buttered paper and lid, then placed in a moderately hot oven to cook. The time required for this depends on size but it is essential that they be just cooked only, i.e. just firm and resilient to the touch, about 15–18 mins. for a suprême of 120g. The cooking juices should always be used in the accompanying sauce and they need to be served as soon as possible. Any overlong delay results in a progressive toughening of the flesh.

Poached poultry is more suited to dinner menus.

Steaming
This method can be successfully applied to older tough poultry such as boiling fowls, always bearing in mind though that it does not produce any stock. Small cuts such as suprêmes may be steamed in a covered perforated container over boiling water or stock; with suitable vegetables this can produce highly nutritious but at the same time very digestible food.

Stewing
Stewing is an appropriate method of cooking for all kinds of poultry although perhaps better when applied to birds which are not so tender.

The white method usually qualified by the prefix 'Fricassée' is only suitable for chicken, young turkey and guinea-fowl. In this case the bird is cut in portions, seasoned and stiffened in butter without colour, sprinkled with a little flour and cooked out. It is then moistened with an appropriate white stock and flavourings added as required. The finishing of the sauce is either with cream or a liaison of cream and egg yolks.

White-fleshed poultry may also be prepared as a blanquette where the portions of poultry are cooked in a white poultry stock which is used with a roux to prepare its accompanying sauce. The sauce is likewise finished with cream or a liaison of cream and egg yolks.

The brown method can be suitably applied to all poultry and follows in general the same techniques as used for stewed meats. The bird should be first cut in portions, sometimes marinated, then seasoned and coloured in butter together with cut vegetables as called for, then usually sprinkled with flour and cooked out. Any brown stock used should always be appropriate and as with the meats the final amount of sauce should not be overabundant or too thick.

Brown and white stews of poultry are suitable for lunch or dinner.

Braising
Although large chicken or turkey may be braised this slow process gives better results when applied to duck, goose, pigeon and guinea-fowl of an older and tougher nature. The method used is in most points the same as that used for the brown braising of joints of meat. That is, the bird is first seasoned, coloured in fat then placed in a braising pan with the necessary vegetables, herbs and seasonings together with sufficient liquid or sauce to come two-thirds of the way up the bird. After covering with a lid, cooking

should take place slowly and gently in a moderate oven. It is essential to baste the bird frequently with its braising liquid and to turn it occasionally so as to build up a nicely glazed surface.

Baking
In general this process relates to a combined method of preparation where the item of poultry is cooked inside a covering of pastry, for example chicken pie.

Poêling or Pot-Roasting
This is an excellent method of cooking for all poultry of first quality and tenderness. The details regarding the poêling of joints of meat are applicable. The specialised preparations 'en Cocotte' and 'en Casserole' are ideally suited to poussins, chicken, guinea-fowl and pigeon. See 1076.

All items of poêléed poultry are suitable for lunch or dinner.

Roasting
There are two methods of roasting, both of which are suitable for all items of prime, tender poultry.

Spit roasting: this is not commonly practised but the process can impart an excellent and authentic quality. It should be carried out with frequent bastings in front of a clear bright fire and the rotation of the spit and its nearness to the fire should be so adjusted as to give a good golden brown colour to the bird when cooked. Various flavourings and seasonings or wines may be added to the drippings in the basting trough to vary the finished flavour of the bird.

Oven roasting: the following general points are particular to the roasting of poultry:
a) All poultry should always be trussed correctly before roasting. This is essential for giving a good shape to the bird and it also facilitates the carving when cooked.
b) Where felt necessary chicken may be barded with slices of fat bacon for extra succulence and flavour. Guinea-fowl on the other hand need to be barded because of the comparative dryness of the flesh.
c) All poultry should be seasoned with salt on the inside from the vent end, and rubbed in on the outside.
d) Any stuffing of poultry should be carried out as near to the start of cooking as possible. It can be dangerous if left too long in a stuffed state especially if the stuffing is composed of raw meat.
e) Various herbs, aromatic vegetables or flavourings may be introduced into the inner cavity of the bird as called for. This can impart a particular required flavour to the flesh.
f) Lay the bird on one side in the roasting tray and coat with a little melted dripping. Butter can be used but great care has to be taken to prevent burning. Place in a hot oven at approx. 220–225°C.
g) The heat of the oven should be adjusted to the size of the bird. As a general rule small items like poussin and pigeon can be started and finished in a very hot oven. Larger birds need to be started in a slightly lower temperature and then to have the temperature reduced progressively after the bird has been turned and coloured on all sides, but never below 165–170°C. Large turkeys or geese may need to be covered with greaseproof or aluminium foil to prevent excessive colouring due to the prolonged cooking times.

h) Basting with its fat and juices should be fairly frequent to ensure even cooking and colouring. Excess fat from duck and goose should be removed, as the process can become more like deep frying if there is too much fat in the tray.

i) Most poultry should be cooked to the degree of being just done, that is no traces of blood evident either in the breast or legs. Any marked overcooking can rapidly result in dryness, especially with turkey and guinea-fowl. However, young pigeon can be left slightly pink at the thickest part and goose can be cooked a little more than just done.

To test for being just cooked, except for turkey: After the calculated cooking time, carefully insert a fork in the leg, tip up the bird and allow a little of the juices to run out from the vent end. This should be clear and free from blood. If stuffed, allow 15–25% more than the calculated times, then prick the leg at the thickest part with a trussing needle and press firmly to squeeze out a little juice; this should not be tinged with blood. Turkey should be tested in this way: If using a meat thermometer this should be inserted into the thickest part of the leg or into the centre of the bird if stuffed. The reading should be between 78 and 80°C.

j) When cooked allow the bird to rest for approx. 15–20 mins. before carving. They are best left on their back in a warm place. Do not stand on either end, this will allow juices to escape unnecessarily – they can be turned on end just before carving and the juices used for the gravy.

k) The roasting pan and its juices should always be deglazed with a stock appropriate to the roasted bird.

Approximate roasting times and degrees of cooking

Poussin, 400g	25 mins. per bird	just cooked
Poussin, 650–750g	35–40 mins. per bird	just cooked
Chicken	15 mins. per 500g plus 15 mins. extra	just cooked
Capon	15 mins. per 500g plus 15 mins. extra	just cooked
Duck	20 mins. per 500g	just cooked
Goose	20 mins. per 500g	fairly well-cooked
Turkey: 3–5kg	2½–3 hours	
5½–8kg	3½–4 hours } approx. 20 mins. per 500g.	just cooked
8½–10kg	4–4½ hours	
Guinea-fowl	15 mins. per 500g	just cooked
Pigeon	25 mins. per bird	slightly underdone

If the poultry is stuffed internally allow an extra 15–25% cooking time, according to size. If stuffed at the breast end only, allow just an extra 10% cooking time.

Grilling

Young chicken up to 1¾kg drawn weight and pigeon can be grilled either split open flat or prepared 'en Crapaudine'. It is best not to remove the inner rib-cage bones or the breastbone before grilling. This can lead to excessive drying and hardening of the flesh. These bones are easily removed just before serving.

The process is carried out in the same way as for meats, using oil or butter as the basting agent. The inner surfaces need to be grilled first then the bird turned over for finishing. The degree of heat should be moderate and always adjusted in relation to the thickness of the item being grilled.

Suprêmes and fillets of young tender poultry as well as unskinned legs or wings may also be grilled. Suprêmes and fillets which have had the skin removed should be seasoned first then floured and brushed preferably with melted butter or oil. The cut side should be grilled first. Care should be taken to baste frequently and to cook to the degree of being just done only. Overcooking will quickly render the flesh dry, stringy and hard.

Chicken livers as components of Kebabs and Brochettes are also grilled.

Grilled poultry is suitable for both lunch and dinner.

Shallow Frying

The many varied applications of shallow frying are well-suited to items of young and tender poultry, particularly chicken.

Sautés of poultry: although these can be finished with brown and white sauces the procedures are almost identical as noted in the following points.
a) The selected bird needs to be cut in suitable portions (1014).
b) Heat the selected fat, ideally butter, or oil if called for, in a heavy sauté pan. Season the poultry and place in the fat when it is hot, skinside down first.
c) The portions can then be cooked to colour on all sides, or almost with no colour if needed for finishing with cream or a white sauce. In some cases after an initial colouring or stiffening various flavourings or seasonings can be added to the pan.
d) The pan should be covered after the initial stage and the cooking completed on a lower heat or in the oven with the temperature adjusted to maintain the required degree of colouring.
e) Care should be taken to ensure equal cooking of any legs; these take extra cooking time because of their relative thickness.
f) When cooked, remove the poultry to a dish. Cover and keep warm.
g) The juices and fat left in the pan can be used to cook added ingredients for any accompanying sauce. Surplus fat needs to be drained and the pan should always be deglazed to utilise any juices, whether caramelised or not, for finishing any accompanying sauce.
h) In some cases it is useful to replace the cooked poultry in the sauce to reheat for 10 mins. or so. This can help to impregnate the poultry with the flavours of a particular sauce. But the sauce should not be boiled as this will tend to toughen the flesh.
i) It is more usual however, to arrange the portions in an orderly and presentable manner. This usually means placing the portions of breast on top of the legs thus making it easy to serve the customer with some of each. The finished sauce can then be ladled over.

Suprêmes and fillets: these can be shallow-fried in two main fashions.
1) In butter or clarified butter. They do not need to be floured but just seasoned and placed uncut side down first in the hot fat. The degree of colouring is determined by its ultimate finishing. This means little to no colouring where the sauce is to be white, or a nice golden brown where the sauce is to be brown. In all cases chicken or turkey should be just done but duck and pigeon can be left a little pink. The pan juices should always be utilised in the preparation of the accompanying sauce.
2) If egg-and-crumbed, in oil or clarified butter. They need to be just cooked to a golden brown, well-drained and served as soon as possible. The range of garnishing is extensive but care should be taken that some sort of compatibility with the cooking method is aimed at. This type of preparation is best for chicken.

Magrets of duck: the breasts of specially-bred and very plump duck with the skin left on or not has been latterly referred to as a Magret. The process of sautéeing is well-applied to this type of poultry but requires that it be cooked very underdone and served thinly sliced on the slant. Again it is essential that the pan juices are utilised for its accompanying sauce.

Sautés à la minute: small thin strips or slices of young tender chicken, duck or turkey breast can be utilised in the making of very quick dishes in the same manner as for meat (see page 274). The same process can be applied to chicken livers.

Raw minced and moulded mixtures: items like Pojarskis and Bitoks of poultry are best moulded with a little flour then shallow-fried in butter. The sediment from the cooking should always be utilised in the preparation of any accompanying sauce. Shallow-fried items as well as sautés of poultry are suitable for lunch or dinner menus.

Deep Frying
As a general principle all items of poultry whether raw or pre-cooked, such as croquettes, need to be coated before deep frying. Mixtures or salpicons of poultry bound with a sauce and moulded are usually egg-and-crumbed. Raw portions of chicken can be deep-fried but need to be floured first. For some dishes this flour can be flavoured with ground herbs and spices. They can also be coated with frying batter. Suprêmes of chicken and escalopes prepared from chicken or turkey breasts may be egg-and-breadcrumbed and deep-fried, a suitable alternative to being shallow-fried. Thin strips or small pieces of chicken, turkey or duck can also be lightly marinated before being coated with frying batter and deep-fried.

In all cases, deep-fried poultry needs to be cooked at fairly high temperatures and should be well-drained and served as soon as possible.

In general, deep-fried items of poultry are more suitable for lunch.

1016 TO CARVE AND PORTION COOKED POULTRY

Poached, poêléed and roast poultry are sometimes carved in the restaurant but are more frequently cut into portions in the kitchen as follows:

Chicken, Poularde, Duck and Guinea-fowl
1) Remove the legs and cut into two pieces. Chop off the lower end of the leg from the drumstick.
2) Carve along the middle of the flesh on each side of the breastbone down to the wing joint. Place the knife between the carcase and the wing joint; cut through and pull each wing portion away.
3) Chop the remaining breast away from the carcase and cut into two lengthways. Serve one piece of leg and one piece of wing or breast per portion.
4) After carving, the bones may be removed completely from the legs and breast.

Capon
Capons may be cut in a similar way to chicken, but cutting each leg into three to four pieces. Remove the two wings and cut the breast into four to six pieces. Large capons may be carved into slices in the same way as turkey.

Turkey
1) Remove the legs and bone out completely. Carve into fairly thick slices.
2) Carve the breast slightly diagonally along the line of the breast. The slices should not be too thin. It is usual to serve slices of leg (dark meat) with slices of breast (white meat) on top, allowing 100–120g in all per portion.

Goose
1) Remove the legs and bone out completely. Carve into fairly thick slices.
2) Carve the breast diagonally if large, or along the length of the breast if small. The slices should not be too thin.
3) It is usual to serve slices of leg with slices of breast on top, allowing 100–120g in all per portion.

SPECIAL POINT
Large poussins and pigeons as well as small chickens or guinea-fowl may be split into halves along the centre of the breastbone.

Volailles – Poultry

The main items of poultry with their average weights, number of portions and suitable cooking methods:

Name	Average Drawn Weight	Approx. No. of Portions	Suitable Cooking Methods and Preparations
1017 Chicken, spring (Poussin)			Roasting, poêling, 'en Cocotte', 'en Casserole', grilling, grilling 'en Crapaudine'.
Single	400–500g	1	
Double	600–750g	2	
1018 Chicken, young small (Poulet de Grain)	1¼–1½kg	3–4	Poaching, stewing, grilling, grilling 'en Crapaudine', roasting, poêling, 'en Cocotte', 'en Casserole', Suprêmes, Fillets and Escalopes for shallow and deep frying, Sautés, Suprêmes and Fillets for shallow poaching, Sautés à la Minute, Stews, Fricassées, Mousselines, Pies, Bitoks, Pojarskis.
1019 Chicken, young medium (Poulet Reine)	1½–1¾kg	4	
1020 Chicken, young fat-tened fowl (Poularde)	2–2½kg	6	Poaching, poêling, roasting.
1021 Capon (Chapon)	2½–3½kg	6–10	Poaching, poêling, roasting.
1022 Boiling Fowl (Poule)	2–3kg	6–8	Boiling, Emincés, Hachis, Vols-au-vent.
1023 Duckling (Caneton)	2–2½kg	2–4	Poêling, roasting, Sautés, Suprêmes for shallow frying.
1024 Duck (Canard)	2½–3kg	4–6	Roasting, poêling, braising, stewing.
1025 Goose (Oie)	4–7 kg	8–14	Roasting, braising, 'en Confit'.
1026 Guinea-fowl, young (Pintadeau)	¾–1kg	2	Roasting, poêling, 'en Cocotte', 'en Casserole', Sautés, Suprêmes for shallow frying.

cont. p.418

Name	Average Drawn Weight	Approx. no. of Portions	Suitable Cooking Methods and Preparations
1027 Guinea-fowl (Pintade)	1¼–1½kg	3–4	Roasting, braising, poêling, 'en Cocotte', 'en Casserole'.
1028 Pigeon, young (Pigeonneau)	350–450g	1–2	Roasting, poêling, 'en Cocotte', 'en Casserole', grilling, grilling 'en Crapaudine', Suprêmes for shallow frying, Sautés.
1029 Pigeon (Pigeon)	450–500g	1–2	Braising, stewing, Pies.
1030 Turkey, young (Dindonneau)	3–5kg	allow 250–300g raw weight	Roasting, poaching, poêling, breasts for deep- and shallow-fried Escalopes, breasts cut in strips for Sautés à la Minute.
1031 Turkey, large hen (Dinde)	6–10kg		Roasting, poêling.

POULET – CHICKEN

1032 Poulet rôti – Roast Chicken

4 portions

1¼ hours

All tender chicken of first quality are suitable for roasting either as they are or stuffed. Poussin, young chicken, poulardes and capons can all be prepared in the same styles and it is only the name of the bird which needs to be altered on the menu. The number of portions and roasting times are naturally variable in relation to size and whether stuffed or not.

The following recipe for a young roast chicken of 1½kg can serve as the standard method for all sizes of chicken.

Stage	Ingredient	Quantity	Method
1	chicken, trussed for roasting (1007) dripping	1 × 1½kg 100g	Season the chicken inside and out with salt and place on one side in a greased roasting tray. Cover with the melted dripping and place in a hot oven at 220°C.
2			Baste occasionally and after 15 mins. turn the chicken over onto its opposite side. After a further 15 mins. turn the chicken onto its back. Baste frequently and allow to roast until golden brown and cooked (total time approx. 50–60 mins). Reduce the heat as necessary. As a guide, allow approx. 15 mins. per 500g plus an extra 15 mins. for the roasting of chicken. To test if cooked, insert a fork into the leg and hold up the chicken to allow some of the juices to run out. These should be clear. Remove the string then place the chicken on a suitable dish. Cover and keep warm.
3	Fonds Brun (97)	3dl	Place the roasting tray on the stove and heat gently allowing the juices and sediment to settle and lightly colour without burning. Drain off the fat, add the brown stock and allow to simmer gently for a few minutes. Correct the seasoning with salt only and pass through a fine strainer into a pan and skim. Do not remove all vestiges of fat.
4	watercress Game Chips (1551) Bread Sauce (205 or 206)	½ bunch 100g 2dl	Send the chicken whole or cut in four portions (1016), and garnished with watercress and game chips. Serve accompanied with one sauceboat of bread sauce and one of the gravy.

1033　Poulet rôti à l'Américaine

Stuff the chicken before trussing (1007) with Farce Américaine (35), then season and cook as for Poulet rôti à l'Anglaise (1034). Garnish with four grilled rashers of back bacon and watercress. Serve accompanied with roast gravy only.

1034　Poulet rôti à l'Anglaise

Stuff the chicken (1009) before trussing with Thyme and Parsley stuffing (45), then season and cook as for Poulet rôti (1032) but allowing extra time for the stuffing. Garnish with watercress and game chips and serve accompanied with sauceboats of Bread Sauce (205 or 206) and the gravy.

SPECIAL POINTS
a) Allow an extra 8 mins. if stuffed at the neck end only, or an extra 15–20 mins. if stuffed internally as well.
b) To test for being cooked, if stuffed inside, pierce the leg at the top end of the drumstick and press. The juices exuded should be clear. Or insert a meat thermometer into the centre of the stuffed bird. This should give a reading of 78–80°C.

1035　Poulet rôti Californienne

Stuff the chicken before trussing (1007) with Farce Californienne (36), then season and cook as for Poulet rôti à l'Anglaise (1034). Garnish with watercress and serve accompanied with roast gravy only.

1036　Poulet rôti au Lard – Roast Chicken with Bacon

Prepare Poulet rôti (1032) and serve with an additional garnish of eight grilled rashers of back bacon.

1037　Poussin rôti

Prepare in any of the ways applicable to Poulet rôti. Serve whole for one portion or, if a good size, cut in half through the breast for two portions.

For a poussin of 400–450g allow approx. 25 mins. cooking time, and if stuffed, an extra 10–15 mins. For a poussin of 650–750g allow approx. 35–40 mins. cooking time, and if stuffed an extra 10–15 mins.

1038　Poularde rôtie

Prepare in any of the ways applicable to Poulet rôti. Serve cut in 4–6 portions according to size. Allow approx. 15 mins. per 500g plus an extra 15 mins. cooking time. If stuffed, allow up to an extra 25% cooking time.

1039　Chapon rôti – Roast Capon

Prepare in any of the ways applicable to Poulet rôti. Serve cut in 6–8 portions as necessary or carve both legs and breast into slices. Allow approx. 15 mins. per 500g plus an extra 15 mins. cooking time. If stuffed, allow up to an extra 25% cooking time.

1040 GRILLS OF CHICKEN

Young tender chicken up to no more than 1¾kg undrawn weight, as well as halves or portions, are suitable for grilling. Anything larger than 1¾kg takes far too long to grill successfully and usually ends up by being overcoloured and dried on the outside surfaces.

1041 Poulet grillé – Grilled Chicken

4 portions
50 mins.

Stage	Ingredient	Quantity	Method
1	chicken, prepared for grilling (1010)	1 × 1½kg	Season well and brush with oil on both sides.
	oil	½dl	
2			Grill gently on both sides until cooked, 18–20 mins., each side, brushing occasionally with oil. To test if cooked, insert the point of a trussing needle into the top end of the drumstick. The juices issuing should be clear and free from blood.
3	watercress	½ bunch	Remove the rib bones and breastbone from the inside of the chicken. Arrange on a suitable dish either whole or cut in portions and garnish with watercress and Pommes Pailles. Offer Sauce Diable or Sauce Champignons as an accompaniment.
	Pommes Pailles (1586)	100g	
	Sauce Diable (125) or Sauce Champignons (121)	2dl	

1042 Poulet grillé à l'Américaine

Prepare Poulet grillé (1041) and garnish with four grilled tomatoes, eight grilled mushrooms and four slices of grilled bacon in addition to the watercress and Pommes Pailles. Serve Sauce Diable separately.

1043 Poulet grillé à la Crapaudine

4 portions
50 mins.

Stage	Ingredient	Quantity	Method
1	chicken, prepared for grilling 'en Crapaudine' (1011)	1 × 1½kg	Season the chicken well and brush with oil on both sides.
	oil	½dl	
2			Grill gently on both sides until almost cooked, approx. 18–20 mins. each side. Remove the rib bones and breastbone from inside the chicken.

3	breadcrumbs,		Sprinkle the top surface of the chicken
	white	50g	with breadcrumbs and the melted butter.
	butter, melted	50g	Grill very gently under the salamander until cooked and golden brown.
4	watercress	½ bunch	Place the chicken on a suitable dish and
	Pommes Pailles		garnish with the watercress and straw
	(1586)	100g	potatoes. Serve accompanied with a
	Sauce Diable (125)		sauceboat of either sauce.
	or Sauce Piquante		
	(132)	2dl	

SPECIAL POINTS

a) Very often two small rounds of cooked egg-white, with a smaller round of truffle set in the centre of each, is placed at the end of the breast of the chicken just before presentation. This has the effect of emphasising its toad-like appearance. It is arguable if this is always appreciated by the customer. Custom and good sense are the best guides in deciding whether to use this technique.

b) The chicken is best when presented to the customer whole and then subsequently carved. However, if necessary, it may be cut in portions and re-formed as neatly as possible before sending to the customer.

1044 Poulet grillé à la Diable – Grilled Devilled Chicken

4 portions
50 mins.

Stage	Ingredient	Quantity	Method
1	chicken, prepared for grilling (1010)	1 × 1½kg	Season well and brush with oil on both sides.
	oil	½ dl	
2			Grill gently on both sides until almost cooked, approx. 18–20 mins. each side. Remove the rib bones and breastbone from inside the chicken.
3	mustard, English	25g	Dilute the mustard with a little water to
	cayenne	touch	a smooth not too stiff paste. Season with a little cayenne.
4	breadcrumbs	50g	Brush the top surface of the chicken
	butter, melted	50g	liberally with the mustard. Sprinkle with the breadcrumbs and melted butter and grill until cooked and golden brown.
5	watercress	½ bunch	Place the chicken on a suitable dish and
	Pommes Pailles		garnish with the watercress and straw
	(1586)	100g	potatoes. Serve accompanied with a
	Sauce Diable (125)	2dl	sauceboat of Sauce Diable.

1045 Poulet grillé au Lard – Grilled Chicken and Bacon

Prepare Poulet grillé (1041) and serve with an additional garnish of eight grilled rashers of back bacon.

1046 Grilled Portions of Chicken

Legs of chicken with the thigh bone removed and breasts of chicken, in either case with the skin left on, and halves of chicken may be grilled and garnished in the same way as for Poulet grillé.

1047 Blanc or Côtelette de Volaille grillé – Grilled Breast of Chicken

Use the suprême of chicken (1012) removed from a 1¾kg drawn chicken and with the wing bone left on. Season, pass through flour and brush with clarified butter. Grill fairly quickly at a moderate heat, brushing frequently with butter until just cooked, i.e. the flesh at the thickest part should feel firm under light pressure. Serve in any of the ways applicable to Poulet grillé. Place a cutlet frill on the wing bone.

SPECIAL POINT
Suprêmes, fillets, cutlets and breast of chicken are traditionally designated as Suprêmes de Volaille, Côtelettes de Volaille and so on. The term poulet is seldom used in this connection.

1048 Chicken Spatchcock or Spatchcocked Chicken

Prepare Poulet grillé (1041) but just before it is completely cooked sprinkle with breadcrumbs and melted butter and grill gently to a golden brown. Serve garnished with watercress only and accompanied with a small dish of large gherkins and a sauceboat of Sauce Robert (136) or Sauce Diable (125).

SPECIAL POINTS
a) It is common practice to serve Poulet grillé à la Crapaudine (1043) as Chicken Spatchcock.
b) The name Spatchcock refers to the old English way of cutting a chicken open through the breast or back then 'spitting' it flat with skewers for grilling.

1049 Poussin grillé – Grilled Spring Chicken

Poussins may be prepared and grilled in the same ways as larger chicken taking into account their size and adjusting cooking times accordingly. See Poulet grillé (1041), Poulet grillé à l'Américaine (1042), Poulet grillé à la Diable (1044), Poulet grillé à la Crapaudine (1043).

The descriptive term 'Poussin' should always be used in the title, e.g. Poussin grillé à l'Américaine.

1050 Ballotine de Volaille braisée

10 portions
2 hours

Stage	Ingredient	Quantity	Method
1	chicken legs	10	Bone out completely without opening the flesh of the drumstick.
2	Farce de Volaille (41)	250g	Stuff the legs with the farce and tie carefully with thin string.

3	butter	75g	Heat in a shallow braising pan, season the ballotines and fry quickly to brown on all sides. Remove the ballotines to one side.

4	carrots ⎫ onions ⎬ sliced celery ⎭ bacon trimmings bayleaf thyme	150g 150g 100g 75g ½ sprig	Cover the bottom of the braising pan with these ingredients then place the ballotines on top. Cover and place in a hot oven for 10 mins. to sweat.

5	Espagnole (111) Fonds Brun (97)	¾ litre ½ litre	Add the Espagnole and sufficient stock to cover a good two-thirds of the ballotines. Bring to the boil and season. Cover with the lid and place in a moderate oven at approx. 170°C and cook until tender (35–40 mins.).

6			Remove the ballotines and discard their strings. Arrange the ballotines in earthenware dishes, cover and keep warm.

7			Skim the fat from the sauce then pass the sauce through a fine strainer into a clean pan. Reduce to a light coating consistency and adjust the seasoning as necessary.

8	parsley, chopped		Make sure the ballotines are hot then ladle the sauce over and sprinkle with chopped parsley.

SPECIAL POINT

Ballotines of chicken may be served with suitable accompaniments and garnishes, for example Nouilles au Beurre, Riz Pilaff, Jardinière, Paysanne etc. and should be designated accordingly on the menu, for example Ballotine de Volaille Jardinière.

1051 Boiled Chicken

6–8 portions
2½–3½ hours

Stage	Ingredient	Quantity	Method

1	boiling fowl,
	   trussed
	water or cold
	   chicken stock
		
		1 × 2½kg
		5 litres
		approx.
			Place in a suitable pot and cover with the water or stock. Bring to the boil and skim carefully.

2	carrots, whole onions, studded (65) celery	250g 250g 200g	Add to the pan, season lightly with salt and simmer gently until the bird is tender (2–3 hours depending on the age of the bird). To test for being cooked,

	Bouquet Garni	1	pierce with a trussing needle at the thick
	peppercorns	10	part of the leg. This should enter and be
			withdrawn without marked resistance; or
			squeeze the end of the drumstick with
			the thumb and forefinger. The flesh
			should give easily under slight pressure.
3			Allow the bird to cool in the cooking
			liquid for 45 mins. or so before using.

SPECIAL POINTS

a) The flesh from boiling fowl can be tender and full of flavour if cooked carefully and is suitable for the preparation of many dishes such as Crêpes, Vols-au-vent and Emincés.

b) Boiling fowl of good quality, especially when carefully cooked in stock, may be skinned, cut in portions and served with a sauce prepared from the cooking liquid, e.g. Sauce Suprême.

1052 Brochette de Foies de Volaille

10 portions

1 hour

Stage	Ingredient	Quantity	Method
1	chicken livers	850g	Carefully remove and discard any gall-bladders and green discolouration from the livers. Trim and cut in half.
2	butter	75g	Heat the butter in a heavy frying-pan. Season half the livers with salt and pepper and fry quickly in the butter to just set the outside surfaces. Remove from the pan to one side. Repeat for the remainder.
3	grilling mushrooms small	40	Wash and trim and fry in the same fat until half-cooked.
4	streaky bacon	350g	Cut into ½cm slices then into 2–3cm squares.
5	breadcrumbs butter, melted	50g 75g	Arrange the livers, bacon and mushrooms equally on ten skewers, sprinkle with a little butter and grill quickly over heat to a good colour keeping slightly underdone. Finish by sprinkling with a few breadcrumbs and more butter and finish grilling until brown. Or alternatively, place on a buttered tray then grill and finish in the same way under the salamander.
6	watercress	1 bunch	Arrange the brochettes on suitable dishes and garnish with a little watercress.

SPECIAL POINTS

a) The use of modern stainless steel skewers will obviate the need to change the skewers prior to service. In any case the skewers are removed in the dining room at the time of actual serving by the waiter.

b) A suitable sauce may be served separately such as Sauce Demi-glace, Sauce Diable or Parsley Butter.

1053 Chapon – Capon

Capons are most suitable for roasting either stuffed or unstuffed. See Roast Chicken (1032). Small capons may be cooked in any of the ways applicable to Poularde (1069–1075).

1054 Chicken à la King

10 portions
1 hour

Stage	Ingredient	Quantity	Method
1	butter	100g	Melt the butter in a shallow pan.
	red pimentos, skinned (78)	100g	Remove the seeds from the pimento and cut in dice. Add to the butter and cook until soft. Add the mushrooms and cook.
	green pimentos, skinned	100g	
	button mushrooms, sliced	200g	
2	cooked white of boiled chicken (1051)	1kg	Cut the chicken into short slices 3–4mm thick; add to the pimentos and mushrooms, lightly season and toss over to heat.
3	sherry	1dl	Add the sherry and reduce slightly.
4	Velouté de Volaille (115)	3dl	Add the velouté to the chicken and bring to the boil. Whisk the cream and egg yolks together and add to the mixture. Mix in quickly, reheat the mixture but do not reboil. Adjust the seasoning.
	cream	1dl	
	egg yolks	3	
5			Serve in earthenware dishes accompanied with hot toast.

1055 Chicken Biryani

10 portions
1¾ hours

Stage	Ingredient	Quantity	Method
1	ghee or clarified butter	100g	Heat the ghee in a shallow pan, add the onions, garlic and ginger and fry gently to a golden brown.
	onions ⎱ finely	200g	
	garlic ⎰ chopped	3 cloves	Season the chicken with salt and add to the pan. Mix to fry and colour on all sides.
	fresh ginger	50g	
	chicken, cut for sauté (1014) and skinned	10 portions	

2	cumin		1 tsp	Add the spices, mix in, and cook slowly
	pepper	all	½ tsp	on the side of the stove for a few
	coriander	ground	2 tsps	minutes to develop their flavours.
	clove	and	½ tsp	
	bayleaf	mixed	pinch	
	cayenne	together	1 tsp	
	mace		pinch	
	cinnamon		pinch	

3	yoghurt	2dl	Add the yoghurt and cook to reduce
	chicken stock	2dl	until almost dry then add the stock and
	cream, double	3dl	cream. Season with salt and simmer
			gently until the chicken is almost cooked,
			approx. 15 mins. Adjust the seasoning as
			necessary.

4	saffron stamens, carefully cut small	pinch	Have the saffron infused in the hot stock for 10 mins. then add to the chicken and mix in together with the lime juice.
	chicken stock (96)	½dl	
	lime juice	1 tbsp	

5	Basmati rice	400g	Wash the rice well two or three times in clean and cold water. Drain then parboil for 12 mins. in boiling salted water. Refresh under cold water and drain.

6	ghee or clarified butter	75g	Heat the ghee, add the onions and cook to a golden colour then add the rice,
	onions, finely chopped	150g	season with salt and fry quickly tossing over and over. Keep on one side.

7			Place half the rice in the bottom of two deep earthenware dishes. Divide the chicken and its liquid between the two dishes and finish with the remaining rice. Cover with the lids and place in a hot oven at 200°C for approx. 30 mins. until rice and chicken are tender.

8	vegetable oil	½dl	Heat the oil in a pan, add the nuts and
	cashew nuts	50g	sultanas and fry. Toss over until lightly
	almonds, halves	25g	coloured. Drain well.
	sultanas	50g	

9			On removing the chicken from the oven sprinkle with the nuts and sultanas.

1056 Chicken Pie

10 portions
3½ hours

Stage	Ingredient	Quantity	Method
1	chicken, cut for pie (1014)	10 portions	Wrap each piece of chicken in a rasher of bacon and place in two 22cm pie
	streaky bacon rashers	20	dishes. Use equal quantities of leg and white in each pie dish.

2	onions, finely chopped	150g	Sprinkle the chicken with the onions and parsley, cover two-thirds of the way up with the cold stock, add a few drops of Worcestershire sauce and season.
	parsley, chopped	1 tbsp	
	Worcestershire sauce	few drops	
	Fonds Blanc de Volaille (96)	5dl	

| 3 | Pâte Feuilletée (1736) | 650g | Roll out the pastry approx. 3mm thick. Eggwash the rims of the pie dishes and cover with 1½cm-wide strips of pastry. Eggwash the strips. Cover the pies with the remainder of the pastry, seal firmly and trim off the surplus paste with a knife. Decorate the edge of the pastry around the pies. Eggwash and decorate with designs of pastry and cut a small hole in the top for the steam to escape. Allow to rest in a cool place for at least 1 hour. |
| | eggwash | | |

| 4 | | | Place the pies in a hot oven at approx. 200°C to lightly brown and set the pastry (approx. 20 mins.). Reduce the temperature to approx. 150°C and cook until the meat is tender (approx. 1½ hours). Cover with a sheet of greaseproof paper if overcolouring seems likely. Clean the pie dishes, place on suitable dishes and surround with pie collars. |

1057 Chicken and Mushroom Pie

Prepare as Chicken Pie (1056), adding 350g sliced button mushrooms at Stage 2.

1058 Chicken Vindaloo

10 portions
6 hours including marination

Stage	Ingredient	Quantity	Method
1	chicken breasts, skinned	1¼kg	Cut the chicken into approx. 2½cm cubes. Place in a china basin.
2	vinegar, white wine	1½dl	Mix all the ingredients with the vinegar to form a fairly liquid paste. Add the chicken, mix in to coat every piece thoroughly then leave in the refrigerator to marinate for 4 hours approx. Turn occasionally or leave overnight if more convenient.
	turmeric	½ tbsp	
	chilli ⎫ all	3 tbsps	
	cumin ⎪ ground	½ tbsp	
	bayleaf ⎬ and	1 tsp	
	fenugreek ⎪ mixed	1 tsp	
	clove ⎪ together	½ tsp	
	cinnamon ⎭	½ tsp	
	salt	1 tsp	

3	oil	1½dl	Heat the oil in a large flat pan, fry the
	onion, finely		onion and garlic until lightly coloured
	chopped	250g	then add the ginger, chillies and
	garlic, finely		cardamom and cook very gently for a few
	chopped	4 cloves	mins. to develop the flavours.
	ginger, finely		
	chopped	25g	
	fresh chillis,		
	whole	4	
	cardamom, ground	½ tbsp	
4			Drain the marinated chicken, add to the pan and fry turning over and over to colour on all sides.
5	Tomates Concassées (90)	300g	Mix the tomato and sugar in with the chicken then add any remaining
	brown sugar	1 tbsp	marinade and sufficient stock to come
	chicken stock (96)	5dl approx.	two-thirds of the way up. Check for salt.
6			Bring to the boil, cover and cook slowly until the chicken is tender. Occasionally turn the chicken over in the sauce. Remove the chillies when cooked. Time approx. 30 mins.
7	fresh coconut, grated	50g	Arrange the chicken in earthenware dishes and sprinkle with the coconut and
	fresh coriander leaves, chopped	1 tbsp	chopped coriander leaves. Serve accompanied with dishes of plain boiled
	rice, long-grain or Basmati, boiled (534) or steam-poached (535)	10 portions	or steam-poached rice.

SPECIAL POINTS

a) The degree of hotness of this curry can be adjusted by adding more or less chilli powder according to taste.

b) Skinned portions of chicken cut for sauté may be used instead of skinned breasts.

1059 Coq au Vin de Bourgogne

10 portions
1 hour

Stage	Ingredient	Quantity	Method
1	butter	125g	Heat the butter in a sauté pan then add
	Lardons, blanched (51)	200g	the lardons, quickly fry brown and remove. Do the same with the onions
	button onions	30	and finally the mushrooms.
	button mushrooms	40	
2	chicken, cut for sauté (1014)	10 portions	Season, place in the same pan and fat and colour quickly on both sides. Drain all the fat then replace the garnish with the chicken.

3	Marc or brandy	1dl	Heat the pan well, then add the Marc or brandy and flamber (32).
4	red wine, Burgundy Fonds Brun (97) garlic, crushed Bouquet Garni	1 bottle 2 cloves 1	Pour over the wine and also if necessary a little stock to just cover. Season with salt and milled pepper and add the garlic and bouquet garni. Cover with a lid, bring to the boil and cook gently in the oven at 180°C for approx. 18–20 mins. until tender.
5			Remove the chicken and garnish and arrange in casseroles. Cover and keep warm.
6	butter ⎫ into Beurre flour ⎭ Manié (11)	50g 25g	Skim off any fat from the cooking liquid then reduce this to about 5dl. Whisk in the beurre manié to thicken to a coating consistency. Simmer gently for 2–3 mins. and adjust the seasoning as necessary. Make sure the chicken is hot then pass the sauce over it through a fine strainer.
7	Heart-shaped Croûtons (26) garlic parsley, chopped	20 1 clove	Surround with the croûtons which have been rubbed with cut halves of garlic and had the tips dipped in chopped parsley.

SPECIAL POINT
The name of the wine used may be included in the title, e.g. Coq au Vin de Chambertin, au Volnay, au Mercurey etc.

1060 Crêpes de Volaille Mornay

10 portions
1¼ hours

Stage	Ingredient	Quantity	Method
1	cooked chicken Sauce Suprême (151) cream	750g 5dl 1dl	Cut the chicken into very small dice. Bring the sauce to the boil; add the chicken and cream and cook gently to a fairly stiff consistency. Adjust the seasoning.
2	Pancakes (71)	20	Lay out on the table. Divide the mixture between the pancakes and roll up.
3	Sauce Mornay (146) Parmesan, grated	7dl 60g	Place a little sauce in the bottom of earthenware dishes, with the pancakes laid diagonally on top, making sure that the ends of the rolling are underneath. Coat with the sauce, sprinkle with grated Parmesan and gratinate to a golden brown in a very hot oven.

SPECIAL POINTS
a) The texture and eating quality of the chicken is always best if it is cut or chopped with a sharp knife. Passing through a mincing machine tends to crush the fibre of the flesh and degrade its texture.
b) The chicken mixture may be varied by the addition of some chopped white mushrooms cooked in a little butter or by replacing one-third of its quantity with lean ham cut in small dice.

1061 Currie de Poulet – Curried Chicken

Prepare in the same way as either recipe for Curried Lamb (720 or 721), using ten portions of chicken cut for sauté (1014).

1062 Emincé de Volaille Argenteuil

10 portions
1 hour

Stage	Ingredient	Quantity	Method
1	Pommes Duchesse (1560)	750g	Using a piping bag and star tube, pipe the Pommes Duchesse along the inner sides of two 25cm oval earthenware dishes or ten single dishes if required. Place under the salamander to dry and very lightly colour.
2	white of boiled chicken	850kg	Cut the chicken into short slices 3–4mm thick.
3	butter button mushrooms, sliced lemon juice	100g 350g good squeeze	Melt the butter in a shallow pan, add the mushrooms and lemon juice and cook gently until soft.
4	white wine, dry fresh tarragon, chopped	1dl ½ tbsp	Add the chicken, season lightly, and toss over carefully to heat, then add the wine and tarragon. Reduce by half.
5	Velouté de Volaille (115) cream, double egg yolks cayenne	3dl 1dl 3	Add the velouté to the chicken, bring to the boil. Whisk the cream and egg yolks together, add to the mixture. Mix in quickly, reheat but do not reboil. Adjust the seasoning plus a touch of cayenne.
6	Asparagus Sprue (1388), buttered	50 pieces	Spoon the mixture into the dishes then place under a hot salamander to colour a light brown. Arrange bouquets of warmed and buttered asparagus sprue on top.

1063 Fricassée de Poulet

10 portions
1½ hours

Stage	Ingredient	Quantity	Method
1	butter chicken, cut for Fricassée (1014)	100g 10 portions	Melt the butter in a sauté pan, season the chicken, place into the pan and stiffen it without colouring.
2	flour	50g	Sprinkle over the chicken and shake the pan to mix in. Cover with a lid and place in the oven at 175°C for 10 mins. Remove and allow to cool.
3	Fonds Blanc de Volaille (96) Bouquet Garni	1½ litres 1	Carefully mix in sufficient stock to just cover the chicken, season, bring to the boil and skim. Add the bouquet garni, cover with the lid and place in a moderate oven approx. 180°C to cook for ¾–1 hour.
4			Discard the bouquet garni and remove the chicken to a clean pan.
5	egg yolks cream	3 1dl	Whisk together in a large basin and add approx. one-third of the sauce, whisking in quickly. Return to the remainder of the sauce, mixing in quickly. Reheat, moving it continuously with a wooden or metal spatula until the liaison thickens taking care that it does not reboil.
6			Adjust the seasoning of the sauce and pass through a fine strainer over the chicken. Carefully reheat without boiling.
7	parsley, chopped Heart-shaped Croûtons (26)	 10	Serve in earthenware dishes, sprinkle with chopped parsley and garnish with heart-shaped croûtons.

1064 Fricassée de Poulet à l'Ancienne

Prepare Fricassée de Poulet (1063) with the addition of 30 button onions cooked à Blanc (1492) and 30 button mushrooms cooked à Blanc (60).

1065 Fricassée de Poulet à l'Ivoire

Prepare Fricassée de Poulet (1063) but add 2 tablespoons of meat glaze (103) to the sauce before adding the liaison of cream and egg yolks. Add 40 button onions cooked à Blanc (1492) and 10 cooked artichoke bottoms (1379) cut in quarters and heated in a little butter.

1066 Kebab de Volaille à l'Orientale

10 portions
2½ hours

Stage	Ingredient	Quantity	Method
1	chicken breasts	10 × 120g	Cut the chicken breasts into thickish slices approx. 3cm square.
2	juice of lime ginger, grated honey, clear vegetable oil thyme, ground	2 tbsps 20g 1 tbsp 1dl 1 tsp	Place the chicken in a shallow dish, season with salt and milled pepper then add the remainder of the ingredients. Turn over carefully to mix and leave to marinate in a cool place for 2 hours. Turn occasionally.
3			Thread the chicken equally on ten skewers then grill gently over a moderate heat to a good colour basting occasionally with the remaining marinade. Or alternatively, place on an oiled tray then grill and finish in the same way under the salamander.
4	Riz Pilaff Safrané (527) yoghurt, natural mint, chopped almonds, finely shredded	10 portions 5dl 1 tbsp 1 tbsp	Dress the Kebabs on a bed of Riz Pilaff Safrané and serve accompanied with a sauceboat of yoghurt seasoned with salt, pepper, a touch of cayenne and mixed with the mint and almonds.

1067 Mousselines de Volaille Alexandra

10 portions
2 hours

Stage	Ingredient	Quantity	Method
1	breast of chicken, free of skin and sinew	750g	Either pound finely or pass twice through the fine plate of a mincer and place in a basin. Chill thoroughly.
2	egg whites, cold	3	Season with a little salt and pepper. Add the whites little by little, beating thoroughly with a wooden spatule until stiff and elastic in texture.
3			Pass the mixture through a fine sieve or food processor, replace in a basin and chill thoroughly in the refrigerator.
4	double cream, cold	5dl	Gradually add to the mixture beating thoroughly with a wooden spatule. Adjust the seasoning.
5			Butter a deep tray and, with a tablespoon, take a twentieth of the mixture. Mould egg-shape with a second tablespoon and remove from the first spoon. Place the mousseline in the tray. Continue until the mixture is finished, 20 pieces in all.

6	Fonds Blanc de Volaille (96)	1 litre	Season lightly, bring to the boil and pour gently around the mousselines. Cover with a buttered paper and poach in a moderate oven at 180°C until slightly firm and resilient to the touch, approx. 15 mins.
7	Sauce Mornay (146) Parmesan, grated	7dl 50g	Drain the mousselines well and arrange in earthenware dishes. Coat with the sauce, sprinkle with the grated Parmesan and gratinate under the salamander.
8	slices of truffle Asparagus Sprue, (1388), buttered	20 50 pieces	Place a slice of truffle on each mousseline and garnish with neat bouquets of buttered asparagus.

SPECIAL POINT

It is advisable to check the consistency of the mixture at Stage 4 when only three-quarters of the cream has been added. Poach a small piece in stock – if the result is too firm, carefully add the remainder; if too soft, add a little more egg white. At all stages of the making of the mixture, vigorous and firm beating is necessary.

1068 Pilaff de Foies de Volaille

10 portions
1 hour

Stage	Ingredient	Quantity	Method
1	chicken livers	1kg	Carefully remove and discard any gall-bladders and green discolouration from the livers. Trim and cut in half.
2	butter	100g	Heat the butter in a heavy frying-pan, season half the livers, and just as the butter turns brown, add the livers. Fry and toss over quickly to colour and cook slightly underdone. Drain off and place in a shallow pan. Use the same fat and repeat with the rest of the livers.
3	Sauce Madère (129)	7dl	Add sufficient of the sauce to just moisten the livers.
4	Riz Rilaff (522)	10 portions	Place the riz pilaff in two earthenware dishes and shape each neatly into an oval mound with a deep depression along its centre.
5	parsley, chopped		Fill the centre of the rice with the livers, surround the rice with a cordon of the Sauce Madère and sprinkle the livers with a little chopped parsley. Serve the remainder of the sauce in sauceboats.

1069 POULARDES

Correctly speaking this descriptive term refers to a young specially fattened fowl of approx. 2–2½kg drawn weight usually sufficient for six people. The poulardes of Bresse and Le Mans are perfect examples of the type, nevertheless large, well-fleshed young birds of equivalent size can be a more than acceptable alternative. Although suitable for roasting, they are perhaps at their best when carefully poached or poêléed then presented whole with a garnish and sauce before carving.

The repertoire for these chickens is extensive and includes many where the bird is stuffed, sometimes being completely or partially boned-out first. The stuffings are frequently based on Riz Pilaff or Farce de Volaille.

1070 Poularde à l'Aurore

6 portions
3 hours

Stage	Ingredient	Quantity	Method
1	poularde, drawn and singed	1 × 2¼kg	Bone out the breast from the inside. First remove the wishbone then insert a small knife through the neck end and carefully detach the collar bones which lie just behind the wishbone. Separate at the wing joints and remove. Cut along each side of the breastbone without piercing the skin. Use the fingers to free the rib bones then separate them from the lower part of the bird by cutting with kitchen scissors. Carefully remove the bones from the inside using the fingers to separate any remaining flesh from the bones. Pull one leg forward from inside, cut around the thigh bone then through the centre joint and remove. Repeat for the other leg. Do not remove the bones from the drumsticks.
2	Farce de Volaille (41)	750g	Mix together, then stuff the prepared chicken. Turn in the parson's nose to enclose the stuffing. Truss for poaching (1007), taking care to pass the needle through the parson's nose when trussing the legs.
	Fondue de Tomates, (91) cold, dry and passed through a fine sieve	75g	
3	Fonds Blanc de Volaille (96)	5 litres approx.	Place the chicken into the lightly seasoned boiling stock. Reboil and skim then simmer carefully until cooked, approx. 1¾ hours. Remove the chicken, untie the string and skin the bird completely. Place in a dish with a little of the cooking liquor, cover and keep warm.

4	Velouté de Volaille (115)	3dl	Strain approx. 3dl of the cooking liquid into a pan, reduce by half then add the velouté, cream and tomato and reduce to a coating consistency. Pass through a fine strainer into a clean pan then shake in the butter away from the fire. Adjust the seasoning as necessary then cover and keep warm.
	cream	2dl	
	tomato purée	1 tbsp	
	butter	75g	
5			Make sure the chicken is hot, drain off any liquid then coat with some of the sauce. Send with the remainder of the sauce in a sauceboat.
			Alternatively, cut the chicken in portions with the stuffing and arrange neatly in an earthenware dish. Coat with some sauce and send the rest separately.

1071 Poularde à la Bressane

6 portions
3 hours

Stage	Ingredient	Quantity	Method
1	poularde, drawn	1 × 2¼kg	Singe and prepare for poêling. Do not truss.
2	butter	50g	Heat the butter in a frying-pan, season the livers then sauté quickly to lightly colour. Tip the liver and fat into a basin. When cold, add the rice and brandy and mix together. Check the seasoning.
	chicken livers, cleaned and cut in small dice	250g	
	Riz Pilaff (522), cold	3 portions	
	brandy	1 tbsp	
3			Season the chicken inside and stuff with the rice. Turn in the parson's nose to enclose the stuffing. Truss for poêling (1007), taking care to pass the needle through the parson's nose when trussing the legs.
4	butter	30g	Butter a deep pan and place in the vegetables, bacon and herbs.
	carrots ⎫ roughly	120g	
	onions ⎬ diced	120g	
	celery ⎭	80g	
	bacon trimmings	50g	
	bayleaf	½	
	thyme	sprig	
5	butter, melted	100g	Season the chicken and place on its back in the prepared pan. Pour the butter over the chicken, cover with the lid and place in the oven at approx. 200°C. Baste occasionally then remove the lid after 1 hour. Continue cooking and basting until the chicken is golden brown and cooked (total time 1¾–2 hours).

6			Remove the chicken and discard the string. Place the chicken in an earthenware dish, cover and keep warm.
7	Madeira Fonds Brun (97) tomato purée arrowroot	½dl 5dl ⅓ tbsp 10g approx.	Place the pan on the stove and allow the juices and vegetables to heat and colour gently without burning. Drain off the fat without disturbing the vegetables and sediment. Add the Madeira and reduce slightly then add the stock and tomato purée and simmer very gently for a few minutes. Lightly thicken with the diluted arrowroot, adjust the seasoning as necessary then pass through a fine strainer into a clean pan. Cover and keep warm.
8	butter, melted	15g	Heat the chicken in the oven for a few minutes, brush with melted butter and send accompanied with the prepared sauce. Alternatively, remove the rice from the chicken and arrange as a neat bed in a dish. Cut the chicken in portions, arrange in a second dish and coat with a little of the sauce. Send the two dishes accompanied with the remainder of the sauce.

1072 Poularde Derby

6 portions
3 hours

Stage	Ingredient	Quantity	Method
1	poularde, drawn	1 × 2¼kg	Singe and prepare for poêling but do not truss.
2	Riz Pilaff, cold (522) foie gras, diced truffles, diced	4 portions 100g 30g	Mix together.
3			Season the chicken inside and stuff with the rice. Turn in the parson's nose to enclose the stuffing. Truss for poêling (1007), taking care to pass the needle through the parson's nose when trussing the legs.
4	butter carrots ⎤ onions ⎟ roughly celery ⎦ diced bacon trimmings bayleaf thyme	30g 120g 120g 80g 50g ½ sprig	Butter a deep pan and place in the vegetables, bacon and herbs.

5	butter, melted	100g	Season the chicken and place on its back in the prepared pan. Pour the butter over the chicken, cover with the lid and place in the oven at approx. 200°C. Baste occasionally then remove the lid after 1 hour. Continue cooking and basting until the chicken is golden brown and cooked (total time 1¾–2 hours).
6			Remove the chicken and discard the string. Place the chicken in an earthenware dish, cover and keep warm.
7	Fonds Brun (97) tomato purée arrowroot	5dl ⅓ tbsp 10g approx.	Place the pan on the stove and allow the juices and vegetables to heat gently and colour without burning. Drain off the fat without disturbing the vegetables and sediment. Add the stock and tomato and simmer gently for a few minutes to reduce slightly. Adjust the seasoning as necessary and lightly thicken with diluted arrowroot. Pass through a fine strainer into a clean pan, cover and keep warm.
8	round Croûtons (26) 4cm in diameter foie gras, raw, and cut in thick collops approx. 4cm in diameter butter	6 6 50g	Lightly sauté the collops of foie gras in a little butter and place one on each of the croûtons. Arrange on the dish around the chicken. Reheat in the oven for a few minutes.
9	slices of truffle	6	Place a buttered slice of truffle on each foie gras and brush the chicken with melted butter. Serve accompanied with the prepared sauce in a sauceboat. Alternatively, remove the rice from the chicken and arrange as a neat bed along the centre of a large dish. Cut the chicken in portions and arrange on top. Surround with the garnish and send accompanied with the sauce in a sauceboat.

SPECIAL POINT
Round slices cut from tinned foie gras may be used.

1073 Poularde Petite-Mariée

6 portions
2½ hours

Stage	Ingredient	Quantity	Method
1	poularde, trussed for poaching (1007)	1 × 2¼kg	Bring sufficient stock to the boil to cover the chicken, add the chicken, reboil and skim. Season lightly with salt and

	Fonds Blanc de		simmer very gently for 1 hour. Add the
	Volaille (96)	5 litres	onions, carrots and potatoes and after a
	button onions	18	further 10 mins. add the peas and
	carrots, turned		continue cooking together (total time
	small	18	approx. 1½ hours).
	potatoes, new or		
	turned small	18	
	peas	100g	
2			Remove the chicken, discard the string and skin the bird completely. Place in a deep cocotte and surround with the cooked garnish. Cover and keep warm.
3	Velouté de Volaille		Strain approx. 3dl of the cooking liquid
	(115)	3dl	into a pan, reduce by half then add the
	cream	2dl	cream and velouté and reduce to a coat-
	butter	75g	ing consistency. Pass through a fine strainer into a clean pan. Shake in the butter away from the fire. Adjust the seasoning as necessary then cover and keep warm.
4			Make sure the chicken is hot then ladle some of the sauce over the chicken and its garnish. Replace the lid and send accompanied with the rest of the sauce in a sauceboat. Alternatively, cut the chicken in portions and arrange neatly in an earthenware dish with its garnish. Coat with a little of the sauce and send the rest separately in a sauceboat.

1074 Poularde poché au Riz, Sauce Suprême –   6 portions
Poached Chicken with Rice and Sauce Suprême 2½ hours

Stage	Ingredient	Quantity	Method
1	poularde, trussed for poaching (1007)	1 × 2¼kg	Bring sufficient stock to the boil, add the chicken, reboil and skim. Season lightly with salt and simmer gently until cooked
	Fonds Blanc de Volaille (96)	5 litres approx.	(approx. 1½ hours).
2			Remove the chicken, discard the string and skin the bird completely. Place in an earthenware dish, cover and keep warm.
3	Velouté de Volaille (115)	3dl	Pass approx. 3dl of the cooking liquor into a pan, add the velouté, mushroom
	mushroom trimmings, white	100g	trimmings and cream. Reduce to a coat- ing consistency and pass through a fine
	cream	1dl	strainer into a clean pan.

4	butter	75g	Shake in the butter away from the fire,
	cream	1dl	add the cream and adjust the seasoning as necessary; cover and keep warm.
5	Riz Pilaff (522)	6 portions	Make sure the chicken is hot, coat with a little of the sauce and send accompanied with a dish of the rice and the rest of the sauce in a sauceboat. Alternatively, cut the chicken in portions, arrange in an earthenware dish and coat with a little of the sauce. Send accompanied with a dish of the rice and the rest of the sauce.

1075 Poularde Stanley

6 portions
2½ hours

Stage	Ingredient	Quantity	Method
1	poularde, drawn	1 × 2¼kg	Singe and prepare for poaching but do not truss.
2	Riz Pilaff (522) truffles, cut in short julienne mushrooms, cut in short julienne and cooked à Blanc (60)	4 portions 30g 250g	Mix together.
3			Season the chicken inside and stuff with the rice. Turn in the parson's nose to enclose the stuffing. Truss for poaching (1007) taking care to pass the needle through the parson's nose when trussing the legs.
4	Fonds Blanc de Volaille (96)	5 litres approx.	Bring sufficient stock to the boil, add the chicken, reboil and skim. Season lightly with salt and simmer gently.
5	onions, sliced curry powder	500g 20g	Place the onions in a pan, barely cover with water. Add the curry powder and boil rapidly for 5 mins. Drain then add the onions to the chicken. Continue to simmer gently until the chicken is cooked (approx. 1¾ hours).
6			Remove the chicken, discard the string and skin the bird completely. Place in an earthenware dish, cover and keep warm.
7			Strain the cooking liquor, pass the onions through a fine sieve. Place 5dl of the cooking liquor and the sieved onions in a pan and reduce by two-thirds.

8	Velouté de Volaille (115)	3dl
	cream	2dl

Add the velouté and cream and continue to reduce to a coating consistency.
Adjust the seasoning as necessary, pass firmly through a fine strainer into a clean pan, cover and keep warm.

9

Make sure the chicken is hot then coat with a little of the sauce. Send accompanied by the rest of the sauce in a sauceboat.
Alternatively, remove the rice from the chicken and arrange as a neat dome-shaped bed in a dish. Cut the chicken in portions, arrange in a second dish and coat with a little of the sauce. Send the two dishes accompanied with the remainder of the sauce.

1076 POULETS 'EN CASSEROLE' AND 'EN COCOTTE'

Technically these two terms relate to the pot-roasting (poêling) of small to medium chickens in earthenware or metal cocottes or casseroles, and in the presentation and serving of the chicken from the utensil it was cooked in.

At one time the cooking of a chicken designated 'en Casserole' signified that it had been cooked with butter only, and was not garnished, whereas 'en Cocotte' denoted a more complicated procedure and was, more often than not, garnished. Modern practice does not allow any arbitrary distinction between these two descriptions. All that is necessary where either term is used is that the chicken, either whole or cut in portions, is presented and served from a cocotte or casserole.

In most cases, for the sake of convenience and to minimise damage or breakage to any earthenware utensils, the cooking is carried out in a covered pan and the chicken is transferred to a cocotte or casserole. It is then sauced and garnished for presentation and service.

It is best for the chicken to be trussed 'en Entrée' (1007) if needed for presenting whole to the customer. If to be cut into portions it is better to remove the lower legs before trussing.

1077 Poulet en Cocotte

4 portions
2 hours

Stage	Ingredient		Quantity	Method
1	butter		25g	Butter a deep pan and place in the
	carrot	roughly diced	125g	vegetables, bacon and herbs.
	onion		125g	
	celery		100g	
	bacon trimmings		60g	
	bayleaf		½	
	thyme		sprig	

2	chicken, trussed for poêling (1007) butter	1 × 1½kg 100g	Season and place the chicken on its back in the prepared pan. Melt the butter and pour over the chicken. Cover with a lid and place in the oven at approx. 200°C. Baste occasionally and remove the lid after 1 hour. Continue cooking and basting until the chicken is golden brown and cooked (total time 1¼–1½ hours). To test if cooked insert a fork into the leg and hold up the chicken to allow some of the juice to run out. This should be clear.
3			Remove the chicken and discard the string. Place the chicken in a cocotte, cover with the lid and keep warm.
4	Fonds Brun (97) Jus lié (113)	1dl 1½dl	Place the pan on the stove and allow the juice and vegetables to heat gently and lightly colour without burning. Drain off the fat without disturbing the vegetables and sediment. Add the stock and jus lié and simmer gently for a few minutes. Adjust the consistency and seasoning and pass through a fine strainer into a clean pan. Cover and keep hot.
5	parsley, chopped		Make sure the chicken is hot, coat with a little of the sauce, sprinkle with chopped parsley, replace the lid and reheat in a hot oven for 5 mins. Send accompanied with the remaining sauce in a sauceboat. Or cut in portions, replace neatly in the cocotte, lightly coat with sauce, sprinkle with parsley, cover and send accompanied with the remaining sauce.

1078 Poulet en Cocotte Bonne-Femme

Prepare Poulet en Cocotte (1077) with the addition of a garnish of Pommes Cocotte (1552), Lardons (51) and Petits Oignons glacés à Brun (1493).

1079 Poulet en Cocotte Champeaux

Prepare in the same way as Poulet en Cocotte (1077) but deglaze with white wine and jus lié instead of brown stock and jus lié. Garnish with Petits Oignons glacés à Brun (1493) and Pommes Cocotte (1552).

1080 Poulet en Cocotte à l'Estragon

4 portions
2 hours

Stage	Ingredient	Quantity	Method
1	chicken, trussed for poêling (1007)	1 × 1½kg	Season the chicken inside and out and push the tarragon inside. Place on its back in a suitably-sized deep pan and pour the butter over the chicken.
	fresh tarragon	small bouquet	
	butter, melted	75g	
2			Cover with a lid and place in the oven at approx. 200°C. Baste occasionally and remove the lid after 1 hour. Continue cooking and basting until the chicken is golden brown and cooked (total time 1¼–1½ hours). To test if cooked insert a fork into the leg and hold up the chicken to allow some of the juice to run out. This should be clear. Remove the tarragon and discard.
3			Remove the chicken and discard the string. Place the chicken in a cocotte, cover with the lid and keep warm.
4	white wine, dry	2dl	Place the pan on the stove and allow to heat gently to lightly caramelise the juices. Drain off the fat, add the wine and tarragon and reduce by three quarters. Add the jus lié, simmer for 2–3 mins. then pass through a fine strainer into a clean pan. Shake in the butter away from the heat and adjust the seasoning. Cover and keep warm.
	butter	50g	
	fresh tarragon, roughly chopped	½ tbsp	
	Jus lié (113)	1½dl	
5	fresh tarragon leaves, blanched	12	Make sure the chicken is hot, coat with a little of the sauce then decorate the breast of the chicken chevron-fashion with the tarragon leaves. Cover with the lid and send accompanied with the remainder of the sauce in a sauceboat. Or cut in portions, replace neatly in the cocotte, lightly coat with sauce, decorate each portion with tarragon leaves, cover and send accompanied with the remaining sauce.

1081 Poulet en Cocotte Grand'mère

Prepare Poulet en Cocotte (1077) with the addition of a garnish of sautéed button mushrooms (61) and baton-shaped croûtons of bread.

1082 Poulet en Cocotte Paysanne

Prepare in the same way as Poulet en Cocotte (1077) but deglaze with white wine and jus lié instead of brown stock and jus lié. Garnish with Lardons (51), Carottes glacées (1400) and Pommes Cocotte (1552).

1083 POULETS SAUTÉS – SAUTÉS OF CHICKEN

This mode of preparation is exceptionally well-suited to young and tender small or medium chickens. Perhaps the most important point to bear in mind is that the chicken, once it has been cooked by shallow frying, should not be boiled in the final prepared sauce. It may be left for 10 mins. or so in the sauce to absorb its flavours but any boiling will tend to toughen the chicken; it will then require further cooking to become properly tender.

For detailed observations see shallow frying under Cooking Methods, page 414.

1084 Poulet sauté Archiduc

10 portions
1 hour

Stage	Ingredient	Quantity	Method
1	butter	100g	Heat the butter in a sauté pan, season
	chicken, cut for	10	the chicken and place in the pan. Set
	sauté (1014)	portions	quickly on both sides without colouring
	onion, finely		then remove. Add the onions and cook
	chopped	100g	without colour. Replace the chicken, cover with a lid and cook gently on the side of the stove taking care not to colour the chicken. Remove the breasts and wings first; the legs will require extra cooking time.
2			Dress the cooked chicken in earthenware dishes leaving the onion in the pan. Cover the chicken and keep warm.
3	brandy	½dl	Drain the surplus butter from the pan,
	Velouté de Volaille		add the brandy and reduce slightly. Add
	(115)	4dl	the velouté and cream and reduce by
	cream	4dl	one-third. Add the squeeze of lemon
	juice of lemon	squeeze	juice and Madeira. Adjust the seasoning.
	Madeira	½dl	
4	slices of truffle	10	Pass the sauce through a fine strainer over the chicken and decorate with the slices of truffle.

1085 Poulet sauté Bercy

10 portions
1 hour

Stage	Ingredient	Quantity	Method
1	butter	100g	Heat the butter in a sauté pan. Season
	chicken, cut for	10	the chicken and when the butter is just
	sauté (1014)	portions	turning brown add the chicken and

colour quickly on both sides. Cover with
the lid and cook more slowly on the side
of the stove. Remove the breasts and
wings first; the legs will require extra
cooking time.

2	butter	60g	Grill the chipolatas. Season and sauté
	chipolatas, small	20	the mushrooms in the butter.
	button mushrooms	40	

| 3 | | | Dress the cooked chicken in earthenware dishes and garnish neatly with the chipolatas and mushrooms. Cover and keep warm. |

4	shallots, finely chopped	150g	Add the shallots to the pan. Cook gently then drain off the surplus butter. Add
	white wine, dry	3dl	the wine and reduce by two-thirds. Add
	Jus lié (113)	6dl	the jus lié and glace de viande and
	Glace de Viande (103)	15g	simmer to correct consistency. Finish the
	juice of lemon	squeeze	sauce with a squeeze of lemon juice and
	butter	75g	shake in the butter away from the fire. Adjust the seasoning.

| 5 | parsley, chopped | | Pour the sauce over the chicken and sprinkle with chopped parsley. |

1086 Poulet sauté Bourguignonne

10 portions
1 hour

Stage	Ingredient	Quantity	Method
1	butter	100g	Heat the butter in a sauté pan and add
	Lardons (51)	200g	the lardons, onions and mushrooms. Fry
	button onions	30	quickly to colour and remove.
	button mushrooms	40	
2	chicken, cut for sauté (1014)	10 portions	Season, add to the sauté pan and colour quickly on both sides. Replace the garnish, cover with a lid and cook more slowly on the side of the stove. Remove the breasts and wings first; the legs will require extra cooking time.
3			Dress the cooked chicken and the garnish in earthenware dishes, cover and keep warm.
4	onion, finely chopped	100g	Add the onion and garlic to the pan and cook. Drain off surplus fat, add the wine
	garlic, finely chopped	1 clove	and reduce by two-thirds. Add the demi-glace and reduce to a light coating
	red wine	3dl	consistency. Adjust the seasoning.
	Demi-glace (112)	5dl	

5	Heart-shaped Croûtons (26) parsley, chopped	10	Pass the sauce through a fine strainer over the chicken and the garnish. Finish with the croûtons which have had the tips dipped in chopped parsley.

1087 Poulet sauté Chasseur

10 portions
1 hour

Stage	Ingredient	Quantity	Method
1	butter chicken, cut for sauté (1014)	100g 10 portions	Heat the butter in a sauté pan, season the chicken and when the butter is just turning brown, add the chicken and colour quickly on both sides. Cover with a lid and cook more slowly on the side of the stove. Remove the breasts and the wings first; the legs will require extra cooking time.
2			Dress the cooked chicken in earthenware dishes, cover and keep warm.
3	button mushrooms, sliced shallots, finely chopped Tomates Concassées (90) white wine, dry tarragon, chopped	350g 50g 250g 2dl ½ tbsp	Add the mushrooms to the pan and fry quickly. Add the shallots and cook gently. Add the tomates concassées, the white wine and the tarragon. Allow to reduce by half.
4	Jus lié (113)	5dl	Add to the pan and reduce to correct consistency. Adjust the seasoning.
5	parsley, chopped		Ladle the sauce over the chicken and sprinkle with chopped parsley.

1088 Poulet sauté aux Fines Herbes

10 portions
1 hour

Stage	Ingredient	Quantity	Method
1	butter chicken cut for sauté (1014)	100g 10 portions	Heat the butter in a sauté pan, season the chicken and when the butter is just turning brown, add the chicken and colour quickly on both sides. Cover with a lid and cook more slowly on the side of the stove.
2	shallots tarragon } finely chervil } chopped parsley	75g 1 tbsp ½ tbsp 1 tbsp	About 10 mins. before the chicken is cooked, sprinkle with the shallots and herbs. Shake the pan to mix in, cover and continue cooking very gently shaking the pan occasionally. Remove the wings and breast first; the legs will require extra cooking time.

3			Dress the cooked chicken in earthenware dishes and keep warm.
4	white wine, dry	3dl	Tip out the fat from the pan, add the wine and dissolve any sediment in the pan. Pass through a fine strainer into a clean pan.
5	Fonds Brun (97) Glace de Volaille (104) butter, soft lemon juice	3dl 2 tbsps 100g squeeze	Reduce the wine by half then add the stock and chicken glaze and reduce further to a light syrupy consistency. Shake in the butter and adjust the seasoning plus the lemon juice.
6	Fines Herbes, chopped	2 tbsps	Make sure the chicken is hot then coat with the sauce and sprinkle with the herbs.

SPECIAL POINT
The sauce for this dish is very concentrated and rich and only needs sufficient to just lightly coat the chicken. If the sauce is needed in less concentrated form or in a larger quantity it is only necessary to add a little excellent jus lié.

1089 Poulet sauté Hongroise

10 portions
1 hour

Stage	Ingredient	Quantity	Method
1	butter chicken, cut for sauté (1014)	100g 10 portions	Heat the butter in a sauté pan, season the chicken, place in the pan, colour lightly on both sides and remove.
2	onions, finely chopped paprika	100g 25g	Add the onions to the pan and cook without colour. Add the paprika and mix in. Replace the chicken, cover with a lid and continue to cook gently on the side of the stove turning the chicken occasionally.
3			Remove the chicken, the breasts and wings first; the legs will require extra cooking time. Cover the chicken and keep warm.
4	Tomates Concassées (90) cream, sour Velouté de Volaille (115)	200g 3dl 3dl	Add the tomatoes to the pan and cook gently. Add the cream and velouté and reduce slightly. Adjust the seasoning then pass through a fine strainer into a clean pan. Cover and keep warm.
5	Riz Pilaff (522) Tomates Concassées (90)	10 portions 200g	Mix the rice and tomatoes together and arrange as a border on suitable oval dishes. Dress the chicken neatly in the centres of the rice and ladle some of the sauce carefully over the chicken. Send the rest of the sauce separately.

1090 Poulet sauté Portugaise

10 portions
1 hour

Stage	Ingredient	Quantity	Method
1	oil, olive	1½dl	Heat the oil in a sauté pan. Season the chicken and when the oil is very hot add the chicken and colour quickly on both sides. Cover with a lid and cook more slowly on the side of the stove. Remove the breasts and wings first; the legs will require extra cooking time.
	chicken, cut for sauté (1014)	10 portions	
2			Dress the cooked chicken in earthenware dishes, cover and keep warm.
3	onions, finely chopped	350g	Add the onions to the pan and fry quickly to lightly colour then add the mushrooms and cook together until also just lightly coloured. Drain off any surplus oil then add the wine, tomatoes, garlic and basil. Season lightly and reduce to a lightly thickened texture. Adjust the seasoning as necessary.
	small button mushrooms, finely sliced	350g	
	Tomates Concassées (90)	750g	
	white wine, dry	3dl	
	fresh basil, chopped	½ tbsp	
	garlic, finely chopped	1 clove	
4	parsley, chopped		Make sure the chicken is hot, ladle over the sauce and sprinkle well with chopped parsley.

1091 Poulet sauté Provençale

10 portions
1 hours

Stage	Ingredient	Quantity	Method
1	oil	1½dl	Heat the oil in a sauté pan, season the chicken and place in the pan. Colour quickly on both sides, sprinkle with the herbs, cover with the lid and cook more slowly on the side of the stove. Remove the breasts and wings first; the legs will require extra cooking time.
	chicken, cut for sauté (1014)	10 portions	
	basil } fresh and	½ tbsp	
	thyme } finely	½ tbsp	
	rosemary } chopped	½ tbsp	
2			Dress the cooked chicken in earthenware dishes, cover and keep warm.
3	green pimentos, skinned (78)	2	Remove the seeds from the pimentos and cut the flesh into julienne. Add to the pan and cook gently. Drain off surplus oil, add the tomatoes concassées and garlic, season lightly and cook gently for a few minutes.
	Tomates Concassées (90)	350g	
	garlic, finely chopped	2 cloves	
4	white wine, dry	3dl	Add the wine and reduce by two-thirds. Add the jus lié, the anchovies and olives,
	Jus lié (113)	4dl	

	anchovy fillets, diced	12	simmer together gently for approx. 10 mins. Adjust the seasoning.
	black olives, stoned and blanched	30	
5	parsley, chopped		Make sure the chicken is hot. Ladle the sauce over the chicken and sprinkle with chopped parsley.

1092 Poussin Polonaise

10 portions
2 hours

Stage	Ingredient	Quantity	Method
1	poussins, drawn	10	Singe and prepare for trussing.
2	breadcrumbs	200g	Soak the breadcrumbs in the milk and
	milk	½ litre	squeeze out the surplus. Place the
	Farce à Gratin (38)	500g	breadcrumbs in a basin with the rest of
	parsley, chopped	1 tbsp	the ingredients, season and mix together.
3			Season the poussins inside and stuff with the mixture. Turn in the parson's noses to enclose the stuffing. Truss for poêling (1008) taking care to pass the needle through the parson's noses when trussing the legs.
4	butter, melted	250g	Season the poussins and place in a braising pan, standing on their backs. Cover with the melted butter and the lid and place in a hot oven at approx. 210°C and cook for 30 mins. Remove the lid and cook until brown, basting occasionally (total time approx. 1 hour).
5	Jus lié (113)	4dl	Remove the poussins, discard the strings and dress in cocottes; surround with the jus lié.
6	butter	300g	Heat the butter in a frying-pan, add the
	breadcrumbs	150g	crumbs and fry until golden brown. Pour over the poussins.
7	juice of lemon	½	Finish with a squeeze of lemon juice and
	parsley, chopped		sprinkle with chopped parsley. Cover with the lids.

1093 SUPRÊMES DE VOLAILLE – CHICKEN BREASTS

The descriptive term 'Suprême' refers to either side of the breast of poultry, especially chicken, removed from the carcase and free of skin; it may also be referred to as a 'Filet'. The two names are interchangeable and either can be used to prevent repetition on the written menu. The older term 'Côtelette' for the suprême with its wing bone left on is generally eschewed by modern practice with 'Suprême' being the most widely used. It is suggested that the wing bone is removed where the suprême is to be coated with sauce.

There are four basic ways of cooking suprêmes: 1) shallow poaching using butter and an absolute minimum of liquid; 2) shallow frying in butter with little or no colour for where the sauce will be of a light to cream colour; 3) shallow frying in butter or oil to a light golden to brown colour where the sauce will be of a basically brown colour; 4) egg-and-breadcrumbed for shallow frying in clarified butter or oil, and for deep frying.

It is essential that suprêmes of chicken be just cooked only, no matter the method used, i.e. the thickest part should be just firm and resilient to pressure. They should be well-drained and in all cases served as soon as possible; any undue delay will result in a progressive toughening of the flesh.

1094 Suprême de Volaille Chivry

10 portions
50 mins.

Stage	Ingredient	Quantity	Method
1	Suprêmes of chicken without wing bones (1013)	10	Remove the small fillets from the suprêmes and make into a Mousseline Forcemeat (39) with the egg white and cream. Season with salt, pepper and a little nutmeg and finally mix in the pistachio nuts.
	egg white	1	
	cream, double, cold	1½dl	
	pistachios, skinned and chopped	50g	
2			Cut a pocket along the thick side of each suprême and stuff with the prepared forcemeat.
3	butter, soft	50g	Butter a shallow pan, lay in the suprêmes, add the stock and lemon juice and lightly season. Cover with a buttered paper and lid and place in a hot oven at 200°C to cook. Approx. 15–20 mins.
	Fonds Blanc de Volaille (96)	1½dl	
	lemon juice	1 tbsp	
4			Remove the suprêmes, drain well, place in earthenware dishes. Cover and keep warm.
5	Velouté de Volaille (115)	3dl	Add the velouté and cream to the pan juices and reduce to a light coating consistency. Pass through a fine strainer into a clean pan then mix in the butter. Season as necessary, cover and keep warm.
	cream, double	3dl	
	Beurre Ravigote (14)	75g	
6	button onions, cooked à Blanc (1492)	30	Make sure the suprêmes are hot then coat with a little of the sauce. Arrange the onions and mushrooms in bouquets around the dishes and just touch these with a little chopped parsley. Send with the rest of the sauce separately.
	button mushrooms, cooked à Blanc (60)	30	
	parsley, chopped		

1095 Suprême de Volaille à la Crème et Champignons

10 portions
40 mins.

Stage	Ingredient	Quantity	Method
1	butter	100g	Heat the butter in a sauté pan, season the suprêmes and place in the butter skinned side down. Cook until coloured very lightly on both sides (7–8 mins.). Remove, drain and dress neatly in earthenware dishes. Keep warm.
	Suprêmes of chicken without wing bones (1013)	10	
2	button mushrooms, sliced	400g	Add to the butter remaining in the sauté pan, lightly season and cook quickly.
3	sherry	½dl	Add the sherry and slightly reduce. Add the velouté and cream and reduce gently to a coating consistency. Adjust the seasoning, then ladle a little of the sauce over the suprêmes. Send the remainder of the sauce separately.
	Velouté de Volaille (115)	3dl	
	cream	3dl	

1096 Suprême de Volaille Doria

10 portions
1¼ hours

Stage	Ingredient	Quantity	Method
1	Suprêmes of chicken (1012)	10	Season the suprêmes and paner à l'Anglaise (72). Lightly flatten, reshape and mark trellis-fashion with the back of a knife.
	flour } for eggwash } crumbing breadcrumbs }		
2	cucumbers	1½	Peel, cut into four lengthways and remove the seeds with a knife. Cut the cucumber into diamond-shaped pieces.
3	butter	50g	Heat in a sauteuse, add the cucumber, season and cover with a lid. Cook gently on the side of the stove without colour. Drain.
4	oil	2dl	Heat in a sauté pan and when hot place in the suprêmes best side downwards and fry to a golden brown on both sides (7–8 mins.).
5			Dress the suprêmes on suitable dishes. Keep warm.
6	Jus lié (113)	3dl	Dress the cucumber in neat bouquets with the suprêmes and surround with a cordon of jus lié.

7	butter	150g	Place the butter in a suitable frying-pan and cook until nut-brown shaking the pan to ensure even colouring. Pour over the suprêmes and place a frill on each wing bone.

1097 Suprême de Volaille à la Kiev

10 portions
1¼ hours

Stage	Ingredient	Quantity	Method
1	Suprêmes of chicken (without small fillets) (1012)	10	Cut an incision along the thickest part of the suprêmes without going right through the flesh. Flatten with a wetted cutlet bat and lightly season.
2	butter, well-chilled	200g	Cut the butter into batons approx. 8 cm long and place one at the edge of each suprême; roll up to completely enclose the butter.
3	flour eggwash breadcrumbs } for crumbing		Season and paner the suprêmes carefully and thoroughly, making sure that the edges are well stuck together then pass them through the egg and breadcrumbs for a second time; roll carefully to make sure the breadcrumbs adhere properly. This is essential to prevent them opening during deep frying.
4	sandwich bread for croûtons clarified butter	150g	Cut the bread into elongated oval shapes ¾cm thick and just slightly larger than the suprêmes and fry in the butter until golden brown. Drain well.
5			Deep fry the suprêmes in hot fat for approx. 5 mins. without over-colouring. Drain well. Place each suprême on a croûton and arrange on an oval dish. Decorate with bouquets of fried sprigs of parsley.

SPECIAL POINTS

a) The above recipe is offered as being a more authentic preparation; other fillings such as herb butter and foie gras although acceptable in their own right should not, correctly speaking, be used if the suprêmes are designated à la Kiev.

b) The use of the croûtons is optional.

1098 Suprême de Volaille Maréchale

10 portions
45 mins.

Stage	Ingredient	Quantity	Method
1	Suprêmes of chicken (1012)	10	Season the suprêmes and paner à l'Anglaise (72). Lightly flatten, re-shape

	flour eggwash }for breadcrumbs }crumbing		and mark trellis-fashion with the back of a knife.
2	oil	2dl	Heat in a sauté pan and when hot place in the suprêmes best side downwards and fry to a golden brown on both sides (7–8 mins.). Drain.
3			Dress the suprêmes on suitable dishes. Keep warm.
4	Jus lié (113) butter	3dl 150g	Surround the suprêmes with a cordon of jus lié. Place the butter in a suitable frying-pan and cook until nut brown shaking the pan to ensure even colouring. Pour over the suprêmes.
5	Asparagus Sprue (1388) slices of truffle	50 10	Garnish the suprêmes with neat bouquets of asparagus tips and place a slice of truffle on each. Place a frill on each wing bone.

1099 Suprême de Volaille Maryland

10 portions
1½ hours

Stage	Ingredient	Quantity	Method
1	flour baking powder egg milk sweetcorn, tinned sugar oil	100g 10g 1 ½dl 250g 10g 2dl	Sift the flour and baking powder into a basin, add the egg and milk and mix to a stiff batter. Add the drained sweetcorn and the sugar and mix together. Heat the oil in a sauté pan and fry ten equal spoonfuls of the mixture in the form of small, thick pancakes. Colour golden brown on both sides.
2	bananas flour eggwash }for breadcrumbs }crumbing	5	Cut in half on the slant. Paner à l'Anglaise (72) and deep fry.
3	tomatoes, small back bacon, rashers	10 10	Prepare and grill the tomatoes and bacon.
4	Suprêmes of chicken (1012) flour eggwash }for breadcrumbs }crumbing	10	Season the suprêmes and paner à l'Anglaise (72). Lightly flatten, re-shape and mark trellis-fashion with the back of a knife.
5	oil	2dl	Heat in a sauté pan and when hot place in the suprêmes best side downwards and fry to a golden brown on both sides (7–8 mins.). Drain.

6	Horseradish Sauce (189)	6dl	Dress the suprêmes on suitable dishes, arrange the garnish of sweetcorn galettes, banana, tomato and bacon around the suprêmes. Place a frill on each wing bone and serve accompanied with the warmed horseradish sauce.

1100 Suprême de Volaille Tessinoise

10 portions
45 mins.

Stage	Ingredient	Quantity	Method
1	Gnocchi Romaine, to Stage 2 (487)	5 portions	Cut the gnocchi into 20 × 4cm diameter rounds. Sprinkle with Parmesan and melted butter and gratinate to a golden brown under the salamander. Place a warmed round of ham on each croûton then a round of the prepared gnocchi on top of this.
	Parmesan, grated	25g	
	butter, melted	50g	
	cooked ham, round slices 4cm in diameter	20	
	round Croûtons (26) cut 4cm in diameter	20	
2	Suprêmes of chicken (1012)	10	Mix the grated Parmesan with sufficient breadcrumbs to paner (72) the suprêmes. Lightly flatten, reshape and mark trellis-fashion with the back of a knife.
	flour		
	eggwash		
	breadcrumbs, white	250g approx.	
	Parmesan, grated	50g	
3	oil	2dl	Heat in a sauté pan and when hot place in the suprêmes best side downwards and fry to a golden brown on both sides (7–8 mins.). Drain. Dress the suprêmes on suitable dishes. Keep warm.
4	butter	150g	Arrange the garnish neatly round the suprêmes. Place the butter in a frying-pan and cook until nut-brown, shaking the pan to ensure even colouring. Pour over the suprêmes and send accompanied with the jus lié in sauceboats.
	Jus lié (113)	5dl	

1101 Suprême de Volaille Tonkinoise

10 portions
45 mins.

Stage	Ingredient	Quantity	Method
1	mango, medium	2	Peel the mangoes, cut to remove the stones then cut the flesh into thickish slices. Place overlapping on a buttered dish, sprinkle with melted butter, dust with a little ginger and sprinkle with a little sugar. Grill to a light brown.
	butter, melted	50g	
	ginger, ground	1 tsp	
	sugar, demerara	50g	

2	butter	100g	Heat the butter in a sauté pan, season the suprêmes and place in, skinned side down. Cook gently until just done and with very little colour on both sides. Remove, drain and keep warm.
	Suprêmes of chicken (1013), wing bones removed	10	
3	onions, finely chopped	75g	Add the onions to the pan and cook until golden. Drain off the surplus fat then mix in the curry powder. Cook gently for a few minutes, add the coconut milk, reduce by half then add the velouté and cream. Simmer to a light coating consistency then pass through a fine strainer into a clean pan. Adjust the seasoning, cover and keep hot.
	curry powder	1 tsp	
	coconut milk	3dl	
	Velouté de Volaille (115)	3dl	
	cream, double	3dl	
4	Riz Pilaff (522)	10 portions	Arrange a bed of the rice to one side of the dishes with the mango neatly over-lapping on top. Place the suprêmes neatly on the other side then coat the suprêmes only with a little of the sauce. Send accompanied with the remainder of the sauce in a sauceboat.

SPECIAL POINT
If fresh coconut milk is unobtainable pour 3dl boiling water over 75g desiccated coconut. Allow to steep for 20 mins. then squeeze firmly through a cloth.

1102 Vol-au-vent de Volaille

10 portions
1 hour

Stage	Ingredient	Quantity	Method
1	boiled chicken (1051)	1 × 2¼kg	Skin, remove the flesh from the bones and cut into approx. 1cm dice.
2	Sauce Suprême (151)	3dl	Place the chicken in a shallow pan, add the sauce and reheat gently to boiling-point. Adjust the seasoning and keep hot.
3	Vol-au-vent cases (1714)	10	Warm the cases and place in hot earthenware dishes. Well fill the cases with the mixture. Place the pastry lids to one side on the Vols-au-vent. Garnish with picked parsley.
	parsley, picked		

1103 Vol-au-vent Toulousaine

Prepare as Vol-au-vent de Volaille (1102), using 500g diced boiled chicken, 200g diced braised sweetbreads (985), 30 Quenelles of Chicken (82) moulded with teaspoons and poached, and 40 small button mushrooms cooked à Blanc (60).

CANARD – DUCK
CANETON – DUCKLING

1104 Aiguillettes de Caneton Bigarade

4 portions
2 hours

Stage	Ingredient	Quantity	Method
1	butter plump well-fleshed duckling, trussed (1007)	75g 1 × 2½kg	Heat the butter in a deep pan, season the duck and colour to a good brown on all sides. Remove to one side.
2	carrots ⎫ roughly onions ⎬ diced celery ⎭ bayleaf thyme	120g 120g 80g ½ sprig	Place the mirepoix in the bottom of the pan and replace the duck on top standing on its back. Cover with the lid. Place in a hot oven at approx. 200°C. Baste occasionally and remove the lid after approx. 1 hour. Continue cooking and basting until the duck is cooked but underdone. Total time approx. 1 hour 20 mins.
3			Remove the duck, discard the string, cover the duck and keep warm.
4	Fonds Brun (97) arrowroot	4dl 10g approx.	Place the pan on the stove and allow the juices and vegetables to colour and heat gently without burning. Drain off the fat without disturbing the vegetables and sediment. Add the stock and allow to simmer gently for a few minutes. Skim carefully any remaining fat. Lightly thicken with the diluted arrowroot, pass through a fine strainer into a clean pan, cover and keep on one side.
5	oranges lemon	3 1	Peel the skin finely from one orange and the lemon, cut into very fine julienne and blanch in boiling water for 5 mins. Drain and keep on one side. Squeeze the juice from the three oranges and half of the lemon only.
6	vinegar, white wine sugar Curaçao	¼dl 30g 1 tbsp	Place the vinegar, sugar and the juices in a small pan. Reduce to a light caramel. Add the prepared sauce, simmer gently, skim and correct the colour if necessary to a rich brown. Adjust the seasoning, pass into a clean pan and add the blanched julienne. Simmer gently for 3–4 mins. then add the Curaçao. Cover and keep warm.

7   Remove the legs from the duckling and reserve for other use. Remove the breasts, cut into long thin slices and arrange overlapping on a flat dish. Coat with a little of the Sauce Bigarade and send the rest separately in a sauceboat.

1105 Aiguillettes de Caneton au Porto

4 portions
1¾ hours

Stage	Ingredient	Quantity	Method

1	butter
	plump well-fleshed
	  duckling, trussed
	  (1007)
		75g
		
		1 × 2½kg
			Heat the butter in a deep pan, season the duck and fry to colour on all sides. Stand on its back then cover with the lid and place in a hot oven at approx. 200°C. Baste occasionally and remove the lid after approx. 1 hour. Continue cooking and basting until the duck is cooked but underdone (total time approx. 1 hour 20 mins.).

2			Remove the duck to one side. Drain off most of the fat in the pan.
3			Remove the legs from the duck and reserve for other uses. Remove the breasts, place on a dish, cover and keep just warm.
4	shallots ⎫ carrots ⎬ chopped celery ⎭ juniper berries, crushed clove, crushed	50g 50g 25g 6 1	Chop the duck carcase into small pieces, replace in the pan together with the vegetables and herbs. Sauté well to colour then completely drain off the fat.
5	port Fonds Brun (97) arrowroot	2dl 4dl 10g approx.	Add the port and reduce by half then add the stock and simmer gently for 10 mins. Pass through a fine strainer into a clean pan, skim off any remaining fat then thicken lightly with the diluted arrowroot. Adjust the seasoning.
6			Remove and discard the skin from the duck breasts. Cut these into thin slices and arrange overlapping on a flat dish. Coat with a little of the prepared sauce and send the remainder of the sauce in a sauceboat.

1106 Canard braisé aux Petits Pois – Braised Duck   4 portions
with Green Peas   2 hours

Stage	Ingredient	Quantity	Method
1	butter	75g	Place the butter in a braising pan, add
	streaky bacon, cut		the lardons and onions and fry brown.
	in lardons (51)	120g	Remove and place on one side.
	button onions	12	
2	duck, trussed for		Season and colour brown on all sides in
	braising (1007)	1 × 2½kg	the remaining fat. Drain off all the fat.
3	Demi-glace (112)	4dl	Add the demi-glace to the duck and
	Fonds Brun (97)	4dl	sufficient stock to half cover the duck. Bring to the boil, cover with the lid and braise in a moderate oven at approx. 175°C until half-cooked (approx. ¾ hour). Baste occasionally.
4	peas	350g	Add the prepared lardons then 20 mins. later add the onions and peas. Finish cooking together. Remove the duck, discard the string, cover the duck and keep warm.
5			Skim the fat from the sauce and peas. Adjust the seasoning and consistency.
6			Carve the duck into portions, arrange in an earthenware dish then ladle the sauce and garnish over.

1107 Caneton poêlé aux Cerises   4 portions
2 hours

Stage	Ingredient	Quantity	Method
1	butter	30g	Butter a deep pan and place in the
	carrots ⎫ roughly	120g	vegetables and herbs.
	onions ⎬ diced	120g	
	celery ⎭	30g	
	bayleaf	½	
	thyme	sprig	
2	duckling, trussed		Season the duckling and place on its
	(1007)	1 × 2½kg	back in the pan. Pour the butter over the
	butter, melted	50g	duckling, cover with the lid and place in the oven at approx. 200°C. Baste occasionally and remove the lid after 1 hour. Continue cooking and basting until the duckling is coloured brown and cooked (total time approx. 1½ hours). Do not overcook.
3			Remove the duckling, discard the string. Cover the duckling and keep warm.

4	Madeira	1dl	Place the pan on the stove and allow the
	Fonds Brun (97)	1dl	juices and vegetables to heat gently and
	Jus lié (113)	3dl	colour without burning. Drain off the fat

Place the pan on the stove and allow the juices and vegetables to heat gently and colour without burning. Drain off the fat without disturbing the vegetables and sediment. Add the Madeira, reduce slightly then add the stock and jus lié. Simmer gently for a few minutes, skim carefully, adjust the seasoning and pass through a fine strainer into a clean pan.

| 5 | cherries, stoned | 24 | Add to the sauce and simmer gently for 5 mins. |

| 6 | | | Carve the duckling into portions, arrange in an earthenware dish and ladle a little of the sauce and cherries over. Send the remainder of the sauce in a sauceboat. |

1108 Caneton poêlé à l'Orange

Prepare and cook as for Aiguillettes de Caneton Bigarade (1104). Carve the duckling into portions instead of slices, coat with the sauce and garnish with warmed segments of orange (66).

1109 Caneton rôti à l'Anglaise – Roast Stuffed Duckling

Stuff the duckling with Sage and Onion Stuffing (44) before trussing and roast in the same way as Poulet rôti à l'Anglaise (1034) allowing approx. 20–25 mins. per 500g. Serve garnished with watercress and accompanied with Apple Sauce (209) and roast gravy.

1110 Caneton rôti, Salade d'Orange – Roast Duckling with Orange Salad

Prepare and roast the duckling as for Poulet rôti (1032). Serve accompanied with roast gravy and Orange Salad (1358).

1111 Caneton sauté Vallée d'Auge

4 portions
1½ hours

Stage	Ingredient	Quantity	Method
1	butter	75g	Heat the butter in a sauté pan. Season
	tender young duckling,		the duckling and fry to a good brown on
	cut for sauté (1014)	1 × 2½kg	all sides. Place in a moderate oven at approx. 190°C until cooked, well-crisped and the maximum of fat is driven off from the pieces of duck. Approx. 25–30 mins.
2	Calvados	½dl	Drain off the fat completely from the pan. Place the pan with duck on the stove then add the Calvados and flamber (32). When the flames have died down remove the duck to an earthenware dish, cover and keep warm.

3	cider, dry	3dl	Add the cider to the pan, reduce by
	cream, double	3dl	two-thirds then add the cream and
			reduce to a coating consistency. Adjust
			the seasoning as necessary and pass
			through a fine strainer into a clean pan.
			Cover and keep warm.
4	apples, firm and		Peel, core and cut the apples into
	sharp	4	quarters. Place on a buttered dish,
	butter, melted	50g	sprinkle with the butter and a little
	sugar	15g	sugar. Glaze brown under the
			salamander.
5			Make sure the duck is hot, coat with a
			little of the sauce and place the apples
			around in bouquets. Send accompanied
			with the rest of the sauce in a sauceboat.

1112 Magret de Canard Bar-le-Duc

4 portions
45 mins.

Stage	Ingredient	Quantity	Method
1	butter	50g	Heat the butter in a sauté pan. Well
	duck breasts, plump		season the duck breasts, colour quickly
	and well-fleshed		on both sides then place in a hot oven
	with skin on	2 × 250g	with occasional basting for approx. 7–8
			mins. Keep well-underdone. Remove,
			cover and keep warm.
2	Port	2dl	Drain off the fat from the pan then add
	redcurrant jelly	1 tbsp	the port and reduce by three-quarters.
	redcurrants, cleaned		Add the redcurrant jelly, heat until
	and washed	75g	melted then add the redcurrants and
	Jus lié (113)	2dl	heat for a few seconds. Add the jus lié
	lemon juice	few drops	and bring just to the boil. Do not
			simmer or cook further. Adjust the
			seasoning as necessary and finish with a
			few drops of lemon juice. Cover and
			keep warm.
3	Armagnac	1 tbsp	Cut the magrets into thinnish slices on
			the slant and arrange overlapping in a
			suitable dish. Add the Armagnac to the
			sauce and ladle a little over the duck.
			Send the rest of the sauce separately.

SPECIAL POINTS

a) The ideal duck breasts for this recipe are those imported from France, vacuum-packed and sold under the name of Magrets of duck. They are cut from a special breed of duck having large, plump, well-formed breasts. They are killed by smothering so as to retain the blood in the tissues of its flesh.

b) If these special duck breasts are unobtainable, use four breasts taken from well-fleshed plump Aylesbury ducklings.

1113 Suprême de Caneton Juan-les-Pins

4 portions
50 mins.

Stage	Ingredient	Quantity	Method

1	butter
	shallots, finely
	    chopped
	duck livers,
	    cleaned
	brandy
		25g
		
		25g
		
		100g
		1 tbsp
			Heat the butter in a frying-pan, add the shallots and cook to a golden colour. Add the liver, season and sauté quickly to lightly colour but keep underdone. Add the brandy and flamber (32). Pass all the ingredients through a fine sieve, mix in a basin and check seasoning.

2	sandwich bread butter, clarified	 75g	Cut four oblong croûtons (26) approx. 12cm in length by 5cm. Shallow fry in the butter to a golden brown and drain. Spread with the prepared liver farce. Place on a dish, cover and reserve.

3	duck suprêmes, skin
	    and wing bones
	    removed
	butter
		
		4
		50g
			Heat the butter in a shallow pan, season the suprêmes and shallow fry them on both sides quickly to colour and cook. Keep just very slightly underdone. Remove, cover and keep warm.

4	brandy grapes, skinned and depipped Jus lié (113)	½dl 32 3dl	Tip out the fat from the pan, add the grapes then add the brandy and flamber (32). Spoon out the grapes into another pan. Add the jus lié to the first pan, simmer for a few minutes then season as necessary and pass through a fine strainer over the grapes. Cover and keep warm.
5			Cut each suprême into thickish slices on the slant and re-form on a prepared croûton. Arrange in an earthenware dish.
6	pine kernels, toasted	 30g	Make sure the duck is hot then coat with the sauce and grapes. Sprinkle with the pine kernels and send.

OIE – GOOSE
OISON – GOSLING

1114 Oie rôtie à l'Anglaise – Roast Stuffed Goose

Prepare, cook and serve in the same way as Caneton rôti à l'Anglaise (1109).

1115 Oie rôtie aux Marrons – Roast Goose with Chestnuts

Stuff the goose with Chestnut Stuffing (43), truss and roast in the same way as Caneton rôti à l'Anglaise. Serve garnished with watercress and Braised Chestnuts (1486). Serve roast gravy separately.

1116 Oison sauté Mâconnaise

6–8 portions
1¼ hours

Stage	Ingredient	Quantity	Method
1	young tender gosling	1 × 4kg	Reserve the liver. Cut the goose into portions for sauté, each leg into 3–4 pieces each, 2 wings, and the breast cut down the centre and then each half into 3–4 pieces.
2	butter	75g	Heat the butter in a heavy sauté pan. Season the pieces of goose well and fry quickly to colour well on all sides. Cover with a lid and place in a moderate oven at approx. 180°C to cook well and slowly and to drive off as much of the fat as possible. Baste occasionally.
3	garlic, finely chopped	3 cloves	After approx. 25 mins. add the seasoned liver, and sprinkle everything with the mixed garlic and herbs. Replace the lid and carry on cooking but with occasional basting for a further 10 mins. approx.
	thyme, ground	1 tsp	
	bayleaf, ground	mixed together ½ tsp	
	rosemary, ground	½ tsp	
	clove, ground	pinch	
4	mushrooms, button	500g	Add the mushrooms. When cooked remove the goose, liver and mushrooms. Arrange the goose neatly in an earthenware dish with the mushrooms. Cut the liver in thick slices and arrange down the middle of the goose. Cover and keep warm.
5	red wine	3dl	Drain off the fat from the pan, deglaze with the wine and reduce by half. Add the demi-glace and reduce to a light coating consistency. Adjust the seasoning and finish with the butter.
	Demi-glace (112)	3dl	
	butter, softened	50g	
6	Heart-shaped Croûtons (26)	8	Make sure the goose is hot then pass the sauce through a fine strainer over the whole. Garnish with the croûtons and sprinkle with chopped parsley.
	parsley, chopped		

PINTADE – GUINEA-FOWL
PINTADEAU – GUINEA-FOWL (YOUNG)

1117 Mignon de Pintadeau en Chausson Bergerac

4 portions
1½ hours

Stage	Ingredient	Quantity	Method
1	butter	25g	Heat the butter in a small pan, add the
	shallots, chopped	50g	shallots and cook until transparent. Add
	mushrooms, cut small		the mushrooms, season and cook, then
	and thinly sliced	250g	add the wine and reduce until almost
	white wine, dry	1dl	dry.
2	cream, double	1dl	Add the cream and reduce until fairly
	basil, finely chopped	good pinch	thick. Finish with the basil and season to taste. Allow to cool completely.
3	butter	50g	Heat the butter in a sauté pan. Season
	Suprêmes (1013) of		the suprêmes and shallow fry on both
	young guinea-fowl,		sides to a light brown. Keep underdone.
	without wing bones	4	Remove and allow to cool.
4	Parma or Ardennes		Lay out the slices of ham on a clean
	ham	4 slices	board. Spread one side of each suprême with a little of the mushroom mixture and place coated side down, to one side of a slice of ham. Cover the top side of the suprême with more of the mixture then fold over the ham and wrap into a neat enclosed parcel.
5	puff pastry (1736)	400g	Roll out approx. 3mm thick and cut out four rounds approx. 15cm in diameter.
6	eggwash		Place a prepared suprême to one side of each round of pastry. Eggwash the edges then fold over and seal well. Place on a dampened baking tray. Crimp the edges and brush with eggwash, then using the point of a small knife neatly score the surface of the chaussons with diagonal lines and make two small holes in the centre to allow steam to escape. Rest in a cool place for 20–30 mins.
7	Sauce Smitaine		Place the chaussons in the oven at
	(212)	2dl	210°C and bake to a golden brown,
	fresh basil, chopped	good pinch	approx. 20 mins. Place on a dish paper and dish and serve accompanied with the Sauce Smitaine mixed with the basil.

1118 Pintade aux Céleris – Guinea-fowl with Celery

Prepare in the same way as Faisan Carême (1170) but using guinea-fowl.

1119 Pintade rôtie – Roast Guinea-fowl

Bard (1) the guinea-fowl with slices of fat bacon. Roast and serve in the same way as Poulet rôti (1032), but remove the fat bacon some ten minutes before the bird is cooked to allow a good colour to develop. Keep just slightly underdone.

1120 Pintadeau sauté Niçoise

4 portions
50 mins.

Stage	Ingredient	Quantity	Method
1	oil	½dl	Heat the oil in a sauté pan. Season the guinea-fowl and place in the oil when it is hot. Colour lightly on both sides, cover with the lid and cook more slowly on the side of the stove. Remove the breasts and wings first; give extra time to the legs. Keep very slightly underdone only. Arrange in an earthenware dish, cover and keep warm.
	young guinea-fowl cut for sauté (1014)	4 portions	
2	onions, chopped	50g	Add the onions and garlic to the pan and cook without colour then add the artichoke bottoms and courgette. Season and toss over to lightly fry. Drain off any surplus oil.
	garlic, finely chopped	1 clove	
	artichoke bottoms (1380) cut in quarters	4	
	courgettes cut in ½cm-round slices	1	
3	Tomates Concassées (90)	250g	Add the tomatoes, olives and wine and simmer gently for a few minutes to reduce by half. Do not overcook. Adjust the seasoning.
	black olives, stoned, blanched and cut in half	12	
	white wine, dry	2dl	
4	tarragon, chopped	good pinch	Place the guinea-fowl in the sauce and allow to heat gently without boiling for 7–8 mins. Transfer the guinea-fowl to an earthenware dish, arrange neatly then cover with the sauce and garnish and sprinkle with the tarragon.

1121 Salmis de Pintade

Prepare in the same way as Salmis de Faisan (1174) but using guinea-fowl.

PIGEON – PIGEON
PIGEONNEAU – PIGEON (YOUNG)

1122 Mignons de Pigeonneau aux Fèves

4 portions
25 mins.

Stage	Ingredient	Quantity	Method
1	butter	75g	Heat the butter in a sauté pan. Season
	breasts of young		the breasts and shallow fry carefully.
	pigeon, free of		Cook with very little colour and keep
	skin and wing bone	8	slightly underdone.
2	Oval-shaped Croûtons		Place each breast on a croûton which
	(26)	8	has been spread with foie gras. The
	foie gras purée	75g	croûtons should be no larger than the
			breasts. Arrange in an earthenware dish,
			cover and keep warm.
3	shallots, chopped	50g	Add the shallots to the butter in the pan
	small broad beans,		and cook without colour. Add the broad
	cooked (1464)	100g	beans to heat then drain off any fat. Add
	white wine, dry	1dl	the white wine, reduce by half then add
	cream, double	2dl	the cream and reduce to a light coating
			consistency.
4	butter, soft	25g	Mix in the butter, adjust the seasoning
	fresh savory,		and finish with the savory.
	chopped	good pinch	
5			Make sure the pigeon breasts are hot
			then coat with the sauce and beans.

1123 Pigeon grillé – Grilled Pigeon

Young pigeon may be grilled in the same ways as for Grilled Chicken; see Poulet grillé (1041), Poulet grillé à la Diable (1044), Poulet grillé à la Crapaudine (1043). Adjust the cooking times and keep slightly underdone.

1124 Pigeon Pie

10 portions
2½ hours

Stage	Ingredient	Quantity	Method
1	pigeons, plump	5 × 450g approx.	Carefully draw and singe the pigeons. Remove the livers and reserve.
2			Cut the pigeons in half and remove all the bones from the inner surfaces and legs.
3	streaky bacon, unsmoked	10 slices	Season the inner surfaces of each pigeon half with a little salt, milled pepper and
	mace, ground		ground mace. Place a piece of the reserved liver in each, fold over then wrap in a slice of bacon.

4	topside of beef	750g	Cut into 20 small slices. Cover the
	eggs, hard-boiled,		bottom of two 22cm approx. pie dishes
	cut in halves	5	with half the slices of beef. Lay five
	onion, finely chopped	100g	pieces of the prepared pigeon in each,
	parsley, chopped	1 tbsp	interspersed with the eggs. Sprinkle with
	mushrooms, button,		the onions and parsley, divide the
	cut in quarters	400g	mushrooms between each dish, then
			cover with the remaining slices of beef.
			Shape the ingredients so that they
			become dome-shaped in the dish.

5	Fonds Brun (97)	5dl	Season the stock and flavour with a few
	cold	approx.	drops of Worcestershire sauce. Cover
	Worcestershire sauce	few drops	the meats two-thirds of the way up with
			this stock.

6	Pâte Feuilletée	650g	Roll out the pastry approx. 3mm thick.
	(1736)		Eggwash the rims of the pie dishes and
			cover with 1½cm-wide strips of pastry.
			Eggwash the strips. Cover the pies with
			the remainder of the pastry, seal firmly
			and trim off the surplus paste with a
			knife. Decorate the edge of the pastry
			around the pies. Eggwash and decorate
			with designs of pastry. Allow to rest in a
			cool place for at least 1 hour.

7			Place the pies in a hot oven to lightly
			brown and set the pastry (approx. 20
			mins.). Reduce the temperature to
			approx. 150°C and cook until the meat is
			tender (approx. 1½ hours).

| 8 | | | Clean the pie dishes, place on suitable |
| | | | dishes and surround with pie collars. |

SPECIAL POINTS
a) The livers of pigeon have no gall-bladders and thus require no cleaning.
b) The bones from the pigeons may be used to produce a more flavoured stock in the
following manner. Colour the bones in a little butter with a little chopped onion,
carrot and celery then cover with the required amount of brown stock, add 2–3 leaves
of sage and 4 crushed juniper berries and simmer gently for one hour. Skim, pass
through a fine strainer and allow to cool before using.

1125 Pigeonneau rôti – Roast Pigeon

Use young, plump pigeons. Draw and singe but leave the liver inside and bard (1) with
fat bacon. Roast in a hot oven as for Poulet rôti allowing 7–8 minutes on each side.
Remove the bard when the bird is stood on its back to colour for a further 7–8 minutes
but keep a little underdone. Garnish with watercress, the fat bacon and game chips, and
serve accompanied with Bread Sauce (205 or 206) and roast gravy.

The liver may be removed, seasoned, mashed with a little butter then spread on
croûtons. These may be used to stand the pigeon on, or arranged at its side.

1126 Salmis de Pigeon

Prepare in the same way as Salmis de Faisan (1174) but using four halves of pigeon.

1127 Pigeonneau en Compote

4 portions
1 hour

Stage	Ingredient	Quantity	Method
1	butter	75g	Heat the butter in a deep pan, add the lardons and onions and fry to colour. Remove to one side then quickly fry the mushrooms and remove.
	Lardons, blanched (51)	100g	
	button mushrooms	100g	
	button onions	16	
2	pigeons, young plump	4	Season the pigeons and colour on all sides in the remaining fat in the pan. Leave standing on their backs. Replace the lardons, onions and mushrooms round the pigeons, cover with the lid and place in a moderate oven at 190°C approx. for approx. 35 mins. Baste occasionally.
3			Remove from the oven and place the pigeons and the garnish in a clean cocotte or casserole.
4	white, wine, dry	1dl	Tip out the fat from the pan, deglaze with the wine, reduce by half then add the jus lié. Simmer gently for a few minutes, adjust the seasoning then pass through a fine strainer over the pigeons and garnish.
	Jus lié (113)	1½dl	
5	parsley, chopped		Cover with the lid and place in a hot oven for ten minutes. Sprinkle with chopped parsley and send.

1128 Suprêmes de Pigeonneau aux Morilles

4 covers
30 mins.

Stage	Ingredient	Quantity	Method
1	butter		Heat the butter in a sauté pan. Season the suprêmes and shallow fry to colour on both sides. Keep very underdone. Remove and keep on one side.
	Suprêmes of young pigeon (1012)	8	
2	morels, trimmed carefully, washed and dried	350g	If necessary cut any large morels into two or three pieces, then place into the remaining fat in the pan. Cook fairly quickly for a few minutes then add the shallot. Mix over and cook until transparent. Drain off any remaining fat.
	shallots, very finely chopped	50g	

3	brandy	½dl	Replace the suprêmes in the pan with the morels, add the brandy and flamber (32). When the flames have died down cover with the lid and cook for a little longer in a hot oven approx. 200°C until the suprêmes are just cooked, about 10 minutes. Remove with the morels to a clean dish. Arrange the suprêmes with the morels in the centre, cover and keep warm.
4	Jus lié (113) butter, soft	1½dl 50g	Add the jus lié to the pan, simmer gently for a few moments then mix in the butter away from the heat. Adjust the seasoning as necessary.
5	parsley, chopped		Make sure the suprêmes are hot then pass the sauce through a fine strainer over the suprêmes only. Sprinkle the morels with a little chopped parsley.

DINDONNEAU – TURKEY (YOUNG)
DINDE – TURKEY (LARGE HEN BIRD)
DINDON – TURKEY (LARGE COCK BIRD)

The French descriptive terms, 'Dindonneau' for a small to medium turkey and 'Dinde' for a larger hen bird, are the most frequently used in menu titling. 'Dindon' for the large male bird is seldom if ever used.

1129 Aileron de Dinde braisé Anversoise

10 portions
2¼ hours

Stage	Ingredient	Quantity	Method
1	turkey winglets, large	10	Trim the winglets clean at each end then tunnel out with a small knife from both ends to remove the bones. Be careful not to damage the outer skin.
2	pork sausage-meat	400g	Use a piping bag and plain tube to stuff the winglets with the sausage-meat. Sew up both ends with thread.
3	butter onion ⎤ sliced carrots ⎦ small garlic, crushed bacon trimmings juniper berries, crushed	100g 450g 250g 1 clove 100g 10	Heat the butter in a braising pan, season the winglets and fry to a good brown colour on both sides. Remove from the pan then place in the vegetables, bacon and herbs. Replace the winglets back on top of these, cover and place in a hot oven at 200°C for 15 mins.

4	dark beer	4dl	Remove the pan from the oven and place
	Fonds Brun (97)	5dl approx.	on the stove. Add the beer and reduce by half, then add sufficient of the stock
	tomato purée	1 tbsp	to barely cover. Mix in the tomato and
	Bouquet Garni	1 large	chestnuts, season and bring to the boil.
	chestnuts, skinned and roughly chopped	300g	Skim, add the bouquet garni, cover with the lid and replace in a moderate oven at approx. 180°C and gently cook until tender, approx. 1 hour.

5			Remove the winglets, discard the thread then place the winglets in two deep earthenware dishes. Cover and keep warm.

6	arrowroot	10g approx.	Discard the bouquet garni then pass the liquid and ingredients through a fine sieve or a food processor. Pass through a medium strainer into a clean pan and lightly thicken with diluted arrowroot if necessary. The texture should be of a good coating consistency. Adjust the seasoning as necessary.

7	Endives braisées (1451)	10 small portions	Garnish the winglets with bouquets of endives and sprouts. Make sure that all is hot then coat the winglets only with a
	Choux de Bruxelles au Beurre (1437)	40 pieces	little of the sauce. Sprinkle with chopped parsley and send accompanied with the
	parsley, chopped		rest of the sauce in a sauceboat.

1130 Dindonneau rôti à l'Anglaise – Roast Stuffed Turkey, English-Style

Prepare and stuff the turkey at the neck end with thyme and parsley stuffing (45) mixed with one-third its weight of pork sausage-meat and 1 fresh egg. Roast as for Poulet rôti à l'Anglaise (1034), basting frequently and allowing approx. 20 mins. per 500g of total weight. Reduce the heat as necessary and cover with foil or greaseproof paper to prevent over-colouring. Do not overcook. Garnish with grilled chipolatas, grilled rolls or rashers of bacon and watercress. Serve accompanied with Bread Sauce (205 or 206), Cranberry Sauce (204) and roast gravy.

1131 Dindonneau rôti aux Marrons or Châtaignes – Roast Turkey with Chestnuts

Prepare and stuff the turkey at the neck end with Chestnut Stuffing (43). Roast as for Poulet rôti à l'Anglaise (1034), basting frequently and allowing approx. 20 mins. per 500g of total weight. Reduce the heat as necessary and cover with foil or greaseproof paper to prevent over-colouring. Do not overcook. Garnish with Braised Chestnuts (1486) and watercress. Serve accompanied with roast gravy.

SPECIAL POINT
According to the fashion of the establishment or the requirements of the customer, it is quite in order to offer, in addition, the same garnishes and sauces as used for Dindonneau rôti à l'Anglaise (1130).

1132 Escalopes of Turkey

Escalopes may be cut and prepared from the breast of turkey and served in any of the ways applicable to Escalopes or Escalopines of Veal (951–962).

1133 Sauté d'Emincé de Dinde aux Amandes et Safran

10 portions
30 mins.

Stage	Ingredient	Quantity	Method
1	turkey breast, skinned butter	1kg 120g	Cut the turkey into thinnish strips approx. 4cm long × 1½cm wide. Heat half the butter in a sauté pan. Season half the turkey and when the butter just begins to brown add the turkey and sauté quickly to a light colour only. Do not overcook. Remove from the pan. Repeat for the remainder of the turkey. Drain the turkey and keep warm. Return the fat to the sauté pan.
2	almonds, shredded	75g	Add the almonds to the remaining fat in the pan and colour lightly.
3	saffron, carefully cut small and steeped in a little hot chicken stock Velouté de Volaille (115) cream, double lemon juice cayenne	good pinch 3dl 2dl squeeze	Drain off the fat then add the velouté, the cream and the saffron and its liquid. Reduce to a coating consistency and adjust the seasoning plus a squeeze of lemon juice and a touch of cayenne.
4			Add the cooked turkey to the sauce and reheat thoroughly.
5	Riz Pilaff (522)	10 portions	Place the turkey in earthenware dishes and send accompanied with separate dishes of the rice.

SPECIAL POINT
6dl of Crème Fraîche may be used instead of the velouté and double cream.

14
Game

For culinary purposes the term 'Game' refers to certain wild birds and animals used as a source of food. Traditionally these birds and animals were hunted both as a sport and as an opportunity for augmenting and replenishing the larder, mostly during carefully regulated seasons of the autumn and winter months.

Both kinds are prized for their particular flavours which derive from their own natural characteristics and also from a period of hanging and maturation which most of them undergo. The flesh of most game birds is easily digested and in many respects can be treated as poultry. Water-fowl, however, are stronger in flavour and in comparison less digestible, although keeping them underdone can help to mitigate this. Game animals provide a much richer flesh of excellent eating qualities which can be prepared in many of the ways applicable to red butcher's meat but it very often requires longer maturation periods and marinating to make it tender; in general the flesh is less digestible than that of game birds.

In recent years game has become more popular as a menu item and this popularity has been attended with a marked increase in the availability of farmed game birds and animals, especially pheasant, quail and deer. The wild boar is now also being farmed in those countries where hunting and the clearance of its natural forest habitats had resulted in their virtual extinction. Flesh from the farmed animal which is almost indistinguishable from the wild species is now becoming available in the United Kingdom.

All forms of game are best obtained through reputable game dealers who have the necessary expertise to supply it in the correct season and condition. A certain amount of imported fresh game and some frozen game is available out of season but there is little demand for it.

In most cases game birds, whatever their preparation, are suitable for lunch or dinner menus, although the various wild duck are best served for dinner. Venison either as joints or small cuts can figure on either menu but hare and rabbit dishes with one or two exceptions, such as the saddle of hare, are best for lunch.

−CLASSIFICATION AND QUALITY POINTS−

Game birds and animals are usually classified as either feathered game or furred game.

Feathered game

Wild game birds are protected by law and have a clearly defined season when shooting is permitted but some birds like the various plovers which were once used as game are now protected species and are rarely if ever available. A quality to look for in all game birds is the absence of excessive damage from lead shot such as shattered bones and areas of congealed blood and bruising. They should be plump and heavy for their size.

Game birds are usually bought ready-plucked and trussed and are sold by number, not by weight.

Blackgame or Blackcock

This is a member of the grouse family but larger. It is of excellent eating quality, delicate and tender and in some respects can compare with grouse. The young adult cock bird can weigh up to 1¾ kg, with the hen approximately half this weight. Look for plump, well-formed breasts with the end of the breastbone slightly pliable. The spurs of the young cock bird are soft at the extreme end.

Capercaillie or Capercailzie

This bird is also a member of the grouse family, very closely related to blackgame but larger still – the cock bird can weigh as much as 5½kg and can be recognised by the scarlet patch of naked flesh over the eyes. The hen bird is smaller and of a more nondescript appearance. Gastronomically speaking, the flesh is not so delicate or fine-flavoured as that of blackgame. The quality points to look for are the same as for blackgame.

Grouse

The true Scotch red grouse is to be found only on the moors of Northern England and Scotland, and to a much lesser extent in Ireland. It has an incomparable flavour whether young or old, or served hot or cold, but the young bird is best served by being roasted. Older birds are useful for braising and for pies and terrines.

The young bird has soft downy feathers on the breast, wings and legs. The spur on the legs should not be pronounced or hard at its extremity. Look for plump pliable breasts and no sign of taint at the vent. The older bird will show well-developed feathering and hard spurs.

Partridge

From the gourmet's point of view the grey-legged partridge is considered to be finer than the so-called French red-legged variety which is more widely distributed and thus more easily obtained at cheaper prices. Quality is determined in the young bird of either variety by plump breasts, pliable breastbones and smooth legs. The older bird has well-developed scales on the legs; these older birds are excellent for braising or for pâtés, terrines or pies.

Pheasant

This popular game bird is usually supplied by the brace, that is one cock bird and one hen. The cock is larger but the hen is considered to be more tender and of a finer flavour.

The young bird makes better eating. Look for plump breasts, pliable breastbones, relatively smooth lower legs and in the cock, small spurs. They tend to reach their best by the middle of November.

Plover

There are three main varieties of this bird, the golden, grey and green plover or lapwing, with pride of place going to the golden plover for its excellent and distinctive gastronomic qualities. As stated previously, they are protected species and thus rarely if ever available. Quality is determined by a plump, well-fleshed body and a firm, fatty vent free of taint.

Quail
They should be used as fresh as possible and are only spoilt by hanging. The flavour is delicate with no gamey overtones. Quality is determined by very whitish skin, evidence of fat especially round the vent and very plump breasts.

Snipe
They are akin to the woodcock though smaller but the feeding habits tend to be dissimilar, resulting in differences in flavour and aroma. The flavour and delicacy of the snipe, however, is generally considered to be inferior to that of the woodcock. Select well-fleshed birds, firm and fatty at the vent. The snipe is usually prepared with its neck and long beak left on, thus there should be no smell of taint in these areas.

Wild Duck
The mallard is the largest and most commonly used with the widgeon being slightly smaller and the teal the smallest of the three. The mallard and teal are aquatic feeders and tend to develop a fishy flavour especially if used out of season, the widgeon on the other hand has a much sweeter flavour because of its liking for meadow grass. The young adult bird is the more tender and better-flavoured. Choose plump well-fleshed birds as a sign of being well-fed and in good condition. The feet and beak should be pliable and tear easily.

Woodcock
It is esteemed as being of high gastronomic quality and by many authorities considered as being second only to grouse. The quality points are the same as for snipe.

Emu
Has dark red meat with a gamey flavour with very tender flesh, farmed in Western Australia. It can be shallow fried and grilled as escalopes, roasted and braised as joints.

Ostrich
Has dark red, very lean meat with a coarse texture and goat flavour, particularly the fillet and leg steaks. Plays an important part in South African cookery, now farmed in the UK and on the continent. It can be shallow fried, stewed and braised.

Furred game

For wild deer the permitted seasons for hunting are regulated by law and these correspond generally to their out-of-breeding seasons which are May–September for the buck, and September–January for the doe. Reject any animal or joint which shows excessive damage from shot such as mangled bones and large areas of bruising.

Hare
The young hare, or leveret, is preferred for its tender and less stringy flesh and its less strong flavour although an older animal with adequate hanging and marination can be acceptable for certain stewed or braised dishes. In the young animal the ears tear easily, the claws are generally short and clean and the hare lip is barely discernible.

Rabbit
There are two types of rabbit used for the table:
Wild rabbit: The young female is always better than the male, especially near the start of the breeding season when the flesh of the male tends to become rank and coarse in

flavour. Quality in the young rabbit is determined by ears which tear easily and the bones of the under jaw which break easily under pressure. The interior of the animal should smell fresh and sweet with no pronounced gamey smell or taint. Kidneys well-covered with fat are a sign of good condition and overall the body should be plump, well-fleshed and of a clean white to pink colour.

Domestic or hutch rabbit: This is a much larger animal in general when compared with its wild cousin and a young specimen of 5–6 months can weigh as much as 4kg. Look for large, small-boned and very plump specimens with almost white flesh. All other quality points as for the wild animal apply.

Venison

This is a general term relating to the flesh of all deer. The flesh of the roe deer is the most esteemed with that of the fallow deer and the red deer closely following. The quality of venison is influenced by such factors as age, sex, general condition, the type of herbage consumed, the method of killing and the subsequent hanging and processing for cooking.
1) The flesh of the male animal (buck) is superior to that of the female (doe).
2) Young animals of up to no more than 4 years of age are excellent but those between 18 months to 2 years are considered the best. The very young animal under 18 months can be very tender but invariably lacks flavour.
3) The carcase should not appear to be emaciated.
4) The colour of the flesh should be dark red in colour and should have a somewhat stronger smell than beef.
5) What little fat there is should be firm and white, the greater its depth being an indication of quality.
6) The inside of the carcase should be relatively dry and not sticky or slimy.
7) Check by smell near and behind the kidneys; this should be clean if a little strong. Reject the carcase if any putrid or rotten smell is detected.

Wild Boar

The young animal up to 1 year old can provide excellent tender flesh but of a strong flavour. Older than this it becomes progressively drier, more stringy and very rank in flavour. The young animal provides a small carcase of up to 14kg in weight. The flesh is dark red but should have no overtly strong or tainted smell. Hanging and marination are essential prerequisites for the best results when cooked. The older animal is the traditional supplier of the festive boar's head although these days the head of the domestic pig is generally used.

Bison

Dark red meat which is sweeter and tastier than beef is suitable for roasting; farmed from North American stock.

Kid

Similar to lamb but with a stronger taste and aroma popular in countries of the Mediterranean and south America; kids and goatlings are reared domestically. They can be roasted, stewed or braised.

Offals

The offals from all kinds of game are dark-coloured but should still be fresh-looking when taken from the bird or animal. They should not be tainted, discoloured or sticky to the touch.

Game animals: The tongue, heart, liver, kidney and lungs of deer can be used for various dishes such as pâtés, terrines, pies and stews. The liver and kidney can be cooked as separate dishes. They should always be removed fresh from the carcase after killing. The offals of hare and rabbit are seldom if ever used separately from the carcase for dishes in their own right. They are usually cooked with the flesh or used in the preparation of accompanying sauces or forcemeat.

Game birds: The liver is removed from game birds for the preparation of forcemeats or pâtés but is frequently left in when the bird is roasted. The remaining giblets are useful in the preparation of game stocks or gravies.

In all cases where the giblets are removed for other uses they should always be as firm and fresh as possible.

———HANGING AND MATURATION———

Most game, with few exceptions, improves from a period of hanging and maturation. This helps to tenderise the flesh and develop the more pronounced flavour prized as one of its special qualities. The length of time tends to vary in relation to the bird or animal but in any case the modern trend is towards shorter times commensurate with a reasonably well-developed flavour. The older demand for game with an overdeveloped taste is no longer so popular, neither is it desirable from the viewpoint of dietary health. In extreme cases, where the flesh becomes almost putrid, it can be toxic and exceedingly dangerous.

As stated before, the correct hanging and maturing of game is best left to the specialist dealer where possible. However, occasions can arise where a customer delivers his own game or a suitable supply of fresh game can be obtained at advantage to the establishment. In these cases it is well to follow certain procedures, to be able to equate the periods of hanging with the particular bird or animal and to carry these out in optimum conditions. The following points need to be borne in mind:

1) Where needed, game birds and hare should be hung before plucking or skinning and drawing, for a certain period of time. Deer and rabbit however, need to be drawn immediately after killing but left unskinned for hanging. This is best carried out in a cold well-ventilated larder or a refrigerated room with fan-assisted circulation and separate from any other foodstuffs. The temperature should not be higher than 8°C.
2) Hang all game birds by the neck, hare by the forelegs and deer and rabbit by the hind legs.
3) The birds or animals should not be hung so that they touch each other. Keep them well-separated so that the air can circulate well around them.
4) After skinning or plucking and drawing, the game can be stored for a further period of time to extend the hanging process where suitable or for holding prior to cooking. Normal refrigeration temperature of 2–3°C is ideal for this.

Hanging Times
The following times are intended as a guide only. Experience related to the use of smell, touch and sight can provide the most useful help in deciding when any item of game is ready. This means being able to discern the possible onset of bad odour, stickiness and discolouration or overdried and blemished surfaces.

Grouse, Blackgame, Capercaillie: As a rule use as fresh as possible but can be hung for no more than two days in feather. Use as soon as possible after plucking and drawing.

Pheasant: Hang for 3–8 days in feather according to requirements. The longer the hanging time the more high and developed the taste and flavour. Do not store for too long after plucking and drawing.

Quail: These do not require hanging and should be used as fresh as possible.

Partridge, Snipe, Woodcock, Plover: Hang for only 3–4 days in feather. Should be used soon after plucking and drawing.

Wild Duck: Hang for no more than two days in feather. After this, water-fowl quickly develop a rank oily taste. Use as soon as possible after plucking and drawing.

Hare: Hang for 5–6 days by the forelegs. After this they are best skinned and drawn. They can then be held for a further 2–3 days in normal refrigerator temperatures, 2–3°C. Be careful not to damage the diaphragm (the skin across the bottom ribs); this contains the blood, lungs and heart which are always used in its final preparation.

Rabbit: The entrails should be removed as soon as possible after killing and the unskinned rabbit should then be hung by the hind legs for no more than 2–3 days with its abdominal flaps kept open by placing a short clean stick of wood between them. Do not remove the heart, liver or kidneys. After skinning use as soon as possible. Any prolonged period of hanging results in an undesirable gamey flavour.

Venison (Deer): Hang in its fur by the hind legs after drawing for no more than 5–6 days then skin it. It can then be hung for a further 8–10 days in normal refrigerator temperatures, 2–3°C, either whole, split into two sides or cut in quarters. Make sure that no stickiness is allowed to develop by wiping carefully and as necessary with a clean cloth.

1134 PLUCKING, DRAWING AND CLEANING OF FEATHERED GAME

In general, all game birds are plucked, drawn and singed after hanging, in the same way as poultry. There are a few exceptions however, as noted in the following:

Grouse (for roasting)
Draw the grouse then replace the liver after removing the gall-bladder. Traditionally, the liver is removed after roasting and mashed with butter and seasoning for spreading on the croûtons served with the bird.

Snipe and Woodcock (for roasting or 'en Casserole')
1) Pluck and singe the bird including the whole of the neck and head. Remove the eyes.
2) Make a small hole with a trussing needle into the inside of the bird just behind the leg. Find the gizzard with the point of the needle and pull it out through the hole. The rest of the entrails should not be removed.

Plover and Quail (for roasting or 'en Casserole')
1) Pluck and singe the bird. Remove the neck and head.
2) Make a small hole with a trussing needle into the inside of the bird just behind the leg. Find the gizzard with the point of the needle and pull it out through the hole. The rest of the entrails should not be removed.

1135 DRAWING AND SKINNING OF FURRED GAME

Venison (Deer)

All deer should be drawn immediately after killing, then skinned after no more than 5–6 days of preliminary hanging.

To Draw (remove the entrails)

1) Cut off the head, remove the tongue and reserve with the other offals if required. Discard the head.
2) Have the carcase hanging by the forelegs.
3) Make a cut through the belly of the animal from the beginning of the breast to between the beginning of the hind legs, taking care not to cut the intestines.
4) Open out, then carefully remove the intestines without any damage so as to prevent soiling of the carcase and fur. Cut cleanly round the anal orifice to remove the end of the large gut.
5) Leave the kidneys in but remove the heart, liver and lungs and reserve with the tongue if needed.
6) Cut through the centre of the breastbones to the neck and along the underside of the neck. Cut clear the opening of where the neck meets the collar bones and remove the windpipe along its length.
7) With a clean cloth wipe the abdominal and breast cavities and the opening along the neck; clean and dry.
8) Wedge open the rib-cage with two or three short sticks so as to assist the circulation of air.

To Skin (after being drawn and hung)

1) Have the carcase hanging by the hind legs.
2) Cut through the skin around the top of the hind legs then down each leg to the cut at the belly. Do not cut into the flesh.
3) Ease the skin away from the flesh of the legs and belly assisting with a sharp knife as needed.
4) Pull the skin down from the back to the breast.
5) Cut through the skin around the top of the forelegs just before the hooves, then cut along the inside of each to the cut in the breast.
6) Ease the skin away from the breast and forelegs and neck.
7) Pull the skin down from the back and detach completely from the carcase.
8) Cut off the hooves at the first joint and discard.
9) As needed, the carcase can now be split into two sides or into quarters for further hanging.

The carcase can then be dissected with minor variations in the same way as for lamb. See the table of joints and small cuts on pages 276–78.

Hare

Hares should be skinned and drawn after 5–6 days of hanging.

To Skin

1) Cut off the feet at the first joint with the legs and lay the hare on its back.
2) Pinch the skin of one of the legs to raise it from the flesh, then insert the point of a small knife and cut along the length of the leg.
3) Using the fingers, ease the leg out of the skin.
4) Repeat with the other leg then cut off the tail under the skin.

5) Pull the skin down from the body to the forelegs.
6) Ease the forelegs out of the skin then pull off the skin to the ears.
7) Cut off the ears close to the head then pull the skin completely from the head.

To Draw
1) Carefully make a cut along the belly from between the legs to just before the breast. Be careful not to pierce the intestines so as to prevent soiling of the carcase.
2) Open out then remove the intestines to a container. Do not remove the kidneys, and take care not to pierce the skin across the rib-cage (diaphragm). This contains the heart, liver and lungs and the blood used in the cooking.
3) Make sure that the anal orifice is cleanly removed.

Rabbit
Rabbits should have their entrails removed as soon as possible after they have been killed and bled.

To Draw and Skin
Proceed as for hare but do not skin first. After drawing they can be hung unskinned for a few days without any undesirable gamey flavour developing. When ready, skin in the same way as for hare.

STORAGE

All drawn and prepared game is a highly perishable commodity, perhaps even more so than poultry, and its quality can soon deteriorate if not handled properly and stored correctly, ideally at a temperature of 2–3°C. Game birds should be placed in single layers on trays and not stacked on top of each other, but it is permissible to lightly cover them with oiled greaseproof to prevent excessive drying of the skin surfaces. In any case they should be used within 3 days.

Venison can be stored and matured after drawing and skinning for up to 10 days in a meat refrigerator at a temperature of 2–3°C. It should be separated from other meats where possible. Care should be continually taken to monitor its progress with special attention paid to preventing any undue drying or stickiness developing or the onset of any unpleasant odour.

Prepared hare and rabbit may be kept for 2–3 days in the meat refrigerator before cutting and cooking. They store better if hung but may be placed side by side on trays and loosely covered with oiled paper.

CUTS AND PREPARATIONS FOR COOKING (FEATHERED GAME)

1136 To Truss

First cut off the winglets near the end of the wing bone and trim the ends of the toes. Except for snipe and woodcock, truss as for poultry (1007). For snipe and woodcock: a) twist the lower legs back and interlock them together; b) pull the head to the side of the bird then pass the beak through the centre of the legs at the joint.

1137 To Bone Out Game Birds for Stuffing

This can be done in the same way as for poultry (1015). The small game birds can be boned out by using the fingers and a small knife and without cutting the bird along the back.

1138 Preparation for Sauté

Young pheasant can be cut for sauté in the same way as chicken (1014). Do not use the drumsticks unless the tendons found there can be successfully removed. Young smaller birds such as grouse and partridge may be cut in half or into quarters, i.e. two legs with the thigh bone removed and two suprêmes.

1139 Preparation for Grilling

Pheasant, grouse and partridge can be prepared for grilling in either of the ways suitable for chicken (1010 or 1011). The small game birds are best if split open and skewered flat.

1140 Preparation for Sautés à la Minute

The breasts of the larger game birds if very tender can be cut into small thin strips for quick sautés.

1141 Preparation of Escalopes and Escalopines

These can be cut to the size required from the skinned breasts of large and tender game birds. Remove the small fillet from under the breast, leave whole or cut in half according to size, then split along the length. Flatten and trim neatly. Cut thickish slices on the slant from the remaining breast of the required weight, flatten and trim neatly.

CUTS AND PREPARATIONS FOR COOKING ——————(FURRED GAME)——————

1142 To Dissect a Skinned and Drawn Hare for Stews, Civets, Sautés etc.

1) Cut off the head close to the trunk.
2) Open up the diaphragm of the hare and drain off the blood into a basin.
3) Remove the liver, heart and lungs and reserve. Clear the liver of its gall-bladder.
4) Cut off the hind legs at the joint with the pelvis and cut each into three or four pieces according to size.
5) Cut off the front legs (shoulders) from the trunk and leave whole or cut into two pieces.
6) Cut off the abdominal flaps and trim the rib-cage up to the flesh of the trunk.
7) Cut square across the lower end of the trunk to remove the bones of the pelvic girdle.
8) Trim the back and inside of the trunk of any sinew then cut the trunk into six pieces. This will give 14–18 pieces in all.

SPECIAL POINTS
a) All the trimmings from the hare including the head can be reserved and used for game stock or soup.
b) If required for a Civet of Hare the liver, heart and lungs can be minced finely and mixed with the blood. This is then used in the finishing of the sauce.

1143 To Dissect a Rabbit for Stews, Fricassées, Sautés and Pies etc.

As rabbits are bled and drawn completely there should be no blood left in the chest cavity.

Cut the rabbit in the same manner as for hare but take account of its smaller size. Cut the hind legs into 2–3 pieces, the front legs leave whole and cut the trunk into 4–5 pieces. The liver and heart can be used in the preparation of stews and pies.

1144 To Prepare a Hare or Rabbit for Roasting

Traditionally, hare and rabbits were trussed to keep the head and legs in position and then roasted whole. In modern practice the hind legs and back, in one piece only, are used.
1) Clean the carcase carefully.
2) Cut off the forepart of the carcase just behind and close to the forelegs and reserve for other uses.
3) Cut off the abdominal flaps and trim the rib-cage close to the trunk. Trim the ends of the legs.
4) With a small knife carefully trim away the sinew and covering skin which runs along the back of the carcase.
5) Cut through the pelvic girdle so that the legs lie flat.
6) Lard (50) the legs and back with fine strips of salt pork fat.
7) If needed, the legs may be locked together by making a small incision through the bottom end of one leg close to the bone then pushing the end of the other leg through this incision.

1145 To Prepare Fillets of Hare or Rabbit for Sauté

1) Remove the hindlegs and cut off the forepart of the carcase just behind and close to the forelegs.
2) Cut off the abdominal flaps and trim the rib-cage.
3) With a small knife carefully trim away the sinew and covering skin which runs along the back of the trunk.
4) Carefully cut away the two long fillets of flesh which lie on each side of the trunk.
5) Cut each fillet into two or three pieces and use whole or split open lengthways, lightly flatten and trim.

1146 To Prepare a Saddle of Hare

1) Remove the legs and cut off the forepart of the carcase just behind and close to the forelegs.
2) Cut off the abdominal flaps and trim the rib-cage.
3) Cut square across the lower end of the trunk to remove the bones of the pelvic girdle.

4) With a small knife carefully trim away the sinew and covering skin which runs along the back of the trunk.
5) Lard (50) along the back with fine strips of salt pork fat.

NOTE
This will give a long saddle sufficient for two portions. It can, however, be separated at the point where the rib-cage begins. The hind part, i.e. that part which corresponds to the saddle of lamb, is the most suitable for single portions. It comprises the small fillets underneath and is the best and choicest part of the whole animal.

1147 Larding and Barding of Furred Game

The flesh of venison is usually very lean and lacks much in the way of natural fat. It also loses the ability to retain its moistness because of the need to trim its outer surfaces and thus tends to be very dry. Joints of venison needed for roasting or poêling can be improved by careful larding of the exposed outer surfaces with fine strips of salt pork fat or fat bacon. It is useful to additionally wrap and tie joints in sheets of pork fat or salt pork fat for a good part of the cooking process.

1148 Marinating of Furred Game

Marination can do much to assist in the tenderising of furred game, especially in the case of venison. The red wine marinade (55) is the most useful but this can be modified by the addition of up to 25% its total volume of good red wine vinegar. In other cases, especially where hare is required for civet, marination with brandy and oil only, plus the usual herbs and aromats, can provide a particular and very distinctive result, totally different to that imparted by a red wine marinade.

──────── COOKING METHODS ────────

In general, game birds and venison when tender are best roasted or poêléed but in many cases the preparations and methods used for poultry and butcher's meat can be successfully applied. The following observations are mainly related to where the treatment and cooking methods tend to be particular to game or differ in detail from those for butcher's meats and poultry.

Boiling, Poaching, Steaming
These methods are seldom if ever applied to venison although poaching and steaming can be suitable for suprêmes and fillets of all game birds, especially if shallow-poached with richly flavoured stocks, prepared from the bones and trimmings of the bird. Mousselines and Quenelles can be prepared from the flesh of all tender game and poached in game stock. In these cases the accompanying sauces need not necessarily be highly flavoured but can be much lighter and more delicate. Those using reductions finished with creams or veloutés as well as light sabayon-finished and glazed sauces can be more appropriate.

Stewing
Hare and the less tender parts of venison can be successfully stewed in the form of civets. This requires marination and particular qualities can be obtained by varying the

wines and/or spirits and flavourings used in the marination. Rabbit can provide excellent Fricassées and Blanquettes as well as the more conventional brown stews. They may be served with any of the garnishes applicable to the equivalent stews of poultry and meats.

Braising
Older game birds and the less tender parts of venison can be suitably brown-braised although it must be said that stewing would always be preferable for tougher venison. Braised joints of venison are best if larded and marinated first.

Baking
This method is usually applied to game in the form of pies, pâtés, terrines or where the item is first prepared then covered with pastry and baked. The latter type of preparation can be excellent when applied to small game birds such as quail, snipe and woodcock. They can be boned and stuffed with various forcemeats and covered with either puff or short pastry. The accompanying sauces are more useful when well-flavoured and highly seasoned.

Poêling
This is also an excellent method of cooking suitable for all game and the process makes it possible to introduce the wide combinations of aromats, herbs and seasonings so suitable for the stronger flavours of game.

Game birds except for water-fowl should be barded, and venison or hare needs to be larded and, where necessary, marinated. The process is the same as for butcher's meat and poultry and can include the use of well-flavoured herbs and vegetables such as juniper, sage, rosemary, fennel and garlic. Wines, especially red, are excellent for deglazing. The cooking juices and spirits, cream, sour cream, game stocks and prepared sauces can vary the final sauce. Fruit juices, flavoured vinegars, lemon, lime and orange juices as well as fruit purées can be utilised and various fruits and their purées make excellent accompaniments, especially for furred game.

The special poêlings termed 'en Casserole' or 'en Cocotte' (1076) are widely applied for game birds, saddle and fillets of hare and for small cuts of venison. Butter should always be used as a basting agent; foie gras, mushrooms, truffles, morels, chanterelles, ceps and olives are excellent as garnishes to be finished in with the cooking, and spirits, wines, meat glazes and light gravies can add the final moistening. What is essential is that everything is done under cover so as to imbue the game with the flavour of the added ingredients. It is very useful to seal the casserole or cocotte with a strip of pastry or dough to ensure minimal loss of flavour.

Roasting
This is undoubtedly the best of all methods for tender game birds and joints of venison. All game birds, except water-fowl because of the comparative dryness of the flesh, are improved if barded first. Venison should be larded and additionally wrapped in slices of salt pork fat for best results; this fat can be removed about three-quarters of the way through the cooking. If from the young animal, venison is better if not marinated but this process can do much to improve the eating qualities of joints of older animals when roasted. In all cases, venison should be cooked underdone unless specifically requested otherwise.

Care should be taken with game birds to ensure that they are not overdone. In most cases just cooked to the bone is sufficient. Grouse and wild duck, however, are better if underdone. Game birds are usually presented and served with traditional accompaniments; see Roast Game Birds (1159). Large, plump and tender rabbit and hare can make excellent roast joints. They can be trussed and roasted whole but are better if just the legs and complete trunk of the carcase are used; see 1144 for this preparation. The larding for this should be carried out meticulously; hare are best underdone and rabbit just done.

Grilling

All game birds can be grilled though some require slightly different treatment. Young and tender pheasant, partridge and grouse may be grilled in any of the ways applicable to grilled chicken. Use butter in preference to oil, baste frequently during the process and keep just done, grouse perhaps a little underdone. Well-flavoured sauces such as Diable, Piquante, Champignons etc. make ideal accompaniments. Quail, snipe, woodcock and wild duck should be split open from the back, skewered open flat and marinated for 30 mins. or so with a little oil, lemon juice, salt and pepper before grilling. The grilling process should be rapid, at a high temperature and only to the point of being just underdone or at the most, just done. Overcooking always results in a dry and tasteless texture. These smaller birds seem to need nothing more than lemon or parsley butter as an accompaniment rather than the more strongly-flavoured sauces more suited to the larger game birds.

The skinned breasts of blackgame and capercaillie may be removed, cut into thickish slices of about 125g each, lightly flattened then marinated for a short time with a little oil, lemon juice, salt and pepper. These are excellent when quickly grilled and underdone. Serve accompanied with well-flavoured sauces.

Grills of venison can provide much in the way of interest for seasonal menus. It is better that the flesh is from the young animal and, in this case, it is not necessary for it to have been too well-hung. The following cuts are suitable: steaks cut from the leg; noisettes and médaillons from the loin; the fillet either whole or split and flattened; and cutlets from the best end. All of these may be plain grilled or marinated first for a short time with oil, lemon juice, salt and pepper. Unless otherwise requested keep underdone. Serve accompanied with the same sauces as noted above for grilled game birds.

The liver and kidneys removed from the freshly killed animal can be plain grilled, kept underdone and served with a well-flavoured composite butter, such as Beurre Maître d'Hôtel or Beurre Bercy.

Shallow Frying

This method of cooking can be successfully applied to all better cuts of tender game.

For game birds, the most suitable cuts and preparations are suprêmes and fillets of pheasant, grouse, partridge and other smaller birds and the breasts of the larger blackgame and capercaillie cut in slices and used as escalopes or cut into small strips for quick sautés.

Young pheasant can be cut in the same way as chicken for sautés and the same garnishes for chicken are applicable.

Fillets, noisettes, médaillons, steaks and cutlets of venison, especially those from the young roe deer, can add much interest and variety to the menu. The hind legs and saddle of young tender hare and rabbit can be cut in portions and prepared as sautés in the same way as sautés of chicken and the back fillets of both animals can be shallow-fried whole or cut in small thick slices for quick sautés.

The following observations may be worth considering in relation to the shallow frying of game:

a) All items should be from young tender birds or animals.
b) No game should be well-cooked unless specifically requested. The dark meats such as venison, hare, grouse and woodcock are best underdone and the white flesh such as pheasant, partridge, quail and rabbit, just done.

c) Butter is almost always the best cooking medium although oil can be useful occasionally where the style of cooking and garnishing suggest a lighter treatment.

d) Some account must be taken of the richness, depth and strength of flavour of the game when deciding on the accompanying sauce and garnish. Although in most cases darker-coloured game flesh can benefit from the compatibility of strongly flavoured and highly seasoned sauces, it can be useful to create contrast by finishing with very light but delicate sauces based on various types of cream.

e) Useful items for the preparation and finishing of sauces related to the deglazing of the pan after cooking are vinegars, wines, spirits, the juices of citrus fruits, game stocks and various creams. Fruits, such as cherries, oranges, pears, quinces, grapes, apples, and berries such as bilberries, mulberries, cranberries, raspberries, redcurrants, blackcurrants, can be utilised as garnishes or to supply flavour or body to sauces in the form of purées.

f) Juniper and rosemary are useful herbs especially for venison and hare; truffles and all varieties of wild mushroom make excellent and compatible garnishes and sauces.

g) The small cuts of dark-fleshed game may be marinated and flavoured for a short period of time before cooking with combinations of various spirits, citrus juices, finely chopped herbs, chopped onions and shallots, pepper and sometimes, very sparingly, with spices.

h) The cooking and finishing should be carried out as quickly as possible; because of its particular qualities game tends to dry and toughen very quickly if held for any undue period of time even at low temperatures.

The flesh of raw game can be prepared as Bitoks or Pojarski, taking into account its relative colour, e.g. Bitoks prepared from venison or Pojarski from pheasant or partridge. In either case they should be just cooked through and not kept underdone.

Deep Frying

In the same way as for poultry, all items of game, either raw or pre-cooked, need to be coated before deep frying. Salpicons or mixtures of game cooked together with such things as mushrooms, truffle and other ingredients can then be bound with suitable sauces and moulded in various shapes. These may be in the shape of cutlets or rissoles and need to be egg-and-crumbed before deep frying.

Small strips or slices cut from the skinned breasts of blackgame and capercaillie or cut from the fillet of hare, rabbit and venison can be marinated with a little lemon or lime juice, oil, various chopped herbs, spices and seasonings then passed through a light frying batter and deep-fried. As with all deep-fried items, preparations of game need to be cooked at fairly high temperatures and must be well-drained and served as soon as possible.

GIBIERS À PLUME – FEATHERED GAME

The main items of feathered game with their seasons, number of portions and suitable cooking methods:

Name	Season	Approx. No. of Portions	Suitable Cooking Methods and Preparation
1149 Blackgame (Petit Coq de Bruyère)	Sept.–Dec.	2–4	Roasting, poêling, 'en Casserole', 'en Cocotte', Suprêmes.
1150 Capercaillie (Grand Coq de Bruyère)	Aug.–Dec.	6–12	Roasting, poêling, breasts for deep and shallow frying, Escalopes, Mousselines, Sautés à la Minute.
1151 Grouse	12 Aug.–20 Dec.	1–2	Roasting, poêling, 'en Casserole', 'en Cocotte', grilling, Suprêmes for shallow frying, Sautés, hot and cold Pies.
1152 Partridge (Perdreau)	1 Sept.–11 Feb.	1–2	Roasting, poêling, 'en Casserole', 'en Cocotte', braising, grilling, grilling 'en Crapaudine', Suprêmes and Fillets for poaching and sauté.
1153 Pheasant (Faisan)	1 Oct.–11 Feb.	3–4	Roasting, poêling, 'en Casserole', 'en Cocotte', Suprêmes for poaching and shallow frying, Sautés, en Pojarski.
1154 Plover (Pluvier)	Oct.–Dec.	1	Roasting, poêling, 'en Casserole', 'en Cocotte', breasts for sauté.
1155 Quail (Caille)	All year	1	Roasting, poêling, 'en Casserole', 'en Cocotte', Suprêmes for shallow frying, stuffed and braised, grilling.

Name	Season	Approx. No. of Portions	Suitable Cooking Methods and Preparation
1156 Snipe (Bécassine)	12 Aug.–10 Feb.	1	Roasting, poêling, 'au Fumet', Sautés.
1157 Wild Duck: Mallard		2	
(Canard Sauvage)	Aug.–Mar.		
Teal (Sarcelle)	Oct.–Feb.	1	Roasting, poêling, 'au Fumet', à la Presse, Salmis.
Widgeon (Canard Siffleur)	Aug.–Mar.	1	
1158 Woodcock (Bécasse)	1 Oct.–10 Feb.	1	Roasting, poêling, 'au Fumet', Sautés.

1159 Roast Game Birds

The following game birds, all of which are suitable for roasting, are listed under the title as they can appear on the menu.

Bécasse rôtie – Roast Woodcock
Bécassine rôtie – Roast Snipe
Caille rôtie – Roast Quail
Coq de Bruyère rôti – Roast Blackgame or Roast Capercaillie
Canard Sauvage rôti – Roast Wild Duck
Faisan rôti – Roast Pheasant
Grouse rôti – Roast Grouse
Perdreau rôti – Roast Partridge
Sarcelle rôtie – Roast Teal

Method for roasting

Blackgame, Capercaillie, Grouse, Partridge, Pheasant:

1) Truss (1136) and bard (1) the bird.
2) Season inside and out with salt and place on its side in a roasting tray. Coat with a little clean melted dripping.
3) Place in a hot oven, approx. 220°C for blackgame, capercaillie and pheasant and 230°C for grouse and partridge. Roast in the same manner as for chicken, taking account of the size of the bird. Remove the bard of fat bacon a little while after turning the bird on its back so as to colour the breast. Baste well during the process.

Plover, Quail, Snipe, Woodcock:

1) Truss (1136) and bard (1) the bird.
2) Season with salt and place standing up on its back in a roasting tray or pan. Coat with a little melted dripping. If more than one bird is placed in the tray take care that they are separated sufficiently for the heat to circulate. Make sure that the tray or pan is not too large but is related to the size or number of the birds.
3) Place in a very hot oven at approx. 240°C to roast. Baste occasionally and remove the bard of fat bacon half-way through the process.

Wild Duck:

1) Truss (1136) the bird but do not bard it.
2) Season with salt, coat with a little melted dripping and place standing on its back in a roasting tray or pan.
3) Place in a very hot oven at approx. 240°C to roast and baste occasionally.

Approximate cooking times, degrees of cooking and number of portions

Name	Approx. cooking time	Degree of cooking	No. of portions
Blackgame	45–55 mins.	slightly underdone	4–6
Capercaillie	20 mins. per 500g	just done	allow 250–300g raw weight per portion
Grouse	20–25 mins.	slightly underdone	1–2
Partridge	20–25 mins.	just cooked	1–2
Pheasant	45–55 mins.	just cooked	3–4
Plover	12–15 mins.	just cooked	1
Quail	10 mins.	just cooked	1
Snipe	8–10 mins.	underdone to just cooked	1
Wild Duck:			
Mallard	20–25 mins.	very underdone	2
Teal	12–15 mins.	very underdone	1
Widgeon	15–18 mins.	very underdone	2
Woodcock	10–12 mins.	underdone to just cooked	1

To test for degree of cooking
This can be effected in two ways:
1) Manually: squeeze the bird at the thick end of the breast and pierce the leg at its thickest part to exude some of its juices. This will give a more than useful guide as in the following.
  Breast firm; juices completely clear: well-cooked.
  Breast slight springiness; juices very slightly pink: just cooked.
  Breast resilient; juices pink to red: underdone.
  Breast, pronounced spongy resilience; juices red to bloody: very underdone.
2) By using a meat thermometer to register the internal temperature of the bird. The approx. readings would be:
  Well-cooked   82.5°C
  Just cooked   78–80°C
  Underdone   68°C
  Very underdone 62–65°C

Roast Gravy – Jus de Rôti
1) When the bird is cooked, remove and keep on one side to rest. Place the roasting tray on the stove and heat gently, allowing the juices and sediment to settle and colour without burning.
2) Drain off the fat without disturbing the sediment.
3) Add game stock (99) as required and allow to simmer gently for a few minutes.
4) Correct seasoning with salt only.
5) Pass through a fine strainer and skim but do not remove every last vestige of fat. Allow approx. 5dl of roast gravy per 10 covers.

Carving and portioning
Roast and poêléed game birds like poultry are very often carved or portioned in the kitchen in the following manner.
  Blackgame: Carve into portions in the same way as chicken (1016). If a good size they can be carved into slices as for turkey.

Capercaillie: Carve as for turkey.

Pheasant: Carve into three or four portions in the same way as chicken. The drumstick can very often have pronounced sinews. These should either be removed together with the bone or not served at all. In the latter case remove the bone from the thigh then cut the flesh into two pieces.

Partridge and Grouse: These are served whole but larger ones may be split into halves through the centre of the breastbone.

Quail, Snipe, Woodcock: More often than not these are served whole.

Wild Duck (Mallard): Remove the breasts from the birds and discard the skin. Carve the breasts into long thin slices. The legs are not served but can be used in the preparation of sauces.

Teal, Widgeon: Remove the breasts and discard the skin. Serve the breasts whole or cut into thinnish slices on the slant.

Presentation and accompaniments

For all roast game birds except wild duck, and whether served whole or carved into portions:
1) Prepare a croûton (26) of a size appropriate to the bird or portion.
2) Spread the croûton with Farce à Gratin (38).
3) Place the whole bird or portion on a croûton on a dish.
4) The bard of fat bacon should be placed on the breast or a cut piece placed on each portion.
5) Garnish with Game Chips (1551) at the breast end and a bouquet of watercress placed at the vent end.
6) Serve accompanied with a sauceboat each of roast gravy, Bread Sauce (205 or 206) and white breadcrumbs fried to a golden brown in butter (21).

For Wild Duck – Mallard, Teal or Widgeon:
Garnish with a bouquet of watercress at the vent end and halves of decorated lemon. Serve accompanied with roast gravy and offer Apple Sauce (209) and redcurrant jelly.

SPECIAL POINTS
a) A little Beurre Noisette (13) may be poured over the bird or portion just prior to service.
b) Heart-shaped croûtons or thickish slices of toasted French bread spread with Farce à Gratin (38) may be placed at the side or round the bird instead of placing it on a larger croûton.
c) It is best to surround a large capercaillie with the requisite number of croûtons spread with game farce instead of placing it on a single large croûton.
d) Instead of using Farce à Gratin on the croûton for roast snipe and woodcock, their entrails can be removed when cooked, mashed with a little butter, spread on the croûton and heated in the oven for a few minutes to lightly cook.

1160 Grilled Game Birds

Blackgame, Grouse, Partridge, Pheasant
These may be grilled and garnished in any of the ways applicable to grilled chicken. Suitable sauces and butters for plain grilled items are Sauce Champignons (121), Diable (125), Piquante (132), Poivrade (133), Beurre Maître d'Hôtel (10), and Bercy (5).

SPECIAL POINTS
a) Use butter as a basting agent in preference to oil and baste frequently.
b) Keep blackgame and grouse just a little underdone; partridge and pheasant just done.

Plover, Quail, Snipe, Woodcock, Wild Duck
Draw and clean the bird then split open from the back without separating it in two halves. Cut off the backbone then skewer open flat. Marinate for approx. 30 mins. with a little oil, lemon juice and salt and pepper. Grill quickly at a fairly high temperature, basting with the remaining marinade. Keep slightly underdone. Garnish with Pommes Pailles (1586), watercress, quarters or halves of lemon and serve accompanied with well-flavoured Beurre Maître d'Hôtel.

SPECIAL POINT
Do not remove the inner rib bones of the bird before grilling or after being cooked. In the first case it would result in the flesh becoming dry and hard and in the second the juices of the bird would tend to run out long before it was placed on the customer's plate.

1161 Grilled Escalope of Blackgame or Capercaillie

Use the skinned breasts of a large bird. Remove the small fillet on the underside of the breast and lightly flatten. Cut the remaining breast into thickish slices approx. 125g and lightly flatten. Marinate for 15 minutes with a little oil, lemon juice and salt and pepper. Grill quickly at a high temperature and keep slightly underdone. Garnish with Pommes Pailles (1586) and watercress and serve accompanied with Beurre Maître d'Hôtel or a suitable well-flavoured sauce.

COQ DE BRUYÈRE – BLACKGAME OR BLACKCOCK, AND CAPERCAILLIE

These birds belong to the same family and their correct names in French are, for Blackgame or Blackcock, Petit Coq de Bruyère, and for Capercaillie, Grand Coq de Bruyère. However, menu titling does not distinguish between the two and the term Coq de Bruyère is invariably used for either bird.

1162 Coq de Bruyère Valenciennes

4–6 portions
2 hours

Stage	Ingredient	Quantity	Method
1	blackgame, cleaned and drawn	1 × 2kg	Keep the liver, remove the gall-bladder and cut the liver in small dice.
2	Riz Pilaff, three-quarters cooked (522)	3 portions	Season the liver, sauté quickly in the butter and add to the rice together with the apricots, dates and coriander. Mix
	butter	25g	well together and adjust the seasoning.
	dried apricots, soaked and cut in small dice	100g	Fill the bird with this mixture leaving a little room for expansion. Turn in the parson's nose to enclose the stuffing.
	dates, cut in small dice	75g	Truss for poêling (1007), taking care to pass the needle through the parson's
	fresh coriander leaves, chopped	½ tbsp	nose when trussing the legs.

3	butter, melted		100g	Butter a deep pan and place in the vegetables and herbs. Season the bird and place on its back in the prepared pan. Pour the remaining butter over, cover with the lid and place in the oven at approx. 200°C. Baste occasionally.
	onion		100g	
	carrot	chopped	100g	
	celery	small	75g	
	fennel		150g	
	thyme		sprig	
4	honey		1 tbsp	After 40 mins. of cooking, brush the breast with the honey and pour over the Pernod. Cover and continue cooking and basting for a further 30 mins. then remove the lid to allow the bird to lightly brown and finish cooking. Total time 1½–1¾ hours. Baste occasionally.
	Pernod		½dl	
5				Remove the bird and place in an earthenware dish. Cover and keep warm.
6	Fonds Blanc de Veau (95)		5dl	Add the stock to the vegetables and juices in the pan, simmer for a few mins. then skim off all fat. Discard the thyme, sieve or liquidise the remainder then pass firmly through a fine strainer into a clean pan. Add the cream and reduce to a coating consistency. Adjust the seasoning as necessary, cover and keep warm.
	cream, sour		3dl	
7	dried apricots, soaked		400g	Place in a pan, cover and cook very gently until just tender. Remove the cinnamon and place the apricots in a suitable dish. Allow to cool. This should be prepared while the bird is cooking.
	honey		2 tbsps	
	water		1dl	
	cinnamon stick		1	
8				Discard the string from the bird, heat in the oven for a few mins. and send accompanied with a sauceboat of the prepared sauce and the dish of apricots. Alternatively, remove the rice from the bird and arrange dome-shape in a dish. Carve the bird in portions, arrange in a second dish and coat with a little of the sauce. Send the two dishes accompanied with the remaining sauce and apricots.

1163 Escalope de Coq de Bruyère aux Champignons

10 portions
45 mins.

Stage	Ingredient	Quantity	Method
1	breast of capercaillie	1¼–1½kg	Cut the breasts into ten thickish slices on the slant each approx. 125g in weight. Lightly flatten, place in a shallow tray and sprinkle with the oil, lemon juice, and season with salt and pepper. Allow to marinate for 30 mins.
	oil	1dl	
	lemon juice	2 tbsps	
	salt		
	pepper		

2	butter	100g	Heat the butter in a sauté pan and just before it begins to brown add the drained escalopes and cook very quickly on both sides to colour. Keep a little underdone. Place on earthenware dishes, cover and keep warm.
3	mushrooms, sliced shallots, finely chopped white wine Demi-glace (112)	450g 50g 2dl 4dl	Add the mushrooms to the remaining fat in the pan, lightly season and sauté quickly until just cooked. Add the shallot and sauté again for a few seconds then add the wine and reduce by half. Add the demi-glace, reduce to a coating consistency and adjust the seasoning.
4	parsley, chopped		Make sure all is hot then cover the escalopes with the prepared sauce. Sprinkle with chopped parsley.

GROUSE

The correct French name for the true Scotch Grouse is Lagopède Rouge d'Ecosse. This term, however, has always been perceived as being cumbersome and because of this the English name Grouse has invariably been used both in the United Kingdom and France for French menu titling.

1164 Grouse Ballantrae

2–4 portions
1¼ hours

Stage	Ingredient	Quantity	Method
1	plump grouse, drawn and cleaned whisky butter thyme back bacon	 2 few drops 30g 2 sprigs 4 slices	Season the inside of the grouse with salt and pepper and sprinkle inside also with a few drops of whisky. Remove the gall-bladder from the livers then replace in the grouse together with a piece of butter and a sprig of thyme. Truss the grouse for poêling then place two slices of the bacon on the breast of each bird and tie on.
2	butter, melted	50g	Place the grouse on their backs in a deep pan, pour over the butter, cover with the lid and place in a hot oven at approx. 240°C. Remove the lid after 20 mins., detach the bacon and place at the side of the grouse. Baste occasionally and carry on cooking to colour the grouse and cook the bacon crispy. Keep slightly underdone. Total time approx. 45 mins.

3			When ready, remove the string and thyme from the grouse and discard. Remove the livers and place on one side. Place the grouse on a suitable dish with the bacon on the breasts. Cover and keep warm.
4	whisky	½dl	Drain off the fat from the pan, add the whisky and flamber (32). Add the stock and reduce by half. Pass through a fine strainer into a clean pan, shake in the butter, adjust the seasoning, cover and keep warm.
	Fonds de Gibier (99)	2dl	
	butter	50g	
5	butter	25g	Mash the reserved livers with the butter, season well then spread on the toasts and sprinkle with a little butter. Keep warm on one side.
	Croûtes de Flûte (310)	4	
6	Pommes Duchesse (1560)	150g	Have prepared 16 small Pommes Croquettes (1556), using the oats instead of breadcrumbs. Deep fry in hot fat and drain.
	flour		
	eggwash } for		
	rolled oats } coating		
7	watercress	1 bunch	Make sure the grouse are hot. Place the watercress at the back end of the grouse, the heated toasts at the other end and the croquettes neatly at the sides. Send accompanied with the sauce in a sauceboat.

1165 Grouse and Steak Pie

10 portions
2½–3 hours

Stage	Ingredient	Quantity	Method
1	grouse, plump	5	Carefully draw and singe the birds. Remove and discard the gall-bladders from the livers. Cut the livers in half and reserve.
2			Cut the grouse in half, remove the bones from the inner surfaces and trim the ends of the legs.
3	rump steak, cut in small slices	750g	Cover the bottom of two 22cm approx. pie dishes with the steak, place five halves of grouse on top of each, then divide the livers, lardons, onion and parsley between them. Arrange the ingredients dome-shape in the dish.
	streaky bacon, smoked, cut in lardons (51)	250g	
	onions, finely chopped	100g	
	parsley, chopped	1 tbsp	

4	Fonds de Gibier, (99) cold	5dl approx.	Season the stock and flavour with a few drops of Worcestershire Sauce. Cover the grouse two-thirds of the way up with this stock.
	Worcestershire Sauce	few drops	
5	Pâte Feuilletée (1736)	650g	Roll out the pastry approx. 3mm thick. Eggwash the rims of the pie dishes and cover with 1½cm-wide strips of pastry. Eggwash the strips. Cover the pies with the remainder of the pastry, seal firmly and trim off the surplus paste with a knife. Decorate the edge of the pastry around the pies. Eggwash and decorate with designs of pastry. Allow to rest in a cool place for at least 1 hour.
6			Place the pies in a hot oven to lightly brown and set the pastry (approx. 20 mins.). Reduce the temperature to approx. 150°C and cook until the meat is tender (approx. 1½ hours).
7			Clean the pie dishes, place on suitable dishes and surround with pie collars.

SPECIAL POINTS
a) This grouse pie is excellent when served cold. In this case finally add 2–3 sheets of gelatine soaked in cold water and drained before covering with the pastry.
b) The bones from the grouse may be used to produce a more flavoured stock in the following manner. Colour the bones in a little butter with a little chopped onion, carrot and celery then cover with the required amount of game stock and simmer gently for approx. 1 hour. Skim, pass through a fine strainer and allow to cool before using.

PERDREAU – PARTRIDGE

1166 Mignons de Perdreau Vigneronne

4 portions
45 mins.

Stage	Ingredient	Quantity	Method
1	plump partridge	4	Remove the breasts without the wing bone from the partridge and skin. Chop the legs and bones small.
2	butter	25g	Colour the chopped bones and legs in the butter together with the vegetables, add the stock and simmer gently for 45 mins. Pass through a fine strainer and skim off fat. Keep on one side.
	shallot ⎫ chopped	25g	
	carrot ⎬ small	25g	
	celery ⎭	25g	
	Fonds de Gibier (99)	6dl	

3	muscatel grapes	32	Skin the grapes and remove the pips. Place in a dish, add the brandy, gently mix, then cover and place in the refrigerator.
	brandy	½ tbsp	
4	butter	50g	Heat the butter in a sauté pan, season the partridge breasts and shallow fry to a golden brown on both sides and until just done.
5	fresh foie gras, cut in small collops	8	Lightly season the foie gras and shallow fry quickly on both sides to lightly colour in the same butter. Remove and arrange on a round dish and place a partridge breast on each. Cover and keep warm.
6	brandy	½dl	Drain off the fat from the pan, add the brandy and flamber (32), then add the grape juice and reduce by half. Add the previously prepared stock and reduce again, until slightly viscous, about 1dl. Pass through a fine strainer into a clean pan and shake in the butter away from the heat. Adjust the seasoning, cover and keep warm.
	grape juice	½dl	
	butter, soft	75g	
7			Make sure the partridge is hot then coat each breast with a spoonful of sauce. Place the chilled grapes in the centre of the dish and send accompanied with the remaining sauce.

1167 Perdreau Brabançonne

4 portions
1¼ hours

Stage	Ingredient	Quantity	Method
1	partridge, cleaned, drawn and trussed	4	Season the partridge, place standing on their backs in a deep pan, cover with the butter and lid and place in a hot oven to cook at approx. 230°C. Baste occasionally and remove the lid after 20 mins. to colour. Keep underdone.
	butter, melted	75g	
2			When ready, remove the strings, and place the partridge in a deep cocotte. Cover and keep warm.
3	white wine, dry	½dl	Drain off the fat from the pan, add the wine and reduce by half, then add the stock and jus lié and reduce to a light coating consistency. Adjust the seasoning as necessary.
	Fonds de Gibier (99)	1dl	
	Jus lié (113)	1½dl	

4	chipolatas, grilled	8	Surround the partridge with the chipolatas and sprouts and pass the sauce through a fine strainer over the partridge and garnish. Cover with the lid and place in a moderate oven for approx. 15–18 mins. to complete the cooking.
	Brussels sprouts, blanched	20	
5	parsley, chopped	½ tbsp	On removing from the oven, sprinkle with chopped parsley and send in the cocotte as it is.

1168 Perdreau aux Choux

10 covers
2½–3 hours

Stage	Ingredient	Quantity	Method
1	partridge, cleaned, drawn and trussed	10	Heat the butter in a suitable braising pan, season the partridge and shallow fry to colour on all sides. Remove the partridge from the pan and place on one side. Allow the fat to remain in the pan.
	butter	75g	
2	cabbage, blanched	1–1½kg	Place a layer of the cabbage in the braising pan and set the partridge on top. Surround with the meats, vegetables and aromats then cover with the remaining cabbage. Season appropriately with salt and pepper then add the stock. Cover with a well-buttered greaseproof paper and the lid.
	carrots, grooved	250g	
	onions, whole	150g	
	streaky bacon	350g	
	smoked pork sausage	350g	
	juniper berries ⎫ in a	10	
	cloves ⎬ muslin	3	
	peppercorns ⎭ bag	10	
	Bouquet Garni	1	
	Fonds Blanc (93)	5dl	
	butter	25g	
3			Heat well then place in the oven at approx. 180°C and braise gently. Remove the bacon and sausage when cooked and leave for sufficient time to cook the partridge. Total time approx. 1½–2 hours.
4			Remove the partridge and discard the strings. Discard the bouquet garni, onions and bag of flavourings.
5			Arrange the cabbage as a bed in earthenware dishes and place the partridge along the centre. Surround with neat rectangles of the bacon and slices of sausage and carrots.
6	Jus lié, flavoured with some well-reduced game stock	6dl	Make sure that all is hot then lightly coat each partridge with a spoonful of sauce. Send accompanied with sauceboats of the sauce.

SPECIAL POINTS

a) This preparation is very suitable for those partridges of a slightly tougher nature which require a more extended cooking time.

b) As an alternative the partridge may be finished in the following manner. Line a buttered deep mould, e.g. a medium charlotte mould, with small rectangles of the bacon and slices of sausage and carrots. Cover with some of the cabbage, place in a partridge, breast downwards, then cover and fill fairly firm with more cabbage. Cover and place in a moderately hot oven for 10–15 mins. Demould onto a suitable dish, sponge up any liquid and surround with a little of the sauce. Send accompanied with a sauceboat of the same sauce.

1169 Perdreau en Cocotte Normande

4 portions
1 hour

Stage	Ingredient	Quantity	Method
1	partridge, cleaned, drawn and trussed	4	Sprinkle the partridge inside with a few drops of Calvados and season. Place standing on their backs in a deep pan and cover with the butter. Cover with the lid and place in the oven at approx. 230°C. Baste occasionally and remove the lid after 20 mins. to colour. Keep slightly underdone.
	Calvados	few drops	
	butter, melted	50g	
2			When ready, remove the strings and place the partridge in a deep cocotte. Cover and keep warm.
3	shallots, finely chopped	75g	Add the shallots to the pan and cook without colour. Add the apples, sprinkle with a touch of mace and cook quickly for a few mins. Drain off surplus fat.
	apples, peeled and sliced	150g	
	mace, ground	pinch	
4	Calvados	½dl	Pour the Calvados over the apples and flamber (32), then add the stock and cream. Season lightly with salt and pepper and cook gently until the apples are soft.
	Fonds de Gibier (99)	1dl	
	cream, double	2dl	
5			Pass the apples and sauce through a fine sieve or liquidise, then firmly through a fine strainer into a clean pan. Adjust the seasoning plus a touch of cayenne. Ladle half of the sauce over the partridge, cover and place in the oven for 9–10 mins. to heat thoroughly.
6	firm, tart apples, cut in quarters	3	Peel and cut the apples into quarters, sprinkle with butter and sugar and glaze a golden brown under the salamander.
	butter, melted	25g	
	sugar, caster	25g	

7   Remove the partridge from the oven and surround with the prepared apples. Send accompanied with the remaining sauce in a sauceboat.

FAISAN – PHEASANT

1170 Faisan Carême

4 portions
1½ hours

Stage	Ingredient	Quantity	Method
1	pheasant, cleaned, drawn and trussed butter	1 50g	Season the pheasant, place in a deep pan on its back and cover with the melted butter. Cover with a lid and place in a hot oven at approx. 230°C. Baste occasionally.
2			Remove the lid after 30 mins. to allow the pheasant to lightly colour, basting occasionally. Total time approx. 1 hour.
3			Remove the pheasant from the oven, discard the string and place the pheasant in a cocotte or casserole.
4	Céleris braisés (1402)	4 portions	Place around the pheasant, cover and keep warm.
5	cream Glace de Viande (103)	3dl 1 tbsp	Place the pan on the stove and allow the juices and sediment to heat gently and colour without burning. Drain off the fat, add the cream and meat glaze and reduce to a coating consistency. Adjust the seasoning and pass through a fine strainer over the pheasant and celery. Cover with the lid and place in the oven for 10 mins. or so to heat thoroughly. Send as it is or carve into portions first before covering with the sauce.

1171 Faisan en Casserole Fermière

4 portions
1½ hours

Stage	Ingredient	Quantity	Method
1	pheasant, cleaned drawn and trussed butter	1 50g	Season the pheasant and place in a deep pan on its back and cover with the melted butter. Cover with a lid and place in a hot oven at approx. 230°C. Baste occasionally.
2			Remove the lid after 30 mins. to allow the pheasant to lightly colour and continue cooking. Keep slightly underdone. Total time approx. 55 mins.

3	butter	50g	Heat the butter in a sauteuse, add the
	carrots ⎫ cut in	50g	vegetables, season with salt, a touch of
	turnips ⎬ thick	50g	sugar and cover with a lid. Cook slowly
	celery ⎭ Paysanne (77)	50g	and without colour for a few mins. until
	button onions, small	12	half-cooked. Prepare these while the
	French beans, cut		pheasant is cooking.
	in diamonds	50g	
	sugar	pinch	
4			When the pheasant is ready, remove from the pan, discard the string and place it in a deep cocotte or casserole. Surround with the prepared vegetables.
5	white wine, dry	1dl	Drain off the fat from the pan, add the wine and reduce by half then add the jus lié and reduce to a light coating consistency. Adjust the seasoning then pass through a fine strainer over the pheasant and vegetables.
	Jus lié (113)	2dl	
6	parsley, chopped	½ tbsp	Cover with the lid and place in a hot oven for 10–15 mins. to complete the cooking. Send as it is sprinkled with the parsley or carve into portions first then cover with the sauce and vegetables.

1172 Faisan sauté à la Catalane

4 portions
50 mins.

Stage	Ingredient	Quantity	Method
1	young tender pheasant, cut for sauté (1138)	4 portions	Heat the oil in a sauté pan, season the pheasant and add to the pan. Colour well on all sides.
	oil	¾dl	
2	garlic, finely chopped	1 clove	Sprinkle with the garlic, mushrooms and tomatoes, cover with a lid and cook slowly on low heat on the side of the stove or in the oven. Shake occasionally to distribute the ingredients well.
	mushrooms, sliced	250g	
	Tomates Concassées (90)	200g	
3			When just cooked remove the pheasant and ingredients to a deep earthenware dish. Arrange neatly, cover with a lid and keep warm.
4	sherry	1dl	Add the sherry to the pan, reduce by half then add the stock and reduce by half. Finally add the demi-glace and reduce to a light coating consistency. Adjust the seasoning as necessary.
	Fonds de Gibier (99)	2dl	
	Demi-glace (112)	2dl	

5	chipolatas, grilled	8	Make sure the pheasant is hot then pass the sauce through a fine strainer over it. Garnish with the chipolatas and onions and sprinkle with chopped parsley.
	Petits Oignons glacés à Brun (1493)	12	
	parsley, chopped		

1173 Faisan Souvaroff

4 portions
1½ hours

Stage	Ingredient	Quantity	Method
1	pheasant, cleaned and drawn	1	Stuff the pheasant with the foie gras and truss with the parson's nose tucked inside.
	foie gras	250g	
2	butter	50g	Season the pheasant, place in a deep pan on its back and cover with the melted butter. Cover with the lid and place in the oven at approx. 230°C.
3			Remove the lid after 30 mins. and allow the pheasant to colour for 10 mins.
4			Remove the pheasant from the oven, remove the string and place the pheasant in a deep cocotte.
5	Fonds de Gibier (99)	1dl	Drain the fat from the pan, add the stock, bring to the boil, reduce by half then pass through a fine strainer over the pheasant.
6	Glace de Viande (103)	30g	Melt the glace de viande, add the truffle, heat and pour around the pheasant. Add the Madeira.
	truffles, diced	75g	
	Madeira	1dl	
7			Place the lid on the cocotte and seal round with a strip of fairly stiff paste made from flour and water. Place in a moderate oven to complete the cooking (approx. 20 mins.). Send without breaking the pastry seal.

SPECIAL POINTS
a) Although it is best to send the pheasant whole, it may be cut in portions at Stage 4 if deemed more convenient.
b) The lid of the cocotte may be sealed with ordinary short paste and eggwashed.

1174 Salmis de Faisan

4 portions
1¼ hours

Stage	Ingredient	Quantity	Method
1	pheasant, cleaned and trussed	1	Season the pheasant and roast it keeping slightly underdone.

2	Glace de Viande		Remove the string. Cut the pheasant into
	(103), melted	15g	four portions and remove the skin. Place
	brandy	¼dl	the pheasant in a cocotte with the
	button mushrooms,		mushrooms and sprinkle with the meat
	sautéed in butter	20	glaze and brandy. Cover with the lid and
			keep warm.
3	shallots, finely		Chop the carcase and skin of the
	chopped	30g	pheasant and place in a small pan with
	peppercorns, crushed	6	the shallots, peppercorns and wine.
	red wine	2dl	Reduce almost completely then add the
	Demi-glace (112)	2dl	demi-glace and stock. Simmer gently for
	Fonds de Gibier (99)	2dl	10 mins. then pass through a fine
			strainer into a clean pan.
4	butter	50g	Reduce the sauce to a coating
			consistency, shake in the butter away
			from the heat, adjust the seasoning then
			pour over the pheasant and mushrooms.
5	slices of truffle	4	Decorate with the slices of truffle,
			replace the lid and reheat in the oven for
			a few minutes.

SPECIAL POINT

Salmis may be prepared in the same way using other game birds such as partridge, woodcock, snipe, wild duck.

1175 Suprême de Faisan au Suc de Mandarines

4 portions
25 mins.

Stage	Ingredient	Quantity	Method
1	suprêmes of pheasant		Heat the butter in a sauté pan, season
	(1012)	4	the suprêmes and shallow fry quickly to
	butter	25g	a golden brown on both sides.
2	brandy	2 tbsps	Tip off the fat, add the brandy and flamber (32). When the flames have died down remove the suprêmes and arrange neatly in a suitable dish.
3	tangerine juice	1dl	Add the juice to the brandy and strain
	butter, soft	75g	into a clean small pan. Reduce until
	lemon juice	squeeze	slightly viscous then shake in the butter away from the heat. Adjust the seasoning as necessary plus a few drops of lemon juice.

4	butter, melted	
	cos lettuce, hearts	4
	segments of tangerine	20
	cream	1dl
	lemon juice	squeeze
	tangerine juice	squeeze
	cayenne	

Make sure the suprêmes are hot, brush with melted butter and place a cutlet frill on each bone. Send with the sauce in a sauceboat and accompanied with hearts of cos lettuce decorated with the tangerine segments and sprinkled with the cream, thinned and flavoured with the juices, a pinch of salt and a touch of cayenne.

1176 Suprême de Faisan Tatiana

4 portions
30 mins.

Stage	Ingredient	Quantity	Method
1	suprêmes of pheasant (1012) without wing bone	4	Heat the butter in a sauté pan, season the suprêmes and shallow fry quickly to a golden brown on both sides. Keep very slightly underdone then arrange in an earthenware dish. Cover and keep warm.
	butter	50g	
2	shallots, finely chopped	25g	Add the shallots to the pan and cook without colour. Drain off excess fat and add the wine. Reduce by half then add the cream. Reduce to a light coating consistency, shake in the glaze, adjust the seasoning and finish with a little lemon juice and a touch of cayenne. Pass through a fine strainer into a clean pan, cover and keep warm.
	white wine, dry	1dl	
	cream, sour	2½dl	
	Glace de Viande (103)	½ tbsp	
	lemon juice	few drops	
	cayenne		
3	button mushrooms, sliced thick	350g	Heat the butter in a pan, add the mushrooms just when the butter is turning brown. Season and sauté quickly. Add the shallots and garlic and sauté again for a few minutes until almost free of liquid.
	butter	50g	
	shallots, chopped	30g	
	garlic, finely chopped	touch	
4	pickled cucumber	8 slices	Arrange the prepared mushrooms to one side of the suprêmes and place two overlapping slices of cucumber on each suprême. Make sure that all is hot then coat the suprêmes only with a little of the sauce. Sprinkle the mushrooms with the dill and send the dish accompanied with the remainder of the sauce in a sauceboat.
	dill, chopped	pinch	

CAILLE – QUAIL

1177 Caille aux Cerises Noires

10 portions
45 mins.

Stage	Ingredient	Quantity	Method
1	quails, cleaned, drawn and trussed	10	Sprinkle the insides of the quails with a few drops of Kirsch and season inside and out. Place in a small deep pan on their backs, cover with the melted butter, cover with the lid and place in a hot oven at approx. 240°C. Baste occasionally and remove the lid after 15 mins. to colour.
	Kirsch	few drops	
	butter, melted	75g	
2			When just cooked, remove the strings, place the quails into casseroles or cocottes, cover and keep warm.
3	port	2dl	Place the pan on the stove and heat gently allowing the juices and sediment to settle and lightly colour. Drain off the fat then add the port and simmer for a few mins. Pass through a fine strainer into a clean pan.
4	black cherries, stoned	400g	Add the cherries, peel, jelly, cinnamon and jus lié to the strained sauce and simmer gently for approx. 5–6 mins. Remove from the heat, discard the peel then shake in the butter and adjust the seasoning as necessary.
	cinnamon, ground	pinch	
	orange peel	2 strips	
	redcurrant jelly	1 tbsp	
	Jus lié (113)	4dl	
	butter	75g	
5	Kirsch	½ tbsp	Make sure the quail are hot then ladle the cherries and sauce over them. Sprinkle with the Kirsch, cover with the lid and send.

1178 Caille fourrée à la Grand Vatel

4 portions
2 hours

Stage	Ingredient	Quantity	Method
1	quails, drawn and cleaned (1134)	4	Cut off the lower legs at the joint with the drumstick. Scald these for a few seconds in boiling water and reserve.
2	brandy	few drops	Bone out the quails completely from inside then sprinkle the insides with a few drops of brandy. Rest for 20 mins.

3	veal, lean and free of sinew	350g	Pass the meat twice through the fine plate of the mincer. Place in a basin, season with salt, pepper and mace and beat together firmly with a wooden spoon. Add the yolk and beat in, then add the cream little by little mixing in well. Finally add the pistachios, truffle and brandy and mix in well. Adjust the seasoning as necessary.
	salt		
	pepper		
	mace, ground	pinch	
	egg yolk	1	
	cream, double	½dl	
	pistachios, chopped	10g	
	truffle, chopped	5g	
	brandy	½ tbsp	
4	butter	50g	Lightly season the inside of the quails then fill with the prepared stuffing. Heat the butter in a pan, season the quails and colour quickly on all sides to a golden brown. Allow to become cold.
5	Bayonne or Parma ham	4 slices	Wrap each quail in a slice of the raw ham. Roll out the pastry to approx. 2mm thick then cut out four circles. Wrap each prepared quail in a circle of pastry neatly sealing it together under the bird. Make a small hole through the top of the pastry and set a small decorated ring of pastry over this hole. Brush with egg-wash and decorate with the point of a small knife. Place on a small baking tray and allow to rest for 30 mins.
	puff pastry (1736)	200g approx.	
	egg wash		
6			Place the quails in a hot oven to set and lightly colour the pastry, approx. 15 mins., then reduce the temperature to approx. 160°C to continue the cooking for a further 30–35 mins.
7	Sauce Périgueux (131)	2½dl	On removing from the oven pour a spoonful of the sauce through the hole on top of the pastry then push two of the reserved legs into the end of each to give the appearance of the bird. For service, place a folded serviette on a round dish and arrange four nice small vine leaves in the centre. Place a quail on each leaf and send accompanied with a sauceboat of the sauce.
	vine leaves, small	4	

1179 Caille à la Grecque

10 portions
45 mins.

Stage	Ingredient	Quantity	Method
1	quails, cleaned, drawn and trussed,	10	Season the quails inside and out. Place in a small deep pan, cover with the
	butter, melted	75g	melted butter and lid and place in a hot

oven at approx. 240°C. Baste occasionally and remove the lid after 15
mins. to colour.

Stage	Ingredient	Quantity	Method
2			When just cooked remove the strings, place the quails on one side, cover and keep warm.
3	white wine, dry	2dl	Place the pan on the stove and heat
	Fonds de Gibier (99)	3dl	gently allowing the juices and sediment
	Jus lié (113)	4dl	to settle and lightly colour. Drain off the
	butter	75g	fat. Add the wine, reduce by half then add the jus lié and stock. Reduce to a lightly thickened consistency then pass through a fine strainer into a clean pan. Shake in the butter, adjust the seasoning as necessary. Cover and keep warm.
4	Riz à la Grecque (524) as a garnish	10 portions	Arrange as a bed along the centre of earthenware dishes. Set the quails on top and place in a hot oven for a few mins. to heat thoroughly. Send accompanied with a sauceboat of the sauce.

1180 Caille aux Raisins

10 portions
45 mins.

Stage	Ingredient	Quantity	Method
1	quails, cleaned, drawn and trussed	10	Sprinkle the insides with a few drops of brandy and season inside and out. Place
	brandy	few drops	in a small deep pan on their backs, cover
	butter, melted	75g	with the melted butter, cover with the lid and place in a hot oven at approx. 240°C. Baste occasionally and remove the lid after 15 mins. to colour.
2			When just cooked, remove the quails, discard the strings and arrange in cocottes. Cover and keep warm.
3	grapes	400g	Skin and remove the pips. Place the
	brandy	few drops	grapes with the quails in the cocottes and sprinkle with the brandy. Cover and keep warm.
4	white wine, dry	2dl	Place the pan on the stove and heat
	Jus lié (113)	4dl	gently allowing the juices and sediment
	Fonds de Gibier (99)	2dl	to settle and colour lightly. Drain off the fat, add the wine and reduce by half. Add the jus lié and stock and simmer gently for a few mins. Adjust the seasoning.

5	juice of lemon	½	Pass the sauce through a fine strainer over the quails and grapes. Sprinkle with the lemon juice and cover with the lid. Place in a hot oven for approx. 5 mins. to heat thoroughly and send.

CANARD SAUVAGE – WILD DUCK

This is a general term which can be used to describe any of the wild duck but in practice it is generally used as a descriptive menu term for the Mallard. Other species such as Teal and Widgeon are worthy of particular mention and should be designated on the menu as such.

The following recipes are suitable for all wild duck and for the sake of convenience are designated using Canard Sauvage – Wild Duck as the standard type. It only remains to take into account the relative size of the different species.

1181 Canard Sauvage à l'Ananas – Wild Duck with Pineapple

4 portions
1 hour

Stage	Ingredient	Quantity	Method
1	wild duck, cleaned drawn and trussed butter, melted	2 50g	Season the duck inside and out, place standing on their backs in a small deep pan, coat with the butter and cover with the lid. Place in a hot oven at approx. 230°C to cook for approx. 20–25 mins. Baste occasionally and keep very underdone.
2			When ready, discard the string, remove the breasts, cover and keep warm. Chop the carcases and legs small.
3	celery } carrot } chopped shallot } small thyme	25g 25g 25g small sprig	Add these ingredients to the pan together with the chopped carcases and legs. Sauté quickly to colour for a few mins. then drain off all the fat from the pan.
4	rum pineapple juice Fonds de Gibier (99)	½ dl 1dl 3dl	Add the rum and flamber (32), then add the juice and stock and simmer for a few mins. Pass through a fine strainer with pressure into a clean pan and reduce quickly by three-quarters.
5	Jus lié (113) butter cayenne	2dl 50g	Add the jus lié and simmer to a light coating consistency. Shake in the butter and adjust the seasoning as necessary plus a touch of cayenne. Cover and keep warm.
6	pineapple slices sugar, demerara	4 25g	Cut each slice of pineapple into four, place on a buttered tray then sprinkle

	butter, melted	25g	with the sugar, butter and a few drops of
	rum	few drops	rum. Glaze under the salamander to a golden brown.

7

Discard the skin from the duck breasts then cut the breasts into long thin slices. Place on a warm dish and coat with a little of the sauce. Surround with the pineapple and reheat without boiling. Send accompanied with the rest of the sauce in a sauceboat.

1182 Canard Sauvage Bigarade

Prepare as Aiguillettes de Caneton Bigarade (1104), taking account of the following: a) keep the wild duck very underdone and b) remove the skin from the breasts before slicing.

1183 Canard Sauvage aux Cèpes Bordelaise

4 portions
1 hour

Stage	Ingredient	Quantity	Method
1	wild duck, cleaned, drawn and trussed butter, melted	2 50g	Season the ducks inside and out, place standing on their backs in a small deep pan, coat with the butter and cover with the lid. Place in a hot oven at approx. 230°C to cook for approx. 20–25 mins. Baste occasionally and keep very underdone.
2			When ready, discard the string, remove the breasts, cover and keep warm. Chop the carcases and legs small.
3	celery ⎱ chopped carrot ⎰ small shallot thyme peppercorns, crushed garlic, crushed	25g 25g 25g small sprig 8 ½ clove	Add these ingredients to the pan together with the chopped carcases and legs. Sauté quickly over heat for a few mins. then drain off all the fat from the pan.
4	Armagnac red wine Fonds de Gibier (99)	½dl 2dl 2dl	Add the Armagnac and flamber (32) then add the wine and stock and simmer for a few mins. Pass firmly through a fine strainer into a clean pan and reduce quickly by three-quarters.
5	Jus lié (113) butter cayenne	2dl 50g	Add the jus lié and reduce quickly to a light coating consistency. Shake in the butter and adjust the seasoning as necessary plus a touch of cayenne.

6	Cèpes Bordelaise (1410)	250g	Discard the skin from the duck then cut the breasts into long thin slices. Place on a warm dish then coat with a little of the sauce. Place the cèpes to one side and reheat without boiling. Send accompanied with the rest of the sauce in a sauceboat.

1184 Canard Sauvage aux Cerises

Prepare as Caneton poêlé aux Cerises (1107), taking account of the following: a) keep the wild duck very underdone, b) use the breasts only, c) discard the skin from the breast and cut the breasts into long thin slices.

1185 Canard Sauvage au Porto

4 portions
1 hour

Stage	Ingredient	Quantity	Method
1	wild duck, cleaned, drawn and trussed butter, melted	2 50g	Season the duck inside and out, place standing on their backs in a small deep pan, coat with the butter and cover with the lid. Place in a hot oven at approx. 230°C to cook for approx. 20–25 mins. Baste occasionally and keep very underdone.
2			When ready, discard the string, remove the breasts, cover and keep warm. Chop the carcases and legs small.
3	celery ⎫ chopped carrot ⎬ small shallot ⎭ juniper berries clove, crushed	25g 25g 25g 4 1	Add these ingredients to the pan together with the chopped carcases and legs. Sauté quickly to colour for a few mins. then drain off all the fat from the pan.
4	port Fonds de Gibier (99)	2dl 4dl	Add the port and reduce by half then add the stock and simmer for 10 mins. Pass through a fine strainer with pressure into a clean pan and reduce by three-quarters.
5	Jus lié (113)	2dl	Add the jus lié and reduce to a light coating consistency. Adjust the seasoning as necessary, cover and keep warm.
6			Discard the skin from the breasts then cut the breasts into long thin slices. Place on a warm dish and coat with a little of the sauce. Send accompanied with the remaining sauce in a sauceboat.

BÉCASSE ET BÉCASSINE – WOODCOCK AND SNIPE

These birds are related species with the woodcock being the slightly larger of the two. For the sake of convenience and because the following recipes are well-suited to both birds, they are designated using woodcock as the standard type.

1186 Bécasse à la Fine Champagne

4 portions
25 mins.

Stage	Ingredient	Quantity	Method
1	woodcock, trussed and barded butter, melted	4 50g	Season the woodcock, place in a small roasting pan, cover with the melted butter and place in a hot oven at approx. 240°C to roast for 12–15 mins. keeping underdone. Baste occasionally.
2			When ready, remove the legs and breasts from the birds, trim, then arrange in a buttered shallow earthenware cocotte. Cover with the lid and keep warm. Reserve the intestines.
3	liqueur brandy	2 tbsps	Tip out the fat from the pan, add the brandy and flamber (32).
4	Fonds de Gibier (99), well-reduced lemon juice cayenne	½dl squeeze	Finely pound the remaining carcases and trimmings, firmly squeeze out their juices and add these to the pan together with the finely chopped intestines and the game stock. Season well plus a touch of cayenne and finish with a squeeze of lemon juice.
5			Make sure the woodcock is hot and pour over the sauce which has been reheated but without boiling.

1187 Bécasse au Fumet

Prepare in the same way as Bécasse à la Fine Champagne, but keeping half the intestines, mash these with a little butter and seasoning, spread on four toasted slices of French bread and place in the oven for a few minutes to lightly cook. Use these to garnish the prepared woodcock.

1188 Mignonnettes de Bécasse Westphalienne

4 portions
1½ hours

Stage	Ingredient	Quantity	Method
1	woodcock, plucked and cleaned	6	Remove the breasts from the birds, discard the skins and keep the breasts on one side. Remove the skin from the legs, bone them out and reserve the flesh.

2	butter	30g	Heat the butter in a pan, add the
	shallots, chopped	30g	vegetables and herbs and cook quickly
	carrot, chopped	30g	with a little colour. Have the carcases
	juniper berries,		pounded, then add to the pan. Mix in
	crushed	4	and cook together quickly for a few
	bayleaf	½	minutes.

3	Fonds de Gibier	6dl	Add to the pan, bring to the boil and
	(99)		simmer very gently for about 30 mins.
			Skim and pass through a fine strainer,
			cover and keep warm.

4	venison, lean and		Remove all sinew from the woodcock
	free of sinew	150g	legs and together with four of the breasts
	cream, double	½dl	and the venison, pass through the fine
	nutmeg		plate of the mincer twice. Season with
	cayenne		salt, pepper, a little nutmeg and a touch
	basil, chopped	good pinch	of cayenne. Mix well then beat in the
			cream a little at a time. Add the basil
			and ensure that the mixture is well sea-
			soned.

5	flour		Mould this mixture with a little flour
			into eight flat oval shapes approx. the
			same size as the woodcock breasts.

6	butter	50g	Heat the butter in a sauté pan and just
			as it begins to turn brown, add the
			moulded items and cook on both sides
			until just done. Arrange on a round dish
			and keep warm.

7			Season the remaining eight woodcock
			breasts and shallow fry quickly in the
			same fat on both sides. Keep underdone.
			Place each on one of the prepared
			moulds. Keep warm.

8	brandy	¼dl	Tip out the fat from the pan then add
	cream	2dl	the brandy and flamber (32). When the
			flames have died down, add the prepared
			stock. Reduce to roughly 1dl then add
			the cream and reduce to a coating
			consistency. Pass through a fine strainer
			into a clean pan.

9	butter	25g	Mix in the butter and adjust the
	basil, chopped	good pinch	seasoning as necessary. Finish with the
	lemon juice	squeeze	basil and a squeeze of lemon. Cover and
			keep warm.

10	Marrons braisés (1486)	12 pieces	Place the chestnuts in the centre of the
	Heart-shaped		prepared breasts. Place a croûton
	Croûtons, small (26)	8	between each. Make sure that all is hot.

butter, melted

Brush the surface of the breasts with melted butter and send the dish accompanied with a sauceboat of the prepared sauce.

1189 Salmis de Bécasse

Prepare in the same way as Salmis de Faisan (1174), using one woodcock per portion and keeping them underdone.

GIBIER À POIL – FURRED GAME

The main items of furred game with their joints, average weights and preparation for cooking.

VENISON – VENAISON

Weight of carcase: according to species and sex, 20–50kg
Seasons: for the buck, May–Sept.; for the doe, Sept.–Jan.

The following details are based on a carcase of approx. 32kg

Joint	Average Weight	Preparation for Cooking
1190 Leg (Gigue or Cuissot)	4½kg	Roasting or Poêling: remove the pelvic bone and trim the end of the leg bone. Carefully trim the surfaces of any dried or discoloured skin. Lard (50) the outer surfaces as necessary, tie with a single string at the thick end of the leg and marinate (55) if needed.
1191 Haunch (Hanche)	7kg	Roasting or Poêling: The haunch consists of the leg and loin in one piece. Remove the pelvic bone and trim the end of the leg bone. Carefully trim the surfaces of any dried or discoloured skin. Cut off any surplus abdominal flap of the loin. Lard (50) the outer surfaces as necessary and marinate (55) if needed. Tie the loin round in two or three places at the thick end of the leg.
1192 Saddle (Selle)	6kg	Roasting or Poêling: remove the kidney and trim the inside. Remove the hip bones then trim the outside of all dry or discoloured skin. Cut off the flanks straight leaving sufficient to fold underneath. Re-form carefully and lard (50) the surface carefully. Marinate (55) if needed.
1193 Loin (Longe)	2½kg	Roasting or Poêling: trim the surface of any dried or discoloured skin and sinew. Bone out, roll and tie. Lard (50) as necessary and marinate (55) if needed.

1194	Best End (Carré)	1¾kg	Roasting or Poêling: trim the surface of any dry or discoloured skin and sinew. Cut off the breast part leaving the thin part 1½ times the length of the eye of the meat. Bare the cutlet bones to within 2cm of the meat and clean the skin from between the cutlet bones. Lard (50) the top surfaces carefully and marinate (55) if necessary.
1195	Middle Neck (Côte découverte)	1½kg	Stewing: trim off any dry surfaces and sinew and bone out completely. Cut in 2cm cubes and marinate (55) as necessary.
1196	Neck (Cou)	3kg	Stewing: trim off any dry surfaces and sinew and bone out completely. Cut in 2cm cubes and marinate (55) as necessary.
1197	Shoulder (Epaule)	3kg	Braising: trim off any dry surfaces and sinew. Bone out completely. Roll carefully and tie. Lard (50) all over and marinate (55).
			Stewing: trim off any dry surfaces and sinew and bone out completely. Cut in 2cm cubes and marinate (55) as necessary.
1198	Breast (Poitrine)	1½kg	Stewing: if meaty, trim carefully of any dry surfaces and fat. Bone out and cut into 2½cm squares. Marinate (55) as necessary.

cont. p.514

The small cuts and offals obtainable from venison and their preparation for cooking:

Name of cut	From which Joint	Average Portion Weight	Preparation for Cooking
1199 Chop	loin	1 × 200g	Trim carefully of any dry or discoloured surfaces and remove the flanks completely. Cut on the bone to the required thickness according to the size of the loin. Trim carefully.
1200 Cutlets (Côtelettes)	best end	1 × 175g or 2 × 80g	Cut between the bones of a prepared but unlarded best end. Trim carefully and bare the end of the cutlet bone. According to size use one or two cutlets per portion.
1201 Fillet (Filet)	saddle	125g	Remove the fillet from the loin and trim clear of any fat and sinew. Leave whole or split open lengthways and lightly flatten. Cut according to size to approx. 125g in weight. The whole fillet may be larded (50) and marinated (55). For grilling or shallow frying, the split fillet may be marinated for 45 mins. or so with a little lemon juice, oil, salt and pepper.
1202 Médaillons	best end or loin	1 × 150g or 2 × 75g	Trim carefully of any dry or discoloured surfaces and bone out completely. Remove all fat and sinew. Cut into one or two thickish slices according to size. Flatten lightly and trim to a nice round or oval shape.
1203 Noisettes	loin	1 × 150g or 2 × 75g	Trim carefully of any dry or discoloured surfaces. Remove the fillet and reserve. Bone the loin out completely then cut into one or two thickish slices on the slant according to size. Lightly flatten and trim cutlet shape.
1204 Steak or Paillard	leg	150g	Trim the leg carefully of any dry or discoloured surfaces. For the small leg bone out completely then cut into thickish slices across the grain and trim as necessary. For the large leg separate the leg at its natural tissues into corresponding pieces as for veal, i.e. topside, silverside, thick flank and rump. Then cut across the grain into the required size and weight. Flatten lightly if too thick.

1205	Heart	100–125g	Trim off any fat and any tubes or gristly parts from the inside.
1206	Kidneys	100–125g	Best only from the female deer and removed immediately after slaughter. Cut open from the outside edge to the core but do not cut in half. Remove the skin and the central core of gristle and fat. Soak in cold water for 3–4 hours so as to get rid of uric acid. Pat dry. Skewer for grilling or cut into small thickish slices for sauté.
1207	Liver	125g	Best from the female deer and removed immediately after slaughter. Cut out any tubes or gristle showing and skin where possible. Wash thoroughly and soak in cold water for 2 hours. Pat dry with a clean cloth. Cut on the slant into slices approx. ½ cm thick.

HARE – LIÈVRE

Average Weights: Young hare (Leveret), 1½–2½ kg; Hare, 3–4kg
Season: 1 Aug.–23 Feb.

Name	Average No. of Portions or Portion Weight	Preparation for Cooking
1208 Hare (Lièvre)	6–8	Stewing: dissect into portions (1142) and marinate in Red Wine Marinade (55) for 24 hours.
1209 Hare, young (Levraut)	5–6	Stewing: dissect into portions (1142) and marinate in Red Wine Marinade (55) for 12 hours. Sauté: remove the forepart of the hare at the start of the rib-cage. Carefully trim the back (saddle) of any sinew, remove the abdominal flap and trim the ends of the legs to the first joint. Use the saddle and legs only, cut into suitably-sized pieces. Roasting: prepare as directed (1144). Can be lightly marinated in Red Wine Marinade (55) for 5–6 hours.
1210 Saddle of Hare (Râble de Lièvre)	150–180g per portion	Roasting or Poêling: prepare the saddle (1146) and lightly marinate for 5–6 hours in a Red Wine Marinade (55) if called for in the recipe and particularly if from an older animal.
1211 Fillet of Hare (Filet de Lièvre)	120g per portion	Shallow frying: remove the back fillets from the hare and trim carefully (1145). Leave whole and lard finely or cut into lengths, split open and lightly flatten. Sautés à la Minute: remove the back fillets (1145) and also the small inside fillets from the saddle. Trim carefully of any sinew then cut across into slices on the slant approx. 1cm thick. May be lightly marinated for ½–1 hour with a little brandy, oil, salt and pepper.

RABBIT – LAPIN

Average Weights: Wild rabbit, 1½–2kg; Hutch rabbit, 2½–3½kg
Season: Jan.–Dec.

Name	Average No. of Portions or Portion Weight	Preparation for Cooking
1212 Rabbit, young (Lapereau)	4–6	Stewing (Blanquettes and Fricassées): dissect into portions (1143) then soak in lightly salted water for 5–6 hours to disgorge and become as white as possible. Wash in clean water then drain and pat dry.
1213 Rabbit (Lapin)	4–8	Sautés and brown stews: dissect into portions as directed (1143). Roasting: prepare as directed (1144). Grilling: prepare as directed for roasting (1144) but do not lard.
1214 Fillet of Rabbit (Filet de Lapereau or Lapin)	125g per portion	Shallow frying: remove the back fillets from the rabbit and trim carefully (1145). Leave whole or cut into lengths, split open and lightly flatten. Or flatten more thinly for breadcrumbing as escalopes. Sautés à la Minute: remove the back fillets and also the small inside fillets from the saddle. Trim carefully of any sinews then cut across, well on the slant, into slices approx. ½–1cm thick.

VENAISON – VENISON

Originally, the term venison (*venaison*) referred to the flesh of all furred game but in these days it is invariably accepted as referring only to the flesh of any species of deer. In cookery, the most commonly used venison is derived from the roe deer (*chevreuil*), the fallow deer (*daim*), and the red deer (*cerf*).

For a knowledgeable and discerning clientele it may be useful to name the particular species of deer on the menu, but for the purposes of this section of the book, the term Venison and its French equivalent Venaison will be used exclusively. The following recipes for Venison are equally suitable for all deer, bearing in mind the relative size of the species and whether obtained from the wild or farmed animal. In general the flesh of the farmed animal can be slightly more tender.

1215 Roast Venison

The following joints are suitable for roasting and their titles are given as they can appear on the menu.

Gigue de Venaison rôtie – Roast Leg of Venison
Cuissot de Venaison rôti – Roast Leg of Venison
Hanche de Venaison rôtie – Roast Haunch of Venison
Selle de Venaison rôtie – Roast Saddle of Venison
Longe de Venaison rôtie – Roast Loin of Venison
Carré de Venaison rôti – Roast Best End of Venison

Joints derived from the young tender animal do not require marinating and are best if just larded or wrapped in slices of salt pork fat or fat bacon where there is an obvious lack of natural fat.

Joints of a tougher nature or from the older animal can profit from a period of marination most suitably using the Red Wine Marinade (55). Added vinegar and longer marination can help to tenderise even the more tougher joints but it is well to remember that marination produces its own particular flavours and eating qualities and this can even be a desirable quality for tender joints.

Portion weights
To calculate the quantity of venison required to serve a given number of covers, the approximate weight of venison prepared for roasting is:

on the bone   e.g. Cuissot de Venaison rôti   200–250g per person
boned and rolled   e.g. Longe de Venaison rôtie   150–180g per person

Method for roasting
For preparation see Table of Joints of Venison and preparation on pages 512–13.
1) Season the joint with salt and a little pepper and rub well into the surfaces. Wrap in slices of salt pork fat or fat bacon if required. If marinated, first drain and dry the joint thoroughly.
2) Place it outer surface upwards in a roasting tray on a trivet or on top of a few venison bones and cover with a little melted dripping.
3) Place into a hot oven at 220–225°C for approx. 20 mins. to set and colour the meat. For thicker and larger joints, for example a leg of venison, reduce the temperature gradually so as to allow the joint to continue roasting without burning.

4) Baste the joint frequently and allow it to roast without becoming overcoloured or dried out by the time it is cooked. Allow approx. 12–15 mins. per 500g plus an extra 15 mins. cooking time and in relation to size and thickness of the joint. Any barding should be removed approx. half-way through the cooking time. The joint should be kept underdone unless otherwise requested.

5) To test when cooked, press firmly to express a little of the juices; these should be quite bloody for underdone. If very slightly pink the joint will be just cooked, if clear, well-cooked. For being correctly underdone the reading on a meat thermometer inserted at the thickest part would be approx. 65°C.

6) Allow the cooked joint to rest for at least 30 mins. in a warm place before carving. This will prevent the meat from shrinking and curling when being carved and also from losing its juices.

Roast Gravy – Jus de Rôti
1) When the roast joint is cooked and removed, place the roasting tray on the stove and heat gently, allowing the juices and sediment to settle and colour lightly without burning.
2) Drain off the fat without disturbing the sediment.
3) Add Game Stock (99) as required and allow to simmer gently for a few mins.
4) Correct the seasoning with salt. There should be no need to colour the gravy.
5) Pass through a fine strainer and skim but it is best not to remove all vestiges of fat. Allow approx. 5dl of gravy per 10 covers.

Accompanying sauces
Roast Venison is frequently accompanied with Sauce Grand Veneur or Sauce Poivrade.

Carving
Leg and Haunch: Carve into thinnish slices. For the leg start just behind the knuckle slicing at an angle towards the bone and at the thickest side until the loin is reached; then carve the loin into slices across its length. The joint should then be turned over and the underneath of the leg carved. Take care to avoid any ends of the ligaments found near the leg joint, mainly on the underside. It is useful to serve a little of the meat from both the leg and loin for each customer.

Saddle: If small, this can be carved in either of the following ways:
a) Carve lengthways either side of the backbone giving long flat strips of meat.
b) Cut down either side of the backbone. Then cut across into slices about ½–¾cm thick. The two filets mignons under the saddle should not be forgotten and should be sliced and served as well.
If the saddle is large, it is best to cut across each side of the saddle as in the second method above. If cut lengthways, the slices can be too long and because it is cut along the length of the grain it tends to exaggerate any possibility of toughness.

Loin (boned and rolled): Carve across the joint into slices about ½cm thick.
Best end: Carve into cutlets by cutting between each rib-bone.

Service of Roast Venison
Carved in the kitchen: Arrange on a suitable dish or plate with just a very little roast gravy, garnish with watercress and send a separate sauceboat of gravy, Sauce Poivrade or Sauce Grand Veneur.

Carved in the restaurant: Send the whole joint on an appropriate dish, garnish with watercress and send also a container of roast gravy, Sauce Poivrade or Sauce Grand Veneur.

SPECIAL POINT
It is usual to offer redcurrant jelly with all joints of Roast Venison. A dish of Purée de Marrons (1534) can be a very suitable accompaniment especially when the venison is served with Sauce Poivrade.

1216 Grills of Venison

The most suitable items of venison for grilling are chops, cutlets and steaks. Médaillons and the fillet split open and lightly flattened may also be grilled but are more suitable for shallow frying. See Small Cuts of Venison on page 514 for preparation of these items.

In all cases a short marination with oil, lemon juice, salt and pepper can be an advantage where variation is required but in general good quality tender venison should be seasoned with salt and pepper, brushed with oil, plain grilled quickly in the same way as lamb (704) and kept underdone. Overcooking renders the flesh very dry and stringy. Any of the garnishes applicable to lamb are suitable and may be accompanied with a suitable sauce or butter such as Sauce Diable (125), Sauce Champignons (121), Sauce Poivrade (133), Sauce Chasseur (123), Sauce Grand Veneur (126), Beurre Maître d'Hôtel (10), Beurre Ravigote (14).

Grills of Venison Offals
Kidneys and liver from the freshly killed animal may be grilled but should be soaked in water first. See Preparation of small cuts, page 515. Kidneys should be just cooked and the liver should be floured first and kept underdone. Garnish with Pommes Pailles (1586) and watercress and serve accompanied with parsley butter.

1217 Civet de Venaison Bourguignonne

For eight portions use 1kg well-trimmed flesh from the shoulder, neck, middle neck and breast of venison, cut in 2½ cm cubes. Marinate for 12 hours in Red Wine Marinade (55). Then proceed as for Civet de Lièvre Bourguignonne (1227). The final thickening with blood is usually omitted because of the difficulty of obtaining blood from the deer but any available blood from hare can make an excellent substitute.

1218 Côtelettes de Venaison au Genièvre   4 portions
25 mins.

Stage	Ingredient	Quantity	Method
1	venison cutlets (1200)	4 × 175g or 8 × 80g	Heat the butter in a sauté pan, season the cutlets and shallow fry quickly on
	butter	50g	both sides. Keep underdone. When ready arrange in a suitable dish, cover and keep warm.
2	gin	½dl	Drain off the fat from the pan, add the gin and flamber (32). When the flames
	juniper berries, crushed	8	have died down add the juniper, pepper
	peppercorns, crushed	6	and demi-glace and simmer gently for a
	Demi-glace (112)	2dl	few mins.
3	cream, double	½dl	Add the cream and simmer to a light
	lemon juice	squeeze	coating consistency. Adjust the seasoning

cayenne		as necessary and finish with a little lemon juice and cayenne. Pass through a fine strainer into a clean pan. Cover and keep warm.
4	Heart-shaped Croûtons (26) 4 Marmelade de Pommes, cold (1695) 2dl	Make sure the cutlets are hot then coat with a little of the sauce. Arrange the croûtons around. Send accompanied with the remainder of the sauce in a sauceboat and a dish of the marmalade of apples.

1219 Côtelettes de Venaison Chasseur

Prepare in the same way as Entrecôte Chasseur (814) using 4 × 175g or 8 × 80g cutlets of venison instead of the sirloin steaks.

1220 MÉDAILLONS AND NOISETTES OF VENISON

The following recipes for médaillons and noisettes are suitable for either and are completely interchangeable

1221 Médaillons de Venaison Conti

4 portions
30 mins.

Stage	Ingredient	Quantity	Method
1	médaillons of venison (1202) butter	4 × 150g or 8 × 75g 50g	Heat the butter in a sauté pan, season the médaillons and shallow fry quickly on both sides. Keep underdone. When ready, arrange in a suitable dish. Cover and keep warm.
2	artichoke bottoms (1379)	4	Colour quickly on both sides in the same fat. Remove and keep with the cutlets.
3	shallots, chopped vinegar, red wine red wine	50g 2 tbsps 1dl	Add the shallot to the pan and cook gently until soft. Drain off the fat then add the vinegar and reduce until about dry then add the wine and reduce by half.
4	Fonds de Gibier (99), well-reduced peppercorns, crushed Demi-glace (112)	½dl 6 2dl	Add and reduce to a light coating consistency. Pass through a fine strainer into a clean pan.
5	redcurrant jelly cayenne butter	½ tbsp 25g	Mix in the redcurrant jelly, adjust the seasoning plus a touch of cayenne then shake in the butter.
6	Purée de Lentilles (1534) 3cm rounds of cooked tongue	2 portions 4	Fill the artichoke bottoms dome-shape with lentil purée and cover each with a round of tongue.

7 | Arrange the médaillons neatly with the filled artichokes, make sure all is hot then coat the médaillons only with a little of the sauce. Send with the remainder of the sauce in a sauceboat.

1222 Médaillons de Venaison Valencia

4 portions
45 mins.

Stage	Ingredient	Quantity	Method
1	orange lemon	3 1	Finely peel the zest from 1 orange and half the lemon. Cut in very fine julienne and blanch for 5 mins. in boiling water. Refresh and drain. Prepare the juice from this orange plus a tablespoon of lemon juice. Keep on one side with the zest. Prepare 16 segments from the remaining oranges and likewise reserve.
2	médaillons of venison (1202) butter	4 × 150g or 8 × 75g 50g	Heat the butter in a sauté pan, season the médaillons and shallow fry quickly on both sides. Keep underdone. When ready, arrange on a suitable dish, cover and keep warm.
3			Drain off the fat from the pan and add the orange and lemon juice. Reduce a little.
4	Fonds de Gibier (99) well-reduced Jus lié (113)	½dl 2dl	Add to the pan and reduce to a light coating consistency. Pass through a fine strainer into a clean pan. Adjust the seasoning as necessary and add the reserved zest. Simmer gently for 2–3 mins.
5	Curaçao	¼dl	Make sure that all is hot. Add the Curaçao to the sauce then lightly coat the médaillons with a little of the sauce. Surround with the warmed segments of orange and send accompanied with the remainder of the sauce in a sauceboat.

1223 Noisettes de Venaison aux Myrtilles

4 portions
25 mins.

Stage	Ingredient	Quantity	Method
1	noisettes of venison (1203) butter	4 × 150g or 8 × 75g 50g	Heat the butter in a sauté pan, season the noisettes and shallow fry quickly on both sides. Keep underdone.

2	brandy	¼dl	Drain off the fat, add the brandy and flamber (32). When the flames have died down remove the noisettes and arrange in a suitable dish. Cover and keep warm.
3	vinegar, red wine Fonds de Gibier (99) bilberries	½dl ½dl 75g	Add the vinegar to the pan and reduce by half then add the stock and bilberries and simmer gently for a few moments.
4	Jus lié (113) redcurrant jelly butter, soft	1½dl ½ tbsp 50g	Add the jus lié and redcurrant jelly then shake in the butter. Adjust the seasoning and keep warm.
5			Make sure the noisettes are hot then coat with a little of the sauce. Send accompanied with the remainder of the sauce in a sauceboat.

SPECIAL POINT

Blackcurrants, redcurrants, mulberries or blackberries may be substituted for the bilberries in the above recipe and following the same procedure.

1224 Noisettes de Venaison aux Poires

4 portions
1¼ hours

Stage	Ingredient	Quantity	Method
1	noisettes of venison (1203) lemon juice oil mixed spice milled black pepper salt	4 × 150g or 8 × 75g 1 tbsp 2 tbsps pinch	Place the noisettes in a shallow tray and sprinkle with the oil, lemon juice and mixed spice and season well with milled pepper and a little salt. Marinate for approx. 45 mins. and turn occasionally.
2	pears cinnamon lemon juice and peel bayleaf sugar	4 1 stick 1 1 50g	Peel, core and cut the pears into quarters, place in a pan with the rest of the ingredients. Barely cover with water and greaseproof paper and poach slowly and carefully. When just soft remove from the heat and keep warm.
3	butter	50g	Heat the butter in a sauté pan and shallow fry the drained noisettes quickly on both sides. Keep underdone. When ready, remove and arrange in a suitable dish. Cover and keep warm.
4	pear brandy Fonds de Gibier (99) well-reduced Demi-glace (112)	½dl ½dl 2dl	Drain off the fat from the pan, add the brandy and flamber (32). Add the stock and demi-glace and reduce to a light coating consistency. Pass through a fine strainer into a clean pan. Cover and keep warm.

| 5 | butter | 50g | Adjust the seasoning and shake in the butter. |
| 6 | redcurrant jelly | 75g | Make sure the noisettes are hot then coat with a little of the sauce. Send accompanied with one sauceboat of the remaining sauce, one sauceboat of redcurrant jelly and a dish of the pears which should be warm and have had the flavourings removed. |

1225 Selle de Venaison Bad-Ragaz

12–15 portions
2¾ hours, excluding
marinating time

Stage	Ingredient	Quantity	Method
1	saddle of venison, larded (1192)	5kg	Season the saddle with salt and rub well in. Place in a suitable receptacle and add the marinade and other ingredients. Allow to marinate for 24–36 hours, turning occasionally.
	Red Wine Marinade (55)	1½ litres approx.	
	brandy	1dl	
	juniper berries, crushed	8	
2	butter, melted	125g	Drain the saddle and wipe dry. Likewise drain the vegetables and place these on the bottom of a buttered braising pan. Reserve the marinating liquid.
3			Place the saddle on top of the vegetables and coat with the remaining butter. Cover with the lid and place in a hot oven at approx. 230°C. Baste occasionally and remove the lid after 1 hour and baste frequently to colour and glaze the joint. Keep underdone. Total time approx. 2 hours.
4			When ready, remove to a suitable dish, cover and keep warm.
5			Place the pan on the stove to settle and lightly caramelise the juices. Drain off the fat then add the marinating liquid. Simmer gently for 15 mins. then pass through a fine strainer into a clean pan. Skim carefully then reduce quickly by three-quarters.
6	Demi-glace (112)	5dl	Add and reduce to a light coating consistency.
	cream, sour	6dl	
	redcurrant jelly	2 tbsps	

7	gherkins, chopped	75g	Season the sauce well with milled pepper
	fresh dill, chopped	2 tbsps	plus salt as necessary then add the
			chopped gherkins and dill.

8	Marrons braisés		Make sure the saddle is hot then coat
	(1486)	10 portions	with a little of the sauce. Arrange a
	Céleris braisés	15 × ½	suitable quantity of the garnish around
	(1402)	portions	and send accompanied with sauceboats
	Choux de Bruxelles		of sauce and dishes of the remaining
	au Beurre (1437)	10 portions	vegetables if to be presented and carved

...in the dining room. Alternatively, the saddle may be carved in portions and garnished in the kitchen.

LIÈVRE – HARE
LEVRAUT – LEVERET (YOUNG HARE)

1226 Civet de Lièvre à l'Anglaise – English-Style Jugged Hare

Prepare Civet de Lièvre (1227) but replace the Bourguignonne garnish of lardons, mushrooms and onions with a garnish of forcemeat balls prepared in the following manner:
1) Chop the hare liver fairly small and mix together with approx. four times its quantity of pork sausage-meat and a little finely chopped onion cooked until soft in butter.
2) Mould in small balls, egg-and-breadcrumb and deep fry in hot fat. Drain.
3) Arrange round the dish of hare together with the croûtons or send the forcemeat balls separately in a dish. In either case accompany with a sauceboat of redcurrant jelly.

1227 Civet de Lièvre Bourguignonne

8 portions
3 hours excluding marinating time

Stage	Ingredient	Quantity	Method
1	hare, skinned	1	Drain the blood from the hare into a
	Red Wine Marinade		basin. Remove the liver and discard the
	(55)	1 litre	gall-bladder. Finely chop the liver, heart and lungs, place with the blood and reserve for use. Cut the hare into portions for stewing (1142), then place into a basin, cover with the marinade and leave for 24 hours.
2	butter	100g	Drain the hare and vegetables. Dry and season the hare. Heat the butter in a frying-pan and just as it turns brown, place in the hare. Fry quickly until brown on all sides and remove to a braising pan. Fry the drained vegetables in the same fat, drain and add to the hare.

3	flour	50g	Sprinkle onto the hare and shake the pan to mix in. Place in a hot oven for approx. 10 mins. and remove.
4	tomato purée	1 tbsp	Add the tomato purée and the liquid remaining from the marinade. Add
	Fonds Brun (97)	1 litre approx.	sufficient stock to just cover the hare.
	garlic, crushed	1 clove	Add the garlic and season. Bring to the boil, skim, cover with the lid, place in a moderate oven at 180°C and cook until tender (2–2½ hours).
5	vinegar	½dl	Remove the hare and place in a clean pan. Remove the fat from the sauce. Mix the vinegar with the blood and chopped offals and whisk it into the sauce. Reheat but do not reboil. Adjust the seasoning and pass through a fine strainer over the hare. Keep hot.
6	Lardons (51)	200g	Blanch the lardons and fry brown in a little fat. Drain. Dress the hare in
	button onions, glacé à Brun (1493)	24	earthenware dishes and garnish with the lardons, onions and mushrooms.
	button mushrooms, sautéed in butter	24	Surround with the croûtons, the points of which have been dipped into chopped
	Heart-shaped Croûtons (26)	8	parsley, and send.
	parsley, chopped		

1228 Civet de Lièvre Flamande

8 portions
3 hours approx.

Stage	Ingredient	Quantity	Method
1	hare, skinned	1	Drain the blood from the hare (1142)
	vinegar	1½dl	into a basin, and reserve if required for other uses. Remove the liver and discard the gall-bladder. Finely mince the liver and heart, place in a basin and mix in the vinegar and reserve. Cut the hare into portions for stewing (1142).
2	butter	100g	Heat the butter in a braising pan. Season the hare, add to the butter and colour well on all sides.
3	flour	35g	Sprinkle with the flour and shake the pan to mix in. Place in a hot oven for approx. 10 mins. mixing occasionally and to brown the flour.
4	red wine	½ litre	Remove from the oven, allow to cool a little then carefully mix in the wine and
	Fonds de Gibier (99)	½ litre	sufficient stock to cover. Add the sugar,

sugar, brown	25g	the onions which have been lightly
onions, finely		sautéed in the butter, the bouquet garni
sliced	600g	and the reserved liver and vinegar.
butter	50g	Season with salt and pepper. Bring to
Bouquet Garni	1 large	the boil, skim, cover with the lid and

the onions which have been lightly
sautéed in the butter, the bouquet garni
and the reserved liver and vinegar.
Season with salt and pepper. Bring to
the boil, skim, cover with the lid and
place in a moderate oven at 180°C. Cook
gently until just tender, approx.
2–2½ hours.

5   Remove the hare from the liquid and
place in a clean pan. Skim the sauce
carefully of all fat and discard the
bouquet garni. Pass the sauce and
onions through a fine sieve and add to
the hare.

6   Heart-shaped Croûtons   Adjust the seasoning as necessary and
    (26)   8   simmer gently for a further 10 mins. or
    redcurrant jelly   1 tbsp   so. Dress the hare in earthenware
dishes, sprinkle with chopped parsley
and surround with the croûtons spread
on one side with redcurrant jelly.

SPECIAL POINT
Kangaroo can also be regarded as a game animal and be jugged as Civet de Kangourou.

1229 Filets de Levraut aux Airelles Rouges
4 portions
35 mins.

Stage	Ingredient	Quantity	Method
1	cranberries, cleaned		Place all the ingredients in a well-tinned
	and stemmed	150g	or stainless steel pan, cover with a lid
	butter	25g	and simmer very gently until just soft.
	redcurrant jelly	2 tbsps	Keep covered and warm in a deep dish
	water	½dl	or timbale.
2	fillets of young		Heat the butter in a sauté pan, season
	hare (1145), larded	8	the hare fillets and shallow fry on all
	butter	50g	sides and keep underdone.
3	brandy	½dl	Drain off the fat from the hare then add
			the brandy and flamber (32). When the
			flames have died down remove the hare
			to an earthenware dish, cover and keep
			warm.
4	Fonds de Gibier		Add the stock to the pan and reduce
	(99)	4dl	until slightly viscous. Shake in the butter
	butter, softened	75g	away from the heat and season well with
	lemon juice	few drops	milled pepper, salt and a touch of
	cayenne		cayenne. Finish with a few drops of
			lemon juice.

5   Make sure that the fillets of hare are hot
                                     then pass the sauce through a fine
                                     strainer over them. Send the dish
                                     accompanied with the dish of
                                     cranberries.

1230 Levraut rôti – Roast Young Hare   4–6 portions
                                                                50 mins.

Stage	Ingredient	Quantity	Method
1	young hare, prepared for roasting (1144) and larded oil	1 1dl	Season the hare with salt and pepper and rub well in. Place in a small roasting tray and cover with the oil.
2			Place in a hot oven at approx. 230°C and baste frequently and keep underdone. Time approx. 25 mins. Test by pressing the flesh, this should be fairly resilient and the juices red. Place on a suitable dish, cover and keep warm.
3	Fonds de Gibier (99)	4dl	Place the roasting tray on the stove and allow the juices to settle and lightly caramelise. Tip off the fat and add the stock. Simmer gently for 2–3 mins. and season with a little salt. Pass through a fine strainer into a clean pan and keep hot.
4	watercress Sauce Poivrade (133), or Sauce Cumberland (183) redcurrant jelly	1 bunch 3dl 100g	Make sure the hare is hot then surround with a little gravy. Garnish with bouquets of watercress and send accompanied with one sauceboat of the remaining gravy and one of redcurrant jelly. Either of the sauces may be offered.

SPECIAL POINT

The hare may be portioned and carved in the kitchen if required. In this case, first cut off the legs and cut each into two or three pieces according to size. Then remove the back fillets and underfillets from the trunk. Cut these into long thickish slices on the slant. Serve a piece of leg with a few slices of the fillet per portion. Place on a dish or plate with a little gravy and a bouquet of watercress, and send accompanied with gravy, sauce and redcurrant jelly.

1231 Râble de Lièvre à l'Allemande   4 portions
                                                                45 mins.

Stage	Ingredient	Quantity	Method
1	saddle of hare (1146), larded Red Wine Marinade (55)	2 × 2 or 4 × 1 ½ litre	Place the saddles in a suitable receptacle and cover with the marinade. Leave for 24 hours and turn occasionally.

2	butter, melted	75g	Carefully drain the saddles and vegetables from the marinade. Place the vegetables on the bottom of a buttered roasting tray. Season the saddles, place on top of the vegetables and coat with the remaining butter. Place in a very hot oven at 230°C to roast. Baste occasionally and keep underdone. Time approx. 15–20 mins.
3			When ready, place the saddles in an earthenware dish, cover and keep warm.
4	cream, sour lemon juice cayenne	3dl squeeze	Completely drain off the fat from the tray and vegetables. Add the cream and reduce to a coating consistency. Adjust the seasoning as necessary and finish with a little lemon juice and a touch of cayenne.
5			Make sure the saddles of hare are hot then pass the sauce without undue pressure through a fine strainer over them.

1232 Râble de Lièvre Baden-Baden

4 portions
50 mins. excluding
marinating time

Stage	Ingredient	Quantity	Method
1	saddle of hare (1146), larded White Wine Marinade (56)	2 × 2 or 4 × 1 ½ litre	Place the saddles in a suitable receptacle and cover with the marinade. Leave for 24 hours and turn occasionally.
2	pears cinnamon stick lemon peel lemon juice sugar white wine	6 1 2 strips 2 tbsps 25g 2dl approx.	Peel, core and cut the pears in quarters. Place in a pan with the rest of the ingredients and just sufficient white wine to barely cover. Cover with greaseproof paper and poach carefully until just soft. Place in a deep dish or timbale and keep warm.
3	butter	75g	Drain the saddles and vegetables and reserve the marinade. Place the vegetables on the bottom of a buttered roasting tray. Season the saddles, place on top of the vegetables and coat with the remaining butter. Place in a very hot oven at 230°C to roast. Baste occasionally and keep underdone. Time approx. 15–20 mins.

4			When ready, place the saddles in an earthenware dish, cover and keep warm.
5	reserved marinade	2dl	Drain off the fat from the pan and vegetables. Add the marinade, simmer for a few mins, then pass through a fine strainer into a clean pan.
6	Jus lié (113) cream lemon juice cayenne	1½dl 1dl squeeze	Add the jus lié and cream and reduce to a light coating consistency. Season as necessary and finish with a little lemon juice and a touch of cayenne.
7	redcurrant jelly		Make sure the saddles of hare are hot and coat with a little of the sauce. Send accompanied with the rest of the sauce in a sauceboat, the dish of pears with the cinnamon and peel removed, and a sauceboat of redcurrant jelly.

LAPIN – RABBIT
LAPEREAU – RABBIT (YOUNG)

1233 Escalopes de Lapin – Escalopes of Rabbit

Remove the back fillets from the rabbit and carefully trim them of any of the sinew which runs along their outside. Cut each across into two, split open along the length and flatten carefully to approx. 3mm thick. Trim carefully. These escalopes may be prepared in any of the ways applicable to Escalopes de Veau (952–961).

1234 Fricassée de Lapin

Cut the rabbit in portions for stewing (1143) and proceed in any of the ways applicable to Fricassée de Poulet (1063–1065).

1235 Lapereau grillé – Grilled Rabbit

Prepare young and tender rabbit as directed for grilling (1213). Season on all sides then brush well with melted butter. Grill at medium heat, first on the underside then turn over and complete the cooking, brushing frequently with butter. Grill until just done, approx. 12–15 mins. each side, then send whole or cut in portions, garnished with watercress and Pommes Pailles (1586). Serve accompanied with a suitable sauce such as Sauce Champignons, Sauce Poivrade or Sauce Diable.

1236 Lapereau rôti – Roast Rabbit

Choose young and tender rabbit, either wild or domesticated. Prepare for roasting (1144) and proceed and serve in the same way as for Roast Hare (1230).

1237 Lapereau sauté Languedocienne

10 portions
45 mins.

Stage	Ingredient	Quantity	Method
1	young tender rabbit, cut for sauté (1143)	10 portions	Heat the oil in a sauté pan, season the rabbit and colour quickly on both sides.
	oil	1½dl	Sprinkle with the herbs, then cover with
	fresh basil ⎫ finely	½ tbsp	the lid and cook more slowly on the side
	fresh thyme⎬ chopped	½ tbsp	of the stove or in a moderate oven.
	garlic ⎭ together	2 cloves	
2			When cooked, remove the rabbit to a dish, cover and keep warm.
3	courgettes, cut in ½cm-thick rounds	200g	Add to the remaining oil in the pan, season and sauté quickly until just
	aubergines, cut in 1cm cubes	200g	cooked. Drain off any surplus oil.
	mushrooms, sliced	250g	
4	Tomates Concassées (90)	350g	Add the tomatoes and wine and reduce the liquid by half, then add the jus lié.
	white wine dry	2dl	Simmer for a few mins. then adjust the
	Jus lié (113)	3dl	seasoning as necessary.
5	fresh basil leaves, roughly chopped	1 tbsp	Return the rabbit to the prepared sauce and reheat gently without boiling. Serve in earthenware dishes sprinkled with the chopped basil.

1238 Lapin à la Moutarde

4 portions
1½ hours excluding
marinating time

Stage	Ingredient	Quantity	Method
1	rabbit, prepared for roasting (1144) and larded	1	Season the prepared rabbit with salt and pepper and marinate with the Madeira for 5–6 hours. Turn the rabbit
	Madeira	2dl	occasionally. When ready, drain and dry the rabbit and reserve the marinade.
2	butter	100g	Heat the butter in a small roasting tray. Season the rabbit and fry quickly to brown on both sides. Remove from the pan.
3	mustard, dry	50g	Dilute the mustard with water to a coat-
	pig's caul, soaked in water, drained and dried		ing consistency. spread the caul flat. Brush the top side of the rabbit well with mustard, lay this side down on the caul then brush the remaining surfaces. Wrap up and enclose completely in the caul, then turn over and replace in the roasting tray.

4			Sprinkle the surface with the butter in the tray then place in a hot oven at approx. 220°C and roast carefully with frequent basting. Turn occasionally and keep just done, approx. 40–45 mins. Remove to a clean dish. Cover and keep warm.
5	cream, double	3dl	Drain off the fat from the roasting tray and deglaze with the reserved marinade. Pass through a fine strainer into a clean pan then add the cream, and reduce to a light coating consistency. Adjust the seasoning as necessary.
6			Serve the rabbit whole or cut in portions coated with the sauce. Or send the sauce separately in a sauceboat.

1239 Lapin aux Pruneaux – Rabbit with Prunes

10 portions
1¾ hours

Stage	Ingredient	Quantity	Method
1	prunes Madeira cinnamon stick	30 2dl 1	Soak the prunes overnight. Drain and remove the stones. Place the prunes in a pan with the Madeira and cinnamon, cover, bring to the boil and simmer gently for 7–8 mins. Remove from the heat and keep on one side.
2	butter unsmoked streaky bacon, cut in lardons (51) young tender rabbit, cut for stewing (1143) ground cinnamon	50g 175g 10 portions pinch	Heat the butter in a braising pan, add the lardons and fry to a light brown and remove to one side. Season the rabbit with salt, pepper and a little cinnamon and sauté to a nice golden brown on all sides in the same fat. Drain off the fat.
3	Fonds de Veau (95)	1 litre approx.	Drain off the liquid from the prunes and add to the rabbit and bacon with sufficient stock to barely cover. Bring to the boil, cover and place in the oven at approx. 180°C to cook gently. After 40–45 mins. when the rabbit should still be firm but needs further cooking, add the prunes and complete the cooking together.
4			When ready, drain and remove the rabbit, bacon and prunes and arrange neatly in earthenware dishes. Cover and keep warm.

5	cream, double	4dl	Reduce the cooking liquid by half then
	redcurrant jelly	1 tbsp	pass through a fine strainer into a clean
			pan. Add the cream and redcurrant jelly
			and reduce to a light coating consistency.
			Adjust the seasoning.
6			Make sure the rabbit and garnish are hot
			then coat with the sauce and send.

1240 Sauté de Lapin aux Champignons

10 portions
2 hours

Stage	Ingredient	Quantity	Method
1	rabbit, cut for sauté (1143)	10 portions	Heat the butter in a shallow braising pan, season the rabbit and fry quickly to
	butter	75g	brown on all sides. Drain off any surplus fat.
2	white wine, dry	3dl	Add the wine to the rabbit, cover and
	Demi-glace (112)	4dl	reduce by half then add the demi-glace
	Bouquet Garni	1	and bouquet garni. Bring to the boil, skim, cover with the lid and cook in a moderate oven at 180°C until just tender. Approx 1–1½ hours.
3			Discard the bouquet garni and remove the rabbit to a clean pan.
4	butter	50g	Heat the butter in a sauté pan, add the
	shallot, finely chopped	75g	shallots and cook without colour. Add the mushrooms, season lightly and sauté
	mushrooms, small button	600g	together until just tender. Add to the rabbit.
5	parsley, chopped		Adjust the seasoning and consistency of the sauce as necessary – it should not be too thick, then pass through a fine strainer over the rabbit and mushrooms. Simmer together gently for approx. 10 mins. then serve in earthenware dishes sprinkled with chopped parsley.

15

Cold Dishes and Buffet Work

Most catering establishments offer cold food in one form or another on their menus, ranging from the provision of cold Hors-d'oeuvre to Sweet Dishes. This section however, is concerned only with 1) items of a savoury nature which can be served as cold dishes in their own right, particularly those of egg, fish, shellfish, meats, poultry and game, and 2) those special related preparations which although having their own distinct qualities nevertheless are an integral part of many of these cold dishes. The range of these cold dishes can be as simple as a choice of cold plated meat and salad to a choice from a grand classical Cold Buffet offering a wide range of decorated joints and dishes.

In some establishments a buffet is prepared each day for display in the restaurant, usually for lunch during the summer months. In others it is featured only for special occasions such as Christmas or Easter, or for functions where it is requested by the customer. In all cases the dishes for a cold buffet must be prepared so as to be attractive to the eye and to the palate, should include as wide a variety as possible and should be well arranged and presented.

There are a large number of cold dishes, most being suitable for presentation on the cold buffet. Some are very simply prepared and do not lend themselves to decoration; others are more elaborate both in their preparation and in their finishing and it is with these that a skilled practitioner can show his good taste and artistic ability. Many of the more elaborate dishes are coated with a sauce, then decorated and finally glazed with a savoury jelly. The finished dishes are often presented on sculpted and decorated bases called Socles which add height and balance. Appropriate decorated garnishes are frequently used in the final arrangement of many dishes.

In addition there are a number of dishes initially prepared hot but which can be successfully and suitably offered as cold items. Fricassées, curries finished with cream and joints such as Boeuf à la Mode or Daube de Boeuf can add interest to the selection of cold dishes.

Other items of cold food can include Mousses of fish, meat or poultry, Pies, Pâtés, Terrines, Galantines and cold deep-fried items such as chicken portions, Rissoles and Croquettes.

———SELECTION OF COMMODITIES———

As with all foodstuffs, quality must be a first consideration when selecting items of food for cold service. In addition some consideration needs to be given to the following:
a) The type and scope of the menu. For example, whether for a grand classical buffet, a small buffet prepared on a daily basis, a special function featuring cold food either

carved in the dining-room or presented already carved and portioned, or perhaps just a selection of cold meats plated to order, and so on.

b) Whether the items are required for presentation whole; in this case extra care should be taken to ensure that the item is of the right size and conformation to present at its best when cooked.

c) The season of the year and weather. Game should always be offered in the winter months particularly for the large classical buffet. The summer months and periods of sustained hot weather can drastically affect the balance of consumption between hot and cold foods, and demand should be assessed in the light of past experience.

d) Quantities need to be carefully judged in relation to the number of covers booked or estimated. Wastage and leftovers should be kept to a minimum but there must be sufficient food and to the customer's choice and expectations.

e) There must always be careful balancing of the menu especially for any special function which features a large cold buffet. Choice from the items of eggs, fish, shellfish, meat, poultry and game has to be decided in respect of the caterer's knowledge of customer preference.

f) Above all, the cold food offered should be suitable for the level of clientele and demand. It would be quite inappropriate, for example, to offer highly decorated and presented items at a carvery specialising in quick turnover.

PREPARATION, COOKING AND PRESENTATION

When needed for presentation whole or as decorated portions for a cold buffet, just that little extra care paid to preparation and cooking of the dishes can do much to enhance their final appearance and eating qualities. The following points are worth noting:

a) Scrupulous attention should be paid to the cleaning, trimming, trussing or tying as appropriate, of all items, bearing in mind the need to present them to their best advantage.

b) Any mixtures, fillings or stuffings used in the preparation should be well-seasoned and well-flavoured. Cold food tends to dull the palate somewhat in comparison with the same food when hot.

c) All roast or poêléed meats or poultry need to be cooked that little extra; on no account should anything, even beef, be so underdone as to drip blood. Beef and furred game should show a nice pink; poultry should show no evidence of pinkness near the bones when carved; game birds again should be just done and the whitish flesh of pheasant and partridge should show no red near the bones when carved; hams should be cooked just to the bone and left to cool in the cooking liquor, ideally showing moistness when carved but no signs of being uncooked. Although poached fish is arguably acceptable when undercooked for hot service, this does not apply when required for cold service. All poached fish for cold should be cooked through and always allowed to cool in its cooking liquor. Poached and soft-boiled eggs should be cooked for a little longer than if for hot – any uncooked white around the yolk can be unpleasant for the majority of customers.

d) Do not cook anything for cold too far in advance; too extended a period under refrigeration whether decorated or not can be deleterious.

e) The time for decoration and presentation should also be kept to a minimum and carried out in cool temperatures. It is better for a neat presentable decor to be carried out quickly then to take an inordinate length of time over too ambitious a decoration. In this last case there is always an increased possibility of contamination and deterioration in quality.

CARVING

The correct carving of cold fish, meat and poultry requires much in the way of skilled experience, firstly to be able to produce slices or portions of the correct thickness or shape and to present it in an appetising and aesthetically pleasing manner and secondly, to produce the maximum number of suitable portions from any item, with portion size being consistent with customer satisfaction.

In general the carving of cold meats is carried out in the same way as for the same roast meats when served hot. Poultry and game birds are portioned in the same manner as when served hot. Producing a smooth surface and an even thickness of the carved slice without ridges is the ideal presentation to aim for.

For carving in front of the customer, good-quality stainless steel knives are to be preferred. They are made in several shapes and sizes, each being suited to a particular type of carving. For example, a fairly long thin and flexible knife for ham and lamb; a fairly wide, long and semi-rigid one for beef; a fairly short and flexible one for saddles of lamb, veal and game. Poultry is best portioned with a medium-sized cook's knife; fish should always be carved with a stainless steel knife, other types of steel tending to impart a metallic taste. At all times the use of a carving fork is recommended. The carving and portioning of cold food should be done to order where possible. If required for presentation in ready-sliced or portioned form, carving should be done as near to the time of service as possible and kept covered and refrigerated until required.

HYGIENE AND HEALTH CONSIDERATIONS

The possibility of contamination is always present at all stages in the preparation, presentation and service of cold food. Strict attention should be paid to normal safe hygiene procedures but the following points have particular relevance to the production and service of cold dishes:

1) Do not cook the food too far in advance; aim to have it cooked as near to requirement as possible, cool it quickly and refrigerate immediately.
2) Do not store cooked meats near raw food. If possible use a separate refrigerator.
3) Keep storage times to a minimum; aim for a quick turnover with as little as possible of toing and froing of the food from the refrigerator.
4) Do not spend prolonged periods of time over the decoration of food in temperatures above 10°C.
5) Savoury jellies and chaud-froid sauces, because of their gelatine content, are highly susceptible to contamination. Use freshly made quantities where possible. If there is need for storage keep this to a minimum, ideally no more than 24 hours, and keep covered and separate from raw foods. If stored, reheat and simmer gently for 10 mins. before using; likewise reboil any jelly or sauce left over from decorating, before storing again.
6) Any cold presentation for the dining-room should be sent as late as possible; it should not be left to deteriorate before the customers arrive.

7) Ideally, the presentation of cold food in the dining-room or servery should be under some type of refrigeration.
8) All food-handlers should be aware of the necessities for personal cleanliness and clean dress. The naked hands should not be used to touch the food; gloves, forks and other implements for handling the food should be used.
9) Remaining food from cold presentations should be used as soon as possible and should not be passed backwards and forwards from the refrigerator and dining-room.

PREPARATION TIMES

In many cases no time has been given for the preparation of the following dishes because of the difficulty of calculating the length of time taken to decorate, artistic licence being the deciding factor.

INITIAL PREPARATIONS FOR BUFFET WORK

1241 GELÉES D'ASPIC – ASPIC OR SAVOURY JELLIES

Many cold dishes, especially those destined for a cold buffet display and whether decorated or not, are glazed with aspic jelly. This helps to make them look more attractive and prevents undue drying of the surfaces. A good jelly should add something to the taste of the dish and where obviously indicated, have a definite relationship to the item which it coats. This means for example, that a chicken aspic jelly is best used for the final coating of chicken dishes and so on. The basic aspic jelly is suitable for egg dishes and meat dishes where the demands for compatibility are not so strong.

The amount of gelatine used in the preparation of a jelly should ensure that the finished jelly is not so weak that it melts in a warm room, nor so stiff that it becomes unpleasant to eat; it must be crystal-clear and the correct colour in keeping with the dish. This can range from an almost colourless chicken aspic to a dark reddish-brown for game or lamb. The colours are best when obtained naturally by the use and variation of ingredients, such as roasted bones and vegetables where appropriate, wines, and extended cooking times which help to develop the depth of colour. The use of artificial colours is not recommended but where essential they should be safe and of the very best quality. The colour of the dish and its jelly should also be compatible, thus a dark-coloured jelly for a white chicken dish would be incorrect and green and blue jelly is wrong for almost any kind of savoury dish. A very light green jelly with its colour obtained from natural vegetable sources can be useful in the preparation of some vegetable dishes such as terrines.

At all stages in the preparation of the stock and subsequent clarification as jelly, the complete and absolute removal of all vestiges of fat is essential. Any fat present in the glazing of any item is deleterious.

1242 Gelée Ordinaire – Basic Aspic Jelly

5 litres
3 hours

Stage	Ingredient	Quantity	Method
1	egg whites	4	Place the egg whites in a pan with ½
	shin of beef,	1½kg	litre of cold water and whisk briskly. Add
	minced		the beef and salt and mix thoroughly
	salt	20g	together.
2	onions	150g	Add and mix in well. Rest for a few
	carrots cut	150g	minutes.
	leek small	100g	
	celery	150g	
	bayleaf	1	
	thyme	sprig	
	peppercorns	10	
3	leaf gelatine	250g	Add the stock to the rest of the
	Fonds de Veau (95)	6 litres	ingredients. Mix in well and add the gelatine previously soaked in cold water and drained. Bring to the boil quickly, keeping the bottom of the pan clean using a metal spatula from time to time and taking care to disturb as little as possible. Remove the spatula immediately it comes to the boil.
4			Simmer very gently for approx. 2 hours then strain through a double muslin. Remove all fat and, if necessary, adjust the seasoning with salt only.

SPECIAL POINT

All aspic jellies should set fairly firm when cold. It is therefore important to check the consistency of the aspic before straining. This can be done by placing a little in a dish in the refrigerator until well-set. If too soft, add extra soaked gelatine as required.

1243 Gelée de Volaille – Chicken Aspic Jelly

Prepare as Gelée Ordinaire (1242), using 1kg of shin of beef only plus 1kg of chicken giblets and carcases at Stage 1.

1244 Gelée de Canard – Duck Aspic Jelly

Prepare as Gelée Ordinaire (1242), using 1kg of shin of beef only plus 1kg of lightly roasted duck giblets and carcases added at Stage 2.

1245 Gelée de Gibier – Game Aspic Jelly

Prepare as Gelée Ordinaire (1242), using 1kg of shin of beef only plus 1kg of roasted carcases, bones and trimmings of game added at Stage 2.

1246 Gelée de Poisson – Fish Aspic Jelly

5 litres
3 hours

Stage	Ingredient	Quantity	Method
1	egg whites	4	Place the egg whites in a pan with
	fillets of whiting,		½ litre of cold water and whisk briskly.
	minced	1½kg	Add the whiting and salt and mix
	salt	20g	thoroughly together.
2	onion ⎫	150g	Add and mix in well. Rest for a few
	leek ⎬ cut small	100g	minutes.
	fennel ⎭	75g	
	parsley stalks	50g	
	peppercorns	10	
3	leaf gelatine	250g	Add the stock to the rest of the
	Fonds de Poisson		ingredients. Mix in well and add the
	(101)	6 litres	gelatine previously soaked in cold water and drained. Bring to the boil quickly, keeping the bottom of the pan clean using a metal spatule from time to time and taking care to disturb as little as possible. Remove the spatule immediately it comes to the boil.
4			Simmer very gently for approx. 2 hours then strain through a double muslin. Remove any traces of fat. Adjust the seasoning if necessary, using salt only.

1247 Glazing with Aspic Jelly

When using a jelly for the final coating of an item, either decorated or not, it is necessary to prepare a much larger quantity than would actually be needed to adhere to the items under preparation. This allows the practitioner to complete each stage of coating the food without having to stop part-way through.

1) Have the items placed on a wire rack or grill with a tray underneath. Keep refrigerated until required.

2) Cool the jelly gradually by placing the container of jelly in a basin of iced water, stir gently and continuously until it becomes slightly viscous. Remove from the iced water and continue stirring gently to the viscosity of a light oil. Take care not to make any air bubbles in the jelly.

3) Bring the prepared items on the tray from the refrigerator then ladle over the jelly in a steady even stream; if this is done the jelly will set on contact and produce a smooth surface. Repeat again then place the grill of items on a clean tray to set properly.

4) Return the surplus jelly to the pan, reheat, strain and cool again in readiness for further coating.

5) Coat the items again to the required degree of thickness and glossiness; the coating of jelly should be no more than 2–3mm thick.

6) When dressing up the glazed finished items, take care to carefully cut away any set drips of jelly or sauce before placing on the service tray.

SPECIAL POINTS

a) A further container of warm jelly can be kept on hand for adding a little at the time to the jelly being used; this can help to control the degree of viscosity needed.

b) If the jelly sets too far it will be necessary to reheat it and cool as before.

c) If the remaining jelly is to be kept after completing the glazing, make sure that it is reboiled gently for a few minutes then strained and cooled quickly before storing covered in a refrigerator. In any case storage time should be no longer than 24 hours. It should never be mixed with any freshly prepared jelly.

1248 Lining or Chemising a Mould with Aspic Jelly

Fill the mould with aspic jelly at near setting-point and place in a container of crushed ice and sufficient water to come almost to the top of the mould. The jelly will quickly start to set around the sides and on the bottom. Allow this coating to set approx. 2–4mm thick according to the size of the mould; this can be judged by gently moving the back of a spoon along the inside of the mould. The thickness of the set jelly becomes evident. At this stage, quickly tip out the unset jelly and place the mould in the refrigerator to set firmly before using.

1249 Coating a dish with Aspic Jelly

Make sure that the dish selected has a flat base – this will prevent the formation of an uneven thickness of jelly showing, particularly bad if of a more pronounced colour. Have the required jelly at a fairly warm temperature then carefully pour into the dish to the required depth, usually 4–5mm. Take care not to form any bubbles in the jelly. Place to set in the refrigerator and adjust the level if necessary to obtain an even depth overall.

1250 Croûtons de Gelée – Savoury Jelly Shapes

Fill a basin with a suitable quantity of the required jelly; allow to set firmly in the refrigerator. When needed, turn out onto greaseproof paper and cut into ¾–1cm-thick slices. Turn each slice over onto the paper and cut into the required size shapes as needed, e.g. triangles, semi-circles, diamonds etc. Use to garnish and decorate the appropriate cold dishes.

Alternatively, the jelly may be set as a ¾–1cm layer in a clean flat shallow dish and then cut to shape as above when needed.

1251 CHAUD–FROID SAUCES

A number of cold dishes are first coated with a sauce to which gelatine in the form of aspic jelly has been added. This is to ensure that it sets to an acceptable firmness commensurate with keeping its place on the food. It should not, however, be too firm when cold but have a texture which softens and melts quickly on the palate. Appearance, flavour and compatibility with the food which it coats are all important. This type of sauce of which there are a number is referred to as a Sauce Chaud-froid. The following are commonly used:

Sauce Chaud-froid à l'Aurore suitable for the coating of poached poultry either whole or as suprêmes.

Sauce Chaud-froid Blanche, suitable for the coating of poached chicken, whole or as suprêmes, galantine and ham.

Sauce Chaud-froid Brune, suitable for the coating of duck, lamb cutlets, boar's head and game.

Sauce Chaud-froid de Poisson, suitable for the coating of poached fillets of sole, turbot, either whole or as suprêmes, and trout.

Sauce Chaud-froid Verte, suitable for the coating of poached poultry either whole or as suprêmes.

1252 Sauce Chaud-froid à l'Aurore – Pink Chaud-froid Sauce

5 litres
25 mins.

Stage	Ingredient	Quantity	Method
1	butter		Melt the butter in a sauteuse, add the
	Tomates Concassées (90)	75g 1½kg	tomatoes and cook to a smooth and fairly dry paste.
2	Chaud-froid Blanche (1253)	4 litres	Bring to the boil, add the tomato paste, mix in thoroughly, season, reboil and pass through a fine strainer.

1253 Sauce Chaud-froid Blanche – White Chaud-froid Sauce

5 litres
30 mins.

Stage	Ingredient	Quantity	Method
1	Velouté de Volaille (115)	4 litres	Place the velouté in a shallow pan and reduce it stirring constantly with a metal
	Gelée Ordinaire (1242)	2 litres	spatule and adding the jelly and cream a little at a time.
	cream	1 litre	
2			Reduce the total by approx. one-third until it reaches a coating consistency. Season and pass through a fine strainer.

1254 Sauce Chaud-froid Brune – Brown Chaud-froid Sauce

5 litres
30 mins.

Stage	Ingredient	Quantity	Method
1	Demi-glace (112)	4 litres	Place the demi-glace in a shallow pan
	Gelée Ordinaire (1242)	3 litres	and reduce it, stirring constantly with a metal spatule and adding the jelly a little at a time.
2	Madeira	1dl	Reduce the total by approx. one-third. Add the Madeira and pass through a fine strainer.

SPECIAL POINTS
a) When using a brown Chaud-froid Sauce for duck, add 2dl of well-reduced duck stock at Stage 1.
b) When using a brown Chaud-froid Sauce for game, add 2dl of well-reduced game stock at Stage 1.

1255 Sauce Chaud-froid de Poisson – Fish Chaud-froid Sauce

Prepare in the same way as Chaud-froid Blanche (1253), using Velouté de Poisson (117) instead of Velouté de Volaille, and Gelée de Poisson (1246) instead of Gelée Ordinaire.

1256 Sauce Chaud-froid Verte – Green Chaud-froid Sauce

5 litres
40 mins.

Stage	Ingredient	Quantity	Method
1	white wine, dry	2dl	Bring the wine to the boil in a small pan,
	chives, roughly		then add the herbs. Bring back to the
	chopped	25g	boil, cover and remove from the heat.
	tarragon leaves	15g	Allow to infuse for 10 mins. Strain
	parsley leaves	15g	through muslin into a clean pan and
	chervil leaves	15g	reduce by half.
	salad burnet leaves	15g	
2	Chaud-froid Blanche		Bring to the boil then add the infusion
	(1253)	5 litres	of herbs, reboil and adjust the seasoning
			as necessary.
3	green vegetable	½ tbsp	Add just sufficient of the colouring to
	colouring (47)	approx.	give a pale delicate green colour to the
			sauce.

1257 Coating with Sauce Chaud-froid

When using Chaud-froid sauce it is necessary to prepare at least double the quantity required. This is to allow for sufficient sauce to flow in a semi-liquid state over the whole item and will allow it to be masked evenly, any surplus draining off. The likely result from having insufficient sauce is that the coating will be uneven.
1) Place the item or items to be coated on a wire rack with a tray underneath. Keep refrigerated until required.
2) Reduce the temperature of the sauce gradually by placing the container of sauce in a basin of iced water. Stir gently and continuously until it just begins to thicken. Remove from the ice and continue stirring gently to a nice flowing consistency. Be careful that no lumps form.
3) Remove the items from the refrigerator then quickly ladle over the sauce in a steady even stream. Take care not to form any ridges or unevenness on the surface. A smooth unblemished surface is required. Place the rack of coated items on a clean tray and return to the refrigerator to set properly.
4) Return the surplus sauce and reheat gently then strain and cool in readiness for further coating as required.

5) Coat the items again as required. It is usual to give two thin coats but the final thickness of the chaud-froid should not in any case exceed 3mm.
6) Keep in the refrigerator until required for decoration and or service.

SPECIAL POINTS
a) Some larger items such as whole chicken or tongue are better and more securely coated if pierced with the prongs of a long roasting fork at the back end. This enables the practitioner to hold it in the left hand and to manipulate the direction and slope of its surfaces while being coated with the sauce. All other previous points hold good.
b) If felt useful to keep the remaining sauce after completing the job, make sure that it is reboiled for a few minutes, strained and cooled quickly before storing in the refrigerator. In any case storage time should be kept to a minimum and the sauce should never be mixed with a freshly prepared one.

1258 Decoration for Cold Buffet work

There is no set pattern for decorating items of cold buffet work; decoration is entirely at the discretion of the practitioner. However, there are a number of rules which need to be followed if the finished result is to be really effective:
1) The item of food to be decorated should have a reasonably smooth surface which, in a number of cases, can be obtained by coating with Sauce Chaud-froid, e.g. decorated ham.
2) Everything used for decorating must be edible.
3) Care should be taken that there is no risk of colour spreading from the decoration onto the surface of the food, e.g. beetroot has a good colour but this always tends to run.
4) Any decoration which needs to be placed on the food should first be dipped in melted aspic jelly; this will ensure that it sticks on and does not become displaced when the final coating of jelly is given.
5) The decoration must be neat and of an appropriate size and relationship to the main item of food on which it is set.

Small cutters are available for cutting different patterns; leaves and flowers can be cut with a small knife. Items which can be used for decorating include truffle, blanched cucumber skin, tarragon and chervil leaves or green of leek; tomato, radish, cooked white of egg, and pimento.

1259 Garnishes for Cold Buffet work

Most of the garnishes for decorated and glazed dishes are best if glazed with aspic jelly before they are arranged on the dish. When the garnish has been arranged on the dish, a final coating of aspic jelly around the items will ensure that they become set on the dish and do not move around when being carried for service. There are very few named garnishes for cold buffet work; hard-boiled eggs – sliced, quartered or stuffed; tomatoes – whole, sliced or quartered, stuffed; cucumber – sliced or cut in shapes and stuffed; bouquets of cooked vegetables – asparagus, broccoli, carrots, cauliflower, French beans, salsifis, Brussels sprouts, turnips, etc., tartlets and barquettes with various fillings, artichoke bottoms filled with peas, asparagus tips or macédoine of vegetables; foie gras; small decorated moulds filled with various mousses or other mixtures; quenelles; mushrooms; chestnuts and so on, may all be used where appropriate. The variety is almost endless, the only rule being that the garnishes are neat, tastefully decorated and in keeping with the item of food which they accompany. The finished dish should not be over-garnished and the number of pieces should be in keeping with the number of portions of the dish. In some cases this would mean keeping a separate dish of the same garnish in reserve.

1260 Hâtelets or Attelets

These are silver skewers of varying lengths usually incorporating an ornamental design at its upper end. Widely used in former times for the decoration of both hot and cold dishes, they are now mainly used to enhance the presentation of special cold buffet items. According to requirements and in keeping with the dish, they are garnished with suitable items of food which are impaled to lie at the upper end of the skewer. Such items . as truffles, decorated mushrooms, cockscombs, crayfish, small decorated tomatoes, small lemons, quenelles etc. can be used as appropriate and for preference should be glazed with aspic jelly when threaded on the skewer. The garnished Hâtelets are then stuck into the item of food in the most aesthetically pleasing position or angle; they may be used singly, or in multiples for a large presentation.

1261 SOCLES

Socles are moulded, edible bases used for cold buffet presentation. Decorated items of food are presented on these to give added height and artistic balance. They may be made from rice, semolina, or mutton fat, in fact anything edible which can be firm enough to stand an item of food on. They may be sculpted, decorated and glazed or first coated with chaud-froid before decorating and glazing.

In some cases shapes cut from large quartern loaves of breads and fried to a golden brown in oil can perform the same function.

1262 Rice Socle

Stage	Ingredient	Quantity	Method
1	long-grain rice	2kg	Wash well in deep water. Place the rice into plenty of boiling salted water and simmer for 5 mins. only. Cool under cold running water and then reheat in hot water. Drain well.
2	pork fat, thin slices	500g	Line a pan with a clean cloth and then line the cloth with the pork fat. Mix the
	powdered alum	10g	alum into the rice and place in the lined
	lard	200g	pan. Add the lard in pieces on top of the rice, cover with the remaining slices of pork fat and cover completely with the cloth.
3			Cover with a lid and place in a cool oven at 130°C for 3 hours. Place the rice into a food processor and work it until the mixture is completely smooth.

4

Grease moulds of the required shape with lard and fill with the mixture taking care to exclude air bubbles. Allow to set and remove from the moulds. Trim if necessary. These socles may be sculpted or decorated and glazed with aspic jelly.

1263 Semolina Socle

Rain sufficient coarse-ground semolina into boiling salted stock mixing with a whisk until a fairly stiff texture is obtained, and cook for approx. 5 mins. Pour into the required dampened moulds and allow to cool thoroughly. Remove from the moulds, coat and decorate as required and glaze with aspic jelly.

1264 Mayonnaise Collée   1 litre

Add 3dl of cool melted Gelée Ordinaire (1242) to 7dl of Mayonnaise (185). Mix together and use before setting. This is mainly used for binding together Salade Russe for cold buffet work.

1265 COLD MOUSSES AND MOUSSELINES

These preparations are suitable for use in cold buffet work, as fillings for chemised dariole moulds, for the re-forming of poultry and for moulded bases on which to place glazed items. They can be served, set in glass bowls, decorated and glazed, or set in large or small chemised (1248) and decorated moulds. In this case they are usually served as an hors-d'oeuvre. When moulded for service in individual portions they should be described as Mousselines.

1266 Mousse de Crevettes Roses – Prawn Mousse   10 portions
1½ hours

Stage	Ingredient	Quantity	Method
1	prawns, cooked	600g	Shell the prawns. Finely pound the shells. Reserve a few of the tails for decoration and make a fine purée of the rest. Reserve also in the refrigerator.
2	butter	25g	Heat the butter in a pan, add the remainder of the ingredients and cook gently without colour.
	shallot, ⎫ finely	25g	
	carrot ⎬	15g	
	parsley stalks ⎭ chopped	5g	
	bayleaf	½	
	thyme	small sprig	
	tarragon, chopped	pinch	
3			Add the pounded shells and cook quickly for a few mins. to extract the flavour.

4	brandy	¼dl	Add the brandy and flamber (32), then
	tomato purée	½ tbsp	add the purée, wine and stock. Simmer
	white wine	1dl	gently for 10–15 mins. then pass firmly
	Fumet de Poisson		through a fine strainer into a clean pan.
	(101)	3dl	
5	Velouté de Poisson		Add the reserved purée of prawns and
	(117)	2½dl	the velouté and bring to the boil. Season
	cayenne		well plus a touch of cayenne then add
	leaf gelatine, soaked	20g.	the gelatine. Simmer gently for 2 mins.
	in cold water and	approx.	then pour into a bowl or basin. Place on
	drained		ice.
6	cream, double	3dl	Stir the mixture until just before setting point. Remove from the ice, then have the cream half-whipped and fold into the mixture. Check the seasoning then turn into glass dishes making sure that the surfaces are level. Allow to set in the refrigerator.
7	Gelée de Poisson		Decorate the surfaces appropriately
	(1246)	2dl	using the reserved prawns as part of the decoration, then cover with a layer of cool melted jelly.

1267 Mousse de Foie – Liver Mousse

1½ kg
30 mins. excluding
soaking time

Stage	Ingredient	Quantity	Method
1	duck and chicken		Season the milk with salt. Add the livers,
	livers, cleaned	1kg	place in the refrigerator and allow to
	milk	½ litre	soak for approx. 12 hours. This will assist in removing the blood and making the livers white. Drain thoroughly.
2	butter	75g	Melt the butter in a pan and add the
	shallot, finely		livers, shallot, thyme and bayleaf. Lightly
	chopped	30g	season with salt and pepper, cover and
	thyme	sprig	stew gently without colouring until
	bayleaf	½	completely cooked.
3			Remove the thyme and bayleaf. Place the liver and the juices into a very fine sieve and pass, or use a food processor.
4	butter, soft	150g	Place the mixture into a basin and allow
	cream, double	2dl	to cool. Mix in the butter and then the cream. Adjust the seasoning.

1268 Mousse de Homard – Lobster Mousse

This is prepared in the same way as Mousse de Jambon (1269) using cooked lobster in place of ham, Sauce Homard (169) in place of Velouté de Veau, and Gelée de Poisson (1246) in place of Gelée Ordinaire. Decorate appropriately with truffle and small cooked lobster claws.

1269 Mousse de Jambon – Ham Mousse

10 portions
1 hour

Stage	Ingredient	Quantity	Method
1	lean ham, cooked and free of fat	600g	Pass through a fine mincer and then through a fine sieve, or use a food processor. Place in a pan.
2	Velouté de Veau (116)	2½dl	Add to the ham, season with salt and pepper and the paprika. Bring to the boil and simmer gently for 2–3 mins. Pour into a bowl or basin.
	Gelée Ordinaire (1242)	2½dl	
	paprika	pinch	
3	cream, double	3dl	Place the bowl of mixture on ice and stir until just before setting-point. Remove from the ice then have the cream half-whipped and fold into the mixture. Check the seasoning and adjust if necessary, then turn into glass dishes making sure that the surfaces are level. Allow to set.
4	Gelée Ordinaire (1242)	2dl	Decorate the surfaces appropriately using small shapes of ham as part of the decoration. Cover with a layer of cool melted jelly and place in the refrigerator to set.

SPECIAL POINT

If the ham is pale it may be necessary to just lightly colour the mixture at Stage 2.

1270 Mousse de Tomates – Tomato Mousse

10 portions
1 hour

Stage	Ingredient	Quantity	Method
1	butter	50g	Heat the butter in a pan, add the onion and cook without colour. Add the wine and reduce by half.
	onion, finely chopped	50g	
	white wine, dry	1dl	
2	Tomates Concassées (90)	600g	Add the tomatoes, season with salt and pepper and paprika. Add the bouquet garni. Stew together gently for approx. 20 mins or until most of the moisture has evaporated. Remove the bouquet garni.
	paprika	good pinch	
	parsley stalks ⎱ Bouquet	10g	
	bayleaf ⎰ Garni	1	
	celery	1 stalk	

3	Velouté de Veau (116)	2dl	Add to the tomatoes, mix together, bring to the boil and simmer gently for 2–3
	Gelée Ordinaire (1242)	2½dl	mins. Pass through a fine sieve or use a food processor, then place in a bowl or basin and place on ice.
4	cream, double	3dl	Stir the mixture until just before setting-point. Remove from the ice, then have the cream half-whipped and fold into the mixture. Check the seasoning and adjust it as necessary then turn into glass dishes making sure the surfaces are level. Allow to set.
5	Gelée Ordinaire (1242)	2dl	Decorate the surfaces appropriately using tomatoes as part of the decoration. Cover with a layer of cool melted jelly and place in the refrigerator to set.

1271 Mousse de Volaille – Chicken Mousse

10 portions
1 hour

Stage	Ingredient	Quantity	Method
1	white of chicken, poached	600g	Clean carefully of any sinew or discoloured parts. Pass through a fine mincer then through a fine sieve, or use a food processor. Place in a pan.
2	Velouté de Volaille (115)	2½dl	Add to the chicken, season with salt and pepper. Bring to the boil and simmer
	Gelée de Volaille (1243)	2½dl	gently for 2–3 mins. Pour into a bowl or basin and place on ice.
3	cream, double	3dl	Stir the mixture until just before setting-point. Remove from the ice, then have the cream half-whipped and fold into the mixture. Check the seasoning and adjust if necessary then turn into glass dishes making sure that the surfaces are level. Allow to set.
4	Gelée de Volaille (1243)	2dl	Decorate the surfaces appropriately then cover with a layer of cool melted jelly. Place in the refrigerator to set.

OEUFS FROIDS – COLD EGGS

1272 Oeuf en Gelée à l'Estragon

10 portions
45 mins.

Stage	Ingredient	Quantity	Method
1	Poached Eggs (473)	10	Place the eggs in individual egg cocottes. Decorate with leaves of tarragon and just cover with cool jelly. Allow to set before serving.
	Gelée Ordinaire (1242)	½ litre	
	tarragon leaves, blanched		

1273 Oeuf mollet froid Yorkaise

10 portions
1 hour

Stage	Ingredient	Quantity	Method
1	Tartlet Cases (1763)	10	Three-quarters fill the tartlet cases with the ham mousse at setting-point.
	Mousse of Ham (1269)	2–3 portions	
2	Eggs, soft-boiled (444)	10	Cut the base of the eggs level and stand them upright on a wire rack. Mask with the chaud-froid, decorate with diamond-shaped pieces of ham and glaze with the aspic. Allow to set thoroughly.
	Sauce Chaud-froid Blanche (1253)	1 litre	
	ham, sliced	50g	
	Gelée Ordinaire (1242)	1 litre	
3			Dress an egg in each of the tartlet cases and carefully fill with aspic jelly at setting-point. Allow to set before serving.

1274 Oeufs de Cailles froids Joinville

10 portions
45 mins.

Stage	Ingredient	Quantity	Method
1	Gelée de Poisson (1246)	½ litre approx.	Coat the inside of ten dariole moulds with a layer of the jelly. Then decorate the insides to choice with a pattern of truffle and egg white.
	truffles	15g	
	egg-white, cooked	25g	
2	Mousse de Crevettes (1266)	5 portions approx.	Prepare the mousse. Before setting place a little in the bottom of each mould. Place one egg sideways on top then cover with a little more mousse and repeat twice more, finishing by covering the last egg and to just fill the mould. Place in the refrigerator to set.
	quails' eggs, hard-boiled	30	

3	Gelée de Poisson (1246)	1 litre	Set a layer of the jelly in a suitable dish. Arrange the asparagus tips in bouquets on a wire rack and also the mushrooms. Glaze all carefully with the jelly and keep in the refrigerator until required.
	asparagus tips (1387), cooked	40	
	mushrooms, grooved and cooked à Blanc (60)	10	
4	prawns, cooked and shelled	125g	Mix the prawns with the mayonnaise and fill into the bouchée cases. Set one of the prepared mushrooms on top of each to replace the pastry lids.
	mayonnaise	1 tbsp	
	Bouchées (1674)	10	
5			Carefully demould the darioles, arrange on the prepared dish and garnish with the bouchées of prawns and asparagus.

SPECIAL POINT

Suitable individual dishes may be used for the presentation of this dish.

POISSONS ET CRUSTACÉS FROIDS – COLD FISH AND SHELLFISH

1275 Dressed Crab

For this preparation see Recipe 267.

1276 Demi-Homard froid – Cold Lobster

10 portions
25 mins.

Stage	Ingredient	Quantity	Method
1	lobsters, cooked (662)	5 × 650g	Split in half lengthways. Remove the claws and legs and black trail from the tail and the sac from the head. Crack the claws and remove the flesh in one piece.
2	capers	100g	Fill the cavities in the head part of the half-lobsters with any flesh from the remaining claw segments, a few capers and cover each with a claw.
3	lettuce	2	Dress the lobsters on lettuce arranged on a suitable dish and garnish with quarters of hard-boiled egg and slices of tomatoes.
	eggs, hard-boiled	5	
	tomatoes, peeled	5	
4	Sauce Mayonnaise (185)	6dl	Serve the lobsters accompanied with the Sauce Mayonnaise.

1277 Mayonnaise de Homard – Lobster Mayonnaise 10 portions
25 mins.

Stage	Ingredient	Quantity	Method
1	lobsters, cooked (662)	5 × 650g	Remove the flesh from the tails and claws. Cut the tails into thick slices and leave the claws whole.
2	lettuce Sauce Mayonnaise (185)	3 7dl	Shred one of the lettuce and place in salad bowls. Dress the lobster neatly on the shredded lettuce and coat with the mayonnaise. Arrange leaves of lettuce around the sides of the salad bowls.
3	anchovy fillets capers green olives, stoned tomatoes, peeled eggs, hard-boiled parsley, chopped	10 30g 10 5 5	Cut the anchovy fillets in half lengthways and arrange trellis-fashion on the mayonnaise. Finish decorating with the capers and olives. Garnish with quarters of tomatoes and hard-boiled egg. Lightly sprinkle with chopped parsley.

1278 Langouste à la Parisienne
10 portions
2 hours

Stage	Ingredient	Quantity	Method
1	crawfish Court-bouillon (538)	1 × 2½kg 10 litres	Tie the crawfish flat to a board and cook in the court-bouillon for approx. 50 mins. Allow to cool in the cooking liquor.
2			Remove from the board and wipe dry. Make two parallel incisions with scissors along the shell of the tail 4–5cm apart. Take off the shell and remove the flesh in one piece. Scoop out the creamy part from the head and pass through a fine sieve. Cut the tail into 20 even slices and arrange on a wire rack.
3	Macédoine de Légumes (1532) Mayonnaise (185)	600g 2dl	Cook the macédoine in boiling, salted water, drain and allow to cool on a clean cloth. Mix it together with the creamy part of the crawfish plus any trimmings from the tail cut in dice. Bind with the mayonnaise. Fill the cavity of the crawfish with the mixture.
4	eggs, hard-boiled Fonds d'Artichauts (1379) small tomatoes, peeled	5 10 10	Cut the eggs in halves zig-zag fashion. Remove the yolks, pass through a sieve, and mix with a little butter and season. Pipe with a star tube into the whites then place them on a wire rack. Place a small tomato in each artichoke bottom and place on the wire rack.

5	Gelée de Poisson (1246)	2 litres	Decorate and glaze the slices of craw-fish. Decorate and glaze the eggs and tomatoes. Set a layer of jelly on a long oval dish.
6	sandwich loaf, large	1	Cut into the form of a ramp, decorate by carving with a knife and deep fry in clean oil to a golden brown. Drain well. Allow to cool.
7	Croûtons of Jelly (1250)	20	Place the socle of fried bread on the dish with the crawfish on it, the head facing upwards. Arrange the médaillons, slightly overlapping, along the back, covering the salad. Ensure that the médaillons are graded in size starting with the largest nearest the head to the smallest at the tail. Arrange the garnish neatly around the dish and surround with croûtons of jelly.

1279 Saumon froid en Bellevue – Cold Decorated Salmon

30 portions
1½ hours
plus cooking time

Stage	Ingredient	Quantity	Method
1	salmon Court-bouillon (538)	4kg 10 litres	Scale, trim the fins, gut, and wash the salmon well. Place on a perforated rack in a salmon kettle. Cover well with the cold court-bouillon, bring to the boil, skim then draw the fish kettle to the side of the stove. Poach gently for 20 mins. and allow the salmon to cool in the cooking liquor.
2			Remove and drain the salmon. Carefully remove the skin.
3	cucumbers prawns, cooked	2–3 400g	Peel the cucumbers, cut in half length-ways and trim 30 boat-shaped pieces. Blanch in boiling salted water for 5 mins., drain and allow to cool on a clean cloth. Arrange the prawns in the barquettes of cucumber and place on a wire rack.
4	small tomatoes peeled	30	Decorate and place on the wire rack.
5	hard-boiled eggs anchovy essence parsley, chopped	15	Cut in halves zig-zag fashion, remove the yolks and pass them through a sieve. Mix the yolks with a little anchovy

			essence and chopped parsley. Pipe the mixture through a star tube into the whites. Place on the wire rack.
6	Gelée de Poisson (1246)	3 litres	Decorate and glaze the salmon. Glaze the cucumbers, tomatoes and eggs. Set a layer of jelly on a long oval flat dish.
7	Sauce Mayonnaise (185) or Sauce Verte (194)	2 litres	Place the salmon on the dish and arrange the garnish neatly around it. If necessary, any remaining garnish can be dished separately. Accompany with the sauce.

SPECIAL POINT

The designation 'en Bellevue' is open to interpretation according to personal taste and means that the dish is well-decorated and presented, providing that the garnish selected is in keeping with the dish.

1280 Mayonnaise de Saumon – Salmon Mayonnaise 10 portions
25 mins.

Stage	Ingredient	Quantity	Method
1	poached salmon, cold	750g	Remove any skin and bone. Lightly flake.
2	lettuce Sauce Mayonnaise (185)	3 7dl	Finely shred one of the lettuce and place in salad bowls. Place the salmon neatly on top and coat with mayonnaise. Arrrange the remaining lettuce in leaves around the sides of the salad bowls.
3	anchovy fillets capers green olives stoned tomatoes, peeled eggs, hard-boiled cucumber, peeled parsley, chopped	10 30g 10 5 5 ¼	Cut the anchovy fillets in half lengthways and arrange trellis-fashion on the mayonnaise. Finish decorating with the capers and olives. Garnish with quarters of tomato, quarters of hard-boiled egg and slices of cucumber. Lightly sprinkle with chopped parsley.

1281 Filet de Sole froid Bagration 10 portions
1½ hours

Stage	Ingredient	Quantity	Method
1	fillets of Dover sole Fonds de Poisson (101) white wine, dry	10 × 100g 2dl 1dl	Butter a shallow tray, and lightly flatten and fold the fillets. Season and poach with the stock and wine for approx. 12–15 mins. in a moderate oven at 195°C. Allow to cool in the cooking liquor, drain and dry the fillets. Place on a wire rack.

2	lobster tails cooked	3	Cut into round pieces, approx. ½cm thick, allowing two per portion. Place on the wire rack.
3	Sauce Chaud-froid de Poisson (1255)	2 litres	Coat the fillets of sole and allow to set.
4	Gelée de Poisson (1246)	2 litres	Decorate the fillets of sole and lobster and then glaze with aspic. Chemise a 12cm charlotte mould and decorate. Set a layer of the jelly on a round flat silver dish.
5	Macédoine de Légumes (1532) Mayonnaise Collée (1264)	600g 3dl	Cook the macédoine in boiling salted water, drain and allow to cool on a clean cloth. Bind it with the mayonnaise, fill the chemised mould with the mixture and allow to set.
6	Croûtons of Jelly (1250)	20	Turn out the mould in the centre of the dish. Arrange the fillets around the mould and place two médaillons of lobster between each fillet. Surround with croûtons of jelly.

1282 Eventail de Truites Yvette

10 portions
2 hours

Stage	Ingredient	Quantity	Method
1	Gelée de Poisson (1246) Mousse de Crevettes (1266)	½ litre approx. 5 portions	Line a 5–6dl capacity charlotte mould with jelly, decorate and allow to set. Fill with the mousse at just before setting-point and reserve in the refrigerator to set.
2	trout	10 × 200g	Clean, scale and gut carefully; trim the tails square and wash.
3	butter Fumet de Poisson (101) white wine, dry	15g 2dl 1dl	Butter a deep tray, place in the trout, all facing left. Season and add the stock and wine. Cover with buttered greaseproof and poach in a moderate oven at 175°C for 15–18 mins. until just cooked. Allow to cool in the cooking liquor.
4			Drain the trout and dry. Cut and remove a neat panel of skin from each fish and with a small knife, carefully clean away any dark flesh on the exposed surface. Place on a wire rack. Decorate the cleaned area of each trout in a like manner. Cover each eye with a small round of egg white or truffle. Place in the refrigerator.

5	cucumber, small	1	Groove the cucumber along its length, cut into ten 2cm lengths and remove part of the centres with a vegetable scoop. Blanch, drain, cool and dry carefully. Place cavity side upwards on a wire rack and fill dome shape with the caviar. Decorate the tomatoes and place on the rack. Fill the drained and dried artichoke bottoms neatly with the prawns and also place on the rack.
	very small tomatoes, blanched and skinned	10	
	artichoke bottoms, cooked (1379)	10	
	black or red caviar	50g	
	prawns, cooked and shelled	125g	
6	Gelée de Poisson (1246)	2½ litres approx.	Set a layer of the jelly on a suitable oval silver or stainless steel dish. Glaze the prepared trout and garnishes with the jelly.
7	Croûtons of Fish Jelly (1250)	20	Demould the mousse of prawns and place at one side of the prepared dish. Set the trout fan-fashion on the dish with their heads towards the edge of the dish. Arrange the garnishes equally between the fish and run a little cool melted jelly round the items to set them in place. Surround the edge of the dish with croûtons of jelly.

VIANDES FROIDES – COLD MEATS

1283 Cold Roast Joints

If for presentation whole on the buffet it is useful to glaze cold roast joints of beef, lamb, veal and venison with aspic jelly so as to improve their appearance. Garnish with bouquets of watercress and serve with a little chopped aspic jelly. An appropriate cold sauce can be offered, e.g. horseradish sauce with beef; mint sauce with lamb; apple sauce with pork; apple, cranberry or Cumberland Sauce with venison.

1284 Cold Meats, sliced

Other than being presented as whole joints on the buffet, cold meats can be pre-sliced and individually plated or dished. Presentations of tastefully arranged sliced meats can sometimes be a more convenient method of serving large numbers from a buffet, particularly where quick service is essential.

The French term Assiette Anglaise refers to a selection of plated or dished cold meats; cold roast beef, ox-tongue, ham, salami, mortadella, galantine or other sliced meats are suitable components.

In all cases the meats should be neatly garnished with chopped or diced aspic jelly and bouquets of watercress. It is useful to offer pickled gherkins as an accompaniment, as well as the cold sauces in the above recipe where appropriate.

1285   Côtelettes d'Agneau en Chaud-froid Bouquetière

5 portions
2 hours

Stage	Ingredient	Quantity	Method
1	best ends of lamb prepared for roasting (684)	2	Roast carefully keeping just done and allow to cool. Cut into ten even-sized cutlets and trim neatly. Place on a wire rack and chill in the refrigerator.
2	carrots } turned turnips } peas French beans cooked artichoke bottoms, small cauliflower	150g 150g 150g 150g 5 200g	Cook the carrots, turnips, peas, beans and cauliflower in boiling salted water. Drain thoroughly and allow to cool completely on a clean cloth. Fill the artichoke bottoms with the peas and place on a wire rack. Also form the rest of the vegetables into neat bouquets on the wire rack.
3	Sauce Chaud-froid Brune (1254)	1 litre	Coat the cutlets with the sauce and return to the refrigerator to set.
4	Gelée Ordinaire (1242)	2 litres	Set a layer of jelly on an oval silver or stainless steel dish.
5			Decorate the cutlets and glaze, also glaze the bouquets of vegetable.
6			Arrange the cutlets along the centre of the dish and garnish neatly with the vegetables. Run a little cool jelly round the items to set them in place. Place a cutlet frill on each cutlet bone.

1286   Selle d'Agneau froide Marly

8–10 portions
2½ hours
plus cooking time

Stage	Ingredient	Quantity	Method
1	saddle of lamb, prepared for roasting (683)	1 × 4kg	Roast the saddle carefully and to just being done. Allow to become completely cold.
2			Make an incision across both sides of the saddle on the slant and about 3cm away from the tail end. Cut down either side of the backbone then remove each side whole. Cut off the top of the back-bone along its length.
3	Macédoine de Légumes, cut small (1532)	750g	Cook the macédoine in boiling salted water, drain and allow to cool on a clean

	red pimentos, grilled, skinned and cut in small dice	75g
	lean ham, cut in small dice	75g
	salami, cut in small dice	75g
	parsley, chopped	1 tbsp
	Mayonnaise Collée (1264)	1½dl

cloth. Place into a basin with the pimento, ham, salami and parsley, and mix together gently then mix together with the mayonnaise.

4

Fill the mixture into both sides of the emptied saddle and smooth to its original shape. Refrigerate to set.

5 red pimento, grilled and skinned (78) — 2
butter, softened — 50g

Cut the removed meat from the saddle into approx. 2mm-thick slices along their length. Lay across the saddle neatly and at even overlapping distance, starting at the tail end, so as to completely cover the filling. Lay a strip of the pimento along the top edge of each slice. Decorate to choice with a little softened butter using a fine tube and cornet. Refrigerate.

6 Socle, decorated and glazed (1262 or 1263) — 1

Have prepared a socle 3–4cm thick and large enough for the saddle.

7 Gelée Ordinaire (1242) — 2 litres

Set a layer of jelly in a suitably-sized oval silver dish. Place the socle in the centre of the prepared dish. Glaze the saddle. Keep everything refrigerated.

8 small red tomatoes, skinned — 10
Farce Duxelloise, cold (37) — 200g
broccoli, boiled, drained and dried — 10 nice bouquets
Gelée Ordinaire (1242) — 1 litre

Remove the top of the tomatoes, discard the seeds, then fill the tomatoes proud with the stuffing, using a piping bag and star tube. Replace the top, sloping at an angle. Place on a wire rack together with the broccoli. Place in the refrigerator to chill, then glaze with the jelly.

9 Croûtons de Gelée (1250)

Set the saddle on the socle, surround with the garnish and float a little more jelly around the dish to set everything in place. Decorate the edges of the dish with the croûtons of jelly.

1287 Daube de Boeuf en Gelée

Prepare ten portions Daube de Boeuf (810) and add 6–7 leaves of soaked gelatine to the liquid at Stage 5. When cooked carefully skim off all fat then pour into a suitable mould. Allow to cool and set in the refrigerator. When ready, turn out onto a dish coated with aspic jelly and surround with cut shapes of jelly. Alternatively, the moulded daube may be cut into thick slices and served individually with a little chopped jelly at the side. In either case offer a dish of gherkins as an accompaniment.

1288 Boeuf à la Mode froid

Prepare ten portions Beef à la Mode (833). When preparing the sauce at Stage 7, be careful to remove all vestiges of fat then add 5–6 leaves of soaked gelatine.

When cold, cut the beef into 20 slices and arrange overlapping down the centre of oval porcelain dishes. Cool the sauce and just before it reaches setting-point, coat the beef with it. Surround with neat bouquets of the button onions and carrots glazed with ordinary aspic jelly.

1289 Langue Ecarlate – Cold Ox-Tongue   12–15 portions

Stage	Ingredient	Quantity	Method
1	ox-tongue, salted	2	Allow to soak overnight in cold water. Place in a pan, cover well with cold water, bring to the boil and allow to simmer gently until tender (approx. 3–3½ hours). Leave in the cooking liquid until cool enough to handle.
2			Remove the skin and bones. Trim the root end square. Press into the shape of slippers, cover with a damp cloth and allow to cool. Refrigerate to chill thoroughly.
3	Gelée Ordinaire (1242) Croûtons of Jelly (1250)	2 litres	Colour the jelly a good reddish-brown and set a layer on a silver dish. Glaze the tongues with the same jelly. When set, place the tongues on the dish and garnish with croûtons of uncoloured jelly.

SPECIAL POINT
A specially made mould can facilitate and improve the shaping of the tongues.

1290 Pressed Beef   16–24 portions

Stage	Ingredient	Quantity	Method
1	boned brisket of beef, salted (87)	2–3kg	Allow to soak overnight in cold water. Place in a pan and cover well with cold water. Bring to the boil and allow to simmer gently until tender for 2–2½ hours.
2			Drain and place in a brisket press while still hot and adjust the pressure until firm.
3			Place in the refrigerator until thoroughly cold. Remove and trim.

4	Gelée Ordinaire		Colour the jelly a good reddish-brown
	(1242)	2 litres	and set a layer on a silver dish. Glaze
	Croûtons of Jelly		the beef with the same jelly. When set,
	(1250)		place the beef on the dish and garnish
			with croûtons of uncoloured jelly.

1291 Jambon froid – Cold Ham

To cook a ham for cold service:
1) Soak the ham for 12 hours in cold running water.
2) Clean and scrape the underside to remove any mould, and saw through the knuckle bone 2–3cm from the end. Place in a pan and cover with plenty of cold water. Bring to the boil, skim and barely simmer until cooked, allowing 20 mins. per 500g plus an extra 20 mins. cooking time. A 5kg ham will take approximately 3½ hours. Allow to get cold in the cooking liquid and remove. Place the ham on a board and turn over. Remove the pelvic bone and trim the underside. Carefully ease out and remove the small bone at the knuckle end. Turn the ham over and remove the skin. Trim the fat to give a smooth surface and bare the knuckle bone.
3) Place on a ham stand for ease of carving.

The following presentations are all suitable for the cold buffet.
a) For its simplest presentation, place the cooked and trimmed ham on a ham stand with a paper ham frill on the bared knuckle bone.
b) Coat the trimmed surface of the cooked ham with white breadcrumbs toasted to a golden brown in a slow oven. Breadcrumbs made from dried crusts or artificially coloured crumbs do not give the best results.
c) Prepare Virginia Glazed Ham (897) to Stage 4 and allow to cool. Place on a ham stand or decorated socle with a paper ham frill on the bared knuckle bone. The dish may be garnished with cold glazed pineapple or peaches.
d) Prepare Jambon en Croûte (896) and allow to cool. Serve accompanied with a suitable sauce, e.g. Sauce Cumberland (183).
e) Coat the trimmed surface of the cooked ham with Sauce Chaud-froid Blanche (1253). Decorate to choice then glaze with Gelée Ordinaire (1242). Place on a ham stand with a paper ham frill on the bared knuckle bone. Alternatively, the decoration may be placed directly on the bare surface of the cooked ham and then glazed.

1292 Jambon en Gelée Persillé – Jellied Ham with Parsley

18–20 portions

Stage	Ingredient	Quantity	Method
1	ham, unsmoked, farm or Wiltshire-type	4 kg approx.	Soak the ham in running cold water for approx. 24 hours. Clean the underside and any cut surfaces. Place in a pan, bring to the boil and blanch for 20 mins. Refresh under cold running water.

2	calf's feet, split		
	and blanched	2	
	white wine, dry	2 bottles	
	shallots	175g	
	tarragon	2 sprigs	
	bayleaf	2	
	thyme	Bouquet	1 sprig
	parsley	garni	
	stalks	15g	
	celery	50g	
	cloves	4	
	peppercorns	10	

Place the ham in a suitable pan with the calf's feet and add the wine and sufficient water to cover. Bring to the boil, skim well then add the remainder of the ingredients and simmer very gently until cooked, approx. 3½ hours. Skim frequently and keep the liquid as clear as possible. To test if cooked, the small bone at the knuckle end of the ham should be easily removable.

3

When cooked, allow the ham to cool slightly in the stock, then remove the skin and trim clean of any unsightly edges and excess fat. Remove the ham completely from the bone and cut into 2–3cm rough cubes. Remove the flesh from the calf's feet and cut into smaller dice. Mix together with the ham and place into deep glass dishes.

4

Pass the cooking liquid through a fine strainer into a clean pan. Skim completely of any fat.

5	egg whites	3
	leaf gelatine	25g

Whisk the egg whites together with a little of the cooking liquid then mix back into the remainder of the liquid in the pan. Bring carefully to the boil, keeping the bottom of the pan clean and clarify carefully. Simmer gently and reduce to a quantity judged to be sufficient to just cover the meat. Pass through a damp folded muslin, reboil, add the gelatine, previously soaked, and check the seasoning.

6	parsley, chopped	5 tbsps
	vinegar, white wine	1 tbsp

Allow the liquid to cool and just when it becomes viscous, mix in the parsley and vinegar. Pour over the ham. Replace in the refrigerator and allow to chill for at least 4 hours.

7

Serve from the dish as it is.

SPECIAL POINTS

a) Traditionally, this dish is moulded in a glass dish and is served from it. However, it may be prepared in a deep mould, turned out when set onto a dish and surrounded with a few salad leaves.

b) This dish is better if chilled overnight.

1293 Cold Sucking-Pig with Apples

Prepare Roast Stuffed Sucking-Pig (901) and allow to become cold. Set a layer of Gelée Ordinaire (1242) on a suitably-sized dish and lightly glaze the pig with the same jelly. Cut a large sandwich loaf into the shape of a gently sloping ramp, decorate by carving with a sharp knife, then deep fry in clean oil to a golden brown. Drain well and allow to become quite cold. Place this on the prepared dish and set the pig on top with the head sloping up. Place an apple in the mouth of the pig. Surround the dish with bouquets of grilled and glazed quarters of apples. Surround the base of the fried socle with a line of picked parsley.

1294 Boar's Head

25–30 portions
2–3 days

Stage	Ingredient	Quantity	Method
1	pig's head, cut off approx. 12cm away from the ears to give a 12cm collar	1 × 6kg approx.	Make sure the head is free from hair and is well-cleaned. Bone out the head carefully. Remove the neck bones first then cut along the underneath of the head to within approx. 10cm of the chin. Remove the tongue then bare the bottom jaw bones and cut through with a saw at the end of the cut. Bone out the rest of the head, turn back the flesh then cut through the snout to the same length as the bottom jaw. This will leave the head boned completely except for approx. 10cm of the front of the lower jaw and snout. Clear the inside of the boned head of any dark blood and blood vessels.
2	salt saltpetre cloves bayleaves juniper berries }pounded together mace thyme, dried	1kg 30g 4 4 12 4 blades 5g	Mix the salt, saltpetre, herbs and spices together. Rub the head inside and out with the mixture and lay open in an enamel or glazed earthenware container together with the tongue. Sprinkle over any remaining mixture. Cover and place in the refrigerator for 2–3 days. Turn the head over occasionally and rub with the salt mixture.
3			When ready, wash well under running cold water for 2–3 hours, drain and dry. Remove most of the meat from the head leaving an even layer under the skin. Cut the removed meat in 1½cm cubes and place in a bowl. Boil the tongue, cool, skin and reserve.

4	veal, lean	500g	Pass the raw meats and fat through the
	pork, lean	1kg	fine plate of a mincer and add to the
	belly of pork	1½kg	reserved meat in the bowl. Add the
	pork back fat	750g	remaining ingredients and the reserved
	ox-tongue, cooked and		pig's tongue, cut in 1cm dice. Season
	cut in 1½cm cubes	500g	well with salt and pepper then mix to-
	truffle, cut in		gether.
	small dice	50g	
	pistachio nuts,		
	blanched	250g	
	brandy	1½dl	
	eggs	3	
	mixed spice	good pinch	

5   Place the prepared head on a board and partly fill with the mixture. Close up and sew up the opening under the jaw, with string, not pulled too tightly. Complete the filling of the head level to the end of neck. Cut off the ears close to the head and keep on one side. Place a large double sheet of foil on the board, then set the stuffed end of the head down on this. Fold 10–12cm of the foil back over the neck; bandage this in place and mould the head in shape, with lengths of cloth.

6	Fonds de Veau	22–25	Bring to the boil, season lightly then add
	(95)	litres	the prepared head. Simmer gently for
		approx.	3½ hours. Add the reserved ears and

continue cooking for a further hour. Leave to cool in the stock for 30 mins. and remove the head and ears. Wash the ears and keep on one side.

| 7 | raw carrot, large | 1 | After 30 mins. remove the cloth from |

the head. Place the carrot in the mouth to keep it open and re-form the shape of the head carefully, using damp 8–10cm-wide cloth bandaging. Leave resting right side up to cool, then refrigerate. When the head is thoroughly cold, remove the wrappings and trim and clean carefully. Trim the ears.

| 8 | Gelée Ordinaire | | Colour the jelly a good reddish-brown. |
| | (1242) | 5 litres | Set a layer of this jelly on a large oval |

silver dish. Glaze the head and ears well with the same jelly. Attach the ears with small skewers in their correct position.

9	butter, soft	150g	Attach imitation eyes and tusks to the
	small lemon or	1	head and decorate the whole tastefully
	apple		with piped softened butter. Remove the
			carrot from the mouth and replace with
			the lemon or apple.

10	Rice Socle, decorated	1 large	Place the socle on the prepared dish
	and glazed (1262)	oval	with the head on top. Pipe a little
	Gelée Ordinaire		chopped jelly around the line where the
	(1242) chopped		head meets the socle and surround the
	Croûtons de Gelée		dish with croûtons of uncoloured jelly.
	(1250)		

11	Hâtelets, garnished		Finish the presentation by fixing three or
	and glazed	3–4	four hâtelets around the top of the neck.
			The garnish should be the same for each
			and can consist of small lemons, small
			tomatoes, cut mushrooms and pickled
			walnuts.

SPECIAL POINTS

a) Correctly speaking, this dish should be made using a wild boar's head but it is acceptably and usually prepared from the head of a domesticated pig.

b) Once cooked and cooled slightly, the head can be pressed in a mould specially made for the job. Artificial eyes and tusks are available commercially.

1295 Selle de Chevreuil froide Grand-Veneur   15–18 portions

Stage	Ingredient	Quantity	Method
1	saddle of venison, larded (1192)	1 × 6kg	Roast the saddle keeping it underdone but not bloody. Remove to a tray when ready.
2	port	2dl	Tip out the fat from the roasting tray,
	redcurrant jelly	200g	deglaze with the port, then pass through a fine strainer into a clean pan. Add the jelly and reduce to a fairly viscous texture. Brush this over the saddle and replace in a hot oven to glaze the surface. Repeat two or three times to give a deep glossy colour. Allow the saddle to become completely cold.
3	Duxelles, cold (29)	350g	Place all the ingredients in a basin, season well and mix together to a
	lean ham, chopped	250g	smooth consistency.
	Pâté de Foie Gras	175g	
	cream, double	1dl	
	parsley, chopped	1 tbsp	

| 4 | | | Remove the string from the saddle. Cut an incision on the slant away from the tail and across both sides of the saddle approx. 3cm from the tail end. Cut down either side of the backbone and remove each side whole. |

5 — Coat the bared bones of the saddle with a little of the mixture. Cut each side of the removed venison into 3–4mm slices on the slant. Spread each slice with a little of the mixture then replace in its original position on the saddle so as to re-form the saddle to its original shape. Make sure the surface is as neat and smooth as possible.

| 6 | ½cm–thick rings of peeled and cored apple | 18 | Sprinkle the rings of apple with a little caster sugar, glaze a light brown under the salamander and cool. Place overlapping down the centre of the saddle with a mushroom on each ring. Place the saddle on a wire grid and chill. |
| | medium button mushrooms, grooved and cooked à Blanc (60) | 18 | |

| 7 | Gelée de Gibier (1245) | 3 litres | Set a layer of jelly on a suitable oval dish. Glaze the prepared saddle and set in the centre of the dish. Keep refrigerated. |

8	Marrons braisés (1486)	60	Place the redcurrants in a basin and add a little cool jelly. When at setting-point, spoon these jellied redcurrants into the tartlets. Place the chestnuts on a wire grid, chill and glaze with the jelly.
	Compote de Groseilles Rouges (1953), drained	450g	
	tartlet cases, small	18	

| 9 | Croûtons de Gelée (1250) | | Arrange the garnish of chestnuts and tartlets around the saddle and surround the dish with the croûtons of jelly. |

VOLAILLES ET GIBIERS À PLUME FROIDS – COLD POULTRY AND GAME BIRDS

1296 Cold Chicken

Cut the chicken into portions or carve in slices, whichever is required. For presentation whole, coat with Chicken Aspic Jelly (1243) at setting-point. In either case garnish with chopped or diced aspic jelly and watercress.

1297 Cold Game Birds

Cold roast game birds such as pheasant, grouse, partridge, blackgame and capercaillie, may be presented on the cold buffet. Brush with Game Aspic Jelly (1245) almost at setting-point and set on a croûton of bread which has been fried in clarified butter and spread with the Farce à Gratin (38). Garnish with Game chips (1551) and watercress.

Alternatively, the game may be cut in portions or carved – pheasant 3–4 portions, grouse and partridge split in half, blackgame, 3–4 portions. Large capercaillie should be carved in the same way as turkey. Garnish with chopped or diced Game Aspic Jelly (1245), Game Chips (1551) and watercress. A small croûton spread with Farce à Gratin should be placed under or at the side of the portion.

1298 Cold Turkey

For presentation whole on the buffet, brush the cold roast turkey with aspic jelly at near setting-point. Garnish with chopped or diced aspic jelly and a bouquet of watercress between the legs.

If required, cut in portions and arrange on plates or dishes. Carve as for hot, i.e. a little of the dark meat from the leg covered with slices of the breast. Garnish with a little chopped or diced jelly and watercress. In either case, offer cold Cranberry Sauce (204).

1299 Canard Sevillaise froid

8 portions
3½ hours

Stage	Ingredient	Quantity	Method
1	ducks, poêléed	2	When cold, remove the breasts from each side of the breastbone taking care not to disturb the legs. Skin and cut the breasts into 16 long slices, four from each breast.
2	Mousse de Foie (1267)	1kg	Remove the breastbone from one of the ducks then re-form the breast with some of the mousse, shaping and modelling it with a wet palette knife. Sandwich the slices of duck together in twos using a little of the mousse. Trim neatly. Place the re-formed duck and the eight portions on a wire rack.
3			Place the remainder of the mousse into a piping bag with a small star tube. Pipe a scroll down the centre of the re-formed duck breast and around both sides to cover the joins of the reshaped breast. Pipe a neat scroll halfway along the centre of each portion of duck. Place the duck and portions in the cold room to chill.

4	orange segments	60	Arrange orange segments neatly overlapping to fill the areas of the breast surrounded by the piped mousse. Garnish each portion of duck with the remaining segments.
5	Gelée de Canard (1244), flavoured with sherry	2½ litres	Set a layer of the jelly on a large oval flat. Glaze the whole duck and the portions with the jelly. Also set a layer of the jelly ¾cm deep in a shallow tray for croûtons of jelly.
6	Socle (1262 or 1263)	1	Place the socle at one end of the dish and set the prepared duck on top, the breast facing towards the unoccupied part of the dish. Arrange the portions neatly around the whole duck. Garnish with croûtons of jelly cut from the reserved layer of jelly.

1300 Canard Sauvage froid aux Cerises – Cold Wild Duck with Cherries

4 portions
1¾ hours

Stage	Ingredient	Quantity	Method
1	wild duck, cleaned and trussed	2	Roast carefully keeping just underdone. Allow to cool then remove the breasts and skin them. Cut each in half lengthways and trim.
2	Mousse de Foie (1267) cherries, stoned port wine	600g 32 approx. 2dl	Remove the centre breastbone of one duck and re-form with some of the mousse. Sandwich the slices of duck together in twos with a little of the mousse. Trim and place on a wire rack together with the re-formed duck. Pipe a scroll of mousse down the centre of the duck breast and round the sides to cover where the mousse meets the legs. Pipe a neat shape along the centre of each portion of duck. Poach the cherries with the port. Allow to cool, drain and dry. Reserve the cooking liquid. Cover the areas of the duck breast with cherries. Place two cherries on the mousse of each of the duck portions. Refrigerate and chill thoroughly.
3	Gelée de Gibier (1245) made using the chopped duck carcase and the port wine from the cherries	1½ litres approx.	Set a layer of jelly on an oval porcelain dish and also a ¾cm-thick layer on a small dish for decoration. Glaze the duck and the portions.

| 4 | Socle (1262 or 1263) | Set the socle at one end of the dish. Place the duck on top of the socle with its breast pointing inwards. Arrange the portions around and float in sufficient jelly to keep everything in place. Place cut shapes of the reserved jelly between the portions. Chill thoroughly. |

SPECIAL POINTS

a) This preparation can be applied equally well to teal, widgeon and Aylesbury duck, bearing in mind the relative size of the birds.

b) This dish may be prepared in the same way using segments of tangerine and sherry-flavoured jelly instead of port wine jelly.

1301 Feuillets de Pintadeau glacés aux Olives

4 portions
2 hours

Stage	Ingredient	Quantity	Method
1	Fonds de Veau (95) young guinea-fowl cleaned and trussed	3 litres 2	Lightly season the stock and bring to the boil. Place in the guinea-fowl and poach them gently. Time approx. 45 mins. Allow to almost cool in the stock then remove.
2			When cold, remove the breasts and carefully clean of all skin. Cover and keep refrigerated. Reserve the legs for other uses. Chop the carcases.
3	egg whites sherry, dry	2 1dl	Whisk the egg whites together with a little of the stock in a pan. Add 1 litre of the stock, the chopped carcases and sherry. Mix together, bring to the boil, keeping the bottom of the pan clean, and clarify carefully.
4	leaf gelatine	6 sheets	Simmer the stock very gently for about 30 mins. then pass through a damp folded muslin. Remove all traces of fat completely; reboil, add the gelatine, previously soaked, then check the seasoning. Allow to cool.
5			Set a layer of the jelly in a suitable glass dish. Cut the breasts of guinea-fowl each into three or four flat, thin slices on the slant and arrange on the jellied dish leaving the centre clear.

6	black olives,		Mix the foie gras and pistachios together
	stoned	16	and fill the olives with the mixture. Place
	green olives,		the black olives in the centre of the dish
	stoned	16	and arrange the green olives round the
	foie gras, purée	30g	edge.
	pistachios, skinned		
	and chopped	15g	
7			Just cover the guinea-fowl and olives with the remaining jelly. Chill and serve.

1302 Mayonnaise de Volaille

Prepare in the same way as Mayonnaise de Saumon (1280), using 750g cooked white of chicken, free of all skin, instead of the salmon.

1303 Mignons de Cailles en Gelée aux Muscats – Quail Breasts in Jelly with Muscatel Grapes

4 portions
1¾ hours

Stage	Ingredient	Quantity	Method
1	Fonds de Veau (95)	1½ litres	Lightly season and bring the stock to the boil. Place in the quails and poach them
	quails, cleaned and trussed	8	very gently. Time approx. 30 mins.
2			Allow the quails to cool in the stock then remove the breasts. Carefully clean of all skin and fat and trim neatly. Arrange neatly in an overlapping circle in a deep glass dish. Cover and refrigerate.
3	egg whites	2	Remove all fat from the stock. Whisk the
	Muscat wine	2dl	whites together with a little of the stock, add the chopped quail bones, the rest of the stock and the wine. Mix together, bring to the boil, keeping the bottom of the pan clean and clarify carefully.
4	leaf gelatine	6 sheets	Simmer very gently for about 30 mins. then pass through a damp folded muslin. Remove any traces of fat completely, reboil, add the gelatine, previously soaked, then check the seasoning. Allow to cool.
5	muscatel grapes, skinned and depipped	40	Arrange the grapes in small bouquets around the edges of the quails and place the remainder in the centre of the dish. Just cover with the jelly just before setting-point. Allow to chill and set in the refrigerator.

1304 Poulet froid à l'Estragon – Cold Chicken with Tarragon

Place a small bouquet of tarragon inside the chicken and roast in the usual manner. When cooked, discard the tarragon, allow the chicken to cool then carefully blot off any fat from the surface with kitchen paper. Chill thoroughly then decorate with blanched tarragon leaves and glaze with tarragon-flavoured aspic jelly. Cut in portions or present whole garnished with chopped or diced tarragon-flavoured aspic jelly.

1305 Suprême de Volaille en Chaud-froid

8 portions
1 hour

Stage	Ingredient	Quantity	Method
1	chickens, poached in chicken stock	2 × 2kg	When cold, remove the breasts from each side of the breastbone taking care not to disturb the legs. Skin and cut the breasts into eight neatly trimmed long ovals (suprêmes).
2	Mousse de Volaille (1271)	750g	When the mousse is set, mix gently to a workable texture. Remove the central breastbone of one of the chicken then re-form it with the mousse, shaping and remodelling it with a wet palette knife. Spread a little mousse dome-shape on each suprême to give a smooth finish. Place the re-formed chicken and the suprêmes on a wire rack. Refrigerate.
3	Gelée de Volaille (1243) Sauce Chaud-froid Blanche (1253)	2 litres 2 litres	Set a layer of jelly on a large oval flat. Coat the chicken and suprêmes with the chaud-froid then decorate and glaze with the jelly.
4	Socle (1263), decorated and glazed	1	Place the socle at one end of the dish and set the chicken on top, the breast facing towards the unoccupied part of the dish. Arrange the suprêmes neatly around the chicken and garnish appropriately.

SPECIAL POINTS
a) Suitable garnishes could include small decorated tomatoes, asparagus tips, chemised dariole moulds filled with chicken mousse or Salade Russe, artichoke bottoms filled with small balls of vegetables.
b) This dish may be prepared using other mousses such as tomato, liver, ham, pimento and so on. Care should be taken that the garnish is compatible.

1306 Suprême de Volaille Jeanne-Marie

8 portions
1½ hours

Stage	Ingredient	Quantity	Method
1	Gelée de Volaille (1243)	½ litre	Line a 5–6dl capacity mould with jelly and decorate with egg-white and truffle.
	Mousse de Jambon (1269)	8 portions	Prepare the mousse and pour two-thirds of it into the prepared mould. Place the
	cooked egg-white truffle		rest in a basin. Place both in the refrigerator to set.
2	chickens, poached in chicken stock	4 × 1½kg	When cold, remove the breasts from each side of the breastbone and without the wing bones. Skin and trim neatly into a nice even shape.
3	lean ham	8 small slices	Coat the underside of each suprême with a little of the reserved mousse. Lay each on a slice of ham and trim round evenly. Place on a wire grill and refrigerate. Reserve the trimmings of ham.
4	Gelée de Volaille (1243) truffle	1 litre approx.	Set a layer of jelly on an oval silver dish. Decorate the suprêmes with diamonds of the ham trimmings and truffle. Place on
	small tomatoes, blanched, top cut off and deseeded asparagus tips, cooked	8 32	a wire rack. Set four asparagus tips in each tomato, place the tops to one side. Place on the rack with the suprêmes. Glaze the suprêmes and tomatoes with jelly. Refrigerate.
5			Demould the mousse and set on one side of the jellied dish. Trim the suprêmes and arrange fan-shape round the mousse. Place a tomato between each suprême.

1307 Suprême de Volaille Jeannette

4 portions
45 mins.

Stage	Ingredient	Quantity	Method
1	chickens, poached in chicken stock	2 × 1¼kg	When cold, remove the breasts from each side of the breastbone and without the wing bones. Skin and trim neatly. Lay on a wire rack and refrigerate.
2	Gelée de Volaille (1243)	1 litre	Set a thin layer of the jelly in an oval porcelain dish. Coat the suprêmes with chaud-froid, decorate with the blanched
	Sauce Chaud-froid Blanche (1253) tarragon leaves, blanched	1 litre	tarragon leaves and glaze with jelly.

| 3 | foie gras | 4 × ½cm slices | Lay the foie gras diagonally along the centre of the dish and place a neatly |
| | Gelée de Volaille (1243) | 5dl | trimmed suprême on each. Coat the whole with the jelly at near setting-point to come two-thirds the way up the suprêmes. Chill and serve. |

1308 PIES, PÂTÉS, TERRINES AND GALANTINES

It should be borne in mind that cold mixtures need to be more highly seasoned than their hot equivalents, but it is better to underseason the mixture in the first instance and to adjust it afterwards. To this end any forcemeats used in the preparation of pâtés, terrines and galantines should be checked before cooking. To do this, poach or shallow fry a small amount and then allow it to become cold. Taste and adjust the seasoning as required. Overseasoning would need the addition of more unseasoned mixture.

1309 Chicken Pie

Prepare Chicken Pie (1056), adding 3–4 leaves of soaked gelatine at Stage 3 to each pie dish. When cooked, allow to cool sufficiently to set the liquid.

1310 Grouse Pie

Prepare Grouse Pie (1165), adding 3–4 leaves of soaked gelatine to each pie dish at Stage 4. When cooked, allow to cool sufficiently to set the liquid.

1311 Pigeon Pie

Prepare Pigeon Pie (1124), adding 3–4 leaves of soaked gelatine at Stage 3 to each pie dish. When cooked, allow to cool sufficiently to set the liquid.

1312 Veal and Ham Pie

10–12 portions
3 hours

Stage	Ingredient	Quantity	Method
1	streaky bacon, cut in thin rashers	350g	Line a 25–26cm pie dish with the bacon leaving the ends overhanging the edges
	veal, cushion	700g	of the dish. Cut the veal and ham into
	raw ham or gammon, lean	700g	approx. ½cm-thick slices. Lightly season the veal only with salt and pepper.
2	onion, finely chopped	50g	Place a layer of veal in the dish, sprinkle
	gelatine, soaked	4 leaves	with a little onion, then cover with a layer of ham. Complete with further layers of veal, ham and onion, finishing with veal. Place the gelatine on top and fold over the ends of the bacon to enclose the meats and to give a nice dome shape.

3	Pâte Feuilletée (1736) 400g eggwash	Roll out approx. 3mm thick. Eggwash the rim of the pie dish and cover with a 1½cm-wide strip of the pastry. Eggwash the strip and cover with the remaining pastry. Crimp and seal the edges and decorate the surface. Eggwash the surface and make a hole in the centre. Allow to rest for 30 mins.
4		Place in a hot oven at approx. 200°C until the pastry is well set and brown, approx. 30 mins. Allow the temperature to fall to approx. 165–170°C and continue baking for a further 1¼–1½ hours. Cover with greaseproof paper or foil if necessary to prevent overbrowning. Remove from the oven and allow to cool.
5	Gelée Ordinaire (1242) 2–3dl	Carefully pour sufficient cool melted jelly through the hole to fill the pie. Refrigerate to set and present on a dish paper on an oval dish. Surround the pie with a pie collar.

1313 Veal, Ham and Egg Pie

Prepare as Veal and Ham Pie (1312), adding five hard-boiled eggs, cut in half lengthways as a centre layer. The amount of veal and ham could be reduced slightly if felt necessary.

1314 Pâté de Veau et Jambon en Croûte – Raised Veal and Ham Pie

12–15 portions
3 hours

Stage	Ingredient	Quantity	Method
1	lard	15g	Lightly grease a 22–23cm hinged oval pie mould with the lard. Remove a quarter of the paste, cover and keep warm. Roughly roll out the remainder to the size of the mould then place in the mould. Work it up with the fingers firmly from the centre of the bottom to cover the sides. Aim to give an equal thickness over the bottom and sides and to make it stand proud for approx. ½cm at the top edge of the mould. Take care to press it firmly into the shaped designs of the mould to prevent air pockets forming. Be careful not to crack the paste.
	hot water paste (1742), warm	750g	

2	veal, lean	600g	Coarsely mince the meats and fat. Place
	raw ham or gammon,		in a bowl, season with salt and pepper
	lean	600g	and add the mace and herbs. Mix well
	pork back fat	750g	together.
	ground mace	pinch	
	fresh sage leaves,		
	finely chopped	½ tbsp	
	fresh thyme leaves,		
	finely chopped	½ tbsp	
3	pork fat, thin slices	400g	Line the pastry with the slices of pork fat leaving the ends to overhang the top edge of the mould. Place the mixture into the prepared mould. Make sure that it goes well into the corners and edges at the bottom. Turn over the fat slices and mould the whole into an even dome-shape, higher than the mould.
4			Eggwash the top edge of the paste in the mould and cover with the remaining paste rolled out to approx. 3mm thick. Crimp the edges together and decorate the surface with pastry shapes. Eggwash the surface and make a hole in the centre. Allow to rest for 20 mins.
5			Place in the oven at 200°C for 20 mins. to set and colour the surface. Reduce the temperature to 165–170°C and continue baking for a further 1½–1¾ hours. Cover with greaseproof paper or foil if necessary to prevent overbrowning. Remove from the oven and allow to cool.
6	Gelée Ordinaire (1242)	2–3dl	Remove the mould and fill the pie with cool melted jelly. Refrigerate to set before presenting on a suitable dish.

1315 Pâté Maison

12–15 portions
3½ hours

Stage	Ingredient	Quantity	Method
1	lard	50g	Heat the lard in a frying-pan. Cut the
	fat bacon	250g	bacon into rough dice and fry quickly in the lard. Remove the bacon and keep on one side.

2	onions, chopped	150g	Fry the onion in the remaining fat
	chicken livers,		without colour and add the rest of the
	cleaned	850g	ingredients. Season with salt, pepper and
	lean pork, diced	350g	mixed spice. Fry quickly to seal without
	garlic, crushed	1 clove	cooking through.
	thyme	pinch	
	bayleaf	2	
	mixed spice	pinch	

| 3 | | | Pass all of the ingredients through the fine plate of a mincer and then through a fine sieve or food processor. Place in a basin and allow to cool. |

| 4 | brandy | ½dl | Add to the mixture. Mix in well and |
| | double cream | 1½dl | adjust the seasoning. |

| 5 | streaky bacon, cut | | Line a 1½ litre-capacity terrine with |
| | in thin rashers | 350g | the bacon leaving the ends to overhang the terrine. Place in the mixture and fold the ends of the bacon over to enclose the mixture. |

| 6 | | | Cover with the lid, place in a deep tray with hot water and cook in the oven at 165–170°C for approx. 1½–2 hours. To judge when the pâté is cooked the juice and fat surrounding it should be quite clear. |

| 7 | bacon fat or lard | 75g | When cooked, cover with a flat dish and weigh it down with a 1kg weight. Allow to cool completely, remove the weight and dish, clean the terrine and cover the pâté with a thin layer of melted bacon fat or lard. |

| 8 | | | Serve accompanied with hot toast. |

SPECIAL POINT
On no account should the liver, pork and bacon be completely cooked through when frying; they must be left raw on the inside otherwise the mixture will not bind together when cooking.

1316 Terrine de Campagne

12–15 portions
3 hours plus
marination time

Stage	Ingredient	Quantity	Method
1	pig's liver	400g	Pass through the medium plate of a
	belly of pork	500g	mincer. Place in a basin.
	pork, lean	250g	
	raw pork fat (flair)	400g	

2	thyme, powdered	pinch	Add to the meats, season with salt and
	bayleaf, powdered	pinch	pepper and mix in. Cover and allow to
	mixed spice	pinch	marinate overnight in the refrigerator.
	garlic, finely		
	chopped	1 clove	
	white wine, dry	2dl	
	brandy	1dl	

3	pork back fat, thinly		Line a 1½ litre-capacity terrine with
	sliced	350g	the slices of fat, leaving the ends to
			overhang the sides of the terrine.

4	butter	50g	Heat the butter in a pan and cook the
	onions, finely chopped	150g	onion without colour. Allow to cool then
	eggs	2	add to the marinated meats together with
	cream, double	1¼dl	the cream and eggs. Mix and beat
			together thoroughly, check the season-ing.

5			Fill the mixture into the prepared terrine and fold the fat over to cover.

6			Cover with the lid, place in a deep tray with hot water and cook in the oven at 165–170°C for approx. 2–2½ hours.

7	bacon fat or lard	75g	When cooked, remove the lid, cover with a flat dish or board and weigh it down with a 1kg weight. Allow to cool completely, remove the weight and cover. Clean the dish and cover the surface of the terrine with a thin layer of melted fat.

8			Serve from the terrine accompanied with hot toast.

1317 Terrine de Canard

10–12 portions
4½ hours

Stage	Ingredient	Quantity	Method
1	duck, cleaned	1 × 2½kg	Bone out the duck including its legs. Skin the breasts and cut each breast in four lengthways. Remove the skin and any sinews from the legs.
2	pork back fat, cut in long ½cm- square strips	150g	Place the cut breasts, legs and strips of fat in a small tray, add the brandy and marinate for 1 hour.
	brandy	½dl	
3	veal, lean	250g	Pass through the fine plate of the mincer
	belly of pork	500g	together with the marinated duck legs.
	duck livers, cleaned	125g	Place in a basin. Reserve the marinating
	pork fat (flair)	250g	liquid.

4	thyme, powdered	pinch	Add to the minced meats together with
	mace, ground	pinch	the reserved marinating liquid and
	orange, juice and		season with salt and pepper. Check the
	grated rind	1	seasoning by cooking a little of the mix-
	Madeira	½dl	ture and taste when cold. Adjust if
	eggs	2	necessary.
5	pork back fat,		Line a 2 litre-capacity terrine with the
	cut in thin slices	350g	pork fat leaving the ends to overhang the
			terrine. Keep one slice to finish.
6			Place a first layer of the mixture in the
			bottom of the terrine. Lay half the
			breasts and strips of fat lengthways on
			top then repeat again, finishing with a
			layer of the mixture. Fold over the pork
			fat from the sides and cover the top with
			the reserved slice.
7			Cover with the lid. Place in a deep tray
			with hot water. Cook in the oven at
			165–170°C for approx. 2–2½ hours.
8			When cooked, remove the lid. Cover
			with a dish or board and weigh down
			with a 1kg weight for 1 hour, then
			remove the weight and cover and drain
			off any fat.
9	Gelée de Canard		Fill the terrine with sufficient warm jelly
	(1244), made with		to cover the surface. Allow to cool in the
	the bones of the		refrigerator to set. Serve from the terrine
	duck	4dl	accompanied with hot toast.

1318 Terrine de Foie de Veau

12–15 portions
3½ hours plus
marination time

Stage	Ingredient	Quantity	Method
1	calf's liver, skinned		Cut the liver in 50g pieces, place in a
	and cleared of any		basin and add the milk. Allow to soak
	gristle and blood		overnight in the refrigerator to whiten.
	vessels	1kg	
	milk	½ litre	
2	brandy	½dl	Drain the liver and dry. Place in a basin
	Madeira	1½dl	with the brandy and Madeira. Season
	mace, ground	good pinch	with salt, pepper and the mace. Allow to
			marinate for 2 hours, then drain.
			Reserve the marinating liquid.
3	belly of pork	600g	Pass the meats and fat through the fine
	lean pork	350g	plate of the mincer. Place in a bowl and
	raw pork fat (flair)	250g	add the truffle, egg, cream and the

	truffle, cut in small dice	50g	reserved marinating liquid. Season with salt and pepper and mix together thoroughly. Check the seasoning by cooking a little. Adjust as necessary.
	egg	1	
	cream, double	1dl	
4	pork back fat or salt pork fat, cut in thin slices	350g	Line a 2 litre-capacity terrine with slices of fat, leaving the ends to overhang the sides of the terrine. Reserve one slice to finish with.
5			Cover the slices of fat at the bottom and sides with a layer of the mixture, place in one-third of the liver then a layer of mixture and repeat twice more, finishing with the remaining mixture. Take care each time to press the layer of mixture firmly on to the liver. Fold over the pork fat from the sides and cover the top with the reserved slice of fat.
6			Cover with the lid. Place in a deep tray with hot water and cook in the oven at approx. 165–170°C for approx. 2–2½ hours.
7			When cooked, remove the lid, cover with a dish or board and weigh down with a 1kg weight. Allow to cool for 1 hour then remove the weight and cover and drain off any fat.
8	Gelée Ordinaire (1242)	3–4dl	Fill the terrine to just cover the surface with warm jelly flavoured with Madeira. Allow to cool then refrigerate to set. Serve from the terrine accompanied with hot toast.
	Madeira	¼dl	

1319 Terrine de Gibier

20–25 portions
3½ hours plus
marination time

Stage	Ingredient	Quantity	Method
1	hare	1 × 2¼kg	Release the blood from the hare into a basin and reserve. Bone out the hare completely and cut the flesh into 1cm cubes. Place in a basin, season with salt, pepper and the spice. Add the brandy and mix together. Place in the refrigerator and marinate for approx. 10 hours.
	brandy	½dl	
	mixed spice	pinch	

2	venison, lean		Pass the venison, pork, liver and fat
	flesh	500g	through the fine plate of the mincer.
	belly of pork	1kg	Place in a bowl then add the shallot,
	chicken livers	250g	thyme, spice and brandy together with
	raw pork fat	250g	the reserved blood from the hare. Mix
	shallot, finely		together thoroughly then place in the
	chopped	75g	refrigerator to marinate for 4 hours.
	thyme, powdered	pinch	
	mixed spice	pinch	
	brandy	½dl	
3	eggs	3	Add to the mixture and mix in well then add and mix in the marinated hare.
4	salt pork fat	850g	Line two 1½ litre-capacity terrines with thin slices of the pork fat, leaving the ends to overhang the sides of the terrines. Keep a few slices for the top and cut the remainder into ½cm-square strips.
5			Place layers of mixture in the terrines with strips of the pork fat on top and along each layer, finishing with a layer of the mixture. Fold over the pork fat from the sides and cover with the reserved slices.
6			Cover with the lids. Place in a deep tray with hot water and cook in the oven at 165–170°C for approx. 2–2½ hours.
7			When cooked remove the lids, cover each terrine with a dish or board and weigh down with a 1kg weight. Allow to cool for 1 hour then remove the weights and covers. Drain off any fat.
8	Gelée de Gibier (1245), made with the bones from the hare	7–8dl approx.	Fill the terrines with sufficient warm jelly to just cover them. Allow to cool then refrigerate to set. Serve from the terrine accompanied with hot toast.

1320 Galantine de Volaille – Chicken Galantine   12–15 portions

Stage	Ingredient	Quantity	Method
1	chicken, cleaned	1 × 2kg	Singe carefully and cut off the winglets and the legs at the first joints. Cut the skin along the back and carefully remove the skin with the point of a sharp small knife taking care not to puncture it. Clean the skin of all fat and flesh and soak in cold water for 30 mins. to whiten it.

2	salt ox-tongue, cooked	150g	Remove the flesh completely from the chicken. Cut the breasts of chicken, tongue and pork fat into long strips approx. ½cm × ½cm thick. Place into a basin with the pistachios, truffle and brandy. Season lightly with a little salt and pepper and allow to marinate until required.
	pork back fat	150g	
	truffles, cut in small dice	50g	
	pistachios, skinned	30g	
	brandy	½dl	

3	veal flesh, trimmed	750g	Remove the tendons from the boned chicken legs. Pass the chicken flesh and veal twice through the fine plate of the mincer together with any trimmings from the chicken breasts. Place into a basin and season with salt, pepper and nutmeg. Mix thoroughly together then slowly beat in the cream. Finally add the brandy from the marination together with the truffle and pistachios. Check the seasoning and adjust if necessary.
	grated nutmeg	pinch	
	cream, double	3dl	

4	pork back fat, cut in very thin slices	400g	Drain and dry the chicken skin, spread it skin side down on a clean damp cloth and cover the skin completely with the slices of pork fat. Place a layer of one-third of the mixture along the centre of the skin and arrange half of the marinated strips on top lengthways. Cover with the second third of the mixture with the remaining strips on top. Finish with the remainder of the mixture.

5			Envelope the mixture completely with the chicken skin. Roll it up in the cloth in the shape of a thick sausage and tie up at both ends and in the middle.

6	Fonds de Volaille (96), lightly seasoned	10 litres	Poach the galantine carefully in the chicken stock for approx. 1½ hours. Remove, retie lightly and allow to cool on a tray under slight pressure.

7	Sauce Chaud-froid Blanche (1253)	2 litres approx.	Coat the galantine with the chaud-froid, decorate, glaze with the chicken aspic and arrange on a silver dish previously set with a layer of jelly. Garnish with croûtons of jelly.
	Gelée de Volaille (1243)	2 litres approx.	
	Croûtons of Chicken Jelly (1250)		

1321 Galantine de Caneton – Duck Galantine   12–15 portions

Stage	Ingredient	Quantity	Method
1	duck, cleaned	1 × 2½kg	Singe carefully and cut off the winglets and the legs at the first joints. Cut the skin along the back and carefully remove the skin with the point of a sharp small knife taking care not to puncture it. Clean the skin of all fat and flesh and soak in cold water for 30 mins. to whiten it.
2	salt ox-tongue	150g	Remove the flesh completely from the duck. Cut the breasts of duck, tongue and pork fat into long strips approx. ½cm × ½cm thick. Place into a basin with the pistachios, truffles, Madeira, brandy and orange. Season lightly with salt and pepper and allow to marinate until required.
	pork back fat	150g	
	truffle, cut in		
	small dice	50g	
	pistachios, skinned	25g	
	Madeira	½dl	
	brandy	¼dl	
	dried orange zest,		
	powdered	½tsp	
3	veal, lean	650g	Remove the tendons from the duck legs. Pass the duck leg flesh and the veal twice through the fine plate of the mincer together with any trimmings from the breasts. Place into a basin with the Farce à Gratin and the egg. Season with salt, pepper, cayenne and spice. Mix thoroughly together then slowly beat in the cream. Finally add the Madeira and brandy from the marination, with the truffle and pistachios. Check the seasoning and adjust if necessary.
	Farce à Gratin		
	(38)	100g	
	egg	1	
	mixed spice	pinch	
	cayenne		
	cream, double	2dl	
4	salt pork fat, cut		Drain and dry the duck skin, spread it skin side down on a clean damp cloth and cover the skin completely with the slices of pork fat. Place a layer of one-third of the mixture along the centre of the skin and arrange half of the marinated strips on top lengthways. Cover with the second third of the mixture with the remaining strips on top. Finish with the remainder of the mixture.
	in very thin		
	slices	400g	
5			Envelope the mixture completely with the duck skin. Roll it up in the cloth in the shape of a thick sausage and tie up at both ends and in the middle.
6	Fonds de Veau (95),		Poach the galantine carefully in the stock for approx. 1½ hours. Remove, retie
	lightly seasoned	10 litres	

lightly and allow to cool on a tray under slight pressure.

7	Sauce Chaud-froid Brune (1254)	2 litres	Flavour the jelly with the Madeira, set a layer on a silver dish and set sufficient for the croûtons of jelly. Coat the galantine with the chaud-froid, decorate and glaze with jelly. Arrange on the prepared dish. Garnish with croûtons of jelly.
	Gelée de Canard (1244) made with the duck bones	2 litres	
	Madeira	¼dl	
	Croûtons of Duck Jelly (1250)		

16

Salads and Salad Dressings

The popularity of salads in one form or another has never been so great as it is today – the latter part of the twentieth century. The eating of salads is perceived by all sections of the population as making a positive contribution to good health and the emphasis on the necessity for some sort of fresh or cooked vegetables as part of the general diet is only to be applauded and encouraged; but it is well to bear in mind that many of the raw vegetables used in salads are not always easily digestible. Because of this the utilisation of cooked or blanched vegetables can sometimes be more acceptable for the latter part of the evening.

Salads provide variety and contrast of texture and colour to the menu. They are suitable for eating at any time of the day or season of the year but make a particularly welcome contribution to the menu in the summer months when a wide variety of fresh home-grown produce is available at reasonable prices. They can be offered as part of the hors-d'oeuvre selection or as an hors-d'oeuvre by itself and as an accompaniment to cold meats, cold dishes or grills and roast meats. A well-presented combination of ingredients can provide a meal in itself and when correctly-selected ingredients are used salads are very popular for vegetarians of all persuasions.

In general, salads are cold preparations made from raw, cooked or blanched vegetables, singly or in combination, and can include other items such as fresh herbs, fruits, nuts and cooked eggs, pasta, rice, fish, meat and poultry; their flavouring and seasoning is effected by the use of a wide variety of dressings or sauces.

There are three main forms in which salads can be served:
1) As simple salads, usually consisting of only one or two ingredients such as the various types of lettuce, asparagus, beetroot, chicory, cucumber, tomatoes, watercress and so on.
2) As composed salads, where they can consist of a selection drawn from raw and cooked vegetables, fruits, nuts and other cooked items. These are frequently garnished with various salad leaves.
3) As warm salads, where the salad consists of ordinary salad leaves finished with a warm or hot dressing instead of one of the more usual cold ones. These types of salad frequently incorporate items of fish, meat or poultry and in this form are useful as an hors-d'oeuvre or light entrée.

1322 CLEANING AND PREPARATION

The possible combinations and permutations of ingredients used in the preparation of salads is almost unlimited and this can give wide scope to the person entrusted with their preparation. It does, however, require a feeling for the compatibility of ingredients and for colour, balance and presentation. Thus attention should be given to careful decoration and garnishing of all salads; a good colour balance is essential for mixed or composed salads using a number of different ingredients.

Care should be given to the following points:

a) All raw salad ingredients should be fresh and of impeccable quality. If required to be held or stored for a time, this should be for preference in a covered container in a refrigerator specially reserved for the purpose. On no account should they be stored close to raw or cooked meat or fish.

b) All leaf salad vegetables should be carefully trimmed of all discoloured or damaged leaves and roots, then washed in cold water, drained and dried thoroughly. They should not be left to soak in water. Watercress may be held, standing in a little cold water.

c) Large salad leaves are best if carefully torn into manageable-sized pieces instead of cutting with a knife.

d) The cutting of vegetables, either raw or cooked, should be carried out as evenly and neatly as possible. This is essential for good presentation. If cut into julienne, this should not be much more than 5cm in length. If too long they can be difficult to manipulate on the plate and awkward to eat.

e) Some items, such as avocado pears, Belgian endives, small raw artichokes and some fruits like banana, tend to discolour quickly when cut. This can be prevented by preparing them at the last minute and using a lemon-based dressing. Alternatively, they may be sprinkled first with a little lemon juice.

f) Some attention should be paid to the optimum period of time required for the marination or maceration of some types of salad. Mixing some ingredients with a dressing strongly flavoured with vinegar or lemon juice will quickly destroy any inherent crispness. For example, a salad of pimento, fennel or celeriac will keep its crispness for 30 mins. or so but will become limp and lifeless if held overnight.

g) Where a number of items are used in the composition of a salad, some thought should be given to the balance of flavours and the possible duplication of vegetables elsewhere in the menu.

h) As a general rule, salads comprising raw green salad leaves should be dressed and mixed at the last possible minute and where practical in front of the customer. In some cases the customer can determine the ingredients and their proportions used in the preparation of the dressing.

i) Most salads can be suitably dressed and presented in glass, china or wooden bowls. The use of crescent-shaped china dishes still has its adherents as far as the formal dinner is concerned; they can be very useful as a side dish where the amount of salad is small and is served as an adjunct to a main course. Certain types of main dish salad consisting of bouquets of already dressed ingredients are best presented on larger shallow dishes.

j) Because of its pungent and all-pervading aroma and taste, the use of garlic as a flavouring ingredient for salads should be treated with respect. For those who like it and are prepared for its consequences, garlic may be added, either chopped or pressed, to the salad or to the dressing. A more subtle and less overpowering way is to rub the salad bowl with a cut clove of garlic before adding the actual salad.

Appendix 2 gives the names and descriptions of the main salad leaves.

1323 SALAD DRESSINGS

In general, salad dressings are based on either vegetable oils, such as olive, groundnut, sunflower, grape seed, sesame seed, walnut and hazelnut, most of which have their own particular flavours but where pride of place goes to the various qualities of olive oil, or various creams and dairy products such as single, double or sour cream, yoghurt, quark, and crème fraîche; and these oils or creams are usually supplemented by an acid, either a vinegar such as cider, sherry, malt, wine, both red and white, raspberry and tarragon, or the juice of citrus fruits such as lemon or lime and occasionally verjuice. All these acids have the qualities of modifying the emollient qualities of oil or cream, adding contrasting sharpness and assisting the digestion.

The wide range of added seasonings and flavourings include sugar; honey; salt; pepper; paprika; cayenne; Tabasco; mustards, dry and made; anchovies; capers; gherkins; fresh cut herbs such as parsley, basil, dill, tarragon, chervil and burnet; sieved hard-boiled eggs; onion; chives; garlic; and sauces such as mayonnaise, soya and Worcestershire.

As with the salads themselves, the possible combinations of the above ingredients can give unlimited scope to the preparation of dressings and thus there are a few worthwhile points to bear in mind when preparing them:

a) Except for the basic oil and vinegar dressings, storage is best kept to a minimum length of time; some ingredients, where texture is part of the inherent quality of the dressings, tend to become soft and lifeless after a few hours and chopped herbs lose their colour. Those made with cream and dairy products should always be freshly made.

b) Attention needs paying to the overall balance and emphasis of ingredients and their suitability to the salad with which they are used. A good dressing will enhance and add quality and contrast to the salad. A poorly-balanced one will ruin it.

c) By and large strong-flavoured salad ingredients can support well-flavoured dressings whereas the more delicate or bland items will benefit more often than not from dressings of a more subtle quality but with a single identifiable flavour.

d) All salad dressings need a final mixing before being used, especially oil-based ones where their emulsified properties tend to separate out if left for any length of time.

The number of dressings in the standard repertoire is extensive; the following are presented as a cross-section of the different types and popular ones. Many of these dressings are also suitable as dips for Crudités, Fondues, Goujonettes of deep-fried fish or poultry.

1324 American Dressing

1 litre
15 mins.

Stage	Ingredient	Quantity	Method
1	egg yolks, hard-boiled	4	Mash the yolks and place in a basin with
	English mustard	½ tbsp	the rest of the ingredients. Mix smoothly
	vinegar	1½dl	together.
	paprika	1 tbsp	
	sugar	1 tsp	
	salt	10g	
	pepper	pinch	
	Worcestershire sauce	few drops	
2	oil, to choice	7½dl	Add the oil and mix together to emulsify.

1325 Avocado Dressing

5dl
15 mins.

Stage	Ingredient	Quantity	Method
1	avocado pears, ripe	2	Peel and stone the avocados and pass through a fine sieve. Place in a basin.
2	cream, single	2½dl	Mix in the cream then add the lemon
	lemon juice	2 tbsps	juice and paprika. Season well with salt,
	paprika	1 tsp	pepper and a touch of cayenne.
	salt		
	pepper, white		
	cayenne		

1326 Cream Dressing

5dl
10 mins.

Stage	Ingredient	Quantity	Method
1	cream, double	4½dl	Add the juice to the cream, mix in well
	lemon juice	½dl	and season with salt, ground white
	salt		pepper and a touch of cayenne.
	pepper		
	cayenne		

1327 Egg Dressing

5dl
15 mins.

Stage	Ingredient	Quantity	Method
1	eggs, hard-boiled	4	Pass the whites and yolks, separately,
	salt		through a sieve. Reserve the sieved whi-
	pepper		tes. Place the sieved yolks in a basin, add
	mustard	pinch	the mustard and vinegar, season with salt
	vinegar, white wine	½dl	and pepper and mix together until smooth.
2	light olive oil	3dl	Add the oil and mix thoroughly together.
	cayenne		Adjust the seasoning as necessary plus a little cayenne. Finally add the reserved whites and mix in.

1328 English Salad Dressing

5dl
15 mins.

Stage	Ingredient	Quantity	Method
1	egg yolks, hard-boiled	4	Pass the yolks through a sieve and place
	made English mustard	1 tbsp	in a basin with the mustard and sugar
	sugar	pinch	and season with salt and pepper. Add
	vinegar, malt	1dl	the vinegar and mix together.
2	oil	1½dl	Mix in the oil slowly then add the
	cream	2½dl	cream. Adjust the seasoning as necessary
	cayenne		plus a touch of cayenne.

1329 French Dressing or Vinaigrette Salad Dressing   1 litre
10 mins.

Stage	Ingredient	Quantity	Method
1	salt	10g	Place the salt and pepper in a basin, add
	milled pepper	pinch	the vinegar and mix in well. Finally, add
	vinegar, wine	2½dl	the oil and mix well together.
	oil, to choice	7½dl	

SPECIAL POINTS
a) The proportion of oil to vinegar can be adjusted as seen fit.
b) According to taste, a little made mustard, finely chopped garlic and chopped herbs to choice may be incorporated.

1330 Italian Dressing   5dl
15 mins.

Stage	Ingredient	Quantity	Method
1	anchovy fillets	25g	Pass the anchovies through a fine sieve
	made English mustard	1 tsp	and place in a basin with the mustard.
	tarragon vinegar	1dl	Mix together then add the vinegar and
	olive oil	4dl	the oil slowly and mixing thoroughly.
2	garlic, very finely chopped	1 clove	Add and mix in the garlic and tarragon. Adjust the seasoning with salt and
	fresh tarragon, finely chopped	1 tbsp	pepper as required.

1331 Lemon Dressing

Prepare in the same way as French Dressing (1329), using 2dl lemon juice only instead of the vinegar and increasing the amount of oil. These proportions can be adjusted according to taste.

1332 Mayonnaise Dressing

Thin the required amount of Sauce Mayonnaise (185) with one-third its quantity of cream. Adjust the seasoning as necessary.

1333 Mignonnette Dressing   5dl
10 mins.

Stage	Ingredient	Quantity	Method
1	salt	5g	Place all the ingredients in a basin and
	milled black pepper	1 tsp	mix together. Leave for 30 mins. or so.
	shallots, finely chopped, washed and squeezed dry	2 tbsps	
	Worcestershire Sauce	few drops	
	red wine vinegar	1dl	

2	oil	3dl	Add the oil and mix in to combine.
	tarragon, chopped	½ tbsp	Adjust the seasoning as necessary then
	parsley, chopped	½ tbsp	finish with the herbs.

1334 Mustard Dressing

5dl
10 mins.

Stage	Ingredient	Quantity	Method
1	English mustard	10g	Place the mustard and lemon juice in a
	or French mustard	1 tbsp	basin and mix together until smooth then
	lemon juice	2 tbsps	mix in the cream and season as
	cream	5dl	necessary with salt, pepper and a touch
	cayenne		of cayenne.

1335 Roquefort Dressing

2½dl
10 mins.

Stage	Ingredient	Quantity	Method
1	Roquefort cheese	50g	Pass the cheese through a fine sieve.
	French Dressing		Place in a basin then gradually mix in
	(1329)	2dl	the French dressing.

SPECIAL POINTS
a) This dressing is best made to order.
b) French dressing made with lemon juice may be used.
c) Other blue cheeses such as Danish blue, Stilton and Bleu de Bresse may be used
   instead of the Roquefort.

1336 Thousand Island Dressing

1 litre
15 mins.

Stage	Ingredient	Quantity	Method
1	salt	10g	Place the salt, pepper and a few drops of
	pepper	pinch	Tabasco in a basin. Add the vinegar,
	Tabasco	few drops	mixing well, then add the oil and mix.
	vinegar	2dl	
	oil	7dl	
2	red pimento,		Add and mix well together. Adjust the
	chopped	100g	seasoning as necessary.
	green pimento,		
	chopped	100g	
	parsley, chopped	25g	
	eggs, hard-boiled		
	and sieved	4	

1337 Yoghurt Dressing

5dl
5 mins.

Stage	Ingredient	Quantity	Method
1	natural yoghurt	450g	Mix the yoghurt and vinegar together
	white wine vinegar	1dl	then season with salt, pepper and a
	salt		touch of cayenne.
	milled white pepper		
	cayenne		

SIMPLE SALADS

1338 Salade de Betterave – Beetroot Salad

Cut cooked beetroot into batons and dress in a salad bowl. Surround with a few leaves of lettuce and serve French Dressing (1329) or Mustard Dressing (1334) separately.

1339 Salade de Champignons – Mushroom Salad

Select very white and firm button mushrooms. Wash quickly, drain and dry thoroughly. Slice 3–4mm thick, place in a basin and mix together with a little Lemon Dressing (1331). Leave to marinate for 10–15 mins. then place in a salad bowl and surround with a few small lettuce leaves. The mushrooms may be sprinkled with a little chopped fresh herbs, e.g. parsley, basil, coriander or dill.

1340 Salade de Chicorée Frisée– Curly Endive Salad

Prepare, wash, drain and dry the nice tender leaves from curly endives. The outer leaves can be reserved for other uses. Arrange in a salad bowl and serve accompanied with Lemon Dressing (1331).

1341 Salade de Concombres – Cucumber Salad

Dress slices of peeled cucumber in a salad bowl and surround with a few leaves of lettuce. Sprinkle with chopped parsley and serve French Dressing (1329) separately.

1342 Salade de Courgettes – Courgette Salad

Select very small crisp courgettes. Trim both ends then cut into 3–4mm slices. Place in a basin and mix together with a little Lemon Dressing (1331). Allow to marinate for 10–15 mins. then arrange dome-shape in a salad bowl. Surround with a few small lettuce leaves and sprinkle with a few chopped fresh leaves of coriander or oregano.

1343 Salade d'Endive Belge – Endive Salade

Trim and wash Belgian endives. Drain, cut into quarters lengthways, rub the cut surfaces with lemon juice, arrange in a salad bowl. Lemon Dressing (1331) or French Dressing (1329) may be served as an accompaniment.

1344 Salade de Feuilles Amères – Bitter Leaf Salad

Prepare a selection of bitter salad leaves such as Belgian endive, curly or frizzy endive, radicchio, Batavian endive, young dandelion, wild chicory. Arrange tastefully mixed in a salad bowl and serve accompanied with Lemon Dressing (1331) or French Dressing (1329).

1345 Salade de Fenouil – Fennel Salad

Select young firm bulbs of fresh fennel. Discard any coarse or discoloured outer stalks. Chop and reserve any young feathery leaves from the top. Slice the fennel, arrange in a salad bowl and mix well with lemon juice, a little excellent olive oil and milled sea salt. Sprinkle with a little chopped basil mixed with the reserved chopped feathery leaves from the fennel.

1346 Salade Française – French Salad

Wash, drain and dry any nice lettuce, such as cabbage lettuce, Little Gem, Webb's Wonder, Iceberg. Arrange the leaves neatly in a salad bowl. Sprinkle with chopped Fines Herbes (31) and serve French Dressing (1329) separately.

1347 Salade de Laitue – Lettuce Salade

Wash lettuce thoroughly, drain, dry and arrange the leaves neatly in a salad bowl. Serve French Dressing (1329) separately.

1348 Coeurs de Laitue – Hearts of Lettuce

Wash lettuce thoroughly, drain, dry, cut into quarters and arrange neatly in a salad bowl. Serve French Dressing (1329) separately.

1349 Salade de Pommes de Terre – Potato Salad

Dress Potato Salad (247) dome-shape in a salad bowl and surround with a few leaves of lettuce. Sprinkle with chopped parsley.

1350 Salade de Romaine – Cos Lettuce Salad

Wash Cos lettuce thoroughly, drain, cut into quarters and arrange neatly in a salad bowl. Serve French Dressing (1329) separately.

1351 Salade de Saison – Seasonal Salad

This salad is composed of any raw salad vegetables in season at the time. Serve French Dressing (1329) separately.

1352 Salade de Tomates – Tomato Salad

Select nicely-shaped firm red tomatoes. Remove the eyes then blanch and skin them. Cut into slices then arrange neatly overlapping in a salad bowl. Sprinkle with a little chopped onion or chives. Sprinkle with chopped parsley, surround with a few leaves of lettuce and send French Dressing (1329) separately.

1353 Salade Verte – Green Salad

This salad is composed of any green salad vegetables, e.g. lettuce, Cos lettuce, chicory, Belgian endive, watercress, mustard and cress, young spinach leaves. Serve French Dressing (1329) separately. A few nice green leaves of fresh basil, coriander, salad burnet or chervil can make an interesting addition.

COMPOSED SALADS

1354 Salade Capriccio

1) Select well-shaped firm red tomatoes. Remove the eyes then blanch and skin them. Cut off the tops of the tomatoes and keep on one side for lids. Empty the tomatoes and season the insides with a little salt and pepper.
2) Prepare equal quantities of fresh pineapple, avocado pear, mango and celery, all cut in small dice, and mix carefully with a little Cream Dressing (1326) and a pinch of paprika. Adjust the seasoning.
3) Fill into the tomatoes dome-shape and set the reserved lids on top at a sloping angle so as to show the filling. Place the tomatoes on a bed of small lettuce leaves for service.

1355 Salade au Chapon d'Ail – Salad with Garlic Crusts

Take a nice crust of French bread or a slice of toast, rub with a cut clove of garlic on both sides and sprinkle with a little olive oil. Cut into small pieces and toss together with the selected raw vegetables or salad leaves before finishing with French Dressing (1329).

1356 Salade Diva

Prepare quarters of crisp lettuce and arrange neatly in a salad bowl. Garnish with peeled and sliced avocado pear and asparagus tips. Sprinkle with sieved hard-boiled egg and serve with a sauceboat of French Dressing (1329) flavoured with paprika.

1357 Salade Florentine

Arrange prepared leaves of young spinach in a salad dish, surround with bouquets of sliced skinned tomatoes and stoned black olives. Sprinkle with pine kernels and send Italian Dressing (1330) separately.

1358 Salade Florida or Salade d'Orange – Orange Salad

Arrange prepared leaves or hearts of lettuce neatly in a salad bowl and garnish with segments of peeled orange. Sprinkle the segments with a very fine julienne of orange zest. Serve with a sauceboat of Cream Dressing (1326).

1359 Salade Gauloise

Arrange quarters of Cos lettuce hearts on a salad dish. Garnish with bouquets of equal quantities of a julienne of apple, celeriac, raw mushrooms and cooked potato. Sprinkle with chopped walnuts and serve with a sauceboat of Cream Dressing (1326).

1360 Salade Japonaise

Neatly arrange prepared quarters of lettuce in a salad bowl. Garnish with segments of orange, diced pineapple sprinkled with lemon juice and diced peeled tomato flesh sprinkled with lemon juice and a touch of sugar. Serve with Cream Dressing (1326) finished with a little orange juice and a touch of paprika.

1361 Salade Lorette

Neatly arrange some prepared corn-salad in a salad bowl and garnish with bouquets of julienne of celery and beetroot. Serve with French Dressing (1329).

1362 Salade Milady

1) Select nicely-shaped firm sharp eating apples, red or green. Cut off the stalk ends complete with stalks, rub with lemon juice and reserve for lids.
2) Using a small thin knife cut round the cut end of the apples approx. 3mm from the edge and down near to the bottom. Push the knife into the apple at the bottom and cut right and left without cutting through the skin or enlarging the cut where the knife first entered. This should allow the whole centre of the apple to be withdrawn.
3) Rub the inside of the apple cases with lemon juice and reserve.
4) Cut the removed apple into short thick julienne, place in a basin and sprinkle well with lemon juice. Add half the quantity of a short julienne of heart of celery, the same amount of small seedless white grapes and half this amount of skinned almonds cut in julienne. Add a little half whipped double cream, a pinch of paprika and season with a little salt and a touch of sugar. Mix carefully together.
5) Fill the mixture into the apple cases dome-shape and set the reserved lids on top at a sloping angle so as to show the filling. Place the apples on a bed of lettuce leaves for service.

1363 Salade Mimosa

Prepare quarters of lettuce and arrange neatly in a salad bowl. Garnish with segments of peeled orange, depipped grapes and slices of banana dipped in lemon juice. Serve with a sauceboat of Cream Dressing (1326).

1364 Salade Niçoise

Neatly arrange prepared leaves of lettuce in a salad bowl. Garnish with bouquets of cooked French beans, slices of cooked potatoes and slices of peeled tomatoes. Decorate with thin strips of anchovy fillets, stoned black olives and capers. Serve with French Dressing (1329) separately.

1365 Salade Panachée – Mixed Salad

Neatly arrange prepared leaves of lettuce in a salad bowl. Garnish with quarters of peeled tomatoes, quarters of hard-boiled egg and sliced beetroot. Serve French Dressing (1329) separately.

SPECIAL POINT
This recipe is offered only as the standard type. The lettuce may be garnished as seen fit with any other cooked or raw salad vegetable, providing colours and flavours are well-balanced.

1366 Salade Russe – Russian Salad

Dress Russian Salad (249) in a salad bowl and surround with a few leaves of lettuce.

1367 Salade Villa d'Este

Arrange some nice leaves of young spinach in a salad bowl and garnish with bouquets of sliced young fennel, sliced peeled tomato, and stoned black olives. Sprinkle with a little grated white truffle and serve with Lemon Dressing (1331) containing a little chopped fresh basil.

1368 Salade Waldorf

Arrange prepared leaves of lettuce neatly in a salad bowl. Garnish the centre with a mixture consisting of 2 parts julienne of raw celery, 2 parts julienne of Bramley apple and 1 part chopped, shelled and peeled walnuts, all mixed with Mayonnaise Dressing (1332).

1369 SALADES TIÈDES – WARM SALADS

This type of salad is usually made from ordinary salad vegetables, dressed with a warm or hot dressing instead of one of the usual cold ones. It is inevitable that the addition of a hot dressing will cause any salad leaves to lose some of their crispness but some people prefer a salad to be purposely wilted by the dressing. If desired, the salad ingredients may be added to the pan of hot dressing and turned over briefly before serving, or the hot dressing can be poured over the salad then covered with a plate and left for a few seconds; this will lightly steam the salad.

In many instances this type of salad is the vehicle for a small item of hot fish or meat such as scallops, slices of foie gras, chicken livers, or suprêmes of game, whereby the fat and juices from the cooking form the basis of the dressing. This form of salad can be served as a hot hors-d'oeuvre or light entrée.

It is essential that these salads are quickly prepared to order and served immediately.

1370 Salade de Chicorée Frisée au Lard – Curly Endive Salad with Bacon

4 portions
10 mins.

Stage	Ingredient	Quantity	Method
1	curly endive	350g	Wash well, drain and dry. Arrange neatly in a salad bowl.
2	oil	2 tbsps	Heat the oil in a frying pan, add the
	Lardons of bacon		lardons and sauté until cooked light

| | (51), cut small and blanched | 100g |
| wine vinegar | 1 tbsp |

brown and crisp. Add the vinegar, away from the heat, season with milled pepper and salt as necessary. Tip over the salad, mix in and serve immediately.

1371 Salade d'Epinards et Mâche aux Croûtons Aillés – Salad of Spinach and Corn-salad with Garlic Croûtons

4 portions 10 mins.

Stage	Ingredient	Quantity	Method
1	corn-salad	150g	Wash well, drain and dry carefully.
	young spinach leaves	150g	Arrange neatly in a salad bowl.
2	slices of bread	2	Discard the crusts and cut the bread into approx. ½cm small dice. Heat the oil in a frying pan, add the diced bread and sauté to a golden brown. Drain well.
	oil	¾dl	
3	oil	2 tbsps	Heat the oil in the same pan, add the garlic and cook gently for a few seconds without colouring. Now add the croûtons, season with salt and pepper and toss over to mix. Pour over the salad.
	garlic, finely chopped	1 clove	
4	vinegar, white wine	2 tbsp	Add to the pan, heat then also sprinkle over the salad.

1372 Salade de Pommes de Terre chaude – Hot Potato Salad

4 portions 35 mins.

Stage	Ingredient	Quantity	Method
1	new potatoes, small	400g	Wash well and cook in boiling salted water until just cooked. Peel quickly, cut into 3mm-thick slices and place in a basin. Add the wine and mix in gently.
	white wine, dry	1dl	
2	oil	1 tbsp	Heat the oil in a frying-pan, add the lardons and sauté until just crisp then add to the potatoes and mix in.
	Lardons of bacon (51), cut very small and blanched	75g	
3	vinegar, white wine	2 tbsps	Heat the vinegar in the same pan, add to the potatoes and mix in. Serve in a salad bowl sprinkled with chopped parsley.
	parsley, chopped		

1373 Salade tiède Bergère

4 portions 12 mins.

Stage	Ingredient	Quantity	Method
1	lettuce	300g	Wash well, drain and dry and arrange neatly on four plates or salad dishes.

2	oil	1dl	Heat the oil in a pan and sauté the
	Lardons of bacon		lardons until just crisp. Add the
	(51), cut small	75g	seasoned chicken livers and mushrooms
	chicken livers,		and sauté together quickly, keeping the
	cleaned and cut in		livers pink, then add the garlic. Toss
	quarters	150g	over quickly then remove the ingredients
	mushrooms, thickly		with a perforated spoon and arrange in
	sliced	100g	the centre of the salads.
	garlic, finely		
	chopped	½ clove	
3	vinegar, red wine	2 tbsps	Add the vinegar to the hot oil then
	parsley, chopped		sprinkle over the salad and garnish.
			Sprinkle with chopped parsley and serve
			immediately.

1374 Salade tiède mélangée – Mixed warm Salad   4 portions
10 mins.

Stage	Ingredient	Quantity	Method
1	mixed salad leaves,		Wash well, drain and dry. Arrange neatly
	(lettuce, endives,		in a salad bowl.
	corn-salad,		
	watercress, etc.)	400g	
2	oil	2 tbsps	Heat the oil in a frying-pan, add the
	lardons of bacon (51)		lardons and sauté until cooked light
	cut small and		brown and crisp.
	blanched	100g	
3	lemon juice	1 tbsp	Add the lemon juice, away from the
			heat, season with pepper and little salt,
			then pour the whole over the salad.

1375 Salade tiède de Pigeon   4 portions
20 mins.

Stage	Ingredient	Quantity	Method
1	pigeon breasts,		Heat the oil in a sauté pan, season the
	skinned and trimmed	4	breasts and cook quickly on both sides
	oil	1dl	keeping underdone. Remove from the
			pan and keep warm.
2	corn-salad, or		Wash, drain and dry and arrange dome-
	other salad leaves		shape on four plates. Cut each pigeon
	to choice	200g	breast into slices on the slant and
			arrange overlapping on the salad.
3	vinegar, white wine	2 tbsps	Add to the oil and cooking juices in the
			pan. Season with salt and milled pepper,
			pour over the pigeon and salad and serve
			immediately.

1376 Salade tiède de Poulet et Coriandre – Chicken 4 portions
Salad with warm Cream and Coriander 20 mins.
Dressing

Stage	Ingredient	Quantity	Method
1	lettuce	400g	Wash well, drain and dry and arrange on four plates or salad dishes.
2	breasts of chicken, skinned	250g	Cut into strips approx. ¾cm by 5cm long.
3	coriander, ground oil	pinch 1dl	Season the chicken with salt, milled black pepper and a little coriander. Heat the oil in a pan, add the chicken and sauté quickly to just cook and colour a light brown. Drain and arrange in the centres of the salads.
4	cream lemon juice cayenne fresh coriander leaves, chopped	1½dl 1 tbsp ½ tbsp	Deglaze the pan with the cream, add the lemon juice and season to taste with salt, pepper and a touch of cayenne. Do not reduce. Spoon over the chicken and lettuce and sprinkle with a little of the coriander.

17
Vegetables

Vegetables play an important part in most people's diet and these days are no longer regarded as merely an adjunct to the main item of a meal; people realise the benefits to be derived from eating vegetables inasmuch as they can supply a significant amount of the vitamins, minerals and fibre needed for healthy living. The modern awareness of the importance of vegetables, together with contemporary moral and ethical attitudes to the eating of animal flesh, has resulted in an increase in the numbers of practising vegetarians and the amount of organically grown produce. This means that the work of those responsible for the cooking of vegetables in the professional kitchen has assumed greater importance and thus greater skill is called for in cooking these, whether the more common or the more expensive ones such as asparagus or aubergines.

It is necessary to know how to cook vegetables correctly so that they retain their original colour, texture, taste and nutritional value. Most vegetables need to be cooked only to the stage where they still possess their authentic character and some degree of firmness of texture. The fashion of blanching vegetables for only a few second so as to retain complete crispness is not necessarily applicable to all kinds of vegetables and not all customers want their vegetables to be served in the nearly raw state. Nonetheless, the taste and texture of a vegetable which is cooked but still firm to the bite is a standard of quality to be aimed for.

The impact of seasons and weather do not now greatly affect the availability of vegetables as modern methods of transport allow them to be imported from many parts of the world where they are available. The novelty of new season's vegetables must be considered however, as many customers welcome new arrivals to the menu as spring comes round each year.

Many establishments nowadays proudly claim that they serve only fresh vegetables but this is not to discount the value of convenience vegetables in the form of frozen, canned and dehydrated products which still have an important part to play in many sectors of the catering industry. However, their use should only be resorted to when fresh vegetables are unavailable.

The vegetable cook then must run his section in an efficient and economical way so that every dish is perfectly cooked and served as fresh as possible and with the minimum of waste. Many of the so-called exotic vegetables are expensive and therefore need great care in preparing and cooking; this means that skill and imagination is required by the practitioner and also makes the job a more interesting and demanding one.

As well as being used to accompany main courses, vegetables are used in the making of hors-d'oeuvre dishes, in soups, as garnishes for entrées of fish and meat poultry, as vegetarian dishes, in many kinds of savoury dishes and occasionally in the preparation of sweet dishes.

——CLASSIFICATION AND QUALITY POINTS——

Roots and Tubers

Artichoke, Jerusalem: a knobbly tuber which is best when not too small or too misshapen; it should not be wrinkled or flabby but firm and crisp.

Beetroot: best when firm, round and not too large; reject if sprouting or wrinkled. Small new season's beetroot are excellent as a vegetable dish.

Carrot: new season's carrots should be of a reasonable size and colour for preparation; old carrots should have a good colour and shape with no signs of splitting, breaking or pest damage. Reject if flabby, wrinkled or having signs of rootlet formation.

Celeriac: select when firm and heavy in relation to size and with no signs of damaged or rotting surfaces.

Parsnip: should be fresh-looking, clean and firm with no signs of brown patches or damage.

Potato, sweet: served more as a vegetable than as a potato. Should be firm, heavy in relation to weight; select when of even size and colour.

Salsify: for white or black varieties, select when even-sized and neither too thick nor too thin; reject if damaged, wrinkled or flabby.

Swede: should be firm, without blemish or signs of pest damage. Select when clean and small; these have the best flavour.

Turnip: essential that they are firm and unblemished with no signs of sponginess or insect damage; new season varieties are crisper and of a better flavour.

Bulbs

Leek: best with long white stems shading to pale then dark green at the top; should be plump, clean, unblemished with no signs of wilting or yellowness; when required as a vegetable select even and small- to medium-sized examples; reject late season examples with signs of the tough central flower stem developing.

Onion: should be firm, dry and compact in shape and of even size; reject if moist or soft to pressure or having signs of sprouting; there are many varieties, the Spanish onion being the mildest in flavour but very prone to decay.

Onion, button: should have no signs of sponginess or sprouting; select when small, of a nice round shape and even-graded size.

Onion, spring: should have a good white colour at the root end ranging to nice dark green stems; reject if showing signs of wilting or discolouration.

Shallot: many varieties ranging from white to light green to pale violet; softness or sponginess is usually a sign of decay; select when firm, not too small and with no signs of sprouting.

Leaves

Brussels Sprouts: should be small, tight and compact and of a bright green colour; select when even-sized and with no signs of discolouration or mould.

Cabbage, green: there are many varieties; select those which have a good colour with unblemished crisp leaves and are heavy in relation to size.

Cabbage, red: should be firm, compact and of a good reddish, purple colour; reject if there are signs of the leaves opening or of being wilted or dried.

Cabbage, spring: select with nicely developing hearts and with the leaves fresh, crisp, unblemished, of a good bright colour.

Cabbage, Chinese: also known as Chinese leaves; should have long, crisp, white leaves shading to pale green at the top; select when fairly compact with no signs of limpness, wilting or growing open at the top.

Chard: variety of beet grown for its leaves; best when young, nice dark green in colour and with white mid-ribs; reject if large and stringy or limp and discoloured.

Chicory or Frizzy Endive: should be white at the base of the leaves to darkish-green tops; select fresh-looking and crisp with a certain tightness of light green leaves at the centre; reject if wilted or with blemished leaves.

Endive, Belgian: should have tightly packed long white leaves shading to a light yellowish-green at the tops only; reject if showing signs of opening, dark green tops or brown on the outside leaves.

Kale, curly: select with crisp and unblemished leaves with a minimum of stalk and attached root.

Lettuce, cabbage: of the many varieties of lettuce these are the best for cooking and serving as a vegetable; should be crisp and with a firm heart; check for rotting leaves and browning at centre of heart and reject if found.

Spinach: the leaves should be crisp with a bright green colour; reject if leaves are yellow or blemished, too much root attached or sandy or dirty.

Flowers, Fruits and Seeds

Artichoke, globe: best when fresh and crisp-looking with tightly-packed heads and a good olive green colour; reject if a dull colour or with limp pliable stalks; select very small and even-sized for cooking and eating completely whole; medium for serving singly, and large for providing the artichoke bottoms.

Aubergine or Eggplant: select plump, firm and glossy with a good well-developed dark purple colour; reject if skin is wrinkled or has discoloured patches.

Broccoli: many varieties of differing colours ranging from white, yellow green to the dark green calabrese, and purple; select well-shaped and close-packed flower heads with no wilting or discoloured leaves on the outside; similar in many respects to cauliflower.

Cauliflower: the unopened flower head is referred to as the 'curd'; this should be well-formed, tightly packed, of a good white to yellowish colour and with no signs of spotting; reject if the flower is open or loosely packed or if the surrounding leaves are discoloured and wilted.

Chestnut: these should be large, plump, even-sized and firm to pressure between the thumb and forefinger; check for discoloured, dry-looking skins and which crack under pressure.

Courgette: small baby marrow, best when not too large, say approx. 12–18cm in length; select when firm with glossy skins and no signs of damage and even-graded size.

Marrow: should be young and firm with a soft skin; select with a good green shiny colour, undamaged, preferably no longer than 30cm.

Pimento: available in green, yellow, red and black and white varieties; should feel firm and crisp, have a bright glossy colour and with no signs of wrinkling or flabbiness.

Sweetcorn: for serving whole on the cob, select when young, well-filled and covered with fresh-looking green leaves; the grains should be milky-looking in colour and soft; reject if the grains are hard and dark yellow to orange in colour.

Tomato: should be firm, of even smooth shape and of the size required; unless fancy colour varieties, the colour should be a good even red with no hard greenish yellow patches near the eye of the tomato.

Squash

There are many varieties of this vegetable which are in general use in other countries and becoming more popular in the UK. Pumpkins are squashes and are used both as a vegetable and a filling for pumpkin pie, the buttermilk squash is a well known kind. Different varieties are available throughout the year and they keep well, summer ones being mild and delicate in flavour.

Legumes or Pods

Beans, broad: best when young and well-filled with small soft beans which do not require skinning when cooked; reject if the beans are hard and black where attached to the pod.

Beans, French: should be straight, flat, crisp and stringless; select small to medium and of an even-graded size; reject if flabby or with the inner bean developing.

Mange-tout: this is a variety of pea which can be eaten whole; the pod should be crisp with no signs of papery inner skin, of a good glossy dark green colour and not too large.

Peas: should be plump and crisp without being too full or tight and of a good green colour; reject if too large and the pod dry and with a netted parchment-like appearance.

Stems and Stalks

Asparagus: select with straight, tight unopened heads; wrinkling and browning at the stalk end is a sign of staleness; good varieties are Lauris, Evesham, Argenteuil, Malines and Genoa. The thinning of asparagus beds are sold in bundles as asparagus sprue.

Celery: best when white and crisp with a well-packed, firm heart; check for discolouration and pest damage to the inside.

Fennel: select when very tight bulbous shape, white and with just a little green showing at top; reject if split, dried or with brown patches at side or base.

Seakale: long, blanched, creamy white stalks which should be crisp and with very small bluish-green leaves at the top; reject if limp, broken and/or with brown edges.

Dried Pulses

These are the dried seeds of various leguminous plants such as broad beans, red beans, haricot beans, lentils, yellow and green peas, chick peas. Select product of the current season which can be guaranteed as no more than 1 year old. This can be checked by looking for plump shiny seeds which are relatively firm but can be easily cut. Reject if very hard and/or having wrinkled skins.

Funguses

Although not vegetables, mushrooms are included here with the vegetables as being customary and for the sake of convenience.

Cep or Flap Mushrooms: select firm and fresh-looking with as little damage as possible; reject if dirty or slimy to the touch.

Chanterelle: yellow in colour and of an irregular funnel shape; inclined to be very fragile so select as undamaged as possible with a good bright colour.

Morel: irregular pitted and conical-shaped cap and pale to dark brown in colour; select when fresh-looking with a fresh smell; should not be too sandy as they are difficult to wash.

Mushroom, cultivated: available in three grades; buttons which should be firm and white with no signs of opening; caps which are larger and partially opened but still white and firm, and flats which are fully opened and darker in colour and larger; select as fresh unbroken, unblemished and not discoloured.

STORAGE

Root vegetables such as carrots, turnip and swede as well as onions and shallots do not deteriorate quickly and may be bought in bulk and stored for a reasonable period of time, preferably not exceeding one week. They should be placed on racks or shelves raised from the floor to ensure adequate ventilation, in a cool dry shaded area out of the way of any direct light and at an even temperature where possible of no higher than 8°C. Failure to do this will result in rapid deterioration and the onset of sprouting. With this probability in mind it may be better to order more frequently.

All other vegetables show marked deterioration in quality very quickly and are best if ordered on a daily basis. Nevertheless, if it is found necessary to store them for a short period of time this is best done by holding them in a refrigerator preferably reserved for vegetables only or at least in a section separate from other commodities. The temperature should be as cool as possible but without the danger of freezing the vegetables.

Frozen vegetables should be stored in a deep freezer at −18°C or less, and ordered and used in strict rotation.

PREPARATION

It is essential that all care is taken with the handling, cleaning and preparation of all vegetables. The actual preparation of vegetables for specific requirements is detailed in the recipes; however the following general preparations and observations should be noted:

a) Root vegetables such as carrots, turnips, swedes and Jerusalem artichokes should be washed before preparing and peeling or cutting.

b) Peel turnips and swedes thickly with a small knife to remove the inner line of peel which is fibrous and tasteless.

c) Peel carrots thinly or, if using a peeling machine, time it correctly to avoid undue waste. Do not keep peeled carrots in water for any length of time; this tends to start incipient germination and alters the taste. Also do not keep them dry after peeling for a long time; this will mean having to peel them again.

d) Green leaf vegetables should be used on the day of the delivery and should not be left in water to soak for any length of time; this will lead to a loss of certain mineral salts and vitamins.

e) Certain clean vegetable trimmings can be used for flavouring stocks and sauces, e.g. trimmings from leek, celery, onion and carrot for stocks, consommés or purée-style vegetable soups, and asparagus trimmings for Crème Argenteuil. Turnip or swede trimmings can be used for thick soups but not for stocks.

PORTION GUIDE

It is usual to serve approximately 100g of prepared vegetable per portion, i.e. 10 portions per 1kg. Preparation losses vary considerably and the following table shows examples of approximate purchase weights to yield 1kg of vegetables prepared for cooking:

Artichokes, Jerusalem	2kg	Leeks	1½kg
Beans, broad	2½kg	Marrow	2kg
Beans, French	1⅛kg	Turnips	1½kg
Beans, runner	1⅛kg	Onions	1¼kg
Broccoli	1½kg	Peas, fresh	3kg
Brussels sprouts	1¼kg	Salsify	1¼kg

Cabbage	1½kg	Seakale	1¼ kg
Chestnuts	1½ kg	Spinach	2kg
Endive (Chicory)	1¼ kg		

Some vegetables are purchased by number or weight and the portion served is usually determined by size or number. The following are common examples:

Vegetable	*Amount per portion*	*Purchasing unit*
Artichoke, globe	1	Number
Asparagus	6–8 sticks	Bundle
Cauliflower	¼–½	Number
Celery	¼–½	Head
Corn on the cob	1	Number
Eggplant	½	Number
Fennel	¼–½	Head
Lettuce	½–1	Number
Tomatoes	2 medium	Weight

COOKING METHODS

The variety and range of vegetables is extensive; some are more suited to a single particular method of cooking while others are more versatile and suited to a number of differing methods. In other cases vegetable dishes can be the result of combined methods of cookery or the amalgamation of two or more different vegetables.

The following details and observations will give some idea of the possible range and scope of the cooking methods suitable for vegetables:

Boiling
This widely used method consists in the main of cooking the vegetable in plain boiling salted water; this should be abundant and salted in the proportion of approx. 50g of salt to 5 litres of water. Too little salt in the water can result in loss of colour and poor texture and flavour, especially in green vegetables. Oversalting will degrade the taste and flavour of any vegetable even if refreshed under running water and then reheated. For green vegetables, bring the water rapidly to the boil, add the vegetables immediately, cover with a lid and bring back to the boil as quickly as possible then remove the lid, remove any scum and boil as required until just cooked and still firm to the bite. In general, most green vegetables such as French beans or cabbage can be boiled fairly quickly but for tender items like asparagus or peas the water should just simmer to prevent damage. In some cases it is advisable to cover vegetables such as cauliflower, marrow and asparagus with clean muslin or cloth so as to ensure that anything floating proud of the water is cooked by the trapped steam.

For older root vegetables such as carrots and swedes, start in cold salted water and bring to the boil, this can help to leach out certain strong flavours, then skim and cook briskly until just still firm to the bite. Young root vegetables are usually better if placed to cook in boiling salted water.

For dried pulses such as haricot beans, lentils and peas, place in cold water, bring to the boil, skim then add just a little salt and any required flavourings and simmer gently until cooked and just soft; any too obvious firmness to the bite is not a desirable quality. If the pulses are of good fresh stock, soaking is not necessary or desirable.

When cooked always drain boiled vegetables carefully and serve immediately; this style of plain cooking is referred to as 'à l'Anglaise' or 'Nature'.

SPECIAL POINT

The use of soda or bicarbonate of soda is not recommended for obtaining a bright colour in green vegetables or to soften and speed up the cooking times for pulses. In all cases their use can degrade the flavour and taste of the vegetables and also lead to the destruction or leaching out of valuable vitamins and mineral salts.

Reheating of boiled vegetables

Ideally, all boiled vegetables should be drained and served immediately they are cooked. In practice however, this can be very difficult where large numbers of customers have to be served over a long period of service time. Green vegetables tend to discolour quickly and all vegetables tend to acquire an overcooked taste if held too long at the required service temperature. This problem can be overcome to some extent by cooking the vegetables frequently in small batches but this can lead quickly to bottlenecks and a slow-down in the speed of service. The following method is recommended for vegetables like peas, French beans, cauliflower, broccoli, seakale, asparagus, artichokes and sprouts.

As soon as the vegetables are only just cooked, place them under cold running water until they are quite cold. Drain thoroughly, place on trays then place in the refrigerator until required. When required for service, bring one tray of vegetables into the kitchen and as orders are received place the required number of portions in a one-handled vegetable strainer and immerse them in a large pan of boiling salted water. After just sufficient time to thoroughly reheat the vegetables, remove the strainer, allow the vegetables to drain thoroughly, then send in warmed vegetable dishes as usual. In this way the vegetables can be served over a long period of time in a fresh condition and with only a minimal loss of flavour. This method is also economical since any vegetable not used for one service period can be utilised for the next.

Cooking 'au Blanc'

Certain vegetables, such as Jerusalem artichokes and salsify, tend to discolour if boiled in plain salted water. Their whiteness can be retained by cooking them in a liquid composed of water, salt, a little flour and lemon juice. This liquid is called a 'Blanc'. See Recipe 15 for method of preparation.

Finishing with butter

This is a suitable improvement for any boiled vegetable and is prepared in the following manner. Well drain the boiled vegetables and toss in a little butter which has been freshly melted in the pan. Season as necessary. On no account should the butter be more than just melted and never heated until it browns – this will result in a sautéed vegetable with a completely different taste. For this see under Shallow Frying on page 604. Neither use clarified butter – this will make the vegetable oily in appearance and to the taste. Finishing with butter is described in menu terms as 'au Beurre', e.g. Haricots Verts au Beurre.

Finishing with cream

For this particular finish for boiled vegetables, always use good-quality double cream and make sure that the vegetables are somewhat less than completely cooked before draining them. To prepare, place the well-drained vegetables in a shallow pan and just cover with cream. Cook gently and slowly on top of the stove, turning or tossing them occasionally until just cooked and the cream reduced to a good coating consistency. Season as required and finish with a little butter and a few drops of lemon juice where appropriate. This is described in menu terms as 'à la Crème'.

Glazing of Vegetables

Root vegetables such as carrots, turnips, swedes and onions are improved in flavour and appearance if they are cooked with a little water, butter, sugar and salt. The water is allowed to evaporate during the cooking of the vegetables. This results in a certain amount of glossy syrup in which the vegetables need to be tossed prior to serving. See Carottes glacées (1400), Navets glacés (1488), Petits Oignons glacés (1492).

Poaching

This method has very little application to the cooking of vegetables. In general most vegetables need the temperature of a boiling liquid even if only gentle simmering to cook them quickly and successfully. However, some very tender items like courgettes, young marrow, cucumber and very tender young turnips and kohlrabi will finish cooking in their water if the pan is removed from the heat after a short initial period of boiling or simmering.

Steaming

This method, when applied to vegetables, produces the same results as when plain boiled ar d drained but with the added advantage of minimal nutritional loss. It is very important that the vegetables are placed in perforated trays or containers to prevent the accumulation of any condensed steam and it is useful to lightly salt the vegetables first.

Low-pressure steaming is ideal for vegetables such as turnips, swedes, carrots, celeriac and kohlrabi, but tends to discolour any green vegetable because of the length of time involved. High-pressure steaming on the other hand is useful for most types of vegetable which otherwise can be successfully boiled; it can preserve the colour of green vegetables well because of the much shorter cooking times needed.

Excellent results can be obtained with the steaming of very young vegetables by placing them in a perforated container which fits tightly over a pan of boiling liquid or stock, then covering with a tight-fitting lid. The vegetables should be lightly salted and the liquid or stock can be highly perfumed with herbs, spices and aromats which can impart very subtle flavours and aromas to the vegetables.

The steaming of fresh vegetables can be even more successful than boiling for the preparation of vegetable purées.

Stewing

Vegetables which have a high water content such as aubergine, courgette, marrow, tomato and mushroom can be successfully stewed especially when prepared as a mixture. The success of this type of cooking is exemplified by such dishes as Ratatouille (1535) and Courgette Provençale (1449).

Cooking 'à l'Etuvée'

This type of preparation is synonymous with the stewing of vegetables inasmuch as it is a gentle cooking with a more or less minimum amount of liquid which is served as part of the dish. It is well-suited to the cooking of legumes, leaf and root vegetables, which usually contain sufficient moisture themselves to effect a satisfactory result. Root vegetables need to be cut small and leaf vegetables either roughly shredded, torn into smaller pieces or left whole if small.

Place the prepared and washed vegetables in a small deep pan and add approx. 25g butter per 500g of vegetables. For those vegetables like carrots and older peas which require longer cooking times, add ½dl of water or white stock. Season with a little salt, cover tightly and cook gently at low heat on top of the stove until only just cooked but firm. Toss over occasionally and adjust the rate of cooking in relation to the estimated time needed for the cooking of the particular vegetable.

Braising
This method of cooking is used mainly for vegetables such as Belgian endive, cabbage, celery, fennel, lettuce and onions. First wash the vegetables thoroughly then blanch them in boiling water for a few minutes to get rid of excess acridity, especially in older vegetables; in the case of cabbage, celery and lettuce, it helps to make them pliable and easy to manipulate. Refresh and drain then place on a bed of roots with the addition of bacon trimmings and herbs as necessary. Season, moisten half-way up with white stock, cover with more bacon trimmings or slices of beef suet. Cover with greaseproof paper and a lid and cook in the oven until tender. Belgian endives should not be blanched as they turn brown if placed in boiling water. It is necessary to add lemon juice to the liquid used for braising them so as to preserve their whiteness.

Chestnuts can also be braised but do not require blanching first; they should be carefully peeled however, and then cooked under cover in the oven with a little white stock.

Roasting and Baking
These methods have few applications. Parsnips and sweet potatoes may be roasted in the same way as potatoes but in general baking is only applied to the preparation of certain vegetables dishes which require a longer period of oven heat for successful cooking and gratination to take place. Examples are Tomate farcie, Courgette farcie and Aubergine farcie.

Grilling
This method is usually applied to the cooking of mushrooms and tomatoes. These are cleaned, placed on an oiled or buttered tray, brushed with a little fat, seasoned and grilled for preference under an over heat grill, i.e. salamander.

Young tender carrots and turnips as well as thickish slices of sweet potato may also be grilled but this is best done over grill bars and using butter. Much care is needed to prevent discolouration from any smoking of dripping fat.

Vegetables such as onions, pimentos, mushrooms, very young maize, aubergines, courgettes, can be cut in suitably-sized pieces, marinated with oil, lemon juice and chopped herbs etc. then threaded on skewers as Kebabs and grilled.

Shallow Frying
This method of cooking is more commonly applied to vegetables which have already been boiled and drained. The normal procedure consists of heating butter in a frying-pan until it just begins to brown then adding the vegetables, seasoning them and shallow frying to a golden brown on all sides, either by turning over in the fat if large enough, or sautéeing by tossing over and over if small. This style of finish is usually designated as 'sauté au Beurre', e.g. Choux de Bruxelles sautés au Beurre, Champignons sautés au Beurre. Raw onions may be sliced and sautéed in the same way and as another example, braised Belgian endives or braised lettuce may be drained, shallow-fried in butter and finished à la Meunière with brown butter, lemon juice and parsley.

Other shallow-fried items are Galettes of vegetables where a quantity of cooked vegetable either as small grain or roughly chopped is added to an equal quantity of a thick batter containing a little baking powder. This mixture is then placed as spoonfuls in hot fat and shallow-fried on both sides. Also Subrics which are similar but where the vegetable is bound with Béchamel, eggs and cream. They are cooked in the same way as Galettes.

Cooked vegetables either singly or as a mixture may be bound with Pommes Duchesse, moulded in various shapes with flour then shallow-fried in hot fat.

Stir-frying

This traditional Chinese method of cooking is in effect a variation on the standard method of sautéeing and is well-applied to vegetables. The technique consists first of cutting larger raw vegetables into bite-size pieces, with other smaller items like bean sprouts and peas being left whole. The prepared vegetables are then added to a little very hot oil in a wok or heavy frying-pan with curved sides. The cooking is then carried out quickly and at a fairly high temperature by stirring and tossing over and over continuously and to give very little colour. When judged to be of the right texture, that is, still crisp and firm, the vegetables may be finished by flavouring with a little stock, soy sauce, vinegar, rice wine and/or special seasonings. The oil may be flavoured just prior to the commencement of cooking by frying such things as a little garlic, ginger root or sesame seeds for a few seconds and then removing them.

Where several different vegetables for a single dish are to be cooked by stir-frying, this should be done by adding the vegetables in a staggered manner. That is, by first adding the vegetable which is deemed to take the longest time to cook because of its hardness and texture; the remaining vegetables are then added in ascending order of tenderness and delicacy of texture so that finally they are all cooked evenly to the same degree.

The essential qualities of a good stir-fried vegetable are crispness, firmness, the original colour retained and the particular flavour of the vegetable still evident.

Deep Frying

This method has a number of applications for vegetables, perhaps the most popular being as Beignets or fritters. With few exceptions these are best when prepared using cooked vegetables such as cauliflower, French beans, salsify, artichoke bottoms, sprouts, small baby maize, and Jerusalem artichokes etc. They should be well-drained and where necessary cut in small pieces, then marinated with a little lemon juice, oil, seasoning and chopped fresh herbs where called for. They should then be passed through frying batter and deep-fried quickly until crisp. Occasionally, raw items such as mushrooms, courgette flowers and onion rings may be prepared in the same way.

Mixtures of cooked vegetables bound with potatoes then moulded in various shapes can be egg-and-breadcrumbed and deep-fried as Croquettes of vegetables. Raw vegetables, such as aubergines, courgettes cut in slices and onion rings, can be passed through milk and then flour, and deep-fried. In a similar fashion the same vegetables may be passed through flour and beaten egg before frying.

In all cases, deep-fried vegetables should be well-drained before serving and should not be covered with a lid as condensation will take place and they will very quickly become soft and soggy. The quality of all deep-fried items deteriorates quickly if held for more than a short time in a hot cupboard.

ARTICHAUTS – GLOBE ARTICHOKES

1377 Artichaut Nature, Sauces Diverses – Boiled   10 portions
Globe Artichoke with Various Sauces   1 hour

Stage	Ingredient	Quantity	Method
1	globe artichokes, medium to large	10	Trim the top of the outside leaves with a pair of scissors. Cut off the stalks level with the bottoms and then cut off the top third of the artichokes.
2	lemon	½	Rub the top and bottom of the artichokes with the lemon to prevent discolouring and tie with string to hold their shape.
3			Place into boiling salted water and boil gently for 15–20 mins. according to size until the bottoms are just tender.
4	Sauce Hollandaise (157), Sauce Mousseline (159) or Beurre Fondu (9)	6dl	Drain well and remove the string. Remove the centre leaves in one piece and carefully scrape out the exposed furry insides (chokes). Replace the centres upside-down, reheat if necessary and dress on a folded serviette accompanied by a suitable sauce.

SPECIAL POINT
To test for tenderness, insert the point of a small knife into the base of the artichoke. This should enter without marked resistance.

1378 Artichauts Barigoule   10 portions
                                                        1½ hours

Stage	Ingredient	Quantity	Method
1	globe artichokes, tender and small to medium in size lemon	20 ½	Remove any tough-looking outside leaves. Cut off the stalks level across the bottom and cut off the top third of each artichoke. Trim off the top of any remaining hard leaves. Rub the top and bottom of the artichokes with the lemon.
2			Place into boiling water and blanch for 5–6 mins. Refresh under cold water, drain then remove the centre furry part (choke) completely.
3	Farce Duxelloise (37) streaky bacon	500g 20 slices	Fill the centre of each artichoke with the stuffing, wrap each, over the stuffing, with a slice of bacon then tie round with string to hold it in place.
4	butter onion, sliced	25g 200g	Butter a suitable braising pan and cover with the vegetables. Place the artichokes

	carrot, sliced	150g	on top, stuffed side upwards, add the
	Bouquet Garni	1	stock, bouquet garni and season lightly.
	Fonds Brun (97)	7dl	Cover with a buttered paper and lid and
			braise gently in a moderate oven until
			tender, approx. 45 mins.
5			Drain well, remove the strings then arrange the artichokes with the bacon in oval earthenware dishes. Cover and keep warm.
6	Demi-glace (112)	4dl	Skim the braising liquid of all fat, add
	butter	50g	the demi-glace and reduce to a light
	parsley, chopped		coating consistency. Pass through a fine strainer into a clean pan, shake in the butter and adjust the seasoning. Make sure the artichokes are hot; ladle the sauce over and sprinkle with chopped parsley.

1379 Fonds d'Artichauts (cuits) – Artichoke Bottoms (cooked)

Select nice fresh globe artichokes medium to large in size. Cut off the stalks and remove all the leaves. Scoop out the furry part of the artichokes with a silver spoon and trim carefully with a stainless steel knife so as to produce hollow rounded bases. Rub well with lemon and cook until just tender in a Blanc (15). Leave in the blanc until required.

1380 Fonds d'Artichauts farcis – Stuffed Artichoke Bottoms

10 portions
45 mins.

Stage	Ingredient	Quantity	Method
1	artichoke bottoms, cooked (1379)	20	Drain the artichoke bottoms well and fill neatly with the stuffing using a piping bag and star tube.
	Farce Duxelloise (37)	500g	
2	breadcrumbs	75g	Sprinkle with breadcrumbs and melted butter. Place in buttered earthenware dishes and gratinate under the salamander or in a very hot oven.
	butter	60g	

1381 Fonds d'Artichauts sautés au Basilic – Sautéed Artichoke Bottoms with Basil

4 portions
20 mins.

Stage	Ingredient	Quantity	Method
1	globe artichokes, tender and small to medium in size	12	Trim carefully to produce hollow rounded bases (1379), rub with lemon juice then cut across into slices about 2mm thick.
	lemon	½	

| 2 | butter | 50g | Heat the butter in a heavy frying-pan and just as it begins to lightly colour, add the sliced artichokes. Season with salt and pepper and sauté quickly tossing over and over until lightly browned and just tender. |
| 3 | lemon juice
fresh basil leaves,
    coarsely chopped | few drops

½ tbsp | Sprinkle over a little lemon juice and then the basil. Toss over quickly then tip into a hot earthenware dish and send. |

ASPERGES – ASPARAGUS

From the culinary standpoint there are two main types of asparagus; the white variety, mainly French, which can be very thick and with green tops shading to a reddish-purple, and the English, exemplified by the Evesham variety which is thinner and mostly an excellent green except for the very bottom part of the stem; the English varieties are deemed to have a better flavour. Perhaps the best asparagus in terms of flavour, colour and size is undoubtedly the Lauris variety.

1382 Preparation of Asparagus for cooking

1) Wash well to remove any sand.
2) Remove the small spurs from the top part of the asparagus with the back of a small knife working away from the head.
3) Thinly peel the lower white stem peeling away from the head.
4) Wash well again.
5) Place the heads level together, in bundles of 6–8 pieces for one portion. Tie in two places, firstly lightly at the green end then tightly at the white.
6) Trim off the white ends evenly with a knife and each bundle to the same length. Use as required.

SPECIAL POINT
It is good economy when preparing asparagus to keep any nice clean stalk ends for the preparation of asparagus soup.

1383 Asperges bouillies, Sauces Diverses – Plain Boiled Asparagus with Various Sauces

4 portions
20 mins.

Stage	Ingredient	Quantity	Method
1	asparagus, cleaned and prepared	4 portions	Place the asparagus into boiling salted water. Cover with a piece of clean muslin and simmer gently until the tips are just tender.
2	Sauce Hollandaise (157), Mousseline (159), Maltaise (158) or Beurre Fondu (9)	 3dl	Lift carefully from the water and place on an asparagus cradle or folded serviette on a suitable dish. Remove the strings. Serve accompanied with a suitable sauce.

1384 Asperges au Gratin

Arrange the cooked asparagus (1383) in rows in buttered earthenware dishes and coat the green part only with Sauce Mornay (146). Sprinkle with grated Parmesan and gratinate.

1385 Asperges Milanaise

Arrange the cooked asparagus (1383) in rows in buttered earthenware dishes. Sprinkle with grated Parmesan, coat well with Beurre Noisette (13) and gratinate under the salamander.

1386 Pointes d'Asperges – Asparagus Tips

Clean the asparagus and tie up in bundles (1382). Cut off the base of the stalks, leaving the tender part and tip approx. 8cm in length. Place in boiling salted water and simmer gently for approx. 15–18 mins. Lift out, drain and serve as an accompanying vegetable. Pointes d'Asperges may also be served au Beurre, au Gratin, or Milanaise. Allow five to six pieces per person.

1387 Pointes d'Asperges à la Tessinoise

4 portions
25 mins.

Stage	Ingredient	Quantity	Method
1	butter	25g	Well butter an earthenware dish and lay
	asparagus tips,		in the asparagus, sideways along the
	cooked (1386)	4 portions	centre.
2	butter	25g	Heat the butter in a pan, add the
	shallots, finely		shallots and cook until just transparent.
	chopped	50g	Sprinkle over the asparagus.
3	Gruyère, grated	75g	Sprinkle the cheese over the asparagus
	cream, double	1dl	then add the cream. Season the surface
	paprika		with milled white pepper and a little
			paprika.
4			Place in a moderate oven at 190°C to
			lightly colour.

1388 Asparagus Sprue

The term 'sprue' denotes the thin green asparagus thinnings which, because of their colour and size, are suitable as a garnish for all types of dishes where called for. Snap off the tough part at the base of the stalks, leaving only the tender green ends. Wash these well and tie into bundles. Cut off the ends into small pieces, approx. 5mm in size, leaving the bundles 6cm long. Place the bundles and the pieces into the boiling salted water and simmer gently for approx. 10–12 mins. Drain. Use the bundles as a garnish. The small pieces can also be utilised for garnishing, e.g. Crème Argenteuil and Omelette aux Pointes d'Asperges.

AUBERGINE – EGGPLANT

1389 Aubergine à l'Egyptienne

10 portions
1 hour

Stage	Ingredient	Quantity	Method
1	eggplants oil	5 1dl	Remove the stalks and the green parts which are attached to them. Cut the eggplants into halves lengthways. Make an incision around the eggplants ½cm from the edge on the cut surface and score the centre criss-cross. Brush well with oil, place on a tray and cook in the oven at 180°C until soft.
2			Scoop out the pulp carefully with a spoon into a basin, leaving the empty skins on the tray.

3	oil
	onions, finely
	  chopped
	cooked mutton,
	  finely chopped
		½dl
		
		150g
		
		400g
			Heat the oil in a sauteuse, add the onion and cook without colour. Finely chop the eggplant pulp and add to the onions with the mutton. Season and cook gently for a few minutes.

4	tomatoes, skinned	10	Fill the empty halves of aubergine with the mixture and smooth the surface level. Slice the tomatoes and cover the fillings with overlapping slices.
5	parsley, chopped oil		Sprinkle the tomatoes with a little oil, lightly season and place in a hot oven at 200°C for 8–10 mins. Serve sprinkled with chopped parsley.

1390 Aubergine farcie – Stuffed Eggplant

10 portions
1 hour

Stage	Ingredient	Quantity	Method
1	eggplants oil	5 1dl	Remove the stalks and the green parts which are attached to them. Cut the eggplants in halves lengthways. Make an incision around the eggplant ½cm from the edge on the cut surface and score the centre criss-cross. Brush well with oil, place on trays and cook in the oven until soft.
2			Scoop out the pulp carefully with a spoon into a basin, leaving the empty skins on the tray.
3	oil onions, finely chopped	½dl 75g	Place the oil in a sauteuse, add the onion and cook without colour. Add the mushrooms and cook for 3–4mins.

	mushrooms, finely chopped	250g	Finely chop the eggplant pulp and add with the tomatoes concassées to the mushrooms. Add the parsley, season and cook gently until the surplus moisture has evaporated.
	Tomates Concassées (90)	250g	
	parsley, chopped	1 tbsp	
4	breadcrumbs	75g	Fill the empty halves with the mixture and smooth the surface dome-shaped. Sprinkle with breadcrumbs and a little oil and gratinate in a hot oven.
	oil	½dl	
5	Demi-glace (112)	3dl	Serve in earthenware dishes and finish with a cordon of demi-glace.

1391 Aubergine frite – Fried Eggplant

10 portions
25 mins.

Stage	Ingredient	Quantity	Method
1	eggplants	5	Remove the stalks and the green parts which are attached to them. Peel the eggplants and cut into ½cm-thick slices.
2	milk	2dl	Pass the slices of eggplant through the milk, then through flour. Place in frying-baskets and shake off surplus flour.
	flour		
3			Deep fry in hot oil at 175°C until golden brown.
4			Drain well, season with a little salt and serve on dish papers on suitable dishes.

BEAN SPROUTS

These are the crisp, tender young sprouts of the mung bean; the young sprouts of the soya bean and others are also widely used in oriental cookery. They tend to deteriorate quickly and should be purchased fresh on a daily basis. Alfalfa, also known as Lucerne, is a similar leguminous plant, much used in Australia.

1392 Sweet and Sour Bean Sprouts

4 portions
15 mins.

Stage	Ingredient	Quantity	Method
1	bean sprouts	450g	Pick over the bean sprouts to remove any seed cases and trim off any long rootlets. Wash well, drain and dry in a cloth.
2	vinegar, sherry	2 tbsps	Place all these ingredients in a basin, mix together and keep ready for use.
	sugar	1 tbsp	
	Tabasco or chilli sauce	few drops	
	soy sauce	1 tsp	
	chicken stock (96)	½dl	
	cornflour	½ tsp	

3	groundnut oil	½dl	Heat the oil in a wok or heavy frying-pan with curved sides. Add the garlic and fry until just turning brown, remove and discard.
	garlic, lightly crushed	1 clove	
4	root ginger, grated	1 tsp	Add to the oil for a few seconds only then add the bean sprouts and stir-fry quickly for 30–40 seconds.
5			Season with salt then add the liquid mixture in the basin. Toss over to mix well together then simmer for approx. 1 min. only. The bean sprouts should be kept nice and crisp. Serve in a vegetable dish.

SPECIAL POINT

The above recipe can be used for most vegetables either singly or in combination, provided that the total weight of vegetables is not exceeded. The vegetables should be cut into short strips or thickish slices and should be stir-fried in a staggered manner, that is, by first adding the vegetable which is deemed to take the longest to cook and then adding each vegetable in ascending order of tenderness and texture, finishing with the most tender.

BETTERAVE – BEETROOT

1393 Betteraves au Beurre – Buttered Baby Beetroot

Select very small new season's beetroot. Wash well and cook gently in boiling salted water until tender. Drain and carefully remove the skin, and trim the tops and bottoms. Melt a little fresh butter in a pan, add the beetroot, season with salt, a little pepper and a touch of sugar and gently toss over to coat. If possible, serve covered in round porcelain cocottes.

1394 Betterave farcie à la Russe

10 portions
1¼ hours

Stage	Ingredient	Quantity	Method
1	beetroots, medium-sized	10	Wash, place on a tray and bake in the oven at 190°C until tender. Remove the skin and trim the top and bottom.
2			Remove the centre of each beetroot by means of a plain pastry cutter and small knife.
3	butter	50g	Heat the butter in a pan, add the lardons and fry to a light brown then add the onions and cook together without colour. Now add the mushrooms. Cook together for a few mins. then add the rice, season well and mix together well.
	onion, finely chopped	50g	
	Lardons, small (51)	75g	
	mushrooms, finely chopped	150g	
	Riz Pilaff (522) cooked	4 portions	

Stage	Ingredient	Quantity	Method
4	cream, sour	2½dl	Fill the beetroots with the mixture. Place in a shallow pan, add the cream, season, cover with a lid and cook in the oven at 190°C for 15 mins. basting occasionally.
5	lemon juice dill, roughly chopped	1 tbsp	When ready, arrange in earthenware dishes, coat with the cream and sprinkle with the lemon juice and dill.

1395 Betteraves à la Viennoise

10 portions
1¼ hours

Stage	Ingredient	Quantity	Method
1	beetroots, small	1¼kg	Wash, place into cold salted water, bring to the boil and allow to simmer until almost tender. Drain, rub off the skin and trim the tops and bottoms.
2	red wine vinegar sugar Sauce Espagnole (111) horseradish, grated	1½dl 15g 3dl 15g	Place the beetroots in a clean pan, add the vinegar and sugar and reduce by half. Add the Espagnole and horseradish, season, cover and allow to cook gently on the stove for a few mins.
3	cream, sour	1dl	Arrange in vegetable dishes with the cooking liquid and pour a thread of cream over the beetroots.

1396 BROCCOLI

The several varieties of broccoli may be cooked and served in any of the ways applicable to cauliflower. Because of their usually smaller size it is not necessary to hollow out the stalk end when preparing them for boiling, a deepish cross-cut in the stalk is normally sufficient. It is also well to remember that in general, broccoli takes a shorter time to cook and if anything can even be left a little firmer than cauliflower.

1397 Stir-fried Broccoli with Ginger

4 portions
15 mins.

Stage	Ingredient	Quantity	Method
1	Calabrese broccoli spears	500g	Wash well and dry. Remove the stalks just below the flower head and cut diagonally into slices no more than 2mm thick. Cut and separate the heads into small florets.
2	fresh ginger root, peeled	10g	Cut the ginger into short thin sticks.

| 3 | oil | ¼dl | Heat the oil in a wok or suitable frying-pan, add the prepared ginger and stir-fry gently for about 10 seconds; do not colour. Add the sliced stalks and stir-fry quickly for 1 min. or so then add the florets and stir-fry quickly for another two or three mins. Season with salt and a pinch of sugar. |
| | sugar | pinch | |

4	cornflour	½ tsp	Have the cornflour diluted with the stock and the soy sauce. Pour over the broccoli, toss over and over to mix and bring to the boil for just a few seconds. Turn into a warm dish and serve.
	Fonds de Volaille		
	(96)	½dl	
	soy sauce	few drops	

CAROTTES – CARROTS

1398 Carottes au Beurre – Buttered Carrots

10 portions
1 hour

Stage	Ingredient	Quantity	Method
1	carrots, peeled	1½kg	Cut the carrots into sections and turn barrel-shape, approx. 3cm in length.
2			Place in a pan, cover with water, season with a little salt and bring to the boil. Skim and simmer gently until tender, approx. 15 mins. Drain well.
3	butter	50g	Melt in a sauteuse, add the carrots and toss over to coat with the butter. Serve in vegetable dishes.

1399 Carottes à la Crème– Creamed Carrots

10 portions
1 hour

Stage	Ingredient	Quantity	Method
1	carrots, peeled	1½kg	Cut the carrots into sections and turn barrel-shape, approx. 3cm in length.
2			Place in a pan, cover with water, season with a little salt and bring to the boil. Skim and simmer gently until not quite cooked, approx. 10–12 mins. Drain well.
3	cream, double	3½dl	Place the carrots in a shallow pan, add the cream, bring to the boil and complete the cooking while reducing the cream to a light coating consistency. Season lightly with a little salt and pepper. Serve in vegetable dishes.

SPECIAL POINT

If desired, the carrots may be plain boiled and mixed with 3dl of Sauce Crème.

1400 Carottes glacées – Glazed Carrots

10 portions
1 hour

Stage	Ingredient	Quantity	Method
1	carrots, peeled	1½kg	Cut the carrots into sections and turn barrel-shape approx. 3cm in length.
2	butter sugar	50g 15g	Place the carrots in a pan and barely cover with water. Add the butter, sugar and a little salt, cover with a lid and allow to boil steadily until almost cooked.
3			Remove the lid and continue cooking to evaporate all the liquid leaving a light syrup in which the carrots need to be tossed.
4	parsley, chopped		Serve in vegetable dishes sprinkled with chopped parsley.

1401 Carottes Vichy

10 portions
1 hour

Stage	Ingredient	Quantity	Method
1	medium-sized carrots, peeled	1kg	Cut the carrots into 2mm-thick slices using a mandolin if possible.
2	butter sugar	50g 15g	Place the carrots in a pan, barely cover with water and add the butter, sugar and a little salt. Cover with a lid and allow to boil steadily until almost cooked.
3			Remove the lid and continue cooking to evaporate all the liquid, leaving a light syrup in which the carrots need to be tossed.
4	parsley, chopped		Serve in vegetable dishes sprinkled with chopped parsley.

CÉLERI – CELERY

1402 Céleri braisé – Braised Celery

10 portions
2½ hours

Stage	Ingredient	Quantity	Method
1	celery heads	5	Remove any outer blemished stalks and trim the roots clean. Cut off the top square, leaving the celery approx. 16cm long. Wash thoroughly and place in boiling water to blanch for 10 mins. Refresh under cold running water and wash again, taking care to remove any soil lodged between the sticks at the root end.
2	butter	30g	Butter a braising pan and cover the bottom with the carrot and onions. Arrange the celery on top, barely cover with stock and season. Cut the suet in thin slices and place on top of the celery. Cover with a greaseproof paper and lid.
	carrot ⎫	100g	
	onion ⎬ sliced	100g	
	Fonds Blanc (93)	1 litre	
	beef kidney suet	250g	
3			Bring to the boil and cook gently in a moderate oven at approx. 180°C until tender (approx. 1½ hours).
4			Remove the celery and drain. Cut in half lengthways and fold the top half underneath. Dress neatly in vegetable dishes with a little of the cooking liquor.

1403 Céleri braisé au Jus

Prepare Céleri braisé (1402). Coat with 2dl Jus lié (113) and sprinkle with chopped parsley when serving.

1404 Céleri braisé à la Moelle

Prepare Céleri braisé (1402) and coat with 2dl of Sauce Moelle (120). Sprinkle with chopped parsley.

1405 Céleri Milanaise

Prepare Céleri braisé (1402). Sprinkle with 75g grated Parmesan and gratinate under the salamander. Cover with 100g of Beurre Noisette (13) when serving.

CÉLERI-RAVE – CELERIAC

1406 Céleri-rave étuvé au Beurre – Buttered Celeriac

10 portions
50 mins.

Stage	Ingredient	Quantity	Method
1	celeriac	1½kg	Wash well, peel then cut into sections and trim in large barrel shapes approx. 5cm in length. Place into water with lemon juice to keep white.
	juice of lemon	2	
2			Place in boiling salted water and blanch for approx. 5 mins. Drain well.
3	butter	75g	Melt the butter in a pan, add the celeriac and stock, lightly season and cover. Cook very gently on the side of the stove turning over occasionally until just tender. Serve in vegetable dishes with a little of the butter.
	Fonds Blanc (93)	1dl	

1407 Céleri-rave à la Crème – Creamed Celeriac

Prepare Celeriac (1406) then mix gently with 3dl of Sauce Crème (143). Serve in vegetable dishes.

1408 Céleri-rave Persillé – Parslied Celeriac

Prepare Céleri-rave étuvé au Beurre (1406) and sprinkle with chopped parsley.

1409 CHAMPIGNONS – MUSHROOMS

In addition to the various grades of cultivated mushrooms, several other varieties are available commercially. These include Chanterelles, Blewits or Wood Blewits, Ceps, Morels, Oyster mushrooms and Shiitake mushrooms. The last two are now available as cultivated mushrooms.

In general the following recipes are interchangeable between any of the edible funguses. The quality of cultivated mushrooms is such that peeling is unnecessary. Field and horse mushrooms have a tougher skin and should be peeled before cooking.

1410 Cèpes Bordelaise

10 portions
20 mins.

Stage	Ingredient	Quantity	Method
1	ceps (flap mushrooms)	1kg	Trim the stalks, wash well, drain and dry. Cut into quarters or slices on the slant.

2	oil	1dl	Heat the oil in a frying-pan and when
	shallots, finely		very hot, add the flap mushrooms.
	chopped	75g	Season and sauté quickly until well-
	breadcrumbs	50g	coloured and a little crisp. Add the
			shallots and breadcrumbs and sauté until
			the breadcrumbs are crisp and coloured.
3	juice of lemon	squeeze	Finish with a good squeeze of lemon
	parsley, chopped	1 tbsp	juice and the parsley and serve in
			vegetable dishes.

1411 Champignons farcis – Stuffed Mushrooms 20 pieces
30 mins.

Stage	Ingredient	Quantity	Method
1	large cup mushrooms	20	Wash the mushrooms and remove the
	butter, melted	50g	stalks. Place on a tray cup side up,
			season and sprinkle with the butter. Grill
			under the salamander until half-cooked,
			keeping them a little firm.
2	Farce Duxelloise		Place the stuffing into a piping bag with
	(37)	500g	a star tube and fill into the mushrooms.
	breadcrumbs	50g	Sprinkle with the breadcrumbs and
	butter, melted	50g	butter. Place in a hot oven at 200°C to
	parsley, picked		finish cooking and gratinate. Serve
			garnished with picked parsley.

1412 Champignons grillés – Grilled Mushrooms 10 portions
15 mins.

Stage	Ingredient	Quantity	Method
1	flat mushrooms	1kg	Wash the mushrooms. Cut off part of
	butter, melted	75g	the stalks if too long, then place the
			mushrooms on a tray dark side upwards.
			Season and sprinkle with the butter.
			Grill under the salamander until soft.
2	parsley, picked		Arrange the mushrooms on flat dishes
			and serve garnished with picked parsley.

1413 Champignons sautés aux Fines Herbes 10 portions
15 mins.

Stage	Ingredient	Quantity	Method
1	button mushrooms, small	1kg	Wash the mushrooms quickly and dry carefully. Trim the stalk ends if too long. Leave the mushrooms whole if small enough or cut into quarters on the slant.
2	butter	75g	Heat half the butter in a heavy frying-
	Fines Herbes (31),		pan and add half the mushrooms just as
	chopped	2 tbsps	it begins to turn brown. Season with salt

and pepper and sauté quickly and at
high temperature until just cooked, then
add the chopped herbs and toss over to
mix. Repeat for the remainder. Serve in
hot earthenware dishes.

1414 Chanterelles à la Crème – Creamed Chanterelles

4 portions
15 mins.

Stage	Ingredient	Quantity	Method
1	chanterelles	450g	Carefully clean the chanterelles of any blemished parts. Wash gently and dry carefully in a cloth. Cut any large ones in half.
2	butter	50g	Heat the butter in a suitable pan, add the chanterelles, season with salt and pepper and sauté quickly until just tender.
3	cream, double cayenne	1½dl	Add the cream and allow to cook quickly and reduce the cream to a light coating consistency. Adjust the seasoning plus a touch of cayenne. Tip into a hot china dish and serve.

1415 Gratin de Morilles

4 portions
25 mins.

Stage	Ingredient	Quantity	Method
1	morels	450g	Wash very carefully and thoroughly to remove all traces of sand. Dry in a cloth then trim carefully of any blemishes. Cut any large ones in half to give fairly even sizes overall.
2	butter shallots, finely chopped	50g 25g	Heat the butter in a heavy sauteuse, add the shallots and cook without colour. Add the morels, season with salt and pepper and cook together fairly quickly until soft.
3	sherry cream, double	¼dl 1½dl	Add the sherry to the morels and reduce by half then add the cream and stew together to reduce to a coating consistency.
4	egg yolk cayenne	1	Remove from the heat and quickly mix in the egg yolk. Adjust the seasoning plus a touch of cayenne. Tip into an earthenware dish.
5	Parmesan, grated butter, melted	25g 25g	Sprinkle with the Parmesan and melted butter and gratinate under a very hot salamander.

1416 CHOU – CABBAGE

Of the many varieties of cabbage available the year round, it is only necessary to distinguish between 1) those which are generally light to dark green in colour and ranging from the early spring cabbage and Primo varieties to later season ones like Savoy and Drumhead; these are mostly useful for cooking and serving as a vegetable, 2) the hard and white Dutch varieties which are more suitable for the preparation of salads and sauerkraut, and 3) the red varieties which can be cooked in various ways and are very useful when pickled for use as a salad vegetable. They should always be selected as fresh as possible, with good firm hearts and except for spring cabbage heavy in relation to size.

The oft-repeated criticisms of overcooked mushy cabbage should not be allowed to keep arising. Different varieties of green cabbage require different cooking times and especially if boiled, care should be taken to check the progress of the cooking and endeavour to halt it just when the leaves are tender but with a definite firmness to the bite. The use of soda or bicarbonate of soda should be eschewed; they are major culprits for producing soft, overcooked cabbage with a debased flavour.

1417 Chou à l'Anglaise – Boiled Cabbage
10 portions
35 mins.

Stage	Ingredient	Quantity	Method
1	cabbage	2kg	Remove any blemished outer leaves and cut the cabbage into quarters. Remove the centre stalks and any large stalks in the leaves. Wash well and drain.
2			Place in plenty of boiling salted water and allow to boil steadily until tender (approx. 8–15 mins according to type and quality), but still firm. Drain in a colander.
3			Place the cabbage between two plates and press firmly to squeeze out most of the liquid. Cut into even-sized portions and arrange in vegetable dishes.

1418 Chou au Beurre – Buttered Cabbage

Prepare Chou à l'Anglaise (1417) and brush with butter before serving.

1419 Chou de Printemps – Spring Cabbage
10 portions
45 mins.

Stage	Ingredient	Quantity	Method
1	spring cabbage	5 × 350g	Remove any blemished outer leaves, trim the stalks square and cut the end criss-cross. Wash well and lightly tie with string so as to hold together while cooking.
2			Place the cabbage into boiling salted water and cook gently until tender but

			slightly firm. Remove from the water and drain.
3	butter, melted	25g	Take off the strings and squeeze each cabbage gently to remove surplus liquid. Cut in half lengthways and fold the tops under to a neat shape. Dress in vegetable dishes and brush with the melted butter.

1420 Petit Chou braisé – Small Braised Cabbage   10 portions
2 hours

Stage	Ingredient	Quantity	Method
1	cabbage	2kg	Remove any blemished outside leaves. Cut the cabbage into half, remove the centre stalk and any large stalks from the leaves. Wash well and drain.
2			Place in boiling water and blanch for 7–8 mins. Drain and spread out to cool.
3			Take the ten largest and greenest leaves and lay them on the table. Place the remainder equally in the centres of the outer leaves and enfold. Place one at a time in a clean cloth and squeeze firmly to remove the water and mould round.
4	butter	25g	Butter a braising pan and cover the bottom with the sliced vegetables. Arrange the small cabbages on top, barely cover with stock and season. Cover with the bacon, a buttered greaseproof paper and a lid. Bring to the boil and cook in a moderate oven at 180°C until tender (approx. 1 hour).
	onion ⎫ sliced	125g	
	carrot ⎭	125g	
	Fonds Blanc (93)	1½ litres	
	bacon rinds or trimmings	150g	
5	Demi-glace (112)	2dl	Remove the cabbages, drain and arrange neatly in vegetable dishes. Coat with demi-glace when serving.

SPECIAL POINTS
a) To prevent the cabbages from breaking open during cooking, it is essential that the braising pan should not be too large; the cabbages should fill the pan and be tightly packed together.
b) The braising liquid may be reduced and added to the demi-glace.

1421 Chou Vert étuvé au Beurre

4 portions
10–12 mins.

Stage	Ingredient	Quantity	Method
1	green cabbage, young and tender	1kg approx.	Remove any blemished or tough-looking outer leaves keeping the more tender parts. Cut into quarters and remove the central stalks and any largish ribs from the leaves. Cut into rough squares of approx. 2cm or very roughly shred. Wash well in cold water and drain.
2	butter	50g	Place the cabbage in a shallow pan, add the butter and season with salt and pepper. Cover with a lid and place over high heat to start cooking, then finish the cooking more slowly so as not to colour the cabbage. Toss over and over occasionally. There should be enough moisture from the cabbage itself and the water adhering from the washing. Keep firm and crisp and serve in a vegetable dish.

1422 Chou-rouge Flamande

10 portions
3¼ hours

Stage	Ingredient	Quantity	Method
1	red cabbage	1½kg	Remove any blemished outer leaves, cut into quarters and remove the centre stalks. Wash and cut into coarse julienne.
2	butter	75g	Coat a braising pan with the butter and add the cabbage, vinegar and bouquet garni. Season, cover with buttered greaseproof paper and a lid and cook in a moderate oven at 175°C for approx. 2 hours.
	vinegar	1½dl	
	Bouquet Garni	1	
3	brown sugar	50g	Add the sugar and apples and continue cooking for approx. ¾ hour more until the cabbage is tender. Serve in vegetable dishes.
	cooking apples, diced	350g	

SPECIAL POINT

The use of aluminium or iron pans for cooking red cabbage will result in discolouration and metallic contamination. It is essential to use a well-tinned copper or stainless steel pan.

1423 Chou-rouge Limousine

10 portions
3 hours

Stage	Ingredient	Quantity	Method
1	red cabbage	1½kg	Remove any blemished outer leaves, cut into quarters and remove the centre stalks. Wash and cut into coarse julienne.

2	lard
	Fonds Blanc (93)
	Bouquet Garni
	brown sugar
	chestnuts, peeled
	  and cut in small
	  dice
		75g
		2dl
		1 large
		25g
		
		350g
			Coat a suitable braising pan and a piece of greaseproof paper with the lard. Mix the cabbage and chestnuts together and add to the pan. Add the sugar, white stock, bouquet garni and season with salt and pepper. Cover with the paper and lid.

3			Place in a moderate oven and cook at 175°C for approx. 2¼ hours until tender. Serve in vegetable dishes.

CHOU-FLEUR – CAULIFLOWER

1424 Chou-fleur à l'Anglaise (Nature) – Boiled Cauliflower

10 portions
30 mins.

Stage	Ingredient	Quantity	Method
1	cauliflowers, medium	2–3	Remove the outer leaves, cut the stalks square and hollow out with a knife. Wash well and place into plenty of boiling salted water. Simmer gently until tender but slightly firm.
2			Drain well and serve whole or cut into portions.

SPECIAL POINT
Plain boiled cauliflower can be served accompanied with a suitable sauce, e.g. Hollandaise, Mousseline, Crème, Beurre Fondu.

1425 Chou-fleur au Beurre – Buttered Cauliflower

Prepare Chou-fleur à l'Anglaise (1424) and cover with 50g of melted butter before serving.

1426 Chou-fleur au Gratin or Chou-fleur Mornay

10 portions
35 mins.

Stage	Ingredient	Quantity	Method
1	cauliflowers, medium	2–3	Remove the outer leaves, cut the stalks square and hollow out with a knife. Wash well and place into plenty of boiling salted water. Simmer gently until tender but slightly firm.
2	Sauce Mornay (146) grated cheese	7dl 75g	Drain the cauliflower well, cut into portions and dress neatly in dishes. Coat with the Sauce Mornay, sprinkle with the cheese and gratinate under the salamander.

1427 Chou-fleur Italienne

10 portions
45 mins.

Stage	Ingredient	Quantity	Method
1	cauliflowers, medium	2–3	Remove the outer leaves, cut the stalks square and hollow out with a knife. Wash well and place into plenty of boiling salted water. Simmer gently until tender but slightly firm.
2	Sauce Italienne (127) breadcrumbs Parmesan, grated butter, melted	7dl 50g 50g 50g	Drain the cauliflower well, cut into portions and dress neatly in dishes. Coat with the Sauce Italienne, sprinkle with the cheese, breadcrumbs and the melted butter. Gratinate in a hot oven at approx. 200°C.

1428 Chou-fleur Milanaise

Prepare Chou-fleur à l'Anglaise (1424) and cut into portions. Dress neatly in dishes, sprinkle with 50g of grated Parmesan and 50g of melted butter and gratinate under the salamander.

1429 Chou-fleur Persillé

Prepare Chou-fleur à l'Anglaise (1424) and cover with 50g of melted butter. Serve sprinkled with chopped parsley.

1430 Chou-fleur Polonaise

10 portions
45 mins.

Stage	Ingredient	Quantity	Method
1	cauliflowers, medium	2–3	Remove the outer leaves, cut the stalks square and hollow out with a knife. Wash well and place into plenty of boiling salted water. Simmer gently until tender but slightly firm.

2	butter	100g	Drain the cauliflower well and cut into portions. Heat the butter in a frying-pan and just as it turns brown add the cauliflower. Fry until lightly browned on all sides and arrange in vegetable dishes.
3	butter	200g	Heat the butter in a frying-pan, add the
	breadcrumbs	150g	breadcrumbs and fry until golden brown.
	hard-boiled eggs,		Add the eggs, toss over to mix and pour
	sieved	3	over the cauliflower. Sprinkle with
	parsley, chopped		chopped parsley.

1431 Chou-fleur sauté au Beurre

Prepare Chou-fleur à l'Anglaise (1424) and cut into portions. Heat 100g of butter in a frying-pan and just as it turns brown add the cauliflower. Fry until lightly browned on all sides and serve in vegetable dishes.

CHOU DE MER – SEAKALE

1432 Chou de Mer (Chou Marin) Nature – Boiled Seakale

10 portions
35 mins.

Stage	Ingredient	Quantity	Method
1	seakale	1¼kg	Trim any damaged stalks and the root. Wash well and tie loosely in bundles.
2			Place in boiling salted water and simmer gently until tender (approx. 15–20 mins.).
3	Sauce Hollandaise (157) or Beurre Fondu (9)	6dl	Drain the seakale well and dress on a folded serviette. Serve accompanied with the sauce.

1433 Chou de Mer Milanaise

Prepare Chou de Mer (1432) and dress neatly in dishes. Sprinkle with 50g of grated Parmesan and 50g of melted butter and gratinate under the salamander.

CHOU-RAVE – KOHLRABI OR CABBAGE TURNIP

1434 Chou-rave à la Crème – Creamed Kohlrabi

10 portions
30 mins.

Stage	Ingredient	Quantity	Method
1	kohlrabi	1½kg	Remove the top leaves and bottom and peel. Wash and either cut into thick slices or trimmed sections.

2	cream, double	3dl	Place in a shallow pan, add the cream
	butter	50g	and butter. Season with salt and pepper, cover and cook slowly on the side of the stove turning over occasionally until the cream is slightly thickened and the vegetable cooked but firm. Serve in vegetable dishes.

1435 Chou-rave Lucernoise

10 portions
45 mins.

Stage	Ingredient	Quantity	Method
1	kohlrabi	1½kg	Remove the top leaves and reserve any which are green. Peel the kohlrabi and cut into ½cm slices. Wash both leaves and slices and blanch for 2–3 mins. in boiling water. Drain.
2	butter	50g	Chop the leaves, mix together with the slices of kohlrabi and place into buttered dishes.
3	white wine, dry	½dl	Sprinkle with the wine and the cream to just below the level of the ingredients. Season with salt and milled pepper then sprinkle with the grated cheese.
	cream, double	3dl	
	Gruyère cheese, grated	100g	
4			Place in a moderate oven at 190°C to cook and gratinate to a golden brown at the same time, approx. 20 mins. Clean the dishes and serve as they are.

CHOUX DE BRUXELLES – BRUSSELS SPROUTS

1436 Choux de Bruxelles à l'Anglaise – Boiled Brussels Sprouts

10 portions
35 mins.

Stage	Ingredient	Quantity	Method
1	Brussels sprouts	1¼kg	Select even-sized sprouts, trim the stalks level and discard blemished outer leaves. Cut a cross in the stalk ends so as to ensure even cooking. Wash well.
2			Place into boiling salted water and allow to simmer gently until tender but slightly firm (approx. 10 mins.).
3			Drain well and serve in vegetable dishes.

1437 Choux de Bruxelles au Beurre – Buttered Brussels Sprouts

Prepare Choux de Bruxelles à l'Anglaise (1436) and toss in 50g of melted butter before serving.

1438 Choux de Bruxelles Grand'mère

10 portions
35 mins.

Stage	Ingredient	Quantity	Method
1	Brussels sprouts	1¼kg	Select even-sized sprouts, trim the stalks level and discard any blemished outer leaves. Cut a cross in the stalk ends so as to ensure even cooking. Wash well then plain boil and drain.
2	butter	75g	Heat the butter in a frying-pan, add the
	Lardons, small (51)	100g	lardons and sauté quickly to a light
	onions, chopped	100g	brown. Add the onions and sauté together without colouring the onions.
3			Add the sprouts, season with salt and milled pepper and sauté together for a few mins. until just lightly coloured. Place in vegetable dishes and sprinkle with chopped parsley.

1439 Choux de Bruxelles au Gratin or Choux de Bruxelles Mornay

10 portions
35 mins.

Stage	Ingredient	Quantity	Method
1	Brussels sprouts	1¼kg	Prepare and cook as for Choux de Bruxelles à l'Anglaise (1436). Drain well.
2	Sauce Mornay (146)	6dl	Place the sprouts into buttered serving
	grated cheese	75g	dishes, coat with the Sauce Mornay, sprinkle with the cheese and gratinate under the salamander.

1440 Choux de Bruxelles Limousine – Brussels Sprouts with Chestnuts

Toss together 2 parts Choux de Bruxelles au Beurre (1441) with 1 part broken pieces of Marrons braisés (1486). Serve in vegetable dishes.

1441 Choux de Bruxelles sautés au Beurre

Prepare Choux de Bruxelles à l'Anglaise (1436), drain well then shallow fry in hot butter tossing over and over until lightly browned. Serve in vegetable dishes sprinkled with chopped parsley.

CONCOMBRE – CUCUMBER

1442 Concombre à la Crème – Creamed Cucumber 10 portions
45 mins.

Stage	Ingredient	Quantity	Method
1	cucumbers	3	Peel, cut into four lengthways and remove the seeds with a knife. Cut into diamond-shaped pieces.
2	butter	75g	Place in a sauteuse and melt. Add the cucumber, lightly season and cover with a lid. Cook gently on the side of the stove without colour.
3	cream	4dl	Add and simmer gently for a few minutes to reduce the cream. Correct the seasoning and serve in vegetable dishes.

1443 COURGETTE – YOUNG MARROW

Courgettes or Zucchini are the names for the young fruits of the many varieties of marrows. From the culinary standpoint the fully grown marrow has little to commend it as a vegetable; its French name Courge when used as a menu term conjures up an impression of a large, fully-grown marrow, with a tough skin, hard seeds, coarse stringy flesh and a nondescript flavour. For this reason it is thought better to use the term Courgette in the singular for denoting a young tender marrow, large enough however to produce a number of portions, and Courgettes in the plural, where one or more are needed for a portion.

1444 Courgette à l'Anglaise (Nature) – Boiled Marrow
10 portions
30 mins.

Stage	Ingredient	Quantity	Method
1	marrows, young	2kg	Remove the stalks, peel and cut in half lengthways. Remove the seeds with a spoon then cut the marrow into pieces approx. 6–7cm square. Wash.
2			Place into boiling salted water and simmer gently until just tender. Drain very well and serve in vegetable dishes.

SPECIAL POINT
Marrow can be served with Sauce Crème (143), Sauce Hollandaise (157) or Beurre Fondu (9).

1445 Courgette au Beurre – Buttered Marrow

Prepare Courgette à l'Anglaise (1444) and butter with 50g of melted butter before serving.

1446 Courgettes farcies – Stuffed Baby Marrows   10 portions
45 mins.

Stage	Ingredient	Quantity	Method
1	baby marrows	10	Trim the stalk ends and cut in half lengthways. Remove the seeds with a small spoon. Wash.
2			Place into boiling salted water and simmer gently until just tender. Drain very well.
3	Farce Duxelloise (37)	650g	Fill the marrows neatly with the stuffing using a piping bag and star tube.
4	breadcrumbs butter	75g 60g	Sprinkle with breadcrumbs and melted butter. Place in buttered earthenware dishes and gratinate in a hot oven.

SPECIAL POINT

Baby marrow (courgettes) may be stuffed with Riz Pilaff (522), forcemeats of meat and suitable vegetable purées such as spinach. They may be gratinated with cheese instead of breadcrumbs.

1447 Courgettes frites – Fried Baby Marrow   10 portions
30 mins.

Stage	Ingredient	Quantity	Method
1	baby marrows	10	Remove the stalks then cut the marrow into ½cm-thick slices.
2	milk flour	2dl	Pass the slices of marrow through the milk and then through flour. Place in frying-baskets and shake off surplus flour.
3			Deep fry in hot oil at 175°C until golden brown.
4			Drain well, season with a little salt and serve on dish papers on flat dishes.

1448 Courgette Milanaise

Prepare Courgette à l'Anglaise (1444). Dress neatly in dishes, sprinkle with 75g of grated Parmesan and 50g of melted butter and gratinate under the salamander.

1449 Courgette Provençale   10 portions
2½ hours

Stage	Ingredient	Quantity	Method
1	oil onions, finely sliced garlic, finely chopped	1dl 200g 2 cloves	Heat the oil in a round braising pan. Add the onion and garlic and cook without colour.

2	marrows, young	1½kg	Remove the stalks, peel and cut in four lengthways. Remove the seeds with a spoon then cut the marrow in ½cm-thick slices.
3	oil	1½dl	Place the oil in a frying-pan and heat. When very hot add the marrow. Season well with salt and pepper and sauté quickly until transparent and lightly coloured. Add to the onions and garlic.
4	Tomates Concassées (90) parsley, chopped	750g	Add, season, cover with a lid and cook in a moderate oven at 165°C for approx. 1½ hours. Serve in vegetable dishes sprinkled with chopped parsley.

1450 Fleurs de Courgettes frites – Fried Courgette Flowers

10 portions
30 mins.

Stage	Ingredient	Quantity	Method
1	courgette flowers	30–40 according to size	Wash, drain and dry carefully.
2	lemon	1	Sprinkle the insides of the flowers very lightly with a few drops of lemon juice and season lightly with salt and pepper. Leave for 5–6 mins.
3	flour Pâte à Frire (76), not too thick	½ litre	Hold the flower by the stalk end, lightly dust with flour, dip into the batter and deep fry in batches in hot fat at 180°C until crisp and golden brown.
4			Drain well on kitchen paper and serve arranged on a dish paper or serviette on a flat dish.

SPECIAL POINT
The flower with a thin stalk attached is the male and is best for frying either by itself or stuffed. The stalk may be left on and held by the customer for eating, but is best removed after frying as it is not particularly pleasant to eat.

ENDIVE BELGE – BELGIAN ENDIVE (CHICORY)

This is a forced and blanched variety of chicory (Cichorium Intibus). The growing shoots are deprived of light to produce tight-packed, white- and yellow-tipped, crisp heads. The best are produced in Belgium and are called Witloof.

1451 Endive braisée – Braised Chicory

10 portions
1½ hours

Stage	Ingredient	Quantity	Method
1	Belgian endives	10 × 100g	Remove any blemished outer leaves, trim the roots and place the endives in a well-buttered braising pan.
	butter	75g	
2	juice of lemon	1	Add the lemon juice and stock and lightly season. Cover with buttered greaseproof paper and a tightly fitting lid.
	Fonds Blanc (93)	1 litre	
3			Cook in a moderate oven at 175°C for approx. 1 hour. Remove, drain and dress neatly in vegetable dishes.

1452 Endive braisée au Jus

Prepare Endive braisée (1451) and coat with Jus lié (113) when serving. Finish with chopped parsley.

1453 Endive Meunière

10 portions
30 mins.

Stage	Ingredient	Quantity	Method
1	butter	75g	Heat the butter in a frying-pan and just before it turns brown add the endives. Fry until light brown on all sides and dress in vegetable dishes.
	Endive braisée (1451)	10	
2	juice of lemon	squeeze	Squeeze a little lemon juice over the endives. Heat the butter in a pan and cook to a light brown shaking the pan to ensure even colouring. Pour over the endives and sprinkle with chopped parsley.
	butter	75g	
	parsley, chopped		

EPINARDS – SPINACH

1454 Epinards en Branches – Leaf Spinach

10 portions
30 mins.

Stage	Ingredient	Quantity	Method
1	spinach	2kg	Remove the stalks and wash the leaves in several changes of cold water. Drain and place in boiling salted water. Allow to boil steadily until just tender (approx. 5 mins.)
2			Refresh under cold water, drain in a colander and squeeze gently into balls to remove the water.

| 3 | butter | 75g | Melt in a sauteuse and add the spinach. Loosen the balls gently with a fork. Season with salt and milled pepper and reheat gently without frying. Serve in vegetable dishes. |

1455   Epinards sautés à l'Ail – Buttered Spinach with Garlic

10 portions
30 mins.

Stage	Ingredient	Quantity	Method
1	spinach	2kg	Remove the stalks and wash the leaves in several changes of cold water. Drain and place in boiling salted water. Allow to boil steadily until just tender (approx. 5 mins.).
2			Refresh under cold water, drain in a colander and squeeze gently into balls to remove water.
3	butter garlic, crushed and finely chopped	75g 1–2 cloves	Heat the butter in a shallow pan, add the garlic and gently cook for a few seconds until transparent but not coloured.
4			Add the spinach, loosen quickly with a fork, season with salt and milled pepper and reheat quickly turning over and over to mix and heat sufficiently. Serve in vegetable dishes.

1456   Purée d'Epinards – Purée of Spinach

10 portions
45 mins.

Stage	Ingredient	Quantity	Method
1	spinach	2kg	Remove only the large coarse stalks and wash the remainder in several changes of cold water. Drain and place in boiling salted water. Allow to boil steadily until well cooked (approx. 10 mins.).
2			Refresh under cold water, drain in a colander and squeeze into balls to remove the water. Pass through the fine plate of the mincer or through a sieve.
3	butter	100g	Melt in a pan, add the spinach, season and reheat mixing with a wooden spoon. Serve dome-shaped in vegetable dishes. Smooth and decorate with a palette knife.

1457 Purée d'Epinards à la Crème – Creamed Purée of Spinach

Prepare Purée d'Épinards (1456) and reheat with the addition of 1dl of cream. Surround with a cordon of warmed cream when serving.

1458 Purée d'Epinards aux Croûtons – Purée of Spinach with Croûtons

Prepare Purée d'Epinards (1456) and reheat with the addition of 1dl of cream. Surround with a cordon of warmed cream and garnish with triangular Croûtons (26).

1459 Subrics d'Epinards

10 portions
45 mins.

Stage	Ingredient	Quantity	Method
1	spinach cooked to end of Stage 2 (1454) butter	1kg 50g	Heat the butter, add the spinach which has been roughly chopped and stir over heat so as to dry it out. Allow to slightly cool.
2	Béchamel (114) cream eggs egg yolks nutmeg	2dl 1dl 2 4 pinch	Add to the spinach, season and mix well together.
3	oil butter	1dl 75g	Heat in a sauté pan. Take tablespoons of the mixture and place in the hot fat without allowing them to touch. Turn over when coloured and colour the other sides. Continue as necessary to use the mixture.
4	Sauce Crème (143)	5dl	Drain the subrics well, arrange in vegetable dishes and serve accompanied with sauceboats of the sauce.

SPECIAL POINT
The use of 5dl of fairly thick pancake batter instead of the ingredients listed in Stage 2 also gives an excellent result.

FENOUIL – FENNEL

1460 Fenouil braisé – Braised Fennel

10 portions
2½ hours

Stage	Ingredient	Quantity	Method
1	fennel	5	Remove any outside blemished stalks, trim the root and cut off the stalks close to the bulbs. Wash thoroughly and place into boiling water to blanch for 10 mins. Refresh under cold water.

2	butter	30g	Butter a round braising pan and cover
	carrot ⎫ sliced	100g	the bottom with the carrot and onion.
	onion ⎭	100g	Arrange the fennel on top. Barely cover
	Fonds Blanc (93)	1½l	with stock and season. Cover with the
	bacon rind or		bacon, a greaseproof paper and a lid.
	trimmings	150g	Bring to the boil and cook gently in a
			moderate oven at 175°C until tender
			(1–1½ hours).
3			Remove the fennel, drain and cut in half
			lengthways. Dress neatly in dishes with a
			little of the cooking liquor.

1461 Fenouil braisé au Jus

Prepare Fenouil braisé (1460), coat with 2dl of Jus lié (113) and sprinkle with chopped parsley.

1462 Fenouil à la Crème – Braised Fennel with Cream

Prepare Fenouil braisé (1460), coat with 3dl of Sauce Crème (143) and sprinkle with chopped parsley.

1463 Fenouil poché, Sauce Hollandaise

10 portions
1¾ hours

Stage	Ingredient	Quantity	Method
1	fennel	5	Remove any outside blemished stalks, trim the root and cut off the stalks close to the bulbs. Wash thoroughly and place into boiling water to blanch for 10 mins. Refresh under cold water.
2	Fonds Blanc (93)	2 litres	Bring the stock to the boil then add the
	juice of lemon	1	fennel, juice, suet and bouquet garni.
	beef suet, chopped	250g	Season with a little salt and cover with a
	Bouquet Garni	1	piece of clean muslin or cloth. Simmer as gently as possible until tender, approx 1–1½ hours.
3	Sauce Hollandaise (157)	5dl	Drain the fennel well, remove any adhering suet and cut in half lengthways. Place in warm earthenware dishes and surround with a little of the strained cooking liquor. Send accompanied with the sauce.

FÈVES (DES MARAIS) – BROAD BEANS

1464 Fèves à l'Anglaise (Nature) – Boiled Broad Beans

10 portions
30 mins.

Stage	Ingredient	Quantity	Method
1	broad beans, shelled	1½kg	Wash and place in boiling salted water. Simmer gently until tender (approx. 20 mins.).
2			Drain and serve in vegetable dishes.

SPECIAL POINT

If the broad beans are large, it may be found that the skins are tough after cooking, in which case they should be removed before serving.

1465 Fèves au Beurre – Buttered Broad Beans

Prepare Fèves à l'Anglaise (1464) and toss in 50g of butter before serving.

1466 Fèves à la Crème – Broad Beans with Cream

Prepare Fèves à l'Anglaise (1464) and place in a sauteuse with 3dl of cream. Simmer until slightly reduced and correct seasoning. Serve sprinkled with chopped parsley.

HARICOTS BLANCS – HARICOT BEANS

1467 Haricots Blancs – Haricot Beans

10 portions
2 hours

Stage	Ingredient	Quantity	Method
1	haricot beans	750g	Wash well, place in a pan and cover with plenty of cold water. Bring to the boil and skim.
2	carrot, whole	100g	Add, season with a little salt and simmer gently until the beans are tender.
	Oignon Piqué (65)	1	
	Bouquet Garni	1	
	bacon bone or trimmings	150g	
3			Remove the flavourings. Drain the beans well and serve in vegetable dishes.

SPECIAL POINT

Good quality haricot beans do not require soaking before cooking.

1468 Haricots Blancs Persillés

Prepare Haricots Blancs (1467). Toss in 50g of butter and serve sprinkled with chopped parsley.

1469 Haricots Bretonne

10 portions
3 hours

Stage	Ingredient	Quantity	Method
1	haricot beans	750g	Wash well, place in a pan and cover with plenty of cold water. Bring to the boil and skim.
2	carrot, whole	100g	Add, season with salt and simmer gently for 1 hour.
	Oignon Piqué (65)	1	
	Bouquet Garni	1	
	bacon bone or		
	trimmings	150g	
3	Sauce Bretonne (207)	1 litre	Remove the flavourings, drain the beans well and place in a braising pan. Add the sauce, shake to mix in well and bring to the boil. Cover with the lid and place in the oven at approx. 150°C. Allow to cook gently until the beans are tender.
4	parsley, chopped		Serve in vegetable dishes sprinkled with chopped parsley.

1470 HARICOTS D'ESPAGNE – RUNNER BEANS

These can be prepared in any of the ways applicable to Haricots Verts. Because of their large size they should be cut into thinnish strips, approx. 7cm long.

1471 HARICOTS FLAGEOLETS – FLAGEOLET OR GREEN KIDNEY BEANS

These are obtainable fresh when in season but mostly in canned or dried form. If fresh, place to cook in boiling salted water. If dried, treat as for Haricots Blancs (1467); whether fresh, dried or canned, these beans may be served in any of the ways applicable to Haricots Blancs (1467–1469).

1472 HARICOTS DE LIMA – LIMA BEANS

These are mostly obtainable in dried form and may be cooked and served in any of the ways applicable to Haricots Blancs (1467). If fresh, place in boiling salted water and simmer gently until cooked and serve as for the dried ones. They are also obtainable in canned form.

1473 HARICOTS ROUGES – RED KIDNEY BEANS

These are mostly obtainable in dried form and may be cooked and served in any of the ways applicable to Haricots Blancs (1467). If fresh, place in boiling salted water and simmer gently until cooked and serve as for the dried ones. They are also obtainable in canned form.

HARICOTS VERTS – FRENCH BEANS

1474 Haricots Verts à l'Anglaise (Nature) – Boiled French Beans

10 portions
40 mins.

Stage	Ingredient	Quantity	Method
1	French beans	1¼kg	Remove the tops, tails and any strings. If small, leave whole; if large, cut in half lengthways and then across giving lengths of approx. 7cm.
2			Wash well, place into plenty of boiling salted water and cook briskly until just tender. Drain and serve in vegetable dishes.

1475 Haricots Verts au Beurre – Buttered French Beans

Prepare Haricots Verts à l'Anglaise and toss in 50g of melted butter. Season as necessary with salt and milled black pepper.

1476 Haricots Verts aux Amandes – French Beans with Almonds

10 portions
40 mins.

Stage	Ingredient	Quantity	Method
1	French beans	1¼kg	Prepare as Haricots Verts à l'Anglaise (1474).
2	almonds, skinned	100g	Cut the almonds in half lengthways.
	butter	50g	Heat the butter in a pan, add the almonds and fry gently until a light brown.
3	lemon juice	few drops	Add the well-drained beans, season as necessary with salt and milled pepper and toss over and over to mix. Finish with a few drops of lemon juice and the chopped parsley. Serve in vegetable dishes.
	parsley, chopped	1 tbsp	

1477 Haricots Verts à la Tourangelle

Prepare Haricots Verts à l'Anglaise (1474), drain well and mix with sufficient well-buttered Sauce Béchamel (114). Serve in vegetable dishes sprinkled with chopped parsley.

LAITUE – LETTUCE

1478 Laitue braisée – Braised Lettuce

10 portions
2 hours

Stage	Ingredient	Quantity	Method
1	lettuce	5	Remove any outer blemished leaves, trim the roots square and wash well. Place into boiling water and blanch for 5 mins. until the leaves are limp. Refresh, drain and press firmly to remove the water.
2	butter	30g	Butter a round braising pan and cover the bottom with the carrot and onion. Arrange the lettuce on top, barely cover with the stock and season. Cover with the bacon, a greaseproof paper and a lid. Bring to the boil and cook gently in a moderate oven at 175°C until tender (approx. ¾–1 hour).
	carrot ⎱ sliced	100g	
	onion ⎰	100g	
	Fonds Blanc (93)	1 litre	
	bacon rinds or		
	trimmings	150g	
3			Remove the lettuce, drain and cut in half lengthways. Fold the top half underneath and dress neatly in vegetable dishes.

1479 Laitue braisée au Jus

Prepare Laitue braisée (1478) and coat with 2dl of Jus lié (113) when serving.

1480 Laitue braisée aux Croûtons – Braised Lettuce with Croûtons

Prepare Laitue braisée (1478), coat with 2dl of Jus lié (113) and garnish with small Heart-shaped Croûtons (26) when serving.

1481 Laitue braisée à la Moelle – Braised Lettuce with Bone Marrow

Prepare Laitue braisée (1478), coat with 2dl of Sauce Moelle (120) and garnish with Heart-shaped Croûtons (26) when serving.

LENTILLES – LENTILS

1482 Lentilles au Beurre – Buttered Lentils

10 portions
1½–1¾ hours

Stage	Ingredient	Quantity	Method
1	lentils, brown	750g	Wash well and discard any which float.
2			Place in a pan with plenty of cold water. Bring to the boil and skim.

3	carrots, whole	100g	Add to the lentils, season lightly with salt
	Oignon Piqué (65)	1	and simmer gently until just tender,
	Bouquet Garni	1	approx. 1 hour. Take care not to
	bacon or ham bones	150g	overcook. Drain and remove the flavourings.
4	butter	50g	Melt in a sauteuse, add the lentils, season with salt and pepper and toss over to mix. Serve in vegetable dishes.

SPECIAL POINT

The brown and brownish-grey European lentils are best for serving as a vegetable as they do not cook to a purée as quickly as red varieties.

1483 Lentilles au Lard – Lentils with Bacon

Prepare Lentilles au Beurre (1482), mix with 150g small fried Lardons of bacon (51) and sprinkle with chopped parsley.

MAÏS – SWEETCORN

1484 Epis de Maïs – Corn on the Cob
10 portions
35 mins.

Stage	Ingredient	Quantity	Method
1	corn on the cob	10	Trim the stalks, wash and place in boiling salted water. Simmer gently until the grains of corn are tender (approx. 20 mins.).
2	Beurre Fondu (9)	4dl	Drain and remove the outer leaves and silky fibres. Turn back the remaining leaves and arrange the corn on folded serviettes on suitable dishes. Serve accompanied with a sauceboat of Beurre Fondu.

1485 Maïs à la Crème – Creamed Sweetcorn
10 portions
45 mins.

Stage	Ingredient	Quantity	Method
1	corn on the cob	10	Trim the stalks, wash and place in boiling salted water. Simmer gently until the grains of corn are tender (approx. 20 mins.).
2			Drain and remove all the leaves and silky fibres. Scrape off the grains of corn into a basin, using a spoon.

Stage	Ingredient	Quantity	Method
3	cream	3dl	Place the grains of corn in a sauteuse, add the cream and sugar and simmer until slightly reduced. Correct seasoning and serve in vegetable dishes.
	sugar	15g	

MARRONS – CHESTNUTS

1486 Marrons braisés – Braised Chestnuts

10 portions
1½ hours

Stage	Ingredient	Quantity	Method
1	chestnuts	1¼kg	Cut a horizontal slit in the shell on both sides of the chestnuts. Place into frying-baskets and dip in very hot fat until the shells split open. Alternatively, place on a tray with a little water and place under a very hot salamander or in a very hot oven, until they split open. Drain and remove the shells and inner skins carefully.
2	butter	50g	Butter a small braising pan and add the chestnuts. Add the stock and celery and season very lightly. Cover with a buttered greaseproof paper and lid. Bring to the boil and cook gently in a moderate oven at 175°C until tender (approx. ½ hour).
	Fonds Brun (97)	5dl	
	celery	1 stalk	
3	parsley, chopped		Remove the chestnuts and reduce the cooking liquor to a syrup. Replace the chestnuts and toss gently to glaze. Serve in vegetable dishes sprinkled with chopped parsley.

SPECIAL POINT

Great care must be taken to ensure that the chestnuts are not overcooked as they tend to break into pieces very quickly.

NAVETS – TURNIPS

1487 Navets au Beurre – Buttered Turnips

10 portions
45 mins.

Stage	Ingredient	Quantity	Method
1	turnips, peeled	1½kg	Cut the turnips into sections and turn barrel-shape approx. 3cm in length. Place in boiling salted water and simmer gently until just tender (approx. 5–8 mins.). Drain.

Stage	Ingredient	Quantity	Method
2	butter parsley, chopped	50g	Melt the butter in a sauteuse, add the turnips and toss gently to coat with the butter. Serve sprinkled with chopped parsley.

1488 Navets glacés – Glazed Turnips

10 portions
50 mins.

Stage	Ingredient	Quantity	Method
1	turnips, peeled	1½kg	Turn the turnips barrel-shape approx. 3cm in length.
2	butter sugar	50g 25g	Place the turnips in a pan and barely cover with water. Add the butter, sugar and a little salt.
3			Cover with a lid and allow to simmer gently until just cooked (approx. 5–8 mins.).
4	parsley, chopped		Remove the turnips and keep on one side. Reduce the cooking liquor to a syrup. Replace the turnips and toss gently to glaze. Serve in vegetable dishes, sprinkled with chopped parsley.

OIGNONS – ONIONS

1489 Oignon braisé – Braised Onion

10 portions
1½ hours

Stage	Ingredient	Quantity	Method
1	onions	10 × 120g	Peel without removing too much of the root end. Place into boiling water and blanch for 10 mins. Drain.
2	butter Fonds Blanc (93) bacon rind or trimmings	20g 1 litre 150g	Butter a braising pan, place in the onions, barely cover with stock and season. Cover with the bacon, a buttered greaseproof paper and a lid. Bring to the boil and cook gently in a moderate oven at 175°C until tender (approx. 1 hour).
3	Jus lié (113) parsley, chopped	2dl	Remove the onions, drain and arrange neatly in vegetable dishes. Coat with the jus lié and sprinkle with chopped parsley.

1490 Oignons frits à la Française – French Fried Onions

10 portions
30 mins.

Stage	Ingredient	Quantity	Method
1	onions	1kg	Peel and cut into rings, approx. 3mm thick. Separate the rings and remove the centre core.
2	milk flour	3dl	Pass the rings of onion through the milk and then through flour. Place in a frying-basket and shake off surplus flour.
3			Plunge into hot fat at 180°C and fry to a golden brown. Drain, lightly season with salt and serve on dish papers on flat dishes.

1491 Oignons sautés (Oignons Lyonnaise) – Fried Onions

10 portions
45 mins.

Stage	Ingredient	Quantity	Method
1	onions	1¼kg	Peel, cut in half vertically and remove the root. Slice finely along the grain of the onion.
2	butter	150g	Melt in a sauteuse, add the onions and season. Cook gently on the side of the stove tossing frequently until tender and golden brown. Serve in vegetable dishes.

1492 Petits Oignons glacés à Blanc – Small White-Glazed Onions

10 portions
1 hour

Stage	Ingredient	Quantity	Method
1	button onions	1¼kg	Peel without removing too much of the root.
2	butter	75g	Place the onions in a pan and barely cover with water. Add the butter and season with salt.
3			Cover with a lid and allow to simmer gently until tender.
4			Remove the onions then reduce the cooking liquor to a syrup. Replace the onions and toss to glaze.

SPECIAL POINT
Small white glazed onions are usually served as a garnish, e.g. Blanquette de Veau à l'Ancienne.

1493 Petits Oignons glacés à Brun – Small Brown-Glazed Onions

10 portions
1 hour

Stage	Ingredient	Quantity	Method
1	button onions	1¼kg	Peel without removing too much of the root.
2	butter	75g	Melt the butter in a sauteuse. Add the
	sugar	15g	onions, sugar and lightly season with salt.
3			Cover with a lid and cook slowly on the side of the stove tossing occasionally to ensure that the onions take on the required brown glaze at the same time as they finish cooking.

SPECIAL POINT
Small brown-glazed onions are usually served as a garnish, e.g. Boeuf braisé Bourgeoise.

OKRA – OKRA OR LADY'S FINGERS

1494 Okras braisés aux Tomates

10 portions
1 hour

Stage	Ingredient	Quantity	Method
1	okras, small and fresh	1¼kg	Carefully trim both ends of the okras without cutting into the seeds. Wash well and drain.
2	oil	½dl	Heat the oil in a shallow pan, add the
	onion ⎱ finely	150g	onion and garlic and cook until soft.
	garlic ⎰ chopped	1 clove	
3			Add the okras and sauté together for a few mins. to lightly colour.
4	Tomates Concassées (90)	450g	Add to the okras and season with salt and pepper. Bring to the boil. Cover
	juice of lemon	½	with a lid and cook in the oven at 190°C
	brown sugar	15g	for approx. 30 mins. or until tender.
5	parsley, chopped		Serve sprinkled with chopped parsley.

PANAIS – PARSNIPS

1495 Panais au Beurre – Buttered Parsnips

10 portions
45 mins.

Stage	Ingredient	Quantity	Method
1	parsnips, peeled	1½kg ·	Cut the parsnips into sections and turn them barrel-shape approx. 5cm in length. Place in boiling salted water and simmer gently until tender (approx. 12 mins.). Drain.
2	butter	50g	Melt in a sauteuse, add the parsnips and toss over to coat with the butter.

1496 Panais à la Crème – Creamed Parsnips

Prepare as Panais au Beurre (1495). Add 3dl double cream and simmer gently to lightly thicken. Adjust the seasoning as necessary.

1497 Panais Persillés – Parslied Parsnips

Prepare Panais au Beurre (1495) and sprinkle with chopped parsley when serving.

1498 PETITS POIS – PEAS

The cooking times in the following recipes for peas are given on the assumption that fresh peas are to be used. Frozen peas, however, are more commonly available at all times of the year and are widely used in the catering industry. If they are to be used for these recipes it remains only to take account of the size and quality of the frozen peas and to adjust cooking times accordingly.

1499 Petits Pois à l'Anglaise – Boiled Peas

10 portions
20 mins.

Stage	Ingredient	Quantity	Method
1	peas, shelled	1kg	Wash and place in plenty of boiling salted water. Simmer gently until tender (approx. 10–15 mins.).
2			Drain and serve in a vegetable dish.

1500 Petits Pois au Beurre – Buttered Peas

Prepare Petits Pois à l'Anglaise (1499) and toss in 50g of butter with a pinch of sugar.

1501 Petits Pois Bonne Femme

10 portions
1¼ hours

Stage	Ingredient	Quantity	Method
1	streaky bacon	150g	Cut into small Lardons (51), cover with cold water and blanch for 2 mins. Refresh, drain and place in a pan.

2	button onions	20	Add the onions and peas to the lardons.
	peas, shelled	800g	Barely cover with stock, season, bring to
	Fonds Blanc (93)	1 litre	the boil, cover with a lid and simmer
			gently until all the ingredients are
			tender.
3	butter⎱ into Beurre	60g	Add to the peas while still simmering
	flour ⎰ Manié (11)	30g	and shake the pan until the liquid
			thickens. Correct the seasoning and
			serve in vegetable dishes.

1502 Petits Pois à la Flamande

Toss together equal quantity of Carottes glacées (1400) and Petits Pois à l'Anglaise (1499) and serve in vegetable dishes.

1503 Petits Pois à la Française

10 portions
50 mins.

Stage	Ingredient	Quantity	Method
1	button onions	20	Place all the ingredients in a pan.
	lettuce, coarsely		
	shredded	2	
	peas, shelled	850g	
	butter	75g	
	sugar	10g	
2	Fonds Blanc (93)	2dl	Add the stock, season and cover with a tight-fitting lid and cook gently on the side of the stove until tender, approx. 35 mins. Shake the pan occasionally.
3	butter	75g	When ready, shake in the butter piece by piece to effect a liaison and to thicken the liquid. Adjust the seasoning as necessary and serve in vegetable dishes.

SPECIAL POINT

If wished, a little flour may be mixed with the butter at Stage 3 then added and simmered for a few seconds.

1504 Petits Pois à la Menthe

10 portions
25 mins.

Stage	Ingredient	Quantity	Method
1	mint	½ bunch	Remove the leaves from the stalks and place into boiling water for 30 seconds to blanch. Refresh and keep on one side.
2	peas	1kg	Wash, place in plenty of boiling salted water together with the mint stalks tied in a bunch. Simmer gently until tender (approx. 10–15 mins.).

| 3 | butter | 50g | Drain the peas and discard the stalks. |
| | sugar | pinch | Melt the butter in a sauteuse, add the peas and a pinch of sugar and toss over to mix. Serve in vegetable dishes garnished with the blanched mint leaves. |

PIMENT DOUX – PIMENTO

1505 Piment farci – Stuffed Pimento

10 portions
50 mins.

Stage	Ingredient	Quantity	Method
1	pimentos, medium-sized, skinned (78)	10	Cut off the tops and reserve as lids. Scoop out the seeds.
2	Riz Pilaff (522), half-cooked	10 portions	Fill into the prepared pimentos and replace the tops.
3	butter	50g	Butter a braising pan and cover the bottom with the sliced vegetables.
	onion ⎫	75g	
	carrots ⎬ sliced	75g	Arrange the pimentos on top standing straight and close together; add the stock. Cover with a buttered greaseproof paper and lid and cook in a moderate oven at 175°C for approx. 45 mins. Remove and drain.
	Fonds Blanc (93)	3dl	
4	Demi-glace	3dl	Arrange the pimentos in suitable dishes and surround with the sauce.

SPECIAL POINT
Duxelles or other kinds of vegetable stuffings may be used.

1506 POIS MANGE-TOUT – MANGE-TOUT PEAS

Mange-tout peas, known also as sugar peas, are a variety of pea with a tender pod free of the parchment-like skin found in the common garden peas. Consequently it is eaten whole after removing the top and tail.

1507 Pois Mange-tout Nature – Plain Boiled Mange-tout Peas

10 portions
15 mins.

Stage	Ingredient	Quantity	Method
1	mange-tout peas	1¼kg	Remove the tops and tails. Wash the pods well.
2			Place into plenty of boiling salted water and cook briskly until just cooked but still crisp, approx. 4–5 mins. Drain and serve in vegetable dishes.

1508 Pois Mange-tout au Beurre – Buttered Mange-tout Peas

Prepare Mange-tout Nature (1507) and toss in 50g of butter before serving.

1509 Pois Mange-tout à l'Etuvée

10 portions
25 mins.

Stage	Ingredient	Quantity	Method
1	mange-tout peas	1¼kg	Remove the tops and tails and wash the pods well then place immediately into a clean pan. There should be enough water adhering to the pods to effect their proper cooking.
2	butter sugar salt	75g 15g	Add the butter, sugar and a little salt and cover with a tight-fitting lid. Cook fairly quickly on top of the stove, shaking now and again to mix. When just tender, serve in vegetable dishes.

POIREAU – LEEK

1510 Poireau braisé – Braised Leek

10 portions
2 hours

Stage	Ingredient	Quantity	Method
1	leeks, medium	10 × 120g	Remove any outer blemished leaves and trim the roots clean. Cut off part of the green top leaving the leeks approx. 18cm long. Make a cross-cut upwards through the top third of the leeks. Wash well under running cold water.
2	butter Fonds Blanc (93) bacon rind or trimmings	30g 1 litre 150g	Tie the leeks into bundles and place in a buttered braising pan. Barely cover with the stock and season. Cover with the bacon rind, a buttered greaseproof paper and lid. Bring to the boil and cook gently in a moderate oven at 175°C for approx. 1 hour.
3			Remove the leeks, drain and discard the string. Fold the top half underneath and dress neatly in vegetable dishes with a little of the cooking liquor.

1511 Poireau braisé au Jus

Prepare Poireau braisé (1510), coat with 2dl of Jus lié (113) and sprinkle with chopped parsley.

1512 RUTABAGA – SWEDE

Swedes may be cooked and served in either of the ways applicable to turnips.

SALSIFIS – SALSIFY

1513 Salsifis au Beurre – Buttered Salsify

10 portions
45 mins.

Stage	Ingredient	Quantity	Method
1	salsify	1¼kg	Wash, peel and cut into 5cm lengths and
	juice of lemon	2	place immediately into water with the lemon juice to prevent discolouration.
2	Blanc (15)	4 litres	Place the salsify into boiling blanc, cover with a piece of muslin and simmer gently until tender (10–15 mins.). Drain well.
3	butter	75g	Melt the butter in a sauteuse, add the salsify and toss over to coat with the butter. Serve in vegetable dishes.

1514 Salsifis à la Crème – Creamed Salsify

Prepare Salsifis (1513) to the end of Stage 2 and mix gently with 3dl of Sauce Crème (143). Serve in vegetable dishes.

1515 Salsifis frits – Fried Salsify

Prepare Salsifis (1513) to the end of Stage 2. Marinate with a little oil, lemon juice, chopped parsley and salt and pepper for 25–30 mins. Pass through flour and frying batter (76). Fry in deep fat at approx. 175°C until golden brown. Drain and dress on dish papers on suitable dishes garnished with picked or fried parsley.

1516 Salsifis Persillés – Parslied Salsify

Prepare Salsifis au Beurre (1513) and sprinkle with chopped parsley when serving.

1517 Salsifis sautés

Prepare Salsifis (1513) to the end of Stage 2, sauté in 100g of butter until brown and serve in vegetable dishes.

TOMATES – TOMATOES

1518 Tomates farcies – Stuffed Tomatoes

10 portions
1 hour

Stage	Ingredient	Quantity	Method
1	tomatoes, medium	20	Wash and remove the eyes of the tomatoes. Cut off the top quarter and

keep on one side. Remove the seeds carefully using a small spoon. Place the tomatoes on a buttered grilling tray and season the insides.

2	butter
	onions, finely
	    chopped
	mushrooms, finely
	    chopped
		100g
		
		100g
		
		500g
			Melt the butter in a sauteuse, add the onions and cook without colour. Add the mushrooms, season and cook until almost dry.

3	white wine, dry Demi-glace (112) breadcrumbs parsley, chopped	1dl 1dl 200g 1 tbsp	Add the wine and reduce by two-thirds. Add the demi-glace and reduce until the mixture is fairly stiff. Add sufficient breadcrumbs to produce a piping consistency. Adjust the seasoning and mix in the chopped parsley.
4			Place the mixture into a piping bag with a star tube and fill the tomatoes well. Place the cut tops back on the tomatoes at an angle so that some of the stuffing is still visible.
5	butter, melted parsley, picked	50g	Brush the tops with butter and cook the tomatoes in a moderate oven at 175°C for 5–6 mins. Dress in vegetable dishes garnished with picked parsley.

1519 Tomates farcies Provençale

10 portions
50 mins.

Stage	Ingredient	Quantity	Method
1	tomatoes, large	10	Wash and remove the eyes of the tomatoes. Cut in half horizontally and remove the seeds carefully with a small spoon. Place on an oiled tray and season the insides.

2	oil
	onions, finely
	    chopped
	garlic, finely
	    chopped
	breadcrumbs
	parsley, chopped
		3dl
		
		100g
		
		2 cloves
		500g
		2 tbsps
			Heat the oil in a sauteuse, add the onions and garlic and cook gently without colour. Remove from the stove and add the breadcrumbs and chopped parsley. Season and mix in well.

3	oil parsley, picked	½dl	Fill the tomatoes dome-shaped with the mixture. Sprinkle with oil and place the tray in a fairly hot oven at 185°C to cook and gratinate the stuffing (5–6 mins.). Dress in vegetable dishes and garnish with picked parsley.

1520 Tomates grillées – Grilled Tomatoes

10 portions
20 mins.

Stage	Ingredient	Quantity	Method
1	tomatoes, medium	20	Wash and remove the eyes of the tomatoes. Place on a buttered grilling tray with the eye side downwards. Cut a shallow incision in the form of a cross on the top.
2	butter	25g	Brush with melted butter and season.
	parsley, picked		Grill gently under a moderately hot salamander until just soft. Dress in vegetable dishes and garnish with picked parsley.

TOPINAMBOURS – JERUSALEM ARTICHOKES

1521 Topinambours Nature – Boiled Jerusalem Artichokes

10 portions
1 hour

Stage	Ingredient	Quantity	Method
1	Jerusalem artichokes	2kg	Wash, peel, trim to an even shape and
	juice of lemon	2	place into water with the lemon juice to prevent their discolouring.
2	Blanc (15)	3 litres	Place the artichokes into the boiling blanc, cover with a piece of muslin and simmer gently until just tender (approx. 10–15 mins.). Drain well and serve in vegetable dishes.

1522 Topinambours à la Crème – Creamed Jerusalem Artichokes

Prepare Topinambours Nature (1521) and mix gently with 3dl of fairly thin Sauce Creme (143). Serve in vegetable dishes.

1523 Topinambours Persillés – Parslied Jerusalem Artichokes

Prepare Topinambours Nature (1521). Toss gently in 50g of melted butter and serve in vegetable dishes sprinkled with chopped parsley.

—————MIXED VEGETABLE DISHES—————

As the title of this section implies, the following vegetable dishes generally utilise two or more vegetables in their preparation; others use more involved preparations which in many cases make them more suitable for serving as dishes in their own right or as vegetarian dishes.

1524 Beignets de Légumes – Vegetable Fritters

This style of preparation involves the deep frying of vegetables dipped in batter. Most kinds of vegetable are suitable and, according to the particular quality of the vegetable, can be finished from either the raw, partly-cooked or cooked state. In most cases they need to be cut or sectioned to a smaller size so as to maintain a reasonable proportion between a softish centre and a crisp outer coating. Marinating for a short time with a little lemon juice, parsley and salt and pepper, helps to improve the flavour and the lemon juice assists in counteracting the oily nature of the process. The frying batter should not be too thick and should be such that it cooks crisply and maintains its crispness.

The following lists the more suitable items together with an outline of their preparation:

Prepared from the raw state: ½cm slices of courgette or aubergine; courgette flowers; whole mushrooms; skinned cherry tomatoes.

Sprinkle first with a little lemon juice, salt and pepper and leave no longer than 5 mins., then lightly flour, pass through batter (76) and deep fry in hot oil at approx. 175°C until crisp and golden brown.

Prepared from the parcooked state: small tender globe artichokes, either whole or cut in half; artichoke bottoms halved or quartered; small Jerusalem artichokes; French beans in small bunches; cauliflower florets; sections of fennel; small baby maize; sections of parsnips; small packets of spinach leaves; whole Brussels sprouts; sections of salsify; pieces of seakale.

All the above should be parcooked as appropriate to their type, until near being cooked but firm and easy to handle. Some, like globe artichokes, French beans, baby maize and salsify, can be used from the cooked state. Make sure that all items are well-drained. Marinate for 30 mins. with a little oil, lemon juice, salt and milled pepper, plus a little chopped parsley for white-coloured items. Drain well, pass through flour then batter and deep fry at 175°C until crisp and golden brown.

For service, drain all items well and present on dish papers on flat dishes. Suitable sauces can be served as an accompaniment, e.g. Coulis de Tomates (179) or Sweet and Sour Sauce (213). Segments of lemon may be offered.

SPECIAL POINTS
a) Beignets of vegetables may be served as a single accompanying vegetable or as a mixture of different vegetables as a dish in its own right.
b) The name of single vegetable fritters should be given in the menu title, e.g. Beignets de Chou-fleur, Beignets de Fenouil, Beignets de Salsifis and so on. If mixed vegetables, they can be designated as Beignets de Légumes panachés or mixtes.

1525 Bouquetière de Légumes

This is a selection of vegetables of contrasting types, colours and textures arranged neatly in separate piles (Bouquets) or rows on a suitable dish. It may be served as a selection for the customer to choose from or may be sufficient for some of each kind to be served to each customer.

The vegetable may be boiled or braised but fried, puréed or stewed items should not be included.

The following are the traditional components when served as a classical garnish: Carottes glacées, Navets glacés, Haricots Verts au Beurre, Petits Pois au Beurre, Pommes Château, and Chou-fleur Nature accompanied with Sauce Hollandaise. In addition to these, the contemporary service of a Bouquetière de Légumes can also include such things as buttered artichoke bottoms, Brussels sprouts, courgettes and baby sweetcorn, braised celery, leeks and fennel, and whole small tomatoes, skinned and lightly cooked in the oven with a little butter.

1526 Croquettes or Côtelettes de Légumes

10 portions
30 mins.

Stage	Ingredient		Quantity	Method
1	carrots	⎫	200g	Blanch all these vegetables in boiling
	cauliflower	roughly	150g	salted water for 7–8 mins. until almost
	celery heart	cut	100g	cooked. Drain well, cool and chop fairly
	French beans	⎭	150g	small.
2	butter		75g	Heat the butter in a large shallow pan.
	onion		75g	Add the onion and garlic and cook
	garlic, finely chopped		½ clove	without colour then add the mushrooms
	mushrooms		200g	and cook until almost dry.
3				Add the chopped vegetables, season lightly, mix together and cook slowly under cover until tender and dry.
4	Pommes Duchesse mixture (1560), stiff		450g	Add the potatoes and chopped herbs to the vegetables, season with salt and pepper and allow to cool.
	parsley, chopped		1 tbsp	
	coriander leaves, chopped		1 tbsp	
5	flour	⎫		Divide the mixture into 20 pieces and
	eggwash	for crumbing		mould into croquettes or cutlet shapes
	breadcrumbs	⎭		with flour then paner à l'Anglaise (72).
6	Sauce Tomate (118) or Sauce Smitaine (212)		5dl	Deep fry in hot oil at 175°C until crisp and golden brown. Drain well and serve on dish papers on flat dishes. Send accompanied with the sauce.

1527 Fleurs de Courgettes farcies – Stuffed Baby Marrow Flowers

4 portions
30 mins.

Stage	Ingredient	Quantity	Method
1	courgette flowers with the baby marrows attached	12	Open the petals wide, wash carefully and dry. Lightly season inside. Trim the stalk ends of the baby marrows.
2	Farce Mousseline de Volaille (39)	250g	Half fill each flower with the farce using a small plain piping tube and bag, then close the petals over to completely enclose the stuffing.

3			Arrange in a buttered colander or wicker steaming-sieve and cover with a round of buttered greaseproof paper and lid and steam for approx. 10 mins. To test, the stuffed flowers should feel firm and resilient.
4	Sauce au Beurre Blanc (164)	2½dl	Cover the bottoms of four hot plates or a dish with a little of the sauce and arrange the stuffed courgette flowers on top, three to the portion. Place a leaf of chervil on each flower and send the rest of the sauce separately.
	chervil leaves, blanched	24	

SPECIAL POINT

The baby marrows may be cut three or four times along the length almost to the flower and then fanned open.

1528 Feuilles de Vigne farcies – Stuffed Vine Leaves or Dolmas

10 portions
1¼ hours

Stage	Ingredient	Quantity	Method
1	vine leaves	30	Remove the stalks from the leaves. Place the leaves into a pan of boiling salted water, blanch for 3–4 mins., refresh, drain and dry.
2	Duxelles (29)	300g	Place in a basin, season and mix
	Riz Pilaff (522)	5 portions	together.
	Ricotta cheese or similar	75g	
	ground coriander	pinch	
	egg yolks	2	
3			Lay out the leaves, season and place a cylinder-shaped piece of the stuffing on each. Fold the leaves over to enclose the filling.
4	butter	30g	Butter a suitably-sized shallow pan and cover the bottom with the carrot and onion. Place the vine leaves close together on top with the joins underneath. Add the stock, lightly season and cover with the fat and a buttered greaseproof paper. Cover with the lid. Braise gently at 175°C for approx. 45 mins.
	carrot ⎱ finely	100g	
	onion ⎰ sliced	100g	
	Fonds Blanc (93)	5dl	
	slices of fat bacon	120g	
5			Remove the stuffed leaves and drain. Arrange the stuffed leaves in suitable dishes, cover and keep warm.

| 6 | egg yolks | 3 | Strain the cooking liquid and reduce by one-third. Grate the rind and squeeze the juice from the lemon. Mix with the yolks and gradually add the cooking liquid, mixing well. Reheat but do not boil, correct the seasoning and serve with the vine leaves. |
| | lemon | 1 | |

SPECIAL POINTS
a) If using salted vine leaves, soak them in cold water for 15 mins. before blanching.
b) Other kinds of fillings of minced meat or poultry may also be used.

1529 Gratin Languedocienne

10 portions
1 hour

Stage	Ingredient	Quantity	Method
1	aubergines	3	Peel the aubergines and cut into 3mm slices. Season, pass through flour and sauté quickly in the hot oil until coloured on both sides. Drain well.
	flour		
	oil, olive	2dl	
2	tomatoes, large red	1kg	Blanch, skin, cut into quarters and discard the seeds. Season and sauté quickly in the same oil. Drain off surplus oil.
3	fresh basil leaves } roughly chopped	1 tbsp	Fill shallow dishes with alternate layers of the aubergines and tomatoes, sprinkling a little of each herb between each layer. Finish with a layer of tomatoes.
	fresh thyme leaves	1 tbsp	
4	Parmesan, grated	50g	Sprinkle the Parmesan and breadcrumbs over the vegetables. Sprinkle with oil and gratinate in a hot oven for approx. 20 mins.
	breadcrumbs, white	50g	
	oil, olive	½dl	

1530 Haricots panachés au Beurre – Buttered Mixed Beans

This can be a selection of mixed, boiled beans, tossed together in a little butter, the more usual combination being equal quantities of French beans (1474) and green kidney beans (flageolets) (1471). Other combinations to include red kidney beans, butter beans, haricots beans, and Lima beans are all permissible.

1531 Jardinière de Légumes

10 portions
45 mins.

Stage	Ingredient	Quantity	Method
1	carrots, peeled	350g	Cut the carrots and turnips into batons approx. 2cm long × 4mm × 4mm. Remove the tops, tails and any strings from the beans and cut into diamond-shaped pieces.
	turnips, peeled	350g	
	peas	250g	
	French beans	250g	

| 2 | | | Cook each vegetable separately in boiling salted water, drain and mix together lightly. |
| 3 | butter | 50g | Melt the butter in a pan, add the vegetables, season if necessary and toss over to mix. |

1532 Macédoine de Légumes

Prepare as Jardinière de Légumes (1531) but cut the carrots and turnips into ³⁄₄cm dice.

SPECIAL POINT

The vegetables for Jardinière or Macédoine de Légumes may be cooked in a staggered fashion in one pan instead of separate pans in the following manner: First place the carrots in boiling salted water and cook for approx. 5 mins. Then add the beans and peas and cook for a further 5 mins. Lastly, add the turnips. A further 4–5 mins. will complete the final cooking of all the vegetables.

A little experience is necessary, however, for judging the relative length of cooking time needed. What is essential is that the vegetables must not be overcooked and that there is an equal firmness in all of them.

1533 Peperonata – Stewed Pimentos and Tomatoes 10 portions
2 hours

Stage	Ingredient	Quantity	Method
1	pimentos, red and yellow, skinned	1kg	Remove the stems and seeds. Cut into approx. 2cm squares.
2	oil	1½dl	Heat the oil in a suitable pan. Add the onion and cook for a few mins. without colour then add the pimentos and garlic and sauté together for a few mins.
	onion, finely chopped	350g	
	garlic, finely chopped	2 cloves	
3	Tomates Concassées (90)	500g	Add to the onion and pimento and mix in. Season well, cover tightly with a lid and cook gently in the oven at 175°C for approx. 1 hour.
	sugar	15g	
4	vinegar, wine	½dl	Sprinkle over the vegetables, return to the oven and continue to cook for a further 30 mins. until the consistency is fairly stiff.
5	parsley, chopped		Serve sprinkled with chopped parsley.

1534 Purées of Vegetables

Purées of fresh or dried vegetables can be served as vegetables in their own right or can be used to garnish other prepared dishes; for example, braised ham can be served with a garnish of spinach purée and could be designated on the menu as Jambon braisé aux Epinards.

To prepare: plain boil the vegetables according to type, drain well then pass through a fine sieve or machine for puréeing. Reheat in a saucepan and dry out any excess moisture then finish with butter and seasoning as necessary. The texture and quality of all purées can be improved with the addition of a little cream and/or Béchamel. In this case, when served as a vegetable, the menu title can take the added suffix 'à la Crème', e.g. Purée de Carottes à la Crème, or Purée de Flageolets à la Crème.

NOTE
Turnips and cauliflower have a high water content and, even when thoroughly drained before passing, still tend to be watery in consistency afterwards. The addition of up to 25% by volume of dry mashed potato will give the desired smooth texture, without altering the particular flavour.

Purées can be served under their own name, e.g. Purée d'Epinards, Purée de Navets and so on, but they can also be served under a descriptive title which implies the name of the vegetable by association. The following list is not comprehensive but gives those most commonly used:

Name of purée	Ingredient
Argenteuil	Asparagus
Bruxelloise	Brussels sprouts
Clamart	Peas
Condé	Red kidney beans
Crécy	Carrots
Dubarry	Cauliflower
Esaü	Lentils
Favorite	French beans
Florentine	Spinach
Freneuse	Turnips
Musard	Flageolet beans
Soissonaise	Haricot beans

1535 Ratatouille Provençale

10 portions
1½ hours

Stage	Ingredient	Quantity	Method
1	oil, olive	½dl	Heat the oil in a casserole, add the onions and cook for a few mins. without colour.
	onions, finely sliced	350g	
2	pimentos, red, seeded and cut in coarse short julienne	4	Add the pimentos and cook for a few mins. then add the tomatoes and garlic. Mix together and keep on one side.
	Tomates Concassées (90)	500g	
	garlic, finely chopped	2 cloves	
3	aubergines, peeled	4	Cut the aubergines into approx. 1½cm cubes and the courgettes into ½cm-round slices.
	courgettes	500g	

4	oil, olive	1½dl	Heat the oil in a frying-pan, add the aubergines, season lightly and sauté quickly to lightly colour. Drain and add to the tomato mixture. Use the same oil and repeat for the courgettes.
5	basil leaves, chopped	1 tbsp	Add to the mixture and season with salt and milled pepper. Cover with a lid, cook in a moderate oven at 175°C for approx. 1 hour. Remove the bouquet garni and serve as required.
	Bouquet Garni	1	
	sugar	5g	

1536 Stir-Fried Vegetables

4 portions
20 mins.

Stage	Ingredient	Quantity	Method
1	spring onions	100g	Wash, drain and dry all the vegetables. Cut the vegetables in the following manner and keep separate. Onions and carrots: cut across and on the slant, approx. 3mm thick. Celery: cut across the stalks approx. 3mm thick. Mange-tout peas: top and tail then cut into two or three pieces diagonally. Mushrooms: cut in quarters.
	young carrots, peeled	125g	
	celery stalks, tender	125g	
	mange-tout peas	125g	
	button mushrooms	125g	
2	chicken stock (96)	1dl	Place in a basin, mix together and reserve for use.
	soy sauce	1 tbsp	
	tomato purée	1 tsp	
	cornflour	½ tsp	
	sugar	pinch	
3	oil	¾dl	Heat the oil in a wok or heavy frying-pan with curved sides. Add the garlic, fry until light brown then remove.
	garlic, lightly bruised	1 clove	
4			Add the onions first and stir-fry for 30 seconds, add the carrots, celery and mange-tout peas at 30-second intervals and finally the mushrooms. Stir-fry continuously and adjust the heat as necessary for a further 1 min. or so.
5	five spice powder	pinch	Season with salt and a pinch of five spice powder. Toss over to mix then quickly stir in the reserved flavoured stock and add to the vegetables. Toss over to mix whilst bringing to the boil and thickening. Simmer gently for 2 mins. The vegetables should all retain their colour and crispness. Serve in dishes as required.

SPECIAL POINT

Other raw vegetables singly or in combination can be used, always making sure that they are stir-fried in order of relative hardness and time required to cook. Suitable vegetables are artichoke bottoms, broccoli, cauliflower, French beans, courgettes, onions, cabbage, Chinese leaves, turnips, bamboo shoots, baby sweetcorn etc.

1537 Succotash

For ten portions, mix together 500g cooked sweetcorn grains (1485) and 500g cooked Lima beans with 2dl Béchamel and ½dl double cream. Add a little sugar, season and simmer gently for a few mins. Serve in dishes as required.

18
Potatoes

Of all vegetables, the so-called humble potato must surely enjoy pride of place for its wide variety of recipes and presentations. Its particular qualities of taste and texture lend themselves to an almost infinite number of combinations with other commodities, and thus it can make an important contribution to almost all sections of the menu. For these reasons alone it is felt that the potato warrants a chapter by itself.

Potatoes contain good nutritional value, they are rich in vitamin C and mineral salts and add bulk and fibre to the diet. Their absence from the menu would leave it in a much diminished form both from the point of variety and nutritional balance. But like all valuable commodities, the potato deserves care in handling; a high degree of knowledge and skill is essential for realising its full possibilities.

VARIETIES

In the last twenty years or so the number of different varieties of potato available to the catering industry has risen markedly. Where once a few sometimes indeterminate varieties were available, now the caterer and chef have recourse to a dozen or more named varieties on a local basis, each having its own particular characteristics and cooking qualities. A good knowledge of their names and their best cooking methods is of the utmost value in selection and ordering for the particular requirements of the menu.

Potatoes are grown and available in the United Kingdom in two main groups, early and second early potatoes from late May to August, and maincrop potatoes from September to May.

In addition, the early crops are supplemented with imported new potatoes which fill the gap between the end of the maincrop varieties and the first of the new potatoes. Recipes which call for firm waxy potatoes, e.g. for salads and certain types of potato cooked in the oven with liquid, are well-served by early British varieties but later in the season this demand can also be met by certain varieties of imported potatoes from the continent such as Linzer Delikatess and Dutch Bintjes.

The following table lists a number of important varieties together with their range of uses where applicable.

POTATO VARIETIES AND USES

Name	Description	Uses
(Early and Second Early Varieties)		
ALCAMARIA	Nice long oval shape; yellow waxy flesh	Boiling, braising, salads.
ESTIMA	Oval shape; firm yellowish flesh	Boiling, baking, braising, deep frying.
HOME GUARD	Roundish oval shape; white flesh	Good for boiling and salads.
PENTLAND JAVELIN	Short oval shape; white waxy flesh	Good for boiling and salads.
ULSTER SCEPTRE	Long oval shape; white and very waxy flesh	Good for boiling, roasting, deep frying.
WILJA	Long oval shape; yellow firm flesh	Boiling, roasting, deep frying.
(Maincrop Varieties)		
CARA	Round oval shape; creamy soft flesh	Baking, boiling, mashing, roasting, deep frying.
DESIREE	Oval and red-skinned; yellowish firm flesh	All-purpose.
KING EDWARD	Oval shape; creamy floury texture	All-purpose.
MARIS PIPER	Oval shape; creamy floury texture	All-purpose
PENTLAND DELL	Long oval shape; whitish floury texture	Baking, roasting, deep frying.
ROMANO	Oval and pink-skinned; creamy and waxy texture	Baking, boiling, roasting.

Potatoes are also available in frozen, canned, powdered, and dehydrated convenience forms.

————QUALITY AND SELECTION————

As with all commodities, potatoes should be purchased from a reputable supplier, able to offer the best quality and any particular varieties and sizes required by the establishment.

In assessing quality, look for clean, firm and well-shaped potatoes, free from damage and blemishes and showing no signs of disease, green skin, sprouting or rotting. There should be no excessive amounts of soil.

New potatoes particularly should be firm and crisp and of an even-graded size; the skin should come off easily when rubbed or scraped. Special attention is needed towards the end of the maincrop season when wrinkling of the skin and sprouting become prevalent; this is usually a sign of poor storage at main distribution points.

STORAGE

New potatoes should be purchased on a day-to-day basis where possible as they tend to deteriorate very quickly if stored for any length of time.

Maincrop potatoes can be stored successfully for up to two weeks or more providing that the storage qualities are ideal. This means, firstly, good-quality potatoes correctly bagged in brown paper sacks, not plastic, and then keeping them on slats in an area which is dark, cool, dry and with a good circulation of air. They should not be adjacent to any strong-smelling item and they should be used in rotation. Dampness can lead to rotting, warmth can start sprouting and exposure to daylight can start them greening; this last can be harmful if eaten.

If covered with clean water in a container, peeled potatoes can be held in a refrigerator overnight but prolonged storage in this state is not to be recommended; it can alter the flavour of the potato and lead to loss of nutrients. On no account should peeled potatoes be left covered with water in a warm place; this can start them fermenting even after three or four hours.

PREPARATION

New Potatoes
For the very early and expensive varieties, careful washing and scraping is without doubt the best method of preparing them for boiling; it retains the maximum of flavour and nutritional quality. If required peeled, careful hand peeling is the best method. Machine peeling is wasteful and damaging to the potato; it is far better to cook them in their skins and then skin them or serve as they are.

Maincrop potatoes
Wash them well to remove any grit before hand peeling with a potato peeler, then remove any eyes or discolouration and place into cold water; use as soon as possible. For machine peeling, do not overload the machine as this will lead to uneven peeling and flattening of the potatoes; on the other hand if there are too few potatoes in the machine these will become badly bruised and damaged. Make sure that it is timed correctly so as to avoid unnecessary loss. Remove any eyes or blemishes then place the potatoes in cold water for use as required.

Trimming and shaping
Where called for, potatoes, especially maincrop, are trimmed or cut into various regular shapes which can result in a certain quantity of trimmings. Expertise in the handling of knives and tools is a requisite for keeping the amount of these trimmings to a minimum. It is possible to utilise them for such things as potato soup but it is not recommended that trimmings be used to bulk up mashed potatoes; this invariably gives a watery and gluey result.

COOKING METHODS

In one form or another most of the standard methods of cooking may be applied to potatoes; in many cases finished potato dishes involve the combination of more than one method.

Boiling

For potatoes, boiling is one of the most widely-used and versatile preparations. Not only are boiled potatoes used as an accompanying vegetable, but also as a garnish and, when cold, as a component of salads and for shallow frying. In addition, boiled potatoes are frequently processed into a purée and subsequently into a wide range of excellent deep-fried dishes, e.g. Pommes Croquettes, Pommes Dauphine, etc.

For new potatoes: wash the potatoes well and either scrape or leave in their skins. Place into boiling salted water. The water should be sufficient to cover them well and to allow for evaporation. Bring to the boil and skim as necessary then allow to simmer very gently until cooked. The time depends on size but taken on average for small new potatoes, 18–20 mins. The larger the potato the longer the cooking time. To test for being cooked, either pierce with a small thin knife which should enter easily or take one potato and press from the sides; it will give easily if cooked.

Draining and serving immediately is the ideal, but the exigencies of service to the customer demand speed and organisation. For this reason new potatoes may be left in their cooking liquid and kept hot for the period of the service but prolonged immersion inevitably leads to an increase of moisture in the potatoes. If the potatoes have been boiled in their skins, drain and peel them then replace in hot salted water for service. In all cases, the potatoes should be thoroughly drained; there should be no evidence of water in the service dish.

For old and maincrop potatoes: it is essential to select potatoes known to keep firm when boiled, not prone to discolouration and of an even shape and size. After washing and peeling the potatoes should be cut to an even small size or trimmed barrel-shape, approx. 5cm in length, then placed to cook in cold salted water. After bringing to the boil the procedures are the same as for new potatoes.

For mashed potatoes and purées: again, the use of the correct potato for the job is of prime importance. Select potatoes of a firm but floury texture and not prone to discolouration. Cut them to an even size then boil as above but taking care that they are properly cooked with no hard centres. Drain them well and dry to remove any excess moisture on the stove, then pass quickly and firmly through a medium sieve or through a potato puréeing machine. It is very important not to rub the potatoes round and round or work them excessively while passing them; this will develop a rubbery texture. Finish by mixing with other ingredients as called for.

Mashed potatoes can be kept hot for the period of service but this should be in a container in a bain-marie and at not too high a temperature. If kept too hot the mashed potatoes will soon lose their fluffy texture and colour and will develop a degraded and overcooked taste.

Steaming

If correctly carried out, this process can produce potatoes almost indistinguishable from correctly boiled potatoes. In many cases the result for the same type of potatoes can be even better. It is very useful for potatoes cooked and served in their skin, for potatoes cooked in their skin and peeled for shallow frying, for potatoes which are likely to break up if boiled, and for good floury potatoes required for mashing or purées. New potatoes, however, are usually best if boiled.

To steam potatoes, cover the bottom of the steaming tray with a clean cloth, place the potatoes on top, either trimmed or cut to equal size, lightly salt them, then cover with a cloth and steam for the required length of time according to the equipment being used. This can vary from 7–8 mins. in a high-pressure steamer to 20–30 mins. in a low-pressure steamer. A few minutes of overcooking is not really noticeable but any excessive time leads to discolouration and a degraded flavour and texture. Obversely, any undercooking can be easily rectified.

When cooked, steamed potatoes can be held for service on a tray covered with a clean wet cloth and kept in a hot cupboard, or they can be left in a low-pressure steaming oven with the door slightly ajar; this will keep them moist and hot but without further cooking taking place. Because of their speed in cooking, high-pressure steamers are ideal for steaming small quantities of potatoes in successive batches.

Braising

In this form of cooking, potatoes cut in various shapes are cooked with a liquid and other ingredients in the oven. The type of potato used should be of a firm waxy texture able to keep its shape and at the same time absorb a certain amount of the liquid with which it is cooking. They are cooked in the oven without covering and the aim is to build up a nice golden brown glossy surface to the potatoes which can be done by occasionally basting the potatoes with the liquid and brushing with butter. When cooked, the majority of the liquid should have been absorbed or reduced; the potatoes should not be turned over; coloured on the top surface only is correct. Pommes Fondantes and Pommes Boulangère are good examples of this type of potato dish.

In other cases potatoes can be cooked and finished with milk and/or cream and finally gratinated with the addition of grated cheese and breadcrumbs. There should be sufficient liquid in a reduced and thickened form to serve with the dish.

Baking

Baked potatoes are used in two main forms; as baked potatoes and in dishes derived from them. Here the selection of suitable potatoes is of the utmost importance; they should have a good even shape, be unblemished and have a creamy floury texture and not be waxy. The ideal baked potato should have a good crisp outer coating and a soft floury interior. This means that the potato should be exposed to all-round dry heat; on the open bars of the oven shelf is by far the best place. Wrapping in foil or paper does not give the true flavour but can be useful where the pulp of the potato only is needed.

There are also a number of potato dishes which are baked either using the pulp of baked potatoes, for example in the making of Pommes Macaire, or using raw potatoes as for Pommes Anna. In either case it is important that the potatoes are put into heated pans or moulds which have been carefully cleaned and seasoned to prevent sticking. Clarified butter is the best fat to use, the liquid and salt in fresh butter tending to make the potatoes stick.

Roasting

Most potatoes excepting early new potatoes are suitable for this purpose. They need to be cut or trimmed to an even size then washed well, drained and dried before using.

Good-quality clean beef dripping is the best fat to use as far as flavour is concerned. The following are the main points to be considered:

a) Use sufficient fat to cover the bottom of the roasting tray well.
b) Heat the fat on the stove until just before a blue haze starts rising.
c) Add the potatoes, season with salt only and mix over and around to make sure that they are all coated with a layer of fat.
d) Keep on the stove until they begin to start sizzling well then place in a very hot oven at 220°C to cook, for approx 50–60 mins. Occasionally baste the potatoes or roll them around in the fat to ensure even colouring and reduce the temperature if any signs of overcolouring become evident.
e) To test for being cooked, squeeze gently with the fingers, they will give easily if cooked.
f) Drain well and serve immediately if possible.

The quality of a good roast potato is determined by a crisp golden brown outside and a soft moist interior. Make sure that they are removed from the oven when just cooked; overcooking will result in a dry shrivelled interior.

Roast potatoes can be held for a period in a hot cupboard or under heated elements but they tend to dry out fairly quickly. Cooking in batches can ensure reasonable quality for the period of service.

It is not necessary to blanch potatoes first for roasting; it does not speed up the cooking process neither does it improve the moistness of the potato. Correctly speaking, roast potatoes should not be buttered or sprinkled with chopped parsley.

Shallow Frying
Potatoes can be shallow-fried from the raw or cooked state; the process is usually referred to as 'sauter', in effect a description of the way in which the potatoes need to be tossed over to ensure even colouring. Heavy metal frying-pans with curved sides are the best for this type of cooking; sauté pans tend to stick and they are more difficult to manipulate for tossing over the contents. Ideally clarified butter is best but when the process is slower, good clean beef dripping can be excellent. Oil should only be used where the recipe calls for it or where it is considered better for health or dietary reasons.

For raw potatoes: these are usually cut into slices or various small shapes such as cubes or balls. They should always be washed, drained and dried before use, and only placed into the fat when it is very hot; if too cool there is always the danger of the potatoes sticking to the pan. Season with salt and cook as required with frequent or occasional tossing as necessary so as to ensure that the potatoes are coloured and cooked at the same time. They should be just soft to a little pressure, well-drained and tossed in a little butter.

For sauté potatoes: select small to medium potatoes of even shape and particularly potatoes which are firm and do not break easily when boiled. Scrub the potatoes well and either boil or steam them in their skins until not much more than three-quarters cooked. After skinning them, they should be left to become quite cold and set before slicing.

Place the cut potatoes into sufficient hot fat to cover the bottom of the pan well, season with salt and sauté quickly, tossing over when the edges of the potatoes are seen to start colouring. Do not overdo the tossing of the potatoes; although a certain amount of breaking is inevitable, when this becomes excessive there is the danger of their becoming a soggy and greasy mess. Endeavour to obtain an overall crisp and golden brown colour. Drain them well then place a little fresh butter in the pan in which to finally toss them over. They will keep well for a short period of service but frequent batch-cooking is to be preferred where possible.

For Galettes and Potato Cakes: whether using a raw potato mix or a cooked mixture, the process is best carried out in a heavy metal frying-pan. Oil is the best medium for raw mixtures and clarified butter for cooked mixtures.

Deep Frying

This is a very popular method for processing potatoes either from the raw state or for moulded and coated mixtures of cooked potato.

For the preparation of items such as Pommes Frites or Pommes Chips the following points are worth noting:

a) All potatoes with the exception of the very early varieties are suitable for deep frying, with the King Edward and Maris Piper varieties being exceptionally good.
b) First-class beef dripping or good-quality oils make the best frying mediums.
c) Make sure that there is the correct amount of fat in the fryer, i.e. half to two-thirds full.
d) Ensure that the fat is at the correct temperature for the particular job. It must be high enough to prevent the potato from absorbing too much fat.
e) After trimming and cutting, the potatoes should be well washed, drained and dried.
f) Most sizes of fried potato need to be parcooked first without colour at a temperature of approx. 170–175°C and then refried crisply and to order at a temperature of approx. 190°C.
g) Game chips, straw potatoes and similar varieties require that they be cooked until completely crisp. This can be done in the one operation at a temperature of approx. 175°C.
h) When cooked and ready, drain all fried potatoes well, for preference on kitchen paper, then shake in a little salt immediately to season.
i) Serve on dish papers on flat dishes where appropriate and do not cover; this would cause condensation and subsequent softening of the potatoes.
j) All fried potatoes except those which are completely crisp like Game Chips should be finished to order. The crisp varieties can be held in a warm place or hot cupboard for service.

The following points need to be observed for the deep frying of moulded and coated potato mixtures:

a) Any flour, egg and breadcrumbing or similar should be carried out carefully; there should be no areas left untouched or uncoated with the egg and its coating otherwise the potatoes will quickly break open when placed in the fat.
b) The frying temperature should be fairly high, approx. 185–190°C, so as to ensure instant sealing and quick colouring. Too low a temperature will lead to greasy potatoes with the danger of them splitting open before they are sufficiently coloured.
c) Any Dauphine mixture, i.e. Duchesse containing chou paste, should be checked first before moulding. Just try a small piece to see whether it holds together and expands properly. If it breaks open in the fat add a little more chou paste or if the mixture is too stiff, a little beaten egg.
d) Moulded Dauphine mixtures require a longer cooking time than breadcrumbed mixtures. Place into hot fat at about 170°C to allow them to cook, swell and colour at the same time. The high egg content will prevent them from absorbing fat even at this low temperature.
e) When cooked, both these types of fried potatoes should be well-drained but do not require salting when finished.

f) Serve on dish papers on flat dishes.

g) Generally speaking, these types of potato are best if finished to order but reasonable quantities may be held in a hot cupboard where the demand is particularly heavy.

PREPARATION LOSSES AND PORTION GUIDE

As a general guide the following represents the average preparation losses for potatoes, bearing in mind that good trimmings of peeled potatoes can be utilised for other preparations:

New potatoes: scraped or peeled after boiling	3–4%
Maincrop potatoes: peeled by hand or machine	12–18%
Trimming and turning of peeled potatoes	25–30%
Preparation of Pommes Parisienne and similar	up to 60%

It is usual to serve on average 100–125g prepared potato per portion.

1538 Pommes à l'Anglaise (Nature) – Boiled Potatoes

10 portions
35 mins.

Stage	Ingredient	Quantity	Method
1	potatoes, peeled	1¾kg	Cut into sections and turn barrel-shape, approx. 5cm in length, allowing three pieces per portion.
2			Place the potatoes into cold salted water, bring to the boil and simmer gently until cooked (approx. 20 mins.).
3			Drain well and serve in vegetable dishes.

1539 Pommes Allumettes

Prepare as for Pommes frites (1565) but cut the potatoes into batons 5cm long × 3mm × 3mm.

1540 Pommes Amandines

10 portions
35 mins.

Stage	Ingredient	Quantity	Method
1	Duchesse mixture (1560)	1kg	Place the duchesse mixture on a floured board and roll into long cylinders. Cut into pieces of approx. 30g allowing three per portion.
2	flour eggwash nibbed almonds	300g	Pass the pieces of potato through the flour, eggwash and roll in the almonds. Mould into pear shapes.

| 3 | parsley | | Place the potatoes into frying-baskets and deep fry in hot fat at approx. 185°C until golden brown. Drain and serve on dish papers on flat dishes garnished with picked parsley. |

1541 Pommes Anna

10 portions
1½ hours

Stage	Ingredient	Quantity	Method
1	potatoes, peeled	1½kg	Trim the potatoes to an even cylindrical shape and cut into approx. 1mm slices.
2	butter, clarified	150g	Heat two Pommes Anna moulds on the side of the stove and well coat the sides and bottom with butter.
3			Place a layer of potatoes neatly overlapping in the bottom of the moulds, butter and lightly season. Continue to arrange layers in the same manner until the mould is almost full and finally well butter the top layer.
4			Heat the pans well on the stove until a sizzling sound can be heard, then place in a hot oven at approx. 220°C to cook, occasionally pressing the potatoes flat and brushing with butter. Time approx. 45–50 mins.
5			When golden brown, knock firmly to release the potatoes from the sides of the mould, then turn over onto a flat tray to allow them to drain for a few seconds of any excess butter. Serve either whole on a round dish or cut into portions in vegetable dishes.

SPECIAL POINTS
a) It is not advisable to wash the potato slices; the starch on the surfaces helps them to stick together and form a nice compact mass in the mould. However, sufficient potato slices for the first layer in the mould may be washed and dried; in this case the removal of the starch helps to prevent this bottom layer sticking to the mould.
b) Heavy omelette pans can be used successfully instead of Anna moulds.
c) The moulds or pans used for this dish should always be kept clean by wiping with kitchen paper or cloth and coating with a little clean fat for later use.

1542 Pommes Arlie

10 portions
1½ hours

Stage	Ingredient	Quantity	Method
1	baking potatoes	10 × 180g	Select smooth even-sized potatoes without blemishes. Wash them well and dry. Lay the potatoes flat and cut a shallow incision around the top quarter of each potato.
2	coarse salt		Place a layer of the salt in a suitable tray then lay the potatoes on top without touching each other. Bake in a hot oven at 220°C for approx. ¾–1 hour, until soft. This can be ascertained by squeezing them.
3			Open the potatoes around the cut line and empty the pulp from the potatoes with a spoon and into a basin. Discard the top skins.
4	butter	50g	Mix the potatoes with a fork or wooden spatule, then mix in the butter, cream and chives and season with salt and milled pepper.
	cream, double	¾dl	
	chives, chopped	2 tbsps	
5	Parmesan, grated	50g	Fill the empty potato cases with the mixture moulding slightly dome-shape with the back of a fork. Sprinkle with the cheese and butter and gratinate in a hot oven. Serve on dish papers on flat dishes.
	Cheddar, grated	50g	
	butter, melted		

1543 Pommes Berny

10 portions
35 mins.

Stage	Ingredient	Quantity	Method
1	Duchesse mixture, (1560)	1kg	Mix together thoroughly.
	truffle, finely chopped	50g	
2	flour		Place the mixture on a floured board and roll into cylinders. Cut into approx. 30g pieces, allowing three per portion.
3	flour		Pass the pieces of potato through the flour, eggwash and roll in the almonds. Mould into round balls.
	eggwash		
	flaked almonds	350g	

4	parsley, picked		Place the potatoes into frying-baskets and deep fry in hot fat at approx. 185°C until golden brown. Drain and serve on dish papers on flat dishes garnished with picked parsley.

1544 Pommes Berrichonne

10 portions
1¼ hours

Stage	Ingredient	Quantity	Method
1	potatoes, peeled	1¾kg	Cut into sections and turn barrel-shape approx. 5cm in length, allowing three pieces per portion.
2	streaky bacon onions, chopped Fonds Blanc (93) butter	250g 200g 1 litre 50g	Cut the bacon into lardons then blanch, refresh and drain them. Place the potatoes in a deep tray with the onions and lardons and add sufficient stock to come half-way up the potatoes. Brush with melted butter and season.
3			Place in a hot oven at approx. 200°C and cook until the potatoes are golden brown on top and the stock almost completely reduced.
4	butter, melted parsley, chopped	30g	Serve in vegetable dishes, brushed with melted butter and sprinkled with chopped parsley.

1545 Pommes Biarritz

Prepare Pommes Purée (1592) and add 100g small dice of cooked ham, 100g small dice of skinned and cooked red pimento and 2 tablespoons of chopped parsley. Mix well and serve dome-shaped in vegetable dishes. Smooth and decorate with a palette knife.

1546 Pommes Boulangère

10 portions
1¾ hours

Stage	Ingredient	Quantity	Method
1	potatoes, peeled onions, finely sliced butter	1¼kg 350g 75g	Cut the potatoes into 2mm-thick slices and reserve the best slices for finishing the dish. Fry the onions lightly in the butter without colour.
2	Fonds Blanc (93) butter, melted	1 litre 50g	Mix the potato and onions together, season and place in buttered earthenware dishes. Barely cover with white stock. Arrange the reserved slices of potatoes neatly overlapping on top and sprinkle well with melted butter.

| 3 | | | Place in a hot oven at approx. 200°C and cook for approx. 20 mins. until lightly coloured. Press the potatoes flat, reduce the temperature to approx. 175°C and continue cooking for a further 1 hour approx. until the stock is almost absorbed and the potatoes soft and golden brown on top. |
| 4 | butter
parsley, chopped | 50g | Brush with melted butter and serve sprinkled with chopped parsley. |

1547 Pommes Bourgeoise

10 portions
35 mins.

Stage	Ingredient	Quantity	Method
1	butter streaky bacon, cut into ½cm dice onion, finely chopped	50g 250g 150g	Heat the butter in a pan, add the bacon and fry until cooked and lightly coloured. Then add the onions and cook together.
2	Duchesse mixture (1560) Tomates Concassées (90)	 850g 150g	Add the cooked onion and bacon to the duchesse mixture and mix together with the tomato. Season well.
3	flour		Using flour, mould the mixture into flat cakes approx. 5cm × 1½cm thick, allowing two pieces per portion. Mark trellis-fashion on top.
4	oil	1½dl	Heat in a heavy frying-pan and when very hot place in the potatoes, decorated side downwards. Fry quickly until golden brown on both sides.
5			Serve overlapping in vegetable dishes.

1548 Pommes Byron

Prepare Pommes Macaire (1572) and place on trays. Make an indentation in the top of the potatoes with a ladle and fill with double cream. Sprinkle with grated Cheddar cheese and gratinate in a hot oven. Serve either whole on flat dishes or cut in portions in vegetable dishes.

1549 Pommes Champignol

Prepare Pommes Fondantes (1563) and sprinkle with grated cheese. Sprinkle with melted butter and gratinate in a hot oven. Serve in vegetable dishes.

1550 Pommes Château

10 portions
1½ hours

Stage	Ingredient	Quantity	Method
1	potatoes, peeled	2kg	Cut into sections and turn barrel-shape approx. 5cm in length, allowing three pieces per portion.
2	clean fat	150g	Place the fat in a roasting tray and heat. Add the potatoes, season with salt and move the potatoes until coated with fat. Place in a hot oven at approx. 200°C and cook until golden brown (approx. 40–50 mins.) and soft.
3	butter, melted parsley, chopped	50g	Remove the potatoes and drain off the fat. Toss the potatoes in the butter and serve in vegetable dishes sprinkled with chopped parsley.

1551 Pommes Chips – Game Chips

10 portions
1 hour

Stage	Ingredient	Quantity	Method
1	potatoes, peeled	1½kg	Trim to an even cylindrical shape and cut into 1mm-thin slices using a mandolin. Wash well under cold running water until crisp then drain and dry them.
2			Place half the potatoes into a frying-basket and lower gently into hot deep fat at approx. 175°C. Shake the basket gently and when the boiling action of the fat subsides carefully tip out the potatoes into the fat. Using a frying-spider, move the potatoes occasionally to separate them and to ensure even colouring.
3			Fry until golden brown and completely crisp. Drain well and lightly season with salt. Repeat with the remainder of the potatoes.

SPECIAL POINT

Pommes Chips are seldom served as a potato dish in their own right. They are normally served as a garnish for roast poultry and game or served at receptions and cocktail bars.

1552 Pommes Cocotte

10 portions
45 mins.

Stage	Ingredient	Quantity	Method
1	potatoes, peeled	2kg	Cut into sections and turn barrel-shape approx. 2½cm in length. Wash and drain.

| 2 | clean fat | 150g | Place the fat in a heavy frying-pan and heat. Add the potatoes, season with salt and fry until golden brown and soft, tossing from time to time. |
| 3 | butter, melted parsley, chopped | 50g | Drain the potatoes well and toss in the melted butter. Serve in vegetable dishes sprinkled with chopped parsley. |

1553 Pommes Collerette

Prepare and cook as for Pommes Chips (1551) but trim the cylinders of potatoes to 3cm in diameter then groove along the sides with a canneler knife before slicing.

1554 Pommes à la Crème

10 portions
1 hour

Stage	Ingredient	Quantity	Method
1	waxy potatoes, small	1½kg	Wash well, place in salted water and bring to the boil. Simmer gently until almost cooked (approx. 15 mins.).
2			Drain, peel the potatoes and cut into ½cm-thick slices.
3	milk	1 litre	Place the potatoes in a shallow pan, season and add the milk. Simmer gently on the side of the stove to finish cooking (approx. 10–15 mins.).
4	cream	2dl	Place the potatoes in earthenware dishes with a little of the milk. Warm the cream, pour over the potatoes and serve.

1555 Pommes Crétan

Prepare Pommes Fondantes (1563), mixing a good pinch of powdered thyme in the stock. When cooked, arrange in vegetable dishes, brush with melted butter and sprinkle with chopped parsley mixed with a few finely chopped fresh thyme leaves.

1556 Pommes Croquettes

10 portions
30 mins.

Stage	Ingredient	Quantity	Method
1	Duchesse mixture (1560) flour	1kg	Place the mixture on a floured board and roll into long cylinders 2cm in diameter. Cut into pieces approx. 5cm in length, allowing three per portion.
2	flour eggwash white bread-crumbs } for crumbing		Pass the pieces of potato through the flour, eggwash and roll in the bread-crumbs. Remould cork-shape with a palette knife.

3	parsley, picked		Place in frying-baskets and deep fat at approx. 190°C until golden brown. Drain and serve on dish papers on suitable dishes, garnished with picked parsley.

1557 Pommes Dauphin

10 portions
1¼ hours

Stage	Ingredient	Quantity	Method
1	butter, clarified	50g	Well butter two Pommes Anna moulds.
	potatoes, peeled	1½kg	Cut the potatoes into julienne.
2	butter, clarified	100g	Season the potatoes with salt and pepper and place in the moulds. Well butter the top of the potatoes.
3			Cook in a hot oven at approx. 220°C occasionally pressing the potatoes flat (approx. 45–50 mins.).
4			When golden brown, turn out of the moulds and serve either whole on round dishes or cut into portions in vegetable dishes.

1558 Pommes Dauphine

10 portions
40 mins.

Stage	Ingredient	Quantity	Method
1	Duchesse mixture (1560)	750g	Mix together thoroughly.
	Chou Paste, general purpose (24)	½ litre	
2	flour		Mould into small balls or cork-shaped pieces approx. 30g in weight using the flour. Place on small sheets of oiled greaseproof paper. Allow three pieces per portion.
3			Hold the paper firmly by the sides and carefully slide the potatoes into hot deep fat at approx. 175°C. Using a spider, move the potatoes occasionally to ensure an even colour.
4	picked parsley		When golden brown, remove and drain. Serve on dish papers on flat dishes garnished with picked parsley.

SPECIAL POINT
Pommes Dauphine may be moulded egg-shape using oiled tablespoons.

1559 Pommes Delmonico

10 portions
1 hour

Stage	Ingredient	Quantity	Method
1	waxy potatoes, peeled	1¾kg	Trim to give straight sides and cut into approx. 1½cm cubes. Place in a shallow pan.
2	milk	1 litre	Add, season and cover. Cook very gently on the side of the stove until the potatoes are just tender.
3	cream	3dl	Place the potatoes in earthenware dishes with a little of the milk. Pour the cream over the potatoes and sprinkle with the breadcrumbs and melted butter.
	breadcrumbs	100g	
	butter, melted	100g	
4			Gratinate in a moderate oven at approx. 175°C.

1560 Pommes Duchesse – Basic Duchesse Mixture

1 kg
50 mins.

Stage	Ingredient	Quantity	Method
1	potatoes, peeled	1kg	Cut into even-sized pieces and place in salted water. Bring to the boil and simmer gently until tender (approx. 20–25 mins.).
2			Drain well, return to the pan and place in the oven to dry out for a few mins. Pass the potatoes through a medium sieve or masher and place in a clean pan.
3	egg yolks	3	Add to the potatoes, season and mix in thoroughly with a wooden spatule over moderate heat.
	butter	50g	
	nutmeg, grated	pinch	

SPECIAL POINT

This is a basic preparation, widely used in the preparation of many other potato dishes as well as being used to garnish fish dishes and the like such as Cabillaud Crème au Gratin and Coquilles Saint-Jacques Mornay.

1561 Pommes Duchesse (as a potato dish)

10 portions
25 mins.

Stage	Ingredient	Quantity	Method
1	Duchesse mixture (1560)	1kg	Place the mixture into a piping bag with a large star tube. Pipe spiral shapes onto a buttered grilling tray approx. 5cm in height and 4cm in diameter at the base. Allow two pieces per portion.
2	eggwash		Place the Pommes Duchesse in a hot oven for a few mins. to dry the outside

surface. Brush with eggwash and return
to the oven to colour a golden brown.

3   Serve in vegetable dishes.

1562 Pommes Elisabeth

10 portions
45 mins.

Stage	Ingredient	Quantity	Method
1	spinach, plain boiled, refreshed and squeezed in balls to remove excess moisture	300g	Chop the spinach fairly fine and heat together with the butter. Season with salt and milled pepper and mix in the cheese. Allow to cool.
	butter	25g	
	Parmesan, grated	25g	
2	Duchesse Mixture (1560)	750g	Mix together thoroughly.
	Chou Paste, general purpose (24)	½ litre	
3	flour		Mould the mixture into balls approx. 30g in weight using the flour. Make a depression in one side of each ball and place a little of the spinach mixture in each. Reshape to enclose and seal the mixture in completely. Place on small sheets of oiled greaseproof paper. Allow three pieces per portion.
4			Hold the paper firmly by the sides and carefully slide the potatoes into hot deep fat at approx. 175°C. Using a spider, move the potatoes occasionally to ensure an even colour.
5	picked parsley		When golden brown, remove and drain. Serve on dish papers on flat dishes garnished with picked parsley.

1563 Pommes Fondantes

10 portions
1¼ hours

Stage	Ingredient	Quantity	Method
1	potatoes, peeled	2kg	Cut into sections and turn barrel-shape approx. 5cm in length, allowing three pieces per portion.
2	Fonds Blanc (93)	1 litre	Place the potatoes in a deep tray and add sufficient stock to come half-way up the potatoes. Brush well with melted butter and season.
	butter	75g	

3			Place in a hot oven at approx. 220°C and cook until the potatoes are golden brown on top and the stock is almost completely reduced. Baste frequently with the stock in the pan and brush with butter to build up a nice gloss.
4	butter, melted parsley, chopped	30g	Serve in vegetable dishes brushed with melted butter and sprinkled with chopped parsley.

1564 Pomme au Four – Baked Potato

10 portions
1¼ hours

Stage	Ingredient	Quantity	Method
1	baking potatoes	10 × 250g	Select smooth even-sized potatoes without blemishes. Wash them well and dry. Prick in a few places with the point of a small knife.
2	coarse salt		Place a layer of the salt in a suitable tray then lay the potatoes on top without touching each other. Bake in a hot oven at 220°C for approx. 1–1¼ hours until soft. This can be ascertained by squeezing them.
3	parsley, picked		Remove any adhering salt then make a cross-cut incision in the top of the potatoes and press to open. Serve between folded serviettes on flat dishes. Garnish with picked parsley.

SPECIAL POINTS
a) A knob of butter may be inserted where the potatoes have been pressed open.
b) The potatoes are best if placed directly on the bars of the oven shelf; this gives a better overall crisp baked quality to the outside of the potatoes which to the true amateur of baked potatoes can be the best part.

1565 Pommes frites – Fried Potatoes

10 portions
30 mins.

Stage	Ingredient	Quantity	Method
1	large potatoes, peeled	2kg	Trim to give straight sides and cut into batons approx. 6cm × 1cm × 1cm. Wash and dry well.
2			Place into frying-baskets and fry in deep fat at approx. 170°C until soft and with little colour. Drain and place on trays until required.
3			When required, place the potatoes in a frying-basket and plunge into hot deep

fat at approx. 190°C until crisp and golden brown. Drain well and shake in a little salt.

4   Serve on dish papers on flat dishes. Do not cover.

1566 Pommes Galette

10 portions
35 mins.

Stage	Ingredient	Quantity	Method
1	Duchesse mixture (1560)	1kg	Using flour, mould the mixture into flat cakes approx. 5cm in diameter × 1½cm thick, allowing two pieces per portion. Mark trellis-fashion on top.
2	clarified butter	180g	Heat in a heavy frying-pan and when very hot place in the potatoes, decorated side downwards. Fry quickly until golden brown on both sides.
3			Serve overlapping in vegetable dishes.

1567 Pommes Gaufrettes

Prepare and cook as for Pommes Chips (1551), but slice the potatoes on the corrugated blade of the mandolin giving a half-turn to the potato between each slicing movement, so as to produce a trellis pattern.

1568 Pommes Gratinées

10 portions
1½ hours

Stage	Ingredient	Quantity	Method
1	baking potatoes	10 × 180g	Select smooth even-sized potatoes without blemishes. Wash them well and dry. Prick in a few places with the point of a small knife.
2	coarse salt		Place a layer of the salt in a suitable tray then lay the potatoes on top without touching each other. Bake in a hot oven at 220°C for approx. ¾–1 hour until soft. This can be ascertained by squeezing them.
3	butter	100g	Cut the potatoes into halves lengthways. Remove the potato pulp with a spoon and place it in a basin. Add the butter, season and mix in well with a fork.
4	Cheddar cheese, grated	100g	Refill the skins with the mixture and place on a tray. Sprinkle with the cheese and melted butter.
	butter, melted	75g	

5	Place the potatoes in a hot oven and gratinate to a golden brown.
6	Serve in vegetable dishes.

1569 Pommes au Lard

10 portions
1½ hours

Stage	Ingredient	Quantity	Method
1	waxy potatoes, peeled	1½kg	Trim to give straight sides and cut into approx. 1½cm cubes.
2	streaky bacon button onions	250g 20	Cut the bacon into lardons and fry together with the onions in a little fat until coloured light brown. Drain.
3	Fonds Blanc (93)	1 litre	Place the potatoes, onions and lardons in a deep tray and add sufficient stock to come half-way up the potatoes. Season and cover with a lid.
4			Place in a moderate oven at approx. 190°C and cook gently until tender (approx. 50–60 mins.).
5	parsley, chopped		Serve in vegetable dishes with a little of the cooking liquor and sprinkle with chopped parsley.

1570 Pommes Lorette

This is made in the same way as Pommes Dauphine (1558), adding 75g of grated Parmesan to the mixture at Stage 1 and moulding cigar-shape.

1571 Pommes Lyonnaise

This consists of two-thirds Pommes sautées (1598) and one-third Oignons sautés (1491), mixed together. Sprinkle with chopped parsley when serving.

1572 Pommes Macaire

10 portions
2 hours

Stage	Ingredient	Quantity	Method
1	baking potatoes	2kg	Wash well and dry, place on a tray and bake in a hot oven for approx. 1 hour until soft.
2	butter	100g	Cut the potatoes in halves and scoop out the pulp into a basin. Add the butter, season and lightly mix with a fork or a wooden spatula.

3	butter, clarified	100g	Well butter two heavy frying-pans approx. 20cm in diameter. Place on the stove to heat then add the potato mixture, press down flat and smooth the surface with a palette knife. Well butter the surface and place in a hot oven at approx. 220°C for 30–40 mins.
4			When golden brown remove from the oven and shake the pans firmly to make sure that the potatoes are not sticking. Turn out from the pans and serve either whole on round dishes, or cut into portions in vegetable dishes.

1573 Pommes Maître d'Hôtel

Prepare Pommes à la Crème (1554) and sprinkle with chopped parsley when serving.

1574 Pommes Marquise

10 portions
30 mins.

Stage	Ingredient	Quantity	Method
1	Duchesse mixture (1560)	1kg	Place in a piping bag with a large star tube. Pipe onto a buttered grilling tray in the form of round nests approx. 6cm in diameter and 2½cm in height. Allow two per portion.
2	eggwash		Place in a hot oven for a few minutes to dry the outside surface, brush with eggwash and return to the oven to colour a golden brown.
3	Tomates Concassées, cooked (91) parsley, chopped	175g	Fill the centre of the potatoes with the hot tomato and sprinkle with chopped parsley.
4			Serve in vegetable dishes.

1575 Pommes Mignonnettes

Prepare as for Pommes frites (1565) but cut the potatoes into batons 4cm × ½cm × ½cm.

1576 Pommes Mireille

10 portions
1¼ hours

Stage	Ingredient	Quantity	Method
1	potatoes, peeled	1¼kg	Trim the potatoes to an even cylindrical shape and cut into approx. 1mm slices.

2	artichoke bottoms, raw (1379) juice of lemon	10 ½	Cut in approx. 2mm slices and place in a little water acidulated with the lemon juice.
3	butter, clarified	150g	Heat the butter in a heavy frying-pan, add the potatoes, season with salt and pepper and sauté quickly tossing over and over to lightly colour. Drain and keep on one side.
4			Drain the artichoke slices well, add to the same fat in the pan and sauté quickly to lightly colour.
5	truffle, cut in julienne	25g	Replace the potatoes in the pan with the artichokes and toss together to mix. Add the truffle and toss together.
6	butter	25g	Place the potato mixture in buttered earthenware dishes. Make sure that the top layer consists only of potatoes, press fairly flat, brush with butter and finish cooking in a hot oven, approx. 25 mins.
7	parsley, chopped		Serve sprinkled with chopped parsley.

1577 Pommes Mont d'Or or Pommes Purée au Gratin

Prepare and dress Pommes Purée (1592). Sprinkle well with grated Cheddar cheese and melted butter and gratinate under the salamander.

1578 Pommes Nana

10 portions
1 hour

Stage	Ingredient	Quantity	Method
1	potatoes, peeled	1kg	Cut the potatoes into julienne 4–5cm long.
2	butter, clarified	125g	Well butter ten dariole moulds. Season the julienne of potatoes with salt and pepper then fill into the moulds. Press in well to leave slightly proud of the top. Sprinkle well with melted butter.
3			Heat the filled moulds well on top of the stove, place on a tray and then into a hot oven at approx. 220°C to cook. Press occasionally to compact the potatoes and brush with more butter if necessary. Time approx. 35–40 mins.

4

When judged to be cooked and a nice golden brown, remove from the oven. Run a small knife carefully round the sides of the potatoes to ensure that they are not sticking and demould onto a flat tray to drain any excess butter. Serve in suitable dishes.

SPECIAL POINT

These moulded potatoes are excellent for the garnishing of large joints.

1579 Pommes à la Neige

Prepare plain boiled potatoes, drain and dry them, then pass through a sieve or potato masher and serve in vegetable dishes without further handling.

1580 Pommes Noisette

Scoop out balls of potato using a pommes noisette cutter and proceed as for Pommes Cocotte (1552).

SPECIAL POINT

Ten portions of Pommes Noisette will require approx. 3kg of large peeled potatoes.

1581 Pommes Nouvelles – New Potatoes

10 portions
35 mins.

Stage	Ingredient	Quantity	Method
1	new potatoes	1¼kg	Wash and scrape off the skins.
2			Place in a pan of boiling salted water and cook until tender.
3			Drain and serve in vegetable dishes.

New potatoes may be washed and boiled in their jackets, then peeled, placed into hot salted water and served as required.

1582 Pommes Nouvelles au Beurre – Buttered New Potatoes

Prepare Pommes Nouvelles (1581) and toss gently in 75g of melted butter. Serve in vegetable dishes.

1583 Pommes Nouvelles à la Menthe – New Potatoes with Mint

Prepare and cook Pommes Nouvelles (1581) with a bunch of mint in the water. Drain, toss in 75g of melted butter and serve in vegetable dishes with blanched mint leaves.

1584 Pommes Nouvelles Persillées – Parslied New Potatoes

Prepare Pommes Nouvelles (1581) and toss in 75g of melted butter. Serve in vegetable dishes sprinkled with chopped parsley.

1585 Pommes Nouvelles rissolées

10 portions
45 mins.

Stage	Ingredient	Quantity	Method
1	new potatoes	1¼kg	Scrape, wash and dry.
2	clean fat	150g	Place in a heavy frying-pan and heat, add the potatoes, season and fry gently until golden brown and soft, tossing from time to time.
3	butter, melted	50g	Drain the potatoes then toss in the melted butter. Serve in vegetable dishes.

SPECIAL POINT
Pommes Nouvelles rissolées may be prepared with boiled and drained new potatoes instead of raw potatoes.

1586 Pommes Pailles – Straw Potatoes

10 portions as a garnish

Stage	Ingredient	Quantity	Method
1	potatoes, peeled	750g	Cut into julienne 6cm long, wash and dry well.
2			Place in a frying-basket and lower slowly into deep fat at approx. 175°C. Shake the basket gently and when the boiling action of the fat subsides, carefully tip out the potatoes into the fat. Using a spider, move the potatoes occasionally to separate them and to ensure even colouring.
3			Fry until brown and completely crisp. Drain well and lightly season with salt.

SPECIAL POINT
Pommes Pailles are seldom served as a potato dish; they are normally served as a garnish for grilled meats.

1587 Pommes Parisienne

Scoop out balls of potato using a parisienne cutter and proceed as for Pommes Cocotte (1552). Before serving roll the cooked potatoes in 2 tablespoons of melted Glace de Viande (103).

SPECIAL POINT
Ten portions of Pommes Parisienne will require approx. 3kg of large peeled potatoes.

1588 Pommes Parmentier

Trim the potatoes to give straight sides and cut in approx. 1½cm cubes. Proceed as for Pommes Cocotte (1552).

1589 Pommes Persillées – Parslied Potatoes

Prepare Pommes à l'Anglaise (1538) and toss gently in 75g of melted butter. Serve in vegetable dishes sprinkled with chopped parsley.

1590 Pommes Pont-Neuf

Prepare as for Pommes frites (1565) but cut the potatoes into large batons 6cm long × 2cm × 2cm.

1591 Pommes Provençale

Place 75g of butter in a heavy frying-pan, add 2 cloves of finely chopped garlic and fry gently without colour. Add Pommes sautées (1598), prepared to the end of Stage 4 and toss over to mix. Serve in vegetable dishes sprinkled with chopped parsley.

1592 Pommes Purée – Mashed Potatoes

10 portions
50 mins.

Stage	Ingredient	Quantity	Method
1	potatoes, peeled	1¼kg	Cut into even-sized pieces and place in salted water. Bring to the boil and simmer gently until tender (approx. 20–25 mins.).
2			Drain well and pass through a medium sieve. Place in a clean pan.
3	milk, hot butter	1½dl 75g	Add to the potatoes, season and mix well with a wooden spatule to obtain a soft creamy texture.
4			Serve dome-shaped in vegetable dishes. Smooth and decorate with a palette knife.

1593 Pommes Purée à la Crème – Mashed Potatoes with Cream

Prepare Pommes Purée (1592) and surround with a cordon of warm cream when serving.

1594 Pommes en Robes de Chambre – Steamed or Boiled Jacket Potatoes

Wash small even-sized potatoes and either steam or boil in salted water. Drain and serve unpeeled on a serviette.

1595 Pommes Robert

This is made in the same way as Pommes Macaire (1572), adding 2 egg yolks and 1 tablespoon of chopped chives to the mixture at Stage 2.

1596 Pommes rôties – Roast Potatoes

10 portions
1¼ hours

Stage	Ingredient	Quantity	Method
1	clean fat	150g	Place the fat in a roasting tray and heat;
	small potatoes,		add the potatoes, season with salt and
	peeled	1½kg	move them until coated with fat.
2			Place in a hot oven at approx. 220°C and cook until golden brown (approx. 50–60 mins.).
3			Remove, drain and serve in vegetable dishes.

1597 Pommes Sablées

10 portions
45 mins.

Stage	Ingredient	Quantity	Method
1	potatoes, peeled	1½kg	Trim the potatoes to give straight sides and cut into 1cm cubes. Wash, drain and dry well.
2	clean fat	150g	Heat in a heavy frying-pan, add the potatoes and season with salt. Fry until golden brown tossing over and over until almost cooked. Drain in a colander.
3	butter	75g	Heat the butter in the frying-pan,
	breadcrumbs, white	75g	replace the potatoes, then add the breadcrumbs and toss over to mix. Carry on cooking, gently tossing over and over so as to finish the cooking of the potatoes and to colour and crisp the breadcrumbs at the same time.
4	lemon juice	squeeze	At the last minute squeeze over a little
	parsley, chopped	1 tbsp	lemon juice and add the parsley. Toss over to mix and serve in vegetable dishes.

1598 Pommes sautées

10 portions
1 hour

Stage	Ingredient	Quantity	Method
1	small potatoes	1¼kg	Wash well, place in salted water and bring to the boil. Simmer gently until almost cooked (approx. 15 mins.).

2			Drain, peel the potatoes and allow them to cool.
3			Cut into 3mm-thick slices.
4	clean fat	200g	Place the fat in a heavy frying-pan and heat. Add the potatoes and fry to a golden brown colour, tossing occasionally. Drain in a colander.
5	butter	75g	Heat in the frying-pan, add the potatoes, season with salt and toss over.
6	parsley, chopped		Serve in vegetable dishes sprinkled with chopped parsley.

1599 Pommes Soufflées

10 portions as a garnish
45 mins.

Stage	Ingredient	Quantity	Method
1	potatoes, peeled	1kg	Trim to give straight sides approx. 6cm long × 4cm wide and cut into slices 3mm thick. Wash and dry.
2			Plunge the slices into deep hot oil at 180°C and remove the friture from the heat. Allow the potatoes to cook for 6–7 mins., moving the potatoes carefully from time to time with a spider to prevent them from sticking together. By the time the potatoes are cooked the temperature will drop appreciably. Remove the potatoes and place on a tray.
3			Reheat the oil to a temperature of 190°C and plunge the potatoes back into the oil. Move them carefully with a spider to ensure even colouring on both sides and fry until well puffed, crisp and golden brown.
4			Remove, drain, sprinkle lightly with salt and use as required.

SPECIAL POINT
Pommes Soufflées are most frequently used to accompany grilled meats.

1600 Pommes St Florentin

10 portions
35 mins.

Stage	Ingredient	Quantity	Method
1	Duchesse mixture (1560)	1kg	Mix together thoroughly.
	lean ham, finely diced	150g	

2	flour		Place the mixture on a floured board and roll into long cylinders 2cm in diameter. Flatten into oblongs and cut into approx. 30g pieces allowing three per portion.
3	flour eggwash vermicelli, broken small	300g	Pass the pieces of potato through the flour, eggwash and roll in the vermicelli. Remould into oblong cakes with a palette knife.
4			Place the potatoes in frying-baskets and deep fry at approx. 185°C until golden brown.
5	picked parsley		Drain and serve on dish papers on flat dishes garnished with picked parsley.

1601 Pommes Vapeur – Steamed Potatoes

10 portions
45 mins.

Stage	Ingredient	Quantity	Method
1	potatoes, peeled	2kg	Cut into sections and turn barrel-shape, approx. 5cm in length, allowing three pieces per portion.
2			Place on a cloth in a steaming tray, lightly salt, cover with cloth and steam for approx. 20–25 mins.
3			Serve in vegetable dishes.

1602 Pommes Voisin

Prepare in the same way as Pommes Anna (1541), but sprinkle with a little grated cheese between each layer of potatoes. Serve either whole on round dishes or cut into portions in vegetable dishes.

1603 Gratin Dauphinoise

10 portions
1½ hours

Stage	Ingredient	Quantity	Method
1	medium-sized, waxy potatoes, peeled nutmeg, grated	1kg	Cut into approx. 2mm slices, season with salt, pepper and a little grated nutmeg and mix together.
2	milk egg cream	4dl 1 3dl	Bring the milk to the boil, cool slightly and mix into the beaten egg then add the cream and strain.
3	garlic butter	½ clove 50g	Rub shallow earthenware dishes with the garlic then coat well with the butter.
4	Gruyère cheese, grated butter, melted	150g 25g	Fill the dishes with layers of the potatoes and three-quarters of the cheese, to a depth of 6cm. Pour the egg and milk

mixture over, sprinkle with the rest of the cheese and the butter and bake slowly at 175°C for 45–50 mins. until golden brown and lightly set. Press down occasionally if necessary.

1604 Potato Latkes

10 portions
35 mins.

Stage	Ingredient	Quantity	Method
1	potatoes, peeled	1kg	Coarsely grate the potatoes. Allow to stand for a short while and squeeze out the moisture. Place in a basin.
2	eggs, beaten	2	Add to the potato, season with salt and pepper and mix together.
	flour	75g	
	bicarbonate of soda	1 tsp	
3	oil	1½dl	Heat in a heavy frying-pan. Place in spoonfuls of the potato mixture, flatten slightly with the back of a spoon and fry on both sides until golden brown. Drain well.
4			Serve overlapping on dish papers on flat dishes.

1605 Potato Nests

1 nest
20 mins.

Stage	Ingredient	Quantity	Method
1	potatoes, peeled	350g	Cut into 6cm-long julienne. Wash, drain and dry well.
2			Dip the pair of nest-shaped wire frying-baskets into hot fat for a few mins. then line the large one with the julienne of potatoes, approx. 1cm thick. Fold over the smaller basket firmly into the centre and clamp together firmly. Fill any spaces around the rim and trim level.
3			Lower the basket slowly into deep fat at approx. 175°C and fry until golden brown and crisp.
4			Drain well and carefully remove from the frying-baskets.

SPECIAL POINTS

a) Potato Nests are used mainly for the presentation of other fried potato dishes.
b) Potatoes cut as for Pommes Gaufrettes (1567) can be used instead of the julienne of potatoes by arranging them closely overlapping in the special frying-basket.

1606 Potato Rösti

4 portions
1½ hours

Stage	Ingredient	Quantity	Method
1	waxy potatoes	1kg	Wash the potatoes well and bring to the boil in a pan of salted water. Simmer very slowly until only just cooked but still very firm.
2			Peel and allow to rest and cool completely then grate coarsely.
3	butter lard	50g 50g	Heat the fats in a 22–24cm heavy frying-pan. Add the potatoes and season with salt and pepper. Cook fairly slowly turning the potatoes frequently until they take on a lightly coloured appearance, then press flat.
4	butter	25g	Cook the potato slowly until golden brown and crisp underneath then slide onto a flat tray. Place the extra butter in the pan and turn the potatoes over back into the pan. Carry on cooking until brown and crisp on this side. When ready, turn onto a round dish and serve immediately.

SPECIAL POINTS
a) The potatoes should always be allowed to cool thoroughly before grating.
b) This potato dish is best when finished to order. It should not be allowed to rest or be held for any lengthy period of time.
c) Such things as grated Gruyère, small lardons of bacon and lightly fried chopped onion may be added to the potatoes.

19

Canapés, Sandwiches and Savouries

This chapter comprises three related areas of cookery although each has its own particular role to play in various parts of the menu; in addition to their individual function they are frequently combined in the form of a thematic menu in which a selection of items from each area of canapés, sandwiches and savouries, both cold and hot, are served. In this form they are ideal for such semi-formal social gatherings as cocktail parties, buffet receptions and finger buffets. With a few suitable additions such as quick sautés of meat, poultry and game, creamed curries, chilli con carne, chicken à la King, fried goujons of fish, small Bitoks, Rissoles, Cromesquis etc., these three areas can be the basis of a fork buffet meal.

1607 CANAPÉS

The term Canapé generally refers to a shape of toasted or fried bread. Of a certain size and covered with game farce they accompany roast game birds; they are used to garnish certain savoury foods and the name is used to designate many of the savouries which are served at the end of a meal. In this section of the chapter though, the term refers to what are popularly known as Cocktail Canapés. These take many forms, but usually consist of small shapes of buttered toast or plain savoury biscuit, covered with a savoury item of food which is then decorated appropriately and, more often than not, glazed with aspic jelly.

These small savoury items are designed to be served as appetisers for consumption before the commencement of a meal; they can also be served at cocktail parties and receptions or as part of a buffet reception. Canapés are not usually regarded as a course of the menu though they are sometimes served in raviers as part of the Hors-d'oeuvre selection or when prepared in the 'de luxe' style, as a single hors-d'oeuvre. They are always served cold.

The following points should be taken into consideration when making canapés:
a) They should be dainty and small enough to be consumed in at most two mouthfuls.
b) Prepare them as near to requirements as possible. Dry tired-looking canapés can mar the proceedings of a reception or spoil one's anticipation of the meal to follow.
c) Ordinary butter is best for spreading on the toast but flavoured and coloured butters can be used where appropriate – these last are especially good for decorating.
d) Any decoration must be tasteful and in keeping with the fillings. The result should be appetising to the eye as well as the palate.
e) The canapés should be cut or fashioned in a variety of shapes mainly determined by the filling, e.g. an elongated triangle for a sardine, asparagus tips on a finger-shape, sliced egg on rounds, etc.

f) The use of aspic jelly to finally glaze the canapés can be useful to improve the appearance and can help to keep them moist. However, the jelly should be of an excellent quality, it should not be of too thick a layer nor too firm in texture. In many cases freshly made canapés are better when served unglazed. Good sense and a critical eye are the best guides here.

g) The garnishing and presentation of canapés with centre-pieces is at the discretion of the practitioner and naturally relates to the custom and standard of service offered by the establishment.

Various titles given to the service of canapés include:

Cocktail or Reception Canapés: These are served as a selection of at least ten different varieties of small shape and size. They are best if glazed with aspic jelly then arranged either in lines or symmetrically, on a folded napkin or tray paper on a suitable dish and garnished with sprigs of parsley.

Canapés Moscovite: This is a general term to denote a dish of canapés made for a special party at a reception before going in to dinner. They would be made of high-quality ingredients such as caviar, foie gras, Parma ham, smoked salmon, prawns, asparagus, quails' eggs and so on, freshly prepared and unglazed. A dish of salted almonds or Pommes Chips may be placed in the centre of the dish.

Canapés à la Russe: This is a general term to denote a service of canapés usually with a selection of other appropriate items such as bouchées with various fillings, sausage rolls, goujons, chipolatas, barquettes and tartlets with various fillings and other suitable items as listed later in this chapter under the heading of savouries. These last items should be made in smaller sizes and some could be offered either hot or cold.

1608 Preparation of Canapés

There are two acceptable methods of making canapés, the first being for large-scale production and the second for producing more expensive items individually and to a higher standard.

Large-scale production
1) Slice a sandwich or tin loaf into 5mm slices and toast on both sides.
2) Immediately lay them on top of each other, press to keep them flat then separate the slices and let them cool.
3) When cold, spread the slices well with butter and place the chosen item on the toasted slices using one kind of ingredient on each slice; press lightly to ensure they are fixed to the butter.
4) Decorate the tops tastefully and ensure that it is spaced between where the canapés will be cut, then place on a wire rack and refrigerate.
5) Have ready sufficient cooling aspic jelly.
6) Bring the canapés from the refrigerator, place the rack on a tray and glaze the slices of canapés with the jelly. Replace in the refrigerator to set.
7) Trim the edges of the slices straight then cut them into different shapes not more than 3cm wide.
8) Arrange the canapés neatly in lines or in a symmetrical fashion on a folded table napkin or dish paper on a dish.
9) Garnish with picked parsley and keep in the refrigerator until required.

Individual production
1) Toast 5mm slices of bread on both sides.
2) Immediately lay the slices of toast on top of each other and press to keep them flat then separate the slices and let them cool.
3) When cold, spread the slices with butter or flavoured butter.
4) Cut the toast with a knife or cutters into individual shapes and sizes just a little larger than above, e.g. ovals, rounds, oblongs, squares and triangles.
5) Arrange the chosen item on each piece of toast ensuring that the shape and size is compatible.
6) Place the decoration on top and pipe with flavoured and coloured savoury butter to form an outline, in dots or motifs.
7) Place the canapés on a tray and refrigerate; do not allow to get damp.
8) Arrange the canapés on a folded or moulded table napkin on a suitable tray to make a colourful and symmetrical display.
9) Garnish with picked parsley and keep in the refrigerator until required for service.

NOTE:
These canapés may be glazed with aspic jelly if desired.

1609   Suitable Items for Making Canapés

Any of the following items may be used alone or in any combinations as desired:
a) Cream cheese; slices of cheese; purée of blue cheese.
b) Slices of hard-boiled egg; sliced cooked egg yolk; quails' eggs.
c) Anchovy fillets; caviar; salmon caviar; smoked cod roe; smoked fish including eel, herring, mackerel, salmon, sturgeon and trout; rollmops; brislings; sardines; prawns; lobster; shrimps; tuna fish.
d) Foie gras; ham; jambon de Parme; liver paste; pressed beef; tongue; salami and other smoked sausages; pastrami; smoked turkey.
e) Asparagus tips; green, red and yellow pimentos; mushrooms; radish; tomato.
f) For decoration: capers; gherkin; olives; hard-boiled white of egg; sieved yolk of hard-boiled egg; peas; truffle; piped savoury butter; mayonnaise and anchovy essence; picked parsley; pickled walnuts.

Additional items which can be used at a reception or finger buffet include the following:
Barquettes: small boat-shaped pastry cases baked and filled with salpicons of fish, shellfish, poultry, mushrooms etc. in an appropriate sauce.
Bouchées: small puff pastry cases made in various shapes and filled with salpicons of fish, poultry, mushrooms etc.
Carolines: small éclairs filled with a savoury mixture and glazed with Sauce Chaud-froid.
Celery: small lengths of celery filled with creamed blue cheese and sprinkled with paprika.
Cornets: triangular slices of ham, tongue, smoked salmon etc., rolled cornet-shape and filled with a suitable savoury purée or mousse.
Croquettes: finely chopped cooked egg, fish, shellfish, meat, poultry or game with mushroom, truffle etc. bound with an appropriate sauce, moulded in various shapes, egg-and-crumbed and deep-fried.
Dartois: finger-shapes of puff pastry spread with a forcemeat with strips of the item used on top, then baked.

Goujons and Goujonettes: small strips of fish or chicken, egg-and-crumbed and deep-fried.

Petits Pâtés: very small patties made with puff pastry and meat, poultry or game fillings.

Quails' eggs: soft- or hard-boiled, placed in a tartlet or bouchée with a hot sauce, or dressed with aspic jelly.

Quichelettes: tartlets filled with a savoury egg custard mixture together with cheese, bacon, ham, mushrooms etc. and baked.

Scampi: dipped in batter or coated with egg and breadcrumbs and deep-fried.

Tartlets: short pastry tartlet cases filled with a salpicon or purée of egg, cheese, fish, shellfish, meat, poultry, game or vegetable in an appropriate sauce.

In addition to the above, many of the savouries in the last section of this chapter are suitable as hot items. It is only necessary that they be prepared in smaller sizes of two to three mouthfuls each.

1610 SANDWICHES

Sandwiches consist of two slices of buttered bread with a filling in between which can usefully be served at any time of the day or night. The word sandwich is also applied to other similar light snacks, some made with only one slice of bread in the form of an open sandwich while others can be made with three or even four slices of bread or toast as in a triple-decker sandwich. Sandwiches can be a dainty component of the afternoon tea, or substantial enough for a meal.

The combination of bread and fillings are countless and the opportunity for creating new ones unlimited, but in all cases some thought must be given to their preparation. The quality of ingredients, balance and preparation are just as important as for any other dish of food. The following details are intended as a guide only; it is left for the practitioner to interpret them as seen fit.

Bread
Many kinds of bread are suitable for making sandwiches. The following are the most commonly used:
1) The sandwich or tin loaf, because of its square shape, is ideal for cutting across in slices or lengthways.
2) French bread, such as the Baguette, can be used for making more robust sandwiches by cutting it into thickish slices on the slant and filling the centre, or by cutting lengthways on one side and filling the opening.
3) Rye bread is suitable for Scandinavian-style open sandwiches; it needs to be sliced fairly thickly in order to support the fillings.
4) Brown bread of all kinds can be used for making sandwiches, indeed some fillings are more suited to brown bread than white, e.g. smoked salmon.

Butter
Butter should be used in preference to any other fat for sandwiches unless specifically prohibited, such as when proscribed by religion or diet. Butter gives a certain richness of taste but also acts as a barrier to prevent moist fillings from making the bread soggy. It must be used at room temperature so as to spread easily, or it may be creamed but not too softly. The practice of extending butter by the addition of thin cream or milk ir not recommended. Flavoured butter such as mustard or garlic butter should not be used indiscriminately.

Fillings
There are several categories of fillings for sandwiches and they can be used in suitable combinations. The most popular fillings include:
Cheese: any kind that can be sliced or spread.
Fish: anchovy paste; caviar; crabmeat; sardine; salmon paste; tuna fish; smoked salmon; shrimp paste.
Meat: roast beef; brisket of beef; corned beef; chicken; turkey; liver pâté; liver sausage; ham; roast pork; salami; Parma ham; ox-tongue; chicken pâté; pâté de foie.
Eggs. sliced hard-boiled egg; sieved hard-boiled egg mixed with mayonnaise; scrambled egg.
Vegetables: avocado pear; cucumber; lettuce; tomato; watercress; mustard and cress.
Fruit and nuts: apricots; bananas; dates; figs; pineapple; raisins; almonds; peanuts; walnuts:
Miscellaneous: honey; chutney; mixed pickle; various proprietary brands of thick sauce.
Soft fillings made as spreads or pâtés should be well-seasoned.
Mayonnaise and cream cheese can be used instead of butter in some kinds of sandwiches.

Seasonings
The usual seasonings for sandwiches are salt and pepper which should be added to all mixtures and added to sliced eggs, meat and vegetables which need them. Seasoning must be complete as people do not expect to have to open a sandwich to add anything further. Mustard of the appropriate kind may be used on sliced meats, and pickles where appropriate.

1611 Preparation of Sandwiches

Sandwiches should be made according to demand of the service ranging from dainty to the more substantial. The method used can be according to volume of sales, individually or in bulk.

Individual sandwiches
Cut two slices of the chosen bread approx. 3mm thick, spread evenly with butter; cover with the chosen filling which must completely cover the bread but not overlap, generous but not wasteful. Season if necessary, cover with the top slice, press to seal and cut as appropriate. According to the custom of the establishment, this means either leaving the crusts on or removing them, then cutting in half diagonally.

Bulk preparation of sandwiches
These can be produced as the required number of individual sandwiches but the following method is more time-saving where very large numbers are called for.

Using a sandwich loaf cut off the top, two sides and one end crust, thus leaving one end and the bottom crust attached. Cut through the end crust down to the bottom but not right through. Using a long slicing knife, cut slices horizontally through the loaf using the end crust as a guard, piling the slices on top of each other on the top crust. Spread half of the total number of slices evenly with the prepared butter laying them out, place the filling on top arranging it near to the edges then butter the remaining slices and invert each onto the filling and press together. Pile on the crust and trim the edges evenly. If for immediate use, cut into triangles, fingers or squares; for future use, wrap the loaf of sandwiches in a clean damp cloth or sheet of dampened greaseproof paper.

Rolled Sandwiches

These are made by spreading a thin slice of buttered decrusted bread with the required filling and rolling it up tightly; or an item such as an asparagus tip, small sardine or slice of smoked salmon can be rolled in a buttered slice of bread. To keep the shape, wrap fairly tightly and refrigerate; trim the ends before serving.

Pinwheel Sandwiches

These are made in the same way as rolled sandwiches using longer slices of bread to give a diameter of approx. 5cm; the roll is then cut into 5mm-thick slices.

Ribbon Sandwiches

These are made by sandwiching alternate slices of white and brown bread with various colours and flavours of fillings; after being refrigerated the block can be cut downwards into approx. 5mm-thick slices.

Afternoon Tea Sandwiches

The traditional fillings are egg and cress, sliced peeled tomato, sliced peeled cucumber, salmon paste, sardine paste, purée of ham and purée of white of chicken. Remove the crusts, cut a pile of rounds into small squares or fingers and trim the corners or cut into triangles, placing sufficient of each variety on a dish on a dish paper and sprinkling with mustard and cress.

1612 HOT SANDWICHES

This kind of sandwich is made with toast, or by making an ordinary round of sandwich with medium-sliced bread and toasting it in a sandwich-toasting machine. Hot sandwiches can be made successfully as single- or double-deckers; if made any higher they become unwieldy to serve and to eat. They should be made to order and served while still hot. It is helpful to serve the sandwich cut into quarters and the contents of each held in place with a cocktail stick. The following are given as examples of their type.

1613 Club Sandwich

Toast two slices of bread and spread each with Mayonnaise (185). On one slice arrange leaves of lettuce, sliced tomato, sliced hard-boiled egg, slices of cooked chicken breast and season. Finish with two slices of grilled bacon and cover with the second slice of toast. Press firmly together, trim the crusts and cut into two diagonally. Serve hot on a dish paper on a flat dish garnished with picked parsley. Because of the thickness of the filling it is good practice to pin each of the halves with a cocktail stick.

1614 Bookmaker's Sandwich

Cut two slices of bread lengthways from a sandwich loaf. Toast and spread with butter. Season a Minute Steak (786) and grill it quickly on both sides. Place it on one of the slices of toast, spread the steak with mustard and cover with the second slice of toast. Trim the crusts, cut into three pieces and reheat quickly. Serve on a dish paper on a flat dish garnished with picked parsley.

1615 Cape Cod Sandwich

Toast two slices of bread and spread one side of each with the brown meat of a dressed crab. On one side, add flaked white crabmeat mixed with a little mayonnaise, sliced peeled tomato and sliced peeled avocado pear. Season these then cover with the top slice and serve as for Club Sandwich (1613).

1616 Denver Sandwich

Toast two slices of bread and spread one side of each with liver pâté; add a 3mm-thick slice of grilled gammon and a small heap of sautéed onion. Cover with the top slice, reheat, cut into four and serve with a portion of coleslaw.

1617 Tongue and Spinach Sandwich

Toast three slices of bread and spread with butter. Place sliced ox-tongue on the bottom slice and arrange some slices of hard-boiled egg on top. Cover with the centre slice which should be buttered on both sides. Spread it with buttered spinach and sliced hard-boiled egg and cover with the top slice. Finish as for Club Sandwich (1613).

1618 Western Sandwich

Toast two slices of bread and spread one side of each with creamed horseradish. Cover the bottom slice with shredded lettuce, slices of roast beef, chopped pimento, pimento-stuffed olives and chopped walnuts. Cover with more roast beef then more shredded lettuce. Finish with the second slice of toast. Trim the crusts, cut into four, reheat and serve with a sauceboat of Guacamole (203).

1619 Smørrebrød or Open Sandwiches

These Scandinavian specialities are fairly substantial sandwiches made with one slice of bread only and with many different toppings and decorations. Rye, wholemeal, pumpernickel or Vienna bread can be used and should be cut into ¾cm-thick slices. The butter must be spread right across the bread and the toppings arranged artistically and generously on top. The crusts are not removed.

Suitable fillings for open sandwiches can include:
Eggs: scrambled; slices or quarters of hard-boiled; sieved egg with mayonnaise; raw yolk.
Cheese: all kinds including sliced, grated, and cream cheese.
Fish: anchovy; caviar; smoked eel; pickled and smoked herring; lobster; smoked mackerel; prawns; salmon – fresh, pickled and smoked; sardines; shrimps; sild.
Meat: bacon rashers; roast beef; brisket of beef; chicken; corned beef; ham; liver pâté; mortadella; roast pork; salami; tongue; turkey.
Vegetables: asparagus; cucumber; endive; lettuce; mushrooms; mustard and cress; onion rings; pimento; radish; spring onions; tomato; watercress.
Fruit: apple; grapes; mandarin and orange segments; pineapple; prunes.
Garnishes: capers; grated carrot; pickled red cabbage; chives; gherkin; grated horseradish; lemon quarters; potato salad; Russian salad; mayonnaise-based sauces; pickles.

1620 SAVOURIES

Savouries are normally served as the last course of a formal meal and are a peculiarly British contribution to the menu. They are served in other countries but more often as part of a selection of items suitable for a reception or cocktail party. As the savoury course these items should be fairly small, well-seasoned and should be served very hot where possible, without being dried up. This means preparing them as near as possible to the time of service.

There is a wide selection of savouries of which a large number are prepared and presented on toast, and which come under the heading of hot Canapés; in addition this section includes savoury Barquettes, Beignets, Bouchées, Dartois, Flans, Soufflés and Tartlettes etc.

Many of these savouries or canapés can be served as hot hors-d'oeuvre and are also suitable for serving hot or cold at receptions and cocktail parties and for finger buffets. In this case, they should be served very small as the customer does not usually sit down at this type of function.

1621 Allumettes d'Anchois – Anchovy Fingers

25 pieces
1½ hours

Stage	Ingredient	Quantity	Method
1	Pâte Feuilletée (1736)	500g	Roll out the pastry into an oblong, approx. 60cm × 15cm, cut in half lengthways and eggwash one half.
2	anchovy fillets	25	Place the anchovy fillets on the eggwashed half, side by side along the length of the pastry, leaving a space at each end and an equal space between each fillet.
3			Cover with the other piece of pastry. Seal by pressing between each fillet and then at the top, the bottom and the ends.
4			Trim the edges square, eggwash and cut into oblong pieces between each fillet. Place on a damp baking tray, allow to rest for 30 mins. in a cool place then bake at approx. 220°C until golden brown.
5			Serve warm, dressed on dish papers on flat dishes.

1622 Anges à Cheval – Angels on Horseback

10 portions
30 mins.

Stage	Ingredient	Quantity	Method
1	oysters	30	Remove the oysters from their shells and season with milled pepper. Roll one oyster in each slice of bacon. Place on skewers.
	bacon, short thin streaky rashers	30	

2			Grill on both sides until golden brown.
3	slices of toast	10	Remove the oysters from the skewers
	butter	75g	and place three pieces on each slice of
	parsley, picked		toast, buttered and trimmed oblong. Serve very hot, dressed on hot dishes, garnished with picked parsley.

1623 Barquettes

These boat-shaped savoury items may be served either hot or cold as required, or according to the filling. They may be filled with a wide variety of mixtures, e.g. diced lobster with lobster sauce, diced chicken in cream sauce, poached soft roes gratinated with Sauce Mornay, diced game with game flavoured demi-glace etc.

1624 Barquettes aux Crevettes

25 pieces
20 mins.

Stage	Ingredient	Quantity	Method
1	prawns, shelled	350g	Mix together, reheat thoroughly and
	Sauce Homard (170)	2½dl	adjust the seasoning.
2	pastry Barquette cases 7cm long (1764)	25	Fill the barquettes neatly with the mixture and serve warm dressed on dish papers on flat dishes. Garnish with
	parsley, picked		picked parsley.

1625 Beignets Soufflés au Fromage – Cheese Fritters

10 portions
45 mins.

Stage	Ingredient	Quantity	Method
1	water	2½dl	Place in a deep pan and bring to the boil
	butter	50g	slowly in order that the butter is melted
	salt	8g	by the time the water boils.
2	flour, strong	160g	Add away from the heat mixing well with a wooden spatula. Return pan to the heat and continue mixing until the mixture becomes smooth and does not stick to the side of the pan. Cool slightly.
3	eggs	3	Add the eggs to the mixture one at a
	Gruyère, cut in small dice	75g	time mixing in thoroughly. Add the cheese and a little cayenne.
	Parmesan, grated	25g	
	cayenne		
4			Using a dessertspoon, scoop out the mixture into 30 pieces the size of a walnut on to two sheets of oiled greaseproof paper.

5	Parmesan, grated	50g	Hold the sides of the paper steady and
	parsley, picked		slide the beignets into hot deep fat, fry

5   Parmesan, grated   50g   Hold the sides of the paper steady and
     parsley, picked   slide the beignets into hot deep fat, fry
                                to a golden brown (approx. 5 mins.).
                                Drain well, sprinkle with grated
                                Parmesan and serve very hot garnished
                                with picked parsley.

1626 Beignets Soufflés au Parmesan

This is prepared in the same way as Beignets Soufflés au Fromage (1625), using 75g of grated Parmesan at Stage 3 instead of Gruyère and Parmesan.

1627 Bouchées

This type of small vol-au-vent may be served hot or cold as required, or according to the filling. They may be filled with a wide variety of mixtures such as diced mushrooms in cream sauce, diced shrimp and mushroom in shrimp sauce, crabmeat in mayonnaise etc.

1628 Bouchées à l'Indienne

25 pieces
10 mins.

Stage	Ingredient	Quantity	Method
1	butter	25g	Heat the butter in a small pan, add the
	shelled prawns	350g	prawns, season and heat for a few seconds.
2	Curry Sauce (208)	2½dl	Add the sauce and heat together thoroughly.
3	Bouchée cases (1674)	25	Neatly fill the warmed bouchée cases with the prawns and just cover the surface of each with a teaspoon of chutney. Replace the lids, arrange on dish papers on flat dishes and garnish with picked parsley.
	mango chutney, warmed	50g	
	parsley, picked		

1629 Bouchées à la Reine

25 pieces
15 mins.

Stage	Ingredient	Quantity	Method
1	Velouté de Volaille (115)	2dl	Place in a small pan and simmer gently
	cream, double	1dl	together to a good coating consistency.
2	butter	25g	Heat the butter in a sauteuse, add the mushrooms, season lightly and add the lemon juice. Cook quickly until almost dry then add the chicken and sauce. Season well plus a touch of cayenne and heat thoroughly.
	white button mushrooms, cut in small dice	125g	
	lemon juice	good squeeze	
	cooked white of chicken, cut in small dice	300g	
	cayenne		

3	Bouchée cases		Neatly fill the warmed bouchées with the
	(1674)	25	mixture, replace the lids and arrange on
	parsley, picked		dish papers on flat dishes, garnished
			with picked parsley.

1630 Buck Rarebit

This is prepared in the same way as Welsh Rarebit (1670) with the addition of a drained, hot poached egg on each rarebit.

1631 Canapé aux Anchois – Anchovies on Toast   10 portions
20 mins.

Stage	Ingredient	Quantity	Method
1	anchovy fillets,		·Butter the toast. Arrange the anchovies
	well-drained	200g	neatly on each toast and trim square.
	slices of toast	10	Season with cayenne and reheat under
	butter	50g	the salamander.
	cayenne		
2	parsley, picked		Serve very hot, garnished with picked parsley.

1632 Canapé Diane   10 portions
30 mins.

Stage	Ingredient	Quantity	Method
1	chicken livers,		Season the livers with milled pepper and
	cleaned and cut		roll each piece in a rasher of bacon.
	in quarters	30 pieces	Thread on skewers.
	bacon, short thin		
	streaky rashers	30	
2			Grill on each side until golden brown.
3	slices of toast	10	Remove the rolled livers from the
	butter	75g	skewers and place three pieces on each
	parsley, picked		slice of toast, buttered and trimmed
			oblong. Serve very hot garnished with
			picked parsley.

1633 Canapé des Gourmets   10 portions
30 mins.

Stage	Ingredient	Quantity	Method
1	butter	50g	Melt the butter in a pan, add the ham
	lean ham, finely		and cream and heat together thoroughly
	chopped	450g	to a well-cohered consistency.
	cream, double	1dl	
2	lemon juice	good	Add the lemon juice and mustard. Mix
		squeeze	in well but do not reboil. Season well
	made English		plus a touch of cayenne.
	mustard	2 tbsps	
	cayenne		

3	slices of toast	10	Butter the toasts, trim square and spread
	butter	75g	the mixture dome-shape on top. Lightly
	parsley, picked		colour under the salamander and serve
			very hot garnished with picked parsley.

1634 Canapé Hollandaise

10 portions
40 mins.

Stage	Ingredient	Quantity	Method
1	smoked haddock	600g	Poach gently, drain, remove all skin and bone and lightly flake the flesh.
2	butter	50g	Melt in a sauteuse, add the flaked haddock and reheat.
3	slices of toast	10	Butter the toast and cut into rounds.
	butter	75g	
4	eggs, hard-boiled	4	Pile the mixture dome-shape on the
	butter, melted	25g	toasts and place two slices of hard-boiled
	cayenne		egg on each. Sprinkle with a little butter
	parsley, picked		and cayenne and reheat under the salamander. Serve very hot garnished with picked parsley.

1635 Canapé Ivanhoe

10 portions
40 mins.

Stage	Ingredient	Quantity	Method
1	smoked haddock	500g	Poach gently, drain, remove all skin and bone and lightly flake the flesh.
2	Béchamel (114)	2dl	Reheat the Béchamel in a sauteuse. Add
	cream	½dl	the flaked haddock and the cream,
	cayenne		season with cayenne and heat together gently.
3	slices of toast	10	Butter the toast and cut into rounds.
	butter	75g	
4	mushrooms, grilled	10	Pile the mixture dome-shaped on the
	parsley, picked		toasts and place a grilled mushroom on each. Reheat under the salamander. Serve very hot garnished with picked parsley.

1636 Canapé Nina

10 portions
30 mins.

Stage	Ingredient	Quantity	Method
1	flat mushrooms, grilled	20	Cut the mushrooms into half on the slant. Cut each tomato into four thick
	tomatoes, peeled	10	slices. Cut each walnut into four slices.
	pickled walnuts	10	

| 2 | slices of toast | 10 | Butter the toast and cut into squares. |
| | butter | 75g | |

3	cayenne		Garnish each slice of toast with four
	parsley, picked		pieces of mushroom, dark side upper-
			most, four slices of tomato and finally
			four slices of walnut. Season with a little
			cayenne, reheat under the salamander
			and serve very hot garnished with picked
			parsley.

1637 Canapé Quo Vadis

10 portions
40 mins.

Stage	Ingredient	Quantity	Method
1	flat mushrooms, grilled	20	Cut the mushrooms in half on the slant.
	soft herring roes	20	Season, flour and shallow fry the roes on
	butter	50g	both sides in the butter.
2	slices of toast	10	Butter the toast and cut into squares.
	butter	75g	
3	cayenne		Arrange the mushrooms and roes neatly
	parsley, picked		on the toast, season with cayenne, reheat under the salamander and serve very hot garnished with picked parsley.

1638 Canapé Ritchie

10 portions
40 mins.

Stage	Ingredient	Quantity	Method
1	smoked haddock	600g	Poach gently, drain, remove all skin and bone and lightly flake the flesh.
2	Béchamel (114)	2dl	Reheat the Béchamel in a pan. Add the
	cream, double	½dl	haddock, cream and cheese, season well
	Cheddar cheese, grated	50g	with cayenne and heat together gently.
	cayenne		
3	slices of toast	10	Butter the toast and trim square. Pile the
	butter	75g	mixture dome-shape on the toasts,
	Parmesan, grated	35g	sprinkle with the Parmesan and gratinate a light brown under the salamander.
4	parsley, picked		Serve very hot garnished with picked parsley.

1639 Cassolette Epicurienne

10 portions
50 mins.

Stage	Ingredient	Quantity	Method
1	Pommes Duchesse mixture (1560)	750g	Using flour, mould into ten round flat galettes approx. 5cm in diameter and
	flour		2cm thick.

2	eggwash breadcrumbs, white	} for crumbing	Paner (72) the galettes carefully then pass through the egg and breadcrumbs a second time. Reshape neatly then cut a circle through the top surface of each with a 4cm plain pastry cutter.
3			Deep fry at 190°C to a golden brown. Drain, then remove the top circles with a small knife and reserve. Empty the cases of the Duchesse mixture.
4	butter	75g	Heat the butter in a frying-pan, season the livers and quickly sauté until just pink. Remove with a perforated spoon and keep on one side. Add the mushrooms to the same fat and sauté until almost dry. Return the livers with the mushrooms, add the meat glaze and toss over together. Add the lemon juice and chopped basil. Check the seasoning and finish with a good touch of cayenne.
	chicken livers, cut in small thick slices	300g	
	small button mushrooms, cut in thick slices	125g	
	Glace de Viande (103)	1 tbsp	
	lemon juice	good squeeze	
	fresh basil, chopped	½ tbsp	
	cayenne		
5	parsley, picked		See that the cases are warm and fill them proud with the chicken mixture. Cover with the reserved lids, sloping to one side and serve on dish papers on flat dishes, garnished with picked parsley.

1640 Champignons sous Cloche

10 portions
30 mins.

Stage	Ingredient	Quantity	Method
1	button mushrooms, white	750g	Wash well and trim off the stalks. Place in buttered fireproof glass dishes.
2	double cream	½ litre	Season the mushrooms and add the cream to half-way up the dishes. Add a few drops of lemon juice and bring to the boil on the stove. Cover with glass lids and draw to the side of the stove. Allow to cook very gently for 8–10 mins. Serve immediately without removing the lids.
	juice of lemon	few drops	

1641 Champignons sur Croûte – Mushrooms on Toast

10 portions
20 mins.

Stage	Ingredient	Quantity	Method
1	flat mushrooms	40	Wash, trim the stalks, and place on a tray dark side uppermost. Season,
	butter	75g	

sprinkle with the melted butter and grill
under the salamander until soft.

2	slices of toast	10	Butter the toast and trim square.
	butter	75g	Arrange the mushrooms dark side
	parsley, picked		uppermost on top, four per slice. Reheat
			under the salamander and serve very hot
			garnished with picked parsley.

1642 Chaussonettes aux Champignons

20 pieces
1¼ hours

Stage	Ingredient	Quantity	Method
1	butter	50g	Heat the butter in a shallow pan and
	shallots, finely		cook the shallot without colour. Add the
	chopped	50g	mushrooms, lightly season and cook
	mushrooms, finely		together until almost dry.
	chopped	450g	
2	ham, finely chopped	250g	Add the ham and cream and cook
	cream, double	½dl	together until lightly thickened then add
	foie gras, purée	75g	the foie gras and parsley. Season as
	parsley, chopped	1 tbsp	necessary plus a little cayenne. Heat
	cayenne		thoroughly and allow to cool.
3	Pâte Feuilletée		Roll out the paste approx. 2mm thick
	(1736)	600g	and cut out 20 rounds approx. 8cm in
	eggwash		diameter. Place equal amounts of the
			mixture to one side of each round.
			Eggwash the edges then fold over and
			seal well together. Place on a dampened
			baking tray. Crimp the edges, brush with
			eggwash and using the point of a small
			knife, score the surface of the
			Chaussonettes to decorate. Make two
			small holes in the centre for the steam to
			escape. Allow to rest for 30 mins.
4	parsley, picked		Place the Chaussonettes in the oven at
			215°C and bake to a golden brown.
			Serve on dish papers on flat dishes,
			garnished with picked parsley.

1643 Croque Monsieur

10 portions
30 mins.

Stage	Ingredient	Quantity	Method
1	ham, slices	10	Place each slice of ham between two
	Gruyère, thin		slices of cheese and then sandwich it
	slices	20	between two slices of bread. Press firmly
	bread, thin		together and cut out with a round cutter
	slices	20	8cm in diameter.

2	butter, clarified	300g	Heat in a pan then fry the croques on
	parsley, picked		both sides to a golden brown. Drain well and serve garnished with picked parsley.

1644 Croûte Baron

10 portions
30 mins.

Stage	Ingredient	Quantity	Method
1	bacon, back rashers	20	Grill the bacon, cut the mushrooms into half on the slant, poach the marrow in a little hot stock and drain.
	flat mushrooms, grilled	20	
	bone marrow, slices	40	
2	slices of toast	10	Butter and trim the toast square.
	butter	75g	
3	cayenne		Dress each slice of toast with four pieces of mushroom, two slices of bacon and finally four slices of marrow. Season with a little cayenne, reheat under the salamander and serve very hot garnished with picked parsley.
	parsley, picked		

1645 Croûte Derby

10 portions
30 mins.

Stage	Ingredient	Quantity	Method
1	Béchamel (114)	2dl	Reheat the Béchamel in a sauteuse. Add the ham and cream. Season with cayenne, mix well and heat thoroughly.
	lean ham, finely chopped	400g	
	cream	½dl	
	cayenne		
2	slices of toast	10	Butter and cut the toast into rounds.
	butter	75g	
3	pickled walnuts	5	Pile the mixture dome-shape on the toast and place half a walnut on each. Reheat under the salamander and serve very hot garnished with picked parsley.
	parsley, picked		

1646 Croûte Windsor

This is prepared in the same way as Croûte Derby (1645), garnishing with a grilled mushroom instead of the pickled walnut.

1647 Croûte Yorkaise

This is prepared in the same way as Croûte Derby (1645), garnishing with a diamond of ham instead of the pickled walnut.

1648 Dartois aux Anchois

25 pieces
1½ hours

Stage	Ingredient	Quantity	Method
1	anchovy fillets Béchamel (114)	150g ½dl	Pass the anchovy fillets through a fine sieve and mix with the cold Béchamel. Season with a little cayenne.
2	Pâte Feuilletée (1736) eggwash	650g	Roll out the pastry into an oblong approx. 50cm × 18cm cut in half lengthways and place one half on a damp baking tray. Eggwash the edges and prick the centre area.
3			Spread the anchovy mixture along the centre of this eggwashed half leaving the edges clear.
4			Fold the other piece of pastry in half lengthways. Make incisions 2½cm long across the folded edge at 7mm intervals.
5			Carefully unfold the cut pastry onto the filled piece. Seal the four edges carefully and trim square. Eggwash and allow to rest for 30 mins. in a cool place. Bake at approx. 220°C until golden brown (20–25 mins.).
6			Remove from the tray and cut across into 25 fingers. Serve warm dressed on dish papers on suitable dishes.

1649 Diables à Cheval – Devils on Horseback

10 portions
25 mins.

Stage	Ingredient	Quantity	Method
1	prunes, cooked chutney, chopped	30 100g	Remove the stones from the prunes, taking care not to damage the flesh, then stuff each with a little chutney.
2	bacon, short thin streaky rashers	30	Roll one prune in each slice of bacon and place on skewers.
3			Grill on both sides until golden brown.
4	slices of toast butter parsley, picked	10 75g	Remove the rolled prunes from the skewers and place three pieces on each slice of toast, buttered and trimmed oblong. Serve very hot garnished with picked parsley.

1650 Flan à la Florentine

8 portions
1 hour

Stage	Ingredient	Quantity	Method
1	Pâte à Foncer (1738)	250g	Line a buttered 20cm flan ring with the pastry and allow to rest for 30 mins.
2	butter	50g	Heat the butter in a pan, add the garlic and cook very gently for a few seconds without colour. Add the spinach and toss over to mix. Allow to cool.
	garlic, finely chopped	1 clove	
	spinach, plain boiled, drained, squeezed and roughly chopped	350g	
3	Parmesan, grated	50g	Spread the spinach over the bottom of the prepared flan and sprinkle with the cheese.
4	eggs	3	Whisk the eggs well, add the cream and season with salt, pepper, and a little cayenne. Mix well together and pour into the flan to within ½cm of the rim of the flan. Dust the surface with a little nutmeg. Bake in a moderate oven at 175°C so as to cook the pastry, set the custard and give a light brown colour to the surface (approx. 35–40 mins.). Serve warm, either whole or cut in sections.
	cream	3½dl	
	cayenne		
	nutmeg, ground	pinch	

1651 Flan Forestière

8 portions
1½ hours

Stage	Ingredient	Quantity	Method
1	Pâte à Foncer (1738)	250g	Line a buttered 20cm diameter flan ring with the paste and allow to rest for 30 mins.
2	butter	75g	Heat the butter in a pan, add the onions and cook until transparent then add the mushrooms, season lightly and sauté together until cooked and almost free from moisture. Allow to cool, then cover the bottom of the flan with the onions and mushrooms. Sprinkle with the chopped parsley.
	small onions, finely sliced	100g	
	button mushrooms, sliced	350g	
	parsley, chopped	1 tbsp	
3	eggs	3	Whisk the eggs well, add the milk and cream, season with salt and a little cayenne and mix well together. Add to the flan to within ½cm from the rim of the flan.
	milk	2dl	
	cream	1½dl	
	cayenne		

4   Bake in a moderate oven at 175°C so as
to cook the pastry, set the custard and to
give a light brown colour to the surface
(approx. 35–40 mins.). Serve warm,
either whole or cut in sections.

1652 Flan aux Fruits de Mer

8 portions
1½ hours

Stage	Ingredient	Quantity	Method
1	Pâte à Foncer (1738)	250g	Line a buttered 20cm diameter flan ring with the paste and allow to rest for 30 mins.
2	butter		Heat the butter in a pan, add the shallots and cook without colour. Add the prawns and mussels and toss over to mix. Allow to cool.
	shallots	50g	
	prawns, shelled	75g	
	mussels, cooked and		
	cut in half	24	
3	scallops	8	Separate the red tongues and cut the white parts horizontally into three slices.
4	butter	50g	Heat the butter in a sauté pan, add the slices of scallop, the red tongues and the scampi, season and toss over to stiffen and set. Allow to cool.
	scampi	8	
5	Lobster Sauce		Heat the lobster sauce and allow to cool in a basin; add the eggs and cream. Season with salt and cayenne and mix thoroughly together.
	(169)	1½dl	
	eggs	3	
	cream, double	2dl	
6	parsley, chopped	1 tbsp	Spread the prawns and mussels over the bottom of the prepared flan, cover with the slices of white scallop meat. Place the scampi equidistant on top and pointing to the centre with a red scallop tongue between each, sprinkle with the parsley.
7			Pass the custard mixture carefully through a fine strainer over the whole to within ½cm from the rim of the flan.
8			Bake in a moderate oven at 175°C so as to cook the pastry and give a light brown colour to the surface, approx. 35–40 mins. Serve warm, either whole or cut in sections.

1653 Laitances sur Canapé – Soft Roes on Toast   10 portions
20 mins.

Stage	Ingredient	Quantity	Method
1	soft herring roes	30	Season, flour and fry the roes to a
	butter	75g	golden brown on both sides in the butter.
2	slices of toast	10	Butter and trim the toast into squares.
	butter	75g	
3	cayenne		Dress three roes on each piece of toast,
	parsley, picked		sprinkle with a little cayenne, reheat under the salamander and serve very hot garnished with picked parsley.

1654 Moelle sur Croûte – Bone Marrow on Toast

Cut beef bone marrow into 7mm-thick slices and poach gently in a little salted stock. Drain and dress neatly on trimmed squares of buttered toast. Sprinkle with a little cayenne and serve garnished with picked parsley.

1655 Paillettes au Fromage – Cheese Straws   60 pieces
1½ hours

Stage	Ingredient	Quantity	Method
1	Pâte Feuilletée (1736)	325g	Roll out the paste approx. 60cm × 30cm. Brush with water to dampen the
	Parmesan, grated	50g	surface then sprinkle evenly with the
	cayenne		cheese and a little cayenne pepper. Lightly roll into the surface. Give a single turn, i.e. fold into three then roll out again to an oblong 30cm × 40cm and approx. 3mm thick.
2	Parmesan, grated	40g	Eggwash the surface. Sprinkle with the
	cayenne		Parmesan and a little cayenne and very
	eggwash		lightly roll in. Cut into strips 1cm wide × 30cm long. Twist each strip several times and fix on a dampened baking tray.
3			Allow to rest for 30 mins. in a cold place and bake at approx. 220°C for 8–10 mins. until golden brown.
4			Trim the ends and cut into approx. 10cm lengths while still warm. Serve on dish papers on silver flats.

SPECIAL POINT

For presentation, take strips of pastry, at Stage 2, 16cm long × 1cm wide, twist them two or three times and form into a circle joining the ends together. Cook with the straws. Place the cooked straws through the circles to give the appearance of sheaves.

1656 Quiche Lorraine

8 portions
1½ hours

Stage	Ingredient	Quantity	Method
1	Pâte à Foncer (1738)	250g	Line a buttered 20cm diameter flan ring with the paste and allow to rest for 30 mins.
2	bacon, streaky	200g	Cut the bacon into small lardons, blanch, lightly fry and drain. Cut the cheese into small dice. Garnish the bottom of the flan with the bacon and cheese.
	Gruyère cheese	100g	
3	eggs	3	Whisk the eggs well, add the milk and cream, season with salt and a little cayenne and mix well together. Add to the flan to within ½cm from the rim of the flan.
	milk	2dl	
	cream	1½dl	
	cayenne		
4			Bake in a moderate oven at 175°C so as to cook the pastry, set the custard, and to give a light brown colour to the surface (approx. 35 mins.). Serve hot.

1657 Quichelette au Jambon

10 pieces
1¼ hours

Stage	Ingredient	Quantity	Method
1	Pâte à Foncer (1738)	250g	Roll out the paste to approx. 2mm thick, and line ten deep tartlet moulds (6½–7cm diameter). Leave to rest for 30 mins.
2	lean ham, cut in 3mm dice	200g	Place equal amounts of ham in the tartlets plus a small pinch of parsley.
	parsley, chopped		
3	eggs	3	Whisk the eggs well, add the cream, season with a little salt and cayenne and mix well together. Add to the tartlets to within 3mm of the tops of the paste.
	cream	3½dl	
	cayenne		
4			Bake in a moderate oven at 175°C so as to cook the pastry, set the custard and to give a light brown colour to the surfaces (approx. 30 mins.). Serve warm.

1658 Ramequin au Gruyère (1)

10 portions
45 mins.

Stage	Ingredient	Quantity	Method
1	milk	2½dl	Place in a deep pan and bring to the boil slowly in order that the butter is melted by the time the water boils.
	butter	50g	
	salt	8g	

2	flour	150g	Add, away from the heat mixing well with a wooden spatule. Return pan to the heat and continue mixing until the mixture becomes smooth and does not stick to the side of the pan. Cool slightly.
3	eggs Gruyère, cut in very small dice Parmesan, grated cayenne	3 100g 25g	Add the eggs to the mixture one at a time mixing in thoroughly. Add the cheese and a little cayenne.
4	butter Gruyère, cut in very small dice	75g 50g	Well butter ten porcelain ramequin moulds and fill with the mixture equally divided between them. Sprinkle with a little of the Gruyère and bake in a moderate oven at 190°C for 15–20 mins. Place on dish papers on suitable dishes and serve immediately.

1659 Ramequin au Gruyère (2)

Proceed in the same way as for Ramequin au Gruyère (1) but at Stage 4 fill the mixture into ten deep tartlet moulds lined with Pâte à Foncer (1738) instead of the ramequin moulds. Place a diamond-shaped slice of Gruyère cheese on top of each and bake at 190°C for 15–20 mins. Place on dish papers on suitable dishes and serve immediately.

1660 Sardines on Toast

10 portions
20 mins.

Stage	Ingredient	Quantity	Method
1	sardines, medium	40	Carefully remove the skins then open up from the back and remove the central bones. Re-form to shape.
2	slices of toast butter parsley, picked	10 75g	Arrange the sardines on squares of trimmed and buttered toast. Sprinkle with a little melted butter and cayenne. Place under the salamander and serve very hot. Garnish with picked parsley.

1661 Sausage Rolls

20 pieces
1½ hours

Stage	Ingredient	Quantity	Method
1	Pâte Feuilletée (1736) sausage-meat flour . eggwash	650g 500g	Roll out the pastry 60cm × 20cm wide and cut in half lengthways. Mould the sausage-meat into two rolls of approx. 60cm length using a little flour. Place along the centre of each piece of pastry. Eggwash the edges of the pastry, fold over and press the edges to seal. Trim the edges square and eggwash.

2			Cut into 6cm lengths, mark with the back of a fork, place on a damp baking sheet and allow to rest for 30 mins. in a cool place.
3			Bake at approx. 220°C until golden brown for 18–20 mins. Serve arranged on dish papers on flat dishes.

1662 Scotch Woodcock

10 portions
30 mins.

Stage	Ingredient	Quantity	Method
1	eggs	10	Scramble the eggs with the butter and
	butter	75g	cream (420).
	cream	½dl	
2	slices of toast	10	Pile dome-shaped on squares of trimmed
	butter	75g	buttered toast.
3	anchovy fillets (thin strips)	40	Arrange the anchovies trellis-fashion over the eggs and decorate with a caper
	capers		in each space. Reheat and serve
	parsley, picked		garnished with picked parsley.

1663 Soufflé aux Champignons – Mushroom Soufflé

8 portions
50 mins.

Stage	Ingredient	Quantity	Method
1	butter	25g	Heat the butter in a pan, add the shallot
	shallot, finely chopped	25g	and cook without colour. Add the mushrooms, season and cook quickly
	mushrooms, finely chopped	350g	until soft and almost dry. Pass through a fine sieve.
2	Béchamel (114)	3dl	Bring to the boil in a pan. Add the mushroom purée and cook to a fairly stiff consistency.
3	egg yolks	5	Remove the mixture from the heat and
	cayenne		whisk in the egg yolks quickly. Season well with salt and cayenne. Mix thoroughly and allow to cool slightly.
4	butter	25g	Well butter two 15cm soufflé moulds.
	egg whites	6	Whisk the whites in a clean copper bowl
	whole button mushrooms, stalks removed and cooked à Blanc (60)	8	with a pinch of salt until just stiff. Add a little of the whites to the mushroom mixture and mix in. Fold in the rest of the whites gently. Pour the mixture into the prepared soufflé moulds. Place four mushrooms on each.

5	Cook the soufflés in the oven at 195°C for 25–30 mins. Remove and serve immediately.

1664 Soufflé Florentine – Spinach Soufflé

Prepare in the same way as Soufflé au Parmesan (1667), mixing in 100g of fairly dry spinach purée (1456) at Stage 2 in place of the Parmesan. Season and add a little grated nutmeg. The finished mixture is poured into soufflé moulds which have been buttered only.

1665 Soufflé au Fromage – Cheese Soufflé   8 portions
                                                      45 mins.

Stage	Ingredient	Quantity	Method
1	Béchamel (114)	3dl	Bring to the boil in a sauteuse.
2	egg yolks	5	Remove the Béchamel from the fire and whisk in the egg yolks quickly. Add the cheeses and season well with salt and cayenne. Mix thoroughly and allow to cool slightly.
	Parmesan, grated	15g	
	Cheddar, cut in very small dice	75g	
	cayenne		
3	butter	25g	Well butter two 15cm soufflé moulds and dust with Parmesan. Whisk the whites in a clean copper bowl with a pinch of salt until just stiff. Add a little of the whites to the mixture and mix in. Fold in the rest of the whites gently. Pour the mixture into the prepared soufflé moulds. Make a star shape with the diamonds of Cheddar on top of each soufflé.
	egg whites	6	
	Parmesan, grated	25g	
	thin diamond shapes of Cheddar	8	
4			Cook in the oven at 195°C for 25–30 mins. Remove and serve immediately.

1666 Soufflé au Jambon – Ham Soufflé   8 portions
                                                  45 mins.

Stage	Ingredient	Quantity	Method
1	lean cooked ham	350g	Chop the ham finely and pass through a sieve or food processor to give a fine purée.
2	Béchamel (114)	3dl	Bring the Béchamel to the boil in a sauteuse. Add the ham and heat well.
3	egg yolks	5	Remove the mixture from the heat and whisk in the egg yolks quickly. Season with salt, pepper and a good pinch of paprika. Mix thoroughly and allow to cool slightly.
	paprika		

4	butter	25g	Well butter two 15cm soufflé moulds.
	egg whites	6	Whisk the whites in a clean copper bowl
	diamond shapes of		with a pinch of salt until just stiff. Add a
	lean ham	8	little of the whites to the mixture and
			mix in. Fold in the rest of the whites
			gently. Pour the mixture into the
			prepared soufflé moulds. Make a star
			shape with the diamonds of ham on top
			of each soufflé.
5			Cook in the oven at 195°C for 25–30
			mins. Remove and serve immediately.

1667 Soufflé au Parmesan

8 portions
45 mins.

Stage	Ingredient	Quantity	Method
1	Béchamel (114)	3½dl	Bring to the boil in a sauteuse.
2	egg yolks	5	Remove the Béchamel from the fire and
	Parmesan, grated	75g	whisk in the egg yolks quickly. Add the
	cayenne		Parmesan and season well with salt and
			cayenne. Mix thoroughly and allow to
			cool slightly.
3	butter	25g	Well butter two 15cm soufflé moulds
	egg whites	6	and dust with Parmesan. Whisk the
	Parmesan, grated	25g	whites in a clean copper bowl with a
			pinch of salt until just stiff. Add a little
			of the whites to the mixture and mix in.
			Fold in the rest of the whites gently.
			Pour the mixture into the prepared
			soufflé moulds.
4			Cook in the oven at 195°C for 25–30
			mins. Remove and serve immediately.

1668 Tarte aux Oignons – Onion Flan

8 portions
1½ hours

Stage	Ingredient	Quantity	Method
1	Pâte à Foncer	250g	Line a buttered 20cm flan ring with the
	(1738)		pastry and allow to rest for 30 mins.
2	butter	75g	Heat the butter in a shallow pan, add the
	streaky bacon, smoked,		lardons and sauté until lightly coloured.
	cut in very small		Add the onions and cook more slowly
	lardons (51)		until the onions are soft and just lightly
	and blanched	100g	coloured.
	onions, thinly		
	sliced	500g	
3	flour	25g	Sprinkle the onions with the flour, mix
			in well and cook slowly for a few mins.
			Allow to cool slightly.

4	milk cayenne nutmeg, ground	3dl	Boil the milk then add to the onions and mix in thoroughly, bring to the boil and simmer gently for a few mins. Season well plus a little cayenne and nutmeg, allow to cool a little.
5	egg yolks	3	Add to the mixture and mix in thoroughly. Allow to cool then place into the prepared flan. Smooth the surface level then place into the oven at 190°C to bake for 35–40 mins. Serve warm.

1669 Tartelettes de Crevettes

Prepare in the same way as Barquettes aux Crevettes (1624), using Tartlet Cases (1763) instead of the barquettes. Other suitable mixtures may be used to fill tartlet cases and should be designated according to the mixture used, e.g. Tartelettes à la Reine using a salpicon of chicken, mushroom and Sauce Suprême or Diane using a salpicon of game, mushroom, truffle and demi-glace.

1670 Welsh Rarebit

10 portions
30 mins.

Stage	Ingredient	Quantity	Method
1	Béchamel (114) Cheddar cheese, grated	2dl 400g	Boil the Béchamel in a sauteuse, add the cheese and mix in thoroughly away from the heat.
2	egg yolks mustard, English Worcestershire sauce cayenne	2 5g few drops	Add, season with salt and a little cayenne and mix in thoroughly.
3	slices of toast butter	10 75g	Butter and trim the toast into squares.
4	parsley, picked		Spread the mixture dome-shape on the toast, place under the salamander and glaze brown. Serve immediately garnished with picked parsley.

SPECIAL POINT
A little reduced beer may be added to the mixture.

20

Pastry and Sweet Dishes

The pastry department plays an important part in the overall operation of a professional kitchen and the standard of its products has a great impact on the reputation of the establishment. If the sweet course is not up to the standard of the previous course the customer is likely to remember this, to the detriment of the meal as a whole. The reason for this is that the sweet course is normally the last course and the one which leaves a lasting impression.

The specialised nature of the work of the pastry department often means that it tends to operate separately from the main kitchen. The techniques used there are very different from those of the main kitchen; although the range of commodities used is perhaps not as wide, they must be understood well in order to produce satisfactory results and in no other department is it so important to use correct ingredients, to weigh them accurately, to mix correctly and to cook at the right temperature.

The pastry department produces the following items: hot sweets such as puddings, pies, soufflés, fritters; cold sweets such as jellies, bavarois, mousses, charlottes; ice-cream dishes; flans, tarts, pastries and gâteaux, petits fours; sweet sauces; yeast products such as bread, rolls, Savarins and Croissants, and a number of items required by the main kitchen, e.g. Fleurons, Vols-au-vent, cheese straws, tartlet cases, and the covering and cooking of pies and so on.

This chapter is devoted mainly to recipes for dishes and other preparations which can figure as items on the menu of a catering establishment. Specialised decorative pastry work, confectionery and the more extended repertoire of bread, rolls, cakes, gâteaux, pastries and buns are not fully covered in this chapter. There is a wide range of specialist pastry books available for these specialised areas and recommended titles can be found in the Select Bibliography (see page 881).

———————————————COMMODITIES———————————————

The following have special applications to pastry work:

Flours

The most important factor which determines the suitability of a particular type of flour for pastry work is the ratio of its gluten-forming protein.

Strong flour: this type of flour has a high gluten protein content which is developed by manipulation and gives a high tensile strength to any dough or paste which is made with it. It is an essential requirement for the production of the yeast-fermented doughs for bread, savarins, buns and croissants, for chou paste and puff pastry and for frying batters which need to produce a crisp outer coating for such things as fritters.

Soft flour: also known as cake flour. This type of flour has a low gluten content and is more suited to the production of cakes, sponges and sweet and short pastry where a high degree of manipulation is not required.

Fats

Butter: this is undoubtedly the best as far as flavour is concerned. It has excellent creaming qualities but tends to become soft if not manipulated at cool temperatures. Unsalted butter of a fairly firm plastic texture is to be preferred to blended salted butter.

Margarines: these are blended from oils and have a good texture and creaming properties. They are mostly neutral in flavour and because of this are not to be preferred to butter.

Pastry margarine: known as puff pastry fat. Has a firm texture and high melting properties and thus excellent for the production of puff pastry but the cooked pastry has a poor flavour and tends to develop a dry and plastic eating quality when very cold.

Lard: has excellent shortening qualities. Used extensively for short, savoury and hot water pastry.

White compound fat: neutral in flavour and colour, this fat creams easily and is useful in the making of bread and pastry and for the greasing of pastry equipment where required.

Sugars

Cube or Lump: traditionally used for boiled sugar as being the most pure.

Granulated: this is useful for any product which requires sweetening but which can be dissolved in a liquid, e.g. stewed fruits. Not best for the making of sweet pastry as the crystals are too large and tend to caramelise in the cooking pastry. These days it is of excellent purity and is now suitable for all sugar boiling.

Caster: this sugar has a fine grain and dissolves quickly. It gives a smooth consistency to pastry products and is used in the recipes in this chapter unless otherwise stated.

Icing: a very fine powdered sugar used mainly for the production of icings, for dredging over items and sometimes for glazing.

Milk

Fresh: this is extensively used in the production of milk puddings and related mixes.

Powdered: this is available as full-cream or skimmed and should only be used to replace fresh milk for reasons of economy. Very useful form of milk to enrich doughs without adding moisture.

Eggs

Fresh: graded by size from 1, the largest, to 7, the smallest. The standard egg, size 3, weighs 60–65g in the shell or 5dl per 10 eggs as a liquid by measure. Should be used fresh where the whole egg or yolk is required. The whites of staler eggs lose moisture and the thicker quality is more useful for the production of meringue etc.

Frozen: these are available as yolks, whites and mixed whole eggs; these save time in cracking eggs but require greater care in defrosting, handling and storage.

Dried albumen: this is used as a substitute for fresh egg white; it is useful for the making of the various kinds of meringue but is really only suitable for very large-scale work.

Cream

Single: this type of cream has an 18% butterfat content and will not thicken when whipped. It is used as a pouring cream but has little application in the making of sweet dishes.

Whipping: this cream has a butterfat content of 35% and will whip to a satisfactory peak with a good increase in bulk. It lacks the richness and colour of double cream but is satisfactory for any sweet dish where whipped cream is called for.

Double: this cream has a minimum butterfat content of 48%, it holds its shape well when whipped and has a particularly rich appearance and taste. Almost always the best for all types of pastry work.

STORAGE AND HYGIENE CONSIDERATIONS

The commodities used in pastry work are very prone to contamination and care should be taken to ensure hygienic storage and refrigeration. Milk, cream and eggs should be stored under separate air-circulated refrigeration and where possible kept in clean covered containers separate from each other so as to avoid any possibility of cross-contamination. Prepared dishes and products such as pastry and batters need good refrigeration, separate above all from other cooked or raw foods and strong smelling items; they can quickly absorb smells and flavours from other food. All dairy produce should be used in rotation.

Dry commodities such as flour, sugar, cereals and nuts etc. are prone to contamination and infestation by insects. They need storing in well sealed containers and the ingredients not just topped up with supplies but finished up and used strictly in rotation. The emptied container should be scrupulously cleaned and sterilised when empty.

Work surfaces, benches, shelves and floors quickly pick up dust from flour and sugar and these quickly attract insects. Scrupulous attention should be paid to ensure the cleanliness of all these surfaces; there should be an adequate supply of hot water and washing facilities.

The pastry department uses a very high proportion of machinery and equipment. These should be adequately and regularly maintained.

BASIC AND MISCELLANEOUS PREPARATIONS

1671 Almonds, to Toast

Spread the whole, nibbed or flaked almonds on a baking tray and place in the oven at 175°C. Turn from the outside to the centre from time to time so as to ensure even colouring. Toast until medium brown in colour. Allow to cool and store in an airtight container.

1672 Apricot Glaze

Boil together four parts of apricot jam with one part of water and pass through a fine strainer. If more water is required to adjust the consistency, the glaze should be reboiled before use.

1673 Biscuits à la Cuillère – Finger Biscuits
30
45 mins.

Stage	Ingredient	Quantity	Method
1	egg yolks caster sugar	5 120g	Place in a basin and whisk until white and creamy.
2	egg whites soft, flour, sieved	4 120g	Whisk the whites until stiff and cut in a quarter of the whites to the creamed yolks and sugar using a metal spoon. Gently fold in the flour, followed by the remaining whites.
3			Place the mixture into a piping bag with a 1cm plain tube and pipe 9cm lengths on greaseproof paper on a baking tray. Sprinkle liberally with caster sugar. Shake off the surplus sugar.
4			Bake at 220°C for approx. 10 mins.
5			To remove from the paper, turn over and sprinkle the reverse side of the paper with water while the biscuits are still warm. Allow to cool on a wire rack.

SPECIAL POINT
It is essential that this mixture is used and baked off immediately.

1674 Bouchées

Prepare in the same way as Vols-au-vent (1714), rolling out the paste 4mm thick and cutting out with a 5cm fancy cutter. Use a 4cm plain cutter to cut half-way through each round.

1675 Brandy Snaps
30
40 mins.

Stage	Ingredient	Quantity	Method
1	butter sugar golden syrup lemon juice	250g 250g 250g 1 tbsp	Melt the butter in a bowl, remove from the heat then add the remaining ingredients and mix in.
2	flour ginger, ground	250g 1 tsp	Sift together and mix slowly and thoroughly into the melted ingredients. Allow to rest for 15 mins.

3	butter	25g	Take equal-sized portions with a dessertspoon and place on a well-buttered baking tray approx. 6–7cm separate from each other.
4			Press each piece slightly flat then bake in a moderate oven at 185°C until golden brown, approx. 10 mins.
5			Allow the snaps to rest on the tray for a few seconds, then remove with a palette knife one by one and either mould to give a tube shape or mould round cream horn tins to give a cornet shape. Remove to a wire grill to set firmly.

1676 Bun Wash

Boil together an equal amount of water and sugar to a light syrupy consistency.

1677 Buttercream (1)

1kg
45 mins.

This preparation is used extensively in the preparation and decoration of gâteaux and pastries. It may be flavoured with, for example, vanilla essence, melted chocolate, coffee as well as liqueurs and spirits such as Kirsch, rum, brandy, Grand Marnier etc., and may also be lightly coloured as required using good-quality food colours.

Stage	Ingredient	Quantity	Method
1	egg yolks	10	Place in a basin and whisk well together.
	caster sugar	350g	Place over a pan of hot water or in a
	water	1dl	bain-marie and whisk continuously until the mixture becomes light, creamy and thick in texture. Remove from the heat and continue whisking until it becomes cold.
2	butter, unsalted	500g	Cream the butter and add to the egg mixture a little at a time beating with a wooden spoon. Store in the refrigerator.

1678 Buttercream (2)

1 kg
10 mins.

Stage	Ingredient	Quantity	Method
1	unsalted butter, soft	500g	Place the butter in a basin and beat with a wooden spatula until light and creamy.
2	icing sugar, sifted	500g	Add the icing sugar slowly, mixing in thoroughly. Finally, beat the mixture vigorously to a light fluffy texture.

1679 Chocolate Shapes

1) Melt the chocolate slowly in a double saucepan or in the bain-marie, stirring continuously with a wooden spoon. Do not overheat but aim for a lukewarm temperature of 38–40°C.
2) Spread thinly, no more than 2mm thick, on greaseproof paper laid on a marble slab. Allow to just set then cut into shapes as required with a knife or using a shaped cutter. Do not cut through the paper.
3) Leave in a cool place until hard then remove from the paper and use as required or store in a covered tin.

1680 Chocolate Shavings

1) Melt the chocolate slowly in a double saucepan or in the bain-marie, stirring continuously with a wooden spoon. Do not overheat but aim for a lukewarm temperature of 38–40°C.
2) Using a long flexible palette knife, spread a layer of the chocolate on a clean marble slab, no more than 2mm thick. Aim to get the layer of an even thickness by using the palette knife at a shallow angle and moving it back and forth.
3) Allow the chocolate to cool a little to where it is still slightly soft but not set hard.
4) Hold the cleaned palette knife in one hand and hold the end of the blade with the thumb and forefingers of the other hand. Cut down and forwards into the chocolate at a shallow angle, and at the same time draw the knife towards the front edge of the slab. Start at one end of the chocolate and work backwards. This will result in the chocolate rolling itself into long shavings. Allow to set then use or store as required.

1681 Cornets

Prepare the same mixture as for Langues de Chat (1693) to the end of Stage 3. Pipe out into rounds approx. 2½cm in diameter. Bake at 220°C until the edges turn brown and the centre is still white. Remove from the oven and, while still hot, twist tightly inside the point of a cream horn tin. Allow to cool in the moulds and remove when set in cornet shape.

1682 Crème Chantilly

Place 1 litre of cold double or whipping cream in a cold basin and add 75g of caster sugar and a few drops of vanilla essence. Whisk until fairly stiff. 1 litre of whipping cream, i.e. 40% fat content, will produce approx. 1½–1¾ litres of Crème Chantilly. 1 litre of double cream will produce approx. 1¼ litres of Crème Chantilly.

1683 Crème Chiboust (Crème St Honoré)   1 litre
                                                            30 mins.

Stage	Ingredient	Quantity	Method
1	egg yolks,	6	Cream the yolks and sugar together then
	sugar, caster	125g	add the flour and beat together
	flour	60g	thoroughly to a smooth paste.
	vanilla essence	few drops	
2	leaf gelatine	25g	Soak in cold water.
3	milk	½ litre	Place in a pan and bring to the boil.
	butter	15g	

4			Add half of the milk to the egg mixture whisking vigorously until smooth then whisk in the remainder.
5			Return the mixture to the pan and bring to the boil to thicken; whisk continuously. Cook whilst whisking for a further 2 mins. approx.
6			Quickly mix in the drained gelatine.
7	egg whites	5	Whisk the egg whites until stiff then
	sugar, caster	50g	whisk in the sugar as for meringue. Quickly fold this meringue into the mixture at boiling temperature when just removed from the heat. Use immediately as required.

1684 Crème Frangipane

¾ litre
30 mins.

Stage	Ingredient	Quantity	Method
1	eggs	2	Cream the eggs and sugar together then
	egg yolks	4	add the flour and beat together
	sugar, caster	100g	thoroughly to a smooth paste.
	flour	100g	
2	milk	½ litre	Place in a pan and bring to the boil.
	butter	25g	
3			Add half of the milk to the egg mixture whisking vigorously until smooth then whisk in the remainder. Bring to the boil and whisk continuously for 2–3 mins. to thicken and cook.
4	macaroons (1694) crushed	35g	Remove from the heat then mix in the macaroons. Use as required, or place in a basin, cover with a buttered paper and keep in the refrigerator.

1685 Crème Pâtissière

¾ litre
30 mins.

Stage	Ingredient	Quantity	Method
1	egg yolks	6	Cream the yolks, sugar and vanilla to-
	sugar, caster	125g	gether then add the flour and beat to-
	flour	60g	gether thoroughly to a smooth paste.
	vanilla essence	few drops	
2	milk	½ litre	Place in a pan and bring to the boil.
	butter	15g	
3			Add half the milk to the egg mixture whisking vigorously until smooth then whisk in the remainder.

4   Return the mixture to the pan and bring
                to the boil to thicken; whisk
                continuously. Cook whilst whisking for a
                further 2 mins. approx. Use as required
                or place in a basin, cover with a buttered
                paper and when cool, keep in the
                refrigerator.

1686 Eggwash, for Pastry Work

Whisk together eggs and milk in the proportions of 2 eggs to ½dl of milk and add a pinch of salt.

1687 Fondant

1) Place 3dl of water, 1kg of loaf or caster sugar and 100g of glucose into a sugar boiling pan. Bring to the boil and skim.
2) Boil gently to 115°C washing down the sides of the pan to remove any crystallised sugar which forms.
3) Pour slowly onto a dampened marble slab, preferably inside oiled iron bars, and allow to cool slightly.
4) Work the syrup with a fishtail scraper until it turns white and creamy.
5) Finish by kneading to a smooth texture.
6) Leave covered with a damp cloth for 1 hour to soften and mature.
7) Reserve for use by placing the fondant in an airtight container or polythene bag.

1688 Fondant, Preparation for Glazing Cakes and Pastries

1) Place sufficient Fondant (1687) in a pan then place in a bain-marie and warm gently, stirring continuously until it reaches blood heat, 37°C. On no account must this temperature be exceeded, otherwise the fondant will lose its gloss.
2) The working consistency should be such that it flows smoothly on the item being glazed. If too thick, a little Stock Syrup (1709) may be stirred in to give the right consistency.
3) Fondant can be coloured and flavoured as required, provided that these are in a liquid form and are added before adjusting the consistency with stock syrup.

1689 Frangipane Filling for Flans and Pastries   1 kg
                                                            20 mins.

Stage	Ingredient	Quantity	Method
1	butter, unsalted	250g	Place in a basin and beat together
	sugar, caster	250g	thoroughly until light and creamy.
2	eggs, beaten	4	Add to the mixture one at a time.
3	flour	60g	Sift the flour and almonds together, add
	ground almonds	250g	to the mixture and mix in lightly.

1690 Fruit Syrup Glazes

These glazes are useful for the finishing of bandes, flans, barquettes and tartelettes of fruit where their flavour and appearance is felt to be more appropriate than the usual apricot and red glazes. They can be prepared from a sugar syrup flavoured with any crushed fruit of second quality, trimmings and clean peelings of fruit, the zest of citrus fruits, or good-quality essences and so on, then thickened with arrowroot. They can be left either clear or lightly coloured as appropriate to the fruit, either yellow/orange or pink/red, and finally passed through a fine strainer and used hot. Syrups from any poached fruits used, or from tinned fruits, can also be utilised in the same manner and with advantage.

The following recipe is offered as an example.

1 litre
25 mins.

Stage	Ingredient	Quantity	Method
1	water	1 litre	Bring to the boil, skim and simmer
	sugar	500g	gently for 7–8 mins.
	pineapple pulp	250g	
	lemon juice and zest	2	
2	arrowroot	50g	Dilute the arrowroot with a little water and stir quickly into the simmering liquid. Boil for 2 or 3 mins. then pass through a fine strainer.
3			The glaze can be lightly coloured yellow/orange and flavoured with a little Kirsch but it must be used hot.

SPECIAL POINT
Arrowroot-thickened glazes are best used hot; they set and gel when cold, which is excellent for the finishing of flans etc. The use of cornflour, although the finished glaze is not so clear, allows them to be used cold if mixed properly but the result in this case is more of a coating sauce without any gelling properties.

1691 Ganache

750g
25 mins.

Stage	Ingredient	Quantity	Method
1	chocolate	500g	Cut into pieces, place in a basin over a pan of hot water and allow to melt. It must not exceed 46°C. Stir occasionally.
2	cream	2½dl	Place in a pan and heat until it comes to the boil. Pour into the chocolate and mix well together. Allow to cool before using then heat slightly and beat thoroughly to give a workable consistency.

Used for the filling and decoration of gâteaux and as fillings for biscuits and Petits Fours.

SPECIAL POINTS
a) Plain or milk chocolate can be used.
b) Use more cream to lighten the texture or less to make it stiffer.
c) Ganache can be flavoured with spirits or liqueurs such as rum, Kirsch and Tia Maria, etc.

1692 Japonaise Mixture for Gâteau and Pastry Bases

3 × 25cm bases
1 hour

Stage	Ingredient	Quantity	Method
1			Lightly grease a baking tray and dust with flour.
2	egg whites	6	Place the whites in a basin with a pinch of salt, whisk to a stiff peak then whisk in the sugar.
	sugar, caster	150g	
3	almonds, ground	250g	Sift these ingredients together to mix, then carefully fold into the meringue mixture.
	sugar, caster	100g	
	cornflour	25g	
4			Use a piping bag with a 1cm plain piping tube and pipe out round bases of the required size on the tray; start from a centre point and make the round shape by piping in a continuous and touching flat spiral.
5			Place in the oven at 125°C and bake for approx. 40–45 mins. or until the Japonaise are a light golden brown and completely crisp. Remove carefully from the tray with a palette knife and allow to cool before using.

SPECIAL POINT
The size and shape of the base may be more precisely obtained by placing a circle of the required diameter cut from cardboard on the floured tray and tracing round it with a pencil or sharp piece of wood.

1693 Langues de Chat

45–50
50 mins.

Stage	Ingredient	Quantity	Method
1	butter	250g	Cream together.
	caster sugar	250g	
2	egg whites	6	Add one at a time beating in well.
3	flour	250g	Add to the mixture, beating well.
	vanilla essence	few drops	
4			Place the mixture in a piping bag with a ½cm plain tube and pipe onto a

| | | greased and floured baking tray, 7cm in length, at approx. 4cm intervals. |

| 5 | | Bake at 220°C until the edges turn brown and the centre is still white. Remove from the tray while hot and allow to cool flat. |

1694 Macaroons

25–30
45 mins.

Stage	Ingredient	Quantity	Method
1	rice paper		Cover a baking tray with rice paper.
2	almonds, ground	250g	Place the almonds in a basin, add the
	egg whites	5	egg whites and mix together well, then
	sugar	500g	add the sugar and essences. Mix
	vanilla essence	few drops	together thoroughly to give a soft moist
	almond essence	few drops	mixture neither too stiff nor wet.
3			Use a piping bag with a 1cm plain piping tube and pipe out small round dome shapes approx. 2cm in diameter, on to the rice paper. Allow enough room between each to allow for spreading when baking.
4			Brush the surfaces of the macaroons very lightly with water to just moisten them. Bake in the oven at 165°C for 20–25 mins until a light brown colour. Remove and allow to cool then separate from the surrounding rice paper and use as required.

SPECIAL POINTS
a) The macaroons can be decorated before baking with half a skinned almond.
b) The mixture may be piped smaller to give small button macaroons which are useful for Petits Fours and for the garnishing and decorating of certain sweet dishes.

1695 Marmelade de Pommes

650g
30 mins.

Stage	Ingredient	Quantity	Method
1	cooking apples	750g	Peel, core and slice the apples. Place in
	water	½dl	a pan, add the water, sugar and lemon
	sugar	350g	juice and bring to the boil. Cook slowly
	juice of lemon	½	to a fairly stiff purée taking care not to burn it. Pass through a sieve and place in a basin for use.

1696 Marzipan

1kg
45mins.

Stage	Ingredient	Quantity	Method
1	water	1dl	Place in a sugar boiling pan, bring to the
	sugar	500g	boil and skim. Cook to 115°C on the
	glucose	50g	sugar boiling thermometer.
2	ground almonds	350g	Add and mix in thoroughly.
3	egg yolks	2	Add the yolks and mix in quickly. Turn
	icing sugar		onto a marble slab and knead well using icing sugar. Wrap in a polythene bag for use as required.

1697 Meringue Italienne

2 litres
45 mins.

Stage	Ingredient	Quantity	Method
1	sugar	500g	Place in a sugar boiling pan and bring to
	water	2dl	the boil. Wash down the inside of the pan and continue to boil steadily until the syrup reaches 140°C on the sugar boiling thermometer.
2	egg whites	8	Whisk the whites in a clean basin to a stiff peak. When the sugar reaches 140°C pour it slowly into the egg whites whisking continuously. Continue whisking until cold.

1698 Meringue (Ordinary)

2½ litres

This type of meringue is mainly used for the preparation of meringue shells, nests, Vacherin cases and various other shapes and designs for decoration, or the garnishing of other sweet dishes.

Attention to the following points is essential for the production of a good quality meringue:
1) All equipment used should be perfectly clean and free of any traces of grease or detergent.
2) Do not use thin watery egg whites.
3) Separate the whites carefully. There should be no trace of egg yolk present in the whites. Fat is deleterious to the aerating qualities of the whites.
4) A pinch of salt added just before whisking plus a pinch of cream of tartar or a few drops of acid, e.g. lemon juice or vinegar, can improve the strength of the aerating properties of the egg whites.
5) Be careful not to overwhisk the whites especially before adding the sugar as this can lead to a breakdown in the structure of the whites; they become granular and liquid separates downwards.
6) Do not bake at too high or too low a temperature. Over 125°C the meringues will colour and acquire a cooked flavour; below 80°C there is always the possibility of the meringues weeping, i.e. exuding sugar in liquid form.

Stage	Ingredient	Quantity	Method
1	egg whites	9	Place the whites in a clean mixing
	lemon juice	few	bowl, add a pinch of salt and the
		drops	lemon juice and whisk to a stiff peak.
	salt		
2	caster sugar	500g	Whisk in half the sugar, keeping the meringue stiff, then fold in the remaining sugar.

1699 Meringue Nests

36
3½ hours

Stage	Ingredient	Quantity	Method
1			Cover a baking tray with greaseproof paper.
2	Ordinary Meringue (1698)	2½ litres	Place the meringue in a piping bag with a 1cm plain or star tube. Pipe out into nest shapes 7–8cm in diameter with raised sides approx. 2½cm high, onto the greaseproof paper.
3			Place into a very cool oven at 110°C and bake until dry and crisp, approx. 3 hours.
4			Remove from the paper and allow to cool. Use as required or store in a sealed container.

1700 Meringue Shells

36
4½ hours approx.

Stage	Ingredient	Quantity	Method
1			Cover a baking tray with greaseproof paper.
2	Ordinary Meringue (1698)	2½ litres	Place the meringue in a piping bag with a 1cm plain tube and pipe out into oval shapes approx. 7–8cm in length onto the greaseproof paper.
3			Place into a very cool oven at 110°C and bake until completely dry and crisp, approx. 4 hours.
4			Remove from the paper, allow to cool and use as required or store in a sealed container.

1701 Peaches and Nectarines, to Skin

Immerse the fruit in boiling water for a few seconds so that the skin can be readily removed. Place immediately into cold water and skin.

1702 Palmiers

20
1 hour

Stage	Ingredient	Quantity	Method
1	Pâte Feuilletée (1736) caster sugar	500g 50g	Sprinkle the board with caster sugar and roll out the paste on this to a rectangle 20cm wide and 2½mm thick.
2	caster sugar	50g	Lightly mark a centre line along its length then brush with water and sprinkle well with the sugar. Fold each side into three towards the centre leaving a gap down the centre of approx. 1½ cm then fold one side onto the other.
3			Flatten slightly to seal together, then cut the strip into 1cm slices. Dip the cut edges into sugar and place on a lightly greased baking tray approx. 7–8cm apart. Allow to rest in a cool place for 30 mins.
4			Place in the oven at 220°C and bake for 10 mins. approx. until lightly caramelised. Turn over with a palette knife and bake for a few mins. more to give a nice golden brown colour. Place on a wire grid to cool.

1703 Pralin

900g
1 hour

Stage	Ingredient	Quantity	Method
1	sugar, caster water lemon juice	500g 1dl few drops	Place into a sugar boiling pan, bring to the boil and skim. Cook to a light caramel colour.
2	almonds } skinned, hazelnuts } toasted and kept hot	200g 200g	Add to the sugar, mix in and continue to cook for a little longer just to develop the colour of the sugar a little more.
3			Turn out onto a lightly oiled marble slab. Allow to become quite cold then crush with a rolling pin to a granular texture. Reserve for use in an airtight container.

1704 Ratafia Biscuits

60
30 mins.

Stage	Ingredient	Quantity	Method
1	egg whites	4	Place in a mixing bowl and mix all the
	sugar	250g	ingredients together thoroughly.
	ground almonds	250g	
	ground rice	30g	
2			Place the mixture in a piping bag with a 1cm plain tube and pipe into 2½cm rounds on a greased and floured baking tray. Bake at approx. 180°C for 10–15 mins.

1705 Red Glaze

Boil together four parts of raspberry or strawberry jam with one part of water and pass through a fine strainer. Colour if necessary. The glaze should be of a coating consistency. Use while still hot.

1706 Rice for Condés

1¼ litres
2½ hours

Stage	Ingredient	Quantity	Method
1	milk	1 litre	Place the milk in a pan, add the vanilla
	vanilla essence	few drops	and sugar and bring to the boil. Rain in
	sugar	150g	the washed rice, stir until it reboils,
	short-grain rice	175g	cover with a lid and cook slowly in the oven at 175°C for approx. 1 hour until tender. Stir occasionally with a wooden spoon. Cook until thick but creamy.
2	egg yolks	4	Remove the rice from the oven, add the
	butter	50g	yolks and butter and mix in quickly. Allow to cool.
3	cream	2dl	Place into a basin and whip. Mix into the cool rice. Use or mould as required.

1707 Royal Icing

½ kg
15 mins.

Stage	Ingredient	Quantity	Method
1	icing sugar	500g	Sieve the icing sugar into a basin, add
	egg whites	3	the egg whites and the lemon juice and
	juice of lemon	1 tsp	mix together with a wooden spoon. Beat well. If too moist, add further icing sugar until the icing is of a creamy consistency. Continue beating until the icing is white and will stand in points. Keep covered with a damp cloth while using.

1708 Sacristans

Stage	Ingredient	Quantity	Method
1	Pâte Feuilletée (1736)	250g	Roll out the pastry into an oblong 7cm wide by 3mm thick.
2	eggwash almonds, finely chopped sugar, icing	 75g 	Eggwash the surface of the pastry, sprinkle evenly with the almonds and lightly roll into the surface of the pastry. Dust well with sifted icing sugar.
3			Cut into 1½cm-wide strips, twist each two or three times to give a spiral shape and fix by the ends to a greased baking tray. Allow sufficient space for expansion. Leave to rest for 30 mins.
4			Place in a hot oven at 210°C for 6–7 mins. until golden brown. Trim the ends evenly and place on a wire grill to cool.

1709 Stock Syrup

Place water and sugar into a pan in the proportions 1 litre of water to 750g sugar. Bring to the boil, skim and reserve for use.

1710 Sugar Boiling

Sugar, with a little water, glucose or acid, and boiled to varying degrees of temperature, is widely used in the making of such things as fondant icing, caramels, nougat, marzipan, meringues, buttercreams and so on. It is also used for the dipping of fruits for Petits Fours and for pulled or blown sugar presentation pieces.

Care must be exercised throughout the process and the following points need to be observed carefully:
1) The utmost care should be taken when boiling sugar. It can reach a temperature as high as 175°C and can be very dangerous and painful if splashed on the hands. Always keep a bowl of iced water near by so that in the event of splashing, the hands can be quickly plunged in. This will prevent any real damage to the skin, if done immediately.
2) All equipment used for sugar boiling should be scrupulously clean and free from fat and detergent, i.e. boiling pan, spoon, thermometer.
3) Use good-quality cube or granulated sugar.
4) The sugar solution must be brought to the boil slowly so that the sugar crystals are dissolved completely before boiling commences. Failure to do this can result in crystallisation of the solution.
5) Splashes on the sides of the pan or thermometer must not be left to crystallise but should be washed clean with a clean brush dipped in water.
6) The solution must not be stirred.
7) Check the required temperature with the sugar boiling thermometer.
8) Any colouring or flavouring essences must be of the right type and quality for the job and should be added just before the sugar reaches the required temperature.

9) When the correct temperature is reached, place the pan in cold water to stop the bubbling action of further cooking, then remove and use as required. The pan may be placed over gentle heat to maintain its temperature and degree of flow particularly when the solution is used for dipping Petits Fours.

Degrees of cooking
Many of the degrees of cooking sugar can be ascertained manually by first dipping the thumb and first two fingers in cold water then quickly in the solution, trapping a little on the fingers, then quickly back into the water. The feel or degree of firmness and/or brittleness can be readily identified by the skilled practitioner but this technique should only be attempted under guidance. Experience is a guiding factor here; the sugar boiling thermometer can give precision.

The following are the usual degrees of boiled sugar:

Manual description	*Temperature*	*Some uses*
Short thread	105°C	candied peel and fruits
Long thread	110°C	crystallised fruits, marrons glacés
Soft ball or feather	115°C	fondant, marzipan
Medium ball	120°C	fudge, soft nougats
Hard ball	125°C	Italian meringue, soft caramels
Soft crack	137–140°C	nougat, toffee, rock sugar
Hard crack	155–160°C	pulled and spun sugar
Caramel	170–175°C	cream caramel

1711 Sugar for Glazing Dipped Petits Fours

Stage	Ingredient	Quantity	Method
1	sugar, loaf or granulated	500g	Place into a sugar boiling pan, bring to the boil slowly to first dissolve the sugar, then skim carefully.
	glucose	50g	
	water	2dl	
	lemon juice	squeeze	
2			Boil rapidly until the sugar boiling thermometer registers 160°C. During the boiling process, frequently wash down the sides of the pan and the thermometer with a brush dipped in water, to prevent the syrup from crystallising.
3			Place the pan in cold water for a few seconds to stop the boiling action, remove and use whilst hot.

1712 Sugar, Spun

1) Have ready two lightly oiled metal or wooden bars or sticks placed approx. 30cm apart and projecting 40cm or so from the side of a table, or between two tables. Place some newspaper on the floor underneath the bars and further back and towards them. This will be to catch any drips.
2) Proceed as for Sugar for Glazing (1711) and take the temperature to 160°C.
3) Dip the pan in cold water to stop further cooking then remove.
4) Dip a sugar-spinning whisk, i.e. a thin wire whisk with the bottom third cut off, or two forks, into the sugar and wave it quickly backwards and forwards over the bars. Repeat as necessary until the mass of thread-like strands can be gathered up and shaped as required.
5) Carry on spinning until sufficient spun sugar has been made. The sugar can be kept at the right consistency by gentle heating.

SPECIAL POINTS
a) Be careful to stand well to one side when making the spun sugar and make sure no one else is near.
b) Any colouring should be added just before the sugar reaches its required temperature.

1713 Syrup for Savarins and Babas

2 litres
15 mins.

Stage	Ingredient	Quantity	Method
1	water	1 litre	Place the water and sugar into a pan
	sugar	700g	with the thinly peeled zest of the orange
	lemon ⎱ zest and	1	and lemon and the remainder of the
	orange ⎰ juice	1	ingredients. Bring to the boil, skim and
	coriander seeds	10	simmer gently for 7–8 mins.
	cloves	4	
	cinnamon stick	1	
2			Strain the syrup and use hot for soaking the prepared savarins and babas.

1714 Vols-au-vent

10
1 hour

Stage	Ingredient	Quantity	Method
1	Pâte Feuilletée (1736)	650g	Roll out the paste ¾cm thick and cut into rounds with an 8cm diameter plain cutter. Place upside down on a damp baking tray. Dip a 6cm diameter plain cutter into hot oil and cut evenly, half-way through each round of paste. Egg-wash the surface and leave to rest in a cool place for 30 mins.
	eggwash		
2			Bake at 215°C until golden brown (approx. 20 mins.).
3			Allow to cool, remove the centres carefully with a knife and reserve for use as

the lids for the vols-au-vent. Empty the
case of any soft dough.

1715 Water Icing

Add sufficient boiling water to sieved icing sugar so as to mix to a smooth paste of the
required consistency. This should be of a flowing consistency for coating and somewhat
thicker for piping.

————SWEET AND BUTTER SAUCES————

1716 Sauce à l'Abricot – Apricot Sauce (1)

1 litre
15 mins.

Stage	Ingredient	Quantity	Method
1	apricot jam	1kg	Place in a pan, bring slowly to the boil
	water	2dl	and allow to simmer gently for 5 mins.
2			Pass through a fine strainer and keep warm.
3	Kirsch	½dl	Add to the sauce just before using.

1717 Sauce à l'Abricot – Apricot Sauce (2)

1 litre
30 mins.

Stage	Ingredient	Quantity	Method
1	fresh apricots, ripe	1kg	Wash the apricots, cut in half and remove the stones. Place the fruit in a
	sugar	400g	pan with the sugar and water, bring to
	water	2dl	the boil, skim and cook gently until the apricots are soft, approx. 20 mins.
2	Kirsch	1½dl	Pass the fruit mixture through a fine sieve then reheat in a clean pan. Add the Kirsch just before serving and if necessary adjust the consistency with sugar syrup.

SPECIAL POINT
Dried apricots can be used when fresh ones are unobtainable; the cooking time will need
to be extended. Tinned apricot halves and their syrup can also be used.

1718 Sauce Anglaise

1 litre
30 mins.

Stage	Ingredient	Quantity	Method
1	milk	1 litre	Place in a pan and bring to the boil.
	vanilla essence	few drops	
2	sugar	125g	Place in a basin, mix together and whisk
	egg yolks	9	in the milk quickly and thoroughly.

3			Return the mixture to the pan and heat gently, stirring with a wooden spoon until it thickens and coats the back of the spoon. Do not allow to reboil as the sauce will curdle. Pass through a fine strainer and keep warm in a bain-marie of warm water.

1719 Butterscotch Sauce

7½dl
25 mins.

Stage	Ingredient	Quantity	Method
1	butter	75g	Place in a pan and allow to melt gently
	sugar, demerara	375g	while stirring. Increase the heat and boil
	golden syrup	2 tbsps	without stirring, for 3 mins.
2	cream, double	3½dl	Remove the pan from the heat. Allow to
	vanilla essence	few drops	cool and mix in the cream and vanilla essence. Serve warm or cold.

1720 Sauce au Caramel – Caramel Sauce

7½dl
15 mins.

Stage	Ingredient	Quantity	Method
1	sugar	200g	Place in a pan, bring to the boil and
	water	1dl	cook to a golden brown colour (175°C on the sugar boiling thermometer). Immediately cool the base of the pan in cold water.
2	double cream	5dl	Pour into the caramel, bring slowly to the boil and mix. Allow to get cold, stirring occasionally.

1721 Sauce au Chocolat – Chocolate Sauce (1)

1 litre
40 mins.

Stage	Ingredient	Quantity	Method
1	plain chocolate	500g	Grate the chocolate and place in a pan
	water	7dl	with the water and sugar. Bring to the
	sugar	120g	boil and simmer very gently for 20 mins.
2	cream	1dl	Add to the sauce, mix in quickly and pass through a fine strainer.

SPECIAL POINT
This sauce is more suitable for serving with profiteroles, ice-cream and coupes.

1722 Sauce au Chocolat – Chocolate Sauce (2)

1 litre
20 mins.

Stage	Ingredient	Quantity	Method
1	milk	1dl	Mix in a basin.
	cocoa powder	80g	
	cornflour	50g	

2	milk	7dl	Place in a pan and bring to the boil;
	sugar	120g	pour onto the diluted cocoa and corn-flour whisking in quickly and thoroughly.
3			Return the mixture to the pan and place on the stove to reboil, stirring contin-uously.

SPECIAL POINT
This sauce is more suitable for serving with steamed puddings.

1723 Sauce au Citron – Lemon Sauce

1 litre
30 mins.

Stage	Ingredient	Quantity	Method
1	lemons	4	Remove the zest from the lemons with a peeler and place on one side.
2	water	1 litre	Place into a pan and add the juice from the lemons. Bring to the boil.
	sugar	250g	
3	cornflour	60g	Dilute with a little cold water and mix into the liquid stirring with a wooden spoon. Reboil and pass through a fine strainer.
4			Cut the lemon zest into a very fine julienne, blanch well in boiling water, drain and add to the sauce.

1724 Coulis de Fruits Frais – Fresh Soft Fruit Sauces

These sauces are simply sweetened purées of fresh soft fruits.

To prepare: Select fruits which are ripe, well-coloured and of excellent quality. Remove any stalks or blemishes, then wash and drain them well. Where appropriate, such as for peaches, apricots or mangoes, remove the skin and stone. Purée or mash them well then pass through a fine sieve or muslin. For each 5dl of purée add approx. 65–75g sifted icing sugar and up to one tablespoon of lemon or lime juice. The amount of sugar and lemon juice can be adjusted up or down according to the degree of sweetness and acidity of the fruit.

The following fruits are all suitable for preparation in this manner and may be mixed in varying proportions to create sauces with differing cross-flavours: apricots, blackberries, blackcurrants, loganberries, mulberries, mangoes, peaches, raspberries, redcurrants, strawberries.

1725 Custard Sauce

1 litre
20 mins.

Stage	Ingredient	Quantity	Method
1	milk	1dl	Mix together in a basin.
	custard powder	60g	

2	milk	7dl	Place in a pan and bring to the boil.
	sugar	120g	Pour into the diluted custard powder, whisking in quickly and thoroughly.
3			Return the mixture to the pan and place on the stove to reboil, stirring continuously.

1726 Jam Sauce

1 litre
15 mins.

Stage	Ingredient	Quantity	Method
1	jam	1kg	Place in a pan and bring to the boil.
	water	4dl	
2	cornflour	50g	Dilute with a little cold water and mix into the sauce stirring with a wooden spoon. Reboil and pass through a fine strainer.

1727 Sauce Melba (1)

1 litre
40 mins.

Stage	Ingredient	Quantity	Method
1	raspberries	1kg	Place into a pan, bring to the boil and simmer gently for 20 mins.
	sugar	450g	
	water	2dl	
2			Pass through a fine strainer and allow to cool thoroughly before using.

1728 Sauce Melba (2)

1 litre
40 mins.

Stage	Ingredient	Quantity	Method
1	raspberry jam	400g	Place into a pan, mix together and bring to the boil. Allow to simmer gently for approx. 5–6 mins.
	redcurrant jelly	400g	
	water	2½dl	
2			Pass through a fine strainer and allow to cool thoroughly before using.

1729 Sauce Mousseline

1 litre
15 mins.

Stage	Ingredient	Quantity	Method
1	water	1¼dl	Place in a pan and bring to the boil. Allow to cool a little.
	sugar	150g	
2	egg yolks	6	Place in a bowl, whisk well and gradually add the prepared syrup.
3			Place the bowl in a bain-marie or over a pan of hot water and whisk vigorously

<table>
<tr><td></td><td></td><td></td><td>and continuously until the mixture is thick and creamy. Remove from the heat and continue to beat until cool.</td></tr>
<tr><td>4</td><td>cream
vanilla essence</td><td>5dl
few drops</td><td>Whip the cream until fairly thick. Blend into the egg mixture and flavour with the vanilla. Serve warm.</td></tr>
</table>

SPECIAL POINT

This sauce may be flavoured with spirits or liqueurs such as Kirsch, rum, brandy, Grand Marnier, Cointreau etc.

1730 Sauce à l'Orange – Orange Sauce

Prepare in the same way as Sauce au Citron (1723), using oranges instead of lemons.

1731 Sauce Sabayon

½ litre
15 mins.

Stage	Ingredient	Quantity	Method
1	egg yolks sugar, caster white wine, dry	8 250g 2dl	Place all the ingredients in a bowl and whisk in a bain-marie or over a pan of hot water continuously. The sabayon is cooked when it clings to the whisk when raised from the mixture.
2			Remove from the heat and pour into a sauceboat for service. If required cold, place the basin of sauce in a container of iced water and whisk until cold before serving.

SPECIAL POINTS

a) The sauce may be flavoured with rum, brandy, Kirsch or other suitable spirit.

b) The sauce may be made with fortified wines such as sherry, Marsala or Madeira, in which case replace the white wine with the selected fortified wine and reduce the amount of sugar by 50g.

1732 Syrup Sauce

1 litre
15 mins.

Stage	Ingredient	– Quantity	Method
1	golden syrup water juice of lemon	600g 3½dl 2	Place in a pan, bring slowly to the boil, mixing occasionally.
2	arrowroot	25g	Dilute with a little cold water and mix into the sauce stirring with a wooden spoon. Reboil, allow to simmer for a few mins. and pass through a fine strainer.

1733 Brandy Butter

500g
15 mins.

Stage	Ingredient	Quantity	Method
1	soft butter,		Place the butter in a basin and add the
	unsalted	250g	sifted icing sugar. Mix together with a
	icing sugar	250g	wooden spoon to a creamy consistency
	brandy	½dl	and add the brandy a little at a time.
2			Serve in a sauceboat.

1734 Rum Butter

Prepare in the same way as Brandy Butter (1733), using rum instead of brandy.

—————————— BASIC PASTES ——————————

1735 Pâte à Chou – Chou Paste

1½ litres
30 mins.

Stage	Ingredient	Quantity	Method
1	water	½ litre	Place in a deep pan and bring to the boil
	butter	200g	slowly in order that the butter is melted
	salt	2g	by the time the water is boiled.
	sugar	15g	
2	flour, strong	275g	Add, away from the fire mixing well with a wooden spatula. Return the pan to the fire and continue mixing until the mixture becomes smooth and does not stick to the sides of the pan. Cool slightly.
3	eggs	8–9	Add to the mixture, one at a time, mixing thoroughly.

Used for éclairs, cream buns, profiteroles, Gâteau St Honoré, etc.

SPECIAL POINT
The correct texture of the chou paste is reached when it folds in on itself when cut through with the wooden spoon. It is useful to check this before adding the last egg and then adding only sufficient to obtain the correct texture; obversely add more egg if too stiff.

1736 Pâte Feuilletée or Feuilletage – Puff Pastry

1¼kg
3 hours

This type of pastry, distinguished by its many-layered flaky texture, has many applications in pastry work, ranging from small Bouchées to gâteaux, pastries and so on. The practical skills involved in the making of a good quality puff pastry rely also on a good understanding of the special properties of the flour and fats used in its production. Although there are a number of differing methods used, all of which can give excellent results, the following recipe and method has been selected as appropriate to the scope of this book.

It is well to bear in mind the following points:
1) Pastry margarine is extensively used in the production of puff pastry. It maintains a firm plastic and workable quality in warm conditions but does not give the excellence of taste and smoothness of texture which is the hallmark of the same pastry made with butter.
2) Good quality unsalted butter of a waxy texture is to be preferred to butter of a soft creamy quality.
3) Cool working temperatures and refrigeration between stages is essential to prevent the butter from becoming too soft. The use of a marble slab for working on is a great help.
4) The butter should be kept cold before being required then kneaded to the same texture of the dough being used.
5) Use the same flour sparingly to dust the slab and paste when rolling out and brush the surface clear of surplus flour before folding.
6) Wrap the pastry in polythene at all the stages of resting and storage so as to prevent drying of the surfaces.
7) Any scraps of pastry left from the production of puff pastry should be placed on top of each other, pressed flat into a compact shape and stored for further use. Do not knead into a ball. They can be used for items where the rise of a full puff pastry is not required, e.g. Palmiers, Sacristans, cheese straws etc.
8) To mark the number of turns the pastry has been given it is good practice to lightly press the number of fingers, corresponding to the number of turns, into the pastry before resting it each time.

Stage	Ingredient	Quantity	Method
1	flour, strong salt butter, unsalted water, cold juice of lemon	500g 5g 50g 2½–3dl 1 tsp	Sift the flour and salt into a basin and rub in the butter. Make a bay in the centre, add the water and lemon juice and mix together. Knead to a smooth dough and roll into a ball. Wrap in polythene and allow to rest in the refrigerator for 30 mins.
2			Cut a cross in the ball of dough half-way down, pull out the four corners in the shape of a star leaving the centre fairly thick. Roll out each corner to a quarter the thickness of the centre.
3	butter, unsalted	450g	Knead the butter to the same consistency and shape as the centre of the paste and place it on the centre. Fold over the rolled-out corners of the paste to enclose the butter completely and to exclude any air.

4	Press the paste with a rolling pin to flatten it slightly then roll it out to an oblong approx. 60cm × 20cm, keeping the sides straight.
5	Fold the pastry into three, seal the edges then roll it out in the opposite direction to that previously done and again fold in three. Wrap it up in polythene and place in the refrigerator for 30 mins. The pastry has now been given two turns.
6	Repeat Stages 4 and 5 twice more, so giving the pastry a total of six turns, resting it for 30 mins. between each two turns. Rest again before using or wrap in the polythene and keep in the refrigerator.

SPECIAL POINT
Instead of giving six turns as in the above recipe, puff pastry can be made with four double turns which are made by folding the two ends of the rolled-out paste to the centre and then folding it over together.

1737 Rough Puff Pastry

1kg
2½ hours

Stage	Ingredient	Quantity	Method
1	flour, strong salt butter	500g 5g 375g	Sift the flour and salt into a basin. Cut the butter, which must be firm, into approx. 2cm cubes and lightly mix into the flour. Make a bay in the centre.
2	water, cold ⎱ mixed juice of ⎰ together lemon	2½–3dl 1 tsp	Add to the flour and mix in lightly to a fairly firm paste.
3			Press the paste with a rolling pin to flatten it slightly then roll out to an oblong approx. 60cm × 20cm, keeping the sides straight. Fold in three and squeeze the edges flush then roll it out again in the opposite direction from before and fold into three. Wrap it up and place in the refrigerator for 30 mins. The pastry has now been given two turns.
4			Repeat the rolling and folding twice more so as to give it six turns, resting it for 30 mins. between each two turns and after it is finished. Use as required or wrap in polythene and store in the refrigerator until needed.

SPECIAL POINTS

a) If desired, 75g of the butter may be rubbed into the flour at Stage 1, and the remainder cut into cubes and added as above.

b) This kind of puff pastry is sometimes called Scotch puff pastry and can be used for items which do not require the amount of rise obtained from ordinary puff pastry, e.g. sausage rolls, pasties, coverings for pies.

c) Four double turns may be given instead of six turns. This is done by folding the two ends of the rolled-out paste to the centre and then folding them over together.

1738 Pâte à Foncer – Short Lining Pastry

850g
30 mins.

Stage	Ingredient	Quantity	Method
1	flour, soft	500g	Sift the flour and salt into a basin and
	butter	125g	rub in the fats to give a granular texture.
	lard	125g	
	salt	pinch	
2	water, cold	1dl	Make a bay in the centre and mix in sufficient water to form the ingredients into a light smooth paste. Rest the paste, covered, for 30 mins. before use.

Used for savoury flans and barquettes.

1739 Pâte à Pâté – Pie Pastry

1kg
30 mins.

Stage	Ingredient	Quantity	Method
1	flour, general purpose	500g	Sift the flour and salt in a basin and rub
	salt	pinch	in the butter to give a granular texture.
	butter	275g	
2	eggs	2	Whisk well together, add to the flour
	water	1dl	and mix to a smooth paste.
3			Knead the paste very well. Wrap in polythene and rest it for at least 1 hour in the refrigerator before using.

Used for pies, Pâtés en Croûte and raised pies.

1740 Pâte Sucrée – Sweet Pastry

1kg
30 mins.

Stage	Ingredient	Quantity	Method
1	flour, soft	500g	Sift the flour and salt into a basin and
	salt	pinch	rub in the butter to give a granular
	butter	250g	texture. Make a bay in the centre.
2	eggs, beaten ⎫ mixed	2	Add and mix the ingredients into a light
	caster sugar ⎬ together	100g	smooth paste. Cover the paste and rest it
	water ⎭	1 tbsp	for 30 mins. before using.

Used for flans, barquettes and for covering fruit pies.

1741 Pâte à Savarin – Savarin Paste

1¼kg
1 hour

Stage	Ingredient	Quantity	Method
1	flour, strong	500g	Sift the flour into a warm basin and
	yeast	20g	make a bay. Mix the yeast and milk and
	milk at 37°C	1dl	place in the bay.
2	eggs	8	Mix together and warm to approx. 37°C.
	caster sugar	20g	Add to the yeast and milk. Draw the flour in from the side and beat well to a smooth light paste.
3	butter, unsalted	250g	Place the softened butter in pieces on top of the paste, cover and allow to prove in a prover until double its size.
4			Beat the butter well into the paste until it forms a smooth elastic dough. Allow to rest for 10 mins. This dough is now ready for further processing into savarins and babas.

1742 Hot Water Pastry

800g
15 mins.

Stage	Ingredient	Quantity	Method
1	flour, general purpose	500g	Sift the flour and salt into a basin and make a bay in the centre.
	salt	5g	
2	water	2dl	Place into a pan and bring to the boil slowly in order that the lard is melted by the time the water is boiled. Pour into the flour and mix with a wooden spatule.
	lard	150g	
3			Knead to a smooth paste. Cover and allow to rest for 10 mins. but use while still warm so that it moulds easily.

Used for raised pies.

1743 Suet Pastry for Sweet Puddings

1kg
30 mins.

Stage	Ingredient	Quantity	Method
1	flour	500g	Sift the flour, baking powder and salt into a basin, add the suet and mix in lightly.
	baking powder	15g	
	salt	pinch	
	beef kidney suet, chopped	300g	

2	caster sugar	50g	Make a bay in the centre, add the sugar,
	water, cold	2½dl	dissolved in the water, and mix lightly to
			form a fairly firm paste. Use as required.

Used for steamed puddings such as jam roll and fruit puddings.

1744 Pâte à Frire – Frying Batter for Pastry Work   1 litre
                                                          15 mins.

Stage	Ingredient	Quantity	Method
1	flour, strong	400g	Sift into a basin and make a bay in the
	salt	pinch	centre.
	sugar	5g	
2	butter, melted	50g	Pour all the ingredients into the bay.
	beer	1½dl	Gradually mix in the flour, whisking to a
	water at 37°C	2½dl	smooth batter. Cover and allow to prove
	egg yolks	2	in a warm place for 1 hour or so.
3	egg whites	2	When the batter is required, place the
			whites in a clean mixing bowl, add a
			pinch of salt and whisk to a stiff peak.
			Fold into the batter gently and use
			straight away.

——————————YEAST GOODS——————————

1745 Babas au Rhum – Rum Babas   18
                                                          1½ hours

Stage	Ingredient	Quantity	Method
1	Pâte à Savarin		Mix the paste and currants together.
	(1741)	1¼kg	Grease well 18 dariole moulds with the
	currants	60g	fat. Fill the moulds one-third full with
	white compound fat	20g	the mixture, cover and allow to prove in
			a warm place until they reach the tops of
			the moulds.
2			Bake at approx. 235°C for approx.
			15 mins. Turn out to cool on wire racks.
3	Savarin Syrup,		Place the babas in the syrup until well
	hot (1713)	5 litres	soaked. Remove carefully and replace on
			the wire rack to drain.
4	rum	½dl	Sprinkle the rum over the soaked babas
	Apricot Glaze		and brush carefully with the hot glaze.
	(1672)	½ litre	
5	Crème Chantilly	½ litre	Place the babas on suitable dishes and
	(1682)		decorate with the cream.

SPECIAL POINT
It is better not to soak babas immediately after baking but to leave them to dry out overnight.

1746 Bread Rolls

(800g) 20
2 hours

Stage	Ingredient	Quantity	Method
1	flour, strong milk powder	500g 10g	Sift the flour and milk powder into a warm basin or on the table and make a bay.
2	white compound fat salt	50g 10g	Break the fat into small pieces and distribute on top of the flour. Place the salt in the centre of the bay.
3	water at 37°C yeast	2¾dl 30g	Pour half the water in the bay to dissolve the salt. Dissolve the yeast in the rest of the water and add to the bay.
4			Draw in the flour from the inside of the bay to form a paste. Mix in the remainder of the flour and knead well to a smooth dough. Cover with a warm damp cloth and leave to prove in a warm place for approx. 20 mins. to allow the dough to rise to double its size.
5			Knead the dough again to knock it back to its original bulk. Cover over and rest for a further 10 mins.
6			Weigh the dough into 80g pieces and divide each piece in half. Mould round and place in a warm baking tray. Place in the prover and allow the rolls to prove to double their size.
7	eggwash		Eggwash the rolls carefully and bake at approx. 240°C for 15–20 mins.

1747 Bread Rolls, brown

(800g) 20
2 hours

Stage	Ingredient	Quantity	Method
1	flour, brown bread flour, strong milk powder	250g 250g 10g	Sift the two kinds of flour and the milk powder together several times until well mixed. Place in a warm basin or on the table and make a bay.
2	white compound fat salt	30g 10g	Break the fat into small pieces and distribute on top of the flour. Place the salt in the centre of the bay.

3	water at 37°C	2¾dl	Pour half the water into the bay to dissolve the salt. Dissolve the yeast in the rest of the water. Add the sugar and pour into the bay.
	yeast	30g	
	sugar	1 tsp	
4			Draw the flour from the inside of the bay to form a paste. Mix in the remainder of the flour and knead to a smooth dough. Cover with a warm damp cloth and leave to prove in a warm place for approx. 30 mins. to allow the dough to rise to double its size.
5			Knead the dough again to knock it back to its original bulk. Cover over and rest for a further 10 mins.
6			Weigh the dough into 80g pieces and divide each piece in half. Mould round and place on a warm baking tray. Place in the prover and allow the rolls to prove to double their size.
7			Bake at approx. 240°C for approx. 20 mins.

SPECIAL POINT
Wholemeal flour may be used instead of brown bread flour.

1748 Bridge Rolls

28
2 hours

Stage	Ingredient	Quantity	Method
1	flour, strong	500g	Sift the flour and salt into a warm basin or on the table and rub the butter into it.
	salt	8g	
	butter	40g	
2	milk at 37°C	2½dl	Dissolve the yeast in the milk, add the sugar and the beaten egg. Add to the flour and knead to a smooth dough.
	yeast	30g	
	sugar	10g	
	egg, beaten	1	
3			Cover the dough with a damp cloth and leave to prove in a warm place for approx. 20 mins. to allow the dough to rise to double its size.
4			Knead the dough again to knock it back to its original bulk. Cover and rest for another 10 mins.
5			Weigh the dough into 30g pieces and mould round. Allow to recover slightly then mould boat-shape with rounded ends.

6	eggwash		Place on a warm greased baking tray, eggwash and place in the prover to double their size.
7			Eggwash again and bake at 230°C for approx. 10 mins. to a light golden brown.

1749 Brioche

24
6½ hours

Stage	Ingredient	Quantity	Method
1	flour, strong	125g	Sift the flour into a basin, make a bay and place in the yeast and water. Mix together to a soft dough. Cut a cross on the top. Cover with a warm damp cloth and leave in a warm place to prove until it is double in size.
	yeast	25g	
	water at 37°C	¾dl	
2	flour, strong	375g	Sift the flour into a basin and make a bay. Beat the eggs together, pour into the bay, add the sugar and salt and mix to a dough. Knead well.
	eggs	6	
	caster sugar	25g	
	salt	10g	
3	unsalted butter, softened	400g	Mix into the flour and egg dough and knead very firmly.
4			Place the 2 doughs together on a cold marble slab and knead well together.
5			Cover and allow to prove in a very cool place at approx. 8°C for 4–5 hours until it is doubled in size.
6	butter	25g	Place the dough on a lightly floured board and knead again thoroughly. Butter 24 small brioche or deep tartlet moulds. Divide the dough into 24 × 50g. Take one piece and cut off one-third. Mould the remainder into a ball and place into one of the moulds. Roll the small piece into a ball and place on top. Proceed in the same manner with the remainder of the dough.
7	eggwash		Allow to prove until they double in size. Brush carefully with eggwash and bake at 235°C for approx. 15 mins.

1750 Bun Dough

900g
1 hour

Stage	Ingredient	Quantity	Method
1	flour, strong	500g	Sift the flour and salt into a warm basin or on the table, add the butter and rub to a fine texture.
	salt	2g	
	butter	60g	

2	yeast	30g	Make a bay in the centre of the flour
	caster sugar	60g	and place the yeast and sugar into the
			bay.
3	milk at 37°C	2¼dl	Pour a little of the milk into the bay and
	egg	1	blend with the sugar and yeast. Beat the
			egg into the remainder of the milk, add
			to the bay and mix in with the other
			liquid.
4			Mix the flour gradually into the liquid
			and work into a dough. Knead it until it
			leaves the sides of the basin clean. Cover
			with a warm damp cloth and allow to
			prove in a warm place until it doubles in
			size. This dough is now ready for further
			processing into fruit buns, Chelsea buns,
			Bath buns etc. It should be used
			immediately.

1751 Bath Buns

16
1¼ hours

Stage	Ingredient	Quantity	Method
1	Bun Dough (1750)	900g	Prepare the dough with the lemon
	lemon essence	few drops	essence added with the milk at Stage 3.
2	sultanas	60g	Work carefully into the dough.
	mixed peel	60g	
3	eggwash		Break the dough into 16 roughly shaped
	nib sugar	100g	pieces. Place on a lightly greased warm
			baking tray, brush with eggwash and
			sprinkle with the nib sugar. Allow the
			buns to prove in a prover until they have
			doubled in size. Bake at 235°C for
			15–20 mins. Place on a wire grid to cool.

1752 Chelsea Buns

16
1¼ hours

Stage	Ingredient	Quantity	Method
1	Bun Dough (1750)	900g	Knead the dough and roll out to a
			square 35cm × 35cm.
2	butter, melted	60g	Brush with the butter and sprinkle with
	mixed fruit	125g	the fruit and the cinnamon sugar. Roll
	cinnamon ⎫ mixed	5g	up, brush with melted butter and cut
	caster sugar ⎭ together	25g	into 16 slices.
3			Place flat on a greased baking tray fairly
			close together. Allow them to prove in a
			prover until they have doubled in size.
			Bake at 235°C for 15–20 mins.

| 4 | Bun Wash (1676)
sugar, caster | | Brush over the buns while still hot and place on a wire grid to cool. Dredge with caster sugar. |

1753 Croissants

18

4½–5 hours

Stage	Ingredient	Quantity	Method
1	Bread Roll Dough (1746) (to end of Stage 4)	800g	Roll out 45cm × 30cm.
2	butter, chilled	250g	Dot the butter evenly over half the dough then fold over the other half to enclose the butter completely.
3			Roll out the dough carefully to 45cm × 30cm, fold in three, cover and allow to rest in the refrigerator for 20 mins.
4			Roll out the dough to the same size but in the opposite direction to that previously done, then fold in three. Allow it to rest then repeat this operation, turning the dough again in the opposite direction. (This gives three single turns in all.)
5			Cover closely and allow to rest in the refrigerator for at least 2 hours but preferably overnight.
6			Roll out the dough approx. 60 × 35cm and cut in half lengthways. Cut each half into triangles having 12cm bases; this will give 18 pieces in all. Using a light dusting of flour roll out from the bases and towards the pointed ends until these are approximately 25cm long; brush off all flour then roll up each piece tightly, starting from the base, stretching and pulling the pointed end of the dough but without using any flour.
7	eggwash		Turn the ends round to give the shape of crescents then place on a warm greased baking tray keeping the tips underneath, brush with eggwash and place in the prover until they have doubled in size. Bake in the oven at 220°C for approx. 15 mins.

1754 Doughnuts

16
1¼ hours

Stage	Ingredient	Quantity	Method
1	Bun Dough (1750)	900g	Knead the dough, divide into 16 even pieces and mould into balls. Place on a greased tray. Allow them to prove in a prover until they have doubled in size.
2			Place into deep fat at 165°C and fry to a golden brown on both sides. (10–12 mins.).
3	raspberry jam cinnamon ⎫ mixed caster sugar⎭ together	200g	Drain, pipe a little jam into the middle of each then roll in the cinnamon sugar.

1755 Fruit Buns

16
1¼ hours

Stage	Ingredient	Quantity	Method
1	Bun Dough (1750) mixed spice	900g 5g	Prepare the dough with the spice added at Stage 1.
2	mixed fruit	125g	Work carefully into the dough.
3			Divide the dough into 16 equal pieces and mould into balls. Place on a lightly greased warm baking tray. Allow them to prove in a prover until they have doubled in size. Bake at 235°C for 15–20 mins.
4	Bun Wash (1676)		Brush over the buns while still hot and place on a wire grid to cool.

1756 Marignans Chantilly

24
1 hour

Stage	Ingredient	Quantity	Method
1	white compound fat Pâte à Savarin (1741)	50g 1¼kg	Grease well 24 × 12cm barquette moulds. Fill the moulds one-third full with the savarin paste and allow to prove in a prover until they reach the tops of the moulds.
2			Bake at approx. 235°C for approx. 15 mins. Turn out to cool on wire racks.
3	Savarin Syrup (1713)	5 litres	Place the marignans in the hot syrup until well soaked. Remove carefully and replace on the wire rack to drain. Cut slits along the marignans on the slant.
4	Apricot Glaze (1672)	4dl	Brush over the marignans.

5	Crème Chantilly (1682)	½ litre	Place the marignans on suitable dishes and decorate with cream in the slits.

SPECIAL POINT

It is better not to soak marignans immediately after cooking but to leave them to dry out overnight.

1757 Savarins

3 × 18cm dry cases
1½ hours

Stage	Ingredient	Quantity	Method
1	flour, strong	500g	Sift the flour into a warm basin and
	yeast	20g	make a bay. Mix the yeast and milk and
	milk at 37°C	1dl	place in the bay.
2	eggs	8	Mix together and warm to approx. 37°C.
	caster sugar	20g	Add to the yeast and milk. Draw the flour in from the side and beat well to a smooth light paste.
3	butter, unsalted	250g	Place the softened butter in pieces on top of the paste, cover and allow to prove in a prover until double its size.
4			Beat the butter well into the paste until it forms a smooth elastic dough. Allow to rest for 10 mins.
5	white compound fat	50g	Grease well three 18cm savarin moulds with white compound fat. Half fill with the savarin dough, cover and allow to prove in a warm place until doubled in size.
6			Bake at 235°C for approx. 20 mins. Remove from the moulds and allow to cool upside down on a wire rack.

1758 Savarin Chantilly

8 portions
25 mins.

Stage	Ingredient	Quantity	Method
1	Savarin case (1757)	1	Place in the syrup until well-soaked. Remove carefully and place on a wire rack to drain thoroughly and cool.
	Savarin Syrup (1713)	2 litres	
2	Apricot Glaze (1672), hot	1½dl	Brush all surfaces of the savarin with the glaze then place it on a round flat dish.
3	Crème Chantilly (1682)	7½dl	Place into a piping bag with a 1cm star tube and use to neatly fill the centre of the savarin and decorate the sides.

1759 Savarin aux Fraises

8 portions
1 hour

Stage	Ingredient	Quantity	Method
1	small ripe strawberries, cleaned	650g	Place the strawberries in a basin, add the Grand Marnier and the sugar and toss over gently to mix. Place in the refrigerator to macerate for 45 mins.
	Grand Marnier	½dl	
	sugar, caster	50g	
2	Savarin case (1757)	1	Place the savarin in the syrup until well-soaked. Remove carefully and place on a wire rack to drain thoroughly and cool.
	Savarin Syrup (1713)	2 litres	
3	Apricot Glaze (1672), hot	1½dl	Brush all surfaces of the savarin with the glaze then place it on a round flat dish.
4	Crème Chantilly (1682)	7½dl	Reserve eight nice strawberries for decoration. Add three-quarters of the Crème Chantilly to the strawberries and fold in carefully. Pile this into the centre of the prepared savarin.
5			Use the remaining cream in a piping bag with a star tube to decorate the middle of the savarin and pipe eight nice rosettes around the sides. Place a reserved strawberry in the centre of each.

1760 Savarin aux Fruits

8 portions
30 mins.

Stage	Ingredient	Quantity	Method
1	Savarin case (1757)	1	Place in the syrup until well-soaked. Remove carefully and place on a wire rack to drain thoroughly and cool.
	Savarin Syrup (1713)	2 litres	
2	Apricot glaze (1672), hot	3dl	Brush all surfaces of the savarin with the glaze, then place it on a round flat dish. Allow the remaining glaze to cool then add to the fruit salad and mix together carefully.
	Salade de Fruits (2007), drained	750g	
3			Fill the fruit into the savarin then decorate the top edges of it with some of the best pieces of fruit.
4	Crème Chantilly (1682)	3dl	Neatly decorate the centre and sides of the savarin with the cream.

1761 Turban de Croûtes aux Fruits

10 portions
20 mins.

Stage	Ingredient	Quantity	Method
1	Savarin case, (1757) icing sugar	1	Cut the savarin into 20 × ¾cm slices. Place on a tray, dust well with icing sugar and glaze in a hot oven or under the salamander.
2			Arrange the slices overlapping in turban-fashion on two round dishes, the thinner sides under the thick. Leave empty centres.
3	Fruit Salad (2007), drained Apricot glaze (1672), cold	900g 2½dl	Carefully mix the fruit and glaze together and divide equally into the centres of the croûtes.
4	Crème Chantilly (1682)	3dl	Decorate to choice with the cream in a piping bag with a star tube.

FLANS, BANDES, TARTS, TARTLETS
——————AND BARQUETTES——————

1762 To Line a Flan Ring

1) Grease the flan ring and place on a greased baking tray.
2) Mould the paste into a ball on a lightly floured board. Use 1740 for sweet, and 1738 for savoury fillings.
3) Lightly dust with flour and roll out the paste to a round shape, a little larger than the ring, approx. 2mm thick.
4) Roll the paste carefully onto the rolling pin and unroll evenly across the ring.
5) Mould the paste to the base and sides of the ring to exclude the air and obtain an even thickness.
6) Allow the surplus paste to fall over the outside edge of the ring, and remove by rolling the pin over the rim.
7) With both thumbs and forefingers bring up the lip of the paste ½cm above the rim of the flan ring and decorate with pastry tweezers or use the thumb and forefinger to give a scalloped edge.
8) Allow the flan to rest for 30 mins. before cooking so as to prevent shrinkage. The lined flan ring may be filled with its particular filling, such as raw or prepared fruit, the whole being baked together.
9) For some flans the lined flan is baked first and the filling added when the flan case is cooked. Baking an empty flan is known as baking 'blind': a sheet of greaseproof paper is placed in the lined flan ring and then filled with raw haricot beans. Bake at 220°C for approx. 15 mins., remove the beans and paper, lift off the flan ring, brush the outside with eggwash and replace in the oven for a further 10 mins. to complete the cooking and to glaze the exterior.

1763 To Line Tartlet Moulds

1) Grease the tartlet moulds.
2) Roll out the paste on a lightly floured board to 2mm thickness. Use 1740 for sweet, and 1738 for savoury fillings.
3) Cut out rings with a fancy cutter slightly larger than the moulds.
4) Turn the pieces of paste upside down and place in the moulds, pressing to the base to exclude air.
5) With both thumbs and forefingers bring up the lips of the paste a little above the rims of the tartlet moulds.
6) Prick the bottoms with a fork.
7) Allow the tartlets to rest for 30 mins. before cooking so as to prevent shrinkage. The lined tartlet may be filled with its particular filling, such as raw or prepared fruit, the whole being baked together.
8) For some tartlets the lined tartlets are baked first and the filling added when the tartlet cases are cooked. Baking empty tartlets is known as baking 'blind': greaseproof paper is placed in the lined tartlets and then filled with raw haricot beans. Bake at 220°C for approx. 15 mins., remove the beans and papers and remove the tartlets from the moulds. Replace in the oven for a further 5 mins. to complete the cooking.

1764 To Line Barquette Moulds

1) Grease the barquette moulds and place close together.
2) Roll out the paste on a lightly floured board to 2mm thickness. Use 1740 for sweet, and 1738 for savoury fillings.
3) Roll the paste carefully onto the rolling pin and unroll evenly over the moulds.
4) Press the paste into the moulds with a small ball of paste.
5) Remove surplus paste by rolling across the surface of the moulds with the rolling pin.
6) Finish as for Tartlet Moulds (1763) from Stage 6.

SPECIAL POINTS
a) After lining flans, tartlets or barquettes for use with fresh fruit, a little Frangipane (1689) may be spread in the bottom before adding the fruit and baking. This will help to prevent the paste from becoming soggy.
b) Flans, tartlets and barquettes which have been baked 'blind' in readiness for filling with fresh soft fruits, such as raspberries and strawberries, may be brushed out with hot Red Glaze (1705). Allow to cool before adding the fruit. This will help to prevent the paste from becoming soggy.

1765 Bakewell Tart

8 portions
1¼ hours

Stage	Ingredient	Quantity	Method
1	Pâte Sucrée		Line a 20cm flan ring (1762).
	(1740)	250g	Spread the bottom with the jam.
	raspberry jam	50g	
2	Frangipane Filling		Fill the frangipane into the flan and
	(1689)	500g	smooth level.

3	eggwash		Rest the flan for 30 mins. then place in the oven at 210°C and bake for 25–30 mins. until golden brown. Remove from the oven and remove the flan ring. Brush the outside of the flan with eggwash, then replace in the oven for a few more mins. to complete the cooking and to glaze the exterior.
4	Apricot Glaze (1672) water icing (1715)	½dl	Brush the surface of the flan lightly with the hot glaze. Allow the flan to cool then lightly coat with the water icing. Place on a doily on a round dish.

1766 BANDES AUX FRUITS – FRUIT BANDS or SLICES

Fruit bands can be prepared in two basic fashions, 1) where the fruit either fresh, poached or tinned is placed on a blind-baked puff pastry base which has been coated with either Crème Pâtissière or Crème Frangipane, or 2) where the fruit is placed in its fresh state on an uncooked puff pastry base and both fruit and pastry are baked together. In both cases they are glazed and decorated as appropriate.

Most soft and hard fruits can be used and although most are best prepared in one fashion only, there are a few such as cherries and apricots which can be satisfactorily prepared in either fashion.

It is also possible to prepare a bande incorporating a number of different fruits. It is only necessary that the fruits are arranged in a tasteful manner and with the different varieties carefully delineated. This will help the customer to make an easy choice.

Fruit bands may be decorated with Crème Chantilly but in this case the name of the band should take the suffix 'Chantilly' and should be so designated on the menu, for example, Bande à l'Ananas Chantilly. On the other hand, it is customary in any case to offer Crème Chantilly separately.

The following popular examples have been selected as being representative of both types of preparation.

1767 Bande aux Abricots – Apricot Band (1)

10 portions
1 hour

Stage	Ingredient	Quantity	Method
1	Pâte Feuilletée (1736)	350g	Roll out the paste into a long strip approx. 40cm long × 15cm wide and approx. 3mm thick. Cut two even-width strips from the length of the paste 1½cm wide and reserve. Reroll the paste lightly and trim to an even oblong shape 40cm × 15cm; place on a dampened baking tray.
2	eggwash		Eggwash along the edges and place the reserved strips of paste along each edge. Press firmly to seal, then scallop the outside edges. Eggwash the surface of the

			edges and prick the centre of the band all over with a fork. Rest for 30 mins. and bake at 230°C for 15–20 mins. until a golden brown. Place on a wire grid to cool.
3	Crème Pâtissière (1685), hot	3dl	Spread along the centre of the band and allow to cool.
4	tinned or poached apricots, well-drained	600g	Arrange the halves of apricots neatly and in an orderly fashion to cover the whole of the area between the edges.
5	Apricot Glaze (1672), warm	2dl	Coat the apricots carefully with the warm glaze, allow to cool.
6			Place the band either whole or cut in portions on a doily on a suitable dish.

1768 Bande aux Abricots – Apricot Band (2)

10 portions
1 hour

Stage	Ingredient	Quantity	Method
1	Pâte Feuilletée (1736)	350g	Roll out the paste into a long strip approx. 40cm long × 15cm wide and approx. 3mm thick. Cut two even-width strips from the length of the paste 1½cm wide and reserve. Reroll the paste lightly and trim to an even oblong shape 40cm × 15cm; place on a dampened baking tray.
2	eggwash		Eggwash along the edges and place the reserved strips of paste along each edge. Press firmly to seal, then scallop the outside edges. Eggwash the surface of the edges and prick the centre of the band all over with a fork.
3	Frangipane Filling (1689)	150g	Spread a thin layer along the centre of the band and to the inside edges of the raised strip.
4	fresh apricots, cut in halves and stones removed	600g	Arrange neatly to cover the whole of the area between the edges then press them down slightly into the Frangipane. Allow to rest for 30 mins.
5			Bake at 210°C for 25–30 mins. until a golden brown. Place on a wire grid to cool slightly.
6	Apricot Glaze (1672), hot	2dl	Coat with the apricot glaze and allow to cool.

7

Place the band either whole or cut in portions on a doily on a suitable dish.

1769 Bande à l'Ananas – Pineapple Band

Prepare in the same way as Bande aux Abricots (1) (1767) but using approx. 600g well-drained canned pineapple. Cut each slice across into thin slices and each slice into four. Arrange neatly overlapping and coat with Apricot Glaze (1672) or a glaze prepared from the juice (1690).

1770 Bande aux Cerises – Cherry Band

Prepare in the same way as Bande aux Abricots (1) (1767) but using 600g stoned poached cherries or as Bande aux Abricots (2) (1768), using 600g stoned fresh cherries. In either case, arrange the cherries with the stalk end, from where the stones were removed, underneath. Coat with Red Glaze (1705) or a glaze prepared from the poached cherry syrup (1690) to finish.

1771 Bande aux Fraises – Strawberry Band

Prepare in the same way as Bande aux Abricots (1) (1767) but using 600g even-sized fresh prepared strawberries. Coat the centre of the band well with the appropriate Red Glaze (1705) instead of Crème Pâtissière. Arrange the strawberries, hulled side downwards, and cover with strawberry-flavoured Red Glaze (1705).

1772 Bande aux Framboises – Raspberry Band

Prepare in the same way as Bande aux Abricots (1) (1767) but using 600g even-sized fresh raspberries. Coat the centre of the band well with the appropriate Red Glaze (1705) instead of Crème Pâtissière. Arrange the raspberries, hulled side downwards, and cover with raspberry-flavoured Red Glaze (1705).

1773 Bande aux Groseilles Vertes – Gooseberry Band

Prepare in the same way as Bande aux Abricots (1) (1767) but using 600g poached and well-drained gooseberries or as Bande aux Abricots (2) (1768), using 600g fresh gooseberries. Coat with Apricot Glaze (1672) or a glaze prepared from the poached gooseberry syrup to finish.

1774 Bande aux Mandarines – Tangerine Band

Prepare in the same way as Bande aux Abricots (1) (1767) but using 600g well-drained segments of tinned mandarins. Arrange neatly, slightly overlapping on the Crème Pâtissière, and coat with a lightly coloured yellow glaze made from the juice of the mandarins (1690).

1775 Bande aux Poires – Pear Band

Prepare in the same way as Bande aux Abricots (1) (1767) but using approx. 600g well-drained poached or canned halves of pears. Cut in even slices and arrange neatly overlapping. Finish with a lightly coloured glaze prepared from the pear syrup (1690).

1776 Bande aux Pommes – Apple Band

Prepare in the same way as Bande aux Abricots (2) (1768) but using 600g cored, peeled and quartered apples, cut into thinnish slices. Arrange neatly overlapping on the frangipane and sprinkle with a little caster sugar before baking. Coat with Apricot Glaze (1672) to finish.

1777 Bandes aux Prunes variées – Various Plum Bands

All varieties of plums, mirabelles, damsons and greengages may be prepared in the same way as Bande aux Abricots (2) (1768) but using approx. 650g of the selected fruit cut in halves and stoned. Arrange the plums, cavity side upwards and slightly overlapping on the slant. Sprinkle with a little caster sugar before baking. Coat with Red Glaze (1705) or Apricot Glaze (1672) as appropriate to the colour of the plum, to finish.

The following titles are given as they can appear on the menu: Bande aux Prunes – Plum Band, Bande aux Mirabelles – Mirabelle Band, Bande aux Reines-Claude – Greengage Band.

1778 Bande à la Rhubarbe – Rhubarb Band

Prepare in the same way as Bande aux Abricots (2) (1768) but using 600g peeled fresh rhubarb cut in 5cm lengths. Arrange side by side along the length of the band and sprinkle with a little caster sugar before baking. Coat with either a clear or light pink Fruit Syrup Glaze (1690) to finish.

1779 Dutch Apple Tart

8 portions
1½ hours

Stage	Ingredient	Quantity	Method
1	Pâte Sucrée (1740)	350g	Line a 20cm flan ring with approx. two-thirds of the paste.
2	cooking apples	750g	Peel, core and slice the apples. Place
	sultanas	60g	into a pan with the remainder of the
	demerara sugar	125g	ingredients and one tablespoon of water
	ground cinnamon	2g	and partly cook. Allow to cool.
	lemon zest, grated	½ tsp	
3			Place the mixture into the lined flan ring. Roll out the remainder of the paste, moisten the edges and cover the apple. Seal the edges and brush with water and sprinkle with caster sugar. Bake at 215°C for 30–35 mins.
4	Sauce Anglaise (1718)	5dl	Place the tart on a doily on a round dish and serve accompanied with the Sauce.

1780 FRUIT FLANS

Fruit flans have much in common with the Fruit Bands inasmuch as they are either blind-baked short pastry cases filled with fresh, tinned or poached fruits or they are uncooked pastry cases filled with raw fruits and uncooked mixtures which are then cooked together. There are a number of variations to the fillings and finishes of flans and sometimes these are variously described as tarts or pies; but in general the observations concerning the Fruit Bands are applicable to the more usual Fruit Flans.

1781 Flan aux Abricots – Apricot Flan (1)

8 portions
1¼ hours

Stage	Ingredient	Quantity	Method
1	Pâte Sucrée (1740)	250g	Line a 20cm flan ring with the paste and bake it blind (1762).
2	Crème Pâtissière (1685)	3dl	Pour into the finished flan case and smooth level.
3	tinned or poached apricots, well-drained	600g	Arrange the halves of apricots round side upwards to neatly cover the pastry cream, starting as a circle round the outer edge.
4	Apricot Glaze (1672), hot	2dl	Coat the apricots evenly with the glaze and allow to cool.
5			Place the finished flan on a doily on a round dish.

1782 Flan aux Abricots – Apricot Flan (2)

8 portions
1¼ hours

Stage	Ingredient	Quantity	Method
1	Pâte Sucrée (1740)	250g	Line a 20cm flan ring (1762) with the paste.
2	Frangipane Filling (1689)	200g	Spread evenly over the base of the flan.
3	fresh apricots, cut in halves and stones removed	600g	Arrange the apricots round side upwards, to neatly cover the frangipane, starting as a circle round the outside edge. Press them lightly into the frangipane then allow to rest for 30 mins.
4	sugar, caster	25g	Sprinkle the apricots with a little sugar then bake the flan at 210°C for 20–25 mins.
5	eggwash		Remove the flan ring, brush the outside of the flan with eggwash then replace in the oven for a few more mins. to complete the cooking and to glaze the exterior.
6	Apricot Glaze (1672), hot	1½dl	Coat the apricots evenly with the glaze and allow to cool.

1783 Flan aux Bananes – Banana Flan

8 portions
1¼ hours

Stage	Ingredient	Quantity	Method
1	Pâte Sucrée (1740)	250g	Line a 20cm flan ring with the paste and bake it blind (1762).
2	Crème Pâtissière (1685)	3dl	Pour into the finished flan case and smooth it level.
3	bananas lemon juice	4 1 tbsp	Cut the bananas into 2mm-thick slices slightly on the slant. Place on a plate and sprinkle with a little lemon juice to prevent browning.
4			Cover the whole surface of the pastry cream with neatly overlapping slices of the banana, starting from the outer edge.
5	Apricot Glaze (1672), hot	1½dl	Coat the bananas evenly with the glaze. Allow to cool. Place the finished flan on a doily on a round dish.

1784 Flan aux Cerises – Cherry Flan

Prepare in the same way as Flan aux Abricots (1) (1781), using 600g stoned poached cherries, or as Flan aux Abricots (2) (1782), using 600g stoned fresh cherries. Arrange the cherries with stalk end underneath. Coat with Red Glaze (1705) or a glaze prepared from the poached cherry syrup (1690).

1785 Flan aux Fraises – Strawberry Flan

8 portions
1¼ hours

Stage	Ingredient	Quantity	Method
1	Pâte Sucrée (1740)	250g	Line a 20cm flan ring with the paste and bake it blind (1762).
2	Red Strawberry Glaze (1690), hot	½dl	Brush the inside of the flan with the glaze and allow to cool.
3	strawberries, cleaned, washed and drained dry	600g	Arrange neatly in the flan case with the points upwards.
4	Red Strawberry Glaze (1690), hot	2dl	Coat the strawberries evenly with the glaze and allow to cool.
5			Place the finished flan on a doily on a round dish.

1786　Flan aux Framboises – Raspberry Flan

Prepare in the same way as Flan aux Fraises (1785), using 600g raspberries. When ready, coat with a raspberry-flavoured Red Glaze (1690).

1787　Flan Normande

8 portions
1½ hours

Stage	Ingredient	Quantity	Method
1	Pâte Sucrée (1740)	250g	Line a 20cm flan ring (1762) with the paste. Allow to rest for 30 mins.
2	dessert apples	750g	Peel, core and quarter the apples then cut into fairly thick sections. Arrange neatly overlapping in the lined flan starting at the outer edge to form a circle. Continue to fill the flan. Bake at 215°C for 15 mins. until the paste is set.
3	eggs	2	Mix the eggs and sugar. Warm the milk,
	sugar	75g	add to the eggs and mix well together.
	milk	3dl	Pass through a strainer over the apple.
	grated nutmeg	pinch	Sprinkle with a little nutmeg.
4	eggwash		Return to the oven at 180°C to set the custard. Remove the flan ring, brush the outside with eggwash and replace in the oven for a few mins. to complete the cooking and to glaze the exterior.
5			Place the flan on a doily on a flat dish.

1788　Flan aux Pêches – Peach Flan

Prepare in the same way as Flan aux Abricots (1) (1781), using 600g approx. well-drained halves of poached or tinned peaches. The halves of peach may be used as they are or cut across in thickish slices and lightly fanned. When ready, coat with Apricot Glaze (1672) or a glaze prepared from the poached or tinned syrup (1690).

1789　Flan aux Poires – Pear Flan

Prepare in the same way as Flan aux Abricots (1) (1781) using 600g approx. well-drained halves of poached or tinned pears. The halves of pear may be used as they are or cut across in thickish slices and lightly fanned. When ready, coat with Apricot Glaze (1672) or a glaze prepared from the poached or tinned syrup (1690).

1790　Flan aux Poires Bourdaloue

8 portions
1½ hours

Stage	Ingredient	Quantity	Method
1	Pâte Sucrée (1740)	250g	Line a 20cm flan ring with the paste and bake it blind (1762).

Stage	Ingredient	Quantity	Method
2	Crème Pâtissière (1685), boiling poached or tinned halves of pears, well-drained	5dl 600g approx.	Half fill the flan case with some of the pastry cream then quickly cover this with the halves of pear, the pointed ends towards the centre; immediately cover smoothly with the remaining pastry cream.
3	Flaked Almonds, toasted (1671) icing sugar	75g	Cover the surface with the almonds then well dust to cover with icing sugar. Lightly glaze under a not too fierce salamander.
4			Place the finished flan on a doily on a round dish.

1791 Flan aux Pommes – Apple Flan

8 portions
1½ hours

Stage	Ingredient	Quantity	Method
1	Pâte Sucrée (1740)	250g	Line a 20cm flan ring (1762) with the paste and allow to rest for 30 mins.
2	cooking apples water sugar juice of lemon	750g ½dl 250g squeeze	Peel, core and slice the apples. Place in a pan, add the water, sugar and lemon juice and bring to the boil. Cook slowly to a fairly stiff purée taking care not to burn it. Pass through a sieve and allow to cool.
3	cooking apples	350g	Place the cold apple purée in the lined flan ring and smooth the surface flat. Peel, core and quarter the apples and cut into neat slices. Arrange neatly overlapping, starting at the outer edge, to form a circle. Continue in the same manner to cover the apple purée.
4	eggwash		Bake at 215°C for 25–30 mins. Remove the flan ring, brush the outside with egg-wash and replace in the oven for a further 5 mins. to complete the cooking and to glaze the exterior.
5	Apricot Glaze (1672)	2dl	Coat the flan evenly with the hot apricot glaze.
6			Place the flan on a doily on a silver dish.

1792 Flan aux Pommes Meringué

8 portions
1¼ hours

Stage	Ingredient	Quantity	Method
1	Pâte Sucrée (1740)	250g	Line a 20cm flan ring and bake it blind (1762). Allow to rest for 30 mins.

2	cooking apples	850g	Peel, core and slice the apples. Place in a pan, add the water, sugar and lemon juice and bring to the boil. Cook slowly to a fairly stiff purée taking care not to burn it. Pass through a sieve and allow to cool.
	water	½dl	
	sugar	250g	
	juice of lemon	squeeze	
3			Place the cold apple purée in the lined flan ring and smooth the surface flat.
4	egg whites	3	Prepare an Ordinary Meringue (1698) with the whites and sugar.
	sugar, caster	175g	
5			Place the meringue in a piping bag with an 8mm star piping tube. First cover the surface of the apple with straight lines then on top of this pipe lines first one way and then across at an angle to give a lozenge effect.
6	icing sugar		Dust well with the sugar then place the flan in a hot oven at 200°C to lightly colour and set the meringue.
7	Red Glaze (1705)	½dl	Place the glazes in small greaseproof paper cornets and fill the lozenge shapes with the glazes and alternating the colours.
	Apricot Glaze (1672)	½dl	
8			Place the finished flan on a doily on a round dish.

1793 Lemon Meringue Pie

8 portions
1½ hours

Stage	Ingredient	Quantity	Method
1	Pâte Sucrée (1740)	250g	Line a 20cm flan ring and bake it blind (1762).
2	water	3dl	Place the water and sugar in a pan, bring to the boil then add the diluted cornflour and reboil while mixing. Remove from the heat. Add the grated lemon rind and the juice and mix in with the butter and yolks. Pour into the prepared flan case and smooth flat.
	sugar	125g	
	cornflour	50g	
	lemons	2	
	butter	25g	
	egg yolks	3	
3			Place the flan in the oven at 165°C to set the filling.
4	egg whites	3	Whisk the whites in a clean basin to a stiff peak and fold in the sugar.
	sugar, caster	175g	
5	icing sugar		Place the meringue mixture in a piping bag with a star tube and neatly decorate

the top of the flan. Dredge with icing
sugar and place in the oven at 200°C
until the meringue is set and lightly
coloured (approx. 5 mins.).

6   Place the pie on a doily on a silver dish.

1794 Pumpkin Pie

8 portions
1½ hours

Stage	Ingredient	Quantity	Method
1	Pâte Sucrée (1740)	250g	Line a 20cm flan ring (1762) with the paste and allow to rest for 30 mins.
2	pumpkin flesh, free of skin and seeds	600g	Place in boiling water and cook until soft. Drain, press out any surplus moisture, then pass through a sieve and allow to cool.
3	eggs	3	Mix together in a basin then mix in the pumpkin purée.
	milk	2½dl	
	sugar, caster	50g	
	sugar, brown	25g	
	cinnamon	pinch	
	ginger, ground	pinch	
	clove, ground	pinch	
	nutmeg, ground	pinch	
4	eggwash		Place the mixture into the prepared flan ring to within ½cm of the top of the paste. Bake at 200°C for 20–25 mins. Remove the flan ring, brush the outside with eggwash then return to the oven for a further 10 mins. or so to complete the cooking and to glaze the exterior.
5			Place the finished pie on a doily on a round dish.

SPECIAL POINT
Whipped cream may be offered as an accompaniment.

1795 Tarte Tatin

8 portions
1½ hours

Stage	Ingredient	Quantity	Method
1	unsalted butter, soft	50g	Brush the sides of a shallow 20cm cake tin with butter then evenly coat the
	sugar, caster	75g	bottom with the remainder; sprinkle this with the sugar.
2	dessert apples	1¼kg	Peel, core and cut the apples into
	cinnamon, ground	good pinch	quarters, mix together with the cinnamon then cover the bottom of the mould with the apples tightly packed in concentric circles.

| 3 | sugar, caster | 50g | Sprinkle the top of the apples with the |
| | butter, melted | 50g | sugar then sprinkle with the butter. |

| 4 | | | Place on a hot stove for a few mins. to start the sugar at the bottom caramelising. This will be noticeable by appearance and smell; do not burn it. Remove from stove to cool. |

| 5 | Pâte Sucrée (1740) | 200g | Roll out the pastry to give an even circle a little larger than the cake tin. Place this over the apples and tuck the edges down into the tin at the sides of the apples. Make two or three holes in the top then allow to rest for 10 mins. |

| 6 | | | Bake at 195°C for approx. 25–30 mins. until the paste is nicely cooked and brown. Remove from the oven and allow to rest for 15 mins. |

| 7 | Crème Fraîche or Sauce Anglaise, cold (1718) | 4dl | Carefully turn upside down on a round dish and serve lukewarm, accompanied with Crème Fraîche or Sauce Anglaise. |

1796 Tartelettes et Barquettes aux Fruits – Fruit Tartlets and Barquettes

Line the tartlet or barquette moulds with Pâte Sucrée (1740) and then prepare and finish in either of the ways as shown for Fruit Flans.

——1797 GÂTEAUX AND PASTRIES——

The number and variety of decorated gâteaux served for the sweet course of a meal or for afternoon tea is vast. Mostly they are based on a Génoise sponge filled and decorated with various kinds of cream and in many cases are sprinkled with a sugar syrup flavoured with a liqueur to give added moistness, flavour and aroma.

Correctly speaking, the descriptive term 'Torte' (pl. Torten) is synonymous with that of 'Gâteau' although a torte is often thought of as being larger than a gâteau, with a higher percentage of filling and frequently marked on its upper surface with a Torten divider, or cut in portions and separately decorated or re-formed. For the purposes of this section the terms 'Gâteau' and 'Torte' will be used where felt to be appropriate.

There is also a wide range of pastries generally based on all the various kinds of pastes with suitable fillings and decorative work. A perusal of any good professional book on gâteaux and pastries will give some idea of the wide range of techniques and artistic skills employed in the production of these highly specialised items (see Select Bibliography, page 881).

The following gâteaux and pastries have been selected as representatives of their type.

1798 Choux à la Crème – Cream Buns   24

1½ hours

Stage	Ingredient	Quantity	Method
1	Pâte à Chou (1735) eggwash nibbed almonds	¾ litre 120g	Place the chou paste into a piping bag with a 1cm plain tube and pipe out balls approx. 3cm in diameter on a lightly greased baking tray. Sprinkle with nibbed almonds and bake at 220°C for 30 mins. until crisp and light brown in colour.
2			Place on a wire rack and allow to cool.
3	Crème Chantilly (1682)	1 litre	Slit open the side of the buns with a knife. Place the cream in a piping bag with a plain tube and fill the buns.
4	icing sugar		Dredge with icing sugar.
5			Place on doilys on silver dishes.

1799 Dartois aux Amandes

Prepare in the same way as Jalousie (1812) using Frangipane Filling (1689) instead of jam.

1800 Cornets Chantilly – Cream Horns   15

1½ hours

Stage	Ingredient	Quantity	Method
1	Pâte Feuilletée (1736)	450g	Roll out the paste 2mm thick and to a width of approx. 30cm. Trim the edges straight. Cut into strips 2cm × 30cm along the width.
2			Brush lightly with water to dampen the surface. Using greased cornet moulds, wind each strip damp side up onto the cornets, starting at the pointed end and rolling round the mould with the edges overlapping. Finish off by smoothing the edge of the paste level with the open under-edge of the mould. Dampen and secure the end of the paste. Check to ensure that the pointed end is covered properly with paste.
3	sugar, caster	75g	Brush the top side of the finished horn with water and dip into caster sugar. Place on a greased baking tray, sugar side up, and allow to rest for 30 mins.

Stage	Ingredient	Quantity	Method
4			Bake at 210°C for 18–20 mins. until crisp and a light golden brown. Remove from the oven then remove the cornets from the moulds. Place on a wire grill to cool.
5	red jam Crème Chantilly (1682)	50g 3dl	Pipe a little of the jam into the end of the cornets then fill completely with the Crème Chantilly using a piping bag and star tube, finishing with a rosette of the cream.
6			Present on a doily on a flat dish.

1801 Eclairs au Café – Coffee Eclairs

18

1½ hours

Stage	Ingredient	Quantity	Method
1	Pâte à Chou (1735)	¾ litre	Place the chou paste into a piping bag with a 1cm plain tube and pipe out 10cm lengths on a lightly greased baking tray. Brush with eggwash and bake at 220°C for 30 mins. until crisp and light brown in colour.
2			Place on a wire rack and allow to cool.
3	Crème Chantilly (1682)	1 litre	Slit open one side of the éclairs with a knife. Place the cream in a piping bag with a plain tube and fill the éclairs.
4	Fondant (1688) coffee essence or extract	500g	Prepare and flavour the fondant with sufficient essence or extract to give a good coffee flavour and colour. Dip the tops of the éclairs into the fondant and remove the surplus. Allow to set.
5			Place on doilys on suitable dishes.

1802 Eclairs au Chocolat – Chocolate Eclairs

Prepare in the same way as Eclairs au Café (1801), using chocolate-flavoured fondant instead of coffee fondant.

1803 Génoise – Genoese Sponge

1 sponge cake

1 hour

Stage	Ingredient	Quantity	Method
1	white compound fat	20g	Grease a 25cm diameter gâteau tin and coat with flour.
2	eggs caster sugar	5 150g	Place in a basin over a pan of hot water or in a bain-marie and whisk until it becomes light, creamy and thick in texture. Remove from the heat and whisk until cold.

3	flour, sifted melted butter at 37°C	150g 60g	Fold the flour very gently into the egg mixture. Add the butter and fold in again. Do not over-mix.
4			Pour the mixture into the mould, level the surface and bake at 195°C for 25–30 mins.
5			Turn out on a wire rack and allow to cool.

1804 Génoise au Chocolat – Chocolate Genoese Sponge

Prepare in the same way as Génoise (1803), using 120g of flour and 30g of cocoa powder sifted together twice instead of the 150g of flour.

1805 Gâteau au Chocolat – Chocolate Gâteau   8–12 portions
35 mins.

Stage	Ingredient	Quantity	Method
1	Chocolate Génoise (1804)	 1	Cut horizontally in half.
2	Buttercream (1677) chocolate couverture	350g 100g	Melt the chocolate and mix into the buttercream.
3			Spread one of the sponge layers with the chocolate buttercream and sandwich the Génoise together. Coat the top and sides smoothly with the same buttercream.

4	Chocolate Squares
	  (1679), or chocolate
	  vermicelli
			Cover the sides with overlapping squares of chocolate or chocolate vermicelli. Decorate the top with piped buttercream or chocolate squares.

5			Set the gâteau on a cake board and place on a suitable round dish.

1806 Gâteau Forêt-Noire – Black Forest Gâteau   12–16 portions
1 hour

Stage	Ingredient	Quantity	Method
1	Chocolate Génoise (1804)	 2	Cut each Génoise horizontally into two rounds.
2	cream, whipping sugar Kirsch	6dl 50g 1 tbsp	Whisk the sugar and cream until fairly stiff then gently whisk in the Kirsch and reserve.

3	black cherries or
	  morello cherries,
	  poached or tinned
	Kirsch
		
		400g
		2 tbsps
			Strain the syrup from the cherries. Place ½dl of the syrup in a small basin with the Kirsch and reserve. Reserve also 12–16 cherries for decoration.

4	cornflour	1 heaped tsp	Place the remaining cherries in a pan with 1½dl only of the remaining syrup, bring to the boil and thicken with the cornflour diluted with a little water.
5			Sprinkle the bottom layer of the Génoise with some of the Kirsch syrup, then spread with some of the cream and spoon over some of the cherries and their sauce, but not quite to the edges. Place the second and third layer on top, treating each in the same way. Sprinkle the underside of the top slice with the remaining syrup and place on top sprinkled side down. Lightly sandwich the whole together.
6	Chocolate Shavings (1680)	250g	Coat the top and sides of the gâteau with more of the cream and coat the sides and ½cm rim around the edge of the top with the chocolate shavings. Pipe 12–16 rosettes of cream on top, just inside the edge of the chocolate shavings and pipe an open ring in the centre of the gâteau; fill this with the remainder of the chocolate.
7			Place a reserved cherry in each rosette of cream. Set the gâteau on a cake board and place on a suitable round dish.

1807 Gâteau Moka – Coffee Gâteau

8–12 portions
35 mins.

Stage	Ingredient	Quantity	Method
1	Génoise Sponge (1803)	1	Cut horizontally in half.
2	Buttercream (1677) coffee essence or extract	450g	Flavour the buttercream with sufficient essence to give a good coffee flavour and a light coffee colour.
3			Spread one of the sponge layers with the buttercream and sandwich the génoise together. Coat the top and sides smoothly with buttercream.
4	flaked almonds, toasted	250g	Cover the sides with the toasted almonds. Place a little of the buttercream in a piping bag with a small plain piping tube and write the word 'Moka' on the centre. Decorate according to taste.
5			Set the gâteau on a cake board and place on a suitable round dish.

1808 Gâteau Nelusko

8–12 portions
35 mins.

Stage	Ingredient	Quantity	Method
1	Chocolate Génoise (1804)	1	Cut horizontally into three slices.
2	Buttercream (1677) } mixed Pralin (1703) } together	250g 50g	Coat the bottom and centre slices of sponge with the buttercream and keep a little for the final decoration. Re-form the gâteau and place on a grill.
3	Fondant (1687) chocolate couverture, melted	400g 100g	Place the fondant in a pan and heat gently, stirring continuously until it reaches blood heat 37°C. Add the chocolate and see that it is a smooth flowing consistency. Add a little Stock Syrup (1709) if too thick.
4			Pour the fondant over the gâteau starting from the centre and to mask it completely.
5	Chocolate Squares (1679) pistachios, blanched and skinned	100g 12	Cover the sides with overlapping squares of chocolate. Decorate the top with rosettes of the remaining buttercream and place a pistachio in the centre of each.
6			Set the gâteau on a cake board and place on a suitable round dish.

1809 Gâteau Praliné

8–12 portions
35 mins.

Stage	Ingredient	Quantity	Method
1	Génoise Sponge (1803)	1	Cut in half horizontally.
2	Buttercream (1677) Pralin (1703)	300g 75g	Mix together.
3			Spread one of the layers of the Génoise with some of the pralin and buttercream, then sandwich the Génoise together. Coat the top and sides smoothly with the same buttercream.
4	Pralin (1703) hazelnuts, skinned and toasted	50g 12	Coat the sides evenly with the pralin. Decorate the top with rosettes of the remaining buttercream and place a toasted hazelnut in the centre of each.
5			Set the prepared gâteau on a cake board and place on a suitable round dish.

1810 Gâteau Printanière

10 portions
1 hour

Stage	Ingredient	Quantity	Method
1	Génoise Sponge (1803)	1	Cut horizontally into three rounds.
2	Buttercream (1677) almond essence raspberry essence	500g	Colour one-third of the buttercream green and flavour with almond essence, one-third pink with raspberry essence and leave the remaining third plain.
3			Spread one layer of the sponge with green buttercream, one with pink buttercream and sandwich the Génoise together. Coat the top and sides smoothly with plain buttercream.
4	flaked almonds, toasted (1671)	250g	Coat the sides with toasted almonds. Decorate the top with small rosettes of the three different buttercreams in an artistic manner.
5			Set the gâteau on a cake board and place on a suitable round dish.

1811 Gâteau St Honoré

10 portions
2½ hours

Stage	Ingredient	Quantity	Method
1	Pâte Feuilletée (1736)	250g	Roll out 3mm thick and cut out a circle 22cm in diameter. Place on a lightly greased baking tray and prick all over with a fork. Allow to rest for 30 mins.
2	eggwash Pâte à Chou (1735)	¾ litre	Eggwash around the edge of the pastry. Place the chou paste in a piping bag with a 1cm tube. Pipe the chou paste around the puff paste ½cm from the edge. Pipe twenty 1½cm diameter small balls of chou paste on another tray.
3			Bake at approx. 220°C until crisp and light brown in colour. The buns will require 18–20 mins., the base approx. 25 mins.
4	leaf gelatine Crème Pâtissière (1685) egg whites sugar	30g 7dl 5 50g	Soak the gelatine in cold water. Remove the pastry cream from the boil and add the gelatine. Mix in thoroughly and keep hot. Whisk the whites until stiff and whisk in the sugar. Mix quickly into the pastry cream.
5			Fill the twenty profiteroles with some of the prepared Crème St Honoré.

6	sugar	250g	Dip the tops of the profiteroles into the boiled sugar. Fix them on top of the raised edge of the gateau by dipping the bases in the sugar and sticking them quickly in place.
	glucose } cooked for	25g	
	water } glazing (1711)	1dl	

7			Place the remaining Crème St Honoré into a piping bag with a star tube and fill the centre of the gâteau dome-shaped.

8			Place on a doily on a round dish.

1812 Jalousie

10 portions
1½ hours

Stage	Ingredient	Quantity	Method
1	Pâte Feuilletée (1736) eggwash	650g	Roll the pastry into an oblong 40cm × 24cm; cut in half lengthways. Place one half on a damp baking tray, eggwash the edges and prick the centre area.
2	jam, to choice	150g	Spread the jam along the centre of the eggwashed half leaving the edges clear. Fold the other piece of pastry in half lengthways. Make incisions 2½cm long across the folded edge at 7mm intervals.
3			Carefully unfold the cut pastry onto the filled piece, seal the four edges carefully and trim square. Eggwash and allow to rest for 30 mins. in a cool place.
4	icing sugar		Bake at 220°C for 20–25 mins. until golden brown. Dredge with icing sugar and return to the oven for a few mins. to glaze. Serve on a doily on a suitable dish.

1813 Linzer Torte

8–10 portions
1¾ hours

Stage	Ingredient	Quantity	Method
1	flour, soft	125g	Sieve, mix together thoroughly and place in a basin.
	sugar, caster	150g	
	almonds, ground	75g	
	hazelnuts, ground	75g	
	mixed spice	good pinch	
	lemon zest	1 tsp	
	salt	pinch	
2	butter, unsalted	150g	Add the butter and rub it in to give a granular texture. Add the eggs and knead to a smooth dough. Cover with a cloth and allow to rest for 15 mins.
	egg yolks	2	

3			Roll out the pastry to approx. ¾cm thick and line a 22cm flan ring (1762). Reserve the trimmings.
4	raspberry jam.	250g	Spread an even layer of jam in the flan.
5	eggwash		Roll out the trimmings approx. 2mm thick and cut into ½cm-wide strips with a fluted pastry wheel. Arrange these strips across the torte 1cm apart, and fixing them at the side then arrange more strips across these to give a lattice effect. Eggwash the surfaces of the strips and top sides of the flan. Allow to rest for 15 mins.
6			Bake at 180°C for approx. 50 mins. then remove the flan ring and eggwash the outside of the flan. Return to the oven for a further 10 mins. to complete the cooking and glaze the outside.
7	icing sugar		Remove from the oven, allow to cool on a wire grill then dredge well with icing sugar. Place on a doily on a round dish.

1814 Mille–Feuille

10 portions
1½ hours

Stage	Ingredient	Quantity	Method
1	Pâte Feuilletée (1736)	650g	Roll out 2mm thick and cut out three circles approx. 22cm in diameter. Place on a damp baking tray, prick all over with a fork and allow to rest for at least 30 mins. in a cool place. Bake at approx. 200°C until crisp and light brown in colour (approx. 15 mins.). Allow to cool.
2	raspberry jam Crème Pâtissière (1685)	200g 3dl	Spread one layer of pastry with the jam and pastry cream, place the second piece of pastry on top and spread this also with jam and pastry cream. Turn the third piece over and place on top. Lightly sandwich together and trim the sides evenly.
3	Apricot Glaze (1672) Fondant (1688)	1dl 500g	Brush the top with a thin layer of glaze. Coat with white fondant and immediately pipe a thin spiral of chocolate-flavoured fondant radiating from the centre to the outside edge. With the point of a small knife, draw straight lines through the fondant from the centre to the outside

edge evenly spaced at approx. 4cm intervals at the outside. Then reverse the process cutting back from the edge, in between the first set of lines to the centre. Clean the knife between each stroke of the feathering. Allow to set.

Stage	Ingredient	Quantity	Method
4	Crème Pâtissière (1685) Flaked Almonds, toasted (1671)	2dl	Spread the sides smoothly with pastry cream taking care not to disturb the fondant. Coat the sides with the flaked almonds.
5			Place on a doily on a suitable dish.

1815 Mince Pies

12–15
1½ hours

Stage	Ingredient	Quantity	Method
1	Pâte Feuilletée (1736)	650g	Roll out the pastry 2mm thick and cut half the paste into 7cm rounds and the other half into 8cm rounds using fancy cutters. Place the small rounds on a damp baking tray.
2	mincemeat eggwash	250g	Pipe a little mincemeat in the middle of each piece of paste, eggwash the edges and cover with the larger pieces of paste. Seal the edges and eggwash. Make a very small incision in the centre of each pie. Allow to rest in a cool place for 30 mins.
3	icing sugar		Bake at 215°C until light brown (approx. 20 mins.). Dredge with icing sugar and serve warm on a doily on a suitable dish.

1816 Palmiers (as a Pastry)

10
5 mins.

Stage	Ingredient	Quantity	Method
1	Palmiers (1702) raspberry jam Crème Chantilly (1682)	20 pieces 100g 2½dl	Pipe a little jam on half of the palmiers then cover with some piped cream. Sandwich together in pairs with the remaining palmiers.
2			Arrange on a doily on a suitable dish.

1817 Pithivier

10 portions
1½ hours

Stage	Ingredient	Quantity	Method
1	Pâte Feuilletée (1736)	650g	Roll out 3mm thick and cut out one circle approx. 22cm in diameter and one 23cm in diameter. Place the smaller circle on a damp baking tray.

2	Frangipane Filling (1689) rum eggwash	250g ¼dl	Mix the rum into the frangipane and spread it on the pastry on the tray, leaving a 1cm border around the edge free. Eggwash this border.
3			Place the larger circle of pastry on top, seal well and scallop around the edge. Brush with eggwash. With the point of a small sharp knife make curved cuts 1mm deep radiating from the centre of the gâteau to the edge. Leave to rest in a cool place for 30 mins.
4	icing sugar		Bake at 215°C for 25–30 mins., then dredge with icing sugar and return to the oven to glaze or glaze carefully under the salamander.
5			Serve on a doily on a round dish.

SPECIAL POINT
It is permissible to add raspberry jam to the pastry base at Stage 2 before adding the frangipane filling.

1818 Rigi-Kirsch Torte

8–12 portions
45 mins.

Stage	Ingredient	Quantity	Method
1	Japonaise bases (1692) Génoise Sponge (1803)	2 × 25cm 1	Neatly trim the Japonaise bases to the same size as the Génoise. Reserve the trimmings. Cut the Génoise in half horizontally.
2	Buttercream (1677), soft Kirsch red colour	450g 1 tbsp	Mix together and colour a very light pink.
3	Stock Syrup (1709) Kirsch	½dl 2 tbsps	Mix together in a basin and reserve.
4			Coat the surface of one Japonaise base with a little of the prepared buttercream. Place one layer of the Génoise on top, sprinkle well with the Kirsch syrup, then coat carefully with a layer of the same buttercream. Well sprinkle the underside of the remaining Génoise with the Kirsch syrup, then turn over on top to sandwich the whole together.
5			Coat the top surface with a little more of the buttercream, then cover with the remaining Japonaise base, its smooth

side upwards. Sandwich the whole together lightly and evenly then trim the Japonaise bases again if required.

6	Pralin (1703)	50g	Coat the sides and top evenly with the remaining buttercream. Crush the reserved trimmings from the Japonaise and mix together with the pralin. Use this to cover the sides of the torte evenly.
7	icing sugar		Well dredge the top surface of the torte with icing sugar. Using the back of a long straight knife, mark the surface of the torte with lines approx. 1½cm apart then mark again diagonally across the lines to give a lozenge effect.
8			Set the torte on a cake board and place on a suitable round dish.

1819 Sacher Torte

8–10 portions
1½ hours

Stage	Ingredient	Quantity	Method
1	butter, melted	10g	Butter a 25cm diameter shallow cake tin and dust lightly with flour.
2	butter, unsalted	150g	Well cream the butter and sugar together then mix in the chocolate and the vanilla essence then finally beat in the egg yolks one at a time.
	sugar, caster	100g	
	plain couverture chocolate, melted	175g	
	vanilla essence	few drops	
	egg yolks	6	
3	egg whites	8	Place the whites in a clean basin with a pinch of salt and whisk to a stiff peak then fold in the sugar.
	sugar, caster	75g	
4	soft flour, sifted	150g	Fold into the egg whites then quickly fold in the prepared chocolate mixture. Do not overmix.
5			Fill into the prepared mould and bake at 180°C for 45–50 mins. until cooked. A thin trussing needle placed into the centre of the sponge should come out clean. Remove from the oven and place on a wire grill to cool.
6	apricot jam, smooth and with no fruit pieces	200g	Cut the sponge in half horizontally. Coat one half with a good layer of jam and sandwich together. Brush the top and sides with a thin layer of the remaining jam, thinned and made hot. Replace on the grill.

7	plain chocolate couverture	175g	Melt the chocolate in a pan over hot water and keep warm. Cook the sugar and water to 105°C on the sugar boiling thermometer. Allow to cool to lukewarm then mix into the chocolate.
	sugar, granulated	175g	
	water	½dl	
8			Pour over the torte starting from the centre so as to give a smooth glossy even coating all over. Allow to set then place on a cake board on a suitable dish.

1820 Swiss Roll

1 roll – 10 portions
45 mins.

Stage	Ingredient	Quantity	Method
1	white fat	15g	Line a Swiss roll tin with greased greaseproof paper allowing sufficient to come up a little above the sides.
2	eggs	4	Place in a basin over a pan of hot water or in a bain-marie and whisk until it becomes light, creamy and thick in texture. Remove from the heat and whisk until cold.
	sugar, caster	120g	
3	soft flour, sifted	120g	Fold very gently into the egg mixture.
4			Pour the mixture into the tin, level the surface and bake at 225°C for 8 mins.
5	sugar, caster	75g	Turn out on a clean cloth sprinkled with caster sugar and remove the paper.
6	jam, warm	250g	Spread the sponge with jam, fold in the nearest edge tightly and roll up the sponge into a roll using the cloth. Trim the ends square.
7			Present either whole or cut in sections, on a doily on a suitable dish.

1821 Swiss Roll, Chocolate

1 roll – 10 portions
45 mins.

Stage	Ingredient	Quantity	Method
1	white fat	15g	Line a Swiss roll tin with greased greaseproof paper allowing sufficient to come up a little above the sides.
2	eggs	4	Place in a basin over a pan of hot water or in a bain-marie and whisk until it becomes light, creamy and thick in texture. Remove from the heat and whisk until cold.
	sugar, caster	120g	

3	soft flour	} sifted together twice	90g
	cocoa powder		30g

Fold very gently into the egg mixture.

4

Pour the mixture into the tin, level the surface and bake at 225°C for 8 mins.

5	sugar, caster	75g

Turn out on a clean cloth sprinkled with caster sugar and remove the paper.

6

Roll up the sponge using the cloth and allow to cool as it is in the cloth.

7	Buttercream (1677)	200g
	chocolate couverture, melted	150g

Mix together thoroughly.

8

Unroll the roll, quickly spread with the chocolate buttercream then reroll it. Allow to cool thoroughly in a cool place. Trim the ends square, and present either whole or cut in sections, on a doily on a suitable dish.

— ENTREMETS CHAUDS – HOT SWEETS —

1822 Abricots Colbert

10 portions
1 hour

Stage	Ingredient	Quantity	Method
1	apricot halves, tinned or poached	60	Drain and dry the apricots. Fill the centres with some of the rice and sandwich two together to re-form as whole apricots.
	Condé rice (1706)	½ litre	
2	flour eggwash breadcrumbs } for crumbing		Paner the apricots à l'Anglaise (72).
3			Place the apricots into frying-baskets and deep fry at 185°C until crisp and golden brown. Drain well.
4	Apricot Sauce (1716)	6dl	Dress the apricots on doilys on round dishes and serve accompanied with the Kirsch-flavoured apricot sauce.

1823 Apfelstrudel

10–12 portions
2 hours

Stage	Ingredient	Quantity	Method
1	flour, strong	250g	Sift the flour and salt into a basin and
	salt	pinch	make a bay. Add the egg, milk and
	egg yolk	1	butter and mix to a smooth dough.
	milk, lukewarm	1¼dl	Cover and allow to rest for 30 mins. in
	butter, melted	30g	a warm place.
2	apples, eating	1½kg	Peel and core the apples and slice thinly
	sugar	150g	into a basin. Add the sugar, sultanas,
	sultanas	175g	cinnamon and apricot jam and mix in.
	cinnamon	2g	
	apricot jam	150g	
3	butter	100g	Melt the butter in a frying-pan, add the
	breadcrumbs	125g	breadcrumbs and fry to a light brown.
4			Roll out the dough into a square as thinly as possible. Place a clean cloth on the table, sprinkle with flour and place the rolled out dough on top.
5	butter, melted	100g	Pull the paste from the sides carefully until it is thin and transparent. Sprinkle the fried breadcrumbs over the paste, almost to the edges. Cover with the apple mixture, sprinkle with the butter and then roll into a thick roll.
6	butter, melted	50g	Place the roll with the leading edge underneath, onto a baking tray, brush with the butter and bake in the oven at approx. 190°C until cooked and golden brown (approx. 40mins.).
7	icing sugar		Dredge with the icing sugar, cut into
	Sauce Anglaise		portions and dress on a dish paper on a
	(1718)	6dl	flat dish. Serve accompanied with the sauce.

1824 BAKED FRUIT OR JAM ROLL

These may be prepared with fillings of fresh fruits such as apples, pears and apricots, dried fruits such as sultanas, figs and dates, either singly or in combination, and jams, syrup, lemon curd and marmalade etc. Fresh fruit will need sprinkling with up to 75g of sugar per 500g of fruit. Sauce Anglaise or custard sauce is always suitable for any baked roll but sauces compatible with the main fillings are to be preferred for jam or syrup rolls, e.g. jam sauce with baked jam roll.

The following recipes are of the standard type. The ingredients for fillings may be varied or mixed as seen fit.

1825 Baked Devonshire Roll

10 portions
2 hours

Stage	Ingredient	Quantity	Method
1	Pâte à Foncer (1738)	850g	Roll out to a rectangle approx. 30cm × 35cm. Thin down 2cm of the short ends to half their thickness. This will give an area approx. 30cm × 39cm.
2	Marmelade de Pommes (1695) cooking apple, peeled, cored, and cut in ½cm dice sultanas sugar, caster cinnamon, ground	200g 350g 75g 50g good pinch	Spread the apple jam all over the paste except for the unthinned edge furthest away. Sprinkle the jam evenly with the diced apple, sultanas and sugar and dust with a little cinnamon. Fold over the thinned-out edges to seal in the filling and roll up loosely towards the uncovered edge which must be brushed with water. Seal completely.
3	eggwash sugar, caster	75g	Place the roll, sealed edge downwards on a greased baking tray. Brush with eggwash, sprinkle well with caster sugar and decorate the surface by scoring with a knife taking care not to expose the filling. Allow to rest in a cool place for 30 mins.
4			Bake at 215°C until the paste is set and then allow the heat to reduce to approx. 175°C. Cook until golden brown (approx. 45 mins.).
5	Sauce Anglaise (1718) or Custard Sauce (1725)	6dl	Serve cut in portions accompanied with either of the sauces.

1826 Baked Jam Roll

10 portions
2 hours

Stage	Ingredient	Quantity	Method
1	Pâte à Foncer (1738)	850g	Roll out to a rectangle approx. 30cm × 35cm. Thin down 2cm of the short ends to half their thickness. This will give an area approx. 30cm × 39cm.
2	jam	300g	Spread the jam all over the paste except for the unthinned edge furthest away. Fold over the thinned out edges to seal in the jam and roll up loosely towards the unjammed edge, which must be brushed with water. Seal completely.

3	eggwash		Place the roll sealed edge downwards on a greased baking tray. Brush with eggwash, sprinkle well with caster sugar and decorate the surface by scoring with a knife taking care not to expose the jam filling. Allow to rest in a cool place for 30 mins.
	caster sugar	75g	
4			Bake at 215°C until the paste is set and then allow the heat to reduce to approx. 175°C. Cook until golden brown (approx. 45 mins.).
5	Jam Sauce (1726)	5dl	Serve cut into portions accompanied by jam sauce.

SPECIAL POINT
If rolled too tightly, the baked jam roll will tend to split during the baking process.

1827 Baked Syrup Roll

Prepare in the same way as Baked Jam Roll (1826), using 300g of golden syrup instead of jam. Warm the syrup slightly to facilitate spreading and sprinkle with 75g of white breadcrumbs before rolling it up. Serve accompanied with heated golden syrup.

1828 Baked Egg Custard

10 portions
1¼ hours

Stage	Ingredient	Quantity	Method
1	milk	1½ litres	Place the milk in a pan and warm. Mix the eggs and sugar in a basin and add the milk while stirring.
	eggs	9	
	sugar	180g	
2	nutmeg, grated	pinch	Pass the custard through a fine strainer into pie dishes. Sprinkle the surface with a little grated nutmeg.
3			Place the pie dishes in a deep tray and half fill the tray with warm water. Place in the oven at approx. 165°C to cook for 40–50 mins.
4			Clean the pie dishes and place on dish papers on oval dishes. Surround with pie collars.

1829 BEIGNETS – FRITTERS

Sweet fritters are of two basic types as follows:
1) Items such as fruits, set creams, slices of savarin, macaroons or biscuits etc., sprinkled with liqueurs, then coated with frying batter and deep-fried.
   For this type of fritter, the batter needs to be fairly thin and should give a crisp light brown coating when cooked. It is essential that the item is completely covered with a

thin layer of batter; lightly flouring the item before passing through the batter will help to ensure this. Failure to do so will give a greasy result, even to the extent of some fat being absorbed by the item of food itself.

When cooked, these fritters should be well-drained on kitchen paper then dusted with icing sugar which can be left as is or glazed in the oven, or under the salamander. The glazing should be just sufficient to melt the sugar to a high gloss; colouring or caramelisation should not be the aim.

2) Sweet and flavoured chou paste moulded in pieces, deep-fried, and sometimes filled with various pastry cream preparations or confitures. These are known as Beignets Soufflés.

The essential quality of souffléed fritters is that they are well-puffed, crisp and dry on the outside and with no uncooked paste inside. This means cooking at a lower temperature and for a longer time than ordinary fritters. The high egg content will prevent any absorption of fat. To finish they need to be well-drained then dredged with icing sugar.

Both types of fritter should be served with a suitable sauce, either fruit-based or a flavoured Sauce Anglaise or Sabayon.

1830 Beignets d'Abricots – Apricot Fritters

10 portions
1½ hours

Stage	Ingredient	Quantity	Method
1	apricots, firm	20	Cut the apricots in half, remove the
	sugar	50g	stones and place the halves in a basin.
	Kirsch	½dl	Sprinkle with the sugar and Kirsch and allow to macerate for approx. 1 hour. Turn them over occasionally.
2	flour		Drain the apricots well, pass through the
	Pâte à Frire		flour and shake off the surplus. Place
	(1744)	1 litre	them in the batter.
3			Remove from the batter one at a time and place into hot deep fat at 180°C. Fry until golden brown on both sides. Drain well.
4	Apricot Sauce (1716)	5dl	Add the liqueur remaining from macerating the apricots to the sauce then pass the sauce through a fine strainer.
5	icing sugar		Place the fritters on a tray and dredge with icing sugar. Glaze under the salamander.
6			Dress the fritters on a dish paper on a flat dish and serve accompanied with the apricot sauce.

1831 Beignets d'Ananas – Pineapple Fritters

10 portions
1½ hours

Stage	Ingredient	Quantity	Method
1	pineapple slices	15	Cut the pineapple slices in half and place the halves in a basin. Sprinkle with the sugar and Kirsch and allow to macerate for approx. 1 hour. Turn them over occasionally.
	sugar	50g	
	Kirsch	½dl	
2	flour		Drain the pineapple slices well, pass through the flour and shake off the surplus. Place them in the batter.
	Pâte à Frire (1744)	1 litre	
3			Remove from the batter one at a time and place into hot deep fat at 180°C. Fry until golden brown on both sides. Drain well.
4	Apricot Sauce (1716)	5dl	Add the liqueur remaining from macerating the pineapple to the sauce then pass the sauce through a fine strainer.
5	icing sugar		Place the fritters on a tray and dredge with icing sugar. Glaze under the salamander.
6			Dress the pineapple slices on a dish paper on a flat dish and serve accompanied with the apricot sauce.

1832 Beignets de Bananes – Banana Fritters

10 portions
45 mins.

Stage	Ingredient	Quantity	Method
1	bananas	10	Cut the bananas in half lengthways, place on a wire rack and coat with the hot pastry cream. Allow to cool.
	Crème Pâtissière (1685), hot	5dl	
2	flour		Pass through the flour and dip in the batter one at a time. Remove and place in hot deep fat at 180°C. Fry until golden brown on both sides (4–5 mins.). Drain well.
	Pâte à Frire (1744)	1 litre	
3	icing sugar		Place the fritters on a tray and dredge well with icing sugar. Glaze under the salamander.
4	Apricot Sauce (1716)	5dl	Dress on a dish paper on a flat dish and serve accompanied with the apricot sauce.

1833 Beignets de Crème Pralinée

10 portions
30 mins.

Stage	Ingredient	Quantity	Method
1	Crème Frangipane (1684), cold Pralin (1703)	500g 75g	Mix together then mould using a little flour into 30 small pear shapes.
2	Pâte à Frire (1744)	1 litre	Carefully pass the creams through the frying batter one at a time and place in deep hot fat at 180°C. Fry until golden brown, carefully moving occasionally to obtain an equal colouring all over. Drain well.
3	icing sugar Sauce Sabayon (1731), flavoured with a little rum	5dl	Dredge with icing sugar and arrange on a dish paper on an oval dish. Serve accompanied with the sauce.

1834 Beignets de Fraises – Strawberry Fritters

4 portions
40 mins.

Stage	Ingredient	Quantity	Method
1	strawberries, large, ripe and even-sized Curaçao sugar, caster	24–32 2 tbsps 15g	Remove the stalks then wash and dry the strawberries. Place in a basin with the Curaçao and sugar and allow to macerate for 30 mins. Turn over occasionally.
2	flour Pâte à Frire (1744)	4dl	Drain the strawberries well then lightly flour. Place in the frying batter.
3			Remove from the batter one at a time and carefully place in hot deep fat at 185°C. Fry quickly until golden brown. Drain well.
4	icing sugar Sauce Sabayon (1731)	2dl	Dredge the strawberries with icing sugar and arrange in a pile on a doily on a round dish. Serve accompanied with the sauce flavoured with the strained Curaçao left from the marination.

1835 Beignets de Pommes – Apple Fritters

10 portions
1½ hours

Stage	Ingredient	Quantity	Method
1	apples, cooking sugar cinnamon Calvados juice of lemon	5 50g pinch ½dl ½	Peel, core and cut the apples into approx. ¾cm-thick rings. Place in a basin and sprinkle with the sugar, cinnamon, Calvados and lemon juice. Allow to macerate for approx. 1 hour. Turn them over occasionally.

2	flour Pâte à Frire (1744)	1 litre	Drain the apples well, pass through flour and shake off the surplus. Place them in the batter.
3			Remove from the batter one at a time and place into hot deep fat at 180°C. Fry until golden brown on both sides. Drain well.
4	icing sugar		Place the fritters on a tray and dredge with icing sugar. Glaze under the salamander.
5	Apricot Sauce (1716)	5dl	Dress the beignets on a dish paper on a suitable dish and serve accompanied with the apricot sauce flavoured with the Calvados from the maceration.

1836 Beignets Soufflés

10 portions
30 mins.

Stage	Ingredient	Quantity	Method
1	Pâte à Chou (1735)	¾ litre	With a dessertspoon take up portions of the paste. Dip another dessertspoon into hot fat and mould off pieces the size of a walnut into hot deep fat at approx. 150°C.
2			Allow to fry until golden brown and cooked (approx. 10–12 mins.). Turn the beignets over in the fat from time to time to ensure even colouring and cooking. Remove and drain well.
3	icing sugar Apricot Sauce (1716)	5dl	Dredge well with icing sugar and dress on a dish paper on a flat dish. Serve accompanied with the apricot sauce.

1837 Beignets Soufflés Parisienne

Prepare Beignets Soufflés (1836). Fill the beignets with rum-flavoured Crème Pâtissière (1685) using a piping bag and a small plain piping tube. Dust with icing sugar and serve with apricot sauce flavoured with rum.

1838 Beignets Soufflés Dijonnaise

Prepare Beignets Soufflés (1836), cut open from the sides, and fill with a little blackcurrant confiture. Serve accompanied with Sauce Anglaise (1718).

1839 Bread and Butter Pudding

10 portions
1½ hours

Stage	Ingredient	Quantity	Method
1	slices of white bread, thin butter, melted	6–7 75g	Remove the crusts, cut each slice into four triangles and dip into the melted butter.
2	sultanas	100g	Wash well then sprinkle them in the bottom of pie dishes. Cover with the triangles of bread neatly overlapping.
3	milk vanilla essence eggs sugar	1½ litres 3–4 drops 9 175g	Place the milk and vanilla essence in a pan and warm. Mix the eggs and sugar in a basin and add the milk while stirring.
4	caster sugar	50g	Pass the custard through a fine strainer over the bread in the pie dishes. Sprinkle with the caster sugar.
5			Place the pie dishes in a deep tray and half fill the tray with warm water. Place in the oven at approx. 170°C and cook for 35–40 mins.
6			Clean the pie dishes and place on dish papers on flat dishes. Surround with pie collars.

1840 Cabinet Pudding

10 portions
1¼ hours

Stage	Ingredient	Quantity	Method
1	Génoise Sponge (1803) glacé cherries, chopped sultanas currants	250g 75g 40g 40g	Cut the Génoise into ½ cm cubes and mix with the fruits.
2	butter sugar, caster	25g 25g	Butter and sugar ten dariole moulds. Place an equal quantity of the mixture of Génoise and fruit in each.
3	milk vanilla essence eggs sugar	1 litre few drops 6 100g	Place the milk and vanilla essence in a pan and warm. Mix the eggs and sugar in a basin and add the milk while mixing.
4			Pass the custard through a fine strainer and fill the moulds almost to the top.
5			Place the moulds in a deep tray and half fill the tray with warm water. Place in the oven at approx. 170°C and cook for approx. 30 mins.

6	Apricot Sauce (1716) or Sauce Anglaise (1718)	5dl	Demould onto a flat dish and serve accompanied with the sauce.

1841 Charlotte de Pommes – Apple Charlotte

2 × 5 portions
2 hours

Stage	Ingredient	Quantity	Method
1	slices of white bread, ½cm thick	14	Remove the crusts from ten slices of the bread and cut three fingers from each slice, 3cm wide. Trim the fingers to the height of the charlotte moulds (2 × 12cm diameter). Soak one side of the fingers of bread in the butter. Arrange them overlapping around the inside of the moulds, with the buttered surface to the moulds. Cut two rounds from the other slices to the size of the bottom of the mould, butter one side and place buttered side downwards in the moulds.
	butter, melted	250g	
2	apples, dessert	2¼kg	Peel, core the slice the apples. Heat the butter in a sauté pan, add the apples, sugar and cinnamon and cook to a well-reduced very thick mixture. Mix in the jam.
	butter	175g	
	cinnamon	good pinch	
	sugar	150g	
	apricot jam, thick	100g	
3			Fill the prepared moulds with the apple mixture making sure that it comes a little higher in the centre. Cover with the remaining two slices of bread, cut to shape and dipped in the remaining melted butter.
4			Place the charlottes on a baking tray and bake at 205°C for 20–25 mins. to start the bread browning then reduce the heat to 175°C and continue cooking for a further 25–30 mins. to set the charlottes well.
5	Sauce à l'Abricot (1716)	5dl	Remove from the oven and allow to rest for 15 mins. then turn out carefully onto round dishes. Serve accompanied with the sauce.

SPECIAL POINT

The apple mixture must be of a good thick consistency and not watery; this would make the bread soggy with the possibility of the charlotte collapsing when being demoulded.

1842 Charlotte Normande

Prepare in the same way as Charlotte de Pommes (1841), adding ½dl Calvados to the apples when cooking the mixture and adding a little Calvados to the sauce at the time of serving.

1843 CHAUSSONS – TURNOVERS

These can be made with short, sweet or puff pastry, the latter giving the best result. Several kinds of fillings can be used, including jam, lemon curd, stiff fruit purées, Frangipane Filing, mincemeat, chestnut purée or Marmelade de Pommes (1965). Any sauce served should be appropriate to the filling.

1844 Chausson aux Pommes – Apple Turnover 10 portions
1½ hours

Stage	Ingredient	Quantity	Method
1	Pâte Feuilletée (1736)	400g	Roll out 3mm thick and cut into ten 12cm diameter rounds using a plain pastry cutter.
2	butter	50g	Peel and core the apples. Cut into approx. ½cm dice. Heat the butter in a pan, then add the apples, sugar and lemon juice and water. Cook until softened but not to a purée. Allow to cool completely.
	apples	1kg	
	sugar	150g	
	lemon juice	good squeeze	
	water	1 tbsp	
3	eggwash sugar, caster		Divide the apple mixture between the rounds of pastry, placing to one side of the centre. Eggwash the edges then fold over and seal well together. Eggwash the tops, make a small hole in the centre for steam to escape, then dip the tops in caster sugar and place sugar side up on a greased baking tray. Allow to rest for 30 mins.
4			Bake at 210°C for approx. 20 mins. until golden brown.
5	Sauce Anglaise (1718)	5dl	Serve the turnovers hot with sauceboats of Sauce Anglaise.

1845 Christmas Pudding 40 portions

Stage	Ingredient	Quantity	Method
1	currants	500g	Wash well, pick over for any stalks then drain and dry. Place in a large stainless steel or glazed earthenware container.
	sultanas	500g	
	raisins, seedless	500g	

2	mixed peel, chopped	500g	Add to the fruits and mix in.
	beef kidney suet,		
	chopped	500g	
	demerara sugar	350g	
	apple, chopped	250g	
	mixed spice	15g	
	ground ginger	10g	
	salt	5g	
	orange ⎱ grated rind	1	
	lemon ⎰ and juice	1	
3	brandy	1dl	Mix together, pour over the mixture and
	rum	1dl	mix in well. Cover with greaseproof
	sherry	1dl	paper and leave in a cool place to mature
	beer	1½dl	for 5–6 days.
4	eggs	5	Whisk together and add to the mixture.
	water	2dl	
5	breadcrumbs, white	750g approx.	Add sufficient to give a fairly stiff texture.
6			Fill the mixture into buttered 1kg-capacity basins. Cover with double sheets of buttered greaseproof and cover these with foil or pudding cloths. Tie down securely. Steam for 4 hours.
7			Demould onto round silver or stainless steel dishes and serve very hot accompanied with a suitable sauce or butter such as Custard Sauce (1725) flavoured with rum or brandy, Brandy Butter (1733), cream, or a Sabayon Sauce (1731) flavoured with rum or brandy.

SPECIAL POINTS
a) If the puddings are to be kept for any length of time, the wet cloths should be taken off and replaced by clean dry ones. Store the puddings in a cool, dry place and steam again for at least 2 hours before serving.
b) The puddings may be coated with sifted icing sugar or sprinkled with nibbed sugar and decorated with a sprig of holly placed in the centre; it can be served flaming by pouring ½dl of warmed brandy or rum over the very hot pudding and igniting it just prior to serving.

1846 Clafoutis aux Cerises

10 portions
2 hours

Stage	Ingredient	Quantity	Method
1	flour, strong	100g	Sift the flour and salt into a basin and
	salt	pinch	make a bay. Add the eggs and half the
	eggs	3	milk. Whisk to a smooth batter.
	egg yolks	1	Gradually add the remainder of the milk,

milk	4dl
liquid honey	50g
Kirsch	2 tbsps

the honey and Kirsch. Allow to rest for 1 hour.

2   butter   15g
       Pâte Sucrée (1740)   350g

Lightly grease ten 10cm shallow patty tins with the butter. Roll out the pastry approx. 2mm thick and line the tins (1763). Leave to rest for 30 mins.

3   cherries, morello
       or small black   600g

Wash and remove the stones.

4

Divide the cherries between the lined moulds then fill with the batter to within 3mm of the top of the paste.

5

Bake in the oven at 200°C for approx. 25–30 mins. until well risen and brown and crisp on top.

6   icing sugar
       Sauce Anglaise
         (1718)   5dl

Remove from the oven, demould, dredge with icing sugar and present on a dish paper on a hot dish. Serve accompanied with the sauce.

SPECIAL POINT

Clafoutis can also be made with other fruit such as pears or apricots, cutting them into fairly small pieces.

1847 CRÊPES – PANCAKES

30

1¼ hours

In general, sweet pancakes should be thin, light and delicate in texture and eating quality; the only exceptions to this are where a double layer of batter is used to enclose some sort of raw fruit or mixture and is then served flat. The following points should be observed:

1) The batter should be made with soft flour and the amount of egg called for in the recipe should not be exceeded. Too much egg will result in the cooked pancake having an oversoft spongy texture which tends to stick to the pan and is too fragile for any sort of manipulation.
2) The prepared batter should be of a flowing consistency which can quickly cover the bottom of the pan in an even thin coating.
3) Clarified butter is best for frying the pancakes as far as taste is concerned but it cannot reach a high enough temperature to ensure the quick cooking so essential to the finished result. A good quality vegetable oil with no pronounced flavour is more than suitable for most purposes.
4) Ideally, pancakes are best when freshly made and served immediately. They can however, be satisfactorily prepared in bulk by placing them as they are cooked, one on top of each other, after sprinkling each with a little caster sugar. They should then be covered to prevent drying and kept just warm only. Storage in a refrigerator for future use results in a chewy and rubbery texture when reheated; this is not to be recommended.

Large-diameter pancakes can be filled and rolled as in the following appropriate recipes for pancakes. They can then be cut on the slant into diamond-shaped pieces and finished as ordinary pancakes. In this form they are known as Pannequets, e.g. Pannequets Créole. See Crêpes Créole (1851).

Stage	Ingredient	Quantity	Method
1	flour, soft	250g	Sift the flour and salt into a basin. Make
	salt	pinch	a bay and add the eggs and sugar. Add
	sugar, caster	30g	the milk slowly and whisk continuously
	eggs	2	to a smooth batter. Cook the butter until
	milk	½ litre	just nut-brown in colour, add to the
	butter	60g	batter and whisk in quickly. Allow to rest for 1 hour.
2	oil	1½dl	Heat the pancake pan, add a little of the
	sugar, caster	50g	oil and reheat until very hot. Tip out the surplus oil, add ⅓dl of batter, sufficient to coat the bottom of the pan. Cook quickly until brown on both sides. Remove the pancake, place on a plate and sprinkle lightly with a little sugar. Continue making the pancakes in the same way, placing them on top of each other, until all the batter has been used. This mixture should yield approx. 30 pancakes.

1848 Crêpes au Citron – Pancakes with Lemon

Prepare pancakes (1847) as required. Fold in half then in half again and arrange overlapping on lightly buttered oval dishes allowing three pancakes per portion. Sprinkle with a little caster sugar and reheat carefully under the salamander or in the oven. Serve accompanied with quarters of lemon.

1849 Crêpes à la Confiture – Jam Pancakes

Prepare pancakes (1847) as required. Spread with the selected jam, slightly warmed, and roll up. Arrange on lightly buttered oval dishes with the joins underneath, allowing three per portion. Sprinkle with a little caster sugar and reheat in the oven. It is useful to mention the particular jam used in the menu title, e.g. Crêpes à la Confiture d'Abricots – Pancakes with Apricot Jam.

1850 Crêpes du Couvent

When making the pancakes, sprinkle the batter in the pan with thin slices of ripe pear which have been macerated with a little sugar. Add a little more of the batter to barely cover then cook to a golden brown on both sides. Serve flat and overlapping on a lightly buttered dish, allowing two per portion. Sprinkle with a little caster sugar and reheat in the oven. Sprinkle with a little Poire William liqueur when sending.

1851 Crêpes Créole

Prepare pancakes (1847) as required. Spread with equal quantities of finely diced pineapple and warm Crème Pâtissière (1685) flavoured with rum and roll up. Arrange on lightly buttered oval dishes with the joins underneath, allowing three per portion. Sprinkle with caster sugar and reheat in the oven.

1852 Crêpes à la Marmelade de Pommes

Prepare pancakes (1847) as required. Spread with warm Marmelade de Pommes (1695) and roll up. Arrange on lightly buttered oval dishes with the joins underneath, allowing three per portion. Sprinkle with a little caster sugar and reheat in the oven.

1853 Crêpes Mimi

Prepare pancakes (1847) as required. Spread with warm Crème Pâtissière (1685) containing one-quarter its amount of finely diced preserved ginger. Roll up and arrange on a lightly buttered oval dish with the joins underneath, allowing three per portion. Coat with a little of the syrup from the ginger and reheat in the oven.

1854 Crêpes Normande

10 portions
1½ hours

Stage	Ingredient	Quantity	Method
1	flour	350g	Sift the flour and salt in a basin. Make a bay and add the eggs and sugar. Add the milk slowly and whisk continuously to a smooth batter. Cook the butter until just nut-brown in colour, add to the batter and whisk in quickly. Finally add the Calvados and mix in. Allow to rest for 1 hour.
	salt	pinch	
	sugar, caster	30g	
	eggs	3	
	milk	7dl	
	butter	60g	
	Calvados	½dl	
2	apples	400g	Peel, core and cut the apples into small dice. Melt the butter in a sauteuse and when hot, add the apple, sprinkle with the cinnamon and sugar and cook quickly until half-cooked. Remove from the heat and keep on one side.
	butter	50g	
	cinnamon	1g	
	sugar	60g	
3	oil	1½dl	Heat the pancake pan, add a little oil and reheat until very hot. Tip out the surplus oil and add ⅓dl of batter, sufficient to coat the bottom of the pan. Sprinkle the surface with a spoonful of the cooked apple and cover evenly with as much batter again. Cook until brown underneath, turn over and cook until the other side is brown. Remove the pancake, place on a plate and sprinkle lightly with sugar. Continue making the pancakes until all the batter has been used. This mixture should yield 20 flat pancakes.
	sugar, caster	50g	

4	sugar, caster		Arrange overlapping on buttered oval
	Calvados	¼dl	dishes allowing two pancakes per person. Reheat in the oven and sprinkle with a little sugar and Calvados when sending.

1855 Crêpes à l'Orange – Pancakes with Orange

Prepare as Crêpes au Citron (1848) but serve accompanied with quarters of orange.

1856 Crêpes au Pralin

Prepare pancakes (1847) as required. Spread with warm Crème Pâtissière (1685) mixed with one-sixth its amount of Pralin (1703). Roll up and arrange on a lightly buttered oval dish with the joins underneath allowing three per portion. Sprinkle with a little pralin and caster sugar, heat in the oven and sprinkle the tops with a little rum when sending.

1857 Crêpes Soufflées Vanille

Prepare pancakes (1847) allowing two per portion. Lay them out flat then place two tablespoons of Vanilla Soufflé mixture (end of Stage 4, Recipe 1897) to cover one half of each pancake. Smooth level then fold the other half of the pancakes loosely over to cover the mixture. Place on a well-buttered silver or stainless steel dish. Dredge well with icing sugar. Place in a hot oven at 210°C for 10–12 mins. to cook the soufflé and lightly caramelise the sugar. Serve immediately accompanied with Sauce Anglaise (1718).

SPECIAL POINT
This type of pancake may be made with other sweet soufflé mixes. Always serve with Sauce Anglaise, flavoured where appropriate.

1858 Eve's Pudding

10 portions
1¼ hours

Stage	Ingredient	Quantity	Method
1	apples	1kg	Peel, core and slice the apples, add the
	sugar	250g	sugar and water and cook to a fairly firm
	water	1dl	purée. Pass through a sieve and divide evenly between two 25cm pie dishes.
2	butter	160g	Place in a bowl and cream together until
	sugar	160g	light and white.
3	eggs, beaten	3	Add grádually, beating in well.
4	flour	240g	Sift the flour, baking powder and salt
	baking powder	10g	and mix carefully into the creamed
	salt	pinch	mixture together with the milk.
	milk	⅓dl	
5			Spread a layer of mixture evenly on top of the apple.
6	Sauce Anglaise		Place the puddings in the oven at 195°C
	(1718)	6dl	and bake for 35–40 mins. Serve accompanied with Sauce Anglaise.

1859 FRUITS FLAMBÉS – FLAMBÉED FRUITS

This type of preparation and presentation of fruit dishes is usually and best carried out in the dining-room where the techniques and professional showmanship required are best appreciated by the customer. In essence, these preparations consist of the flavouring and heating of either fresh or poached fruits to which suitable spirits or liqueurs are added and which are then ignited. The cooking juices can include butter; sugar, both white and demerara; sugar syrup, sometimes lightly thickened with arrowroot; flavourings of citrus fruits; wines or fruit syrups.

As with most dishes, the amount of finished sauce should be kept to a minimum.

See Select Bibliography on page 881, for recommended titles relating to this specialised branch of cookery.

The following recipes are given as examples of their type.

1860 Ananas flambé au Kirsch

2 portions
15 mins.

Stage	Ingredient	Quantity	Method
1	Stock Syrup (1709)	1dl	Pour three-quarters of the syrup in a shallow pan and bring to the boil. Add the prepared slices of pineapple and start to baste them frequently and to sprinkle with the sugar as the syrup reduces. Turn the pineapple over, add the rest of the syrup and let them lightly caramelise.
	pineapple slices	4	
	sugar	25g	
2	Kirsch	¼dl	Pour over the pineapple and flamber (32). Serve at once spooning the cooking liquid over.

1861 Banane flambée au Rhum

2 portions
15 mins.

Stage	Ingredient	Quantity	Method
1	bananas	4	Peel and cut in half lengthways.
2	butter	25g	Heat the butter in a chafing pan, lightly flour the bananas and add. Dredge with sugar and cook on both sides until lightly caramelised. Remove to hot serving dishes.
	flour		
	sugar, demerara	50g	
3	Stock Syrup (1709)	¾dl	Add the syrup to the pan and allow to reduce slightly. Pour around the bananas.
4	rum	¼dl	Sprinkle over the bananas and flamber (32) for immediate service.

1862 Pêche flambée au Cognac

2 portions
15 mins.

Stage	Ingredient	Quantity	Method
1	peaches	2	Dip into boiling water for a few seconds and remove the skins. Cut in halves and discard the stones.
2	Stock Syrup (1709)	1dl	Heat the syrup and butter in a chafing pan. Add the peaches and baste frequently and sprinkle with sugar occasionally. Prick the peaches with a fork to allow the syrup to penetrate. Cook until the peaches are well glazed, adding a little more syrup if necessary and allow to lightly caramelise.
	butter, unsalted	25g	
	sugar	25g	
3	Cognac brandy	¼dl	Pour over the peaches and flamber (32) for immediate service.

1863 FRUIT PIES AND PUDDINGS

Fruit pies and puddings can be made from any fresh fruit singly or in combination. Tinned fruits can be used but it is not recommended to do so unless absolutely necessary; the length of cooking has to be reduced to take account of the already-cooked state of the fruit and the finished result is never so good.

Preparation of the fruit
This should be attended to carefully; blemishes, insects and maggots as well as stalks and flower stems need to be rigorously removed. The following are the main fruits used for these dishes together with the essential needs of preparation and cleaning:

Apples: peel, core and cut into quarters or medium slices. Wash. If being prepared in large quantities it may be necessary to keep them in water with a little lemon juice to prevent discolouration. Apples lose approximately one-third of their original weight in preparation.

Apricots: remove stalks, wash and drain. Use either whole or cut in half with the stone removed.

Blackberries: remove any stalks, pick out any damaged fruit and wash in salted water to get rid of any maggots. Rinse in clean water and drain.

Blackcurrants and Redcurrants: remove the stalks and pick off the flower ends where possible. Wash and drain.

Cherries: remove the stalks, wash and drain. If desired, remove the stones.

Gooseberries: remove the tops and tails, wash and drain.

Plums, Damsons and Greengages: remove the stalks, wash and drain. If desired, cut in half and remove the stones.

Rhubarb: remove any leaves, the coarse skin and the root end. Cut into 5cm pieces. Wash and drain.

1864 Fruit Pie

10 portions
1½ hours

Stage	Ingredient	Quantity	Method
1	fruit to choice water sugar	1¼kg 2dl 250g	Divide the fruit equally between two 25cm pie dishes. Add 1dl of water and 125g of sugar to each dish.
2	Pâte à Foncer (1738) eggwash	500g	Roll out approx. 3mm thick, eggwash the rim of the pie dish and cover with a 1½cm-wide strip of paste. Eggwash the strip and cover the pies with the remainder of the paste. Seal firmly and trim off the surplus with a knife. Decorate the edge of the paste around the pie. Allow to rest in a cool place for 30 mins.
3	sugar, caster	25g	Brush the surface of the paste with water and sprinkle with sugar. Place the pies in the oven at 215°C to lightly brown and set the pastry (approx. 15 mins.). Reduce the temperature to approx. 190°C and allow to cook for a further 30 mins.
4	Sauce Anglaise (1718) or Custard Sauce (1725)	6dl	Clean the pie dishes, place each on a dish paper on a flat dish and surround with a pie collar. Serve accompanied with the sauce.

SPECIAL POINTS
a) When using apples by themselves, add a few cloves.
b) For rhubarb, add an extra 60–75g sugar.

1865 Fruit Pudding

10 portions
4 hours

Stage	Ingredient	Quantity	Method
1	Suet Paste (1743)	750g	Line two 17cm buttered pudding basins with three-quarters of the paste.
2	fruit to choice water sugar	1¼kg 2dl 250g	Divide the fruit equally between the two basins. Add 1dl water and 125g of sugar to each basin.
3			Roll out the remainder of the paste to the size of the puddings. Moisten the edges, cover and seal firmly. Cover with buttered greaseproof paper and pudding cloths. Tie securely. Place in a steamer and cook for 2½–3 hours.

4	Sauce Anglaise (1718) or Custard Sauce (1725)	6dl	Remove the cloth and papers and clean the basins. Place on doilys on round dishes and fasten folded serviettes around the basins. Serve accompanied with the sauce.

SPECIAL POINTS
a) When using apples by themselves, add a few cloves.
b) For rhubarb, add an extra 60–75g sugar.

1866 OMELETTES, SWEET

There are three clearly defined categories of sweet omelettes:
1) Omelettes aux Confitures – Jam Omelettes.
2) Omelettes aux Liqueurs – Omelettes flamed with a liqueur or spirits.
3) Omelettes Soufflées – Souffléed Omelettes.

In addition there are a number of omelettes which do not fall into these categories because of their particular fillings.

The following are examples of the standard types.

1867 Omelette à la Confiture d'Abricots – Apricot Jam Omelette

1 portion
10 mins.

This type of omelette may be filled with any jam to choice or with a stiff fruit purée which has been cooked with half its amount of sugar, in effect a smooth jam without any pieces of fruit being evident (Fr. Marmelade). In some cases they are flamed with spirits or liqueurs to finish. It is always useful to designate or imply the particular jam used as in the above recipe title.

1) Break two eggs in a basin, add a small pinch of salt and a good pinch of sugar. Beat with a fork so as to blend the whites and yolks thoroughly.
2) Prepare as a plain omelette (446), placing a tablespoonful of warm apricot jam inside the omelette before folding oval-shape.
3) Turn out on a warm buttered dish, sprinkle liberally with caster sugar and mark trellis-fashion with a red-hot poker.

1868 Omelette Normande

1 portion
10 mins.

1) Break two eggs in a basin, add a small pinch of salt and a good pinch of sugar. Beat with a fork so as to blend the whites and yolks thoroughly.
2) Prepare as a plain omelette (446), placing a good tablespoon of warm Marmelade de Pommes (1695) inside the omelette before folding oval-shape.
3) Turn out onto a warm buttered dish, sprinkle liberally with caster sugar and mark trellis-fashion with a red-hot poker.
4) Warm the dish, pour over ¼dl of Calvados and set alight.

1869 Omelette au Rhum – Rum Omelette

1 portion
10 mins.

This type of omelette may be flamed with any suitable liqueur or spirit to choice and this should always be designated on the menu. The flaming of sweet omelettes is usually carried out in the dining-room where it is best appreciated by the customer.

1) Break two eggs in a basin, add a small pinch of salt and a good pinch of sugar. Beat with a fork so as to blend the whites and yolks thoroughly.
2) Prepare as a plain omelette (446).
3) Turn out on a warm buttered dish, sprinkle liberally with caster sugar and mark trellis-fashion with a red-hot poker.
4) Warm the dish, pour over ¼dl of rum and set alight.

1870 Omelettes Soufflées

There are two forms of Souffléed omelette, 1) where the stiffly beaten whites are added to the yolks then cooked flat in an omelette pan, filled with a suitable mixture and folded, and 2) where the stiffly beaten egg whites are added to well-whisked egg yolks and sugar. This mixture is then moulded on a dish and cooked in the oven.

1871 Omelette Soufflée Viennoise

2 portions
15 mins.

Stage	Ingredient	Quantity	Method
1	egg yolks	3	Place in a basin and whisk until thick.
	sugar	20g	
2	egg whites	3	Whisk until firm and fold carefully into the egg yolk mixture.
3	butter	15g	Heat a large omelette pan. Add the butter and move the pan so as to coat the base and sides completely. Add the mixture, stir lightly with a fork and when set underneath, allow to colour lightly then place under the salamander to slightly set the top.
4	warm jam, to choice	2 tbsps	Place the jam along the centre of the omelette, fold over and turn out on a warm buttered dish.
5	icing sugar		Sprinkle well with icing sugar.

1872 Omelette Soufflée Créole

Prepare and finish as Omelette Soufflée Viennoise (1871) but fill with two tablespoons of warm small dice of pineapple mixed with a little apricot jam and flavoured with Kirsch.

1873 Omelette Soufflée George Sand

Prepare and finish as Omelette Soufflée Viennoise (1871) but fill with two tablespoons small dice of pear, pineapple, Fraises des Bois and Marrons glacés mixed with a little sweetened apricot purée and flavoured with Kirsch.

1874 Omelette Soufflée au Grand Marnier

4 portions
25 mins.

Stage	Ingredient	Quantity	Method
1	Macaroons (1694)	5	Cut the macaroons in very small dice,
	Grand Marnier	½dl	and pour over the Grand Marnier to be soaked up.
2	egg yolks	4	Place in a basin and whisk to a thick
	sugar, caster	175g	creamy texture. Mix in the prepared macaroons.
3	egg whites	6	Place in a basin with a pinch of salt and whisk to a stiff peak. Fold quickly into the egg yolk mixture.
4			Reserve a little of the mixture in a piping bag and large star tube. Place the remainder on a large oval buttered dish and smooth and mould quickly with a palette knife to a low oval shape. Decorate the sides with the side of the palette knife and pipe a scroll or rosettes of the mixture around the bottom edge.
5			Place in a moderately hot oven at 185°C for 15–18 mins. to cook then dredge well with icing sugar and return to the oven to glaze and colour its surface.
6	small button macaroons (1694)	12	On removing from the oven arrange the macaroons which have been sprinkled
	Grand Marnier	¼dl	with a little of the liqueur around the soufflé. Sprinkle the omelette with the remaining Grand Marnier and serve immediately.

SPECIAL POINTS
a) This type of omelette may be prepared with any flavouring, spirit or liqueur as seen fit and decorated and garnished in an appropriate manner.
b) It is essential that it be served immediately. Any untoward delay can result in the omelette collapsing.

1875 Omelette Soufflée Jamaïque

Prepare and finish as Omelette Soufflée Viennoise (1871) but fill with two tablespoons of warm Crème Pâtissière (1685) flavoured with rum.

1876 Omelette Framboisette

1 portion
10 mins.

1) Break two eggs in a basin, add a small pinch of salt and a good pinch of sugar. Beat with a fork so as to blend the whites and yolks thoroughly.
2) Prepare as a plain omelette (446), placing one good tablespoon of small raspberries, which have been macerated with a little sugar and Curaçao, inside the omelette before folding oval-shape.
3) Turn out on a warm buttered dish, sprinkle liberally with caster sugar and mark trellis-fashion with a red-hot poker or bar.
4) Surround with a little warm Coulis de Framboises (1724) flavoured with the remaining Curaçao from the macerating of the raspberries.

1877 Pomme Bonne-Femme – Baked Apple

10 portions
1 hour

Stage	Ingredient	Quantity	Method
1	cooking apples, medium-sized	10	Wash, remove the cores and make a shallow incision around the middle of the apples.
2	sugar butter	150g 100g	Place the apples in earthenware dishes and fill the centres with the sugar and butter. Cover the bottom of the dish 2–3mm deep with water.
3			Place in the oven at 190°C and cook gently until soft. Allow the tops of the apples to colour lightly.
4	Sauce Anglaise (1718) or Custard Sauce (1725)	6dl	Remove from the oven and clean the sides of the dishes. Place on dish papers on suitable dishes accompanied with the sauce.

1878 POUDINGS AU LAIT – MILK PUDDINGS

These puddings are very acceptable as lunchtime sweets and can be made with rice, macaroni or other Italian pastas, sago, semolina and tapioca. Rice is the only one which can be successfully baked with milk from the raw state, the others having to be cooked by gentle simmering with milk on the stove before being apportioned out, preferably into individual pie dishes, then coloured under the salamander or in the oven.

1879 Pouding au Macaroni – Macaroni Pudding

10 portions
1 hour

Stage	Ingredient	Quantity	Method
1	milk sugar vanilla essence	1½ litres 150g few drops	Place in a pan and bring to the boil.
2	short-cut or elbow macaroni	150g	Add the macaroni and stir to the boil. Simmer gently at the side of the stove stirring frequently until tender, approx. 40–45 mins.

| 3 | butter | 50g | Ladle into buttered pie dishes, dot with butter and place in a hot oven until coloured brown on top. |
| 4 | | | Remove the puddings, clean the dishes and place on dish papers on oval dishes. Surround with pie collars. |

1880 Pouding au Riz à l'Anglaise – Rice Pudding (baked)

10 portions
2¼ hours

Stage	Ingredient	Quantity	Method
1	short-grain rice	150g	Wash the rice and place in two 25cm pie
	sugar	150g	dishes. Add half the milk and sugar to
	milk	1½ litres	each pie dish then dot equally with
	butter	30g	butter and a pinch of nutmeg.
	nutmeg, grated		
2			Place the pie dishes on a baking tray and place in a moderate oven at 180°C until the milk begins to simmer. Reduce the temperature to approx. 150°C and cook very slowly (approx. 2 hours). The top should be a light brown.
3			Remove the puddings, clean the dishes and serve on dish papers on oval dishes. Surround with pie collars.

1881 Pouding au Riz – Rice Pudding (boiled)

10 portions
1½ hours

Stage	Ingredient	Quantity	Method
1	milk	1½ litres	Place the milk in a pan, add the sugar
	short-grain rice	150g	and bring to the boil. Rain in the washed
	sugar	150g	rice and bring to the boil stirring continuously. Cook very slowly until tender, stirring frequently.
2	butter	50g	Ladle the rice pudding into suitable pie
	nutmeg, grated		dishes, dot with butter and sprinkle with a little grated nutmeg. Place in a hot oven until coloured brown on top.
3			Remove the puddings, clean the dishes and serve on dish papers on oval dishes. Surround with pie collars.

1882 Pouding au Riz à la Française – Rice Pudding (French method)

10 portions
2 hours

Stage	Ingredient	Quantity	Method
1	milk	1½ litres	Place the milk in a pan and bring to the boil. Rain in the washed rice, stir until it reboils, cover with the lid and place in the oven at 150°C for approx. 1 hour until tender. Stir occasionally. Remove from the oven.
	short-grain rice	150g	
2	egg yolks	5	Mix together in a basin.
	sugar	150g	
	butter, soft	75g	
	vanilla essence	few drops	
3			Add two or three ladles of the cooked rice to the mixture of egg yolks, mixing in quickly. Return it to the rice and mix in quickly. Do not reheat.
4	egg whites	5	Place in a basin with a pinch of salt and whisk to a stiff peak. Fold quickly and carefully into the rice.
5			Pour the mixture into buttered pie dishes and place in the oven at 175°C until risen and brown on top.
6			Remove the puddings, clean the dishes and serve on dish papers on oval dishes. Surround with pie collars.

1883 Pouding au Sagou – Sago Pudding

10 portions
1 hour

Stage	Ingredient	Quantity	Method
1	milk	1½ litres	Place the milk in a pan, add the sugar and vanilla essence and bring to the boil.
	sugar	150g	
	vanilla essence	few drops	
2	sago	125g	Rain in the sago, stirring continuously, and simmer gently until cooked (15–20 mins.), stirring frequently. Remove from the stove.
3	egg yolks	3	Mix in the yolks and butter quickly then pour the pudding into buttered pie dishes.
	butter, soft	50g	
4			Brown in a hot oven or under the salamander. Serve on dish papers on oval dishes. Surround with pie collars.

1884 Pouding au Semoule – Semolina Pudding

Prepare in the same way as Pouding au Sagou (1883) but using 125g semolina instead of sago.

1885 Pouding au Tapioca – Tapioca Pudding

Prepare in the same way as Pouding au Sagou (1883) but using 125g tapioca instead of sago.

1886 Pouding au Vermicelle – Vermicelli Pudding

Prepare as Pouding au Macaroni (1879) but using 150g vermicelli crushed to short lengths instead of macaroni. Simmer in the milk for 12–15 mins. only.

1887 Pouding Mexicaine

10 portions
1 hour

Stage	Ingredient	Quantity	Method
1	milk	5dl	Place the ingredients into a pan and
	sugar	75g	bring slowly to the boil.
	plain chocolate, grated	100g	
	butter, unsalted	50g	
	vanilla essence	few drops	
2	cornflour	50g	Dilute the cornflour with the milk then stir into the boiling milk. Bring back to the boil and simmer for 3–4 mins., stirring continuously.
	milk	1dl	
3			Pour the chocolate cream into ten lightly buttered single pie dishes, sufficient to half fill them. Rest them for a few mins.
4	Tapioca Pudding (1885) to stage 3	5 portions	Carefully ladle in the tapioca pudding to fill the dishes completely. Sprinkle with a little grated nutmeg and well dredge with icing sugar.
	nutmeg, grated		
	icing sugar		
5			Place under the salamander to glaze and caramelise the surface. Place on dish papers on suitable dishes.

1888 POUDINGS SOUFFLÉS – PUDDING SOUFFLÉS

This type of soufflé differs from the preparation of the more delicate oven-baked varieties in the following ways:
1) The cooking of pudding soufflés is carried out 'au Bain-marie', i.e. the filled moulds are placed in a deep tray with hot water half-way up the moulds. They have an initial boiling on the stove and the tray with the soufflés is then placed to finish in the oven.
2) Pudding soufflés are best cooked in single-portion dariole moulds but can be cooked in charlotte moulds for two, three or four persons. Larger than this is not advisable

because of the difficulty of serving each customer satisfactorily with a clean and clearly defined portion.

3) The base mixture before the eggs are added is of a more heavy texture. This helps the cooked soufflés to maintain shape and lightness for a reasonable period of time providing that they are kept in a bain-marie of simmering water. It is thus possible to cook a number of portions in advance but cooking in batches is to be preferred for any lengthy Table d'Hôte service.

4) The soufflés are always demoulded for service and accompanied with a suitable sauce.

1889 Pouding Soufflé Vanille – Vanilla Pudding Soufflé or Pouding Soufflé Saxon

10 portions
1 hour

Stage	Ingredient	Quantity	Method
1	butter	25g	Butter and sugar ten dariole moulds.
	sugar	25g	
2	butter	100g	Place the butter in a basin and mix. Add
	sugar	100g	the sugar and flour and mix to a paste.
	flour	100g	
3	milk	3dl	Place the milk and vanilla essence in a
	vanilla essence	few drops	pan and bring to the boil. Whisk the milk into the mixture, return to the pan and cook, stirring continuously until the mixture thickens. Remove from the fire and allow to cool slightly.
4	egg yolks	5	Add the yolks and mix in well.
5	egg whites	5	Place in a clean bowl and whisk until stiff. Add a quarter to the mixture and mix in. Fold the remainder of the whites in gently. Divide the mixture between the moulds.
6			Place the moulds into a tray of hot water, bring to the boil and simmer for 5–6 mins. until the mixture starts to rise in the moulds. Place in the oven at approx. 200°C to cook for 15–20 mins.
7	Sauce Anglaise (1718)	6dl	Turn out onto hot dishes and serve accompanied with Sauce Anglaise.

1890 Pouding Soufflé au Citron – Lemon Pudding Soufflé

Prepare as Pouding Soufflé Vanille (1889), using the grated rind of two lemons instead of vanilla. Serve accompanied with Sauce Citron (1723).

1891   Pouding Soufflé au Chocolat – Chocolate Pudding Soufflé

Prepare as Soufflé Vanille (1889) but adding sufficient grated plain chocolate to the milk to colour and flavour it well. Serve accompanied with Sauce Chocolat (1722).

1892   Pouding Soufflé au Café – Coffee Pudding Soufflé

Prepare as Pouding Soufflé Vanille (1889) but adding sufficient coffee extract to the milk to colour and flavour it well. Serve accompanied with Sauce Anglaise (1718).

1893   Pouding Soufflé Montmorency

Prepare Soufflé Vanille (1889) but mixing in 75g very small dice of glacé cherries, macerated with a little Kirsch, to the mixture just before folding in the egg whites. Serve accompanied with Sauce Anglaise flavoured with Kirsch or Maraschino.

1894   Pouding Soufflé à l'Orange – Orange Pudding Soufflé

Prepare as Pouding Soufflé Vanille (1889), using the grated rind of two oranges instead of vanilla. Serve accompanied with Sauce Orange (1730).

1895   Pouding Soufflé Praliné – Praline Pudding Soufflé

Prepare as Pouding Soufflé Vanille (1889), adding 75g Pralin (1703) to the mixture just before folding in the egg whites. Serve accompanied with Sauce Anglaise (1718).

1896   Pouding Soufflé Saxon

See Pouding Soufflé Vanille (1889).

1897   Queen of Puddings

10 portions
1½ hours

Stage	Ingredient	Quantity	Method
1	milk	1¼ litres	Place the milk in a pan and warm. Mix
	eggs	9	the eggs and sugar in a basin and add
	sugar	180g	the milk while stirring.
2	white breadcrumbs	250g	Place in two 25cm buttered pie dishes. Pass the egg custard through a fine strainer over the crumbs.
3			Place the pie dishes in a deep tray and half fill the tray with warm water. Place in the oven at approx. 180°C to cook for 35–40 mins. Remove from the oven and allow to cool.
4	egg whites	3	Whisk the whites and salt in a clean
	salt	pinch	bowl to a stiff peak. Whisk in half the
	caster sugar	175g	sugar, and fold in the remainder. Place

the meringue in a piping bag with a star tube and decorate the top of the puddings in a lattice pattern.

| 5 | Red Glaze (1705) | 100g | Place the puddings in a hot oven to brown the meringue. Pipe the glazes alternately into the squares of the lattice pattern. |
| | Apricot Glaze (1672) | 100g | |

| 6 | | | Place the puddings on dish papers on flat dishes and surround with pie collars. |

1898 Rabotte de Pomme – Baked Apple Dumpling 10 portions
2 hours

Stage	Ingredient	Quantity	Method
1	cooking apples, medium to small	10	Peel, core, wash the apples and place in a basin of cold water with a little lemon juice.
	juice of lemon	½	
2	Pâte à Foncer (1738)	750g	Roll out approx. 2mm thick and cut into 12–14cm squares.
3			Dry the apples and place in the centres of the squares of paste.
4	sugar	150g	Fill the holes in the apples with sugar. Eggwash the edges of the paste and fold over carefully to completely enfold the apples. Seal the four edges neatly.
	eggwash		
5			Place the apples on a greased baking tray. Decorate each top with a small round of paste cut out with a fancy cutter. Eggwash and make a small hole in the top. Allow to rest in a cool place for 30 mins.
6			Place in a hot oven at 220°C to set and lightly colour the paste, then reduce the temperature and allow to cook for approx. 30 mins.
7	Sauce Anglaise (1718) or Custard Sauce (1725)	6dl	Serve on hot dishes accompanied with the sauce.

1899 Sabayon au Marsala – Zabaglione alla Marsala 4 portions
15 mins.

Stage	Ingredient	Quantity	Method
1	egg yolks	5	Place in a suitable mixing bowl and mix together thoroughly with a balloon whisk.
	sugar	175g	

| 2 | Marsala | 1½dl | Add to the egg mixture. Place the bowl in a bain-marie or over a pan of hot water and whisk vigorously and continuously, keeping the sides of the bowl clean. The sabayon is sufficiently cooked when it clings to the whisk when it is raised from the bowl. It should be light and fluffy. |
| 3 | Biscuits à la Cuillère (1673) | 8 | Pour the sabayon carefully into glass goblets. Place on a doily on a dish and serve accompanied with a suitable biscuit, e.g. Biscuits à la Cuillère. |

1900 SOUFFLÉS, SWEET

These light delicate entremets are excellent for serving at the end of a meal, more particularly for dinner. There are two basic types of sweet soufflés:
a) Those made using a panada, prepared from flour, butter, sugar and milk, which can be flavoured to choice then finished with egg yolks and stiffly beaten whites.
b) Those made from a base of fruit purée mixed with a cooked sugar solution, which can be flavoured as required then finished with stiffly beaten whites.

Although soufflés are not over-complicated preparations, attention to the following important points is necessary if good results are to be attained:
1) The soufflé moulds should be carefully and thoroughly buttered and sugared. Failure to do so can result in uneven rising and deformity of shape.
2) Whichever base mixture is used should be smooth and free from lumps.
3) Care should be taken to ensure that the egg whites to be used are clean and completely clear of any egg yolk. The mixing bowl and whisk should likewise be clear of any traces of grease or detergent. Any fat present will result in imperfectly whisked whites with fatal consequences for the soufflé.
4) The condition of the whisked whites used for a soufflé is crucial; being too soft or over-whipped and granular can lead to insufficient lift. Aim for a texture which allows the whisked whites to maintain a smooth volume and shape when lifted with the whisk from the bowl.
5) One-quarter of the whisked whites needs to be mixed into the base mixture first. This is to ensure a soft texture for the folding-in of the remainder. This must be done quickly and evenly to secure as much aeration as possible in the soufflé.
6) Do not open the oven door during the initial stages of cooking, and when it is opened later for the glazing of the soufflé, this should be done slowly and closed again carefully. Do not bang or knock the soufflé at any stage of the cooking. Send and serve the soufflé immediately it is cooked.

1901 Soufflé Vanille – Vanilla Soufflé

4 portions
50 mins.

Stage	Ingredient	Quantity	Method
1	butter	15g	Carefully butter and sugar a 15cm
	sugar, caster	15g	soufflé mould.

2	milk	1dl	Place the milk and vanilla in a pan and
	vanilla	few drops	bring to the boil. Cream the butter and
	butter	40g	sugar in a basin and mix in the flour to a
	sugar	60g	smooth paste. Add the milk slowly,
	flour	30g	whisking in well. Return the mixture
			to the pan and stir to the boil. Cook
			gently for 2–3 mins. Remove from the
			stove and allow this panada to cool
			slightly.
3	egg yolks	3	Mix well into the panada.
4	egg whites	4	Place in a clean bowl and whisk to a stiff
			peak. Add a quarter to the mixture and
			mix in. Fold the remainder of the whites
			in carefully then pour into the prepared
			soufflé mould.
5	icing sugar		Place the soufflé in the oven at 195°C
			for approx. 25–30 mins. Dredge the
			surface with icing sugar and cook for a
			further 5 mins. to glaze.
6			Place on a doily on a dish and serve
			immediately.

1902 Soufflé au Chocolat – Chocolate Soufflé

Prepare as Soufflé Vanille (1901), adding 30g of grated chocolate to the milk and using one extra egg white.

1903 Soufflé au Citron – Lemon Soufflé

Prepare as Soufflé Vanille (1901), replacing the vanilla with the grated zest of one lemon.

1904 Soufflé au Grand Marnier

Prepare as Soufflé Vanille (1901) with the addition of ¼dl of Grand Marnier added to the finished panada.

1905 Soufflé à l'Orange – Orange Soufflé

Prepare as Soufflé Vanille (1901), replacing the vanilla with the grated zest of one orange.

1906 Soufflé Arlequin

This is prepared with half vanilla and half chocolate soufflé mixtures. A simple way of obtaining a clear division of the different flavours is to place across the middle of the mould a piece of card cut to its exact diameter and a little higher than the rim. Pour in the mixtures one either side of the card and then remove the card by lifting upwards carefully.

1907 Soufflé Rothschild

Prepare as Soufflé Vanille (1901) with the addition of 30g of finely diced candied fruits which have been macerated in ¼dl of Kirsch, both fruits and Kirsch being added to the finished panada.

1908 Soufflés aux Fruits – Fruit Soufflés

These soufflés may be prepared using a thick purée of any fresh or cooked fruit. If necessary the purée can be thickened by reducing carefully on the stove. Once the purée is combined with the cooked sugar solution at 138°C and reboiled, the mixture should then be checked and cooked to 120°C on the sugar-boiling thermometer if below this temperature. If cooked fruit is used, account should be taken of the sugar content and the initial sugar solution temperature of 138°C should be adjusted slightly downwards.

The purée/sugar mixture may be flavoured with a suitable spirit or liqueur as appropriate, such as Kirsch, Mirabelle, Eau de Vie de Framboises, Curaçao and so on.

The following recipe is of the standard type.

1909 Soufflé aux Fraises – Strawberry Soufflé

4 portions
50 mins.

Stage	Ingredient	Quantity	Method
1	butter	15g	Carefully butter and sugar a 15cm
	sugar, caster	15g	soufflé mould.
2	water	1dl	Place in a pan, bring to the boil. Skim,
	sugar	250g	brush down the inside of the pan with
	glucose	25g	water to prevent crystallisation and
	juice of lemon	squeeze	continue to boil steadily until the syrup reaches 135°C on the sugar-boiling thermometer.
3	thick strawberry purée	250g	Quickly mix the hot syrup into the purée, return to the pan and bring back to the boil. Check with the sugar thermometer and boil to 120°C if below this. Allow to cool for a few mins.
4	egg whites	5	Place in a clean bowl and whisk to a peak. Add the fruit mixture and gently mix together. Pour into the prepared soufflé mould.
5	icing sugar		Place the soufflé in the oven at 195°C for approx. 20–25 mins. Dredge the surface with icing sugar and cook for a further 5 mins. to glaze.
6			Place on a doily on a dish and serve immediately.

1910 STEAMED PUDDINGS

These are nourishing and substantial puddings which are worthy of inclusion on lunch-time menus, especially during cold weather. They should be served with a suitable hot sauce or with one of the flavoured sweet butters. Although there are many variations there are only two basic methods of making them, 1) a pudding made of suet paste with various fillings, 2) a sponge pudding mixture made by the creaming method with the addition of dried fruit, jam or other preserve, or a flavouring such as lemon, chocolate, vanilla, etc.

Both types of pudding should be covered properly and carefully steamed for no longer than called for in the recipe; overcooking will spoil the light texture which is a desirable quality in the finished product.

1911 Steamed Sponge Pudding

10 portions
2 hours

Stage	Ingredient		Quantity	Method
1	butter		240g	Place in a bowl and cream together until
	sugar		240g	light and white.
2	eggs, beaten		4	Add gradually, beating in well.
3	flour	sifted	350g	Add the flour, baking powder and salt
	baking powder	together	15g	and mix carefully into the creamed mix-
	salt	twice	2g	ture together with the milk.
	milk		½dl	
4	butter		30g	Place the mixture in buttered and
	sugar, caster		30g	sugared pudding basins or individual dariole moulds. Cover with buttered greaseproof papers and steam for approx. 1½ hours for pudding basins and approx. 40 mins. for dariole moulds.
5	Jam Sauce (1726) or Custard Sauce (1725)		6dl	Turn out on suitable dishes and serve with the sauce.

1912 Steamed Black Cap Pudding

Prepare as Steamed Sponge Pudding (1911), covering the bottom of the moulds with golden syrup and washed currants before placing in the sponge mixture. Serve accompanied with Sauce Anglaise (1718) or Custard Sauce (1725).

1913 Steamed Cherry Sponge Pudding

Prepare as Steamed Sponge Pudding (1911), adding 100g of chopped glacé cherries to the finished mixture before placing it in the moulds. Serve accompanied with Sauce Anglaise (1718) or Custard Sauce (1725).

1914 Steamed Chocolate Sponge Pudding

Prepare as Steamed Sponge Pudding (1911), replacing 60g of flour with 60g of cocoa powder. Serve accompanied with Chocolate Sauce (1722). Add a little extra milk to the sponge mixture to compensate for the cocoa.

1915 Steamed Ginger Sponge Pudding

Prepare as Steamed Sponge Pudding (1911), adding 15g of ground ginger to the flour and 100g of chopped preserved ginger added to the finished mixture before placing it in the moulds. Serve accompanied with Sauce Anglaise (1718) or Custard Sauce (1725).

1916 Steamed Golden Sponge Pudding

Prepare as Steamed Sponge Pudding (1911), covering the bottom of the moulds with golden syrup before placing in the sponge mixture. Serve accompanied with hot golden syrup.

1917 Steamed Jam Sponge Pudding

Prepare as Steamed Sponge Pudding (1911), covering the bottom of the mould with jam before placing in the sponge mixture. Serve accompanied with Jam Sauce (1726).

1918 Steamed Lemon Sponge Pudding

Prepare as Steamed Sponge Pudding (1911), adding the grated rind of two lemons to the mixture before placing it in the moulds. Serve accompanied with Lemon Sauce (1723).

1919 Steamed Orange Sponge Pudding

Prepare as Steamed Sponge Pudding (1911), adding the grated rind of two oranges to the mixture before placing it in the moulds. Serve accompanied with Orange Sauce (1730).

1920 Steamed Vanilla Sponge Pudding

Prepare as Steamed Sponge Pudding (1911), adding a little vanilla essence to the mixture before placing it in the moulds. Serve accompanied with Sauce Anglaise (1718) or Custard Sauce (1725).

1921 Steamed College Pudding

10 portions
1¾ hours

Stage	Ingredient	Quantity	Method
1	soft flour	250g	Sift all the ingredients together twice
	baking powder	10g	into a mixing bowl.
	mixed spice	good pinch	
	salt	pinch	
2	beef kidney suet, finely chopped	250g	Add to the flour and mix together lightly. Make a bay in the centre.

	white breadcrumbs	250g	
	sugar, caster	150g	
	currants	200g	
	mixed peel, chopped	50g	
	lemon, grated rind	1 tsp	
3	eggs, beaten⎱ mixed milk ⎰ together	2 1½dl	Add the milk and egg and mix gently to a light dropping consistency.
4	butter	25g	Divide the mixture between ten individual greased pudding moulds. Cover with buttered greaseproof paper and steam for approx. 1 hour.
5	Sauce Anglaise (1718) or Custard Sauce (1725)	6dl	Turn out of the moulds and place on suitable dishes. Serve accompanied with either sauce.

1922 Steamed Jam Roll

10 portions
2½ hours

Stage	Ingredient	Quantity	Method
1	Suet Paste (1743) jam	850g 300g	Roll out the paste to a rectangle approx. 30cm × 35cm. Spread the jam all over to within 1cm of the edges. Damp the edges, roll up loosely into a roll and press the ends and edges to seal.
2			Roll in greased greaseproof paper and tie lightly in a pudding cloth, or place in a greased pudding sleeve.
3	Jam Sauce (1726) or Custard Sauce (1725)	6dl	Steam for approx. 2 hours. Untie, remove the paper and serve the roll either whole or cut in portions on suitable dishes. Serve accompanied with either sauce.

1923 Steamed Sultana Roll

10 portions
2½ hours

Stage	Ingredient	Quantity	Method
1	flour baking powder salt beef kidney suet, finely chopped	500g 15g pinch 300g	Sift the flour, baking powder and salt into a mixing bowl. Add the suet and mix in lightly.
2	sugar, caster sultanas water	150g 200g 2½dl	Make a bay in the centre of the flour, add the sugar, sultanas and water and mix lightly to form a fairly firm paste.

3			Mould the paste into a thick roll, then roll in a greased greaseproof paper and tie in a pudding cloth, or place in a greased pudding sleeve.
4	Custard Sauce (1725)	6dl	Steam for approx. 2 hours. Untie, remove the paper and serve the roll whole or cut in portions in suitable dishes. Dredge with caster sugar and serve accompanied with the custard sauce.

1924 Steamed Suet Pudding

10 portions
1¾ hours

Stage	Ingredient	Quantity	Method
1	flour, soft baking powder salt	275g 10g pinch	Sift together twice into a mixing bowl.
2	breadcrumbs, white beef kidney suet, finely chopped caster sugar	275g 275g 150g	Add these ingredients to the flour and mix lightly together. Make a bay.
3	eggs, beaten\ mixed milk / together	2 2dl	Place the eggs and milk in the centre of the ingredients and gently mix to a light dropping consistency.
4	butter	25g	Divide the mixture between ten individual greased pudding moulds. Cover with buttered greaseproof paper and steam for approx. 1 hour.

5	Custard Sauce (1725)
	  or Jam Sauce
	  (1726)
		6dl	Turn out of the moulds and place on suitable dishes. Serve accompanied with either sauce.

SPECIAL POINT

Variations of the above recipe can be made by 1) placing ½ tablespoon of jam, golden syrup or marmalade in the bottom of the mould before adding the mixture, or by 2) adding 175–200g of dried fruit, such as currants, sultanas, dates or figs cut small, to the mixture at Stage 2 and a little mixed spice sifted with the flour.

In all cases the puddings should be accompanied with custard sauce or a sauce in keeping with the ingredients, e.g. Jam Sauce with Steamed Jam Pudding.

—ENTREMETS FROIDS – COLD SWEETS—

1925 Ananas Créole

10 portions
2¼ hours

Stage	Ingredient	Quantity	Method
1	milk vanilla	1 litre few drops	Place the milk in a pan, add the vanilla and sugar and bring to the boil. Rain in

	sugar	150g	the washed rice and stir until it reboils. Cover with a lid and cook slowly in the oven at 175°C for approx. 1 hour until tender. Stir occasionally with a wooden spoon. Remove from the oven.
	short-grain rice	180g	
2	leaf gelatine	25g	Allow the mixture to cool slightly, soak the gelatine in cold water, drain, add and mix in. Pour the rice into a basin and allow to cool until almost set.
3	cream	2dl	Place into a basin and whip. Mix into the rice. When on setting-point, mould on two flat dishes into the shapes of half-pineapples cut lengthways. Allow to set in a refrigerator.
4	pineapple slices, thin	20	Cut into half-rings and arrange neatly overlapping to completely cover the moulded rice.
5	Apricot Glaze (1672)	½ litre	Coat the pineapple with the glaze also covering the bottom of the dishes around the moulded pineapples.
6	angelica	100g	If using tinned pineapple decorate one end of the créole with strips of angelica to represent the green leaves of the pineapple. If using fresh pineapple use the top leaves of the pineapple instead of the angelica.

1926 BAVAROIS

These light delicate cream entremets can be prepared in two basic fashions, 1) as a flavoured Crème Anglaise containing gelatine and lightly whipped cream, or 2) as a fruit purée mixed with a sugar syrup, a little gelatine and which, likewise, is then finished with lightly whipped cream. Both types of mixture are moulded, allowed to set, then served demoulded, decorated, and garnished where appropriate. Fruit purée Bavarois may be satisfactorily prepared in either fashion.

A soft, smooth creamy texture which melts quickly in the mouth is the quality to be aimed for; the addition of stiffly beaten egg white to aerate or bulk out the mixture is not in keeping with these particular qualities. In this case, the resultant texture is more akin to the light airy texture of cold soufflés.

A nicety of judgement has to be exercised for ensuring that the base mixture is of the right consistency before adding the lightly whipped cream. It should just show signs of thickening. If it should start to set the result will be lumpy; if too thin the Bavarois will separate out in the mould to a layer of firm custard or fruit purée and a layer of softish cream with a much reduced volume.

The use of highly decorative moulds for Bavarois is not recommended. They are best reserved for jellies. Charlotte moulds are suitable for most purposes and when turned out have a nice flat base on top and sides suitable for most types of decoration. Deep funnel moulds afford a central hollow space appropriate for filling with fruit garnishes.

Allow Bavarois to set in the refrigerator for a minimum of at least 2 hours before demoulding.

1927   Bavarois au Café – Coffee Bavarois

Prepare as Bavarois Vanille (1938), using sufficient coffee extract instead of vanilla to colour and flavour the mixture. Decorate with candied coffee beans and Crème Chantilly.

1928   Bavarois au Chocolat – Chocolate Bavarois

Prepare as Bavarois Vanille (1938), adding 150g of grated chocolate to the milk when bringing it to the boil. Decorate with chocolate shapes and Crème Chantilly.

1929   Bavarois au Citron – Lemon Bavarois

Prepare as Bavarois Vanille (1938), but instead of the vanilla infuse the zest of two lemons in the milk for 5 mins. and colour a light yellow. Add the juice from the lemons to the mixture just before adding the cream.

1930   Bavarois aux Fraises – Strawberry Bavarois (1) 10 portions
1½ hours

Stage	Ingredient	Quantity	Method
1	milk	2½dl	Place in a shallow heavy pan and bring to the boil.
2	egg yolks	3	Place in a large basin and whisk
	sugar, caster	150g	together. Add the milk slowly whisking in well. Return the mixture to the pan and cook gently, stirring continuously with a wooden spoon until the mixture thickens and coats the back of the spoon. Take care not to overheat.
3	leaf gelatine, soaked in cold water	25g	Drain the gelatine, add to the hot mixture and stir until it has dissolved. Pass through a fine strainer into a bowl and allow to cool, stirring occasionally.
4	strawberries	500g	Remove the stalks, wash and drain the strawberries then pass through a fine sieve and add to the mixture.
5	cream, double	3dl	Place the cream in a basin and whip
	almond oil		lightly. Fold into the mixture just as it reaches setting-point. Pour into moulds which have been very lightly coated with almond oil. Place the Bavarois in the refrigerator and allow to set.
6	Crème Chantilly (1682)	2dl	Shake the moulds and turn out the
	strawberries	10	Bavarois onto suitable dishes. Decorate with the cream and strawberries.

1931 Bavarois aux Fraises – Strawberry Bavarois (2) 10 portions
1½ hours

Stage	Ingredient	Quantity	Method
1	water	2dl	Place in a pan, bring to the boil and
	sugar	150g	skim. Remove from the heat.
2	leaf gelatine, soaked in cold water	25g	Drain the gelatine and mix into the hot syrup to dissolve. Allow to cool.
3	strawberries	500g	Remove the stalks, wash and drain the strawberries then pass through a fine sieve and add to the mixture.
4	cream, double almond oil	5dl	Place the cream in a basin and whip lightly. Fold into the mixture as it starts to thicken, and just before setting-point. Pour into two moulds very lightly coated with almond oil. Place the Bavarois in the refrigerator to set.
5	Crème Chantilly (1682) strawberries	2dl 10	Shake the moulds and demould the Bavarois onto suitable dishes. Decorate with the cream and strawberries.

1932 Bavarois aux Framboises – Raspberry Bavarois

This can be prepared in either of the ways applicable to Bavarois aux Fraises (1930 and 1931), using raspberries instead of strawberries.

1933 Bavarois Nesselrode
10 portions
2 hours

Stage	Ingredient	Quantity	Method
1	chestnuts, shelled	450g	Bring the milk to the boil with the
	milk	5dl	vanilla and chestnuts. Cover and simmer
	vanilla pod	½	very gently until the chestnuts are soft and tender. Drain carefully.
2	milk as required		Remove the vanilla, pass the chestnuts through a fine sieve and reserve. Pass the milk through a fine strainer into a clean heavy shallow pan. Make up to 4dl with added milk and bring to the boil.
3	egg yolks	4	Mix together in a large basin then add
	sugar, caster	150g	the milk slowly, mixing in well. Return the mixture back into the pan and cook slowly, continuously stirring with a wooden spatule, until the mixture thickens and coats the back of the spatule. Take care not to overheat.

4	leaf gelatine, soaked in cold water	30g	Drain the gelatine, add to the hot mixture and stir in to dissolve. Pass through a fine strainer into a bowl. Mix in the chestnut purée and allow to cool, stirring occasionally.
5	cream, double almond oil	5dl	Place the cream in a basin and whip lightly. Fold into the mixture as it starts to thicken but just before setting-point. Pour into two moulds which have been lightly coated with almond oil. Place the Bavarois in the refrigerator to set.
6	Crème Chantilly (1682) marrons glacés	2dl 5	Shake the moulds and turn out the Bavarois onto suitable dishes. Decorate with rosettes of the cream and halves of the marrons glacés.

1934 Bavarois à l'Orange – Orange Bavarois

Prepare as Bavarois Vanille (1938), but instead of the vanilla, infuse the zest of two oranges in the milk for 5 mins. and colour a light orange. Add the juice from the oranges to the mixture just before adding the cream. Decorate with orange segments.

1935 Bavarois Praliné

Prepare as Bavarois Vanille (1938), adding 75g Pralin (1703), together with the cream. Decorate with Crème Chantilly (1682) and toasted hazelnuts which have been dipped in sugar at caramel stage. See sugar boiling (1711).

1936 Bavarois Religieuse

Prepare half the recipe of Bavarois Vanille (1938). Chill the moulds well and, when the mixture is just at setting-point, line the moulds instead of filling them. Allow to set in the refrigerator. Fill the centres with half the recipe of Bavarois au Chocolat (1928), allow to set and finish in the usual manner.

1937 Bavarois Rubané

This is prepared with layers of different coloured and flavoured Bavarois, e.g. layers of chocolate, vanilla and strawberry Bavarois. Allow each layer to set before adding the next.

1938 Bavarois Vanille – Vanilla Bavarois   10 portions
1½ hours

Stage	Ingredient	Quantity	Method
1	milk vanilla essence	5dl few drops	Place in a shallow heavy pan and bring to the boil.
2	egg yolks sugar	5 150g	Place in a large basin and whisk together. Add the milk slowly whisking well. Return the mixture to the pan and

cook gently, stirring continuously with a wooden spoon until the mixture thickens and coats the back of the spoon. Take care not to overheat.

3	leaf gelatine, soaked in cold water	25g	Drain the gelatine, add to the hot mixture and stir until it has dissolved. Pass through a fine strainer into a bowl and allow to cool, stirring occasionally.
4	cream, double almond oil	5dl	Place the cream in a basin and whip lightly. Fold into the egg mixture as it thickens but just before setting-point. Pour into moulds which have been very lightly coated with almond oil. Place the Bavarois in the refrigerator and allow to set.
5	Crème Chantilly (1682)	2dl	Shake the moulds and turn out the Bavarois onto suitable dishes. Decorate lightly with the Crème Chantilly.

1939 Blancmange, Vanilla

10 portions
2 hours

Stage	Ingredient	Quantity	Method
1	cornflour milk cream sugar butter vanilla essence	125g 1 litre 3dl 125g 50g few drops	Place the cornflour in a large basin and mix with 1dl approx. of the milk. Place the rest of the milk and other ingredients into a pan. Bring to the boil then whisk quickly into the prepared cornflour. Return to the pan and continue stirring over heat until the blancmange thickens then simmer for just a few mins.
2			Pour into two dampened jelly moulds. Allow to cool and refrigerate to set well.
3			Loosen around the top edges of the moulds, shake carefully to loosen the blancmanges and turn out onto suitable dishes.

SPECIAL POINTS
a) The milk may be flavoured and coloured with chocolate or coffee, flavoured by infusing with various citrus zests and colouring appropriately, or flavoured with good quality essences and colouring appropriately.
b) If desired, the blancmange may be made without using the cream or butter but naturally the result will not be so rich and creamy.

1940 Charlotte Eugénie

1) Set a ½cm layer of strawberry jelly flavoured with Cointreau on the bottom of two charlotte moulds.

2) Line the sides of the moulds with close-fitting Biscuits à la Cuillère (1673), the rounded surfaces facing to the moulds.
3) Have prepared 250g of small ripe strawberries cut in quarters and macerated with ½dl Cointreau.
4) Prepare a Bavarois aux Fraises (1930) and just before setting, quickly mix in the strawberries together with the macerating liqueur. Fill into the moulds.
5) Refrigerate to set well; trim the ends of the biscuits level with the Bavarois. Dip the top of the moulds very quickly in hot water, dry then demould on to suitable dishes. Be careful not to melt the jelly by overheating the mould.

1941 Charlotte Montreuil

1) Line the sides only of two charlotte moulds with close-fitting Biscuits à la Cuillère (1673), the rounded surfaces facing to the moulds. Leave the bases clear.
2) Prepare Bavarois Vanille (1938) and just after folding in the cream, fold in 250g of diced fresh peaches which have been sprinkled with a little lemon juice and sugar to preserve their colour.
3) Pour into the prepared moulds just before the Bavarois reaches setting-point.
4) Refrigerate to set well; trim the biscuits level with the Bavarois. Turn out onto round dishes and decorate the top of each with a rosette of sliced peaches which have been previously soaked in lemon juice and sugar.

1942 Charlotte Royale

1) Set a ½cm layer of raspberry jelly on the bottom of two charlotte moulds.
2) Line the sides and bottom of the moulds with slices of Swiss roll (1820) cut ¾cm thick. (The diameter of the Swiss roll should be approx. 3½cm.)
3) Fill the lined moulds with Bavarois Vanille (1938) or Bavarois aux Fraises (1930) at just near setting-point.
4) Refrigerate to set well then turn out on suitable dishes.

1943 Charlotte Russe

10 portions
2 hours

Stage	Ingredient	Quantity	Method
1	Biscuits à la Cuillère (1673)	36	Trim sufficient of the biscuits into small fan-shaped pieces to line the base of two charlotte moulds in the form of a rosette, the points to the centre and the rounded surface downwards. Line the sides with close-fitting biscuits, trimmed as necessary, the rounded surfaces facing to the mould.
2	Bavarois Vanille mixture (1938)	10 portions	Pour into the lined moulds just before it reaches setting-point. Place in the refrigerator to set.
3			Trim off any ends of the biscuits which are projecting above the mould. Turn out onto suitable dishes.

1944 Chartreuse de Bananes

10 portions
2 hours

Stage	Ingredient	Quantity	Method
1	lemon jelly	½ litre	Chemise two charlotte moulds (see 1248) with the jelly and set a thin layer on two round flat dishes.
2	bananas	4	Cut into thin slices, dip in a little melted jelly and arrange overlapping to cover the bottom and sides of the jellied moulds. Allow to set well.
3	Bavarois Vanille mixture (1938)	10 portions	Pour into the prepared moulds just before it reaches setting-point. Place in the refrigerator and allow to set well.
4			Dip the moulds into hot water for 2–3 seconds, dry the moulds and turn out onto the jellied dishes.

1945 COMPOTES DE FRUITS – POACHED AND STEWED FRUITS

The word compote denotes fresh or dried fruits poached or stewed in a sugar syrup which can be flavoured with such things as cinnamon, cloves, the zest of citrus fruits and in some cases wines, spirits or liqueurs.

Fresh fruits are best for poaching when not quite ripe; this helps them to retain their shape. Hard fruits such as pears and apples can be very gently simmered but soft and stone fruits are best when cooked slowly at low poaching temperatures. Fruits like raspberries and redcurrants only need to be covered with a hot sugar syrup and then allowed to cool. In many cases the poaching process can be carried out either on the stove or by placing the container of fruit in a warm to moderate oven.

Dried fruits must be well-washed then soaked in water for approx. 12 hours. They can then be drained, simmered slowly in the syrup which can be usefully flavoured with cinnamon and lemon zest. The cooking times are usually longer than for fresh fruit.

Any specially flavoured poaching liquids are noted in the recipes where applicable.

SERVICE
Whether poached or stewed, the fruits should be chilled and presented for service in shallow glass fruit bowls or served in individual shallow glass coupes or dishes.

A compote of fruit is popularly served as it is at breakfast but is also appropriate as a light lunch-time sweet, served plain with a little of the poaching liquid. Sauce Anglaise or cream, together with a sweet dry biscuit, can be offered in this case.

1946 Stock Syrup for Compotes

The standard proportions are: 750g of sugar and the juice of 2 lemons to 1 litre of water; bring to the boil, skim and use as required. The sugar content of the syrup may be increased to 1kg for poaching any sour or unripe fruit such as rhubarb or early season's gooseberries.

1947 Compotes de Fruits frais – Poached Fresh Fruits

These fruits have been grouped together where the preparation and poaching for them is the same.

1948 Compote d'Abricots – Poached Apricots

Remove the stalks, wash and drain then place the apricots in a shallow pan. Cover with hot stock syrup and greaseproof paper. Bring almost to the boil and place a plate or lid on top of the greaseproof paper to prevent the fruit from floating above the surface. Remove from the direct heat and allow to poach slowly until soft. Allow to cool in the cooking liquid.

1949 Compote de Cerises – Poached Cherries

Remove the stalks and stones. Wash and drain the cherries and place in a shallow pan. Cover with hot stock syrup and greaseproof paper. Bring almost to the boil and place a plate or lid on top of the greaseproof paper to prevent the fruit from floating above the surface. Remove from the direct heat and allow to poach slowly until soft. Allow to cool in the cooking liquid.

1950 Compote de Figues – Poached Figs

Wash well, drain and place in a shallow pan, cover with stock syrup flavoured with vanilla and greaseproof paper. bring slowly almost to the boil and remove from the heat. Allow to cool in the cooking liquid.

1951 Compote de Fraises – Poached Strawberries

1952 Compote de Framboises – Poached Raspberries

1953 Compote de Groseilles Rouges – Poached Redcurrants

1954 Compote de Mûres – Poached Blackberries

Hull the strawberries, raspberries or blackberries, or remove any stalks or flower ends from the redcurrants. Wash and drain well then place in a deep tray or shallow pan and barely cover with boiling stock syrup and greaseproof paper. Allow to cool in the liquid.

1955 Compote de Groseilles Noires – Poached Blackcurrants

Clean the fruit, wash and place in a shallow pan. Cover with hot stock syrup and greaseproof paper, bring almost to the boil and remove from the heat. Allow to cool in the cooking liquid and serve well-chilled in a glass bowl.

1956 Compote de Groseilles Vertes – Poached Gooseberries

Remove the tops and tails, wash and drain. Place the gooseberries in a shallow pan. Cover with hot stock syrup and greaseproof paper. Bring almost to the boil and place a plate or lid on top of the paper to prevent the fruit from floating on the surface. Remove from the direct heat and allow to poach very slowly until soft. Allow to cool in the cooking liquid.

1957 Compote de Mirabelles – Poached Mirabelle Plums

1958 Compote de Prunes – Poached Plums

1959 Compote de Reines-Claude – Poached Greengages

Remove the stalks, wash and drain. Place the fruit in a shallow pan. Cover with hot stock syrup and greaseproof paper. Bring almost to the boil and place a plate or lid on top of the paper to prevent the fruit from floating above the surface. Remove from the direct heat and allow to cool in the cooking liquid.

1960 Compote de Nectarines – Poached Nectarines

1961 Compote de Pêches – Poached Peaches

Skin the fruit (1701) and place into hot vanilla-flavoured stock syrup either whole or cut in half with the stones removed. Bring almost to the boil, cover with greaseproof paper and place a plate or lid on top of the paper to prevent the fruit from floating above the surface. Remove from the direct heat and allow to poach slowly until just soft. Allow to cool in the cooking liquid.

1962 Compote de Poires – Poached Pears

Peel and either leave whole with the stalk attached and with the core removed from underneath, or cut into halves or quarters and remove the cores. Wash in clean water and place in a deep pan. Cover with hot stock syrup flavoured with vanilla, and greaseproof paper. Bring almost to the boil and place a plate or lid on top of the paper to prevent the fruit from floating above the surface. Remove from the direct heat and allow to poach slowly until soft. Allow to cool in the cooking liquid.

1963 Compote de Pommes – Poached Apples

Peel, cut into halves or quarters and remove the cores. Place in a pan and cover with hot stock syrup flavoured with extra lemon juice and cloves, and greaseproof paper. Bring almost to the boil and place a plate or lid on top of the greaseproof paper to prevent the fruit from floating above the surface. Remove from the direct heat and allow to poach slowly until just soft. Allow to cool in the cooking liquid.

1964 Compote de Rhubarbe – Poached Rhubarb

Remove any leaves, the coarse skin and the root end. Cut into approx. 5cm-long pieces, wash well and place neatly in a deep tray. Just cover with hot stock syrup and greaseproof paper and poach gently by placing in the oven at 150°C until soft. Allow to cool in the cooking liquid.

1965 Compotes de Fruits secs – Stewed Dried Fruits

All dried fruits should be washed well, covered with cold water and allowed to soak for 9–10 hours or overnight before cooking in a flavoured stock syrup; for this, add some strips of orange and lemon zest and cinnamon stick to the standard Stock Syrup (1709), simmer gently for 10 mins., strain and allow to cool.

1966 Compote d'Abricots secs – Stewed Apricots

1967 Compote de Figues sèches – Stewed Figs

1968 Compote de Poires sèches – Stewed Pears

1969 Compote de Pommes sèches – Stewed Apples

1970 Compote de Pruneaux – Stewed Prunes

Drain the soaked fruit and place in a pan. Cover with the prepared stock syrup (1965), bring to the boil and simmer gently until tender. Allow to cool in the cooking liquid.

1971 Crème Beau-rivage

10 portions
2½ hours

Stage	Ingredient	Quantity	Method
1	butter	50g	Well butter two savarin moulds, add the
	Pralin (1703)	90g	pralin and shake to coat the insides of the moulds.
2	milk	1 litre	Place the milk in a pan and warm. Mix
	vanilla	few drops	the eggs, sugar and vanilla in a basin and
	eggs	8	add the milk while stirring.
	sugar	120g	
3			Pass the mixture through a fine strainer into a basin and ladle the mixture carefully into the prepared savarin moulds.
4			Place the moulds in a deep tray and half fill the tray with warm water. Place in the oven at approx. 165°C to cook and set (35–40 mins.). Remove and allow to cool in a refrigerator.
5	Cornets (1681)	10	Turn out the moulded custards onto
	Crème Chantilly		round flat dishes. Fill the cornets with
	(1682)	1 litre	some of the cream and pipe the
	crystallised violets	10	remainder of the cream into the centre of the custards. Place the cornets on top of the cream with their points to the centre. Place a violet in the centre of the cream in each cornet.

1972 Crème Brulée

10 portions
1½ hours

Stage	Ingredient	Quantity	Method
1	milk	5dl	Place the milk, cream and vanilla
	cream	5dl	essence in a pan and warm.
	vanilla essence	few drops	

2	eggs	6	Mix the eggs, egg yolks, sugar and milk in a basin and add the warm milk and cream, stirring in thoroughly. Pass through a fine strainer.
	egg yolks	4	
	sugar	120g	
	milk	1dl	
3			Pour the custard into ten individual pie dishes. Place the dishes into a deep tray and half fill the tray with warm water. Place in the oven at approx. 165°C to cook until set (35–40 mins.).
4	icing sugar		Dredge the creams with the icing sugar and glaze under the salamander to a golden brown. Clean the dishes and serve on a doily on a suitable dish accompanied with the biscuits.
	Ratafia Biscuits		
	(1704)	30	

1973 Crème Caramel – Caramel Cream

10 portions
2½ hours

Stage	Ingredient	Quantity	Method
1	sugar	200g	Place the sugar and 1dl of the water in a sugar-boiling pan, bring to the boil and cook to a golden brown caramel. Carefully add ½dl boiling water and boil to mix. Pour into the bottoms of ten dariole moulds.
	water	1½dl	
2	milk	1 litre	Place the milk into a pan and warm. Mix the eggs, egg yolks, sugar and vanilla in a basin and add the milk while stirring.
	vanilla	few drops	
	eggs	6	
	egg yolks	4	
	sugar	120g	
3			Pass the mixture through a fine strainer into a basin and fill into the prepared moulds.
4			Place the moulds in a deep tray and half fill the tray with warm water. Place in the oven at 165°C to cook and set (35–40 mins.). Remove and allow to cool in the refrigerator.
5			Loosen around the top edges of the moulds, shake carefully to loosen the creams and turn out onto a round dish making sure that all the caramel is utilised.

SPECIAL POINTS
a) Caramel creams are best left for a few hours to chill and set thoroughly before turning out.
b) Caramel creams may be prepared in charlotte moulds instead of dariole moulds.

1974 Crème Opéra

10 portions
2½ hours

Stage	Ingredient	Quantity	Method
1	butter Pralin (1703)	50g 75g	Well butter two savarin moulds, add the pralin and shake to coat the insides of the moulds.
2	milk vanilla eggs sugar	1 litre few drops 8 125g	Place the milk in a pan and warm. Mix the eggs, sugar and vanilla in a basin and add the milk while stirring.
3			Pass the mixture through a fine strainer into a basin, skim then ladle the mixture carefully into the prepared savarin moulds.
4			Place the moulds in a deep tray and half fill the tray with warm water. Place in the oven at approx. 165°C to cook and set (35–40 mins.). Remove and allow to cool then refrigerate.
5	small even-sized strawberries Kirsch sugar, caster	250g ¼dl	Macerate the strawberries with the Kirsch and sugar while the cream moulds are being prepared and cooked.

6	double cream, cold
	Meringue Shells
	  (1700), crushed
	  in small pieces
		6dl
		
		6
			Place the cream in a basin and whisk to a fairly stiff peak. Add the Kirsch from the maceration of the strawberries and the crushed meringue.

7	Pralin (1703)	25g	Turn out the moulded creams onto round dishes. Fill the centres with the whipped cream and mould dome-shaped. Surround the base of the cream with the strawberries and sprinkle with the pralin.
8	Spun Sugar (1712)		Cover each mould with a nice veil of pink-coloured spun sugar.

1975 Crème Viennoise

10 portions
2 hours

Stage	Ingredient	Quantity	Method
1	milk sugar water	1 litre 200g 1dl	Place the milk in a pan and warm. Place the sugar and water in a sugar boiling pan, bring to the boil and cook to a golden brown caramel. Immediately add to the warmed milk and bring to the boil gently so as to dissolve the caramel.

2	eggs	6	Mix together in a basin and add the milk
	egg yolks	4	while stirring. Pass through a fine
	sugar	100g	strainer into a basin and fill ten dariole
			moulds.
3			Place the moulds in a deep tray and half fill the tray with warm water. Place in the oven at 165°C to cook and set (35–40 mins.). Remove and allow to cool in the refrigerator.
4			Loosen around the top edges of the moulds, shake carefully to loosen the creams and turn out onto a round dish.

1976 Fraises Romanoff

10 portions
1½ hours

Stage	Ingredient	Quantity	Method
1	strawberries	1kg	Remove the stalks, wash the strawberries
	sugar	150g	and drain well. Place in glass bowls and
	Curaçao	1dl	add the sugar and Curaçao. Allow to macerate in the refrigerator for 1 hour, turning the strawberries occasionally.
2	Crème Chantilly (1682)	8dl	Place in a piping bag with a star tube. Make sure the strawberries are level in the dishes and pipe the cream in neat lines to completely cover the strawberries. Decorate the edges with scrolls of the cream.
3	Biscuits à la Cuillère (1673)	20	Serve the strawberries accompanied with the biscuits.

1977 Fraises Zelma Kuntz

10 portions
1½ hours

Stage	Ingredient	Quantity	Method
1	strawberries	1kg	Remove the stalks, wash the strawberries
	sugar, caster	50g	and drain well. Place in glass bowls and sprinkle with the sugar. Allow to macerate in the refrigerator for 1 hour, turning the strawberries occasionally.
2	raspberries	200g	Clean the raspberries then wash and drain them well. Pass through a fine hair sieve.
3	double cream, cold	5dl	Place in a cold basin, whisk until fairly
	sugar, caster	50g	stiff then fold in the raspberry purée.
	vanilla essence	few drops	

4			Place the cream in a piping bag with a star tube. Make sure the strawberries are level in the dishes then pipe the cream in neat lines to completely cover the strawberries. Decorate the edges with scrolls of the cream.
5	Pralin (1703)	25g	Sprinkle the surface of the cream with the pralin and serve accompanied with the Biscuits à la Cuillère or other suitable biscuits.
	Biscuits à la Cuillère (1673)	20	

1978 FRUIT CONDÉS

This type of sweet dish consists of fruit, either fresh, poached or tinned, arranged on a base of short-grain rice which has been cooked with milk and sugar, flavoured with vanilla and finished with egg yolks and whipped cream. The fruit is coated with apricot sauce and then decorated with Chantilly cream, glacé cherries and angelica. As an essential quality of this dish, the rice mixture should be light and fluffy with no evidence of hard uncooked grains.

The most suitable fruits for this dish are apples, apricots, pineapples, peaches and pears. It is more usual to use halves of apples, apricots, peaches and pears but if thought more suitable the last three may be sliced. Presentation can be in individual coupes or small fruit bowls and for a number of portions in larger shallow glass bowls.

The following recipe for Apricot Condé is offered as the standard type; it is only necessary that the particular fruit is designated in the menu title, e.g. Ananas Condé, Poire Condé, and so on.

1979 Abricot Condé

10 portions
2 hours

Stage	Ingredient	Quantity	Method
1	Rice for Condé (1706)	1¼ litres	Place the mixture as soon as finished into individual coupes or larger glass bowls.
2	apricot halves, poached or tinned	20	Drain well then arrange neatly on the rice.
3	Sauce à l'Abricot (1716), cold	3dl	Coat the apricots carefully with the sauce then decorate with rosettes of cream, cherries and angelica. Chill then arrange on doilys on suitable dishes for service.
	Crème Chantilly (1682)	3dl	
	glacé cherries	10	
	angelica	50g	

1980 FRUIT FOOLS

In general, fools are prepared from poached fruits, appropriately sweetened and flavoured, which are well-drained, passed through a fine sieve then mixed with half its quantity of whipped double cream. Soft berried fruits such as raspberries, strawberries and blackberries can also be used in their raw state.

Fruit fools are best served in glass coupes or goblets. Decoration is not essential but, if desired, a rosette of Crème Chantilly may be piped in the centre of the fool.

1981 Apple Fool

10 portions
1 hour

Stage	Ingredient	Quantity	Method
1	apples, cooking	1kg	Peel, core and slice the apples. Place in
	sugar	250g	a pan with the sugar, water and lemon
	water	1dl	juice. Allow to cook slowly to a fairly
	juice of lemon	1	stiff purée, pass through a sieve into a
			basin and allow to cool thoroughly.
2	cream, double	½ litre	Place into a basin and whip. Add to the apple purée and mix in carefully. Ladle into glass coupes and smooth the surface level. Allow to chill and set in the refrigerator.
3	Crème Chantilly (1682)	2dl	Decorate the apple fools with rosettes of cream and serve accompanied with the
	Biscuits à la Cuillère (1673)	20	biscuits.

1982 Gooseberry Fool

Prepare as Apple Fool (1981) without lemon juice and using cleaned gooseberries. Increase the sugar content to 350g.

1983 Blackberry/Loganberry/Raspberry/ Strawberry Fool

10 portions
1 hour

Stage	Ingredient	Quantity	Method
1	soft fruit to choice, cleaned, washed and drained	750g	Pass the fruit through a fine sieve and mix in the sugar.
	icing sugar	250g	
2	cream, double	½ litre	Place into a basin and whip. Add to the purée and mix in carefully. Ladle into glass coupes and smooth the surface level. Allow to chill and set in the refrigerator.

3	Crème Chantilly		Decorate the fools with rosettes of cream
	(1682)	1½dl	and serve accompanied with the biscuits.
	Biscuits à la		
	Cuillère (1673)	10	

SPECIAL POINT
Add a little red colour to strawberry purée if it should appear too pale.

1984 GELÉE – JELLY

The quality of most proprietary brands of sweet jelly is of a sufficiently high standard that it is no longer common practice to make jelly in the traditional manner. Packet jellies and jelly crystals are available in a wide variety of flavours and are very easy to prepare by following the instructions given. However, the following traditional recipes for Lemon and Raspberry Jelly are offered as examples of their type.

To present jellies, pour the liquid into jelly moulds and place in the refrigerator to set. To turn out, dip the mould into hot water for 2–3 seconds, wipe the mould, shake and turn out on a suitable flat dish. Decorate with Crème Chantilly (1682) if desired.

1985 Gelée au Citron – Lemon Jelly   1 litre
1¼ hours

Stage	Ingredient	Quantity	Method
1	lemons	4	Peel the rind thinly without pith from two of the lemons and squeeze the juice from them all.
2	water	7½dl	Place in a pan together with the lemon rind and bring to the boil. Allow to cool slightly then add the juice from the lemons.
	sugar	200g	
	cinammon stick	small	
	cloves	2	
	coriander seeds	10	
3	leaf gelatine, soaked in cold water	35g	Drain and add to the prepared liquid. Stir to dissolve.
4	egg whites	2	Whisk in a clean pan adding some of the prepared liquid, stir in the remainder and bring to the boil quickly, keeping the bottom of the pan clean by gently stirring with a wooden spatule. Remove the spatule immediately it comes to the boil. Allow to simmer very gently for 10 mins. then allow to rest for a further 20 mins.
5			Strain the jelly carefully through a jelly bag or a folded teacloth which has been well-washed in clean water and well-wrung out. Use as required.

1986 Gelée aux Framboises – Raspberry Jelly

1 litre
1¼ hours

Stage	Ingredient	Quantity	Method
1	raspberries, cleaned and washed	450g	Crush or liquidise the raspberries and place in a basin.
2	water lemon juice sugar	7dl 2 tbsps 250g	Place in a pan, bring to the boil and skim.
3	leaf gelatine, soaked in cold water	35g	Drain the gelatine, add to the syrup, stir to dissolve then pour this over the raspberry pulp. Mix well together, cover and leave for 10 mins.
4	egg whites water	3 1dl	Whisk together with the water then add to the raspberry mixture and mix thoroughly.
5			Place in a pan and bring to the boil, keeping the bottom of the pan clean by gentle stirring with a wooden spatule. Remove the spatule immediately it comes to the boil. Simmer very gently for 10 mins. only, then strain carefully through a jelly bag or a folded teacloth which has been well-washed in clean water and well-wrung out. Use as required.

SPECIAL POINT
100g or so of raspberries may be used to garnish the jelly in the same way as a Fruit Jelly (1987).

1987 Gelée aux Fruits – Fruit Jelly

Line the mould with the selected jelly and arrange suitable fruits in a pattern in the base and around the side. The fruit should be affixed by dipping in near-setting jelly. Refrigerate to set well. Add more of the same fruit to the setting jelly and fill this into the prepared moulds.

An alternative method is to set a layer of the jelly in the bottom of the mould, arrange a pattern of fruit on this, set in place with a layer of jelly to cover, then repeat this technique to fill the mould. Finish with a thin layer of jelly.

The jellies are then demoulded as usual but are best if left undecorated. Crème Chantilly may be offered separately.

1988 Gelée Rubanée

This is made by setting even layers of several different colours and flavours of jelly in a mould allowing each layer to set before adding the next.

1989 Ile Flottante

10 portions
2 hours

Stage	Ingredient	Quantity	Method
1	butter	20g	Butter two 14cm charlotte moulds and dust with flour.
2	caster sugar egg yolks vanilla essence	200g 7 few drops	Place in a bowl and whisk until white and creamy.
3	flour cornflour	90g 90g	Sift the flour and cornflour together and fold into the egg mixture.
4	egg whites salt	7 pinch	Place in a bowl and whisk to a peak. Mix half the whites into the egg mixture using a metal spoon and fold in the remainder.
5			Fill the prepared moulds two-thirds full with the mixture. Place in the oven to bake at approx. 185°C for 35–40 mins. Turn out and allow the sponges to dry overnight.
6	Kirsch apricot jam currants, washed and dried	1dl 150g 75g	Cut the moulded sponges horizontally into 1½cm-thick slices and sprinkle each slice with Kirsch. Coat each slice, except the top one, with apricot jam and sprinkle with a few of the currants. Sandwich the slices together to re-form the sponges into their original shape.
7	Crème Chantilly (1682) pistachios, skinned almonds, skinned glacé cherries	 3dl 50g 50g 10	Place the re-formed sponges in glass bowls. Coat the top and sides with the cream. Decorate the top and sides of the sponges with the pistachios, almonds and cherries.
8	Sauce Anglaise (1718)	 7dl	Chill the sauce and pour around the decorated sponges just before serving.

1990 Junket

10 portions
1 hour

Stage	Ingredient	Quantity	Method
1	milk sugar rennet	2 litres 60g 4 tsps	Place the milk and sugar in a pan and heat to 37°C. Add the rennet and stir in gently.
2	grated nutmeg		Pour into ten individual dishes, sprinkle with a little nutmeg and leave in a warm place to set.

SPECIAL POINT
Any suitable flavouring essence may be used in making junket.

1991 Meringue Chantilly

10 portions
20 mins.

Stage	Ingredient	Quantity	Method
1	Meringue Shells (1700)	20	Place the cream in a piping bag with a star tube and pipe out onto the flat side of one meringue shell and sandwich together with a second meringue. Proceed in the same way to sandwich all the meringues.
	Crème Chantilly (1682)	8dl	
2			Place on a doily on a flat dish and decorate by piping more cream over the joins.

1992 Mont Blanc

10 portions
1¾ hours

Stage	Ingredient	Quantity	Method
1	chestnuts	1kg	Cut horizontal slits in the shells on both sides. Place on a tray with a little water and put in a hot oven until the shells burst open. Remove the shells and inner skins carefully.
2	milk	1 litre	Place in a pan, add the chestnuts, bring to the boil and simmer gently until the chestnuts are soft. Drain well and pass the chestnuts through a fine sieve into a basin. Allow to cool.
	sugar	100g	
3	Buttercream (1677)	250g	Mix into the chestnut purée. Place in a piping bag with a 2–3mm plain tube and pipe random-fashion into two savarin moulds so as to imitate bird's nests. Allow to set in the refrigerator.
4	Crème Chantilly (1682)	1 litre	Turn out the moulded nests onto cold round dishes and fill the centres with the neatly piped cream.

1993 Mousse au Chocolat – Chocolate Mousse

10 portions
1½ hours

Stage	Ingredient	Quantity	Method
1	chocolate, grated	250g	Place into a pan and heat to allow the chocolate to dissolve.
	milk	1dl	
	sugar	150g	
2	leaf gelatine	15g	Soak in cold water, drain, add to the diluted chocolate and stir to dissolve. Allow to cool.

Stage	Ingredient	Quantity	Method
3	cream, double	7dl	Place in a basin, whip lightly and fold into the chocolate mixture just before it reaches setting-point.
4	almond oil		Pour into moulds which have been very lightly coated with almond oil. Place the mousses in a refrigerator and allow to set.
5	Crème Chantilly (1682)	2dl	Shake the moulds and turn out the mousses onto suitable dishes. Decorate with the cream.

1994 Mousse au Citron – Lemon Mousse

10 portions
1½ hours

Stage	Ingredient	Quantity	Method
1	lemons	4	Grate the zest and place in a pan with the juice from the lemons, the sugar and water. Heat to dissolve the sugar and add a few drops of yellow colour.
	sugar	250g	
	water	1dl	
2	leaf gelatine	25g	Soak in cold water, drain, add to the lemon syrup and stir to dissolve. Allow to cool.
3	cream, double	7dl	Place in a basin, whip lightly and fold into the lemon mixture just before it reaches setting-point.
4	almond oil		Pour into moulds which have been very lightly coated with almond oil. Place the mousses in a refrigerator and allow to set.
5	Crème Chantilly (1682)	2dl	Shake the moulds and turn out the mousses onto suitable dishes. Decorate with the cream.

1995 Mousse aux Framboises – Raspberry Mousse

10 portions
1½ hours

Stage	Ingredient	Quantity	Method
1	raspberries	1kg	Remove any stalks, wash the raspberries and pass through a fine sieve into a basin. Add the sugar and mix in.
	icing sugar	200g	
2	leaf gelatine	30g	Soak the gelatine in cold water. Place the lemon juice and water in a pan and heat. Add the drained gelatine and stir to dissolve. Allow to cool slightly, add to the raspberries and mix in quickly and thoroughly.
	juice of lemon	½	
	water	1dl	

3	cream, double	4dl	Place in a basin, whip lightly and fold into the mixture just before it reaches setting-point.
4	almond oil		Pour into moulds which have been very lightly coated with almond oil. Place the mousses in a refrigerator and allow to set.
5	Crème Chantilly (1682) raspberries	2dl 10	Shake the moulds and turn out the mousses onto suitable dishes. Decorate with the cream and the raspberries.

1996 Mousse aux Fraises – Strawberry Mousse

Prepare in the same way as Mousse aux Framboises (1995), omitting the lemon juice and using strawberries instead of raspberries.

1997 Oeufs à la Neige

10 portions
2 hours

Stage	Ingredient	Quantity	Method
1	egg whites salt caster sugar	8 pinch 450g	Place the whites in a clean basin, add the salt and whisk to a stiff peak. Whisk in half the sugar and fold in the remainder.
2	milk vanilla sugar	1¼ litres few drops 200g	Place in a shallow pan and heat to just below boiling-point.
3			Using two tablespoons mould the meringue into egg-shaped pieces and place in the hot milk. Poach very carefully on both sides until firm, remove and drain. Continue to poach twenty pieces of the meringue.
4	egg yolks	10	Mix in a basin and add the strained milk from the cooking of the meringues, whisking thoroughly. Replace in a clean pan and heat gently, stirring with a wooden spoon until it thickens. Do not reboil.
5	flaked almonds, toasted (1671)	50g	Pass the sauce through a fine strainer into two glass bowls and allow to cool thoroughly. Place the poached egg-shaped meringues on the custard and sprinkle with the almonds.

1998 Pavlova

10 portions
2 hours

Stage	Ingredient	Quantity	Method
1	egg whites	8	Place the whites in a clean mixing bowl, add a pinch of salt and whisk to a stiff peak. Whisk in half the sugar, keeping the meringue stiff. Fold in the remaining sugar, then the cornflour and the vinegar.
	sugar, caster	450g	
	cornflour	25g	
	white vinegar	1 tsp	
2			Place two 22cm diameter flan rings on a baking tray on a sheet of non-stick baking paper. Fill each with half of the meringue, dipping it at the centre and building up the sides.
3			Bake in a cool oven at 150°C for approx. 1 hour until crisp.
4			Allow the meringue bases to cool. Remove from the rings and place on doilys on dishes.
5	Crème Chantilly (1682)	1 litre	Spread some of the cream on the bases and fill neatly with the fruits. Decorate with rosettes of cream.
	bananas, sliced and sprinkled with lemon juice	3	
	kiwifruit, peeled and sliced	4	
	raspberries	250g	
	strawberries	250g	

SPECIAL POINTS
a) The cream may be flavoured and coloured with a little purée of passion fruit. The fruit may be sprinkled with a suitable liqueur such as Kirsch or Cointreau.
b) All soft, berried or stone fruits in season either singly or in combination can be used.
c) If required, individual nest shapes can be moulded or piped.

1999 Petit Pot de Crème au Café

Prepare as Petit Pot de Crème à la Vanille (2001) with the addition of sufficient coffee extract to flavour and colour, instead of the vanilla essence.

2000 Petit Pot de Crème au Chocolat

Prepare as Petit Pot de Crème à la Vanille (2001) with the addition of 150g of grated chocolate added to the milk in Stage 1.

2001 Petit Pot de Crème à la Vanille

10 portions
1½ hours

Stage	Ingredient	Quantity	Method
1	milk cream	5dl 5dl	Place into a pan and warm.
2	eggs egg yolks sugar vanilla essence	6 4 125g few drops	Mix the eggs, egg yolks, sugar and vanilla in a basin and add the milk while stirring carefully. Pass through a fine strainer into a basin and fill into individual Petits Pots moulds.
3			Place the moulds in a deep tray and half fill the tray with warm water. Place in the oven, cover the moulds with a tray and cook at 165°C for 30–35 mins. until set. Remove and allow to cool in the refrigerator.
4			Serve as they are in the moulds dressed on doilys on round dishes.

2002 Poire Marie-Rose

10 portions
2 hours

Stage	Ingredient	Quantity	Method
1	Condé Rice (1706)	1 litre	Place into two glass dishes and smooth the surface level.
2	whole pears, poached (1958)	10	Cut off the stalks. Remove the cores from underneath with a small vegetable scoop.
3	Crème Pâtissière (1685) Pralin (1703)	2dl 60g	Mix together. Fill the cavities of the pears with the mixture. Stand the pears on the rice.
4	raspberries icing sugar cream	500g 250g ½ litre	Pass the raspberries through a very fine sieve and mix with the sugar. Place the cream in a basin and whip slightly. Add to the purée of raspberries and mix in.
5	angelica Crème Chantilly (1682)	20g 3dl	Coat the pears with the raspberry cream and place a small piece of angelica in each pear to represent the stalk. Decorate with rosettes of cream.

2003 Poire au Vin Rouge – Pear in Red Wine

10 portions
1 hour

Stage	Ingredient	Quantity	Method
1	pears, medium	10	Peel, cut in half and remove the cores, or leave whole with the stalk attached and remove the cores from underneath. Wash and place in a deep pan.

| 2 | red wine,
full-bodied
sugar
lemon zest
cinnamon | 1 bottle
250g
1 strip
½ stick | Pour the wine over the pears, add the sugar and cinnamon and zest. Bring almost to the boil and cover with grease-proof paper. Place a plate or lid on top to prevent the pears from floating above the surface. Reduce the heat and allow to poach slowly until soft. |
| 3 | brandy | 1 tbsp | Place the pears in shallow glass bowls or individual fruit dishes. Strain the cooking liquid into a clean pan and reduce to approx. 4dl. Add the brandy and pour over the pears. Serve cold or hot. |

2004 Pouding Diplomate

10 portions
2½ hours

Stage	Ingredient	Quantity	Method
1	lemon jelly glacé cherries angelica	4dl 10 50g	Set a layer of jelly in the bottom of two 13cm charlotte moulds and on two round dishes. Decorate the bottom of the moulds with cherries and diamonds of angelica set in place with a little jelly.
2	milk vanilla essence	5dl few drops	Place in a pan and warm.
3	egg yolks sugar	5 150g	Place in a basin and mix together. Add the milk slowly stirring in well. Return the mixture to the pan and cook gently, stirring with a wooden spoon until the mixture thickens and coats the back of the spoon. Take care not to overheat.
4	leaf gelatine	25g	Soak in cold water, drain and add to the hot mixture. Stir until the gelatine has dissolved. Pass through a fine strainer into a bowl and allow to cool stirring occasionally.
5	Biscuits à la Cuillère (1673) currants, washed Kirsch	15 60g 1dl	Cut the biscuits into dice and place in a basin with the currants. Sprinkle with the Kirsch.
6	cream	5dl	Place in a basin and whip lightly. Fold into the egg mixture just before it reaches setting-point. Fold in the soaked biscuits and currants immediately.
7			Pour the mixture into the prepared moulds and place in the refrigerator to set.

8			Dip the moulds into hot water for 2–3 seconds. Wipe the moulds, shake and turn out the puddings on the prepared dishes.
9	Apricot Sauce (1716)	5dl	Serve the puddings accompanied with the cold Kirsch-flavoured apricot sauce.

2005 Profiteroles au Chocolat

10 portions
1 hour

Stage	Ingredient	Quantity	Method
1	Pâte à Chou (1735) eggwash	½ litre	Place the chou paste in a piping bag with a 1cm plain tube and pipe thirty 1½cm diameter balls on a lightly greased baking tray.
2			Bake the profiteroles at approx. 220°C until crisp and light brown in colour (18–20 mins.). Remove from the oven and cool on a wire rack.
3	Crème Chantilly (1682)	½ litre	Place in a piping bag with a small plain tube and fill the profiteroles from underneath.
4	Sauce au Chocolat (1721)	8dl	Pile the profiteroles dome-shaped in glass bowls and cover with the cold chocolate sauce.

SPECIAL POINT
The chocolate sauce may be served separately in which case the profiteroles should be dusted with icing sugar.

2006 Riz à l'Impératrice

10 portions
2 hours

Stage	Ingredient	Quantity	Method
1	raspberry jelly	4dl	Set a layer of jelly in the bottom of two 13cm charlotte moulds and on two round dishes.
2	Condé Rice (1706) crystallised fruits (cut in small dice)	½ litre 75g	Mix together.
3	milk vanilla essence	2½dl few drops	Place in a pan and warm.
4	egg yolks sugar	3 75g	Place in a basin and mix together. Add the milk slowly stirring in well. Return the mixture to the pan and cook gently, stirring with a wooden spoon until the mixture thickens and coats the back of the spoon. Take care not to overheat.

5	leaf gelatine	15g	Soak in cold water, drain, add to the hot mixture and stir until the gelatine has dissolved. Pass through a fine strainer into a bowl and allow to cool, stirring occasionally.
6	cream	1½dl	Place in a basin and whip lightly. Fold into the egg mixture just before it reaches setting-point.
7			Add the egg mixture to the prepared rice and mix in thoroughly but lightly. Pour into the prepared moulds and place in the refrigerator to set.
8	Crème Chantilly (1682)	2dl	Dip the moulds into hot water for 2–3 seconds, wipe the moulds, shake and turn out on the prepared dishes. Decorate with the cream.

2007 Salade or Macédoine de Fruits – Fruit Salad

Fruit salad can be prepared from any fruits in season using a wide variety in more or less equal proportions of different fruits. Unless forced by circumstances, it is best not to mix fresh and tinned fruits.

In addition to the more usual fresh fruits there are now available many of the more exotic fruits from the tropics and the Far East. Improved air transport has made it possible to obtain these in prime condition and the possibilities of variety and change in the compilation of a fruit salad have never been greater. However, if these fruits are used they should never overwhelm the balance of the traditional components of the salad but should be used with discrimination.

To prepare fruit salad
1) Make a syrup using the proportions of 750g of sugar and the juice of 2 lemons to 1 litre of water. Bring to the boil and allow to cool.
2) The fruit should be washed, then prepared as follows, placed into the syrup and mixed together.
   Apples and Pears: peel, core and cut into thin slices.
   Apricots: cut in half, remove the stone and cut the flesh in thick slices.
   Bananas: peel and cut into slices. These are best prepared just prior to service.
   Cherries: remove the stones, leave whole.
   Grapes: these may be skinned and the pips removed or cut in half and the pips removed.
   Kiwifruit: peel and cut in slices. Useful for decoration.
   Melon: cut in half, remove the seeds, remove the skin and cut the flesh into dice.
   Oranges and other citrus fruits: peel and cut into segments (66).
   Peaches and Nectarines: place in boiling water for a few seconds then remove the skin, cut in half, remove the stone then cut in thickish slices.
   Pineapple: remove the skin, cut into slices and remove the centre core. Cut into small wedges.
   Plums, all varieties: cut in half, remove the stone and cut the flesh in thick slices.

Raspberries, Strawberries and other berry fruits: may be mixed in but are fragile and some will colour the syrup; useful for decorating at the last moment.

Tropical and Far Eastern fruits

Cape gooseberries: detach the parchment-like covering and use whole.

Mango: remove the stone and cut in slices.

Pawpaw: skin, cut in half, remove the seeds and cut in slices.

Persimmon: remove the stalk, cut in half and then in slices.

Starfruit: remove the sharp edge of the star with a knife and cut in slices; useful for decoration.

3) Allow approx. 175g of unprepared fruit per portion to yield approx. 125g of finished fruit salad per portion.

4) Service: fruit salad is best served well-chilled in glass bowls. It may be flavoured with suitable liqueurs, e.g. Kirsch, Maraschino, Curaçao. It is usual to serve either ordinary or whipped cream with the fruit salad. Suitable biscuits, such as Biscuits à la Cuillère, may be served as an accompaniment.

2008 Salambos à la Marquise

10 portions
1½ hours

Stage	Ingredient	Quantity	Method
1	Pâte à Chou (1735) eggwash	¾ litre	Place the chou paste in a piping bag with a 1cm plain tube and pipe out thirty 4cm lengths on a lightly greased baking tray. Brush with eggwash and lightly groove along their lengths with a fork.
2			Bake at approx. 220°C until crisp and light brown in colour (18–20 mins.). Remove from the oven and cool on a wire rack.
3	Crème Pâtissière (1685) rum	½ litre ½dl	Mix together, place in a piping bag with a small plain tube and fill the salambos from underneath.
4	sugar ⎱ glucose ⎰ for glazing water ⎰ (1711)	250g 25g 1dl	Dip the tops of the salambos into the boiled sugar.
5	Sauce au Chocolat (1721) Crème Chantilly (1682)	5dl 3dl	Pour the cold sauce into two glass bowls and float the salambos on top. Decorate with the cream between the salambos.

2009 Soufflé froid aux Fraises – Cold Strawberry Soufflé

10 portions
1½ hours

Stage	Ingredient	Quantity	Method
1			Tie a band of greaseproof paper around the outside of two 15cm soufflé moulds so that the paper comes approx. 5cm above the rims.

2	strawberries, cleaned, washed and drained sugar, icing	450g 100g	Reserve ten nice strawberries for decoration. Pass the remainder through a fine sieve and mix with the sugar.
3	gelatine, soaked in cold water juice of lemon juice of orange	30g 1 1	Warm the juices in a small pan, add the drained gelatine and mix to dissolve.
4	egg yolks sugar	5 150g	Place in a sufficiently large bowl and place over a pan of hot water or in a bain-marie. Whisk continuously until the mixture thickens and whitens. Remove from the heat, add the dissolved gelatine and strawberry purée and whisk from time to time until nearly cold. Add a little red colour if the mixture appears too pale.
5	cream, double	5dl	Place in a basin and lightly whip. Prepare this while the mixture is cooling.
6	egg whites sugar	5 50g	Place the whites in a basin and whisk until nearly stiff. Add the sugar and continue whisking until fairly stiff. Prepare this while the mixture is cooling.
7			Fold the cream into the mixture just before it reaches setting-point, then fold in the whites. Pour the mixture into the soufflé moulds, place in the refrigerator and allow to set.
8	nibbed almonds Crème Chantilly (1682)	100g 2dl	Remove the paper from the moulds and coat the exposed sides of the soufflés with the almonds. Decorate with the cream and the reserved strawberries. Present on doilys on round dishes.

2010 Soufflé froid au Grand Marnier

10 portions
2 hours

Stage	Ingredient	Quantity	Method
1			Tie a band of greaseproof paper around the outside of two 15cm soufflé moulds so that the paper comes approx. 5cm above the rims.
2	leaf gelatine, soaked in cold water juice of orange	30g 2	Warm the orange juice in a small pan, add the drained gelatine and mix to dissolve.
3	egg yolks sugar, caster	6 200g	Place in a sufficiently large bowl and place over a pan of hot water or in a

			bain-marie. Whisk continuously until the mixture thickens and whitens. Remove from the heat, add the dissolved gelatine and whisk from time to time until nearly cold.
4	Grand Marnier	1dl	Add to the mixture and mix in.
5	cream, double	½ litre	Place in a basin and lightly whip. Prepare this while the mixture is cooling.
6	egg whites sugar, caster	6 50g	Place the whites in a basin and whisk until nearly stiff. Add the sugar and continue whisking until stiff. Prepare this while the mixture is cooling.
7			Fold the whipped cream into the egg mixture just before setting-point, then fold in the whites. Pour the mixture into the soufflé moulds, place in the refrigerator and allow to set.

8	nibbed almonds,
	   toasted (1671)
	Crème Chantilly
	   (1682)
	glacé cherries
	angelica
		100g
		
		2dl
		10
		15g
			Remove the paper from the moulds and coat the exposed sides of the soufflés with the almonds. Decorate the surface of the soufflés with the cream, cherries and angelica. Present on doilys on round dishes.

2011 Soufflé froid Milanaise

10 portions
2 hours

Stage	Ingredient	Quantity	Method
1			Tie a band of greaseproof paper around the outside of two 15cm soufflé moulds so that the paper comes approx. 5cm above the rims.

2	leaf gelatine,
	   soaked in cold
	   water
	juice of lemon
		
		30g
		2
			Warm the lemon juice in a small pan, add the drained gelatine and mix to dissolve.

3	egg yolks sugar, caster juice of lemon	6 250g 2	Place in a sufficiently large bowl and place over a pan of hot water or in a bain-marie. Whisk continuously until the mixture thickens and whitens. Remove from the heat, add the dissolved gelatine and whisk from time to time until nearly cold.
4	cream, double	½ litre	Place in a basin and lightly whip. Prepare this while the mixture is cooling.

5	egg whites	6	Place the whites in a basin and whisk
	sugar, caster	50g	until nearly stiff. Add the sugar and
			continue whisking until stiff. Prepare this
			while the mixture is cooling.

6			Fold the whipped cream into the egg
			mixture just before setting-point, then
			fold in the whites. Pour the mixture into
			the soufflé moulds, place in the
			refrigerator and allow to set.

7	nibbed almonds,		Remove the paper from the moulds and
	toasted (1671)	100g	coat the exposed sides of the soufflés
	Crème Chantilly		with the almonds. Decorate the surface
	(1682)	2dl	of the soufflés with the cream and
	pistachio nuts,		pistachio nuts. Present on doilys on
	blanched	20g	round dishes.

2012 Summer Pudding

10 portions
1 hour (plus
setting time)

Stage	Ingredient	Quantity	Method
1	blackcurrants ⎫ cleaned,	450g	Place all the fruit in a pan with the sugar
	redcurrants ⎬ washed,	450g	and water and cook gently until the fruit
	raspberries ⎭ drained	450g	is soft but still in shape, approx. 3 mins.
	dessert apples		
	peeled, cored		
	and thinly sliced	500g	
	sugar	300g	
	water	1dl	
2			Strain the fruit keeping it separate from the juices.
3	slices of day-old		Cut off the crusts and reserve four
	sandwich bread	14–16	slices. Cut the rest into three lengthways.
4			Place a round shape of bread in the base of two charlotte moulds or pudding basins. Dip the slices one at a time into the cooled fruit juice and arrange overlapping to line the sides of the moulds.
5			Fill the moulds proud with the cold fruit then cover each with a round shape of the reserved bread. Place a clean plate and a 250g weight on each to press down slightly. Refrigerate overnight.
6	Crème Chantilly (1682)		Turn out the puddings onto suitable
	or clotted cream	6dl	dishes and serve accompanied with sauceboats of cream.

SPECIAL POINT
Strawberries, stoned cherries, loganberries, mulberries and gooseberries can also be used to make this pudding.

2013 Syllabub

10 portions
3 hours (including macerating time)

Stage	Ingredient	Quantity	Method
1	white wine, sweet	3dl	Place in a basin and allow to macerate in
	sherry, sweet	1½dl	the refrigerator for approx. 2 hours.
	sugar, caster	150g	Remove the zests and discard them.
	lemon zest	2 strips	
	orange zest	1 strip	
	lemon juice	2 tbsps	
2	double cream, cold	7dl	Place in a basin and half whip, then add to the prepared wine. Whisk vigorously until light and fluffy.
3	Biscuits à la Cuillère (1673)	20	Pour into goblets and chill in the refrigerator. Arrange on doilys on suitable dishes and serve accompanied with the finger biscuits.

2014 TRIFLES

The following recipes for trifles use Biscuits à la Cuillère and Crème Anglaise to finish. This gives an excellent result in terms of taste, texture and appearance. However, where economy dictates, Génoise sponge and custard sauce made with custard powder give perfectly acceptable results.

2015 Fruit Trifle

Prepare as Sherry Trifle (2016). Omit the sherry but add tinned or poached fruits cut in small dice with sufficient juice to soak the biscuits.

2016 Sherry Trifle

10 portions
2 hours

Stage	Ingredient	Quantity	Method
1	Biscuits à la Cuillère (1673)	30	Sandwich the biscuits together with the jam. Cut each into three and place into glass bowls or coupes.
	raspberry jam	100g	
2	sherry	1dl	Sprinkle over the biscuits.
3	milk	1 litre	Place in a pan and bring to the boil.
	vanilla essence	few drops	

4	sugar	125g	Place in a basin, mix together and whisk
	egg yolks	12	in the milk quickly and thoroughly.
			Return the mixture to the pan and heat
			gently, stirring with a wooden spoon
			until it thickens. Do not allow to reboil
			as the sauce will curdle.
5			Pass the sauce through a fine strainer
			into a basin and ladle over the biscuits in
			the bowls or coupes. Allow to cool and
			then chill thoroughly in the refrigerator.
6	Crème Chantilly		Place the cream in a piping bag with a
	(1682)	3dl	star tube and decorate the trifles. Finish
	glacé cherries	10	decorating with the cherries and
	angelica	60g	angelica.
7			Serve on doilys on round dishes.

2017 Vacherin aux Fraises

10 portions
3 ½hours

Stage	Ingredient	Quantity	Method
1	egg whites	8	Place the whites in a clean mixing bowl,
	caster sugar	450g	add a pinch of salt and whisk to a stiff
			peak. Whisk in half the sugar, keeping
			the meringue stiff and fold in the
			remaining sugar.
2			Place the meringue in a piping bag with
			a 1cm tube and pipe onto greaseproof
			paper on a baking tray. Start from the
			centre and pipe round in spiral fashion
			to form a circular base approx. 18cm in
			diameter. Pipe a circle onto the base
			around the edge, so as to form a rim
			4cm high. Pipe out another case. Place
			into a cool oven at 110°C and bake until
			completely dry. Allow to cool, remove
			from the paper and place on doilys on
			round dishes.
3	strawberries	800g	Fill the vacherin cases with the cleaned
	Sauce Melba (1727)	4dl	and prepared strawberries and coat care-
	Crème Chantilly		fully with the sauce. Decorate with
	(1682)	2dl	rosettes of the cream.

2018 Vacherin aux Framboises

Prepare as Vacherin aux Fraises (2017) but using raspberries instead of the strawberries.

2019 Vacherin aux Mandarines

Prepare as Vacherin aux Fraises (2017) but using well-drained tangerine segments instead of strawberries and coating with Apricot Glaze (1672) to finish.

GLACES ET ENTREMETS À GLACE – ICES AND ICE-CREAM SWEETS

Ices are a popular sweet at any time of the year and are equally suitable for lunch and dinner. They are light on the palate, smooth in texture and easily digested; their flavour and sweetness should be pronounced. Ices can be served in many ways from the very plain and unadorned to very elaborate presentations. The quality of ices produced on the premises can be of an excellence far surpassing that of most factory-produced varieties. They can be made using a machine which mechanically churns the mixture during the freezing process and results in a very smooth creamy texture; these can be referred to as freeze-churned ices. They can also be made by freezing the mixture without any agitation at all; in this case the mixture needs to be of a different formulation to ensure an acceptable texture with minimal ice-crystal structure when frozen. These ices can be referred to as unchurned or still-frozen ices.

Ices can be classified in the following varieties:

Freeze-Churned Ices
1) *Cream Ices:* these are the most widely used kind which are made from a cooked egg custard mixture (Crème Anglaise) with the addition of a third to half its quantity of cream, plus the basic flavouring which can be an essence or flavouring, a fruit purée or added ingredient such as pralin.
2) *Fruit Ices:* these ices are made from cooked sugar syrups with juices or purées of fruit, plus the thinly peeled zest of citrus fruits. This kind is also called water-ice or fruit water-ice.
3) *Sorbets:* these light and refreshing kinds of ice can be served between the two main courses of a substantial meal and also as an iced sweet. They are made of sugar syrups of varying densities plus flavouring of fruit or liqueurs and colouring where needed. They are finished with Italian meringue.
4) *Granités:* these are made from a sugar syrup and flavouring which can be a sweet wine, liqueur or spirit, churned until it takes on a slightly granular texture. The syrup should register 14° on the saccharometer and the resultant ice is usually served to refresh the palate between courses.
5) *Marquises:* these ices are suitable for serving as an iced sweet. A sugar syrup at 17° on the saccharometer with the addition of Kirsch or other liqueur is churned until it begins to freeze then approx. one-third its quantity of whipped cream is added and the churning completed to give a slightly granular texture. If made with a purée of fruit, e.g. pineapple, the purée is added at the same time as the cream.

Unchurned or Still-Frozen Ices
6) *Bombes:* this kind of ice-cream takes its name from the shape of the mould in which it is frozen, without the mixture being churned. They can be made from a whisked yolk, sugar and water mixture with the addition of cream as in the basic bombe mixture, or from a sugar syrup whisked into egg yolks and whipped cream. The mixture can be flavoured with essence, flavouring, liqueur or fruits.

7) *Biscuits Glacés:* these ice-creams are made by whisking yolks and sugar to the ribbon stage then incorporating an equal amount of Italian meringue and double its amount of whipped cream. They can be flavoured with an essence or flavouring, a liqueur, pralin, or chocolate etc. The distinguishing feature of this type of ice is the brick-shaped mould in which they are frozen.

8) *Parfaits Glacés:* these are rich and delicate kinds of ice-cream which are made by whisking yolks of egg and sugar to the ribbon stage then incorporating approximately the same quantity of whipped cream, or they can be made with the addition of a purée of fruit. They are made in a similar way to the basic bombe mixture, frozen in any kind of mould or served in scooped portions.

9) *Iced Mousses:* iced mousses can be made with a purée of fruit combined with an equal amount of sugar syrup at 32° on the saccharometer, plus the addition of double its quantity of whipped cream, or they can be made from egg yolks and sugar whisked to the ribbon stage then lightened with whipped cream and whisked egg whites. They are sometimes made by incorporating approximately one-third the quantity of Italian meringue into a basic bombe mixture. They are frozen in chilled dariole or charlotte moulds.

10) *Iced Soufflées:* these can be made from a fine purée of fruit which is mixed into one and a half times its quantity of whipped cream and an equal quantity of Italian meringue, or they can be made by whisking yolks and sugar to the ribbon stage with double its quantity of whipped cream and an equal quantity of meringue. They are set in individual or large moulds so as to come above the rim to give the effect of having risen.

In addition to the above, there are a number of categories in which the ices listed above are used in various forms; they include Coupes, Omelettes en Surprise etc. and are included in the section headed Ice-cream Sweets.

Making and Storing Ice-Cream
Great care is required in the safe hygienic production and storage of ice-cream and catering establishments are well-advised to adhere to current legislation and to seek the approval of the local environmental health office. The following points should be noted:

a) All utensils, equipment and machines must be sterilised and maintained in a perfect state of hygienic cleanliness.

b) The mixture must be frozen as soon as possible after being made, stored at a temperature of not above −20°C and not allowed to rise above this until required for service.

c) For service, the container should be taken from its storage of −20°C to an ice-cream service conservator operating at approx. −10°C.

d) It should be remembered that freezing will not destroy any bacteria that may be present in the ice-cream either from a contaminated ingredient or unsterilised equipment; ice-cream is an ideal environment for the development of micro-organisms.

e) An excess of sugar in the mixture will lower its freezing-point and so retard the freezing process and limit the amount of aeration thereby spoiling the texture and eating quality of the finished ice.

f) Too much butterfat in the form of cream will produce a hard texture.

g) If stored over an extended period, fruit-based water ices will become hard-frozen and acquire a debased texture.

Service and Portion Control

It is usual to serve ordinary ices by means of an ice-cream scoop which produces easily controlled portions in the shape of a neat scooped ball; these are referred to as 'Rochers' in French. When served on its own it is usual to give two scoops of ice per portion using a No. 10 scoop which works out at 10 portions per 1 litre of ice-cream.

Ordinary ice-cream can be served in single portions in well-chilled coupes or in a silver timbale for several portions; crushed ice should be placed in the outer container. Ice-cream on its own should be served with wafers or suitable biscuits.

The scoop used for serving ice-cream must be sterilised before use and kept in a container of clean cold water frequently changed during the service period.

GLACES À LA CRÈME – CREAM ICES

2020 Glace Vanille – Vanilla Ice-cream

3½ litres
1 hour

Stage	Ingredient	Quantity	Method
1	milk	2 litres	Place in a pan and bring to the boil.
	vanilla essence	few drops	
2	caster sugar	550g	Place in a basin and whisk together. Add the milk, whisking continuously. Return the mixture to the pan and cook gently, stirring with a wooden spoon until the mixture thickens and coats the back of the spoon. Take care not to overheat.
	egg yolks	20	
3			Pass the custard through a fine strainer into a bowl and cool down quickly, stirring occasionally.
4	cream, double	6dl	Add to the mixture and mix in thoroughly. Pour into the container of the ice-cream machine and churn-freeze. When ready, remove and store if necessary at −20°C.

2021 Glace à la Banane – Banana Ice-cream

Pass five bananas through a fine sieve and proceed as for Glace Vanille (2020), adding the banana at the end of Stage 3. If desired ¼dl of banana liqueur or ½dl of Crème de Banane may be added.

2022 Glace au Café – Coffee Ice-cream

Prepare as Glace Vanille (2020), using sufficient coffee extract to colour and flavour instead of vanilla essence.

2023 Glace au Chocolat – Chocolate Ice-cream

Prepare as Glace Vanille (2020), adding 250g of grated chocolate to the milk and vanilla essence when heating.

2024 Glace aux Fraises – Strawberry Ice-cream
3 litres
1 hour

Stage	Ingredient	Quantity	Method
1	milk	1 litre	Place in a pan and bring to the boil.
2	sugar, caster egg yolks	600g 10	Place in a basin and whisk together. Add the milk whisking continuously, return the mixture to the pan and cook gently, stirring with a wooden spoon until the mixture thickens and coats the back of the spoon. Take care not to overheat.
3			Pass the custard through a fine strainer into a bowl and cool down quickly, stirring occasionally.
4	strawberries lemon juice red colouring	1kg 2 tbsps few drops	Clean and wash the strawberries and pass through a very fine sieve. Add to the mixture with the juice and a little red colour if necessary.
5	cream, double	6dl	Add to the mixture and mix in thoroughly. Pour into the container of the ice-cream machine and churn-freeze. When ready, remove and store if necessary at −20°C.

2025 Glace aux Framboises – Raspberry Ice-cream

Prepare as Glace aux Fraises (2024), using raspberries instead of strawberries.

2026 Glace au Gingembre – Ginger Ice-cream
2 litres
1 hour

Stage	Ingredient	Quantity	Method
1	milk fresh ginger, peeled and grated	1 litre 25g	Place in a pan, bring to the boil and infuse for 5 mins.
2	sugar, caster egg yolks	250g 10	Place in a basin and whisk together. Add the strained milk whisking continuously. Return the mixture to the pan and cook gently, stirring with a wooden spoon until the mixture thickens and coats the back of the spoon.
3	syrup from preserved ginger	1dl	Add the syrup to the custard then pass through a fine strainer into a bowl and cool down quickly, stirring occasionally.

| 4 | cream, double preserved ginger, chopped very fine | 5dl 250g | Add to the mixture and mix in. Pour into the container of the ice-cream machine and churn-freeze. When ready, remove and store if necessary at −20°C. |

2027 Glace à la Pistache – Pistachio Ice-cream

Prepare as Glace Vanille (2020). Omit the vanilla essence and add to the milk 75g of blanched pistachios and 25g of blanched almonds, pulverised to a fine paste. Colour the mixture a pale green before freezing.

2028 Glace Pralinée – Praline Ice-cream

Prepare as Glace Vanille (2020), adding 125g of Pralin (1703) at the end of the churning process.

2029 Glace au Rhum et Raisins – Rum and Raisin Ice-cream

Place 250g small seedless raisins to soak in 1½dl rum for 2 hours. Add the rum and raisins to Glace Vanille (2020) near the end of Stage 4.

GLACES AUX FRUITS – FRUIT WATER ICES

2030 Glace à l'Abricot – Apricot Water Ice
2½ litres
1 hour

Stage	Ingredient	Quantity	Method
1	water sugar	1 litre 600g	Place the sugar and water into a pan and reduce until the syrup registers 32° on the saccharometer. Allow to cool thoroughly.
2	apricots, ripe	1½kg	Wash, remove the stones and pass the flesh through a sieve, add to the syrup and mix in. Colour carefully if necessary to a light orange.
3			Place the mixture into the container of the ice-cream making machine and churn-freeze. When ready, remove and store if necessary at −20°C.

2031 Glace à l'Ananas – Pineapple Water Ice
2½ litres
1¼ hours

Stage	Ingredient	Quantity	Method
1	water sugar	1 litre 600g	Place the sugar and water in a pan and reduce until the syrup registers 32° on the saccharometer. Allow to cool thoroughly.

2	pineapple, skinned		Chop very finely in a food processor
	and cored	1kg	machine, add to the syrup and mix in
	Kirsch	2 tbsps	together with the Kirsch.
3			Place the mixture into the container of the ice-cream machine and churn-freeze. When ready, remove and store if necessary at −20°C.

2032 Glace aux Cassis – Blackcurrant Water Ice

2½ litres
1¼ hours

Stage	Ingredient	Quantity	Method
1	water	1 litre	Place the sugar and water in a pan and
	sugar	600g	reduce until the syrup registers 32° on the saccharometer. Allow to cool thoroughly.
2	blackcurrants,		Pass through a fine sieve and add to the
	picked and washed	1kg	syrup together with the lemon juice and
	lemon juice	2 tbsps	liqueur.
	Crème de Cassis		
	liqueur	½dl	
3			Pour the mixture into the container of the ice-cream machine and churn-freeze. When ready, remove and store if necessary at −20°C.

2033 Glace au Citron – Lemon Water Ice

2½ litres
1¼ hours

Stage	Ingredient	Quantity	Method
1	water	2 litres	Place in a pan, bring to the boil and
	sugar	1kg	reduce until the syrup registers 22° on
	lemon juice	3dl	the saccharometer. Pass through a fine
	zest of lemons	4	strainer and cool completely.
2			Pour the syrup into the container of the ice-cream machine and churn-freeze. When ready, remove and store if necessary at −20°C.

2034 Glace aux Mandarines – Tangerine Water Ice

Prepare as Glace à l'Orange (2036), using tangerine juice and zest instead of the orange juice and zest and colouring the syrup a light orange.

2035 Glace à la Mangue – Mango Water Ice

2½ litres
1¼ hours

Stage	Ingredient	Quantity	Method
1	water	1 litre	Place in a pan, bring to the boil and
	sugar	600g	reduce until the syrup registers 32° on

			the saccharometer. Allow to cool thoroughly.
2	mangoes, ripe fresh lime juice	5 ½dl	Cut the mangoes in half, discard the stones and peel the flesh. Pass this through a fine sieve and add the lime juice.
3			Add the purée to the syrup. Place into the container of the ice-cream machine and churn-freeze. Remove and store if necessary at −20°C.

2036 Glace à l'Orange – Orange Water Ice
2½ litres
1¼ hours

Stage	Ingredient	Quantity	Method
1	water sugar	1 litre 600g	Place in a pan, bring to the boil and reduce until the syrup registers 32° on the saccharometer.
2	zest of oranges zest of lemon	5 1	Add to the boiling syrup then allow to stand until it becomes cold.
3	orange juice lemon juice	5dl ½dl	Add the juices then pass through a fine strainer.
4	Curaçao	1dl	Add to the syrup and colour if necessary to give a good orange tint. Pour into the container of the ice-cream machine and churn-freeze. Remove and store if necessary at −20°C.

2037 SORBETS

The finished sorbet mixture, ready for churn-freezing, should register 15–16° on the saccharometer; if it is higher adjust down by adding a little cold boiled water, if lower adjust upwards by adding a little cold stock syrup.

A sorbet is best when served in a frosted goblet or coupe, just as it has been freshly made and is still of a soft texture. A little of the wine, spirit or liqueur used in the making of a sorbet, may be sprinkled over the sorbet in the goblet just before serving to the customer.

2038 Sorbet à l'Ananas – Pineapple Sorbet
2 litres
1½ hours

Stage	Ingredient	Quantity	Method
1	water sugar	7½dl 500g	Place in a pan, bring to the boil and reduce until the syrup registers 22° on the saccharometer. Cool completely.
2	fresh pineapple juice sherry, sweet	7½dl ¼dl	Add to the syrup which should now register approx. 15–16°. Colour a light yellow if necessary.

Stage	Ingredient	Quantity	Method
3	Meringue Italienne (1697)	4dl	Place the mixture into the container of the ice-cream machine and commence to freeze-churn. At the point where it begins to thicken, add the meringue and continue to freeze until it is light and fluffy.
4			Serve the sorbet in frosted glass coupes or goblets. Place on doilys on dishes.

2039 Sorbet au Champagne – Champagne Sorbet

2 litres
1½ hours

Stage	Ingredient	Quantity	Method
1	water sugar juice of lemon	1 litre 500g 1	Place in a pan, bring to the boil and reduce until the syrup registers 22° on the saccharometer. Cool completely.
2	Champagne, demi-sec	½ bottle	Add to the syrup which should now register approx. 15–16° on the saccharometer.
3	Meringue Italienne (1697)	4dl	Pour the syrup into the container of the ice-cream machine and commence to freeze. At the point where it begins to thicken, add the meringue and continue to freeze the sorbet until light and fluffy.
4			Serve the sorbet in frosted glass coupes or goblets. Place on doilys on suitable dishes.

2040 Sorbet au Citron – Lemon Sorbet

2 litres
1½ hours

Stage	Ingredient	Quantity	Method
1	water sugar juice of lemons zest of lemons	1 litre 500g 6 2	Place in a pan, bring to the boil and reduce until the syrup registers 15–16° on the saccharometer. Pass through a fine strainer and cool completely.
2	Meringue Italienne (1697)	4dl	Pour the syrup into the container of the ice-cream machine and commence to freeze. At the point where it begins to thicken add the meringue and continue to freeze the sorbet until light and fluffy.
3			Serve the sorbet in frosted glass coupes or goblets. Place on doilys on suitable dishes.

2041 Sorbet au Citron Vert – Lime Sorbet

Prepare as Sorbet au Citron (2040), using the juice of eight limes and two lemons and the zest of three limes.

2042 Sorbet aux Framboises – Raspberry Sorbet   2 litres
1¼ hours

Stage	Ingredient	Quantity	Method
1	raspberries, washed and drained water sugar	1kg 2dl 75g	Mash or crush the raspberries to a pulp. Place in a pan with the water and sugar, and bring to the boil. Skim and simmer for 5 mins. only.
2			Squeeze firmly through a fine strainer to give approx. 7½dl of juice. Allow to cool.
3	water sugar	7½dl 500g	Place in a pan, bring to the boil and reduce to 22° on the saccharometer.
4			Cool completely and add to the raspberry juice. Add a little red colouring if necessary.
5	Meringue Italienne (1697)	4dl	Place the mixture into the container of the ice-cream machine and commence to freeze-churn. At the point where it begins to thicken, add the meringue and continue to freeze until it is light and fluffy.
6			Serve the sorbet in frosted glass coupes or goblets. Place on doilys on dishes.

2043 Sorbet à l'Orange – Orange Sorbet

Prepare as Sorbet au Citron (2040), using oranges instead of lemons and colouring the syrup a light orange.

2044 BOMBES

Bombes are moulded ice-cream sweets, the name of which is derived from the shape of the mould in which they are frozen. This is a slightly elongated dome shape. The moulds are usually made of copper and the inner surface should be well-tinned. At the rounded end there is a small pedestal screwed into the mould which allows it to be stood upright during the freezing process and when removed facilitates the demoulding of the bombe.

The bombe mould is usually lined with a thick coating of ice-cream and the centre filled with the selected bombe mixture. In some cases the filling can be a number of layers of differing mixtures or with an extra central filling.

The moulding of bombes
1) Freeze the bombe mould.
2) Spread a layer of the required ice-cream approx. 1½cm thick inside the mould using the back of a spoon, then freeze firm again.

3) Fill the centre with the selected bombe mixture.
4) Cover with greaseproof paper, cover with the lid and freeze.

Service of bombes
Remove the lid and paper. Dip the mould into hot water for 2–3 seconds. Dry the mould and remove the pedestal. De-mould onto a well-chilled dish. Decorate to taste and in keeping with the contents of the bombe, using Crème Chantilly, glacé fruits, crystallised roses or violets, nuts, etc.

2045 Pâte à Bombe – Basic Bombe Mixture

2 litres
45 mins.

Stage	Ingredient	Quantity	Method
1	egg yolks	18	Place all the ingredients in a bowl, whisk together thoroughly. Place over a pan of hot water or in a bain-marie and whisk continuously until it becomes thick. The mixture is ready when it clings to the whisk when it is raised from the bowl. Remove from the heat and whisk until cold.
	sugar, caster	500g	
	water	½ litre	
2	double cream	7dl	Place in a basin and whip.
3			Add the cream to the egg mixture and fold in. Add the required essence, flavour, colour, liqueur or garnish, e.g. crystallised fruits, pralin. Use as required.

The following is a small selection of the very large repertoire of bombes.

2046 Bombe Aïda

Line the mould with Strawberry Ice-cream (2024) and fill the centre with Bombe Mixture (2045) flavoured with Kirsch. Freeze.

2047 Bombe Archiduc

Line the mould with Strawberry Ice-cream (2024) and fill the centre with Bombe Mixture (2045) flavoured with vanilla and pralin. Freeze.

2048 Bombe Celia

Line the mould with Chocolate Ice-cream (2023) mixed with chopped walnuts and fill the centre with Bombe Mixture (2045) flavoured with Crème de Menthe liqueur and coloured green. Freeze.

2049 Bombe Ceylan

Line the mould with Coffee Ice-cream (2022) and fill the centre with Bombe Mixture (2045) flavoured with rum. Freeze.

2050 Bombe Cyrano

Line the mould with Praline Ice-cream (2028) and fill the centre with Bombe Mixture (2045) flavoured with Kirsch and chopped glacé cherries and coloured pink. Freeze.

2051 Bombe Diplomate

Line the mould with Vanilla Ice-cream (2020) and fill the centre with Bombe Mixture (2045) flavoured with Maraschino and mixed with some diced crystallised fruit. Freeze.

2052 Bombe Nelusko

Line the mould with Praline Ice-cream (2028) and fill the centre with Bombe Mixture (2045) flavoured and coloured with melted chocolate. Freeze.

2053 Bombe Reine

Line the mould with Vanilla Ice-cream (2020) and fill the centre with Bombe Mixture (2045) mixed with diced marrons glacés. Freeze.

2054 GRANITÉS

The following recipe is of the standard type; it is only necessary to ensure that the prepared syrup, ready for freeze-churning, is at 14° on the saccharometer. Any suitable white wine, liqueur or fruit juice may be used and this should be named in the menu title, e.g. Granité au Monbazillac. Granités should not be made for storage or future use.

2055 Granité au Barsac

2 litres
1½ hours

Stage	Ingredient	Quantity	Method
1	water	7½dl	Place in a pan and reduce to approx. 18°
	sugar	500g	on the saccharometer. Allow to cool
	lemon juice	¼dl	completely.
2	Barsac	1 bottle	Add to the syrup and adjust to 14°. Add more water if too high or more syrup if too low.
3			Place the syrup into the container of the ice-cream machine and freeze-churn. The texture should be lightly granulated. Do not overmix. Serve in frosted coupes or goblets on doilys on dishes.

2056 Marquise aux Fraises

1 litre
1¼ hours

Stage	Ingredient	Quantity	Method
1	water	7½dl	Place in a pan and reduce to give a
	sugar	500g	reading of 18° on the saccharometer. Allow to cool.

2	Kirsch	¾dl	Add to the syrup. Colour a light pink.
	lemon juice	¼dl	

3	strawberries, hulled, cleaned and drained	350g	Rub the strawberries through a fine sieve and fold into the cream.
	Crème Chantilly (1682)	4dl	

4			Place the Kirsch and syrup into the container of the ice-cream machine and commence to freeze-churn. At the point where it has developed a fairly firm texture add the strawberry cream mixture and churn to mix well for a few more mins.

5	Kirsch		Serve in frosted glass coupes or goblets. Place on doilys on dishes and sprinkle with a few drops of Kirsch at the last minute.

2057 BISCUITS GLACÉS

The shape of this moulded ice-cream is similar to a brick but it can, however, be moulded in other shapes. The mixture is moulded and frozen without being churned and is often made with two or three different-coloured layers in the one mould. The mixture can be flavoured with liqueurs, spirits, coffee, chocolate, fine fruit purées, crushed pistachios, pralin and so on. Colour the mixture as appropriate.

The moulding of Biscuits glacés
The moulds are a flat brick shape with removable top and bottom lids. Line the bottom lid with sufficient greaseproof paper to overhang the sides. Press this lid back firmly onto the main mould. Fill the mould with the prepared mixture and firmly affix the top lid, likewise lined with greaseproof paper. Place in the freezing cabinet to freeze.

Service of Biscuits glacés
Dip the mould for a few seconds into hot water, wipe dry then remove the top and bottom lids. If necessary run a thin knife round the sides of the mould and allow the Biscuit to slide out. Cut into slices 2–3cm thick, place each on an ice wafer and place on a dish paper on a chilled dish. Decorate with rosettes of Crème Chantilly and an appropriate garnish determined by the flavour of the ice, e.g. crystallised roses and violets, sugared strawberries, raspberries, marrons glacés and so on.

2058 Biscuit glacé Vanille

8–10 portions
1½ hours

Stage	Ingredient	Quantity	Method
1			Line the top and bottom lids of a Biscuit mould with greaseproof paper. Place the body of the mould firmly on the bottom lid.

2	egg yolks	7	Place in a bowl and whisk together
	sugar	250g	thoroughly. Place over a pan of hot water
	vanilla essence	1 tsp	and whisk continuously until the mixture
			becomes thick and clings to the whisk.
			Remove from the heat and whisk until
			cold.
3	Meringue Italienne		Fold into the egg mixture.
	(1697)	2dl	
4	double cream,		Fold into the mixture.
	whipped	6dl	
5			Fill the mixture into the mould and
			cover with the lid. Freeze until hard.
6	wafer biscuits	10	To serve, demould the Biscuit, cut into
	Crème Chantilly		2–3cm slices and serve on wafers on a
	(1682)	2dl	dish. Decorate with the cream and any
	crystallised roses		appropriate garnish.
	or violets	10	

SPECIAL POINT

Biscuit glacés can be made with a Bombe Mixture (2045) instead of the above mixture.

2059 Biscuit glacé Praliné

Prepare as Biscuit glacé Vanille (2058), folding in 75g Pralin (1703) with the whipped cream.

2060 Biscuit glacé au Cointreau

Prepare as Biscuit glacé Vanille (2058) mixing ¾dl Cointreau into the cold egg yolk mixture before adding the meringue and cream.

2061 PARFAITS

These were originally moulded in tall round sloping-sided moulds with a dome-shaped top. Modern service allows the use of other plain moulds including the bombe mould and smaller individual shapes.

Traditionally Parfait ices are made in one flavour only and are never mixed or lined in the same way as bombes, or contain a garnish, although it is in order to decorate them lightly when demoulded. They are prepared from a bombe mixture.

2062 Parfait au Café

Flavour and colour Bombe Mixture (2045) with sufficient coffee extract added at the end of Stage 1. Mould and freeze in the usual manner. Demould and decorate with rosettes of Crème Chantilly (1682) and candied coffee beans.

2063 Parfait à la Crème de Menthe

Add 1dl Crème de Menthe to the Bombe Mixture (2045) at the end of Stage 1. Add a little green colour if necessary. Mould and freeze in the usual manner. Demould and decorate with rosettes of Crème Chantilly (1682) and small crystallised mint leaves.

2064 MOUSSES GLACÉES – ICED MOUSSES

Iced mousses can be made in many colours and flavours, singly or in contrasting combinations. The various kinds of essence, fruit purées and flavourings can be used as well as most liqueurs. The mousses can be set in moulds and turned out for service or frozen in moulds suitable for service.

The two following recipes are examples of the standard types.

2065 Mousse glacée aux Fraises – Iced Strawberry Mousse
10 portions
1½ hours

Stage	Ingredient	Quantity	Method
1	water	2dl	Place in a pan, bring to the boil and reduce until the syrup registers 32° on the saccharometer. Cool completely.
	sugar	150g	
2	strawberries, hulled, washed and drained·	450g	Reserve ten nice small strawberries. Pass the rest through a fine sieve and add the lemon juice and syrup. Mix together and add a little red colour if necessary.
	lemon juice	1 tbsp	
3	double cream, whipped	5dl	Fold the cream into the fruit mixture and fill this into single dariole or charlotte moulds. Place to freeze.
4	Crème Chantilly (1682)	2dl	Demould the mousses onto chilled dishes. Decorate with the cream and the reserved strawberries dipped in sugar at the last minute.

2066 Mousse glacée à la Vanille – Iced Vanilla Mousse
10 portions
1½ hours

Stage	Ingredient	Quantity	Method
1	egg yolks	8	Place into a basin and whisk together thoroughly. Place over a pan of hot water and whisk continuously until it becomes thick and clings to the whisk. Remove from the heat and whisk until cold.
	sugar	150g	
	water	1¾dl	
	vanilla essence	1 tsp	
2	double cream, whipped	4dl	Mix the cream into the egg mixture then fold in the whisked whites. Fill into dariole or other moulds and place to freeze.
	egg whites, whisked to a light peak	3	

3	Crème Chantilly (1682)	2dl	Demould the mousses onto dishes and decorate with the cream.

2067 SOUFFLÉS GLACÉS – ICED SOUFFLÉS

These soufflés can be made with the basic bombe mixture, with a basic Bavarois mixture together with whipped cream and Italian meringue or with a base of yolks and sugar whisked to the ribbon stage plus cream and whisked egg whites. All these can be flavoured with a liqueur, coffee, chocolate, pralin, etc. A fruit version of the Iced Soufflé is made with sugar added to a purée of the chosen fruit which is lightened with cream and Italian meringue. The following recipes are examples of the standard types.

2068 Soufflé glacé au Drambuie – Iced Drambuie Soufflé

10 portions
2½ hours

Stage	Ingredient	Quantity	Method
1			Tie a band of greaseproof paper around the outside of two 15cm soufflé moulds so that the paper comes approx. 5cm above the rims.
2	milk	5dl	Place in a pan and bring to the boil.
3	egg yolks caster sugar	5 150g	Place in a large basin and whisk together. Add the milk slowly whisking well. Return the mixture to the pan and cook, stirring gently with a wooden spatule until the mixture thickens and coats the back of the spoon. Take care not to overheat.
4	leaf gelatine, soaked in cold water	15g	Drain and add to the hot mixture. Stir until the gelatine has dissolved. Pass through a fine strainer and whisk from time to time until nearly cold.
5	Drambuie	1dl	Add to the mixture.
6	double cream, whipped Meringue Italienne (1697)	½ litre ½ litre	Fold the cream into the egg mixture then carefully fold in the meringue. Pour the mixture into the prepared soufflé moulds and place to freeze.
7	nibbed almonds, toasted Crème Chantilly (1682)	100g 2dl	To serve, remove the paper from the moulds and coat the bared sides of the soufflés with the almonds. Decorate the surface with the cream.

2069 Soufflé glacé aux Framboises – Iced Raspberry Soufflé

10 portions
2½ hours

Stage	Ingredient	Quantity	Method
1			Tie a band of greaseproof paper around the outside of two 15cm soufflé moulds so that the paper comes approx. 5cm above the rims.
2	raspberries	450g	Wash the raspberries and drain. Reserve 20 nice ones for decoration and pass the remainder through a fine sieve. Add the sugar and lemon juice.
	sugar, icing	150g	
	lemon juice	½	
3	cream, double	½ litre	Place in a basin and whip lightly.
4	Meringue Italienne (1697)	½ litre	Fold the raspberry purée into the cream then fold in the meringue. Pour into the prepared moulds and place to freeze.
5	flaked almonds	100g	To serve, remove the paper from the moulds and coat the bared sides of the soufflés with the almonds. Decorate the surface of the soufflés with rosettes of the cream and garnish with the reserved raspberries, rolled in sugar at the last moment.
	Crème Chantilly (1682)	2dl	

2070 Soufflé glacé Tutti-frutti

10 portions
2½ hours

Stage	Ingredient	Quantity	Method
1			Tie a band of greaseproof paper around the outside of two 15cm soufflé moulds so that the paper comes approx. 5cm above the rims.
2	crystallised fruit, cut in small dice	100g	Place in a basin and allow to macerate until required.
	Kirsch	½dl	
3	egg yolks	8	Place in a large basin and whisk together thoroughly. Place over a pan of hot water or in a bain-marie and whisk continuously until it becomes thick. The mixture is ready when it clings to the whisk when raised from the bowl. Remove from the heat and whisk from time to time until cold.
	sugar	200g	
	water	¾dl	
4	double cream	5dl	Place in a basin and whip lightly. This can be prepared while the mixture is cooling.

5	egg whites	5	Place the whites in a basin with a pinch
	sugar, caster	50g	of salt and whisk until nearly stiff then

5   egg whites   5   Place the whites in a basin with a pinch
sugar, caster   50g   of salt and whisk until nearly stiff then add the sugar and whisk until stiff. This can be prepared while the mixture is cooling.

6   Fold the cream into the egg mixture then fold in the whites, and lastly, fold in the crystallised fruits and the Kirsch.

7   Crème Chantilly (1682)   2dl   Fill the mixture into the soufflé moulds and place to freeze. To serve, remove the paper and decorate the surface of the soufflés with the cream, cherries and angelica.
glacé cherries   10
angelica   15g

2071 ENTREMETS À GLACE – ICE-CREAM SWEETS

The following include many of the well-known desserts incorporating the various kinds of ices already dealt with. Because of their varied nature they are included here under a general heading.

2072 COUPES

This is a descriptive term given to single or mixed flavours and colours of ice-cream, with or without the addition of fruits and cold sauces, usually finished with whipped cream and presented in a shallow silver or crystal coupe. They should be served with wafers or a suitable biscuit.

The following are a selection of the most popular ones.

2073 Coupe Alexandra

Place diced fresh fruit in the coupe, sprinkle with Kirsch and place a ball of Strawberry Ice-cream (2024) on top. Decorate with rosettes of Crème Chantilly (1682) and fresh strawberries.

2074 Coupe Andalouse

Place segments of oranges in the coupe, sprinkle with Maraschino and place a ball of Lemon Water Ice (2033) on top. Decorate with rosettes of Crème Chantilly (1682).

2075 Coupe Camargue

Place small segments of pineapple in the coupe, sprinkle with brandy and place a ball each of Vanilla Ice-cream (2020) and Coffee Ice-cream (2022) on top. Decorate with rosettes of Crème Chantilly (1682).

2076 Coupe Edna May

Place poached cherries in the coupe and a ball of Vanilla Ice-cream (2020) on top. Coat with Melba Sauce (1727 or 1728) and decorate with raspberry-flavoured whipped cream smoothed to the shape of a cone.

2077 Coupe Jacques

Place diced fresh fruit salad in the coupe, sprinkle with Kirsch and place a ball of ice-cream on top consisting of half Strawberry Ice-cream (2024) and half Lemon Water Ice (2033). Decorate with rosettes of Crème Chantilly (1682) and place a grape in the centre.

2078 Coupe Janine

Place pieces of Marrons glacés in the coupe, sprinkle with rum and place a ball of Coffee Ice-cream (2022) on top. Coat with chocolate sauce and decorate with rosettes of Crème Chantilly (1682).

2079 Coupe Jamaïque

Place diced fresh pineapple in the coupe, sprinkle with rum and place a ball of Coffee Ice-cream (2022) on top. Decorate with rosettes of Crème Chantilly (1682) and crystallised coffee grains.

2080 Coupe Léonora

Place broken pieces of Marrons glacés in the coupe and a ball each of Vanilla Ice-cream (2020) and Chocolate Ice-cream (2023) on top. Decorate with Crème Chantilly (1682) and place a whole marron glacé in the centre.

2081 Coupe Rêve d'Amour

Place strawberries macerated with Curaçao in the coupe and place a ball of Vanilla Ice-cream (2020) on top. Coat the ice-cream with a spoonful of Sauce Melba (1727 or 1728) and decorate with rosettes of Crème Chantilly (1682).

2082 Coupe Savoy

Fill the coupe with raspberries and sprinkle with Anisette Liqueur. Place a ball each of Praline Ice-cream (2028) and Coffee Ice-cream (2022) on top and garnish with crystallised violets.

2083 Coupe Vénus

Place a ball of Vanilla Ice-cream (2020) on the bottom of the coupe. Cover with a poached half of peach. Decorate with rosettes of Crème Chantilly (1682) and place a fresh strawberry in the centre.

FRUIT ICE-CREAM SWEETS

2084 Cerises Jubilée

4 portions
30 mins.

Stage	Ingredient	Quantity	Method
1	cherries, cleaned and stoned	300g	Place in a pan and gently poach. When the cherries are tender, drain off the

	water	1dl	juice and place the cherries in a deep
	sugar	50g	metal dish or timbale.
2	arrowroot	1 tsp	Reduce the juice from the cherries by boiling for a few mins. and thicken it with the arrowroot diluted in a little cold water. Strain it over the cherries.
3	Kirsch	¼dl	At the moment of service pour the
	Vanilla Ice-cream		warmed Kirsch over the cherries and
	(2020)	8 scoops	flamber (32). Serve accompanied with the ice-cream in a separate timbale.

SPECIAL POINT
If desired the cherries may be served in individual containers.

2085 Fraises Cardinal

Place whole strawberries in either a timbale or glass bowl, coat with Sauce Melba (1727 or 1728) and sprinkle with toasted flaked almonds. Serve accompanied with balls of Vanilla Ice-cream (2020) dressed in a timbale or glass bowl and decorated with rosettes of Crème Chantilly (1682).

2086 Fraises Femina

Sprinkle whole strawberries with sugar and Grand Marnier and allow to macerate for 30 mins. Place on a bed of Orange Ice (2036) in a timbale or glass bowl. Decorate with Crème Chantilly (1682).

2087 Fraises Melba – Strawberry Melba

Place a bed of Vanilla Ice-cream (2020) in a chilled timbale or glass bowl, cover with a layer of strawberries and coat with Sauce Melba (1727 or 1728). Decorate with rosettes of Crème Chantilly (1682).

2088 Framboises Melba – Raspberry Melba

Place a bed of Vanilla Ice-cream (2020) in a timbale or glass bowl, cover with a layer of raspberries and coat with Sauce Melba (1727 or 1728). Decorate with rosettes of Crème Chantilly (1682).

2089 Orange en Surprise

10 portions
1½ hours

Stage	Ingredient	Quantity	Method
1	oranges, medium-sized	10	Cut a circle into the skin around the top quarter of an orange with a small knife but do not cut into the flesh. Introduce the curved handle of a dessert spoon between the rind and the orange flesh. Work round and round carefully until the top can be detached as a lid. Turn the orange over and use the handle of the spoon to release the orange in one piece from the remaining three-quarters of the skin; this leaves an empty orange case and its lid. Repeat for the rest of the oranges.
2			Place the orange cases and lids into the freezer to freeze hard.
3	sugar, caster Curaçao	25g ½dl	Cut segments from the skinned oranges and place in a glass dish with the sugar and Curaçao and macerate.
4	Orange Water Ice (2036)	1 litre approx.	Fill the empty orange cases with the ice and return to the freezer.
5	Italian Meringue (1697) ready-prepared	4dl	Place in a piping bag with a star tube, take the filled oranges from the freezer and cover the ices only, neatly and completely.
6	sprigs of young mint		Place the oranges into a very hot oven to quickly colour the meringue. Cover with the lids to one side and decorate with the mint. Place on doilys on dishes and serve immediately, accompanied with the macerated orange segments.

2090 Pêche Cardinal

Place whole skinned peaches in either a timbale or glass bowl, coat with Sauce Melba (1727 or 1728) and sprinkle with toasted flaked almonds. Serve accompanied with balls of Vanilla Ice-cream (2020), dressed in a chilled timbale or glass bowl and decorated with rosettes of Crème Chantilly (1682).

2091 Pêche Dame-blanche

Place a bed of Vanilla Ice-cream (2020) in a chilled timbale or glass bowl. Cover with thin slices of pineapple and sprinkle with Kirsch. Cover with halves of skinned peaches and decorate with Crème Chantilly (1682).

2092 Pêche Melba – Peach Melba

Place a bed of Vanilla Ice-cream (2020) in a chilled timbale or glass bowl. Cover with whole or halves of skinned peaches and coat with Sauce Melba (1727 or 1728). Decorate with rosettes of Crème Chantilly (1682).

2093 Poire Belle Hélène

Place whole poached pears with a little of their syrup in either a timbale or glass bowl. Serve accompanied with balls of Vanilla Ice-cream (2020) arranged in a chilled timbale or glass bowl and a sauceboat of Hot Chocolate Sauce (1721).

ICE-CREAM SWEETS WITH MERINGUE

2094 Meringue glacée au Chocolat

Place a bed of Vanilla Ice-cream (2020) in a small chilled glass bowl, arrange two Meringue Shells (1700) one on each side of the dish and neatly pipe an arrangement of whipped cream well-coloured and flavoured with melted chocolate and a little Crème de Cacao liqueur, over the ice-cream.

2095 Meringue glacée Vanille

Sandwich two Meringue Shells (1700) together with Vanilla Ice-cream (2020), place on a doily on a suitable dish and decorate with Crème Chantilly (1682). Meringues glacées may be prepared with any appropriate flavour of ice-cream.

2096 OMELETTES EN SURPRISE

This type of sweet dish consists of an ice-cream with or without fruit, placed on a Génoise base, then coated with meringue and glazed quickly in a hot oven. A little suitable spirit or liqueur can be sprinkled over the Génoise base and the finished omelette can also be sprinkled with a little of the same spirit or liqueur when removed from the oven and sent to the dining-room, or it can be flamed.

With a little ingenuity and understanding of the necessary ingredients, it is possible to create a wide variety of Omelettes en Surprise. The following are popular examples.

2097 Omelette en Surprise Brésilienne

10 portions
30 mins.

Stage	Ingredient	Quantity	Method
1	Génoise Sponge (1803)	1 × 15cm diam.	Hollow the centre slightly and fix with a little apricot jam in the middle of a large round silver dish approx. 30cm in diameter.
2	egg whites	8	Place the whites in a clean mixing bowl,
	sugar, caster	450g	add a pinch of salt and whisk to a stiff peak. Whisk in half the sugar keeping the meringue stiff and fold in the remaining sugar.

3	rum Coffee Ice-cream (2022), very firm	¼dl 20 balls	Sprinkle the rum over the Génoise then pile on the ice-cream starting round the edge of the Génoise and arranging in the form of a tallish cone.
4			Mask the whole with three-quarters of the meringue and smooth to a truncated cone shape. Place the remaining meringue in a piping bag with a star tube and decorate the omelette.
5	sugar, icing		Dust with icing sugar, clean the dish very carefully and place in a very hot oven to colour a golden brown.
6	rum, warmed	½dl	Pour the rum round the omelette and set alight at service in the dining-room.

2098 Omelette en Surprise Norvégienne

10 portions
30 mins.

Stage	Ingredient	Quantity	Method
1	Génoise Sponge (1803)	1	Trim oval-shape and slightly hollow out the centre. Fix in place in the centre of a large oval silver dish, using a little apricot jam.
2	egg whites sugar, caster	8 450g	Place the whites in a clean mixing bowl, add a pinch of salt and whisk to a stiff peak. Whisk in half the sugar keeping the meringue stiff and fold in the remaining sugar.
3	Kirsch Vanilla Ice-cream (2020)	2 tbsps 20 balls	Sprinkle the Kirsch over the Génoise base and place the ice-cream on top.
4			Mask three-quarters of the meringue over the ice-cream and smooth to a neat oval shape with a palette knife. Place the remaining meringue in a piping bag with a star tube and decorate the omelette.
5	glacé cherries angelica sugar, icing	10 25g	Finish decorating the omelette with the cherries and angelica. Dredge with icing sugar, clean the dish and place in a very hot oven to colour a golden brown. Serve immediately.

2099 Omelette en Surprise Milady

Prepare as Omelette en Surprise Norvégienne (2098), sprinkling the Génoise with Maraschino instead of Kirsch and using 10 balls only of Raspberry Ice-cream (2025) instead of vanilla ice-cream. Cover the ice-cream with halves of peaches.

2100 Omelette en Surprise Milord

Prepare as Omelette en Surprise Norvégienne (2098), adding halves of poached pears to 10 balls only of vanilla ice-cream.

─────────── PETITS FOURS ───────────

Petits Fours is the name given to describe a selection of small bite-size confections served at the end of a meal, more usually dinner. The selection consists in the main of a) Petits Fours Secs which are biscuit and wafer products and items made from various kinds of pastry, and b) Petits Fours Glacés, which are glazed varieties and include items dipped in boiled sugar or coated with fondant. In addition, there are items made from marzipan, chocolate, nougat, marshmallow, nuts and so on. The range of both types of Petits Fours is bewilderingly large and their preparation can involve a wide spectrum of techniques and artistic ability.

To be effective, Petits Fours should be made fairly small in a range of flavours, colours, texture and shapes, and presented in a balanced variety of the several kinds. Presentation should always be neat and attractive; for this purpose their particular qualities can always be enhanced by using special baskets or presentation caskets and stands of Pastillage or pulled sugar. It is essential that all items, except for some of the dry biscuit types, are served in small paper cases. Above all it is best that they are freshly made on the premises; excellence in quality, decoration and presentation can do much to enhance the reputation of the establishment.

Petits Fours may also be described on the menu, where perceived as being fitting, as Mignardises, Friandises, Frivolités, Caprices des Dames, Délices des Dames, Douceurs and so on.

The following recipes and suggestions are only a fraction of the wide repertoire of possible items. They have been selected as being some of the more popular and least complicated and are intended as a guide.

2101 Boiled Sugar-glazed Petits Fours

Fruit for glazing must be firm and dry and have unbroken skin, otherwise it will start to weep and spoil the glaze. It must be allowed time to dry out properly, laid out on a wire rack.

Suitable fruits include: black or white grapes on short lengths of stalk; pairs of cherries joined on the same stalk; carefully separated segments of orange, tangerine and mandarin; stoned dates or prunes stuffed with different-coloured marzipans; whole strawberry with the stalk; halves of walnuts sandwiched with marzipan; glacé cherries cut in half and sandwiched with marzipan.

To Glaze
Boil the sugar syrup to hard crack at 157–160°C (1710) and dip the base of the pan in cold water for a few seconds to prevent any further cooking. Immerse each item separately using a dipping-fork or holding the fruit by the stem. Remove the surplus by drawing lightly across the side of the pan. Place on an oiled slab or tray to set.

NOTE
The sugar may be kept over a low heat to maintain its working temperature.

2102 Chocolate-dipped Petits Fours

Chocolate couverture needs to be tempered before use which is done by firstly melting it to 45°C, cooling to 27°C then re-warming to 32°C stirring gently; it should not then exceed this heat. Ordinary chocolate coating needs only to be melted to 40°C.

The prepared centres of marzipan, ganache, pralin, nuts, biscuits etc. may be dipped in the prepared chocolate by means of a dipping-fork, or coated by placing on a wire rack and pouring the chocolate over; they should not be left to go completely hard before removal from the rack.

2103 Fondant-dipped Petits Fours

This kind of glazed Petit Four is made by warming fondant to 43°C and thinning it slightly if necessary with a little stock syrup and colouring to choice, then dipping prepared items into it; it sets after a short time.

Items included in this category must be thoroughly dry.

Physalis (Cape gooseberry): draw back the petals and dip the bulb into pastel shades of fondant.
Strawberries: leave the hull on and dip the fruit in pink-coloured fondant.
Cherries: leave on the stalk and dip the fruit into pink-coloured fondant.
Glacé Fruit: glacé pineapple, cherries etc. dipped into the appropriate coloured fondant.
Small Génoise Fancies: cut a length of Génoise in half lengthways and sandwich it with buttercream, jam, ganache, etc. Cut into various shapes, place on a wire rack and coat with various colours of fondant. Allow to set and decorate with different-coloured fondant piped in various patterns. If buttercream is used in the centre the pieces must be chilled before being coated.

2104 Marzipan Petits Fours

These can be made in several forms:
Dipped
a) Roll out marzipan approx. 6mm thick and cut out with various shapes of small fancy cutters. Place on a wire rack and coat with coloured and flavoured fondant or with melted chocolate.
b) Sandwich two halves of glacé cherries with a small round of marzipan; press half a walnut into a round of marzipan; remove the stone from dates and replace with a piece of marzipan. These can be dipped in sugar syrup cooked to hard crack at 155°C.

Toasted
Roll out marzipan approx. 1cm thick and mark the surface crisscross-fashion. Brush with eggwash, allow to dry then cut into various small shapes. Dredge well with icing sugar and glaze under the salamander. Marzipan may be moulded into miniature shapes, eggwashed and glazed lightly under the salamander.

Sliced
Colour marzipan in up to four contrasting colours, roll out 1cm thick, cut into strips and join together to give a checkerboard or other variegated pattern then cut into approx. 6mm slices.

Modelled
Various kinds of miniature fruits and vegetables can be modelled from appropriate coloured and flavoured marzipan.

2105 Chocolate Brandy Truffles   48

30 mins, plus resting time

Stage	Ingredient	Quantity	Method
1	chocolate, plain	500g	Cut into pieces, place in a basin over a pan of hot water to melt.
2	butter, softened	60g	Add all these ingredients to the chocolate while it is still warm and mix to a smooth paste. Allow to rest overnight.
	cream	2dl	
	egg yolks	5	
	ground almonds	250g	
	vanilla essence	few drops	
	brandy	2 tbsps	
3	cocoa powder ⎫ sifted	50g	Divide the truffle mixture into walnut-sized pieces and coat with the mixed cocoa and sugar.
	icing sugar ⎭ together	100g	

2106 Marquises

Mix 60g Pralin (1703) into 200g Ganache (1691) and use it to sandwich two Langues de Chat (1693) together. Dip both ends into melted chocolate and allow to set. Instead of dipping the ends, the word 'Marquise' can be written in chocolate on each biscuit.

2107 Marshmallows   48

30 mins. plus resting time

Stage	Ingredient	Quantity	Method
1	sugar, granulated	350g	Place in a pan and bring to the boil slowly. Cook until it reaches 127°C on the sugar boiling thermometer.
	glucose	½ tbsp	
	water	1½dl	
2	leaf gelatine	20g	Soak the gelatine in the water and dissolve over heat. Keep warm.
	water	1dl	
3	egg whites	2	Place in a mixing machine and whisk to a stiff peak. Pour the syrup slowly into the centre whisking continuously. Add the dissolved gelatine and continue whisking briskly until the mixture becomes thick, creamy and its bulk is noticeably increased.
4			Pour into a tray previously lined with oiled greaseproof paper. Smooth the surface evenly to approx. 2cm thick and allow to cool and set in a cool place for 4 hours.

Stage	Ingredient	Quantity	Method
5	chocolate, melted (2102) desiccated coconut, toasted icing sugar } sifted cornflour } together	300g 100g 50g 50g	Turn out the marshmallow onto a lightly oiled slab. Cut into cubes and either, a) dip into melted chocolate, placing onto greaseproof paper and removing when set, b) roll into the toasted coconut, or c) roll into the sifted sugar.

2108 Nougat Montélimar

48

40 mins. plus resting time

Stage	Ingredient	Quantity	Method
1	sugar, granulated glucose water	400g ½ tbsp 2dl	Place in a pan, bring to the boil and cook until it reaches 132°C on the sugar boiling thermometer.
2	clear honey, warmed	100g	Add to the syrup and continue cooking to 137°C.
3	almonds, skinned, toasted and halved pistachios, skinned glacé cherries, halved	100g 50g 75g	Have these ready, placed in a basin and kept warm.
4	egg whites	1½ (40g)	Place in a mixing machine and whisk to a stiff peak. Slowly pour the syrup as soon as ready, into the centre whisking continuously. Remove from the machine and mix in the prepared nuts and fruit.
5			Pour the nougat into a 25 × 18 × 2cm deep tray lined with rice paper. Cover with a second sheet of rice paper and a board and weigh it down with a 1kg weight. Leave for 6 hours to set then cut into 2cm squares or oblongs.

2109 Othellos

40

30 mins.

Stage	Ingredient	Quantity	Method
1	egg yolks sugar flour	5 25g 100g	Whisk the yolks and sugar briskly then fold in the flour.
2	egg whites sugar flour	8 100g 100g	Whisk the egg whites with a small pinch of salt to a soft peak. Whisk in half the sugar and continue whisking to a peak. Fold in the rest of the sugar and the flour.
3			Combine the meringue into the yolk mixture.

4 Place the mixture into a piping bag with a 1cm plain tube and pipe 3cm diameter rounds onto a greased and floured baking tray. Bake at 240°C for approx. 5 mins.

NOTE
Two Othellos may be sandwiched together with vanilla-flavoured buttercream.

2110 Palets de Dames   48

30 mins.

Stage	Ingredient	Quantity	Method
1	butter	200g	Cream the butter and sugar until light
	sugar	200g	and fluffy. Add the eggs one at a time,
	eggs	4	mixing in well.
2	flour	275g	Fold the flour into the creamed mixture
	vanilla essence	few drops	and add the vanilla and currants.
	currants	25g	
3			Pipe the mixture through a 1cm plain tube into 3cm diameter discs on a greased baking tray. Bake at 205°C for 8–10 mins.

2111 Parisian Rout Biscuits   48

30 mins. plus resting time

Stage	Ingredient	Quantity	Method
1	sugar, icing	250g	Mix all the ingredients together to a
	ground almonds	250g	smooth consistency.
	whites of egg	2	
2			Place the mixture into a piping bag with a 1½cm fancy tube. Pipe out onto a greased and floured tray into various fancy shapes.
3	glacé fruits	50g	Decorate each biscuit with small pieces
	almonds, flaked	25g	of the fruit, e.g. angelica, glacé cherries, pineapple, or with flaked almonds. Allow the biscuits to rest for approx. 8 hours.
4			Bake the biscuits at 245°C for a few mins. until tinged a golden brown.
5	water	1½dl	Place in a pan and bring to the boil to
	gum arabic powder	25g	dissolve. Brush over the biscuits immediately they come from the oven.

NOTE
Rice paper may be used to line the baking tray.

2112 Peppermint Creams

48
40 mins.

Stage	Ingredient	Quantity	Method
1	Fondant (1687)	750g	Place in a basin in a bain-marie or over a pan of hot water. Allow to melt, stirring gently until it registers 60°C on a sugar boiling thermometer.
2	peppermint essence	few drops	Add to the fondant to give a fairly good taste and aroma.
3			Use a cone dropper or paper cornet to drop the mixture onto a wax paper lined tray making 3cm circles approx. ½cm thick. Allow to set.

SPECIAL POINT
These creams may be dipped or half-dipped in chocolate.

2113 Rum Truffles

48
30 mins.

Stage	Ingredient	Quantity	Method
1	cake crumbs	600g	Mix together in a basin.
	sugar	100g	
	cocoa powder	50g	
2	apricot jam, smooth	100g	Soften the jam with the rum. Add to the crumb mixture and work to a smooth paste.
	rum	2 tbsps	
3	chocolate vermicelli	150g	Mould the mixture into walnut-sized pieces and roll in the vermicelli to cover.

2114 Sablé Biscuits

48
40 mins.

Stage	Ingredient	Quantity	Method
1	butter	175g	Cream the butter and sugar until light and fluffy. Add the yolks one at a time, mixing in well.
	sugar	125g	
	egg yolks	3	
2	flour	200g	Sift together and fold into the creamed mixture.
	ground almonds	50g	
3			Pipe rosettes of the mixture onto a greased and floured baking tray, allowing space between for them to spread.
4	glacé cherries	12	Place a piece of cherry rounded side up in the centre of each biscuit. Bake at 190°C for approx. 10 mins. until lightly browned around the edges.

2115 Tuiles

48

40 mins.

Stage	Ingredient	Quantity	Method
1	egg whites	4	Whisk the egg whites and sugar until slightly frothy. Gently fold in the flour, almonds and butter.
	sugar	200g	
	flour	100g	
	almonds, finely shredded	75g	
	butter, melted	75g	
2	sugar, icing		Place dessertspoonfuls of the mixture on a lightly greased baking tray, leaving space between for them to spread. Sprinkle with icing sugar.
3			Bake the biscuits at 240°C for 4–5 mins. Remove and lay over rolling pins pressing lightly to take the shape. Leave until cool.

2116 Turkish Delight

48

30 mins. plus resting time

Stage	Ingredient	Quantity	Method
1	cornflour	55g	Dilute the cornflour with 1dl of the water. Place the remaining water in a pan with the sugar. Bring to the boil and cook to approx. 112°C on the sugar boiling thermometer. Add the lemon juice, shake to mix in then remove from the heat to cool a little.
	water	3dl	
	sugar, granulated	375g	
	lemon juice	1 tbsp	
2			Pour and quickly mix in the diluted cornflour with the syrup. Stir to the boil and simmer gently for 3–4 mins.
3	leaf gelatine	15g	Have the gelatine ready soaked in the water, dissolved over heat and kept warm; then add to the syrup and simmer gently for 2–3 mins. more.
	water	1dl	
4	rosewater or other flavouring and appropriate colour		Flavour and colour the syrup as required, allow to cool a little then pour into a suitable tray oiled and dusted with icing sugar, approx. 2cm deep. Allow to set in a cool place for at least 6 hours.
5	icing sugar ⎱ sifted	50g	Dust a board with some of the sifted sugar. Turn out the Turkish delight on top, sprinkle with more sifted sugar, then cut into approx. 2cm cubes. Roll in the remaining sugar. Use as required or store in a closed container mixed with the remaining sugar. Keep in a cool place.
	cornflour ⎰ together	50g	

2117 Vanilla Fudge

48

30 mins.

Stage	Ingredient	Quantity	Method
1	sugar	1kg	Place all the ingredients into a pan. Heat slowly and stir until it comes to the boil. Allow to simmer for 2 mins. then cook until it registers 115° on the saccharometer.
	butter	100g	
	golden syrup	100g	
	evaporated milk	2½dl	
2	vanilla essence	few drops	Add to the mixture and beat it vigorously until it becomes creamy. Pour into a shallow tin approx. 20cm × 15cm lined with greaseproof paper.
3			Allow to set then cut into 2½cm squares.

SPECIAL POINT

Chopped nuts or glacé cherries may be added to the mixture and it may be flavoured at Stage 2 with chocolate or coffee essence or any suitable liqueur or spirit.

2118 Viennese Fingers

36

40 mins.

Stage	Ingredient	Quantity	Method
1	butter	350g	Cream the butter and sugar until light. Sift the flour and cornflour together and mix into the butter. Mix well together.
	sugar, icing	100g	
	flour	250g	
	cornflour	100g	
2			Fill the mixture into a piping bag with a 1cm fancy tube and pipe approx. 5cm lengths on a tray lined with greased greaseproof paper. Bake at 180°C for approx. 12 mins.
3	chocolate, melted (2102)	150g	Allow the biscuits to cool then dip both ends into the melted chocolate and allow to set.

Glossary

The following list is intended to be used as a source of further information to that already given or insufficiently described in the recipes.

abatis: specifically the giblets of poultry or game birds

abats: the offals of the animal carcase such as the heart, liver, kidneys and tripe etc.

aiguillettes: long thin slices of cooked meat more usually cut from the breast of poultry and game birds

ail: garlic aileron: winglet of poultry

aloyau: a whole unboned sirloin of beef including the fillet

amuses-bouches: fanciful name used to describe an assortment of cocktail canapés and small savoury appetisers

appareil: a prepared mixture of food made ready for further processing

aromats or aromates: aromatic vegetables and herbs used to impart flavour

aspic: originally an entrée moulded in savoury jelly but now used as a short descriptive term for the clear savoury jelly itself

assiette anglaise: a selection of sliced cold meats

bain-marie: container of hot water for keeping prepared food hot or for slowing down a cooking process

ballotine: a boned, stuffed and tied item of meat, poultry or game. The leg of chicken and the shoulder of lamb are frequently prepared in this manner

balsamic vinegar: rich, sweet and sour vinegar made with the juice of Trebbiano grapes, *aged for several years*

balti: the cookery of Pakistan and the wok-shaped pan it is cooked and served in, mainly highly-spiced curries

bean curd: thick paste made of soya beans set with gypsum; not much natural taste but high in protein much used in Southeast Asian cookery

to bard: to cover with thin slices of fat bacon or salt pork fat; commonly applied to items of meat, poultry and game

baron: a double sirloin together with the rumps of beef as a whole joint; also the whole saddle and two legs of lamb. In either case as one whole joint

to beard: to remove the surrounding frilly part from shellfish such as mussels, oysters and scallops

à blanc (cuisson): the cooking of items of food in such a manner as to preserve or enhance their light colour

à la broche (rôti): roasted on a spit in front of or over an open fire, e.g. Poulet rôti à la Broche (Spit-roasted Chicken)

au beurre: buttered, or cooked with butter

au blanc (cuisson): the cooking of items such as salsifis or calf's head in an acidulated liquid called a Blanc (15) so as to prevent discolouration

Bombay duck: this refers to the bummaloe fish, native to the coastal waters of India; it is opened out, the central bone is removed and it is then sun-dried. Used as an accompaniment to curry

boulangerie: the bakery department

bresaola: cured, air-dried quality beef carved very thinly and served as an appetizer with oil and lemon

brine: a salted and flavoured liquid used for the salt curing of meat

au bleu (cuisson): a method for cooking freshly killed freshwater fish, especially trout, in an acidulated liquid which results in the natural coating of the fish becoming a smoky blue.

brochette: a skewer; also used as a term to describe items of food threaded on a skewer and grilled

broil: to grill. An alternative American word

en buisson: to dress small items of food on top of each other in a pile

bündnerfleisch: salt-cured and air-dried beef, cut in very thin slices and served as an hors-d'oeuvre. Originates from the alpine valleys of the Grisons in Switzerland

cajun: simple but hearty cuisine dating from the French occupation of Louisiana, USA. It uses alligator, rabbit and racoon and is especial to New Orleans

Calvados: French apple brandy distilled from cider

carapace: the shell of any crustacean such as lobster or crab etc.

carpaccio: very thin slices of raw fillet of beef served with oil and lemon juice as an appetiser; shavings of Parmesan may be added

caul: fatty membrane lining the cavity of the abdomen; that from the pig is widely used to enclose savoury salpicons or other mixtures, e.g. Cromesquis, faggots, crépinettes

cassolette: small individual earthenware or porcelain fireproof dish in which food can be cooked and served; also refers to a small pleated paper case

cep: a large, edible fleshy fungus, known also as the flap mushroom (Fr. cèpe)

chanterelle: delicate mushroom with a fragrant flavour and aroma; trumpet-shaped and yellowish in colour

charcuterie: items of pork butchery

chatrer: to gut or remove the trail, especially of crayfish

chef de partie: a chef in charge of a secdon in the kitchen

chemiser: to line a mould or coat an item of food with jelly

chilli: pod of the many varieties of Capsicum Frutescens; they have a very hot peppery and pungent taste. Used fresh, dried or processed into flakes or as cayenne paper

to clarify: to clear of impurities and sediment as in the making of consommé

collop: meat or fish cut into thin or thick round slices and of the required size

concasser: to roughly chop

contrefilet: a boned-out sirloin of beef

coquille: the shell of any mollusc such as oyster, scallop, mussel etc.

cordon: indicates a line or circle of sauce poured round an item of cooked food when placed on its serving dish

coulis: cullis; a concentrated sauce or liquid purée prepared from the ingredients used in the making of the sauce

couscous: Moroccan speciality of coarsely ground millet or semolina moistened with water and steamed over a panful of stock, lamb, beef, chicken, vegetables and chickpeas

crème fraîche: bland, slightly sour cream made in varying degrees of fat content

creole: French, Spanish, African and USA-inspired cuisine based on New Orleans produce

cru: raw

cuisson: the process of cooking; also a general term for a cooking liquid

cuissot: a large leg, e.g. of pork or venison

Curaçao: liqueur made from bitter oranges

dariole mould: a small deep round mould with sloping sides

decant: to pour off a liquid after allowing any sediment or particles to settle

decorticate: to remove the shell, e.g. to shell prawns

déjeuner: lunch

al dente: descriptive Italian term to indicate the cooking of pasta to the stage where it still retains a firmness of bite, 'to the teeth'

diablé: devilled; a hot peppery taste given to food

doily: a decorative round dish paper

dorer: to colour or cook to a light golden brown

émincer: to slice thinly or cut into small thinnish pieces

emu swaggies: proprietary brand pie made with rice noodle pastry filled with well-peppered chopped emu meat, deep fried

entrée: a light main dish of meat, poultry or game prepared and garnished and distinct from a joint or large item for a number of people

entremets: sweet dishes

entremettier: the vegetable chef

estouffade: brown stock; also the name given to a particular type of brown beef stew

en éventail: a method of arranging food fan-shape on the serving dish

faux-filet: a boned and trimmed sirloin of beef

fécule or fecula: starch such as arrowroot, cornflour or potato flour

Filo pastry: made by mixing 4dl of warm water with 1dl olive oil, adding it to 600g strong flour sifted with 1tsp salt to form a dough. After resting for 1 hour it is rolled out tissue paper thin, preferably using a rolling machine. It dries quickly and should be used immediately, or frozen for future use. Also spelt Phyllo, it is used for Greek-style pies and flans both savoury and sweet and in the syrup-drenched pastries and cakes such as Baklavà

fines herbes: the fine herbs; usually considered to be chives, chervil, tarragon and parsley.

flair pork fat: first quality pork fat which covers the inner sides of the loins and encloses the kidneys

au four (cuisson): cooking or baking in the oven, e.g. Pommes au Four (Baked Potatoes)

fourrer: to fill or stuff an item of food, e.g. when filling an omelette with a garnish

frappé: well-chilled

friandises: another name for petits fours

fromage frais: soft fresh cheese made from the curds of skimmed, pasteurised milk

fumet: a stock having a fairly concentrated and dominant flavour and aroma derived from a particular ingredient, e.g. Fumet de Caille; in this case the quail provides the dominant flavour and aroma, and names the fumet

garde-manger: the larder chef

gaufrettes: wafers as served with ice-cream

ghee: a type of clarified butter used extensively in Indian cookery

gigue: descriptive term specifically for the leg of venison

givre: frosted

to glaze: this descriptive term has many applications; the following are the most common:
1) to coat a food with aspic jelly
2) to colour food under the salamander, especially certain types of sauce
3) to cook vegetables with a little sugar, stock or water until evaporated and imparting a glossy coating
4) to sprinkle with sugar and to cook to a glossy coating in the oven or under the salamander.

au gratin: sprinkled with grated cheese or breadcrumbs and browned in the oven or under the salamander

gravlax or gravlaks: fresh raw salmon cured with salt, sugar and dill and sometimes with other flavourings and spirits. Served raw, cut in thin slices

grillardin: the grill chef

gross sel: coarse salt

hâtelet: ornamental skewer mainly used in the decoration of large cold buffet items

haunch: the hindquarter of venison consisting of the leg and loin

haute cuisine: the finest of high-class cookery

incise: to make shallow cuts in the flesh of whole fish for grilling or shallow frying to assist even cooking

to infuse: to extract the flavour and aroma of an ingredient by covering it with a boiling liquid and allowing it to stand for a suitable time

jus: gravy, as in Jus lie (thickened gravy); juice, as in jus de citron (lemon juice)

kangaroo swaggies: as emu swaggies using kangaroo meat, reheated for serving; a proprietary brand name

Kirsch: clear white spirit distilled from a base of wild cherries

korma: mild milk-flavoured curry of chicken, lamb or prawns

liaison: a thickening or binding agent such as egg yolk or egg yolks and cream

luter: to seal the lid of a cooking utensil with a strip of dough or pastry so as to minimise loss of moisture and aroma from the cooking process when placed in the oven

to macerate: to steep in wine or liqueur, especially fruit, which allows an interchange of flavours; the fruit and its liquid are usually served together

magrets: these are the plump well-formed breasts obtained from specially reared breeds of French ducks and geese.

mandolin: utensil used for slicing vegetables

Maraschino: liqueur made from a base of the juice and crushed kernels of the sour Marasca cherry

Marc: spirit distilled from a base of the skins and pips left after the crushing of grapes

to marinate: to tenderise and flavour food, especially meat, by placing in a liquid such as wine with aromats and herbs

marmite: earthenware or porcelain container used for the cooking and serving of soups; also refers to the stock-pot

matelote: type of fish stew

médaillon: round or oval, flat-shaped cut of meat or fish

mignardises; anodler name for petits fours

mignonnette pepper: coarsely milled pepper

mirin: Japanese rice wine used for cooking purposes similar to sweet sherry

mitan: middle-cut of fish especially of salmon

morel: an excellent-flavoured fungus having a pitted brown, conical-shaped cap

mortifier: to hang meat or game for a predetermined period of time so as to tenderise and develop its flavour

à la nage: indicates a style of preparation particular to crustaceans in which the shellfish is cooked and served in a court-bouillon

napper: to coat food with a sauce

natives: menu term denoting English oysters; the flat oyster (Ostrea Edulis) raised from indigenous stock in English waters

panaché: mixed or variegated

paner: to egg-and-breadcrumb

en papillote: a method of cooking and presenting food in a paper or foil case

Pauillac: refers to milk-fed lamb from the district of that name in France

petit-salé: brine-cured belly of pork

petits fours: an assortment of sweetmeats served at the end of a meal

physalis: another name for the cape gooseberry

pine nuts: the seeds from the cone of the stone pine

pistachio: small nut with reddish-brown skin and pale green flesh

plat à sauter: shallow pan with straight sides used for shallow frying; referred to commonly as a sauté pan

poêle: frying-pan

pralin: almonds and sometimes hazelnuts added to sugar at caramel stage, then cooled and crushed. Used in pastry work. Not to be confused with praline. See the following

praline: a sugared almond, a speciality of French confectionery

praliné: pralined; descriptive of pralin being incorporated in the preparation of a dish and in its tide, e.g. Gateau Praliné or Glace Pralinée

pré-salé: descriptive term applied to lamb reared on salt meadows near the coast

primeurs: young spring vegetables

prosciutto: name given to cured ham served raw, e.g. Prosciutto di Parma (Parma ham)

purée: foods reduced to a smooth pulp

quark: soft, smooth and very bland cheese made from the curds of whole or skimmed milk

quatre épices: mixture of ground spices commonly used in the proportion of 12 parts white pepper, 3 parts ginger, 3 parts nutmeg and 1 part cloves

racines: root vegetables such as carrots, turnips and swedes etc.

rapé: grated

ravier: small dish used for the service of hors-d'oeuvre

réchauffer: to reheat

relevé: relates to braised, roast or poêléed joints of meat, poultry or game, specifically with a garnish; highly spiced or seasoned

refresh: to cool; or cool rapidly under cold running water

rennet: secretion from the calf's stomach used to set milk for junket

rocher: menu term used to denote a scoop of ice-cream

rognures: trimmings of puff pastry used where the rising of full puff pastry is not required or necessary

rondeau: a large round shallow pan

saccharometer: an instrument used for measuring the density of a syrup

saffron: the dried stamens of the Crocus Sativus, a member of the iris family. Used for flavouring and colouring

sago: starchy pith of the sago palm processed into granules

salmis: a brown, feathered game stew

salpicon: a mixture of diced meats, vegetables or fruit etc. usually mixed together with a sauce and used as a filling

sauerkraut (Fr. choucroute): shredded and salted white cabbage

sauter: to shallow fry; to toss over while frying

sauteuse: shallow pan with sloping sides

score: to cut shallow incisions in an item of food

semolina: first grinding of wheat before it becomes flour

soya bean: a legume having a high protein content; used as a base for the making of soy sauce and Textured Vegetable Protein

soy sauce: flavouring liquid much used in Oriental cookery speck: salt pork fat

Tabasco: proprietary brand of pepper sauce

tapioca: starchy substance from the root of the cassava plant

terrine: deep earthenware or porcelain fireproof dish, usually oval or round and with a lid

timbale: deep round silver dish used for the serving of food tourner: usually denotes trimming to a barrel shape tranche: a slice or cut

tofu: pressed paste made of fermented soya beans with smooth texture and delicate flavour; can be eaten raw, sut into slices and fried or grilled; available as firm or silky in texture

tortilla: cornmeal pancakes made into taco shells which are deep fried and filled with chicken, lettuce, guacamole burritos stuffed with re-fried beans, egg, cheese, etc. and folded

à la vapeur (cuisson): cooking by steam, e.g. Pommes à la Vapeur (Steamed Potatoes)

vegan: person who is a vegetarian but in addition eats no dairy products or eggs

vegemite: concentrated yeast extract rich in B vitamins used as flavouring in savoury pastries, sandwiches, etc., as a healthy drink and vegetarian stock

vegetarian: a person whose diet excludes all meat, fish, poultry and game

vésiga: dried spinal cord of fish, particularly the sturgeon and allied species; used in Russian cookery

vindaloo: hot-tasting curry soured with tamarind liquid and vinegar, usually of pork or chicken with potatoes and pimentos

voiler: to veil, as in the case of covering or surrounding a sweet dish with spun sugar

vol-au-vent: puff pastry case formerly made in a size sufficient for 4–6 persons. Now more usually made in individual sizes

wild rice: aquatic plant producing seeds which have the general appearance of brown rice. It is not a true rice

wok: round-bottomed pan that fits in the open stove top. Particular to Chinese cooking

Xérès: the correct name in French of sherry

yoghurt: milk cultured with a lactobacillus to produce an acidic taste and a thick to semi-solid consistency

zabaglione: a sweet dish made of whisked egg yolks, sugar and wine or liqueur

zest: the outer rind of any citrus fruit such as orange or lemon, completely free of pith

Appendix 1

The following list gives the names, suitable cooking methods and best season for the most popular fish found in the waters in and around Australia and New Zealand.

Name	Suitable cooking methods	Best season
Barramandi	all recipes for cod	Oct.–Mar.
Blue Grenadier (called Hoki in New Zealand)	baking, deep and shallow frying, grilling	Mar.–Oct.
Boarfish (4 varieties)	baking, braising, poaching	all year
Cod (9 varieties including freshwater)	as for UK	all year
Dart	baking, shallow frying	Oct.–May
Dhufish	grilling, poaching, shallow frying	autumn and winter (Australia)
Emperor	baking, braising, frying, grilling, poaching	all year
Flathead	deep and shallow frying, baking	Apr.–Jun.
Garfish	boiling, frying, grilling	all year
Gemfish	as for hake	Jun.–Aug.
Gurnard	baking, deep and shallow frying, poaching, stewing	Jul.–Feb.
Hapuka (similar to Sea Bass, previously called Groper)	roasting	Apr.–Aug.
Jewfish	all methods	all year
Kingfish (2 varieties)	baking, braising, grilling, poaching	all year
Leatherjacket	baking, deep and shallow frying, grilling	Dec.–Mar.
Luderick (like River Bream)	baking, braising, shallow and deep frying, roasting	Mar.–Jul.
Morwong (like Sea Bream)	as for luderick	Mar.–Jul.
Mulloway	as for cod	all year
Oriental Bonito	as for tuna	all year
Parrot Fish	baking, braising, deep and shallow frying, poaching, grilling	all year best during Jun.
Pomfret	baking, braising, frying, grilling, poaching	all year
Redfish	baking, braising, deep and shallow frying, grilling	all year
Ribbonfish	baking, deep and shallow frying, grilling (usually cut into darnes)	Apr.–Aug.
Shark (8 varieties)	in fillets is sold as flake	all year

Name	Suitable cooking methods	Best season
Snapper (3 varieties)	baking, braising, grilling	all year
Tailor	as tuna	Nov.–Apr.
Trevally (4 varieties)	baking, braising, grilling, deep and shallow frying	all year
Trumpeter	all methods	all year
Tuna	baking, braising, shallow frying, grilling	all year
Warehou (2 varieties)	as trevally	all year
Wrasse (also called parrot fish)	(see parrot fish)	all year

Australian shellfish are as follows, available raw, cooked and frozen:

Crustaceans

    Bugs (3 varieties) – like lobsters

    Crabs (7 varieties)

    Marron, Redclaw and Yabbie are freshwater crayfish.

    Prawns (9 varieties)

    Rock Lobsters (4 varieties) – crawfish

    Scampi – similar to Dublin Bay Prawns

    Shrimps are imported

Molluses

    Abalone (4 varieties)   ear-shaped shell with a row of holes

    Beche-de-Mer   elongated body; the dried body is known as trepang

    Calamari   Italian name for cuttlefish

    Clams   burrowing bivalve, requires beating to tenderise it

    Cockles   has rounded shell with radiating ribs

    Cuttlefish   a cephalopod with a broad, flattened body and cuttlebone

    Mussels (2 varieties)   blue bivalve shells, most popular cooked mollusc

    Octopus   cephalopod mollusc with soft oval body and 8 tentacles

    Oysters (5 varieties)   reared in pure coastal waters; usually eaten raw

    Paua   similar to abalone

    Pipi   similar to cockle

    Scallops (3 varieties)   fluted fan-shaped shell, white flesh with red tongue

    Squid   torpedo-shaped body similar to cuttlefish with tentacles

    Sea Urchin   spiny globular body found in shallow waters

Appendix 2

The following list gives the names and descriptions of the main salad leaves:

Amaranti Spinach: heart-shaped pointed leaves with purple veins and green edge and strong flavour

Baby Tatsoi: mild, earthy flavour sold as plants and as leaves much used in Asian salads.

Burnet: round, indented small leaves with a strong cucumber smell and flavour

Chard: available as green, red and yellow leaves with a sappy taste which adds some sharpness to mixed salads

Chrysanthemum: long leaves with deep grooves and an intense flavour much used in Thai dishes

Endive: frizzy endive has curly, pale green leaves with a firmness and slightly sharp flavour; Belgian endives are known as chicory and are white, bulbous and bitter

Erba Stellar: leaves of an attractive pale green colour and mild flavour

Kale: sharp, peppery taste which stands out; purple or white leaves with frilly ends

Lettuces: available as Cabbage, the round kind; Cos, the elongated dark green one; Little Gem, which look like baby cabbage lettuces; iceberg, which is firm, crisp and large; Webb's Wonder, which is crisp and tasty and Chinese cabbage

Mizuna: elongated, spiky leaves deeply indented with a mild flavour and mid-green colour, also spelt Mibuna

Monet: mild-flavoured large flat leaves which have a long central stalk

Nasturtium: peppery taste that adds piquancy to a salad; the flowers can also be used

Neva: deep flat leaves with a mild flavour and green to purple colour

Radicchio or red-leaved chicory: red and variegated green in colour, full, bitter flavour often used as a garnish with food as well as in salads.

Red Coral: available as green or browny-purple leaves with tightly frilled edges

Red Festival: available as red and lime-green leaves with a mild flavour; often used to decorate foods

Red Velvet: dark, deep red leaves with a mild, grassy flavour

Rocket: available as cultivated and wild, deep, pointed indentations in the dark green leaves with sharp, peppery taste; the cultivated leaves are wider than the uncultivated

Spinach: baby spinach with tender, delicate leaves is ideal for salad making

Wild Fennel Leaves: deep green feathery strands with a slight aniseed flavour

Select Bibliography

The following list of books is given for the use of those readers who wish to extend their knowledge of any particular aspect of cooking beyond the scope of this book or who want to study in greater detail any particular culinary technique.

REFERENCE

AXFORD, L. B., *English Language Cookbooks 1600–1973*, Gale Research, 1976.
BICKEL, W. (ed.), *Hering's Dictionary of Classical and Modern Cookery*, Virtue, 1980.
ESCOFFIER, A., *The Complete Guide to the Art of Modern Cookery*, Heinemann, 1979.
MONTAGNE, P., *New Larousse Gastronomique*, Hamlyn, 1977.
SAULNIER, L., *Le Répertoire de la Cuisine*, Jaeggi, All editions.

NATIONAL, ETHNIC AND SPECIAL SUBJECT COOKERY

BACHMANN, W. (ed.), *Continental Confectionery*, Maclaren, 1955.
BOYD, L. (ed.), *British Cookery*, Croom Helm, 1976.
BRADSHAW, G., *Cooking at the Table*, New English Library, 1971.
BRUN, P. and le PRAT, A., *Russian Cooking*, Hamlyn, 1990.
CARNACINA, L., *Great Italian Cooking*, Hamlyn, 1969.
ELLIOT, P., *Vegetarian Cooking*, Collins, 1988.
FANCE, W. J. (ed.), *The New International Confectioner*, Virtue, 1976.
FULLER, J., *Guéridon and Lamp Cookery*, Hutchinson, 1987.
GRANGER, A. (ed.), *A Taste of the Orient*, Macdonald, 1987.
GRIGSON, J., *Fruit Book*, Penguin, 1982.
GRIGSON, J., *Vegetable Book*, Penguin, 1979.
GUERARD, M., *Cuisine Gourmande*, Macmillan, 1978.
ITALIAN ACADEMY OF COOKERY, *The Italian Cookery Book*, Pelham Books, 1987.
KRAMER, R. (ed.), *Meat Dishes in the International Cuisine*, Virtue, 1983.
LAMBERT ORTIZ, E., *Caribbean Cookery*, Penguin, 1977.
LEONARD, L., *Jewish Cooking*, André Deutsch, 1968.
LETO, M. J. and BODE, W. K. A., *The Larder Chef*, Heinemann, 1989.
LUARD, E., *European Peasant Cookery*, Bantam Press, 1986.
LUI, H. J. and T., *Chinese Gastronomy*, Nelson, 1982.
MANJON, M., *Gastronomy of Spain and Portugal*, Garamond, 1989.
MORRIS, S., *South-East Asian Cookery*, Grafton, 1989.
ROBBINS, C., *The Healthy Caterers' Manual*, Dorling Kindersley, 1989.
RODEN, C., *New Book of Middle East Food*, Viking, 1985.
SAHNI, J., *Classic Indian Cookery*, Dorling Kindersley, 1986.

SIMMS, A. E. (ed.), *Fish and Shellfish*, Virtue, 1973.
SMALL, M. (ed.), *Buffets and Receptions*, Virtue, 1978.
TOZUKA, I. (ed. consultant), *Japanese Cooking Class Cookbook*, Windward, 1984.
TROISGROS, T. and P., *The Nouvelle Cuisine*, Macmillan, 1980.
WAKEMAN, A. and BASKERVILLE, G., *Vegan Cookery*, Faber & Faber, 1986.
TIME LIFE, *Foods of the World Library*, All editions.

Index

This index uses both English and French terms. Where appropriate, groups of dishes have been entered under separate general headings with their range of recipe numbers given in parentheses.

Recipe

A

(1822)	Abricots Colbert	777
(710)	Agneau Boulangère, Carré	284
(724)	Agneau Boulangère, Epaule	292
(731)	Agneau Boulangère, Gigot	294
(732)	Agneau Bretonne, Gigot	294
(742)	Agneau Clamart, Longe	300
(743)	Agneau Dubarry, Longe	300
(744)	Agneau Niçoise, Longe	300
(741)	Agneau poêlée, Longe	299
(760)	Agneau poêlée Cadmos, Selle	307
(745)	Agneau Saint-Mandé, Longe	301
(706)	Agneau, Blanquette	283
(707)	Agneau, Blanquette à l'Ancienne	283
(708)	Agneau, Blanquette à la Menagere	284
(709)	Agneau, Carré Persillé	284
(711)	Agneau, Chop braisé	285
(713)	Agneau, Coeur braisé	286
(1285)	Agneau, Côtelettes en Chaud-froid Bouquetière	556
(714)	Agneau, Côtelettes Maintenon	287
(715)	Agneau, Côtelettes Milanaise	288
(716)	Agneau, Côtelettes Napolitaine	288
(717)	Agneau, Côtelettes panées	288
(718)	Agneau, Côtelettes Réforme	288
(720)	Agneau, Currie	289
(725)	Agneau, Epigrammes	292
(726)	Agneau, Filets Mignons	293
(727)	Agneau, Filets Mignons Persane	293
(728)	Agneau, Foie	293
(729)	Agneau, Fricassée	294

Recipe

(730)	Agneau, Fricassée à l'Ancienne	294
(737)	Agneau, Kebab	297
(739)	Agneau, Langue braisée aux Cornichons	298
(740)	Agneau, Langue Poulette	299
(748)	Agneau, Navarin	302
(750)	Agneau, Noisettes Choisy	303
(751)	Agneau, Noisettes Clamart	304
(752)	Agneau, Noisettes Dubarry	304
(753)	Agneau, Noisettes Mascotte	305
(754)	Agneau, Noisettes Niçoise	305
	Agneau, Ris	305
(755)	Agneau, Rognons sautés	306
(756)	Agneau, Rognons sautés au Madère	306
(757)	Agneau, Rognons sautés Turbigo	306
(759)	Agneau, Selle	307
(1286)	Agneau, Selle froide Marly	556
	Aiglefin	190
(1105)	Aiguillettes de Caneton au Porto	457
(1104)	Aiguillettes de Caneton Bigarade	456
(1129)	Aileron de Dinde braisé Anversoise	468
(180)	Aïoli	76
	Alfalfa	611
	Alligator	182
(1621)	Allumettes d'Anchois	696
(1671)	Almonds, to toast	717
(1324)	American Dressing	584
(1925)	Ananas Créole	812
(1860)	Ananas flambé au Kirsch	793
(201)	Anchoïade	81
(1621)	Anchois, Allumettes	696
(1631)	Anchois, Canapé	699

Recipe

(1648)	Anchois, Dartois	705
(1631)	Anchovies on Toast	699
(4)	Anchovy Butter	20
(227)	Anchovy Fillets	91
(1621)	Anchovy Fingers	696
(162)	Anchovy Sauce	69
(1622)	Angels on Horseback	696
(1622)	Anges à Cheval	696
(541)	Anguille à la Bourguignonne, Matelote	190
(542)	Anguille à la Normande	190
(300)	Anguille Fumée	106
(1823)	Apfelstrudel	778
(1776)	Apple Band	757
(1841)	Apple Charlotte	786
(1898)	Apple Dumpling, baked	805
(1791)	Apple Flan	761
(1981)	Apple Fool	827
(1835)	Apple Fritters	783
(209)	Apple Sauce	84
(1844)	Apple Turnover	787
(1877)	Apple, Baked	799
(42)	Apple, Raisin and Walnut Stuffing	29
(1963)	Apples, poached	821
(1969)	Apples, stewed	822
(1767)	Apricot Band (fresh fruit)	754
(1768)	Apricot Band (poached or tinned fruit)	755
(1979)	Apricot Condé	826
(1782)	Apricot Flan (fresh fruit)	758
(1781)	Apricot Flan (tinned or poached fruit)	758
(1830)	Apricot Fritters	781
(1672)	Apricot Glaze	718
(2030)	Apricot Water Ice	849
(1948)	Apricots, poached	820
(1966)	Apricots, stewed	822
(1377)	Artichaut Nature, Sauces Diverses	606
(215)	Artichauts à la Grecque	88
(216)	Artichauts à la Grecque, Fonds	88
(1378)	Artichauts Barigoule	606

Recipe

(253) Artichauts for
Hors-d'Oeuvre 95
(1379) Artichauts, Fonds 607
(1380) Artichauts, Fonds farcis 607
(1381) Artichauts, Fonds
sautés au Basilic 607
(1379) Artichoke Bottoms 607
(1381) Artichoke Bottoms
sautéed with Basil 607
(1380) Artichoke Bottoms,
stuffed 607
(1377) Artichoke, Globe,
boiled with various
sauces 606
(253) Artichokes, Globe for
Hors-d'Oeuvre 95
Artichokes, Globe
(1377–81), *see also*
under Artichaut
Artichokes, Jerusalem
(1521–3), *see also under*
Topinambours
(1521) Artichokes, Jerusalem
boiled 650
(1522) Artichokes, Jerusalem,
Creamed 650
(1523) Artichokes, Jerusalem,
parslied 650
Asparagus (1382–8), *see*
also under Asperges
(254) Asparagus for
Hors-d'Oeuvre 95
(1388) Asparagus Sprue 609
(1386) Asparagus Tips 609
(1383) Asparagus, boiled with
various sauces 608
(387) Asparagus, Cream of 133
(1382) Asparagus, preparation 608
(1384) Asperges au Gratin 609
(1383) Asperges bouillies,
Sauces Diverses 608
(254) Asperges for
Hors-d'Oeuvres 95
(1385) Asperges Milanaise 609
(1386) Asperges, Pointes 609
(1242) Aspic Jelly, basic 538
(1243) Aspic Jelly, chicken 538
(1249) Aspic Jelly, coating à
dish 540
(1244) Aspic Jelly, Duck 538
(1246) Aspic Jelly, Fish 539
(1245) Aspic Jelly, Game 538
(1247) Aspic Jelly, glazing with 539
(1248) Aspic Jelly, lining or
chemising a mould 540
(1260) Attelets 544
(1389) Aubergine à
l'Egyptienne 610
(1390) Aubergine farcie 610
(1391) Aubergine frite 611
(414) Avocado and Tomato
Soup, chilled 144
(1325) Avocado Dressing 585
(255) Avocado Pear with

Recipe

French Dressing 96
(256) Avocado Pear with
Prawns 96
(256) Avocat aux Crevettes 96
(257) Avocat Côte d'Azur 96
(255) Avocat Vinaigrette 96

B

(1745) Babas au Rhum 743
(1745) Babas, Rum 743
Bacon joints, weights
and preparation
(871–5)
Bacon, small cuts
(876–7)
(1877) Baked Apple 799
(1825) Baked Devonshire Roll 779
(1828) Baked Egg Custard 780
(1824) Baked Fruit or Jam
Roll 778
(1826) Baked Jam Roll 779
(1827) Baked Syrup Roll 780
(1765) Bakewell Tart 753
(1050) Ballotine de Volaille
braisée 423
(1783) Banana Flan 759
(1832) Banana Fritters 782
(2021) Banana Ice-cream 847
(1861) Banane flambée au
Rhum 793
(1769) Bande à l'Ananas 756
(1778) Bande à la Rhubarbe 757
(1767) Bande aux Abricots
(fresh fruit) 754
(1768) Bande aux Abricots
(poached or tinned
fruit) 755
(1770) Bande aux Cerises 756
(1771) Bande aux Fraises 756
(1772) Bande aux Framboises 756
(1773) Bande aux Groseilles
Vertes 756
(1774) Bande aux Mandarines 756
(1775) Bande aux Poires 756
(1776) Bande aux Pommes 757
(1766) Bandes aux Fruits 754
(1777) Bandes aux Prunes
variées 757
(543) Bar au Beurre Blanc 191
(544) Bar grillé au Fenouil 192
Barbue 192
(1) Barding 19
Barnsley Chop 278
(1764) Barquette Moulds, to
line 753
(1624) Barquettes aux
Crevettes 697
(1796) Barquettes aux Fruits 764
(1623) Barquettes, savoury 697
Bass *see also under* Bar
(544) Bass, grilled with
Fennel Sauce 192
(1751) Bath Buns 747

Recipe

(76) Batter, frying 37
(1744) Batter, frying (for
pastrywork) 743
Bavarois (1926–38)
(1934) Bavarois à l'Orange 816
(1927) Bavarois au Café 814
(1928) Bavarois au Chocolat 814
(1929) Bavarois au Citron 814
(1930) Bavarois aux Fraises
(with Crème Anglaise) 814
(1931) Bavarois aux Fraises
(with sugar syrup) 815
(1932) Bavarois aux
Framboises 815
(1933) Bavarois Nesselrode 815
(1935) Bavarois Praliné 816
(1936) Bavarois Religieuse 816
(1937) Bavarois Rubané 816
(1938) Bavarois Vanille 816
(1392) Bean Sprouts, Sweet
and Sour 611
Beans, Broad (1464–6),
see also under Fèves
(1471) Beans, Flageolet 636
Beans, French
(1474–7), *see also under*
Haricots Verts
(1471) Beans, Green Kidney 636
Beans, Haricot
(1467–9) *see also under*
Haricots Blancs
(1472) Beans, Lima 636
(1530) Beans, Mixed, Buttered 654
(1473) Beans, Red Kidney 636
(1470) Beans, Runner 636
(1186) Bécasse à la Fine
Champagne 509
(1187) Bécasse au Fumet 509
(1188) Bécasse, Mignonnettes
Westphauenne 509
(1189) Bécasse, Salmis 511
Beef Baby 364
Beef dishes, *see also*
under Boeuf
Beef Médaillons, *see*
under Tournedos
(831) Beef Olive 331
(237) Beef Salad 93
(799) Beef, boiled French
Style 316
(832) Beef, braised 332
(809) Beef, Curried 321
Beef, Fillet (821–7)
(797) Beef, grills 315
Beef, main joints,
weights and
preparations (761–79)
Beef, offals (790–4)
(1290) Beef, Pressed 558
(795) Beef, Roast 313
(804) Beef, Sirloin 320
Beef, small cuts
(780–9)
(836) Beef, stewed 335

Recipe

Beef, Tournedos
(848–53)

Beetroot (1393–5), *see
also under* Betterave

(1338) Beetroot Salad   588

 (236) Beetroot Salad for
Hors-d'Oeuvres   93

(1393) Beetroot, Baby,
buttered   612

(1829) Beignets   780

(18303 Beignets d'Abricots   781

(1831) Beignets d'Ananas   782

(1832) Beignets de Bananes   782

(1833) Beignets de Crème
Pralinée   783

(1834) Beignets de Fraises   783

(1524) Beignets de Légumes   651

(1835) Beignets de Pommes   783

(1836) Beignets Soufflés   784

(1625) Beignets Soufflés au
Fromage   697

(1626) Beignets Soufflés au
Parmesan   698

(1838) Beignets Soufflés
Dijonnaise   784

(1837) Beignets Soufflés
Parisienne   784

(1394) Betterave farcie à la
Russe   612

(1395) Betteraves à la
Viennoise   613

(1393) Betteraves au Beurre   612

   (6) Beurre à la
Bourguignonne   20

   (5) Beurre Bercy   20

  (14) Beurre Chivry   21

   (7) Beurre Clarifié   20

   (3) Beurre d'Ail   19

   (4) Beurre d'Anchois   20

   (8) Beurre de Crevette   20

   (9) Beurre Fondu   20

  (10) Beurre Maître d'Hôtel   20

  (11) Beurre Manié   20

  (12) Beurre Noir   21

  (13) Beurre Noisette   21

  (14) Beurre Ravigote   21

(2060) Biscuit Glacé au
Cointreau   857

(2059) Biscuit Glacé Praliné   857

(2058) Biscuit Glacé Vanille   856

(1673) Biscuits à la Cuillère 718

(2057) Biscuits Glacés,
moulding and service   856

(1673) Biscuits, Finger   718

(2111) Biscuits, Parisian Rout 871

(1704) Biscuits, Ratafia   729

(2114) Biscuits, Sablé
Bison   872
                         474

 (401) Bisque de Crabe   138

 (400) Bisque de Homard   137

 (798) Bitok de Boeuf   316

(1344) Bitter Leaf Salad   589

(1806) Black Forest Gâteau   767

(1954) Blackberries, poached   820

Recipe

(1983) Blackberry Fool   827

(2032) Blackcurrant water ice 850

(1955) Blackcurrants, poached 820

(1161) Blackgame, grilled
Escalope   490

(545) Blackgame, *see also
under* Coq de Bruyère

  (15) Blanc   21

(1047) Blanc de Volaille grillé 423

 (545) Blanchailles Diablées   192

 (546) Blanchailles frites   193

  (16) Blanching   21

(1939) Blancmange, Vanilla   817

 (706) Blanquette d'Agneau   283

 (707) Blanquette d'Agneau à
l'Ancienne   283

 (708) Blanquette d'Agneau à
la Menagere   284

 (938) Blanquette de Veau   371

 (939) Blanquette de Veau à
l'Ancienne   372

  (17) Blinis   22

 (558) Bloaters   199

 (202) Blue Cheese, Celery
and Chive Sauce   82

(1294) Boar's Head   561

 (834) Boeuf à la
Bourguignonne   334

(1288) Boeuf à la Mode froid   558

 (799) Boeuf bouilli à la
Française   316

 (832) Boeuf braisé   332

 (802) Boeuf Flamande,
Carbonnade   319

 (798) Boeuf, Bitok   316

 (804) Boeuf, Contrefilet   320

 (806) Boeuf, Cromesquis   320

 (807) Boeuf, Cromesquis à la
Polonaise   321

 (808) Boeuf, Croquettes   321

 (809) Boeuf, Currie   321

 (810) Boeuf, Daube à la
Provençale   321

(1287) Boeuf, Daube en Gelée   557

 (820) Boeuf, Estouffade,
Bourguignonne   325

 (822) Boeuf, Filet au Madère
et Champignons   327

 (823) Boeuf, Filet
Bouquetière   327

 (824) Boeuf, Filet Dubarry   328

 (825) Boeuf, Filet Nivernaise 328

 (826) Boeuf, Filet Richelieu 328

 (827) Boeuf, Filet Wellington 328

 (828) Boeuf, Goulash
Hongroise   329

 (830) Boeuf, Langue au
Madère   330

 (831) Boeuf, Paupiette   331

 (835) Boeuf, Queue braisée   335

 (836) Boeuf, Ragoût   335

 (837) Boeuf, Sauté Hongroise 336

 (838) Boeuf, Sauté
Stroganoff   337

Recipe

(799) Boiled Beef, French
Style   316

(1051) Boiled Chicken   424

 (891) Boiled Gammon   355

 (733) Boiled Leg of Mutton   295

 (800) Boiled Silverside and
Dumplings   317

(2046) Bombe Aïda   854

(2047) Bombe Archiduc   854

(2048) Bombe Celia   854

(2049) Bombe Ceylan   854

(2050) Bombe Cyrano   855

(2051) Bombe Diplomate   855

(2045) Bombe mixture, basic   854

(2052) Bombe Nelusko   855

(2053) Bombe Reine   855

Bombes (2044–53)

(2044) Bombes, moulding and
service   853

  (18) Bone Marrow   22

(1654) Bone Marrow on Toast   708

 (346) Bortsch Polonais   118

(1628) Bouchées à l'Indienne   698

(1629) Bouchées à la Reine   698

(1674) Bouchées, cases   718

(1627) Bouchées savoury   698

 (645) Bouillabaisse   239

  (19) Bouquet Garni   22

(1525) Bouquetière de
Légumes   651

 (832) Braised Beef   332

(1106) Braised Duck with
Green Peas   458

 (895) Braised Ham, Madeira
Sauce   356

 (835) Braised Oxtail   335

 (801) Braised Steak   318

(1733) Brandy Butter   738

(1675) Brandy Snaps   718

(1839) Bread and Butter
Pudding   785

(1746) Bread Rolls   744

(1747) Bread Rolls, brown   744

 (206) Bread Sauce (optional)   83

 (205) Bread Sauce
(traditional)   83

 (305) Bread, Pitta   108

  (72) Breadcrumbing   37

  (20) Breadcrumbs   23

  (21) Breadcrumbs, Fried   23

(1748) Bridge Rolls   745

 (87) Brill   192

 (87) Brine Pickling   40

(1749) Brioche   746

(1466) Broad Beans with
Cream   635

(1464) Broad Beans, boiled   635

(1465) Broad Beans, Buttered   635

(1396) Broccoli   613

(1397) Broccoli, Stir-fried with
Ginger   613

 (547) Brochet, Quenelles au
Vin Blanc   193

(1052) Brochette de Foies de

Recipe

Volaille 425
(646) Brochette de Poisson à l'Orientale 240
(348) Broth, Chicken 120
(349) Broth Mutton 120
(350) Broth Scotch 121
(22) Brunoise 23
Brussels Sprouts (1436–41), *see also under* Choux de Bruxelles
(1440) Brussels Sprouts with Chestnuts 627
(1436) Brussels Sprouts boiled 626
(1437) Brussels Sprouts, Buttered 627
(1630) Buck Rarebit 699
(1750) Bun Dough 746
(1676) Bun Wash 719
(1751) Buns Bath 747
(1752) Buns Chelsea 747
(1798) Buns, Cream 765
(1755) Buns, Fruit 749
(164) Butter Sauce 69
(4) Butter, Anchovy 20
(1733) Butter Brandy 738
(13) Butter Brown 21
(3) Butter, Garlic 19
(10) Butter Parsley 20
(1734) Butter Rum 738
(8) Butter, Shrimp 20
(1677) Buttercream, with egg yolks 719
(1678) Buttercream, with icing sugar 719
(1393) Buttered Baby Beetroot 612
(1418) Buttered Cabbage 620
(2) Butters 19

C

Cabbage (1416–23), *see also under* Chou Cabbage Turnip (1434–5)
(1417) Cabbage, boiled 620
(1418) Cabbage, buttered 620
(1420) Cabbage, small braised 621
(1419) Cabbage, Spring 620
(552) Cabillaud au Beurre d'Anchois, Suprême 196
(548) Cabillaud Crème au Gratin 194
(553) Cabillaud frit, Suprême 197
(550) Cabillaud poché, Darne 195
(551) Cabillaud Portugaise, Darne 195
(1840) Cabinet Pudding 785
(1179) Caille à la Grecque 504
(1177) Caille aux Cerises Noires 503
(1180) Caille aux Raisins 505
(1178) Caille fourée à la

Recipe

Grand Vatel 503
(1303) Cailles, Mignons en Gelée aux Muscats 568
(1274) Cailles, Oeufs froids Joinville 549
(648) Caissette de Turbot et Saumon Granvillaise 241
(980) Calf's Feet 391
(981) Calf's Foot, grilled 391
Calf's Head (1002–4)
(1004) Calf's Head, Sauce Vinaigrette 401
(966) Calf's Liver with Bacon 382
(965) Calf's Liver with Blackcurrants 382
(937) Calf's Offals, grills 371
(984) Calf's Sweetbreads 392
(652) Calmars Royannaise 248
(182) Cambridge Sauce 77
(1631) Canapé aux Anchois 699
(1633) Canapé des Gourmets 699
(1632) Canapé Diane 699
(1634) Canapé Hollandaise 700
(1635) Canapé Ivanhoe 700
(1636) Canapé Nina 700
(1637) Canapé Quo Vadis 701
(1638) Canapé Ritchie 701
(1607) Canapés 689
(1608) Canapés, preparation 690
(1609) Canapés, suitable items 691
(1106) Canard braisé aux Petits Pois 458
(1181) Canard Sauvage à l'Ananas 506
(1185) Canard Sauvage au Porto 508
(1183) Canard Sauvage aux Cèpes Bordelaise 507
(1184) Canard Sauvage aux Cerises 508
(1182) Canard Sauvage Bigarade 507
(1300) Canard Sauvage froid aux Cerises 566
(1299) Canard Sevillaise froid 565
(1112) Canard, Magret Bar-le-Duc 460
(1108) Caneton poêlé à l'Orange 459
(1107) Caneton poêlé aux Cerises 458
(1109) Caneton rôti à l'Anglaise 459
(1110) Caneton rôti, Salade d'Orange 459
(1111) Caneton sauté Vallée d'Auge 459
(1105) Caneton, Aiguillenes au Porto 457
(1104) Caneton, Aiguillettes Bigarade 456
(1113) Caneton, Suprême Juan-les-Pins 461
(520) Cannelloni au Jus 175

Recipe

(141) Caper Sauce 63
(1161) Capercaillie, grilled Escalope 490
Capercaillie, *see also under* Coq de Bruyère
(1053) Capon 426
(1039) Capon, Roast 420
(1973) Caramel Cream 823
(1720) Caramel Sauce 734
(802) Carbonnade de Boeuf Flamande 319
(1399) Carottes à la Crème 614
(1398) Carottes au Beurre 614
(1400) Carottes glacées 615
(1401) Carottes Vichy 615
(710) Carré d'Agneau Boulangère 284
(709) Carré d'Agneau Persillé 284
(360) Carrot Soup 126
Carrots (1398–1401)
(1398) Carrots buttered 614
(1399) Carrots Creamed 614
(1400) Carrots, glazed 615
(1639) Cassolette Epicurienne 701
Cauliflower (1424–31), *see also under* Chou-fleur
(240) Cauliflower Salad 93
(1424) Cauliflower boiled 623
(1425) Cauliflower buttered 623
(390) Cauliflower, cream of 134
(258) Caviar 96
(1402) Céleri braisé 616
(1404) Céleri braisé à la Moelle 616
(1403) Céleri braisé au Jus 616
(1405) Céleri Milanaise 616
Celeriac (1406–8)
(239) Celeriac Salad 93
(1406) Celeriac, buttered 617
(1407) Celeriac, creamed 617
(1408) Celeriac, parslied 617
(1407) Céleri-rave à la Crème 617
(1406) Céleri-rave étuvé au Beurre 617
(1408) Céleri-rave Persillé 617
(217) Céleris à la Grecque 89
(1402) Celery, braised 616
Celery (1402–05)
(388) Celery, Cream of 133
(1410) Cèpes Bordelaise 617
(308) Cereals for Soups 111
(2084) Cerises Jubilée 862
(1846) Cerises, Clafoytis 788
(940) Cenelle de Veau au Beurre Noir 372
(2039) Champagne Sorbet 852
(1409) Champignons 617
(218) Champignons à la Grecque 89
(1411) Champignons farcis 618
(1412) Champignons grillés 618
(1413) Champignons sautés aux Fines Herbes 618
(1640) Champignons sous

Recipe

Cloche 702
(1641) Champignons sur
Croûte 702
(1642) Champignons
Chaussonettes 703
(1414) Chanterelles à la
Crème 619
(1414) Chanterelles, creamed 619
(723) Chapatis 291
(1053) Chapon 426
(1039) Chapon rôti 420
(259) Charcuterie as a Single
Hors-d'Oeuvre 97
(225) Charcuterie for
Hors-d'Oeuvre Variés 90
(288) Charentais Melon with
Port 104
(1841) Charlotte de Pommes 786
(1940) Charlotte Eugénie 817
(1941) Charlotte Montreuil 818
(1842) Charlotte Normande 787
(1942) Charlotte Royale 818
(1943) Charlotte Russe 818
(1944) Chartreuse de Bananes 819
(727) Chateaubriand 315
(1254) Chaud-froid Sauce,
Brown 541
(1255) Chaud-froid Sauce,
Fish 542
(1256) Chaud-froid Sauce,
Green 542
(1252) Chaud-froid Sauce,
Pink 541
(1253) Chaud-froid Sauce,
White 541
Chaud-froid Sauces
(1251–6)
(1844) Chausson aux Pommes 787
(1642) Chaussonettes aux
Champignons 703
(1843) Chaussons 787
(146) Cheese Sauce 64
(1655) Cheese Straws 708
(1752) Chelsea Buns 747
(1949) Cherries, poached 820
(1770) Cherry Band 756
(1784) Cherry Flan 759
(419) Cherry Soup 147
(43) Chestnut Stuffing 29
(1486) Chestnuts, braised 640
(1295) Chevreuil, Selle froide 563
Grand-Veneur
(1054) Chicken à la King 426
(1057) Chicken and
Mushroom Pie 428
(1243) Chicken Aspic Jelly 538
(1055) Chicken Biryani 426
(348) Chicken Broth 120
Chicken dishes, *see also*
under Poularde, Poulet
and Volaille
Chicken en Cocotte
(1076–82)
(41) Chicken Forcemeat 29

Recipe

(1320) Chicken Galantine 578
(104) Chicken Glaze 47
(1044) Chicken grilled
Devilled 422
Chicken grills (1040–9)
(1271) Chicken Mousse 548
(1309) Chicken Pie, cold 571
(1056) Chicken Pie, hot 427
(1376) Chicken Salad with
warm Cream and
Coriander 595
Chicken Sautés
(1083–91)
(1048) Chicken Spatchcock 423
(115) Chicken Velouté 53
(1058) Chicken Vindaloo 428
(1051) Chicken, boiled 424
(1296) Chicken, cold 564
(1304) Chicken, cold with
Tarragon 569
(398) Chicken, Cream of 136
(1061) Chicken, curried 431
(1041) Chicken, grilled 421
(1047) Chicken, grilled breast 423
(1046) Chicken, grilled
portions 423
(1045) Chicken, grilled with
Bacon 422
(1074) Chicken, poached with
Rice and Sauce
Suprême 439
(1032) Chicken, roast 419
(1036) Chicken, Roast with
Bacon 420
Chicken, Suprêmes
(1093–1101)
Chicory (1451–3)
(1451) Chicory, braised 631
(23) Chiffonade 23
(309) Chiffonades for Soups 111
(803) Chilli con Carne 319
(1928) Chocolate Bavarois 814
(2105) Chocolate Brandy
Truffles 869
(1802) Chocolate Eclairs 766
(1805) Chocolate Gâteau 767
(2023) Chocolate Ice-cream 848
(1993) Chocolate Mousse 831
(1891) Chocolate Pudding
Soufflé 804
(1721) Chocolate Sauce (with
chocolate) 734
(1722) Chocolate Sauce (with
cocoa powder) 734
(1679) Chocolate Shapes 720
(1680) Chocolate Shavings 720
(1902) Chocolate Soufflé 807
(711) Chop d'Agneau braisé 285
(1417) Chou à l'Anglaise 620
(1418) Chou au Beurre 620
(1420) Chou braisé, Petit 621
(1433) Chou de Mer
Milanaise 625
(1432) Chou de Mer nature 625

Recipe

(1419) Chou de Printemps 620
(1432) Chou Marin Nature 625
(1735) Chou Paste (for
pastrywork) 738
(24) Chou Paste (general
purpose) 23
(1421) Chou Vert étuvé au
Beurre 622
(1424) Chou-fleur à l'Anglaise 623
(1425) Chou-fleur au Beurre 623
(1426) Chou-fleur au Gratin 624
(1427) Chou-fleur Italienne 624
(1428) Chou-fleur Milanaise 624
(1426) Chou-fleur Mornay 624
(1424) Chou-fleur nature 623
(1429) Chou-fleur Persillé 624
(1430) Chou-fleur Polonaise 624
(1431) Chou-fleur sauté au
Beurre 625
(1434) Chou-rave à la Crème 625
(1422) Chou-rouge Flamande 622
(1423) Chou-rouge Limousine 623
(882) Choucroute garnie 352
(1798) Choux à la Crème 765
(1436) Choux de Bruxelles à
l'Anglaise 626
(1437) Choux de Bruxelles au
Beurre 627
(1439) Choux de Bruxelles au
Gratin 627
(1438) Choux de Bruxelles
Grand'mère 627
(1440) Choux de Bruxelles
Limousine 627
(1439) Choux de Bruxelles
Mornay 627
(1441) Choux de Bruxelles
sautés au Beurre 627
(219) Choux-fleurs à la
Grecque 89
(1845) Christmas Pudding 787
(712) Chump Chop
Champvallon 286
Civet de Kangarou 527
(1226) Civet de Lièvre à
l'Anglaise 525
(1227) Civet de Lièvre
Bourguignonne 525
(1228) Civet de Lièvre
Flamande 526
(1217) Civet de Venaison
Bourguignonne 520
(1846) Clafoutis aux Cerises 788
(406) Clam Chowder 140
(7) Clarified Butter 20
(347) Clear Oxtail Soup 119
(345) Clear Turtle Soup 118
(1249) Coating a dish with
Aspic Jelly 540
(351) Cockie Leekie 121
(25) Cockscombs and
Kidneys 24
(261) Cocktail de Crabe 97
(260) Cocktail de Crevettes 97

Recipe

(262) Cocktail de Fruits de Mer 97
(263) Cocktail de Homard 97
(198) Cocktail Sauce for Fish and Shellfish (1) 81
(199) Cocktail Sauce for Fish and Shellfish (2) 81
(261) Cocktail, Crab 97
(276) Cocktail, Florida 101
(274) Cocktail, Grapefruit 101
(263) Cocktail, Lobster 97
(278) Cocktail Melon 101
(277) Cocktail Orange 101
(260) Cocktail, Prawn 97
(262) Cocktail, Seafood 97
(273) Cocktails, Fruit 100
Cod (548–53), *see also under* Cabillaud
(549) Cod Steak, grilled 195
(304) Cod's Roe Relish 107
(553) Cod, Fried 197
(550) Cod, poached 195
(713) Coeur d'Agneau braisé 286
(1348) Coeurs de Laitue 589
(1927) Coffee Bavarois 814
(1801) Coffee Eclairs 766
(1807) Coffee Gâteau 768
(2022) Coffee Ice-cream 847
(1892) Coffee Pudding Soufflé 804
(1258) Cold Buffet Work, Decoration 543
(1259) Cold Buffet Work, Garnishes 543
(1304) Cold Chicken with Tarragon 569
(1279) Cold decorated Salmon 552
Cold dishes, carving 536
Cold dishes, hygiene and health 536
Cold dishes, preparation, cooking and presentation 535
Cold dishes, selection of commodities 534
(1297) Cold Game Birds 565
(1291) Cold Ham 559
(1284) Cold Sliced Meats 555
(1298) Cold Turkey 565
(226) Coleslaw 90
Colin 197
(1948) Compote d'Abricots 820
(1966) Compote d'Abricots secs 822
(1949) Compote de Cerises 820
(1950) Compote de Figues 820
(1967) Compote de Figues sèches 822
(1951) Compote de Fraises 820
(1952) Compote de Framboises 820
(1965) Compote de Fruits secs 821
(1955) Compote de Groseilles Noires 820
(1953) Compote de Groseilles

Rouges 820
(1956) Compote de Groseilles Vertes 820
(1957) Compote de Mirabelles 821
(1954) Compote de Mûres 820
(1960) Compote de Nectarines 821
(1961) Compote de Pêches 821
(1962) Compote de Poires 821
(1968) Compote de Poires sèches 822
(1963) Compote de Pommes 821
(1969) Compote de Pommes sèches 822
(1970) Compote de Pruneaux 822
(1958) Compote de Prunes 821
(1959) Compote de Reines-Claude 821
(1964) Compote de Rhubarbe 821
(1127) Compote, Pigeonneau 467
(1947) Compotes de Fruits frais 820
(1946) Compotes, stock syrup 819
(1442) Concombre à la Crème 628
(1979) Condé, Apricot 826
(1978) Condés, Fruit 826
(264) Confit d'Oie 97
(339) Consommé au Tapioca 117
(340) Consommé au Vermicelle 117
(326) Consommé aux Ailerons 115
(327) Consommé Brunoise 115
(328) Consommé Carmen 115
(329) Consommé Célestine 116
(330) Consommé Colbert 116
(331) Consommé Crécy 116
(332) Consommé Croûte-au-Pot 116
(323) Consommé de Gibier 114
(324) Consommé de Poisson 115
(322) Consommé de Volaille 114
(337) Consommé des Pêcheurs 116
(342) Consommé des Viveurs 117
(333) Consommé Diane 116
(411) Consommé en Gelée aux Vins 144
(410) Consommé froid en Gelée 143
(334) Consommé Julienne 116
(335) Consommé Madrilène 116
(412) Consommé Madrilène en Gelée 144
(336) Consommé Niçoise 116
(321) Consommé Ordinaire 113
(338) Consommé Royale 116
(341) Consommé Viennoise 117
(343) Consommé Xavier 117
(322) Consommé, Chicken 114
(324) Consommé, Fish 115
(323) Consommé, Game 114
Consommés (321–43)
(325) Consommés aux Fumets 115

(413) Consommés froids aux Fumets 144
(413) Consommés, cold flavoured 144
(325) Consommés flavoured 115
(410) Consommés, Jellied 143
(804) Contrefilet de Boeuf 320
(1059) Coq au Vin de Bourgogne 429
(1162) Coq de Bruyère Valenciennes 490
(1163) Coq de Bruyère, Escalope aux Champignons 491
(647) Coquille de Poisson Mornay 241
(653) Coquilles St Jacques Bercy 248
(654) Coquilles St Jacques frites au Lard 249
(655) Coquilles St Jacques Mornay 250
(656) Coquilles St Jacques Parisienne 250
(1484) Corn on the Cob 639
(805) Corned Beef Hash 320
(1681) Cornets 720
(1800) Cornets Chantilly 705
(883) Côte de Porc Flamande 352
(884) Côte de Porc Milanaise 353
(885) Côte de Porc Napolitaine 353
(886) Côte de Porc Provençale 353
(942) Côte de Veau au Basilic 373
(948) Côte de Veau au Romarin 375
(943) Côte de Veau Bonne-Femme 373
(947) Côte de Veau en Papillote 374
(944) Côte de Veau Milanaise 373
(945) Côte de Veau Napolitaine 373
(946) Côte de Veau panée 374
(949) Côte de Veau sautée 375
(950) Côte de Veau Vallée d'Auge 376
(437) Côtelette d'Oeufs Forestière 153
(1047) Côtelette de Volaille grillée 423
(1285) Côtelettes d'Agneau en Chaud-froid Bouquetière 556
(714) Côtelettes d'Agneau Maintenon 287
(715) Côtelettes d'Agneau Milanaise 288
(716) Côtelettes d'Agneau Napolitaine 288
(717) Côtelettes d'Agneau panées 288
(718) Côtelettes d'Agneau

Recipe

Reforme 288
(1526) Côtelettes de Légumes 652
(1218) Côtelettes de Venaison au Genièvre 520
(1219) Côtelettes de Venaison Chasseur 521
(941) Côtes de Veau 372
(584) Coulibiac de Saumon 207
(1724) Coulis de Fruits Frais 735
(178) Coulis de Poivrons 75
(179) Coulis de Tomates 75
(176) Coulis Moravienne 74
(177) Coullis Palermitaine Coulis, savoury (176–9) 74
(2073) Coupe Alexandra 861
(2074) Coupe Andalouse 861
(2075) Coupe Camargue 861
(2076) Coupe Edna May 861
(2077) Coupe Jacques 862
(2079) Coupe Jamaïque 862
(2078) Coupe Janine 862
(2080) Coupe Léonora 862
(275) Coupe Miami 101
(2081) Coupe Rêve d'Amour 862
(2082) Coupe Savoy 862
(2083) Coupe Vénus 862
(2072) Coupes 861
(1443) Courgette 628
(1444) Courgette à l'Anglaise 628
(1445) Courgette au Beurre 628
(1450) Courgette Flowers, fried 630
(1448) Courgette Milanaise 629
(1449) Courgette Provençale 629
(1342) Courgette Salad 588
(1446) Courgettes farcies 629
(1447) Courgettes frites 629
(1527) Courgettes, Fleurs farcies 652
(1450) Courgettes, Fleurs, frites 630
(540) Court-bouillon, for white fish 188
(261) Crab Cocktail 97
(401) Crab Soup 138
(657) Crab, boiled 251
(267) Crab, Dressed 99
(658) Crabe Calaisienne, Quenelles 251
(204) Cranberry Sauce 82
Crayfish, freshwater 253
(1326) Cream Dressing 585
(1800) Cream Horns 765
(387) Cream of Asparagus 133
(388) Cream of Celery 133
(143) Cream Sauce 63
(1414) Creamed Chanterelles 619
(1434) Creamed Kohlrabi 625
(2112) Creams, Peppermint 872
(538) Court-bouillon, vinegar 187
(539) Court-bouillon, white wine 188
(2001) Crème à la Vanille, Petit Pot 835

Recipe

(387) Crème Argenteuil 133
(1999) Crème au Cafe, Petit Pot 834
(2000) Crème au Chocolat Petit Pot 834
(1971) Crème Beau-rivage 822
(1972) Crème Brulée 822
(1973) Crème Caramel 823
(1682) Crème Chantilly 720
(1683) Crème Chiboust 720
(388) Crème de Céleri 133
(389) Crème de Champignons 133
(392) Crème de Laitue 134
(394) Crème de Pois frais 134
(397) Crème de Tomate 135
(398) Crème de Volaille 136
(390) Crème Dubarq 134
(391) Crème Favorite 134
(1684) Crème Frangipane 721
(1974) Crème Opéra 824
(393) Crème Palestine 134
(1685) Crème Pâtissière 721
(395) Crème Pompadour 135
(396) Crème Portugaise 135
(1683) Crème St Honoré 720
(1975) Crème Viennoise 824
(399) Crème Washington 136
(387) Crème d'Asperges '133
(1855) Crêpes à l'Orange 792
(1849) Crêpes à la Confiture 790
(1852) Crêpes à la Marmelade de Pommes 791
(1847) Crêpes (sweet) 789
(1848) Crêpes au Citron 790
(1856) Crêpes au Pralin 792
(679) Crêpes aux Fruits de Mer Princesse 262
(1851) Crêpes Créole 791
(1060) Crêpes de Volaille Mornay 430
(1850) Crêpes du Couvent 790
(1853) Crêpes Mimi 791
(1854) Crêpes Normande 791
(1857) Crêpes Soufflées Vanille 792
(25) Cretes et Rognons de Coq 24
(265) Crevettes, Roses 98
(1624) Crevettes, Barquettes 697
(659) Crevettes, Currie 253
(1669) Crevettes, Tartelettes 714
Crocodile 182
(1753) Croissants 748
(806) Cromesquis de Boeuf 320
(807) Cromesquis de Boeuf à la Polonaise 321
(1643) Croque Monsieur 703
(438) Croquettes d'Oeufs 153
(808) Croquettes de Boeuf 321
(1526) Croquettes de Légumes 652
(1644) Croûte Baron 704
(1645) Croûte Derby 704
(1646) Croûte Windsor 704

Recipe

(1647) Croûte Yorkaise 704
(310) Croûtes de Flûtes 111
(1761) Croûtes, Turban aux Fruits 752
(26) Croûtons 24
(1250) Croûtons de Gelée 540
(311) Croûtons for Soups 111
(266) Crudités 98
(415) Cucumber and Mint Soup, chilled 144
(242) Cucumber Salad for Hors-d'Oeuvre 93
(1442) Cucumber, Creamed 628
(1341) Cucumber, Salad 588
(183) Cumberland Sauce 77
(720) Curtie d'Agneau 289
(809) Currie de Boeuf 321
(659) Currie de Crevettes 253
(1061) Currie de Poulet 431
(721) Curried Lamb, Indian Style 290
(1061) Curried Chicken 431
(719) Curry 289
(208) Curry Sauce 84
(974) Cushion of Veal 386
(1725) Custard Sauce 735
(1828) Custard, baked Egg 780

D

(549) Darne de Cabillaud grillée 195
(1799) Dartois aux Amandes 765
(1648) Dartois aux Anchois 705
(810) Daube de Boeuf à la Provençale 321
(1287) Daube de Boeuf en Gelée 557
(1258) Decoration for Cold Buffet Work 543
(27) Deglazing 24
(112) Demi-glace 52
(1276) Demi-Homard froid 550
(125) Devilled Sauce 57
(1649) Devils on Horseback 705
(1649) Diables à Cheval 705
(312) Diablotins 111
(1129) Dinde, Aileron braisé Anversoise 468
(1133) Dinde, Sauté d'Emincé aux Amandes et Safran 470
(1130) Dindonneau rôti à l'Anglaise 469
(1131) Dindonneau rôti aux Marrons 469
(28) Disgorging 25
(1528) Dolmas 653
(1750) Dough, Bun 746
(1754) Doughnuts 749
(2068) Drambuie Soufflé, iced 859
(267) Dressed Crab 99
(1324) Dressing, American 584
(1325) Dressing Avocado 585
(1326) Dressing Cream 585

Recipe

(1327) Dressing, Egg 585
(1328) Dressing English 585
(1329) Dressing French 586
(1330) Dressing, Italian 586
(1331) Dressing Lemon 586
(1332) Dressing Mayonnaise 586
(1333) Dressing, Mignonnette 586
(1334) Dressing Mustard 587
(1335) Dressing Roquefort 587
(1336) Dressing, Thousand Island 587
(1329) Dressing, Vinaigrette 586
(1337) Dressing, Yoghurt 588
Dressings, Salad (1323–37)
(1244) Duck Aspic Jelly 538
(1321) Duck Galantine 580
(1106) Duck, braised with Green Peas 458
(1181) Duck, Wild with Pineapple 506
Duck, *see also under* Canard and Caneton
(1110) Duckling, roast with Orange Salad 459
(1109) Duckling, stuffed and Roast 459
(89) Dumplings 41
(1779) Dutch Apple Tart 757
(29) Duxelles 25

E

(1801) Eclairs au Café 766
(1802) Eclairs au Chocolat 766
(1801) Eclairs, Coffee 766
Ecrevisses 253
(660) Ecrevisses à la Bordelaise 253
(661) Ecrevisses à la Nage 254
Eel (541–2), *see also under* Anguille
(300) Eel, Smoked 106
(152) Egg and Butter Sauces 66
(437) Egg and Mushroom Cutlet 153
(438) Egg Croquettes 153
Egg Dishes, classification 148
(1327) Egg Dressing 585
(285) Egg Mayonnaise as a single Hors-d'Oeuvres 103
(231) Egg Mayonnaise for Hors-d'Oeuvre Variés 91
(173) Egg Sauce 73
(482) Egg, poached on toast 162
(439) Egg, Scotch 154
Eggplant (1389–91), *see also under* Aubergine
(1391) Eggplant, fried 611
(1390) Eggplant, stuffed 610
Eggs in Cocotte (427–33), *see also under* Oeufs en Cocotte

Recipe

(434) Eggs, boiled 151
Eggs, Cold (1272–4)
(442) Eggs, French fried 155
Eggs, fried (441–3)
(443) Eggs, fried, Andalouse 155
(293) Eggs, Gulls' 105
Eggs, hard-boiled and stuffed (435–40)
(441) Eggs, pan-fried 154
Eggs, poached (473–82) *see under* Oeuf poché
(291) Eggs, Quails' 104
Eggs, scrambled (420–6), *see also under* Oeufs brouillés
(444) Eggs, soft boiled 155
(292) Eggs, Stuffed 104
Eggs, sur le Plat (465–72), *see under* Oeuf sur le Plat 104
(1686) Eggwash, for pastry work 722
(1062) Emincé de Volaille Argenteuil 431
Emu 473
(1451) Endive braisée 631
(1452) Endive braisée au Jus 631
(1453) Endive Meunière 631
(1343) Endive Salad 588
Endive, Belgian (1451–3)
(1340) Endive, Curly, Salad 588
(1328) English Salad Dressing 585
(817) Entrecôte au Poivre 324
(813) Entrecôte aux Champignons 323
(X12) Entrecôte Bordelaise 323
(814) Entrecôte Chasseur 323
(815) Entrecôte Marchand de Vins 324
(816) Entrecôte Mirabeau 324
(818) Entrecôte Tyrolienne 325
(819) Entrecôte Vert-Pré 325
Entrecôtes (811–19)
Entremets à Glacé (2071–100)
(724) Epaule d'Agneau Boulangère 292
(725) Epigrammes d'Agneau 292
(1454) Epinards en Branches 631
(1455) Epinards sautés à l'Ail 632
(1456) Epinards, Purée 632
(1457) Epinards, Purée à la Crème 633
(1458) Epinards, Purée aux Croûtons 633
(1459) Epinards, Subrics 633
(1484) Epis de Maïs 639
(1163) Escalope de Coq de Bruyère aux Champignons 491
(953) Escalope de Veau à la Crème 377
(954) Escalope de Veau à la

Recipe

Crème et Champignons 377
(956) Escalope de Veau au Madère 378
(957) Escalope de Veau au Marsala 379
(957) Escalope de Veau au Porto 379
(957) Escalope de Veau au Xérès 379
(952) Escalope de Veau Cordon Bleu 376
(955) Escalope de Veau Holstein 378
(958) Escalope de Veau Milanaise 379
(959) Escalope de Veau Napolitaine 379
(960) Escalope de Veau panée 379
(961) Escalope de Veau Viennoise 379
(1161) Escalope of Blackgame or Capercaillie 490
(1233) Escalopes de Lapin 530
(951) Escalopes de Veau 376
(887) Escalopes of Pork 354
(1233) Escalopes of Rabbit 530
(1132) Escalopes of Turkey 470
Escalopes of Veal (951–62)
(962) Escalopines de Veau 380
(269) Escargots à la Bordelaise 100
(268) Escargots à la Bourguignonne 99
(270) Escargots à la Chablaisienne 100
(111) Espagnole 51
(97) Estouffade 45
(820) Estouffade de Boeuf Bourguignonne 325
(1858) Eve's Pudding 792
(1282) Eventail de Truites Yvette 554

F

(1170) Faisan Carême 498
(1171) Faisan en Casserole Fermière 498
(1172) Faisan sauté à la Catalane 499
(1173) Faisan Souvaroff 500
(1174) Faisan, Salmis 500
(1175) Faisan, Suprême au Suc de Mandarines 501
(1176) Faisan, Suprême Tatiana 502
(38) Farce à Gratin 27
(35) Farce Américaine 26
(36) Farce Californienne 27
(40) Farce de Poisson 28
(41) Farce de Volaille 29
(37) Farce Duxelloise 27

Recipe

(39) Farce Mousseline　28
(34) Farces　26
(30) Fat Clarification　25
Fennel (1460–3), *see also under* Fenouil
(1345) Fennel Salad　589
(177) Fennel Sauce　74
(1460) Fennel, braised　633
(1462) Fennel, braised with Cream　634
(1462) Fenouil à la Crème　634
(1460) Fenouil braisé　633
(1461) Fenouil braisé au Jus　634
(1463) Fenouil poché, Sauce Hollandaise　634
(220) Fenouils à la Grecque　89
(1344) Feuilles Amères, Salade　589
(1528) Feuilles de Vignes farcies　653
(1736) Feuilletage　738
(1301) Feuillets de Pintadeau glacés aux Olives　567
(1464) Fèves à l'Anglaise　635
(1466) Fèves à la Crème　635
(1465) Fèves au Beurre　635
(271) Figs, for Hors-d'Oeuvre　100
(1950) Figs, poached　820
(1967) Figs, stewed　822
(271) Figues, for Hors-d'Oeuvre　100
(822) Filet de Boeuf au Madère et Champignons　327
(823) Filet de Boeuf Bouquetière　327
(824) Filet de Boeuf Dubarry　328
(825) Filet de Boeuf Nivernaise　328
(826) Filet de Boeuf Richelieu　328
(827) Filet de Boeuf Wellington　328
(888) Filet de Porc Hongroise　354
(889) Filet de Porc Normande　355
(964) Filet de Veau aux Fenouils　381
(963) Filet de Veau Esterhazy　380
(227) Filets d'Anchois　91
(1229) Filets de Levraut aux Airelles Rouges　527
Filets de Sole (595–629), *see under* Sole
(726) Filets Mignons d'Agneau　293
(727) Filets Mignons d'Agneau Persane　293
Fillet of Beef (821–7)
(31) Fines Herbes　25
(554) Finnan Haddock, poached　197

Fish and Shellfish, Cold (1275–82)
(1246) Fish Aspic Jelly　539
Fish, Australian and New Zealand　881
(649) Fish Cakes　242
(40) Fish Forcemeat　28
(105) Fish Glaze　47
(286) Fish Mayonnaise　103
Fish Portion Guide　189
(83) Fish Quenelles　38
(117) Fish Velouté　54
Fish, classification　181
(536) Fish, cleaning and preparation　183
Fish, cooking methods　188
(537) Fish, cuts and special preparations　185
Fish, quality points　182
(299) Fish, Smoked　106
(1859) Flambéed Fruits　793
(32) Flamber　26
(1650) Flan à la Florentine　706
(1782) Flan aux Abricots (fresh fruit)　758
(1781) Flan aux Abricots (tinned or poached fruit)　758
(1783) Flan aux Bananes　759
(1784) Flan aux Cerises　759
(1785) Flan aux Fraises　759
(1786) Flan aux Framboises　760
(1652) Flan aux Fruits de Mer　707
(1788) Flan aux Pêches　760
(1789) Flan aux Poires　760
(1790) Flan aux Poires Bourdaloue　760
(1791) Flan aux Pommes　761
(1792) Flan aux Pommes Meringué　761
(1651) Flan Forestière　706
(1787) Flan Normande　760
(1762) Flan Ring, to line　752
(1668) Flan, Onion　713
(1780) Flans, Fruit　757
Flétan　197
(33) Fleurons　26
(1527) Fleurs de Courgettes farcies　652
(1450) Fleurs de Courgettes frites　630
(276) Florida Cocktail　101
Flounder　211
(1527) Flowers, stuffed Baby Marrow　652
(728) Foie d'Agneau　293
(890) Foie de Porc　355
(966) Foie de Veau au Lard　382
(965) Foie de Veau aux Cassis　382
(967) Foie de Veau Lyonnaise　383
(272) Foie Gras　100
(1052) Foies de Volaille,

Brochette　425
(1068) Foies de Volaille, Pilaff　434
(1687) Fondant　722
(1688) Fondant, preparation for glazing pastries　722
(93) Fonds Blanc　44
(94) Fonds Blanc de Mouton　45
(95) Fonds Blanc de Veau　45
(96) Fonds Blanc de Volaille　45
(97) Fonds Brun　45
(98) Fonds Brun de Veau　45
(1379) Fonds d'Artichauts　607
(1380) Fonds d'Artichauts farcis　607
(1381) Fonds d'Artichauts sautés au Basilic　607
(99) Fonds de Gibier　46
(100) Fonds de Légumes　46
(101) Fonds de Poisson　47
(91) Fondue de Tomates　42
(1980) Fools, Fruit　827
(34) Forcemeats and Stuffings　26
(2085) Fraises Cardinal　863
(2086) Fraises Femina　863
(2087) Fraises Melba　863
(1976) Fraises Romanoff　825
(1977) Fraises Zelma Kuntz　825
(2088) Framboises Melba　863
(1689) Frangipane filling for pastries　722
(244) French Bean Salad　94
(1476) French Beans with Almonds　637
(1474) French Beans, boiled　637
(1475) French Beans, Buttered　637
(391) French Beans Cream of　134
(1329) French Dressing　586
(1346) French Salad　589
(968) Fricandeau de Veau　383
(729) Fricassée d'Agneau　294
(730) Fricassée d'Agneau à l'Ancienne　294
(1234) Fricassée de Lapin　530
(1063) Fricassée de Poulet　432
(1064) Fricassée de Poulet à l'Ancienne　432
(1065) Fricassée de Poulet à l'Ivoire　432
(969) Fricassée de Veau　383
(970) Fricassée de Veau à l'Ancienne　384
(21) Fried Breadcrumbs　23
(1391) Fried Eggplant　611
(654) Fried Scallops and Bacon　249
(1835) Fritters, Apple　783
(1830) Fritters, Apricot　781
(1832) Fritters, Banana　782
(1625) Fritters, Cheese　697
(1831) Fritters, Pineapple　782
(1834) Fritters, Strawberry　783

Recipe

Fritters, sweet
(1829–38), *see also*
under Beignets
(1524) Fritters, Vegetable 651
 (650) Friture des Pêcheurs 243
 (651) Frogs' Legs 243
(1766) Fruit Bands 754
(1796) Fruit Barquettes 764
(1755) Fruit Buns 749
 (273) Fruit Cocktails 100
(1978) Fruit Condés 826
(1780) Fruit Flans 757
(1980) Fruit Fools 827
(1987) Fruit Jelly 829
(1864) Fruit Pie 795
(1863) Fruit Pies and
Puddings 794
(1865) Fruit Pudding 795
(2007) Fruit Salad 838
(1908) Fruit Soufflés 808
(1690) Fruit Syrup Glazes 723
(1796) Fruit Tartlets 764
(2015) Fruit Trifle 843
 (679) Fruits de Mer
Princesse, Crêpes 262
(1652) Fruits de Mer, Flan 707
 (680) Fruits de Mer,
Vol-au-Vent 263
(1859) Fruits Flambés 793
Fruits stewed and
poached (1945–70), *see*
also under Compote
(1965) Fruits, dried, stewed 821
(1947) Fruits, poached, fresh 820
(1744) Frying Batter (for
pastrywork) 743
(2117) Fudge, Vanilla 874
 (101) Fumet de Poisson 47

G

(1321) Galantine de Caneton 580
(1320) Galantine de Volaille 578
(1320) Galantine, Chicken 578
(1321) Galantine, Duck 580
(1245) Game Aspic Jelly 538
Game Birds and
Poultry, cold
(1296–1307)
(1297) Game Birds, cold 565
(1160) Game Birds, grilled 489
(1141) Game Birds,
preparation for
escalopes and
escalopines 479
(1139) Game Birds,
preparation for grilling 479
(1138) Game Birds,
preparation for sauté 479
(1140) Game Birds,
preparation for sauté à
la minute 479
(1159) Game Birds, roast 487
(1137) Game Birds, to bone

Recipe

out 479
(1136) Game Birds, trussing 478
(1551) Game Chips 671
Game, classification
and quality points 471
 (323) Game, Consommé 114
Game, cooking
methods 481
Game, Feathered 471
Game, Feathered; main
items, seasons and
portions (1149–58)
(1134) Game, Feathered;
plucking, drawing and
cleaning 476
Game, Furred 473
(1135) Game, Furred; drawing
and skinning 477
(1147) Game, Furred- larding
and barding 481
(1148) Game, Furred;
marinating 481
Game, hanging and
maturation 475
Game, Offals 474
Game, storage 478
 (891) Gammon, boiled 355
 (892) Gammon, grilled 356
 (893) Gammon, grilled with
Pineapple or Peaches 356
(1691) Ganache 723
 (722) Garam Masala 291
  (3) Garlic Butter 19
 (46) Garlic, to prepare 30
(1259) Garnishes for Cold
Buffet 543
(1805) Gâteau au Chocolat 767
(1806) Gâteau Forêt-Noire 767
(1807) Gâteau Moka 768
(1808) Gâteau Nelusko 769
(1809) Gâteau Praliné 769
(1810) Gâteau Printanière 770
(1811) Gâteau St Honoré 770
Gâteaux and Pastries
(1797–1821)
 (417) Gazpacho Andalouse 146
(1985) Gelée au Citron 828
(1986) Gelée aux Framboises 829
(1987) Gelée aux Fruits 829
(1244) Gelée de Canard 538
(1245) Gelée de Gibier 538
(1246) Gelée de Poisson 539
(1243) Gelée de Volaille 538
(1242) Gelée Ordinaire 538
(1988) Gelée Rubanée 829
(1250) Gelée, Croûtons 540
(1984) Gelée, sweet 828
(1241) Gelées d'Aspic 537
Gemfish 197
(1803) Génoise 766
(1804) Génoise au Chocolat 767
 (228) Gherkins 91
 (731) Gigot d'Agneau
Boulangère 294

Recipe

 (732) Gigot d'Agneau
Bretonne 294
 (733) Gigot de Mouton
bouilli 295
(2026) Ginger Ice-cream 848
(2031) Glace à l'Ananas 849
(2030) Glace à l'Abricot 849
(2036) Glace à l'Orange 851
(2021) Glace à la Banane 847
(2035) Glace à la Mangue 850
(2027) Glace à la Pistache 849
(2022) Glace au Café 847
(2023) Glace au Chocolat 848
(2033) Glace au Citron 850
(2026) Glace au Gingembre 848
(2029) Glace au Rhum et
Raisins 849
(2032) Glace aux Cassis 850
(2024) Glace aux Fraises 848
(2025) Glace aux Framboises 848
(2034) Glace aux Mandarines 850
 (105) Glace de Poisson 47
 (103) Glace de Viande 47
 (104) Glace de Volaille 47
(2028) Glace Praliné 849
(2020) Glace Vanille 847
Glacés aux Fruits
(2030–6)
(1672) Glaze, Apricot 718
(104) Glaze, Chicken 47
(105) Glaze, Fish 47
(103) Glaze, Meat 47
(1705) Glaze, Red 729
 (897) Glazed Virginian Ham 357
(1690) Glazes, Fruit Syrup 723
(102) Glazes, Savoury 47
 (483) Gnocchi 163
 (486) Gnocchi Carravese al
Sugo 164
 (490) Gnocchi de Pommes de
Terre 165
 (485) Gnocchi Florentine 164
 (490) Gnocchi Italienne 165
 (489) Gnocchi Palermitaine 165
 (484) Gnocchi Parisienne 163
 (491) Gnocchi Piémontaise 166
 (487) Gnocchi Romaine 164
 (488) Gnocchi Ticinese 165
 (492) Gnocchi Venitienne 166
 (264) Goose, Preserved 97
(1115) Goose, roast with
Chestnuts 462
(1114) Goose, stuffed and
roast 461
Goose, *see also under*
Oie and Oison
(1956) Gooseberries, poached 820
(1773) Gooseberry Band 756
(1982) Gooseberry Fool 827
 (577) Goujonettes de Plie
frites 203
 (631) Goujonettes de Sole
frites 229
 (576) Goujons de Plie frits 203

Recipe

(630) Goujons de Sole frits 229
(632) Goujons de Sole Murat 230
(828) Goulash de Boeuf Hongroise 329
(2055) Granité au Barsac 855
(2054) Granités 855
(279) Grapefruit 102
(274) Grapefruit Cocktail 101
(280) Grapefruit, grilled 102
(1603) Gratin Dauphinoise 686
(1415) Gratin de Morilles 619
(1529) Gratin Languedocienne 654
(281) Gravlax 102
(113) Gravy, Thickened 52
(368) Green Pea Soup 128
(394) Green Peas (fresh), Cream of 134
(194) Green Sauce 80
(47) Green Vegetable Colouring 31
(1959) Greengages, poached 821
(971) Grenadin de Veau braisé 384
(651) Grenouilles (Cuisses de) 243
(1047) Grilled Breast of Chicken 423
(1041) Grilled Chicken 421
(1044) Grilled Devilled Chicken 422
(1161) Grilled Escalope of Blackgame 490
(1161) Grilled Escalope of Capercaillie 490
(1160) Grilled Game Birds 489
(892) Grilled Gammon 356
(893) Grilled Gammon with Pineapple or Peaches 356
(1123) Grilled Pigeon 465
(1235) Grilled Rabbit 530
(1049) Grilled Spring Chicken 423
(797) Grills of Beef 315
(1040) Grills of Chicken 421
(880) Grills of Pork 351
(881) Grills of Pork Offals 351
(936) Grills of Veal 370
(1216) Grills of Venison 520
(1165) Grouse and Steak Pie 493
(1164) Grouse Ballantrae 492
(1310) Grouse Pie, cold 571
(203) Guacamole 82
(1118) Guinea-Fowl with Celery 464
(1119) Guinea-Fowl, Roast 464
Guinea-Fowl, *see also under* Pintade and Pintadeau

H

(555) Haddock Monte Carlo 197
Haddock, Finnan 197
Haddock, fresh 190
Haddock, smoked 197
Hake 197

Recipe

Halibut 197
Ham (894–7)
Ham dishes, *see also under* Jambon
(1269) Ham Mousse 547
(894) Ham, braised with Spinach 356
(1291) Ham, cold 559
(897) Ham, Glazed Virginian 357
(1292) Ham, Jellied with Parsley 559
(284) Ham, Parma 103
(878) Ham, preparation 349
(829) Hamburg Steak 330
(1142) Hare, dissection for stews and sautés, etc. 479
(1226) Hare, Jugged, English Style 525
(1144) Hare, preparation for roasting 480
(1145) Hare, preparation of fillets for sauté 480
(1146) Hare, preparation of saddle 480
Hare, weights, small cuts, portions and preparation (1208–11)
(1230) Hare, young, Roast 528
Hare, *see also under* Lièvre and Levraut
(557) Hareng grillé 198
(224) Harengs à la Portugaise 89
(381) Haricot Bean Soup 129
(1467) Haricot Beans 635
(734) Haricot de Mouton 295
(1467) Haricots Blancs 635
(1468) Haricots Blancs Persillés 635
(1469) Haricots Bretonne 636
(1470) Haricots d'Espagne 636
(1472) Haricots de Lima 636
(1471) Haricots Flageolets 636
(1530) Haricots panachés au Beurre 654
(1473) Haricots Rouges 636
(1474) Haricots Verts à l'Anglaise 637
(1477) Haricots Verts à la Tourangelle 637
(1475) Haricots Verts au Beurre 637
(1476) Haricots Verts aux Amandes 637
(1260) Hâtelets 544
Herring, *see also under* Hareng
(557) Herring, grilled 198
(303) Herrings, Soused 107
(663) Homard à l'Américaine 255
(664) Homard Cardinal 256
(665) Homard grillé 256
(666) Homard grillé au Pernod 257
(667) Homard Mornay 257

Recipe

(668) Homard Newburg 257
(669) Homard Thermidor 258
(214) Hors-d'Oeuvre à la Grecque 88
(223) Hors-d'Oeuvre à la Portugaise 89
(200) Hors-d'Oeuvre Dips 81
(189) Horseradish Sauce 79
(1742) Hot Water Pastry 742
(738) Hot-Pot, Lancashire 298
(670) Huitres Florentine 259
(671) Huitres Mornay 259
(672) Huitres pochees 259
(283) Huitres, raw as Hors-d'Oeuvre 103

I

Ice-Cream Sweets (2071–2100)
(2021) Ice-Cream, Banana 847
(2023) Ice-Cream, Chocolate 848
(2022) Ice-Cream, Coffee 847
(2026) Ice-Cream, Ginger 848
(2027) Ice-Cream, Pistachio 849
(2028) Ice-Cream, Praline 849
(2025) Ice-Cream, Raspberry 848
(2029) Ice-Cream, Rum and Raisin 849
(2024) Ice-Cream, Strawberry 848
(2020) Ice-Cream, Vanilla 847
(2064) Iced Mousses 858
Ices and Ice-Cream Sweets 845
Ices, Cream (2020–9)
Ices, Fruit Water (2030–6)
(1707) Icing, Royal 729
(1715) Icing, Water 733
(1989) Ile Flottante 830
(735) Irish Stew 296
(1330) Italian Dressing 586

J

(1812) Jalousie 771
(1826) Jam Roll, Baked 779
(1922) Jam Roll, steamed 811
(895) Jambon braisé au Madère 356
(894) Jambon braisé aux Epinards 356
(284) Jambon de Parme 103
(896) Jambon en Croûte 357
(1292) Jambon en Gelée Persillé 559
(1291) Jambon froid 559
(897) Jambon glacé à la Virginienne 357
(899) Jambon, Mousselines Florentine 359
(1692) Japonaise for Gâteaux and pastry bases 724
(48) Jardinière 31

Recipe

(1531) Jardinière de Légumes 654
(1292) Jellied Ham with
    Parsley 559
    Jellies, Aspic (1241–46)
(1241) Jellies, Savoury 537
(1250) Jelly Shapes, savoury 540
(1984) Jelly, sweet 828
(1521) Jerusalem Artichokes
    boiled 650
 (393) Jerusalem Artichokes,
    Cream of 134
(1522) Jerusalem Artichokes,
    Creamed 650
(1523) Jerusalem Artichokes
    parslied 650
    John Dory, *see under*
    Saint-Pierre
(1226) Jugged Hare, English
    Style 525
 (307) Juice, Tomato 108
  (49) Julienne 31
(1990) Junket 830
 (113) Jus Lié 52

K

 (405) Kangarou Tail Soup 120
 (737) Kebab d'Agneau 297
(1066) Kebab de Volaille à
    l'Orientale 433
 (736) Kebabs 297
 (556) Kedgeree 198
    Kid 474
 (404) Kidney Soup 139
    Kidney, Lamb, *see*
    under Rognon d'Agneau
    Kidney, Veal, *see under*
    Rognon de Veau
 (559) Kippers 199
    Kohlrabi (1434–5)
(1435) Kohlrabi Lucernoise 626
(1434) Kohlrabi, creamed 625

L

    Lady's Fingers 643
(1653) Laitances sur Canapé 708
(1478) Laitue braisée 638
(1481) Laitue braisée à la
    Moelle 638
(1479) Laitue braisée au Jus 638
(1480) Laitue braisée aux
    Croûtons 638
    Lamb and Mutton
    offals (698–702)
    Lamb and mutton,
    main joints, average
    weights and preparation
    (681–9)
    Lamb and mutton,
    small cuts (690–7)
 (711) Lamb Chop, braised 285
    Lamb Cutlets
    (714–18)
    see also under Côtelettes
    d'Agneau

Recipe

    Lamb dishes, *see also*
    under Agneau
    Lamb Loin (741–5), *see*
    also under Longe d'Agneau
    Lamb Noisettes
    (749–54)
    Lamb Rosettes
    (749–54)
 (713) Lamb's Heart, braised 286
 (728) Lamb's Liver 293
 (705) Lamb's Offals, Grills 283
 (739) Lamb's Tongue,
    braised with Gherkins 298
 (721) Lamb, Curried Indian
    Style 290
 (720) Lamb, Curry 289
 (704) Lamb, Grills 281
 (703) Lamb, Roast 280
 (759) Lamb, saddle 307
 (738) Lancashire Hot-Pot 298
(1278) Langouste à la
    Parisienne 551
 (739) Langue d'Agneau
    braisée aux Cornichons 298
 (740) Langue d'Agneau
    Poulette 299
 (830) Langue de Bœuf au
    Madère 330
(1289) Langue Ecarlate 558
(1693) Langues de Chat 724
(1235) Lapereau grillé 530
(1236) Lapereau rôti 530
(1237) Lapereau sauté
    Languedocienne 531
(1238) Lapin à la Moutarde 531
(1239) Lapin aux Pruneaux 532
(1234) Lapin, Fricassée 530
(1240) Lapin, sauté aux
    Champignons 533
  (50) Larding 31
  (51) Lardons 32
 (516) Lasagnes 173
 (357) Leek and Potato Soup 124
 (365) Leek and Potato Soup
    (purée) 127
(1510) Leek, braised 647
    Leek, *see under* Poireau
(1929) Lemon Bavarois 814
(1331) Lemon Dressing 586
(1985) Lemon Jelly 828
(1793) Lemon Meringue Pie 762
(1994) Lemon Mousse 832
(1890) Lemon Pudding
    Soufflé 803
    Lemon Sole 199
(2040) Lemon Sorbet 852
(1903) Lemon Soufflé 807
(2033) Lemon Water Ice 850
  (52) Lemons 32
(1482) Lentilles au Beurre 638
(1483) Lentilles au Lard 639
(1483) Lentils with Bacon 639
(1482) Lentils, Buttered 638
    Lettuce (1478–81), *see*

Recipe

    also under Laitue
(1347) Lettuce Salad 589
(1350) Lettuce Salad, Cos 589
(1478) Lettuce, braised 638
(1481) Lettuce, braised with
    Bone Marrow 638
(1480) Lettuce, braised with
    Croûtons 638
 (392) Lettuce, Cream of 134
(1348) Lettuce, Hearts 589
(1230) Levraut rôti 528
(1229) Levraut, Filets aux
    Airelles Rouges 527
(1226) Lièvre, Civet à
    l'Anglaise 525
(1227) Lièvre, Civet
    Bourguignonne 525
(1228) Lièvre, Civet Flamande 526
(1231) Lièvre, Râble à
    l'Allemande 528
(1232) Lièvre, Râble
    Baden-Baden 529
 (106) Liaisons 48
    Limande 199
(2041) Lime Sorbet 853
(1813) Linzer Torte 771
(1267) Liver Mousse 546
 (966) Liver, Calf's, with
    Bacon 382
 (965) Liver, Calf's, with
    Blackcurrants 382
 (728) Liver, Lamb's 293
 (890) Liver, Pig's 355
    Lobster (662–9), *see*
    also under Homard
 (263) Lobster Cocktail 97
(1277) Lobster Mayonnaise 551
(1268) Lobster Mousse 547
 (170) Lobster Sauce 72
 (169) Lobster Sauce, Basic 71
 (400) Lobster Soup 137
 (662) Lobster, boiled 254
(1276) Lobster, Cold 550
 (665) Lobster, grilled 256
(1983) Loganberry Fool 827
    Loin of Lamb (741–5)
    Longe d'Agneau
    (741–5)
 (742) Longe d'Agneau
    Clamart 300
 (743) Longe d'Agneau
    Dubarry 300
 (744) Longe d'Agneau
    Niçoise 300
 (741) Longe d'Agneau poêlée 299
 (745) Longe d'Agneau
    Saint-Mandé 301
 (898) Longe de Porc aux
    Pruneaux 358
 (560) Lotte à la Bordelaise 199
 (562) Lotte à la Provençale 200
 (561) Lotte aux Concombres,
    Médaillon 200

Recipe

M

(2007) Macédoine de Fruits 838
(1532) Macédoine de Légumes 655
(1879) Macaroni Pudding 799
(1694) Macaroons 725
Mackerel, *see under*
Maquereau
(563) Mackerel, grilled 201
(129) Madeira Sauce 58
(1112) Magret de Canard
Bar-le-Duc 460
(1485) Maïs à la Crème 639
(229) Maïs à la Crème (for
Hors-d'Oeuvre) 91
(1484) Maïs, Epis 639
(399) Maize, Cream of 136
Mange-tout Peas
(1506–9), *see also under*
Pois Mange-tout
(1508) Mange-tout Peas,
Buttered 647
(1507) Mange-tout Peas, plain
boiled 646
(2035) Mango Water Ice 850
(563) Maquereau grillé 201
(564) Maquereau Meunière,
Filet 201
(1756) Marignans Chantilly 749
(57) Marinade, Cooked 33
(54) Marinade, Quick 32
(55) Marinade, Red Wine 33
(56) Marinade, White Wine 33
(53) Marinating 32
(1695) Marmelade de Pommes 725
(2056) Marquise aux Fraises 855
(2106) Marquises 869
(1486) Marrons braisés 640
Marrow (1443–50), *see
also under* Courgette
(1527) Marrow, Baby, Flowers,
Stuffed 652
(IW7) Marrow, Baby, fried 629
(1444) Marrow, boiled 628
(1445) Marrow, buttered 628
(1446) Marrow, stuffed Baby 629
Marrow, Young
(1443–50)
(130) Marsala Sauce 59
(2107) Marshmallows 869
(1696) Marzipan 726
(2104) Marzipan Petits Fours 868
(541) Matelote d'Anguille à la
Bourguignonne 190
(185) Mayonnaise 78
(1264) Mayonnaise Collée 545
(285) Mayonnaise d'Oeufs as
a single Hors-d'Oeuvre 103
(231) Mayonnaise d'Oeufs for
Hors-d'Oeuvre Variés 91
(1277) Mayonnaise de Homard 551
(286) Mayonnaise de Poisson 103
(1280) Mayonnaise de Saumon 553
(1302) Mayonnaise de Volaille 568

(1332) Mayonnaise Dressing 586
(286) Mayonnaise of Fish 103
(1277) Mayonnaise, Lobster 551
(1280) Mayonnaise, Salmon 553
(230) Mayonnaises for
Hors-d'Oeuvre 91
(103) Meat Glaze 47
Meats, Cold (1283–95)
(1284) Meats, cold sliced 555
Meats, cooking
methods 267
Meats, hanging and
conditioning 266
Meats, portion guide 275
Meats, quality points 264
Meats, storage 266
(992) Médaillons de Ris de
Veau Maréchale 395
(993) Médaillons de Ris de
Veau Saint-Germain 395
(972) Médaillons de Veau à
l'Estragon 385
(973) Médaillons de Veau
Musette 385
(1221) Médaillons de Venaison
Conti 521
(1222) Médaillons de Venaison
Valencia 522
Megrim 211
(287) Melon 103
(288) Melon Charentais au
Porto 104
(278) Melon Cocktail 101
(289) Melon et Jambon de
Parme 104
(289) Melon with Parma
Ham 104
(1991) Meringue Chantilly 831
(209~) Meringue glacée au
Chocolat 865
(2095) Meringue glacée
Vanille 865
(1697) Meringue Italienne 726
(1699) Meringue Nests 727
(1700) Meringue Shells 727
(1698) Meringue, ordinary 726
(565) Merlan à l'Anglaise 201
(566) Merlan Colbert 201
(567) Merlan en Colère 202
(569) Merlan frit à la
Française, Filet 202
(568) Merlan frit, Filet 202
(570) Merlan Meunière, Filet 202
Microwave Cooking 18
(1117) Mignon de Pintadeau
en Chausson Bergerac 463
(1333) Mignonnette Dressing 586
(1188) Mignonnettes de
Bécasse Westphalienne 509
(1303) Mignons de Cailles en
Gelée aux Muscats 568
(1166) Mignons de Perdreau
Vigneronne 494
(1122) Mignons de

Pigeonneaux aux Feves 465
(1878) Milk Puddings 799
(1814) Mille-Feuille 772
(1815) Mince Pies 773
(352) Minestrone 122
(186) Mint Sauce 78
(1957) Mirabelle Plums,
poached 821
(58) Mirepoix 34
(746) Mixed Grill 301
(1374) Mixed Warm Salad 594
(402) Mock Turtle Soup 138
(18) Moelle 22
(1654) Moelle sur Croûte 708
Monkfish (560–2), *see
also under* Lotte
(1992) Mont Blanc 831
(59) Monter au Beurre 34
(1415) Morilles, Gratin 619
(673) Moules frites en
Buisson 259
(674) Moules Marinière 260
(675) Moules Poulette 260
(747) Moussaka 302
(1993) Mousse au Chocolat 831
(1994) Mousse au Citron 832
(1996) Mousse aux Fraises 833
(1995) Mousse aux Framboises 832
(1266) Mousse de Crevettes
Roses 545
(1267) Mousse de Foie 546
(1268) Mousse de Homard 547
(1269) Mousse de Jambon 547
(1270) Mousse de Tomates 547
(1271) Mousse de Volaille 548
(2066) Mousse Glacée à la
Vanille 858
(2065) Mousse Glacée aux
Fraises 858
(1271) Mousse, Chicken 548
(1269) Mousse, Ham 547
(1267) Mousse, Liver 546
(1268) Mousse, Lobster 547
(1266) Mousse, Prawn 545
(39) Mousseline Forcemeat,
Fine 28
(899) Mousselines de Jambon
Florentine 359
(633) Mousselines de Sole au
Vin Blanc 230
(1067) Mousselines de Volaille
Alexandra 433
(1265) Mousselines, cold 545
(290) Mousses for
Hors-d'Oeuvre 104
(2064) Mousses Glacées 858
Mousses, cold savoury
(1265–71)
(733) Mouton bouilli, Gigot 295
(734) Mouton, Haricot 295
(403) Mulligatawny 139
(1339) Mushroom Salad 588
(121) Mushroom Sauce
(brown) 56

Recipe

 (142) Mushroom Sauce
   (white) 63
  (37) Mushroom Stuffing 27
       Mushrooms (1409–15),
       see also under
       Champignons
(1641) Mushrooms on Toast 702
  (60) Mushrooms, Cooked à
       Blanc 34
 (389) Mushrooms, Cream of 133
(1412) Mushrooms, grilled 618
  (61) Mushrooms, Sautéed 34
(1411) Mushrooms, stuffed 618
 (409) Mussel Soup 142
       Mussels, *see under*
       Moules
(1334) Mustard Dressing 587
 (172) Mustard Sauce 72
 (349) Mutton Broth 120
 (733) Mutton, boiled leg 295
 (704) Mutton, Grills 281
 (703) Mutton, Roast 280

N

 (748) Navarin d'Agneau 302
(1487) Navets au Beurre 640
(1488) Navets glacés 641
(1960) Nectarines, poached 821
(1701) Nectarines, to skin 728
 (749) Noisettes and Rosettes
       of Lamb 303
 (750) Noisettes d'Agneau
       Choisy 303
 (751) Noisettes d'Agneau
       Clamart 304
 (752) Noisettes d'Agneau
       Dubarry 304
 (753) Noisettes d'Agneau
       Mascotte 305
 (754) Noisettes d'Agneau
       Niçoise 305
(1223) Noisettes de Venaison
       aux Myrtilles 522
(1224) Noisettes de Venaison
       aux Poires 523
 (974) Noix de Veau 386
 (975) Noix de Veau braisée
       (brown braised) 386
 (976) Noix de Veau braisée
       (white braised) 387
 (977) Noix de Veau
       Neuchâtelloise 388
 (978) Noix de Veau poêlée 389
 (510) Noodle Paste 172
 (512) Noodle Paste green 173
 (513) Noodle Paste Tomato 173
 (515) Noodle Paste,
       Wholemeal 173
 (514) Noodle Paste, Yellow 173
 (509) Noodles 171
 (511) Noodles with Butter 172
(2108) Nougat Montelimar 870
 (509) Nouilles 171

Recipe

 (511) Nouilles au Beurre 172

O

(1273) Oeuf mollet froid
       Yorkaise 549
 (474) Oeuf poché Argenteuil 161
 (475) Oeuf poché
       Benedictine 162
 (476) Oeuf poché Bombay 162
 (477) Oeuf poché Florentine 162
 (478) Oeuf poché Mornay 162
 (473) Oeuf poché Nature 161
 (479) Oeuf poché à la Reine 162
 (480) Oeuf poché Viroflay 162
 (481) Oeuf poché
       Washington 162
 (465) Oeuf sur le Plat 160
 (466) Oeuf sur le Plat Bercy 160
 (467) Oeuf sur le Plat au
       Beurre Noir 160
 (469) Oeuf sur le Plat au
       Jambon 160
 (470) Oeuf sur le Plat au
       Lard 161
 (468) Oeuf sur le Plat aux
       Foies de Volaille 160
 (471) Oeuf sur le Plat
       Lorraine 161
 (472) Oeuf sur le Plat Opéra 161
 (421) Oeufs brouillés aux
       Champignons 149
 (422) Oeufs brouillés aux
       Croûtons 150
 (423) Oeufs brouillés aux
       Foies de Volaille 150
 (424) Oeufs brouillés aux
       Pointes d'Asperges 150
 (425) Oeufs brouillés aux
       Tomates 150
 (420) Oeufs brouillés nature 149
 (425) Oeufs brouillés
       Portugaise 150
 (291) Oeufs de Cailles 104
(1274) Oeufs de Cailles froids
       Joinville 549
 (435) Oeufs durs 152
 (429) Oeufs en Cocotte à la
       Crème 151
 (432) Oeufs en Cocotte à la
       Reine 151
 (430) Oeufs en Cocotte au
       Jus 151
 (428) Oeufs en Cocotte
       Bergère 151
 (427) Oeufs en Cocotte
       Nature 150
 (431) Oeufs en Cocotte
       Portugaise 151
 (433) Oeufs en Cocotte
       Soubise 151
 (292) Oeufs farcis 104
 (436) Oeufs farcis Chimay 152
 (442) Oeufs frits à la

Recipe

       Française 155
 (441) Oeufs frits à la Poêlé 154
 (443) Oeufs frits Andalouse 155
(1272) Oeufs en Gelée à
       l'Estragon 549
 (444) Oeufs mollets 155
 (293) Oeufs de Mouettes 105
(1997) Oeufs à la Neige 833
 (440) Oeufs à la Tripe 154
 (881) Offals of Pork, grills 351
 (937) Offals, Calf's, grills 371
(1114) Oie rôti à l'Anglaise 461
(1115) Oie rôti aux Marrons 462
(1489) Oignon, braisé 641
  (65) Oignon Clouté 35
  (65) Oignon Piqué 35
 (221) Oignons à la Grecque 89
(1490) Oignons frits à la
       Française 642
(1491) Oignons Lyonnaise 642
(1491) Oignons sautés 642
(1668) Oignons, Tarte 713
(1116) Oison sauté
       Maconnaise 462
(1494) Okras braisés aux
       Tomates 643
 (232) Olives 91
(1867) Omelette à la Confiture
       d'Abricots 796
 (456) Omelette à la Reine 158
 (447) Omelette Arnold
       Bennen 157
 (451) Omelette au Fromage 157
 (452) Omelette au Jambon 157
 (454) Omelette au Parmesan 158
(1869) Omelette au Rhum 797
 (448) Omelette aux
       Champignons 157
 (453) Omelette aux Pointes
       d'Asperges 158
 (457) Omelette aux Rognons 158
 (458) Omelette aux Tomates 158
 (449) Omelette Chasseur 157
(2097) Omelette en Surprise
       Brésilienne 865
(2099) Omelette en Surprise
       Milady 866
(2100) Omelette en Surprise
       Milord 867
(2098) Omelette en Surprise
       Norvégienne 866
 (459) Omelette Espagnole 158
 (460) Omelette Fermière 159
 (450) Omelette Fines Herbes 157
(1876) Omelette Framboisette 799
 (453) Omelette Lyonnaise 157
 (464) Omelette Mousseline 159
 (446) Omelette Nature 156
(1868) Omelette Normande 796
 (462) Omelette Parmentier 159
 (461) Omelette Paysanne 159
 (458) Omelette Portugaise 158
(1874) Omelette Soufflée au
       Grand Marnier 798

Recipe

(1872) Omelette Soufflée
Créole 797
(1873) Omelette Soufflée
George Sand 798
(1875) Omelette Soufflée
Jamaïque 798
(1871) Omelette Soufflée
Viennoise 797
(463) Omelette Suissesse 159
(452) Omelette Yorkaise 157
(1867) Omelette, Apricot Jam 796
(455) Omelette, Asparagus 158
(451) Omelette, Cheese 157
(452) Omelette, Ham 157
(457) Omelette, Kidney 158
(448) Omelette, Mushroom 157
(453) Omelette, Onion 157
(446) Omelette, plain 156
(459) Omelette, Spanish 158
(458) Omelette, Tomato 158
Omelettes (445–64)
(2096) Omelettes en Surprise 865
(1870) Omelettes Soufflées 797
(1866) Omelettes, Sweet 796
(1489) Onions, braised 641
(1668) Onion Flan 713
(147) Onion Sauce (white) 64
(65) Onion, Studded 35
(63) Onion, to chop 35
(64) Onion, to slice 35
Onions (1489–93), *see*
also under Oignons
(1490) Onions, French fried 642
(1491) Onions, fried 642
(1493) Onions, small
brown-glazed 643
(1492) Onions, small
white-glazed 642
(62) Onions, to peel 35
(1934) Orange Bavarois 816
(277) Orange Cocktail 101
(2089) Orange en Surprise 864
(1894) Orange Pudding
Soufflé 804
(1358) Orange Salad 590
(1730) Orange Sauce 737
(66) Orange Segments 35
(2043) Orange Sorbet 853
(2036) Orange Water Ice 851
(979) Ossi Buchi alla
Milanese 390
Ostrich 473
(2109) Othellos 870
(1289) Ox-Tongue, cold 558
(347) Oxtail Soup, clear 119
(405) Oxtail Soup, thick 140
(835) Oxtail, braised 335
(672) Oysters, poached 259
(283) Oysters, raw as
Hors-d'Oeuvre 103
Oysters, *see under*
Huitres

Recipe

P

(533) Paella 178
(1655) Paillettes au Fromage 708
(2110) Palets de Dames 871
(1702) Palmiers 728
(1816) Palmiers (as a pastry) 773
(70) Panada, Bread 36
(68) Panada, Flour 36
(67) Panadas 36
(6B) Panade à la Farine 36
(69) Panade à la Frangipane 36
(70) Panade au Pain 36
(67) Panades 36
(1496) Panais à la Crème 644
(1495) Panais au Beurre 644
(1497) Panais Persillés 644
(1849) Pancakes with Jam 790
(1848) Pancakes with Lemon 790
(1855) Pancakes with Orange 792
(71) Pancakes, plain 36
(313) Pancakes, Savoury 111
Pancakes, sweet
(1847–57), *see also*
under Crêpes
(72) Paner à l'Anglaise 37
(2063) Parfait à la Crème de
Menthe 858
(2062) Parfait au Café 857
(2061) Parfaits 857
(284) Parma Ham 103
(289) Parma Ham with
Melon 104
(10) Parsley Butter 20
(148) Parsley Sauce 65
(73) Parsley, Chopped 37
(74) Parsley, Fried 37
(75) Parsley, Picked 37
(1495) Parsnips, Buttered 644
(1496) Parsnips, Creamed 644
(1497) Parsnips, parslied 644
Partridge, *see also under*
Perdreau
(495) Pasta, cooking of 167
(494) Pastas 166
(314) Pastas for Soups 111
(496) Pastas, sauces for 167
(517) Pastas, Stuffed 173
(512) Paste, Green Noodle 173
(510) Paste, Noodle 172
(1741) Paste, Savarin 742
(513) Paste, Tomato Noodle 173
(515) Paste, Wholemeal
Noodle 173
(514) Paste, Yellow Noodle 173
Pastry, basic and
miscellaneous
preparations
(1671–1715)
Pastry, basic pastes
(1735–43)
Pastry, commodities 715
(1742) Pastry, Hot Water 742
(1739) Pastry, Pie 741

Recipe

(1736) Pastry, Puff 738
(1737) Pastry, rough Puff 740
(1738) Pastry, short lining 741
Pastry, storage and
hygiene 717
(1743) Pastry, Suet (for sweet
puddings) 742
(89) Pastry, suet, for
Dumplings and
Puddings 41
(1740) Pastry, Sweet 741
Pastry, Yeast Goods
(1745–61)
(2045) Pâte à Bombe 854
(1735) Pâte à Chou (for
pastrywork) 738
(1738) Pâte à Foncer 741
(76) Pâte à Frire 37
(1744) Pâte à Frire (for
pastrywork) 743
(510) Pâte à Nouilles 172
(1739) Pâte à Pâte 741
(1741) Pâte à Savarin 742
(1736) Pâte Feuilletée 738
(1740) Pâte Sucrée 741
(1314) Pâte de Veau et Jambon
en Croûte 572
(1315) Pâte Maison 573
(294) Pâtés and Terrines 105
Pauillac Lamb 280
(831) Paupiette de Boeuf 331
(982) Paupiette de Veau 392
(1998) Pavlova 834
(77) Paysanne 37
(1788) Peach Flan 760
(2092) Peach Melba 865
(1961) Peaches, poached 821
(1701) Peaches, to skin 728
(1775) Pear Band 756
(1789) Pear Flan 760
(2003) Pear in Red Wine 835
(1962) Pears, poached 821
(1968) Pears, stewed 822
Peas (1498–1504), *see*
also under Petits Pois
(1499) Peas, boiled 644
(1500) Peas, Buttered 644
(2090) Pêche Cardinal 864
(2091) Pêche Dame-blanche 864
(1862) Pêche flambée au
Cognac 794
(2092) Pêche Melba 865
(1533) Peperonata 655
(2112) Peppermint Creams 872
(1168) Perdreau aux Choux 496
(1167) Perdreau Brabançonne 495
(1169) Perdreau en Cocotte
Normande 497
(1166) Perdreau, Mignon
Vigneronne 494
(187) Pesto 79
(1420) Petit Chou braisé 621
(2001) Petit Pot de Crème à la
Vanille 835

Recipe

(1999) Petit Pot de Crème au Café — 834
(2000) Petit Pot de Crème au Chocolat — 834
(344) Petite Marmite — 117
Petits Fours — 867
(2101) Petits Fours, boiled sugar glazed — 867
(2102) Petits Fours, chocolate dipped — 868
(2103) Petits Fours, fondant dipped — 868
(2104) Petits Fours, Marzipan — 868
(1492) Petits Oignons glacés à Blanc — 642
(1493) Petits Oignons glacés à Brun — 643
(1499) Petits Pois à l'Anglaise — 644
(1503) Petits Pois à la Française — 645
(1504) Petits Pois à la Menthe — 645
(1500) Petits Pois au Beurre — 644
(1501) Petits Pois Bonne-Femme — 644
(1502) Petits Pois Flamande — 645
Pheasant, *see also under* Faisan
(1057) Pie, Chicken and Mushroom — 428
(1309) Pie, Chicken, cold — 571
(1056) Pie, Chicken, hot — 427
(1864) Pie, Fruit — 795
(1165) Pie, Grouse and Steak — 493
(1310) Pie, Grouse, cold — 571
(1793) Pie Lemon Meringue — 762
(1311) Pie Pigeon, cold — 571
(1124) Pie, Pigeon, hot — 465
(1794) Pie, Pumpkin — 763
(758) Pie, Shepherd's — 307
(840) Pie, Steak (cooked filling) — 338
(835) Pie, Steak (raw filling) — 337
(841) Pie, Steak and Kidney — 338
(842) Pie, Steak, Kidney and Mushroom — 338
(1312) Pie, Veal and Ham — 571
(1313) Pie, Veal, Ham and Egg — 572
(1815) Pies, Mince — 773
Pies, Pâtés, Terrines and Galantines (1308–21)
(834) Pièce de Boeuf à la Bourguignonne — 334
(832) Pièce de Boeuf braisée — 332
(833) Pièce de Boeuf braisée à la Mode — 332
(981) Pied de Veau grillé — 391
(900) Pieds de Porc Gribiche — 360
(900) Pieds de Porc Vinaigrette — 360
Pieds de Veau (980–1)
(890) Pig's Liver — 355
(900) Pig's Trotters — 360

Recipe

(1123) Pigeon grillé — 465
(1311) Pigeon Pie, cold — 571
(1124) Pigeon Pie, hot — 465
(1125) Pigeon, Roast — 466
(1375) Pigeon, Salade tiède — 594
(1126) Pigeon, Salmis — 467
(1127) Pigeonneau en Compote — 467
(1125) Pigeonneau Rôti — 466
(1128) Pigeonneau, Suprêmes aux Morilles — 467
(1122) Pigeonneau, Mignons aux Fèves — 465
Pike, *see under* Brochet
(1068) Pilaff de Foies de Volaille — 434
(1505) Piment farci — 646
(79) Pimento as a Garnish — 38
(246) Pimento Salad — 94
(1505) Pimento, stuffed — 646
(78) Pimento, to skin — 38
(1533) Pimentos and Tomatoes, Stewed — 655
(1769) Pineapple Band — 756
(1831) Pineapple Fritters — 782
(2038) Pineapple Sorbet — 851
(2031) Pineapple Water Ice — 849
(1118) Pintade aux Céleris — 464
(1119) Pintade rôtie — 464
(1121) Pintade, Salmis — 464
(1120) Pintadeau sauté Niçoise — 464
(1301) Pintadeau, Feuillets glacés aux Olives — 567
(1117) Pintadeau, Mignon en Chausson Bergerac — 463
(2027) Pistachio Ice-cream — 849
(1817) Pithivier — 773
(305) Pitta Bread — 108
Plaice (571–7), *see also under* Plie
(571) Plaice, fried Fillet — 203
(572) Plaice, grilled Fillet — 203
(575) Plie à l'Orly, Filet — 203
(571) Plie frit, Filet — 203
(572) Plie grillé, Filet — 203
(573) Plie Meunière, Filet — 203
(574) Plie Niçoise, Filet — 203
(577) Plie, Goujonettes frites — 203
(576) Plie, Goujons frits — 203
(80) Pluches — 38
(315) Pluches for Soups — 112
(1777) Plum Bands, various — 757
(1958) Plums, poached — 821
(482) Poached Egg on Toast — 162
(473) Poached Eggs — 161
(1386) Pointes d'Asperges — 609
(1387) Pointes d'Asperges Tessinoise — 609
(2003) Poire au Vin Rouge — 835
(2093) Poire Belle Hélène — 865
(2002) Poire Marie-Rose — 835
(1510) Poireau braisé — 647
(1511) Poireau braisé au Jus — 647
(222) Poireaux à la Grecque — 89

Recipe

(1509) Pois Mange-tout à l'Etuvée — 647
(1508) Pois Mange-tout au Beurre — 647
(1507) Pois Mange-tout nature — 646
(983) Pojarski de Veau Smitaine — 392
(1877) Pomme Bonne-Femme — 799
(1538) Pommes à l'Anglaise — 666
(1554) Pommes à la Crème — 672
(1579) Pommes à la Neige — 681
(1539) Pommes Allumettes — 666
(1540) Pommes Amandines — 666
(1541) Pommes Anna — 667
(1542) Pommes Arlie — 668
(1564) Pommes au Four — 676
(1569) Pommes au Lard — 678
(1543) Pommes Bemy — 668
(1544) Pommes Berrichonne — 669
(1545) Pommes Biarritz — 669
(1546) Pommes Boulangère — 669
(1547) Pommes Bourgeoise — 670
(1548) Pommes Byron — 670
(1549) Pommes Champignol — 670
(1550) Pommes Château — 671
(1551) Pommes Chips — 671
(1552) Pommes Cocone — 671
(1553) Pommes Collerene — 672
(1555) Pommes Crétan — 672
(1556) Pommes Croquettes — 672
(1557) Pommes Dauphin — 673
(1558) Pommes Dauphme — 673
(1561) Pommes Duchesse (as a potato dish) — 674
(1560) Pommes Duchesse (basic mixture) — 674
(1349) Pommes de Terre Salade — 589
(1559) Pommes Delmonico — 674
(1562) Pommes Elisabeth — 675
(1594) Pommes en Robes de Chambre — 683
(1563) Pommes Fondantes — 675
(1565) Pommes Frites — 676
(1566) Pommes Galene — 677
(1567) Pommes Gaufrettes — 677
(1568) Pommes Gratinées — 677
(1570) Pommes Lorette — 678
(1571) Pommes Lyonnaise — 678
(1572) Pommes Macaire — 678
(1573) Pommes Maitre d'Hôtel — 679
(1574) Pommes Marquise — 679
(1575) Pommes Mignonnettes — 679
(1576) Pommes Mireille — 679
(1577) Pommes Mont d'Or — 680
(1578) Pommes Nana — 680
(1580) Pommes Noisette — 681
(1581) Pommes Nouvelles — 681
(1583) Pommes Nouvelles à la Menthe — 681
(1582) Pommes Nouvelles au Beurre — 681
(1584) Pommes Nouvelles

Recipe

Persillées 682
(1585) Pommes Nouvelles rissolées 682
(1586) Pommes Pailles 682
(1587) Pommes Parisienne 682
(1588) Pommes Parmentier 683
(1589) Pommes Persillées 683
(1590) Pommes Pont-Neuf 683
(1591) Pommes Provençale 683
(1592) Pommes Purée 683
(1593) Pommes Purée à la Crème 683
(1577) Pommes Purée au Gratin 680
(1595) Pommes Robert 684
(1596) Pommes rôties 684
(1597) Pommes Sablées 684
(1598) Pommes sautées 684
(1599) Pommes Soufflées 685
(1600) Pommes St Florentin 685
(1601) Pommes Vapeur 686
(1602) Pommes Voisin 686
(898) Porc aux Pruneaux, Longe 358
(883) Porc, Côte Flamande 352
(884) Porc, Côte Milanaise 353
(885) Porc, Côte Napolitaine 353
(886) Porc, Côte Provençale 353
(888) Porc, Filet Hongroise 354
(889) Porc, Filet Normande 355
(900) Porc, Pied Gribiche 360
(900) Porc, Pied Vinaigrette 360
(903) Porc, Rognons Liègeoise 362
(901) Porcelet, Pomeranienne 360
(902) Pork Chow Mein 361
Pork dishes, *see also under* Porc
(880) Pork Grills 351
Pork joints, weights and preparation (856–60)
(887) Pork, Escalopes 354
Pork, offals (865–70)
(879) Pork, Roast 350
Pork, small cuts (861–4)
(904) Pork, Sweet and Sour 362
(353) Potage Bonne-Femme 122
(369) Potage Bretonne 128
(359) Potage Bruxelloise 125
(370) Potage Choiseuil 128
(371) Potage Condé 128
(372) Potage Conti 128
(360) Potage Crécy 126
(361) Potage Cressonière 126
(354) Potage Cultivateur 122
(373) Potage Dartois 128
(374) Potage Egyptienne 129
(375) Potage Esaü 129
(376) Potage Faubonne 129
(402) Potage Fausse Tortue 138
(355) Potage Fermière 123
(362) Potage Freneuse 126
(363) Potage Garbure 126

Recipe

(377) Potage Gentilhomme 129
(407) Potage Germiny 141
(408) Potage Goanèse 142
(364) Potage Julienne d'Arblay 127
(378) Potage Lamballe 129
(379) Potage Longchamps 129
(380) Potage Maria 129
(365) Potage Parmentier 127
(356) Potage Paysanne 123
(357) Potage Poireaux et Pommes 124
(347) Potage Queue de Boeuf Clair 119
(405) Potage Queue de Boeuf Lié 140
(366) Potage Santé 127
(381) Potage Soissonaise 129
(367) Potage Solferino 127
(368) Potage St Germain 128
(1604) Potato Latkes 687
(1605) Potato Nests 687
(1606) Potato Rösti 688
(1349) Potato Salad 589
(247) Potato Salad for Hors-d'Oeuvre 94
(1564) Potato, Baked 676
(1538) Potatoes, boiled 666
Potatoes, cooking methods 662
(1565) Potatoes, fried 676
(1592) Potatoes, Mashed 683
(1593) Potatoes, Mashed with Cream 683
(1581) Potatoes, New 681
(1582) Potatoes, New Buttered 681
(1584) Potatoes, New Parslied 682
(1583) Potatoes, New with Mint 681
(1589) Potatoes, Parslied 683
Potatoes, preparation 661
Potatoes, preparation losses and portion guide 666
Potatoes, quality and selection 660
(1596) Potatoes, roast 684
(1601) Potatoes, steamed 686
(1594) Potatoes, steamed or boiled Jacket 683
Potatoes, storage 661
(1586) Potatoes, Straw 682
Potatoes, varieties 659
Potatoes, *see also under* Pommes
(295) Potted Meats and Fish 105
(297) Potted Shrimps 105
(296) Potted Smoked Salmon 105
(1879) Pouding au Macaroni 799
(1881) Pouding au Riz 800
(1880) Pouding au Riz à l'Anglaise 800
(1882) Pouding au Riz à la Française 801

Recipe

(1883) Pouding au Sagou 801
(1884) Pouding au Semoule 802
(1885) Pouding au Tapioca 802
(1886) Pouding au Vermicelle 802
(2004) Pouding Diplomate 836
(1887) Pouding Mexicaine 802
(1894) Pouding Soufflé à l'Orange 804
(1892) Pouding Soufflé au Café 804
(1891) Pouding Soufflé au Chocolat 804
(1890) Pouding Soufflé au Citron 803
(1893) Pouding Soufflé Montmorency 804
(1895) Pouding Soufflé Praliné 804
(1896) Pouding Soufflé Saxon 804
(1889) Pouding Soufflé Vanille 803
(1878) Poudings au Lait 799
(1070) Poularde à l'Aurore 435
(1071) Poularde à la Bressane 436
(1072) Poularde Derby 437
(1073) Poularde Petite-Mariée 438
(1074) Poularde poché au Riz, Sauce Suprême 439
(1038) Poularde rôtie 420
(1075) Poularde Stanley 440
Poulardes (1069–75)
(1077) Poulet en Cocotte 441
(1080) Poulet en Cocotte à l'Estragon 443
(1078) Poulet en Cocotte Bonne-Femme 442
(1079) Poulet en Cocotte Champeaux 442
(1081) Poulet en Cocotte Grand'mère 443
(1082) Poulet en Cocotte Paysanne 444
(1304) Poulet froid à l'Estragon 569
(1041) Poulet grillé 421
(1042) Poulet grillé à l'Américaine 421
(1043) Poulet grillé à la Crapaudine 421
(1044) Poulet grillé au Diable 422
(1045) Poulet grillé au Lard 422
(1032) Poulet rôti 419
(1033) Poulet rôti à l'Américaine 420
(1034) Poulet rôti à l'Anglaise 420
(1036) Poulet rôti au Lard 420
(1035) Poulet rôti Californienne 420
(1084) Poulet sauté Archiduc 444
(1088) Poulet sauté aux Fines Herbes 446
(1085) Poulet sauté Bercy 444
(1086) Poulet sauté Bourguignonne 445
(1087) Poulet sauté Chasseur 446
(1089) Poulet sauté Hongroise 447

Recipe

(1090) Poulet sauté Portugaise 448
(1091) Poulet sauté Provençale 448
(1061) Poulet, Currie 431
(1063) Poulet, Fricassée 432
(1064) Poulet, Fricassée à
l'Ancienne 432
(1065) Poulet, Fricassée à
l'Ivoire 432
(1076) Poulets en Casserole 441
(1076) Poulets en Cocotte 441
(1083) Poulets sautés 444
Poultry and Game
Birds, cold
(1296–1307)
(1016) Poultry, carving and
portioning 415
Poultry, cooking
methods 410
Poultry, main items,
weights and portions
(1017–31) 418
(1006) Poultry, plucking,
drawing, singeing and
cleaning 404
(1010) Poultry, preparation for
grilling 408
(1011) Poultry, preparation for
grilling 'en Crapaudine' 408
(1014) Poultry, preparation for
Sauté, Fricassée and
Pies 409
(1013) Poultry, preparation of
Fillets 409
(1012) Poultry, preparation of
Suprêmes 409
Poultry, quality points 403
Poultry, storage 404
(1015) Poultry, to bone out for
stuffing 410
(1009) Poultry, to stuff for
roasting 408
(1049) Poussin grillé 423
(1092) Poussin Polonaise 449
(1037) Poussin rôti 420
(1703) Pralin 728
(2028) Praline Ice-cream 849
(1895) Praline Pudding Soufflé 804
(260) Prawn Cocktail 97
(1266) Prawn Mousse 545
(265) Prawns 98
(659) Prawns, curried 253
(1290) Pressed Beef 558
(81) Printanière 38
(2005) Profiteroles au
Chocolat 837
(316) Profiteroles for Soups 112
(1970) Prunes, stewed 822
(1889) Pudding Soufflé,
Vanilla 803
Pudding Soufflés
(1888–96)
(1839) Pudding, Bread and
Butter 785
(1840) Pudding, Cabinet 785

Recipe

(1845) Pudding, Christmas 787
(1858) Pudding, Eve's 792
(1865) Pudding Fruit 795
(1879) Pudding Macaroni 799
(1880) Pudding, Rice (baked) 800
(1881) Pudding, Rice (boiled) 800
(1882) Pudding, Rice (French
method) 801
(1883) Pudding, Sago 801
(1884) Pudding, Semolina 802
(843) Pudding, Steak and
Kidney 338
(844) Pudding, Steak, Kidney
and Mushroom 339
(845) Pudding, Steak, Kidney
and Oyster 339
(1912) Pudding, steamed
Black Cap 809
(1913) Pudding, steamed
Cherry Sponge 809
(1914) Pudding, steamed
Chocolate Sponge 810
(1921) Pudding, steamed
College 810
(1915) Pudding, steamed
Ginger Sponge 810
(1916) Pudding, steamed
Golden Sponge 810
(1917) Pudding, steamed Jam
Sponge 810
(1918) Pudding, steamed
Lemon Sponge 810
(1919) Pudding, steamed
Orange Sponge 810
(1911) Pudding, steamed
Sponge 809
(1924) Pudding, Steamed Suet 812
(1920) Pudding, steamed
Vanilla Sponge 810
(2012) Pudding, Summer 842
(1885) Pudding, Tapioca 802
(1886) Pudding, Vermicelli 802
(796) Pudding, Yorkshire 314
Puddings, Milk
(1878–1886)
(1897) Puddings, Queen of 804
Puddings, steamed
(1910–24)
(1736) Puff Pastry 738
(1737) Puff Pastry, rough 740
(1794) Pumpkin Pie 763
(1456) Purée d'Epinards 632
(1457) Purée d'Epinards à la
Crème 633
(1458) Purée d'Epinards aux
Croûtons 633
(1534) Purées of Vegetables 655

Q

(1303) Quail Breasts in Jelly
with Muscatel Grapes 568
Quail, *see also under*
Caille

Recipe

(1897) Queen of Puddings 804
(547) Quenelles de Brochet
au Vin Blanc 193
(658) Quenelles de Crabe
Calaisienne 251
(83) Quenelles de Poisson 38
(82) Quenelles for garnish 38
(317) Quenelles for Soups 112
(835) Queue de Boeuf
braisée 335
(347) Queue de Boeuf Clair,
Potage 119
(1656) Quiche Lorraine 709
(1657) Quichelette au Jambon 709

R

(1239) Rabbit with Prunes 532
(1143) Rabbit, dissection for
stews, sautés, fricassés,
etc. 480
(1233) Rabbit, Escalopes 530
(1235) Rabbit, grilled 530
(1144) Rabbit, preparation for
roasting 480
(1236) Rabbit, roast 530
Rabbit, weight, small
cuts, portions and
preparation (1212–14)
Rabbit, *see also under*
Lapin and Lapereau
(1231) Râble de Lièvre à
l'Allemande 528
(1232) Râble de Lièvre
Baden-Baden 529
(1898) Rabotte de Pomme 805
(233) Radis 91
(233) Radishes 91
(836) Ragoût de Boeuf 335
(578) Raie au Beurre Noir 204
(1658) Ramequin au Gruyère 709
(1659) Ramequin au Gruyère
(in tartlet cases) 710
(1952) Raspberries, poached 820
(1772) Raspberry Band 756
(1932) Raspberry Bavarois 815
(1786) Raspberry Flan 760
(1983) Raspberry Fool 827
(2025) Raspberry Ice-cream 848
(1986) Raspberry Jelly 829
(2088) Raspberry Melba 863
(1995) Raspberry Mousse 832
(2042) Raspberry Sorbet 853
(2069) Raspberry Soufflé, iced 860
(1704) Ratafia Biscuits 729
(1535) Ratatouille Provençale 656
(518) Raviolisu Jus 173
(266) Raw Vegetables 98
(241) Red Cabbage, Pickled 93
Red Mullet (580–2) *see
also under* Rouget
(580) Red Mullet, grilled 205
(175) Red Wine Sauce 73
(1953) Redcurrants, poached 820

Recipe

(135) Reform Sauce 61
(1964) Rhubarb, poached 821
(1778) Rhubarb Band 757
(521) Rice 175
(1706) Rice for Condés 729
(1880) Rice Pudding (baked) 800
(1881) Rice Pudding (boiled) 800
(1882) Rice Pudding (French method) 801
(248) Rice Salad 94
(1262) Rice Socle 544
(534) Rice, boiled 179
(535) Rice, poach-steamed 179
(1818) Rigi-Kirsch Torte 774
(298) Rillettes 106
(988) Ris de Veau à la Crème 394
(987) Ris de Veau Bonne-Maman 394
(985) Ris de Veau braisé 393
(986) Ris de Veau braisé au Madère 393
(989) Ris de Veau Financière 395
(992) Ris de Veau Maréchale, Médaillons 395
(990) Ris de Veau pané 395
(991) Ris de Veau Princesse 395
(993) Ris de Veau Saint-Germain Médaillons 395
(529) Risotto 177
(531) Risotto alla Milanese 178
(530) Risotto Milanaise 177
(532) Risotto Piémontaise 178
(521) Riz 175
(524) Riz à la Grecque 176
(2006) Riz à l'Impératrice 837
(526) Riz à la Turque 177
(523) Riz Créole 176
(525) Riz Egyptienne 177
(522) Riz Pilaff as à garnish 176
(52i) Riz Pilaff Safrané 177
(534) Riz Poché 179
(528) Riz Valenciennes 177
(795) Roast Beef 313
(1032) Roast Chicken 419
(1159) Roast Game Birds 487
(1115) Roast Goose with Chestnuts 462
(1119) Roast Guinea-Fowl 464
(1283) Roast Joints, cold 555
(703) Roast Lamb 280
(703) Roast Mutton 280
(879) Roast Pork 350
(1236) Roast Rabbit 530
(1109) Roast Stuffed Ducklmg 459
(1114) Roast Stuffed Goose 461
(901) Roast Stuffed Sucking Pig 360
(935) Roast Veal 369
(1215) Roast Venison 518
(1653) Roes, Soft on Toast 708
(995) Rognon de Veau à la Fine Champagne 396
(994) Rognon de Veau

Recipe

Dijonnaise 396
(996) Rognonnade de Veau aux Salsifis 397
(755) Rognons d'Agneau sautés 306
(756) Rognons d'Agneau sautés au Madère 306
(757) Rognons d'Agneau sautés Turbigo 306
(903) Rognons de Porc Liègeoise 362
Roker 204
(234) Rollmops 92
(1746) Rolls, Bread 744
(1748) Rolls, Bridge 745
(1747) Rolls, Brown Bread 744
(1335) Roquefort Dressing 587
Rosettes d'Agneau 306
(635) Rouelle de Thon Mentonnaise 232
(582) Rouget en Papillote 205
(579) Rouget Grenobloise 204
(580) Rouget Grillé 205
(581) Rouget Niçoise 205
(2111) Rout Biscuits, Parisian 871
(107) Roux Blanc 48
(108) Roux, Blond 49
(109) Roux, Brown 49
(109) Roux Brun 49
(107) Roux, White 48
(1707) Royal Icing 729
(318) Royale 112
(319) Royale Crécy 112
(1745) Rum Babas 743
(1734) Rum Butter 738
(1869) Rum Omelette 797
(2029) Rum and Raisin Ice-cream 849
(2113) Rum Truffles 872
(1366) Russian Salad 592
(249) Russian Salad for Hors-d'Oeuvre 94
(1512) Rutabaga 648

S

(84) Sabayon 39
(1899) Sabayon au Marsala 805
(2114) Sablé Biscuits 872
(1819) Sacher Torte 775
(1708) Sacristans 730
(44) Sage and Onion Stuffing 30
(1883) Sago Pudding 801
(583) Saint-Pierre en Papillote Arnaudy 206
Salad Dressings (1323–37)
(1355) Salad with Garlic Crusts 590
(237) Salad, Beef 93
(1338) Salad, Beetroot 588
(236) Salad, Beetroot (for Hors-d'Oeuvre) 93

Recipe

(1344) Salad, Bitter Leaf 589
(240) Salad, Cauliflower 93
(239) Salad, Celeriac 93
(1376) Salad, Chicken with warm Cream and Coriander 595
(1350) Salad, Cos Lettuce 589
(1342) Salad, Courgette 588
(1341) Salad, Cucumber 588
(1340) Salad, Curly Endive 588
(1370) Salad, Curly Endive with Bacon 592
(1343) Salad, Endive 588
(1345) Salad Fennel 589
(1346) Salad French 589
(244) Salad, French Bean 94
(2007) Salad, Fruit 838
(1353) Salad, Green 590
(1372) Salad, Hot Potato 593
Salad Leaves 883
(1347) Salad, Lettuce 589
(1348) Salad, Lettuce Hearts 589
(1365) Salad, Mixed 592
(1339) Salad, Mushroom 588
(1358) Salad, Orange 590
(246) Salad, Pimento 94
(1349) Salad, Potato 589
(248) Salad, Rice 94
(1366) Salad, Russian 592
(1351) Salad, Seasonal 589
(1371) Salad, Spinach and Corn salad with Garlic Croûtons 593
(1352) Salad, Tomato 589
(1374) Salad, warm mixed 594
(1355) Salade au Chapon d'Ail 590
(238) Salade Bretonne 93
(1354) Salade Capriccio 590
(1343) Salade d'Endive Belge 588
(1371) Salade d'Epinards et Mâche aux Croûtons Aillés 593
(1358) Salade d'Orange 590
(1338) Salade de Betterave 588
(236) Salade de Betterave for Hors-d'Oeuvre 93
(237) Salade de Boeuf 93
(239) Salade de Céleri-Rave 93
(1339) Salade de Champignons 588
(1340) Salade de Chicorée Frisée 588
(1370) Salade de Chicorée Frisée au Lard 592
(240) Salade de Chou-fleur 93
(241) Salade de Chou-rouge 93
(1341) Salade de Concombres 588
(242) Salade de Concombres for Hors-d'Oeuvre 93
(1342) Salade de Courgettes 588
(1345) Salade de Fenouil 589
(1344) Salade de Feuilles Amères 589
(2007) Salade de Fruits 838

Recipe

(244) Salade de Haricots
    Verts 94
(1347) Salade de Laitue 589
(246) Salade de Piments 94
(1349) Salade de Pommes de
    Terre 589
(1372) Salade de Pommes de
    Terre chaude 593
(247) Salade de Pommes de
    Terre for
    Hors-d'Oeuvre 94
(248) Salade de Riz 94
(1350) Salade de Romaine 589
(1351) Salade de Saison 589
(1352) Salade de Tomates 589
(250) Salade de Tomates for
    Hors-d'Oeuvre 95
(1356) Salade Diva 590
(243) Salade Fécampoise 94
(1357) Salade Florentine 590
(1358) Salade Florida 590
(1346) Salade Française 589
(1359) Salade Gauloise 591
(245) Salade Italienne 94
(1360) Salade Japonaise 591
(1361) Salade Lorette 591
(1362) Salade Milady 591
(1363) Salade Mimosa 591
(1364) Salade Niçoise 591
(1365) Salade Panachée 592
(1366) Salade Russe 592
(249) Salade Russe for
    Hors-d'Oeuvre 94
(1373) Salade tiède Bergère 593
(1375) Salade tiède de Pigeon 594
(1376) Salade tiède de Poulet
    et Coriandre 595
(1374) Salade tiède Mélangée 594
(1353) Salade Verte 590
(1367) Salade Villa d'Este 592
(1368) Salade Waldorf 592
    Salades Tièdes
    (1369–74)
(235) Salads for
    Hors-d'Oeuvre 92
(1322) Salads, cleaning and
    preparation 582
    Salads, Composed
    (1354–68)
    Salads, Simple
    (1338–53)
    Salads, Warm
    (1369–74)
(86) Salaison à Sec 40
(87) Salaison Liquide 40
(2008) Salambos à la Marquise 839
(1189) Salmis de Bécasse 511
(1174) Salmis de Faisan 500
(1126) Salmis de Pigeon 467
(1121) Salmis de Pintade 464
    Salmon (584–90), *see
    also under* Saumon
(1280) Salmon Mayonnaise 553
    Salmon Trout 236

(1279) Salmon, cold decorated 552
(586) Salmon, grilled 209
(588) Salmon, poached 210
(301) Salmon, Smoked 106
(1514) Salsifis à la Crème 648
(1513) Salsifis au Beurre 648
(1515) Salsifis frits 648
(1516) Salsifis Persillés 648
(1517) Salsifis sautés 648
    Salsify (1513–17)
(1513) Salsify, Buttered 648
(1514) Salsify, Creamed 648
(1515) Salsify, fried 648
(1516) Salsify, parslied 648
(85) Salt Curing and
    Pickling 39
(86) Salt Curing, Dry 40
(1614) Sandwich, Bookmakers' 694
(1615) Sandwich, Cape Cod 695
(1613) Sandwich, Club 694
(1616) Sandwich, Denver 695
(1617) Sandwich, Tongue and
    Spinach 695
(1618) Sandwich, Western 695
(1610) Sandwiches 692
(1612) Sandwiches, hot 694
(1619) Sandwiches, Open 695
(1611) Sandwiches,
    preparation 693
(251) Sardines 95
(1660) Sardines on Toast 710
(1716) Sauce à l'Abricot 733
(1717) Sauce à l'Abricot (with
    fresh apricots) 733
(1730) Sauce à l'Orange 737
(139) Sauce Allemande 62
(181) Sauce Andalouse 77
(1718) Sauce Anglaise 733
(140) Sauce Aurore 63
(164) Sauce au Beurre Blanc 69
(1720) Sauce au Caramel 734
(1721) Sauce au Chocolat
    (with chocolate) 734
(1722) Sauce au Chocolat
    (with cocoa powder) 734
(1723) Sauce au Citron 735
(130) Sauce au Marsala 59
(134) Sauce au Porto 61
(174) Sauce au Vin Blanc 73
(175) Sauce au Vin Rouge 73
(204) Sauce aux Airelles 82
(162) Sauce aux Anchois 69
(141) Sauce aux Câpres 63
(166) Sauce aux Crevettes 70
(173) Sauce aux Oeufs 73
(147) Sauce aux Oignons
    (white) 64
(209) Sauce aux Pommes 84
(153) Sauce Béarnaise 66
(114) Sauce Béchamel 53
(163) Sauce Bercy (for fish) 69
(119) Sauce Bercy (for grilled
    meats) 55
(497) Sauce Bolognaise 167

(498) Sauce Bolognaise (with
    red wine) 168
(120) Sauce Bordelaise 55
(207) Sauce Bretonne 83
(165) Sauce Cardinal 70
(121) Sauce Champignons
    (brown) 56
(142) Sauce Champigons
    (white) 63
(159) Sauce Chantilly 68
(122) Sauce Charcutière 56
(123) Sauce Chasseur 56
(124) Sauce Chateaubriand 57
(1252) Sauce Chaud-froid à
    l'Aurore 541
(1253) Sauce Chaud-froid
    Blanche 541
(1254) Sauce Chaud-froid
    Brune 541
(1255) Sauce Chaud-froid de
    Poisson 542
(1256) Sauce Chaud-froid
    Verte 542
(1257) Sauce Chaud-froid
    coating with 542
(155) Sauce Choron 67
(143) Sauce Crème 63
(208) Sauce Currie 84
(112) Sauce Demi-glace 52
(125) Sauce Devilled 57
(125) Sauce Diable 57
(111) Sauce Espagnole 51
(282) Sauce for Gravlax 102
(156) Sauce Foyot 67
(167) Sauce Génevoise 70
(126) Sauce Grand Veneur 57
(168) Sauce Gratin 71
(184) Sauce Gribiche 77
(157) Sauce Hollandaise 67
(170) Sauce Homard 72
(169) Sauce Homard de Base 71
(144) Sauce Hongroise 63
(127) Sauce Italienne 58
(145) Sauce Ivoire 64
(128) Sauce Lyonnaise 58
(129) Sauce Madère 58
(158) Sauce Maltaise 68
(185) Sauce Mayonnaise 78
(1728) Sauce Melba (with
    fresh fruit) 736
(1727) Sauce Melba (with jam) 736
(186) Sauce Menthe 78
(120) Sauce Moelle 55
(500) Sauce Monégasque 169
(146) Sauce Mornay 64
(171) Sauce Mornay (for fish) 72
(159) Sauce Mousseline 68
(1729) Sauce Mousseline
    (sweet) 736
(172) Sauce Moutarde 72
(499) Sauce Niçoise 168
(160) Sauce Paloise 68
(131) Sauce Périgueux 59
(148) Sauce Persil 65

Recipe

(132) Sauce Piquante 60
(133) Sauce Poivrade 60
(210) Sauce Portugaise 85
(149) Sauce Poulette 65
(188) Sauce Provençale (cold) 79
(211) Sauce Provençale 85
(189) Sauce Raifort 79
(190) Sauce Ravigote 79
(135) Sauce Réforme 61
(191) Sauce Remoulade 80
(136) Sauce Robert 61
(1731) Sauce Sabayon 737
(212) Sauce Smitaine 85
(150) Sauce Soubise 65
(151) Sauce Suprême 65
(192) Sauce Tartare 80
(118) Sauce Tomate 54
(138) Sauce Tortue 62
(193) Sauce Tyrolienne 80
(156) Sauce Valois 67
(194) Sauce Verte 80
(190) Sauce Vinaigrette 79
(196) Sauce Vincent 80
(137) Sauce Xérès 62
(162) Sauce, Anchovy 69
(209) Sauce, Apple 84
(1716) Sauce, Apricot 733
(1717) Sauce, Apricot (with
    fresh apricots) 733
(169) Sauce, basic Lobster 71
(202) Sauce, Blue Cheese,
    Celery and Chive 82
(206) Sauce, Bread (optional) 83
(205) Sauce, Bread
    (traditional) 83
(111) Sauce, Brown 51
(128) Sauce, Brown Onion 58
(164) Sauce, Butter 69
(1719) Sauce, Butterscotch 734
(182) Sauce, Cambridge 77
(141) Sauce, Caper 63
(146) Sauce, Cheese 64
(204) Sauce, Cranberry 82
(143) Sauce, Cream 63
(183) Sauce, Cumberland 77
(208) Sauce, Curry 84
(1725) Sauce, Custard 735
(173) Sauce, Egg 73
(177) Sauce, Fennel 74
(282) Sauce, Gravlax 102
(194) Sauce Green 80
(189) Sauce Horseradish 79
(1726) Sauce, Jam 736
(1723) Sauce, Lemon 735
(170) Sauce, Lobster 72
(186) Sauce, Mint 78
(121) Sauce, Mushroom
    (brown) 56
(142) Sauce, Mushroom
    (white) 63
(172) Sauce, Mustard 72
(147) Sauce, Onion (white) 64
(1730) Sauce, Orange 737
(148) Sauce, Parsley 65

Recipe

(134) Sauce, Port Wine 61
(175) Sauce, Red Wine 73
(137) Sauce, Sherry 62
(166) Sauce, Shrimp 70
(213) Sauce, Sweet and Sour 86
(1732) Sauce, Syrup 737
(499) Sauce, Tomato and
    Basil 168
(114) Sauce, White 53
(174) Sauce, White Wine 73
Sauces based on
    Béchamel and Veloutés
    (139–51)
Sauces based on
    Demi-glace and Jus Lié
    (119–38)
(110) Sauces, Basic 51
Sauces, Chaud-froid
    (1251–6)
(197) Sauces, Cocktail 81
Sauces, cold (180–203)
Sauces, Egg and Butter
    (152–61)
Sauces, Fish (162–75)
(1724) Sauces, Fresh soft
    Fruit 735
Sauces, Miscellaneous
    (204–13)
Sauces, Sweet and
    Butter (1717–34)
(590) Saumon à l'Oseille,
    Suprême 211
(585) Saumon Chambord 208
(589) Saumon Condorcet,
    Suprême 211
(1279) Saumon froid en
    Bellevue 552
(301) Saumon Fumé 106
(586) Saumon grillé, Dame 209
(588) Saumon poché 210
(587) Saumon poché, Darne 210
(584) Saumon, Coulibiac 207
(1661) Sausage Rolls 710
(1133) Sauté d'Emincé de
    Dinde aux Amandes et
    Safran 470
(837) Sauté de Boeuf
    Hongroise 336
(838) Sauté de Boeuf
    Stroganoff 337
(999) Sauté de Filet de Veau
    aux Chanterelles 399
(1240) Sauté de Lapin aux
    Champignons 533
(1000) Sauté de Veau à la
    Portugaise 399
(998) Sauté de Veau aux
    Champignons 398
(1381) Sautéed Artichoke
    Bottoms with Basil 607
(1083) Sautés of Chicken 444
(997) Sautés of Veal 398
(1759) Savarin aux Fraises 751
(1760) Savarin aux Fruits 751

Recipe

(1758) Savarin Chantilly 750
(1741) Savarin Paste 742
(1757) Savarins 750
Savouries (1620–70)
Scallops (653–6), *see
    also under* Coquilles St
    Jacques
(654) Scallops, fried and
    Bacon 249
(676) Scampi frits 261
(677) Scampi Meunière 261
(678) Scampi Provençale 262
(676) Scampi, fried 261
(350) Scotch Broth 121
(439) Scotch Egg 154
(1662) Scotch Woodcock 711
(426) Scrambled Eggs on
    Toast 150
(424) Scrambled Eggs with
    Asparagus Tips 150
(423) Scrambled Eggs with
    Chicken Livers 150
(422) Scrambled Eggs with
    Croûtons 150
(421) Scrambled Eggs with
    Mushrooms 149
(425) Scrambled Eggs with
    Tomatoes 150
    Sea Urchin 247
(262) Seafood Cocktail 97
    Seakale (1432–3)
(1432) Seakale, boiled 625
(759) Selle d'Agneau 307
(1286) Selle d'Agneau froide
    Marly 556
(760) Selle d'Agneau poêlée
    Cadmos 307
(1295) Selle de Chevreuil
    froide Grand-Veneur 563
(1225) Selle de Venaison
    Bad-Ragaz 524
(1884) Semolina Pudding 802
(1263) Semolina Socle 545
    Shellfish Australian 882
    Shellfish, classification 244
    Shellfish, cleaning and
    preparation 245
    Shellfish, quality points 244
    Shellfish, storage 245
(758) Shepherd's Pie 307
(137) Sherry Sauce 62
(2016) Sherry Trifle 843
(8) Shrimp Butter 20
(166) Shrimp Sauce 70
(297) Shrimps, Potted 105
(800) Silverside of Beef,
    boiled, and Dumplings 317
(804) Sirloin of Beef 320
(813) Sirloin Steak with
    Mushrooms 323
    Sirloin Steaks (811–19)
(578) Skate with Black Butter 204
(304) Smoked Cod's Roe
    Relish 107

Recipe

(300) Smoked Eel 106
(299) Smoked Fish 106
(301) Smoked Salmon 106
(296) Smoked Salmon,
Potted 105
(302) Smoked Trout 107
(1619) Smørrebrød 695
Snails, *see under*
Escargots
Snipe, *see* Bécasse and
Bécassine
(1262) Socle, Rice 544
(1263) Socle, Semolina 545
(1261) Socles 544
(619) Sole à l'Orly, Filet 223
(623) Sole à la Russe, Filet 226
(592) Sole au Gratin 212
(627) Sole au Vin Blanc, Filet 228
(633) Sole au Vin Blanc
Mousselines 230
(628) Sole au Vin Rouge,
Filet 228
(614) Sole Belle-Meunière,
Filet 222
(596) Sole Bercy, Filet 214
(597) Sole Bonne-Femme,
Filet 215
(598) Sole Bretonne, Filet 215
(599) Sole Bréval, Filet 216
(600) Sole Caprice, Filet 216
(601) Sole Cléopâtre, Filet 217
(591) Sole Colbert 212
(602) Sole Cubat, Filet 217
(595) Sole d'Antin Filet 214
(603) Sole Dieppoise, Filet 217
(604) Sole Doria, Filet 218
(605) Sole Dugléré, Filet 218
(606) Sole Florentine, Filet 218
(607) Sole François Ier, Filet 219
(608) Sole frit Filet 219
(609) Sole Gailliéra, Filet 220
(610) Sole Grenobloise, Filet 220
(611) Sole grillé, Filet 220
(593) Sole grillée 213
(612) Sole Marguery, Filet 221
(594) Sole Meunière 213
(615) Sole Meunière aux
Aubergines, Filet 222
(616) Sole Meunière aux
Câpres, Filet 222
(613) Sole Meunière, Filet 221
(617) Sole Mornay, Filet 222
(632) Sole Murat, Goujons 230
(618) Sole Nelson, Filet 223
(620) Sole Otéro, Filet 224
(621) Sole Palace, Filet 224
(622) Sole Polignac, Filet 225
(624) Sole Saint-Germain,
Filet 226
(625) Sole Suchet, Filet 226
(634) Sole Sylvia, Paupiette 231
(626) Sole Véronique, Filet 227
(629) Sole Walewska, Filet 229
(1281) Sole, Filet froid

Recipe

Bagration 553
(608) Sole, Fried Fillet 219
(631) Sole, Goujonettes frites 229
(630) Sole, Goujons frits 229
(593) Sole, grilled 213
(611) Sole, Grilled Fillet 220
(2038) Sorbet à l'Ananas 851
(2043) Sorbet à l'Orange 853
(2039) Sorbet au Champagne 852
(2040) Sorbet au Citron 852
(2041) Sorbet au Citron Vert 853
(2042) Sorbet aux Framboises 853
Sorbets (2037–43)
(1905) Soufflé à l'Orange 807
(1906) Soufflé Arlequin 807
(1902) Soufflé au Chocolat 807
(1903) Soufflé au Citron 807
(1665) Soufflé au Fromage 712
(1904) Soufflé au Grand
Marnier 807
(1666) Soufflé au Jambon 712
(1667) Soufflé au Parmesan 713
(1663) Soufflé aux
Charnpignons 711
(1909) Soufflé aux Fraises 808
(1664) Soufflé Florentine 712
(2010) Soufflé froid au Grand
Marnier 840
(2009) Soufflé froid aux
Fraises 839
(2011) Soufflé froid Milanaise 841
(2068) Soufflé glacé au
Drambuie 859
(2069) Soufflé glacé aux
Framboises 860
(2070) Soufflé glacé
Tutti-frutti 860
(1907) Soufflé Rothschild 808
(1901) Soufflé Vanille 806
(1665) Soufflé, Cheese 712
(1666) Soufflé Ham 712
(1663) Soufflé Mushroom 711
(1664) Soufflé, Spinach 712
(1908) Soufflés aux Fruits 808
Soufflés glacés
(2067–70)
Soufflés, cold sweet
(2009–11)
Soufflés, hot sweet
(1900–9)
(2067) Soufflés, iced 859
(1888) Soufflés, Pudding 802
Soup, Classification 109
Soup, Quantity Guide 113
(358) Soupe à l'Oignon
Gratinée 124
(419) Soupe aux Cerises 147
(409) Soupe aux Moules 142
(404) Soupe aux Rognons 139
Soups; Bisques (400–1)
Soups; brown (402–5)
Soups; Clear (321–47)
Soups; cold (410–19)
Soups; Consommés

Recipe

(321–43)
Soups; Cream (387–99)
Soups; Potages,
Soupes, and Broths
(348–58)
Soups; purée-based
(359–81)
Soups; special
unclassified (406–9)
Soups; Veloutés
(382–6)
(303) Soused Herrings 107
(502) Spaghetti Bolognaise 170
(503) Spaghetti Carbonara 170
(501) Spaghetti Italienne 169
(504) Spaghetti Milanaise 170
(505) Spaghetti Monégasque 171
(506) Spaghetti Napolitaine 171
(507) Spaghetti Niçoise 171
(508) Spaghetti Sicilienne 171
(1048) Spatchcocked Chicken 423
(493) Spätzle 166
Spinach (1454–9), *see
also under* Epinards
(1457) Spinach Purée,
Creamed 633
(1458) Spinach Purée with
Croûtons 633
(1455) Spinach, buttered with
Garlic 632
(1454) Spinach, Leaf 631
(1456) Spinach, Purée 632
(1804) Sponge, Chocolate
Genoese 767
(1803) Sponge, Genoese 766
(1049) Spring Chicken, grilled 423
Squash 598
Squid, *see under* Calmar
(841) Steak and Kidney Pie 338
(843) Steak and Kidney
Pudding 338
(840) Steak Pie (cooked
filling) 338
(839) Steak Pie (raw filling) 337
(846) Steak Tartare 339
(801) Steak, braised 318
(829) Steak, Hamburg 330
(842) Steak, Kidney and
Mushroom Pie 338
(844) Steak, Kidney and
Mushroom Pudding 339
(845) Steak, Kidney and
Oyster Pudding 339
(1912) Steamed Black Cap
Pudding 809
(1913) Steamed Cherry
Sponge Pudding 809
(1914) Steamed Chocolate
Sponge Pudding 810
(1921) Steamed College
Pudding 810
(1915) Steamed Ginger
Sponge Pudding 810
(1916) Steamed Golden

Recipe

Sponge Pudding 810
(1922) Steamed Jam Roll 811
(1917) Steamed Jam Sponge
Pudding 810
(1918) Steamed Lemon
Sponge Pudding 810
(1919) Steamed Orange
Sponge Pudding 810
(1911) Steamed Sponge
Pudding 809
(1924) Steamed Suet Pudding 812
(1923) Steamed Sultana Roll 811
(1920) Steamed Vanilla
Sponge Pudding 810
(735) Stew, Irish 296
(836) Stewed Beef 335
(1965) Stewed dried fruits 821
(1536) Stir-fried Vegetables 657
Stir Frying 17
(1709) Stock Syrup 730
(1946) Stock Syrup for
Compotes 819
(97) Stock, Brown 45
(98) Stock, Brown Veal 45
(101) Stock, Fish 47
(99) Stock, Game 46
(100) Stock, Vegetable 46
(93) Stock, White 44
(96) Stock, White Chicken 45
(94) Stock, White Mutton 45
(95) Stock, White Veal 45
(1951) Strawberries, poached 820
(1771) Strawberry Band 756
(1930) Strawberry Bavarois
(with Crème Anglaise) 814
(1931) Strawberry Bavarois
(with sugar syrup) 815
(1785) Strawberry Flan 759
(1983) Strawberry Fool 827
(1834) Strawberry Fritters 783
(2024) Strawberry Ice-cream 848
(2087) Strawberry Melba 863
(1996) Strawberry Mousse 833
(2065) Strawberry Mousse,
iced 858
(1909) Strawberry Soufflé 808
(2009) Strawberry Soufflé,
cold 839
(42) Stuffing, Apple, Raisin
and Walnut 29
(43) Stuffing, Chestnut 29
(44) Stuffing, Sage and
Onion 30
(45) Stuffing, Thyme and
Parsley 30
Stuffings (34–45)
(519) Stuffings for Ravioli
Cannelloni, etc. 175
(1459) Subrics d'Epinards 633
(1537) Succotash 658
(1293) Suckmg Pig with
Apples, cold 561
(901) Sucking Pig, Roast
Stuffed 360

Recipe

(1743) Suet Pastry (for sweet
puddings) 742
(89) Suet Pastry for
Dumplings and
Puddings 41
(88) Suet, Chopped 41
(1710) Sugar Boiling 730
(1711) Sugar for glazing Petits
Fours 731
(1712) Sugar, spun 732
(1923) Sultana Roll, steamed 811
(2012) Summer Pudding 842
(1113) Suprême de Caneton
Juan-les-Pins 461
(1175) Suprême de Faisan au
Suc de Mandarines 501
(1176) Suprême de Faisan
Tatiana 502
(1095) Suprême de Volaille à
la Crème et
Champignons 451
(1097) Suprême de Volaille à
la Kiev 452
(1094) Suprême de Volaille
Chivry 450
(1096) Suprême de Volaille
Doria 451
(1305) Suprême de Volaille en
Chaud-froid 569
(1307) Suprême de Volaille
Jeannette 570
(1306) Suprême de Volaille
Jeanne-Marie 570
(1098) Suprême de Volaille
Maréchale 452
(1099) Suprême de Volaille
Maryland 453
(1100) Suprême de Volaille
Tessinoise 454
(1101) Suprême de Volaille
Tonkinoise 454
(1128) Suprêmes de
Pigeonneau aux
Morilles 467
(1093) Suprêmes de Volaille 449
(1512) Swede 648
(1392) Sweet and Sour Bean
Sprouts 611
(904) Sweet and Sour Pork 362
(213) Sweet and Sour Sauce 86
Sweet Dishes, cold
(1925–2019)
Sweet Dishes, hot
(1822–1924)
Sweet Flans, Bandes
Tarts, Tartlets and
Barquettes (1762–96)
Sweetbreads, calf's
(984–93), *see also under*
Ris de Veau
Sweetbreads Lamb's
Sweetcorn (1484–5) 305
(1485) Sweetcorn, creamed 639
(229) Sweetcorn, creamed for

Recipe

Hors-d'Oeuvre 91
(1820) Swiss Roll 776
(1821) Swiss Roll, Chocolate 776
(2013) Syllabub 843
(1713) Syrup for Savarins and
Babas 732
(1827) Syrup Roll, baked 780
(1732) Syrup Sauce 737
(1709) Syrup, stock 730

T

(509) Tagliatelli 171
(1774) Tangerine Band 756
(2034) Tangerine Water Ice 850
(1885) Tapioca Pudding 802
(304) Taramasalata 107
(1765) Tart, Bakewell 753
(1779) Tart, Dutch Apple 757
(1668) Tarte aux Oignons 713
(1795) Tarte Tatin 763
(1796) Tartelenes aux Fruits 764
(1669) Tartelenes de Crevettes 714
(1763) Tardet Moulds, to line 753
(1316) Terrine de Campagne 574
(1317) Terrine de Canard 575
(1318) Terrine de Foie de
Veau 576
(1319) Terrine de Gibier 577
(294) Terrines and Pates 105
(1003) Tête de Veau en
Tortue 400
(1002) Tête de Veau Poulette 400
(1004) Tête de Veau
Vinaigrette 401
(106) Thickening Agents 48
(252) Thon à l'Huile 95
(635) Thon Mentonnaise
Rouelle 232
(1336) Thousand Island
Dressing 587
(45) Thyme and Parsley
Stuffing 30
(847) Toad in the Hole 340
(90) Tomatoes Concassées 41
(91) Tomatoes Concassées
Cooked 42
(1518) Tomates farcies 648
(306) Tomates farcies for
Hors-d'Oeuvre 108
(1519) Tomates farcies
Provençale 649
(1520) Tomates grillees 650
(416) Tomato and Basil
Soup, chilled 145
(307) Tomato Juice 108
(1270) Tomato Mousse 547
(1352) Tomato Salad 589
(250) Tomato Salad for
Hors-d'Oeuvre 95
(118) Tomato Sauce 54
(397) Tomato, Cream of 135
Tomatoes (1518–20)
(90) Tomatoes, Chopped or

Recipe

Diced 41
(1520) Tomatoes, grilled 650
(1518) Tomatoes, stuffed 648
(306) Tomatoes, stuffed for
Hors-d'Oeuvre 108
(1522) Topinambours à la
Crème 650
(1521) Topinambours nature 650
(1523) Topinambours Persillés 650
(1813) Torte, Linzer 771
(1818) Torte, Rigi-Kirsch 774
(1819) Torte, Sacher 775
(345) Tortue Claire 118
(849) Tournedos Chasseur 340
(850) Tournedos Choisy 341
(851) Tournedos Choron 341
(852) Tournedos
Montpensier 342
(848) Tournedos or
Médaillons 340
(853) Tournedos Rossini 342
(2015) Trifle, fruit 843
(2016) Trifle, Sherry 843
(2014) Trifles 843
(855) Tripe and Onions 343
(855) Tripes à l'Anglaise 343
(854) Tripes Provençale 343
Trout (636–40), *see also*
under Truite
(637) Trout, grilled 234
Trout, Rainbow 233
(302) Trout, Smoked 107
(92) Truffles 42
(2105) Truffles, Chocolate
Brandy 869
(2113) Truffles, Rum 872
(636) Truite au Bleu 233
(640) Truite au Vin Blanc 235
(302) Truite Fumée 107
(637) Truite grillée 234
(638) Truite Meunière 234
(639) Truite Meunière aux
Amandes 235
(1282) Truite, Eventail Yvette 554
Truite-Saumonée 236
(1007) Trussing 406
(1008) Trussing (single string) 407
(2115) Tuiles 873
(252) Tunny Fish 95
Tunny, *see under* Thon
(1761) Turban de Croûtes aux
Fruits 752
(641) Turbot à la Normande 236
(648) Turbot et Saumon
Granvillaise, Caissene 241
(642) Turbot grillé, Tronçon 237
(643) Turbot poché, Tronçon 238
(644) Turbot Trouvillaise,
Médaillon 238
(642) Turbot, grilled 237
(643) Turbot, poached 238
(1298) Turkey, Cold 565
(1132) Turkey, Escalopes 470
(1131) Turkey, Roast with

Recipe

Chestnuts 469
(1130) Turkey, Stuffed and
Roast, English Style 469
Turkey, *see also under*
Dindonneau
(2116) Turkish Delight 873
(362) Turnip Soup 126
(1487) Turnips, Buttered 640
(1488) Turnips, glazed 641
(1843) Turnovers 787
(345) Turtle Soup, clear 118
(2070) Tutti-frutti Soufflé,
iced 860

V

(2017) Vacherin aux Fraises 844
(2018) Vacherin aux
Framboises 844
(2019) Vacherin aux
Mandarines 845
(1938) Vanilla Bavarois 816
(1939) Vanilla Blancmange 817
(2117) Vanilla Fudge 874
(2020) Vanilla Ice-cream 847
(2066) Vanilla Mousse, iced 858
(1889) Vanilla Pudding,
Soufflé 803
(1901) Vanilla Soufflé 806
(1312) Veal and Ham Pie 571
(1314) Veal and Ham Pie,
raised 572
(942) Veal Cutlet with Basil 373
Veal Cutlets (941–50)
Veal dishes, *see also*
under Veau
Veal Escalopes
(951–62)
Veal joints, weights and
preparations (905–18)
Veal Offals (927–34)
(1001) Veal Saddle 400
(997) Veal Sautés 398
(116) Veal Velouté 54
(936) Veal, grills 370
(1313) Veal, Ham and Egg Pie 572
(935) Veal, Roast 369
Veal, small cuts
(919–26)
(971) Veau braisé, Grenadin 384
(975) Veau braisée, Noix
(brown braised) 386
(976) Veau braisée, Noix
(white braised) 387
(1314) Veau et Jambon, Pâte
en Croûte 572
(977) Veau Neuchâtelloise,
Noix 388
(938) Veau, Blanquette 371
(939) Veau, Blanquette à
l'Ancienne 372
(940) Veau, Cervelle au
Beurre Noir 372
(942) Veau, Côte au Basilic 373

Recipe

(948) Veau, Côte au Romarin 375
(943) Veau, Côte
Bonne-Femme 373
(947) Veau, Côte en Papillote 374
(944) Veau, Côte Milanaise 373
(945) Veau, Côte Napolitaine 373
(946) Veau, Côte panée 374
(949) Veau, Côte sautée 375
(950) Veau, Côte Vallee
d'Auge 376
(953) Veau, Escalope à la
Crème 377
(954) Veau, Escalope à la
Crème et Champignons 377
(956) Veau, Escalope au
Madère 378
(957) Veau, Escalope au
Marsala 379
(957) Veau, Escalope au
Porto 379
(957) Veau, Escalope au
Xérès 379
(952) Veau, Escalope Cordon
Bleu 376
(955) Veau, Escalope
Holstein 378
(958) Veau, Escalope
Milanaise 379
(959) Veau, Escalope
Napolitaine 379
(960) Veau, Escalope panée 379
(961) Veau, Escalope
Viennoise 379
(962) Veau, Escalopines 380
(964) Veau, Filet aux
Fenouils 381
(963) Veau, Filet Esterhazy 380
(966) Veau, Foie au Lard 382
(965) Veau Foie aux Cassis 382
(967) Veau Foie Lyonnaise 383
(968) Veau, Fricandeau 383
(969) Veau Fricassée 383
(970) Veau Fricassée à
l'Ancienne 384
(972) Veau, Médaillons à
l'Estragon 385
(992) Veau, Médaillons de
Ris Maréchale 395
(993) Veau, Médaillons de
Ris Saint-Germain 395
(973) Veau, Médaillons
Musette 385
(978) Veau, Noix poêlée 389
(982) Veau, Paupiene 392
(981) Veau Pied grillé 391
(983) Veau Pojarski Smitaine 392
(984) Veau, Ris 392
(988) Veau Ris à la Crème 394
(987) Veau Ris
Bonne-Maman 394
(985) Veau Ris braisé 393
(986) Veau Ris braisé au
Madere 394
(989) Veau Ris Financière 395

Recipe

(990) Veau Ris pané 395
(991) Veau, Ris Princesse 395
(995) Veau, Rognon à la Fine
　　　Champagne 396
(994) Veau, Rognon
　　　Dijonnaise 396
(996) Veau, Rognonnade aux
　　　Salsifis 397
(1000) Veau, Sauté à la
　　　Portugaise 399
(998) Veau, Sauté aux
　　　Champignons 398
(999) Veau, Sauté de Filet
　　　aux Chanterelles 399
(1001) Veau, Selle 400
(1003) Veau, Tête en Tortue 400
(1002) Veau, Tête Poulette 400
(1004) Veau, Tête Vinaigrette 401
　　　Vegetable Dishes,
　　　mixed 650
(1524) Vegetable Fritters 651
(320) Vegetable Garnishes for
　　　Soups 113
(1534) Vegetable Purées 655
(363) Vegetable Soup 126
(100) Vegetable Stock 46
　　　Vegetables,
　　　classification and
　　　quality 597
　　　Vegetables, cooking
　　　methods 601
　　　Vegetables, portion
　　　guide 600
　　　Vegetables, preparation 600
(1536) Vegetables, Stir-fried 657
　　　Vegetables, storage 599
(382) Velouté Agnès Sorel 130
(383) Velouté Dame Blanche 130
(117) Velouté de Poisson 54
(116) Velouté de Veau 54
(115) Velouté de Volaille 53
(384) Velouté Doria 130
(385) Velouté Fédora 131
(386) Velouté Marie-Stuart 132
(115) Velouté, Chicken 53
(117) Velouté, Fish 54
(116) Velouté, Veal 54
(1218) Venaison, Côtelettes au
　　　Genièvre 520

Recipe

(1219) Venaison, Côtelettes
　　　Chasseur 521
(1217) Venaison, Civet 520
(1221) Venaison, Médaillons
　　　Conti 521
(1222) Venaison, Médaillons
　　　Valencia 522
(1223) Venaison, Noisettes aux
　　　Myrtilles 522
(1224) Venaison, Noisettes aux
　　　Poires 523
(1225) Venaison, Selle
　　　Bad-Ragaz 524
(1216) Venison, Grills 520
(1220) Venison, Médaillons 521
　　　Venison, main items,
　　　joints, weights and
　　　preparation (1190-8)
(1220) Venison, Noisettes 521
　　　Venison, offals
　　　(1205-7)
(1215) Venison, Roast 518
　　　Venison, small cuts and
　　　preparation
　　　(1199-1204)
(1886) Vermicelu Pudding 802
(418) Vichyssoise 146
(2118) Viennese Fingers 874
(1329) Vinaigrette Salad
　　　Dressing 586
(1528) Vine Leaves, Stuffed 653
(680) Vol-au-Vent de Fruits
　　　de Mer 263
(1102) Vol-au-Vent de Volaille 455
(1103) Vol-au-Vent
　　　Toulousaine 455
(1047) Volaille grillé, Blanc 423
(1047) Volaille grillée,
　　　Côtelette 423
(1050) Volaille, Ballotine
　　　braisée 423
(1060) Volaille, Crêpes
　　　Mornay 430
(1062) Volaille, Emincé
　　　Argenteuil 431
(1066) Volaille, Kebab à
　　　l'Orientale 433
(1302) Volaille, Mayonnaise 568
(1067) Volaille, Mousselines

Recipe

　　　Alexandra 433
(1305) Volaille, Suprême en
　　　Chaud-froid 569
(1307) Volaille, Suprême
　　　Jeannette 570
(1306) Volaille, Suprême
　　　Jeanne-Marie 570
(1102) Volaille, Vol-au-Vent 455
(1714) Vols-au-Vent 732

W

(1368) Waldorf Salad 592
(1715) Water Icing 733
(361) Watercress and Potato
　　　Soup 126
(1670) Welsh Rarebit 714
(93) White Stock 44
(174) White Wine Sauce 73
(545) Whitebait Devilled 192
(546) Whitebait fried 193
　　　Whiting (565-70), *see
　　　also under* Merlan
(567) Whiting, curled 202
(565) Whiting, fried English
　　　style 201
(568) Whiting fried fillet 202
(569) Whiting, fried fillet,
　　　French style 202
(1005) Wiener Schnitzel 401
　　　Wild Boar 474
(1300) Wild Duck with
　　　Cherries, cold 566
(1181) Wild Duck with
　　　Pineapple 506
　　　Wild Duck, *see also
　　　under* Canard Sauvage
　　　Woodcock, *see also
　　　under* Bécasse

Y

　　　Yabbies 253
(1337) Yoghurt Dressing 588
(796) Yorkshire Pudding 314

Z

(1899) Zabaglione alla Marsala 805